OTHER BOOKS BY JAMES KNOWLSON

D0447947

CRITICISM

Universal Language Schemes in England and France 1600–1800

Samuel Beckett: An Exhibition

Light and Darkness in the Theatre of Samuel Beckett

Frescoes of the Skull:
    The Later Prose and Drama of Samuel Beckett
    (with John Pilling)

Samuel Beckett: Krapp's Last Tape. Theatre Workbook I (ed.)

EDITIONS

Happy Days/ Oh les beaux jours
    by Samuel Beckett

Drunken Boat:
    A Translation by Samuel Beckett
    of Arthur Rimbaud's *Le Bateau ivre*
    (with Felix Leakey)

Happy Days: Samuel Beckett's Production Notebook

The Theatrical Notebooks of Samuel Beckett

  VOL. I: *Waiting for Godot*
    (with Dougald MacMillan)

  VOL. II: *Endgame*
    ed. S. E. Gontarski

  VOL. III: *Krapp's Last Tape*

  VOL. IV: *The Shorter Plays*
    ed. S. E. Gontarski

Damned to Fame

The Life of Samuel Beckett

JAMES KNOWLSON

A TOUCHSTONE BOOK
Published by Simon & Schuster

TOUCHSTONE
Rockefeller Center
1230 Avenue of the Americas
New York, NY 10020

Copyright © 1996 by James Knowlson
All rights reserved,
including the right of reproduction
in whole or in part in any form.

First Touchstone Edition 1997
Published by arrangement with Bloomsbury Publishing Limited

TOUCHSTONE and colophon are registered trademarks
of Simon & Schuster Inc.

Beckett's writings in English are quoted by permission of the Beckett
Estate, Faber and Faber Ltd. and the Calder Educational Trust,
London, and Grove/Atlantic Inc. in the United States of America and
Canada, who hold the copyright to his published work. His writings
in French are quoted by permission of the Beckett Estate and Les
Editions de Minuit.

The poem of James Joyce printed in note 66 of chapter 7 is published
by courtesy of the Estate of James Joyce.

Frontispiece photograph by Barbara Jackson, 1966.

Designed by Edith Fowler

Manufactured in the United States of America

10 9 8 7 6 5 4 3 2 1

Library of Congress Cataloging-in-Publication Data

Knowlson, James.
   Damned to fame : the life of Samuel Beckett / James Knowlson.
     p.   cm.
   Includes bibliographical references and index.
   1. Beckett, Samuel, 1906–   —Biography.   2. Authors, Irish—
20th century—Biography.   3. Authors, French—20th century—
Biography.   I. Title.
PR6003.E282Z764   1996
848'.91409—dc20
[B]   96-23702   CIP

ISBN 0-684-80872-2
     0-684-83658-0 (Pbk)

Acknowledgments

I am happy to acknowledge the help that I have received in researching and writing this book. My chief debt of gratitude is to the late Samuel Beckett. He helped in many different ways, above all with five months of crucial interviews. His nephew Edward Beckett provided important unpublished material and supported me throughout what became a rather long haul. His niece Caroline Beckett Murphy also helped with photographs and other information. The chapters on Beckett's early years could scarcely have been written without the help of the author's cousins Morris Sinclair, whom I cannot thank enough for his constant advice and help, and the late Sheila Page Roe. John Beckett, Samuel's musician cousin, also gave me important insights, as did John's sister, Ann. I was also helped by Deirdre Hamilton Sinclair, John Beckett (Harold Beckett's son), Desmond Beckett, and Charles Horner Beckett.

Among Beckett's own close friends, I want to single out for special thanks his publisher and literary executor, Jérôme Lindon; Josette Hayden; Avigdor and Anne Arikha; his English-language publishers, John Calder and Barney Rosset; Georges Belmont; Ruby Cohn; Denise Deleutre; Edith Fournier; Marthe Gautier; Jocelyn Herbert; Mary Manning Howe (Mrs. Adams); Jean Martin; Pamela Mitchell; Elisabeth van Velde; and Billie Whitelaw. Gottfried and Renate Büttner in Kassel, Aléxis Péron in Paris, and Walter Asmus in Hanover and Berlin were of special assistance to me.

I have been helped with research for short periods of time by several assistants who are also good friends, most importantly by Emily Lemoing Emerson in Paris—and I thank Emily and Arnaud for the warmth of their hospitality—Krystyna Illakowicz in New York, Jane Walling Wefelmeyer in Germany, and Susan Schreibman in Dublin. Monika Seidl researched brilliantly for me in Hellerau-Laxenburg, coming up with some remarkable results. Rebecca Creasy, Julie Goodwin, Marie-Louise Muir, Jan Willem Reiksma, Suzanne Willadt, Prue Winnett, and Dagmar Wobser helped me more briefly. My friend and colleague Wolfgang van Emden translated German texts for me.

Many of the following have given me important help and advice, and I thank them all most warmly. I list them according to countries.

France: Fernando Arrabal; Geneviève Asse; Simone Benmussa; Danielle van Bercheycke; André Bernold; Etienne Bierry; Jean Bourdier; Barbara Bray; Robert Carlier; Sergio de Castro; Pierre Chabert; Alberto Chiarini; Philippe Clidière; Olivier Corpet; Jean Coulomb; Anne Cremin; John Crombie; Marc Dachy; Jacques Deniau; André Derval; Maurice Dirou; Claude Duthuit; Nicole Greub; Denise Hayter; Philippe Hautefeuille; Matias Henrioud; Eléonore Hirt; Emmanuel Jacquart; Erik Kahane; Hermine Karagheuz; Roger Kempf; Rémi Labrusse; Claude Lasibille; Yvonne Lefèvre; Emma Lévin–Le Chanois; Aléxis Léon; Annette Lindon; Michael Lonsdale; Simone McKee; Marysette Mayoux; Deryk Mendel; Michèle Meunier; Maurice Nadeau; Jacques Noël; Lynda Peskine; Jean Piel; Valérie Poinsotte; Jacques and Catherine Putman; Nathalie Sarraute; Pierre Schneider; Delphine Seyrig; Anne Simonin; Jack Thieuloy; and David Warrilow. I benefited from the information of the following former *normaliens:* Paul Bénichou; Roger Bernard; Pierre Chambon; Emile Delavenay; Roger Dumaine; Renée Evrard; Claude Jamet; Camille Marcoux; Ulysse Nicollet; Henri Queffélec; Lucien Roubaud; and Jean Weill. I thank members of the Resistance for their invaluable information: Henri Boussel; Andrée Jacob; André Jarrot; Jean Laroque; Roger and Bernadette Louis; Anise and André Postel-Vinay; Violette Rougier-Lecoq; Germaine Tillion; Pierre Weydert; and Mme. Denise Vernay (Secrétaire Générale of the Association Nationale des Anciennes Déportées et Internées de la Résistance). In London, the SOE adviser, Gervase Cowell, and Mark Seaman of the Imperial War Museum gave me important help. On Beckett's stay in Roussillon, I was advised by Hélène Albertini (née Gulini); Fernand Aude; Elie Blanc; Claude Blondel; Emile Bonhomme; André Bonhomme; Mme. Bonnelly; Edith Champbeix (formerly Mme. Fidler); Valérie Cravagnolo; Mayor Jean David; Juliette Ferrier; Eugène Fidler; Maryse Finel; Elie Icard; Paulette Icard; M. Lagier; Yvonne Lob; and M. and Mme. Vitter.

Germany: Boleslaw Barlog; Dr. Henning Bock; the director of the Gemäldegalerie at Dahlem, Ernst Bollmann; Dr. Rolf Breuer; Pastor Hans Freitag; Dr. Walter Georgi; Klaus Herm; Nancy Illig; Rosemary Koch; Michael Kuball; Henning Kühner, the pastor of the Andreaskirche in Brunswick; Dr. Helmut Leppien, the director of Hamburg's Kunsthalle; Jim Lewis; Dr. Magdalena Moeller of the Brücke Museum, Berlin; Dr. Reinhart Müller-Freienfels; Dr. Barbara Neu of S. Fischer Verlag; Dr. Dina Panneck of the Nationalgalerie, Berlin; Kevin Perryman; Eva-Katharina Schultz; Erika Tophoven; Dr. Siegfried Unseld of Suhrkamp Verlag; Dr. Klaus Völker; Dr. Reinhold Wex and Anne Harmssen of the Herzog-Anton-Ulrich Museum in Brunswick. At the Akademie der Künste in Berlin, Dr. Wolfgang Trautwein, Dr. Dagmar Wünsche, and Frau Ingeborg Lübold.

Great Britain: Dame Peggy Ashcroft; Philip Baker; Michael Bakewell; Shulamith Behr; Francesca Bion; Peter Boxall; David Bradby; Brenda Bruce; Stuart Burge; James Campbell; Alan Clodd; Denise Coffey; Melanie Daiken; Paul Daneman; Betty Dimond; Geoffrey Elborn; Jack Emery; Martin Esslin; Leonard Fenton; Michael J. Fitt; John Fletcher; Julian Garforth; Peter Gidal; David Gothard; Sir Alec Guinness; Peter Glenville; Michael Hamburger; Robbie

Hendry; Robert Hinshelwood; Robin Holley; Michael Horovitz; Rory Johnston; Bettina Jonic; Pearl King; Marion Leigh; Peter Lennon; Oscar Lewenstein; Jane Lidderdale; Pauline McWhinnie; Juliet Maguinness; John Minihan; Charles Montieth; Peter Murphy; Graham Nicholls; John Osborne; Siân Phillips; Malcolm Pines; Rosemary Pountney; Tristram Powell; Ronald Pickup; Adam Piette; Frank Pike; Nick Rawson; Vera Poliakoff Russell; Andrew Murray Scott; Duncan Scott; Stephen Stuart-Smith; Ursula and Miona Thompson; Dorothy Tutin; Mita and Edmund Tuby; Anne Leventhal Woolfson; Irene Worth; Katharine Worth; and Peter Woodthorpe. While visiting Folkestone to research Beckett's wedding, I was helped by Christine Labrosciano (information office), Keith Rosenz, Pauline Davey (art and libraries assistant), and Robert Paine.

Ireland: James Barrett; David A. Bowles; Sheila Brazil; Lily Condell; Valerie Costello; William Cunningham; Gerry Dukes; Margaret Farrington; Jim Fields; Arthur Finegan; James Guilford; J. D. Gwynn; Lieutenant Colonel D. J. Healy; Aidan Higgins; Noel Hughes; Ernest Keegan; John McCormick; Barry McGovern; Anna McMullan; John Manning; James Mays; Eilís Mercier; Bernard Mitton; John Montague; Eoin O'Brien; Christoir O'Duinn; Patrick O'Dwyer; Richard O'Sullivan; Roger Parris; Suzanne Pegley; Donald Perrin; Geoffrey Perrin; Hilary Pyle; Marjorie Reynolds; Elizabeth Ryan; Andrée Skeffington; Elsie Smiley; Cornelius F. Smith; Joe Sweeney; Elizabeth Steen; Carolyn Swift; Mervyn Wall; John O. Wisdom; Barbara Wright; F. G. Yoakley. For help on Campbell College, Belfast: Miles Delap; Keith Haines; Rona McAlpine; Rev. Dr. G. B. G. McConnell; Dr. R. J. I. Pollock; Joan Powell; Professor Colin Radford. For invaluable help on Beckett's stay at Portora Royal School: Richard Bennett; Victor Brennan; Dr. E. S. Dorman; Lieutenant Colonel G. Graham; John Graham; Cyril Harris; D. B. McNeill; Hugh D. Pim; Colonel Mark Scott; John S. S. Sealy; Patricia Simms. For information on Beckett at Trinity College, Dublin: Professor Terence Brown; Phyllis Killingley (née Ffrench); Arthur Hillis (my unpaid consultant); Professor Roger Little; Lady Violet Pike; Gerald Pakenham Stewart; Professor David Webb; Dr. Trevor West; and Mrs. Eileen Williams (née Adamson).

The United States of America and Canada: Edward Albee; Paul Auster; the estate of William Barrett; Helen Bishop; Tom Bishop; Herbert Blau; Helaine Blum; Georges Borchardt; Kay Boyle; Enoch Brater; Jane Lougee Bryant; Joe Chaikin; Rick Cluchey; Kandy Codish; Tom Cousineau; Hume Cronyn; Judith Douw; Raymond Federman; Martha Fehsenfeld; Morton Feldman; Lois Friedberg-Dobry; S. E. Gontarski; Mel Gussow; Israel Horowitz; Bill Irwin; Eugene Istomin; Jonathan Kalb; Hugh Kenner; Charles Klabunde; John Kobler; Charles Krance; Daniel Labeille; Rosette Lamont; Jay Levy; Alan Mandell; Steve Martin; Claudia Menza; Edna Meyers; Peter Murphy; Fred Neumann; J. D. O'Hara; Lois Overbeck; Donn Pennebaker; John Reilly; Laura Rièse; Rubin Rabinovitz; Andra Samelson; Elliseva Sayers; Robert Scanlan; Richard and Jeannette Seaver; Martin Segal; Lawrence Shainberg; Jean Schneider; Frederik Smith; Elizabeth Stockton; Jessica Tandy; Sheila Harvey Tanzer; William Targ; Bud Thorpe; David Wheeler; and Nicol Williamson.

Australia and New Zealand: Colin Duckworth; Lawrence Held; and B. Wongar. Austria: Hans Hiebel. Holland: Marius Buning and Karlijn Stoffels. Israel: Yossi Alfi; Mira Avrech; and Shimon Levy. Italy: Keir Elam; Guido Ferrarini; Gabriele Frasca; Luigi Majno; Connie Ricono; and Aldo Tagliaferri. Malta: John Bezzina. Poland: Jacek Gasiorowski; Marek Kedzierski; Antoni Libera. Portugal: Carlos Jardim (Madeira). Russia: Igor Pissarev. Spain: Patrick Bowles; Julio Castronuovo; Manolo Masti Fandos; Antonia Rogriguez-Gago; and John de St.-Jorre. Sweden: Beppe Arvidsson; Jan Jonson; Lüfti Özkök; and Percival. Switzerland: Wolfgang Fischer.

The staff of the following libraries and other institutions were most helpful and friendly: Mrs. J. Adams, Central Royal Parks; the estate of Richard Aldington; Patricia H. Allderidge, archivist and curator, Bethlem Royal Hospital; Robert J. Bertholf, curator, and Michael Basinski, Poetry/Rare Books Collection, University Libraries, State University of New York at Buffalo; Roger and Marie-Claire Boulez, Ecole Normale Supérieure; François Chapon, Bibliothèque Jacques Doucet; Phil Cronenwett, Dartmouth College Library, Hanover, New Hampshire; Julia Collieu, Museum Arts and Records Service, Leicestershire; Betty L. Corwen, Performing Arts Research Center, New York Public Library; Carolyn A. Davis, Syracuse University Library, Syracuse, New York: Kathryn DeGraff, Special Collections Librarian, De Paul University, Chicago; Gilian Furlong, University College, London, Library; Vincent Giroud, curator, The Beinecke Rare Book and Manuscript Library, Yale University; Bob Grattan, director, American Library in Paris; Elizabeth Gumerman, Grunwald Center for the Graphic Arts, University of California, Los Angeles; the late Holly Hall, Washington University Libraries, St. Louis, Missouri; Sidney Huttner, curator of Special Collections, and Lori Curtis, assistant curator, McFarlin Library, University of Tulsa; Jacqueline Kavanagh of the BBC Written Archives in Caversham; the estate of James Joyce; David Kochs, director of Special Collections, Karen Drickmayer, curator, and Shelley Cox, rare-book librarian, and her assistant, Bob Loewe, Morris Library, Southern Illinois University, Carbondale, Illinois; Gerard Lyne, Department of Manuscripts, National Library of Ireland; Alexandra Mason, Kenneth Spencer Research Library, University of Kansas Libraries, Lawrence, Kansas; Bernard Meehan, keeper of manuscripts, and Felicity Mahoney, Trinity College, Dublin Library; Timothy D. Murray, head, Special Collections, University of Delaware Library; Jeanne T. Newlin, curator, Harvard Theater Collection, Harvard College Library; Robert K. O'Neill, Burns Librarian, Boston College; Marek P. Prokop, head of the Département des Manuscrits, Bibliothèque Polonaise, Paris; Tom Staley, director, Carlton Lake, executive curator, Linda Ashton, John Fitzpatrick, and Kathy Henderson, Harry Ransom Humanities Research Center, University of Texas at Austin; Saundra Taylor, curator of manuscripts, Lilly Library, Indiana University, Bloomington, Indiana; and Dr. Geoffrey Wexler, University of California, San Diego. I also want to thank most warmly the Bibliothèque Nationale, Paris; the Boston University Library; Chatto and Windus; the Kent State University Library, Ohio; McMaster University, Hamilton, Canada; the Henry W. and Albert A. Berg

Collection at the New York Public Library; the Princeton University Library; Routledge; Secker and Warburg; The Board of Trinity College, Dublin; the Library, Victoria College, University of Toronto; and the Dublin Writers' Museum and Irish Writer's Centre.

Beckett's writings in English are quoted by permission of the Beckett Estate, Faber and Faber Ltd., and The Calder Education Trust, London, in England, and Grove/Atlantic Inc. in the United States of America and Canada, who hold the copyright to his published work. His writings in French are quoted by permission of the Beckett Estate and Les Editions de Minuit.

On a more personal level, I thank my former doctor, David Blomley, for medical advice on Beckett's various illnesses, and the always welcoming Corrayer family and staff at the Grand Hôtel des Balcons for never failing to find me a room even at late notice on my dozens of visits to Paris. I owe a huge debt of gratitude to my colleagues at the University of Reading, especially to John Pilling and Mary Bryden, for our frequent discussions about Beckett, and thank them for their advice on early drafts of chapters in this book. I am grateful to Michael Bott, the archivist, and his assistants, Francesca Hardcastle and Frances Miller, for their unfailing helpfulness and support. John Wieczorek, John Sandford, Graham Jackman (German), Zig Baranski (Italian), and Tim Ryder (Classics) have helped me with German, Italian, and Latin queries; Toby and Cecilia Bainton helped with Spanish and Portuguese. The previous vice chancellor, Dr. Ewan Page, allowed me leave to work on this book, and the present one, Professor Roger Williams, has maintained his predecessor's interest and support. The staff of the University Photographic Department, especially Simon Johnson and I. Maclean, have taken a keen interest in the illustrations for this book and done some admirable work on them. I have been helped at various times by Tony Warden, Ron Goodenough, and Roger Mansbridge, and by Brian Holden and his staff. My colleagues in the French Department and the secretarial staff have treated my prolonged absence with tolerance, on the surface at least. I thank Buddy Liyanage, Paul Janota, and Bob Redknap for their friendly advice and for keeping my computer systems going. Our friends Malcolm and Roberta Stewart and Rolf and Iris Kruger read an early draft and have given me invaluable advice. I thank them for their friendship. Anthony Harwood and Sally Riley have been a constant support. I am delighted to thank my editor at Bloomsbury Publishing plc in London for her enthusiastic support and her dedicated work on the book in its various stages, and Alice Mayhew and Roger Labrie, my splendid copy editors, Jolanta Benal and Lydia Buechler, and designer, Edith Fowler, at Simon & Schuster for seeing it into print in the United States. Finally, the second-largest debt that I have, next to that owed Samuel Beckett himself, is to my wife, Elizabeth, who left her own university post to become my full-time assistant. I cannot thank her enough for all her help both with the research and with the cutting of a lengthy first draft.

This list of acknowledgments is inevitably a long one with so large a book. But I am certain to have missed some whom I should have thanked. I can only apologize to them and promise to remedy the omission in a second edition.

FOR ELIZABETH

"THE USES OF POETRY"
by Anne Atik

For S.B. (13 April 1906–22 December 1989)

I

A Bible-reading man, he came and left
between two holy days he didn't much observe:
the Good Friday of his birth, near the Christmas of his death.
His life between, a pilgrim's progress with a smile
for what he saw along the way and wrote of,
oversleeping, age and hope and sloth.
Then saw, and wrote of, wrenched along the way,
age and hope and helpless weeping. But
he would have, reading those two states, rejected both
as most remotely holding but one part
or more than minute dose
of the inexpressible, whole truth
of how it is, it was.

II

He showed the shortest way to get across
a line like this:
crossed out such words as these to get to
speechlessness.
He crossed out rivers to get to their stones.
To get to the bottom, when the crisis is reached
and truth-telling begins.
Whatever he knew he knew to music.
He found the pace for misery,
matched distress to syncope, and joke
to a Beethoven stop at the punch line.
But thought that he'd failed to find failure's pulse.
What that says about failure,
music and us.

Contents

Preface

THIS BIOGRAPHY of Samuel Beckett could be said to have started its life twenty-five years ago. Organizing an exhibition to honor Beckett's work after he had been awarded the Nobel Prize for Literature and founding the Beckett Archive in the University of Reading, I met Beckett and got to know him — increasingly well over the years. As early as 1972, an American publisher invited me to write his biography. I declined when Beckett indicated that he would prefer me not to do this. He always hoped that it would be his work rather than his life that was placed under the microscope. So, over the next two decades, fascinated by his writing and particularly by his stage and television plays, I went on to write about that work, corresponding with him regularly and meeting him many times every year. In the meantime, a first biography was written by Deirdre Bair, which was published in 1978.

Approached again about writing his biography in 1989, I wrote to Beckett saying that this time, too, I would not proceed without an unambiguous yes from him. He replied with a one-line note: "To biography of me by you its Yes." When we met to discuss this, he told me that he regarded his life as separate from his work but that, since someone else would certainly be commissioned to write a new biography, he had decided to cooperate very fully with me, expressing satisfaction that his biographer would at least be someone who knew his work well. Finally, he wrote formally to my publisher that this was to be "his sole authorized biography" and pledged his active support. For five months we had weekly interviews and he provided me with letters of support, many names and addresses, and other vital sources of information. He allowed me to visit his cottage in Ussy and work in his study at 38 boulevard Saint-Jacques. Generously, as well as self-protectingly, he wrote that he did not want the book to be published until after his death and that of his wife, "because it will give you more freedom." Sadly, he died six months after I began research on the book.

Since then, no attempt has been made to censor or change what I have written. If the book is authorized, then, it is certainly not sanitized. His heirs, Edward and Caroline Beckett, and his literary executor and publisher, Jérôme Lindon, kindly continued the help that Beckett gave by lending me his student notes, a 1931–32 workbook, the notes that he made in the mid-1930s on his readings in philosophy, psychology, and literature, his appointment books from 1964 to 1986, many family photographs, and some material related to his work with the French Resistance. This was in addition to the scores of manuscripts and notebooks that Beckett had already donated to the Beckett Archive in Reading—now a charitable trust, the Beckett International Foundation—which were, of course, close at hand. The most exciting major new source, however (for Chapter Ten of this biography), was discovered by Edward Beckett in a trunk in Beckett's cellar after the writer's death. It consists of six long, tightly written notebooks, a detailed diary that Beckett kept of his travels in Germany in 1936–37.

Beckett kept scarcely any of the thousands of letters addressed to him. But his friends, with only two or three exceptions, made his letters to them available to me and, with his encouragement, talked to me freely in over a hundred interviews. So, as some measure of compensation for the absence of friends who had died in the period between the earlier biography and my own, I have had access to many more private letters and documents, as well as to correspondences only recently acquired by libraries (Alan Schneider's, at Boston College; A. J. Leventhal's, Ethna MacCarthy's, and Kay Boyle's, at the Harry Ransom Humanities Research Center in Austin, Texas; Nick Rawson's, at Trinity College, Dublin) and to the vast archive of Les Editions de Minuit. Believing that important issues have so far been passed over somewhat hastily, I have also used the major correspondence between Beckett and his friend and confidant Tom MacGreevy, rather differently from his earlier biographer, focusing on its relevance to his work.

Access to another major source of information helped to soften the blow that Beckett's death represented for me as his biographer. In the early 1960s, Beckett was friendly with Lawrence Harvey, an American professor of French and Italian. Harvey talked long into the night with Beckett on dozens of occasions about his life and his beliefs for his book, *Samuel Beckett, Poet and Critic*, and for a potential biography. Harvey took detailed notes on all his conversations and his widow, Sheila Harvey Tanzer, generously offered me unlimited use of this material. It made a difficult task much easier and I am most grateful to her.

In the first interview with Beckett intended specifically for this book, I said that although I understood perfectly well what he meant when he spoke of a separation between his life and his work, I could not agree that such a separation was as absolute as he claimed. I then adduced some of the images of his childhood in Ireland that appear often in his work, even in his late prose texts: a man and a boy walking hand in hand over the mountains; a larch tree turning green every year a week before the others; the sounds of stonecutters chipping away in the hills above his home. Dozens of such images could be cited, I maintained, which bridge his life and his work. At this point, Beckett nodded in agreement: "They're obsessional," he said, and went on to add several others.

In spite of his antipathy toward naturalism in literature, much of his early work quite unsurprisingly draws, like that of many a young writer, from his own personal experiences. But there is a vast difference between the way that such experiences are used and transformed in his earliest work and in his post–World War II writing. When I look at the relations between his life and his work, I have tried to make my approach respond to such changes, finding sources of inspiration at a much deeper level. In the later period, he does indeed seek to escape from any direct depiction of life by writing himself out of the text, by making the text self-referential or even, in some cases it would seem, virtually self-generating. Yet the life material remains. It is simply located at several removes below the surface. Beckett's late work seeks to explore the nature of being and is consequently less concerned with the superficial and the transitory. He has often been treated as if he were a cold formalist dealing in abstractions. Yet there is an intense concern in his writing with the physical, the concrete, the here and now. As the Irish novelist John Banville wrote in 1969: "Now that the Fifties murk has lifted and the labels—Absurdist, Existentialist, whatnot— have fallen into disuse, we can see how firmly his writings are rooted in the solid, the commonplace. . . . In his work the thing shines. All is immanence, thereness. The *moment* in Beckett carries an extraordinary weight" *(The Observer*, December 31, 1969). One of Beckett's best friends, the painter Bram van Velde, once said that "Beckett never wrote anything that he had not lived." By this van Velde was not alluding to simplistic life-work equivalences but, as I am, to experience at a deep level.

This book must speak for itself. I hope, however, to have brought out something new, in three areas in particular. The interests of Beckett that have been least explored in the past forty years of Beckett criticism are music and art. He was a passionate connoisseur of painting and sculpture, and his startling post-modern images appear to have been influenced by his love of the work of the Old Masters: Dürer, Rembrandt, Caravaggio, Mantegna, Antonello, Giorgione, Blake, Jack B. Yeats. While stressing the radically innovative nature of Beckett's writing, I have aimed to place it in an artistic as well as a literary continuum.

Beckett has often been labeled apolitical, and his attitudes have sometimes been misunderstood or misinterpreted. When, as an Irishman, he could have been neutral in World War II, he chose to join a Resistance cell of the British SOE and won the Croix de Guerre and the Médaille de la Reconnaissance Française. He was deeply committed to human rights; he firmly and totally opposed apartheid and was hostile from an early age to all forms of racism; he supported human rights movements throughout the world, including Amnesty International and Oxfam; he supported the freedom movement in Eastern Europe; and, although as a foreigner living in France he was wary of having his residential permit withdrawn, he was involved in a number of specific political cases.

Beckett has frequently been regarded as an arch-"miserabilist." This seems to me to be a misrepresentation of the man and a distortion of his work. Though he was intense and often depressed, the hundreds of letters from which I quote reveal a Beckett whom his friends knew extremely well: a witty, resilient man whose reflex response to adversity was often humor and the determination to go on. His work was his prime concern and his prime reason for keeping going: weighing every word, balancing every phrase, listening for every false note. This did not prevent him, however, from giving his understanding and undivided attention to his many friends. While devoting a lot of space to his work, I have tried to present the private man more than the public figure: complex, genuinely intellectual yet dismissive of pretentiousness, self-critical yet tolerant of others, and capable of inspiring deep affection in his friends and admirers.

Beckett would not have wanted to be treated like a saint. And I have not attempted to do so. If my own affection for him shines through in this book, it is, at least I hope, counterbalanced by the wish to paint the fuller portrait that he would have expected from me.

1

Images of Childhood
1906–15

1

SAMUEL BARCLAY BECKETT, who was to become one of the major writers of the twentieth century, was born at Cooldrinagh in Foxrock, County Dublin, on Good Friday, 13 April, 1906. There has been a lot of debate as to whether this was or was not the true date of his birth. His birth certificate records the date as the thirteenth of May, not April. And his father registered the event on June 14 —a month later, it is argued, than he would, or at least should, have done, if the birth had been in April. So it has been claimed that Beckett deliberately created the myth that he was born on Friday the thirteenth—and a Good Friday at that: a fitting date for someone so conscious of the Easter story and so aware of life as a painful Passion.[1]

The truth is much less dramatic. A mistake was clearly made. Everyone who knew Beckett as a child thought of his birthday as being on April 13. This never changed. But fortunately—and surely conclusively, even for those who believe in Beckett's propensity for myth-making—the birth was announced in the "Births and Deaths" columns of *The Irish Times* of April 16, 1906, that is a month before he was officially recorded as having been born. The confusion is ironic, but no more significant than that. One explanation is that his father simply forgot to register the birth, which is by no means impossible; a second is that there was some doubt as to whether the child would survive or not; a third is that the registrar of Stillorgan District Registry Office wrote down May instead of April. Beckett himself could throw no light on the reasons for the discrepancy, except to say that he could remember his mother telling him about it as an error when he was a child and to repeat that his birthday had always been celebrated on April 13.[2]

More interesting, and far more revealing, is how Beckett spoke about his birth. He claimed to have clear prenatal memories of life within his mother's womb. The womb is commonly thought of as a sheltered haven, where the fetus is protected from harm. Occasionally, that is how it is reflected in Beckett's writing; in the poem "Sanies I," for instance, which looks back to his birth, he writes nostalgically, "ah to be back in the caul now with no trusts / no fingers no spoilt love."[3] Yet the memories that, as an adult, he claimed to have of the womb, deriving probably from the period shortly before birth, were associated more often with feelings of being trapped and unable to escape, imprisoned and in pain.[4]

In his writings, Beckett has offered several different versions of his own birth. Characteristically, all of them are imbued with pain: "where I was born with a pop with the green of the larches / . . . oh the larches the pain drawn like a cork."[5] And the pain is associated not only with the single event of a difficult childbirth, but with the beginning of a long and painful odyssey. In the fullest account, in his late prose text *Company*, his father goes off alone on Good Friday morning for a lengthy tramp in the mountains south of Dublin. On that particular day he is inspired, however, not just by his love of walking and wild scenery, but by his general aversion to the "pains and general unpleasantness of labour and delivery."[6] He carries a flask and a package of his favorite egg sandwiches. At midday, he stops to rest and to relish the sandwiches, gazing out to sea from the summit of a mountain. On his return home at nightfall, he learns from the maid that the labor, which has been in progress for ten hours, is still in full swing. So he walks into the garage and sits in his car, wondering anxiously what can possibly be happening. Eventually, a maid runs out of the house to tell him that it is all over at last. "Over!" comments the narrator of this story ironically.

Although the coincidence of his own birth with Good Friday, the thirteenth, was not created by Beckett, it was assimilated by him into a view of life that sees birth as intimately connected with suffering and death and that sees life as a painful road to be trod.

2

BECKETT'S FIRST NAME, Samuel, came from that of his grandfather on his mother's side, Samuel Robinson Roe. No one in the family seems to know where his middle name, Barclay, came from. Samuel Roe, a large, jovial man with an enormous beard, was widely respected in the farming community of County Kildare and much revered on the corn exchange in Dublin.[7]

The Roe family can be traced back locally in Leixlip as far as the late seventeenth century.[8] Several of Grandfather Samuel's forebears appear to have been land surveyors. But his own father was the Reverend Samuel Roe, and one of his brothers was the vicar of Gartree.[9] Samuel himself became a miller and owned a grain mill, Newbridge Mills, in Celbridge. On the outskirts of Leixlip, he also owned a very grand house, almost a mansion, dating from 1760, with imposing pillars at the front door, a flight of stone steps and a cast-iron balustrade, stables, a large, walled garden, and an orchard, overlooking the river Liffey with the famous Salmon Leap (from which Leixlip takes its name) at the foot of its sixty-five acres of grounds. The house, known locally as Roe Hall, was actually called Cooldrinagh House,[10] a name that comes from the Gaelic and means "the back of the blackthorn hedge (or copse)."[11] So when the man who was to become Samuel Beckett's father decided to build a substantial house for himself and his bride, May Roe, in 1902 in Foxrock, a fashionable village to the south of Dublin, they named the house after her family home. In the 1870s, when Beckett's mother was a girl, the family was exceedingly well-to-do and employed many servants and gardeners.[12]

Samuel Robinson Roe's wife, Anne or Annie, was known to her grandchildren as "Little Granny," in contrast to "Big Granny," who was Beckett's father's mother, Frances, née Crothers. Physically, this was apt since, as a family photograph taken about 1910 shows, she was a tiny, frail woman. Born in December 1839, she was seventy when Beckett was four.[13] After her husband died, she always dressed somberly and primly in black. She was an extremely devout Christian. Her grandchild Sheila Roe Page could remember saying to her once how much she adored chocolates. "You shouldn't love something to eat, my dear," answered Little Granny. "You should only love God."[14]

It was with the Roe side of the family that Beckett identified a Quaker background, although he descended both on his mother's and his father's side from Protestant families living in a mainly Catholic society. Annie Roe survived for several decades after her husband's death and kept in constant touch with Beckett's mother. Beckett recalled that "she used to come and see us. And actually came to stay in the house — and died in the house. Granny. 'Little Granny.' A little, wizened woman, always embroidering."[15] Annie Roe also came from a well-to-do Leixlip family called Belas. Her father, George Henry Belas, was a solicitor. She married Samuel Robinson Roe in July 1863.[16] In 1934, when Samuel Beckett was looking for a name with which to sign his pseudonymous article "Recent Irish Poetry," he chose that of Andrew Belis, going back three generations on the Roe side.[17]

Little Granny gave birth to a large family. Beckett's mother, who was christened Maria Jones Roe but was known widely as May, was born on March 1, 1871.[18] She had three older brothers, George Henry (born 1865), John Littledale, born the following year, and Edward Price (born 1869), who was the nearest in age and the closest to her in her affections.[19] In later years, he became the Roe uncle best known to May's own two children. They called him Uncle Ned. He was the father of Molly, Sheila, and Jack, three cousins who were to play an important part in Beckett's early life.[20] But May also had a sister called Annie Frances (born in 1873) and another called Esther Maiben, who was seven years younger than May.

The death of Samuel Roe, at the age of fifty-four, in Cooldrinagh House on 14 October, 1886 dramatically changed the life of Beckett's mother, May. It has been suggested that, as the daughter of a well-to-do gentleman, she did not need to work and could have confined herself to working for charities, as many gentlewomen did.[21] Before her father's death, that would probably have been true. After it, Beckett said it certainly was not.[22] Although the Roe family was indeed once wealthy, Samuel's grain business took a serious downward turn in the early 1880s. When he died, it was believed in the family that he left sizable debts, although a record in the Index of Wills and Administrations in the National Archives shows that the sum of £17,500 was granted to his solicitors. But this was probably assigned to pay off his creditors, for when his wife, Annie Roe, died in 1924, she left only £130.

His granddaughter Sheila Page explained the reversal in the family fortunes by changes that had occurred in the world trade in grain: in the late 1870s and early 1880s, the Americans and Canadians began to export grain in huge quantities to flood a European market that traditionally had been the main customer for the grain grown in Ireland. This increased competition and brought down world prices.[23] To this explanation of the Roes' fall into comparative hard times, Samuel Beckett added that, in order to compete more efficiently,

> the old man, Samuel, had just invested a lot of money in new equipment and then he died, leaving quite a numerous family, with my mother not the youngest. I don't know exactly where she came. But they were left without much money. So, at the age of fifteen, she had to make a living. That's how she came to be a nurse in the Adelaide Hospital where she met my father. That's how from the family prosperity they were all brought down.[24]

May Roe was educated in Ballymena at the Moravian Mission School, where, by all accounts, she was not an easy pupil. Samuel's somewhat rebellious nature and stubborn streak of independence probably had their source in May's own mercurial temperament. May seems to have been sent home — whether temporarily or more permanently is not clear from this distance in time — for chatting to a young man over the school wall.[25] Such behavior was not condoned in so strict an environment. And it is most unlikely from what is known of Little Granny that her daughter would have received anything other than disapproval and possibly even further punishment when she returned home. As she grew older, May herself was to become extremely strict and demanding.

May grew tall with a long face, a large nose and ears, and a formidable glare. Even as a young woman she appeared somewhat masculine. She had an imposing bearing, a regal elegance, and a strong, forceful personality. She suffered fools badly and could be very forthright in her criticisms when she felt that someone was in the wrong. But she had a keen sense of the ridiculous, laughed at her husband's jokes, and was capable herself of the occasional shaft of acerbic wit. She was an eminently practical woman, and when she married Bill Beckett in 1901, she ran the new Cooldrinagh with ruthless efficiency and a rod of iron. She had "a dramatic kind of temperament"[26] and a violent temper and used to have fierce arguments with one of her two maids, Mary Foran, when they would shout at each other at the top of their voices in scenes that May's parlor maid described as "holy murder between them."[27] Then she would dismiss Mary, only to take her back a few days later, for her outbursts of temper subsided almost as quickly as they flared up. She also had a genuine strain of unselfishness and kindness, giving practical help to her relatives, visiting sick neighbors, or maintaining a friendship with a widow long after the husband, who had been a friend of Bill, had died. Her behavior seems to have been dominated, however, by a rigid code of conduct and a concept of decorum that promised trouble once her second son started to behave in rather wild, bohe-mian ways of which she strongly disapproved. She used to have moods of dark depression that would last for days on end, when she was extremely difficult to deal with: "strange," "ill-tempered," "bottled up," "tricky," and "difficult" were among the words used by those trying to convey this side of her personality.[28]

3

MAY'S HUSBAND, Bill Beckett, also came from a largish family of five boys and one girl. The third child in order of birth, Henry Herbert, called Harry, born in 1880, was hardly ever talked about in the family.[29] "He wasn't mentioned. I think I met Harry once," said Beckett. "A thin grey man. Not a bit like the jovial brothers."[30] But Beckett knew the other members of his father's family well and, because they stayed in Ireland, they played a far more important part in his life than did the Roe uncles and aunts, who emigrated to Honolulu, Canada, Africa, or England and, with the single exception of Edward Price Roe, were scarcely known to him.

The Becketts descended from Huguenots who emigrated from France probably in the eighteenth century. Beckett's great-great-grandfather William rose rapidly to become head of Richard Atkinson and Company, "Poplin Manu-facturers to the Queen, Her Royal Highness the Duchess of Kent, His Excel-lency the Lord Lieutenant, the Irish Court and the Most Illustrious Order of St. Patrick." From 31 College Green, Dublin, it produced "gold and silver tissue poplins for gentlemen's waistcoats," "brocaded poplin vestings," and "silk for clergymen's and lawyers' gowns."[31] William Beckett married Elizabeth Hartston. Their son James, born in 1803, followed his father as a weaver of silk and poplin. He married Eleanor Whitehead in 1826 and had eleven children by her, the first five of whom (four girls and a boy) died as children, two as infants. The family were by this time extremely well-to-do and had their own family crest, with "Prodesse Civibus" ("Serve the Citizens") as its motto. The genial, heavily sideburned James was a pillar of Dublin society, so well respected for his integ-rity that he served for ten years as the secretary of the Liberal Friendly Brothers Society.[32]

William Frank Beckett, born in November 1843, was the fourth of Elea-nor's children to survive. William was the grandfather whom Samuel Beckett knew in Ballsbridge when he was a small boy and who used to come to the Foxrock Cooldrinagh from time to time to dine with the family. A Beckett family photograph shows him at sixty, burly in build, with a full beard, looking benign and proud in the presence of his whole family.

Both William and his elder brother, James, became master builders, main-taining the respectable image that the earlier weaver Becketts had established in middle-class Dublin society. In partnership for a long time as J. and W. Beckett Builders, one of their first big contracts was to build part of Dublin's Adelaide Hospital.[33] Later, they constructed several important civic buildings in the city, including the National Library of Ireland and the Science and Art Museum (now the National Museum) which still stand imposingly on Kildare Street.[34] By the turn of the century, both James and his brother William had amassed a considerable amount of money.

The partnership between the two brothers was dissolved, however, soon after the completion of the National Library.[35] Then Beckett's grandfather William went on to concentrate on buying land and building large, impressive houses on it in the city of Dublin and its growing suburbs.[36] He handed on many of his professional contacts in the building trade and with architects, as well as his keen business acumen, to his first surviving son, Samuel Beckett's father, Bill. "Willie," as he was widely known, was to become a busy and respected quantity surveyor, estimating building costs and buying materials.

Beckett's grandfather married Frances Crothers. Frances, known as Fannie Beckett, had a sensitive, artistic face with a piercing stare that was inherited by her eldest son and by his sons. She was extremely musical and wrote songs herself, as well as adapting pieces for the piano and setting to music various poems, including Alfred, Lord Tennyson's "Crossing the Bar."[37] But she lost three children who died in infancy. It is said that she was shut up with them in strict quarantine while they were ill and dying to prevent the illness from spreading any further.[38] After the deaths, she was often found wandering around the streets of Dublin quite distraught and much the worse for whiskey: "Do you blame her for being driven to drink after all that?" Beckett used to ask members of his family.

Grandmother Beckett passed on her musical interests and her talent to two of her children, Gerald and Frances, also known as Fanny (or, more commonly, Cissie, to distinguish her from her mother). Gerald studied medicine at Trinity College, Dublin, and became the county medical officer for Wicklow. He was a talented pianist, who enjoyed playing piano duets with his young nephew Samuel. Gerald's son John (a pianist, the conductor of Musica Reservata, and a composer), remembered them playing together:

> My father was a good pianist, a very good sight-reader, but also the sort of person who could go to a cinema and hear a song and come back and play it. The piano was in the dining-room of our house and he and Sam would play for hours. My father didn't really approve of Sam's playing because he used to play the bass part. For the catch is that the bass-player controls the sustaining pedal which must catch sound at the right moment and, even more important, must release it at the right moment, otherwise you get a shambles. And Sam didn't understand that. This used to offend my father — not that he said anything about it. . . . They would have played what we had in the house. We had volumes of Haydn symphonies, Haydn quartets, Mozart symphonies, Beethoven symphonies and our favourites were arrangements for four hands of the late quartets of Mozart. I remember the oblong volumes, in blue binding; we loved those particularly.

. . . I also remember we had a volume of Mozart symphonies, again oblong.[39]

The daughter, Aunt Cissie, also played the piano well. She loved Mozart and Beethoven sonatas and Chopin's piano pieces. But she was particularly good at picking out popular music-hall numbers, songs like "I Feel So Funny When the Moon Comes Out."[40] She played, mostly by ear, songs chosen from a vast repertoire of Irish and English songs. But she displayed even more talent as an artist and was sent to the Dublin Metropolitan School of Art, where she was a fellow pupil of Beatrice and Dorothy Elvery and Estella Solomons and was taught painting by Walter Osborne and William Orpen.[41] Contrary to the wishes of her family, she married a Jewish art dealer, William "Boss" Sinclair, and she and the Boss were to play what was probably a crucial part in Beckett's own early artistic development.

Beckett's athletic prowess was prefigured in his uncles, "the jovial brothers" Gerald and James, as well as in his father, who won cups for his swimming. Both of his uncles were excellent sportsmen. Gerald played rugby, first for Wesley College, then for Ireland. He was a scratch golfer too, good enough to be captain of the golf club at Greystones. But he seems to have had a relaxed, uncompetitive approach to sports that was similar to that of his nephew. His daughter Ann summed up this attitude rather well:

> He swam for the love of swimming rather than beating people. Jim was much more competitive than he was. Father was a rather solitary athlete, if you know what I mean. He liked ambling around, walking and playing golf. He used to love coming home from work and going off to the outer nine in the golf links at Greystones just, as he used to say, to knock a ball about for a few hours.[42]

Gerald was a quiet, thoughtful man with wide-ranging interests for whom Beckett felt a great deal of affection. He had a dry sense of humor and, like Beckett's own father, had the habit of applying humorous nicknames to local people. He called his young nephew Samuel "the frog footman" because of his way of walking with his feet splayed outward. He was quite irreligious and used to describe life morbidly as "a disease of matter."[43]

Gerald's brother James was highly competitive and won numerous trophies, cups, and medals, which were kept in a display case in their house on Fitzwilliam Place. He "was captain of the Old Wesley [Rugby] team that won the Leinster Cup two years running; he captained the Dublin hospitals against the London hospitals at least twice, played several times for the province of Leinster and later, in the 1920s, was an international referee."[44] But swimming was his real strength. He represented Ireland at water polo internationally for twenty-five years and held national records over all distances in the first decade of the century.[45] The hundred-yard freestyle record he set in 1909 was not equaled for thirty-five years. Beckett's close friend A. J. Leventhal, always known as Con, used to say, "All the Becketts can either sing or swim."[46] James had a wicked sense of humor and used to delight in the ridiculous. Like Gerald, he studied medicine at Trinity College, but went on to become an anesthetist. Samuel Beckett never felt as close to him as he did to Gerald.[47]

The youngest brother, Howard, was called the Kraken by his elder brothers, Poyntz by James, and Eyebrows Beckett by the younger generation, on account of his very bushy eyebrows. He was far less outgoing than his two sporting brothers ("He was a loner; he wasn't the hail-fellow-well-met the others were," commented Beckett) and was rather looked down on by the other members of the family.[48] He had been in the Ambulance Corps during the First World War and witnessed horrors that were thought to have affected him deeply. Beckett could "remember him coming home on leave. Coming to Cooldrinagh in uniform. He had a dreadful time. He was more or less pushed into it, black-mailed into it by the family. To join up."[49] Like many young unmarried men of the time, Howard lived for a long time with his father, the retired building contractor, until he married late and had one son.

Beckett became quite fond of his uncle Howard, who played a distinctive role in developing some of the more intellectual of his nephew's interests when he was in his teens. For Howard was an excellent chess player and acquired a high reputation in Dublin by beating the famous chess grandmaster, José Raúl Capablanca y Graupera, the Cuban diplomat who was world chess champion from 1921 to 1927. This happened during an exhibition match in Dublin, when Capablanca was, admittedly, playing against several opponents at the same time. Nevertheless, it represented a remarkable achievement for a local player. Samuel Beckett, who had been taught to play the game by his brother Frank, and had quickly become an addict, used to play chess with his uncle when he went to call on his grandfather in Ballsbridge or whenever Howard accompanied his father to Cooldrinagh. Many of his best moves were learned from Howard. Chess was to play an important part in Beckett's life and appears several times in his writing. His uncle also encouraged Beckett's early interest in the cinema by taking him and his brother to films showing in Dublin or in a little cinema in Dún Laoghaire.[50] Film, too, remained one of Beckett's enduring interests.

4

SAMUEL BECKETT'S FATHER, Bill Beckett, was in his late twenties when he first met May Roe. He was handsome and thickset, almost six feet tall, with a thick, dark mustache. Like his younger brothers, he was very athletic, an excellent swimmer and a fair tennis player and golfer.[51] He was very much of a man's man, a hail-fellow-well-met.[52] A close friend of Bill's firstborn son, Frank, said of his father that he "was a terrific character, a charmer, a real charmer. . . . Tremendously energetic, large in figure, heavily built. All he knew about was to get on with things."[53] He had a highly developed sense of humor, a ready wit, and a bonhomie that more sensitive souls found somewhat overbearing. This was accompanied by a fiery temper that could flare up quickly from time to time. "He was known to have found a cat in his bed and [loathing cats as he did] thrown it out of the window. . . . He'd get angry very easily." [54] Beckett himself described his father as "absolutely non-intellectual. He left school at fifteen. He was taken away. Couldn't stay. And was put to work. He had a big case of books, Dickens and Encyclopedias that he never opened. He used to read Edgar Wallace." [55] And it was with a mixture of amusement and envy that he described his father's way of reading in his early novel *Dream of Fair to Middling Women*:

> His father assembled his arsenal of cold pipes, turned on the book, connected up, and it did the rest. That was the way to read — find out the literary voltage that suits you and switch on the current of the book. That was the mode that everyone had known, the corduroy trousers and bunch of blue ribbon mode. Then it goes. . . . To the convalescent, well again and weak, the old mode may come back; or in winter, in the country, at night, in bad weather, far from the cliques and juntas. But his Father had never lost it. He sat motionless in the armchair under the singing lamp, absorbed and null. The pipes went out, one after another. For long spells he heard nothing that was said in the room, whether to him or not. If you asked him next day what the book was like he could not tell you. [56]

In the early decades of the century it was customary for men of a certain social standing in Dublin to meet for drinks and a friendly chat in gentlemen's clubs, rather than drink in pubs, which remained the preserve of the working class. A lot of business was done in the clubs, too. Beckett's father, like his own father before him, was a member of several such clubs. When he went in to work, for instance, he used to leave his sports Delage at the Royal Irish Automobile Club on Dawson Street and go there for a drink or a pot of tea after work. May was also a member and used to meet him there sometimes to be driven home after she had been shopping in Dublin. [57] Or he would lunch at the Kildare Street Club, where he was also a member, with a friend like the architect Fred Hicks, or another good family friend called Fry. In the early years of his marriage, according to Beckett, he would entertain some of his male friends at home: "My father used sometimes to have bridge parties when I was young with his men friends. I remember them sitting round the card-table with plenty of drinks by the fire. I was sometimes allowed to sit and watch. That was before he took to going up to his little room to smoke his pipe and read his Edgar Wallace." [58]

Bill found a lot of satisfaction in his work, throwing himself with apparently inexhaustible energy into creating his business contacts once Medcalf, the senior partner in the quantity surveying firm, had died. Fortunately, he was not deskbound, as his job took him out to building sites, where he found even more pleasure in keeping up with the progress that was being made on a house and admiring its completed appearance than he did in arranging the initial deal.

After working hard, he used to relax by playing golf at Foxrock Golf Club (where he was captain in 1920) and at Carrickmines, or, on Saturday night, playing more bridge in a regular bridge school at the golf club.[59]

He was interested in horse racing, although his son commented:

> I don't remember him betting. He liked the races. But he wasn't a regular there. He knew Fred Clarke, the Clerk of the Course. He gave my father permission to take a little back entrance of the racecourse. Then he walked through it on his way home. But I don't remember him betting on the horses. I remember being on the bridge at Foxrock Station. You could see the horses well from there. They came very close to the station at that point. The railings were nearby.[60]

When Bill Beckett went to the races with Fred Clarke, who became general manager of the racecourse and moved into nearby Leopardstown House, they used to watch the racing from a privileged official position in the stand. Sometimes Beckett accompanied him. In *All That Fall*, Beckett's first radio play, Mrs. Rooney reflects his familiarity with the Leopardstown Racecourse when she evokes "the entire scene, the hills, the plain, the racecourse with its miles and miles of white rails and three red stands, the pretty little wayside station."[61]

Bill Beckett adored the great outdoors. He used to dive from the rocks at Sandycove into the famous, deep "Gentlemen Only" Forty-Foot, or he would swim, often with his two sons, at some of the numerous bathing places around Dublin Bay. But his regular pastime was walking. He loved the Dublin mountains and, on Sunday mornings and public holidays, accompanied by the family's Kerry Blue terrier, he used to go for walks in the country that were three or four times longer than most people could manage. When first married, and before he bought a car to drive in to Dublin to his office at number 6 Clare Street, according to Beckett, he regularly used to take the train as far as Rathfarnham and then complete the hour-and-a-half-long walk home in time to sit down to a hearty dinner.

It was for his straightforwardly affectionate, uncomplicated, chummy relationship with his two sons and for the simple things that they shared that Beckett best remembered his father. "They sort of understood each other," said Sheila Page. "They played golf together and went for wonderful walks. They were absolutely tuned in."[62] One of the most moving images in Beckett's late prose is that of an old man and a boy walking hand in hand across the foothills.[63]

Although, like many heads of Edwardian families, Bill Beckett kept his feelings mostly under strict control and was not overtly affectionate, he was not lacking in emotion. Before he ever met Beckett's mother, he had fallen head over heels in love with a young woman named Eva Murphy, the daughter of a fairly wealthy Catholic, William Martin Murphy. Mary Manning, a friend of the family, recalled how her mother, Susan, then a Bennett, had similarly fallen in love with Eva Murphy's brother. The Murphys were fiercely opposed to either of their children marrying into two such deeply Protestant families: "The Murphy man said he would despise his son who was a lawyer if he married my mother and his daughter could go on to the streets, he would never talk to her again, if she married Bill Beckett. It ruined both their lives. Bill never got over it, never, and neither did mother. They were madly in love, both of them."[64] She recounted how Bill would call for her mother and herself and take them out for a drive in his car, long after both of them were married and after her own father had died. As they drove past a castellated mansion near Rathgar, she heard her mother announce angrily that this was "where the murder took place." "What murder?" Mary asked her mother. "William Martin Murphy's house. He murdered love. Didn't he, Bill?" The driver nodded in silent agreement. Apparently not only had both son and daughter been forbidden from marrying the Protestants but the daughter had then been married off to an old widower who, Mary Manning heard her mother mutter darkly, "did certain things with her . . . not only in bed but on the dining room table." "Dirty wretch," growled Bill Beckett.[65]

The wound went deep; a stay in the Adelaide Hospital may have resulted from a depression occasioned by the abrupt guillotining of this misbegotten love affair. It was at the hospital that Bill first met May Roe, who was working there as either a nurse or a nursing aide on his ward. May was at her best in periods of crisis, and her practical skills, no-nonsense approach, and genuine kindness and thoughtfulness seem to have quickly won over someone who was vulnerable to the attentions of this capable woman who offered him support as well as affection — and who came from a respectable Protestant family. She responded to his friendly banter, and in a matter of weeks they were engaged, and, within the year, married.

They shared a love of the countryside, although May was not a great walker like Bill. And so, early in their marriage, Bill bought a motorbike and sidecar, a Sparkbrook, in which May used to travel with a scarf tied firmly around her head, while one of the boys rode pillion. Later on, Bill acquired a Fiat two-seater car and, in the 1920s and early 1930s, he bought the far more expensive Delage.[66] The impression given by Bill and May as a couple was of a marriage that was never seriously under strain but was based on habit as much as on affection, with each of them, increasingly, pursuing his or her own interests: Bill in his business, sports, walking, and playing cards; May in the running of the household, the welfare of her sons, the affairs of Tullow Parish Church, and local events such as dog shows. She enjoyed gardening and kept pets: her dogs and a donkey called Kish.[67]

5

THEIR FIRST CHILD, Frank Edward, was born on July 26, 1902, soon after they moved into the new house in Foxrock; their second son, Samuel Barclay, was born almost four years later. The new Cooldrinagh was a fine house in which to bring up two lively boys. It had large, beautiful gardens, lawns, and a tennis court. There was an acre of land, with a summerhouse, a double garage, and outbuildings in which May kept her donkey. To the left of the house was a little spinney in which the children built tents out of branches covered by leaves and a rug; they played at wigwams or lay there reading their storybooks.[68] The larches growing in the garden figure prominently in Beckett's poetry, prose, and drama. They denote the season of Beckett's birth ("Born dead of night. Sun long sunk behind the larches. New needles turning green"[69]). But they also remind him of his childhood ("Larches however he knew, from having climbed them as a little fat boy, and a young plantation of these, of a very poignant reseda, caught his eye now on the hillside"[70]). As in his novel *Watt*, one of the larches really did, according to Beckett,[71] turn "green every year a week before the others" in the spring and "brown a week before the others"[72] in the autumn.

The spacious, Tudor-style house was built on a favored corner site at the junction of Kerrymount Avenue and the Brighton Road. It was designed by Beckett's father's friend Frederick Hicks, a well-known architect and surveyor with an office in South Frederick Street in Dublin.[73] Around the red-tiled outside porch grew a heavily scented lemon verbena that is evoked many times in Beckett's writing.[74]

The sitting hall, as it was called on the original plans, had (and still has) a large, elegant fireplace with small rectangular dark green tiles both on the hearth and on the fireplace itself; an elaborately carved wooden surround frames an open fire. Heavy curtains were drawn across the room to separate the hall from the doorway when the family wanted to sit on the huge settee that stood in the bay window in front of a log fire. Leopardskins were spread across the polished wooden floor, and on the wall hung the long spiral horns of the kudu that May's brother Edward Price Roe had brought back from Africa. On one wall were a pair of large crossed swords and a brass helmet.[75] When the curtains were drawn to shut out drafts, the hall managed to feel quite cozy, in spite of the dark brown wooden paneling. On the side of the hall opposite to the staircase, Sam and Frank scratched their signatures, which are still faintly discernible. To the left on the ground floor was the drawing room, in which the piano was kept, next to a dining room with a large table and a few conventional pictures, including one of a vase of yellow tulips. May Beckett loved flowers, and the sitting room was often perfumed by a large blue bowl of sweet peas.[76]

The room in which May gave birth to the two boys was on the second floor. It has a large bow window that extends the bow of the drawing room below. As Beckett wrote in *Company*, the window "looked west to the mountains. Mainly west. For being bow it looked also a little south and a little north. Necessarily. A little south to more mountain and a little north to foothill and plain."[77] The two brothers shared an attic bedroom on the top floor where first the nurse, then the maid also had a room. Close by, said Beckett, "there was a place with the water tank, where the water supply was stored. Frank turned it into a workshop. And he used to shut himself there and make things: you know, wood and so on."[78] Frank was by far the more practical of the two boys, and Sam's role often turned out to be one of holding things for his older brother, watching him devotedly as he worked, and learning from him all he knew about woodwork.

For the first three years of his life, Beckett's brother was looked after by a nurse called Annie Bisset. Then, when Annie left to get married and Sam was born, May employed a young woman named Bridget Bray, who came from the neighboring county of Meath. She was known as Sam's nurse and remained with the Becketts for almost twelve years before she too left, to marry a gardener called Cooney. During Sam's childhood, she lived in the house at Cooldrinagh and exercised an important influence on her young charge.

Bridget was a friendly, loquacious Catholic, rich in stories, folktales, and homespun wisdom. She was a big woman with a "strawberry nose" and an expression that, in Beckett's own words, had "the quality of ruined granite."[79] She sucked cloves or peppermint. The boys used to call her Bibby, a name that figures several times in Beckett's writings: in Winnie's story of Milly and the mouse in *Happy Days*, for example, and again in *Texts for Nothing III*, where, nostalgically, the narrator recreates her baby talk: "She'll say to me, Come, doty, it's time for bye-bye. I'll have no responsibility, she'll have all the responsibility, her name will be Bibby, I'll call her Bibby, if only it could be like that. Come, ducky, it's time for yum-yum."[80]

More than half a century later, Beckett still remembered some of his nurse's common sayings and remonstrances. As a small child, he was often taciturn and would reply to her questions with a hesitant, irritating "Well, well . . ." "How many wells make a river?" Bibby would ask him sharply. He was often obstinate too, refusing stubbornly to eat his dinner whenever he did not feel like it. Her picturesquely alliterative response first intrigued, then annoyed him: "One day you'll follow a crow for a crust," she used to say.[81] Along with his mother, she was the main source for the commonplace sayings that appear (and are ironically undercut) in Beckett's writing: "If a thing was worth doing at all it was worth doing well, that was a true saying" and "We live and learn, that was a true saying."[82] Yet Bibby had a great sense of fun; rainy days were made sunny as she taught Beckett to recite rhymes and catches. "Rain, rain, go to Spain" was one that they chanted in unison, the little boy dancing around the nursery.[83] Sometimes she went too far and, instead of amusing the children, terrified them — as when, on one occasion, she dressed up as an old man in a dark overcoat and hat and chased them around the garden.[84] At night, Bibby told her charge fairy tales of old Meath that are alluded to in Beckett's poem "Serena II":

> the fairy-tales of Meath ended
> so say your prayers now and go to bed
> your prayers before the lamps start to sing behind the larches
> here at these knees of stone
> then to bye-bye on the bones[85]

Every night, the two boys recited their prayers before climbing into bed. One was the Lord's Prayer; the other was "God bless dear Daddy, Mummy,

Frank, Bibby and all that I love and make me a good boy for Jesus Christ sake Armen," which is reproduced almost verbatim in *Dream of Fair to Middling Women*.[86] Beckett was taught his prayers by his devout mother, who mostly supervised prayer time herself. A photograph of Beckett aged two or three, kneeling in a nightshirt on a chintz cushion at his mother's knee, his tiny hands clasped firmly together in hers, shows this nightly ritual being practiced.[87]

6

As HE GREW UP, Sam was told of several occasions when his mother and his nurse had been seriously concerned about the state of his health. As a baby he was usually very quiet. But one day he cried inconsolably. His mother, a former nurse, realized that something was physically wrong with the infant but could not establish what. It was some time before a doctor could call, who, after a prolonged examination, eventually diagnosed otitis, a very painful inflammation of the ear. More seriously, when still young enough to be sleeping in a cradle, Beckett was discovered lying unconscious at the foot of the steep wooden staircase that led up to the children's rooms. How he had fallen remained a total mystery. But it was, of course, poor Bibby who received the blame for not watching him carefully enough.[88]

As a little boy, Samuel became very nervous at night and would go to sleep only with a night-light and his favorite teddy bear. "He had a teddy-bear called 'Baby Jack' and they had brass bedsteads. And it was always tied to the top of the bed, with almost no stuffing left in it at all," said Sheila Page.[89] These details find their way almost unaltered into Beckett's account of Jacques Moran Junior in *Molloy*:

> My son's window was faintly lit. He liked sleeping with a night-light beside him. I sometimes felt it was wrong of me to let him humour this weakness. Until quite recently he could not sleep unless he had his woolly bear to hug. When he had forgotten the bear (Baby Jack) I would forbid the night-light.[90]

He and Frank used to lie in their beds listening to sounds that stayed with Beckett all his life: "the barking of the dogs, at night, in the clusters of hovels up in the hills, where the stone-cutters lived, like generations of stone-cutters before them;"[91] the clanging of the iron gates in a storm at the end of the drive; the clatter of horses' hooves on the road beyond the garden; even the sighing of every tree close to the house. Beckett seems to have shared the extraordinarily acute sense of hearing that he ascribed to the narrator in *Malone Dies:* "I could tell from one another, in the outcry without, the leaves, the boughs, the groaning trunks, even the grasses and the house that sheltered me. . . . There was nothing, not even the sand on the paths, that did not utter its cry."[92]

On weekday mornings, he was wakened by the chink of a metal can on a big brown-and-white pottery jug as the cheery, whistling milkman ladled out the daily pints—he never forgot the extra ladleful, or "tilly," for the dog—on the doorstep of the tradesmen's entrance to Cooldrinagh or by the sound of the postman skidding up the gravel drive on his bicycle. This often brought Samuel to the window to see which of the Foxrock postmen was delivering the mail. For one of them, Thompson by name, cycled with his longhaired spaniel balanced on the front carrier of his bicycle. This postman was called Pop-a-lot in the village, for after a heavy night's drinking he was usually left with a residue of wind that escaped regularly and noisily from him as he lifted his leg over the crossbar and settled down again onto the saddle.[93] The other postman was Bill Shannon, known to be very musical and prone to whistling loudly as he delivered the morning mail with its colorful stamps on letters from May's relatives in several different countries.[94]

Foreign stamps were swooped on eagerly by the boys, who spent a lot of time collecting. Following in Frank's footsteps again, although with less dedication, Beckett started his first stamp album at the age of nine. That album still exists. It was handed on to a younger schoolboy named Dick Walmesley-Cotham, who used to visit his grandfather during the holidays at a house called Cardonagh, which faced Cooldrinagh. Inside the front cover, the album bears Beckett's childish signature with the date 25 August 1918. A table inside the back cover notes that, on October 24, 1915, he had only 71 stamps but that, on April 10, 1917, a few days before his eleventh birthday, he had as many as 574 stamps.[95] Already the young Samuel Beckett was displaying the meticulousness that was to be one of his most striking characteristics as an adult.

He and Frank used to sit together at the big dining room table or sprawl, legs outspread, on the carpet earnestly studying, then delicately mounting their stamps into separate stamp albums with the traditional tools of the stamp collector: magnifying glass, tweezers, perforation gauge, and gummed mounts. It was Frank who taught Sam how to reveal hidden watermarks by placing the stamp in a little black tray filled with spirit. Together, they pored over the pages of the latest catalogue from the famous London stamp sellers, Stanley Gibbons. They also used to accompany each other to Mountrath, the house of a near neighbor, Mr. Coote, who managed an insurance company. Mrs. Coote was a good friend of their mother and the source for the "small thin sour woman" who comes to tea to be served "wafer-thin bread and butter" sandwiches in *Company*.[96] Mr. Coote was a dedicated, highly professional philatelist and obtained many of Frank's rarer stamps for him.[97] For Beckett remembered his brother as being a much keener collector than he ever was himself.[98]

Memories of such hours spent browsing, but also bickering, with Frank over their favorite stamps insinuate themselves into Beckett's mature writing. Jacques Moran asks in *Molloy*:

> Do you know what he was doing? Transferring to the album of duplicates, from his good collection properly so-called, certain rare and valuable stamps which he was in the habit of gloating over daily and could not bring himself to leave, even for a few days. Show me your

new Timor, the five reis orange, I said. He hesitated. Show it to me! I cried.[99]

The Timor five-reis orange stamp is a real stamp, although it is not valuable, and Moran finds two other, equally authentic, stamps as he searches through his son's collection: "I put down the tray and looked for a few stamps at random, the Togo one mark carmine with the pretty boat,[100] the Nyassa 1901 ten reis, and several others. I was very fond of the Nyassa. It was green and showed a giraffe grazing off the top of a palm-tree."[101]

As he grew up, Samuel Beckett seems to have had a positive genius for acquiring cuts and bruises. One of the more serious of these incidents happened when he was about ten years old. Playing in the garden, he found a discarded gasoline can lying by the kitchen door. Without telling anyone, he fetched a box of Swan Vesta matches from the kitchen and dropped a lighted match into the can, leaning over and peering into it, curious to see what would happen. At the bottom a small amount of gasoline remained; the vapor promptly ignited and flared up right into his face, burning his skin and singeing his eyebrows. He was very hurt but also very ashamed of himself, much too ashamed to reveal to his mother what he had done. So he lay low for some time in an outbuilding before creeping silently upstairs to the bathroom to douse his face in cold water. Since neither the pain nor the burns would subside, in the end he was forced to confess his foolishness. Although, as a former nurse, his mother knew exactly what, according to received medical opinion, needed to be done for the burns, she was horrified, angry, and extremely upset at the sight of her son's burnt face. He was put to bed, his face swathed in oily rags. It was many days before the soreness abated and a couple of weeks before his skin and eyebrows began to look at all normal again.[102]

Many of these accidents resulted from Beckett's intrepid, even reckless behavior. He relates in *Company* how, as a young boy, he used to throw himself down with arms outstretched from the top of a sixty-foot-high fir tree, relying on the lower branches to break his fall before hitting the ground.[103] Finding that they always did, he repeated this dangerous game again and again. Terrified of what he was doing, his mother lashed her son fiercely with her tongue, although not, according to Beckett himself, with a stick. Sheila Page, who lived with the Becketts during the holidays for many years, also did not remember seeing May beat her younger son.[104] But her elder sister, Molly, said the opposite — and, considering the then prevalent wisdom of "Spare the rod and spoil the child," it would be most surprising if Beckett's mother had not chastised him from time to time.[105] Whatever was said or done, even as a small child Beckett was determined and independent, and he was to give up his attempts at a kind of "free fall" only when he tired of the game or found the results too painful.

Such potentially suicidal behavior probably only reflected, along with a child's failure to recognize his own mortality, Beckett's quickly acquired passion for diving. His memory of learning to swim was of his father in the sea below inviting him to dive in from the rocks of the Forty-Foot at Sandycove. Diving through the air was an experience that entered into his dreams in his childhood and returned to him often in adult life. Dream frequently turned into nightmare as he saw himself diving into too narrow a pool between the jagged walls of a rock face. In life, he loved to throw himself off heights into a pool or into the sea and particularly enjoyed diving off the highest boards. Diving probably had that element of freedom, danger, and excitement that, privately, sometimes even secretly, and in a quiet, undemonstrative way, he was to seek out in his life.

7

EVERYDAY LIFE at Cooldrinagh was regulated as much as it was in May Beckett's power to control it. It reflected *le grand style*. Everything had to be properly done as she attempted to live up to the standards of the big house in which she had been brought up, although with fewer staff. The parlor maid explained, for example, how she

> had to wear a white apron and a cotton frock in the morning and a white cap and in the afternoon I had a black frock with rubber cuffs and rubber collar and a small little cap with black velvet just across the front. And you couldn't go to the door in the afternoon without being dressed. If somebody came with a letter you had a silver tray and they put it on the tray.[106]

This was conventional enough at the time for such a comfortably off, middle-class Dublin family. But with May decorum often became obsessional. At mealtimes everything had to be done immaculately. "I used to do all the rounds," the maid went on, "with little finger bowls if they had grapes or anything. Little doilies and little glass dishes that you had to leave with a little drop of water to wipe their fingers."[107] Enormous stress was laid on cleanliness. "If you went into the house with muddy shoes, the maids were crawling about cleaning the floor behind you," said Sheila Page.[108]

May Beckett had very strict standards of behavior and the children had to conform or risk her anger and punishment. Given such pressure, it was difficult to avoid acquiring excellent manners. So the children stood up whenever a visitor came into the room, opened doors for guests and pulled out chairs for them at dinner, and were scrupulously polite in greeting people and answering their questions. "Our table manners were terribly Victorian," reminisced Sheila Page.[109]

Yet, in spite of all these inhibitions and prohibitions, Beckett's childhood was mainly a happy one. There seemed to be so much to do and plenty of time to do it in: long walks with Wolf, his Kerry Blue terrier, games of tennis or croquet at Carrickmines, or, later on, golf at Carrickmines and Foxrock, long, thoughtful games of chess with Frank, and swimming with their father in the Forty-Foot. The two boys did quite a lot of cycling, playing cycle polo in a field not far from Cooldrinagh, just as their father had done earlier in a team run by a man called Wisdom Healy.[110] The scene in Beckett's novel *Dream of Fair to Middling Women*, where the two brothers go off on their bicycles to the sea, recalls a poignant memory of his childhood:

> That was in the blue-eyed days when they rode down to the sea on bicycles, Father in the van, his handsome head standing up out of the great ruff of the family towel, John in the centre, lean and gracefully seated, Bel behind, his feet speeding round in the smallest gear ever constructed. They were the Great Bear, the Big Bear and the Little Bear; aliter sic, the Big, Little and Small Bears. . . . Many was the priest coming back safe from his bathe that they passed, his towel folded suavely, like a waiter's serviette, across his arm. The superlative Bear would then discharge the celebrated broadside: B-P! B-P! B-P! and twist round with his handsome face wreathed in smiles in the saddle to make sure that the sally had not been in vain. It had never been known to be in vain.[111]

May Beckett aimed to mold her children to her own design. But she did not always succeed, particularly with her younger son. Everyone who knew them spoke of the fierce bond of affection that seemed to bind them together, but also of the stormy conflicts that would blow up between them, sometimes, apparently, over nothing at all. Even as a young boy, Sam struggled hard not to be dominated in this conflict of wills. A streak of stubbornness was added to a strong love of independence. The more his mother tried to make him do things, the more he fought to have his own way, as Sheila Page recalled:

> How she agonised over Sam. I suppose she loved him so much. Sam seems to have been an anxiety with her. All his life. A naughty boy. Of course he was a bit of a rebel. I remember in the War, the First World War, we only had margarine to eat. And he absolutely refused to eat it. Those sort of things. If he didn't want to do anything, he didn't.[112]

May won these conflicts only by threats or punishment. But punishment often had little or no effect on Samuel. He made dreadful scenes, for instance, when he was forced to go to children's parties (which he loathed), trying to escape by hiding in the outbuildings or shutting himself in his room. When found and made to go, he would sulk and speak to nobody. Later, as he grew older, the conflicts became even more tempestuous, as May's power to influence her son or impose her view of what he should or should not do simply diminished.

But, although she could be difficult and lose her temper, May was by no means an ogre. Even her anxiety about Samuel stemmed from what he later described as her "savage loving."[113] Equally, it was not that Beckett disliked his mother or did not care what she thought of him. Rather he loved her almost as strongly and cared too much for her. So conflicts of will became heartrending struggles with that loving side of himself as well as with his mother, as he saw her determinedly and diametrically opposed to him in her judgments or her expectations. And to feel the weight of her moral condemnation and disappointment, as well as to be distanced from her affection, was an additional burden for him to bear. For they rarely saw eye to eye on anything concerning himself.

This outwardly happy childhood had its fair share of fears and horrors. One such fear was of Balfe, the road repairman in Foxrock, whose terrifying stare was enough to make Beckett quake as a small boy and scuttle indoors. "I remember the roadman," said the eighty-three-year-old Beckett, "a man called Balfe, a little, ragged, wizened, crippled man. He used to look at me. He terrified me. I can still remember how he frightened me."[114] The Foxrock roadman makes several fleeting, yet memorable cameo appearances in Beckett's work, where he is associated either with childhood fear or with decay. "The day I saw the look I got from Balfe, I went in terror of him as a child," he wrote in *From an Abandoned Work*.[115] And some years later, in the text "Afar a bird" in *For to End Yet Again*:

> I'll put faces in his head, names, places, churn them all up together, all he needs to end, phantoms to flee, last phantoms, to flee and to pursue, he'll confuse his mother with whores, his father with a roadman named Balfe, I'll feed him an old curdog, a mangy old curdog, that he may love again, lose again, ruinstrewn land, little panic steps.[116]

Another childhood horror focused on a hedgehog that he saved as a small child by putting it in an old hat box with some worms. Congratulating himself on having rescued it, he left it for days or perhaps even weeks before returning to check on its welfare, out of fear of what he might find. "You have never forgotten what you found then. . . . The mush. The stench."[117]

8

By THE TIME of Beckett's birth, the village of Foxrock was becoming a high-class neighborhood for retired local dignitaries and for businessmen who wanted to live outside Dublin but still have easy access to their offices in the city. On the Brighton Road, in the immediate vicinity of the Beckett home, there lived, for instance, two justices of the peace, a banker, several solicitors and barristers, a knight, and a colonel in fine houses that were rated at little more than the fifty-two-pound, five-shillings taxable value of Cooldrinagh. At the center of the village was a group of poor rented cottages, called Orchard Cottages, the station, the post office, and Findlater's Stores.

This branch of the family grocery firm Findlater's stood at the junction of the Brighton, Westminster, and Torquay roads. A large, substantial building, imitation Tudor in style, it housed a roomy shop with, between thick pillars, big glass windows that overlooked the approach to the station. A high-class shop, it had first a horse-drawn, then a motorized van delivering provisions to the neighborhood. When he was an old man, Beckett recalled cycling, as a child, past the tall hedges of Cooldrinagh, down the Brighton Road to fetch items of food for his mother from Findlater's or calling at the shop on his way home from school, as he alighted from the Dublin train. The opening picture in *Dream of Fair to Middling Women* is of the young Belacqua,

> an overfed child pedalling, faster and faster, his mouth ajar and his nostrils dilated, down a frieze of hawthorn after Findlater's van, faster and faster till he cruise alongside of the hoss, the black flat wet rump of the hoss. Whip him up, vanman, flickem, flapem, collop-wallop fat Sambo. Stiffly, like a perturbation of feathers, the tail arches for a gush of mard. Ah . . . ![118]

May Beckett patronized more regularly, however, a smaller store, that of "William Connolly, grocer, tea, wine and provision merchant" in nearby Cornelscourt. With a minimum of accompanying chit-chat—Bill Beckett was more genial and chatty on the telephone than she was—Beckett's mother used to ring through her order for daily delivery by Connolly's motor van.[119] In *Company*, the narrator remembers that as "A small boy you come out of Connolly's Stores holding your mother by the hand"[120] and in the radio play *All That Fall*, Mrs. Rooney cries out, "Heavens, here comes Connolly's van,"[121] as Mr. Tyler is almost knocked off his bicycle.

On Sunday mornings, the bell of Tullow Church called all good local Protestants to worship. May Beckett was an assiduous attender at the church and ensured that, from an early age, her two sons accompanied her regularly. They had, Beckett remembered, a pew close to the pulpit, which they shared with a market gardener called Watt Tyler, and across the aisle from another well-known Foxrock family, the Orpens.[122] Beckett was never happy at having to go to church and hated wearing the hard, chafing collars that "Sunday best" entailed. So he used to sit scowling at Beatrice Orpen and at the world in general.[123] His father never came with them to Tullow Church. Instead, he used to say "that he'd go to church with the birds up the mountains"[124] and take himself off into the Dublin hills, alone or with one of his many friends. Later on, Beckett used to accompany him on these Sunday morning walks. But, sometimes, in the evening, according to Beckett, his father would "condescend to go to church but not at Tullow Parish Church. He'd go to a church near Monkstown down at Blackrock, 'All Saint's Church,' where the parson [the Reverend Henry B. Dobbs, B.A.] was a friend of my father's."[125] Bill Beckett was not deeply religious ("not a churchman," Beckett said of him) and on his occasional visits Bill went to the church alone or with Sam, while Frank accompanied his mother to Tullow.

9

FROM THE AGE of five until he was nine, Beckett attended a small kindergarten school run by two German-born, naturalized sisters, Misses Ida and Pauline

Elsner. The school was on the Leopardstown Road between Foxrock and Stillorgan in a house called Taunus, which belonged to their widowed mother, Mrs. Elise Elsner.[126] Beckett could remember that the school had a big garden[127] with a lawn where, between lessons, his brother and he used to play a game in which they dragooned the other children into joining hands to form a line, which they would then burst through vigorously, after getting their speed up with a good run.[128] The number of children who were at the school at any one time seems to have varied from fourteen or fifteen down to one.[129] While Sam —or Sammy, as he was known in the school—was a pupil there, his father acted as the surveyor for a new building that the Elsners had constructed at the rear of their garden for use as a gymnasium.

At first, either Sam's mother or his nanny, Bridget Bray, used to walk hand in hand with him, in the morning, along the Brighton Road to the school. In the afternoon, May Beckett would collect him, sometimes bringing him home in a little trap harnessed to her donkey. But his elder brother, Frank, attended the school for at least a year with Beckett and they would often have walked back along the quiet road to Cooldrinagh together. As he grew a little older, Sam used to ride to school on a bicycle so tiny that other children laughed at him as he pedaled furiously past. His pride was hurt by their laughter and, many decades later, he could still remember what it felt like to be an object of mockery.[130]

The Elsner sisters had a cook called Hannah and an Aberdeen terrier called Zulu. Sisters, cook, and dog all figure in *Molloy*, which Beckett wrote in French shortly after the Second World War:

> She would call Hannah, the old cook of the Elsner sisters, and they would whisper together for a long time, through the railings. Hannah never went out, she did not like going out. The Elsner sisters were not bad neighbours, as neighbours go. They made a little too much music, that was the only fault I could find with them. . . . Everything remained to be planned and there I was thinking of the Elsner sisters. They had an aberdeen called Zulu. People called it Zulu. Sometimes, when I was in a good humour, I called, Zulu! Little Zulu! and he would come and talk to me, through the railings.[131]

Both Elsner sisters taught music and Miss Pauline also gave piano lessons at 21 Ely Place in Dublin, just as their father and mother had done before them.[132] Whenever he referred to the Elsner family, Beckett took great pleasure in pointing out that Chopin's first great piano teacher in Poland had been called Elsner.

The sisters also taught general subjects. Sam's own teacher was Miss Ida. She was registered in *Thom's Directory* as a teacher of languages and Beckett began to learn not German but French from her at a very early age. Known locally as Jack because of her mannish, rather dominant nature, she was something of a character in Foxrock village. Some fifty years later, Beckett described her as "eccentric and rather remarkable; not too lovable but very intelligent."[133]

She rode a bicycle all her life and, as she got older, was inclined to fall off; cursing vigorously, she would lie sprawling by the roadside until a passerby came along to help her up.[134] This eccentric behavior was well known in Foxrock in the late 1930s; Beckett may well have had this story in mind when he created the character of Maddy Rooney in his 1956 radio play *All That Fall*, in which Mrs. Rooney expresses the desire to "just flop down flat on the road like a big fat jelly out of a bowl and never move again! A great big slop thick with grit and dust and flies, they would have to scoop me up with a shovel."[135]

When he was very young, Sam, blond and pretty, was not considered exceptionally bright, but he learned to read very quickly and was a thoughtful child. He was very fond of being alone, at his happiest when he could curl up by himself with, at first, a picture book or, later, a proper book to read.[136] It did not matter whether this was in the house or in the garden. To the consternation of his parents, from an early age he would occasionally wander much farther afield into the nearby countryside to read, losing all sense of time as he devoured his stories. Beckett said that he read avidly (mostly rubbish, he conceded) until he was about seventeen, when he became far more critical and less easily absorbed in what he was reading.[137] He retained this love of reading until the last few weeks of his life.

10

AT COOLDRINAGH, LIFE changed radically with the death of Rubina, the wife of May's brother, Edward Price Roe, in October 1913.[138] Rather than take his three motherless children, Molly, Sheila, and Jack, out to Africa, where he was an accountant with the British Central Africa Company in Blantyre in Nyasaland (now Malawi), Uncle Ned opted to send them to boarding schools in Dublin. Jack, whom May Beckett used to call Velvet Bunny, became the sole boarder at Earlsfort House School, where Sam and Frank were also day pupils. Sheila and Molly attended Morehampton House, a boarding and day school for girls, on the Morehampton Road. The school had originally been run by three spinster sisters and was commonly known in Dublin as Miss Wade's.[139] In the mid-1960s, Beckett recalled this name, when in his short play *Come and Go* one of the three female characters asks that they should all "Just sit together as we used to, in the playground at Miss Wade's."[140] But during the First World War, when Sheila and Molly Roe were boarders there, the school was run by two elderly ladies called Miss Irwin and Miss Molyneaux. A fellow pupil, Mary Manning, who knew both Roe girls, wrote:

> After morning prayers, even if the weather was polar, we sang God Save the King with the windows open so that the IRA would know exactly where we stood. Over the war years, we were compelled to knit frightful khaki scarves and socks for the brave boys fighting in France. During our hours of travail, Miss Molyneaux would read us

such works of literature as "Jessica's First Prayer," "Froggy's Little Brother," and "The Schoolboy Baronet."[141]

The spinsters were exceptionally kind to the Roe girls, taking them shopping, buying them clothes, and giving them little treats. But, with their father back in Central Africa, they would have had no home to go to during the holidays, except for the kindness of the Becketts. May Beckett very generously took them under her wing at Cooldrinagh. Jack also used to come to stay with them from time to time, although his stays tended to be less frequent than those of Molly and Sheila, as he often spent the holidays with his mother's relatives, who were farmers in Kerry. Suddenly, instead of being a family of four, they were often six or seven, two of whom were girls.

Holidays now became hectic affairs. The Roe girls stayed with the Becketts from Christmas 1913 for five or six years, until their father remarried and they moved to North Wales. When their mother died, Sheila was nearly eight, Molly two years older. Sam was six. As a young child, he found the name Sheila too difficult to pronounce; so she became first "Ela" then "Eli," a name he continued to use for her all his life. The girls had one of the bedrooms on the second floor. The children's playroom was on the same floor. They did jigsaws, painted and drew, and played a simplified child's version of bridge. All of the family had bicycles, and May often used to take them off for picnics in the country. Christmas was an especially exciting time. Bill and May went to great lengths to ensure that the girls and their brother had just as many presents as their own boys. "We had wonderful Christmases," said Sheila Page. "On Christmas morning, Father Christmas was supposed to be at one of the doors with a sack of presents. And, of course, we always went to the wrong door."[142]

Every year May took them to the annual pantomime at the Gaiety Theatre in Dublin. These shows and the Gilbert and Sullivan productions by the visiting D'Oyly Carte Opera Company were Beckett's first introductions to the theater. Beckett used to play Sullivan's music on the piano at home; a friend recalled that "he sang irreverent, ribald Beckett *libretti* in substitution for Gilbert's words."[143] The same local friend remembered that the Becketts had a set of gramophone recordings of the D'Oyly Carte operas that they would play whenever rain interfered with the tennis at Cooldrinagh. Frank was also a very good pianist, specializing in popular songs, which he used to play to the delight of the extended family. The boys played piano duets together. A surviving copy of Diabelli's Duet in D with the name Samuel Barclay Beckett written in a childish hand on the cover and the date "Sam & Frank 15 Dec 1914" on the top of the sheet music indicates the brothers' progress as they practiced the piece through the opening months of 1915.[144] All the children used to take turns practicing on the piano in the drawing room. "We used to queue up for this," said Sheila Page. "Sam used to sing madly with a quavering voice when he played. And we'd all be roaring with laughter out in the hall. But he was very musical."[145]

Part of the summer holidays was usually spent in a rented house by the seaside, mostly at Greystones, a small fishing village in County Wicklow within easy reach of Foxrock. May would go to the house with a maid to help her look after the children. Bill stayed at home during the week so that he could continue to go in to the office but used to take the train to join his large family at the weekends. In spite of Frank's hasty temper and Sam's recurrent moodiness, the boys generally got on well together and, for games, Frank used to team up with Molly and Sam with "Eli."

Greystones was then a predominantly Protestant, Anglo-Irish holiday village. Its Grand Hotel (later the La Touche Hotel) was patronized at the beginning of the century by some of Dublin's most prominent businessmen, who played golf on what at the time was a pleasant nine-hole course. The Beckett and Roe children used to play on the stony beach with its large gray and pink pebbles or run along the harbor wall to watch the masted schooners unloading their cargo of Welsh coal to be carted away by heavy workhorses to Arthur Evans's Coal Depository by the harbor. On the beach, local fishermen sat mending their whelk pots and repairing their fishing nets. When the children tired of watching all this activity, they jumped or dived into the little dock to the south side of the harbor. At Greystones, the entire family was able to relax and enjoy the freedom of a simpler way of life far removed from the constraints of school and business or the social conventions that were adhered to rigidly at Cooldrinagh. May and Bill loved this little seaside village. At night, the children could hear the waves crashing against the rocks and, through the windows overlooking the harbor, see the light of the Bailey Lighthouse near Howth flashing across Dublin Bay. These sights and sounds, together with those from Foxrock, Dún Laoghaire, and the Forty-Foot, were to stay deeply etched in Beckett's memory. He always loved the Irish countryside and its mountains. The County Dublin coastline with its lighthouses, harbors, viaduct, and islands permeated his imagination and pervaded his work. These recurrent images were, to use his own word, "obsessional."

May and Bill Beckett noted their younger son's need for solitude. For the most part, he would play quite contentedly with the other children. Then he would wander off alone along the beach or stand motionless gazing out to sea. It was on these occasions that he indulged in what he described as his "love" for certain stones. He recounted how he used to take stones of which he was particularly fond home with him from the beach in order to protect them from the wearing away of the waves or the vagaries of the weather. He would lay them gently into the branches of trees in the garden to keep them safe from harm. Later in life, he came to rationalize this concern as the manifestation of an early fascination with the mineral, with things dying and decaying, with petrification. He linked this interest with Sigmund Freud's view that human beings have a prebirth nostalgia to return to the mineral state.[146] And in Beckett's later work, there is an obsession with decay and with petrification, with stone and with bone: Molloy permutates the sucking stones that he has gathered on the beach, moving them from pocket to pocket via his mouth; Malone is to tell three stories, one about a thing, "a stone probably";[147] Lucky's monologue tells of a world of stones and repeats wildly the phrase "the skull, the skull";[148] Estragon looks out from the stage and sees in the auditorium only skeletons in a charnel house.[149] Had they lived long enough to read or see his mature novels and plays, Beckett's parents would have been as baffled by his later interpretation of the meaning of his actions as they were by his early writing. As it was, they looked with great affection at their slim nine-year-old son, as, standing alone on the beach, he threw sticks for Wolf to retrieve or skimmed small, flat stones across the surface of the sea, watching them bounce as they hit the waves before they sank.

2

School Days

1915–23

1

IN 1915, AT THE AGE OF NINE, Beckett left the Misses Elsners' Academy to attend a larger school in Dublin called Earlsfort House. This was not just a preparatory school, as Beckett himself referred to it at times, since it not only took juniors (boys from nine until thirteen), but also took some seniors (boys from thirteen until eighteen) through to university entrance. The school occupied two large houses numbered 3–4 Earlsfort Place, now the site of 63 Adelaide Road, and was only a few minutes' walk from the Harcourt Street railway station. Every day, at first with his older brother, then alone once Frank was away at boarding school, Beckett took the train on the Dublin and South-Eastern line (the "inner line," known locally as the Dublin Slow and Easy) from Foxrock Station to the terminus at Harcourt Street, from where he walked down the road to the school.

This Dublin railway station with its "pretty neo-Doric colonnade,"[1] still in existence but no longer operating as a station, figures in a number of Beckett's works including *Texts for Nothing, That Time,* and *Watt.* The station staff offered a mixture of fascination and fear to the young, highly impressionable schoolboy. Several were to appear only slightly transformed in *Watt,* which Beckett wrote during the Second World War, while he was cut off from Ireland. The incident in which Watt bumps into a porter who is wheeling a milk churn was probably based on an actual platform encounter, for Beckett admitted that one of the porters terrified him; the eloquent curses that are laid on the offending Watt — "The devil raise a hump on you" and "Mute on top of blind,"[2] sound as if they were taken from real-life memories.

Beckett bought his favorite comic papers from a little lock-up newsagent's stall on the platform, run by an acerbic individual called Mr. Evans, whom he later vividly described in *Watt:*

> One noticed his cap, perhaps because of the snowwhite forehead and damp black curly hair on which it sat. The eye came always in the end to the scowling mouth and from there on up to the rest. His moustache, handsome in itself, was for obscure reasons unimportant. But one thought of him as the man who, among other things, never

left off his cap, a plain blue cloth cap, with a peak and knob. For he never left off his bicycle-clips either. These were of a kind that caused his trouser-ends to stick out wide, on either side.[3]

Having bought his weekly copy of *The Union Jack*, Beckett would sit on a seat out on the platform when it was warm or in the third-class waiting room when it was cold, totally engrossed in the stories of Sexton Blake and his assistant, Tinker. The narrator of one of the *Texts for Nothing* asks rhetorically:

> And what if all this time I had not stirred hand or foot from the third class waiting-room of the South-Eastern Railway Terminus, I never dared wait first on a third class ticket, and were still there waiting to leave, for the south-east, the south rather, east lay the sea, all along the track, wondering where on earth to alight, or my mind absent, elsewhere. The last train went at twenty-three thirty, then they closed the station for the night. What thronging memories, that's to make me think I'm dead, I've said it a million times.[4]

Beckett spent four active and, on the whole, happy years at Earlsfort House. In theory, the school was run by its first headmaster, a Monsieur Alfred E. Le Peton.[5] "Lep," as he was widely known throughout the school, had a French father but had been brought up in Manchester, so his English had developed a fairly strong Lancashire accent. But he spoke excellent French and helped Beckett keep up the French that he had started to learn with Miss Elsner.

In practice, it was Lep's partner and coprincipal, a master who mainly taught Latin and mathematics to the senior boys, "a serious fellow" named William Ernest Exshaw (nicknamed by Beckett's father "Eggshell"[6]) who kept the school ticking over and became its sole headmaster in 1922, when either he or Lep broke up the partnership and Le Peton left to found his own school, Sandford Park, in the Dublin suburb of Ranelagh.

Le Peton, a "very likeable bouncy little man,"[7] seems to have been very strict but still managed to remain popular with the boys, although several of them found him to be a very strange fellow. One of the pupils, Andrew Ganly, put it bluntly:

> The headmaster was a rogue. We loved him but he was a rogue. Curiously, he inspired us with a certain sense of honour. He hadn't got it himself and how he gave it to us, I just don't know. And he used to say at Speech Days: "God sends me the boys but the Devil sends me their parents," which, of course, went down very well with the boys.[8]

Beckett voiced even greater doubt about Lep, probably combining his father's suspicions with his own instinctive response. He remembered M. Le Peton as being "not too reliable a character. I think (though I don't want to speak ill of the dead) that he was a bit of a rogue, a 'bad egg.' I remember once he tried to borrow money from my father. I think he was a homosexual. He liked friendly physical contact, you know."[9]

Beckett remembered some of the teachers at the school as being very good. Several were graduates of Trinity College, Dublin, and one or two, like Walter Starkie, were on the staff of Trinity and came in part-time to teach special subjects and so add to their stipend. It was at Earlsfort House that Beckett first began to take a serious interest in his studies, realizing, at the age of eleven or twelve, that what he liked best was English composition. His English essays there regularly received high marks.

He was always extremely good at games. He played quite a lot of tennis at school, mostly against the other boys but sometimes against Mr. "Eggshell" ("I was quite good at tennis until I was about fourteen, I guess," he said[10]). But he also played with Frank at Carrickmines Tennis and Croquet Club, where they entered, and often won, tournaments. On a brick of the second porch at Cooldrinagh to the left of the bow window Beckett wrote: "S Roe and S Beckett won Juvenile Tennis Tournament August 1920."[11] It was at Carrickmines that Beckett won the Junior Boys' Final and his cousin Sheila won the Junior Girls' Final. When Frank was away at school or when Beckett needed to play with a junior boy of his own age, his partner was usually a friend called Geoffrey Perrin, who also lived on Kerrymount Avenue. Perrin wrote:

> We partnered each other in the handicap doubles in both the Co. Dublin and Co. Wicklow championship tournaments for two years. We were about the youngest pairing and must have been reasonably competent as we were never given a fancy handicap. + or − 0.2 was usually our level.[12]

Tennis parties were a permanent feature of life at Cooldrinagh in the summer. The family had a grass court that Beckett remembered helping Christy, the gardener, mark out. In spite of the age gap, Frank and Sam played against each other, and at the weekends they sometimes played with their father. Visitors, too, like Mary Manning and her brother, John, came to play. John said that Beckett "was born with the sportsman's eye" and that he never managed to beat him. On these occasions Sam's mother used to come out of the house with large pottery jugs full of thirst-quenching orange or lemon juice and a tray loaded with neat little sandwiches prepared by the cook or herself. But Beckett loathed the social side of these gatherings. He spoiled them for at least two of his visitors by remaining almost totally silent, particularly with the girls, doubtless out of a mixture of embarrassment and disdain for the standard of their tennis.[13]

Bill Beckett took each of his sons in turn to buy tennis rackets and cricket bats from William Elvery's sports shop at 2 Lower Abbey Street, next door to Mooney's public house (where in *Murphy*, Neary drowns his sorrows and thinks longingly of Miss Counihan). The boys had bats and rackets almost from the time that they could physically wield them. But it was a proud moment for Beckett when, at the early age of ten, he was taken by his father to purchase his first set of basic golf clubs. Soon after this, he began to take the first of many golfing lessons from James Barrett, the professional at Carrickmines Golf Club, where he tried to play as often as he could.[14] When he could find no one to play against, he used to follow one ball with another, enjoying being out on the course alone. At Earlsfort House, Beckett was also in the school cricket and rugby teams. Several of the masters were good cricketers (one, probably A. D. Cordner, playing for a distinguished team called The Gentlemen of Ireland) and Beckett received some excellent coaching, which stood him in good stead later when he went on to represent Portora Royal School and Trinity College.

During the summer term, when the light was good, the boys of Earlsfort House cricket team played some of their matches late on into the evening on the Landsdowne Road ground where international rugby is now played. On match days, Beckett used to travel to school with an impressively large cricket bag containing his bat, whitened boots, neatly pressed cream flannels, cricket sweater, and cap. The bag was in truth much too big and heavy for him to carry at all easily. After the game, he would normally not arrive home until nine o'clock, tired out and hungry, having eaten nothing since his lunchtime sandwiches. He used to take a tram from the cricket ground to Harcourt Street station, then board a train (for which he had a season ticket) for the twenty-minute journey to Foxrock.

On one such occasion, however, when he was about twelve, having performed rather well in the game, he took the tram in the best of spirits, looking forward to describing to his father some of the delicate shots that he had executed during the match. As he was approaching Harcourt Street station, he felt casually in his pockets for his season ticket. The ticket was not there. Carefully he went through every pocket of his blazer and trousers and emptied his cricket bag. To no avail. With his last remaining penny, he took the return tram back to the cricket ground and retraced his steps to see if he could have left the ticket in the pavilion. No one was there, and the ticket was nowhere to be seen.

He was much too terrified of the station porter to go back to Harcourt Street and explain what had happened about the ticket and, being either too independent or too obstinate to call at his grandfather's house in Ballsbridge to obtain the price of his fare, he decided to walk the eight miles home. About a mile from home, weary from carrying the heavy bag so far, he flopped down exhausted by the roadside. He was discovered there just before midnight by his anxious father, who had come out to search for him. Together they walked the rest of the way, his father carrying the cricket bag, saying almost nothing. His mother, on the other hand, frantic with worry, had plenty to say on their arrival home and sent him off to bed without any supper. Soon afterward, as he lay in bed feeling ravenously hungry, Beckett could hear the creaking of the steep wooden stairs that led up to his room. It was his father bringing him something to eat. "I suppose he understood," commented Beckett over forty years later. "I don't remember any form of severity from him. But," he added quickly and generously, "that is not to disparage my mother. She was sick with anxiety."[15]

At this time too Beckett played a successful part in school athletics: "I did a lot of running there. I was a fairly good runner at middle to long distances. I remember winning a race, coming into the sports ground and seeing my father leaving. He had to go to a meeting just before I went up to the tape."[16] He also learned how to box. Boxing was considered formative for the character as well as useful as a means of self-defense. So the Earlsfort House boys would go once or twice a week to the cricket pavilion of the Leinster Cricket Club, where they could feel the knots in the floorboards through the soles of their sneakers, the wood around the knots having been worn down by the studs of countless cricket boots. They were taught how to box by a Sergeant Parsons, whose most common words of advice were "Now spar natural! Spar natural!"[17]

By his own admission, Beckett was quite often involved in fights at Earlsfort House outside the ring as well as inside. He remembered being beaten three or four times by Le Peton for various offenses such as "scrapping," carving pieces out of a desk, or breaking bounds. In theory, discipline had an important part to play in Le Peton's English-public-school philosophy. But this was not sustained in practice throughout the school. It was undermined first by some of the senior boys, who abused the system by indulging in quite serious bullying. In the basement of one of the two schoolhouses, for instance, several of the more sadistic seniors ran what was called the Dancing Class. Juniors who were thought to have offended their elders and betters were taken down there, and stones or small pieces of concrete were thrown at their feet to make them dance.[18] One or two of the masters also were incapable of keeping order and were ragged unmercifully by the boys.

Two separate sets of incidents from his time at Earlsfort House remained firmly imprinted in Beckett's mind. Both show a profound distaste for any form of cruelty. Even allowing for a degree of compassionate hindsight, they are very revealing. The first concerned a teacher of mathematics called Lister who, though a brilliant mathematician, had failed Trinity's fellowship examination — one of the hardest examinations in the world, according to Beckett — and was "reduced to teaching inky schoolboys in a Prep school."[19] This master had the bulging eyes of a sufferer from Graves' disease and he found keeping discipline almost impossible. He was mocked, ragged, and taunted unmercifully by the boys until, in Beckett's words, his "nerves [were] shot" and he was driven nearly mad.[20] The master appeared totally defenseless against such unrelenting collective baiting. Beckett recalled being horrified by the unfairness of the cruelty of his classmates, and not only refused to join in but tried to stop the malicious sport of Lister-baiting.[21] This did not prevent him, however, as he got older and perhaps bolder, from taking part in what he regarded as some wittier, more sophisticated japes when he reached Portora Royal School.

Another example of cruelty and inhumanity that affected him deeply centered on an incident with a dog. At the end of a normal school day, a rabid dog was discovered running wild in the school garden, raging, foaming at the mouth, and threatening to bite anyone who approached it. The boys were told to stay indoors but Beckett and a friend, anxious to catch the train home, decided to make a run for it. As they raced through the gate, they spotted the dog crouching in a corner of the garden. Walking along the road toward Harcourt Street, they encountered a very large policeman who had been summoned to deal with the animal. Curious as to how he was going to handle the situation, they followed him back to the school. The officer took out his truncheon and went into the garden where the dog was cornered. The man started to lash out viciously at it. It jumped up at him and was beaten down again. Beckett looked on with horror as the policeman literally beat the dog to death. Half a century later, he said that it "made a terrible effect on me." [22]

Although memories of his school days were hardly ever reflected directly in his work, two aspects of Beckett's life at Earlsfort House do appear to have exerted a deep influence on his later attitudes and behavior. The school was deliberately multidenominational and, unusually in the Irish context, although it had a large majority of Protestants, it accepted Catholics, Jews, and freethinkers as well. Tolerance for religious differences and an emphasis on equality were drummed into the boys, to such a degree that Le Peton once threatened to "flay anyone alive" who treated Edward Solomons, a Jewish boy who was about to join them, any differently from anybody else.[23] Arrangements were made for each group to have its own form of religious instruction — or lack thereof. So, although the Protestant boys knew perfectly well who the Catholic and Jewish pupils were, it made relatively little difference to attitudes or friendships within the school. Such an ethos, in which religious beliefs matter little by comparison with the personal qualities of the individual, stayed with Beckett throughout his life. In the early 1930s, his close friends included A. J. Leventhal, who was Jewish, and Tom MacGreevy, who was Catholic, as well as numerous Protestants and unbelievers. Later on, his tolerance was to be transformed into a much more active antiracism.

The second attitude within the school that marked Beckett just as it did so many of the boys was the emphasis placed on loyalty, honor, integrity, politeness, and respect for others. School reinforced the values that Beckett had absorbed from his earliest years at home. These were the positive values that members of the Protestant middle class proclaimed and to which they aspired, even if in practice they only too often fell short. There was also a great emphasis in the school on esprit de corps.[24]

2

IN 1916, DUBLIN WAS IN TURMOIL after the bloody fighting and the deaths in the Easter Uprising. Frank was sent away to school, partly perhaps to get away from the troubles while still remaining in Ireland. Sam, the parents concluded, was not yet old enough to live away from home but would be able to join his brother as soon as he was thirteen. They chose Portora Royal School, a prominent boarding school in Enniskillen in the northern county of Fermanagh, favored throughout the nineteenth century by well-to-do Protestant families. Ireland was partitioned during Beckett's second year at the school. And although he himself felt that the event scarcely impinged on him at the time, passing across the border at the beginning and end of each term, seeing British troops stationed nearby, and then returning to the capital of a new country that was in the process of forming itself must have had some impact on his developing political awareness.

Portora Royal School had a tradition that dated back almost three hundred years. Several of Bill Beckett's professional colleagues in Dublin and neighbors in Foxrock had already sent their sons to the school. It had an excellent academic record and a long-established link with Trinity College, Dublin. But it also had a good reputation for sports, which was important for two such athletic boys. Discipline in the school was said to be strong, even though the book of rules and regulations announced rather grandly that "Discipline must come from within. Self-discipline is discipline in its highest form."

Portora is built in one of the most beautiful areas of the Irish lake district. It stands impressively on a steep little hill looking down on the county town of Enniskillen. From the cricket ground behind the school you can see Lower Lough Erne and all its islands stretching out of sight to the north. Behind the slope of the hill to the left lies the Narrows, a kind of strait through which the Erne passes on its way from Enniskillen to the lower lake. To the west, Mount Belmore rises on the horizon. Nearby are the stately homes of Castle Coole and Florence Court. There are lovely walks through the forest and along the lakeside, which the boys were allowed, even encouraged to take at weekends.

Any social mix at the school was provided by the day boys (mostly on scholarship) who were the sons of local shopkeepers, tradesmen, and farmers. They were called the day dogs and were taught separately from the boarders, who were virtually all the sons of businessmen, bank managers, lawyers, army officers, civil servants, or clergymen of the Church of Ireland (who paid reduced fees for the education of their sons). The "day dogs" were looked down on by the boarders. The higher landed gentry mostly sent their sons to England, where fees at a top public school were about twice as high as those at Portora, so there were few double-barreled names and even fewer "honourables" in residence. But although Portora had its own distinctive Irish characteristics and flavor, it resembled the famous English public schools in several important respects: an emphasis on sports; a military Officer Training Corps (which Beckett and a friend, Geoffrey Thompson, adamantly refused to join); regular morning prayers in the Remembrance Hall, with the school song, "Floreat Portora," which echoed Eton's "Floreat Etona," and Sunday morning service in the cathedral for Church of Ireland boys; mediocre to appalling food, with lifesaving "grub boxes" from home kept locked in the basement "grub room"; school and house prefects and begowned masters; school uniforms with distinctive blazers and caps for those who had been awarded their sporting colors.

During his first term at the new school, the Easter term of 1920, Beckett was desperately homesick.[25] It was the first time he had ever lived away from home. And it was not a lot of help to him that his elder brother was a boarder at the same school. He soon learned that he had to fight his own battles. For Frank was three years ahead of Samuel. He was also one of five or six prefects and had his own small circle of friends among the senior boys. So, inevitably, however well disposed he felt toward his younger brother, he was far more remote from him than he had ever been at home.

Beckett suffered quite a lot at first from the bullying and baiting that happened routinely to new boys. He remembered very vividly an incident in his first term when he was bullied in the library by a gang led by a boy called Clark. Unknown to the bullies, Beckett had a violent temper, which erupted only once in a while. On this occasion, the taunting and teasing infuriated him so much that he went almost berserk, lashing out with fierce blows at the ringleader. Having learned how to box at Earlsfort House and being slightly heavier than Clark, he gave the boy a terrible beating; in Beckett's own words, he "nearly killed him." [26] After this, and in view of his developing prowess as a boxer, he was left strictly alone. But his main memory of that first term remained one of looking forward to getting to bed, "away from the whole bloody mess." [27]

Much of his homesickness lifted in his second term. But he still regarded Portora as a tough school ("They were a pretty rough lot, you know," he commented [28]), where life was hard and where it often seemed cold and damp. There was a fairly strict regimen, with numerous rules and regulations. If an account written about a period only a few years after Beckett's stay at the school is to be believed, the food was poor and inadequate:

> Our staple diet was bread-and-butter and tea; jam we provided ourselves, except on Sundays. This was varied by, at breakfast, either burnt porridge, or one burnt rasher, or one burnt sausage. Cheap as porridge is, we only got it on the days when we didn't get fry. As for lunch, it was usually uneatable. The meat, which was poor to begin with, was roasted until all the juices had left it, or else was made into an incredibly messy stew. The potatoes were soapy or rotten, the cabbage overcooked and the water not strained off at all. Hungry as we were, we often could not eat a bite, and the sweet was little better. Over and over again I have lunched on one piece of dry bread and a glass of water. Tea consisted simply of bread-and-butter and your own jam again. If you wanted a boiled egg, you had to pay extra for it, or have eggs sent from home. [29]

The greatest advantage of being in the school sports teams, of which Beckett was almost immediately a member, was that the boys had what he described as "special rations for training." [30]

Once he settled down, Beckett found that he was not unhappy at Portora. He made a number of very good friends, either in his own year or in the "blue dormitory" of Connaught House, to which he belonged: Geoffrey Thompson, Oliver McCutcheon, Charles Jones, Tom Cox, Herbert Gamble, and, mostly through sports, Courtney Deverell. One of these good friends, who became General Sir Charles Jones, recalled what Beckett was like at the time:

> Although withdrawn and sometimes moody, he was a most attractive character. His eyes, behind his spectacles, were piercing and he often

sat quietly assessing in a thoughtful, and even critical way what was going on around him and the material that was being presented to him. However, he had a keen sense of the ridiculous and a great sense of humour; from time to time his face would light up with a charming smile and change his whole appearance.[31]

There was some degree of agreement among his contemporaries that he could be moody, withdrawn, and introspective.[32] Clearly, he already had something strangely reserved, enigmatic, even aloof about him. Yet his good friends discovered then, as they did later, that when he emerged from these periods of withdrawal, he could be an excellent, witty companion. There remained enough doubt, however, about his sociability for an obituary by the present headmaster to conclude that "despite his natural ability and sharp intelligence, he never seems to have fitted easily into the schoolboy community."[33]

His closest friend at Portora was Geoffrey Thompson, who was to play an important role later in his life. He and Geoffrey felt themselves to be "kindred spirits."[34] They both came from the south and, according to Beckett, had a very clear sense of the difference between themselves and the northerners. Far less hardy and resilient than Beckett, Thompson remembered his school days with more resentment: "I just battered my way through them all right," he commented later.[35] He was quiet and retiring like Beckett, with whom he shared a highly developed sense of humor and a similar sardonic wit. Beckett admired his friend's razor-sharp intelligence and greatly enjoyed his company. Although Thompson was brilliant at science — he was to go on to become first a physician in Dublin and then a psychiatrist in London — he was also keenly interested in literature, read widely, and wrote extremely well himself. Beckett remembered having been beaten into second place by him on several occasions in school essay competitions, although other pupils could equally well remember Beckett winning the Seale Prize for an English essay on a number of occasions.[36]

The headmaster was the Reverend Ernest G. Seale, the twelfth clergyman to hold that office since the school's foundation in 1618. Seale was known among the boys as the Boss or even Ned Boss.[37] Members of the staff were collectively known as the Gangers.[38] A near contemporary of Beckett described Seale in the following way:

He was, and always must have been, even before his hair went white, a remarkably handsome and dignified-looking man. Yet he had a list of disabilities which should have made him a mere figure of fun. He had a club foot, his right arm was partially paralysed, there was a nervous twitch in his cheek — particularly when he was angry — and he had a peculiar, almost barking voice. All of these infirmities we imitated when his back was turned, but we feared and respected his presence, and when he was angry and stamped his foot on the dais of the Big Schoolroom and called us "cads," it was like Jehovah thundering from the top of Mount Sinai. This word "cads" . . . was his worst term of abuse.[39]

Mathematics and the sciences were taught by a graduate of St. Catherine's College, Cambridge: W. M. Tetley, the senior master, who also coached the boys at cricket. He had the nickname "Bolo," from his habit of saying "Bowl away" when umpiring.[40] Tetley, who specialized in the study of mosses, was "a burly, rather forbidding figure with a heavy moustache and gold rimmed spectacles," thick eyebrows, and thin gray hair with an immaculate middle parting.[41] He had a mean-looking face with small, ferrety eyes.[42] Beckett detested him. Good relations were not fostered by the fact that Beckett was dreadful at physics and chemistry, although he was much better at mathematics. Geoffrey Thompson recalled Tetley saying:

"Beckett, I can't understand how a person of your intelligence doesn't seem to be able to understand the basic principles of chemistry and physics." Sam didn't say anything to that. But his response, a couple of days later, was absentmindedly to pour a bottle of sulphuric acid down the sink. He didn't distinguish clearly enough between sulphuric acid and water.[43]

On the other hand, Beckett did much better, though by no means outstandingly, at arts subjects.[44] He was taught French first by a talented, kindly woman, Miss Evelyn Tennant, who "had a round, rather old face and wore rimless pince-nez which gave her a rather severe appearance,"[45] then by a tall, angular Miss Harper, who, in spite of vain attempts to be strict, tended to be teased by the boys. Mr. Breul, "a large fat man with a lordly paunch,"[46] taught English, though his father was German. The boys distrusted Breul and were "suspicious of his familiarity and motives."[47] The much respected Mr. A. T. M. Murfet, known throughout the school as Mickey, was a former scholar of Peterhouse in Cambridge and was president of Connaught House. He taught Beckett Latin and Scripture. "Murfet was a small quiet man with a tendency to sarcasm which did his popularity no good but [he was] an outstanding classics teacher," said Beckett's cousin, who attended the school a few years after him.[48] Beckett received an excellent grounding in Latin, first from Murfet, then from the headmaster, who was a good classical scholar and taught senior classes in Latin (which was a compulsory subject).[49] This allowed Beckett later to tackle some very difficult Latin texts and to quote easily from classical authors. But he did not study either Greek or German at school.[50]

As schoolboys, Beckett and Geoffrey Thompson shared the same literary interests: principally Conan Doyle's stories and the work of the English-born Canadian humorist Stephen Leacock.[51] Leacock's playful wit, somewhat unsubtle games with the reader, amusing parodies, wordplay, and interest in unusual words would certainly have appealed to two bright adolescents.[52] But, again with the invaluable benefit of hindsight, intriguing parallels emerge between Leacock's humorous, extravagant toying with logic and reason, and Beckett's later novels *Murphy* and *Watt*. The opening paragraph of "Gertrude the Governess: or, Simple Seventeen" illustrates the kind of writing that amused the young Beckett and, at the same time, hints at a possible link with his own later upending of some of the conventions of fiction:

> *Synopsis of Previous Chapters:*
> *There are no Previous Chapters.*
> It was a wild and stormy night on the West Coast of Scotland. This, however, is immaterial to the present story, as the scene is not laid in the West of Scotland. For the matter of that the weather was just as bad on the East Coast of Ireland.
> But the scene of this narrative is laid in the South of England and takes place in and around Knotacentinum Towers (pronounced as if written Nosham Taws), the seat of Lord Knotacent (pronounced as if written Nosh).
> But it is not necessary to pronounce either of these names in reading them.[53]

Beckett and his friend also read poetry together. Thompson remembered a country stroll one Sunday afternoon ("On fine Sunday afternoons, the School buildings are out of bounds from 2.30 until 3.30 o'clock," read the school rules), when they stopped to sit under a tree and learned by heart the "Ode to a Nightingale."[54] Keats's poem is alluded to several times in Beckett's writing, most strikingly in his early story "Dante and the Lobster," where the narrator appropriately quotes the line "Take into the air my quiet breath" as a lobster collected by Belacqua from the fishmonger is plunged alive by his aunt into boiling water.[55] Such an episode occurred in reality at Beckett's own aunt Cissie's house in Howth.[56]

3

FITTING IN TO SCHOOL LIFE was, of course, made much easier for Beckett because of his abilities as an all-around athlete. Public schools like Portora have always claimed that sports develop leadership and notions of fair play. So two afternoons every week were devoted to rugby football, rowing, swimming, cricket, and boxing. Beckett did not row, but he performed well at every other sport, except track. He became light-heavyweight boxing champion of the school.[57]

At cricket, he displayed an excellent eye as a left-hand batsman ("I batted left-handed because my brother taught me that way," he told me)[58] and some early talent as a right-arm bowler of off-breaks. He went straight into the first eleven in his first summer at the school, at the age of fourteen. He and Geoffrey Thompson soon became established as the school's regular opening batsmen. The school magazine described Beckett in his final season at the school, in which he made a top score of 40: "Scores freely once he gets set, but takes time to settle down. Only on two or three occasions has he produced his true form.

Has improved his play on the off, and can punish balls on the leg side. A dangerous bowler on his day. A first-rate fielder." [59]

Swimming completed Beckett's wide range of sports. The Portoran boys used to swim regularly in nearby Lough Erne. A diving board had recently been installed on a stone parapet,[60] and Beckett was one of a small group of early morning bathers who dived into the cold waters of the lough before a quick swim across the Narrows. There were also highly competitive races across the Narrows, as well as a longer race of 420 yards. Beckett showed more speed in the sprints than he did endurance in the longer races, although he still managed to win the Junior Long Race in 1921.[61]

Most of his free time when he was not studying or on the playing fields was spent either reading or playing bridge and chess with his friends. One of these, Charles Jones, remembered him as "a keen and effective bridge player." [62] Chess was rapidly becoming a passion, and he seized every opportunity for a game. He was also one of the very few boys in the fifth and sixth years who took regular music lessons, although he was somewhat critical of the woman who gave him piano lessons, dismissing her as "not very good." [63] But his interest in music and in verse at the time led him to have the reputation of being "almost word perfect over the whole range of Gilbert and Sullivan operas." [64] There are also signs that a real interest in books was beginning to develop while he was at Portora, for he became one of the librarians assisting Mr. Breul and he donated at least one book to the library. In his second year, he was elected to the committee of the Literary and Scientific Society and, in spite of a deep-seated shyness, participated in the debates by delivering a "violent and eloquent speech" that opposed a motion attacking women's emancipation. He and another boy lost the vote by a majority of ten.[65]

Although Beckett did not admit to writing for the school magazine, he was quite proud of some lavatorial lines that he penned, he said, in his mid-teens.[66] They impressed several of his friends sufficiently for them to learn the ode by heart.[67]

> Come away, my love, with me
> To the Public Lavatory
> There is an expert there who can
> Encircle twice the glittering pan
> In flawless symmetry to extend
> Neatly pointed at each end.

These and another fourteen lines stem from a vein of earthy humor that runs through Beckett's mature fiction, where a schoolboy pleasure in scatology has been transformed into a wry (and very Joycean) mocking of the natural functions, expressed in language that refuses to be censored and maintains its right to explore every nook and cranny of human experience.

4

BECKETT WAS no plaster saint at Portora, any more than he had been at Earlsfort House. Charles Jones wrote that "he was just as naughty as the rest of us in tormenting Mr. Breuil [Breul] to a pitch of rage which gave us vast enjoyment but must have brought him almost to the point of a coronary on many occasions."[68] He either initiated or took a leading part in several practical jokes. At seven o'clock every evening, the "Wee Bell" summoned ninety or so frisky Irish boys, the boarders of Portora Royal, to do their "prep" in the Big School, or large study hall. Halfway along one side of the room on a small dais sat the duty master, who was there to keep order. But on one particular night the duty master was known to all the boys as an utterly ineffectual disciplinarian, whom they ragged mercilessly. A tall, gaunt man with a straggly mustache, Thomas Tackaberry wore khaki riding breeches, leather leggings, and a tweed jacket. He was one of life's failures. His wife had left him somewhere along the way and, good scholar though he was,[69] in his fifties, he was still only a junior master at a time when, because of the decimation of the male population by the First World War, almost every decent teacher had been snapped up for a senior post by some headmaster somewhere.

That evening, in addition to the usual range of impertinent questions, illicit whisperings and conversations, and desks being opened and shut more loudly than was necessary, two enterprising members of a bright fifth form decided to liven up the evening with some organized, precisely orchestrated community singing. One of the boys was Claude Sinclair, who, after a few years as an ordained clergyman of the Church of England, wrote several novels of Irish life, now forgotten; the other was Samuel Beckett. Under the alliterative title "The Singular Sing-Song Singers," they had issued in advance a list of songs to be sung. The signal for the "spontaneous" outburst of each number was given by Beckett, whose desk at the side of the central aisle was visible to everyone.

The "concert" went exactly as planned. With the raising of Beckett's index finger, ninety voices started singing in noisy unison. Unfortunately, the furious Tackaberry spotted who was orchestrating the singing; leaving his dais, he strode furiously across the room toward Beckett. As he arrived at the desk, something seemed to snap in the master and he began to rain blows on the boy with both fists. Beckett, who boxed regularly, put up his guard and protected his head from the punches until, ashamed of what he was doing, the master stopped hitting him. Beckett dropped his guard, looked up, and delivered the coup de grâce: amid a stunned silence, he said quietly: "Why don't you hit somebody your own size!" The combined effect on the master of his own attack and the boy's remark was devastating: Tackaberry walked slowly back to the dais, put his head into his hands, and started to weep. Through his sobs, the boys could hear him muttering: "To think I've come to this—a convenient piss-pot for the whole school!" Then he got up abruptly and walked out of the room, leaving the boys as shocked by the dramatic effects of their practical joke as by the master's words.[70]

Beckett seems to have been dreadfully upset by what at first had appeared to be an entertaining, harmless prank. He told his friend Lawrence Harvey of Dartmouth College that he felt pity for the defenselessness of the master. He was certainly much too sensitive as a boy not to have connected this ragging with his own experience of being bullied.

Once, Beckett himself felt hurt at being unjustly punished. Sixty years later he could still remember every detail as if it were yesterday:

> Frank was Headboy or Senior Prefect and in charge of our dormitory. He had his own little room or cubicle. One night he had supposed to have checked that we were all in bed. And I had gone into a friend called Gamble's bed. I knew nothing about sex at the time. It was to tell him a Conan Doyle story. The Headmaster, Seale, came in with a torch in his hand and found me in bed with this other boy. Of course it was his bed. So I was the guilty one. Seale had me in his room the next morning and asked me what I was doing in Gamble's bed. I told him I was telling him a story. "A story, what story?" he said. So, I told him it was the Sherlock Holmes' story, *The Speckled Band.* He gave me six of the best for my trouble. "That will teach you not to tell stories," he said.[71]

Although hurt at the injustice of being punished for something that he had not done, in general Beckett felt great respect for the headmaster. "The soul of honour himself," said one former pupil, "he [Seale] expected an impossible standard of honour from us, and we often deceived him. If you looked him straight in the eye, he would believe anything you said."[72]

The stress placed on honor, loyalty, and integrity reinforced the emphasis laid on these qualities in Beckett's previous school. Retrospectively, this might seem an ethos that Beckett would have found stuffy and boringly conformist. As an adult he found the notion of the "gentleman" much too English for his liking. Yet it is doubtful if that was how he regarded it at the time. For whatever reservations he might have had about the rather crude way in which these standards were imposed, it seems likely that, by the time he left Portora at the age of seventeen, they were deeply imprinted in his nature, perhaps in spite of an instinctive individualism and impatience with the pompous moralizing that often accompanies the public proclamation of such values. Although he would probably have disowned any causal link between his later behavior and his education, the standards held out to the boys of Portora remained an important and greatly underestimated element in his formation. In later life he displayed an old-style politeness and an almost unfailing kindness and courtesy toward people to whom, often, he had no special obligations. And he remained totally loyal to his friends. Honesty, integrity, and loyalty seem to have remained intact within him, to be transformed later in his life into a personal ethic motivated by pity, compassion, or guilt and not by public school tradition or bourgeois conformism. His standards made him exceptionally vulnerable to those less scrupulous than himself. And, when he felt that he himself had fallen short of his own demanding standards, his strongly puritanical conscience pricked him into paroxysms of often quite unnecessary remorse. Clashes of this kind between conscience and inclination were to lead in his life to many deeply disturbing tensions and to a powerful sense of guilt.

3
The Growth of a Mind
1923–26

1

BECKETT WAS A SHY, retiring seventeen-year-old when he went up to Trinity College as an undergraduate in October 1923 to study for an arts degree. He was slim and quite tall for his age, although still a couple of inches below the six feet of his maturity. His short reddish-brown hair was brushed severely across to the right. But the sternness of his appearance was contradicted by an unruly parting that he later abandoned altogether. His short haircut tended to empha- size the size and protrusion of his ears, which, like his strikingly aquiline nose, seemed over the years to grow even larger and dominate his face. He had bright blue eyes and a piercing stare. That, at least, never changed. He wore small round metal-framed spectacles, which lent him a most studious air, but this was counterbalanced by the physique of the athlete. And yet, although he was still involved in some sports, it was his passion for words, literature, and art that was to develop most dramatically at Trinity College. In this, he was enormously influenced by two of his teachers.

He had not been at university for very long before Thomas Brown Rud- mose-Brown, the professor of Romance languages, began to take a keen interest in his progress. Rudmose-Brown had a reputation in the college for having firm favorites. Equally, he could be actively hostile to those he did not like. One of his students, Eileen Williams, for instance, a contemporary of Beckett, took a much less favorable view of their professor than he did. "I must say I was never very fond of 'Ruddy' as a person," she said. "He was unreliable and changeable. He took a fancy to somebody and that person was everything at the time and the rest of us were very small fry. He let his personal feelings interfere greatly with academic standards."[1]

Although he was known as a ladies' man, prone to laying on the charm lavishly with attractive young women undergraduates (although married with children, he was reputed to have had a number of affairs), occasionally, and for purely intellectual reasons, his favorite would be a man. Beckett was one of the favored few. Classes in the arts at Trinity were small. So the lecturers knew their honors students very well. In any case, even in his first ("junior freshman") year, Beckett's aptitude for French and English literature, his thoughtful appreciation of the texts that they were studying, and his unusual essays, as well as his silent, brooding manner, brought him to the professor's notice. Much later, Beckett acknowledged that Rudmose-Brown "opened all kinds of doors for me."[2] As late as 1983, he wrote with great warmth of his debt to him: "Much needed light came to me from 'Ruddy,' from his teaching and friendship. I think of him often and always with affection and gratitude."[3]

Ruddy, as he was known to his friends and foes alike, was in his mid-forties when Beckett first met him. He had a kind, friendly face, a slightly bulbous nose, sensual lips, and a high color. He suffered badly from catarrh, which caused him to sniff most unattractively. He was tall and heavily built, with massive, stooping shoulders. His forehead protruded beneath a large, domed, bald head. He liked to suggest that the unusual shape of his upper head, with a marked protuberance in front of a dipping fontanelle, was found among the Lapps and the Eskimos and boasted that he was descended from ancient Scandinavian — or, as Beckett remembered him maintaining — Icelandic stock.[4] Tracing his lineage to more recent times, he spoke of having a copy of a grant of arms from 1488 that had belonged to an ancestor on his mother's side; he also used to claim proudly: "My father's mother was a Stewart of royal descent."[5]

Although he had been a professor at Trinity College since 1909, Rudmose-Brown was a highly unorthodox, even controversial figure, who was never part of the academic establishment. In those days, there were two quite separate categories of members of staff: the fellows, elected young after passing the very difficult fellowship examinations and providing firm evidence of distinguished scholarship; and the teaching professors, who mostly tended to be regarded as second-class citizens by the fellows and especially by the provost. In spite of having a respectable number of publications to his name,[6] Ruddy had not convinced the fellows that they should elect him, and he never became one of their number. Such a change of status would in any case have been extremely rare.[7] Beckett described him as a "voluptuary"[8] and Con Leventhal spoke of Rudmose-Brown's "individual and independent outlook" and "forceful personality."[9] None of this would have endeared him to the more orthodox or more austere of the fellows.

Retrospectively, Beckett spoke of Ruddy as a witty, disillusioned man. But, as a young student, he was highly intrigued and vastly entertained by some of his professor's more outrageous idiosyncrasies and fiercely held prejudices, as well as flattered by the interest that he was taking in him. Rudmose-Brown, who was a great talker, was, for instance, rabidly anticlerical. He argued interminably about religion with the many clerics on the Trinity College staff. He used to swear like a trooper and was full of cleverly barbed witticisms and sharply etched epigrams. Once he defined the best government as the one "that charges you the least blackmail for leaving you alone"; Beckett never forgot this cynical turn of phrase.[10]

Ruddy was, in Beckett's words, a "free spirit."[11] He spoke to students as equals and not only had them around to tea, as many of the tutors did, but also used to accompany them to concerts, the theater, and even to pubs. Although his family home was in Malahide, he had rooms in Dublin where occasionally he gave parties for students. Sixty years later, Beckett chuckled mischievously as he talked about these parties, commenting that they were "very sexy" affairs: when the party was in full swing, much to the amusement of his student guests —and to the delight of some—Rudmose-Brown tactfully used to turn out all the lights. Beckett also said that he often went for drives in the hills around Dublin in Rudmose-Brown's car—"not always talking about literature," he added.[12] When his father bought him his own little sports car, he was able to return his professor's kindness and hospitality. On a couple of occasions, he even took him back to Cooldrinagh to meet his parents and was surprised at how well Rudmose-Brown seemed to get on with them.[13]

Rudmose-Brown strongly influenced Beckett's own tastes in literature and undoubtedly affected his attitudes to life. It was he who inspired Beckett with his deep love for Racine's plays but equally passed on to him his antipathy to Corneille's.[14] Much of Beckett's knowledge of nineteenth-century French poets such as Leconte de Lisle, José-Maria de Heredia, the Symbolist Henri de Regnier,[15] whom Rudmose-Brown almost idolized, and Paul Verlaine, some of whose poems Rudmose-Brown was anthologizing while Beckett was his student,[16] derived from the enthusiasms of his mentor. Ruddy loved Ronsard, too, and passed on to Beckett his great affection for the "Sonnets pour Hélène" and for the poetry of Petrarch and his sixteenth-century follower Louise Labé. (In Dream of Fair to Middling Women, the Polar Bear, a character who is a caricature of Ruddy, pontificates: "Now Louise Labbé [sic] . . . was a great poet, a great poet, perhaps one of the greatest of all time, of physical passion, of passion purely and exclusively physical."[17] He also recognized the importance of her friend the elegist Maurice Scève, and guided Beckett carefully through the poems in Délie, objet de plus haute vertu (1544).[18]

Rudmose-Brown was unusual for his time in that he actually taught— and clearly relished teaching—modern authors such as Proust, Gide, Francis Vielé-Griffin, Léon-Paul Fargue, Valery Larbaud, Louis Le Cardonnel, and Francis Jammes rather than confining himself to the time-honored literary canon.[19] More interestingly to Beckett, Ruddy either knew or corresponded with a number of practicing French poets and kept closely in touch with what was happening in current French writing. He had corresponded with the writer Stuart Merrill, and probably met Francis Jammes. And, after a sustained correspondence with the French writer and admirer of James Joyce Valery Larbaud, in the last year of Beckett's studies Ruddy finally went to Vichy to meet the French writer.[20]

Undoubtedly, Rudmose-Brown fostered Beckett's love for poetry in general and encouraged his growing interest in contemporary poetry. It was he who was responsible for Beckett starting to do his post-graduate work on a contemporary French poet, Pierre-Jean Jouve, and, in the late 1920s and early 1930s, this led to Beckett translating Surrealist writers like Paul Eluard, André Breton, and René Crevel.[21] But Rudmose-Brown was also a poet himself, who wrote in French as well as English. Some of his poems in the two languages had been published some years before in a slim volume entitled Walled Gardens.[22] It seems likely that Beckett was encouraged to start writing creatively by his professor.

The wider impact of Rudmose-Brown on Beckett in terms of his attitudes to life was probably just as crucial. Rudmose-Brown's memoirs show him to have been a staunch believer in individual freedom: "that is why I am neither Fascist nor Communist, Imperialist or Socialist," he wrote.[23] He was totally opposed to any kind of narrow patriotism or nationalism and could become apoplectic with rage when speaking about the increasing stranglehold that he saw the Catholic Church exerting on the newly created Irish state: "I accept no dogma and deny none. I allow everybody complete freedom of belief. But when the Church — any Church — takes upon itself to lay down the law on what does not concern it, I protest and I oppose. . . . I cannot accept the interference of a Church in politics, social economy and ethics."[24]

In several of his early occasional pieces, Beckett adopted a very similar position to that of Rudmose-Brown when he confronted issues relating to the interference of church and state in matters to do with personal freedom. In a little article entitled (after Voltaire's *Candide*) "Che sciagura," published in *T.C.D.: A College Miscellany* in 1929, and in "Censorship in the Saorstat" (which was written for *The Bookman* in 1934 but never appeared there because *The Bookman* merged with another review) he attacked respectively the ban on contraceptives and the banning of books by the Free State, whose legislation was coming to be dominated more and more by the strict morality of the Catholic Church.[25] Talking regularly to so interested, committed, and forthright a spokesman for individual freedom as Ruddy must have shaped as well as sharpened Beckett's own opinions.

Rudmose-Brown clearly considered his student a fellow freethinker. When Beckett went to Paris in 1928, he recommended him to Valery Larbaud as a "grand ennemi de l'impéralisme, du patriotisme, de toutes les Eglises" (a "great enemy of imperialism, patriotism, and all the Churches").[26] And he would have tried to set Beckett against all systems and all orthodoxies, whether religious, philosophical, or ethical: "Every one of us must strive, unflinchingly, to be himself," he said.[27] Beckett's entire career could be regarded as an illustration of that particular precept.

Yet Beckett did not idealize Rudmose-Brown. The shambling figure of the Polar Bear in *Dream of Fair to Middling Women* and in *More Pricks Than Kicks* is a grotesque, "a big old brilliant lecher."[28] He is tightfisted and gross, with a propensity to catarrh, and he makes highly unwelcome advances to young women. In the story "A Wet Night," the Polar Bear spews out witty but pretentious anti-Christian sentiments, never using "the English word when the foreign pleased him better."[29] And in *Dream of Fair to Middling Women*, he proves this by cursing vigorously in a mixture of French and English: " 'God b——— the bastards' he snarled, 'merde and remerde for the bastards.' He snatched off his huge old hat and his head shone high above the crowd. He was an enormous stout block of a man. 'Merde' he snarled 'merde, merde.' "[30]

2

THE SECOND MAJOR INFLUENCE on Beckett during his student days was not a Trinity College lecturer at all but a small, plump, middle-aged Italian lady called Bianca Esposito, a private tutor who gave him regular Italian lessons. "You had to do two languages at the time," said Beckett, "so I chose Italian as my second language. It was my good luck to meet Bianca Esposito. She helped me with my literature as well as my Italian language." [31] As well as conversing in Italian, they analyzed in great detail the writers he was studying in his final two years at the university: Machiavelli, Petrarch, Ariosto, Carducci, and D'Annunzio, and, above all, Beckett's greatest love among Italian writers, Dante, studying the *Divina commedia* and the *Vita nuova*. [32] He took copious notes on Dante's great poem and went into its allusions as well as its overall vision. He seems to have discovered the nineteenth-century poet of pessimism, Leopardi, either by himself or guided by Rudmose-Brown. For, although he was taught Italian literature both by Rudmose-Brown and by the equally colorful Walter Starkie, if you were a favorite of Ruddy you were unlikely to be an admirer of Starkie, for the two professors failed to see eye to eye on anything. Beckett never had much esteem for Starkie and felt that he learned nothing worthwhile from him.

Private classes in Italian were held in a small school of languages and music at 21 Ely Place, a four-story red-brick building with a handsome stone portico. It was natural that Beckett should seek help from this private language school, not only because Bianca Esposito had a reputation in Dublin as a first-rate teacher and a highly intelligent woman but also because the music teacher there was Miss Pauline Elsner, the sister of his former kindergarten teacher, Miss Ida Elsner, who herself taught occasionally at Ely Place. [33] French and German were also taught. And so a couple of times a week, Beckett used to stride up Grafton Street or Dawson Street from Trinity College across St. Stephen's Green and down the short Hume Street for his Italian class with Signorina Esposito.

The layout of the language school closely resembled the one that is described by Beckett in the opening story of *More Pricks Than Kicks*, "Dante and the Lobster." This opens with its antihero, Belacqua, failing to understand Beatrice's explanation of the spots on the moon in cantos two to four of Dante's *Paradiso*. [34] Students walked into a largish entrance hall in which stood a hat and coat stand and a small oak table. What was called the Italian Room opened off the hall at the front of the house, with the French Room behind it; the German Room was somewhere else in the house, Beckett wrote indifferently—since he was less interested at the time in German than he was in the Romance languages.

Again, according to Beckett, it was Bianca Esposito, not his Trinity College Italian professors, who nurtured his love for Dante's *Inferno* and *Purgatorio* (he found the *Paradiso* much less compelling reading).[35] For his love of Dante remained with Beckett until the end of his life and deeply influenced his own writing at several different points in his career. He had a constant and apt reminder of his debt to Signorina Esposito. When, following a serious fall in his eighties, he had to live in an old people's home in the rue Rémy-Dumoncel, he took with him the little edition of Dante's *Divina commedia* that he had under-lined and annotated in class with her. Inside the book, he kept a card with a faded miniature reproduction of a painting by Giotto of St. Francis feeding the birds. On it is a message in Italian from his teacher wishing him a speedy recovery from an illness that had put him to bed at Cooldrinagh a few days before his twentieth birthday. Beckett had been using the card as his Dante bookmark for sixty-three years.[36]

Belacqua's Italian teacher in "Dante and the Lobster," "Signorina Adriana Ottolenghi," was closely modeled on Bianca Esposito.[37] The fictional Italian teacher comes, we learn in the story, from Naples ("But Neapolitan patience has its limits," comments the narrator[38]) and Esposito is indeed a common Neapolitan name. The name of Ottolenghi, on the other hand, comes from the north of Italy and was borrowed by Beckett from that of his landlady at the pensione in Florence where he stayed during his first visit to Italy in 1927.[39]

Bianca Esposito also had a most unusual voice, to which Beckett alludes in "Dante and the Lobster," where he uses the word "ruined." This was later to become one of the defining characteristics of the voice of an old man, Krapp, in the first manuscript draft of the play *Krapp's Last Tape*. In the same play, autobiographical traces persist as Beckett chooses "Bianca" for the name of one of Krapp's lovers, although mainly on account of its associations with light in a play that is full of black and white contrasting imagery. And so the thirty-nine-year-old Krapp records on his tape recorder: "At that time I think I was still living on and off with Bianca in Kedar Street," Kedar being not a real street but an anagram of "darke."[40]

The youthful, shy, retiring Beckett had no sort of amorous entanglement with Bianca, who was much too old for him anyway. But she was someone for whose intelligence, judgment, wisdom, and wit he had enormous respect. His admiration creeps into the detail of the opening story of *More Pricks Than Kicks*: "His Professoressa was so charming and remarkable. . . . He did not believe it possible for a woman to be more intelligent or better informed than the little Ottolenghi."[41] Beckett used to look forward to his Italian classes with great excitement, as much for Signorina Esposito's witticisms as for the subjects they discussed. For she could coin a neatly rounded, aphoristic turn of phrase in English as well as in Italian, and this ability tickled him inordinately. In "Dante and the Lobster," when Belacqua asks the Italian teacher where they were, after their lesson has been interrupted, Signorina Ottolenghi, in all likelihood again echoing Bianca Esposito, replied weightily as well as wittily: "Where are we ever? . . . where we were, as we were."[42]

3

BECKETT'S HONORS SUBJECTS at Trinity College were French and Italian. But he also studied other subjects. For leading up to the "Littlego" examination he was obliged to take mathematics — geometry and algebra — in which he did not do particularly well,[43] and he followed the Latin classes of Kenneth Bailey and E. H. Alton. More important is that he also completed two full years of English literature, doing well in most of his examinations.[44] He laid the groundwork for his close knowledge of Shakespeare's major plays. In spite of Professor W. F. Trench's dour emphasis, in his Shakespeare lectures,[45] on versification and on demonstrating how metrical evidence could be used to date the plays, in reading the texts Beckett still seems to have responded in a lively, direct way to Shakespeare's language and imagery and was soon able to call readily to mind quotations from the plays.

Passages like *Macbeth*'s "Life's but a walking shadow; a poor player / That struts and frets his hour upon the stage, / And then is heard no more" and phrases like "Sleep that knits up the ravell'd sleave of care," from the same play, thrilled him. Allusions to *Hamlet, The Tempest, Romeo and Juliet,* and *Macbeth* (all of which he studied) are intricately woven into the tapestry of his stories in *More Pricks Than Kicks* and of the novels *Dream of Fair to Middling Women* and *Murphy.* The title of one of the early stories, "Ding-Dong," probably derives from Ariel's dirge in *The Tempest*; in "Fingal," the narrator, commenting on Belacqua and Winnie's climb up one of the martello towers at Portrane, borrows Hamlet's ironic linking of his late father's funeral and his mother's wedding. "The tower began well; that was the funeral meats. But from the door up it was all relief and no honour; that was the marriage tables."[46] And "Draff" hints at how keenly the imagery of *Romeo and Juliet* had touched Beckett ("but the livery of death, leaving aside its pale flag altogether, was too much for her").[47] In his later writing he used Shakespearean allusions and echoes more naturally and more casually.

Rudmose-Brown taught English literature as well as modern languages, and Beckett attended his lectures on Spenser's *Colin Clouts Come Home Againe,* as well as *The Faerie Queene.* (Parallels have been drawn between Molloy's sojourn with Lousse in Beckett's postwar novel *Molloy* and the enchanted garden scene in *The Faerie Queene.*[48]) In his second year, he studied two terms of Chaucer, including the Prologue to *The Legend of Good Women.* The title of Beckett's novel *Dream of Fair to Middling Women,* written seven years later, is partly borrowed from the Prologue and partly from Tennyson's "Dream of Fair Women." Beckett also used a quotation from the Chaucer text as an epigraph to the same book.[49]

Beckett found himself captivated by the Miltonic world, when he was introduced (again by Rudmose-Brown) to Milton's *Paradise Lost, Comus,* and *Lycidas.* And he revealed that, when he was a student, he really did once try to explain Milton's cosmology to his father "away up in the mountains, resting against a huge rock looking out to sea," as *From an Abandoned Work* suggests.[50] Thirty years later, in *Happy Days*, a play shot through with light and dark images of Miltonic resonance, Winnie, now buried up to her neck in the earth under a scorching sun, opens the second act with an ironic "Hail, holy light" consciously borrowed by Beckett from *Paradise Lost*. In his English classes, Beckett also studied More's *Utopia*, Bacon's *Essays*, Donne's sermons as well as his poems,[51] Pope's *Rape of the Lock*, and Swift's *Drapier's Letters*, and read other books by some of these authors. For the English course almost forced the student to do a lot of additional reading, since the examination questions were framed in such a way that a wide-ranging knowledge of an author's work was needed in order to answer them at all properly.

However richly innovative much of his own later writing was to be, Beckett always saw himself as belonging to and drawing from a wide European literary tradition.[52] Discussion of his formative influences has tended to concentrate on Joyce or Dante. Yet, although both were vitally important to him, it was also his good fortune to study Balzac — mostly so that he could reject his entire approach as a novelist — and to have Racine (for the drama) and Diderot as well as Stendhal (for the novel) among his forerunners. Nor did he object to being placed in the company of Rabelais, Swift, Fielding, and Sterne.[53] Although after the war years he was to turn away from the quest for more knowledge to the exploration of impotence and ignorance, he remained one of the most erudite writers of the twentieth century, with a range of easy reference that extended widely over many literatures.

4

BECKETT LIVED AT HOME until the summer of 1926, traveling to Trinity College either by train, just as he had done when going to school at Earlsfort House, or, until he got a car, by motorcycle. His social life in college tended to be restricted at first to a small group of male friends who had come up with him to Trinity from Portora Royal School: Geoffrey Thompson, who studied medicine; Oliver McCutcheon, who read French and German; and Tom Cox, who read classics. He often went to the Abbey Theatre with Thompson, who was almost as fascinated by the theater and literature as he was by medicine. Beckett and he always tried to occupy the same seats at the Abbey. Beckett explained: "The balcony was semi-circular with two aisles, a central triangle and two aisles. And if you got a seat at the centre end of the aisles, you were as well off as you were sitting in the centre. You got just as good a view. It also only cost you one and six for a side seat as opposed to three shillings in the centre."[54]

It was a very rich time in Irish theater. Beckett could remember very clearly seeing premieres of Sean O'Casey's *Juno and the Paycock* and *The Plough and the Stars* at the Abbey. But he also went to Lennox Robinson's *The White Blackbird*, T. C. Murray's *Autumn Fire*, and Brinsley Macnamara's *Look at the*

Heffernans! [55] There were some wonderful character actors in the Abbey company, among them F. J. McCormick, W. O'Gorman, and M. J. Dolan. Michael Dolan in particular impressed Beckett. He saw him in the role of a modern Job in T. C. Murray's *Autumn Fire*, remarking to his new Trinity College golfing friend, Bill Cunningham, "how much his [Dolan's] hands came into expressing his feelings, when, as a man who was maimed and stricken, he had all these tragic occurrences falling upon him." [56] Surprisingly, by the age of eighteen or nineteen, Beckett was already intrigued by the power of gesture. In 1931, lecturing at Trinity College on Molière, he stressed the importance of "muscular dialogue generated by gesture." [57] Then, several decades later, directing his own plays, he was to discover how powerful gesture could remain even when reduced to a few essential, repeated movements. In his final two years as an undergraduate, Beckett saw W. B. Yeats's two versions of Sophocles' *Oedipus the King* and *Oedipus at Colonus*. Oedipus' wretched plight is echoed (or parodied) by Hamm's first rhetorical question in *Endgame*: "Can there be misery — *(he yawns)* — loftier than mine?" [58]

Yet the revivals of John Millington Synge's plays at the Abbey were of greater significance to Beckett than the work of any other Irish dramatist. When I asked him who he himself felt had influenced his own theater most of all, he suggested only the name of Synge. [59] He saw *The Playboy of the Western World*, *The Well of the Saints*, and *The Tinker's Wedding*. He was drawn to Synge's unusual blend of humor and pathos, his stark but resilient tragicomic vision, his imaginative power and clear-sighted pessimism. And he was impressed by the rich texture and vitality of Synge's theatrical language and the striking, bold simplicity of his verbal and visual imagery. [60] His first encounter with Synge's plays at the Abbey Theatre was a memorable event.

But Beckett went to other theaters in Dublin as well as the Abbey, particularly in his last two years as an undergraduate. The Gaiety, the Olympia, or the Theatre Royal put him in touch with a lighter kind of theater that grew out of the revues and music-hall sketches of the "illegitimate" theater or the circus and that differed entirely from the realistic style that was currently holding sway at the Abbey. At the same time, he continued to go to the cinema, enjoying the early silent feature films of Buster Keaton: *Sherlock Jr.*, *The Navigator*, *Go West*, *Battling Butler*, and the famous *The General*, as well as some of Keaton's earlier shorts. He also saw a lot of Charlie Chaplin films at this time, enjoying particularly *The Kid*, *The Pilgrim*, and *The Gold Rush*. This love of old music-hall and circus routines was to remain with him and resurface later in the tricks to which the tramp-clowns of *Waiting for Godot* have recourse in a desperate attempt at "holding the terrible silence at bay" [61] and in the precisely timed comedy routine with the cat and dog in *Film*, the film he made with Buster Keaton. But a Keaton film like *Go West* was also noted for what James Agee called a "freezing whisper not of pathos but of melancholia." [62] Its unsmiling protagonist, Friendless by name, resembles a Beckett hero, lost and alone in the world. [63]

Beckett's education was not entirely literary, theatrical, or cinematographic. For although he followed no formal art history classes and appears to have been largely self-taught, he was captured at this time by a deep love of painting. He visited the National Gallery of Ireland regularly both as a student and, later, as a lecturer in Trinity. So he was nursed on the gallery's eclectic collection of Old Masters and developed an abiding passion for seventeenth-century Dutch painting: Salomon van Ruysdael's *The Halt*, in which sixty years later he could still describe the little boy urinating against the wall by the lower right-hand frame; Jan van Goyen's A *View of Rhenen on the Rhine*. He was so familiar with van Goyen that later he would occasionally refer to an actual landscape as being "very van Goyen." He found the Merrion Square Rembrandts splendid, the *Portrait of a Young Lady* (now thought to be from the studio of Rembrandt, although still catalogued in 1981 as by Rembrandt), the astonishing *Rest on the Flight into Egypt*, and, by an imitator of Rembrandt, the *Portrait of an Old Gentleman*. These were the first of many paintings he saw by an artist whom he loved for a long time.

It was in the Irish National Gallery too that Beckett encountered his first member of the Brueghel family, the son, Pieter Brueghel II — Hell Brueghel, as he was known — in the form of *The Peasant Wedding*. Nicolas Poussin's *The Entombment* stunned the young Beckett with its lyrical blue and purple; and Adriaen Brouwer's *The Corn Doctor*, Aelbert Cuyp's *Milking Cows*, and Titian's *Ecce Homo* impressed him so much that they became important points of reference or comparison on his wider safaris into the European galleries. For this deep love of painting remained with him for the rest of his life and influenced him in startling ways as a writer.

5

DURING HIS UNDERGRADUATE years, Beckett first fell in love. It is almost impossible to discover exactly when he succumbed to the spell of Ethna MacCarthy, although it was probably soon after his arrival at Trinity College. Ethna was a year ahead of him as a student. But, in terms of experience of the world, she was light-years ahead in maturity. She too was studying modern languages, although she specialized in French and Spanish, while, after the first two years, he was studying French and Italian. But the students who started their courses in 1922 and 1923 respectively often attended French lectures together. The shy, retiring Beckett used to sit silent with his head down, scarcely addressing a word to anyone.[64] He was very ill at ease with women whom he did not know well and never made advances to the women students.

The emphasis at the time on the segregation of the sexes was hardly conducive to easy relationships between men and women. Although they took classes with the men, women were not allowed, for example, to talk to male students in Trinity Square, and had to leave the college site by six o'clock. They were excluded from most male activities like dining on Commons and had to receive special permission from the junior dean of students before they could attend an evening function such as a recital or a concert at the college. A porter was on the alert at the front gate and women had to display their passes before they were allowed in. Men and women students used to mingle, of course, in cafés such as the modest little Pâtisserie Belge near the back gate of Trinity and the old Westland Row railway station or, if they had enough money, at Switzers or the Bonne Bouche at 51 Dawson Street.[65] Beckett only rarely frequented such cafés himself. But Ethna, who was not in the least retiring, was a favorite of Rudmose-Brown; she was invited to many of the same parties as Beckett and would have chatted animatedly to the enigmatic young man from Foxrock. There were other social gatherings outside Trinity when he must have met her — at Susan Manning's soirées, for instance, which provided him with the raw material for his satirical picture of such a gathering at Casa Frica in the story "A Wet Night." Even though he hated the pretentiousness and false conviviality of such occasions, it was sometimes difficult to refuse to attend, since the Mannings were such old childhood friends.

Ethna was a remarkable woman for her time, a feminist *avant la lettre*. Intelligent and independent-minded, she was determined to carve out her own career, although for a long time she was uncertain exactly what that career should be. She was also most attractive physically. Small and dark-haired, she had beautiful, dark, expressive eyes with long, curling lashes, and a devastating smile. "She was so lovely and so graceful and nice," said one of her friends. "She had such a lovely manner, no affectation about her at all. She was just naturally lovely. She didn't try to be; she just was."[66] She dressed fashionably and elegantly, often wearing blue, although she was immortalized by Beckett in his poetry and prose writing as being sheathed in vivid scarlet or "flamingo."[67]

The Irish playwright Denis Johnston had been one of Ethna's earlier admirers. In a letter written to him in 1959 when she knew she was dying, she described him as "my first love in what seemed the springtime of the world."[68] Almost forty years before, each of them had penned a character study of the other. Although clearly written to tease her and prick her conscience, Denis's revealing analysis shows how easily, if she had tried, she would have been able to twist not only himself but also the totally inexperienced Beckett around her tiny little finger:

> From her earliest youth upwards she has been admired and adored both by family and by outsiders. Now adoration is the normal, expected thing. She looks to be given first place and first attention everywhere and — sadly for herself — almost invariably gets it, for the simple reason that she deserves it. She has never been friendless and it is doubtful if she ever experienced what it is to be lonely.
>
> Consequently she has never been shy, can be frank and outspoken to a degree, is absolutely fearless, intolerant of mediocrity and finds it difficult to suffer fools gladly.[69]

Beckett, on his own admission, adored Ethna, but said that the relationship with her never became a sexual one. "She was a wonderful person," he added.[70] All the evidence suggests that she swept him completely off his feet. Unfortunately, as Denis Johnston's character study and diary reveal, she did much the same to most of the young men she met. Naturally flirtatious, she was usually to be found at the center of a whole gaggle of captivated young men: medical students, rugby players, professors, poets, and musicians. When they did not feel jealousy at her success, women respected her. Many men besides Beckett tried to court her. She was escorted, for instance (to Johnston's as well as Beckett's annoyance), by a medical student, Donald O'Connor, the son of a judge, who was a fellow Catholic and a family friend.[71] And when the elegant young Frenchman Alfred Péron arrived in the autumn of 1926 to take up his post as *lecteur* at Trinity College, he too fell in love with Ethna. By then she had finished her degree but was still around Trinity writing a research essay.[72]

A later *lecteur* and French friend of Beckett, Georges Pelorson, gave a striking personal account of the magnetic effect that Ethna used to have on young men:

> I had the impression of a kind of panther, you know, ready to jump. That's the reputation she had. Extraordinarily intelligent, extraordinarily witty and with a command of French that was absolutely wonderful. She was not exactly pretty — she was small, she was rather fleshy shall we say, not fat, but rather small and almost corpulent. She had a very beautiful face, lovely eyes, extraordinary eyes — very penetrating, very sagacious and almost black. Her hair was almost black too. Beautiful forehead. I met her not more than three times, but the first time, that's why I felt immediately like this [nervous and on edge], because she was aggressive in a not unpleasant way; she was "going at you" immediately. I remember she said to me something like "What kind of a Frenchman are you?" And immediately I thought: "Oh-oh." She was very talented. She was prodigiously witty, and witty in French as well because she had such a command of the language. I was amazed.[73]

Something had happened earlier, however, while Ethna was still an undergraduate, that dashed any hope Beckett, Johnston, Péron, or any of a dozen or so other young men might have had of winning her affections: she became passionately involved with an older man who was both married and a professor at the college. She was happy enough to be surrounded by adoring young men and to be escorted by Beckett to concerts, the cinema, or the theater. But, by comparison with her older, more experienced lover, Ethna must have found him very small fry indeed.

Beckett's feelings for Ethna ran very deep. And once he had gained sexual experience himself, in Germany and France, her unwillingness to allow their relationship to develop into a physical love affair seems to have preoccupied and troubled him for many years. In the early 1930s, he constantly had to reassure himself that he could bear to see her, when she had embarked on a love affair with one of his best friends, Con Leventhal, who was also married at the time. The image that he retained of this "wonderful person" remained inviolable over the years. Eventually, in 1956, after the death of his wife, Leventhal married Ethna; Beckett stayed an adoring friend until her premature death in May 1959.

What was it about this flirtatious, highly intelligent, articulate young woman that guaranteed that she would stay so deeply imprinted on Beckett's mind? She was probably the first woman for whom he felt real love. And the fact that this love was never consummated, as his later amorous relationships with women mostly were, and that she was able to offer him only her friendly affection, may well have ensured that his own feelings would remain in a different category from the rest. The young Beckett had considerable difficulty in reconciling the lusts of the flesh with the yearnings of the spirit. Perhaps more than anything, Ethna represented for him a glimpse of a possible harmony of flesh and spirit, in which the loved one could be both desired and admired at the same time. She appeared as the "feminine incarnate" for Beckett and inspired two of his most beautiful poems, "Alba" and "Yoke of Liberty" (also called "Moly"); more fleetingly, she appears in her "old black and flamingo" dress as the "dauntless daughter of desires" in the poem "Sanies I."[74] She entered deeply into his fantasy to become the model for one of the major characters in his youthful prose.

6

BECKETT CONTINUED PLAYING various sports at Trinity College. Mostly playing with a handicap of seven, he represented the college at golf. He also joined the Carrickmines Golf Club as a student member and, during the holidays, would often complete as many as seventy-two holes in a day. Golf was for him, he told Lawrence Harvey, "all mixed up with the imagination," with the impact on him of the ocean, which one could see from the local course, and the landscape of the Dublin foothills.[75] He knew, he said, "every blade of grass." At night, when he could not sleep, even many years later in France, he would play over again in his mind all the holes on the pretty bracken and heather course. Sometimes, to add a little spice to games at Carrickmines, he used to challenge Jim Barrett, the club's professional, with whom he was on easy, relaxed terms, for the enormous sum in those days of seven shillings and sixpence. A friend who accompanied him on two such occasions commented: "Had Sam won, he would have been lucky to be paid. Barrett hardly had the price of a bottle of stout, to which he was very partial. His victories over Sam must have felt rather like paradise."[76]

Beckett also played a lot of cricket and, during the summer vacation, was contacted by the writer Joe Hone to play for his cricket team in matches throughout the county.[77] The highest standard of cricket in which he competed, however, was undoubtedly played on Dublin University's two tours of England in the summers of 1926 and 1927. A game against the English county side, Northamptonshire, was the climax of a short tour that also included a match against the Royal Engineers. The county game was thought of by the university cricketers as by far their most demanding fixture. And it was through these games that Beckett became the only Nobel Prize winner to be included in the pages of the cricketers' bible, *Wisden*.

Beckett also took an active part in chess matches with the college eight, playing at number seven for a couple of years.[78] And he played a lot of billiards while he was at Trinity, a game that he enjoyed playing for many decades with friends in Parisian cafés after he left Ireland.[79]

But Beckett's enjoyment of competitive sports or games took him into more adventurous territory. As a student, he owned a two-and-three-quarter-horsepower A.J.S. motorcycle. He told me, "I had two of them. My father bought me them. It was a four-stroke motor bike, I remember. My brother had a Douglas. . . . I used to ride the A.J.S. into Trinity College from Foxrock. I remember once bumping into Sir Robert Tate [one of his lecturers in Italian, and the junior dean] with all my gear on."[80] As a member of the Dublin University Motor Cycle Club, he raced the A.J.S. in motorcycle trials. Early in March 1925, for instance, he took part in an open novices' trial that started from Donnybrook and covered sixty-three miles through pine forests and mountains.[81] Beckett did not win but, unlike two of the starters, he did complete the entire course. According to John Manning, who used to ride pillion with him from time to time,[82] Beckett was an intrepid motorcyclist, driving too fast for his own (and his passenger's) safety. Over the years he had many spills as he took corners much too sharply; in several of these accidents he was slightly injured.

He also tried his hand, memorably, at roller skating, which had become the latest craze in Dublin in the 1920s when a number of new ice-skating and roller-skating rinks were opened. So, always ready to have a go at a new sport, Beckett went along with his brother to the Plaza to test his balance. Gerald Pakenham Stewart, his roommate at Trinity, reported:

> There his efforts on the skates caused such a disturbance that the management accused him of being drunk and demanded that he leave the premises. Sam, protesting that he was in no way intoxicated, eventually agreed to leave without making trouble provided the management gave him back his entrance money, and this they did with relief. The thing that gave Sam considerable satisfaction in this incident was, as he related to me later, that he had obtained entry to the rink without paying anything.[83]

Before the scholarship examination that he took early in the summer of 1926, Beckett was taken ill with an infection that his friend Tom Cox remembered as pneumonia.

> He was out of action for some time. He felt he had to make up for lost time and the last six weeks before the Scholarship examination he worked day and night, so much so that we were afraid he would knock himself up. That seemed to be a turning point with Sam because after

that he withdrew more into himself. I and the Portora crowd, he still kept in touch with them nearly as closely as before I think, but from the others he withdrew. And I remember one thing we thought was very odd, he suddenly started reading Nat Gould and declared he was the finest writer of English that ever had been. Nat Gould wrote racing novels such as *Kissing Cups Race*, things like that, where at the last moment, despite all the attempts to nobble the horse, the horse won.[84]

Nat Gould's books probably offered Beckett the kind of escape that he found later in French *série noire* thrillers. They were a soporific that helped him switch off his mind when he was driving himself very hard.

7

INSOMNIA WAS ONLY ONE of a disturbing set of physical symptoms that now began to afflict Beckett. In April 1926, while he was still living at Foxrock, he first experienced what he later came to describe as "the old internal combustion heart."[85] During the night his heart started to race faster and faster, fast enough to keep him awake. At first, this caused him relatively little anxiety. But, later, the attacks were to become more frequent and far more distressing. Soon they were accompanied by dreadful night sweats and feelings of panic that eventually became so serious that Beckett felt he was being paralyzed by them and was forced to seek medical help. The problem was to plague him for very many years. For the time being, however disturbing he found this new, mostly nocturnal phenomenon, it did not prevent him from working. And hard work brought its just rewards. In the summer, he was one of only sixteen students out of the entire year in all subjects who succeeded in securing a College Scholarship.

After this success, he decided that he would like to spend August 1926 visiting France. His chief intention was to improve his spoken French. But at the same time he wanted to see some of the fine old towns of Touraine and the châteaus of the Loire. He was also eager to pay homage to the memory of the Renaissance poet Pierre de Ronsard.[86] So he planned to go to see the Ronsard family home at La Poissonnière and make a pilgrimage to the poet's grave at Prieuré de Saint-Côme-les-Tours.

From Greene's bookshop opposite his father's office in Clare Street, he purchased a copy of Henry Debraye's *En Touraine et sur les bords de la Loire* (translated into English as *Touraine and Its Châteaux)*[87] and carefully mapped out a tour of the region, deciding how many miles he could reasonably expect to cover each day on his bicycle, while still allowing himself plenty of time to visit the châteaus and the churches. The tour fitted in well with his literary interests, for so many great writers had either been born or lived in "this privileged land," including Rabelais at Chinon and La Devinière; Joachim du Bellay at "le petit Liré"; Ronsard at La Poissonière, Vendôme, and Saint-Côme-les-

Tours; "Descartes at La Flèche, Alfred de Vigny at Loches, and Honoré de Balzac in the valley of the Indre, at Tours, Saumur, and Vendôme."[88] It was Beckett's first visit to France and the first of several literary or artistic pilgrimages that he was to undertake in the next ten years.

Tours became both his starting and his finishing point.[89] He took a train from Paris to the beautiful old town, then hired a bicycle and, for the first night, took a room in a little pension called "le petit Belmont," on a hillside just outside the town. In the middle of the morning, he was standing in the lovely garden looking out over the Loire at the elegant twin towers of the Cathedral of St-Gatien and at Charlemagne's Tower, when he noticed a young man leaning against his bicycle on the road outside. The man asked Beckett in perfect French what the pension where he was staying was like. From Beckett's reply, he quickly detected that he was not French. So he explained that his name was Charles Clarke and that he was an American postgraduate student from Yale University vacationing in France. The reason his French was so good, he explained to a surprised Beckett, was that he had a Belgian mother and he spoke the language regularly at home. His father also happened to be a professor of French at Yale.[90]

Beckett went off to visit the town and returned to find that the American had taken a room in the pension. Over dinner they talked, finally deciding that they would tour the region together. As far as possible, they followed Beckett's plan based on Debraye's little volume, visiting a dozen or so of the surrounding châteaus, Ronsard's tomb, and some of the places with other literary associations in the region, especially Rabelais's birthplace in La Devinière and his residence in Chinon. At the end of an exciting trip in which Beckett's enthusiasm for things French and enjoyment of speaking real French with the local residents in cafés and pensions grew apace, they agreed that Clarke would come over to Ireland and stay at Cooldrinagh as soon as it could be arranged after Beckett's final examinations.

On his return to Ireland, Beckett moved into rooms at 39 New Square that he had agreed to share with Gerald Pakenham Stewart. The set of rooms, which went with their newly elected status as "Scholars," was on the ground floor left, in the second square of Trinity College, New Square. "We had one large living room and each had our own bedroom," Stewart explained. "There was also a small kind of 'scullery,' where we could boil a kettle and wash dishes."[91] Every day, a manservant or "skip" came in to clear out the grate and stoke up the fire, make the beds, and generally clean up for the young men. Early in his final year, Beckett rented a piano, which stood in the sitting room. He played it only before close friends like Geoffrey Thompson or when no one was there. One of his enthusiasms at this time was French music. "He was quite a good pianist and he was particularly interested in the music of Debussy," said Thompson. "I remember he used to play Debussy preludes and other piano pieces. 'La Fille aux cheveux de lin' was one of his favourites."[92] His roommate's "only memory of him playing was one night he came in after I had gone to bed and sat there playing, what he described as 'sad chords' in the dark."[93]

8

HIS FINAL ACADEMIC SESSION was transformed for Beckett by the arrival from Paris of the new exchange *lecteur*, Alfred Péron. Two years older than Beckett, Péron was elegant, witty, and urbane. A student at the Ecole Normale Supérieure since 1924, he had shared a study there with Jean-Paul Sartre and Paul Nizan. Someone who knew both Sartre and Péron in the mid-1920s described Péron as being at the time "every bit as charming as Sartre was disagreeable."[94] Péron had started at the Ecole studying classics but had then changed his field to English language and literature. He was also widely read in French literature and seems to have offered Beckett exactly the right blend of personal friendship and intellectual questioning that he needed to extend his mind at this stage of his studies. He also helped enormously with Beckett's spoken and written French. The friendship between the two young men lasted throughout the 1930s and was to have momentous consequences for them both during the Second World War.

In spite of Péron's liveliness, Beckett still went into a period of growing introspection, depression, and withdrawal. This probably resulted from a combination of factors: first, the natural tendency he had had from childhood on to sit back, observe, and listen, noting the oddities of what others said and the idiosyncrasies or follies of their behavior; second, his keen awareness of his own intelligence and sensitivity. These characteristics were ultimately to contribute to Beckett's success as a writer. But during his time as a student, they seem to have led only to an unhappy separation from all but a few close friends. When he went on tour with the cricketers to Northampton, he said that, instead of going off whoring or drinking in the local pubs with the others, he went on his own around local churches.[95] He was still strictly teetotal and a nonsmoker. He confessed later to feelings of superiority and contempt, which led to a depression that came to seem, to use the word he used himself, "morbid."

But another factor came into play. He became acutely aware at this time in his life of the poverty, pain, and suffering that were visible almost everywhere around him in the big city. Living in a prosperous suburb had protected him from exposure to all but the most blatant examples of human misery. And, like so many of the well-to-do (and not only they), he had probably operated his own filter system, refusing to notice, turning away or shutting out what was not pleasant to contemplate. Now, no longer returning home to Foxrock at the end of the day, he began to wander around the streets, observing how wretched the lives of so many of his fellow men could be: beggars, tramps, ex-soldiers wounded or gassed in the First World War; the blind paralytic, wheeled daily into his place "near the corner of Fleet Street and in bad weather under the shelter of the arcade."[96] It seems highly likely that Beckett witnessed at this period an incident like that in which, in the story "Ding-Dong," a little girl is tragically run down by a bus in "long, straight Pearse Street."[97] Beckett "could never understand," Gerald Pakenham Stewart wrote, "why God allows decent, harmless people to suffer so much and when, in his sports car, he ran over and killed his own Kerry Blue terrier, he was heart-broken."[98]

It was on the key issue of pain, suffering, and death that Beckett's religious faith faltered and quickly foundered. This happened, according to him, when he was a student. It may have resulted partly under the influence of the free-thinking, anticlerical Rudmose-Brown and partly from his intellectual encounters with a number of skeptical authors who were taught in the modern languages program. But one revealing incident suggests that his loss of faith occurred primarily as a result of the kind of personal experiences just described.

One evening, he went with his father to All Saints' Church at Blackrock to hear his father's friend Canon Dobbs deliver a sermon about his pastoral visits to the sick, the suffering, the dying, and the bereaved. "What gets me down," said the minister, "is pain. The only thing I can tell them is that the crucifixion was only the beginning. You must contribute to the kitty." Beckett was horrified by the logic of the cleric's position: not merely an open admission of total failure to cope with the problem of apparently undeserved suffering and an overt acceptance of the fact that it is the human lot to suffer, but a grisly justification for it. "When it's morning, wish for evening," Dobbs went on. "When it's evening, wish for morning."[99] His sad litany of human suffering was close enough to Beckett's own feelings at the time to strike a vibrant if chilling chord in the young scholar who had recently read *Candide* with its remorseless, if ironic, piling up of human misfortunes and natural disasters.

How, Beckett argued with himself, could one possibly justify pain and death as making a "contribution" to anything? The "kitty" was simply a senseless accumulation of pain. How then could pain and suffering have any moral value? And how cynical it seemed to him to regard such suffering as somehow preparing one for an afterlife that would be all the better for the suffering that preceded it. Canon Dobbs seemed perilously close here to Dr. Pangloss with his argument that evil, pain, and suffering are all part of a divine plan that we simply cannot understand (in Alexander Pope's words, "All discord, harmony not understood / All partial evil, universal good"). And the bitter pill of Dobbs's medicine struck Beckett as Pope's words had struck Voltaire: as an appalling affront to the suffering of the individual.

Such an undiluted acceptance of suffering lies behind a bitterly ironic poem like "Ooftish" — undoubtedly written much earlier than 1938, when it was published — and behind a statement like Hamm's in *Endgame*: "Use your head, can't you, use your head, you're on earth, there's no cure for that!" that Beckett was to pen much later in his career.[100] Gerald Stewart could recall Beckett as a student coming back to their rooms in Trinity College one day "with an aluminium strip from one of the printing machines which used to grace the platforms of railway stations, on which he had inscribed the words 'PAIN PAIN PAIN' and which he affixed to the wall."[101]

4

Academic Success and Love

1927–28

1

OVER THE CHRISTMAS VACATION of 1926–27, there was much animated discussion at Cooldrinagh as to what Beckett should do when he finished his degree the following autumn. Taciturn as usual when he himself was the subject of the conversation, Beckett said as little as possible. He had a clear idea of what he did not want to do, which included law and chartered accountancy, the subjects that his tutor, the philosophy don A. A. Luce, had written on his tutorial card as the careers that Beckett had indicated he might follow on his arrival at Trinity College—perhaps for the sake of having something to write down.[1]

School teaching did not appeal to him either. His father, who had suggested earlier that he should join the Guinness brewing company ("a cushy job, early retirement and plenty of Guinness," commented Beckett[2]), could no longer see him taking a job in business. He also recognized that his second son had no inclination to follow him into the family firm of quantity surveyors or to become a building contractor like his grandfather. The close bond of sympathy and affection between them meant, however, that Bill Beckett did not press him too hard, although he worried periodically about his future. May, on the other hand, her head buzzing with her own ideas for Sam's future career, was more persistent in her questions and far less tolerant of his protestations that he and the worlds of business and finance were utterly incompatible. However, pressed by his parents to discuss possibilities with the staff at Trinity, Beckett turned for advice to Rudmose-Brown rather than to his tutor.

Ruddy had been delighted with the success of his favorite student in becoming one of the "Scholars of the House" the previous summer. (This was the highest award that an undergraduate could achieve at Trinity, for at any one time there were only seventy Scholars in all subjects throughout the entire college.) Moreover, Beckett had underlined his success in "Schols" by coming top of his class in the recent autumn examinations in Modern Literature, and Rudmose-Brown was convinced that he would do outstandingly well in the final Moderatorship examinations.

Believing that his protégé would eventually enhance the standing of the School of Modern Languages, he suggested that, as a first step on the path to becoming an academic, Beckett should allow his name to be put forward as

Trinity College's exchange Lecturer in English for the coming year at the Ecole Normale Supérieure in Paris. He could then be appointed at a later date to the Modern Language School at Trinity as Rudmose-Brown's assistant. Although privately Beckett had seen quite enough of university life to have serious reservations about it, he agreed, having nothing better in mind. So, at the end of March, on Rudmose-Brown's recommendation, the Board of Trinity College formally recommended "S. B. Beckett (Scholar)" for the post to the distinguished academic literary critic Gustave Lanson, the Director of the Ecole Normale.[3]

At this point an almighty rumpus blew up over Beckett's nomination that was to have important repercussions on both his personal life and his career.[4] Trinity's exchange lecturer for the academic year 1926–27 had been William McCausland Stewart. But, in January, Stewart was appointed to a lectureship in French at Sheffield University. This created a vacancy that was filled, on a temporary basis, by a former Moderator in History from Trinity College, Thomas MacGreevy.[5]

MacGreevy, an affable, talented all-rounder who spoke French much better than he wrote it,[6] got on extremely well with both students and staff alike at the Ecole Normale and, having met James Joyce, his family, and his circle soon after his arrival there, was enjoying his life in Paris. So, believing that Trinity officials had no one whom they wished to appoint for the coming academic year, MacGreevy asked Lanson if he could continue in his post. Grateful to MacGreevy for helping them out and well disposed toward him personally, Lanson led him to believe that he would favor his reappointment.

On hearing this, Rudmose-Brown wrote a curt, ill-tempered letter to MacGreevy accusing him of trying to retain the post unfairly, even though he knew that he had been appointed as a stopgap, and stressing that the Modern Languages School would insist that its own nominee, "S. B. Beckett," be appointed. MacGreevy complained and wrote to the Board as well as to Rudmose-Brown pleading his total innocence and asking for Trinity's backing to stay on. Stewart also wrote a letter of support to the college, saying that MacGreevy had given up the assistant editorship of *The Connoisseur* in London on the understanding that the Ecole Normale post would be free for another year.[7] But Dr. Louis C. Purser, the secretary of the Board, replied that the School of Modern Languages was adamant that Beckett, "a young man of great ability and promise with high academical distinctions," should be appointed.[8]

The matter dragged on for several months. However, in the end, Lanson kept his word to MacGreevy, even though it meant flying in the face of the Trinity board. It was a frustrating time for Beckett. He could do nothing but listen to Rudmose-Brown huff and puff and finally fail to get him appointed to the Paris post. Instead, early in July, he was told that, if he were to apply, he would almost certainly be offered an alternative appointment as *lecteur* at the University of Besançon.

As it happened, Beckett was touring in England with the university cricket team at the time this alternative offer arrived and could have met the application deadline only with great difficulty.[9] In any case, the idea of an appointment at a provincial university did not appeal to him at all. And Rudmose-Brown simply would not hear of it. Paris was, after all, not just a mecca for writers and painters but also for aspiring university professors anxious to meet these writers and painters and savor the cultural riches of the French capital. The Ecole Normale was also considered a prestigious academic appointment. So it was decided that Beckett's name should go forward again as Trinity's nominee for the Ecole post for the following academic year, but with a prior understanding that he would definitely be appointed.[10] What is most ironic about this whole dispute is that, once Beckett finally took up the Paris post, following what was for him an irritating delay, the usurper MacGreevy became his closest friend and confidant. Their friendship lasted until MacGreevy died in 1967.

2

WHILE THESE NEGOTIATIONS were continuing concerning his postgraduate future, Beckett still had to prepare for his undergraduate examinations in French and Italian. During the summer term, he visited Italy for the first time. "My father let me go to improve my Italian before my final exam," he explained. "I stayed in Florence."[11] Astutely, he borrowed notes on the lectures he missed from the brightest student of his year, Vida Ashworth, who had beaten him in most earlier examinations and whom he then promptly beat to take first place in finals.[12] He chose Florence partly because of its artistic splendor, but mainly because Bianca Esposito had a sister, Vera, who had returned to Italy from Dublin five years earlier and was looking after her mother in a little house at 24 Via Fra Guitone near Fiesole.[13]

Beckett stayed in Florence at a pensione run by a Signora Ottolenghi, paying thirty lire for a small room and three meals a day. The pensione, at 14 Via Campanella, was close to the Piazza Oberdamm and not far away from the Campo di Marte. Most days, after visiting galleries and churches in the morning, Beckett would make the short journey to see Vera and her seventy-six-year-old Russian mother, whom he thought a fascinating woman.[14]

Vera interested him too. She had been married to an Irishman, Maurice Dockrell, the son of Sir Maurice and Lady Dockrell, who — or so Beckett remembered having been told — drank heavily and beat her badly. Consequently the marriage had broken up. She had lived for twenty years in Dublin when, having become involved with the IRA, she was forced to leave the country sometime after the civil war in 1922. In the early years of the century, she had acted with the National Theatre Society. Later, at the Abbey Theatre in the early 1920s, she played female roles that called for a Continental accent.[15]

Beckett and Vera used to go for long walks in Fiesole or sit for hours over lunch talking about the old days in Dublin. Vera found that he spoke Italian "very fluently, but with a strong Irish accent."[16] Beckett said that he interspersed his vocabulary from time to time with archaic phrases from Dante that the

Italians no longer used, such as "Non meno caler" instead of "[Per] me é uguale" for "It doesn't much matter." [17] He was offered local wine at the Espositos'; still a total abstainer at that time, he firmly declined. [18]

Vera recounted to Beckett a story about James Joyce. More than twenty years before, she said, they had called on James Joyce with her father, Michele, a musician, while Joyce was staying briefly with his friends James and Gretta Cousins in Ballsbridge. Her father had been greatly impressed by Joyce's voice as he sang (to his own accompaniment) the ballad of "Turpin Hero" and a couple of sentimental songs. A year later, Beckett met Joyce in Paris and passed on to him — to Joyce's obvious delight — Commendatore Esposito's lavish praise of his fine tenor voice. Vera or her mother could scarcely have resisted telling Beckett either about an incident in the same year, when, coming out of a theater rehearsal together, they had stumbled over Joyce's drunken, prostrate body lying in a passageway, from which he was unceremoniously thrown out into the street. [19]

Vera and Bianca had a brother called Mario, who was a well-known medieval scholar, paleographer, and bibliophile in Dublin and Paris, publishing several studies of early Latin manuscripts in Ireland and two inventories of Irish and Swiss ancient manuscript collections. [20] While living with his father and Bianca in Dublin, it seems that he had also been leading a secret life, operating as a Sinn Fein agent, traveling to the Continent on IRA business. [21] He, too, had to leave Ireland on account of his IRA connections after the civil war. Beckett told me that he had little knowledge of either of the Espositos' political activities.

Beckett was joined in Florence by his American friend from the previous year, Charles Clarke. Together, they paid a visit to Venice, where they went to the Accademia and Beckett stood, smoking a pipe, in the Piazza San Marco feeding the pigeons, while his friend took his photograph. Once Clarke had left, Beckett took a short holiday with Mario Esposito, staying near Lake Como in the north of Italy. [22] An account of the holiday given by Mario has survived in the surprising form of a letter to James Joyce's biographer Richard Ellmann. The account is very revealing about Beckett's extreme "touchiness" as a young man and about how he drew (selectively) on such incidents in his personal life for his early writing. Mario Esposito recalled that

> Beckett's adventure on Monte Generoso in July 1927 was a ludicrous fiasco. He damaged his feet badly and spent the rest of his sojourn in the house of a peasant woman who had let us two rooms in her house. Every few hours she bathed his feet in hot water and herbs which she said would cure him, and did. He got angry with me and a doctor who lived in the same house for joking about him.... On returning to Ireland he wrote me two letters which I have, apologizing for his rude behaviour to me and the doctor. [23]

This ill-fated walking expedition by Lake Lugano under the peaks of Monte Generoso and Monte Galbiga figures prominently in Beckett's 1932 novel, *Dream of Fair to Middling Women*. In this book, the chief character, whose name is taken from Dante's figure Belacqua, in the *Purgatorio*, arrogantly refuses to wear two pairs of thick socks or to bandage his feet with rags prior to the ascent, even though he has bought a new pair of "mighty nailed boots for climbing." Soon he finds himself "utterly fatigued, the new boots sprawled in the ditch where he had cast them from him, the bloated feet trembled amongst the little flowers, with his socks he had staunched them, the bells of the cattle high above under the crags asperged him, he cried for his Mother."[24] Beckett mocks Belacqua and, implicitly, himself here. But he does not draw on the more embarrassing elements of his experience: being confined to the peasant's house waiting for his bleeding feet to heal, and being mocked by his friend and the doctor.

Yet this painful and humiliating experience forms the basis for a passage that evolves into an exercise in style, part mock-pastoral, part mock-erudite: "A fat June butterfly, dark brown to be sure with the yellow spots, the same that years later on a more auspicious occasion, it was inscribed above on the eternal toilet-roll, was to pern in a gyre about a mixed pipi champêtre, settled now alongside his degradation."[25] The passage ends with a learned parallel with Dante, a small copy of which, according to Mario Esposito,[26] Beckett always carried in his pocket: "under the laggard moon, eternal pearl of Constance and Piccarda, of Constance whose heart we are told was never loosed of its veil, of Piccarda alone but for her secret and God, he picked his steps home as a barefoot hen in a daze would down the steep Calvary of cobbles to the village in the valley where he lived."[27]

Beckett tramped for hours around the sunlit streets of Florence. A few years later, he recalled this most beautiful of cities in the story "A Wet Night." A walk down Dublin's Pearse Street, past the red, castellated, Florentine tower of the fire station on the corner of Tara Street and Pearse Street, brings back for the central character, again Belacqua, fond memories of the Piazza della Signoria and a firework display on the Feast of St. John; the Palazzo Vecchio; the parapets overlooking the river Arno; and what he called "the sinister Uffizi" gallery where Beckett spent many days looking at the vast collection of paintings.[28]

He visited the Pitti Palace, from which memories of paintings such as Titian's *The Penitent Magdalen* with her upturned face, long, thick tresses, and right arm held diagonally across her breasts were to stay firmly lodged in his mind. While generally Beckett preferred the Dutch and Flemish painters to the Italians, he was not insensitive to the wonders of the Florentine Titians, Giorgiones, Peruginos, Uccellos, and Masaccios. Eager to learn more about early Italian art, he bought a copy of Vasari's *Lives of the Most Eminent Italian Architects, Painters, and Sculptors*, which traces the history of Renaissance art from Giotto to Michelangelo.[29]

With his voracious appetite for architecture, painting, and sculpture, he visited most of the museums, galleries, and churches: the Accadémia, to see, among other masterpieces, Michelangelo's *David*; the church of Santa Maria Novella, to look at Uccello's *Deluge* and, in the choir, the Ghirlandaio frescoes;

the Brancacci Chapel of the Santa Maria del Carmine, to see Masaccio's famous frescoes.[30] Florence was a breathtaking revelation for someone already in
love with painting.

He returned home elated by the great art that he had seen, even more
fluent in Italian, less depressed, and eager to work hard for the final moderatorship examinations, which in those days were held after the long vacation in
October. Dante, Machiavelli, D'Annunzio, Racine, Balzac, Stendhal, Gide,
and Proust—he worked on them for the rest of the summer, focusing on the
kind of questions Rudmose-Brown and Starkie liked to set.[31] He was so successful in the examinations that he came out first of first, ending, in the words of
his tutor, "in a blaze of glory and [with] a large gold medal in Modern Literature
in Michaelmas 1927."[32]

3

DURING HIS FINAL undergraduate year, inspired by Rudmose-Brown's enthusiasm, he had become very keen on the early poetry of Pierre-Jean Jouve and
Jules Romains and interested in the literary movement called Unanimism that
centered on Romains and his friends. He had enjoyed reading Romains's collection of poems La Vie unanime (1908) and had developed, he confessed later,[33]
a "passion" for the poems that Jouve had written before the First World War and
before his conversion to Catholicism.[34] He had also read at least two of Jouve's
novels, Le Monde désert and Polina, and some of the work of the little-known
Unanimist poet G. Chennevière.[35]

Now with his final examinations successfully behind him, he stayed on in
his rooms at 39 New Square until January 1928, working in the Long Room of
the library on a research essay that he chose to write on Jouve, Romains, and
Unanimism.[36] Unanimism starts from the writers' intense feeling that they belong to some kind of collective existence: the life of a city, a barracks, a church
service, a crowded theater auditorium, or a café, for example. "The world lives
and works by these social or group events; in a sense, without them we could
not go on to develop our private and individual experiences, which, though far
from negligible, are not ultimately so decisive."[37] The emphasis in the early
poems of Romains or Jouve (although Jouve left the group at a very early stage)
is, then, on a collective life shared by the individual. For being in a group of
what Romains calls Unanimes, or collective beings, leads one to participate in
an individuality greater than one's own: the individuality, personality, or soul of
a group.

It might appear surprising at first that Beckett, who was to become so much
of an individualist, should have taken a special interest in the early unanimist
poems of Jules Romains and in his stories, some of which take as their subjects
groups of people; Beckett liked Romains's Les Copains and Mort de quelqu'un
in particular. Les Copains was very much an "in" book among undergraduates
at that time.[38] An outlook that sees the individual as finding some degree of

solace in a collective must have held some attraction for a young man who at the time was feeling increasingly his own sense of isolation. Jouve appealed to Beckett because, in spite of the waves of communal feeling that surge powerfully in his poems, he does not so much seek out the soul of the crowd as focus on his own sensations and reactions, relating everything to them. Even in some of Romains's early poems, such as "Je ne suis pas heureux," the solitude of a man who sits unhappily at his table feeling the sadness of his isolation from others is not so far removed from that of the "man in a room" of Beckett's own late plays or prose works. But Beckett's *solitaire* has not merely reconciled himself to his solitude. He has actively sought it out, having found no consolation in the outside world. The mood was close enough to Beckett's own feelings as he sat in his room at Trinity for it to appeal to him.

There is also a stark simplicity of language in Romains's poems, and a quality of humor in the novels and stories, that would have pleased the young Beckett. But as he looked more closely into the theories and ideals of the Unanimists, he may well already have considered their collectivist emphasis and idealized aspirations not just passé but also as romantic youthful chimeras. For, although quite capable personally of being swayed by his emotions, even as a young man he had a clear-sightedness about easy consolations, not to say panaceas, that was disconcertingly precocious.

It has been claimed that whatever research Beckett did for his essay on Jouve and Unanimism—which he later described as "a ridiculous essay"[39] and a "scrappy work"[40]—was done later in Paris and that he never actually finished it, producing his study of Proust instead.[41] However, although the essay has not yet surfaced (and any copy may simply have been lost or destroyed over the years), he insisted that it was indeed completed during the summer of 1928.[42] Ridiculous and scrappy or not, the money that the research prize from Trinity College brought him—either fifty or a hundred pounds, Beckett could not remember which, but it was probably the lower figure—undoubtedly helped him later in the year with the initial expenses involved in moving to Paris.

4

AFTER CHRISTMAS, helped again by a recommendation from Professor Rudmose-Brown, he obtained a teaching post in French and English at Campbell College, Belfast, the largest residential public school in Northern Ireland. A quite imposing, red-brick building with a clock tower, the school was built in the 1890s on beautiful, spacious grounds on the outskirts of Belfast, near Stormont. The pupils either belonged to the Church of Ireland or were Presbyterian. There were no Catholics. Beckett taught at the public school for only two terms, the Hilary (or spring) term and the Trinity (or summer) term of 1928. During the first term, he occupied furnished rooms in Belfast, traveling out to the college by tram to the terminus at Belmont. But, throughout the second term, he lived in the college rent free, in exchange for some residential duties.

The teaching post served its purpose only inasmuch as Beckett managed to accrue a hundred and fifty pounds that year. This included the research prize he received from Trinity College for his essay on Unanimism. For he spent little in Belfast, finding the city hideously dull, lacking in culture, and far too industrial and commercial for his taste.[43] Admittedly, there were the Opera House and the Empire and Alhambra theaters. But good theater and music were relatively rare, and what there was appeared to Beckett pitifully parochial. However, there was a grand piano in the Central Hall of the school, and, as a former master recalled, several other pianos for music practice elsewhere that Beckett could have played to relieve his boredom.[44] In the summer term, Beckett remembered, "he played cricket with the boys"[45] and the school magazine, *The Campbellian*,[46] reveals that he also represented a losing staff side against the school cricket team.[47]

Apart from enabling him to save money, Beckett's brief spell as a schoolmaster was not a resounding success. The school held few surprises for him, since Portora Royal, which he had left less than five years before, resembled it fairly closely in both attitudes and routine. After the intellectual excitement of his final year at Trinity College, he found it hard to adjust to teaching elementary French grammar and translation and took little pleasure in reading Shakespeare with fifteen-year-olds. He was, of course, totally inexperienced as a teacher. But, above all, he was emotionally quite unprepared for the shock of self-exposure that was involved in teaching and unhappy at the need to keep a constantly wary eye on discipline.

He did not get on particularly well either with the highly respected headmaster, William Duff Gibbon, M.A., D.S.O., M.C., widely known in the school as Scottie or Duffy Gibbon.[48] The present historian of Campbell College writes: "He was a kindly but firm man, who was keen to produce 'useful Christian citizens' (as one Old Campbellian told me). He understood boys, and tried to adapt the school to meet the needs of the most non-conformist pupil, if he could."[49] But Gibbon was, above all, a firm disciplinarian who had a number of brushes with Beckett concerning his own conduct and discipline in general. Beckett recounted how, on one occasion, some of the boys had so horrified the headmaster by their outrageous behavior that he ordered him as master on duty to beat them all soundly. To the headmaster's disgust, Beckett refused and, throughout the whole of his brief stay at Campbell College, never agreed to administer corporal punishment, confessing that he simply could not bring himself to do it.[50] He also found it hard to get up in time for the first lesson, even though he regularly missed breakfast. And when Gibbon discovered that he had persuaded one of the maids to bring him breakfast in bed on Sundays so that he could have a lie-in, the headmaster is said to have responded: "This is not a bloody hotel, you know, Beckett."[51] After Beckett had written some particularly acerbic comments on the Easter end-of-term reports, Gibbon commented that the boys whom he was lucky enough to be teaching represented "the cream of Ulster." "Yes, I know," replied Beckett promptly, "rich and thick."[52]

In spite of his shyness and love of solitude, Beckett always seemed able to make friends. Even his relationship with Gibbon cannot have ended on really bad terms: four years later, when he was seeking a post from a London educational agency, he asked for and received a testimonial from the headmaster.[53] His best friend at the school was Philip Arthur Tyrer Chrimes, a graduate in engineering science from Keble College, Oxford, who had arrived recently at the school to teach mathematics. Although Beckett liked the twenty-three-year-old Chrimes very much, they lost touch with each other after Beckett left Ireland for a two-year stay in Paris, and were never to meet again.[54] It was probably with Chrimes that he managed to get away sometimes on Saturday afternoons (for there was morning school on Saturdays) to the North Antrim coast to play golf on the attractive seaside courses such as Portrush (whose Palais de Danse, or Arcadia Ballroom, which Beckett may have sampled, is mentioned later in *More Pricks Than Kicks*).[55] He enjoyed these half days out, but at the end of the summer term was ready to leave, concluding that Belfast was "a dreary place" and had "no grace."[56]

5

ON HIS RETURN to Dublin in the summer of 1928, he met his young cousin Peggy Sinclair. She was the daughter of Beckett's aunt Cissie, who had married the Jewish art and antiques dealer William Sinclair, and lived in Howth before moving to Kassel in Germany in the early 1920s. Beckett had been in touch with the Sinclairs occasionally before their departure, although his parents did not encourage their son to visit his aunt, whose marriage had dismayed the entire Beckett family. In any case, Peggy was then only a young girl. Now aged seventeen, she came over from Germany to Ireland to stay with her uncle, Harry Sinclair, her father's twin brother, at Dalkey Lodge.[57] At more or less the same time, Charles L. Clarke, the American whom he had met two years earlier in France, came on his promised visit to Cooldrinagh. Beckett found himself torn between this captivating young woman and his friend. He often compromised by taking both Peggy and Clarke out for drives in his car, sometimes with Peggy's young sister, Deirdre, who had also come to stay with her uncle. They drove along the quiet, winding country lanes and through the little villages around Dublin and went to the beach at Killiney or farther afield. Deirdre recalled what happened:

> I think he fell in love with Peggy in Dalkey. He had a little car with a dicky-seat, I think it was a Swift, and used to go out driving. I must have been a bit of a pest to them because I was 9 and probably quite unaware that there was a love affair going on and I was put in the dicky-seat and Peggy and Sam sat in the front. An American friend often sat in the back with me and told me stories about grizzly bears.[58]

Charles Clarke's widow could remember her husband telling her about this German-speaking little girl who paid him amusing compliments like "You've got a funny face. . . . But it's a nice face." [59] Meanwhile, in the front of what was really only a two-seater sports car, Peggy and Sam, oblivious to everything else, laughed distractedly at each other's jokes.

But once Clarke had returned to America and Uncle Harry and his companion could be persuaded to "baby-sit" for Deirdre, Beckett was able to take Peggy off alone for drives into the Wicklow mountains or to the many beaches nearby, where they sometimes took out a boat. One such occasion provided the inspiration for a scene in *Dream of Fair to Middling Women*, when Belacqua is with the Smeraldina-Rima, a character who, according to Beckett, is closely modeled on Peggy.[60] The narrator dreams of

> the shining shore where underneath them the keel of their skiff would ground and grind and rasp and stay stuck for them, just the pair of them, to skip out on to the sand and gather reeds and bathe hands, faces and breasts and broach the foothills without any discussion, in the bright light with the keen music behind them.[61]

For, like the Smeraldina-Rima with Belacqua, the first "Dublin edition" of Peggy with her "intact little cameo of a bird-face, so moving" [62] totally bewitched Beckett. In this case, as so often with Beckett's early work, fiction followed fact very closely. For the shy, thoughtful, twenty-two-year-old student, on his own admission, had fallen promptly and passionately in love with his delightful, touchingly naïve, laughing "Smeraldina."

Born in Dublin on March 9, 1911, Ruth Margaret Sinclair, to give her her full name, had gone to Germany at the age of eleven with her parents and family. She had been educated at a German school. As a result, she spoke English with a slight Teutonic accent and made funny grammatical and syntactical slips when it was corrupted by her German. But she had an irrepressible sense of fun and would dissolve into great peals of laughter at the slightest provocation. Beckett's account in *Dream of Fair to Middling Women* of the Smeraldina-Rima's capacity to make others laugh is, again on his own admission, inspired by Peggy.[63]

> When she was in form, launched, she could be extremely amusing, with a strange feverish eloquence, the words flooding and streaming out like a conjurer's coloured paper. She could keep a whole group, even her family, convulsed with the ropes and ropes of logorrhoea streaming out in a gush. Her own Mammy used to foam at the mouth. . . .[64]

Surprising though it may seem, Samuel Beckett could be most at ease with someone who was extroverted and took the lead in conversation. And he soon fell into an easy, relaxed relationship with this lively, attractive, different young woman, although it was not to be very long before their rather frail skiff sailed into much choppier waters.

Peggy had a fresh, freckled face with a nose that was a little too large for her ever to be called beautiful. She wore her hair unfashionably long. But she had most attractive green eyes that were to haunt Beckett, hypersensitive to eyes, for many years to come. She often dressed in green too, though not exclusively so. She was highly conscious of fashion, in her younger brother's eyes perhaps even somewhat ahead of it.[65] A portrait of her, painted three years later by the artist Karl Leyhausen, a friend of her father's and a visitor to their flat in Kassel, shows her wearing a green beret-type hat with a smart green blouse, a green-and-brown skirt, and a green necklace.[66] The Smeraldina-Rima in *Dream of Fair to Middling Women* wears such a beret. "The sun had bleached it from green to a very poignant reseda and it had always, from the very first moment he clapped eyes on it, affected him as being a most shabby, hopeless and moving article."[67] And, looking back on just such a hopeless affair as the one between Beckett and Peggy, Krapp asks in *Krapp's Last Tape*: "What remains of all that misery? A girl in a shabby green coat, on a railway-station platform? No?"[68]

In a natural, relaxed sepia photograph of this period Peggy is seen wearing a light-colored blouse with a beige, or possibly gray, tweed two-piece suit, carrying a handbag with a blue-and-gray flap in patchwork leather, "vaguely cubist" in style.[69] Her keen sense of humor was complemented by a quality of wistfulness that lent her an air of mystery. It was this unusual mixture that captivated Beckett so intensely.

For her part, Peggy was very taken with this shy, gentle, good-looking, blue-eyed Irishman, with whom she seemed at times to get on so well and who was happy to spend large parts of his days in her company. At other times, she found him infuriatingly withdrawn, sullen, and elusive. She was only seventeen when they first met, and Beckett must have seemed extraordinarily complex for someone as open and straightforward as Peggy. At first, her affections seem to have been divided between her cousin and the talented young Irish painter Cecil Salkeld, whom she had known for some time in Kassel. She kissed both of them. But, on returning to Germany, it was Beckett who increasingly filled her thoughts. She began to write to him regularly and lovingly. As for Beckett, he spent a lot of his time thinking about how he could see her again before he took up his Paris appointment. He began to apply himself assiduously to learning German. What he felt after Peggy's return to Kassel is summed up retrospectively and with wry humor in *Dream of Fair to Middling Women*, where the main protagonist feels "alone and inconsolable," seeing "her face in the clouds and in the fire and wherever he looked or looked away and on the lining of his lids, such a callow wet he was then."[70]

But the world quickly intruded on such romantic yearnings. His parents were horrified when they realized that a romance had developed. Even if the extent of Sam's involvement with Peggy had not become apparent to them during the summer, the symptoms of youthful infatuation could scarcely have stayed hidden for very long, with the regular arrival of letters from Germany and in the face of Beckett's equally prompt responses. Peggy's father had too much of a reputation for wild extravagance combined with penury for May Beckett to feel at all happy at the prospect of her son staying for any length of time in Kassel or having a serious relationship with his cousin. Sinclair's Jewish origins may also have played a part in their disapproval. The Jewish community has never had an easy time in Ireland. Far more significantly, however, both his mother and his father would have been horrified at the dangers involved in an intimate liaison between first cousins. Fear was very great at something regarded, at the time, as close to incest.

When Beckett made clear that his own feelings were very much involved, his parents expressed their total disapproval and were hostile to his plans to go to see Peggy. The first in a whole series of monumental rows then blew up between Beckett and his mother; as a result, Beckett briefly left home. Gerald Stewart, who had shared rooms with him at Trinity during his last year there, wrote:

> Sam turned up once at my home in Dublin and asked if we could put him up. It transpired that he had fallen in love with a cousin of his who lived in Germany and his mother disapproved and refused to take him seriously. We took him in and he had a bed in my room for a while. The girl went back to Germany and Sam worked his way on a liner to a port in France and then traveled third-class by rail to Germany. I know no more about this event except that a long time later I asked Sam how the affair was going and he replied by saying that he had become a misogynist! [71]

Almost two years later, Beckett was to mark a passage in his own copy of Proust's A l'ombre des jeunes filles en fleur that related to the pain of separation and the death of the old self with the marginal note "Mail Boat—Aug 1928." [72] This almost certainly alludes to the sad, painful experience of separating from his family and from Ireland when he left to go to see Peggy—an experience made even sadder by the upsetting row with his mother.

The "mail boat" entry suggests that Beckett went to Kassel to see Peggy sometime in late August. It would be reasonable to surmise that he passed through Paris on his way back to meet the director and secretary and perhaps to see his room at the Ecole Normale. It was at this time that he may have met Thomas MacGreevy for the first time. The marginal note and Gerald Stewart's testimony are, however, the only indications we have of such a flying visit to Kassel. And if it did occur, Beckett must have returned to Foxrock in late September to pack his trunk and bags at least, for what turned out to be a two-year stay in Paris.

6

IN MID-SEPTEMBER, Peggy enrolled for a program of study at a well-known school of music, dance, and movement in Austria. Her fees were paid by her grandfather in Dublin. Contrary to the wishes of his parents, Beckett visited her there at the beginning of October, staying until the end of the month. [73] The school, called the Schule Hellerau-Laxenburg, was in the village of Laxenburg, nine miles south of Vienna. Classes were held in the Altes Schloss, a part of the fourteenth-century Laxenburg Palace, which had been the summer residence of the Emperor Franz Joseph and Empress Maria Theresia.

Beckett was to base a whole section of *Dream of Fair to Middling Women* on his stay in Laxenburg. The part of the book concerning the "Schule Dunkelbrau" derives not only in its broad outline but in its most minute detail from his memories of — or, more likely, his notes on — what he saw and experienced at the Schule Hellerau-Laxenburg. Even the fictional name "Schule Dunkelbrau" (*dunkel* = "dark") merely reverses the actual name of Hellerau (*hell* = "light").

Hellerau was originally the name of a garden city outside Dresden to which a Swiss teacher, Emile Jaques-Dalcroze, had transferred his school of "Eurythmics" and music from Geneva in 1911. Dalcroze was forced to leave Germany during the First World War. Courses continued, however, under new management until, ten years later, the school had to vacate the Hellerau buildings because they were unable to afford the rent. It was while the dancers and musicians of the school were touring in Austria that the managers were able to negotiate successfully with the trustees of the Habsburg estates and move the whole enterprise into the Altes Schloss of the Laxenburg Palace, where female students and members of staff also lived. The palace is set in a magnificent park of seventeen hundred acres with lakes, watercourses, lawns, and small woods. In Beckett's novel his fictional school is set in just such a park, which he called by the name of Mödelberg, perhaps suggested by the town of Mödling about six miles away.

The students at the Schule Hellerau-Laxenburg were mostly young women who had just left school. It was, commented Peggy's younger brother,

> quite a well known place. They went in for music combined with dancing, total approach to art — not really a professional school for people who were going into music professionally, but rather for artistic development. One of the things I remember about it was that the students had a special whistle by which they recognized each other, an extremely difficult whistle, which involved a chromatic scale. Peggy showed off this whistle, she had it pat. . . . I remember as well two physical exercises Peggy brought back from Hellerau Laxenburg: first, keeping one's feet together and swaying with one's whole rigid body in circles as big as one could manage, and, second, without using one's thumbs, snapping one's four fingers onto the palm of one's hand. The Sinclair children duly imitated.[74]

The "Dunkelbrau gals" in Beckett's novel, the "Apfelmus" (apple purée) that was a staple of their diet, and the Swiss teacher of improvisation (Dr. Gustav Guldenstein in reality, Herr Arschlochweh in the fiction) were all borrowed directly from Peggy's life at the school.[75] It was, comments the narrator,

> All very callisthenic and cerebro-hygienic and promotive of great strength and beauty. In the summer they lay on the roof and bronzed their bottoms and impudenda. And all day it was dancing and singing

and music and douches and frictions and bending and stretching and classes — Harmonie, Anatomie, Psychologie, Improvisation, with a powerful ictus on the last syllable in each case.[76]

A look at the prospectus shows how closely Beckett follows the actual classes that were held in the school: Dalcroze's method of rhythmics ("Rhythmics aspire to develop the individual in his entirety and to lead the pupils to grasp both bodily and musical rhythm according to their special needs"[77]), gymnastics, dance, music, educational psychology, percussion, and costume design.

The "gals" at the school were indeed "very Evite and nudist and shocked even the Mödelbergers when they went in their Harlequin pantalettes, or just culotte and sweater and uncontrollable cloak, to the local Kino."[78] One local Laxenburg resident claimed that the school porter used to take money for tours of the palace attic, from the windows of which visitors had a fine view of the terrace where the girls used to sunbathe in the nude.[79] The "local Kino" that they attended was, in reality, in the grounds of the summer palace and used to be the building in which the Habsburgs kept their silver and tableware.

Beckett stayed, just as his fictional character Belacqua did, in the "big blue Hof" (it was called the Blauer Hof) of the former Habsburg palace which stood off the last street in the village, the Wiener Strasse.

> On the fringe of the village, empty, invested with dilapidation, squatted the big blue Hof, four-square about a court-yard of weeds. There he lived, in a high dark room smelling of damp coverlets, with a glass door opening on to the park. To get to his room he could enter the Hof from the last village street and walk across the court-yard, or better still make the circuit of the corridors, or again he could come at it deliberately from the other side, from the park.[80]

The building still exists today and the layout is exactly as described here. At the time the Blauer Hof was also very run-down, so it is likely that Beckett actually stayed in a room smelling of damp, where the rats slithered and slid behind the sweating wallpaper. As in *Dream*, Beckett's room was "ten minutes' walk through the park" from the school. Even the hedge, through a breach in which Beckett made his way after kissing Peggy good night "under the arch of the school buildings," and the clump of bushes where he regularly stopped to urinate as he walked back to his room, were there at the end of the 1920s, although the hedge has now been removed.[81]

Almost everything about the layout of the school and Belacqua's experiences there is fact, then, rather than fiction. What is totally unverifiable is whether the rape of the man by the woman actually took place in real life and whether it marked the beginning of a significant change in their relationship as it does in the novel. Quite clearly the fictional woman, having herself initiated the sexual stage of the relationship, wants it to continue. The fictional man for his part, committed to a purer love of the mind, does not want to become enmeshed in so physical a way. The fictional woman wants sex only with a man whom she loves, and she says that she loves Belacqua: "Looking babies in his eyes, the ———, that was her game, making his amorosi sospiri sound ridiculous."[82] But the man does not want anything that could lead to such commitments, not only because of the practical consequences, but because he separates the lusts of the flesh from the love of the spirit.

But how does all this relate to Beckett and Peggy? If Peggy was, as she is said to have been, a sexy kind of girl, openly physical with someone with whom she was very much in love, and wanting the relationship to continue in a passionate sexual way, this would certainly have led to problems. Beckett was going away very soon to Paris. And even though he did not yet seriously envisage himself becoming a writer, he certainly would not have seen himself settling down at twenty-two with a wife and a child. And the girl he loved was after all, as his mother pointed out to him interminably, his first cousin. It would not be surprising then if fears not just of conception but of the possibility of an ill-fated, defective, or mentally ill offspring should have frightened him too. But, more important, there are many indications throughout Beckett's life that — in this respect, at least, not unlike his character Belacqua — he saw the sexual act as not necessarily related to love. In the novel "it was always on that issue [of sex] that they tended to break and did break."[83] Disagreements over sex were responsible for the affair between Beckett and Peggy breaking up, she wanting such a physical relationship, he not. In spite of their quarrels, however, the affair did not end in Vienna and, at the end of October, Beckett took himself off on the train to Paris. In the novel, "The Smeraldina bit her lip with great skill and did the brave girl until the Platznehmen of the porters became final. Then her tears fell fast and furious. A hiccup convulsed the train. Off flew the green helmet . . ."[84]

5
The Paris Years
1928–30

1

ON 1 NOVEMBER, 1928, Beckett woke to face his first day in Paris. He had arrived by train from Vienna the previous evening for the beginning of the autumn term at the Ecole Normale Supérieure.[1] His room — once he was able to move in, for on the day of his arrival it was still occupied by his predecessor, Tom MacGreevy — lay in the front part of the old Ecole building on the second floor to the right of the big central doorway facing onto the rue d'Ulm. From his bed, he looked out through the rain-streaked windowpanes at the view that he evoked in *Dream of Fair to Middling Women*:

> the bare tree, dripping; then, behind, smoke from the janitor's chimney-pot, rising stiff like a pine of ashes; then, beyond, beyond the world, pouring a little light up the long gully of the street that westers to the Luxembourg, half blinded by the sodden boughs, sending a little light into the room where he [Belacqua] lay spreadeagled on the hot bed.[2]

The Ecole Normale was a surprise to Beckett. It appeared exceedingly elitist. Yet many of the students were there only because they had passed the difficult, highly competitive entrance exams and been awarded grants, not because their parents were necessarily well off. There were enormous advantages for a young Frenchman in attending the Ecole Normale: its fine scholarly reputation; use of a splendid old library; personal guidance (rather than formal lectures) from the highly intelligent scholars in residence; prospects of an excellent appointment in the French educational system; and, above all, the knowledge that, as a *normalien*, he belonged to the crème de la crème of young intellectuals.

Normale Supérieure was far more of a residential institute than an actual center of learning. After receiving intensive tuition at school from some of the most distinguished teachers in the French educational system in what were termed *khâgnes*, the students at the Ecole were then left very much to their own devices. It had some of the characteristics of an inward-looking institution: ivory-towerdom, self-satisfaction, and complacency. At the Sorbonne, where they took most of their classes, the *normaliens* were often disliked by the ordinary students for their arrogance and assumption of superiority. Over the next two years, Beckett, the least gregarious of people, was nonetheless to make one or two good friends at the Ecole and to discover that some of them were very clever indeed.

Student numbers were kept deliberately small.[3] Beckett had only one *conscrit* (that is, "conscript," or first-year student) studying English for a degree. The *lecteurs* also helped those preparing for the highly competitive national examination, the *agrégation*. Among these were Beckett's friend Alfred Péron, back from Trinity College, Dublin, and another candidate, Emile Delavenay, who was away much of the time teaching as a *lecteur* in French in Cambridge.

Whenever Delavenay was in Paris, the two postgraduate students, or *agrégatifs*, used to arrange informal meetings, first with MacGreevy, then with Beckett —"when we could lay our hands on him (he also was not an early riser)," wrote Delavenay[4]—working mainly on prose translations into English, but also discussing some of their literary texts.[5] Péron worked with a number of friends, including his girlfriend, Maya (or, as Beckett wrote it, Mania) Lézine, whom he later married. Mania, whom Beckett called Péron's "subtle Russian sweet,"[6] was to play a key role in his life during the Second World War.

However privileged the *normaliens* were, their living conditions were poor. They had to share dormitories with cubicles separated one from another only by an ugly partition wall and a dark curtain. They worked in studies called *turnes* that were shared by several students. Washing facilities were primitive and the toilets were squalid.[7] The food and the coffee were appalling. Students used a form of in-house slang to which Beckett soon became accustomed. There was also quite a lot of traditional but fairly juvenile horseplay: songs of insult were hurled across the refectory by members of one year at those of another and a Masonic style of initiation ceremony took place at the beginning of each academic year. In this ceremony the *conscrits* were led into the "palace" of the *archicubes* (or third-year students), where a traditional song about a "spider in love with a louse" was sung; new entrants were then blindfolded and led through the cellars, up the stairs, and out onto the flat section of the roof. The night ended with the *normaliens* shouting insults in unison across the roofs at the military students in the Ecole Polytechnique several blocks away: "Sabre-wielders, tigers thirsty for blood," they bayed.[8] Although immune, as a lecturer, to this kind of treatment, Beckett must have wondered, at times, what kind of institution he was in.

The lecturers were more comfortably housed than the students. At least they had the privacy of having their own rooms, which were spacious and warm.[9] But the water in which they washed was every bit as cold in the morning and the food in the small lecturers' dining room was hardly any improvement on what was being served in the students' refectory. And so lecturers and students alike ate out in nearby cafés and restaurants—whenever they could afford it, for the English lecturers were very badly paid.[10] A *garçon* or "skip" cleaned and washed up for them. Beckett's skip was a tiny figure, a heavy drinker called Ferdinand. The rooms were furnished with spartan simplicity: a bed, a table, an armchair, a few shelves for books; cups, plates, spoons, two knives, a few glasses, and a couple of saucepans. Before Beckett's arrival, MacGreevy moaned to his own predecessor, William McCausland Stewart, about the beetles and cockroaches in the tiny kitchen that no one seemed able to get rid of.[11]

2

SOMEWHAT SURPRISINGLY in view of the fuss that had been made about the appointment, MacGreevy was allowed to keep a room at the Ecole for two more years, living down the corridor from Beckett, doing a little teaching and acting as secretary to the English-language edition of *Formes*, a journal of the visual arts. In spite of the unpromising start of their relationship, Beckett was quickly won over by his fellow Irishman's cordiality, wit, and helpfulness. MacGreevy offered him companionship on tap whenever he needed it, and made everyday life much easier by passing on vital bits of information: to give his dirty washing to the *lingère* every Monday morning; to tip the janitor five francs from time to time; and to give an equal amount to the bearded concierge, Jean, who brought up the letters and took incoming phone calls.[12]

Born in Tarbert, County Kerry, in 1893, Tom MacGreevy was thirteen years older than Beckett.[13] He was commissioned as a second lieutenant in the Royal Field Artillery in the First World War, and was wounded on two occasions. After the end of the war, he took a degree in political science and history at Trinity College, Dublin, and, as a student, became an active member of the Dublin United Arts Club and the Dublin Drama League.[14] A dapper little man with a twinkling sense of humor and a store of splendid, sometimes quite risqué anecdotes, MacGreevy conveyed an impression of elegance, even when, as was often the case, he was virtually penniless. He had two identical navy blue suits and always wore a clean white shirt and, often, a smart bow tie.[15] He was as confident, talkative, and gregarious as Beckett was diffident, silent, and solitary. Everyone who knew MacGreevy spoke of how likable he was and remarked on his great gift for friendship. For a born talker, he seems to have had an unusual talent for listening.

Beckett described MacGreevy as "a living Encyclopedia"[16] and was impressed by his unusually wide-ranging interests. On an intellectual level, it was probably their common passion for painting and love of music and theater that drew them close to each other. But for some years MacGreevy also seems to have provided Beckett with a role model as an all-rounder: poet, essayist, literary reviewer, and art critic, even novelist (although he never published his own novel), all rolled into one.[17] It was several years before Beckett gave up all thoughts of emulating even more modestly the activities and range of his learned friend.

Yet it was MacGreevy's personal qualities of liveliness, wit, and ready sympathy that attracted Beckett most of all and won his confidence and affection. He had the ability to draw Beckett out of his cocoon of shyness and silence with his effervescent, challenging, yet reassuring talk. So successful was he at establishing a real bond of friendship between them that, until the Second World War at least, he was Beckett's only true confidant. There were crucial differences of character and viewpoint that could easily have become barriers to their friendship. MacGreevy was an ardent Catholic, for instance, while Beckett, coming from a firmly Protestant background, was profoundly skeptical by that time in matters of religion. But MacGreevy was sufficiently open-minded and tolerant, and Beckett interested enough in religious ideas, for this never to have become a problem. They simply argued or begged to differ. Quite often they disagreed strongly about literature and painting as well. But theirs was a genuine dialogue, in which for a long time Beckett was passionately involved.

Although MacGreevy had served in the British army and retained a British passport, by 1928 he had become vehemently anti-British. Brought up in a fervently loyalist and royalist family, Beckett was probably led by MacGreevy to identify more fully with his own Irishness, which MacGreevy constantly stressed, although, like Beckett, he could not bear some of the increasingly stifling features of the new Irish Free State. He himself opted for a period of exile before returning to Dublin during the war and taking up the post of director of the National Gallery of Ireland in 1950. Both men were keenly responsive to European traditions in literature and art, just as both were opposed to all kinds of narrowness in ideas or culture.

Almost as impressive to Beckett as MacGreevy's knowledge and achievements were the people he knew: Lennox Robinson, Stephen McKenna, George Russell ("A.E."), and W. B. Yeats in Dublin; T. S. Eliot in London; James Stephens, Richard Aldington, and James Joyce and his inner circle in Paris. Among his friends were Jack Butler Yeats and the Spanish painter Joan Junyer, and he knew the stained-glass artist Harry Clarke. He was open and generous with his introductions. He eased Beckett's entry into the Ecole by introducing him to his elegant, effeminate friend, the secrétaire-général, Jean Thomas, and the librarian of the Ecole, Monsieur Etard. He took the trouble to take Beckett to meet the garçon in the library, a Breton former tailor called Quere, who helped readers to locate their books, and Jean, the concierge. Then he set about introducing him to his friends living in Paris, many of them Irish, British, or American expatriates.

A true night owl, MacGreevy loved the animation and sociability of Parisian cafés and was happy to stay out talking into the early hours, sometimes until breakfast. Consequently neither he nor Beckett arranged to meet his students in the morning. Work was done mostly in the afternoon and at night. In the evening they used to eat out in a number of different restaurants in the Latin Quarter. They used to go, when they were in funds, to the Cochon de Lait by the side of the Odéon theater in the rue Corneille,[18] where Beckett loved to speak Italian with the waiters, Mario and Angelo.

When they were up in time, they took a late breakfast or "brunch" in the Café Mahieu (now a McDonald's) on the corner of the rue Gay-Lussac and the boulevard Saint-Michel.[19] They often met their students there or in the less resplendent Café du Départ opposite the Gare de Sceaux (later called the Gare du Luxembourg).[20] After dinner, they used to drift for late-night drinks into the Mahieu to meet two other Irish friends of MacGreevy, Captain Alan Duncan[21] and his tiny Rathmines-born wife, Belinda. Beckett said: "I saw a lot of the Duncans in Paris. We used to go to the café together. He would swill beer in enormous quantities. Her maiden name was Belinda Atkinson and they had a house near Foxrock, on the way to Stillorgan."[22] Beckett was irritated by Duncan's avid hero-worship of George Bernard Shaw as an essayist and a playwright. But his friendship with the Duncans, although strained at times, lasted for many years. Other haunts included the bar of the famous but more expensive Closerie des Lilas, as well as the Dôme, Les Deux Magots, and the Sélect in Montparnasse.

MacGreevy introduced Beckett to the American poet Walter Lowenfels, who, with Michael Fraenkel, founded the short-lived *anonyme* movement. But a more important contact for Beckett was Eugene Jolas, friend of Joyce and editor of the journal *transition*, which had begun publishing Joyce's *Work in Progress* and soon published some of Beckett's early work. He was also to meet, again through MacGreevy, the painter and celebrated French designer of tapestries, Jean Lurçat.

Soon after Beckett's arrival in Paris, MacGreevy took him down the hill to meet Sylvia Beach at her famous English bookshop and lending library, Shakespeare & Co., at 12 rue de l'Odéon, to which Alfred Péron and he were constant visitors. Beckett had heard of Miss Beach's legendary kindness and great devotion to James Joyce and was delighted to meet the courageous publisher of *Ulysses*.[23] The bookshop with its open fireplace, its well-stocked bookshelves, its dozens of photographs of writers, and, above all, its welcoming owner was to become one of Beckett's favorite ports of call, although he seems not to have borrowed books from her lending library.

3

BECKETT STARTED TO DRINK in Paris, at first fairly modestly, then toward the end of his two-year stay much more heavily. He rarely drank before five o'clock, a habit he retained throughout his life. After the years of total abstinence while he was a student, he now began to experiment with several different drinks. MacGreevy and he used to love to down a couple of bottles of Chambertin over a meal at the Cochon de Lait. But mostly Beckett preferred to drink dry white wines. However, he sometimes experimented with a variety of other drinks, apéritifs, and digestifs: "the potent unpleasant Mandarin-Curaçao, the ubiquitous Fernet-Branca that went to your head and settled your stomach and was like a short story by Mauriac to look at, oxygéné and Real-Porto, yes, Real-Porto."[24] For someone as retiring and inhibited as he was, the feeling of relaxation and release that alcohol offered helped him to cope with the nervousness that he felt when meeting someone whom he did not know well or stiffened his resolve on more formal occasions. Sometimes, however, he drank for the sheer pleasure of drinking. One day toward the end of his stay he wrote to Tom MacGreevy that he had been so drunk the previous night that he could not find his glasses the next day and was forced to wear his steel-framed ones instead.[25] Such occasions were not all that rare.

Beckett made a great impression on the permanent staff of the Ecole Normale by the lateness of the hours he used to keep. Long after the gates had been locked (midnight), whenever he had forgotten or lost the key to which he was entitled, he would make a well-practiced, athletic entry up and over the railings at the front of the Ecole, walking, often unsteadily, across the courtyard and through the big entrance doors of the main building.[26] Looking out of the little windows of his gate lodge, the concierge would catch a glimpse of Beckett coming into the Ecole in the small hours, as did the night porter on his regular rounds.[27] The bearded, limping janitor, known to *normaliens* as Louvois (after Louis XIV's severe minister of war, the Marquis de Louvois, who restored order and discipline to the king's army; his predecessor had been called Colbert) spent most of his day in the "Aquarium," a little glass capsule in the vestibule. During Beckett's stay at the Ecole, Louvois was a down-to-earth Breton, Yves Guélou, who strongly disapproved of the two Irishmen's habit of getting up at lunchtime. Beckett would creep furtively out of his room and along the corridor in his dressing gown and carpet slippers. He was usually fast asleep when Louvois or the concierge tried to rouse him to take a morning phone call by shouting up at his window from the front courtyard, and was hardly ever up to receive the first delivery of mail.[28]

But Beckett did not confine himself to escapades while in Paris. He worked hard and he played hard. In Dublin, categories had seemed (to him at least) more starkly differentiated. You could not drink and smoke and play sports. These activities appeared mutually exclusive. In Paris, there was less rigidity, more fluidity. He kept up his sporting interests but in a more relaxed, less stern way. Sports and physical fitness had been something of a fetish at Portora Royal. At Trinity College he had continued to devote himself determinedly and dourly to his sporting activities. Now he played rugby occasionally, and far less seriously, with a team from the Ecole Normale. Matches took place every fortnight on Sunday afternoons, often against local teams in the suburbs of Paris. Beckett played center three-quarter. One of his teammates, Camille Marcoux, remembered that he could be outstandingly fast, vigorous, and highly effective in turning defense into attack for the opening fifteen or twenty minutes of the game. After that he tended to fade; "il s'écroulait dans les pâquerettes" ("he flopped among the daisies") was the picturesque French expression Marcoux used to describe Beckett's loss of energy or enthusiasm. The same teammate explained that, in Ireland, games were played on Saturday afternoon and what was sometimes called the third half was played on Saturday night in the pubs of Dublin. Beckett had, it was alleged, merely been carrying on the Irish tradition in the bars of Montparnasse (though he had not practiced it in Ireland) but, unfortunately, on the night before the Sunday game.[29] This, it was claimed, limited the extent of his sporting exploits.

A more charitable and probably more accurate explanation for Beckett's early loss of energy is offered by Ulysse Nicollet, a classicist and the team's "hooker," who described Beckett in action:

> I have a very clear memory of his way of attacking. He ran quite fast with his knees pumping up and down, high in the air. Since he wasn't wearing his glasses, he could not make out his opponents' movements very clearly and he charged ahead blindly with grim determination. This made his attacks very penetrating but exposed him to some brutal tackles. Marcoux told me that he had heard him complain after these painful collisions: [in English] "Never again, never again" as he picked himself up.[30]

It would have taken few such vigorous tackles for Beckett's strength to be sapped.

He also played tennis regularly during the summer. Sometimes he and Alfy Péron used to play on a court at the Ecole Normale. More often, they took the train from Saint-Lazare to a private tennis club just outside Paris, where Péron was a member. In 1929 Beckett met there a Frenchwoman who was studying the piano: Suzanne Deschevaux-Dumesnil. He and Péron used to play against Suzanne and her partner. At the time, Beckett thought little of his encounters with this handsome twenty-eight-year-old woman, who a decade later was to become his lover. At the time she struck him as merely likable and interesting.

At the Ecole Normale, weird, nocturnal wailings could often be heard emanating from Beckett's room. Richard Aldington was alluding to this when he wrote that Beckett "wanted to commit suicide, a fate he nearly imposed on half the faculty of the Ecole by playing the flute."[31] MacGreevy's friend Jean Coulomb, who had a room near Beckett, objected to the nocturnal serenading when he was trying to sleep. In fact, it was not a flute Beckett played at all: "I used to play the tin whistle," he said. "A rusty old tin whistle. I had a tin whistle and I used to tweetle on it."[32] MacGreevy speaks almost with nostalgia of companionable moments when, having bought a jar of Cooper's marmalade from a grocery store near the Madeleine, they would have it for breakfast,

> maybe with Stokowski and the Boston Symphony playing the Leonora no 3 on the gramophone — or, while I was boiling the kettle for an extra cup of tea to go with the bread and excellent marmalade with Sam fetching his tin whistle from his room down the passage at the Ecole and trying out once again the Serenade from the Kleine Nacht Musick.[33]

Although no great performer on the whistle, Beckett had plenty of opportunity in Paris to advance his interest in music. On the ground floor, opposite the little lodge where Louvois mounted guard, a glass door led to a piano room that *normaliens* could use; Beckett's slim torso could often be seen hunched over the piano, pounding a little heavily on the keys.

A student named Guy Harnois also had a gramophone in his room and he and a friend, Lucien Roubaud, invited Beckett several times to listen to their recordings of American black spirituals and translate the words for them. Roubaud remembered Beckett accompanying his impromptu translations with skeptical remarks about the trust that the slaves put in religion to save them and about the picturesque differences between "American English" and "English English."[34] Beckett also went to a number of concerts and the occasional opera during his two years in Paris.[35]

One thing changed very little for him at the Ecole Normale. At school and Trinity College, he had been really friendly with a very few individuals. This suited his shy, retiring nature and allowed him to choose carefully those with whom he wanted to spend his time. As a young man he was intolerant of those who irritated him and suffered fools badly. When bored or annoyed, he would lapse into deep uncomfortable silences that people interpreted (often correctly) as rudeness and lack of civility. Yet, because he had been brought up to believe in courtesy and good manners, he became upset when he knew he had been impatient, rude, or discourteous. At the Ecole Normale, he was just as selective in his choice of friends. Most of the students, even those with rooms near his, knew him hardly at all. Beckett's sole first-year student of English, Georges Pelorson, described his first meeting with Beckett:

> The day after I settled in, I found a note in pencil in my mailbox. It said, "I am your English lecturer and I think that we should meet, so could you come to my place tomorrow morning at 11 o'clock." So the next day I came up the stairs, knocked on the door and there was no answer, so I knocked again and again — no answer. I tried the knob, it worked and the door opened slightly. I saw an open window with shutters half-closed, the sun was pouring through that and falling right on the bed. On that bed, half-naked, was stretched a tall young man, very fair, and who seemed even fairer because of the sun falling on him as he slept. I was impressed by this spectacle. I didn't want to wake him so I scribbled a note to say that I had come to see him but as he was asleep, I had returned to my studies.[36]

They met for lunch the following day and, returning to Beckett's room, decided uncertainly that they would try reading through *The Tempest* together. Since this did not seem to be a very effective way of learning English, they finally opted to meet in bars and restaurants and simply talk. Pelorson's enthusiasms — for the music of Wagner, for instance; for avant-garde literature, especially for Surrealism; and for beautiful women — tickled Beckett enormously and they soon found their way into *Dream of Fair to Middling Women*.

Another member of the select group of Beckett's friends at the Ecole

Normale Supérieure, particularly during his second year as lecturer in English, was a flamboyant, highly articulate student of philosophy called Jean Beaufret. Beckett recalled his friendship with him:

> A man I knew at the Ecole Normale fairly well was Jean Beaufret, who was the Heidegger expert, a very well-known philosopher and a specialist on Heidegger. He came to the defence of Heidegger against the accusations of being a Nazi and so on, you know. We used to go about together when I was at the Ecole Normale. He taught at the Henri IV near the Panthéon.[37]

Born in the Creuse and a year younger than Beckett, Beaufret came to the Ecole Normale in 1928. By associating his name with the French word *beaupré*, which means the mast of a sailing ship, Beckett and his friends called him affectionately the Bowsprit; so they would "launch the Bowsprit" and so on. Beaufret was probably introduced to Beckett by Georges Pelorson, who had been at the Lycée Louis-le-Grand with him and was of the same *promotion*, or year of matriculation.

Beckett sought Beaufret's help in catching up on his reading of some of the major classical and more modern European philosophers. Traces of this help can be detected in his correspondence, his library, and his work. In a letter to Tom MacGreevy in the summer of 1930, he wrote that "the Bowsprit comes and talks abstractions every second day and déniche [unearths] books for me in the library."[38] On his death, Beckett's library still contained a copy of the selected writings of Descartes that had once belonged to Beaufret and included the latter's handwritten notes on the *Treatise on the Passions*. At the Ecole Normale, Beaufret was particularly interested in Greek thought and may well have introduced Beckett to the ideas of Parmenides on "being" and "nonbeing" and on change and changelessness, as well as to the thought of Heraclitus, Parmenides' opponent, and to the paradoxes of Zeno of Elea, which were to preoccupy Beckett later in his work. Even more transparently than Pelorson, Beaufret became the model for one of the more eccentric, colorful characters in *Dream of Fair to Middling Women*.

4

BUT ONE FRIENDSHIP in Paris outshone all the others. Beckett was first introduced to James Joyce by Tom MacGreevy and was to remain unfailingly grateful to his new friend for this. He had come to Paris with an introduction from his uncle by marriage, Harry Sinclair, who had known Joyce in the old days in Dublin.[39] But it is unlikely that he would have been made quite so welcome in the Joyce family circle if MacGreevy had not recommended him so enthusiastically. Throughout 1928, MacGreevy had become one of Joyce's inner circle of friends who read to him or for him and helped him in a variety of other ways.

For Joyce was a demanding taskmaster who, according to his wife, would soon have had God running errands for him, if he had come down to earth.[40] Mac-Greevy came from the West of Ireland, as did Nora Joyce; with his easygoing friendliness and warmth of manner, he soon became a good friend of hers, something Beckett never really achieved. Beckett was simply not very interested in Nora, probably made this much too obvious, and found her somewhat distant with him in return.

Beckett wanted to meet Joyce, mainly because of his intense admiration for *Dubliners, Portrait of the Artist as a Young Man, Ulysses,* and some of his poems. We cannot be sure exactly when he first got to know Joyce's work. Mario Esposito maintained that when Beckett came to visit his family in Florence in the early summer of 1927, he knew nothing about Joyce or the Irish literary movement in general and that he, Mario, was responsible for pointing him in that direction.[41] His sister Vera also claimed quite independently that Beckett "did not appear to know anything about Joyce then."[42] But there is no doubt that, during that same summer vacation, he felt sufficiently enthusiastic about Joyce's poems to give his golfing partner, Bill Cunningham, a copy of *Pomes Penyeach* signed "Yours ever, Sam Beckett July 1927."[43] This suggests that it was, at the very latest, in his last few months at Trinity and during his postgraduate year, spent first in Dublin and then in Belfast, that Beckett's crucial encounter with Joyce's writing took place.

There was much in the background and personality of the older Irish writer to attract Beckett. They both had degrees in French and Italian, although from different universities in Dublin. Joyce's exceptional linguistic abilities and the wide range of his reading in Italian, German, French, and English impressed the linguist and scholar in Beckett, whose earlier studies allowed him to share with Joyce his passionate love of Dante.[44] They both adored words—their sounds, rhythms, shapes, etymologies, and histories—and Joyce had a formidable vocabulary derived from many languages and a keen interest in the contemporary slang of several languages that Beckett admired and tried to emulate.

They shared, too, a fervent anticlericalism and a skepticism in all matters to do with religion, although their mutual preoccupation with religious imagery still ran very deep and their knowledge of the Scriptures was almost word-perfect. They had many interests in common: a love of Schubert's lieder, although Joyce's musical interests were almost exclusively vocal and operatic, while Beckett, who had no liking for opera, loved instrumental music; a mutual interest in the painting of Cézanne, although Joyce had none of MacGreevy's talent for talking about pictures; a liking for the plays of John Millington Synge; and a fondness for the films of Charlie Chaplin.

Beckett found his first meeting with Joyce "overwhelming."[45]

I was introduced to him by Tom. He was very friendly immediately. I remember coming back very exhausted to the Ecole Normale and, as usual, the door was closed; so I climbed over the railings. I remember that. Coming back from my first meeting with Joyce. I remember walking back. And from then on we saw each other quite often.[46]

He soon agreed to help Joyce by doing some research for his "Work in Progress," which became *Finnegans Wake*. He used to stroll along to Joyce's apartment in the square Robiac in the late afternoon, often exchanging a few minutes of awkward preliminary small talk with Nora and their daughter, Lucia, before he settled down with Joyce to a period of intensive work before dinner. Beckett's own memories of the geography of the square some sixty years later would enable a visitor to Paris to find the apartment today with little difficulty.

> It's a little street off the rue de Grenelle; this goes from the Latin Quarter to the avenue Bosquet near the Ecole Militaire. Just before it comes to the end of the rue de Grenelle near the avenue Bosquet, before it "debouches" on the avenue Bosquet, there's a little street on the right-hand side. It was an impasse in those days. It still exists but it's a square now. The square Robiac. I remember it as an impasse. You go in to the right off the rue de Grenelle. It was very short. And on the right-hand side was the house where Joyce had his flat.[47]

Beckett's work with Joyce mainly consisted of reading aloud from books that the "Penman," as Joyce's friends called him, thought might be helpful to him. But, very occasionally, Joyce dictated to him. For by this time Joyce's eyesight was failing badly, and he was trying to avoid eyestrain as much as he possibly could. Joyce's biographer Richard Ellmann described the scene: "Joyce sat in his habitual posture, legs crossed, toe of the upper leg under the instep of the lower; Beckett, also tall and slender, fell into the same gesture."[48] Frequently he came away from Joyce's apartment with books to read and report on. Among Beckett's personal papers some notes appear to have been made for Joyce, including detailed ideas from mythology and history relating to "The Cow" and notes on the history of Ireland.[49]

Writers on Beckett and Joyce have often spoken about Beckett's contribution to *Finnegans Wake*. He is said to have taken down as dictation the words "Come in," as someone knocked at the door and, when Joyce insisted that the phrase should be included, let it stand. Yet it has proved hard for scholars to find the unintended words in the finished text.[50] A further anecdote attributes to Beckett the line "Another insult to Ireland" as a comment on the story of an Irish man, Buckley, shooting a Russian general in the Crimean War as he wiped his bottom on the turf (the line appears in the text as "At that instullt to Igorladns"). Finally, the apparent hidden allusion to Beckett and his work in the lines "Sam . . . I bonded him off more as a friend and a brother. . . . Illstarred punster. . . . 'Twas the quadra sent him and Trinity too. . . . He'll priskly soon hand tune your Erin's ear for you"[51] is not one at all, since most of the passage was published before Beckett ever met Joyce.

Just over a month after they met, Joyce asked Beckett to write about his "Work in Progress." Beckett explained:

It was at his suggestion that I wrote "Dante . . . Bruno. Vico . . Joyce"
—because of my Italian. I spent a lot of time reading Bruno and Vico
in the magnificent library, the Bibliothèque of the Ecole Normale.
We must have had some talk about the "Eternal Return," that sort of
thing. He liked the essay. But his only comment on it was that there
wasn't enough about Bruno; he found Bruno rather neglected. They
were new figures to me at the time. I hadn't read them. I'd worked on
Dante, of course. I knew very little of them. I knew more or less what
they were about. I remember reading a biography of one of them.[52]

Joyce was right. From Bruno, Beckett borrowed only his principle of identified contrarities: "Maximal speed is a state of rest. The maximum of corruption
and the minimum of generation are identical: in principle, corruption is generation. And all things are ultimately identified with God, the universal monad,
Monad of monads." Instead he developed, under Joyce's own guidance but
based on his reading of the *Scienza Nuova*, the relationship between Joyce's
writing and the view of the "practical, round-headed Neapolitan" Giambattista
Vico of the development of human society into three ages, which were adapted
by Joyce "as a structural convenience — or inconvenience" as Birth, Maturity,
and Corruption, leading to Generation. Beckett shows how in "Work in Progress," Joyce has adopted Vico's theory of cyclical "progression — or retrogres-
sion." But Beckett is at his best, with and without the help of Vico's poetics, on
Joyce's use of language ("When the sense is sleep, the words go to sleep . . .
when the sense is dancing, the words dance") and in a comparison between
Dante's Purgatory and that of Joyce ("Dante's is conical and consequently
implies culmination. Mr. Joyce's is spherical and excludes culmination"). Already there is much of the later Beckett in this essay: literature is not for the
bookkeeping kind of critic; English is abstracted to death as a language; and
"form *is* content, content *is* form."[53]

Working for Joyce made considerable inroads into Beckett's time, although
he was only one of seven friends who helped Joyce with various tasks connected
with his new book.[54] But the young man admired Joyce so much that he was
happy to help. He even suggested at this time to the *directeur-adjoint* of the
Ecole Normale, a Professor Bouglé, who had replaced Gustave Lanson, that he
might register for a French doctorate, taking the work of Proust and Joyce as his
subject.[55] But the French tradition had always been to wait until a writer was
dead, buried, and consecrated by time before any such serious academic investigation should begin. Proust had died only eight years before, and Joyce was
vigorously alive. So Bouglé discouraged Beckett strongly and the proposal was
promptly dropped.

Joyce's apartment lay only five hundred meters away from the Seine, and a
favorite Sunday morning walk for Beckett and Joyce was to saunter together
west along the quai de Branly and the quai de Grenelle as far as Bir-Hakeim,
then stroll along the narrow, tree-lined Allée des Cygnes (or Isle of Swans),
which extends in midstream near the pont de Grenelle. Their footsteps echo

years later in Beckett's short play *Ohio Impromptu*: "From its single window he could see the downstream extremity of the Isle of Swans. . . . Day after day he could be seen slowly pacing the islet. Hour after hour."[56] He and Joyce often paced the Isle of Swans in silence. Beckett said:

> There wasn't a lot of conversation between us. I was a young man, very devoted to him, and he liked me. . . . I was very flattered when he dropped the "Mister." Everybody was "Mister." There were no Christian names, no first names. The nearest you would get to a friendly name was to drop the "Mister." I was never Sam. I was always "Beckett" at the best.[57]

According to Nino Frank, Beckett did not joke with Joyce as his other helpers Paul Léon or Stuart Gilbert did.[58] He was probably too much in awe of the master. After all, he was only twenty-two years old, a time for hero-worship. He used to ape Joyce's way of dressing and adopted some of his habits or mannerisms — wearing shoes that were too narrow for him, drinking white wines, and holding his cigarette in a certain way.

Sixty years later, he could still remember Joyce's phone number without a moment's hesitation: Ségur 95-20. "I used to come down sometimes in the morning from the Ecole Normale to the concierge and he used to say 'Monsieur Joyce a téléphoné et il vous demande de vous mettre en rapport avec lui' ['Mr. Joyce phoned and he wants you to get in touch with him']. And it was usually to do with going for a walk or going for dinner."[59] Beckett would phone to make an appointment or to find out what errand Joyce wanted him to run. Sometimes the call was to ask him to bring him a particular book or look up a reference for him, or, occasionally, to escort him to a party, for Joyce's failing vision made him fearful of going out alone. Beckett used to take his arm tenderly, although a little gingerly, as they crossed the street or walked to a seat in a café, for Joyce did not like being treated as if he were blind.[60] This combination of vulnerability and apparent self-confidence appealed to a young man who was intellectually arrogant yet still unsure of himself. Significantly, one of the things Beckett stressed to Richard Ellmann was that Joyce was nothing like as confident as he may have appeared: "I may have oversystematized *Ulysses*," Beckett quoted him as saying once.[61] For his part, Joyce rated Beckett very highly. According to Lucie Léon Noel, he felt that he was the most talented of the young men around him,[62] and Maria Jolas confirmed that Joyce had great confidence in Beckett's keen intelligence.[63]

But, as Lucie Léon Noel put it, being a member of the Joyce circle was "like sinking into cotton-wool."[64] This meant for Beckett being absorbed into a ready-made circle of Joyce's intimate friends or acquaintances — Paul and Lucie Léon; Eugene and Maria Jolas; Stuart and Moune Gilbert; Nino Frank; Sylvia Beach and Adrienne Monnier. It also meant many social occasions — anniversary dinners or birthday parties — at the Joyces' apartment or in their favorite restaurants. Beckett's own memories of Nora Joyce's dinner parties were very vivid: "when he had these at home parties, receptions at home, with various friends, when he had enough taken, he would sit down at the piano and sing, with his marvellous remains of a tenor voice: 'Bid adieu, adieu, adieu / Bid adieu to girlish days,' "[65] the song being a setting of Joyce's own poem from *Chamber Music* (1907). On 27 June, 1929, Beckett was one of the group of friends who accompanied Joyce in a charabanc to the Hôtel Léopold at Les-Vaux-de-Cernay to celebrate the publication of the French translation of *Ulysses* and the twenty-fifth anniversary of Bloomsday, the sixteenth of June. After this, Joyce wrote to Valery Larbaud that

> there were two riotous young Irishmen and one of them Beckett whose essay you will find in the *Exag* [Beckett's essay published in *Our Exagmination* etc] fell deeply under the influence of beer, wine, spirits, liqueurs, fresh air, movement and feminine society and was ingloriously abandoned by the Wagonette in one of those temporary palaces which are inseparably associated with the memory of the Emperor Vespasian [in other words, a urinal].[66]

When I asked Beckett where he was in the group photograph of the occasion, he replied: "Probably under the table."[67]

Being a member of the inner circle also meant for Beckett being the listener to Joyce's anxieties concerning his own and Nora's health,[68] and his worries about his son Giorgio's career and love life. Very soon Beckett found himself enmeshed in a complex web of attitudes relating to the two children, Giorgio and Lucia.

5

BECKETT FIRST MET Lucia Joyce at her father's flat early in November 1928. The image of her that emerges from books on Joyce has, hardly surprisingly, been distorted by knowledge of the mental illness from which she suffered in the early 1930s. It is difficult to imagine her as she would have appeared to young men when Beckett first met her. Several photographs of her survive, alone or with her family. Many show clearly enough the squint of which she was extremely conscious. But some also reveal the "beautiful, vibrant girl" with the "tall slender graceful" body that several young men admired. "She was pretty," wrote Joyce's niece, Bozena Berta Delimata, "with dark, curly shoulder-length hair and blue eyes with a slight cast but . . . attractive in spite of it."[69] According to one of her first lovers, Albert Hubbell, she had a solemn expression that could suddenly erupt into a monkeyish grin; she also had "a way of standing close to you and, for a moment, confiding herself to your care."[70] She would often sing in French, German, Italian, or English. One of her favorite songs was DeSylva, Brown, and Henderson's current hit, "You're the Cream in My Coffee."[71]

She had studied dancing from about 1926 to 1929, taking courses such as that of Jaques Dalcroze—the principles of which were familiar to Beckett from

Peggy's studies at the school in Laxenburg—and with Raymond Duncan's dance school near Salzburg. And just before Beckett met her, she danced on the stage of the Vieux-Colombier theater in *La Princesse Primitive*. Beckett accompanied the Joyces with Tom MacGreevy and the Duncans when she danced publicly at the Bal Bullier across the road from the Closerie des Lilas on May 28, 1929. Lucia looked enchanting in a shimmering silver fish costume: "It was in silver sequins edged with green. One leg was covered to the heel and the other came right through the costume, so that when she put one behind the other, she created the illusion of a fish tail. Green and silver were entwined in her hair." [72] According to Beckett, she danced Schubert's "March" that evening in the solo dance contest. She did not win but, to Joyce's immense delight, members of the audience called out loudly as the result was announced, protesting: "Nous réclamons l'Irlandaise! Un peu de justice, messieurs!" ("We're calling for the Irish girl! Be fair, gentlemen!") Beckett described her dancing as excellent. In the apartment when Joyce used to play the piano and sing, Lucia would sometimes be in the background dancing, trying to catch Beckett's eye. Because she lacked the stamina, she gave up dancing soon after the Bal Bullier evening, although she cried for a month with regret. [73]

Lucia was very interested in men and had already had a number of crushes before focusing her amorous attention on Beckett. He used to call at the apartment to work with her father and he and MacGreevy would quite often eat out with the entire family. At the end of February 1929, while her mother was in hospital having a hysterectomy and her father was sleeping in the hospital, Lucia had plenty of opportunity to see Beckett alone on numerous occasions, even though Joyce's benefactor, Miss Weaver, had come over to Paris to help the Joyce family to cope. Indeed Beckett's letters from Paris reveal that she used to stop by to have tea with him at the Ecole Normale, and they certainly went to restaurants (often to the Brasserie Universelle) and to the theater and the cinema together.

Giorgio Joyce was having a love affair at the time with Helen Fleischman, and once Nora and Joyce became reconciled to this relationship, Beckett often made up the family group of three couples—escorting Lucia, for instance, with James and Nora, to hear their son make his singing début in April 1929. Like Belacqua in *Dream of Fair to Middling Women*, Beckett tried to avoid going to the opera. But Joyce could be very persistent and dragged him along sometimes with the rest of his family. He went, for instance, with a party of some eight to ten guests of Joyce to hear John Sullivan sing, when Joyce called out in a loud voice "Up Cork!" Afterward there was a big dinner at the Café de la Paix with champagne and cold chicken. [74]

There were numerous occasions when it seemed to friends as if Beckett was present not as a friend of Joyce but as Lucia's companion. On his arrival at the Joyce apartment, Lucia was usually waiting by the door to greet him and tried to keep him talking as long as possible. She gazed passionately at him across the dining table and constantly tried to engage him in private conversation. He continued to take her out to restaurants and theaters, but this was more in an attempt to bind himself to Joyce than out of any great desire to be with Lucia, who was already beginning to show wild and disturbing fluctuations of mood. It is unlikely, however, that he would have allowed his relationship with her to become a sexual one, although he admitted to finding her "very good-looking."[75] He had far too much to lose with Joyce and was in any case emotionally involved at the time with Peggy Sinclair. Albert Hubbell, who admitted to having had a physical affair with Lucia at the end of 1930, several months after Beckett had made his lack of romantic interest in her clear, claimed that Lucia assured him that, until then, she was still a virgin.[76]

Beckett certainly allowed the situation to drag on much longer than he should have done before making it clear to her in May 1930, while her parents were away in Zurich, that he came to the apartment only to see her father and that he was not interested in her amorously.

> Lucia was distraught. Nora, when she returned from Switzerland, was furious. She blamed Beckett for leading the girl on in order to ingratiate himself with Joyce. Nora rounded upon Joyce and told him that his daughter's affections had been trifled with. Joyce (who, absorbed in his book, may not have noticed before) accepted his role as the outraged father. He delivered the message. Beckett's visits were to cease; he was *persona non grata* at Square Robiac.[77]

Beckett was devastated by his rift with Joyce, which was never totally repaired until Joyce came to recognize how ill his daughter was and how impossible a true love affair with her would have been. For these Paris years were primarily the "Joyce years" for Beckett, and his friendship with the master of language counted as much as anything else that happened to him there.

Joyce's literary influence on Beckett in these early years was vital. Beckett himself regarded this influence as primarily a moral one. He said:

> When I first met Joyce, I didn't intend to be a writer. That only came later when I found out that I was no good at all at teaching. When I found I simply couldn't teach. But I do remember speaking about Joyce's heroic achievement. I had a great admiration for him. That's what it was, epic, heroic, what he achieved. But I realised that I couldn't go down that same road.[78]

In 1980 he wrote more elliptically: "heroic work, heroic being."[79] It must have been fascinating for him to see Joyce's inventiveness, his intoxication with words, and his working methods at such close quarters. And it is hardly surprising if, after such an experience, he should have found it a herculean task to rid himself of a Joycean approach.

Certain parallels between Beckett's early methods and those of Joyce are fairly obvious. Joyce took meticulous care with his research, reading books primarily for what they could offer him for his own writing. (Indeed, many people who knew him, including Beckett, have claimed that he read almost exclusively for this purpose.) Though he was inspired more by disinterested intellectual and scholarly curiosity than Joyce was, Beckett's notebooks show that he too plundered the books he was reading or studying for material that he could then incorporate into his own writing. Beckett copied out striking, memorable, or witty sentences or phrases into his notebooks. Such quotations or near quotations were then woven into the dense fabric of his early prose. It is what could be called a grafting technique, and at times it almost runs wild. He even checked off the quotations in his private notebooks once they had been incorporated into his own work. This technique was not specifically adopted by Joyce, but it was very Joycean in its ambition and its impulse. Beckett also drew, as Joyce did, from many languages and literatures for his quotations or part-quotations. But he carried this even further than Joyce had done, at least until *Finnegans Wake*. There are signs that Beckett may also have acquired from Joyce some of his practice of introducing echoes into his writing, as if in music. It was a technique that he developed much more fully even than Joyce, particularly in his later prose and theater.

Although there are entire passages in *Dream of Fair to Middling Women* that either imitate or parody late Joyce (for there were many different Joyce styles, to which Beckett was sensitive at different moments), Beckett certainly felt, from early on in their relationship, that it was essential for him to separate himself from Joyce as a writer and establish a distance between them. Yet the basic impetus in his early writing remained accretive and accumulative, just as Joyce's art was based on absorbing everything into itself. But already, by the middle years of the 1930s, there are clear signs that Beckett is reaching toward an approach to writing that is radically different from Joyce's, even though it took him until after the Second World War to discover his own road.

6

PARIS ITSELF was a revelation to Beckett. Coming from the prescriptive gentility of Foxrock and the academic stuffiness of Trinity College, he experienced a great sense of release, not entirely dissociated with guilt. The remark in *Dream of Fair to Middling Women* that "Money came from the blue eyes of home, and he spent it on concerts, cinemas, cocktails, theatres, apéritifs" suggests something of the world of exciting new possibilities that opened up tantalizingly before him.[80] During these years Beckett laid the foundations of an enduring personal relationship with "Paris our Mistress"[81] and became fascinated with avant-garde literature, painting, and theater.

He went to the theater, as he had in Dublin. He saw one of Racine's plays, probably *Bérénice*, at the Odéon[82] and talked excitedly to Kay Boyle about Machiavelli's *Mandragola* in the winter season of 1929.[83] Mostly, however, we do not know which plays he saw. There was certainly no shortage of choice. Although Jacques Copeau's Vieux-Colombier theater had closed down five years before, the "Cartel" of directors—Gaston Baty, Charles Dullin, Louis Jouvet, and Georges Pitoëff—was still very active. The Pitoëffs were offering a foreign repertoire at the Théâtre des Arts—in 1929, Chekhov, Shaw, Bruckner, and O'Neill; Dullin was mounting his adaptations of foreign classics; Jouvet was directing some stunning productions of Molière and more modern authors like Jean Giraudoux; Firmin Gémier was active at the Odéon, until his resignation in February 1930.

As for poetry, in which Beckett took a keen interest, Dada may already have been dead, but André Breton's 1924 *Manifeste du surréalisme* was reprinted in 1929, and the latest poems of Tristan Tzara and René Crevel, André Breton and Paul Eluard were appearing in some of the little magazines. He could not feel close to the Surrealists, largely because, with the single exception of Philippe Soupault, they were distinctly cool, if not actively hostile, to Joyce's own "revolution of the word." But Beckett shared in the thrilling atmosphere of experiment and innovation that surrounded Surrealism. Just as exciting to him, however, was the appearance in the smaller Parisian art galleries of work by painters belonging to the German "Die Brücke" group and members of the Bauhaus. But while he was fascinated by what was most modern in the art world, he also visited major galleries like the Louvre, where he familiarized himself with the Rembrandts and the Poussins and learned from Tom MacGreevy (who acted as an occasional lecturer and guide there) about Italian art. He was imbibing a very heady mixture indeed.

Another exciting thing about Paris in 1928–29 was its proliferation of private presses and little magazines, where with talent and the right social contacts a young or prospective writer could place his work. For Beckett, who was not to write creatively in French for another ten years, the existence of Nancy Cunard's small publishing house, the Hours Press, Eugene Jolas's review, *transition*, and Edward Titus's *This Quarter* meant that there was a source of future commissions. Jolas seems to have printed Beckett's work mainly because of the latter's connection with Joyce. In 1929, he published Beckett's first critical essay, "Dante . . . Bruno. Vico . . Joyce" in *transition*, together with a first piece of fiction entitled "Assumption." But, in the spring of 1930, Beckett already started branching out on his own by translating some Italian texts for Titus's associate editor, Samuel Putnam.[84]

7

WHILE SO MUCH was happening to him intellectually, Beckett's emotional life was in turmoil. He had spent the greater part of the summer of 1928 in the company of Peggy, who had initiated, then led, their sexual explorations. But he was confused about sex. And the regular flood of passionate letters that followed their separation in Vienna could hardly have lessened his confusion. "Absence makes the heart grow fonder is a true saying," he quipped in *Dream of Fair to Middling Women*.[85] Coming from a stratum of Dublin society where sex was scarcely admitted as a force in life at all and where it was almost never discussed, he now found himself living in a city where it was accepted, even paraded openly on the streets and catered to commercially in the brothels. "We set our principal boy down in this gay place and at the same time insist that he eschewed its bawdy houses," comments the narrator ironically in *Dream of Fair to Middling Women.*[86]

The less discreet parts of Beckett's correspondence, as well as his own evidence and that of friends, confirm that his need to satisfy sexual hunger, regarded as an appetite like any other—and commonly, although not always, dissociated from love—was not confined to the various affairs that he conducted with exquisite discretion throughout most of his life. From this two-year stay in Paris onward, he clearly consorted occasionally with "ladies of the night." The poems "Dortmunder" and "Sanies II," as well as the novel *Murphy* and the postwar short story *First Love*, show a familiarity with the figure and the ways of the prostitute. And we can be quite sure, in view of his puritanical upbringing, that such encounters would have led to intense feelings of guilt and self-disgust.

An entire section of *Dream of Fair to Middling Women* discusses (and none too obliquely at that) whether, since Belacqua is in love with a girl who cannot be with him in Paris, it is preferable in her absence to enter "the bawdy houses," in which he finds himself unable to avoid defiling or nullifying the image of the loved one that inevitably accompanies him there, or whether it is better to practice "narcissism" (meaning masturbation)—and there are many euphemisms for this in the novel—by which the loved one can remain intact in spirit even though violated in carnal fantasy. Certainly whatever convolutions of thought and language Beckett applied to the analysis of this dilemma in his novel, it is unlikely that the conclusion reached there—"So he refrained, during this period, from entering houses of ill-fame"—was anything like as straightforward in real life.[87]

One important factor, however, makes a purely biographical reading of these passages inadequate. Before writing *Dream*, Beckett immersed himself deeply in the *Confessions* of St. Augustine. He copied out dozens of passages, mostly verbatim, from the text. Many of these quotations refer to the wonder, majesty, and goodness of God, one for all time, "incorruptible, uninjurable, unchangeable." In the novel, Beckett applies all of these terms to his spiritual image of the woman Belacqua loves, concluding: "She is, she exists in one and the same way, she is everyway like herself, in no way can she be injured or changed, she is not subject to time, she cannot at one time be other than at another."[88] These are the precise words that St. Augustine uses to define true Being. So Belacqua's loved one becomes the incarnation of spirit which, in the *Confessions*, is also threatened by the temptations of the flesh, spelled out there almost as clearly as they are in Beckett's novel. A private notebook of Beckett gives chapter and verse to his many borrowings from St. Augustine. It is not that he plagiarizes; he makes no attempt to hide what he is doing. Anyone familiar with St. Augustine's book would recognize the passages involved. He merely uses the quotations to underline the contrasting demands of flesh and spirit and to add levels of philosophical allusion for his own delight and for the pleasure or amusement of the reader.

According to Beckett, he made several trips to Kassel throughout 1929. He rushed there as soon as the term was over, mainly to see Peggy. He enjoyed himself with the Sinclairs. There was a lot of laughter, many practical jokes, and much billing and cooing. The apartment at 5 Landgrafenstrasse always seemed to be filled with music too. Beckett played the piano (Granados, Mozart, Casella, MacDowell); Peggy sang; Beckett and Peggy or Beckett and Cissie played four-handers; Peggy's younger brother Morris practiced the violin and began to play violin and piano sonatas by Mozart; Cissie sang a medley of popular songs to her own accompaniment.[89] During the summer, the family visited Kragenhof on the Fulda, where they had lived for some time and where they swam in the river near the ferry or sunbathed on the riverbank. Beckett got on extremely well with his aunt Cissie, who, because she was aware that her nephew now knew its author personally, was reading *Ulysses* during his stay and was anxious to discuss with him both the book and Joyce himself. Peggy had no interest at all in books and could not, Beckett commented, be persuaded that illiteracy is a crime.[90] She was infuriated by discussions that excluded her. Nevertheless, between his many visits (Christmas 1928; Easter and the summer of 1929) she continued to write him hundreds of passionate letters.

The Christmas vacation of 1929–30 marked a watershed in their relationship. An episode in *Dream of Fair to Middling Women* that begins on New Year's Eve in a bar and ends in a café at dawn on Kassel's Wilhelmshöhe, with Belacqua spending the whole of the night apart from the Smeraldina (with a prostitute, it is implied) reflects the deterioration in their relationship at a time when, increasingly, they seem to have started to quarrel over more or less everything and agree upon virtually nothing. Beckett returned to Paris and the affair broke up. Beckett concentrated on his books, while Peggy acquired another boyfriend, Heiner Starcke, who, having been an artist, worked in Kassel for a food processing firm called Hohenlohe, then for the Kurverwaltung in Bad Wildungen. Beckett went back several times later to stay with the Sinclairs, met Heiner, whom he regarded as a very "strange fellow," and continued to regard Peggy as a close friend.[91]

8

INSPIRED BY JOYCE and MacGreevy, Beckett started to write in Paris, first the essay on Joyce, then "Assumption." This is a highly innovative story. It is only three and a half pages long and avoids most traditional methods of storytelling, using metaphor and paradox instead of narrative plot, dialogue, or characterization. It tells of a young man, "an artist who strives to create a work that, without itself interrupting silence, will suggest silence to others."[92] Feeling a well of pent-up emotion within himself, he remains silent, until he receives the visit of a woman who through her devotion, or through sex, brings him to a form of release, so that he becomes "irretrievably engulfed in the light of eternity, one with the birdless cloudless colourless skies, in infinite fulfilment."[93] Mind and body, sense and spirit, silence and scream are paired powerfully, though obscurely.

"Assumption" reflects Beckett's own life and interests; there are allusions to chess, which he loved to play, to Romains's Unanimism, which he had been studying, to Michelangelo's tomb in Florence's Santa Croce, which he had seen two years before, and perhaps even to "the faded green felt hat" and green eyes of Peggy Sinclair in the woman who brings a kind of consuming release. The emphasis on the impulse of the scream also suggests an Expressionistic device borrowed from Munch's painting, which Beckett would have seen in reproduction, for the piece is in a strange way intensely visual. But such biographical echoes fade in comparison with the aesthetic concerns that lie at the heart of the little story: "the struggle for perfection; the reduction of significance; the refusal to pamper readers with sensational effects, or with what is merely pretty; the conviction that beauty cannot be achieved easily."[94] At the very core of the story is the anguished contrast between the repressed scream and "the storm of sound" that appears to lead to death ("they found her caressing his dead hair"). However difficult the story may be, it is powerful stuff and anticipates not only some of the themes but also the pain of Beckett's later work. It has often been described as a Joycean story in the vein of *Dubliners*. On the contrary, it seems to be very much Beckett's own, with the young disciple already, perhaps, trying to distance himself from the master.

His first separately published work was a long poem, "Whoroscope." He wrote it in a matter of hours on June 15, 1930. The idea of composing it at all was suggested to him by Tom MacGreevy, who called at his room the same afternoon. MacGreevy had learned that the novelist Richard Aldington and the poet-publisher Nancy Cunard were sponsoring a contest for a poem of not more than one hundred lines on the subject of time. He also knew that Nancy Cunard hoped to publish the poem, provided that it reached a high enough standard. But what was just as important to Beckett at the time was the prize of ten pounds awarded to the winning poem. It might allow him to stay on longer in Paris during the summer. Earlier in the day, MacGreevy had seen Aldington, who had told him that Cunard and he were disappointed at the quality of the poems already received.[95] With a wry smile, MacGreevy suggested to Beckett that, although it was virtually the last moment, he might still write a poem and take it personally to Nancy Cunard's office at the Hours Press in the rue Guénégaud before the competition closed officially at midnight.

Beckett had been working for some months on the philosopher René Descartes in the Ecole Normale library and with books borrowed from his friend Jean Beaufret.[96] Acting on MacGreevy's suggestion, he leafed through his notes on Descartes, wondering whether it would be possible to shape the varied material already assembled into something suitable for the competition. Soon he started to map out his poem: it would be narrated by Descartes; it would contain allusions to the philosopher's life, work, and times; most idiosyncratically, it would revolve around Descartes's curious penchant for eating eggs only when they had been hatched for between eight and ten days; there would be pain as well as humor in it; and time would be there as its theme, lurking scarcely visible beneath the surface. In a letter to Nancy Cunard, Beckett summarizes how quickly he wrote the poem. He recounts how he wrote the "first half before dinner, had a guzzle of salad and Chambertin at the Cochon de Lait, went back to the Ecole and finished it about three in the morning. Then walked down to the rue Guénégaud and put it in your box. That's how it was and them were the days."[97]

"Whoroscope" is witty, erudite, even arcane. You would need to be a specialist on Descartes or to have read the books that Beckett had read to pick up many of the more obscure allusions. To be fully comprehensible, it certainly needs more extensive notes than Beckett added for its publication. He was probably aware of this difficulty, and the fact that he provided such limited information suggests that he saw it not just as an imitation but as a deliberate send-up of T. S. Eliot's footnoting of *The Waste Land*. It also represents a cursory nod in the direction of academicism and only partially hides a haughty "make sense who may" attitude.

Beckett was only twenty-four when he wrote "Whoroscope." He was the product of an academic system that he was quite happy to mock but to which he was due to return, although without any great enthusiasm. And he was not at all averse to dismissing ignorance and philistinism in a way that was later to appear to himself as well as to others as more than a little superior.[98] And, even though he was soon to reject academic life and pour scorn from time to time on critics and criticism, he never really abandoned scholarship. His first long poem, with its display of erudition combined with a jocular tone and implicit mockery, seems to reflect the ambiguity of his position. But it is a remarkable effort for anyone, no matter how clever, to have produced in a matter of hours. For reflections of serious arguments on the doctrine of transubstantiation and proofs of the existence of God, as well as on scientific controversies in the seventeenth century, are set alongside or sometimes specifically raised by witty allusions to Descartes's private life.

Beckett's ninety-eight-line poem impressed both Nancy Cunard and Richard Aldington and promptly won the prize. Nancy Cunard later expressed her own enthusiasm most effusively—revealing, incidentally, how impressed she had been by the poem's very obscurity: "What remarkable lines, what images and analogies, what vivid colouring throughout! Indeed what technique! This long poem, mysterious, obscure in parts . . . was clearly by someone very intellectual and highly educated. Our enthusiasm was great and the fact of its having arrived at the last moment made it all the sweeter."[99]

Aldington and Cunard sent for Beckett the next day to congratulate him and present him immediately with the prize — in cash. He was delighted at his success and grateful for the much-needed windfall. He is said to have invited Richard Aldington with Bridget Patmore and Tom MacGreevy out to a celebration dinner the same evening, typically spending a large part of the money, appropriately enough again at the Cochon de Lait.[100] Two days later, Richard Aldington wrote to his good friend Charles Prentice of the publishers Chatto and Windus, passing on a suggestion from MacGreevy that Beckett would be an excellent person to write an essay on Proust for their new Dolphin Books series.[101]

9

IT IS OFTEN SAID that *Proust* was commissioned from Beckett by Chatto and Windus. This is not quite true. Correspondence between Aldington and Prentice shows that Aldington had warned MacGreevy (and through him, Beckett) that his essay could not be commissioned by the publishers. "You are right," wrote Prentice, "we must not commission any Dolphins. Thank you for telling MacGreevy so. If Samuel Beckett has no objection to taking a chance with the Proust essay by all means let us consider it." [102] Beckett wrote the study, therefore, not knowing whether it would be published. However, Tom MacGreevy was already engaged on an essay on T. S. Eliot for the same series (on the same noncommissioned basis), and it was because of MacGreevy's involvement and personal friendship with Charles Prentice—the prime mover of the Dolphin Books at Chatto and Windus—that Beckett was encouraged to feel that there was at least a good chance of the essay being accepted.

Dolphin Books was an interesting, innovative, highly varied series with some distinguished contributors.[103] The aim was to provide a variety of genres quite cheaply in a uniform, attractive format with a maximum length of seventeen thousand words. Design was an important feature, with the charming dolphin image adopted both as a vignette on the title page and as a major identifying feature of both the boards and the dust jacket designs.[104] Variety came with the color of the binding, although the dust jacket was kept uniform. Considerable thought went into the choice of the kind of binding and the price: light boards at two shillings per copy, rather than paper covers at one shilling.

In the case of better-known authors, the publishers also printed a large-format, limited, signed edition for the collectors' market. But neither MacGreevy nor Beckett was well enough known at the time to justify the expense of such an edition. Charles Prentice could only be honest when he wrote to Beckett in October offering him a contract: "We are rather doubtful whether we would be successful with a Large-Paper edition of your Proust, as your name is not yet before the collecting and bibliophilic public; a failure to sell such an edition now would not help you with the booksellers later on." [105] In accepting his offer, Beckett could not resist an acerbic if rather witty riposte:

> No, of course, the library rats wouldn't buy a swagger edition stained by such an attribution. But wouldn't the drawing-room rattesses love to expose a more declamatory testimonial than a 2/- pamphlet? Or is the race of undershot Proustian lèche-fesses [arse-lickers] extinct? Don't take any notice of this bad-tempered irrelevancy.[106]

It is time for justice to be done. The first commercial publisher to "discover" Samuel Beckett was undoubtedly Charles Prentice, the studious classical scholar and senior partner at Chatto and Windus. It was he who published Beckett's study of Proust and later accepted his book of stories *More Pricks Than Kicks.* Although he confessed several times to Beckett that he could not always follow him in his more innovative flights and had to turn down some of his later work,[107] Prentice never lost his enthusiasm for Beckett's writing or his conviction that Beckett had "really something in him" and might one day produce "something really good."[108] His firm lacked the patience, however, to wait just a little longer for Prentice's astute prognosis to be proved correct, and let Beckett go in the mid-1930s. But it is easy to talk with hindsight and difficult for a publisher who is running a commercial firm to persist with an author when few readers are buying his books.

For a few years, in common with Richard Aldington, Aldous Huxley, Norman Douglas, and, for a time, Wyndham Lewis, Beckett became a good friend of Prentice. On their first meetings in 1930, he quickly warmed to this shy but friendly, kind, and hospitable man. He used to meet Prentice when he was in London and dined with him several times when he was living there in 1934–35; he also corresponded with him for many years.[109] In the last year of his life, Beckett remembered the publisher with great affection and recalled that he had been one of his leading supporters in the early days.[110] Richard Aldington wrote of Prentice:

> His kindness was genuine and disinterested. He was a scholar, particularly devoted to Greek studies, yet enthusiastic for some modern authors. . . . He was unmarried, and in spite of his amiable qualities rather a lonely man, living in lodgings in Earl's Terrace, Kensington, in a chaos of books, boxes of cigars, wines and pictures by Wyndham Lewis.[111]

An astute Scot, Prentice had a flair for nosing out new authors and for encouraging established ones to produce their best. John Fothergill described him as "a genius in eiderdown clothing"[112]; in his history of Chatto and Windus, Oliver Warner offered several clues as to why Beckett enjoyed his company so much:

> Prentice had an air of Mr. Pickwick, who was in fact one of his favourite characters in fiction. There was, however, a sharp difference. Prentice was shrewd; he had no illusions about life in general—he felt, like Conrad's Winnie Verloc, that it didn't bear looking into; he was a scholar; and both in literary matters and in book design he had wonderful taste.[113]

Whenever Prentice turned down Beckett's work (as he did with the early poems, the story "Sedendo et Quiescendo," and *Dream of Fair to Middling Women*) he wrote with honesty, delicacy, and tact. His criticisms were shrewd and he never forgot to praise and encourage at the same time. He was certainly someone whom Beckett rated as a friend and respected as an admirable judge of a book.

10

BECKETT STAYED ON at the Ecole Normale through the summer of 1930 instead of traveling again, as he had thought he might, to Germany. His intention was to finish two pieces of work. One was a translation of a fragment—the first third —of "Anna Livia Plurabelle," part of Joyce's "Work in Progress," which was suggested to Alfred Péron and himself by Philippe Soupault, who was attending to its proposed publication in the review *Bifur*. The other was his essay on Marcel Proust.

Péron and he used to meet in the evening either in Beckett's room or in a café in the Latin Quarter to work on the Joyce translation. As July raced by, Beckett grew increasingly irritated because they were unable to devote enough time and energy to the work to do it properly. He was anxious to please Joyce by producing a good French version of so difficult a piece of writing, particularly since the rift with Lucia had introduced such a freeze into their relations. He grumbled to Tom MacGreevy that he and Alfy were meeting only when both of them were too tired to work at all well. He also regretted that, because Péron was so intimately involved with his girlfriend, Mania, he was often not available and was due to spend most of August away in the Auvergne. But, although Beckett was happy with neither the arrangements nor the timetable,[114] in the end a draft was produced and sent to Joyce and to *Bifur*.

Beckett celebrated *Le Quatorze juillet* (Bastille Day) in the company of Nancy Cunard and her black American lover, the pianist Henry Crowder. It was a drunken evening, with Beckett getting even drunker, he claimed, than his friends, before collapsing exhausted into a taxi. Earlier in the evening, he had presented Henry Crowder with a seventeen-line poem that he had written specially at Nancy Cunard's request for Henry to set to music. He dismissed the poem himself at the time as "the Rahab tomfoolery" and never thought highly of it. Its title was "From the Only Poet to a Shining Whore": the "only poet" was Dante, while the "shining whore" was Rahab, the harlot of Jericho. After Nancy Cunard had read the poem through aloud, Crowder thanked Beckett very warmly for it, repeating several times that it was "very very bootiful" and "very very fine indeed."[115]

The three of them went on to one of Nancy Cunard's favorite haunts in Paris, the Cigogne, which was probably the older habitués' name for Le Boeuf sur le Toit in the rue Boissy-d'Anglas.[116] This had an excellent reputation for American jazz and, invited to perform by the patron and encouraged by Nancy and Beckett, Henry Crowder "played the piano at the Cigogne where," said Beckett, once again imitating Joyce, "I described arabesques of an original pattern."[117] Although his normal persona was quiet and reserved, Beckett was quite capable — after consuming a good deal of alcohol and in the company of friends with whom he felt relaxed — of becoming fairly wild and uninhibited.

Over the summer months, he worked with tremendous concentration on his study of Proust's long novel. He found the book strangely uneven. His early judgments of *Du côté de chez Swann* reveal not only a keen sensitivity to the dangers that lie in loquacity and artificial symmetry but an interesting and unusual recognition that there is a danger, too, in a total mastery of form:

> There are incomparable things — Bloch, Françoise, Tante Léonie, Legrandin — and then passages that are offensively fastidious, artificial and almost dishonest. It is hard to know what to think about him. He is so absolutely the master of his own form that he becomes its slave as often as not. Some of his metaphors light up a whole page like a bright explosion, and others seem ground out in the dullest desperation. He has every kind of subtle equilibrium, charming trembling equilibrium and then suddenly a stasis, the arms of the balance wedged in a perfect horizontal line, more heavily symmetrical than Macaulay at his worst, with primos and secundos echoing to each complacently and reechoing . . . And to think that I have to contemplate him at stool for 16 volumes.[118]

He worked feverishly in the Ecole Normale library or in his room, sometimes until dawn, taking notes on various critical studies on Proust that had come out in France in the previous few years, although he did not always name his sources.[119]

As a relaxation, he reread with great pleasure the poems of John Keats. In a letter to Tom MacGreevy he wrote that he liked

> that crouching brooding quality in Keats — squatting on the moss, crushing a petal, licking his lips and rubbing his hands "counting the last oozings, hours by hours." I like him the best of them all, because he doesn't beat his fists on the table. I like that awful sweetness and thick soft damp green richness. And weariness: "Take into the air my quiet breath."[120]

Quotations of Keats reappear, together with phrases that Beckett used about him in his correspondence, almost verbatim in Beckett's discussion of "Proust's floral obsessions."[121] In *Proust*, he evokes a picture of the almost will-less Marcel sitting up all night staring at a branch of apple blossom that is laid beside his lamp; Beckett contrasts this with "the terrible panic-stricken stasis of Keats, crouched in a mossy thicket, annulled, like a bee in sweetness, 'drowsed with the fume of poppies' and watching 'the last oozings, hours by hours.' "[122]

He also followed up allusions to Giorgione's paintings in Proust's novel (*The Country Concert* and *The Tempest* in particular) by reading Gabriele D'Annunzio on Giorgione. He pulled no punches in commenting on the Italian novelist, whom he had read at Trinity College:

I was reading d'Annunzio on Giorg[i]one again and I think it is all balls and mean nasty balls. I was thinking of Keats and Giorg[i]one's two young men — the Concert and the Tempest — for a discussion of Proust's floral obsessions. D'A. seems to think that they are *merely* pausing between fucks. Horrible. He has a dirty juicy squelchy mind, bleeding and bursting, like his celebrated pomegranates.[123]

Beckett's irritated antagonism to what he saw as a vulgar misreading surfaces in *Proust,* where he finds "the remote, still, almost breathless passion of a Giorgione youth" misinterpreted by D'Annunzio "when he sees in the rapt doomed figure of the Tempesta a vulgar Leander resting between orgasms."[124]

But the reading that affected his approach to Proust most significantly while he was preparing his study was that of Schopenhauer. In July, he wrote to Tom MacGreevy:

I am reading Schopenhauer. Everyone laughs at that. Beaufret and Alfy etc. But I am not reading philosophy, nor caring whether he is right or wrong or a good or worthless metaphysician. An intellectual justification of unhappiness — the greatest that has ever been attempted — is worth the examination of one who is interested in Leopardi and Proust rather than in Carducci and Barrès.[125]

What is most interesting here is that Beckett should have been seeking for "an intellectual justification of unhappiness" at that time. And Schopenhauer profoundly marks the essay, not only where Beckett explicitly stresses his influence on music in the work of Proust, nor in the final notion of life as a *pensum* (a task to be accomplished) that "reveals the meaning of the word: 'defunctus,'" but in the generally dark, pessimistic tone of Beckett's own reading of Proust.[126] The essay is by turns illuminating — particularly strong on involuntary memory and the role of habit in human life — and exasperating in its ostentatious display of learning and its extravagant style.

Beckett delivered *Proust* by hand to Charles Prentice at Chatto and Windus toward the end of September 1930, passing through London on his way home to Dublin. On the boat train from Paris and during a bad crossing to Folkestone, he dozed, reading fitfully D. H. Lawrence's *St. Mawr,* in which he found "lovely things as usual and plenty of rubbish."[127] In London he felt very self-conscious because of a rash on his face and scalp. It looked so bad that a woman, who announced that she came from Cork, stopped him on the pavement in London, "and declaimed at the top of her voice that I had *Barber's Itch* or *Coiffeur's Rash,* that she knew, that she had a couple of lads of her own, that I must wash it from time to time. Then she asked me had I been drinking. So I left her, feeling that she had exhausted the subject."[128]

She had said enough, however, to make him wonder how his mother was going to react to his appearance. On his return to Dublin, he looked, he wrote, like "a scrofulous gargoyle."[129]

6

Academe:
Return and Flight
1930–31

1

BECKETT RETURNED HOME to take up his appointment as Lecturer in French at Trinity College. Although the welcome he received from his parents was warm enough, his mother was shocked by his appearance and tried to discourage him from leaving the house until his face had considerably improved. His father advised him to have his head shaved and to consult a skin specialist. Tired as he was, he needed little encouragement to be lazy and at first accepted without protest the fuss his mother made over him. He wrote to MacGreevy:

> To-day I am sitting by the fire listening to the rain and the trees and feeling ideally stupid. I suppose I will read the Strand Magazine until it is time for tea and then the Illustrated London News until it is time for dinner and then listen to Liebestraum and . . . the TSF [French for wireless] until it is time for bed. When I have put on 2 or 3 stone and achieved a complexion like Beaufret's, I may be released.[1]

Few things disturbed his first days back at Cooldrinagh. He was concerned that he had left two boxes of Peggy's love letters behind in his room at the Ecole Normale and wrote immediately to ask MacGreevy to ensure that they were burned. But, in the main, he was content to "sit in an armchair and listen for the gong" for meals.[2]

His ironic enjoyment of his life of ease at home lasted no more than a couple of weeks. His mother's excessive fussing annoyed him and going into college introduced other irritations. He wrote in dismay: "This life is terrible and I don't understand how it can be endured. Quip—that most foul malady—scandal and KINDNESS. The eternally invariable formulae of cheap quip and semi-obscene entirely contemptible potin [tittle-tattle] chez Ruddy and in the Common Room Club, and kindness here at home, pumped into me at high pressure."[3] He was torn between his liking for Rudmose-Brown and feelings of debt toward him, on the one hand, and on the other hand his aversion to having to listen uncomplainingly to the latter's constant anticlerical, antimilitary, and anti-Romantic outpourings. He was exasperated by the *"little* jokes—the kind that dribble into a subtle smile."[4] To someone listening, as he was now, with a critical ear, scholarly wit and sarcasm sounded all too often like exhibitionism, bitchiness, and character assassination.

He came rapidly to the conclusion that he would be unlikely to stand this kind of life for more than a year. He hoped to exploit the independence that a move into rooms at Trinity College gave him to do as much reading, if not writing, as he could. For, he asked rhetorically, "How can one write here, when every day *vulgarizes* one's hostility and turns anger into irritation and petulance?"[5]

Early in November 1930, Beckett gave a witty lecture in French to Trinity's Modern Language Society "on a nonexistent French poet—Jean du Chas."[6] The talk, entitled "Le Concentrisme," has been preserved.[7] There are plenty of clues in both the content and the tone to indicate that he is indulging his keenly developed sense of humor in this parody of the learned literary lecture. The talk begins, for example, with a discussion of du Chas's obsession with "the concierge"—a French institution that provides him, it seems, with the cornerstone of his whole literary edifice. In a play on the title of Descartes's famous treatise, du Chas is said to be the author of a *Discours de la Sortie* ("Discourse on Exits") —ironically for someone who, Beckett claimed, had committed suicide in a little hotel in "comic Marseille."[8]

Beckett invented an entire biography for his imaginary poet. He conferred on him his own date of birth, April 13, 1906. Indeed, although an extravagant creation, du Chas is related to Beckett's own life and character. He passes the summer months of his childhood in Kragenhof, where Beckett remembered only too well having been scorched by the sun on a visit with the Sinclairs;[9] he is by nature indolent; he resents "university hiccups—*reductio ad obscenum,* he called them, [which] made him wince and collapse in hysterics"; and he knows his Descartes, his Racine, and his Proust. The flavor of the piece is well caught in this translation by the Beckett scholar John Pilling:

> A variety of conclusions could be drawn from the Concentriste Manifesto sketched by Chas in his Journal. It is the kind of articulation which happily tolerates the obscene aspiration towards domains of order and clarity of each and every one of us. You could, for example, interpret this *Discours de la Sortie* as the artistic expression of the evasions that presage suicide, with "door, please!" as the single definitive act of the individual who ultimately does more than justice to himself. This would be a very modest *cogito ergo sum.* And the concierge who lets him out? As you will, God or fatigue, a spasm or Racinian clearsightedness. The decay of floosies descending a staircase. And there you are. . . . But what is crystal clear is that, if you insist on rigidifying the Idea of which he speaks, on concretizing Kant's Thing-in-itself, you would be devaluing to the level of a vaudeville by Labiche the art which, like a resolution of Mozart's, is perfectly intelligible and perfectly inexplicable.[10]

Beckett enjoyed using his imagination again, sharpening his wits and writing in French. But he also delighted in spelling out to his staff and student listeners his view, often repeated later, that true art has nothing to do with the Cartesian "clear and distinct" and that ultimately it stirs in the murky waters of the inexplicable. It has been thought that the talk was taken seriously at the time. "No," said Beckett. "Everyone was well aware that it was a spoof." [11]

In retrospect the "Concentrisme" lecture looks like a desperate attempt by Beckett to take his mind off his other problems: exasperation with the academic community, frustration at writing nothing acceptable himself, and, above all, a growing dissatisfaction with teaching.

2

EARLY IN JANUARY 1931, some members of the modern languages staff of Trinity College met informally with a few students to discuss which play they should put on at the Peacock Theatre in Dublin as the annual presentation of the Modern Languages Society. It was traditional at Trinity for staff, including the French exchange *lecteur*, as well as student members, to be involved in the production. The dynamic young *lecteur* for the two academic years 1929–31, Beckett's student friend from Paris Georges Pelorson, had directed Jean Giraudoux's *Siegfried* the previous spring with great success in the same theater and was again put in overall charge of the program.

Numerous ideas were tossed around; the society finally opted for a year of innovation. A varied trilogy of plays would be performed: one in Spanish; one an almost contemporary French play; and one a burlesque of Pierre Corneille's sevententh-century four-act tragedy *Le Cid*, called *Le Kid*. A tradition has grown up in Beckett criticism that this burlesque was an early, now lost work by Beckett himself. It is easy to see why: the tandem of high literature and popular knockabout, Don Diègue combined with Charlie Chaplin, makes a perfect vehicle for the future author of *Waiting for Godot* to start to ride. Unfortunately for myth, the truth is more complex and less symmetrical.

According to Georges Pelorson, the idea of the play was his alone and the cutting up of Corneille's text which produced the one-act burlesque was also done almost entirely by himself, with very little help and advice from Beckett.[12] Only the title was Beckett's own — after the film *The Kid*, which Charlie Chaplin had made ten years earlier with Jackie Coogan. The play remains of interest, however, as one of Beckett's earliest practical incursions into drama in which he played, as far as we know, his only acting part.

The evening opened with *La Quema*, a one-act comedy in Spanish by the Alvarez Quintero brothers, directed by the dapper little professor of Italian, Walter Starkie, with the help of his wife. There followed a short play called *La souriante Mme. Beudet*, written by Denys Amiel and André Obey and first produced in Paris in 1921. This was suggested by Beckett, who had either read or seen it in Paris the previous year and who was responsible for obtaining copies of the text for the cast. The choice was a controversial one. Several members of the society (including Pelorson, who thought it a most surprising selection for Beckett to have made) considered the play a pale and rather tedious reflection of Flaubert's *Madame Bovary*, with Beudet, the Charles Bovary figure, as "a gross, beef-witted merchant tailor who cannot understand his sensitive, temperamental wife." [13] Beudet likes to play with an unloaded revolver which he places to his temple and, to frighten his wife, squeezes the trigger. One day, unable to bear the mortal tedium of living with him anymore, she places a bullet in the gun and watches him as he acts out his little scene. The bullet fires but misses Beudet's head and hits a vase. Ironically, Beudet assumes that his wife intended to kill herself because he pays her too little attention. And so all she has managed to do is to create an even worse hell of marital boredom for herself. With somewhat misplaced enthusiasm the Modern Languages Society was praised rather snootily by *T.C.D.*, the college's own magazine, for "choosing a serious and difficult piece from the most important contemporary literature of modern Europe, instead of some stale commercial scribble thirty years out of date, as the tradition of College drama seems to require." [14]

Le Kid was described on the program as a "Cornelian nightmare," but Beckett preferred to think of it as a blend of Corneille and Bergson, because of the importance given to time. [15] The script does not appear to have survived, but from what one can learn of it from its main author, it radically and comically compressed Corneille's play, used actual speeches from the original text, and introduced a lot of visual jokes and comic byplay, dreamed up again by Pelorson, not Beckett. "Here," wrote the *Irish Times* reviewer, "we had classicism held up in the distorting mirror of expressionism. The heroes of Corneille suddenly assumed grotesquely comic shapes." [16] Don Fernand, the King of Castile, treated as a mild, harmless geriatric, spent the entire play in a Bath chair; a silent Infanta drifted twice across the stage to the music of Ravel's Pavane [17] as if wandering around in "mute Cartesian bewilderment"; [18] all the men wore modern dress, with the Kid himself sporting flannel trousers; and Don Diègue (played by Beckett in a long white beard à la Old Father Time) carried an umbrella instead of a sword and, like Clov in Beckett's 1956 play, *Endgame*, an alarm clock. Pelorson played Chimène's father, Don Gomès, decked out in the uniform of a German general, with pointed helmet, big boots, and saber, a costume from the previous year's play, *Siegfried*. [19] Rattles were whirled and balloons were burst onstage or were thrown into the audience. Don Gomès jumped down from the stage and chased the balloons into the auditorium, bursting as many as he could with his saber. Finally, the play was brought to its conclusion by a barman announcing, "Time, gentlemen, please."

Time supplied one of the main visual jokes. The classical unity of time, according to which all of a play's action occurs (or could be imagined as occurring) within a span of twenty-four hours, was shown being observed literally by "a silent figure seated on a ladder and smoking a pipe [playing] Einsteinian tricks with time" [20] by moving the hands of a large clock attached to a painted backdrop. The silent actor was supposed to fall asleep from time to time and be roused by one of the others shouting at him or shaking the ladder; waking with a jolt, he then moved the hands of the clock frantically forward. It was Beckett's own idea to bring an alarm clock on stage with him for Don Diègue's mono-logue in the first act: he knelt down, placed the clock very carefully on the floor, and was midway through his famous "O rage! ô désespoir! ô vieillesse ennemie!" speech when the alarm went off, infuriating him and waking up the man on the ladder. This, combined with the speeded-up movements of the hands of the big clock, forced him to go faster and faster until he built up a wild, crazy momentum, producing a torrent of sound that has aptly been compared with the effect of Lucky's extravagant monologue in *Waiting for Godot*.[21]

Three performances of the plays were given at the Peacock Theatre on February 19–21, 1931. Beckett found the first night acutely embarrassing. At the end there was a terrible scene. Professor Rudmose-Brown, who had played no part in the choice of the plays, insulted both Pelorson and Beckett and stormed away, apoplectic with rage and disgusted by what he regarded as a stupid, shameful charade that reflected badly on the entire department.[22] By the second night, Beckett had come to feel that the whole thing was a terrible mistake and dreaded having to face an audience again. The Friday and Saturday night performances were even more tense than the first night. Pelorson com-mented: "The truth is that Beckett got terribly depressed with a deep sense of the vanity of the whole thing (typical of him) — I am pretty sure of that — and a feeling of guilt. He had been terribly affected by Ruddy's *sortie* the first night (though of course he would never have admitted to this)."[23] He drank heavily before the second performance and had to be extricated from his rooms by Pelorson, who argued angrily that he would be letting the others down badly if he did not turn up. He was almost dragged along to the Peacock Theatre. He got through the performances somehow, commenting later that "They might have gone worse" but adding pompously that "The inevitable vulgarisation leaves one exhausted and disgusted."[24]

The play was not a howling success. But it did arouse a certain amount of controversy, which was after all Pelorson's intention, and was far from being unpopular with everyone. If Rudmose-Brown was horrified, W. F. Trench, the Professor of English, was delighted. The college magazine asked: "Really wasn't it rather naïve? It reminded us forcibly of those grand old parodies that used to be shown at the Gaiety some forty years past, 'Carmen Uptodata' and the like — unless you happened to hate Corneille very, very heartily it was rather a strain on the digestion."[25] However, rather than following in the tradition of the Gaiety Theatre parodies, *Le Kid* was, as Pelorson himself recognized, much more of an intellectual *canular*, a product of the Ecole Normale kind of mind: clever, avant-garde, and rather Surrealistic, but with a mixture of the effete, the preten-tious, and the puerile.[26] The *Irish Times* reviewer described it, however, as "an excellent *jeu d'esprit*." And, in his allusion to Expressionism, he was probably right in reminding us that *Le Kid* should be seen as adopting some of the distortion techniques of German Expressionism (such as are found, for instance, in Ivan Goll's play *Methusalem: or the Eternal Bourgeois*), and as exuding the irreverent, iconoclastic (if by then somewhat jaded) spirit of some of the early theatrical experiments of Dada.

Beckett virtually never went to rehearsals for *Le Kid*, which took up most of Pelorson's free time in the Lent term; typically, he preferred to rehearse by himself in his rooms.[27] Apart from reading in the library for his lectures on Racine and Gide, he found it extremely hard to settle down to any serious work, although he did find time to read with great fascination the meticulous self-analysis of Jules Renard's *Journal intime*. He wrote virtually nothing of his own at this time.[28] "You know I can't write at all," he wrote plaintively to Tom MacGreevy. "The simplest sentence is a torture. I wish we could meet and talk — before I become inarticulate or eloquently suave."[29]

One of the major reasons for what Beckett described as his "paralysis" was his sheer hatred of lecturing. Only three weeks after he began teaching in October, he described it as "this grotesque comedy of lecturing."[30] "I don't get on well with my classes," he wrote to MacGreevy on 14 November, 1930, "and that flatters me and exasperates my pride. . . . How long it will drag on, my dear Tom, I have no idea."[31] Early in March 1931, he protested vehemently: "I don[']t want to be a professor (it[']s almost a pleasure to contemplate the mess of this job)."[32] A major problem for him was that standing up to speak in public was excruciatingly painful. He experienced extreme embarrassment and utterly lacked any exhibitionistic streak that might have helped to counter the natural self-consciousness that affects so many speakers, who manage, in spite of their nerves, to sound confident. Beckett lacked confidence, too, in what he felt capable of offering to his students and has often said that he gave up his job because "he could not bear teaching to others what he did not know himself." His Michaelmas term lecture notes on Gide and Racine (preserved by one of his students, Rachel Burrows) show that his lectures were impressively wide-ranging and full of fascinating insights. But they may have been pitched over the heads of the duller undergraduates.

His shy, diffident manner did little to disguise his disdain for the shallowness, paucity of interest, and lack of literary sensitivity of most of those he was teaching. A mixture of defensiveness, hurt pride, and contempt comes through in his account of how, while lecturing on Rimbaud, he tried to explain about the "eye suicide" of the poet only to find the students "guffawing" when he quoted the lines "Noire bise, averse glapissante / Fleuve noir et maisons closes." "So," he went on, "I repeated. Titter. I, in my innocence, couldn't understand, and wondered could 'maisons closes' [bordellos] have tickled their repressions."[33] Puzzled, Beckett asked Pelorson about the incident; Pelorson explained that the joke lay not only in the *maisons closes* but in the fact that the word *glapissante* contained *pissante*, which means "pissing."

This kind of juvenile humor and immaturity depressed Beckett. He told Lawrence Harvey that, when he had taught at Campbell College, he had been prepared for such childish behavior with associated problems of discipline. But when he went to teach at Trinity he had expected more from his students. Instead, he found that these sons and daughters of wealthy families "simply

5. II. 71.

© *Avigdor Arikha*

"Samuel Beckett, Double Profile," February 5, 1971, goldpoint on blueish coated paper.

Courtesy of John Beckett

The Beckett family, *c.* 1896. Back row: Samuel Beckett's father, William Beckett; and his aunt, Frances "Cissie" Sinclair. Front row, left to right: Gerald Beckett; William Frank Beckett (Samuel's grandfather); Howard Beckett; Frances Beckett *née* Crothers (Samuel's grandmother); James Beckett; and Harold Beckett.

"Little Granny," Samuel Beckett's maternal grandmother, Annie Roe, with a Roe family group, *c.* 1910. Back row: May Beckett (Samuel's mother); her mother, Annie Roe; Rubina Roe, the wife of Edward Price Roe; Samuel Beckett; and Molly Roe (Beckett's cousin). Front row: Mabin Fry (May's nephew, son of Esther Roe); Sheila Roe (Beckett's cousin); and Frank Beckett (Beckett's brother).

Courtesy of Dartmouth College

Courtesy of Edward and Caroline Beckett

May Beckett, Samuel's mother, on
the window seat at Cooldrinagh,
c. 1920.

The successful businessman, William Beckett, Samuel's father,
c. 1922.

Courtesy of Edward Beckett

Courtesy of Caroline Beckett Murphy

Samuel Beckett at the age of about three with his brother, Frank, aged around seven.

Below left: Beckett's family home, Cooldrinagh, in Foxrock, showing the bow window of the bedroom where he was born. The extension to the right of the house was added later.

Below: Beckett's school, Portora Royal, Enniskillen, in the 1920s.

Photograph by Michael Jacob

Courtesy of the headmaster, Richard Bennett

The young cricketer. Beckett in 1920.

The rugby team at Portora Royal School. Beckett stands fifth from the left.

Two photographs: courtesy of the headmaster, Richard Bennett

Beckett as a student.

Beckett the golfer, with his TCD and Carrickmines Golf Club partner, Bill Cunningham, standing to his left.

Courtesy of Edward Beckett

Courtesy of William Cunningham

Beckett feeding the pigeons in Piazza San Marco, Venice, in the summer of 1927. The photograph (taken by Beckett's American friend Charles Clarke) was described on its reverse by Beckett's mother.

Courtesy of Edward Beckett

Ethna MacCarthy, whom Beckett loved and admired and who was the inspiration for the character of the "Alba."

Below left: Beckett's professor, friend, and mentor, Thomas Brown Rudmose-Brown, photographed with a student, Eileen O'Connor, at Trinity College, Dublin.

Below: Beckett's close friend, A. J. "Con" Leventhal, in the garden, *c.* 1931.

Portrait by Seán O'Sullivan, courtesy of Anne Wolfson Leventhal

Courtesy of Eileen Williams

Courtesy of Anne Wolfson Leventhal

"Boss" Sinclair, Beckett's uncle by marriage, 1932.

Below: Peggy Sinclair, Beckett's cousin, with whom he had his first real love affair.

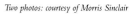

Two photos: courtesy of Morris Sinclair

Above left: Georges Pelorson, Beckett's friend and his first student at the Ecole Normale.

Above right: Jean Beaufret, another friend at the Ecole Normale, with whom Beckett talked philosophy during 1928–29.

The Ecole Normale Supérieure, rue d'Ulm, Paris, in the 1920s, where Beckett was Lecturer in English. In the foreground stands the tree that Belacqua saw from his bedroom window in Beckett's novel *Dream of Fair to Middling Women*.

Three photos: courtesy of the Ecole Normale

Beckett's close friend and confidant, Thomas MacGreevy, at the Ecole Normale, *c.* 1928.

James Joyce in the 1930s.

Courtesy of Margaret Farrington and Elizabeth Ryan

Courtesy of Edward Beckett

Samuel Beckett in the early 1930s.

Courtesy of University College, London Library

Courtesy of Edward Beckett

Above left: Lucia Joyce after her breakdown in the early 1930s.

Above right: Bill and May Beckett with their niece, Sheila Page Roe, and her daughters, Jill and Diana, *c.* 1932.

Below left: Suzanne Deschevaux-Dumesnil, Beckett's future wife, on the beach in Tunisia.

Below right: Suzanne Deschevaux-Dumesnil in her twenties.

Two photos: courtesy of Mita and Edmund Tuby

Courtesy of the Beckett International Foundation, The University of Reading

Beckett at Peggy Guggenheim's Yew Tree Cottage in 1938. In the foreground: Beckett holding a tin whistle, next to George Reavey. In the background, left to right: Pegeen, Peggy's daughter; Geer van Velde (with a pipe); Gwynned Reavey; and Elisabeth van Velde.

Samuel Beckett relaxing on the beach in Donegal with his brother, Frank, in 1937.

Courtesy of Dartmouth College

Courtesy of Edward Beckett

May Beckett, holding her Kerry Blue terrier in her arms, chats with a neighbor *c.* 1937.

Beckett's friend, the painter Bram van Velde.

Photographer unknown

Two photos: courtesy of Aléxis Péron

Alfred and Mania Péron, both close personal friends of Beckett. Péron is wearing his army uniform.

Alfred Péron. Photograph taken by the Gestapo after his arrest in August 1942.

couldn't care less." [34] The contrast between these halfhearted students and the French *normaliens*, who traditionally prided themselves on belonging to an intellectual elite, must have seemed very striking. And if anyone had pointed out a resemblance between the Trinity students' lavatorial humor and Pelorson and Beckett's broad burlesque of Corneille, the comparison would doubtless have been brushed aside with a gesture of intellectual superiority.

3

UNTIL THE SECOND WEEK in March 1931, Beckett was still planning to spend the Easter vacation in Germany. He had considered for some time traveling to Hamburg, although the thought of staying there alone frightened him. [35] But eventually someone, in all probability Sylvia Beach, wrote to invite him to come over to Paris for an evening to be held at Adrienne Monnier's bookshop, La Maison des Amis des Livres, in the rue de l'Odéon to honor Joyce, focus attention on his *Work in Progress*, and read the French version of the "Anna Livia Plurabelle" section. Since Beckett had produced a first version of the French text with his friend Alfred Péron, he was naturally curious to find out how the finished translation, described by Joyce to Harriet Shaw Weaver as "one of the masterpieces of translation," had turned out. [36] So, at the very last moment, [37] he caught the boat and took himself off to Paris, spending only the night of 25 March in London at the Shaftesbury Hotel. [38]

At Adrienne Monnier's, Joyce was the guest of honor and the focus of attention. He sat looking extremely dignified but pleased throughout, surrounded by his friends, associates, and admirers. Among these were Edouard Dujardin, the venerable author of *Les Lauriers sont coupés*, to whom Joyce had acknowledged a debt for the interior monologue; Harriet Shaw Weaver, who had come over from London especially for the event; Sylvia Beach; Philippe Soupault; Paul Léon; Eugene and Maria Jolas; Robert McAlmon; Mina Loy; Mary Colum; Samuel Beckett; and Adrienne Monnier herself. The Joyce family was also there. As well as the specially invited guests, there were a few newcomers like Leon Edel, who later described the evening for the *Canadian Forum*. [39]

It was a solemn, even reverential occasion. The back rooms of the rue de l'Odéon bookshop were crowded with, McAlmon maintained, about two hundred people. [40] The program was organized and introduced by Adrienne Monnier. She began by recounting how she had first met James Joyce at André Spire's house in 1920, how his reputation and influence had grown in France in those intervening years, and what her own opinion was of *Ulysses*. Philippe Soupault then went on to describe how the translation of "Anna Livia Plurabelle" had been produced. [41] The roles of Beckett and Péron were described only cursorily at the beginning of his account, and their translation was referred to as a "premier essai," or first attempt, which had then been subject to a further correction by Paul Léon, Ivan Goll, and Joyce himself. The Frenchman focused on the way in which, during a third stage of revision, he, Léon, and Joyce had *rejected* what they felt were inappropriate renderings in the earlier version and had worked hard to improve the text both in its rhythm and in its sense. Since Beckett considered what he and Péron had done as much more than a first draft, he sharply resented this but, in the company of Joyce and the other collaborators, felt obliged to hide his true feelings.

After Beckett's return to Dublin, Joyce sent him an autographed copy of the *Nouvelle Revue Française* containing the translation, together with a signed copy of *Haveth Childers Everywhere*.[42] In thanking him, Beckett could not resist the comment that "it was impossible to read his text without understanding the futility of the translation," adding even more acidly to MacGreevy that he could not "believe that he [Joyce] doesn't see through the translation himself, its horrible quip atmosphere and vulgarity."[43] Fortunately, the Beckett-Péron version has been preserved and can be compared with the published text.[44]

As the third item in the program, Adrienne Monnier played Joyce's own recording of "Anna Livia Plurabelle" in English on Sylvia Beach's gramophone. Immediately afterward she read the French translation in a rapid, unemotional, singsong voice.[45] Robert McAlmon, who had turned up rather reluctantly with a doctor just back from exploring South America, described the scene as resembling Madame Tussaud's waxworks; he was intensely irritated by the reverential air of those whom he described as the "dumbly worshipful."[46] So, indicating these feelings mutely to his guest, he raised his hands in the air in a gesture of mock prayer. At this point Edouard Dujardin, who thought that McAlmon had been looking at his wife's very thick ankles and was commenting by his gesture on their size, got up, walked across the room, and slapped him sharply on the face. This sudden dramatic action caused an enormous buzz of excitement all around the room and, since Dujardin walked out immediately without explaining himself, the puzzlement as to what could have prompted his extraordinary action continued at a reception held afterward in the apartment over the shop. It was not until the following day that the true explanation emerged and that Dujardin in his turn learned the real reason for McAlmon's gesture.

While he was in Paris, Beckett again met Samuel Putnam, who was interested in publishing some of his poems in the Irish section of a first volume (and the only one to appear) of *The European Caravan: An Anthology of the New Spirit in European Literature*.[47] It was decided that Beckett would send him four poems, one of which, "Yoke of Liberty," may have been written and sent on later. The other poems were "Hell Crane to Starling," "Casket of Pralinen for a Daughter of a Dissipated Mandarin," and "Text." Putnam used the last poem again in the first issue of his *New Review*. Beckett also hoped to obtain more commissions for translations from Putnam, Edward Titus, and Eugene Jolas.

Several of Beckett's friends were in town: George Reavey, whom he had met in Paris in 1930, Jean Thomas, and Jean Beaufret. And, of course, Joyce himself was there. Although Beckett still found him extremely cool, the fact that, after he returned to Dublin, he received signed copies of Joyce's two publications and a card at Whitsun with the Joyces' Campden Grove address in

London[48] suggests that the visit had at least served to improve relations between them, as he had hoped it would.

Immediately after his Paris visit, he went to stay again with the Sinclairs in Kassel. On his way there, he had to spend part of a bleak, uncomfortable night in the third-class waiting room in Nuremberg railway station from three o'clock in the morning until his train arrived. He found that the Sinclairs were very worried about Peggy, whose health had declined in the past few months, and anxious about their worsening financial position. Yet they were still prepared to listen with concern to his complaints about teaching and his wish to leave the university. The time raced by, and soon he had to return to Ireland with a heavy heart to do a job that he hated.

4

IN THE SUMMER TERM, Beckett was able to teach for only a few weeks before he was struck down by a severe attack of pleurisy at the end of May.[49] Rudmose-Brown and Pelorson were obliged to take over his classes and it was several weeks before he was well enough to return to work. Probably in order to help him to recover fully, Beckett and his brother planned to spend a month's holiday together in France starting at the end of June. They intended to make their way to the Mediterranean, then travel along the coast until they reached Le Lavandou in Var. There they had arranged to meet Tom MacGreevy, who, in the hope of writing his novel, was staying for a couple of months at the Villa Koeclin as the guest of Richard Aldington and Bridget Patmore. On the return journey, they wanted to tour the vineyards of Burgundy.

Before this could happen, however, a dreadful scene took place between Beckett and his mother that was to shatter the fragile peace of Cooldrinagh. Correspondence between Beckett, MacGreevy, and Prentice allows us to piece together a fairly coherent picture of what happened, although there remains some doubt as to its precise cause.[50] MacGreevy left his family home in Tarbert on 8 June to travel to London via Dublin on his way to France. En route he joined Beckett in Trinity College, but found him still quite ill, so he stayed only a couple of days. After MacGreevy's departure, it seems likely that Beckett went back home to Foxrock to recover completely before their holiday. One day, while her son was out walking, May Beckett came across some of his writing that he had left out on a table. She cast a casual eye on it, then started to read with a mixture of growing horror and disgust.

When Beckett returned to the house, he found his mother in a state of blind fury. A blazing row ensued in which she told him that she was appalled at what she had just read and that she would not have him writing such monstrous work under her roof. Nothing that Beckett could say would placate her. When Frank and his father returned home from the office, it was to find a distraught May not speaking to an unhappy Beckett, who was waiting to leave, his bags already packed with the offending work. Attempts to intercede on his behalf by his father and his brother came to nothing; his mother was adamant that he could not stay. So a stunned, miserable Beckett found himself fleeing back to his rooms in Trinity College two weeks before the projected holiday.

The question poses itself as to what could possibly have shocked his mother so much. She would certainly have disliked intensely some of the poems that Seamus O'Sullivan (the editor of the *Dublin Magazine*) had turned down, because of phrases like "give us a wipe for the love of Jesus." But they are hardly likely to have provoked so violent a reaction. The stories that he was working on at the time are more plausible contenders: "Sedendo et Quiescendo," which was later absorbed into his novel *Dream of Fair to Middling Women*, or "Walking Out," a story that was published three years later in *More Pricks Than Kicks*. May Beckett would have been shocked enough at the "peeping Tom" activities and subsequent fight in "Walking Out" and at the cynical treatment of Lucy by her indolent fiancé, Belacqua, who is only too happy to see her take a lover so as to leave him to his inner peace. Even phrases like "what the hell she wanted" would have upset someone of May's straitlaced Protestant background. But she may also have picked up a manuscript notebook that dates from 1931.[51] In this Beckett wrote out lists of words and phrases from "erotic" literature, phrases like "a claque on the seat of honour" or "as badly off as the friar's arse." But these flagellatory images or allusions, many of which he wove into his poem "Sanies II" and into a section of *Dream of Fair to Middling Women*, were often highly recondite or were written in foreign languages that his mother would not have understood.

There were rumors in Dublin a year later that he was writing a novel of "unparalleled obscenity;"[52] six months after that, while in the Merrion Nursing Home recovering from an operation, he certainly experimented with writing some "obscene Spenserian stanzas."[53] The so-called obscene novel may, however, have been an early draft of *Dream of Fair to Middling Women*, a portion of which was clearly written many months before the period January–July 1932 to which it is usually assigned. And Mrs. Beckett may indeed have come across the pages of *Dream* that contain a thinly veiled transposition of Beckett's own sexual experiences with Peggy and, most shocking of all, his use of a love letter from his cousin. This would certainly go a long way toward explaining her horrified response.

There was a lot of to-ing and fro-ing from Foxrock to Trinity College in the two weeks before the holiday but no shift in May's position. And in spite of the emotional turmoil created by the rift, the brothers duly set off for France at the end of June. They stopped in Rouen to tour the cathedral and look at the town's famous big clock, staying overnight at the Hôtel du Nord,[54] before traveling south to Charolles and Mâcon in the Saône-et-Loire, where they called at several vineyards to taste the local wines. To Beckett's surprise the famous Nuits St.-Georges and the Gevrey-Chambertin, which they sampled on the return journey, and from which they had hoped "for great things," seemed quite "plain and tawdry"[55] in comparison with the fine wines of the "Mâcon country."[56] Their brief visit to the town of Mâcon, where the Romantic poet Alphonse de Lamartine was born, inspired Beckett soon after their return to pen the following nicely ironic piece of dialogue in his story "Fingal." Belacqua and his girlfriend Winnie are looking out over the countryside of Fingal, which Belacqua compares with the scenery of the Mâcon region of France:

> "When it's a magic land" he sighed "like Saône-et-Loire."
> "That means nothing to me" said Winnie.
> "Oh yes" he said, "bons vins et Lamartine, a champaign land for the sad and serious, not a bloody little toy Kindergarten like Wicklow."
> You make great play with your short stay abroad, thought Winnie.
> "You and your sad and serious" she said. "Will you never come off it?"
> "Well" he said "I'll give you Alphonse."
> She replied that he could keep him. Things were beginning to blow up nasty.[57]

Having picked up MacGreevy's address at Le Lavandou from the *poste restante* in Toulon, Beckett and Frank moved farther along the Côte d'Azur to stay for almost a week at Canadel-sur-Mer, close to Richard Aldington's rented house. They visited the Villa Koeclin twice (having lunch on one occasion with MacGreevy, Aldington, and Bridget Patmore) and then had MacGreevy to dinner. Conversation focused on MacGreevy's novel and on the story "Sedendo et Quiescendo," which Beckett had just completed; later, MacGreevy commented astutely that Beckett "went Joyce in it—though he denies that it is Joyce."[58] But however convivial Beckett tried to be and however unforthcoming he was in the presence of his brother, it was clear to MacGreevy that the break with his mother had made him desperately unhappy. Beckett and Frank then traveled back north via Digne, Grenoble, and Annecy, passing the Lac du Bourget, where Lamartine wrote "Le Lac," to Dijon and Troyes.

They returned to Dublin at the end of July via Paris and London. Staying for a few days at the Hôtel Corneille, Beckett was able to look up some of his French and expatriate friends again. The first person they met in the Latin Quarter was Beckett's old friend and drinking companion Giorgio Joyce, now "drinking Vittel on the terrace of the Deux Magots."[59] The previous December, Giorgio had married Helen Fleischman (whom Beckett often called Fleshwoman in his correspondence) and Beckett was curious to see how their controversial marriage appeared to be working out. For Helen was ten years older than Giorgio, and both Nora (at first) and Lucia had strongly disapproved of the marriage. Beckett and Frank were invited to dinner where conversation centered on Giorgio's father, mother, and sister, whom Beckett promised he would visit in London the following week.

Nancy Cunard, whom Beckett was anxious to see partly at least in order to secure more commissions for literary translations, was unfortunately away in America, reunited again, however turbulently, with Henry Crowder; she was, joked Beckett, "comparing colours" there.[60] But his friends from the Ecole Normale, Jean Thomas, the *secrétaire-général* (who had promised to write letters of reference for him when he applied for jobs), and Jean Beaufret, were in town again and he lunched or dined with them both. Frank and he went out, too, with Alan and Belinda Duncan for what Beckett described as a "Grand Gui-gnol" dinner at La Rivière restaurant before accompanying them for drinks at the Flore with two other expatriates, Tom McKenna and his wife.[61]

They crossed the Channel to London, where Beckett stayed on alone for a few days after Frank's return home. He went to Joyce's house at 28B Campden Grove in Kensington in a state of acute anxiety. The breakup with Lucia was recent enough for him to feel that tension was almost inevitable. With the ice already broken in Paris, he wanted time to talk to Joyce alone, but complained later that he hardly managed to see him because of Nora and Lucia. He also found the "usual fucking complications and flight"—whether because Lucia was once more being embarrassingly attentive or sullen and resentful, it is impossible to determine, although it was probably the former. Later in the week, he had "a rather miserable dinner," once again, unfortunately, with all three of them.[62] Although he found Joyce fired up with fury and threatening litigation against the *Frankfurter Zeitung* on account of an article that the newspaper had wrongly printed under his name,[63] he thought that James and Nora were in good enough form, and looking forward to a holiday in Kent. But Lucia, he thought, looked dreadful. "Foutue" was the word he used to describe her state,[64] "knackered" being almost strong enough as a translation.

Another potentially important meeting for Beckett was with Charles Pren-tice of Chatto and Windus. They met for dinner and discussed Beckett's own plans for further work as well as Greece and Greek culture, on which Prentice was something of an expert. "For the sake of something to say more than anything else," wrote Beckett, "and knowing bloody well I would (could) never do it," he proposed writing an essay on Dostoyevsky, whom he had been reading for some time.[65] After what both of them independently described as "a very pleasant evening," Beckett took round his story "Sedendo et Quiescendo" the following day, only for Prentice to reject it a few days later.

5

BECKETT RETURNED TO DUBLIN on the first of August. But he went back to his rooms in Trinity College, not to his parents' home in Foxrock. Neither he nor his mother was to be easily reconciled and the rift between them remained for several months. This was only partly because of his mother's obduracy. Beckett was deeply wounded, and the wound was kept open by his hurt pride and inherent stubbornness.

> Daddy says come off it for the love of God, come out and dine, I'll give you a drink, kiss and make friends. God bless dear Daddy Mummy Frank Bibby and all that I love and make me a good boy for Jesus Christ's sake armen. So I said something quiet and flat and blank but I won't. No sir. Nothing would induce me to.[66]

He met his father from time to time in Dublin; "Father stands me a Turkish bath and a dry Martini once a week and I appreciate that," he wrote.[67] His brother, too, visited him quite often and worried about him constantly, paying the first two months' rent on his rooms and, in October, hiring a piano for him in an attempt to cheer him up.[68] But there is no evidence that he saw his mother at all until mid- to late November. The tone of Beckett's comments on this indicates that this mattered a lot to him. He was clearly upset, not just by his dramatic expulsion from home but by the emotional gulf that this had created between his mother and himself.

Trinity College was almost deserted during the latter part of the summer vacation. Rudmose-Brown came in, but Beckett saw him rarely. When he did, the Professor seemed only capable of speaking about jobs that Beckett might conceivably apply for: a lectureship in Cape Town or a similar post at Cardiff University. He also told Beckett that Walter Starkie had applied for the Italian chair at Oxford; if he were hired, that would free the Chair of Italian at Trinity College, to which Beckett might well then be appointed. "That'll be the real pig's back," commented Beckett.[69]

Occasionally he saw Con Leventhal, with whom he became increasingly friendly at this time. He also saw a lot of Ethna MacCarthy. But seeing her becoming emotionally involved with Con inflicted sharp stabs of pain on his bruised and still-tender ego. In August 1931, he wrote two of his most beautiful poems, inspired by his love for Ethna. The poems "came together one on top of the other, a double-yolked orgasm in months of dispermatic nights and days," he wrote;[70] both poems were great favorites of his.[71] "Alba," the Italian word for dawn, was the title of the first poem and the name he gave to the woman based on Ethna in his stories. It was accepted by Seamus O'Sullivan for publication in the *Dublin Magazine*. "I was told," wrote Beckett, "he and his bloody committee examined it longitudinally and diagonally for fear of an obscene anagram."[72] The second poem, once called "Moly" and published a few months later as "Yoke of Liberty" in *The European Caravan*, was turned down by O'Sullivan—probably, surmised Beckett, because the editor presumed that the opening line, "The lips of her desire are grey," referred to the woman's genitalia. Beckett explained both the title "Yoke of Liberty" (borrowed from Dante's "Il giogo della libertà") and its main theme in remarking that "he [the poet] will not be caught in this trap but not to be caught is a burden."[73] The closing lines develop this résumé:

> But she will die and her snare
> tendered so patiently
> to my tamed and watchful sorrow
> will break and hang
> in a pitiful crescent.[74]

Clearly he was far from being cured of his love for Ethna.

Until his return to France in the second week in October, Georges Pelorson was still living at number 1 in the old square of Trinity College, whereas Beckett was in New Square. Pelorson was one of the few people able to get through to Beckett at this time. Partly this was because he was bubbling over with enthusiasm for books he was reading and poems that he was writing. He was himself thinking of giving up his studies at the Ecole Normale, so he could listen with understanding to Beckett's complaints about teaching, students, and the academic community in general. Beckett enjoyed his company and seems to have absorbed quite a few of Pelorson's lively or unusual turns of phrase or images into his early work. The poem "Enueg II," written during that summer, has some striking images: "feet in marmalade / perspiring profusely / heart in marmalade / smoke more fruit / the old heart the old heart."[75] Pelorson, who was sleeping badly at the time and smoking far too much, often used the expression "J'ai les pieds en marmalade" ("My feet are in marmalade") transforming something his grandmother used to say to him, "J'ai les pieds en compote" "My feet are in jam"). Interestingly, another common expression that Pelorson used was "mon vieux coeur" ("my old heart").[76] Six years later, in a letter to Mary Manning, Beckett wrote

> Pelorson used to talk about the stone in his heart. I didn't know what he meant till I felt it myself. Cardiac calculus. I remember after a walk in the Fiendish Park his pausing on the stairs of his rooms in Trinity and inviting me to feel his heart. I placed my hand tenderly on the place. He wore a pullover knitted by the lady who is now his wife, or was when I heard last. His sternum was concave.[77]

Pelorson had fallen madly in love at the time with a young woman named Marcelle who taught in a school outside Dublin, so he was mostly not free to see Beckett during the evening. But he would often drop in to Beckett's rooms unannounced at eleven o'clock or midnight and they would talk into the early hours, sitting in large wicker armchairs, one on each side of the turf fire, with a glass in his hand and a bottle of Jameson whiskey on the floor between them.

Pelorson's visits used to break what Beckett described as a curious *quies rerum.* With his keen awareness of complexity and paradox, Beckett saw this transitory peace and silence as something that he could savor as well as fear. For, although he undoubtedly felt isolated and depressed — feelings aggravated by the emotional distance that separated him from his mother — he also deliberately cultivated and explored his isolation, like the depths of some dark, familiar, comforting pool. For he already felt that he needed solitude and peace. So he avoided the Dublin literati and artists — Austin Clarke, Liam O'Flaherty, Arland Ussher, and painter Harry Kernoff. This meant staying away from the city pubs and drinking either alone in his room (to "booze my heart quiet") or in village pubs where he was not known.[78] But it also meant cutting himself off from his friends, except for those who, like Pelorson and Leventhal, went to the trouble of going round to his rooms and hooking him out. It is this kind of quest for peace and tranquillity that is described in a remarkable passage of *Dream of Fair to Middling Women,* in which he spoke of the main character as having scooped out a cup or a tunnel away from the outer world:

He lay lapped in a beatitude of indolence that was smoother than oil and softer than a pumpkin, dead to the dark pangs of the sons of Adam, asking nothing of the insubordinate mind. He moved with the shades of the dead and the dead-born and the unborn and the never-to-be-born, in a Limbo purged of desire. . . . If that is what is meant by going back into one's heart, could anything be better, in this world or the next? The mind, dim and hushed like a sick-room, like a chapelle ardente, thronged with shades; the mind at last its own asylum, disinterested, indifferent, its miserable erethisms and discriminations and futile sallies suppressed; the mind suddenly reprieved, ceasing to be an annex of the restless body, the glare of understanding switched off.[79]

Such a passage is a precursor of the strange limbo world of Beckett's much later prose texts *Imagination Dead Imagine*, *The Lost Ones*, and *Ping*. The attempt to exist in such a distant inner terrain, however, gradually became more threatening to Beckett's mental well-being as the term wore on.

There were still moments of less intense, quiet, lonely pleasure. On the first Sunday in November, for instance, he walked for many miles from Rathfarnham to Enniskerry through the Pine Forest, ending up drinking flat stout in the Powerscourt Arms, where one could get a drink on a Sunday because it was a hotel. Unlike Rimbaud, who used to compose poems while he was out walking, Beckett wrote that on his walks "the mind has a most pleasant and melancholy limpness, is a carrefour of memories, memories of childhood mostly, moulin à larmes" ["mill of tears"].[80] But often the weather served up one of those dark, dank Dublin Sundays that he disliked so much, when there was "mist and rain and chimes and teetotal" and "nothing at all to be done and nobody at all to go and see."[81]

He managed little work apart from invigilating, marking examination scripts, and giving lectures. He translated a few unpublished pieces by French Surrealists like Breton and Crevel for Nancy Cunard's *Negro Anthology*, for which he was paid twenty-five pounds; he also produced some Tristan Tzara translations. He felt quite unable to function creatively in his present circumstances; he was, he wrote graphically, in "one of the knots in my life teak. I can't write anything at all, can't imagine even the shape of a sentence, nor take notes . . . nor read with understanding, goût or dégoût" ["taste or distaste"].[82]

The sole exception was one long, somber poem or "Enueg" (funeral lament) that he wrote in the late autumn. An apt reflection of his mood at the time, it is full of images of putrefaction, desolation, and exile. According to Beckett, it is based on an actual walk that he took from the Portobello Private Nursing Home westward along the Grand Canal out of the city, then back along the river Liffey.[83] Many local topographical features appear: the barges near Parnell Bridge; the Fox and Geese; the village of Chapelizod; the hurlers at Kilmainham.[84] Autobiographical elements also creep in: "ruined feet," which forced Beckett to have an operation on his hammer toe a year later; "a bush of gorse on fire in the mountain after dark," which recalled a scene he witnessed as a child with his father on one of their many walks together in the hills. There are also allusions, some half-hidden, to his reading: an ironic reference to "a little wearish old man, Democritus," the "laughing philosopher"; an evocation of Dante's *Inferno* in "the pit of the Liffey"; and a reminiscence of Arthur Rimbaud in the phrase "the arctic flowers that do not exist." Perhaps the lines that sum up the mood of the poem best of all are

> *The great mushy toadstool,*
> *green-black,*
> *oozing up after me,*
> *soaking up the tattered sky like an ink of pestilence,*
> *in my skull the wind going fetid*
> *the water . . .*[85]

6

ALTHOUGH BECKETT judged himself incapable of reading intelligently at this time, in reality he read widely, if indiscriminately. And however depressed he may have become, his judgment, although idiosyncratic, does not seem to have been in the least impaired. He read two novels by T. F. Powys — *Mark Only* and *Mr. Tasker's Gods* — "not knowing his work at all, and was very disappointed. Such a fabricated darkness and painfully organised unified tragic completeness. The Hardy sin caricatured. Everybody had been telling me what a great writer he was. And what a style!"[86] It is ironic that Beckett who, in his own later writing, was too often regarded as the personification of hopelessness and miserabilism, should have judged Powys so harshly for his "unified tragic completeness."

He had earlier read Tom MacGreevy's critical essay *Richard Aldington*, which appeared in late September. He enjoyed his friend's bold analogies and imaginative parallels, such as that linking Aldington and the French painter Jean Lurçat as "adepts of *natures vivantes*" in contrast to T. S. Eliot's *natures mortes*. He liked the book much less, however, than MacGreevy's earlier study of Eliot, admitting by way of either explanation or polite excuse that he was more in sympathy with the latter than with Aldington, whose poetry at least he found "lamentable stuff." In September, he became totally wrapped up in Homer's *Odyssey*, reading it in Victor Bérard's French translation and recovering, he wrote, "something of the old childish absorbtion [sic] with which I read *Treasure Island* and *Oliver Twist* and many others."[87] This was yet another experience that he shared with MacGreevy, for whom Bérard's *Odyssée* had "turned [his] days to gold."[88] But Beckett's reading at this time seems to have been lacking in purpose, just as his whole life was, in appearance at least, lacking in direction.

An excursion alone into Dublin's red-light district, called the Kips, was reflected later in his poetry. One night in early October, he walked into a

Dublin brothel kept by a famous madam, Becky Cooper. Several attempts had been made to rid the area of its formerly licensed brothels since the first big police raids of 1925. But a number of establishments continued to operate more covertly, and Beckett knew of their existence. A visit to a brothel was, of course, a more commonly accepted part of the healthy male's life at that time (although it would, of course, have been total anathema to Beckett's mother) than it has come to be considered in recent years. Beckett's two-year stay in Paris had set him in a city in which brothels were legal, even fashionable, places where it was not unusual to spend an evening drinking with one's friends.[89] Customers could either sample the wares by going upstairs with the women or simply stay and look as long as they liked — provided, of course, that they kept on ordering drinks. On this occasion at least (for there is every reason to believe that it was not his first such call) Beckett ordered a bottle of stout and simply looked around him.

What he saw there and his reaction to it became an important feature of the poem "Sanies II," which he wrote some months later in Paris. In the poem, a whole series of brothel and flagellation images, derived from his reading, is set alongside much more innocent images. Names like Gracieuse, Belle-Belle, and Percinet "all have [a] brothel feeling about them,"[90] as well as calling to mind Perrault's and the Countess d'Aulnoy's fairy tales, which, as a personal notebook shows, he was reading at the time.[91] A client who has clearly offended the madam of the house by breaking into contemptuous, sacrilegious laughter is threatened with various tortures. Beckett explained the nature of the offense when he told Lawrence Harvey that he had seen "a print on [the] wall of [a] Dublin brothel and was thrown out when [he] started laughing" at the ironic incongruity.[92] In a letter to MacGreevy, he confessed that, during his visit to Becky Cooper's, he had "sneered at the coloured reproduction of Dante Beatrice — Lungarno intersection,"[93] although he fails to mention that he had been thrown out on account of the sneer. In the poem he alludes to the same reproduction ("Dante and blissful Beatrice are there"), identifies the same offense ("lo Alighieri has got off au revoir to all that / I break down quite in a titter of despite"), and offers compensation for the affront:

> *oh Becky spare me I have done thee no wrong spare me damn thee*
> *spare me good Becky*
> *call off thine adders Becky I will compensate thee in full.*[94]

7

ONE OF BECKETT'S more regular and respectable ports of call at this time was the National Gallery of Ireland. Paintings that he had known for several years, like Salomon van Ruysdael's *The Halt*, had come to seem like old friends. But a new friend had just appeared on the scene. In 1931, at an auction at Christie's in London, the gallery bought Perugino's beautiful *Pietà*. This was promptly put on display, and Beckett immediately rushed round to Merrion Square to view it. "I've been several times to look at the new Perugino Pietà in the National Gallery here," he wrote. "It's buried behind a formidable barrage of shining glass, so that one is obliged to take cognisance of it progressively, square inch by square inch."[95]

He spent literally hours examining the painting and concluded that, although it was "all messed up by restorers," the dead Christ and the women in the picture were "lovely":

> A clean-shaven, potent Xist [his way of writing "Christ"] and a passion of tears for the waste. The most mystical constituent is the ointment pot that was probably added by Raffaela. Rottenly hung in rotten light behind this thick shop window, so that a total view of it is impossible, and full of grotesque amendments. But a lovely cheery Xist full of sperm, and the woman touching his thighs and mourning his secrets.[96]

"The woman" in the center of the picture, who bears the body of Christ on her knees and holds his right thigh, is of course the Madonna herself. The "grotesque amendments" are probably two coats of arms (of the Claude Gouffier and Jacqueline de la Tremouille families) added later on the arches of the portico.[97] Beckett is right that, although a Calvary scene with the cross and a ladder leaning against it has been added in the far distance between the porticos, the Christ in the Dublin picture is a human rather than a mystical representation, as compared with the same artist's other *Pietà*, which he had seen earlier in Florence. The Dublin Christ is not the bearded figure with a crown of thorns of Titian's *Ecce Homo* either, but a serene, vigorous, "spunky" young man; even the marks of the nails on his hands and feet are barely noticeable.

When Beckett came to write his story "Love and Lethe" for *More Pricks Than Kicks*, it was only natural that the Perugino *Pietà* should come to his mind, after a spell of such concentrated attention on the painting. He allows a comparison between Ruby Tough's appearance and "the Magdalene in the Perugino Pietà in the National Gallery of Dublin" to stand in lieu of a description of Ruby, adding the phrase "always bearing in mind that the hair of our heroine is black and not ginger."[98]

The *Pietà* was not the only new painting in the National Gallery to which Beckett paid particular attention in the course of his many visits. Two canvases by the Irish painter William Orpen had recently been bequeathed to the gallery by Lady Poe. Orpen had died only a few months before, and the local newspapers had been full of gushing obituaries and tributes to him. Beckett looked at these latest additions to the collection with a keen personal interest since he knew that his aunt Cissie had been a pupil of Orpen at the Dublin Metropolitan School of Art, and the painter had been a good friend and a boon drinking companion of her husband, Boss Sinclair.[99] But he damned the paintings to MacGreevy, saying: "I thought Orpen's Ptarmigan and Wash House nearly as bad as Keating."[100]

8

HIS LAST VISIT to the gallery, in mid-December, was by way of a fond farewell. For he had finally decided that he could no longer stand teaching at Trinity College, or his life in Dublin in general. He had been aware for some time that he was at a crisis point. His letters reveal him vacillating wildly between a vain attempt to persuade himself that he should and could settle down in his job at Trinity, and the growing conviction that he would have to get away and perhaps quit his post definitively. There was a great temptation to accept the status quo and settle for the "quiet life":

> I'm too tired and too poor in guts or spunk or whatever the stuff is to endow the old corpse with a destination and buy a ticket and pack up here. The 'pottamus waits for his angels. And really I can't seriously suppose that there's anything I want to rid myself of or acquire, no growth of freedom or property that can't be shed or assumed with as absurd a coefficient of plausibility here in the miasma as anywhere else.... A nice quiet life punctuated with involuntary exonerations (Albas). [He meant the poems that he had just written.] And isn't my navel worth 10 of anyone else's, even though I can't get a very good view of it.[101]

Yet he is clearly floundering, as he sets out the pale attraction of inertia and the lethargic pleasure of contemplating one's navel.

He knew that, in giving up his post at Trinity, he would cause practical problems for the college and disappoint his supporters, for instance Rudmose-Brown. But he also knew that he would desperately upset his parents. Even before taking up his appointment, he had realized that the "acceptance of this thing makes flight and escape more and more complicated, because if I chuck Dublin after a year, I am not merely chucking Dublin—definitely—but my family, and causing them pain."[102] The problem was that he cared very much what they felt even if he could not accept and live by their ideas and their values. Half a century later, he could still remember his father's pride as he accompanied him through the little gate into Trinity College grounds that could be opened by a key held only by members of staff. He spoke, too, of the remorse he still felt at the thought of having let his father down.[103] For Bill Beckett would have seen him as running away from his responsibilities and giving up a worthwhile career for nothing; and his mother, so alienated already by having recently read and disapproved of what he had written, would have seen him as a washout.[104] In the end it took a compelling mixture of desperation and willpower to make the decisive break. Even then, he lacked the courage to do it openly. He spoke to no one at Trinity about his impending departure and resignation.

When he wrote to MacGreevy on December 20, his ticket for the boat from Dublin to Ostend was already booked:

> am off, malgré tout et malgré tous [in spite of everything and everybody], immediately after Noel, via Ostend, somewhere into Germany, as far as Cologne anyway, next Saturday night [i.e., December 26] from North Wall, not to return I hope (and entre nous) for many months, though I have not resigned from Trinity. If I have to let them down, tant pis [so much the worse]. Some charming little cunt of a gold medallist will be nominated deputy for a term until they can get some really *responsible* person, and won[']t that be a happy surprise for the New Year. . . . It's madness really to go away now with the exchange u.s.w. [*und so weiter:* "and so on"] but it really is now or never. And as usual I'm not burning any boats! I'm hoping to be able to spit fire at them from a distance.[105]

His resolve finally to resign from Trinity was strengthened by an appalling episode that made him feel doubly anxious to get away. The incident added shame to the remorse he felt at letting down his parents. Just before Christmas, with his ticket for the night ferry to the Continent on Boxing Day already purchased, he drove Ethna MacCarthy home to Sandymount after farewell drinks in Dublin. It was probably a mixture of tiredness, depression, drink, emotional upset at saying good-bye to Ethna, and sheer bravado that made him drive the car much too fast as he approached the Ringsend basin of the Royal Canal. As he came to the dangerous, narrow, "terrible humped Victoria Bridge,"[106] he tried to brake but his speed was too great and he crashed into the middle intersection of the bridge, hitting the passenger side of the vehicle. Beckett himself suffered only a few minor cuts and bruises. But Ethna MacCarthy was badly hurt and had to be taken to the hospital. The incident was an intensely traumatic one for him. Over thirty years later, he confessed to Lawrence Harvey that he would "never forget the look in her father's eye afterwards" and that the episode remained a nightmare, which he still could not bear to talk about.[107] That look was to travel with him on the boat to Germany, a further addition to the burden of guilt that he was already carrying in his baggage.

7

Dream of Fair to Middling Women
1932–33

1

SAMUEL BECKETT went to Germany for Christmas 1931. He feared being there alone and, needing a good deal of friendly support after his sudden flight from Trinity College, decided to stay in Kassel with Cissie and Boss Sinclair rather than travel on to any other German town.[1] He knew that, however difficult his personal position was, he could still count on a warm welcome from the Sinclairs. For both Cissie and the Boss were extremely fond of their sensitive, intellectual, artistic young nephew. Since the Boss had himself left Ireland in difficult circumstances almost ten years before, Beckett probably felt that he would receive understanding and backing, which he would never have been given at home for his decision to leave the country and quit his teaching post.

Intensely preoccupied though he was with resigning from Trinity College —a decision already made but not yet executed—Beckett found the Sinclair family with serious problems of their own. Boss Sinclair had run into even graver financial trouble; the money that the family had brought over from Ireland had run out many years before and the English lessons that he was giving brought in little by way of income. His dealing in modern German paintings was having scant success, for he could find no buyers for the Boccioni, Feininger, and Campendonk paintings he owned. (Today, these canvases would be worth a fortune.) Anti-Semitism was growing rapidly in Germany, and the Boss could foresee a situation in which, partly because of debts and partly on account of racial prejudice and harassment, he and his family would be forced to leave the country.

But the greatest anxiety was reserved for Peggy's health. She had been obliged to leave the Hellerau-Laxenburg school near Vienna before completing her studies. Now she looked pale and run-down; she had lost weight; she grew increasingly short of breath; and she was subject to more and more frequent night sweats, as well as an erratic temperature during the day. A worrying dry cough accompanied these attacks. Doctors advised her to get plenty of fresh air and rest. The conjunction of these symptoms and this common medical advice inevitably raised the ever-present specter of pulmonary tuberculosis. But little was said of the dread that was haunting them. Beckett could do nothing but worry with the others about Peggy. Although she was now engaged to Heiner Starcke, he was still extremely fond of her. He felt helpless. He was much too badly off himself to help the Sinclairs out financially, and too preoccupied with his own feelings of guilt to offer them much support.

He was due back for the Hilary term at Trinity College early in January and needed to resign formally before he could even begin to contemplate an alternative life to that of a university teacher. So after he dispatched a telegram to the college resigning from his teaching appointment, he sat down and wrote two of the most difficult letters of his life: to his parents and to Professor Rudmose-Brown. The recipients were shocked and dismayed by his decision.[2]

Although it has been suggested that Beckett spent the first six months of 1932 in Kassel, the evidence indicates that he stayed there a month at most.[3] He needed time to pull himself together and to consider how he was going to earn his living, but he did not want to be an additional burden on his aunt and uncle at so difficult a time. So he left for Paris at the end of January and, apart from a short break with his aunt's family at Easter, stayed in France until July 12. He told Lawrence Harvey that he spent from February until early July living in a little room like a *chambre de bonne* at the top of the Trianon Palace Hôtel, run by a M. and Mme. Poisson, at 1 *bis* and 3 rue de Vaugirard, on the corner of the rue de Vaugirard and the rue Monsieur-le-Prince.[4] Charles Prentice wrote to him at that address on February 8 to arrange a joint meeting in Paris with him and MacGreevy for the following week.[5] And Richard Aldington sent his good wishes to "Sam," whenever he wrote to MacGreevy in Paris from February until June.[6]

It was for practical as well as sentimental reasons that Beckett chose Paris as the place to stay. MacGreevy was already there with a small but devoted circle of friends. Beckett also hoped that Titus, Jolas, Putnam, and Nancy Cunard would come up with more translating work.[7] James Joyce, who made a great fuss about the celebration of birthdays, was to be fifty on the second of February and Beckett badly wanted to be within easy reach of Joyce, so that the thaw that had set in during the previous summer in their recently very icy relationship could be allowed to continue.

At the Trianon Palace, Beckett concentrated almost exclusively on writing the extraordinary *Dream of Fair to Middling Women*.[8] He composed a large part of the book in Paris from February until the early summer. It was finished by the end of June.[9] In his unpublished memoirs, MacGreevy writes of this period of their lives:

> When, for a time at the Ecole Normale in Paris and later, for a short period at the hotel in the Quarter, Samuel Beckett and I had adjoining rooms and breakfasted together, Sam could go straight from his morning tea or coffee to his typewriter or his books, his biblical concor-

dance, his dictionaries, his Stendhal. I, on the contrary, had to go out and make sure that the world was where I had left it the evening before.[10]

2

DREAM OF FAIR TO MIDDLING WOMEN deals with the experiences, ideas, and inner life of a young man called Belacqua, who is named after the waiting figure in Dante's *Purgatorio*. The structure of the novel is complex and fragmented; its plot deliberately lacks linear form and unity ("The only unity in this story is, please God, an involuntary unity," comments the narrator);[11] and its surface reality is quite consciously distorted. It has been labeled picaresque and episodic, but neither term does justice to the book's deliberate lack of coherence, let alone its verbal extravagance and stylistic bravura.

Coherence, artifice, and unity were regarded by Beckett as belonging to the "chloroformed world" of Balzac's novels, where, he claimed, characters are turned into "clockwork cabbages"; the novelist can "rely on their staying put wherever needed or staying going at whatever speed in whatever direction he chooses."[12] Beckett renounced such easy control over both his plot and his characters, for a variety of reasons. He clearly saw that in everything that matters, life is simply not like that—living creatures are too complex, mysterious, and unknowable to be classified or controlled in such a crudely mechanistic way. He was also composing a work of self-conscious fiction in which there are different rules, which offer a much wider range of possibilities for both the author and the reader. It is as if he were playing a game with the reader, talking to him, teasing him, even taunting him. And he actively relished dismantling the props and supports of the conventional novel.

Beckett was a very clever young man, and was very aware of this fact. So there is a lot of showing off in the novel. As one reviewer wittily put it, when the book was eventually published in 1992,

> to cope with this book you will need some French and German [he could have added Italian, Spanish and Latin], a resident exegete of Dante, a good encyclopedia, OED, the patience of Job and your wits about you. What an addition to company they would be! It's uphill all the way, but then so was Calvary, and the view from the top redeems the pains taken.[13]

As well as using dictionaries and reference books, Beckett wove into his novel hundreds of quotations from other works of literature, philosophy, and theology. For if he is consciously trying to rid himself of Joyce's influence in this novel— even to the point of parodying Joyce's "Work in Progress" in one section—it remains very Joycean in its ambition and its accumulative technique. Almost the entire novel—for it is a highly uneven piece of writing—is animated by

Beckett's enormous intellectual vitality and highly individual, irrepressible sense of humor. It is a very funny, if daunting book.

The overall structure derives from Belacqua's experiences with three young women: the Smeraldina-Rima, the Syra-Cusa, and the Alba. In this, and almost only in this, the novel is very simple. It also contains a flashback to the time when Belacqua first met the Smeraldina in Ireland, and a love letter from the young woman in question. But the plot is too fragmented to resemble the sonata form in which, according to the narrator, he might well have written a shorter story about these three women. Instead, *Dream* shifts its terrain, its time scheme, and its focus very rapidly; the narrator plays a self-consciously playful, often self-deprecating role in the plot, bantering with the reader and himself in a way that is reminiscent of Sterne or Diderot in the eighteenth century, rather than assuming the position of apparently unobtrusive, yet in fact highly manipulative, nineteenth-century narrator.

Detailed characterization, background information, and factual descriptions are consciously avoided, again as belonging to the traditional novel against which Beckett is reacting. Yet the narrator is still very much concerned with an outer reality, of people as well as of place, and, as author, Beckett does not always take account of his own strictures. For many of the figures who appear in the novel are closely based on people whom he knew—in some cases much too closely for this not to have been a source of embarrassment to the older Beckett, who, after several initial attempts to get it published, became extremely reluctant to see it appear during his own and their lifetimes.

However, as the scholar Rubin Rabinovitz has pointed out,[14] Beckett does not provide explicit descriptions of these people. Instead he uses highly figurative language to evoke the sense of a character's appearance. The novel is not, strictly speaking, a roman à clef, but it comes very close at times to that genre. The imagination transforms real-life material, often quite radically, and efforts have been made to disguise some of the more directly autobiographical elements. Yet *Dream* remains closer to reality than any of Beckett's later writing, close enough for one to be able to identify most of the characters with some degree of certainty.

The three main female characters—"our capital divas," the narrator calls them[15]—correspond fairly closely to the three women who had figured in Beckett's life up to that time. The first mentioned, the Smeraldina-Rima ("Smerry," for short) has long been known to be based on Beckett's cousin and youthful love, Peggy Sinclair. Many of the incidents in the novel involving this character actually involved Peggy: their first meeting in Ireland; Beckett's visit to Laxenburg, where she was studying music and dance; his later visit to Kassel, when their relationship went irretrievably awry; and the flood of love letters that she sent him, one of which he included as the "Smeraldina's Billet Doux"—"a mixture of fact and fiction" was the way Beckett described it[16]—in *Dream* and which, to both the Sinclair and Beckett families' dismay, was published later in *More Pricks Than Kicks.*

Many of the external details used to portray the young woman in the novel were taken from Peggy: her pale complexion, with "the dim fanlight of the brow under the black hair growing low and thickly athwart the temples";[17] her green faded beret, which moves Belacqua as she waves it in a fond farewell; her talent for improvisation, both in music and in talk; and, as we have seen, "the loveliest little pale firm cameo of a bird face he ever clapped his blazing blue eyes on."[18] But in *Dream* the Smeraldina is also depicted in terms of painting: "she was the living spit he thought of Madonna Lucrezia del Fede. Ne suis-je point pâle? Suis-je belle? [Am I not pale? Am I beautiful] . . . We suppose we can say she looked like an ulula in pietra serena, a parrot in a Pietà. On occasions that is."[19] In this way, the narrator tries to convey the essentials of her impact on Belacqua through image and allusion. The emphasis is as much on the subjective associations that she evokes as on the young woman herself.

She is placed, however, in an authentic, Bohemian family setting of Irish exiles in Germany. "Smerry's" mother and father, "Mammy" and "The Mandarin" as they are called, echo Cissie and Boss Sinclair's qualities, talents, and attitudes. Mammy has little more than a supportive maternal role to play; she is a "multipara,"[20] the hardworking, loving mother of four daughters, like Cissie breathing concern and compassion. The Mandarin is more fully developed. But he is used to pursue further the distinctions made in the book between love and physical sex. A spokesman for the need to live fully and relish hedonistically the good things in life, he argues against what he calls Belacqua's "literary mathematics."[21] He does not accept the reality of the young man's "incoherent reality" and, to put it in the blunt, earthy terms that he uses, he can see no problem in "you and Beatrice happy in the Mystic Rose at say five o'clock and happy again in No. 69 [clearly denoting the brothel] at say one minute past."[22]

What seems to be a description of Peggy in repose is used to illustrate the clash between the image of chaste, idealized, spiritual love, extolled by the medieval troubadour (perhaps based on a fusion of Dante's Belacqua and Sordello with the German poet Walther von der Vogelweide)[23] and the lascivious, tempting young woman making her own demands while still imposing her own conditions and erupting with somewhat grotesque reality into his pure, still world:

> So she had been, sad and still, without limbs or paps in a great stillness of body, that summer evening in the green isle when first she heaved his soul from its hinges; as quiet as a tree, column of quiet. Pinus puella quondam fuit. Alas fuit! So he would always have her be, rapt, like the spirit of a troubadour, casting no shade, herself shade. Instead of which of course it was only a question of seconds before she would surge up at him, blithe and buxom and young and lusty, a lascivious petulant virgin, a generous mare neighing after a great horse, caterwauling after a great stallion and amorously lay open the double-jug dugs. She could not hold it. Nobody can hold it. Nobody can live here and hold it. Only the spirit of the troubadour, rapt in a niche of rock, huddled and withdrawn forever if no prayers go up for him, raccolta a se, like a lion.[24]

The authentic Madonna face is set on a "porpoise prism" of a body that is treated by Beckett as an occasion for some exuberantly alliterative wordplay: "Poppata, big breech, Botticelli thighs, knock-knees, ankles all fat nodules, wobbly, mammose, slobbery-blubbery, bubbub-bubbub, a real button-bursting Weib, ripe." [25] The affair with Peggy was, of course, over when Beckett composed this particular little essay in rumbustious grotesque. And she was already ill with tuberculosis. The real-life Peggy was, in any case, merely the starting-point for this extravagant exercise in language.

But who was the starting-point for the Syra-Cusa? It has been suggested that this was Nancy Cunard, with whom Beckett was friendly in 1930. [26] This is highly unlikely. Nothing in the text supports such an identification: no physical description matching even the poorest Identikit portrait; no allusions to her notorious ivory bracelets and heavy necklaces; nothing about her addiction to African masks and sculpture; and no reference whatsoever to her love of books and activities as a poet-publisher.

On the other hand, there are many clues that point to Lucia Joyce as Beckett's model for certain facets of this character. The young woman has the body and supple grace of the dancer that was Lucia:

> The Syra-Cusa: her body more perfect than dream creek, amaranth lagoon. She flowed along in a nervous swagger, swinging a thin arm amply. The sinewy fetlock sprang, Brancusi bird, from the shod foot, blue arch of veins and small bones, rose like a Lied to the firm wrist of the reins, the Bilitis breasts. Her neck was scraggy and her head was null. [27]

In his fictional portrait, the narrator introduces a striking reservation about the Syra-Cusa's eyes: "Her eyes were wanton, they rolled and stravagued, they were laskivious and lickerish, the brokers of her zeal, basilisk eyes. . . . Eyes—less good, to be frank, than we make out, our pen carried us away." [28] Lucia, of course, not only had such rolling eyes, but a squint in one of them that detracted from her otherwise pretty looks.

Like the Syra-Cusa, Lucia had a lovely body and something of a reputation for being provocative: "from throat to toe she was lethal, pyrogenous, Scylla and the Sphinx . . . the body like a coiled spring, and a springe, too, to catch woodcocks." And if the Syra-Cusa had "a lech on Belacqua, *she gave him to understand as much,*" it was no more intense than the "lech" Lucia had for Beckett. More precisely, in the novel, the young woman "was prone, when brought to dine out, to puke, but into her serviette, with decorum, because, supposedly, the craving of her viscera was not for food and drink." [29] In real life, according to Beckett, Lucia "even before her breakdown, would sometimes come to dinner, not eat too much, disappear, and vomit." [30]

Beckett also gave Lucia Joyce his copy of Dante as a present. [31] She then promptly left it behind in a café. In *Dream,* Belacqua presses upon the Syra-Cusa "as a gift and a mark of esteem (mark of esteem!) a beautiful book, one that he loved." The Syra-Cusa thinks so little of this book that, to Belacqua's disgust, she too leaves it behind in a café and loses it. That this book is an edition of the *Divina commedia* is shown by the copy that Belacqua is left with: "Now he has only the Florentia edition in the ignoble Salani collection, horrid, beslubbered with grotesque notes, looking like a bank-book in white cardboard and a pale gold title, very distasteful."[32] This is a perfect description of Beckett's own student edition, even to the "grotesque notes" that he made when he was studying it with Bianca Esposito.[33]

Finally, Beckett slips in his own learned nod and a wink to the literary cognoscenti as to the identity of the Syra-Cusa: in the *Divina commedia*, Lucia is one of the "tre donne benedette" (three blessed women), and, one of his student notebooks records, she comes from Syracuse.[34] In spite of all these affinities, the Syra-Cusa is, not surprisingly, a much more fictional creation than either the Smeraldina-Rima or the Alba. Not wishing to upset Joyce any more than he had already done by rejecting Lucia, Beckett would presumably have tried to garb the character based on her in a modest, fairly opaque cloak of anonymity.

"From the extreme Smeraldina and the mean Syra," the narrator of *Dream of Fair to Middling Women* relates, "you could work out the Alba for yourselves, you could control our treatment of the little Alba."[35] Yet so complex is "the little Alba" as a personality that, without a striking model, she would have been far more difficult for Beckett to invent than any of the other characters in the novel. She is an exceptional woman, and a very modern one: she drinks brandy regularly (three-star Hennessy, and doubles at that), smokes heavily, is well-educated, speaks fluent French and Spanish ("hijo de la puta blanca!"[36] as she calls for a drink) and can recognize most of Belacqua's erudite or literary allusions and return them in kind. She has fiercely independent views, a scathing wit, and a talent for not pulling any punches with her criticisms. "You brood like a sick hen," she tells Belacqua, and is pleased "that she had pricked him into elucidating, i.e. defending, a position."[37]

All of these features of the Alba were borrowed from Ethna MacCarthy, with whom Beckett had been so besotted. He even names Ethna in cryptic form in the book: one day when Belacqua found her ill at home, he "said her name, once, twice, incantation, abracadabra, abracadabra, and saying it felt the tip of his tongue between his incisors. Dactyl-trochee dactyl-trochee, he said it wetly, biting at one and four on the viscid tip."[38] You do not have to put the tip of your tongue between the teeth to pronounce "Abracadabra" but you do to intone "Ethna MacCarthy" and — for Beckett had, of course, learned his versification at the feet of Trinity College's two specialists, Professors Trench and Rudmose-Brown — you bite at the first and the fourth rhythmic beats.

When he writes about the Alba in *Dream of Fair to Middling Women*, Beckett is harking back only a matter of months to the time when he agreed to go to a party so that he could spend the evening with Ethna or to the day when he took her down to the cove known as Jack's Hole and they lay on the beach together. Consequently there is far less distance and far more minute analysis of her and of his relationship with her than there is of the affairs with Peggy or (such as it was) with Lucia Joyce. The Alba has the same self-knowledge that Ethna appears to have had; she is aware of her power over men, yet knows only too well how complicated any affair with a cerebral male like Belacqua (or Beckett) would quickly become. "I have to make it a mess and a knot and a tangle," she admits.[39] A feeling of genuine involvement with a woman who still fascinates Beckett comes through. Yet he was spelling out the truth of their situation when he wrote: "He has not lain with her. Nor she with him."[40]

Some of the more minor characters are readily identified. The massive figure of the Polar Bear is so clearly recognizable as to be mildly libelous, had the book been published in the 1930s. No one on the staff of Trinity College would have been in the slightest doubt that it was Professor Rudmose-Brown who had unwittingly posed for this particular portrait. His physical description, fervent anticlerical views, swearing, meanness, and lechery all make him eminently identifiable.

Dream's young Frenchman, Lucien, is modeled on Jean Beaufret, Beckett's philosophy student friend at the Ecole Normale. In the novel, this character discusses Leibniz, Galileo, and Descartes with Belacqua, just as Beaufret did with Beckett, and uses a striking phrase that Beaufret wrote in a letter to Beckett from Berlin: "le diamant du pessimisme" ("the diamond of pessimism").[41] Beaufret was fleshy for a young man and had a pink, girlish complexion; he talked brilliantly, intently, and rapidly. He was homosexual and, finding Beckett good-looking as well as capable of sustaining a lively discussion on philosophical matters, devoted himself to cultivating the Irishman's friendship, often meeting him unannounced at the station on his return to Paris from Dublin, Vienna, or Kassel, when Beckett had been to visit his ladylove, Peggy Sinclair. Beckett appreciated Beaufret's devotion, even though he found that his emotionalism wore a trifle thin.

Like Beaufret, Lucien gesticulates extravagantly.[42] The description of his gestures begins almost dispassionately, with "the hands lifted, plucking and poking at the air in a futility of slow heavy stabs, then lowered on to a support, placed tentatively on his knees or a table and held there, stiff and self-conscious."[43] But, later on, these gestures are transformed into the repellent convulsions of some tentacular marine creature: "the gestures, the horrid gestures, of the little fat hands and the splendid words and the seaweed smile, all coiling and uncoiling and unfolding and flowering into nothingness, his whole person a stew of disruption and flux."[44] Lucien's smile "[was] terrible, as though seen through water. Belacqua wanted to sponge it away. And he would not abandon the gesture that had broken down and now could never be made to mean anything. It was horrible, like artificial respiration on a foetus still-born."[45] But, as other parts of *Dream* show, this portrayal is not representative of Beckett's feelings for Beaufret. It has some basis in the real-life character, but no more. Beaufret becomes merely the occasion for an expression of a sense of alienation from the body. Beckett prefigures here the existential concern with the viscosity of being that was found in Jean-Paul Sartre's *La Nausée*, published four years later. And, even more like Sartre, "Another day, catching sight of his hand in a glass, he began to whinge. That was more in Belacqua's own line and did not discompose him in the same way. Lucien did not know how to deal with his hands."[46]

With Lucien's friend Liebert and the poet Jean du Chas we are dealing with composite figures. Like many a young writer, Beckett borrows features from a number of his friends and contemporaries and puts different combinations of them together to form two distinct characters. Belacqua is dragged by Liebert, for instance, to a performance of Wagner at the National Academy of Music, only for them to be turned away because Liebert is wearing plus-fours: "Belacqua laffed and laffed."[47] Now, although Georges Pelorson never actually forced Beckett "to see . . . the Valkyrie à demi tarif,"[48] he was a fervent admirer of Wagner. Yet it was Beckett's other French friend at the time, Alfred Péron, not Pelorson, who had come back from Ireland sporting a pair of plus-fours, which were all the rage in Dublin but objects of ridicule in France.

In another passage about music, Beckett wrote:

> He [Liebert] appeared one night with a portable gramaphone [sic] and put on the . . . Kleine Nachtmusik and then Tristan and *insisted on turning out the light.* That was the end of that. . . . He remembered how Liebert used to visit Musset in the Père Lachaise and sitting by the tomb make notes for a meditation and then come home in the bus and pull out photographs of the current pucelle who was so wonderful (elle est adorable, oh elle est formidable, oh elle est tout à fait sidérante) and who drove him so crazy and had such a powerful effect on him and gave him such a lift. He detailed the powerful effect, he set forth the lift, with piscatorial pantomime.[49]

Witnesses identified the sources of these details. Georges Pelorson recognized himself in the circumstances of the gramophone playing—his taste for Wagner emerging once again—and in his tendency to praise a woman's beauty extravagantly. He denied, however, that he had a passion for Musset or ever visited the poet's grave. But he could remember telling Beckett about a fellow student at his *lycée* called Henri Evrard who did precisely what Liebert is said to do.[50] Beckett probably did not have to rely on hearsay, however, since Evrard became an English student at the Ecole Normale in 1929 and was taught by Beckett, while Pelorson was away in Dublin.[51] In this way, Beckett conflated different facets of three of his real-life friends: Pelorson, Péron, and Evrard.

There is more freedom and poetic license in the treatment of the imaginary poet, Jean du Chas from Beckett's earlier spoof lecture, who reappears in the novel. Yet even for so apparently fictitious a creation, Beckett borrowed several aspects of du Chas's personality and behavior from different friends. Chas's enthusiasm for the girl whom he has met and fallen in love with, "Ginette Mac Something" (an unusual amalgam of French and Scottish), sounds like that of Pelorson for his future wife, whose name was Marcelle Grahame. But the elegant, precious side of Jean du Chas derives from Beckett's playful mockery of his friend Alfred Péron. The reflections of Belacqua and du Chas on French poetry, with their quotations from Racine's *Phèdre* and *Bérénice*,[52] as they walk along the shore, owe everything to his talks with Péron.

There remain the somewhat cruel portraits of the Fricas, mother and daughter.[53] Are these based on real people too? Beckett's own correspondence reveals that they were. In a letter to Tom MacGreevy, Beckett writes that his friend Dr. Geoffrey Thompson is staying with people he referred to as the Fricas in 1934.[54] John Manning confirmed that Thompson lodged with his mother, Susan, and his sister, Mary, that summer. The Mannings, mother and daughter, provide the starting point for another striking exercise in grotesque caricature. Certain characteristics, the shape of a woman's face, for instance, or an open-minded interest in sexual matters, form the raw materials for passages in which the original is left far behind in a self-indulgent but riotously comic accumulation of horsey images, one giving birth to another.

Dream of Fair to Middling Women also has a very strong sense of place. It roams widely from Dublin to Vienna, to Paris, to Kassel, to the north of Italy, before finally returning to Dublin, which so often makes Belacqua (and a jaundiced Beckett) feel morose:

> For his native city had got him again, her miasmata already had all but laid him low, the yellow marsh fever that she keeps up her sleeve for her more distinguished sons had clapped its clammy honeymoon hands upon him, his moral temperature had gone sky-rocketing aloft, soon he would shudder and kindle in hourly ague.[55]

The "Dunkelbrau" school was modeled on the Hellerau-Laxenburg school near Vienna, and the French section of the book takes place in the Latin Quarter of Paris, where Beckett lived and worked. Anyone who knows Kassel would recognize too — in spite of the destruction caused by heavy bombing during the Second World War — where Belacqua and Smerry are when they drive in a taxi within sight of the Hercules monument on the Wilhelmshöhe, with the water cascade and the castle beneath. Beckett even recreates his everyday life at the Sinclairs'. In explaining, for instance, why Belacqua took Smerry out so rarely, he writes (wittily parodying German sentence structure):

> Indeed what with his slugging-a-bed in the morning and soaks with the Mandarin in the evening and in the afternoon his absorption in a Vasari he had found in his host's library and the latest pictures hanging on his host's wall and the ineffectual darts he was liable to make at the piano at any hour of the day or night and his objection to going out to be frozen to death when there was nothing to prevent him from hatching a great thought over the stove, he was only able, in the week that elapsed between his arrival and Silvester, three times to promenade her, and two of these times Mammy, whose Spreegeist infuriated the Madonna beyond measure, came with.[56]

Beckett is recalling here the Landgrafenstrasse flat with its paintings, its piano, and, apparently, its stove. For Morris Sinclair pointed out that

> in the living room, which was also used by the "Boss" to give his English lessons, there was a coal-burning stove with a window (made of layers of mica I think) through which a glow could be faintly perceived. Sam would have preferred an open fireplace but used to sit in front of the stove holding up his hands to the glow, then dropping them at the wrist, only to raise them up again after a while. My father remarked affectionately on this rhythm and saw some significance in it. I now think that it was dictated by the amount of heat absorbed by the front and then by the back of his hands.[57]

The Irish sections of the novel also are full of references to specific locations in and around Dublin: the greens, the bridges, and the buildings of the city; the trams running from the center to nearby villages; Dún Laoghaire's Carlyle Pier; the mountains of Big Sugarloaf, Djouce, and the Three Rock; and the Silver Strand and Jack's Hole.[58] Unsurprisingly, Beckett transforms places much less than he does people. Places, for one thing, take less offense than people.

However uneven *Dream of Fair to Middling Women* is as a piece of writing, it is a remarkable tour de force. It displays an astonishing erudition and a precocious command of language and languages. But it is also unusually explicit about Beckett's ideas on art, anticipating some of his most cherished themes and prefiguring in some respects his later development as a writer.

3

THE FRIENDSHIP between Beckett and James Joyce resumed in the first few weeks of 1932.[59] Although Beckett went round less often now to the Joyce apartment so as not to upset Lucia,[60] he met her father again for their regular Sunday morning walks along the Allée des Cygnes. He also used to dine or drink with Joyce, sometimes in the company of Tom MacGreevy, in some of Joyce's favorite cafés and restaurants: Les Trianons, the Café Francis, or Chez Fouquet.

At this period Beckett's life and that of Joyce converged at several different points. There was their mutual concern for Lucia, who still appears to have been strongly disturbed by Beckett's renewed presence in Paris. It was widely assumed that this was the reason for her turbulent outburst on Joyce's birthday, when she hurled a chair across the room at her mother. She blamed Nora for coming between her and Beckett, although those who knew the family situation well believed it more likely that the cause of her violence was jealous fury at the marriage and forthcoming parenthood of her brother, Giorgio.

Early in March, in an attempt at a more or less arranged marriage, Alex Ponisovsky, Paul Léon's brother-in-law, proposed to Lucia (more, it seems, to please Léon than because he loved Lucia). She accepted his proposal. But a few days later, following a formal engagement party at the Restaurant Drouand, Lucia "went to the Léons' flat and lay down on the sofa. To their horror she remained there, inert, catatonic."[61] This marked the beginning, for Lucia, of a series of endless, fruitless consultations with doctors, stays in clinics, injections, and operations and, for Joyce, of the obsessive concern with his daughter's health and mental state that preoccupied him for the rest of his life.

What Beckett heard about Lucia's illness differed radically from father to son; from Joyce, he learned of plans for Lucia's treatment and cure and of hopes for involving her in work on more of her designs of lettrines for a decorative alphabet; from Giorgio, he received a somber, realistic, blow-by-blow account of her crises and bouts of irrationality and violence. In the final year of his life, Beckett commented, with reluctant admiration for Joyce's determined hopefulness, that he was the only one who, despite all contrary indications and advice, retained his optimistic belief that she would get well again.[62]

This tragic twist in the Joyce family fate could easily have alienated Beckett from Joyce, who might well have blamed him for some part in his beloved daughter's breakdown. But this does not appear to have been the case. Instead, as Richard Ellmann explained, Joyce identified very closely with Lucia and held himself, and perhaps the irregular family life that she had led on account of him, responsible for her mental breakdown. He said: "Whatever spark of gift I possess has been transmitted to Lucia and has kindled a fire in her brain."[63] But he may also have come to recognize that Beckett had been right in his protestation that the "affair" had been mainly in Lucia's own mind and that he had done almost nothing (except come to visit Joyce) to encourage it.

Beckett was closely involved in both the sad and the joyful moments in Joyce's life. The writer's father, John Joyce, died on December 29, 1931. Joyce was grief-stricken. He wrote to Harriet Shaw Weaver that "it is not his death that crushed me so much but self-accusation." Weeks had passed, he said, "in prostration of mind."[64] For he felt bitter regret that he had never returned to Ireland to see his father before he died. This sadness and remorse used to creep into his conversations with Beckett.[65]

Joyce's deep sadness was broken by the birth of his grandson, Stephen Joyce, on February 15. In Joyce's mind, the proximity in time of the birth to his father's death brought the two events into a close alliance, new life counterbalancing death. And it was on the day that Stephen was born that he wrote one of his most beautiful and moving poems, "Ecce Puer." This poem celebrated his grandson's birth but also acknowledged the remorse that he felt at having "forsaken" his father. Beckett took a keen interest in the poem when Joyce either showed it or recited it to him. The last two lines—"O Father forsaken / Forgive your son!"—epitomized for Beckett, too, his own feeling of remorse at having "forsaken" his family and, in his mind, let his father down so badly by resigning from his post at Trinity College. He knew the poem by heart in a version of his own and, revealingly, in his eighty-third year, when speaking of the remorse that he still felt more than fifty years after the resignation, he began to recite part of it aloud, unprompted, just as he remembered it:

> *New life is breathed*
> *Upon the glass,*
> *That which was not*
> *Has come to pass.*
>
> *A child is born,*
> *An old man gone.*
> *Father forsaken,*
> *Forgive thy son.*[66]

Beckett was also concerned with MacGreevy in Joyce's struggles against censorship. In the opening months of 1932, Joyce was trying to get an ordinary, unexpurgated edition of *Ulysses* published in the United States and Great Britain. The publishers were afraid of being prosecuted for publishing an obscene item. But, when Random House eventually agreed to publish the book in the United States unabridged and unaltered and to face and finance a court challenge to the ban, Joyce encouraged his friends to find out whether a publisher in Britain would similarly risk prosecution by publishing the book there. London publishers, eager to retain their personal freedom, had been terrified by the recent successful prosecution of a young man named Count Geoffrey de Montalk.[67]

Since T. S. Eliot and Geoffrey Faber, who had published Joyce in England, concluded that they could not risk prosecution, Joyce set about trying to find another publisher. Through his friends, he began to take soundings. MacGreevy wrote to Harold Raymond at Chatto and Windus to ask what his advice would be as to the possibility of publishing *Ulysses* safely in England, even in a limited, high-priced edition. Raymond expressed the view that the judicial mind in Britain regarded *Ulysses* as "the supreme example of high-brow pornography" and that he had heard that an undergraduate had been prosecuted for having a copy of it in his luggage at Dover customs. He added that it was "iniquitous that a book like *Ulysses* should not be available in this country in some shape or form, but it will be a courageous man who undertakes it."[68] Various compromises were suggested to Joyce. But he would accept nothing short of unexpurgated publication.

Beckett's interest in Joyce's publishing problems stemmed not only out of concern for his friend but also from firm principles that they shared. He could foresee similar difficulties arising with his own novel, as a letter from Richard Aldington suggests:

> He [Beckett] ought to do something quite remarkable [with *Dream of Fair to Middling Women*]. Pino [i.e. Giuseppe Orioli] can't do it if its [sic] illegal, it's too dangerous after the hullabaloo about Lady C [D. H. Lawrence's *Lady Chatterley's Lover*] and Gian Gastone.... Sam had better publish in Paris, take out European copyright, and not attempt to circulate publicly in U.S. or British Empire.[69]

Joyce's refusal to bow to censorship affected Beckett deeply. The older writer's integrity, determination, and defiance affected, or at the very least reinforced, his own attitudes.

From his twenties on, Beckett was to be a resolute opponent of all kinds of censorship and an active supporter of freedom of expression for writers in all countries. He consistently opposed all kinds of censorship of his own writing. He would have agreed wholeheartedly with Joyce's remarks to Sisley Huddleston on the possibility of an expurgated text of *Ulysses* being printed:

> To consent would be an admission that the expurgated parts are not indispensable. The whole point about them is that they cannot be omitted. Either they are put in gratuitously without reference to my general purpose; or they are an integral part of my book. If they are mere interpolations, my book is inartistic; and if they are strictly in their place, they cannot be left out.[70]

Whenever any proposal was made to Beckett to publish his work provided that cuts were made for reasons of alleged obscenity or indelicacy, he always refused to allow publication, and for the same reasons as Joyce. And if, unknown to him, any cuts were made, he was invariably furious.

While Beckett was being drawn once again into Joyce's personal orbit, he was also becoming increasingly conscious of the need to distance himself from him in his writing as an essential step toward finding his own voice. The previous August, sending his story "Sedendo et Quiescendo" to Charles Prentice at Chatto and Windus, he had written that "of course it stinks of Joyce in spite of most earnest endeavours to endow it with my own odours."[71] In June 1932, he wrote to Samuel Putnam: "I vow I will get over J.J. ere I die. Yessir."[72] He must, then, have been delighted when, later on, sections of *Dream of Fair to Middling Women* elicited this eulogy from Charles Prentice. "You're at your best there, right away from Joyce, and on your own, and the beauty and precision of the language moved me from the feet up."[73]

4

PAUL DOUMER, the French president, was assassinated on May 7, 1932, by a White Russian fanatic, Paul Gorguloff. As a result, the authorities decided to check the papers of all foreigners living in Paris. Since Beckett did not possess a valid *carte de séjour*, he was forced to leave the Hôtel Trianon and, as he could not legitimately register elsewhere, he spent a few nights sleeping on Jean Lurçat's studio floor. But he had to leave the country. Having little money, he called round to see Edward Titus and persuaded him to buy his English translation of Arthur Rimbaud's poem "Le Bateau ivre." Beckett asked him for a thousand francs for the translation. In the end he received seven hundred or eight hundred francs for the poem, which gave him just enough to finance a short stay in England.[74]

He took the July 12–13 overnight boat-train to London and rented a room from a Mrs. Southon, in a lodging at 4 Ampton Street, off the Gray's Inn Road.[75] He paid seventeen shillings and sixpence a week and did his own cooking on a gas stove with saucepans lent to him by Mrs. Southon. At the end of the road was "an enormous pub" where he whiled away his time during the hot summer months.[76] In mid-August, the temperature touched a sweltering ninety-two degrees in the shade.

His main reason for choosing London after Paris was to see if there was any prospect of carving out a niche for himself in literary journalism and reviewing. As a fallback position, he thought of taking a temporary teaching appointment.[77] He wanted to see Charles Prentice to discuss the possibility of writing future literary essays for Chatto and Windus,[78] to try to get *Dream of Fair to Middling Women* published,[79] and to interest him in a collection of his poems.[80]

He received the distinct and, it soon turned out, correct impression that the publisher had grave doubts as to *Dream*'s viability as a publishing venture. In turning the book down, Prentice wrote:

> It isn't a question of a few hard words here and there; we don't think that we would be of much use to you in putting the book across. It is rather an agony to have to confess it, for with parts of the book I and the other reader connected up at once, and we think them most extraordinarily good, but we fail over others, and our failure somehow colours our feelings regarding the whole.[81]

Later on, in a positive flurry of activity, Beckett brought his novel and poems to the Hogarth Press ("the Hogarth Private Lunatic Asylum", he called it),[82] rang the critic Desmond MacCarthy for help,[83] and made an appointment with an educational employment agency, Truman and Knightley. But nothing came of any of these approaches, and he soon became deeply discouraged and depressed.[84]

For most of his time in London Beckett felt incapable of writing creatively. So he read instead, widely and eclectically, first in the British Museum, then, when he tired of the Reading Room, in his lodgings. The museum lay only a short walk from Beckett's room and we know that, in late July, he read there Plato, the Gnostics, Aretino, and Aristotle on the Greek philosopher Thales.[85] He bought Darwin's *Origin of Species* for sixpence — judging that he had "never read such badly written cat lap" — read Thackeray's *Vanity Fair*, and dismissed Aldous Huxley's best-selling novel *Point Counter Point* (which he called picturesquely "Cunt Pointer cunt") as "a very pains-talking work," commenting: "The only thing I won't have forgotten by this day week is Spandrell flogging the foxgloves." He found Melville's *Moby Dick* much more exciting fare: "That's more like the real stuff. White whales and natural piety."[86]

It was his first lengthy stay in London and, when he was not reading, he walked in the parks (Kenwood, part of Hampstead Heath, Hyde Park, and Kensington Gardens), and visited churches and monuments. He climbed the spiral staircase of the monument built by Sir Christopher Wren to commemorate the Great Fire of London,[87] and gazed west to St. Paul's and beyond, remembering Alexander Pope's lines about the tall obelisk on which he stood:

> *Where London's column, pointing at the skies,*
> *Like a tall bully, lifts the head and lies.*[88]

He wandered alone into St. Paul's Cathedral, but found it hideous. So he promptly left and walked around the outside of the Tower of London and sat on the wharf, watching the little steamers dip their funnels as they went under Tower Bridge and the two sections of the bridge being opened to allow a bigger boat to pass through.

Another day, feeling miserable and unable to work, he went to the zoo in Regent's Park. Inside, he walked disconsolately around past cage after cage, casting a jaundiced eye on the monkeys on the monkey hill, the elephants, and the exotic birds from Africa, Asia, and South America: a colorful weaverbird, a bored condor, and a morose harpy eagle. The purple bottom of the baboon reminded him that his nanny had regularly used the letters "b.t.m." as a euphemism for "bottom." But the memory failed to cheer him up at all.[89] Watching a snake slowly devour a large white rat, he was haunted by the inherent cruelty of nature itself and of man's unnecessary claustration of animals. He hated zoos.

These varied experiences, which happened over a period of several days, were all compressed into one new poem, "Serena I," which he wrote soon after returning to Dublin.[90] Above all, this poem captures his feelings of loneliness and misery and has been described as "a series of physical flights from one spectacle of suffering after another."[91]

Apart from a very short visit from MacGreevy soon after his arrival in London, he was alone. He wrote to his friend: "I haven't opened my mouth except in bars and groceries since you left this day week; to haughty bar-persons and black-souled grocers . . . That's all I do now — go out about 2 and find some place to sit till the pubs open and get back here about 7 and cook liver and read the Evening News."[92]

One day, in St. James's Park, he was moved almost to tears by the sight of "a little boy playing at 'empty buses' with a nurse who had exactly the same quality of ruined granite expression as mine had before she married her gardener."[93] He quickly mocked his own nostalgia, but viewed his sentimental overreaction as a worrying symptom. "I'm depressed," he wrote, "the way a slug-ridden cabbage might be expected to be."[94]

By the third week in August, he had run out of both cash and willpower. "This month of creeping and crawling and sollicitation has yielded nothing but glib Cockney regrets," he wrote.[95] Neither *The Spectator* nor *The New Statesman* could offer him books for review, although, as he said, they must have had some. And any teaching posts that the agency offered him did not tempt him in the slightest.[96] The little self-confidence that he had briefly assumed had been completely destroyed as he received *Dream* and the poems back from the Hogarth Press. Prentice also returned his poems from Chatto and Windus (thought of by Beckett now as "Shatton and Windup") with a note saying that they were "a new and strange experience" and "if only he could escort me on longer flights. So sorry, very very sorry."[97] Edward Garnett read the novel for Jonathan Cape, while he was on holiday in Land's End, reporting privately:

> I wouldn't touch this with a barge-pole. Beckett probably is a clever fellow, but here he has elaborated a slavish and rather incoherent imitation of Joyce, most eccentric in language and full of disgustingly affected passages — also *indecent:* this school is damned — and you wouldn't sell the book even on its title. Chatto was right to turn it down.[98]

To upset him even more, Beckett heard from Rudmose-Brown that Ethna MacCarthy had taken Con Leventhal under her wing, where "he snuggles up for dear death."[99] His morale reached rock bottom when a last five-pound note sent to him by his father was stolen from his room, probably by a temporary lodger at Mrs. Southon's. Reluctantly he was forced to write to ask his parents to send him his fare to Dublin.[100] "I crawled home," said Beckett thirty years later, "with my tail between my legs."[101]

5

BACK IN THE BOSOM of his family by the end of August, he was first welcomed, then cosseted. "This is all right," he wrote, "as long as I can keep the menfoutisme ["couldn't-care-less-ism"] up to the good-humoured mark. . . . Father real. Mother comico-real. My need for anaesthetic of caress comico-real."[102] As he had no income of his own, he was dependent on his father for money. He tried to feel that he was earning some by helping in the garden. But, not for the first time, he felt out of place and a burden on his parents. Whatever he did was primarily a strategy for coping with the isolation that he inevitably felt at Cooldrinagh: He sawed wood, walked the dogs down the hill, and played the piano after breakfast — shifting "Mozart in his grave," as he described it.[103] He particularly enjoyed playing the A Minor Piano Sonata and looked forward every week to a piano lesson with "a beautiful old lady" who helped him with his Mozart, sending him home "full of silver."[104] He bathed at the Forty-Foot and accompanied his father on long walks or to the Turkish baths in Dublin.

But he rarely went into town because of his feelings of guilt at having resigned from Trinity and his fear of meeting former colleagues.[105] He was prone to exaggerate his social isolation. For, in spite of Beckett's recent resignation, Rudmose-Brown continued to meet him and tried to get him translations or other "grinds" (private lessons), as Beckett called them. Ruddy's kindness made him regret basing the character of the Polar Bear so closely on his former professor. He also met the artist Seán O'Sullivan and visited the National Gallery.[106] He was invited to Cappagh by Percy (later Arland) Ussher; there he met R. N. D. Wilson, who read some of his poems; the three of them talked of literature.[107] On such occasions, he was ill at ease, for he found the small talk disconcertingly parochial (Austin Clarke and Monk Gibbon seeking definitions of obscenity; George Russell [A.E.] and W. B. Yeats playing croquet together at Rathfarnham; and so on). He spent one evening with Joe Maunsell Hone and his wife, Vera, in Killiney,[108] when they talked about Swift and the book that Hone was writing on him in collaboration with Mario Rossi.[109]

Far more important to Beckett were his meetings with the painter and writer Jack B. Yeats. Yeats was a close friend of Tom MacGreevy and, as with Joyce, it was Tom who told the painter about him. He first met with Yeats in November 1930. He did not always go alone. "Last Sunday I went with Pelorson to see Jack Yeats. He was alone and we had two entirely delightful hours looking at a lot of pictures we had not seen and talking. He wanted a definition of cruelty, declaring that you could work back from cruelty to original sin. No doubt."[110]

Throughout the 1930s, Yeats remained one of the people in Dublin whom Beckett tried to see regularly. Only a few weeks before his death, Beckett recounted his memories of these meetings:

> I used to go to his "at homes" in Fitzwilliam Square. You used to go up there, and he was very hospitable. His wife never appeared. He'd greet you in his studio. . . . And he would go behind a sort of screen and bring out a painting and put it on the easel for me or anyone to look at. Then he would produce some sherry I think it was. I remember the gesture he used when he served the sherry. He would squeeze a lemon with a gesture of his hand. And we used to go for walks. Through the Park. We didn't talk very much.[111]

Yeats's paintings exercised a powerful impact on Beckett's imagination and inspired him to think about the relations between the artist and the world.

> His paintings were wonderful. He used to say that he was completely impervious to influence. I think he thought he was the only painter. He said all the painting must have some "ginger of life" in it. . . . I would make an appointment to go for a drive or for a walk. We'd drive out to a park and leave the car then we'd walk. To Leixlip or somewhere. Then have a meal together and then walk back. Then I'd drive him back along the quays.[112]

For it was as much Yeats's presence and his quiet wit ("I said to Jack Yeats: 'This inhuman landscape evokes — provokes — the inhuman in oneself.' He said: 'Invokes, I think' ")[113], his self-sufficiency, and his determination to follow his own path as a painter that impressed Beckett.

But such inspiring meetings could not offset the problems Beckett was experiencing in placing his own work. He sent his early poems to the London publisher Wishart, and fretted that another publisher, Grayson, had not yet returned the typescript of *Dream of Fair to Middling Women*. A copy of his story "Dante and the Lobster" was with Edward Titus in Paris, but he heard nothing about it for a long time. Irritated, he wrote: "I'm tired [of] being held up by discourteous bastards who won't let me know where I am."[114] Ellis Roberts, the editor of *The New Statesman*, had expressed some interest in an essay that Beckett proposed on André Gide, on whom he had lectured at Trinity College. As a possible subtitle, he suggested *"paralysed in ubiquity."*[115] But he was unable to concentrate on such an academic essay in Foxrock and composed only a few lines.[116]

Instead he worked hard at his creative writing. One main route that he followed was to read voraciously, seeing what he could learn from other writers and sampling a wide range of prose styles. One of the most significant items on his reading list was Henry Fielding's *Joseph Andrews*, which he described as Diderot's *Jacques le fataliste* and Goldsmith's *The Vicar of Wakefield* wrapped into one.[117] He probably learned a lot from Fielding's novels (for he went on to read *Tom Jones*[118]) while he was writing the stories of *More Pricks Than Kicks*. Fielding's influence can still be detected in *Murphy* and continued even into the postwar novel trilogy. It can be seen in what Beckett describes as "the giving away of the show pari passu with the show,"[119] in a balance and an elaborateness of phrase, and (continuing here the influence of Diderot and Sterne) in the playful or ironic comments of a self-conscious narrator who makes regular intrusions into the text of his narrative. In addition to reading Fielding, Swift,[120] and Hardy (*Tess of the d'Urbervilles*, without enthusiasm), Beckett also reread Proust and Rousseau, as well as Sainte-Beuve's novel *Volupté*. But he also read some bad novels, like Rahel Sanzara's *The Lost Child*, finding, however, that it contained the kind of sentence that he loved, "Suffer and trust in God, that's the idea," not because of its message, but because it included both "rescued and rescuer" in one double clause.[121]

He also worked consistently hard at this time to enlarge his vocabulary even further, consulting etymologies as well as dictionaries. His poems display this delight in language. "Sanies," which he used in the title of "Sanies I," written in 1933, means "a blood-tinged seropurulent discharge from ulcers or infected wounds"; the same poem incorporates words that he acquired on the Continent: "a filthy slicker" (a raincoat, an American word that he had picked up from his friend Charles Clarke in France a few years before); German words like *Ritter* (a medieval knight on horseback), *müde* (weary), and *Stürmers* (slang for "lady-killers") that he had learned in Kassel. He continued to enter quotations that delighted him or words and phrases that caught his attention into a writer's notebook, ready to be woven into his own work.

6

HEALTH PROBLEMS bothered him constantly. Eventually he worked himself up to consult a doctor about a painful cyst that had developed on his neck.[122] This was diagnosed as " 'a deep-seated septic cystic system,' " Beckett preferring the alliteration to the diagnosis. He was advised to have an operation in order, or so he was assured, to clear up his trouble once and for all. On Thursday, December 1, 1932, he was operated on in the Merrion Nursing Home and, while under anesthetic, had the joint of a painful hammertoe removed as well. "I have an agreeable room, full of sun all morning. And it is pleasant enough lying in bed sleeping and reading and feeling vaguely spoilt and victimized and comic all at the same time. All in a hail of vitamines and iron and arsenic injections." [123] At a time when there were no antibiotics, these injections, administered in the buttocks, as there was insufficient muscle in his arm, were intended to improve the anemic state of his blood which was, he had been told, a disgrace.

Beckett's stay in the clinic lasted much longer than he anticipated since, after almost a fortnight of injections and dry dressings, his neck began to discharge again and needed further attention. [124] He spent the days gazing out at the pale winter sunlight, reading, writing letters, and receiving visitors. Mostly it was his mother, his father, and his brother, Frank, who came to see him, laden with books that he had asked them to bring.

He observed carefully what was happening to him in the hospital, paying meticulous attention to all the preparations for his operation. And a couple of days after the surgery, he jotted down notes on what he remembered of his experiences and feelings about the occasion. These notes provided him with the raw material for his story "Yellow." Belacqua has the same double operation as Beckett, and information and medical vocabulary that he had gleaned in the hospital reappear, although with a large measure of ironic distance, in the story.

Characteristically at this time, Beckett borrowed many elements of his stories from his daily life, even though—taking a poor view of realism in literature—he went on to transform them imaginatively in his writing. In both the story "What a Misfortune" and the poem "Serena II," he borrows details from a trip he made to Galway and County Mayo with his brother in October. [125] On December 26, 1932, he went for a bicycle ride in the rain to Donabate and the Portrane Lunatic Asylum, which lie north of Dublin, and met an old man who was a native of nearby Lambay Island. Beckett asked him what the tower was that they could see in a field nearby. "That's where Dane Swift came to his motte," said the old man. "What motte?" asked Beckett, not recognizing the unusual word for mistress. "Stella" was the reply. This inspired Beckett to think of composing a poem about Swift, describing the process as "poem scum fermenting" and as the "first flicker in the mash-tub" for some time. The poem came to nothing, but the anecdote concerning Dean Swift meeting his mistress, Stella, in that very tower was soon incorporated almost verbatim into the story "Fingal." [126] Instead, the poem that he first called "Weg du Einzige!" then later entitled "Sanies I" was inspired by a chance meeting in the street with Ethna MacCarthy, a reminder that he had been born on Good Friday, and a bicycle ride on the Saturday of Easter weekend 1933 "through Malahide and round the estuary to Portrane and back by Swords." [127]

But his concerns in the Merrion Nursing Home were not exclusively focused on his own health or on garnering material for his writing. News of family troubles reached him from his aunt Cissie Sinclair in Kassel. [128] She wrote sympathetically concerning his operation and invited him to recuperate with her family for Christmas. But she also referred to the desperate state of their own finances, with the Boss forced to sell off the piano and his pictures to repay some of their debts. If only he had a hundred pounds, dreamed Beckett, to buy some of the pictures that he so admired and that would be going for a song, leaving the Boss with only "a little off the minus side." [129] The Sinclairs' position sounded desperate, as Peggy was now bedridden and her younger brother, Morris, was having transient heart trouble. Much as he would have liked to get away to Germany, Beckett knew that a trip to Kassel was out of the question: He had no money and, in any case, his mother would not let him out of her sight unless she was convinced that he had fully recovered. And he had not.

7

THE BREAD-AND-BUTTER WORK of translating pieces from French for Nancy Cunard's *Negro Anthology* helped him to feel at times that he had not entirely severed his links with literary life in Paris. At others, the work had quite the opposite effect, merely emphasizing his sense of isolation and distance. The truth is that his feelings about Paris fluctuated wildly with his mood and his feelings about home. "The sensation of taking root, like a polypus, in a place," he wrote, "is horrible, living on a kind of mucous [sic] of conformity. And in this of all places." [130] Titus did not write, he grumbled; nor did Jolas. He often envied MacGreevy his courage in taking himself off to Paris with nothing but his ticket. But at least MacGreevy had friends there, he moped, including Jean Lurçat, with whom he could stay for nothing. His feelings of isolation were not helped when Seán O'Sullivan offered him an extra ticket for a friend to attend a Royal Academy exhibition preview, then promptly hurt him by commenting that he had forgotten that Beckett didn't go in for the luxury of friendship. [131] The remark hurt him deeply. That he needed such friendship very badly indeed is clear from the tone of his letters to Tom MacGreevy.

Months after the operation, his neck still refused to heal completely. When she was not nursing Frank, who was having a very severe bout of flu, May Beckett fussed over him. But he felt that "implied reproaches [were] translated in an excess of concern and fondling." [132] And much of her anxiety about him focused on what he was going to do with his life. Earlier, he had applied for a job in Milan, which came to nothing. Now he toyed with attempting another spell of academic life by applying for a job as "lecteur" (as he wrote it) in French at Manchester University. Finally he decided that he simply could not face such a post again.

On May 3, 1933, Beckett had to have the cyst on his neck lanced once again, under a local anesthetic this time. The incision was stitched but suppurated for several days into the fomentations that his mother applied regularly with loving care. Those days were spent in bed. It was as he was lying there, at a low ebb, that he was shocked to learn that his cousin and former love, Peggy, had died of tuberculosis in Bad Wildungen in the early hours of the day of his operation.

Peggy, he was told, had died peacefully after a fit of coughing that followed the administration of a sleeping potion. Her death was not at all expected by the family. Only days before, she had been back to Kassel to see a doctor, who had told her that she was much better and could venture to lie out in the sun. As a result, she and her fiancé had been making optimistic plans for their marriage. The fiancé was inconsolable.

Beckett was horrified and depressed by Peggy's death. He thought with great sadness of the lively, laughing, happy-go-lucky young woman whom he had known and for a time loved in Dublin, Laxenburg, and Kassel, and he shuddered at this latest and most terrible blow that life had inflicted on his poor aunt Cissie. The family debts must seem very unimportant now, he thought, by comparison with this dreadful tragedy.

The atmosphere at home improved a little as his mother and father concentrated on building up their son's health. They encouraged him to eat well; his mother even approved of his drinking stout regularly to improve the state of his blood and put on weight. They stopped talking about his getting a job. But the tensions did not go away because they were unexpressed. And Beckett's financial problems were underlined by letters — typed in red — from a Mr. Seán Cagney of the income tax office threatening him with distrainment if he did not pay five guineas of tax due within a week.[133] Since he could not pay and had no effects of his own to be distrained, he visited the office to beg for respite.

It was with such pressures in mind that Beckett made several further attempts to write and to sell more of his work. He wrote two more short stories about Belacqua Shuah, so that by May 13 he had five stories finished.[134] And, at Joe Hone's suggestion, he saw a young commissioning editor from Methuen and, since Gollancz had not yet returned *Dream*, offered him the poems and two of his stories. In return, Beckett said, he expected only the lobster and the Chablis consumed for lunch at the Shelbourne Hotel. And that, in the end, was what he got.

Throughout May and June, as his work on the stories dried up, Beckett became increasingly frustrated and depressed. To counter this frustration and to combat the feelings of claustrophobia and ennui that he experienced at home, he started to drink heavily again. One evening he arrived home very drunk indeed. He quarreled with his mother and began to throw plates from the kitchen table. Finally he threw a pudding into the veronica hedge near the kitchen door.[135] Not surprisingly, his actions upset the entire household. And his mother was not one to forgive or forget easily what she considered outrageous behavior. So, for everyone's good, including his own, Beckett felt that he ought to prepare the way for him to leave home. He thought of asking his father for an allowance to permit him to live in Spain or Germany and, with the former possibility in mind, set to work to learn Spanish.

Throughout this period of what he called "the old round of unhappenings,"[136] Beckett's father remained a great source of strength to him. Bill Beckett was in his sixty-second year. His son noticed, of course, that he was aging—although Bill behaved as if he were twenty years younger, playing golf, swimming, and walking up mountains—and he admired the bluff, relativistic way with which his father was approaching old age and death:

> Lovely walk this morning with Father, who grows old with a very graceful philosophy. Comparing bees and butterflies to elephants and parrots and speaking of indentures with the Leveller! Barging through hedges and over the walls with the help of my shoulder, blaspheming and stopping to rest under colour of admiring the view. I'll never have anyone like him.[137]

Then, in mid-June, Bill Beckett collapsed with a heart attack. This first attack did not kill him. But it put him to bed for, the doctor proposed, several weeks at least of complete rest; it also made him feel very weak, miserable, and helpless.[138] Beckett washed him and shaved him. An active man all his life, Beckett's father found such a regime intolerable. But it was not to last for long.

On the morning of Monday, June 26, Dr. Abrahamson came to Cooldrinagh to visit his patient and pronounced him much better. To celebrate the good news and probably to cheer up his father, Beckett put on the brightest clothes he could find in his wardrobe. But hardly had the doctor left the house than Bill Beckett collapsed with another massive heart attack. He suffered badly for several hours and then, with all his family gathered around him, he died about four o'clock in the afternoon. Sam was never to forget his father's final words to him: "Fight fight fight" and (with massive understatement) "What a morning."[139]

8

The London Years

1933-35

1

DEVASTATED BY THE LOSS of his father, Beckett could find no words to express his grief: "I can't write about him, I can only walk the fields and climb the ditches after him." [1] Memories of their walks together haunted him and he recalled, with tears now, Joyce's lines "Father forsaken, forgive thy son"; he felt a crushing sense of guilt at having, as he saw it, let his father down.

Bill Beckett was buried in Redford Protestant Cemetery, "a little cemetery on the Greystones side of Bray Head, between the mountains and the sea." [2] Unforgettable images of the preparations for the funeral survive in Beckett's writing. In the short story "Draff," written later in the summer of 1933, Belacqua's grave is decorated by his former best man, Hairy, and the Smeraldina. In reality, this was done by Beckett in the company of his mother:

> In the cemetery the light was failing, the sea moonstone washing the countless toes turned up, the mountains swarthy Uccello behind the headstones. The loveliest little lap of earth you ever saw. . . . Well, to make a long story short, the pair of them between them, she feeding him from above, upholstered the grave: the floor with moss and fern, the walls with the verdure outstanding. Low down the clay was so hard that Hairy had to take his shoe to the tholes. However they made a great job of it, not a spot of clay showed when they had done, all was lush, green and most sweet smelling. [3]

Also the same summer, Beckett wrote a poem that he referred to as "The Undertaker's Man." It evokes the measuring, coffining, and removal of his father's body. In the poem, the son unsuccessfully tries to protect his mother from the most painful moments. The literary allusions—the undertakers are compared to the "clawed demons," or *malebranche*, in Dante's *Inferno*, one of which, Malacoda, provides him with his title—do not detract from the suffering that is felt in its repetitions: "hear she may see she need not." [4]

After his father's death, the family home became like a mausoleum. The Becketts were, wrote Sam several weeks after the funeral, "up to the eaves in the vile worms of melancholy observance." [5] It had long been a tradition for the blinds in a house and in neighboring houses to be lowered when someone died and to remain down until after the funeral. But May insisted on the blinds remaining down in Cooldrinagh for weeks on end. Grieving for his father every bit as much as his mother was, Beckett felt stifled by this ostentatious display of prolonged reverence and suffocated by the atmosphere in the "blank silent house." [6]

To escape from what he regarded as a surfeit of the trappings of mourning, he set up a rudimentary apartment in the top room of his father's office at 6 Clare Street, "for fear I should wreck my Mother's despair of mind by whistling in the house or drawing back a blind to see." [7] This allowed him to spend his days in town, returning home every evening with Frank, who had agreed to carry on his father's firm, in time for a melancholy dinner with their mother. After dinner, Frank retired regularly to his room to work for the Surveyors' Institute membership examination the following March. With no such excuse, Beckett was left to sit on silently with his mother.

As he grieved for his father, his health began to deteriorate very seriously. There were physical troubles that appeared on the surface to have little or nothing to do with his mental state. In July, a cyst or abscess that was growing on his palm responded badly to lancing; then, in late August, he sustained painful injuries to his right arm and hip when he was knocked off his motorcycle by a car. But, most worrying of all, his heart "started its jigs again," with night sweats and panic attacks. [8] In desperation, he sought help from his doctor friend, Geoffrey Thompson. Remembering this period, Beckett said:

> After my father's death I had trouble psychologically. The bad years were between when I had to crawl home in 1932 and after my father's death in 1933. I'll tell you how it was. I was walking down Dawson Street. And I felt I couldn't go on. It was a strange experience I can't really describe. I found I couldn't go on moving. So I went into the nearest pub and got a drink just to stay still. And I felt I needed help. So I went to Geoffrey Thompson's surgery. Geoffrey wasn't there; he was at Lower Baggot Street Hospital; so I waited for him. When he got there, I was standing by the door. He gave me a look over and found nothing physically wrong. Then he recommended psychoanalysis for me. Psychoanalysis was not allowed in Dublin at that time. It was not legal. So, in order to have psychoanalysis, you had to come to London. [9]

It was to be several months before he could act on Thompson's advice. Meanwhile, in an attempt to take a fresh grip on her own life, his mother, who had been living on "housework, holy dying and private tears," decided at the beginning of October to rent a little house by the sea just beyond Dalkey Harbour. Beckett accompanied her, laden with his books, manuscripts, and typewriter. But he never settled there; he questioned "how people have the nerve to live so near, *on* the sea. It moans in one's dreams in the night." [10] He made an effort to sort out his own life, applying for a job as assistant curator at the National Gallery in London, naming Jack Yeats and Charles Prentice as references. But nothing came of the application.[11]

One exhilarating piece of news reached him in the mail. On September 25, Charles Prentice accepted his collection of short stories, which he eventually called *More Pricks Than Kicks*, for publication by Chatto and Windus.[12] Beckett was overjoyed. And while staying at the seaside, he wrote an additional story to satisfy Prentice, who suggested that another five or ten thousand words might help the book's sales. But the story, "Echo's Bones," in which Belacqua is resurrected, proved totally unacceptable to Chatto and Windus.[13] In rejecting it, Prentice pulled no punches:

> It is a nightmare. Just too terribly persuasive. It gives me the jim-jams. The same horrible and immediate switches of the focus, and the same wild unfathomable energy of the population. There are chunks I don't connect with. I am so sorry to feel like this. Perhaps it is only over the details, and I may have a correct inkling of the main impression. I *am* sorry, for I hate to be dense, but I hope I am not altogether insensitive. "Echo's Bones" certainly did land on me with a wallop. . . . "Echo's Bones" would, I am sure, lose the book a great many readers. People will shudder and be puzzled and confused; and they won't be keen on analysing the shudder. I am certain that "Echo's Bones" would depress the sales very considerably.[14]

On returning to Foxrock, Beckett started to go to concerts and the theater again and read widely, including Leibniz and, a little unwisely, Jeremy Taylor's *Holy Living* and *Holy Dying*.[15] But nothing seemed to calm his nerves. He was disturbed, sad, depressed, and, above all, desperately anxious about his health. Geoffrey Thompson's decision to go to London to study psychoanalysis and his view that Beckett might benefit from psychotherapy there finally persuaded him to do something about it. And, after some tense discussions with his mother about his finances — for he was currently living on a pound a week — he decided to go to London for a prolonged stay.

2

BECKETT STARTED his course of intensive psychotherapy shortly after Christmas 1933.[16] This was a terrible time for him in every way. He was, he said, dreadfully unhappy.[17] Fortunately, his close friend Tom MacGreevy was already living in London; over the next few months, their friendship was to represent a constant lifeline for them both. There were periods during Beckett's two-year stay in London when MacGreevy was the only person that he was seeing, apart from his psychotherapist.[18] And when, early in January 1935, MacGreevy had to return to Ireland after his eighty-year-old mother suffered a serious stroke, Beckett found himself on his own again. At such times he tended to retreat into himself, spending large parts of each day walking disconsolately around the streets and parks or sitting by the radiator reading a book, huddled in an arm-chair,[19] sipping lime juice (a taste that he had just acquired) and Kia-Ora (an orange cordial drink)[20] in the summer or something much stronger in the cold winter months.

Although the reason for his residence in London was disquieting, the stay began well enough. MacGreevy found a furnished room for him in a boarding-house at 48 Paulton's Square, a handsome square built in the 1830s. It was less than four hundred yards from 15 Cheyne Gardens, where MacGreevy was staying as a virtual nonpaying guest of Hester Dowden, the daughter of Edward Dowden, a distinguished literary critic and former professor of English at Trinity College, Dublin.[21] As a result, the two friends saw each other regularly. Some-times they met in the "cavernous Tudoresque interior of the Six Bells, where once (it was rebuilt in 1900) Rossetti, Whistler and others used to drink"[22] or in the gabled, pinnacled World's End, a neo-Elizabethan-style public house. They visited London's art galleries together, but only on days when admission was free, for both men were dreadfully short of money.

The fees for Beckett's protracted course of psychotherapy were being paid by his mother. He explained: "It was going to cost about two hundred pounds. So, of course, there was no question of my financing the course myself. My mother paid for my course of treatment; she decided that she would finance me. The allowance from my father's will wasn't enough to pay the fees. So my mother gave me the money."[23] Even so, once his rent, food, and drink were paid for, he had very little money left for luxuries. MacGreevy was even worse off than Beckett, often struggling simply to survive. On at least one occasion, he did not even have the money to buy a postage stamp.[24] Beckett helped him out whenever he could, sending him what he referred to as "a miserable quid"[25] to bail him out with the message: "Let there never be any talk of debts and loans and all the other lousinesses of give and take entre ennemis [between enemies] between us." Then he went on, with a young man's heightened sense of drama and hyperbole: "When it's there it's there and when it's not it's not and basta. What matter which of us uses it to extenuate the affair of dying."[26]

3

ON THE ADVICE of Geoffrey Thompson, Beckett attended the Tavistock Clinic on Malet Place, where he was assigned to one of the younger therapists, Dr. Wilfred Ruprecht Bion.[27] Beckett presented himself to Bion with severe anxiety symptoms,[28] which he described in his opening session: a bursting, apparently arrhythmic heart, night sweats, shudders, panic, breathlessness, and, when his condition was at its most severe, total paralysis.[29] He saw Bion privately three times a week.[30] Although he could remember going to see the therapist only for about six months,[31] in reality his treatment lasted nearly two years.[32]

Bion had enough in common with Beckett to make their relationship friendly as well as professional. Like Beckett, he came from a moderately well-off

family, was educated at a fee-paying school (Bishop's Stortford College), and
excelled at sports.[33] More important for Beckett at this stage of his career,
however, were Bion's various intellectual and literary interests. While Bion was
at Queen's College, he came under the influence of H. J. Paton and studied the
philosophy of Kant. Then, after graduating, he spent a year at the University of
Poitiers studying French literature, which he loved; he read French fluently,
although his spoken French was much weaker. After teaching history and literature for a short spell at Bishop's Stortford College, he went to medical school in
his late twenties at University College Hospital, London (where he was awarded
the Gold Medal for Surgery) and, after qualifying as a doctor in 1930, undertook
to have psychotherapy himself. With no previous training in psychotherapy, he
joined the Tavistock Clinic as an assistant in 1932, only two years before Beckett
became a patient there. As a therapist, he was, then, relatively inexperienced,
although he was promoted to the senior staff in 1933.[34]

Broad-shouldered and athletic in build, Bion had a piercing look and a
small, dark, neatly trimmed mustache; he was thirty-seven, and his hair was
receding rapidly. Beckett liked him. He could be so sharply critical of others at
this time that an absence of unfavorable comments in his correspondence can
be taken as tacit approval. He even pokes gentle, affectionate fun at his therapist,
calling him "the covey" and laughing, for instance, at his penchant for chunky
knitted Scottish sweaters.[35] "Bion off the job is pleasant," he wrote, "but against
a background of Toc H [an interdenominational Christian fellowship] and Tank
Corps that makes me tremble."[36] He respected Bion as a therapist, however, and
obviously felt that he was deriving some benefit from the sessions since he
continued them for so long. Their relationship was an unusually friendly one
for therapist and patient. On October 2, 1935, for example, Beckett went to
dinner with Bion at the Etoile restaurant on Charlotte Street, before going as
his guest to hear the third lecture in a series of five given by C. G. Jung for the
Institute of Psychological Medicine at the Tavistock Clinic. The lecture stayed
in his mind for many years.[37]

The methods of therapy practiced at the Tavistock Clinic in 1934 and
1935, when Beckett was a patient, were highly eclectic. Ideas were borrowed
from both Freud and Jung, but Adlerian hypotheses were used as well. According to the historian of the Tavistock, the group of therapists there was "rather
empirical and non-doctrinaire" and an "eclectic and enquiring spirit" was encouraged.[38] Bion probably employed with Beckett his own version of "reductive
analysis"—a term coined by J. A. Hadfield, the most influential figure at the
Tavistock Clinic at that time—rather than full, rigorous analysis, although the
number of consultations that Beckett had qualified him as a long-term patient
and suggest that his therapist could have gone quite deep.[39] Bion was an innovative thinker and it is probable that, even as early as this, he may have been
borrowing from different sources for his methods. "Reductive analysis" aimed to

discover the dynamic links between the symptom and its causes in the
past. The search was by free association and dream analysis for what

Hadfield termed "nuclear incidents." These need not necessarily be grossly traumatic, but were crises or turning-points in the inner life of the child, as recollected on the couch. The patient relived and realized a repression of one attitude — for example, dependence — by adopting a new attitude — for example, defiance — and a splitting off of his need for love, etc.[40]

Beckett's own account of what happened with his therapist suggests that a form of reductive analysis was indeed being used:

> I used to lie down on the couch and try to go back in my past. I think it probably did help. I think it helped me perhaps to control the panic. I certainly came up with some extraordinary memories of being in the womb. Intrauterine memories. I remember feeling trapped, of being imprisoned and unable to escape, of crying to be let out but no one could hear, no one was listening. I remember being in pain but being unable to do anything about it. I used to go back to my digs and write notes on what had happened, on what I'd come up with. I've never found them since. Maybe they still exist somewhere. I think it all helped me to understand a bit better what I was doing and what I was feeling.[41]

Bion also encouraged Beckett to note down details of his dreams when he woke: "Bion is now a dream habitué," he wrote to MacGreevy in January 1935.[42] Beckett's correspondence shows that he found his therapy sessions totally absorbing. "It is the only thing that interests me at the moment," he wrote to his cousin after the first few sessions, "and that's as it should be, because these kind of things require you to dedicate yourself to them to the virtual exclusion of everything else."[43]

In the course of his therapy, Beckett read widely on the subject of psychology and psychoanalysis. R. S. Woodworth's *Contemporary Schools of Psychology* provided him with the general framework he needed.[44] His detailed notes on this book still exist. In it, he read about behaviorism, gestalt psychology,[45] Freud, Jung, Adler, and William McDougall. It is from Woodworth, for example, that he derived the somewhat arcane knowledge of the Külpe school of psychology which he displays, ostentatiously but wittily, in *Murphy*, the novel that he partly wrote in London: "Murphy had some faith in the Külpe school. Marbe and Bühler might be deceived, even Watt was only human, but how could Ach be wrong." Murphy invokes Külpe's technical terminology, with delightful incongruity, to order a cup of tea and a packet of assorted biscuits in a Lyons tea shop. After saying "Bring me" to the waitress, he stops giving "this preparatory signal [in order] to let the fore-period develop, that first of the three moments of reaction, in which, according to the Külpe school, the major torments of response are undergone."[46] These technical terms are lifted directly from Woodworth.[47]

He also read the lengthy, somewhat indigestible Freudian *Papers on Psychoanalysis* by Ernest Jones (whom he called Erogenous Jones) on which he took twenty pages of single-spaced typewritten notes, and books by Alfred Adler,[48] Otto Rank, Karin Stephens, and Wilhelm Stekel[49] as well as a commentary of Freud (whom he called Freudchen) entitled "Treatment of the Neuroses."

Beckett's notes, discovered in a trunk in the cellar after his death, reveal the depth of his interest and the intensity of his personal involvement. While typing out the characteristics of anxiety neurosis and hysteria as described by Freud, for example, he notes "Dungeons in Spain"—"Castles in Spain" transformed into Beckett's own subterranean mode—and adds, in brackets: "mine own." A little later, after "Peter-Panitis," he writes, again in brackets: "mine own." There are also lines in red ink in the margin indicating that he returned to the notes to emphasize things of particular interest to him, several exclamation marks, and once, a sarcastic "Macché!" ("So what!").

There were sections of these books with which Beckett connected immediately: Otto Rank's "Anxiety of child left alone in dark room due to his unconscious being reminded (er-innert) of intrauterine situation, terminated by frightening severance from mother," for example, and Alfred Adler's "Neurotic insomnia is a symbolic attempt to escape from the defencelessness of sleep and to keep in mind the securities against 'beneath,' 'underneath.' "[50]

The notes do not indicate, however, the kind of neuroses that were uncovered and explored during Beckett's own therapy sessions.[51] The key to understanding Beckett, said Dr. Geoffrey Thompson—who, with Wilfred Bion himself, was the one most likely to know—was to be found in his relationship with his mother.[52] And reductive analysis must have focused on the intensity of his mother's attachment to him and his powerful love-hate bond with her.

Bion wanted Beckett to give himself time before returning to Ireland to extricate himself from the unfortunate consequences of a fierce tug-of-war that seems to have been going on between an almost umbilical dependence on and a desire for independence from his mother. The "Peter-Panitis" that Beckett mentioned was one likely facet of his dependence on her. During breaks in Foxrock in January and late April 1935, he himself linked the return of his night sweats and his "periods of speechless bad temper" with his presence back in the family home.[53] And the letters he wrote when he returned to Dublin and then went on holiday in England with her in July 1935 reveal him to be almost obsessively preoccupied with the progress and nature of their relationship. One aim of his therapy would have been to help him to understand his feelings about his mother, and then find ways of combating their adverse effects on him by resolving the negative feelings and encouraging more positive, less extreme ones.

Another equally important aspect of Beckett's extended therapy is better documented. One remarkable letter to Tom MacGreevy, written on March 10, 1935, after almost a hundred and fifty meetings with Bion, is immensely revealing of what Beckett had been brought to recognize as a principal cause of his distressing physical symptoms and is pivotal to an understanding of his growing control not only of his panic attacks but of his own life. This, one of the half-dozen most important of his letters to survive, also offers perhaps the first convincing explanation of how the arrogant, disturbed, narcissistic young man of the early 1930s could possibly have evolved into someone who was noted later for his extraordinary kindness, courtesy, concern, generosity, and almost saintly "good works."

MacGreevy had written expressing his deep concern about Beckett's black moods and "bubbling heart" and had recommended a way of life that might find comfort in "goodness and disinterestedness," drawing on Thomas à Kempis's *Imitation of Christ.* In his reply, Beckett admits that, although well acquainted with the Kempis text—he quotes it in both Latin and English and comments astutely on it—for him it had served only to reinforce a deliberate immersion in self and isolation from others, what he describes as "an abject self-referring quietism." Then, writing with lucid self-enlightenment, he links his physical symptoms with his isolation, apathy, and feelings of superiority:

> For years I was unhappy, consciously and deliberately ever since I left school and went into T.C.D. [Trinity College, Dublin], so that I isolated myself more and more, undertook less and less and lent myself to a crescendo of disparagement of others and myself. But in all that there was nothing that struck me as morbid. The misery and solitude and apathy and the sneers were the elements of an index of superiority and guaranteed the feeling of arrogant "otherness," which seemed as right and natural and as little morbid as the ways in which it was not so much expressed as implied and reserved and kept available for a possible utterance in the future. It was not until that way of living, or rather negation of living, developed such terrifying physical symptoms that it could no longer be pursued, that I became aware of anything morbid in myself. In short, if the heart had not put the fear of death into me I would be still boozing and sneering and lounging around and feeling that I was too good for anything else.[54]

He had gone first to Thompson in Dublin, then to Bion in London with a specific fear and a specific complaint, only to discover, he wrote, that the fear and the complaint were the "least important symptom of a diseased condition that began in a time which I could not remember" and that

> the fatuous torments which I had treasured as denoting the superior man were all part of the same pathology. That was the picture as I was obliged to accept it, and that is still largely the picture, and I cannot see that it allows of any philosophical or ethical or Christlike imitative pentimenti, or in what way they could redeem a composition that was invalid from the word "go" and has to be broken up altogether.

Referring to his physical symptoms, he continues graphically: "If the heart still bubbles it is because the puddle has not been drained, and the fact of its bubbling more fiercely than ever is perhaps open to receive consolation from the waste that splutters most when the bath is nearly empty."[55]

By this stage, Beckett was more than halfway through his therapy. Some further digging into his past still had to be done, with Bion's help. But he was already clearly convinced that his physical problems were caused in part by his own attitude of superiority and an isolation from others that resulted from a morbid, obsessive immersion in self. It is easy to see how what he called his mother's "savage loving" might have contributed to this attitude.[56] By setting him on a pedestal as a child, she had fostered his sense of superiority, while at the same time smothering him claustrophobically and demanding conformity to her own rigid (and for him unacceptable) standards and values. Now, with MacGreevy's recommendations of "goodness and disinterestedness" in mind, Beckett asks pertinently:

> I cannot see how "goodness" is to be made a foundation or a beginning of anything. Am I to set my teeth and be disinterested? When I cannot answer for myself, and do not dispose of myself, how can I serve? Will the demon — pretiosa margarita! [precious pearl] — disable me any the less with sweats and shudders and panics and rages and rigors and heart burstings because my motives are unselfish and the welfare of others my concern? Macché! Or is there some way of devoting pain and monstrosity and incapacitation to the service of a deserving cause? Is one to insist on a crucifixion for which there is no demand?[57]

At this stage in his therapy, Beckett could see only the negative effects of his isolation and was correspondingly cruel to himself. But, with Bion's help, he was slowly led away from ethical judgments of his own behavior to consider pragmatically how to control its unfortunate symptoms. Without accepting the religious connotations of MacGreevy, Beckett had to learn to counter his self-immersion by coming out of himself more in his daily life and taking a livelier interest in others. A basis for this already existed in the kindness and concern that he felt for his family and his friends. He could build on these positive foundations. Initially, this shift in his attitudes occurred for purely pragmatic, therapeutic reasons. Yet the evidence of his friends suggests that what may once have been a search for a tolerable modus vivendi evolved into a far more natural, spontaneous sharing in the problems, pains, and sufferings of others.

But Bion was an intellectual himself, interested (as his own fine autobiographical writings show) in the processes of artistic creation.[58] And he probably helped Beckett to see how his solipsistic attitudes could be mined fruitfully in his writing. By externalizing some of the impulses of the psyche in his work — the feelings of frustration and repressed violence, for example — he would find it easier to counter the self-absorption that had seemed morbid and destructive in his personal life. Writing thus became essential to his later mental and physical well-being.

The writing Beckett produced while living in London already shows the influence of his own psychotherapy and his reading around the subject. This influence is much more obvious and direct than it was later to become. A short story published in The Bookman in August 1934 as "A Case in a Thousand," although based on a true case that Beckett learned of from Geoffrey Thompson late in 1933, reflects his own psychological preoccupations. In the real-life incident, a mother stayed all day in the hospital ward with her very sick son. When asked to visit him at limited hours only, she came back to wait and watch outside the hospital all day and every day. When her son died, she returned after the funeral to carry on her daily vigil, sitting on a shooting stick on the towpath of the canal. This strange devotion moved Thompson.

The focal point of Beckett's story, however, becomes the relationship between the physician, Dr. Nye, and his old nurse, Mrs. Bray, who, in the fiction, is the mother of the boy in question. The hub of the story is a traumatic event in the doctor's childhood which both he and the nurse recollect, although he can recall it only obscurely. The story is clearly Oedipal, the nurse substituting for the mother, the doctor wanting, as a small boy, to grow up so that he could marry her. But the trauma in question, described by Beckett in the language of the therapist as "the trauma at the root of this attachment," is never elucidated and remains a mysterious, missing element, played down finally as "a matter connected with his earliest years, so trivial and intimate that it need not be enlarged on here, but from the elucidation of which Dr. Nye, that sad man, expected great things." [59]

The story has several autobiographical features. The doctor has some of Beckett's own characteristics: his melancholia and "his heart that knocked and misfired for no reason known to the medical profession." Beckett's own nurse was Bridget Bray, and she, too, had the "strawberry mottle of the nose and the breath smelling heavily of clove and peppermint." We cannot know, however, whether any of Beckett's own "traumas" revolved around an incident in the past with his nanny. What matters is that the mystery — of the doctor's case as well as that of the fictional Mrs. Bray — is left unresolved. With Beckett, writing explores but does not explain away. Implied is the pessimistic suggestion that, although therapy might well uncover the traumatic events of childhood, it does not necessarily heal wounds that have been inflicted on the psyche. Whether Beckett found this story too autobiographical for comfort or too obvious in its use of psychological material, he never allowed it to be reprinted during his lifetime.

4

BECKETT'S VOLUME of ten linked short stories, *More Pricks Than Kicks*, was published in London on May 24, 1934 — "Empire Day," Beckett noted sardonically. [60] He had corrected the proofs in December 1933, before he left Dublin. To the proofs he had added a short passage at the end of the final story, "Draff" (a provisional title also for the whole collection), [61] about the groundsman in the cemetery, which appealed to Charles Prentice. [62]

Chatto made every effort to sell the stories to an American publisher in advance of their publication in England. *More Pricks* was offered to Viking

Press, to Stanley Rinehart of Farrar and Rinehart, to Harrison Smith and Haas,[63] and to Doubleday Doran and Gundy. The pitch quoted Chatto's spring list: " 'the utterance of a very modern voice,' and a brilliant one, too." [64] But none of the American publishing houses was interested and Chatto and Windus decided therefore to go ahead with the publication alone.

Beckett's feelings about the publication of the stories were highly ambivalent; they included excitement at the prospect of seeing his first volume of creative writing appear in print, and hope that this might well lead to other commissioned work — but also worry that the stories would offend relatives and friends. His aunt Cissie and the Boss had been forced to return from Kassel on account of bad debts and anti-Semitism and were now living on the hill of Howth, around the bay north of Dublin. He feared that they would be very upset at the inclusion of "The Smeraldina's Billet Doux," a love letter, written in a massacred Teutonic English, which they would recognize as based on one of Peggy's letters to him. This was made all the more poignant by the fact that it was only a year since Peggy had died. In the circumstances, it seems cruel of him to have used the letter. "I didn't know what I was undertaking," he wrote to Peggy's younger brother, Morris, "peinlich [painful] no matter what angle contemplated." [65] Fifty-four years later, he told me that he "still regretted it." [66] Beckett had carried over several characters and a large section of the text of *Dream of Fair to Middling Women*, and he had genuine fears that other friends in Dublin would recognize themselves in his book as well, as they gazed through the rather flimsy veils in which he had clothed his characters.

Above all, there was his mother to worry about. The proofs and letters from Charles Prentice about the book had been posted to 6 Clare Street, so it had been a simple matter to ensure that his mother did not see them. But now that the stories were about to be published, Beckett could scarcely prevent her from reading them, if she so chose. Although he was convinced that she would totally disapprove, he hoped that her attitude might soften somewhat, if by any chance the book were to be well received and succeed commercially. And he reasoned that, since it would soon be on sale in Dublin's bookshops anyway, it would be best if she and Frank were to receive their copies from him rather than learn of its existence from friends or, worse still, read about it first in the Irish newspapers.

In the end, his worries concerning members of his family and his friends proved largely unwarranted. There was initial resentment and coolness from the Sinclairs. His uncle seems to have understood better than his aunt the needs of fiction, and not been too cross. As for Cissie, she was very upset at first. But she quickly forgave him after he wrote a letter pleading with her to see him during his summer trip home.[67] The reconciliation was so successful that, after meeting her during the summer, he could write to MacGreevy that all was well "with only minimum of constraint with Smeraldina's Ma." [68] And, on his next trip to Ireland at Christmas, fences had been so thoroughly mended that he spent a weekend with the Sinclairs at Howth. Rudmose-Brown took his caricature as the shambling figure of the Polar Bear in good part and, as time was to show,

Mary Manning, herself an open-minded, freethinking writer, did not break off relations with him, although she and her mother were not exactly overjoyed at being used as a basis for the Fricas.

May Beckett had her own technique for coping with the publication. This was to ignore it completely. So it was several months before the Cooldrinagh copies of *More Pricks Than Kicks* ever appeared on the house shelves. The book was never even discussed during his return visits home.[69] This impenetrable wall of silence may have been upsetting, but it was preferable to the open hostility and disgust that was its alternative. Disgust was common enough among those members of the reading public who borrowed from Switzer's Lending Library the only copies that were available in August in Dublin.[70]

This "very modern voice" aroused a bewildering diversity of responses from Irish and English reviewers. Those favorable to the book perceptively situated Beckett in "the tradition of Fielding and Sterne."[71] One stressed that, although clearly influenced by James Joyce, he "is no fashionable imitator."[72] Edwin Muir of *The Listener* wrote: "Mr. Beckett makes a great deal of everything; that is his art. Sometimes it degenerates into excellent blarney, but at its best it has an ingenuity and freedom of movement which is purely delightful."[73] And the *Times Literary Supplement* critic spotted "a definite fresh talent at work in it, though it is a talent not yet quite sure of itself."[74] But many reviews were hostile. "Very strange and puzzling," commented *The Morning Herald* (under the head "Irish Mystification").[75] "The meaning of *More Pricks Than Kicks* completely eludes me," admitted *The Morning Post*.[76] Reviewers saw affinities with T. S. Eliot, Wyndham Lewis, and Ronald Firbank. And the debt to James Joyce was often judged adversely: "Mr. Beckett has imitated everything in James Joyce — except the verbal magic and the inspiration," one reviewer commented harshly.[77] "The whole book is a frank pastiche of the lighter, more satirical passages in *Ulysses*," wrote another.[78]

Suggestions that the stories were "a farce for highbrows"[79] and "unlikely to appeal to a large audience"[80] affected sales. As early as June, Charles Prentice wrote to Richard Aldington that "Sam Beckett's short stories are, I fear, cutting no ice."[81] And, when Beckett acknowledged his first dismal financial statement early in November with an apology to the publishers, Prentice wrote reassuringly:

> It was charming of you to write about the account. God knows, I would the sales had been larger — but I do hope you won't be depressed, and you certainly mustn't worry about Chattos. I have shown your letter to the other partners, and they are completely at one with me. We are very glad indeed to have published *More Pricks Than Kicks*, and such regrets as we have are chiefly for you. After all, it is taking a chance to publish literature, and though we don't welcome disappointment, we are steeled against it. The author's position is much worse, and we do beg you again not to take your own disappointment to heart. It may appear to be a melancholy thing to say that history repeats itself in the case of the large majority of real books, but on the other hand, other

writers have put these blows behind them and go on. So please, when the time comes and you are free, take up pen once more with enhanced vim. Don't for a moment think that we regret having published *More Pricks Than Kicks*.[82]

Beckett took a month-long break from therapy in August 1934 and returned to Foxrock. He used his vacation to make his peace with the Sinclairs. But he was also able to test his feelings about Ethna MacCarthy, who was now in the throes of an affair with his good friend Con Leventhal. He saw them together several times and was able to affirm, too confidently to be convincing: "That has become easy too — as pie."[83]

Principally, however, his return home gave him the chance to see whether his consultations with Bion had helped him to cope with the stresses and strains that seemed endemic to living in the same house as his mother. In this respect too, he found himself much encouraged. "Somehow things at home seem to be simpler," he wrote to MacGreevy. "I seem to have grown indifferent to the atmosphere of coffee-stall emotions, and that in spite of Mother's conscientious cafard [black mood]."[84] Ten days later, he still found it "Much easier with Mother also. I am more than content to take her as she comes and waive her as she does not, and she seems to feel it and be easier in consequence."[85] But his assurances again lacked conviction, and the peace could survive only such relatively short tests.

Concerns about his health remained. At the beginning of his month-long stay, Beckett suffered from acute pains in his abdomen, which he thought might be caused by gallstones or a hernia. So he consulted Geoffrey Thompson, who had not yet quit his job to go to London. X rays showed that there was nothing organically wrong with him.[86] At night, he slept with Frank to help him to control his anxiety and feelings of panic, an unusual arrangement for a man of twenty-eight.[87] Gradually, the abdominal pains subsided and the night panics lessened in their severity. "I am obliged to accept the whole panic as psychoneurotic — which leaves me in a hurry to get back and get on," he wrote.[88] For, after seven months of therapy, he believed that, at long last, his sessions with Bion were beginning to do him some good.

5

ALTHOUGH HE WAS IN LONDON for most of 1934, the focus of much of Beckett's interest and attention remained, naturally enough, Ireland. He was intensely involved with everything that was happening to his family in his absence. He worried about whether his mother should let Cooldrinagh and whether she could afford to go on paying for his therapy.[89] He was anxious now about Boss Sinclair — his uncle was admitted to a hospital with tuberculosis in April 1935[90] — and worried that things were going badly with Harry Sinclair's shop.[91] He took a great interest in how his cousin, Morris, was preparing for the entrance examination into Trinity College, and was concerned about Morris's health, which forced him to go to Spain for three months to benefit from the dry climate.[92] Having lost one daughter to tuberculosis, the Sinclairs were taking no chances with their son. And he thought a lot about his brother Frank's welfare, business affairs, and love life.

He hated London and was infuriated by the patronizing English habit of addressing him in the pubs and shops as "Pat" or "Paddy." His male friends in London were almost all Irish: MacGreevy and, at the beginning of 1935, when he finally arrived in England, Geoffrey Thompson. Fellow poets Brian Coffey and Denis Devlin paid him fleeting visits, as did the artist Seán O'Sullivan. Con Leventhal also came over for a longer stay and they talked of Ethna. Occasionally he saw the critic Desmond MacCarthy.

His female friends, too, were Irish. In September 1933 in Dublin, he had met an attractive young woman called Nuala Costello, to whom he had first been introduced at Giorgio Joyce and Helen Fleischman's flat in Paris. Nuala used to go for tea with James and Nora Joyce and was friendly with Lucia. Beckett saw Nuala often—according to Nuala herself, they dined together once a week.[93]—and he thought for a while that he might even be falling in love with her. It is likely that it was Nuala to whom he was referring, when he wrote to Tom MacGreevy at the beginning of December 1933, "Je suis de nouveau amouraché, fais la cour sans conviction" ("I am a little smitten again, and court without conviction").[94]

Nuala was an intelligent, cultured woman who had been educated at a school in Paris; she graduated in French and history from University College, Dublin, then did postgraduate work at the Sorbonne.[95] Beckett corresponded with her from London throughout the first six months of 1934. His two surviving letters are long, clever, full of fireworks, but forced and self-consciously witty. He makes no concessions, displaying his erudition (though he sometimes mocks himself). He tells her about what he is reading and discusses films with her. They met again when he was back in Foxrock from London in the summer of 1934.

Beckett next saw Nuala when she came to stay in London and he started to see her occasionally over the following few months. The affair, such as it was, ended by the beginning of February 1935, when he wrote that "Costello seems to have cast me off."[96] On her return from Las Palmas in September, however, he saw her again, taking her out for a meal at Poggioli's in Soho, then cooling his ardor by escorting "such an unclitoridian companion" to a Spanish film (in color) called La Cucaracha.[97] According to Beckett, the affair never became a sexual one,[98] although he remained fond of Nuala and kept in touch with her for some time to come.[99]

Earlier in the year, he managed to avoid rekindling his unsatisfactory past nonaffair with the now very disturbed Lucia Joyce, who was staying in Grosvenor Square, although Beckett's comment to MacGreevy that the "Lucia ember flared up and fizzled out" suggests that this did not happen without some of the acrimonious scenes customarily associated with her.[100] It was probably with a great sense of relief that he remained uninvolved and (mostly) celibate. Occasionally, he wandered into the seamier parts of London—and not by accident. He was, after all, twenty-eight years old and was probably not having a regular physical relationship with a woman at the time. It was not uncommon for him, therefore, as he had done over the past six years, to avail himself of the services of prostitutes.[101]

He talked incessantly with MacGreevy about the daily news from Ireland in the *Irish Times* and discussed literary articles as they appeared in the *Dublin Magazine*. This magazine, edited by Seamus O'Sullivan, remained an already established outlet for Beckett's poems and reviews, although O'Sullivan did not accept or like everything that Beckett sent him. But while he was in London Beckett contributed the four-line poem "Gnome" and an enthusiastic review of MacGreevy's *Poems* to the August–September issue of 1934. He was still trying to carve out a niche for himself, as was MacGreevy, in the world of literary journalism, and hoped that his contacts with MacCarthy, Hugh and Ross Williamson of *The Bookman*, and Prentice would lead to more commissions in the English literary press and in the London publishing world. During the year, as part of this strategy, he had written a number of acute, erudite literary reviews for *The Spectator* and *The Bookman* and one for T. S. Eliot's *The Criterion*.[102]

The Williamsons, who edited *The Bookman*, suggested to Beckett that he should write an article on recent Irish poetry for their special Irish issue. He published it under a pseudonym, "Andrew Belis" (the surname of his maternal grandmother), either because his short story "A Case in a Thousand" was appearing in the same issue under his own name or because he thought his article might offend those Irish poets whom he criticized adversely as "antiquarians, delivering with the altitudinous complacency of the Victorian Gael the Ossianic goods." [103]

The essay, written between May and July 1934, looks at first like a lavish and rather cheeky tribute to Beckett's own friends: Tom MacGreevy,[104] Lyle Donaghy, Arland Ussher, Denis Devlin, and Brian Coffey. The last two are described by Beckett as "without question the most interesting of the youngest generation of Irish poets." [105] And yet the piece ought not to be read as a form of poetic nepotism but as an attempt to identify those poets (all, coincidentally, friends) who can be grouped together because of their attitude toward their art and their European outlook. They look for inspiration toward French poets like Tristan Corbière, Arthur Rimbaud, Jules Laforgue, and the Surrealists, and to Eliot and perhaps Pound. Distinguishing them from the "antiquarians" or "Celtic twilighters," Beckett sees them as representing "the new" in Ireland.

But for Beckett "the new thing that has happened" in recent Irish poetry is "the breakdown of the object, whether current, historical, mythical or spook . . . rupture of the lines of communication." [106] His recognition of those aware of this breakdown between subject and object leads him to mark out their territory in an exciting way:

The artist who is aware of this may state the space that intervenes between him and the world of objects; he may state it as no-man's land, Hellespont or vacuum, according as he happens to be feeling resentful, nostalgic or merely depressed. A picture by Mr Jack Yeats, Mr Eliot's "Waste Land," are notable statements of this kind.[107]

Beckett is well enough informed about the "old things": Oisín, Cuchulain, Maeve, *Tir na nOg*, the *Taín Bó Cuailgne*, Yoga, and the Crone of Beare.[108] But to fit some of the alleged antiquarians who handled such Irish themes into this category means distorting what a poet like Austin Clarke, for instance, thought he was doing. (Beckett is particularly hard on Clarke and his *Pilgrimage* poems.) It also means disparaging the mythologizer in Yeats. Beckett does this, however, only with the intention of highlighting a challenging, more subtle Yeats. He always loved and admired much of Yeats's poetry, while finding certain (though not all) of his plays as dull as ditchwater. ("I saw Yeats's two latest— *Resurrection* and the *King of the Great Clock Tower* at the Abbey on Saturday," he wrote to MacGreevy in August 1934. "Balbus building his wall would be more dramatic."[109])

John Harrington suggests that Beckett was less revolutionary in this article than he thought he was being:

> Beckett's praise in "Recent Irish Poetry" of something other than anti-quarianism is less innovation than affiliation with a critique of cut-and-dried Ossianic goods virtually as old as those goods themselves. By attacking antiquarianism, Beckett did not relinquish his own involve-ment in local culture. Instead, he joined a dissenting faction of impec-cable credentials that had been an important feature of modern Irish literature in all but its crudest revival forms or most exigent aims.[110]

But this sees Beckett's piece only in terms of the "Ossianic goods" and ignores the radical emphasis on "rupture" that lies behind his praise of what was new in the younger Irish poets. Increasingly, Beckett was to look out for signs of this "no-man's-land" in literature and painting, which for him represented "the new thing that had happened." "My no-man's-land" came to be a phrase that he related to his own work. And in this, the rupture becomes not merely one between subject and object but between man and man, and between man and himself.

Soon after writing this witty, polemical piece, Beckett suggested to *The Bookman*'s editors that he should contribute an article on either Gide or Rim-baud. Instead, they proposed a piece on "the 'wicked' Censorship in Ireland."[111] He accepted the commission without enthusiasm.[112] But he still ground out a withering attack on the 16 July, 1929 Act (a bill introduced to suppress obscene publications) in about ten days, working again from the little room over his brother's office at 6 Clare Street.[113] He pours scorn first of all on the definitions of indecency used, remarking:

A plea for distinction between indecency obiter and ex professo did not detain a caucus that has bigger and better things to split than hairs, the pubic not excepted. "It is the author's expressed purpose, it is the effect which his thought will have as expressed in the particular words into which he has *flung* (eyetalics mine) his thought that the censor has to consider." (Minister for Justice).[114]

Next, he attacks the constitution of the Censorship of Publications Board and the principle of having "five fit and proper persons" on the board. "Fit and proper persons" here meant "specialists in common sense." However, having pointed out that this comes dangerously close to the principle that "for the artist as for the restaurateur the customer is always right," Beckett also abhors the idea expressed by several members of the committee of inquiry that the censor does not have to read the whole of a book before condemning it.[115] He bewails the fact that, in principle, anyone who is prepared to submit to the board five copies of the book that is being challenged can lodge a complaint, although he sees that—more worryingly because of this proviso—a body like the Catholic Truth Society will be more likely to be the chief complainant. The problem is an obvious one. Morally vested interests will be pressing the small unrepresentative board to ban books that they may not have read either properly *or* improperly.

Beckett also drew attention to the restrictions on the reporting of judicial proceedings and on the prohibition of publications advocating the use of contraceptives. The act was such, he commented, that even Dean Swift's Grand Academy of Balnibarbi could hardly have improved on it as a piece of idiotic legislation. His conclusion was devastatingly dismissive:

> Finally to amateurs of morbid sociology this measure may appeal as a curiosity of panic legislation, the painful tension between life and thought finding issue in a constitutional belch, the much reading that is a weariness exorcized in 21 sections. Sterilization of the mind and apotheosis of the litter suit well together. Paradise peopled with virgins and the earth with decorticated multiparas.[116]

The Bookman ceased publication at the end of 1934, when it merged with *The London Mercury* and was edited by R. A. Scott-James instead of the Williamsons. Beckett's was one of the commissioned pieces to be dropped in the amalgamated review. In May 1936, Beckett sent the piece, which he revised lightly to include some examples from the latest September 1935 register of banned books, to George Reavey for submission to Eugene Jolas for *transition* magazine.[117] But the article, in which Beckett, though adopting a bantering tone, was as explicit as he had ever been about a subject on which he felt very strongly, was not published until 1983. It is tough, uncompromising, and contemptuous. And one feels that Beckett was proud to be able to conclude the revised version of his article with his own censorship number for *More Pricks Than Kicks:* Number 465.

6

BECKETT'S LIFE IN LONDON was not quite as arid nor, as the months went by, as exclusively obsessed with his mental and physical disarray as he frequently suggested. Tom MacGreevy's landlady, Hester Dowden, was partly responsible for the comparative richness of his musical life at this time, although he was probably too unsettled psychologically to appreciate this fully. She was a "medium and psychic investigator." Sixty-six years old when Beckett first met her, she had been divorced from a distinguished Dublin physician, Dr. Travers-Smith, for the past eighteen years. She had one daughter, Dolly, who had married the Irish playwright Lennox Robinson and was working as a stage designer at the Abbey Theatre in Dublin. Hester had an angular face, wispy gray hair, a large nose, a mannish chin, and a piercing stare. She wore long, loose, black shift-style dresses. Beckett used to go round to Cheyne Walk Gardens, where he played piano duets with Hester on the Steinway, which stood in the inner part of a large double drawing room. It was the only opportunity he had in London of practicing on a grand piano.[118]

As they played the piano or sipped tea from Hester's delicate china cups, they were surrounded by Siamese cats and snappy little Pekingese dogs which padded in and out of the room much as they pleased. Beckett disliked this feature of the household intensely. There was even an oil painting by Dolly of two of the Pekingese hanging in a prominent position in the drawing room. Beckett also found that he got "terribly tired of all the psychic evidence, [and] wonder what it has to [do] with the psyche as I experience that old bastard."[119] But MacGreevy's landlady provided a friendly group for Tom and his taciturn friend and it was through Hester that he met a likable painter called Holmes Raven-Hill. "Raven," as he was known, was a doctor who had quit medicine to become a landscape and portrait painter. He lived next door at number 17 and came round for Sunday lunch sometimes when Beckett was invited, as he was on several occasions.[120] Beckett loved talking about painting and music with Raven and MacGreevy.

As a musical enthusiast and pianist of talent herself, Hester was well informed about the concerts that were worth attending in London, and used to hold her own musical entertainments from time to time for friends and guests at her Sunday soirées. We know from Beckett's letters that, in spite of his crippling shyness in company, he attended a number of these evenings, even when MacGreevy had returned to Ireland. It was at 15 Cheyne Walk Gardens, for instance, that he met the concert pianist Maryjo Prado and her husband. Prado played, Beckett commented,

> some things well, a Rameau gavotte and variations that I did not know, Scriabin, the Vie de Brevet, Prokoviev's Tentations Diaboliques [sic], and some flashy Dohnyani [that is, Ernő Dohnányi]. But her Chopin

and Debussy were dragged out by the scruff of the neck, very disagreeable. She sits perched up above the keyboard like Mme. Mahieu [in
Proust's *Du côté de chez Swann*] at the seat of custom. Her left hand
in the Scriabin was extremely scrupulous and good.[121]

What is so striking about Beckett's comments on Prado's playing is how su-
premely confident he is in his musical judgments. Surprisingly for someone
who was to become the apostle of doubt and for whom "perhaps" was such a
crucial word, not a trace of self-doubt emerges in the twenty-nine-year-old's
judgments on music, or, for that matter, on literature and art.

At first, Beckett was overwhelmed by the rich fare of classical music available in London, although his pleasure in savoring such an opulent feast was
tempered by a very real need not to overspend. His judgment of what he heard
was idiosyncratic, assured, and at times highly critical. Of the prestigious Léner
Quartet's playing of Beethoven's three Rasoumovsky quartets that he heard at
the Queen's Hall on 9 March, 1935, he wrote, for instance, that he was
"very disappointed. Their playing seemed dry and finickety to the point of Old
Maidishness and Ludwig never so Rembrandtesque."[122]

Nor was he impressed by Wilhelm Furtwängler, the controversial conductor of the Berlin Philharmonic Orchestra, whom he had been to hear some weeks
before.[123] Furtwängler had been reported in the English press as having some
links with the Nazis,[124] which did nothing to endear him to Beckett. In a letter
to his cousin Morris Sinclair, about Furtwängler's interpretation of Beethoven's
Seventh Symphony (Beckett's favorite), he asks rhetorically what one can expect
from a recent convert to Nazism but an absence of mystery and a disintegration
of formal structures. The concert was not improved, in his opinion, by Furtwängler's choice of Bach's Suite for Orchestra in B minor to open the program.
Beckett simply did not like Bach. His musician cousin John Beckett thought that
this was probably because of the composer's "seamlessness and short, endlessly
repeated, musical phrases."[125] "He hated Bach," said the singer Bettina Jonic.
"He said it was like an organ grinder churning out musical phrases."[126]

But there was much for Beckett to enthuse about, too, notably in a series
of concerts of Beethoven's string quartets given in February 1934 by the Busch
Quartet. He booked for one, he said, especially to listen to the Third String
Quartet of 1825 (Opus 130 in B flat),[127] which he contrasted favorably to the
Pastoral Symphony; the latter, he felt, embodied everything that was vulgar and
facile in Beethoven.[128] He also expressed his intention to buy a ticket for the
final concert in the chamber music series which included the famous Opus 135
Quartet in F major. In the same letter to his cousin, Beckett copied out the
words written by Beethoven on his manuscript, "Der schwer gefasste Entschluss"
("The difficult resolution") together with the musical phrases that are based on
a musical inversion of the grave "Muss es sein" ("Must it be") to become the
allegro "Es muss sein" ("It must be"); these phrases have been taken to represent
Beethoven's questioning acceptance of death. This echoes the moving line in
the poem "Malacoda" that Beckett had written only a few months earlier about

his father's death: "must it be it must be it must be."[129] The phrase was to become one of Beckett's most chilling leitmotifs, repeated in letters to friends at several of the most painful moments of his life.

Music was a constant and important ingredient in Beckett's life. His early writing contained many witty allusions to music or musical form, as in *Dream of Fair to Middling Women:* "Brahms! That old piddler! Pizzicatoing himself off in the best of all possible worlds. Brahms!"[130] But, later in his career, he was to use music directly in a number of his plays.[131] Indirectly, he was to draw on his knowledge of musical techniques and terminology, reshaping musical structures and working with repetition and repetition with variation, counter-point, and changes of key, rhythm, tempo, and pitch. The debt is a subtle one and the affinities and transpositions made are hardly ever self-evident.[132]

During his two-year stay in London, Beckett also went to a number of different ballets. He reasoned that, since some of the finest companies in the world were on show there, he ought to make an effort to see them. And so, in his first year, he saw the famous Ballets Russes in a revival at Covent Garden of Manuel de Falla's *The Three-Cornered Hat*, with décor and costumes by Picasso, choreographed by Léonide Massine during his first period with the famous company.[133] Massine himself danced the part of the Miller opposite Tamara Toumanova, with David Lichine dancing the Corregidor.

Later, in the company of Arthur Hillis, a contemporary of his from Trinity whom he had met quite by chance in the street, he went to more concerts and a number of ballets. At the Coliseum he saw Leon Woizikowsky's program of *Les Sylphides, L'Amour Sorcier, Le Spectre de la Rose*, and *Petrushka*.[134] Having seen Massine dance the same role in *Petrushka* only the year before, Beckett found that Woizikowsky did not dance as surely as the great dancer-choreographer. So, characteristically, he focused his attention on the philosophy behind the ballet, commenting that "the Petrushka as philosophy was elucidated without any attempt to do so having appeared, the man of low humanity wor-shipping the earthball, and the man of high execrations his creator."[135]

Most of the time, Beckett found ballet a distraction from his passionate involvement with music. He wrote to Morris Sinclair, himself quite a talented violinist:

> Don't imagine that ballet is music. It is precisely because the music plays a subordinate role in it that ballet annoys me. . . . To represent music in a particular way through dance, gestures, décors, costumes and so on, is to degrade it, by reducing its value to that of pure anecdote. There are those who can only find satisfaction visually. As far as I'm concerned, and doubtless this is my misfortune, I can only escape with my eyelids closed.[136]

Yet, in spite of this difficulty, it was at this period of his life that the groundwork for his later interest in choreographing movements onstage was laid. When he came to direct his own plays in the 1960s and 1970s, he brought to his task the intense concentration and meticulous precision of the choreographer.

The one cultural event conspicuously absent from Beckett's diary was opera. He simply never liked opera, perhaps because it was such a mixture of music, singing, and acting, but also because for him it was too grandiose and unsuggestive an art form. It is typical that he should have heartily disliked Wagner (in spite of Pelorson's best efforts to convert him) and Richard Strauss, while tolerating, even enjoying Debussy's *Pelléas et Mélisande*, probably because of its understated nature. And according to Bettina Jonic, he had an enormous admiration for Alban Berg's opera *Wozzeck*, which he regarded as a masterpiece of the twentieth century.[137]

7

BECKETT'S ENJOYMENT of music was rivaled only by his passionate love of painting. While living in London, he was a regular visitor to the major London art galleries, often in the company of Tom MacGreevy: the National Gallery, the Tate Gallery, the Victoria and Albert Museum, Dulwich Picture Gallery, the Wallace Collection, and Hampton Court. In personal notes made at this time, some conveniently dated, he wrote out the titles of paintings that he wanted to remember from his visits to Hampton Court and the Wallace Collection, as well as to the Victoria and Albert Museum. In the middle of June 1934, he took a short trip to Paris with his brother, where again he made lists of pictures that captured his attention in the Louvre — Poussin and the Dutch primarily — and on a day in Chantilly.[138] On his August vacation in Dublin, he whiled away entire afternoons in the National Gallery of Ireland.[139] According to his close friend Avigdor Arikha, he could spend as much as an hour in front of a single painting, looking at it with intense concentration, savoring its forms and its colors, reading it, absorbing its minutest detail. Often it was the tiny narrative or human aspects that he picked out and, later, could remember seeing in a canvas.[140]

Beckett's interest in painting was highly serious and long-lasting. His earlier application for a post at the National Gallery in London indicates how professional he was in his approach. He studied books on the history of art, including R. H. Wilenski's *An Introduction to Dutch Art*, bought many catalogues,[141] and made extensive notes on paintings. In his own early writing, a particular painting is sometimes used as a point of comparison, evoking a mood captured by a face, as, for instance, when he conveys the changes that occur in the Alba's eyes in *Dream of Fair to Middling Women*:

> Her great eyes went as black as sloes, they went as big and black as El
> Greco painted, with a couple of good wet slaps from his laden brush,
> in the Burial of the Count of Orgaz the debauched eyes of his son or
> was it his mistress? It was a remarkable thing to see. Pupil and white
> swamped in the dark iris gone black as night.[142]

Some of his sharpest, most enduring memories of paintings in the work date from his two-year stay in London. Although Murphy, in the eponymous novel, has difficulty in calling to mind the faces of his own mother and father, he has a vivid recollection of a face in a painting: "He saw the clenched fists and rigid upturned face of the Child in a Giovanni Bellini Circumcision, waiting to feel the knife." [143]

But paintings meant far more to Beckett than a mere set of visual allusions. At this time of his life in particular, certain images became sharply etched in his mind's eye: Rembrandt's heads set against a dark background; Caravaggio's powerful compositions; Adam Elsheimer's [144] and Gerrit van Honthorst's striking use of spotlighting in their canvases. [145] Later he found that he could draw on these images at will in his own writing — just as naturally, perhaps even as unconsciously, as he did on his memories of Dante or Milton, Racine or Leopardi, Shakespeare or Hölderlin. Sometimes he recognized this influence; sometimes he did not. A man who consumes large quantities of garlic does not always realize how his breath, even the pores of his skin, emit its powerful odor.

But such images are transformed by an approach to the world that is strikingly modern. For Beckett also enthused in the 1930s about the German Expressionists: Kirchner, Feininger, Kandinsky, and Nolde. Techniques of distortion, fragmentation, isolation, and alienation were therefore familiar to him through painting. Even so, if we could take X rays of some of Beckett's own later plays, we would surely be able to detect some of the ghostly images of the Old Masters lurking beneath the surface.

Crucially, painting helped Beckett to think deeply about the relationship between the artist, his work, and the outside world. What he saw happening in twentieth-century art reinforced his own view of the world and encouraged him to search for new ways of finding an appropriate form to accommodate reality in his own work. After looking at Cézanne's paintings in the Tate Gallery in 1934, for example, he contrasted Cézanne's treatment of landscape with that of painters from an earlier age:

> What a relief the Mont Ste. Victoire after all the anthropomorphised landscape — van Goyen, Avercamp, the Ruysdaels, Hobbema, even Claude, Wilson and Crome Yellow Esq., or paranthropomorphised [sic] by Watteau so that the Débarquement seems an illustration of "poursuivre ta pente pourvu qu'elle soit en montant," or hyperanthropomorphised by Rubens — Tellus in record travail, or castrated by Corot; after all the landscape "promoted" to the emotions of the hiker, postulated as *concerned* with the hiker (what an impertinence, worse than Aesop and the animals), alive the way a lap or a *fist* is alive. [146]

It made no difference that he loved many of the earlier "anthropomorphised" landscapes that he invokes here. For in defining what he saw as Cézanne's recognition that landscape had nothing to do with man, that man was quite separate from and alien to it, he was defining a view that was excitingly close to his own and to the "no-man's-land" that he had just written about in his piece on recent Irish poetry. "Cézanne," he wrote, "seems to have been the first to see landscape and state it as material of a strictly peculiar order, incommensurable with all human expressions whatsoever. Atomistic landscape with no velleities of vitalism, landscape with personality à la rigueur, but personality in its own terms, not in Pelman's, *landscapality*."[147]

Then, using as an example a painting that he admired by Ruysdael, he went on to express a subtle yet clear perception of man severed from the outside world:

> Ruysdael's *Entrance to the Forest* — there is no entrance anymore nor any commerce with the forest, its dimensions are its secret and it has no communications to make. . . . So the problem . . . of how to state the emotion of Ruysdael in terms of post-impressionist painting must disappear as a problem as soon as it is realised that the Ruysdael emotion is no longer authentic and Cuyp's cows as irrelevant as Salomon's urinator in Merrion Square [he means *The Halt* by Salomon van Ruysdael, in the National Gallery of Ireland] except as a contrivance to stress the discrepancy between that which cannot stay still for its phases and that which can. . . . How far Cézanne had moved from the snapshot puerilities of Manet and Cie when he could understand the dynamic intrusion to be himself and so landscape to be something by definition unapproachably alien, unintelligible arrangement of atoms, not so much as ruffled by the kind attentions of the Reliability Joneses.[148]

This exhilarating piece of analysis was continued the following week in another letter to Tom MacGreevy. Beckett goes even further now, extending his view of the alien quality of landscape in Cézanne to an alien view of man himself. "What I feel in Cézanne," he wrote, "is precisely the absence of a rapport that was all right for Rosa or Ruysdael for whom the animising mode was valid, but would have been fake for him, because he had the sense of his incommensurability not only with life of such a different order as landscape, but even with life of his own order, even with the life . . . operative in himself."[149] It was to be a dozen years more before Beckett found his own way of expressing this "incommensurability" of man with himself.

9

Murphy

1934–36

1

BECKETT RETURNED FROM DUBLIN to London at the beginning of September 1934 to find new lodgings. He moved into a large bed–sitting room at 34 Gertrude Street, still in Chelsea, with an elderly couple, Mr. and Mrs. Fred Frost. The wife, whose maiden name was Queeney and who came from Athlone, was "the midinette complete with weak eyes that I had given up all hope of." She had served as a maid to "some of the extinct nobility," and her husband had retired from working as chauffeur with the same family. For Beckett, she became "a kind of mother on draught, you pull the pull and she appears with tea, Sanatogen, hot water to stupe a stye [he had a bad stye on his eye when he arrived back in London, which forced him to cancel his first consultation with Bion], every variety of abstract succour and a heavy sane willing presence altogether."[1]

The great advantage of this "mother on draught" was that she voiced none of the strictures and made none of the emotional demands of his own mother. Some of the ways of gentility had rubbed off onto her and her husband, and "she didn't flinch when I produced my Lapsang in favour of her Lipton's," Beckett told MacGreevy.[2] In *Murphy*, Miss Carridge brings Celia a cup of "Choicest Lapsang Souchong," saying: "Drink it before it coagulates."[3] And, in Beckett's later play *Play*, one of the characters burps idiosyncratically, saying "Personally I always preferred Lipton's" — in memory of Mrs. Frost.[4] Beckett was "made free of the kitchen regions, which is better than a million golden gasrings, and my collapses into an atmosphere of home-made jam and the Weekly Telegraph are encouraged without being solicited."[5]

His room had a vast linoleum floor with a design "like Braque seen from a great distance."[6] The size of this room and the analogy with Braque were conferred later on the room that he invented for Celia and Murphy in Brewery Road:

> The room was large and the few articles of furniture it contained were large. The bed, the gas cooker, the table and the solitary tallboy, all were very large indeed. Two massive upright unupholstered armchairs, similar to those killed under him by Balzac, made it just possible for

them to take their meals seated. . . . The vast floor area was covered
all over by a linoleum of exquisite design, a dim geometry of blue,
grey and brown that delighted Murphy because it called Braque to his
mind.[7]

The Frosts slept in the room next door to him. Directly above him lived
for a time two more lodgers. They were a young married couple; he was a waiter
at the Cadogan Hotel, and she a maid to an old lady in Hans Crescent. Beckett
used to give this couple the stamps on his letters from Ireland and France.[8] As
he lay awake at night, fearful of his panicking, arrhythmic heart, he could hear
them making noisy love. The Frosts had a grown-up son, also called Fred, about
whom he wrote: "Fred Frost Jr. dentist's mechanic and person of incredible
handiness about a house, installing baths and closets without the least aid or
assistance, has just fixed up a reading lamp for me with which I can visit the
remotest corners of the room."[9]

During the cold winter of 1934–35, Beckett appreciated more than anything else the coal fire in his room at the Frosts'. Sometimes it froze so hard
that he did not want to set foot out of doors in the evenings. MacGreevy, whom
he missed badly, was in Tarbert with his mother and sister. And in his absence
Beckett saw Hester Dowden far less frequently. Frank went back with him
briefly to London from Dublin in January 1935; with a group of business friends,
they went to Daly's Theatre to see the popular play *Young England*, which
Beckett felt constrained to sit through: "an exasperation beyond all description,"
he wrote.[10] Then James Guilford, a good friend of his brother, came over for a
week in February. But, although he and Guilford knew each other from Foxrock
days, they had never been good friends; Beckett treated the visit as an unavoidable intrusion. George Reavey paid fleeting visits from Paris to set up a branch
of his literary agency, The European Literary Bureau, and to develop his contacts in London both as an agent and as a publisher.[11]

Beckett divided his time between his three consultations a week with Bion,
visiting art galleries, walking, reading, and going to concerts. Although he felt
some improvement after more than a year with his therapist, he wrote resignedly: "I see no reason why it should ever come to an end. The old heart pounces
now and then, as though to console me for the intolerable symptoms of an
improvement."[12] There were odd diversions to spark his interest. Seamus O'Sullivan's wife, Estella Solomons, for example, sent him an invitation to a joint
exhibition with Louise Jacobs and Mary Duncan, "Landscapes from Donegal
and Yorkshire," at the Arlington Gallery at 22 Old Bond Street. But it was
Louise Jacobs's paintings, not Stella Solomons's, that appealed to Beckett.
O'Sullivan was over in England for the exhibition and talked vaguely of publishing Beckett's four-line poem "Da Tagte Es" in a coming issue of the *Dublin
Magazine*.

On a day-to-day basis, however, Beckett often felt thoroughly miserable and
sorry for himself: "Of myself there is nothing to tell, except that the feeling of
relief and vitality of the first week after my return has quite gone, and now I feel

beyond description worthless, sordid and incapacitated." [13] And yet, although his misery cannot be doubted, again it would be too easy to take his complaints and lamentations entirely at face value—MacGreevy was, after all, his sounding board, the person to whom he could complain knowing that he would receive ready sympathy and understanding in return—and only too easy to ignore the real intellectual work that he was doing. New words excited his interest; books fascinated him; he was gripped by philosophical ideas and inspired by music and art. People seemed in no way essential in this ferment of intellectual and aesthetic activity. He felt his solitude, sometimes very acutely. But it was a solitude that he also cultivated, obscurely aware that something was happening within him, as, eclectically, he accumulated knowledge.

2

IN APRIL 1935, he returned to Dublin for a short spring break from therapy. Again "the first few days were difficult, the night sweats worse than for a long time and periods of speechless bad temper that were difficult to negotiate." [14] It was a sad, painful reimmersion into the world of his own family. Frank seemed lost and at loose ends outside his work. Boss Sinclair was a patient now, first in the Adelaide Hospital, having been diagnosed as suffering from tuberculosis, then in the Newcastle Sanatorium. When his uncle was sent there to benefit from the country air, Beckett accompanied Cissie and Deirdre to see him. The same morning he took his aunt to the Academy, where she burst into tears as she talked of Peggy. Beckett felt a huge swell of sympathy for a favorite relative, whom life was treating so cruelly.

He wrote to Tom MacGreevy, "I have spent most of the time at home, playing the piano, cutting the grass and taking the dogs walking. It is a more pleasant form of stupefaction than any to be had near Dublin. I hope to borrow or hire a car and drive Mother to the various cemeteries." [15] For, out of affection and as some kind of compensation for his fourteen months of absence, he tried to spend a lot of time with her, driving her to Greystones to plant heather on his father's grave in a bitterly cold northeast wind. But the visits to the grave on the little hillside overlooking the village harbor and the bay upset him terribly, as he recalled the days when he and his brother used to swim there with their father.

The long walks to Three Rock and Two Rock, then back by Glencullen, alone except for the two Kerry Blue dogs, brought back more poignant memories. In January, on an earlier visit home and a similar walk, he had stood at the top of Two Rock and

> could hear a solitary accordeon played down near the Glencullen
> river, miles away. I thought of a Xmas morning not long ago standing
> at the back of the Scalp with Father, hearing singing coming from the
> Glencullen Chapel. Then the white air you can see so far through,

giving the outlines without the stippling. Then the pink and green sunset that I never find anywhere else and when it was quite dark a little pub to rest and drink gin in.[16]

To love a scene so much and yet to miss someone so essential to it was doubly heartbreaking.

Some of his purest pleasure came from art, from visits to the National Gallery and Charlemont House, but also from calls on Jack Yeats. He wrote: "Yesterday afternoon I had Jack Yeats all to myself, not even Madame, from 3 to past 6, and saw some quite new pictures. He seems to be having a green period. The one in the Academy—*Low Tide*—bought by Meredith for the Municipal is overwhelming."[17] But these occasional delights could not compensate for the increasingly tense atmosphere at Cooldrinagh.

After three weeks, he returned to London for fear things would blow up badly between his mother and himself if he stayed on much longer. Yet in July, less than two months later, he had an outbreak of conscience and invited her to spend a three-week holiday with him in England.[18] He hired a little car to drive her on what he called a "lightning tour" of pretty market towns and cathedral cities: St. Albans (to see the cathedral with its "superb" central tower and "fine fragments of fresco on the nave columns, especially a dark crucifixion"),[19] Canterbury, Warwick, Winchester, Bath, Wells, Bristol, Gloucester, Tewkesbury, Stratford, and Lichfield.[20] In the West Country, they stayed overnight in Porlock Weir, then in Wells, spending the morning admiring the cathedral with its "extraordinary frieze of [the] West front."[21] From there, they drove up the little winding road to the gorge and caves of nearby Wookey Hole. They went through the only three chambers of the caves then open to the public; these caves had been illuminated by electricity in 1929.

They spent almost a week in North Devon, staying at the comfortable Glen Lyn Hotel in Lynmouth,[22] opposite the cottage where, in 1812, Shelley is said to have written seditious pamphlets, put them into bottles, and launched them into the sea.[23] The hotel was their base for excursions along the coast and through Exmoor: to Ilfracombe and Clovelly, and into the *Lorna Doone* valley. Beckett found driving in the hilly country around Lynton and Porlock challenging with its "demented gradients, 1 in 4 a commonplace"; he worried, as he tackled the steepest, Porlock Hill, that the rented car would break down under the strain.[24] Over dinner in the hotel, the question of how his psychotherapy was going inevitably came up, his mother asking him what he was planning to do with his future once his stay in London was over. The conversation revolved in the usual tight circles. For once, though, it did not lead to acrimonious quarrels.

His mother was in a calm, mellow mood. She watched him devotedly as he swam off the North Devon beaches and listened patiently to the parallels that he drew between the places they were visiting and famous books. To please her, he took her to places with very well known literary connections: Oare, where, from the single light window of the tiny parish church, Carver Doone by tradition shot at Lorna in *Lorna Doone* as she was about to marry John Ridd; Bideford, where Charles Kingsley had written part of *Westward Ho!*; and the bathing place of Westward Ho! itself (named after the book) on Bideford Bay, where Rudyard Kipling had been educated at the United Services College and had drawn on his school experiences in *Stalky and Co.*[25]

Of more interest to Beckett himself were places connected with Jane Austen, Shakespeare, and Dr. Johnson. They visited Winchester, where Jane Austen lived and died; she is buried in the north aisle of the cathedral's nave. And they went on to Bath, where "the divine Jane" had lived first at 1 The Paragon, then at 4 Sydney Terrace for several years following her father's retirement. Beckett had been reading *Sense and Sensibility* in February (feeling that Austen had "much to teach him"),[26] and it was fascinating for him to visit Bath's Pump Rooms and Assembly Rooms, where scenes from *Persuasion* and *Northanger Abbey* took place. On the other hand, he found Stratford-on-Avon "unspeakable, everything His Nibs up to the vespasienne universelle [public lavatory]."[27]

Dr. Johnson was especially important to him. So he reserved his pilgrimage to Lichfield, Johnson's birthplace, for when, having seen his mother safely onto the train at Rugby to return home with her brother and niece, he could savor it alone. Many years later, this visit was to stay sharply etched in his mind. Although, typically, he did not sign the visitors' book at Dr. Johnson's house, his pilgrimage to Lichfield fostered his devotion to the "Great Cham" and inspired him to think of writing a play about Dr. Johnson and Mrs. Thrale.[28]

He returned to London at the end of July 1935 to welcome friends passing through: Seán O'Sullivan, Denis Devlin, Brian Coffey, and Nuala Costello. He wrote regularly to his mother and occasionally to Cissie, Boss, and Morris Sinclair; he sent copies of the *Times Literary Supplement* and the *Telegraph* to Tom MacGreevy and renewed his library books for him.[29] He went to the cinema and worked hard revising his poems. But the intellectual ferment that he had been experiencing for the past few years was about to boil over into a phase of intense, deeply creative work. Beckett saw the "boiling over" image in terms of threat and panic: "I have as little to write as to say, or can write as little as say the immensity. As though the brain were full of milk that the least act of interested thinking brought to the boil. Then you can do nothing with it, only snatch away the pan in a hurry. You know the milk boiling over panic."[30] Yet, ironically, it was as he was writing in this fearful vein that the ferment was finding its own outlet. And, in the event, a more appropriate metaphor would be not that of a saucepan on a flame but of a volcano erupting.

3

"I AM HERE A YEAR Tuesday, so Mrs. Frost informs me, and the 'never again a year like the last' as fervent and absurd as ever," he wrote at the end of August.[31] The manuscript of "Sasha Murphy," as his new novel was first entitled, was actually begun at 34 Gertrude Street on August 20, 1935.[32] It progressed slowly in September but, as Fred Frost's reading lamp was put to regular late-night use, it gained pace throughout the autumn and winter.[33] Beckett threw himself obsessionally into his book, at the expense of almost everything else. "I have not been to a gallery for weeks," he wrote in late September. "Preoccupation with the writing sucks all the attention I have out of me. If one could even look forward to going to bed!"[34] In the new book, he drew in the most intensive way on his reading, on his recent experiences in London, and on his intimate knowledge of Dublin.[35]

During the day, he trudged for hours on end around the streets and parks. He walked briskly — partly, he told his cousin, because he wanted to tire himself out so that he would sleep; partly because the regularity of the movement acted as a kind of anesthetic, easing his troubles.[36] He got to know the area down by the Embankment in West Brompton and Chelsea, where he lived, particularly well and used to cross the Thames by Battersea Bridge or the Albert Bridge to circle nearby Battersea Park with its subtropical garden and boating lake. But he could cover as much as twenty miles in a day and knew the more distant Hyde Park and Kensington Gardens like the back of his hand. If his habits two years later in Germany are anything to judge by, as he walked around he would have jotted down notes on things that might be of use in his future writing: the names of streets or local businesses and factories that appealed to him for the humorous associations of their signs (the Perseverance and Temperance Yards, the Vis Vitae Bread Co., and the Marx Cork Bath Mat Manufactory all appear in *Murphy*[37]); details of the entrances to Hyde Park, its walks, and the statues of Queen Victoria, G. F. Watts's statue *Physical Energy*, and Jacob Epstein's stone Rima.[38]

Beckett made extensive use in *Murphy* of his knowledge of London. As any street map reveals, the London episodes focus on three distinct areas of the city, together with one farther afield, in Beckenham. A prostitute, Celia, first notices a motionless figure, who turns out to be Murphy; she soon embarks on a love affair with him.

> She had turned out of Edith Grove into Cremorne Road, intending to refresh herself with a smell of the Reach and then return by Lot's Road, when chancing to glance to her right she saw, motionless in the mouth of Stadium Street, considering alternately the sky and a sheet of paper, a man. Murphy.[39]

All of these streets are literally around the corner from Paulton's Square, where Beckett spent the first seven months of his 1934–35 stay, and from Gertrude Street, where he lived for the next fifteen months. The waste-paper barges on the Thames, the funnel of a boat "vailing" to take Battersea Bridge, an "Eldorado hokey-pokey [ice cream] man," a Chelsea Pensioner in his scarlet tunic from the nearby Chelsea Hospital,[40] were all familiar sights to Beckett as he walked along the Embankment. But there is a Dantesque atmosphere about this setting (with some hints of Hell, Purgatory, and Paradise) as it is described in *Murphy* that lifts it above the purely local and the humdrum.[41]

The second location where Celia rents a room for Murphy and herself is "in Brewery Road between Pentonville Prison and the Metropolitan Cattle Market."[42] This was only a short walk for Beckett, up either the Caledonian Road or York Road, from the room he had occupied in 1932 on Ampton Street off the Gray's Inn Road. The situation of Celia and Murphy's room between a cattle market and a prison is not a geographical coincidence. Pens, prisons, and cages are found everywhere in the book, picking up the theme of isolation and claustration: Murphy's "medium-sized cage of north-western aspect commanding an unbroken view of medium-sized cages of south-eastern aspect";[43] the "four caged owls" of Battersea Park;[44] the padded "cells" of the insane at the "Magdalen Mental Mercyseat"; and the garret dwelling in which Murphy's life comes to an end. These recurring images help to structure a novel that functions primarily through repetition, echo, and allusion.

Missing the fields and hills around Dublin,[45] Beckett sought out London's largest expanse of green (over 630 acres) for his wanderings and made it the third main setting in *Murphy*. Like the protagonist of his novel, he became a regular visitor to the Cockpit in Hyde Park (where sheep really did graze freely at the time[46]) and strolled by the Serpentine and the Long Water. The Round Pond to the west side of Kensington Gardens was a favorite stopping-off place for both Beckett and Murphy. Key scenes in the novel owe their details to the author's frequent leisurely meanderings and careful observations in the park.

But Beckett does not use these settings as a nineteenth-century novelist like Balzac would have done. Precise topographical details do not ground his characters in an apposite world, let alone explain them away. They underline the attempted separation of the "little world" of Murphy's inner self from the "big buzzing confusion" of the outer world. The amount of detail that is offered on such real places contrasts with the deliberately inadequate information that the reader is offered about the characters in the novel — we never learn, for example, what Murphy himself actually looks like — and the studied unreliability of many elements of the narrative. Facts in *Murphy*, as one critic put it, "provide obstacles to be sidestepped, irrelevancies to be hurdled."[47] Sometimes minor mistakes, probably deliberate ones, are introduced. Yet, in what is still his most traditional novel, Beckett drew, often directly, on milieus that were familiar to him and on events that he had either experienced himself or had heard or read about. It is intriguing to see how such autobiographical material is reshaped by the twenty-nine-year-old writer to become the stuff of fiction.

One particular incident referred to in Beckett's correspondence illustrates rather well how idiosyncratically he used and reshaped real-life events in *Murphy*. It centers on a minor character called "the old boy." The real-life incident concerned "the 'old boy' of the house opposite," whom Beckett used to watch in Gertrude Street putting crusts out for the birds several times a day and who, so Beckett was informed, died of a seizure, leaving his cup standing outside on the windowsill where he had placed it only a few moments before his death.[48] In *Murphy*, Beckett constructs an entire episode around the old boy, taking his death by seizure as its starting point. But he uses the event to play with conventional narrative technique and to weave an elaborate set of circumstances around it.

Murphy returns home to find Celia spread-eagled on her face on the bed. "A shocking thing had happened" is the way chapter five ends. It is not until the beginning of chapter eight that this shocking thing is explained as the death of the old boy. Miss Carridge, another minor and picturesquely named character, who runs a boardinghouse, imagines how, crawling about on the floor with an open cutthroat razor in his hand in an attempt to find the cap of his shaving cream, the old boy "falls on his face with the razor under him, zzzeeeppp!" and cuts his throat.[49] The incident is developed into a comic pastiche of the human tendency to invent stories or to elaborate rational explanations to account for uncomfortable or unpalatable events. Beckett parodies the deductive logic of the Conan Doyle stories that he used to love when he was a boy. All of Miss Carridge's deductions — conjured up to justify an accident rather than a suicide, since the latter would reflect badly on her boardinghouse — are radically undercut by the narrator who interjects the word "Lies" after each further revelation. Many such real-life incidents are reworked in *Murphy*.[50]

Beckett himself describes one more significant incident. One late summer afternoon, he was standing by the Round Pond in Kensington Gardens, where, to his surprise, he was transfixed by the sight of

> the little shabby respectable old men you see on Saturday afternoon and Sunday, pottering about doing odd jobs in the garden, or flying kites immense distances at the Round Pond, Kensington. Yesterday there was a regular club of the latter, with a sprinkling of grandchildren, sitting in a crescent waiting for a wind. The kites lying in the grass with their long tails beautifully cared for, all assembled and ready. For they bring them in separate pieces, the sticks and tail rolled up in the canvas and a huge spool of string. Some have boats as well, but not the real enthusiasts.[51]

He observed the kite flyers closely to see how the old men went about their hobby; he saw them unfurl their kites and handle the winches, then observed how they got the kites to take off. He overcame his natural reticence to ask a total stranger what the kites were made of. "Either silk or nainsook" was the reply. "Nainsook" is a word that Beckett relishes and uses in *Murphy*. There was, he wrote in a letter,

> then great perturbation to get them off at the first breath of wind. They fly them almost out of sight, yesterday it was over the trees to the south, into an absolutely cloudless iridescent evening sky. Then when the string is run out they simply sit there watching them, chucking at the string, the way coachmen do at a reins, presumably to keep them from losing height. There seems to be no competition at all involved. Then after about an hour they wind them gently in and go home. I was really rooted to the spot yesterday, unable to go away and wondering what was keeping me. Extraordinary effect too of birds flying close

to the kites but beneath them. My next old man, or old young man, not of the big world but of the little world, must be a kite-flyer.[52]

What Beckett records here is an actual moment of inspiration: the next old man of his creative "little world" was indeed to be the kite flyer of *Murphy*, Mr. Willoughby Kelly. For, in his very next letter, describing a stormy day at the same venue, Beckett wrote: "The kites at the Round Pond yesterday were plunging and writhing all over the sky. The book closes with an old man flying his kite, if such occasion ever arise."[53] By this date, he had written only nine thousand words of "the book," which was to become *Murphy*. Yet he could already foresee how it was going to end. This scene provided him with a powerful image of freedom and release that related it in his mind to one of the most fundamental themes of the novel.

The kite-flying episode was one of three main sources of inspiration for *Murphy*. Another was the horoscope. As he was writing *Murphy*, Beckett also learned, doubtless with surprise, that the famous psychologist C. G. Jung—one of whose lectures he attended with Bion— insisted that his patients have their horoscopes cast.[54] Bion also is reputed to have taken a keen interest in his patients' horoscopes, and Beckett may have arranged to have his own drawn up at Bion's request. In a little burgundy hardback notebook, on the front cover of which he wrote "Whoroscope," Beckett noted down how such a horoscope could be related to the life of his main character, called then simply X. "H," the oracle or horoscope, provides a "corpus of motives"[55] and so works on him that it gradually acquires the authority of fatality, "no longer a guide to be consulted but a force to be obeyed."[56]

When Murphy sees the circumstances surrounding the job of medical orderly as conforming precisely to what the horoscope recommends, he leaves Celia, takes the job, and seals his fate. And the horoscope, first described as a "fake jossy's sixpenny writ to success and prosperity,"[57] leads him inexorably to his death by fire in his garret room and to Celia's return to plying her mercenary trade on the streets of London. As in the plays of Racine, which Beckett had lectured on a few years before and which he had very much in mind while he was planning the structure of his narrative,[58] something has "taken its course" and the characters are brought to a preordained ending.[59]

Beckett found his third important source of inspiration at the Bethlem Royal Hospital in Beckenham. Geoffrey Thompson started work at the hospital as a senior house physician on February 4, 1935, and Beckett managed to visit him there on a number of occasions between February and October, when he left the post.[60] According to Beckett's previous biographer, he never told his friend that he was writing a novel with a mental hospital as its setting, or even that he was writing a novel at all.[61] Nevertheless, since he was being psychoanalyzed himself at the time and had always taken a great deal of interest in illnesses, other people's as well as his own, his visits to the mental hospital added additional authenticity to this part of the novel.

"I was down at Bedlam this day week," Beckett wrote to MacGreevy, "and went round the wards for the first time, with scarcely any sense of horror, though I saw everything, from mild depression to profound dementia." [62] *Murphy* demonstrates not only that Beckett knew about the different categories and names of the mental illnesses but that he had registered very precisely how the individual patients behaved:

> Melancholics, motionless and brooding, holding their heads or bellies according to type. Paranoids, feverishly covering sheets of paper with complaints against their treatment or verbatim reports of their inner voices. A hebephrenic playing the piano intently. A hypomanic teaching slosh to a Korsakow's syndrome. An emaciated schizoid, petrified in a toppling attitude as though condemned to an eternal *tableau vivant*, his left hand rhetorically extended holding a cigarette half smoked and out, his right, quivering and rigid, pointing upward. [63]

Three decades later, Beckett could still remember very clearly "standing five or six feet away from a schizophrenic who was 'like a hunk of meat. There was no one there. He was absent.' " [64]

A myth has grown up that Beckett himself actually worked for some time as a male nurse at the mental hospital. The blurb on the cover of the English paperback edition of *Murphy* states: "A very Irish novel both in its background and conception, it draws heavily on the author's experiences in Dublin and London as a young man, especially on his time spent as a male nurse in a mental hospital." [65] This simply never happened. Geoffrey Thompson was Beckett's main source of information on hospital routines and what actually happened there, as distinct from what was supposed to happen. But a comment in Beckett's personal notebook, where he writes down a detailed account of the duties of a male nurse, shows that he also quizzed one of the nurses on the ward: his information was, he writes, "endorsed by nurse." So detailed information in his notebook relating to the night rounds (the judas hole through which the patients are checked; the "tab," information that is given to a nurse so that he or she can ensure that a patient does not commit suicide; the power of the night nurse; and the various euphemisms for the padded cell) is incorporated almost verbatim into *Murphy*. [66]

"The Bethlem Royal Hospital served only as a point of departure for Beckett's story, and . . . his description of the [Magdalen Mental] Mercyseat and of its buildings is purely fictitious," wrote one critic of the novel. [67] But did it? And was it? On closer investigation, it emerges that much of Beckett's description of the Mercyseat corresponds to the actual location, layout, and appearance of the real Bethlem Royal Hospital. In this respect, Beckett follows descriptive techniques of place that he had adopted in his earlier books. And again he either made detailed notes or remembered clearly what he saw. One part of the real hospital, for example, really does lie in Surrey, while one ward is situated in Kent, although Beckett exaggerates the nearness for comic effect: "In order to die in the one sheriffalty rather than in the other some patients had merely to move up, or be moved up, a little in the bed." [68] Although he made up the name of "Skinner's House," where Murphy toiled on the "male side, first floor," the building on which Skinner's was based was very much as Beckett describes it:

> Skinner's was a long, grey, two-storied building, dilated at both ends like a double obelisk. The females were thrown all together to the west, the males to the east, and on the strength of this it was called a mixed house, as distinct from the two convalescent houses, which very properly were not mixed. Similarly, some public baths are called mixed where the bathing is not.[69]

The "bijou edifice of mellow brick with a forecourt of lawn and flowers, its façade a profusion of traveller's joy and self-clinging ampelopsis, set in a bay of clipped yews"[70] turns out with deliberate irony to be the mortuary. While the description is based on a building that is still used by the hospital as a mortuary, it has been aptly embroidered upon by the writer's imagination: The "profusion of traveller's joy" has Hamlet's "bourne from which no traveller returns" in mind, and the "self-clinging" is a subtle touch! The archivist and curator of the Bethlem Royal Hospital writes: "It *does* still have a yew hedge in front of it, but I don't think it can ever have had grass and flowers, and although it could be said to be set in a bay, it is rhododendron not yew around the back and sides."[71] But even here Beckett may be "conflating the mortuary and gate lodge which is at the corner of the same road and is extremely 'bungaloid' "[72] in appearance, as the building is described when his friends come to inspect Murphy's charred body.

The medical staff at the Magdalen Mental Mercyseat have eccentric names that are characteristic of Beckett's enjoyment of wordplay. The name of the medical superintendent, "Dr. Angus Killiecrankie, the Outer Hebridean R.M.S.,"[73] speaks for itself; *krank* is the German word for "ill," so he is Dr. "Kill the Ill." And the intimidating head male nurse and male "sister" are twins known by the names of Bim and Bom, Russian clowns.[74] Both the senior physician and the assistant physician at the Bethlem Royal, whom Beckett probably met, were Scots, David Robertson and John Hamilton.[75]

A small postscript can be added to these key sources of inspiration. Beckett was an ardent chessplayer and would play with anyone good enough to give him a game, whether a relative, friend, or total stranger. Whenever Geoffrey Thompson was free, they tried to fit in a keenly fought game, and they certainly played during Beckett's visits to the Bethlem Royal Hospital. But the game that Murphy plays against Mr. Endon in the novel ("Murphy for Mr Endon was no more than chess") is one especially contrived to fit in with its themes.[76] It is an exercise in total noncommunication, with Mr. Endon playing Black. The mental patient fails to acknowledge Murphy's existence and finishes with his own pieces ranged symmetrically very much as he began. Murphy resigns unnecessarily after the forty-third move.[77] The experience of playing against this mentally unseeing opponent leads Murphy himself into a transient state of positive peace, "when the somethings give way, or perhaps simply add up, to the Nothing, than which in the guffaw of the Abderite [That is, Democritus, who was born in Abdera] naught is more real."[78] Beckett's love of chess and his interest in Democritus and the pre-Socratic philosophers merge here into a bizarre amalgam.

4

BECKETT HAD LEARNED a bitter lesson from the publication of *More Pricks Than Kicks*. He had discovered that people become extremely upset when they recognize either themselves or those dear to them in characters who are cruelly or unsympathetically portrayed. And he had found that he cared far more than he ever believed he would. His dismay at the pain that he had caused the Sinclairs undoubtedly encouraged him to move further away from depicting recognizable real-life characters in *Murphy*.

One solution was to create characters who, with the exception of Murphy, have only enough reality to exist as "puppets" (to employ the narrator's own term) and who are, in the words of one critic, "all painted surface and mechanical gesture."[79] "All the puppets in this book whinge sooner or later, except Murphy, who is not a puppet," comments the narrator.[80] Another solution was to borrow characteristics from people known to Beckett personally, allow the imagination to transform them, and then add additional elements from his reading of literature, philosophy, and myth.

Murphy's former guru, Neary, for example, has much of the "Oriental sage" about him. His name is an anagram of the verb "yearn." But it also echoes Neary's Bar in Dublin, where the eccentric, hard-drinking, tough-talking Professor H. S. Macran, Hegelian scholar and Professor of Moral Philosophy at Trinity College, used to hold court. (" 'Perhaps you hadn't heard,' said Wylie, 'Hegel arrested his development.' "[81]) Macran, something of a legend in Dublin academic circles, was a familiar of Beckett's own teachers, Walter Starkie (who wrote about him), Rudmose-Brown, and A. A. Luce.[82] But, as he is being created, Neary absorbs other characteristics and ideas: from Gestalt psychology, for example, or from Thomas Dekker's comedy *Old Fortunatus*, which Beckett read just before he wrote *Murphy*.[83] Neary cannot, then, be equated totally with Macran any more than Mr. Willoughby Kelly can be equated totally with James Joyce because of "the yachting cap, the endless work in progress (in bed), the Icaran kite-flying and the attempt to join heaven and earth."[84]

Celia Kelly is both whore and muse, sky (Latin *caelum*) and doubtful aspiration (Beckett punning on "Celia" and French *s'il y a*, "if there is").[85] He borrows widely here again: Celia's "green eyes" are from Peggy Sinclair, her vital statistics from the Venus de Milo, her status as a reformed whore from another Thomas Dekker play,[86] and, after Murphy's death, her stature as ambivalently grieving Madonna from a "Pietà" painting.[87] And what of Miss Counihan? It has been claimed that she echoes the legendary Yeats figure Cathleen ni Houlihan, chased around the circumference of a circle in a plot resembling

Racine's *Andromaque*, in which one character loves another, who loves another, who loves another.

Two of the minor characters owe much more to real life, however, than to literature or myth: the medium, Miss Rosie Dew, and the hospital orderly, Austin Ticklepenny. With her dog, Nelly, and her spirit control, "a panpygop-totic Manichee of the fourth century, Lena by name, severe of deportment and pallid of feature, who had entertained Jerome on his way through Rome from Calchis to Bethlehem,"[88] Miss Rosie Dew has her origins in Tom MacGreevy's landlady, Hester Dowden. Hester was regularly consulted as a medium in her own home, where she often used a Ouija board.[89] By the time Beckett got to know her, she had been communicating for fourteen years with a spirit control from beyond the grave, a certain Johannes, a Greek born in 200 B.C., who had spent much of his life in Alexandria.[90] In his novel, Beckett changes the woman's physical characteristics, blessing her with Duck's Disease, a colloquial expression for someone who is short-legged, for which Beckett coined the word "Pan-pygoptosis," meaning "all bottom visible disease"! (Wittily, the medium's spirit control is made to suffer from the same disease as the medium herself.) He also cunningly transforms Hester's snuffly little Pekingese into an equally small, low-slung dachshund or "sausage dog," and has it consume all but one of Murphy's biscuits in the park.

Hester Dowden had clients among the aristocracy. Probably for this reason, Beckett refers to Rosie Dew as "by appointment to Lord Gall of Wormwood" (using a name borrowed from his rejected story "Echo's Bones").[91] In an attempt to contact his father in the spirit world, Lord Gall sends the medium one of his father's boots and a pair of his socks. Beckett's account of Miss Dew's methods as a medium closely resembles what he had either witnessed or overheard at 15 Cheyne Walk Gardens. And his own attitude emerges in the narrator's combination of amused and slightly irritated skepticism:

> Miss Dew was no ordinary hack medium, her methods were original and eclectic. She might not be able to bring down torrents of ecto-plasm or multiply anemones from her armpits, but left undisturbed with one hand on a disaffected boot, the other on the [Ouija] board, Nelly in her lap and Lena coming through, she could make the dead softsoap the quick in seven languages.[92]

But the most blatant example of a character borrowed from life is Austin Ticklepenny, the "puppet" who hands over his job as a medical orderly in the mental hospital to Murphy. There are numerous parallels between this "distinguished indigent drunken Irish bard," Ticklepenny, and the Irish poet Austin Clarke:[93] Ticklepenny is known in the novel, for instance, by the name of Austin;[94] at one point, he says to Murphy quite gratuitously, "no offence meant, you had a great look of Clarke there a minute ago" — the narrator adding by way of explanation that "Clarke had been for three weeks in a catatonic stupor."[95] Clarke was also reputed to be a heavy drinker, like Ticklepenny. Beckett had drunk with him several times in 1931 in bars off Grafton Street and was also aware that Clarke had spent some time in St. Patrick's Hospital, suffering from a complete nervous breakdown.

The closest identification of the two figures, however, lies in Beckett's uncharitable remarks about Ticklepenny's verse: "as free as a canary in the fifth foot (a cruel sacrifice for Ticklepenny hiccupped in end rimes) and at the caesura as hard and fast as his own divine flatus and otherwise bulging with as many minor beauties from the gaelic prosodoturfy as could be sucked out of a mug of Beamish's porter."[96] This closely resembles what, under his pseudonym, Beckett had written of Clarke only a few months before, in "Recent Irish Poetry." And it echoes even more directly what Clarke himself had written about cross rhymes and vowel rhyming in a note in his *Pilgrimage and Other Poems* (1929).[97]

The Irish poet was in Beckett's mind just before he wrote *Murphy* for a number of different reasons.[98] Almost a clinching factor in the identification was a letter that Beckett wrote to Arland Ussher after *Murphy* was published, saying "Con [Leventhal] sends a message to the effect that Austin Clarke is going through the book with his pubic comb for libellous reference to himself."[99] This suggests that Beckett knows that such references lurk in the novel like lice waiting to be discovered. But Ticklepenny is made into a fawning, irritating, rather unpleasant character, who is also homosexual. This would have appeared in 1936, as James Mays points out, as a gratuitous slur on someone who, though his first marriage, which lasted less than two weeks, was reputed not to have been consummated,[100] was not known to be homosexual.

Why Beckett should have thought of insulting Clarke in this way is not easy to explain. It is impossible to believe that he did not know what he was doing. He had no serious old scores to settle, unless there were some unknown personal slights. He was probably simply unable to resist poking fun at Clarke and his views on versification. But this is no justification for so unkind a portrait. And it may be that, having decided for reasons of the plot to make Ticklepenny into the medical orderly and to link him with Clarke, he may have thought that by developing the homosexual side of the character's role he would lead the reader away from identifying Ticklepenny too closely with the Irish poet.

Basing the character on Clarke could have been a very expensive mistake. The portrayal was thought sufficiently identifiable at the time for Oliver St. John Gogarty to urge Clarke to bring an action against Beckett for libel when *Murphy* was eventually published.[101] According to James Mays, Arland Ussher took it for granted that everyone in Dublin literary circles recognized Clarke as the target of Beckett's satire. Having merely glanced (he claimed) through the book, Clarke decided against suing Beckett because, he said, few people would ever manage to read all the way through the novel.[102] A libel case probably seemed much too risky a venture. The "catatonic stupor" remark and the homosexual slur would certainly have made such a case embarrassing and unpleasant for Clarke to pursue. It is difficult, however, to disagree with Mays that Beckett's joke was in rather poor taste. And we should not be too surprised. Privately, the young Beckett could be very cruel and scathing in his comments about writers whom he held in low esteem.

What, finally, are we to make of Murphy himself, the only character who, the narrator claims, is not a puppet? He undoubtedly reflects many of Beckett's own attitudes and interests (particularly the philosophical ones), without, of course, being Beckett. On the most humdrum of levels, landladies, pubs, cafés, and parks play an important part in his life, as they did in Beckett's own at the time. Murphy's sufferings with a heart that races wildly out of control offer a graphic reflection of the author's own medical symptoms. There is no better description of his symptoms in his letters than in this novel:

> For Murphy had such an irrational heart that no physician could get to the root of it. Inspected, palpated, auscultated, percussed, radiographed and cardiographed, it was all that a heart should be. Buttoned up and left to perform, it was like Petrushka in his box. One moment in such labour that it seemed on the point of seizing, the next in such ebullition that it seemed on the point of bursting.[103]

When Celia, trying to wheedle Murphy into seeking gainful employment, is said to be attempting "to make a man of him," she quotes the exact words that Beckett's mother used to him. And Murphy's reply vents the frustration and tension that had built up between Beckett and May:

> "Ever since June," he said, "it has been job, job, job, nothing but job. Nothing happens in the world but is specially designed to exalt me into a job. I say a job is the end of us both, or at least of me. You say no, but the beginning. I am to be a new man, you are to be a new woman, the entire sublunary excrement will turn to civet, there will be more joy in heaven over Murphy finding a job than over the billions of leatherbums that never had anything else."[104]

But, above all, Murphy expresses in a radical and sharply focused way that impulse toward self-immersion, solitude, and inner peace the consequences of which Beckett was attempting to resolve in his personal life through psychoanalysis.

That Beckett thought long and hard about his own relationship to Murphy is revealed in his answer to a letter from MacGreevy in which his friend had clearly expressed reservations about the wisdom of allowing the novel to run on with the lengthy scene in the mortuary and then with Celia and Mr. Kelly after Murphy's death. He deliberately chose, he replied, to

> keep the death subdued and go on as coolly and finish as briefly as possible. I chose this because it seemed to me to consist better with the treatment of Murphy throughout, with the mixture of compassion, patience, mockery and "tat twam asi" [Schopenhauer's "thus thou art"] that I seemed to have directed on him throughout, with the sympathy going so far and no further (then losing patience) as in the

short statement of his mind's fantasy on itself. There seemed to me always the risk of taking him too seriously and separating him too sharply from the others. As it is I do not think the mistake (Aliosha [of *The Brothers Karamazov*] mistake) has been altogether avoided.[105]

His concern appears to be that he might still be too close to Murphy, and that Murphy is certainly too close to him.

5

MURPHY evolved as much out of Beckett's reading as of his experience of people and places. He read widely: in the British Museum Reading Room again, in the Chelsea Library, and in his own room at the Frosts' with books borrowed from MacGreevy, Thompson, and Hester Dowden. Sometimes he took copious notes. And he always continued his habit of jotting down the occasional word or phrase that impressed him in a notebook.

Some of his reading was specifically aimed at improving his techniques as a novelist. We have seen that he read Jane Austen early in 1935, feeling that she had "much to teach" him,[106] and he reread Stendhal's *Armance* in April. Now he picked up his earlier reading of eighteenth-century literature: the poets Pope and Gay — and, with self-improvement in mind, above all the novelists: Fielding, Smollett, and Swift.[107] He read Fielding's *Amelia* in May,[108] having earlier spent some time reading *Tom Jones* and admiring *Joseph Andrews*. He took a concentrated look at the picaresque novel, reading Lesage's *Gil Blas* and Cervantes's *Don Quixote* with the intention, as this fascinating passage from his notebook shows, of deliberately reversing them in *Murphy*:

> The picaresque inverted. *Gil Blas* is realised by his encounters and receives his mission from them. X [the character who evolves into Murphy] is realised by his failure to encounter and his progress depends on this failure being sustained. If he made terms with people the story would come to an end. He seems to and it seems to. Then H. [the Horoscope] to the rescue.[109]

Some books came alive for him in a special way — Rousseau's *Confessions* and the *Rêveries du promeneur solitaire*, for instance;[110] a great passage in Thomas Mann's *Buddenbrooks* provided him with a basis for quietism.[111] Burton's *Anatomy of Melancholy* was another book he much admired. On the other hand, he reacted negatively to some novels, like Balzac's *La Cousine Bette*: "The bathos of style and thought is so enormous that I wonder is he writing seriously or in parody. And yet I go on reading it."[112] He concluded that Balzac was "a Stock Exchange Hugo."[113] He also read some surprising books: George Peabody Gooch's *Germany and the French Revolution* and Albert Sorel's *La Révolution française*, for instance.[114]

His extensive reading is reflected in casually erudite allusions in *Murphy*:

Sephestia's refrain from Robert Greene's *Menaphon*, "Weep not, my wanton, smile upon my knee, / When thou art old there's grief enough for thee,"[115] for instance, and George Peele's "Love is a prick, love is a sting / Love is a pretty pretty thing"[116] are in both *Murphy* and Beckett's typed notes on the "University Wits." These notes show that Beckett read some little-known plays, giving himself a crash course in Elizabethan and Jacobean drama (Nashe, Peele, Dekker, Marlowe, Marston, and Ford), doubtless to compensate for gaps in his English studies at Trinity College.[117] But he relished Ben Jonson's two much better known *Every Man* plays, *The Poetaster* and *Volpone*, and hoped to see *The Alchemist* at the Embassy Theatre, after reading it in advance.[118]

Some of the knowledge of myth and antiquity that he acquired around this time was introduced, rather self-consciously, into *Murphy*. "Was Ixion under any contract to keep his wheel in nice running order?" the narrator asks. "Had any provision been made for Tantalus to eat salt?"[119] And there are notes on both Ixion and Tantalus in Beckett's notebooks. The biblical story of Dives and Lazarus from Luke 16 is also written out in his notes (quoting the story in both French and Italian!) in which Father Abraham speaks up for the beggar Lazarus. This story is referred to on two separate occasions in *Murphy*.[120]

Several books were crucial to Murphy's evolution. In July 1935, just before going on holiday with his mother, Beckett bought the Génie de France edition of Rabelais's *Pantagruel*, which he read on his return to London. He took twenty-three pages of notes on it, writing out quotations ranging from large sections to single phrases, as well as paraphrasing some of its more genial, uproarious moments. Even though he "got stuck in the Rabelais again, on the voyage round the world to consult the oracle of the Boule,"[121] his reading of the curate of Meudon coincided precisely with the composition of the first ten thousand words of *Murphy*. The account "Of the original and antiquity of the great Pantagruel" in Rabelais's second book may have suggested to Beckett the idea of situating Murphy and his actions in terms of the signs of the zodiac and the movements of the heavenly bodies. But, more generally, the blend of erudition and humor, wordplay and coinages in Beckett's novel, together with the pleasure in the sound of difficult or archaic words, puts one very much in mind of Rabelais. On *Murphy*'s publication in 1938, Herbert Read spotted this immediately, writing to T. M. Ragg at Routledge that the book "is in the true Rabelaisian vein — that is to say, it is the rare and right combination of learning and license."[122] But his perception has been almost totally ignored ever since.

Chapter six of *Murphy* has as its epigraph a quotation from the fifth part of Spinoza's *Ethics*: "Amor intellectualis quo Murphy se ipsum amat" ("The intellectual love with which Murphy loves himself") in which Beckett has merely substituted the name of Murphy for that of God. In this chapter, Murphy pictures his mind as a closed system, "a large hollow sphere, hermetically closed to the universe without."[123] He feels himself to be split in two, a body and a mind, and cannot comprehend how the two can communicate. He then divides the mind into three separate zones of being: light, half-light, and dark. This important chapter — in fact, the whole section of the book relating to Murphy's retreat into the dark zone of his mind—arises from the convergence of Beckett's readings in psychology, psychoanalysis, and philosophy.

During the October 1935 lecture that Beckett attended with Bion, Jung recalled a diagram that he had used earlier, "showing the different spheres of the mind and the dark centre of the unconscious in the middle. The closer you approach that centre, the more you experience what Janet calls an *abaissement du niveau mental:* your conscious autonomy begins to disappear, and you get more and more under the fascination of unconscious contents." [124] A page of Beckett's own psychological notes sets out and defines the "Id, Ego and Superego" and contains a little sketch of the "perceptual-conscious," the "preconscious," and the "unconscious" in their relations with the id, ego, and superego."

It is not that Beckett adopts either a Jungian or a Freudian model in his account of the topography of Murphy's mind. Instead, his model is probably borrowed from his parallel philosophical reading. But it is doubtful whether he would ever have made Murphy's descent into the dark zone, "more and more in the dark, in the will-lessness," [125] as crucial to his narrative as he did without the insights that he had gleaned from his psychological reading and from his own descent into the depths of the psyche with Bion. Even Murphy's dependence on the horoscope can be seen as an external substitute for Adler's inner "life plan" of the neurotic. And the creation of the mental patient Mr. Endon owes as much to Beckett's readings about the unconscious as it did to the patient whom he saw in the mental hospital where Geoffrey Thompson was working.

Beckett had been working on philosophy intermittently ever since his Ecole Normale days. He took a great interest in the pre-Socratic philosophers (and particularly in Democritus, for Murphy in his zone of darkness is portrayed as seeking to become a Democritean "mote in its absolute freedom"),[126] and in the problem of the separation of mind and body which, in the writings of Malebranche and Occasionalists like Arnold Geulincx, can be brought together only by God.

But, as the epigraph to chapter six suggests, Beckett had also been grappling with Spinoza. During the summer of 1936, in Dublin, Beckett met the poet and scholar Brian Coffey, who "talked attractively of Spinoza." When Beckett confessed of Spinoza's *Ethics* that he "had tried it in vain in English," Coffey lent him Léon Brunschvicg's *Spinoza et ses contemporains* ("Spinoza and His Contemporaries") and the French translation of the *Ethics* in the Classiques Garnier series, with the facing Latin "which I have had time only for enough to give me a glimpse of Spinoza as a solution and a salvation (impossible in English translations)." [127]

One revelation occurred to Beckett as he wrote *Murphy.* In mid-January, following his return to Dublin, he wrote about connections that he saw between his novel and the Belgian Occasionalist philosopher Geulincx:

I shall have to go into TCD after Geulincx, as he does not exist in National Library. I suddenly see that *Murphy* is [a] break down between his: *Ubi nihil vales*[,] *ibi* [*etiam*] *nihil velis* (position) ["Where you are worth nothing, you will wish for nothing"] and Malraux's *Il est difficile à celui qui vit hors du monde de ne pas rechercher les siens* (negation). ["It is hard for someone who lives outside society not to seek out his own"].[128]

He was not discovering Geulincx for the first time. Since getting to know Beaufret at the Ecole Normale, he had already read quite a lot about Descartes and the late Cartesians, of whom Geulincx was one. But it was the first time that he had read the original of Geulincx's *Ethics*. And he read it in the original Latin, taking detailed notes in Latin as well. These notes — more than fifty pages of single-spaced typescript — still exist. Even though he did not finish the book, they show a remarkably determined piece of work. And Geulincx's vision fascinated Beckett.

I have been reading Geulincx in T.C.D., without knowing why exactly. Perhaps because the text is so hard to come by. But that is rationalisation and my instinct is right and the work worth doing, because of its saturation in the conviction that the *sub specie aeternitatis* [from the perspective of eternity] vision is the only excuse for remaining alive.[129]

In future, he was to refer scholars to Geulincx's statement about worth and will as being one of the keys to an understanding of *Murphy*.

6

THERE WERE SEVERAL PERIODS during the first few months of writing *Murphy* when Beckett found himself with writer's block or when events interrupted his flow. On the first of November 1935, for example, Geoffrey Thompson and his fiancée, Ursula Stenhouse, called for Beckett in a hired car to drive down to Dorset, where he was to act as best man at their wedding in West Lulworth. He had agreed to be Geoffrey's witness when he thought that the wedding was to take place in a registry office, and now he dreaded "lording the hat," as he put it, at a more onerous and far more social church wedding.[130] But he could not let down a friend of such long standing, and one who had been particularly good to him of late. So he gritted his teeth and made the best of it.

The journey took them nearly four hours. Beckett had forgotten to bring an overcoat with him and sat shivering stoically in the backseat of a freezing cold car.[131] He stayed overnight with Geoffrey at a local hotel. And, that evening in the bar, he met some of Geoffrey's family, who had come over from Ireland for the wedding. It was a convivial night. The next morning, when Beckett escorted the bridegroom to the little village church, gold wedding ring safely ensconced in his pocket, he was relieved to discover that the wedding party was quite small, with only a few more on the bride's side of the church than on the groom's. After the service, they all walked the short distance from the church to Ursula's parents' home for a small reception, Beckett smiling as he overheard Geoffrey saying to his bride that "the fighting *Téméraire* has now been towed to its last berth," alluding to Turner's painting in the National Gallery of the proud fighting ship being towed to its moorings by a tug to be broken up.[132] At the reception, Beckett proposed a toast but, characteristically, made no speech. On their return to London, he was relieved that it was all over. He hated the feeling of being on show at such social occasions as these.

7

SINCE BECKETT HAD TRIED placing his collected poems with a number of London publishers three years before, he had written a number of new poems and reworked several of those written earlier, sometimes quite radically. Then, early in 1934, his friend George Reavey, who was living in Paris, asked Beckett if he could publish a small collection of his poems in a series of poetry books under the imprint of his new publishing house, a miniature cottage industry called grandly Europa Press. The press operated from "a small room just above a Russian bookstore at 13 rue Bonaparte."[133] Having by then given up all hopes of securing more commercial publication, Beckett accepted this decidedly uncommercial offer. George Reavey explained exactly how he came to be the publisher:

> I was very fed up with English publishers at the time. They were always turning down books of poems, not only by me, but by various other of my poet friends. So I decided to see what I could do about it myself. At the same time, I was very closely in touch with Stanley William Hayter, the famous engraver, who ran the Atelier 17 in Paris, and my idea was to get some books of poems illustrated by people out of the school at the beginning. In fact four of my editions in Europa Press were illustrated by people out of the Atelier 17: John Buckland Wright and two Hayters and there was also a Tchelitchew illustration to one of the books. . . . But Sam didn't like the idea of having his book of poems illustrated. So I suggested to him that the book should have an engraving, but he didn't want it. So it came out very plainly, without illustration.[134]

At the beginning of December 1935, Beckett's poems were finally published in a small edition of 327 copies, of which twenty-five were signed by the author. Originally, he had been going to entitle his collection simply "Poems." But, in March 1935, he changed his mind. "Not *Poems* after all," he wrote to the publisher, "but *Echo's Bones, and Other Precipitates.* C'est plus modeste [It is more modest]."[135]

Beckett chose to publish only those poems of which he approved, jettisoning a number of them—for example, "Hell Crane to Starling," "Casket of

Pralinen for the Daughter of a Dissipated Mandarin," and "Text," all of which had appeared earlier in Samuel Putnam's anthology *The European Caravan*.[136] He hesitated longest over the beautiful little poem "Yoke of Liberty," which had previously been published in the same anthology. After deciding to exclude it from the collected volume, he must have had second thoughts; on November 1, 1934, he dispatched it under the title of "Moly" with three other poems to *Poetry* magazine in Chicago. They were soon rejected.[137]

He also left out of *Echo's Bones* several other poems that have remained unpublished, like the long "Spring Song," an early version of which he had sent to Charles Prentice at Chatto and Windus in 1931, and "It is high time lover."[138] Beckett had earlier defined what ideally would have been his own principle for inclusion in a brutally honest, self-critical letter after sending one of his poems to Tom MacGreevy:

> To know you like the poem cheers me up. Genuinely my impression was that it was of little worth because it did not represent a necessity. I mean that in some way it was *"facultatif"* [optional] and that I would have been no worse off for not having written it. Is that a very painless way of thinking of poetry? Quoi qu'il en soit [Whatever may be] I find it impossible to abandon that view of the matter. Genuinely again my feeling is, more and more, that the greater part of my poetry, though it may be reasonably felicitous in its choice of terms, fails precisely because it is *facultatif* whereas the 3 or 4 I like, and that seem to have been drawn down against the really dirty weather of one of these fine days into the burrow of the "private life," *Alba* and the long *Enueg* and *Dortmunder* and even *Moly*, do not and never did give me that impression of being *construits* [constructed]. I cannot explain very well to myself what they have that distinguishes them from the others, but it is something arborescent or of the sky, not Wagner, not clouds on wheels; written above an abscess and not out of a cavity, a statement and not a description of heat in the spirit to compensate for pus in the spirit.[139]

In the end, he was forced to be more tolerant of his own work than this and include some poems in *Echo's Bones* which he did not rate so highly. The different versions that have been preserved (of "Enueg I," "Dortmunder," and the title poem, "Echo's Bones") show how heavily he revised some of these before their publication. "Malacoda," the poem based on his father's funeral, gave him the most difficulty of all. This was radically changed, even on the proofs, which did not arrive from Reavey until October 1935.[140]

The poems in *Echo's Bones* are personal and highly autobiographical. But they are, as one critic has described them, "intimate at arm's length."[141] Even the titles had personal associations for Beckett. The *"enueg,"* the *"serena,"* and the *"alba"* are all Provençal poetic forms that Beckett had studied at Trinity College with Professor Rudmose-Brown. "Sanies," of which there are two, is a bloody discharge, and a tone of morbidity and pain, characteristically Beckettian, runs through not only the two poems with this title but both "enuegs" and several other poems in the collection as well.

Many of the poems relate, as we have seen, to experiences in Beckett's own life or to books or particular poems that inspired him. And they take topographical features of Dublin and its surrounding countryside and transform them into dense patterns of images that relate to certain themes: separation, abandonment, pain, and suffering. But the literary allusions that occur or are echoed more obliquely in the poems are collectively almost as important as these personal experiences: Ovid (the poem "Echo's Bones" itself), Dante ("Malacoda"), Goethe's "Dem Geier gleich" ("The Vulture"); the German troubadour poet Walther von der Vogelweide ("Da Tagte Es"). And there are dozens of fleeting allusions to the Bible, *Tristan und Isolde*, Perrault, Shakespeare, Defoe, Pope, and Rimbaud. Behind the multilingual mixture of erudite language and slang and some of the rhythms of the verse, the presence of James Joyce is evident, but not perhaps much more conspicuously than that of the T. S. Eliot of "Rhapsody on a Windy Night" or the Ezra Pound of the *Cantos*. More than half a century later, the shorter poems, such as "Alba," "Da Tagte Es," and "Echo's Bones," seem both more approachable and more successful than the longer, complex, allusive poems.

Beckett never turned his back on the poems of *Echo's Bones*, as he did for a long time on his early stories. Yet, even though his own judgment that they are the "work of a very young man who had nothing to say and the itch to make" may be too radical a condemnation, too often they need detailed elucidation (of the kind that, guided by Beckett himself, Lawrence Harvey was able to bring to them), before they begin to mean very much to the nonspecialist reader.[142] And Beckett quickly became aware of this himself.

8

HIS RETURN TO COOLDRINAGH from London before Christmas 1935 was not blessed with good fortune. He fell ill almost immediately with an attack of pleurisy and was obliged to remain in bed for over a week. This placed him in the position of being almost totally dependent on his mother, who was happy to nurse him devotedly. It was an unwelcome start to his renewed stay at home.

Frank was kindness itself, trying desperately to make him feel at home by buying him a gramophone record of the pianist Alfred Cortot—but playing Liszt, whom Beckett disliked—then borrowing a whole album of records of Beethoven quartets for Beckett to play on the electric radiogram (a combination radio and gramophone) that his elder brother had built for the family the previous year. There were other concerned callers: Cissie and Deirdre Sinclair; Morris Sinclair; Susan Manning; and Dr. Alan Thompson, who treated Beckett medically in the absence of his brother, Geoffrey, but also came out to play the odd game of chess with him.[143] When Beckett was well enough to go out, he was sent to the Richmond Hospital for X rays of his lungs. But the plates showed that the lungs were clear and that the pleurisy had caused no damage to the lung tissue. Meanwhile, at home, he read avidly whatever he could lay his hands on: even a child's history of France kept him amused for a time while he was ill.[144]

By the second week of January, he had almost entirely recovered from his physical illness. No sooner was this over, however, than the panic attacks started up again at night, leading him to despair that nothing had been resolved by two whole years of analysis. And, looking at the growing pile of notebooks containing his novel, he wrote to Tom MacGreevy, who was back in London again: "The only plane on which I feel my defeat not proven is the literary waste."[145] Right from the beginning of the year, his commitment to living in the family home appeared to him as only temporary: "Perhaps the flight will be sooner than I expect, but no more Bion. As I write, think, move, speak, praise and blame, I see myself living up to the specimen that these 2 years have taught me I am. The word is not out before I am blushing for my automatism."[146]

He thought that his mother was keeping him deliberately short of money, so that he would be obliged to stay and obtain "gainful employment." But he could not resist buying a painting by Jack Yeats called *Morning* for the sum of thirty pounds, borrowing most of the money from his mother and Frank.[147] In trying to get him committed to life in Ireland, his family was doing everything it could — except, of course, to accept him for what he was and what he did. No one, not even Cissie, uttered a single word, for example, about the publication a month before of *Echo's Bones*, even though he had given his mother three copies. There was, he wrote, a "revolted silence."[148] It was very discouraging. By May, he wrote of his relations with his mother: "We seem to have settled down at home to a kind of reciprocal gentleness and reserve that is the best we can do."[149]

He seems to have made a deliberate attempt at this time to get out and see people, having been encouraged earlier by Bion to do this to combat the consequences of his isolation. Rudmose-Brown was in the hospital and hors de combat while convalescing, so Ethna MacCarthy, who was studying medicine at Trinity College at the same time, agreed to give his classes on Provençal poetry. Beckett helped her by taking detailed notes on the *félibres* writers and Frédéric Mistral's poems, particularly *Lou Trésor dóu Félibrige*.[150] His cousin Morris was preparing again for the scholarship examination into Trinity, and Beckett gave him a French lesson every week.

Socially too, he did things that he might well have hesitated to do earlier: With his mother, he went to Sir Thomas Beecham's London Philharmonic concert and a recital by Cortot; he introduced Morris Sinclair to Jack Yeats.[151] He even chatted amiably enough at a Gate Theatre first night to M. et Mme. Jammet — owners of a well-known Dublin restaurant — and their friends, and went next day to their Blackrock outpost. But he was very conscious of the gap that separated their different worlds.[152]

Beckett never liked groups. But he seems to have made a real effort at this time to play at least a walk-on part on the stage of literary Dublin, although he felt dreadfully ill at ease whenever he found himself front stage. "No, he didn't have any time for it," said Mary Manning. "In fact he was like his mother, he was not a relaxed social person at all. He was a loner." [153] Nonetheless, he went to Seamus O'Sullivan's at-homes, sometimes with Cissie, who was an old friend of Seamus and Stella. Later in 1936, after his review of Jack Yeats's *The Amaranthers* had been printed in the *Dublin Magazine* and one of his best poems had been accepted, O'Sullivan proposed to Beckett that he should take over the magazine's editorship. He declined, even though Seamus promised to pay for all of the printing costs for three years. (It is revealing that someone whom Beckett regarded as being very much of the "old school" should have had sufficient respect for the quality of his mind to make him such an offer.) He also called on the Salkelds, where he read some of Cecil's poems and was most impressed.[154]

There were occasions when he took genuine pleasure in the company of fellow writers and artists, especially at Jack Yeats's Saturday afternoons, which he started frequenting again. His greatest pleasure was to see the latest painting and to talk to the painter, of whom he was clearly in awe. But there were some Saturdays when he met other interesting callers — the painter Henry Tonks, for instance, who was there with Dermod O'Brien.[155] And he had a small circle of friends; he met Denis Devlin for lunch, dined with the Coffey family, and went for walks with Brian Coffey. There were other old friends whom he liked or whose work he respected but whom he saw more rarely; he went to see Arland Ussher, for example, at Cappagh with Joe Hone.[156] And when George Reavey came down from Belfast one day, they drove out in Frank's car to visit the novelist Francis Stuart.[157]

But his heart was not really in local matters anymore. His most important task was, he felt, to complete *Murphy*. So he fitted out a bedroom at Cooldrinagh as a study, having brought his books back from his brother's office, and added those carried from London. He was always adept at fitting bookshelves with the help of Frank's tools. He worked there most days on his novel, although sometimes he made little progress. Even so, by February 1936, there remained only three chapters of what he called "mechanical writing" to be done; [158] by the beginning of May, the manuscript was "near its first end"; [159] and by the third week of June, it was finished and he had three copies to send away to publishers.[160]

His mother's constant goading him into employment at least had the effect of making him consider possible alternative careers to that of perhaps permanently poverty-stricken writer and reviewer. He had always been very interested in cinema. And at this time he borrowed many books on the subject, reading about the director Vsevolod Pudovkin and the theoretician Rudolf Arnheim and going through back numbers of *Close-Up*. He even seriously considered going to Moscow to the State Institute of Cinematography, writing a letter to Sergei Eisenstein in which he asked him to take him on as a trainee.[161] He thought that the possibilities for the silent film had been far from exhausted and that, with the development of the color talkie, "a backwater may be created for the two-dimensional silent film that had barely emerged from its rudiments when it was swamped. Then there would be two separate things and no question of a fight between them, or rather of a rout." [162] The approach to Eisenstein, of course, came to nothing. On one "pie in the sky" day, he even wondered half seriously whether he might train to be a pilot, ignoring entirely the deficiencies in his eyesight. [163]

9

BECKETT'S POEMS AND PROSE show an impressive knowledge of German literature and thought. By the mid-1930s, he was reading widely in German (Goethe and Hölderlin most obviously, but also the linguistic thinker Fritz Mauthner and the philosopher Arthur Schopenhauer). He never studied the language formally, either at Portora Royal School or at Trinity College, but as with Spanish — in 1933 he started to "work hard at Spanish" — he studied it on his own. [164] He was helped by his cousins the Sinclairs; he exchanged letters in German with Morris and, more importantly, visited the family regularly in Kassel between 1928 and 1932. As early as 1932, in a typed testimonial for Beckett, T. B. Rudmose-Brown could write without risk of perjury that, as well as being fluent in French and Italian, "He also knows German." [165]

Throughout his stay at 48 Paulton's Square in 1934, Beckett worked on his German language, using a small beige "College" exercise book. Following his move to 34 Gertrude Street, he started making detailed notes in German on histories of German literature. He read a lot of Goethe during 1935 and, having borrowed Hester Dowden's copy of Goethe's autobiography *Dichtung und Wahrheit*, took forty-one pages of notes in German. He also typed out Goethe's poem "Prometheus" at this time. [166] Later, he read *Tasso* and *Iphigenie*, "then Racine's [*Iphigénie*] to remove the taste." [167] In the summer of 1936, he studied Goethe's *Faust*, on which he took extensive notes, also in German. [168]

From noting down related words and phrases, he quickly moved on to writing passages in German. The notebooks show signs of his having been helped by some unknown person, who occasionally corrects his compositions. But there is no evidence that he followed classes at all systematically. Thanks to his logical mind and keen musical ear, language learning was relatively easy for Beckett. Toward the end of the "College" notebook, his German vocabulary and syntax have become much more sophisticated; by August 1936, he was already trying his hand at writing short pieces in German, including a clever, ironic pastiche of the story of Rinaldo and Angelica (based on *Orlando Furioso*) and a translation into German of one of his own poems.

But his motives in acquiring additional languages were not exclusively intellectual. For he was coming to recognize that he could not bear for much longer the stresses and strains of living alone with his mother in Foxrock. And his mastery of languages looks increasingly like the deliberate acquisition of a passport to another life somewhere on the continent of Europe.

10

AS THE YEAR PROGRESSED, Beckett's letters revealed a feeling of increasing restlessness at living in Cooldrinagh. There appears to have been no major upheaval with his mother for several months, simply the growing certainty that he must get away again. Then, during the summer, something happened that made flight essential. A year before, his childhood friend Mary Manning had married Mark de Wolfe Howe. She was living in Boston and came over for the summer, being joined in Dublin by two young Bostonian friends, Elizabeth (Betty) Stockton and Isabella (Belle) Gardner, who had been staying with the Stockton family in a rented house on the southwest coast of County Cork.

On their own admission, the young women came to Dublin to meet some men and kick up their heels in a lively if innocent way. They stayed at the Shelbourne Hotel. Belle had a charming, romantic date who wore a shiny blue serge suit. His name was Erskine Childers and he later became the president of Ireland.[169] Betty's date was a tall, good-looking, blue-eyed, charming but reticent Dubliner called Sam Beckett. He was invited to tea at the end of June to meet Mary's young American friends, and was immediately attracted by this lively, laughing, twenty-year-old, who seemed so excitingly different from anyone he had ever met before. She left him reeling. Sometimes they went out for drives together. On one occasion, they were invited to tea with a Mr. O'Leary. It was an awkwardly formal occasion, with some of the male guests standing stiffly to attention around the room, their hands folded in front of them. The formality of the occasion began to amuse the American girls when their host walked over carrying an enormous plate heaped high with cakes and said: "And will you have a cookie?"

> That was the catalyst. All four of us broke into uncontrollable laughter. The group of men stirred, stared and seemed to fold their hands a little tighter. We were appalled by our lack of manners, but this sobering notion could not stem the tide of our laughter. It became apparent that our only recourse was to leave. And leave we did, in the rain, with no surcease in sight. We drove to a grey and stony beach along the Irish Sea. Sam threw rocks at England. An activity that eventually calmed us.[170]

Betty Stockton enjoyed Beckett's company and they became good friends. But she was simply not interested romantically in this quiet, deep, moody Irishman who was so obviously bowled over by her looks, her liveliness, and her charm. One of his most personal and directly accessible poems, "Cascando," was written under her spell in July. A few lines reveal how utterly enchanted he was:

> a last even of last times of saying
> if you do not love me I shall not be loved
> if I do not love you I shall not love
>
> the churn of stale words in the heart again
> love love love thud of the old plunger
> pestling the unalterable
> whey of words.[171]

But Betty did not respond and the affair (which had never really been one) ended its short, one-sided existence. Afterward he wrote her several letters, which she admitted she did not understand and to which she did not reply. Beckett was disappointed and intensely upset.

So, on the rebound, he sought consolation later in the summer in the arms of Betty's friend, Mary Manning de Wolfe Howe, a more experienced, married woman whom he had known since they were children and whose witty company he enjoyed. She summarized the likely causes of their wild affair: "Both of us were frightened and lonely. I was terribly frightened. I got married in a hurry over here [in the U.S.A.] and I didn't know whether I was right or not. . . . It was two frightened, lonely people about the same age, the same society, the same background, suddenly in crisis and that was it."[172]

They went out with each other regularly for the rest of the summer. It was obvious that a sexual affair was going on, and both their mothers were frantic with worry. May Beckett called Susan Manning, saying, "Please God when is she going home?" Susan responded: "Oh, God I hope she goes soon, God forgive me." In the first week of September, Molly, as she was known, took the boat back to Boston, and everyone breathed a huge sigh of relief. Beckett had already planned his own departure. By September 19, he could write that "The prospect of getting away is a great relief," although he had no specific plans except to travel to Germany and then "selon le vent" ("as the wind takes me").[173]

10
Germany:
The Unknown Diaries
1936–37

1

BECKETT BADE A TENSE though fond farewell to his mother on the front porch of Cooldrinagh on the morning of September 28, 1936. Not wanting to reveal the extent of her sadness or the depth of her anxiety at his departure, she smiled as she watched him drive slowly away with Frank on the first stage of his journey to Germany. As for Beckett, when he left his brother at Waterford station to take the train on to Cork, he felt as if he were deserting him.[1] He had promised his mother that he would write home regularly and, over the next few months, he was as good as his word.

He spent the early part of the evening in Cork visiting the graveyard of the red Shandon church of St. Ann, where he discovered the tombstone of the nineteenth-century writer known as Father Prout, in reality Reverend Francis Mahony, best known for his poem "Bells of Shandon."[2] Then he walked disconsolately on to Fitzgerald Park with a down-and-out to whom he gave a shilling. "I'll say a prayer for you," said the tramp by way of thanks. "Oho noho," wrote Beckett in his diary.[3]

He stayed in a shabby little hotel in Cóbh so as to be up before the lark to catch the four-fifteen morning tender to the U.S. Lines ship, the S.S. *Washington.* He found himself in a flea-ridden bed and unable to sleep, for not only was he excited and apprehensive at the prospect of the trip ahead but also the church bell nearby chimed the quarters as well as the hours and the halves. And the boots boy, with a logic entirely his own, woke up all the passengers to explain that he would be waking them an hour later than had been previously agreed, because the ship's departure had been delayed.[4]

On board, Beckett had a cabin to himself and woke the next morning to discover the boat had berthed for the day in Le Havre. He tired himself out wandering around the town ("But what will Germany be, for 6? months, but walking around, mainly?" he asked anxiously in his diary), ending the day by drinking a final Pernod in the Café de la Poste by way of saying an affectionate *au revoir* to France.[5] Between leaving Le Havre and arriving for German customs control at Cuxhaven, he played chess in the saloon, losing twice to a Czech and winning three games out of four against a Viennese on his way home from Java. Alone in his cabin, he read Céline's *Mort à crédit (Death on the Installment Plan)* which he found "very Rabelais (in technique). Positions flogged into a frenzy" and "superbly overwritten."[6] He quoted from it in French in his diary: "What is essential is not to know whether we are wrong or right — that is quite unimportant. What is important is to discourage the world from concerning itself with us. All the rest is vice."[7] This sentence echoed his own tendency to quietistic self-effacement.

After the boat docked, Beckett spent his first few nights in Hamburg in the Lloyd's Hotel, opposite the main railway station, then moved into a pension owned by a Herr Otto Lembke at 47 Colonnaden. But there was no running water and no central heating and he took an instant dislike to the room.[8] So, a few days later, he moved in with a family called Hoppe at 44 Schlüterstrasse, where he hoped at least to speak quite a lot of German. The Hoppes' comfortable pension was in a handsome, tree-lined street on the corner of Schlüterstrasse and Binderstrasse. Although the façade of number 44 (now an apartment house facing a new part of the university) has been entirely rebuilt after bomb damage in the Second World War, it is clear from the neighboring five-floor houses, with their characteristic stone lion heads and Pan gargoyles, cast-iron grille balconies, and elaborately ornamented pediments, that the area was and remains a fairly well-to-do one. The Hoppes' was no "sleazy boarding house,"[9] but a high-class pension frequented by professors and lecturers visiting the university, as well as patronized by a number of regular paying guests. On the other side of the road to the right towered the large, New Gothic–style post office with its churchlike entrance. Hallerstrasse Hochbahn station lay only a few minutes away and the two "lovely" Alster lakes could be reached by a brisk ten-minute walk: "made me wish College Park was under water, Kook of Bells [playing on the Book of Kells] and all," wrote Beckett in his diary.[10]

Knowing no one during his first week in Hamburg, except for the hosts and residents of the pension, he went out every day on a series of lengthy walks around the city, noting down details of his route in a little notebook. The same evening, he meticulously recorded in his diary everything that he had done during the day. He walked for hours on end in an aging hat and a large leather coat or a mackintosh, sometimes in the pouring rain, and at first with a streaming cold; he felt, at times, desperately lonely and miserable. Back at the centrally heated pension, he consoled himself by smoking a cigar — his mother sent him his father's cigar case when he lost his own — drinking beer, and eating a bunch of bananas that he had bought. Like anyone alone in a strange city, he was intensely preoccupied with where he should eat and drink. When he found somewhere reasonably good to eat, he went regularly to that restaurant, taking a newspaper (the *Frankfurter Zeitung* for preference) or a book to read, so as not to feel too ill at ease and lonely. Since he had a weak bladder — "it is the second devil, after my heart, both sworn enemies," he wrote — he was also often preoccupied with where he could urinate.[11] He was also concerned for his entire stay with making his money last as long as possible, so often ate cheaply or refrained from buying books to keep his expenses under strict control.

Early on in his stay, he went on a desolate pilgrimage to Altona to find the grave of the eighteenth-century poet and dramatist Friedrich Klopstock, "under a shedding lime [and] grown over with ivy" in the Christiankirche churchyard, copying out in his diary the biblical lines of St. John that were engraved in German on the tombstone: "He who then liveth and believeth in me shall never perish."[12] As he gazed around him at the other gravestones and thought of his own father lying far away in the little cemetery on the hillside near Greystones, he found no consolation whatsoever in the promise of everlasting life. And, later on, in the Petrikirche, with the organ playing mournfully, he looked beyond the altar to the stained-glass window based on Dürer's *Apostles* in Munich and thought again of his father: "ça me tue" ("It kills me"), he confided to his diary that evening.[13] He visited the Michaeliskirche, by repute one of the finest Baroque churches in northern Germany, and thought it "unbelievably awful and functional inside."[14] He located the fourteenth- to fifteenth-century churches of St. Jacob and St. Katharine and visited the Nikolaikirche, which, except for its high tower, was to be gutted during the heavy bombing of the Second World War.

Yet, once he had seen the few artworks that interested him in the churches and noted their main architectural features, he used their tall spires or towers only to orient himself in the city.[15] The Hamburg Kunsthalle or art gallery had far more to offer him, and he soon became a regular visitor there, recognized by the attendants as well as the custodians. At the opposite aesthetic extreme, he found the "Reeperbahn extraordinary, long boulevard running west with kinos, bars, cafés, dancings, etc., all the way along both sides. It would want to be night. A rise of Montparnasse to nth."[16]

At dinner with the Hoppes and their paying guests, Beckett felt very isolated at first by the limitations of his spoken German:

> Even to listen is an effort, and to speak ausgeschlossen [impossible]. Anyway the chatter is a solid block, not a chink, interruption proof. Curse this everlasting limpness and melancholy. How absurd, the struggle to learn to be silent in another language! I am altogether absurd and inconsequential. The struggle to be master of another silence! Like a deaf man investing his substance in Schallplatten [gramophone records], or a blind man with a Leica.[17]

Yet he made every effort to improve his knowledge of the language, working systematically in his room on German vocabulary and grammar, reading in the Staatsbibliothek, having private conversation classes, and talking whenever he could over dinner and at drinks afterward. What is astonishing about Beckett's stay in Hamburg (and, later, in Dresden) is how intensely sociable he was for someone who was fundamentally so shy and who loved so much to be alone. "How I ADORE solitude," he wrote one day of a walk that he had just taken through the Tiergarten in Berlin, watching the "ducks in dusk, taking wing from the water with the sound of consternation and settling again with a long liquid râle, flying fiercely in pairs down the axes of water, so different in the air than afloat."[18]

At first, Beckett's social life centered on the Hoppes and their small circle of paying guests: Luther, an amusing journalist on the *Hamburger Tageblatt*;[19] Martion, a "typical young German sentimental Kaufmann [businessman] . . . wringing nervous hands,"[20] who worked in a hosiery department in Hamburg; Fräulein Schön, who lent Beckett huge piles of German books to read or consult;[21] and other less regular residents and callers at the pension. Herr Hoppe found jobs for people in Hamburg, especially for foreigners, and during the tourist season he also acted as a travel guide. He introduced Beckett to a number of his business contacts. "He knowing everyone in Hamburg, speaks with complacence of his Verbindungen [contacts]. He is a very decent little man. Comic walk, between a mince and a steamroller," Beckett noted picturesquely.[22]

But Beckett's circle of acquaintances quickly expanded. Through what he described as the *Auslandstelle*, he arranged conversational exchanges with a tiny dark-haired young woman named Klaudia Ascher, "quite a pleasant schoolmistress, living with her widowed mother."[23] He went to the art gallery and various lectures with her and took her out occasionally to the cinema or the theater. He even helped her to translate a dry-as-dust article entitled "The Car and Its Driver" from the *British Journal of Physical Medicine*. In return, she suggested improvements to one of his poems, "Cascando," which he had translated into German before leaving Dublin.[24] She recommended or lent him several books in German, but it soon became clear that their tastes differed radically.[25] She and Beckett were clearly never destined to become intimate friends. She had the courage, however, to challenge his pessimism, urging him to overcome the distance that he interposed between himself and life and encouraging him to plunge into a much more active involvement in it.[26] He did not thank her for this advice and, ultimately, she was neither sufficiently interesting nor pretty enough to hold his attention. She also suffered from bad breath!

Another young woman in Hamburg, Ilse Schneider (whose mother was English), to whom he was greatly attracted and who accompanied him to a concert given by the Berlin Philharmonic Orchestra,[27] soon made it crystal clear that she was not at all interested in him. Suffering from herpes on his lip (an affliction which recurred throughout his German stay) and a sore nose, he was far from being physically at his best.

The Hamburger Kunsthalle — "the building is magnificent and the pictures admirably presented (one line hanging against matt white throughout)"[28] — soon became a focal point for Beckett and as much of a haven as the National Gallery had been in London two years before. Though he was initially disappointed, his interest was then captured by the excellent Dutch and Flemish collections, especially paintings by van Goyen, Everdingen, Elsheimer, Wouwerman, and van der Neer.[29] On the other hand, the German romantics, like Graff, von Kobell, Feuerbach, and Böcklin, even Menzel, filled him "mainly with loathing": he dismissed a whole roomful of Philipp Otto Runge (whom Fräulein Schön adored) as "Quatsch" (rubbish).[30] Such paintings caught his attention only when they assumed some personal significance; one of the Tyrol paintings of Rudolf Friedrich Wasmann, for instance (of Frau Pastorin Hübbe) made him think nostalgically of the picture of the old lady hanging in a window nook in his parents' home, and Wilhelm Leibl's portrait of Dr. Rauert reminded him of Cecil Salkeld.[31] Surprisingly, he made no comment at all at this time on the gallery's dozen works by Caspar David Friedrich, an artist for whom he later developed a tremendous admiration.

The modern Germans whose works were still on display in the north gallery — Heckel, Kirchner, Schmidt-Rottluff, Modersohn-Becker — as well as the Norwegian Munch were far more to his taste, although here too he revealed a keen sense of discernment in his likes and dislikes. The ease with which Beckett could compare paintings that he had seen in other galleries or spot affinities between paintings from quite different periods of time suggests that he almost certainly possessed a photographic memory. From his wide readings in art history and his earlier visits to galleries, he had acquired the knowledge and discernment of a connoisseur; he showed himself particularly knowledgeable in his judgments of seventeenth-century Dutch painting. But his comments on the modern paintings that he saw are also sensitive and discriminating. In the *Magazin* [store] in Hamburg, he enthused in front of Nolde's *Christ and the Children:*

> Nolde's *Christus und die Kinder*, clot of yellow infants, long green back of Christ (David?) leading to black and beards of Apostles. Lovely eyes of child held in His arms. Feel at once on terms with the picture, and that I want to spend a long time before it, and play it over and over again like the record of a quartet.[32]

As he left the restricted collection, he swapped judgments with the young man in charge about the different paintings they came across:

> Before the 2 Runge mornings, he tries to convert me. But they make me feel ill. He says he is the best portrait painter of the turn of the 17th–18th centuries [error for 18th–19th]. I say I prefer Ingres. I make a hit with my comparison of the Meister Franke Christ with a Bellini. It has already been made, and the similarity had much to say with the acquisition. He thinks of a Bellini in Ravenna. I bring him to the Wouwerman magic *[Reiter an der Düne (Riders on the Dunes)]*: He obviously doesn't feel it, and prefers the Schimmel *[Bauer und Pferde (Peasant and Horses)]*. He agrees that the Brouwers ascription is more doubtful.[33]

Beckett's life in Hamburg became much more hectic when he was introduced to several well-known private collectors of modern art. There began a final few, frenetic weeks when he sometimes felt unable to cope with the number of people whom he had arranged to see. Thanks to his newly made contacts, he attended lectures by Hermann Spehr and by Professor Dr. Mercklin at the Art and Industry Museum and went to hear (mostly with boredom or disgust) the fifty-three-year-old painter Friedrich Ahlers-Hestermann reading from his unpublished memoirs about his artistic life in Paris: "How I hate the impeccable tedium of 1900–1910 Paris aesthetic," he wrote in his diary after the talk.[34]

A private collector, a Frau Fera (first mentioned to Beckett by Klaudia Ascher and later described by him as "the best of her sex I have met and will meet in this country, or in most countries")[35] was one of the first to introduce him to other well-known members of Hamburg's artistic or scholarly community. It was at the Feras' home, for instance, that he met a sympathetic Jewish scholar, Professor Dr. Diederich, who knew Thomas Mann and his sister and who was the first German to have written biographies of Zola and Daudet.[36] Again it was Frau Fera who arranged for him to visit the widow of the distinguished art critic, gallery director, and private collector Max Sauerlandt. Beckett enjoyed looking at Sauerlandt's splendid collection of paintings and watercolors by Schmidt-Rottluff, Kirchner, Nolde, and Ballmer, but found Frau Sauerlandt and her son oddly pedantic, as they made every observation into a little disquisition. However, he was delighted that Frau Sauerlandt agreed to sell him a copy of her husband's book, which could no longer be obtained from the booksellers. (Ultimately, though, he judged it "a poor book on Nolde which he called Art of the past 30 years."[37]) He was also invited to visit Gurlitt's gallery to look at modern paintings, where he saw some Otto Dix etchings that prompted him to comment: "a nightmare talent, a Georg Grosz of mutilation."[38] Quite independently of the art collectors, he became very friendly with a Herr Albrecht who was an assistant to a bookseller named Saucke and advised him on books that he might or might not obtain on modern art. He bought several, including one on Ernst Barlach, and, when told that Barlach and Nolde were about to be banned, commented, "i.e. buy Nolde quick."[39]

Two even more important contacts for Beckett were a Frau Durrieu, who "talked like a Maxim gun,"[40] and an "elderly Jewish art-historian"[41] and modern-art collector, Dr. Rosa Schapire. Frau Durrieu held regular drawing parties that were attended by professional as well as amateur artists. On one such occasion, a highly embarrassed Beckett sat dejectedly for hours as a model, being drawn, as he put it irritably, by "a lot of bloody virgin squaws,"[42] as well as by a well-known painter, the fifty-year-old Erich Hartmann, who already had one painting in the Kunsthalle collection. Beckett disliked the experience intensely and found the drawings of his head, even the one by Hartmann, "unspeakable."[43] What is surprising is that he ever agreed to sit at all.

Dr. Schapire, a fervent admirer and active supporter of the Brücke group of painters,[44] showed Beckett the collection of modern paintings, etchings, woodcuts, and art objects that she had assembled in her own apartment, as well as escorting him to another well-known private collection, that of Herr Hudtwalcker. (It was in Hudtwalcker's apartment on the Elbchaussee that Beckett saw one of the best Munch paintings he claims ever to have seen, one of three women on a bridge over dark water.[45]) Rosa Schapire's own apartment was filled to overflowing with Schmidt-Rottluff's work and appeared like a shrine to her friend and idol: oils, watercolors, even furniture designed and painted by him; "cigarette boxes, ash-trays, table covers, cushions, bedspreads. All carved or designed or worked from designs by S.R."[46] "If she went in for spitoons in her Hamburg home," Beckett joked to MacGreevy, "they would be designed by Schmidt-Rottluff."[47]

Beckett looked for a long time at a *Frauenkopf* of a woman with red hair streaming back, a long nose, and "lip lifted in a dribble of bitter cultivation"[48] painted by Schmidt-Rottluff, before realizing that, like several others in the flat, it was a portrait of Schapire herself. It was while discussing this painting that Beckett found himself drawn into restating his own criterion of true art, in which he not only repeated his view that the authentic poem or picture was a prayer but developed the image further than he had ever done up to that point: "The art (picture) that is a prayer sets up prayer, releases prayer in onlooker, i.e. *Priest*: Lord have mercy upon us. *People*: Christ have mercy upon us."[49] This is an attitude that few readers will associate with Beckett, yet it was essential to his view of art at the time, whether this was the art of the writer, painter, or musician.

2

IT WAS THROUGH SCHAPIRE, Durrieu, or Sauerlandt's son that Beckett managed to meet some of the most interesting painters then working in Hamburg: Karl Kluth, Willem Grimm, Karl Ballmer, Hans Ruwoldt, Paul Bollmann, Gretchen Wöhlwill, and Eduard Bargheer. In the last two weeks of his stay, he visited these artists in their studios, talking to them for hours on end about their painting and about the difficulties that they were experiencing with the Nazi authorities.

Until now little has been known of Beckett's attitude to what was happening politically in Germany at the time. His diaries show that he had many animated discussions with the residents of the Pension Hoppe and with others whom he met later in Berlin and Dresden about German foreign policy: her right to have colonies, the *Selbständigkeit* (Independence) campaign, and so on. He listened to anti-Jewish sentiments with acute distaste. His diaries also reveal an amused disdain for what he almost invariably mocked as the "interminable harangues" of Hitler, Göring, and Goebbels; he found it comical to see how, during one of Hitler's speeches on the radio, one after another member of the listening group in his pension gradually drifted off to bed while the Führer was still in full flow. Later, speaking of a couple whom he had met in Berlin, he described them as "appallingly Nazi."[50] He moaned regularly to his diary about those who preached the "NS [National Socialist] gospel" and the constant "Heil Hitler" greetings irritated him.[51] Later a friend he made in Berlin, Axel Kaun, analyzed the new Germany as being half sentimental demagogics and half the "brilliant obscurantics of Dr G [Goebbels]" with his dangerous, ranting propaganda.[52] But

Beckett was not as interested in political theories as he was in the human injustices being perpetrated by the Nazi régime.

The treatment meted out to painters whom he met shocked him. Earlier that year, during the period of the Olympic Games held in Berlin, Hitler had been keen to present the world with a falsified image of a fair and tolerant society. So for months there had been acres of window-dressing. During the games, for instance, an exhibition called "Contemporary Art from Corinth to Klee" had been staged at Berlin's National Gallery. However, just before Beckett's visit to Hamburg, orders had been passed on from the Führer and the minister for a "liberation" in cultural affairs, which meant that a fight against "decadent art" could be ruthlessly pursued. On November 5, 1936, in the middle of Beckett's stay in Hamburg, a directive was sent out to all gallery directors that they should remove their decadent modern art pictures. The Commission of Confiscation did not arrive until July 1937 but, while Beckett was actually traveling around Germany, pictures were being removed, then later appropriated, destroyed, or sold. Sometimes to his surprise, as in Halle and Erfurt, he found the work of "decadent" artists still openly on public display. But, at other galleries in Berlin and Dresden, the modern painting rooms were closed or paintings had already been removed and stacked in the cellars (where one needed a special permit to see them) or were not visible at all.[53] At the Zwinger gallery in Dresden, he found that, even though he attempted to pull strings with the chief custodian, he was unable to see the "disgraced" pictures.[54]

It was from the Hamburg painters that Beckett gained his clearest insight into the forms that Nazi persecution of them and their work was taking. Like many people, he could not foresee the terrors that Nazism held in store; in one of his letters to Tom MacGreevy from Berlin, he described himself as unwilling to listen any more to complaints from these "great proud angry poor putupons in their fastnesses, and I can't say yessir and nosir any more."[55] But by that time he was ill and jaded with the efforts that he had made over the past three months to be sociable. In any case he had heard the same complaints over and over again. His diaries show that while he was actually meeting these painters, he felt genuine concern at the constraints under which they were working and at the restrictions that had been imposed on their freedoms.

He learned how the non-Nazi "Malerei und Plastik" exhibition held at the Kunsthalle at the end of July had been closed down only ten days after its opening. Gretchen Wöhlwill, who was Jewish, explained to him that she was "naturally excluded from all professional activities. She may have a closed exhibition to which only Jews may be invited. She may sell only to Jews etc. etc."[56] Karl Kluth told Beckett that he could exhibit only watercolors, and those only at Gurlitt's gallery. The Swiss-born Karl Ballmer told him that he had not been allowed to exhibit at all since 1933, that he had received hostile visits from Nazi officials, and that his personal library had been seized. Eduard Bargheer spoke of "difficulties with authorities, demands on all sides to have work removed, flow of inspectors to site, etc."[57] Even the art historian Rosa Schapire commented with heavy irony that "she is fortunate not [to be] of pure Aryan descent, and therefore cannot publish nor give public lectures."[58]

Among the artists whom Beckett met in Hamburg, Karl Kluth, in whom he detected a "very strong Munch influence,"[59] did not interest him particularly. He greatly enjoyed his visit to the studio of the thirty-five-year-old Eduard Bargheer, a "small, taut, choleric, ruddy, graceful" man, "appallingly alive and possessed, frightful energy."[60] Although he found Bargheer's painting "of enormous competence and earnestness, yet he and his painting say nothing to me. It is the bull of painting by the horns."[61] He much preferred the "stillness and the unsaid" of Willem Grimm's and Karl Ballmer's work.[62] On two consecutive days, he visited them both in their studios. He found Grimm, often maligned among some of the private collectors in Hamburg, the "most interesting I have yet seen, of [the] Hamburg group . . . Munch influence seems worked out. Toulouse-Lautrec. Exquisite colour and composition."[63] Beckett also admired Karl Ballmer's work very much and, in a postwar piece on the artists Bram and Geer van Velde, described him as this "great unknown painter."[64] He admired his mildness, "lost almost to point of apathy and indifference," and meditated interestingly on his painting, linking it with Leibniz's monadology and his own poem "The Vulture" in *Echo's Bones:*

> Transparent figures before landscapes, street, town reproduced in Sauerlandt not there. Wonderful red Frauenkopf, skull earth sea and sky, I think of Monadologie [of Leibniz] and my Vulture. Would not occur to me to call this painting abstract. A metaphysical concrete. Nor Nature convention, but its source, fountain of Erscheinung [Appearance]. Fully a posteriori painting. Object not exploited to illustrate an idea, as in say Léger or Baumeister, but primary. The communication exhausted by the optical experience that is its motive and content. Anything further is by the way. Thus Leibniz, monadologie, Vulture, are by the way. Extraordinary stillness. His concern with Renaissance tradition.[65]

Beckett got on very well personally with both Grimm and Ballmer and regretted that he had met them so late in his stay. He vowed to return to Hamburg to see them again later. He never did, although both painters survived the war. (Grimm left Hamburg to live and work on a farm; most of the prewar paintings that Beckett might have seen were destroyed by the bombing of his Hamburg studio.[66] And Ballmer quit the country altogether in 1938 to live and paint in his native Switzerland.)

News from home came in regular letters from his mother. She often enclosed copies of *The Irish Times*, sometimes drawing his attention to items of German interest with the exhortation or implication that he might earn money by writing articles on his experiences.[67] In fact, characteristically, he considered writing something, but a poem rather than an article, about the famous cemetery and crematorium at Ohlsdorf. He walked through the vast cemetery for hours on end on two separate occasions. "Because I thought a poem would be there,

I feel nothing. The noise of my steps in the leaves reminds me of something, but can't find what," he wrote in his diary.[68] The poem about the cemetery was never realized. Yet his memories of Ohlsdorf were sharp and resurfaced in his story First Love, composed shortly after the war.

> I infinitely preferred Ohlsdorf, particularly the Linne section, on Prussian soil, with its nine hundred acres of corpses packed tight, though I knew no one there, except by reputation, the wild animal collector Hagenbeck. A lion, if I remember right, is carved on his monument, death must have had for Hagenbeck the countenance of a lion. Coaches ply to and fro, crammed with widows, widowers, orphans and the like. Groves, grottoes, artificial lakes with swans, offer consolation to the inconsolable. It was December, I had never felt so cold, the eel soup lay heavy on my stomach, I was afraid I'd die, I turned aside to vomit, I envied them.[69]

The last few days of his stay in Hamburg were thoroughly blighted by a festering finger and thumb, which came up "like a blind boil"[70] and were extremely sore. At Frau Durrieu's he bathed them in camomile and she bandaged them for him. But, although still in pain, he insisted on moving on. After spending the night in Hanover and paying a fleeting visit during the morning of December 5 to the Landesgalerie in the Landesmuseum of Lower Saxony,[71] he took the train on to Brunswick the same afternoon expressly to see the Duke of Brunswick's famous collection of Old Masters.

It was in the Herzog-Anton-Ulrich Museum gallery that he saw a painting that was to echo in his imagination for many years to come. This was Giorgione's intense, brooding self-portrait, which "hits the moment one enters the room and is good enough to be by him and has the profound reticence that is his only."[72] The image obsessed him and he returned to look at it on three separate occasions. He saw there an "expression at once intense and patient, anguished and strong" and described the image as "an antithesis of mind and sense."[73] He purchased two large reproductions of it, one of which he sent to Tom MacGreevy, and the other he kept for himself, pinning it above the mantelpiece in his room in Berlin, describing it "as a light in the dark."[74] Looking at the picture with hindsight, we can see the head, with its "knitted brows" and "anguished eyes"[75] emerging from the dark background, as resembling one of Beckett's own late compelling dramatic images.[76]

Beckett was in acute pain as he trailed around Brunswick in the lightly falling snow. Not wanting to call in medical help, and having tried a needle without success, he finally lanced his sore finger himself with a razor blade. Yet he forced himself to visit the churches and monuments of the old town, entering his comments every night in his diary — criticizing, for instance, the "distressing blemish" of the unfinished towers of the otherwise fine Dom and calling the Burg Dankwarderode "deplorable 19th century Romanesque," while admiring the sheer simplicity of Henry the Lion's Lion Monument in the Burgplatz.[77] He forced himself to climb the tall tower of the Andreaskirche in fear and trembling, lest I should break a leg, be attacked by vermin, lose the key, [toiling up] a succession of crazy ladders in the gloom, 365 steps to the gallery (for which I have 2nd key) 70 m. above ground. Tiny platform; 1½' from base of wall to railing. I cower against former, and scarcely dare look at view. Force myself to make the circle round with quick sickening glances at the ground.[78]

Today, the tower still has to be climbed by the same series of ladders and is every bit as frightening as it was then for someone who is afraid of heights.[79] Once you reach the top, however, the view from the narrow platform is indeed stupendous: "a sea of red roofs, Martinikirche looking magnificent, Petrikirche, Katherinenkirche and the big Hagenmarkt and the clotted Dome and fake Dankwarderode greatly improved by distance."[80]

While in Brunswick, Beckett took the opportunity to go by train to nearby Wolfenbüttel where he visited the house of the dramatist Lessing and the Augusta Bibliothek, where Lessing was librarian from 1770 to 1781. He bought from a local bookshop a complete set of Lessing, which he had posted directly to his home in Foxrock.[81] Throughout his German trip, determinedly curious, he followed indications in his Baedeker guide or other travel books and local guides that he bought as he went along and undertook quite a number of such literary or artistic pilgrimages. After a stay in Berlin that had to be extended because of illness, for instance, he stopped off in Weimar to take detailed notes on the houses of Goethe and Schiller.

3

BECKETT ARRIVED IN BERLIN on December 11, 1936. His life there differed radically from that which he had been leading in Hamburg. He deliberately chose not to contact any of the painters—Nolde, Schmidt-Rottluff, and Heckel—whose addresses he had been given, probably because he felt unable or unwilling to face up to the stress of socializing with which he had been coping for the past month. It was only toward the end of his stay in Berlin that he looked up a young man called Axel Kaun, "a young bookseller's improver who has just been taken on by the publisher Ruhwoldt [Rowohlt], who does Hackett, Fleming, Wolf and Romains," or went out anywhere with other people.[82] In retrospect, Berlin looks like a deliberate pause in what had earlier been a very hectic schedule.

He began by staying for a few days at the Hotel Deutsche Traube at 32 Invalidenstrasse, close to Friedrichstrasse station, but then chose to live in a pension at 45 Budapeststrasse (opposite the Zoological Gardens) which offered half board with only one meal a day. Thus he avoided too much company. He also spent most of his time visiting the different galleries and museums, always alone. The Kaiser-Friedrich-Museum (now the Bode-Museum) and Deutsches Museum, the Nationalgalerie, the Pergamon-Museum and the Neues and Altes museums, superbly sited on Museum Island, soon became as familiar to him as the buildings of Trinity College, Dublin.

A good indication of how low his morale had sunk at this time and how wretched he felt is given in a letter that he wrote to Mary Manning only two days after reaching Berlin.

> The trip is being a failure. Germany is horrible. Money is scarce. I am tired all the time. All the modern pictures are in the cellars. I keep a pillar to post account [that is, the diaries used here], but have written nothing connected since I left home, nor disconnected. And not the ghost of a book beginning. The physical mess is trivial, beside the intellectual mess. I do not care, and don't know, whether they are connected or not. It is enough that I can't imagine anything worse than the mental marasmus, in which I totter and sweat for months. It has turned out indeed to be a journey *from*, and not *to*, as I knew it was, before I began it.[83]

The "physical mess" took yet another turn for the worse a few days into his stay in Berlin. Just as his septic fingers were improving, a lump appeared under his scrotum, as he put it, "between wind and water" to give him more pain and discomfort.[84] By the middle of January, he was forced to stay in bed with a more acute reappearance of the same infection in the same unfortunate place; "getting up is like for an execution," he wrote; and he was unable to walk or even sit down without being in agony.[85] He had to eat "in the Roman fashion, the only one in which lump does not ache." [86] For a long time he showed enormous, probably foolhardy, determination and courage in persisting with his program of study. For it is clear that this is what he had embarked on in coming to Germany: an extended tour of its major galleries and art collections, so that he could look at leisure at the pictures that he had always wanted to see and extend his range into areas on which he was not already an expert. After all, Berlin, like Dresden and Munich, held so many gems in its major collections.

He found early Dutch art in the Kaiser-Friedrich-Museum that he didn't know at all. And he seems to have made a real effort, in spite of his deep-rooted prejudices, to find out more about German nineteenth-century painting, buying and studying diligently Karl Scheffler's book on the subject.[87] The painters of the Italian Renaissance had always been Tom MacGreevy's special love. But, in Berlin, Beckett found Italian paintings about which he too could enthuse spontaneously: eight Botticellis, "with a 'Simonetta' portrait looking something like a blonde Ethna [MacCarthy] when young";[88] a "wonderful roomful of Signorellis";[89] the Masaccio panels "lovely";[90] "the Domenico Veneziano Adoration of the Kings magnificent." [91] In a loan exhibition he admired an Elsheimer night landscape, which he thought "exquisite." [92] The paintings of the sixteenth-century German Altdorfer were "a revelation" to him, "sacred subjects [a] pretext for landscape, not at all like Elsheimers, gay rather, but immediately suggesting Elsheimer. Lovely Crucifixion and Rest on the Flight [from Egypt]." [93] His diary positively quivers with excitement at such moments, as

Beckett wanders day after day around the mostly small but very tall rooms of the Kaiser-Friedrich gallery.[94]

But if the prose races as he describes these pictures, he uses the facing pages of his diary to note down in English highly prosaic details of the painters' dates, schools, and influences, which are mostly extracted almost verbatim from the German catalogue of the collection. This constituted, of course, partly a translation exercise for Beckett. But he also had an obsession with dates and facts which was part of a coherent, reasoned, if idiosyncratic view of human knowledge and its limits. Speaking to Axel Kaun and a friend of Kaun called Meier, who physically resembled Dr. Goebbels,[95] about books on history, Beckett said:

> I am not interested in a "unification" of the historical chaos any more than I am in the "clarification" of the individual chaos, and still less in the anthropomorphisation of the inhuman necessities that provoke the chaos. What I want is the straws, flotsam, etc., names, dates, births and deaths, because that is all I can know. . . . Meier says the background is more important than the foreground, the causes than the effects, the causes than their representatives and opponents. I say the background and the causes are an inhuman and incomprehensible machinery and venture to wonder what kind of appetite it is that can be appeased by the modern animism that consists in rationalising them. Rationalism is the last form of animism. Whereas the pure incoherence of times and men and places is at least amusing.[96]

In practice, this meant that Beckett liked chronologies, loved tiny, verifiable details of individual human lives, and had no time for broad sweeping analyses of motives or movements.

> I want the oldfashioned history book of reference, not the fashionable monde romancé that explains copious[ly] why e.g. Luther was inevitable without telling me anything about Luther, where he went next, what he lived on, what he died of, etc. I say the expressions "historical necessity" and "Germanic destiny" start the vomit moving upwards.[97]

More interestingly, his argument hinges on an acceptance of incoherence and chaos in human affairs and a distrust of all rational attempts to impose shape on this chaos that anticipate some of his later comments on form and content in modern art.

A new and somewhat surprising element entered into Beckett's life in Berlin with his interest in the Egyptian, Islamic, and Indian collections of the various great museums. There is one obvious reason for this: He had rented his room at the pension for a whole month and the days had to be filled somehow, since he could not always be looking at paintings. Yet there is a more aesthetic explanation. The Hamburg artists Grimm and Ruwoldt had spoken to him of their enthusiasm for miniatures and for the ancient sculptures in the Tell Halaf Museum and the Asian section of the Kaiser-Friedrich-Museum. Beckett also reminded himself in his diary that Rembrandt collected and copied Indian miniatures.[98] So he looked at these sculptures and ceramics with a fresh eye, finding a lot to fascinate him in the myths that lay behind the objects as well as in the intricate details of the artifacts themselves. He described a Geertgen tot Sint Jans painting of John the Baptist as "sitting very gloomy in a landscape, in rather the attitude of the hermit listening to the music in the Indian miniature, with winding stream."[99]

Every so often, Beckett felt the need to escape from the bustle of a city. One such excursion to the Grunewald forest was his solution to the problem as to what to do on a cold Christmas Day, when everyone else was at home with their family. Another outing was to Frederick the Great's summer residence of Sans Souci in Potsdam. In his diary he records a delightful account of his initial impressions of the summer palace:

> Bright and cold. First view of terraces faced with glass frames for vines disconcerting, but soon accepted. Trimmed yews very effective. Terrace perhaps too steep and heavy for the palace, which disappears at the foot of every flight. Palace exquisite, and big summer house, faultlessly proportioned, the shallow green cupola resting like a flower on the yellow front, and the caryatids laughing under the lightness of their load. Not in the least Versailles or Watteauesque, but truly an architecture without care.[100]

After a rapid guided tour of the various rooms of the palace (including the "exquisite comedy of the Voltaire-Zimmer with its fantastic bird and flower decoration")[101] and a visit to the picture gallery, where he vowed he "never saw so much barock smut assembled in one place,"[102] he took himself off on an exhilarating walk through the vast grounds, going first through the Sicilian, then the Nordic Gardens, past the "ugly 19th century Orangerie"[103] on to the Neues Palais and the facing Communs, and finally walking as far as the Marmorpalais, Frederick Wilhelm II's favorite residence, at the water's edge. Pictures seen in the gallery filled his mind as he walked, but also space, light, and color: "suddenly with mist fallingly wonderful red light like an extension of the leaves that a group of women are raking together, against the grey néant of the Jungfernsee."[104]

After such a blend of light, poetic evocation, it comes as a shock to realize the Beckett had been in great pain throughout the day. Yet, as he discovered back in his room in central Berlin while preparing to go out to see Werner Krauss ("a great actor, the best I have seen")[105] in Friedrich Hebbel's tragedy *Gyges und sein Ring*,[106] he had returned from the higher realms of the mind, only to find the ills of the body busy reasserting themselves with the lump under his scrotum growing bigger and bigger.

Pain and — following his day out at Potsdam and the theater — confinement to his room for several days, stimulated Beckett to ponder interestingly some of the questions raised by what he had seen or read. Hebbel's play prompted him to formulate his objections to poetical drama, which were vital to his own later way of dealing with poetry in the theater. In spite of the brilliance of Werner Krauss, he saw enough in Hebbel to convince him that "the poetical play can never come off as play, nor when played as poetry either, because the words obscure the action and are obscured by it." [107] He argued that the play is "such good poetry that it never comes alive at all," poetic speeches being "too self-sufficient to be merely phrases of a dramatic expression." [108] Racine, he maintained, "never elaborates the expression in this sense, never stands by the word in this sense, and therefore his plays are not 'poetical' i.e. undramatic, in this sense." [109] Beckett's own solution with his postwar play *Waiting for Godot* was to reduce the conventional dramatic action to near stasis and to create, in Artaud's sense, a poetry *of* the theater rather than poetry *in* the theater. In *Godot*, speech rhythms take their vitality not from poetic forms or metaphors but from the music hall and circus, and action and gesture create their own kind of intricate, balletic choreography. The entire waiting situation is a poetic metaphor. Beckett was to take ever greater risks in his late plays as he refocused attention on language but took care to set up tensions within the language and create powerful visual images, often modeled on paintings, that either sustain or undercut it.

Unable to move very far, he read in bed two of the books that Axel Kaun lent him: Hermann Hesse's *Demian: die Geschichte einer Jugend (Demian: The Story of a Youth)* and Walther Bauer's *Die notwendige Reise (The Necessary Journey).*[110] What began as an apt comment on the need to avoid defining a book even by its title (the danger is immediately apparent with Bauer's title — "the critic has merely then to elaborate the contrary" [111]) led him to analyze his own novel, *Murphy.* He surprised himself by what he discovered there, as he focused on the significance of Murphy tying himself into his chair to escape from the contingent world. He found in both German novels "the inevitable business about the journey to self," but argued that:

> Journey anyway is the wrong figure. How can one travel to that from which one cannot move away? *Das notwendige Bleiben* ["the necessary staying put"] is more like it. That is also in the figure of Murphy in the chair, surrender to the thongs of self, a simple materialisation of self-bondage, acceptance of which is the fundamental unheroic. In the end it is better to perish than be freed. But the heroic, the nosce te ipsum [know thyself], that these Germans see as a journey, is merely a different attitude to the thongs and chair, a setting of will and muscle and fingers against them, a slow creation of the desire and power to stand up and walk away, a life consecrated to the possibility of escape, if not necessarily the fact, to a real freedom of choice when the fire comes. Murphy has no freedom of choice, i.e. he is not free to act *against* his inclination. The point is that the *nosce te ipsum* is no more mobile than the *carpe te ipsum* [gather thyself] of Murphy. The difference is that in the one motionless there is the seed of motion, and in the other not. And so on. And so on. It is pleasant to find something in the book that I did not know was there.[112]

Beckett's diaries may give the initial impression that he has almost forgotten about the publication of *Murphy*. Yet his irritation as it wended its way very slowly from publisher to publisher bursts through from time to time and is registered far more explicitly in heavily ironical letters to George Reavey, who was seeking to place the book, and to Mary Manning, who was helping him to get it published in the United States. Soon after arriving in Hamburg, he learned that *Murphy* had been turned down by Simon and Schuster "with the usual kind words, brilliance, 5% appeal and ruisselant avenir [dazzling future]. Houghton and Mifflin now have it. Nott has not yet made up his mind. Perhaps he must get in touch with Mme Beeton before he can reach a decision." [113] A Houghton Mifflin editor named Greenslet required heavy cuts, especially of chapter six (on "Murphy's mind") and asked for a new title, provoking a howl of protest from Beckett: "Do they not understand that if the book is slightly obscure, it is so because it is a compression, and that to compress it further can only result in making it more obscure?" [114] Each section was, he argued to Reavey, essential to the whole. The demands for cuts also inspired Beckett to produce a sustained piece of inventive, lavatorial wit in a letter to Mary Manning, in which his irritation glows white-hot:

> Reavey wrote enclosing a letter from Greensletandhindrance. I am exhorted to oblate 33.3 recurring to all eternity of my work. I have thought of a better plan. Take every 500th word, punctuate carefully and publish a poem in prose in the Paris *Daily Mail*. Then the rest separately and privately, with a forewarning from Geoffrey [Thompson], as the ravings of a schizoid, or serially, in translation, in the *Zeitschrift für Kitsch*. My next work shall be on rice paper wound about a spool, with a perforated line every six inches and on sale in Boots. The length of each chapter will be carefully calculated to suit with the average free motion. And with every copy a free sample of some laxative to promote sales. The Beckett Bowel Books, Jesus in farto. Issued in imperishable tissue. Thistledown end papers. All edges disinfected. 1000 wipes of clean fun. Also in Braille for anal pruritics. All Sturm and no Drang. [115]

He adopted a tone of feigned ignorance and innocence at the thought that Stanley Nott "was apparently prepared to take on the book if an American mug could be found; and Mifflin if an English mug. It seemed to me, unfamiliar with the niceties, that my agent had merely to bring the mugs together and the abuse would begin to pour in. It seems I was wrong again." [116]

Finding anyone in either country to publish *Murphy* proved much more difficult than this and Beckett learned with growing dismay of rejection after rejection as he traveled around Germany. It was turned down by literally dozens of publishers in the course of the year. Beckett sent Reavey a photograph of two apes playing chess, which he had seen in the *Daily Sketch* before he left for Germany and now saw reprinted in a German illustrated magazine. How, he asked Reavey, should he set about obtaining permission to use the photograph as a frontispiece to his novel? Writing to Reavey again, he commented sarcastically: "The last thing I remember is my readiness to cut down the work to its title. I am now prepared to go further and change the title, if it gives offence." [117] In his diary, he wrote: "Don't give a bugger who publishes the blasted book, provided I have proofs to shelter me and the fuss of a publication when I am home." [118] *Murphy* was eventually accepted by T. M. Ragg for Routledge but only toward the end of 1937.

Beckett's last few days in Berlin were spent in a lively round of cinema and theatergoing, often alone but sometimes in the company of his landlord, Kempt, and another guest at the pension, a film actor called Josef Eichheim. [119] The three of them went together to see two films in which Eichheim had roles, *Der Lachende Dritte* and *Jäger von Fall*. Beckett then went on his own to see Werner Krauss star in the film *Burgtheater*, and dragged himself along to the Schauspielhaus to see Schiller's *Maria Stuart*, which, he wrote to Mary Manning, "stays alive for 4 acts without betraying how it contrives to do so." [120] Once he felt well enough to stir, these cultural activities brought down the final curtain on his extended stay in Berlin. He was not to return for nearly thirty years — and then to a very different, mostly rebuilt, but divided city.

4

HE MOVED TO DRESDEN, making four separate stops on the way: Halle, Weimar (with a brief excursion to Erfurt), Naumburg, and Leipzig. Just before leaving Berlin, he met "a charming stage decorator and Händel expert" named Porep, who was going to Halle to prepare some set and costume designs for the theater. [121] Porep, who had lived for some time in Mexico, knew Dolly Travers-Smith (Hester Dowden's daughter) from Dublin, and had known the composer Darius Milhaud in Paris, invited Beckett to contact him later. Beckett liked Porep so much that he seems to have included Halle in his itinerary mainly in order to see him again. He took the train there with the designer's assistant.

To Beckett's surprise, in the Moritzburg gallery in Halle, where, almost inevitably, he spent as much time as he could, he found some excellent modern paintings that had not yet been removed from public display. Porep also arranged for him to view a fine private collection of modern art in the Weise house in Händelstrasse, where, after looking at paintings by Kirchner, Munch, Heckel, Schmidt-Rottluff, and Müller, Beckett sat on for a moment in an upstairs room, talking animatedly with the pleasant Frau Weise about the "widening gulf between the artist, official and public from 19th century on. Dreadful situation, aesthetic (the shadow of expressionism) and material, of young artist in Germany." [122] Before he left Halle, Porep gave him letters of introduction to one of Germany's leading dancers, Gret Palucca, in Dresden, and to a dentist friend of his, Dr. Zarnitz, in Munich. Beckett was to meet them both later and they, in their turn, were to introduce him to others.

He broke his journey to visit the houses of Goethe and Schiller in Weimar from which he made a day trip to Erfurt where, again to his utter delight, he found that some excellent modern pictures of Kirchner, Kandinsky, Feininger, Heckel, Schmidt-Rottluff, Nolde, even Dix, had not yet been removed. Then, allowing only enough time in Naumburg "in the thick snow and sterilising cold"[123] to visit the "stupendous" Dom,[124] he went on the same evening to Leipzig. He found the town ugly, although with the abscess coming up again, he admitted to being in a very "cantankerous mood."[125] He attended a concert in the Gewandhaus that he described to MacGreevy as "an insult to the senses and the understanding"[126] and a big Max Klinger exhibition in the museum in Augustusplatz that failed to impress him. Encouraged by having found some modern paintings on the walls in Halle and Erfurt, he searched, but in vain, for Nolde, Heckel, and Pechstein pictures that should have been in the permanent collection.[127] Adding discomfort to his pain, the weather turned bitterly cold and he froze in a hotel room that was unheated for most of the day. He left Leipzig with a sense of relief and arrived in Dresden on January 29, 1937; there, his mood (or his luck) was to change for the better. "Lovely first impression of Dresden, sense of freedom and space after the thickets of Leipzig,"[128] he wrote on his arrival in what he called either "Florence on the Elbe"[129] or the "Porcelaine Madonna."[130] Even so, he stayed for only three weeks.

In Dresden, as in Hamburg, astonishingly, doors were once again opened for him by art lovers and private collectors. A few days into his stay (on the recommendation of Gret Palucca, whom he telephoned shortly after his arrival), he met Will Grohmann, the former director of the Zwinger gallery, who had been dismissed three years earlier from his post there and from the *gymnasium* because he was Jewish. Beckett, who arrived early for his appointment, found him hanging pictures by Klee, Kandinsky, Picasso, Miró, and Schlemmer. He was charmed by the eminent art historian and overwhelmed by his deep knowledge of modern German art. Grohmann also interested Beckett with his arguments for staying on in Germany after his dismissal and with a Jewish intellectual's perspective on a deteriorating situation:

> Says it is more *interesting* to stay than to go, even if it were possible to go. They can't control *thoughts*. Length of regime impossible to estimate, depends mostly on economic outshot. If it breaks down it is fitting for him and his kind to be on the spot, to go under or become active again. Already a fraternity of intellectuals, where freedom to grumble is less than the labourer's, because the labourer's grumble is not dangerous.[131]

Beckett had the opportunity to observe for himself the Dresden fraternity of intellectuals at work and play and to benefit personally from their friendly welcome, remarkable kindness, and warm generosity. He found himself caught up again in a social group; this one centered on the famous art collector Ida Bienert, her son, Friedrich, and a group of white Russian émigrés, among whom were Prince Obolensky, who worked as a guide in Florence, and his sister, a charming lady married to a German called von Gersdorff. Only a few days after his arrival, he was whisked away one evening in a chauffeur-driven car to Friedrich Bienert's house, where he met Obolensky, the von Gersdorffs, and a number of their friends:

> Frau v. Gersdorff takes me in hand, talks English, says I am earnest, asks questions, communicates the life story of a white emigrant. She has 4 children and her husband teaches Russian in a military barracks! She writes articles for the paper and illustrates them. The redhaired woman [an actress] is now drunk and insists on acting fragments from her repertory, in which I am involved. Obolensky amusing glum throughout, with short burst of articulation. Herr v. Gersdorff plays Russian tunes. I start Mac Donald [the song "Old MacDonald had a farm"] and give it up. Break up about 2, when all the cognac is drunk.[132]

This meeting led Beckett into two quite dissimilar sets of activities with members of a group with whom he described himself as "so agreeably entangled":[133] one, looking at paintings and drawings that he loved; the other, attending lectures, concerts, and parties in which he felt much less at ease.

He liked Ida Bienert very much. He found her "pleasant almost to the point of jollity," but with a slightly rough, forthright side to her of which he also approved. The sole defect, he noted in his diary, was an unpleasant tendency to recite the "Nazi litany."[134] Her son, on the other hand, was not a Nazi sympathizer. Beckett visited Ida first for "tea and cakes in the gloaming"[135] in her palatial abode at 46 Würzburgerstrasse, with beautiful period furniture displayed in a modern setting. The paintings on the walls of every room were magnificent.[136] Frau Bienert invited him back to lunch to see the collection again, this time in daylight, when he admired a wonderful Kandinsky, the *Träumerische Improvisation*, and a beautiful Renoir with a "figure lovely and very Watteauesque."[137]

He accompanied Grohmann and Palucca, who was the divorced daughter-in-law of Bienert, to a concert by the Quartetto di Roma of Mozart, Beethoven, and Verdi, at which he met most of the same people; then he went with the von Gersdorffs to hear Prince Obolensky lecture on Florence and Florentine art. The lecture was followed by a "horrible huge party" in the Italienisches Dörfchen, which, in the company of so many former Russian aristocrats, made him "feel wholeheartedly Communist most of the evening."[138]

The warmth of his welcome into such a tightly knit fraternity served, however, only to highlight his own profound sense of isolation and exile. That evening he poured out his feelings in his diary in a remarkable mixture of fierce self-criticism and intense self-pity:

> I am always depressed and left with [a] sense of worthlessness at the beautifully applied energy of these people, the exactness of documentation, completeness of equipment . . . and authenticity of vocation. In comparison I am utterly alone (no group even of my own kind)

and without purpose alone and pathologically indolent and limp and opinionless and consternated. The little trouble I give myself, this absurd diary with its list of pictures, serves no purpose, is only the act of an obsessional neurotic. Counting pennies would do as well. An "open-mindedness" that is mindlessness, the sphincter of the mind limply for ever open, the mind past the power of closing itself *to everything but its own content*, or rather its own treatment of a content.

I have never thought for myself. I have switched off the incipient thought in terror for so long that I couldn't think now for half-a-minute if my life (!) depended on it.[139]

Yet in this orgy of self-flagellation, he can still be found clinging almost desperately to the hope that from the wreckage he might at some time create literature: "Perhaps I am this equal," he wrote, "to the relatively trifling act of organisation that is all that is needed to turn this dereliction, profoundly felt, into literature. Spes unica. [Only hope]."[140] It was to be ten years before he discovered exactly how to use "this dereliction."

Beckett was not temperamentally drawn to opera. But in Dresden he went on his own to see Mozart's *Marriage of Figaro*, and, for once, relished the performance:

Theatre radiant. Small public. Admirable orchestra, conducted by Böhm. Exquisite inszenierung [production]. Wonderful costumes. Figaro excellent. Susanna and Chérubin lovely and excellent, especially latter. Barbarina also. Gräfin Almaviva the tragic relief. Her high point the Recitative and Aria in Act III. Last act Watteau enough to be not in the least Watteau. A more puerile world than Watteau's, where the interest even in sexual congress has lapsed. They are all Chérubin.[141]

It was, he confessed, "the first opera that I was sorry to have over."[142] As in Berlin, he also escaped from the city on a number of occasions, once to Augustus the Strong's 1720s summer palace at Pillnitz and once to Meissen, where he spent longer looking at the cathedral with its "lovely, simple and cool"[143] interior than at the manufacture and painting of the famous porcelain, although he came away with a powder box as a present for his mother.

But his main purpose in visiting Dresden was to see the art collections, particularly the Old Masters in the Zwinger gallery. So he spent days in a building that he found much restored, but well restored.[144]

I don't know what to say about the gallery. I suppose to us even the more discriminating royal collection of the 18th century, which it remains essentially, must have more defects than merits. There is a terrible lot of late Italian rubbish, no primitives, practically no Flemish of the great period, and rooms and rooms full of Mengs and Rosalba pastels and Bellotto views of Dresden. And it is badly lit and hung. I should not think for a moment of comparing it with the Kaiser Friedrich.[145]

Yet he found plenty of fine paintings to admire in the permanent collection: a "stupendous" Antonello da Messina (a St. Sebastian the details of which he could remember more than a decade later),[146] the "indescribably lovely" Vermeer *Kupplerin, (Procuress)* and a Poussin Venus, which he considered "beyond praise and appraisement," to mention only three of his favorites. He was particularly drawn to Brouwer's paintings of low peasant life: "Brouwer, dear Brouwer," he called him.[147]

As well as visiting the Zwinger on nine separate days, he spent another entire day in the Alte Akademie, where the Caspar David Friedrichs caught his eye; he confessed to having a "pleasant predilection for 2 tiny languid men in his landscapes, as in the little moon landscape, that is the only kind of romantic still tolerable, the bémolisé [in a minor key]."[148] His predilection for this painting of two men observing the moon was to assume added significance after the war, when he began to write *Waiting for Godot.*

5

BECKETT HAD BEEN PLANNING the final phase of his German trip for some while. It was modified several times in the light of recommendations he received, but he wound up going from Dresden to Munich via Freiberg (especially to see the Goldene Pforte, the Golden Portal, there), Bamberg, Würzburg, Nuremberg, and Regensburg. In every town he was an avidly curious spectator, following his Baedeker handbook or books on buildings in the Deutsche Bauten series, which he bought as he went along, asking questions of guides or local people and seeking to buy postcards of sculptures, doorways, and altarpieces.[149]

Near the Alte Residenz in Bamberg, he met a part-time guide who provided him with a lot of detailed information about that building and others in the town. On impulse, Beckett invited him to dinner that evening. Over the meal, it emerged that the man was a tailor by profession. He poured out a stream of woes to Beckett: his illnesses, his war wound, his debts, his difficulty in developing his business because he could not afford to offer credit, and so on. Beckett felt sorry for him but at the same time felt an instinctive distrust of someone who was so adept at playing on his troubles.

Compassion won out over suspicion, however, and though worried about his own financial position, he asked the tailor if he would make him a "midnight blue" suit. A special cloth was recommended; it would have to be sent away for; and it would cost one hundred and twenty marks; Beckett had previously sold his big leather coat for ten marks. He was measured, paid the first thirty-five marks down, then arranged for a fitting on Sunday morning in Nuremberg, following which he would pay the rest by post after receiving his next lot of money from home in Munich. Beckett saw the tailor several times more before he left Bamberg, commenting revealingly in his diary: "Curious that I can court a person that essentially I shudder away from. My need of the sick and evil."[150]

The intuition that he was about to be swindled did not leave him as he had to stay on in Nuremberg for an extra two nights, there being no news of the man or the fitting. The tailor eventually called to tell him the train on which he was coming; Beckett went to the station to meet him. The man was not there, but he turned up a few minutes after Beckett had returned to his hotel. He had come, he said, by an "extra" train. By this time Beckett began to feel sure that he was being conned. The man was, he confided to his diary that evening:

> Full of excuses and explanations. Mixture of insufferably hideous and pitiable. Every second phrase a lie, every third a try on and every sixth a grovel and all?!! Good. Only has coat with him. Says no need to try on the trousers, though of course they are ready! The stuff came only this morning. Suddenly occurs to me that the stuff never came at all, perhaps never was ordered, and that what he has used is inferior. Telepathically he starts to praise the stuff, woof, weight, etc. His next own suit will be of no other. He had meant to bring the sample so that I could compare, but etc. . . . It is so flagrant as to be diverting. It is diverting to be thought to be done. One is done but not in the eye. The difference between being done and done in the eye is in first case one knows and in second not. He thinks he is doing me in the eye, whereas he is only doing me. That is the diverting position, that I would not spoil with the least show of discernment.[151]

This account of the evening—which ended with the tailor commenting that it was a long time since he had met anyone to whom he had felt such a strong and immediate attachment—casts an interesting light on Beckett's attitude to being conned. Later in his career, when he was much better off financially, his willingness to be touched for money or even for material possessions became notorious and his friends tried to protect him from his own generosity and vulnerability. At the time of the German trip, Beckett clearly still enjoyed the sense of intellectual superiority that recognizing that he was "being done" gave him. Later, however, this seems to have become submerged in a deep feeling of pity for someone whose circumstances or nature could force him or her into adopting fraudulent or dubious tactics. This incident also echoes the story that Nagg tells in *Endgame* of the tailor and the pair of trousers that he first botches for the client, then compares with God's less impressive creation. Eventually, Beckett's own suit arrived in Munich by post. It was "of grotesque cut, coat too big and trousers too short, but blue."[152] The same day he went out and bought a white fake-silk shirt to go with the suit. Later in the day he wrote a card to the tailor saying that "the suit is lovely except that it doesn't fit anywhere." Then he tried on the shirt, finding it "too big and beastly cut, but white."[153] Humor was to sustain Beckett in far worse situations than this.

6

HIS STAY IN MUNICH, where he arrived from Regensburg on March 4, 1937, was less congenial than in Dresden. He was already tired when he arrived. It had been a long, cold winter and he was sickeningly weary of traveling and living in unfamiliar rented rooms. Munich itself did not inspire him: "The Isar is a poor kind of a piddle after the lyrical Main in Würzburg and the heroic Danube in Regensburg, taking the Regen without a ripple, and the reinforced concrete of Museum Island doesn't help it. How does one scuttle an island?" [154]

He lodged at the Pension Romana, facing the colossal Akademie with its blackened statues of Castor and Pollux and Minerva. After a few "pig stupid" days when he drank too much and exhausted himself by walking too far, he went to the Alte Pinakothek, where his fatigue miraculously lifted and he rediscovered some of his freshness and enthusiasm. It was a thrill for him to see some of the paintings that he had already studied in reproduction when his cousin Morris Sinclair had brought him the illustrated catalogue of the Alte Pinakothek the previous year:[155] "the stiff-legged Cranach Crucifixions," [156] Hans Burgkmair's *Crucifixion*, described by Beckett as "with Virgin, JB [John the Baptist] and Magdalene, between repentant thief with Lazarus and unrepentant with Martha. . . . Unrepentant thief with back to beholder. The picture that in reproduction gave me idea for a Christ crucified with back to beholder." [157] And he found many other paintings to admire: the "wonderful" Christ in Botticelli's *Entombment*;[158] the St. Paul in Dürer's *The Four Apostles*, which Beckett considered was "Dürer's . . . best work, better than anything in the Baumgartner altar";[159] the wonderful *Resurrection* by Dieric Bouts the Elder, with an "interesting type for Christ, approaching Boschian, half idiot, half cunning. The remoteness almost of schizophrenia." [160]

A few of these paintings were to become so much part of his mental world that they resurfaced when he came to create his own visual images for the stage or to realize his plays onstage as his own director. Antonello da Messina's *Virgin of the Annunciation* from the Alte Pinakothek ("head and shoulders. Superb. With the aghast look, consternated skivvy") [161] is strangely echoed in the posture of May, the pacing figure in *Footfalls*; Beckett, directing, had the actress Billie Whitelaw clasp her hands across her body in a gesture that seemed to encapsulate her whole being. This was stored away with other memorable images from earlier in his artistic pilgrimage: Antonello's *St. Sebastian*; Caspar David Friedrich's *Two Men Observing the Moon* from Dresden; and Giorgione's extraordinary self-portrait from Brunswick.

Beckett soon decided to look up the people whose names he had been given in Hamburg, Dresden, and Halle. Three quite separate avenues quickly led to a number of other contacts. The first, Dr. Hans Rupé, the director of the Bayerisches Nationalmuseum, had been a friend of Rilke and reminded Beckett of his own old friend the scholarly Pickwickian publisher Charles Prentice; he had even translated Sappho, something that Beckett could imagine the English classical scholar doing. Rupé invited Beckett to his house and revived his flagging spirits with Rhine wine, brandy, cigars, and lively, interesting conversation. Their talk at one point anticipated an important shift in Beckett's writing. They spoke, wrote Beckett, "about the nature of language. Every language once ripe, then falls behind, i.e. once congruent with its provocation, then eclipsed. I boost the possibility of stylelessness in French, the pure communication."[162] And, after the Second World War, when Beckett began to write in French rather than in English, he offered by way of explanation the fact that French allowed him to write "without style."

Dr. Rupé was responsible for putting Beckett in touch with Günther Francke, who ran a private art gallery at 8C Briennerstrasse and was the only man in Munich who still dared to exhibit Marc and Nolde. Beckett called round at his Graphisches Kabinett to meet the plump young gallery owner, who, in a private room, showed him a lot of late Nolde watercolors. Francke was friendly and helpful. He showed Beckett the first powerful Brücke-style paintings he had seen of Max Beckmann, whose work had been dismissed as decadent by the Nazis in 1933 and who was to leave the country shortly before the notorious "Degenerate Art" exhibition mounted in Munich a few months after Beckett left Germany. Francke introduced him to the painter Griebel, whose work he was currently exhibiting in his gallery. Griebel's paintings were not at all to Beckett's taste. He dismissed them as "appalling" and "very flat and Greek vasey";[163] he found their creator "as dull as ditch[water]."[164] Francke also gave him the names and addresses of other painters, two of whom invited Beckett along to see their work: one was "the one and only German surréaliste, one Ende";[165] the other was Josef Mader. Beckett did not like the paintings of either of them.[166]

He was disappointed. What had seemed to offer a promising entrée into the modern Munich art scene through the exciting, precarious — and even, by this date, dangerous — world of collecting and dealing in modern painting had petered out into a few cursory, uninspiring meetings with painters whose work totally failed to excite him. During the last two weeks of his stay, however, he met an actor and theater director, Eggers-Kastner, whose name and address he had been given by the painter Kluth. Beckett enjoyed his company more than that of anyone he had met since Dresden and was intrigued by "the touch of histrionics in his gestures and words."[167] But what interested him most was to learn that Eggers was a personal friend of Karl Ballmer and knew Kluth well. The actor owned some admirable pictures, including a beautiful Ballmer portrait of his children and three or four paintings by Kluth. And he talked admiringly of Ernst Barlach as a playwright, when Beckett knew him only as an artist.

Discussing theater and cinema with Eggers-Kastner, Beckett found himself drawn into making discoveries of his own. He was provoked, for example, into an interesting analysis of James Joyce's *Work in Progress*:

Long discussion about theatre and film, which Eggers condemns, calls at the best intellectualism. Won't hear of possibility of word's inadequacy. The dissonance that has become principle and that the word cannot express, because literature can no more escape from chronologies to simultaneities, from Nebeneinander to Miteinander, . . . [than] the human voice can sing chords. As I talk and listen realise suddenly how *Work in Progress* is the only possibility [possible] development from *Ulysses*, the heroic attempt to make literature accomplish what belongs to music — the Miteinander and the simultaneous. *Ulysses* falsifies the unconscious, or the "monologue intérieur," in so far as it is obliged to express it as a teleology. I provoke loud amusement by description of a man at such a degree of culture that he cannot have a simple or even a predominating idea. I say how can one in such a case be of any opinion, i.e. how can one see anything "simple and whole," because perception is opinion (a very doubtful logic that is let pass). Could have gone on to say that the attempt to "purify" vision from judgment had only resulted in the crassest naturalism.[168]

Although he was often silent, Beckett's ideas on the inadequacy of language and the superiority of music as an art form, on the relation between the subject and the object in art, and on the notion that rationalism was an aberration and naturalism in art was an impoverishment could flow with so much passion that he was embarrassed by his own fervor, even his wildness. He was aware of the difficulty of what he was groping to express, for himself as well as for others.[169]

Beckett also used his letter of introduction from Porep to his dentist friend, Dr. Zarnitz, "a hearty little man," who invited Beckett to meet many of his friends: "the bookseller Severing, painter Achmann, a redfaced gent of haberdashing quality and a bearded religious maniac."[170] Then, through the helpful bookseller, who provided Beckett with information on recent German fiction as well as on books on painting, he met the German writer Paul Alverdes. Beckett remembered that his Hamburg bookseller friend Albrecht had rated Alverdes as high as Thomas Mann, and he had purchased *Pfeiferstube* and *Reinhold im Dienst* and read them in the course of his travels. He thought *Pfeiferstube* "excellent. In spite of kiss of peace at end"[171] but found the second book "inferior to *Pfeiferstube*. The same tricks of narration, new introductions, flash backs; physiognomic chinoiserie almost, dying falls."[172]

Beckett met the writer, whom he described as "slight, quiet, very tasteful talent,"[173] on consecutive days. But he found both meetings something of a disappointment.[174] He gave Alverdes a typescript of his own German translation of his poem "Cascando" and a copy of *Echo's Bones*, and showed him some photographic reproductions that Jack Yeats had sent him of his recent paintings. In turn, Alverdes asked Beckett if he would write about the contemporary lyric for the literary review that he edited. They talked about politics, Alverdes expressing his hope that the stranglehold might be broken from within the Nazi party itself and stating his belief that Goebbels was entirely competent to judge what was good and what was not. But the chemistry was wrong, Beckett concluding that Alverdes was a "pleasant little man but not especially impressive. Says he is lazy and without ambition. Better than being lazy and with ambition. The best could be industrious without ambition." [175]

If Beckett did not take to Munich as a city, he still had some intriguing experiences there. One evening, instead of going to bed, he went out alone to the Benz Cabaret to watch the famous comic Karl Valentin perform in a "half-witted electrician act with Liesl Karlstadt. Real quality comedian, exuding depression, perhaps past his best. Physically something like Jack Yeats. Don't follow half of his dialect. Reduced here and there to knockabout." [176] Then, on the very last day of his stay, the film actor Eichheim, who had turned up in Munich, arranged for Beckett to meet Valentin personally. It was a brief, bizarre meeting; "crazy" was the word Beckett used. With a torch in one hand and a toothpick with a little white fur in the other, Valentin led them through a maze of dark corridors "in his new museum," which had the maddest old junk lying all over the place. He rambled on in his difficult dialect about Madame Tussaud's waxworks museum, talked of a form of neurosis, and said that "if he went to London again he would have a long white beard before he got there . . . that the propeller would fall off, etc." [177] Suddenly he excused himself, leaving Beckett and Eichheim disconcerted and yet intrigued. But it was the performance, not the personal encounter, that Beckett would recall thirty-five years later in response to a question as to whether he saw Valentin: "Yes, I saw K.V. in a shabby café-théâtre outside Munich. Evil days for him. I was very moved." [178] It is fascinating that Beckett should have been struck by the element of depression that Valentin's act exuded, for it has been suggested that the nature of the dialogue between Valentin and Liesl Karlstadt may well have combined with the more labored delivery of Laurel and Hardy and the comic repartee of English or Irish music-hall comics to produce the somber though lively exchanges of Estragon and Vladimir. [179]

Although the weather started to improve in late March, as the final weeks of Beckett's stay in Germany wore on his diary records fewer of those poetic moments that he had experienced earlier, watching a dramatic sunset or a flock of birds taking wing. By the third week of his stay, he could write to MacGreevy: "The journey is over, mentally as usual long before physically, and from now on I shall simply be hanging round waiting to get into the air." [180] A less resolute or less resilient person would have given up long before. But in Munich his mood of depression became more and more acute: "Apathetic and melancholy. Nothing now and nothing ahead but age and ugliness and nothing past but grief and remorse," he wrote decisively, if melodramatically, in his diary. [181] "I was never yet so limp, stupid and without hope for the future." [182] He was saddened to learn from his mother on March 12 that his Kerry Blue bitch, Wolf, his companion on so many walks in the hills, was very sick, and was tapped to discover that she had "fibrous growths" [183] It was time to go back home.

He decided to fly back rather than take the long train journey. Traveling by air meant that he could buy a ticket through to England and pay for it entirely in German marks. His bags were sent on by train to London in advance, heavy with books, catalogues, guidebooks, and reproductions. The following day, April 1, 1937, Beckett said good-bye to Nazi Germany with a sense of relief. He took the plane to Croydon, flying via Frankfurt and Amsterdam. He was desperately weary. Yet the memories of the magnificent paintings that he had had the chance to see in the German galleries were to remain etched indelibly in his mind for the rest of his life.

He had chosen to go to Germany when he did partly out of nostalgia for the days spent in Kassel with Peggy and the Sinclair family. But he also sensed that, as things were going, visiting Germany would soon become impossible. "They *must* fight soon (or burst)," he wrote in his diary only a few days after his arrival in Germany, after he had listened to the "apoplexy" of Adolf Hitler's and Goebbels's broadcast speeches.[184] And it was not to be long before Beckett had a chance to display his anti-Nazi credentials.

11

A Permanent Home

1937–39

1

BECKETT FOUND HIS RETURN HOME TRAUMATIC. At first, his mother fussed over him, doing all she could to make him feel welcome, even pampered: "I have been in a daze since returning, very stupid and fairly comfortable," he wrote.[1] For a short while he tried to convince himself that he might even settle down at Cooldrinagh with some degree of bovine contentment. Yet his feelings already sound ambivalent:

> I feel now that I shall meet the most of my days from now on here and in tolerable content, not feeling much guilt at making the most of what ease there is to be had and not bothering very much about effort. After all there has been an effort. But perhaps I am wrong. Perhaps it is Dr. Johnson's dream of happiness, driving rapidly to and from nowhere.[2]

Over the past five years, he had spent only a few consecutive months in Ireland, and it was not long before he again became irritated by what he saw as parochialism and narrow-mindedness. More significantly, the old bones of contention between himself and his mother, covered recently by a light sprinkling of earth, rose inexorably to the surface.

It is not hard to understand her impatience and annoyance. He was thirty-one, unmarried, living at home, and without a job; worse still, he showed no inclination at all to search for one. His mother had never understood why he had resigned his lectureship five years before, throwing away an excellent academic career. Now, three potential posts came up within a few months. He was actually offered the first by a friend of his brother: "I was offered a job as agent to an estate (Lord Rathdowne's?) near Carlow. £300 per an. And a free house," he wrote.[3] Frank thought that the job would allow him to write as well as administer the estate. But Beckett merely passed on the details to Arland Ussher and Joe Hone and turned the post down as totally unsuitable for himself. Then, after dragging his heels for several weeks, he decided not to apply for a lectureship in English in Buffalo, New York.[4] When he did apply, on April 29 1937, for a lectureship in Italian at the University of Cape

Town, it was with the greatest reluctance and because the job was recommended by his old professor, Rudmose-Brown. In spite of Beckett's earlier resignation from Trinity and the Polar Bear caricature, Ruddy provided him with a glowing reference.[5] But Beckett did not really want to teach again, or to resume a life that he had already rejected. More than this, he wanted to write.

Yet if he intended to be a writer, in his mother's eyes he seemed to be going about it in a very bizarre kind of way. *Murphy* had been turned down many times and he had nothing else in his drawer to offer a publisher. But, having just returned from Germany with extensive notes on his experiences, why, she asked, did he not use this material to write a book or newspaper articles about Germany that would sell? Even when requested by Rowohlt Verlag in Berlin to make a selection of Joachim Ringelnatz's poetry and translate it for a Faber and Faber "Miscellany," he turned the offer down on the grounds that the German writer was "worse than I thought."[6] Such a gesture must have been incomprehensible and exasperating to a practical, down-to-earth woman like May.

Beckett soon found himself almost penniless. His small monthly check barely covered normal living expenses — books, train fares into Dublin, beer, and tobacco — and his mother, having already paid for his psychotherapy in London and heavily subsidized his trip to Germany and his flight home, was unwilling to give him more money. Neither *Proust* nor *More Pricks Than Kicks* brought in any royalties, since they had not yet exceeded their advances. So, when he had to buy presents for George Reavey's wedding and for his friend Mary Manning's baby daughter, Susan, he found that he was already broke by the beginning of the month, with three weeks still to go before the next check was due.[7] It was a humiliating position to be in.

Frank remained very protective toward his younger brother, helping him as much as he possibly could, morally as well as financially. Over the Whitsun holiday, for instance, he took Sam on a walking tour to Clonmel and the Galtees. And he regularly lent him money. In fact, Frank emerges from Beckett's correspondence as the unsung hero of these difficult years. Yet their attitudes and interests diverged radically now. And, under great pressure at work, Frank had problems of his own. He was naturally very preoccupied with his forthcoming marriage to Jean Wright and with buying a house, Shottery, in Killiney.

Several incidents in his family contributed to Beckett's growing unhappiness and feelings of frustration.

The old bitch I was so fond of was destroyed (chloroformed) last Saturday week, unbeknown to me, while I was at Jack Yeats. I was very upset, as I had wanted to be with her at the end, to try and make it perhaps a little easier. Mother was prostrated, in bed for 2 days after it, and it was very hard work indeed getting her to take a reasonable view of what oneself could not take a reasonable view of.[8]

His mother was deeply attached to Wolf,[9] and, knowing of her son's even greater devotion to the bitch and of his own fragile state of health, she may well have been trying to spare him the pain of being involved in and responsible for the dog's end.[10]

There was worse to come. Boss Sinclair, with whom he had spent so many happy hours in Kassel, was terminally ill. The family had thought he was dying the previous August, before Beckett's departure for Germany.[11] But he had rallied. Now Beckett drove Cissie devotedly to the hospital to visit her husband. It was profoundly upsetting for him to see his uncle in his final days: "His last words to me were an apology for his poor company," he wrote.[12] The visits brought back too many painful memories of his own father's death, which never failed to tear him apart. And it was heartbreaking to see Cissie, ill herself by now with Parkinson's disease as well as arthritis, coping bravely, almost numbly, with the second death from tuberculosis in her family in four years.

Boss Sinclair died on May 4. Beckett wrote "some 100 lines hurriedly on Boss Sinclair for the "Irish Times" which were not interested."[13] Instead, Harry Sinclair wrote a warm appreciation of his brother, which was accepted — something else that, although he made light of it at the time, represented yet another rejection for Beckett. After her husband's death, Cissie opted to take two of her daughters, Nancy and Deirdre, to Graaff Reinet in South Africa to join her youngest son, Sonny, who had been sent to live on a farm in the semidesert Great Karoo region after suffering a bad attack of pleurisy while he was studying at Trinity College. He had been advised to stay in South Africa over the winter for the sake of his health.[14] Beckett commented of his aunt, "I dread to think how she will return, so rapidly does her 'Parkinsonism' get worse."[15] For him it meant saying farewell to someone else for whom he had enormous affection and with whom he always felt at ease.

2

IN COOLDRINAGH, almost every day Beckett experienced his mother's active disapproval. Although looked on with affection in the village, May was noted at home for her tendency to melodrama and histrionics, even over relatively minor matters relating to the family or the family home. The younger, surviving Kerry Blue terrier, Mac, for instance, got into numerous vicious scraps, attacked and killed a neighbor's cat, and one night came home with a blood vessel severed just underneath his tail. By the morning, the dog had bled all over the carpet, sofa, and armchairs. Eventually, it had to be muzzled to put a stop to such upsetting incidents.[16] Mary Farren, the cook and housemaid, often took Mac out for walks and sometimes, unwisely if kindly — for she regarded the practice of muzzling dogs as cruel—she unmuzzled him and let him off the leash. When, as a result, the dog got into further fights, Mrs. Beckett used to erupt like a volcano and another interminable row took place.

Disputes between May and her son were inevitably more devastating, for both were equally strong-willed and stubborn and the fierce affection that existed between them made disagreements strike more deeply and last longer than with anyone else. The most lightly barbed exchanges could flare up in a matter of moments into blazing rows. After a particularly violent quarrel, Beckett wrote that "Even mother suggests my leaving this country, une fois pour toutes [once and for all]. It isn't of course to be taken very seriously. It has happened so often before and will again. But I suppose each time there is a little less to rebound."[17] Once again, he began to experience his night panics and a racing heart:

> The heart bursts about one night in the seven (or, in the old saving clause, about one night in the seven I remember its having done so) and the pubic bone pain never quite stops its whispering and I have brief dissolvings in panic without their ever working up to the dithers of the old days. I am quite convinced, with that barren numb conviction of birth having sprung the trap, that at this rate it is only a matter of a few years before a hideous crisis compared to which the last was a cold in the nose and which I shall be as little fit to deal with as a bull calf with its castrators.[18]

This had happened only rarely while he was on his own in Germany, and he felt intense anxiety that it would lead to another terrible crisis such as had occurred four years before.

In the early summer, May Beckett fell ill with influenza and acute laryngitis, so, for a short time, she became dependent on him. Frank, too, had to be hospitalized and operated on for a septic hand when the poisoning went on to affect his entire arm. On Frank's discharge from the Merrion Nursing Home, Beckett found himself fully occupied dressing his brother and driving him about, gradually easing him back into work before the wedding and the honeymoon.[19]

But then, a few days before Frank's wedding on August 24, Beckett went "on the blind," as he put it,[20] going to a bottle party with Seán O'Sullivan at Charlie Gilmore's chaotic rented house in the Glencree valley in Wicklow. Beckett knew the hostess; Lilian Donaghy was now estranged from her husband, the poet Lyle, and she and her children were living with Gilmore. Beckett arrived there having already drunk several whiskeys and with a bottle of Jameson, bought with borrowed money, tucked under his arm. And he kept on drinking steadily throughout the evening. The writer Mervyn Wall, who met Beckett for the first time that night, remembered the voice of their hostess coming from underneath the table saying: "You mustn't be making love to me, Sam!"[21] He looked down to see a disheveled, disconsolate, and inebriated Beckett crawling out from under the table.

At about two o'clock in the morning, some of the men went for a swim in the pool, in the course of which Beckett fell and cut his head. When the party eventually ended, he left behind his watch, half a bottle of whiskey, and a lovely velour hat that he had bought in Germany. Although he was able to retrieve the hat and the watch the next day, the gash on his head could not be hidden, and his mother was horrified that he had to turn up at the wedding bearing such visible signs of his wild excesses. Worse still, she knew that he had been driving the car while drunk and feared, as in his more sober moments he did himself, for his physical safety. All this was anathema to the ultrarespectable May.

Beckett reacted to Frank's wedding with very mixed feelings. He was pleased to see his brother happier than he had been for a long time, although appalled by the way in which a love affair was "socialized":

> Watching the presents come along has been painful. The awful unconscious social cynicism that knows that what the relationship comes down to in the end is gongs and tea-trolleys, that without them there is no "together." Till it seems almost a law of marriage that the human personal element should be smothered out of existence from the word go, reduced to a mere occasion for good housekeeping and house chat, the eggcup in the pie of domestic solidity.[22]

His feelings were swayed by knowing that the marriage meant less contact with his brother, of whom he was extremely fond. "Another gone. From me I mean of course," he wrote revealingly, as inevitably he thought also not just of how much his mother would miss Frank but of how all her attention would now be focused exclusively, almost unbearably, upon himself.[23] The tensions in their relationship became more intense; their quarrels became more frequent; his response was to drink more heavily.

3

YET TO ACCEPT at face value Beckett's own judgment that he was "deteriorating now very rapidly"[24] and "going to the dogs" would be to ignore aspects of his life, and particularly of his intellectual life, that were crucial in keeping him going and were to have an enormous impact on his writing. One of his main lifelines was art. He frequently visited Jack Yeats in his studio to look at his latest paintings,[25] and invited Yeats, his wife, Cottie (Mary Cottenham Yeats), and the writer Joe Hone to Cooldrinagh for tea with his mother and himself.[26]

Beckett found Yeats's recent painting thrillingly innovative. Commenting on it to MacGreevy, he picked up what he had said two years earlier about Cézanne's treatment of landscape as being totally indifferent to man:

> What I feel he [Yeats] gets so well, dispassionately, not tragically like Watteau, is the heterogeneity of nature and the human denizens, the unalterable alienness of the 2 phenomena, the 2 solitudes, or the solitude and the loneliness, the loneliness in solitude, the impassable

immensity between the solitude that cannot quicken to loneliness and the loneliness that cannot lapse into solitude.[27]

Looking at Jack Yeats's painting in a way that the painter himself would probably not have recognized as his own, Beckett went on to extend this solitude to human beings, who are irretrievably cut off not just from nature but each other:

> I find something terrifying for example in the way Yeats puts down a man's head and a woman's head side by side, or face to face, the awful acceptance of 2 entities that will never mingle. And do you remember the picture of a man sitting under a fuchsia hedge, reading, with his back turned to the sea and the thunder clouds? One does not realize how still his pictures are till one looks at others, almost petrified, a sudden suspension of the performance, of the convention of sympathy and antipathy, meeting and parting, joy and sorrow.[28]

Speaking many years later of his continued admiration for Yeats, Beckett was to write to his friend the editor Georges Duthuit: "Ce n'est donc pas avec moi qu'on puisse parler art et ce n'est pas là-dessus que je risque d'exprimer autre chose que mes propres hantises" ("So you can't talk art with me; all I risk expressing when I speak about it are my own obsessions").[29] For, when he writes about Yeats, Beckett is clearly voicing his own bleak, uncompromising vision of human separateness and loneliness, a view anticipated seven years before in *Proust*, when he wrote (pushing Proust's own pessimism further than most readers would allow): "We cannot know and we cannot be known."[30] The true significance of the vision that he was formulating becomes clear, however, only when it informs the figures and characters of his own mature prose and drama: two figures wandering across an alien landscape at the beginning of his novel *Molloy*; Estragon and Vladimir in *Waiting for Godot*, together as they wait, but fundamentally alone; Krapp, separated from earlier versions of himself; Winnie, condemned to chatter away the rest of her existence to a largely unhearing, self-preoccupied, brutish companion; and the protagonist in *That Time*, listening to three discrete accounts of different moments in his lonely life.

Beckett's need for intellectual stimulus was answered by reading philosophy. It is symptomatic of his state of mind, however, that while he was ill with gastric influenza in early September 1937, he

> found the only thing I could read was Schopenhauer. Everything else I tried only confirmed the feeling of sickness. It was very curious. Like suddenly a window opened on a fug. I always knew he was one of the ones that mattered most to me, and it is a pleasure more real than any pleasure for a long time to begin to understand now why it is so. And it is a pleasure also to find a philosopher that can be read like a poet.[31]

He immersed himself deeply in Schopenhauer, who continued to influence his outlook, providing a clear justification for his view that suffering is the norm in human life, that will represents an unwelcome intrusion, and that real consciousness lies beyond human understanding.[32] In a letter to MacGreevy dated August 30, 1937, that is reminiscent of Murphy's lowest zone of mind, he wrote:

> The real consciousness is the chaos, a grey commotion of mind, with no premises or conclusions or problems or solutions or cases or judgments. I lie for days on the floor, or in the woods, accompanied and unaccompanied, in a coenaesthesic of mind, a fullness of mental self-aesthesia that is entirely useless. The monad without the conflict, lightless and darkless. I used to pretend to work, I do so no longer. I used to dig about in the mental sand for the lug-worms of likes and dislikes, I do so no longer. The lug-worms of understanding.[33]

Yet, in spite of his "coenaesthesic of mind," in the months after he returned from Germany he did a tremendous amount of work in the National Library of Ireland. Although his attention often wandered, as he watched the seagulls "stalking high overhead" and bringing a bone or a stone onto the glass roof of the reading room, most of the time he concentrated on reading about Dr. Samuel Johnson and his circle.[34]

He had been interested in Dr. Johnson for many years.[35] But the idea of sitting down to write an actual play about him and Mrs. Thrale seems to have occurred to him only during the late summer of 1936, before he left for Germany, or even in Germany itself.[36] He wrote to Mary Manning from Berlin that he had "often thought what a good subject was there, perhaps only one long act. What interested me especially was the breakdown of Johnson as soon as Thrale disappeared."[37]

His original intention was to construct his play around the relationship between Dr. Johnson and Mrs. Hester Thrale, thirty-one years younger. He wanted it to cover the period after Mr. Thrale's death in 1781 and before Hester decided to marry the Italian music teacher Gabriel Mario Piozzi in July 1784. Beckett entertained a number of theories about Johnson. One was that the good doctor had been in love with Mrs. Thrale for all the fifteen years that he had been living with the Thrales at Streatham Park and Southwark. Another, for which he admitted there was no text, was that Johnson was impotent:

> What interests me above all is the condition of the Platonic gigolo or house friend, with not a testicle, auricle or ventricle to stand on when the bluff is called. His impotence was mollified by Mrs Thrale so long as Thrale was there, then suddenly exasperated when the licensed mentula was in the connubial position for the first time in years, thanks to *rigor mortis*.[38]

He filled three bound octavo notebooks with extensive notes on the life of the Great Cham and his entourage.[39] And only in the final notebook and in separate typescripts did he try to "whittle the material down to a scenario for the intended play," to be called "Human Wishes" after Johnson's poem "The Vanity of Human Wishes."[40] However much reading on Johnson he may have done earlier, Beckett's focused research was conducted in Ireland between April and the early autumn of 1937.[41]

The manuscript notes and his letters to friends show Beckett grappling with two rather different themes: the love of Johnson for Mrs. Thrale, but also the image of Johnson in decline, physically ill and morbidly preoccupied with his own physical deterioration, dying, and death. As he worked, he lost some of his initial enthusiasm for the first theme (particularly as his confidence in the hypothesis about Johnson's impotence ebbed away), in favor of an increased concentration on the more private, solitary Johnson, afraid of going mad at several points in his life, charting his own physical decline, and lost in loneliness and dread.[42] He assured Mary Manning, with whom he continued to correspond:

> There won't be anything snappy or wisecracky about the Johnson play if it is ever written. It isn't Boswell's wit and wisdom machine that means anything to me, but the miseries that he never talked of, being unwilling or unable to do so. The horror of annihilation, the horror of madness, the horrified love of Mrs Thrale, the whole mental monster ridden swamp that after hours of silence could only give some ghastly bubble like "Lord have mercy upon us." The background of the *Prayers and Meditations*. The opium eating, dreading-to-go to bed, praying-for-the-dead, past living, terrified of dying, terrified of deadness, panting on to 75 bag of water, with a hydracele on his right testis. How jolly.[43]

His letters even reveal his first subject transforming itself into his second: "His horror at loving her I take it was a mode or paradigm of his horror at ultimate annihilation, to which he declared in the fear of his death that he would prefer an eternity of torment."[44]

In spite of the many differences between them, Beckett seems to have recognized in Dr. Johnson not merely a great writer and a fascinating case study, but a soul mate. For he, too, had long been interested in physical and mental illness, loneliness, and decline, and obsessed with solitude and death. And, as this decaying, solitary, self-conscious[45] Johnson figure swam more sharply into focus, so Beckett found it increasingly difficult to pursue the original biographical love drama on which he had embarked.[46]

His three main preoccupations during what was to be his final year in Ireland—his interpretation of Jack Yeats's painting, his immersion in the philosophy of Schopenhauer, and his study of the life of Johnson—all derive, then, from Beckett's personal obsessions: with the isolation of man from nature and man from man; with a reduction in the role of human will; and with solitude, illness, and death. And in retrospect, his work on Johnson can be seen to prefigure the concerns of his later writings. He wrote presciently to Mary Manning: "I have not written a word of the Johnson blasphemy. I trust that acts of intellection are going on about it somewhere. Which will enable me eventually to see how it coincides with the Pricks, Bones and Murphy, fundamentally and fundamentally with all I shall ever write or want to write."[47]

After all he says about his "Johnson fantasy" in his letters, the fragment of a scene that he did actually manage to write, perhaps written as late as 1940 — eleven and a half typed pages in all — is disappointing. It reveals little about Dr. Johnson, who is never mentioned by name and never appears. Even so, from the mouths of some members of what he called the doctor's "seraglio," he recreates indirectly some of Johnson's most constant concerns: his "vile melancholy"; his aversion to "merriment"; "the peevishness of decay"; his fascination with lexicography and especially recondite words. And Beckett's wider reading still makes its mark in such a short text. One of the characters, Miss Carmichael, for example, reads a passage about death from a favorite book of Dr. Johnson, Jeremy Taylor's *The Rule and Exercise of Holy Dying*, which Beckett had been reading four years before.[48] Another, Mrs. Williams, talks of her friends dying one after another, just as Proust did in *A la recherche du temps perdu* (Beckett had quoted this passage admiringly in his essay). But there is an added level of compassion now that probably stems from the deaths of his own father, of Peggy, and, more recently, of Boss Sinclair.

The play fragment also points forward: to the elegant, old-fashioned language and formalized syntax of the three women in *Come and Go*; to Clov deceiving the blind Hamm in *Endgame*, just as Miss Carmichael deceives the blind Mrs. Williams; and, above all, to *Waiting for Godot*, with conversations going nowhere, long silences pointing to "a sub-text that is never articulated in the dialogue."[49] One of the preparatory Johnson notebooks may even offer an unspotted source for the "Pozzo-Bozzo" exchanges, as Beckett copies out from the *Dictionary of National Biography* entry on Mrs. (Thrale) Piozzi the fact that Peter Pindar ridiculed her with a piece of wordplay on "Bozzy-Piozzi."

4

AT THE BEGINNING of September 1937, with Frank and Jean away on their honeymoon in Scotland and Beckett recovering from gastric flu, May was remarkably patient with him, posing few questions and making no scenes. One day, a Gypsy came to the door and read her palm. The woman reassured May that she would live to be over ninety and never be a burden on anyone, and that she should not worry anymore about her second son because he had "crossen the cross."[50] But this lull in their angry disputes was not to last for very long.

It is difficult to know exactly what precipitated their final and most bitter quarrel, which caused Beckett to leave Cooldrinagh and Ireland, never to live there again. If it was a single event rather than a slow buildup of annoyances and disputes, then it occurred between September 21 and September 28. On the earlier day, he could comment calmly that his mother's plans to rent the big house and move into somewhere smaller had fallen through and that she might go away for a holiday; if this happened, he would probably stay on at Cooldrinagh, he said, "with the cook and the dog."[51] The massive quarrel had clearly not yet taken place. But, by September 28, he wrote to MacGreevy from the Imperial Hotel in Waterford, where his brother had gone on a job:

> It is a great relief to me to get away from home, where the position between mother and me has become impossible. So impossible that I intend not to sleep at home again until I leave the country, which will be I hope early next week. . . . I was wrong in thinking I was well enough to deal with her and with myself in relation to her. Now I give up une fois pour toutes [once and for all].[52]

The break may have been caused by Mrs. Beckett's reaction to a car accident he had. On his first day out driving following his ten-day bout of gastric flu, he was involved in a serious collision with a truck. He was not injured but the car had to be written off. Beckett did not think that he had been driving dangerously, but the Gardai thought otherwise and brought a prosecution against him. Since he had only third-party insurance, no money could be claimed from the insurance company and, because of the prosecution, a claim for compensation against the driver or owners of the truck would stand no chance at all of succeeding. So the car was a total loss. May would have been upset and angry, especially if she believed he had been drinking. But she was probably even more annoyed by Beckett's determination to make a court appearance and defend himself, instead of pleading guilty and paying the fine. In her eyes, this would mean a public ignominy that could easily have been avoided.

The court case may have proved to be the last straw, or the last but one. For Beckett had also agreed to appear as a witness in a libel case that Harry Sinclair was bringing against Oliver St. John Gogarty. And May was resolutely opposed to his involvement. Judging by her subsequent behavior — she would have nothing at all to do with the Sinclairs after the trial — there is no doubt that she rated the damage done to her family's name and reputation as very grave. Boss Sinclair's son Morris wrote: "Knowing May, one understands that having her son pilloried in public and contaminated by a Dublin gutter scandal was almost more than she could bear."[53] Added to Beckett's recent wild behavior and refusal to conform to what she saw as decent standards, the two court cases brought things to a head. An angry yet hurt letter that he wrote after the quarrel suggests that she also invoked his father's memory to condemn him:

> I am what her savage loving has made me, and it is good that one of us should accept that finally. As it has been all this time, she wanting me to behave in a way agreeable to her in her October of analphabetic gentility, or to her friends ditto, or to the business code of father idealised and dehumanised — ("Whenever in doubt what [to] do, ask yourself what would darling Bill have done") — the grotesque can go

no further. It is like after a long forenoon of the thumb-screws being commanded by the bourreau [the torturer] to play his favorite song without words with feeling.[54]

The result was a terrible scene that made Beckett finally decide to leave both his home and the country of his birth—and at a most inconvenient time for him, when he knew he would have to return very soon for the Sinclair-Gogarty trial. Immediately after the quarrel, May left Cooldrinagh temporarily, perhaps in the hope that he would change his mind—about leaving Ireland at least—if he was left completely alone for a while.[55] But he was determined to go.

Although Beckett loved the Irish countryside and its ordinary people, and his writings are full of Ireland, he had become convinced that he could never function properly there as a writer. Morris Sinclair explained:

Living in Ireland was confinement for Sam. He came up against the Irish censorship. He could not swim in the Irish literary scene or in Free State politics the way W. B. Yeats did. . . . But the big city, the larger horizon, offered the freedom of comparative anonymity (Belacqua seeking the pub where he was unknown) and stimulation instead of Dublin oppression, jealousy, intrigue and gossip.[56]

The "larger horizon" was Paris. He felt at home there. He knew that he would have to eke out a precarious, hand-to-mouth existence. His modest allowance would barely allow him to survive on his own, without commissions as a writer, reviewer, and freelance translator, that, in the past, had simply not been forthcoming. Despite the guilt that he felt at leaving his mother's problems in the hands of his already overburdened brother, the strain of staying exceeded the fear and guilt of leaving. He probably rationalized his departure by telling himself that his family would be better off without him anyway.

He left for Paris in the middle of October, staying in London only a few days en route. There he saw MacGreevy, the newly wed Reaveys, and Geoffrey and Ursula Thompson. "Nothing changes the relief at being back here," he wrote from Paris. "Like coming out of gaol in April."[57] Paris was to be his permanent home for the next fifty-two years.

5

HIS FIRST FEW WEEKS in Paris were spent looking for somewhere more permanent to live than a pension or a hotel room. Everything was much more expensive than he had anticipated. Apartments cost four and a half thousand francs a year to rent, when two and a half thousand francs would have been feasible for his pocket. After spending a few days in a room at 12 rue de la Grande-Chaumière, he lived, while he searched, on the third (or fourth) floor of the small Hôtel Libéria on the same street, at number 9. It was just off the boulevard du Montparnasse with its familiar bookshops and cafés, the Dôme, the Sélect, and the Coupole.

He looked up old acquaintances who were going to matter if, as he now intended, he was to settle in Paris: Alan and Belinda Duncan, the Jolases, Georges and Marcelle Pelorson, and, above all, Alfred Péron and the Joyces. Brian Coffey was over from Dublin, living at the Cité Universitaire, and Beckett saw a lot of him, having several fairly "wild" evenings with him and the Duncans, mostly playing billiards or dining together.[58] Living in a hotel room, he was obliged to eat his meals, or mostly the one meal a day to which he restricted himself, in restaurants. He also started to call again at Shakespeare and Company in the rue de l'Odéon; in December, Sylvia Beach introduced him to the burly figure of Ernest Hemingway. Hemingway alienated Beckett almost immediately by dismissing Joyce's "Work in Progress." Beckett remembered: "I met him once in Sylvia Beach's bookshop. And he was very disdainful. He didn't approve at all of *Finnegans Wake*. I remember him saying, which I didn't like at all, 'We mustn't be too hard on the old man. *Ulysses* tired him out.' "[59] Beckett never had the slightest desire to meet Hemingway again.

He started to see the Dutch painter Geer van Velde and his wife, Elisabeth (or Lisl, as she was widely known). Lisl could remember the first meeting, arranged by George Reavey, between Beckett, the tall, good-looking Geer, and Geer's brother, the melancholy, silent, ruminative Bram. This was followed by a flood of visits to Geer's boulevard Arago studio and meetings for drinks and meals. Beckett and Geer played chess a lot together; the Dutchman was an excellent player, with whom Beckett had some engrossing contests. He was particularly fascinated by the small gouaches that Geer was producing at the time, nonfigurative yet with a recognizable figure, its head tilted to one side in a manner that Beckett found tender and touching.[60]

Geer was eight years older than Beckett. He had a great deal of personal charm and a dry sense of humor that appealed to Beckett, who did all he could in the next two years to promote his friend's work. After the war, as Geer and Beckett seemed to grow further apart in their attitudes to life, Beckett's affection and active support focused increasingly on Bram, with whom he felt he had more in common aesthetically. In the company of such new as well as old friends, Beckett started to feel at home and much more relaxed.

6

TRAUMATIC EVENTS SOON OCCURRED, however, which disrupted the excitement of being back in Paris and made Beckett's worries about his finances and flathunting fade into insignificance. Harry Sinclair's libel action was eventually brought before the High Court in Dublin between the twenty-third and twenty-seventh of November 1937. So, to give evidence, Beckett had to return to Ireland shortly after he had left. He could not afford to do this but paid his own return fare on the promise of a refund out of the damages, if the case were won. It is doubtful whether the money was ever repaid.

A few weeks before his death in May, Boss Sinclair had read some passages in Dr. Oliver St. John Gogarty's book *As I Was Going Down Sackville Street*, which he believed clearly libeled their grandfather Morris Harris, as well as himself and Harry. The grandfather had established a jewelry and antique shop at 47 Nassau Street,[61] and, on his death in 1909, he had handed on the shop to his twin grandsons.[62]

Harry agreed with Boss that he should sue Gogarty and the other defendants, Rich and Cowan, the London publishers responsible for publishing the book at the end of 1936.[63] Beckett also promised Boss on his deathbed that he would appear as a witness in support of the libel accusations. The passages complained of, on pages 70 and 71, of Gogarty's book concerned an

> old usurer who had eyes like a pair of periwinkles on which somebody had been experimenting with a pin, and a nose like a shrunken to-mato, one side of which swung independently of the other. The older he grew the more he pursued the immature, and enticed little girls into his office. That was bad enough; but he had grand-sons and these directed the steps of their youth to follow in grandfather's footsteps, with more zeal than discrimination.[64]

There followed a reference to "twin grandchildren." Earlier, on page 65, were some verses that formed a further part of Harry Sinclair's complaint. The first stanza went:

> *Two Jews grew in Sackville Street*
> *And not in Piccadilly.*
> *One was gaitered on the feet,*
> *The other one was Willie.*

A stanza later, in the American edition only, the poem went on:

> *They kept a shop for objects wrought*
> *By Masters famed of old*
> *Where you, no matter what you bought*
> *Were genuinely sold.*[65]

> *But Willie spent the sesterces*
> *And brought on strange disasters*
> *Because he sought new mistresses*
> *More keenly than old Masters.*

These were followed by other lines of verse that end with the words: "Thus did the twin grandchildren of the ancient Chicken Butcher."[66]

The Sinclair grandchildren were indeed twins, although not identical twins. "Harry, rounder, was tie-pin and pin-stripe, whereas Boss, craggier, was more tweed and open-shirt when he was still on the go."[67] Harry was the one who often sported gaiters; Willie was the "Boss." Although their father, John, was a Protestant, their mother was Jewish and the twins had been brought up in the Jewish faith, at the insistence, it is said, of the grandfather, who had been vice president and treasurer of the Jewish congregation in Dublin. Boss Sinclair's son Morris wrote: "Harry always considered himself a member of the Jewish community. Not so my father who used to inveigh against religion."[68] As the final element in the alleged Identikit portrait, both Sinclair brothers dealt in pictures as well as antiques and jewelry, but Willie was the one who specialized in paintings. "They made some very remarkable discoveries," said Beckett. "I remember they discovered a Rembrandt somewhere in the country."[69]

The Gogarty-Sinclair trial itself has been described several times before.[70] Yet it has not, perhaps, been realized quite how exposed and vulnerable Beckett was right from the outset of the case. "I am in it up to the neck. And gladly so in so far as Boss wanted it done," Beckett wrote[71] soon after the injunction against continuing publication of the book was sought in May, months before the actual trial.[72] Only two affidavits were filed at that time — one from the plaintiff, Henry Morris Sinclair, and the other from "Mr Samuel Beckett."[73] Beckett's personal affidavit, which was signed by him on May 12, 1937, filed on May 13, and resubmitted to the actual trial in November, included the claim:

> On reading the paragraphs at pages 65 and 70 and 71 I instantly inferred that the lines commencing "Two Jews in Sackville Street" at page 65 referred to Mr. Henry Morris Sinclair and the late Mr. William Abraham Sinclair, and that words "old usurer" and "grandsons" referred to the late Mr. Morris Harris and his said two grandsons. I also considered that the words constituted a very grave charge against the said Henry Morris Sinclair and his late brother.

In his formal judgment, the judge laid a great deal of emphasis on Beckett's affidavit, stating:

> the evidence of Mr Beckett is more important [than that of the plaintiff] as being that of an outsider and he states in the most unequivocal manner that on reading the book he understood these passages to refer to the plaintiff, his brother William, and their grandfather. He knew to some extent the circumstances and relationship of the Sinclair and Harris family, and it is clear that there are sufficient *indicia* in the passages to give any one who knew the family the necessary clue to their identity.[74]

The judge agreed that there was good cause for an injunction restraining further publication pending the trial, and his judgment was upheld by five judges, including the chief justice, C. J. Sullivan, of the Irish Supreme Court. Even at this early stage, Beckett was therefore a major player. As a consequence, he became a key witness for the plaintiff at the trial, and his judgment, reliabil-

The house at La Croix in Roussillon d'Apt where Beckett and Suzanne lived after their escape from the Gestapo.

The Irish Red Cross Hospital group in Saint-Lô in front of the lorry that Beckett used to drive, September 1945. Standing, foreground, left to right: A. W. Darley; a French military guard; Samuel Beckett; F. F. McKee; J. C. Gaffney; M. B. Killick; Colonel T. J. McKinney; and Tommy Dunne. In the lorry are German prisoners of war.

Courtesy of Mary Bryden

Courtesy of Dartmouth College

Courtesy of Dartmouth College

Beckett's mother, May, a year or two before her death in 1950.

Beckett with his niece, Caroline, and nephew, Edward, *c.* 1950.

Courtesy of Caroline Beckett Murphy

Beckett with Suzanne and his brother, Frank, at Ussy in 1953.

Beckett with his brother, Frank, during the latter's terminal illness, 1954.

Two photos: courtesy of Caroline Beckett Murphy

Left: Beckett in the Luxembourg Gardens in Paris, 1956.

Below: Beckett with his American publisher, Barney Rosset, in 1956, pictured at the foot of the statue of Auguste Comte in the Place de la Sorbonne.

Opposite: Samuel Beckett at Trinity College for the award of his honorary D.Litt., July 1959.

Two photos: courtesy of Syracuse University Library

Courtesy of the Irish Times

Photograph by Georges Pierre, courtesy of Avigdor Arikha

Courtesy of Margaret Farrington and Elizabeth Ryan

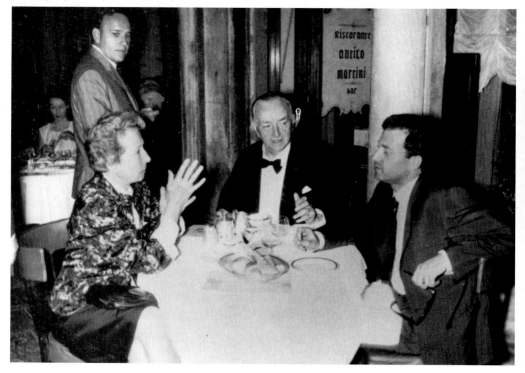

Opposite top: Samuel Beckett with his friend the painter Avigdor Arikha in Giacometti's studio, Paris, 1961.

Opposite bottom: Suzanne Beckett, Tom MacGreevy, and Matias dining in a Venice restaurant in 1962.

Beckett in the snow outside his cottage in Ussy sur Marne, winter 1962.

Courtesy of Dartmouth College

Courtesy of Josette Hayden

Beckett with his friends the painter Henri Hayden (on the left) and the actor Jean Martin, at a private viewing of an exhibition of Hayden's paintings at the Suillerot gallery in Paris.

Beckett leaning against his work desk in Ussy, *c.* 1965.

Courtesy of Dartmouth College

Courtesy of Lili Foldes

Samuel and Suzanne Beckett congratulate the concert pianist Andor Foldes in Paris, 1967. Foldes played all five of Beethoven's piano concertos on two evenings.

On the day he became seriously ill with an abscess on his lung, Beckett stands alone looking at Henri Hayden's paintings at the Musée National d'Art Moderne in Paris, May 1968.

Courtesy of Josette Hayden

Photograph by André Morain, courtesy of Avigdor Arikha
Beckett at the opening of Avigdor Arikha's exhibition at CNAC, Paris, December 1970.

Agence de Presse Bernand

Beckett's two actor friends, Jean Martin as Lucky and Roger Blin as Pozzo, in the world premiere of *En Attendant Godot,* 1953.

Samuel Beckett rehearses with Rick Cluchey and Michael Haerdter in his studio at the Akademie der Künste in Berlin.

Photograph by Ingeborg Lommatzsch, courtesy of Rick Cluchey

© 1956 Elliott Erwitt/Magnum Photos

Bert Lahr as Estragon, with E. G. Marshall as Vladimir, in *Waiting for Godot,* directed by Herbert Berghof, John Golden Theater, New York, April 1956.

Hume Cronyn as Krapp in *Krapp's Last Tape,* Vivian Beaumont Theater, Lincoln Center, New York, November 1972.

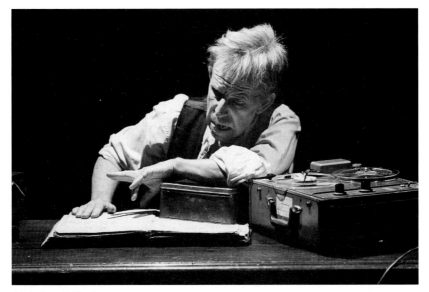

Martha Swope © Time Inc.

Martha Swope © Time Inc.

Photograph by John Haynes

Jessica Tandy in *Happy Days,* with Hume Cronyn as Willie, Vivian Beaumont Theater, Lincoln Center, New York, November 1972.

Billie Whitelaw in *Footfalls,* directed by Samuel Beckett, Royal Court Theatre, London, 1976.

Alvin Epstein, Daniel Wirth, and Rand Mitchell in *What Where,* Harold Clurman Theater, New York, 1983. Directed by Alan Schneider.

David Warrilow as Reader (on right) and Rand Mitchell as Listener in *Ohio Impromptu,* Harold Clurman Theater, New York, June 1983.

Three photos: Martha Swope © Time Inc.

An Off-Broadway revival of *Endgame* at the Samuel Beckett Theater, New York, 1984. Alice Drummond and King Donovan as Nell and Nagg, Peter Evans as Clov, and Alvin Epstein as Hamm. This production was designed by Beckett's friend Avigdor Arikha.

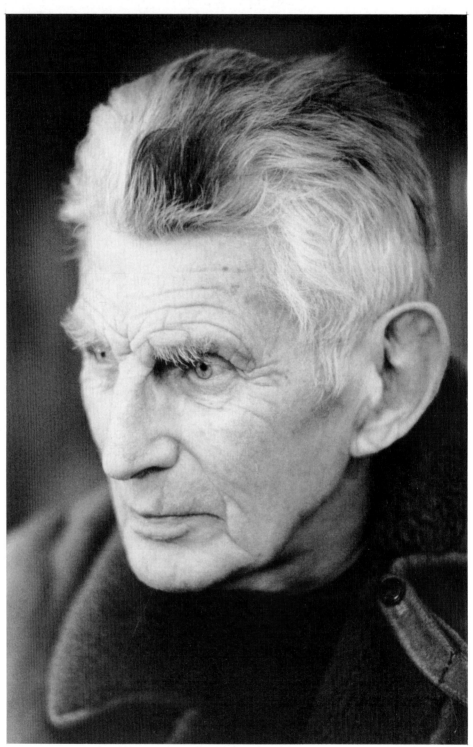

Samuel Beckett at 82.

Photograph by Beppe Arvidsson

ity, and integrity had to be undermined. This explains the defendants' counsel's rough tactics during the later questioning. Beckett was warned in advance that an attempt would be made to discredit him: "All kinds of dirt will be raked up," he wrote, "and I suppose they will try and discredit me as author of the *Pricks*."[75]

Gogarty's biographer, Ulick O'Connor, sets the physical scene for the November trial:

> The case created a sensation in Dublin. There is an illusion common among Dubliners, that they are potential writers or barristers. The opportunity of seeing both professions simultaneously on display was not to be missed. There were queues for seats in the gallery of the court. The action was tried in Court No. 4 of the High Court, which is one of four court rooms forming a circle under the copper dome in the front of the Four Courts. This building, designed by Richard Gandon in 1781, is only a road's width from the Liffey's edge, where a graceful curving balustrade sets it off against the brown tide with its drifting swans.[76]

Beckett took the stand as a witness after the plaintiff, his uncle Harry, had set out the reasons why his grandfather could be identified with Gogarty's "old usurer" with "a nose like a shrunken tomato." This meant, of course, admitting not only that Morris Harris had had a bulbous nose but that he had been accused of enticing young girls into his shop. It also meant claiming that he and his late brother could easily be identified as the "twin grandsons." The defense put little effort into undermining Sinclair's evidence or attacking his integrity.

But Beckett, as the so-called impartial witness, was treated far more roughly by J. M. Fitzgerald, King's Counsel. First, it was indicated to him during the cross-examination that no reference had been made in his affidavit to the fact that he was in any way related to the plaintiff and, consequently, could not be considered at all objective. Then, he was asked whether he had written a book on Marcel "Prowst." Beckett duly corrected counsel, as Fitzgerald knew he would, on the pronunciation of the name. The barrister went on to ask whether Proust had "indulged in the psychology of sex" and how long it had taken for Beckett's book to be banned by the censorship of Ireland. To the first question, Beckett answered that he had not been aware of Proust's indulgence, but, in answer to the second, he had to admit that it took "about six months" for his own book to be banned. Fitzgerald suggested that it was banned because it was blasphemous and obscene; "I never discovered why it was banned," replied Beckett.[77]

The counsel for the defense then switched his line of attack, as had been anticipated, to the 1934 stories, *More Pricks Than Kicks*. The title alone — the book had been listed among the items filed by the defense[78] — would probably have been enough to put off any sensitively pious juror. Fitzgerald read aloud for the jury the following passage, spoken by the Polar Bear to a Jesuit priest in an argument about religion conducted in a bus:

"The Lebensbahn" . . . of "the Galilean is the tragi-comedy of the solipsism that will not capitulate. The humilities and retro me's and quaffs of sirreverence are on a par with the hey presto's, arrogance and egoism. He is the first great self-contained playboy. The cryptic abasement before the woman taken red-handed is as great a piece of megalomaniacal impertinence as his interference in the affairs of his boy-friend Lazarus . . ."[79]

Then Fitzgerald asked Beckett whether this passage represented a blasphemous caricature of Jesus Christ. Beckett replied that both the character who spoke these words and the priest who heard them were fictitious, and that, as a writer, he could put words into their mouths that he did not agree with.[80] The defense counsel asked Beckett whether he would describe himself as a Christian, a Jew, or an atheist, to which Beckett replied, "None of the three." Fitzgerald also asked him if he was the author of a book called "horoscope" but printed with a "W" — that is, "Whoroscope." Beckett admitted that he was and that it had been privately printed for circulation among friends — the suggestion being that this was yet another book with immoral contents.

Further witnesses for the prosecution followed, claiming that they also recognized the complainants in Gogarty's book.

On the second day of the trial, Gogarty himself was called to the stand. He claimed that he had never thought of the lines that were the subject of the complaint as relating to the Sinclairs, that William Sinclair was universally known as Boss, not as Willie, that the name was chosen simply because it rhymed with "Piccadilly," that he had known both the Sinclair brothers but did not know that they were twins, and that his portrait of the "old usurer" was a composite one aimed at moneylenders in general and not at any identifiable person in Dublin. In his speech for the defense, Fitzgerald referred to a phrase that the counsel for the plaintiff, Albert Wood, K.C., had used earlier, "a côterie of bawds and blasphemers," and suggested that if the term applied to anyone present it was surely the chief witness for the plaintiff, Samuel Beckett. They, the members of the jury,

> would like to know why, of all the respectable people he knew, Mr Sinclair should select that "bawd and blasphemer" from Paris to make an affidavit in the case to lead to the belief that an ordinary reasonable man reading the book would have identified Mr Sinclair. Could they imagine "that wretched creature" making representations to the High Court as an ordinary reasonable man?[81]

The exchanges were widely reported in the press, and a column subheading of *The Irish Times* the next day read "Bawds and Blasphemers."[82]

The case was won by Harry Sinclair, who was awarded damages of nine hundred pounds plus costs. The trial cost Oliver St. John Gogarty around two thousand pounds in all and undoubtedly hastened his departure from Dublin. But Beckett, who was on the winning side, came out nothing if not a loser.

Even the judge, Justice O'Byrne, in his summing up to the jury, expressed the view that he "did not strike me as a witness on whose word I would place a great deal of reliance."[83]

Beckett found the experience totally distasteful; he loathed the publicity that the case had aroused and bitterly resented being humiliated. The entire episode left a very nasty taste in his mouth that no amount of reassurance or friendly support from friends like Brian Coffey, who came over with him from Paris, or Seán O'Sullivan could disguise. And, although he rarely discussed the case in his correspondence or with friends, his remarks about Ireland became more and more vituperative after his return to Paris, as he lambasted its censorship, its bigotry, and its narrow-minded sexual and religious attitudes, from which he felt he had suffered. The trial and the publicity it attracted made the situation with his mother, who would have been horrified at what was being written about her son in the press, worse rather than better, and he did not stay with his family while he was in Dublin. Indeed, although he saw Frank on several occasions alone, he left the country without seeing his mother even once. It was a horrendous episode, which he wanted to put far behind him.

7

THE COURTROOM DRAMA WAS OVER. Real-life drama was still to come. It happened just over a month later, on Twelfth Night, at about one o'clock in the morning, according to Beckett.[84] The details of the incident remained sharply etched on his mind, even after fifty years:

> I was bringing them [the Duncans] back home to the Coeur-de-Vey [a small dead-end street] off the avenue d'Orléans, now the avenue Général-Leclerc. We'd just had supper in that big restaurant that still exists under the same name on the corner. We had just spent the evening together, Duncan, his wife and myself, the three of us. And this pimp emerged and started to pester us to go with him. We didn't know who he was until later, whether he was a pimp or not. This was established later when I identified him in hospital. They brought photographs to the Hôpital Broussais. Anyway he stabbed me; fortunately he just missed the heart. And I was lying bleeding on the pavement. Then I don't remember much of what happened.[85]

After stabbing Beckett, the man ran quickly away. Beckett fell to the ground; after a few seconds, he felt his left side and discovered blood on his hand. He called out that he was bleeding. Alan and Belinda managed to get him to their flat, where they undressed him and were horrified when they saw the wound. As they did not know the name of a doctor, they phoned the police and Beckett, unconscious by now, was rushed off by ambulance to the nearest hospital, the Hôpital Broussais in the rue Didot.[86]

The following day, Brian Coffey, who was due to meet Beckett, instead read in the newspaper that his friend had been stabbed the previous night. He telephoned the Duncans and heard their account. Coffey suggested that they should contact James Joyce at once and get him to use his influence to ensure that Beckett received the best possible treatment. As soon as they heard what had happened, the Joyces went along to find Beckett coming out of a coma, looking very weak and in great pain, but quite lucid. Beckett could remember vividly his return to consciousness:

The next thing I knew I came to what remained of my senses in the Hôpital Broussais. I came to in a Salle Commune, a big room. When I came to, the first thing I remember was Joyce standing at the end of the ward and coming to see me. And it was thanks to Joyce and his crazy woman doctor, Fontaine, that he got me a private room.[87]

The knife had entered his left side, missing the lung and the heart by a hairbreadth but piercing the pleura. The wound was serious and there was concern at first for his life, then fear of further hemorrhaging or of complications such as pneumonia setting in. The doctors were unable to see the full extent of the bleeding, since they could not risk moving Beckett to the X-ray room on another floor. On January 13, 1938, Beckett wrote to George Reavey:

It appears that I shall be all right, tho' no proper X Ray can be taken till I can get up and down to X Ray room. They never vouchsafe a confidence to me, just drift in, together and singly, shake hands, look at the chart, ask for 33, give a few disgusted taps like a connoisseur asked to examine fake Meissen and drift out. So I don't know when I'll be let up. The médecin chef nearly assaulted me today because I had the window opened. What a system.[88]

In Dublin, the news of the stabbing was splashed across the billboards and the shrill soprano voices of the newsboys called out: "Irishman stabbed in Paris."[89] Beckett's brother, mother, and sister-in-law immediately rushed over to Paris to be with him, staying until they were assured that he was out of danger and was going to make a successful recovery. The incident effected the long-delayed reconciliation with his mother. He had written earlier, asking that they might at least correspond. And she had already sent him a Christmas present of a tie — anonymously. While she was by his bedside, Beckett was very moved by her genuine affection and deep concern and overwhelmed with his own fondness for her: "I felt great gusts of affection and esteem and compassion for her when she was over," he wrote. "What a relationship!"[90]

Beckett was touched to see how many other visitors flocked to the hospital to see him. The Duncans were, he said, angelic, "coming every day, sometimes twice, and ready to do anything for me"[91] and "dealing with police and keeping reporters away."[92] Joyce was kindness itself. He asked Thérèse Fontaine, the forty-one-year-old doctor who had looked after Nora and himself for the past ten years, to take a special interest in Beckett, which she did most conscientiously throughout his illness. Joyce also paid all the expenses of his private room. He took Beckett a reading lamp, and Nora cooked him a custard pudding and fussed over him. When the van Veldes went to visit him one day they found Joyce waiting outside his door, cradling a large bouquet of yellow roses in his arms.[93]

Many others came to call on him with flowers, fruit, books, and magazines: Brian Coffey, Alfred and Mania Péron, Georges and Marcelle Pelorson, Peggy Guggenheim, and others whom he had not seen for several years, like Henri Evrard, a former student of English at the Ecole Normale, and his wife, who had read about the stabbing of the former *lecteur d'anglais*. The Evrards' visit astounded and confused Beckett so much that he seemed displeased rather than pleased to see them.[94] The Irish ambassador, Cornelius Cremin, also came with his pretty wife, Patricia, who had never met Beckett before but with whom he remained on friendly terms for many years afterward. While he was still in the hospital, the police came to his room with a book of photographs of known offenders. Beckett was able to pick out one Prudent, who was a professional pimp with four previous convictions.

On January 21, Beckett reported to MacGreevy in a letter written in pencil from the hospital that it still hurt him to breathe but that he had been able to get up briefly, have the long-delayed X ray, and see Dr. Fontaine, who told him that he ought to be able to leave the following day but that it would take some time for him to get "back to average and . . . [I] will be the proud possessor of a pleural barometer for years to come."[95]

Breathing continued to be painful for some time, but exercises and rest gradually helped him to regain his strength. By mid-February, he was able to resume his search for an apartment and was well enough to go out to dinner with Nancy Cunard at Lipps where, as in Winnie's story in *Happy Days*, a mouse ran up Beckett's leg—fortunately on the outside of his trousers.[96] He was also fit enough to attend Joyce's birthday party at the Jolases' in Neuilly the same month. His fellow guests Maria Jolas and Sullivan "bawled their heads off afterwards." The dinner party was a large one, consisting of fifteen people, and Joyce danced after dinner in the old style.[97] For a moment it seemed as if the Sinclair-Gogarty trial were a past nightmare and as if the stabbing had never happened. Yet the scars of both remained to prove the opposite.

And, in March, in spite of his wish to let the matter drop, the police insisted on pressing charges against the pimp. This would be Beckett's third court case in a matter of months. He met Prudent in the entranceway and asked him why he did it. "Je ne sais pas, Monsieur," answered the pimp, adding a polite but incongruous "Je m'excuse"[98] ["I don't know why, sir. I'm sorry"]. "The desperado got off with 2 months," wrote Beckett, "not bad for a *5th* conviction. I am still without my clothes, taken away from me at the time as pièces de conviction and never produced. I have now to prove that they ever belonged to me."[99] Prudent was sent to the Santé prison, Beckett reporting to Arland Ussher that "there is no more popular prisoner in the Santé. His mail is enormous. His poules [prostitutes] shower gifts upon him. Next time he stabs someone they will promote him to the Legion of Honour. My presence in Paris has not been altogether fruitless!"[100]

Beckett never did get his clothes back.

8

OVER CHRISTMAS and the New Year 1937–38, around the time of the stabbing, Beckett complicated his personal life by becoming involved with three women at more or less the same time. Two of them pursued him. This was a novel experience. As a result he behaved at times naïvely, clumsily, even foolishly. The experience of lovemaking without love (what he called "taking coffee without brandy")[101] directly inspired a poem he wrote in English after returning to the hotel from the hospital in the third week in January:

> *they come*
> *different and the same*
> *with each it is different and the same*
> *with each the absence of love is different*
> *with each the absence of love is the same.*[102]

One of the women was Irish, the other American, the third French. The Irishwoman was over in Paris, staying for a time at the Hôtel Meurice. In all probability, she was Mrs. Adrienne Bethell, the owner of a little antique shop in Dún Laoghaire.[103] Beckett and she seem briefly to have taken up a flirtation (or possibly an affair) in Dublin. Beckett admitted to Peggy Guggenheim that he slept with the lady in question.[104] But Mrs. Bethell appears to have faded out of the picture very quickly after her return to the safe distance of Ireland.

His second affair was with the American heiress Peggy Guggenheim. This took place at the time when she was setting up her Guggenheim Jeune art gallery in London.[105] The relationship was to last much longer as an odd kind of friendship than as a sexual affair, although Guggenheim's feelings for Beckett became an obsessive passion: "I was entirely obsessed for over a year by the strange creature, Samuel Beckett," she frankly confesses in her memoirs.[106]

The story of their affair has been related before, most fully by Peggy herself. But her letters to her friend and former secretary Emily Coleman, and the evidence of a close witness, Lisl van Velde, add to what is known. Beckett and Peggy had met casually a few times in Paris. But the affair proper began the day after Christmas 1937, when they were both dining with the Joyces at Fouquet's restaurant. After dinner, they went back to Helen Fleischman's house, and Beckett asked Peggy if he could escort her home, where they ended up in bed together, spending the whole of the next day making love and drinking champagne. Soon after this, Peggy moved into her friend Mary Reynolds's house while the owner was hospitalized and, when she bumped into Beckett again in Montparnasse, he joined her there, staying for over a week and going back to his hotel only to collect his mail.

Peggy was not a particularly attractive woman. She had a high brow, a bulbous nose (partly the result of facial surgery that had gone wrong),[107] and thin, spindly legs; she often wore socks and sandals. But she was sexually liberated, with a marked tendency to promiscuity. Since she made it abundantly clear that she had fallen passionately in love with Beckett, it must have been hard for him to resist her. But it may not only have been the lure of the flesh. Beckett was attracted to strong, liberated women with independent minds and original outlooks. And Peggy was very dynamic in her way. She talked openly of her most intimate feelings and desires, unlike Beckett, who only "unraveled himself," as she put it, after copious amounts of alcohol.[108]

She was beginning to take a passionate interest in art; as an admirer of Kandinsky, for example, Beckett was fascinated to hear about the exhibition that she was arranging for the painter in London. She was also starting to collect paintings for her own private collection and flattered Beckett by asking him for advice on whom she should or should not collect. She could also offer him work translating for the catalogues of her gallery or writing pieces for E. L. T. Mesens's *London Bulletin*. It was another novel experience for him to be going out with a woman as rich as Peggy, who had plenty of money to spend on art and who owned (or hired) interesting, fast cars, which she enjoyed seeing him drive.[109]

But Beckett was too complex, too intellectual, and too demanding to settle down with Peggy and, even without the arrival on the scene within a matter of days of a French lady friend, the affair would never have lasted: Peggy was too predatory, too volatile, and infringed too much on his time, energy, and privacy. Daily life with her was too turbulent for someone who was himself trying to reach calmer water. They often quarreled, mainly because she would never give him enough space. And she persisted in trying to get him to do what he did not want to do. Reading between the lines of her personal account, we can detect how quickly he lost patience with her infantile teasing and how wearisome he found her stories of other lovers, both those resurrected from her picturesque past and those in the present with whom she tried to make him jealous — like his good friend Brian Coffey, to whom, to her horror, he eventually "gave her."[110] Coffey, it should be said, then promptly and very sensibly got married to Bridget Baynes, who, ironically, had been introduced to him by Peggy.

Even allowing for male sexual susceptibility, it seems likely that Beckett stayed on close terms with her for as long as he did, not so much for his own sake as for the help Guggenheim could and did give his friend Geer van Velde, and other artists whom he admired. Lisl van Velde certainly felt that Peggy, for her part, clung to Geer and herself because this allowed her to attach herself, limpetlike, to Beckett.[111]

In April 1938, the van Veldes came over to London for the Geer van Velde exhibition that Peggy Guggenheim had arranged at Beckett's request at the Guggenheim Jeune Gallery, 30 Cork Street. They came by train and stayed for almost three weeks with George and Gwynned Reavey, who helped to organize the exhibition. But Beckett, who had recovered by now from the stabbing, came over by airplane, his ticket almost certainly paid for by Peggy, two days before the opening and stayed for a few days at MacGreevy's lodgings in London. To everyone's surprise, he brought no luggage with him at all, except for a box of Voltigeur cigars purchased as a present for Geer. Both he and Geer enjoyed smoking this particular brand.[112] He wore his notorious "midnight blue" German suit, suitably recut in Ireland, and had just purchased a pair of shiny new black shoes that pinched his toes as he walked.

Beckett introduced the van Veldes to Tom MacGreevy, who took charge of the painter, whisking him off immediately for a guided tour of the National Gallery. Then Beckett escorted them and MacGreevy to Hampton Court, which he knew so well from his two-year stay in London. Looking at pictures with Beckett was a delight, wrote Peggy Guggenheim, since he was so knowledgeable about art.

The Geer van Velde exhibition itself was not a great financial success for the painter. Peggy bought several of his paintings under assumed names to make it appear that he was doing much better than he actually was,[113] and — to please Beckett — she made a further deal with Geer that provided him with enough money to enable him to paint for a year.[114]

After the exhibition, Geer, Lisl, Peggy, and Beckett stayed for a couple of days at Peggy's retreat, Yew Tree Cottage, in Petersfield. The Reaveys and Peggy's daughter, Pegeen, were also there. Peggy gave up her bedroom for the Reaveys and, according to Peggy herself, slept in the dining room. Lisl van Velde remembered on the contrary that she slept in a corridor between Beckett's room and the bathroom, ready to pounce on him as he passed.[115] From the cottage, Peggy Guggenheim, Geer and Lisl van Velde, and Beckett drove to the seaside, with Beckett driving Peggy's red sports Delage. On the stony beach, Beckett and van Velde each picked up flat stones that they threw as far as they could out to sea. This soon developed into a friendly contest in which, to Beckett's surprise, van Velde managed to outthrow him in terms of distance, although — the hours spent as a child on the beach at Greystones serving him well — Beckett excelled at skimming the flat stones across the surface of the waves.

They returned to Yew Tree Cottage for drinks and dinner and to have their photographs taken in the garden: van Velde, in relaxed mode, smoking his pipe in a sports jacket, flannels, and slip-on shoes; Beckett, more formally dressed in his suit, black lace-up shoes, a dark shirt, and the tie with a myriad of stars, his mother's anonymous Christmas present; in his hand he is holding a small tin whistle (a relic of the Ecole Normale days) on which he tootled snatches of Schubert or an Irish air.

In the early summer of 1938, Peggy Guggenheim continued to try to attach herself to Beckett through his friendship with the van Veldes. There was the occasional *dîner à quatre* at Le Coq Hardi, a chic restaurant on the outskirts of Paris, followed, on one occasion, by a midnight trip to Chartres to look at the cathedral in the moonlight.[116] Then, a little later, Beckett and Peggy drove the van Veldes again in Peggy's car to Marseilles and along the Côte d'Azur to Cagnes-sur-Mer. On the way back, Peggy Guggenheim relates how, in Dijon,

Beckett booked a double room for them both because it was cheaper than two singles but insisted on sleeping in one of the two single beds alone, slipping out of his own and into the other one when she crawled in beside him.[117]

There seems little doubt that Peggy Guggenheim was in love with Beckett after her fashion. As late as July 1938, she wrote to Emily Coleman: "I love being with him. It is more and more my real life. I have decided now to give up every thing else even sex if necessary and concentrate on him. I am very happy when I am away from him and when we are in the same city and together but he gives me an awful time. However I know he can't help it."[118]

What is certain is that Beckett was never in love with her, except perhaps very briefly during the initial days, when the lines between love and fascination may well have been as hard to draw as the cliché implies. But, as Peggy's letters to Emily Coleman show, he went on seeing her from time to time, long after embarking on his relationship with the woman who, twenty-three years later, was to become his wife. At one point, Peggy even confessed to her friend that she lent him her car to drive his French girlfriend to Normandy and Brittany, so that he would not be in Paris to churn up her own emotions.[119]

The French girlfriend was a thirty-seven-year-old woman, Suzanne Deschevaux-Dumesnil. She and her partner (an excellent musician and a member of a family of famous music publishers with offices near the Madeleine) had played tennis against Beckett and Péron almost ten years before, when he was at the Ecole Normale. She read in the newspaper that he had been stabbed and called several times to visit him in the Hôpital Broussais. As she was alone by then, she took a keen interest in this tall, shy, good-looking Irishman, showing tender concern for his welfare and seeing him once he was back in circulation. Soon after his return to the Hôtel Libéria, they began to meet regularly for dinner and went to concerts and exhibitions together.

In the Hôtel Libéria, Beckett was paying seven hundred and fifty francs a month for a room in which there was little light and no possibility of housing all the books that he had left behind at Cooldrinagh. So, eventually, in the second week of April, he decided to settle for a modest unfurnished apartment for four hundred francs at 6 rue des Favorites in an unfashionable area off the long rue de Vaugirard, a long walk away from the Latin Quarter but near enough to be acceptable. Vaugirard, said Beckett, meant "Valley of Gerald" and reminded him with pleasure of his favorite uncle Gerald.

"I am promised that corner stone of every apartment—a bed—" he wrote on April 14, "but not for a week, so expect to sleep in the bath till then. It is not a bad little place—studio, soupente, bedroom, bathroom, necessary house and kitchenette—on the 7th floor and well away from the Gare Montparnasse."[120] A few days later, he told MacGreevy: "I have been camping here for the past week. People have been good with presents to get me started [the Joyces offered him a shabby settee, for instance, which he kept very proudly for many years, together with one or two smaller items of furniture], but it is a terribly expensive business. I like the place, it is bright and comfortable, and I like the quarter, well away from the stage artists."[121]

The quarter was much more picturesque when Beckett moved in than it is today; there was even "an old fellow who had goats who used to walk around the back streets selling shoes made from goatskin."[122] There was a lift up to the seventh floor and "a staircase to stagger up at night."[123] The door into the apartment had a low lintel, under which someone of Beckett's height needed to stoop every time he entered.

The main room was a living room–cum–study in which Beckett's writing desk stood in front of the window, looking out at the sky. He felt very miserable when he was deprived of light. By the side of the table was a big wastepaper basket in which he used to keep a bottle of John Jameson whiskey.[124] Three crates of books arrived from Ireland early in June and he rigged up bookshelves himself. He was thrilled to have his own home at last and, with a new sense of pride, invited friends like MacGreevy and Reavey to stay with him when they came to Paris. The painter Avigdor Arikha remembered the studio from his visits there in the mid-1950s:

> It was a small studio, a real *atelier de peintre* [painter's studio]. Not large, rather small in fact, but good . . . good light and upstairs was a gallery . . . a loggia, but the loggia was a bedroom. Kitchen downstairs and the atelier. Bedroom and bathroom upstairs. It was a room with books going down each side. They were all very neat and then behind there was a *cagibi* [or storage nook]; everything was very neat.[125]

There were disadvantages, of course: a "terrible wireless"[126] that played all day long next door; a baby crying in a nearby apartment; and, for many years, no telephone. But Beckett was comfortable and more content than he had been for years.

Though shy and reserved, he soon developed his own circle of friends.[127] Many of these were painters and engravers: the forty-two-year-old Polish artist Jankel Adler;[128] the founder of "Atelier 17," Stanley William Hayter;[129] the New Zealander John Buckland-Wright and his wife;[130] and he also knew Otto Freundlich and a German Surrealist, Wolfgang Paalen, who gave him an "automatic" picture.[131] He saw and played chess occasionally with Marcel Duchamp,[132] for Beckett knew Duchamp's companion, Mary Reynolds, well through Peggy Guggenheim. He also met Francis Picabia and his separated wife, Gabrielle Buffet-Picabia, and their daughter, Jeannine. At the end of 1939, he at last met Kandinsky, whom he described as a "sympathetic old Siberian."[133]

Close friends never found Beckett's shyness a problem. Con Leventhal spoke of spending whole evenings together when they might not exchange more than a few sentences; and yet their silence was companionable. Beckett met people in the Montparnasse cafés or wrote letters or even poems there; he loved the food and the wine and often drank too much of it. He found the musical and artistic life of Paris stimulating. In particular, he started to go to the Louvre again, admiring a little Fabritius picture and writing to MacGreevy that he found "the Verrochio Virgin and Child were lovely and the Mantegnas all of a sudden extraordinarily disappointing, except the Sebastian."[134]

From time to time he saw Georges Pelorson, his old friend from the Ecole Normale and Trinity College. But he soon began to feel out of sympathy with the direction that Georges was taking in his editorials for the right-wing review *Volontés*, which he edited and more or less codirected with Raymond Queneau. One of Pelorson's stock themes at this time, according to Noël Arnaud, was the decadence of Europe and an obsession with the will to power, a *"volonté de grandeur."* [135] Beckett would never have been happy with such an aspiration.

His closest French friend now was Alfred Péron. Beckett lunched with him every Tuesday before going on to the club for their weekly game of tennis. Péron soon became closely involved with Beckett's work. He translated the poem "Alba" into French and committed himself to the huge task of translating *Murphy* with Beckett's active help. [136]

Beckett saw a lot of Joyce, his family, and his circle (Stuart and Moune Gilbert, Nino Frank) in the two years immediately preceding the war. Before Christmas 1937, he had helped Giorgio to correct the proofs of parts one and three of *Finnegans Wake*, for which Joyce paid him two hundred and fifty francs for about fifteen hours' work. "He then supplemented it with an old overcoat and 5 ties! I did not refuse. It is so much simpler to be hurt than to hurt." [137] Yet, after another dinner with the Joyces in early January, Beckett's enormous affection for him shines through: "He [Joyce] was sublime last night, deprecating with the utmost conviction his lack of talent. I don't feel the danger of the association any more. He is just a very lovable human being." [138] He again became very wrapped up in Nora's and Joyce's domestic worries: trying to pour oil on troubled waters, when Helen decided to leave for New York, where her father was very ill, taking Giorgio with her; [139] sympathizing with Joyce as he worried deeply and incessantly about Lucia, and advising him to consult Geoffrey Thompson in London if he so wished; [140] and becoming even more closely involved with Joyce's work schedule. As Joyce's eyesight deteriorated more and more seriously, so Beckett continued to read and take notes on books for him, very much as he had done a decade before. He took notes on a study in German of Indian myth. [141] And it may be that the notes that he made in his "Whoroscope" notebook on Fritz Mauthner's critique of language were also intended partly for Joyce. [142]

9

COINCIDENTALLY, BECKETT'S LUCK as a writer seems to have changed with his arrival in Paris. After finishing *Murphy* in June 1936, he sent it first to his earlier publishers, Chatto and Windus. [143] He might reasonably have expected a favorable reception in spite of Charles Prentice's retirement from the firm in 1934. The book was read first by Oliver Warner, then by Ian Parsons. It was turned down, in spite of Warner's praise for the book's humor, poetry, and innovative use of language, because he also reported that it "hadn't a chance of commercial success." [144]

However, this was not quite the end of the affair. Richard Church, who worked at the Dent publishing company, to which the book was later offered, urged Harold Raymond, a partner at Chatto and Windus, to have another look at it, suggesting that "having taken up this man you would be well advised to stick to him, and have faith in him for a bit longer. To my mind he is a thoroughly well equipped writer and there is no knowing what he may not do. I say this realising the practical difficulties from the publishing point of view."[145] Raymond read the novel and concluded that his partners had been right to reject it earlier:

> I agree with much that you say about this book and I certainly do not feel happy at letting go of Samuel Beckett. Yet I feel pretty confident that the recondite nature of so much of his writing would prevent this book from selling more than a few hundred copies, and if we are right, the loss involved would be a high price to pay for an option on his next work.[146]

Beckett was disappointed, but persisted in sending out copies to other publishers in Britain and, through Mary Manning Howe, who continued to assist him, in the United States. Then he offered the book to George Reavey to handle as his literary agent, keeping a list, as reports came in, in his "Whoroscope" notebook of the publishers whom he knew had rejected it. He almost lost count.

The story of how Routledge came to accept the novel at the beginning of December 1937 has been widely misunderstood. It was thought, even by Beckett himself, that Herbert Read had recommended it to the firm. What actually happened is that Jack Yeats, whose own novel *The Charmed Life* was being published at the same time by Routledge, wrote to T. M. Ragg of that firm:

> A friend of mine, Sam Beckett, has the manuscript of a novel "Murphy" which is to be submitted to your firm. I have not seen it, but his other novel [*More Pricks Than Kicks*] I read and I thought it the real thing. There was inspiration in it. It was published a year or two ago and I daresay by now the public readers have crept under its inspiration. But even if this has lept away in front of that, perhaps the hour has come when the public Dunderheads can be induced to stoop their noses to something more alive than the old printers-ink-aniseed-bag — "something to read. The same as the Last." I write to ask you, if you cannot read Beckett's Ms yourself just now, to give it to some very open minded reader.[147]

The novel was sent on to Ragg by George Reavey. Ragg read it himself in a single day while ill with gastric flu and responded with spontaneous enthusiasm: All the miseries of his complaint were forgotten in his immense enjoyment, he said. And, in replying to Jack Yeats, he added: "I want to publish it, and I am seeing Reavey tomorrow to talk the matter over with him. I am afraid there is no doubt that it is far too good to be a big popular or commercial success. On the other hand it, like your own book, will bring great joy to the few. Thank you very much for introducing it to me."[148]

On December 9, 1937, Beckett received a telegram from George Reavey telling him that, at last, Murphy was to be published and a contract was prepared and signed. Herbert Read was consulted only after the contract was signed and the page proofs were printed.[149] He responded very enthusiastically, saying it was "a perfect example of surrealist humour. It is very funny and at the same time very grim. I hope enough people will discover its extraordinary merits."[150]

The publication of Murphy straddled Beckett's stabbing: The contract was signed before Christmas, and the page proofs arrived on January 17, while he was still recovering in the Hôpital Broussais.[151] He corrected them in bed, asking Geer van Velde to bring his chess set along to his hospital room so that they could verify together the moves made in the chess game between Mr. Endon and Murphy. He was deeply disappointed that his "cherished idea" for the book's cover, a photograph of two apes playing chess, had been set aside[152] and grumbled about the blurb, insisting to Reavey that it "will not appear actually between the boards of the book."[153] But the novel was out at last—to his immense relief. Now he confidently expected that it would be accepted by an American publisher. It was not. Proud as ever, he was unwilling to have Joyce put in a word for him with Viking Press.[154] The novel was not published in the United States until 1957, when Barney Rosset of Grove Press reprinted it from the Routledge text.

Early in February 1938, Jack Kahane, the founder of Obelisk Press, whom Beckett had met at the Joyces', rang Beckett with the proposal that he should translate the Marquis de Sade's Les 120 Jours de Sodome. Beckett was very interested in Sade's book, which was for him "one of the capital works of the 18th century."[155] And he badly needed the money Kahane was offering. His main concern was that, since he would never agree to translate it anonymously, it might affect his "own future freedom of literary action in England and USA." And he asked, "Would the fact of my being known as the translator, and the very literal translation, of 'the most utter filth' tend to spike me as a writer myself? Could I be banned and muzzled retrospectively?"[156] Since in the end Beckett never did the translation,[157] the main interest of the proposal was to provoke his thoughts on this controversial work:

> I have read 1st and 3rd vols. of French edition. The obscenity of surface is indescribable. Nothing could be less pornographical. It fills me with a kind of metaphysical ecstasy. The composition is extraordinary, as rigorous as Dante's. If the dispassionate statement of 600 "passions" is Puritan and a complete absence of satire juvenalesque, then it is, as you say, puritanical and juvenalesque. You would loathe it whether or no.[158]

10

A FEW MONTHS after his arrival in Paris, Beckett started to write poetry in French.[159] The shift from one language to another has commonly been regarded as taking place immediately after the war. Although this remains true for the prose fiction and drama, Beckett did rather more than dip his toe into French waters in 1938–39. Writing poetry in French allowed him to get away, most of the time at least, from the dense allusiveness, wide erudition, and "intimate at arms-length" quality of his English poems. As early as the beginning of April, he wrote to MacGreevy: "I wrote a short poem in French but otherwise nothing. I have the feeling that any poems there may happen to be in the future will be French."[160]

A dozen of the poems Beckett wrote in French were not published until after the war. Although difficult and oblique at first sight, they are more directly personal than any of his earlier English poems except the most recent, "Cascando." They spring from Beckett's own feelings about love, sex, death, separation, solitude, and society. Love is often absent. Sex is there, but as an appetite, an erotic need or a temporary relief. Death takes different forms: disintegration, decay, premature ending, death in life. The poet, motionless, contemplative, and mostly alone, even when with another, contemplates the world and finds it alien and uninviting.

Many details of the poems are taken from Beckett's immediate everyday life.[161] And his most abiding themes come through: a split in the self, with the notion of the "double" in "Arènes de Lutèce"; life as a *pensum,* to be lived through in the permanent shadow of premature death (at thirty-two, Beckett had already lost his former love, his father, and his uncle); man as a prisoner of time, the arch-villain.

But he also wrote a number of other short poems in French, known so far only to a few of his closest friends. He refers in letters to something that he has written called "Petit sot" ("Little Fool"). We can be sure that one twenty-four-line poem about a "Petit sot" was written by Beckett, because the manuscripts in his hand and typescript were given by him personally to Avigdor Arikha.[162] Twenty additional short poems exist, however, which form an independent cycle based again on the figure "Le Petit sot."[163] The first poem is actually called "Le Petit sot," and the others follow him (always in the first person) in a variety of guises: as horse rider, traveler, lion, moth, singer, searcher after the moon, and so on. The poems recreate the games or fantasies of a little boy. They are simpler in vocabulary, syntax, and ideas than any of the other poems of Beckett at that time and look at first sight like stylistic exercises. Beckett wrote: "There are two very long ones that do not belong at all to the series, being quite straightforward descriptive poems (in French) of episodes in the life of a child. I do not know what they are worth. The few people I have shown them to liked them, but they are friends."[164] This description aptly applies to the poem that he gave to Arikha and suggests that, although highly unusual for him, the other, shorter poems are genuinely his. Indeed, while asking Reavey to send back his "P.S.," he says that "il me tarde de le mettre en morceaux" [165] ("I long to take it to pieces"), probably meaning to break up the longer poem into much shorter units with separate titles. Although the discovery of these new poems does not drastically change our view of Beckett as a poet, it helps to see him consciously reaching toward a greater simplicity and directness, freeing himself from too much complexity of form and expression. Taken as a whole, the unpublished cycle along with the published poems show him already evolving in 1938–39 into a specifically *French* writer.

11

BECKETT DESCRIBED THIS TIME as a "period of lostness, drifting around, seeing a few friends — a period of apathy and lethargy." [166] He was probably thinking of how little he managed to achieve in terms of his work. Yet important things were happening to him. He was in contact with painters and writers who were at the cutting edge of avant-garde art. As a correction to Beckett's own picture of his indolence, we find him reading eclectically but critically: "Kant, Descartes, Johnson, Renard and a kindergarten manual of science" (in French). To these, we can add Sartre's *La Nausée* in May 1938, which he found "extraordinarily good," [167] Goncharov's *Oblomov*, Vigny's *Journal*, which bored him, Sterne's *Tristram Shandy* ("which irritated me in spite of its qualities"), [168] Wyndham Lewis's *"Blasting and Bombardiering*, 4 pages at a time, with considerable disgust," and Djuna Barnes's *Nightwood*, which he enjoyed in spite of its "early Mann verballistics." [169]

He made two important decisions at this time. First, he resolved the problem of what he could do about his mother, which was crucial to his own well-being as well as hers. That he still cared very deeply for her is revealed by his reaction when he learned that she had burned her hands badly while reading with a candle in bed: "I feel sorry for her often to the point of tears. That is the part that was not analysed away, I suppose." [170] So he made the decision to return to Foxrock for a month every year; this would enable him to see her while retaining his own independence. Except during the war years, he kept his promise, visiting her every year until she died.

His second major decision was to link his life more closely with that of Suzanne Deschevaux-Dumesnil. He did not talk about her in his letters to friends until 1939, when he wrote to MacGreevy in April: "There is a French girl also whom I am fond of, dispassionately, and who is very good to me. The hand will not be overbid. As we both know that it will come to an end there is no knowing how long it may last." [171] "Dispassionately" and "very good to me" suggest more a growing companionship than a passionate, sexual affair. Peggy Guggenheim oversimplified when she wrote that the difference between them was that Suzanne made curtains, while she made scenes. But the thoughtful, calm, caring side of Suzanne counted for a lot in a relationship that became increasingly close.

Six years older than Beckett, she was attractive in a slightly masculine way. She dressed smartly, if soberly. She was a strong, mature, independent woman of decisive left-wing opinions. Although her mother lived in Troyes, Suzanne had spent part of her girlhood in Tunisia. She was an accomplished pianist with an interest in literature and theater and had a voracious appetite for music and concertgoing. She had studied at the Ecole Normale de Musique in the 1920s, where she was taught by a distinguished pianist, Isidor Philipp, for whom she had a great admiration. Students did a lot of theoretical work at the Ecole, so Suzanne had an excellent grounding in music. She also had perfect pitch: "You could play any note of music, and she would immediately tell you what it was," said a close friend, and she could identify every note when several were played together.[172] She even gave a few lessons in harmony to piano students in the late 1920s. She loved walking. And she played bridge.

She was popular and had many good friends, with whom she stayed in touch for the rest of her life.[173] She was an unusual mixture: practical, a first-rate dressmaker, yet totally uninterested in cooking; down-to-earth, yet with a belief in some of the most bizarre practices of "alternative" medicine. Generous and kind to the poor and underprivileged, she sympathized with failure and hated success. Yet she could be jealous and intolerant, sharp and dismissive of anyone whom she did not like.

Suzanne has been seen as taking over the role that Beckett's mother had played in his life. Certainly she grumbled, as his mother used to grumble, about his excessive drinking, for she did not drink herself. But there were crucial differences; above all, she had enormous respect for Beckett's talents and total belief in his genius. When things were going very badly, she never lost this faith and was ready to do all that she could to help him. At first, she was remarkably tolerant, putting up with his late nights, his bouts of irritability, and his moods of black despair when his writing would not advance. She also understood and shared his need for silence: "The way people go on *saying* things . . . ! Who shall silence them, at last?" the narrator had asked in *Dream of Fair to Middling Women*.[174] One phrase in Beckett's letter to MacGreevy, "there is no knowing how long it may last," was understandably cautious, yet, in the end, remarkably prescient, since their relationship was to last until their deaths, he surviving her by only a few months.

12

Exodus, Occupation, and Resistance

1940–42

1

THROUGHOUT 1938 AND 1939, the threat of war hung menacingly over Europe. Already in September 1938, Beckett had "promised Péron, in event of mobilization, to evacuate in his car his children, his mother-in-law, his aunt-in-law. . . . Here there is a great afflux of tenderness, even in the commune of Vaugirard." [1] He still joked occasionally about the Nazi threat, passing on to Arland Ussher the latest definition of an Aryan: "He must be blond like Hitler, thin like Goering, handsome like Goebbels, virile like Roehm—and be called Rosenberg" [2] and remarking, "I heard Adolf the Peacemaker on the wireless last night. And thought I heard the air escaping—a slow puncture." [3] But with Neville Chamberlain's announcement on April 1, 1939, pledging Britain to defend Poland against any threat from Germany, jokes were no longer funny. The die seemed cast. On April 18, Beckett wrote: "If there is a war, as I fear there must be soon, I shall place myself at the disposition of this country." [4]

In the event, when Hitler invaded Poland on September 1, 1939, and, two days later, Chamberlain broadcast that Britain was consequently at war with Germany, Beckett was staying with his mother in a little rented house by the harbor at Greystones. He heard the speech on her radio. France was also at war with Germany from five o'clock on September 3. Beckett deliberately chose to return to France the very next day. He had to travel through England. When he arrived at Newhaven to take the boat to Dieppe, he was told that he would not be allowed on the boat without an exit permit, for which he would have to apply in London. Beckett bluffed his way through, arguing with the officials that, since he was a citizen of Erin, this could not apply to him. Finally, after much discussion, he was allowed on the boat. [5] On the train back home to Paris, he noticed that all the windows were blacked out in the houses they were passing. He was in a country at war.

With the Germans attacking Belgium and Holland on May 10, 1940, and the invasion of France occurring only a few days later, it became clear in Paris from about May 20, in spite of a strict news censorship, that the situation in France was very grave. Belgium fell on May 28 and a British Expeditionary

Force of 338,226 Allied troops, including 26,175 French soldiers, had to be evacuated from the beaches and harbor of Dunkirk in the first few days of June. On June 4, Winston Churchill, in a speech to Parliament, delivered his famous words of no surrender: "We shall fight on the beaches, we shall fight on the landing-grounds, we shall fight in the fields and in the streets, we shall fight in the hills; we shall never surrender." But with Kleist's, Hoth's, and Guderian's Panzer corps pushing south at unexpected speed (and Italy joining Germany by declaring war on France on June 10), it seemed only a matter of days, even hours before Paris fell to the Germans.[6]

Beckett had made his commitment to France by volunteering to drive an ambulance.[7] But his offer was overtaken by events. With the German invasion, he and Suzanne decided that the only sensible thing to do was to join the exodus of people fleeing the capital. They headed south only forty-eight hours before the Germans marched in triumph down the Champs-Elysées. Beckett clutched a couple of heavy bags crammed full of clothes, a few belongings, and his French translation of *Murphy*; Suzanne carried a rucksack on her back bulging with clothing and personal effects. With only enough money for their train fare and a few days' food, they took one of the last trains to leave the Gare de Lyon.[8] As the train pulled out of the station, they saw hordes of people on the roads fleeing from the capital: cars and trucks piled high with suitcases and boxes containing personal possessions; people pushing little handcarts or bicycles. Those who had no vehicle walked, laden like human packhorses. For they took away as much as they could carry, not knowing when or if they would return.

On June 12, Beckett and Suzanne arrived in Vichy, where they knew James and Nora Joyce were staying. Beckett described the circumstances of their brief stay there:

> It was at the beginning of the war in 1940. We went to see James Joyce, who was staying in a hotel in Vichy, for the last time. Suzanne and I stayed in the same hotel [the Hôtel Beaujolais] as Joyce. Then [with the fall of Paris] the hotel was requisitioned to be used by the Vichy government. Maria Jolas ran a language school in Vichy [or nearby in the village of Saint-Gérand-le-Puy]. Joyce moved out of the hotel and they went to stay in Maria's school. So that left Suzanne and myself in the hotel by ourselves. And of course we weren't going to stay there. But we were completely out of money. So, with an introductory letter from Joyce, I went on my own to see Valery Larbaud. He had a very big estate. He was quite rich. . . . He was paralysed at the time. I remember his wife opening the door and taking me in to see him; he was sitting in his wheelchair. My memory of the occasion is that he couldn't speak because of the paralysis, so his wife spoke to me for him. But the end result was that he lent us twenty thousand francs that saved our bacon. I remember repaying him; in fact I think he had died by then, so I repaid his family after his death.[9]

In view of the uncertain circumstances of the war, Larbaud's generous loan would have been offered with little prospect of its ever being repaid. It was for this reason doubtless, as well as in memory of Joyce, that Beckett insisted on paying the money back to Valery Larbaud's estate at the end of the war.

Beckett said his farewells to Joyce, Nora, and Giorgio (who had joined his mother and father while Beckett was there) and he and Suzanne set out from Vichy, at first on foot. Reaching a railway station south of town, they caught a train and, after a long, painfully slow journey, eventually arrived in Toulouse.[10] They found the train packed to overflowing with refugees and soldiers from the fleeing French army, mostly still wearing their uniforms. In Toulouse, they were directed to a refugee center. As an alien, Beckett had been trying for many months to get his papers processed in Paris in order to show clearly his neutral status as an Irishman and as a freelance writer. But, since the papers had never come through,[11] he felt that he could not risk any encounter at this stage with hypersensitive officialdom; once caught up in the system, he felt that it might become difficult to avoid being detained indefinitely as an unregistered alien. So they slept (or at least attempted to sleep) out on a bench. It was, as Beckett put it elliptically, "awful."[12]

A couple of days later, they decided to head west toward the sea. They caught a bus, then a train in the direction of Bordeaux. But, at Cahors, everyone was forced to leave the train when it stopped and would go no farther. Outside the station, the rain was pelting down. It was dark and they had nowhere to spend the night. They were tired and hungry. Exhausted, Suzanne, in Beckett's words, eventually "gave out," saying she could take no more. Eighteen years later, Beckett wrote to a friend, Stuart Maguinness: "The last time I wept was in Cahors, in 1940. Well, nearly the last."[13] Seeing a light in a window, they stood in the street and shouted up at it. Finally, someone came to the door and Suzanne, taking the initiative, quickly explained their predicament. They were allowed to sleep on the floor of what turned out to be a shop selling religious artifacts, or what Beckett called "bondieuserie."

2

BEFORE LEAVING PARIS, Beckett had visited Peggy Guggenheim with Giorgio Joyce at Mary Reynolds's house.[14] Mary was not in residence. Now he remembered, or was reminded by Giorgio in Vichy, that she had left Paris with Marcel Duchamp to live in Arcachon on the Atlantic coast. So, knowing that Mary was both wealthy and well disposed toward Beckett, he and Suzanne set off the next morning to find her. They were dismayed to learn that no one was being allowed to leave the town. Luckily, they managed to find a trucker who had a legitimate reason for driving to Arcachon. After some persuasion, backed by a small financial inducement, he agreed to hide them in the back of his truck.

In this way, hungry and exhausted, after a very bumpy journey, they arrived in Arcachon. They presented themselves at the main post office and asked for Mary Reynolds's address. In spite of Suzanne's desperate pleas, the French officials remained cold and unmoved, adamantly refusing to divulge where Reynolds lived. Somehow, however, by asking local people whether they knew of an American lady who lived there, they managed to locate the house and, thanks to Mary Reynolds's kindness and generosity, were able to find a room in the seaside town.

A little later, with the help of Larbaud's loan, topped up by what they borrowed from their American friend, they rented a house overlooking the Atlantic: the Villa Saint-Georges, 135 *bis* boulevard de la Plage. The house, which still exists today, was rented by Beckett from its owner, a Mme. d'Ambrière.[15] Set at the top of a few steps, the white stone house has a red-tiled roof with a churchlike pinnacle over the left-hand bedroom. It is only a few feet from the sandy beach.[16]

They stayed there for the remainder of the summer, eating meals occasionally with Mary Reynolds, Marcel Duchamp, and the painter Jean Crotti and his second wife, who were staying with Duchamp. Crotti, a sixty-two-year-old naturalized Frenchman, had met Duchamp in New York in 1915 and married his sister, Suzanne, four years later. A former contributor to Dada reviews and creator of Futurist-inspired works, he intrigued Beckett, who was delighted to find that, in one move, he had acquired two new chess partners. So lengthy games of chess in a seafront café helped to while away the long, dreary days. Once when Duchamp and Beckett were playing chess together, Duchamp pointed out, to Beckett's great excitement, that the world chess champion, Alexander Alekhin (a chess genius, according to Beckett) had just walked in.[17] Duchamp was still too good for Beckett and regularly won their games, but Beckett found that he was a match for Crotti. Beckett spent the rest of the time swimming in the sea or translating, in desultory fashion, bits of *Murphy* into French.

All three couples soon realized that they could not stay there indefinitely and that a decision had to be made as to whether they should try to escape from the country or return to Paris. Leaving the country now was not going to be at all easy, however, for the Germans had quickly occupied the entire Atlantic coastline from Dunkirk in the north to Bayonne in the south. In fact, German troops moved into Arcachon, according to Beckett, the day after he and Suzanne managed to trace Mary Reynolds and Duchamp.

That Beckett seriously considered trying to return to Ireland at this stage through Spain or Portugal was confirmed by George Reavey and documented by a letter to him from the Irish legation in Madrid. Reavey explained how he contacted the legation on behalf of his friend, whom he had last seen at a dinner with the Joyces in Paris in January 1940, when Reavey was making his way to Madrid to become secretary and registrar of the British Institute there:

Suddenly, in 1940, in the summer after the fall of France, I received a postcard from Arcachon, in which Beckett implied that he needed help. He had reached Arcachon and I thought that he wanted to come out of the country, so I went to the Irish consulate or the Irish legation in Madrid and told them about Beckett's situation and about his having relatives in Dublin and so on. Apparently they were able to put the relatives in touch with him — Ireland was, of course, neutral — and he was able to receive money from Ireland, but he never came out as I expected. I thought he would appear in Madrid at any moment.[18]

It was Beckett's brother, Frank, who made the arrangement whereby checks could be payable in Arcachon. Beckett spoke of money also being sent "through a wine man there,"[19] who presumably had commercial contacts in Dublin. In this way, Suzanne and he were able to live not too uncomfortably for the three and a half months of their stay. The remainder of the occupation would, Beckett admitted later, have been far more tolerable if they had simply stayed where they were: food would have been more plentiful and the effects of the German presence less dramatic for them. But they felt that Paris was their home; all of their books and pictures were there; and, of course, many of their French friends had stayed on or returned after a few months' absence. Reports reaching them from the capital suggested that the Germans had been behaving fairly decently in this, a honeymoon period. So, early in September, Duchamp and Mary Reynolds decided to return to Paris. And a few days later, probably with some financial help from Mary Reynolds, Beckett and Suzanne followed their example.

3

ONE OF THE FIRST THINGS they had to do on their arrival, having established that their apartment had been neither damaged nor looted, was line up to have their ration cards validated at the Mairie — the town hall — so that they could obtain food tickets and join the first of many lines at the few local bakeries and groceries that had reopened. For Paris still seemed deserted. Beckett pestered the Irish legation at its provisional chancellery at 8 place Vendôme for a formal statement authenticating his profession. Finally, on 28 November, 1940, he extracted a letter. It read (in French):

I, the undersigned, Minister Plenipotentiary and Special Counsellor at the Irish Legation, certify that Monsieur Samuel Beckett, an Irish citizen, 6 Rue des Favorites, Paris (15ème) exercises the profession of writer. His writings, of which one notably is on Marcel Proust, have been published in London since the year 1931.[20]

With this letter, signed by Count Gerald O'Kelly de Gallagh, proving that he had an occupation, and with his Irish passport, Beckett was able to obtain all the normal food allowances of the ordinary Parisian resident. At first, these amounted to 350 grams of bread a day, 500 grams of sugar, 360 grams of meat a week (when there was any at the butcher's) and only 300 grams of coffee and 140 grams of cheese a month.[21] Beckett was affected by the restrictions that were imposed later in 1941 on tobacco and wine: six packets of cigarettes a month and one liter of wine per week per person. There were a few exceptionally good days — on February 18, 1941, for example, a cargo of Moroccan eggs got through the blockade imposed by Allied ships. Throughout the war, Beckett continued to receive his allowance from his father's estate through his bank in Dublin. But the money did not go very far now. So for him and Suzanne, as for so many Parisians, who had not the means to pay inflated prices for black-market goods, obtaining enough food to live was a constant preoccupation. Rations were cut still further after the failure of the 1940 autumn harvest and the bitterly cold winter of 1940–41. Exchanges, anticipating and inspiring those concerning carrots, radishes, and turnips between Estragon and Vladimir in the postwar play *En attendant Godot*, became common enough between Suzanne and himself.[22] Instead, the infamous rutabaga (normally fed only to cattle) came into its own as one of the commonest vegetables. The second major problem was how to keep warm. Because of the lack of fuel, there was no heat in Beckett's apartment. So he constructed a canvas tent within the high-ceilinged studio, and in this they used to sit to read or write, dressed in several layers of clothing.[23]

Finding out who had or who had not returned to Paris was a major source of interest. Geer and Lisl van Velde were in Cagnes-sur-Mer, where they were to remain throughout the war. Joyce, Nora, Giorgio, and Stephen were in St. Gérand-le-Puy, then in Zurich, where Joyce died of a perforated ulcer on January 13, 1941.[24] Lucia was in the Delmas clinic at Pornichet, south of La Baule in Loire-Atlantique. Bram van Velde was living in abject poverty with Marthe Kuntz in the Paris suburb of Montrouge. Mary Reynolds had returned. Importantly for Beckett, Alfred Péron was also back. Having been demobilized from the army, he was teaching again at the Lycée Buffon in Paris. So they were able to start meeting regularly, to talk, play the odd game of tennis, and work together on the translation of *Murphy*. Soon they came to share in a much more hazardous activity.

4

PÉRON WAS RESPONSIBLE for recruiting his Irish friend into the Resistance movement.[25] Beckett needed little persuading. He had followed the rise of Nazism in the 1930s with fascination, growing disgust, and, finally, horror. He had dipped with revulsion into Hitler's *Mein Kampf* and recognized the racial hatred that lay at the roots of national socialism. During his extended visit to Germany in 1936–37, he had witnessed at first hand the impact of anti-Semitism on individual painters whom he had met in Hamburg, persecuted simply because they were non-"Aryan."

Now, back in occupied Paris in 1940, Jewish friends were being stigmatized and abused, even assaulted. Beckett was disgusted by the Statut des Juifs introduced in October 1940 to discriminate against Jews and appalled when they were forced to wear the Star of David. When Jewish-owned properties were daubed with anti-Semitic slogans, then attacked and burned down, he was deeply shocked and repelled by the crude visual symbolism and by the verbal messages of anti-Semitic posters. The taking and execution of hostages in 1941, when some of the Jewish people he knew were rounded up and arrested, horrified him.[26] This was months before "la Grande Rafle" (the Big Roundup) of mid-July 1942, when 12,844 Jews were arrested. Whether all this was being done by French anti-Semitic groups out of indigenous Vichy-inspired hatred (as much of the anti-Jewish violence in the very early days of the occupation was)[27] or by the Germans themselves was a specious distinction for Beckett. It was sufficient that it was inhumane. As an Irishman, he was in principle neutral during the war, but "you simply couldn't stand by with your arms folded," he commented.[28]

One of the key factors in his decision to join the Resistance cell of which Péron was an important member was the arrest and disappearance to a concentration camp of Joyce's friend, unpaid secretary, and helper, Paul Léon. Like many of Léon's friends, Beckett had expressed concern that he and his wife and family should remain in Paris at a time so dangerous for anyone Jewish. Beckett recounted how he met Léon in the street in August 1941 and told him with alarm that he should leave at once. "I have to wait until tomorrow when my son takes his *bachot* [school examination]," replied Léon.[29] The following day he was arrested and interned near Paris. Throughout the next few months, Beckett expressed his concern for his friend by handing over his rations to Paul Léon's wife, Lucie, to be sent to the internee. Lucie Léon relates:

> In 1941, my husband Paul Léon was arrested and was being starved and tortured by the Germans (we were all in Paris at that time). I was trying to get food packages together and it was an almost impossible task. Sam Beckett used to bring me his bread ration and also his cigarette ration, so I could get them through to the camp. I will never forget this great kindness on his part. At that time he was probably in almost as much trouble as we were, and he certainly needed those rations himself.[30]

Léon was arrested on August 21, 1941, and, according to official documents, Beckett formally joined the Resistance on the first day of September.[31]

5

THE CELL THAT BECKETT JOINED was called Gloria SMH. The letters reversed the initials of "His Majesty's Service." "Gloria" was also the code name by which one of the founders of the group, Jeannine Picabia, was known, while "SMH" was the symbol of her coorganizer, Jacques Legrand.[32] By the time Beckett joined the cell, it had already become part of the British SOE (Special Operations Executive) and took its instructions from London, although, like a number of other networks, it had begun its life as a Polish group.[33] Jeannine Picabia worked with several different groups, but primarily with a parent cell named Etoile, which was set up as early as August 1940. But, by November 1940, an embryonic Gloria SMH was already in existence; it began life arranging the escape of British airmen shot down over the occupied zone and of Allied prisoners into the unoccupied zone.[34] Gloria SMH soon developed, however, primarily into an information network, although a few of its members continued to be involved in sheltering escapees or in sabotage activities.

Gloria was one of several specialized cells that, though centered on the Parisian region, gathered information widely over the whole occupied zone.[35] The cell grew until it had eighty members. It was more or less autonomous. For although, in the early days of the movement, members of some cells who knew each other well used to meet quite openly, it was soon recognized that it was better if members of one cell, or small groups within each cell, knew as little as possible about the others. In that way, if a member was uncovered or betrayed, the damage could, in principle at least, be limited to a more restricted circle. Agents could not reveal under torture what they did not know. However, for certain facilities, such as railway transportation or radio transmission, contacts and cooperation between different groups remained essential. Groups that, like Gloria, did not specialize in escape needed to know others to whom they could hand over Allied airmen shot down over France, or other escapees who made contact with them.

When Gloria SMH was first set up, it was run solely by Jeannine Picabia, the tiny twenty-seven-year-old daughter of the painter Francis Martinez Picabia. Christened Gabrielle Cécile Martinez Picabia, she was known in the family as Jeannine and worked with a number of Resistance groups under several different aliases, as well as that of Gloria. She also worked for the British intelligence service (SIS). A few months later, the Gloria cell was run jointly by Jacques Legrand and Jeannine. Legrand, a small, stocky figure, worked as a scientist in a laboratory; in his spare time he was an amateur sailor.[36]

Two other important figures in the cell were Beckett's own close friend Alfred Péron, known to the group as Dick (or, amusingly, as Moby) and his friend Suzanne Roussel (known as Hélène), who was slender with curly, slightly chestnut-colored hair, very feminine and witty. She was also sometimes called La Chatte on account of her large eyes; she was the treasurer of the group and used to issue money for expenses. A third key member was Hélène's best friend, Simone Lahaye, a tall, erect, heavily built teacher of philosophy (later, in the Ravensbrück concentration camp, she was known as the Countess),[37] who became the secretary of the cell and was responsible for its northern sector.[38] Péron and Suzanne Roussel taught English at the time at the Lycée Buffon in Paris[39] and, like Jeannine Picabia and Jacques Legrand, both of them played an active role in recruiting additional agents to the cell. Samuel Beckett was one of these.

In order to survive, Gloria needed specialists. Engraving and printing of false papers were done for the cell, for example, by a sixty-year-old printer, Georges Ozéré, and by an engraver, Victor Stey, twenty years his junior. A silversmith made the stamps for the identity cards. In overall charge of documentation, according to SOE files, was a woman called Sophie Baudouin Zacharoff. Another agent was Gilbert Thomason, a young engineer with the public works department at the Porte d'Orléans who worked with the service responsible for Paris's catacombs. This enabled Resistance members to hide things underground if necessary. Two agents, Pierre Turc and Gaston Passagez, were railway engineers who communicated with Henri Boussel's railway cell, "Rail," in Paris, while two other members of the cell who worked for the railway in Brest reported on movements of troops and on all railway traffic.

Messages came in from agents working in the field. The agents needed a cast-iron cover story and, in the case of carriers of information, the possibility of building up contacts in different parts of the country. The Gloria agent Pierre Weydert, for instance, had a VAP (Commercial Traveler) card which showed him to be the representative of a confectionery company in Paris. This allowed him to travel widely in Normandy and Brittany. One of his contacts was Jean Lucien, the owner of a Dieppe café-tabac called the Café Cayeux, from which all German ship movements in the harbor could be observed. Another two agents, Jean Saluden and Jean le Gad, worked for a chemist named Alanic in Brest, again situated conveniently to note any unusual naval activity in the port. They were two of the agents who worked in the "Secteur de Brest" and who reported when two of the most effective German vessels, the battleships Scharnhorst and Gneisenau, were immobilized in the harbor together with the heavy cruiser Prinz Eugen. Soon after these reports reached London, the ships were heavily bombed by the RAF.[40]

Another agent in Lorient, an architect, provided plans of the German fortifications and harbor installations there. Others took photographs or made detailed line drawings of potential targets such as electricity generating stations or antiaircraft defense systems and barrage balloons. Information also came from naval engineers working in the shipyards at Rouen and Le Trait about the boats that were built or being built in France for the German navy and the extent of the damage done by Allied bombers. Resistance cells also had dozens of people, young and old alike, who recognized, sketched, or described the insignia on Nazi vehicles that they saw in their area. From these reports, British intelligence could work out where various divisions of German troops were located or the places to which they were going.[41] Reports were sometimes deposited in what were called boîtes aux lettres, "letter boxes." These needed to be places such as a doctor's, dentist's, or lawyer's office — someplace where frequent comings and goings would arouse little or no attention or comment. There was, for instance, the bookshop in the rue des Beaux-Arts called (after Balzac's novel of that name) La Peau de Chagrin, where the bookseller, Pierre Périchard (working name Berger), his female companion, and his assistant, the writer André Frank, all worked for the cell. And there was the surgery of Dr. Louis Girard, an ear, nose, and throat specialist in the rue des Eaux in well-to-do Passy, whose eighteen-year-old daughter, Anise, also worked for the cell collecting information.[42]

6

BECKETT'S ROLE IN GLORIA was somewhat vaguely called liaison or secretarial work. SOE in London has the following apt description of him in its files: "Age 38 [this was in 1944]. 6 ft. Well built, but stoops. Dark hair. Fresh complexion. Very silent. Paris agent. Acted as secretary and got reports photographed. An Irishman known to GLORIA [Jeannine Picabia] before the war."[43] More precisely, Beckett's work involved the typing and translation of information reports that were brought to him in different forms and from various sources. Beckett explained:

> Information came in from all over France about the German military movements, about movements of troops, their position, everything that concerned the occupying forces. They would bring this information to me on various bits, scraps of paper. . . . It was a huge group. It was the boy-scouts! They brought it all in to me. I would type it all out clean. Put it in order and type it out, on one sheet of paper as far as was possible. Then I would bring it to a Greek who was part of the group. He lived in what is now the avenue René Coty, I think. And he would take photographs. And my sheets would be reduced to the size of a match-box. All the information. Probably unreadable but it could be magnified. And then he would give them to Madame Picabia, the [former] wife of Picabia, the painter. She was a very respectable old lady; nothing could be less like a Resistance agent. And she could get over to the other zone, the so-called unoccupied zone, without any difficulty. And so it was sent back to England.[44]

Characteristically, Beckett plays down here, as he always did, the significance of his role in the cell. It was, nonetheless, quite an important one. For most of the material that he received was written in French and needed to be classified, organized, and often translated. In many cases, too, as he implied, it had to be carefully condensed before it could be taken to a photographer to be miniaturized and sent on to London. As an intellectual who had translated numerous articles, prose texts, and poems in the 1930s from French into English for Nancy Cunard, Edward Titus, and Eugene Jolas, he was well suited to this task. Not only did Beckett have the necessary translation skills, but, as Péron clearly recognized when he recruited him, he also had astonishing powers of concentration, a meticulous attention to detail, and the ability to organize, reduce, and sift very diffuse material so as to make it succinct and intelligible for the British SOE and SIS. As noted in the SOE files, Beckett could also be very silent and secretive when he wanted to be, another great advantage for a Resistance agent.

The information compiled and typed by Beckett was then microfilmed by a photographer and secreted away by a courier in one form or other. A common method used by agents for hiding film or written or printed messages was to take out the bottom of a box of matches, place the message or the film underneath, then replace the bottom of the box. Another favorite method of carrying secret material was to have the message printed on thin cigarette paper, which was rolled around a needle and inserted deeply into a cigarette.[45] As for carrying secret messages, all kinds of methods were devised.[46] A train driver or a stoker could hide documents under the coal itself, as one of Gloria's agents regularly did on the main line between Paris and Lyons. For these reasons, an information cell like Gloria SMH needed to cast its recruitment net as wide as possible and incorporate members from many different professions and social strata. Gloria SMH also tended to recruit agents irrespective of political persuasion. From various accounts, it would seem, however, that it was primarily to Jacques Legrand, Jeannine Picabia, Alfred Péron, Suzanne Roussel, and Simone Lahaye that most of the reports were brought before being handed on to Beckett or others for processing or, alternatively, before being sent for direct transmission by radio to London.

Although he did not run the same risks as agents or couriers, Beckett's own involvement was still highly dangerous. The danger arose at three separate stages: the original delivery to him of the scraps of paper, which could have caused a lot of suspicious traffic to his flat; the physical presence of clandestine material there, while he was processing it; and, finally, and most dangerous of all, since the material had not yet been miniaturized, the transportation of the sheets of typed information to his own contact. The first of these dangers was reduced by having one or two people only deliver the information to his apartment. Péron was the regular carrier. His cover story, if challenged, had the advantage of being true: he was working with his friend, an Irish writer (neutral, he would have stressed, in the war), on a French translation of the latter's novel *Murphy*. As to the second danger, all that Beckett could do was to keep things out of sight as much as possible, hoping that the flat was not thoroughly searched before compromising material could be destroyed. Beckett emphasized that he himself was responsible for the third stage, the delivery. As a letter from Beckett about the liquidation of the cell reveals, Suzanne shared in the risks that he ran.[47]

Beckett was very insistent that he was not responsible for the photography, as has been claimed.[48] Instead, as he explained in the above interview, he delivered his typed sheets to a man known to him only as Jimmy the Greek. The photographer of Gloria was André (in reality Hadji) Lazaro, who indeed had a Greek father and was also known within the group as Tante Léo (Aunt Léo).[49] Lazaro lived, as Beckett said he did, in the avenue du Parc de Montsouris, now known as the avenue René Coty.[50] It was he, Beckett said, who produced the miniaturized film for dispatch to London.[51]

Once the messages had been photographically reduced, they often needed to be taken over the line to the unoccupied zone by courier. For the courier, it was essential "to be inconspicuous, not to stand out in a crowd, never to attract a second glance."[52] The woman who Beckett knew took many of his messages across the line was Jeannine's tiny, sixty-year-old mother, Gabrielle Buffet-Picabia, who was, as Beckett commented, an ideal agent for this most dangerous of jobs. She used to hide documents in a shopping bag that she carried like a peasant going to market or even conceal them in her underwear. Beckett had met the Picabias, both mother and daughter, before the war.[53]

Gabrielle Picabia was a remarkable woman.[54] She was extremely active in the Resistance movement, yet she has rarely been mentioned in its histories.[55] She contributed to the Allied cause first by helping hundreds of escapees and others who wanted to get to England. Almost every week someone sheltered in her apartment at 11 rue Chateaubriand and was fed by her: Belgians, Englishmen, parachutists, escaped prisoners of war. She also carried documents to the unoccupied zone for the Belgian Secret Service, as well as for Gloria SMH. She used to get up at five o'clock in the morning, fetch a bag from a café near the Gare du Nord, and take an early train to Chalon-sur-Saône; often she did not get back until early the following day, going without food or sleep. If challenged, as she once was by a young Gestapo officer at Montchanin while she was waiting for the last train back to Paris, her cover story was that she had been visiting relatives in the country.[56]

It was through Jeannine that Gabrielle Buffet became involved as a courier going to Chalon-sur-Saône. Jeannine recounted in her debriefing interview with SOE how her own first major contact there was made:

> One day quite by accident I met a young garage-owner on the line just three kilometres from Chalon and asked him if he knew of a way to cross over. He said he would take me over and I went in his car in the luggage place [that is, the trunk]. I asked if he would go on doing it for me and he accepted. His name was André Jarrot (working name Dédé). He went on helping us.[57]

André Jarrot (a member of the French Senate after the war and former minister of the quality of life) lived in a little village called Lux in the unoccupied zone. His contact for almost two years in the occupied zone was another garage owner called Camille Chevallier, who was arrested and shot by the Germans in June 1942. Since Jarrot used to transport mail and documents regularly from one depot of the Société des Pétroles Tonnelines on each side of the line to the other, he had gasoline and could cross between the two zones without too much difficulty.[58] He remembered very clearly smuggling Jeannine Picabia across the line in one of two identical six-horsepower Renault cars that he and two of his friends had built especially for this purpose.[59] He and Chevallier also established a remarkably successful organization for taking people, documents, film, and equipment across the line. After Chevallier's arrest, the secret service bags had to be rerouted. But the system for escorting people across the line at night with *passeurs* continued.

7

IT WAS ONLY NATURAL that the leaders of Gloria SMH should have recruited agents at first from among friends whom they felt they could trust. This could be dangerous, however, since it meant that names and addresses were known to too many people. Although there are different views as to how well organized and well run Gloria was, Beckett certainly felt that too many people knew who the others were, and that meetings were too casually arranged for a clandestine operation.[60] This is hardly surprising since they were all amateurs. But betrayal, when it came, did not occur because of a casual slip of the tongue or as a result of social gatherings of close friends like Beckett and Péron or Suzanne Roussel and Simone LaHaye. Judas came from outside; ironically, in the person of a Catholic priest.

Fifteen miles southeast of Paris, in the parish of La Varenne Saint-Hilaire in the Val-de-Marne, lived the local *vicaire* (assistant to the *curé*) Robert Alesch.[61] Alesch was born in Aspelt in Luxembourg on March 6, 1906. He had studied theology in Freiburg and was ordained into the priesthood at Davos in Switzerland in 1933. He had been *vicaire* at La Varenne St.-Hilaire since 1935. A small man with a receding hairline and steely blue eyes, he preached sermons that seemed to his parishioners sometimes dangerously anti-Nazi and anticollaborationist. Claiming to be the son of a Lorraine French patriot who had been tortured by the Germans in 1917, he managed to infiltrate a Resistance group recruited and organized by Pierre-Maurice Dessinges. The group was mainly involved in secreting escapees or Allied airmen who had been shot down across the line into the unoccupied zone.

What no one knew at the time was that Robert Alesch was already working for the German Abwehr (military intelligence) as Agent Number 162. Since he was bilingual in French and German, he saw the German occupation of France as an ideal opportunity to make himself rich. According to a German major named Schaeffer, who was called by the defense to give evidence for Alesch at his trial, Alesch contacted the Gestapo himself in 1941 and was sent to work under Oskar Reile, chief of the Abwehr-III-Paris, from 1941 for a fixed monthly sum, which was then topped up by a horrifyingly macabre system of bonuses paid out for every member of the Resistance whom he betrayed. He is said to have been paid a regular sum of six hundred marks, or about twelve thousand francs, a month and his two mistresses, Geneviève Cahen-Guillemin and Renée Martin-Andry, were paid another five thousand francs between them.[62] It has been estimated that, with his various bonuses and expenses, Alesch was probably earning in the region of twenty-five thousand francs a month, when the average earnings of a worker were one thousand francs.

He led an extraordinary double life. He would take mass at La Varenne, then change into ordinary clothes and dash into Paris, where he used to spend his nights drinking and fornicating. He even rented a room in the rue Spontini so that he could stay overnight with one of his mistresses. Only with the money gained from his sequence of betrayals in various parts of France could he have supported such an extravagant life-style.

Sex certainly seems to have played a dominant role in Alesch's life. But whether it was financial greed and sex alone that motivated him is difficult to establish. He also seems to have enjoyed the act of treachery itself as well as the fruits of his betrayal. One of his victims, Germaine Tillion, spoke of the look of triumph that came into his eye as he watched her being arrested as a direct result of his betrayal.[63] At his trial, the question of advancement within the church was also raised as a possible motivating factor, Alesch claiming to have wanted the bishopric of Cologne as a reward for his services after the war.[64] The defense lawyers wavered between presenting Alesch as a French patriot who had been maneuvered into betrayal by the Gestapo after threats had been made against his parents' lives and, as the evidence built up against him, shifting their ground to claim that he was actually German and ought to be judged by a military tribunal.

Germaine Tillion was an intelligent, courageous woman who was one of the leaders of a Resistance cell later to be called the Musée de l'Homme. She lived with her mother in Saint-Maur des Fossés, the parish neighboring that of Alesch. Together she and her mother sheltered many escapees in their large three-story house and took part in a variety of other Resistance activities. One day, the Abbé Alesch, dressed in his clerical robe, knocked at her door and introduced himself as coming from one of her coworkers in the Resistance, Maurice Dessinges. He told her that he wanted to work with her group in the cell. Suspicious at first, she made a number of inquiries about him from another member of the cell and from a nun called Sister Ernestine, who worked locally as a nurse. The answers that she received were unequivocal. Alesch was indeed what he said he was, namely the *vicaire* of La Varenne, where he lived at the presbytery. More than that, he was known in the village to be a French patriot and a fervent opponent of Nazism. Above all, he was a priest. This was a virtual guarantee of probity.

However, some months before, at the end of April 1942, a key member of British SOE in the occupied zone, Pierre de Vomécourt (known in the Resistance first as Lucas, then as Sylvain) had been arrested together with his brother and one of his agents. They were being interrogated in Fresnes prison. There was considerable disquiet at this development. Jacques Legrand heard of the arrest while he was in Marseilles and came back to Paris a few days later to see if he could do something about it.[65] Both SIS and SOE desperately wanted to contrive the de Vomécourts' escape. A coded message to consider all possible means of doing this was sent to Jacques Legrand and Gloria SMH. It is believed that a phrase such as "at no matter what cost" was used concerning the need to engineer an escape. Legrand even considered at one time the feasibility of organizing an armed assault on the prison.[66]

Mme. Tillion had met Jacques Legrand so that she could pass on to him and to London her conviction that the members of her own cell, such as the Colonel Duteil de la Rochère and the Colonel Hauet, had been betrayed by another traitor called Gaveau. Seven of her former colleagues had been executed on February 23, 1942. She also hoped that Legrand might be able to "neutralize" (that is, assassinate) Gaveau. It was at this point that Abbé Alesch came up with an audacious plan for effecting the escape of de Vomécourt from Fresnes prison. He told Madame Tillion that he knew one of the German guards there, a young officer who was engaged to a French girl in his parish. The German, Alesch went on, had just learned that he was about to be sent off to fight on the Russian front and consequently he wanted to escape from his commitments and be spirited away with his girlfriend.[67]

Germaine Tillion passed on this information from Alesch to Jacques Legrand, who thought long and hard in view of the huge risks involved. There was time only for the most cursory of investigations, conducted by trying to exchange some messages through the so-called guard with Resistance inmates. What Alesch said checked out. So he was told to go ahead with his plan. This involved, he had explained, the need not only to "buy" the guard but also to pay for intermediaries to hide the couple and then get them out of the country. This would take an awful lot of money, he explained. SOE (probably with the backing if not the active involvement of SIS) conferred and, doubtless after much deliberation, agreed that the plan should be tried. Finally, in mid-August, two separate sums of three hundred thousand francs and one hundred thousand francs were asked for. A magistrate and old sailing companion of Jacques Legrand, named Jean Laroque, who had worked with Legrand for Gloria SMH reporting the movements of ships off the Normandy coast and in the ports, put him in touch with an old school friend of his called Robert Labbé, whose family partially owned the Banque Worms.[68] The bank agreed to put up the money — which Jacques Legrand handed over to Alesch so as to set his plan in motion — on the understanding that they would be reimbursed by British Intelligence.[69] Alesch seems to have pocketed the money and promptly handed over the names of the leaders of Gloria SMH to the Abwehr. The value of such a sum of money at the time was more than an average skilled worker could expect to earn in an entire lifetime. In 1950, according to Jean Laroque, the sum had not yet been repaid.[70]

8

GERMAINE TILLION was the first to be arrested, at the Gare de Lyon on August 13, as she accompanied Alesch and another agent working for Gloria, Gilbert Thomason. "Hélène" Roussel was arrested on August 15. Alfred Péron was picked up the following day in Anjou. On him, the Abwehr found, according to Jeannine Picabia, a letter and instructions in her handwriting, as well as maps of the Fresnes, Cherche-Midi, and La Santé prisons.[71] Further arrests followed, including that of Jacques Legrand. Gabrielle Buffet-Picabia claimed in her debriefing with the SOE that Legrand "when arrested, had on him a notebook containing many names and addresses."[72] It is difficult to know how she could have known this fact at this time and no independent corroboration has been forthcoming. However, one member of the cell quickly broke down and, on his own later admission, wrote out the names of members known to him, who were then picked up one by one over the next few months. Another either talked herself, or else documents containing names and addresses were discovered hidden in her chimney. Of the entire group, more than fifty members of Gloria SMH were picked up; most of them, as a glance down the list of those arrested and deported shows, were captured in August or September 1942.[73] Many of those arrested were kept for months in Fresnes or Romainville prisons before being deported to concentration camps at Ravensbrück, Mauthausen, or Buchenwald. Some survived to tell the tale. Beckett's good friend Alfred Péron did not; he died on May 1, 1945, soon after he was liberated by the Swiss Red Cross. He is buried with seven other victims of the concentration camps in the cemetery of Samedan near St. Moritz.

After the initial shock of learning of her husband's arrest, Mania Péron's first thought was that she must warn Sam Beckett. So she promptly sent a telegram warning him and Suzanne that they should make their escape. The telegram was bold but deliberately ambiguous: "Alfred arrêté par Gestapo. Prière faire nécessaire pour corriger l'erreur" ("Alfred arrested by Gestapo. Beg do what is necessary to correct mistake").[74] Beckett and Suzanne quickly threw a few belongings into a suitcase and a couple of bags — "We took what we could," said Beckett[75] — and, only a matter of hours after receiving the telegram, they left their flat. Before this, however, Beckett tried to warn other members of the group. He telephoned to a chef who he knew worked with them but was unable to reach him; the young man was soon arrested and tortured.[76] He also risked calling on his chief contact, the Greek photographer, who did not take Beckett's warning seriously enough and delayed his escape. He, too, was soon picked up by the Gestapo.[77] Suzanne went to "Hélène" Roussel's apartment to warn her and was arrested briefly by the Gestapo. She managed, however, to convince them that her visit was totally innocent, and she was released.[78] Had she and Beckett not then left immediately they would have been arrested when the Gestapo came to their flat and left men on guard at the door, waiting in case they should return.

Beckett and Suzanne had no money and no idea where they might go. They immediately contacted Mary Reynolds, who had helped them in Arcachon. Her companion, Marcel Duchamp, had been in New York since June, but Mary had stayed on in Paris and was later to escape across the Pyrénées.[79] She allowed the fugitives to spend the first night in her house in the rue Hallé. Then, according to Beckett, they contacted "some Communist friends of Suzanne,"[80] who hid them out in various parts of Paris or its environs, including an apartment in Montmartre and another in Vanves, where a trustworthy concierge was favorable to the Resistance.

Various friends helped them out with money. They moved several times into small hotels where they hoped they would not be recognized. They adopted false names, and Beckett grew a mustache so as to disguise himself. They took the view that it was probably better not to spend too long in the same place. In one small hotel, just as they were preparing to go to bed, Beckett suddenly swore loudly. Then, in a hushed, tense voice, he admitted that, in registering downstairs in the hotel, he had mistakenly used his real name. This meant, of course, that they had to pack their belongings immediately and find somewhere else to spend the night. Appalled at his dangerous slip, Suzanne found it hard to believe that he could be so foolish. After the war she often quoted this story to friends as an extreme example of Sam's wholly impractical nature. Her own quick intelligence and practical nature saved them on a number of occasions.

While they were on the run, Beckett and Suzanne also hid out for ten days with the writer Nathalie Sarraute.[81] Madame Sarraute and her husband, Raymond, were spending the summer out of Paris in a cramped gardener's house belonging to a Monsieur Mariage. The pretty but rustic cottage, which lay in the grounds of the estate of the widow of the celebrated Russian bass Chaliapin, was, and still is, on the square of the village of Janvry in the Vallée de la Chevreuse.

When Mania Péron secretly contacted her Russian-born childhood friend Nathalie Sarraute, and asked her if she would take in Beckett and Suzanne, the Sarrautes already had a full house: in addition to two of their own three children, themselves, and Nathalie Sarraute's mother, they were also sheltering a young Jewish girl called Nadine Liber, who was living with them under the assumed name of Gauthier-Villars. In spite of this, they kindly agreed to take in the escapees. Raymond Sarraute worked for another Resistance cell and both of them felt that in the circumstances they could hardly refuse. So the girls moved into a dark little room that normally served as a dining room, where they slept on mattresses on the floor. Beckett and Suzanne were allocated their sunny bedroom.

Conditions in the house were fairly primitive. There was running water only in the kitchen; consequently, everyone had to carry large jugs of water and wash in large bowls in their rooms. The lavatory was at the bottom of the garden, and to avoid a nocturnal expedition to what was known in the family as "la punition du Ciel" ("the punishment of the gods"), chamber pots were much in demand. One problem was that both Beckett and Suzanne were extremely late risers. So Beckett used to wander through the kitchen at about one o'clock with a chamber pot in his hand, just as the others were sitting down to lunch. The fact that he did this every day irritated Nathalie Sarraute's mother, who considered their guests to be very badly brought up indeed. "Here comes the madman," she would comment aloud to her daughter in Russian, as Beckett crept silently and sheepishly through the kitchen.

The cramped conditions and crowded nature of the house meant that tension between its occupants was inevitable. It was not helped by the fact that Mme. Sarraute and Beckett did not take to each other. Indeed, fifty years later,

Nathalie Sarraute spoke with considerable bitterness of Beckett and Suzanne's behavior at the time and of his subsequent lack of gratitude for what she and her husband had done for them. She considered Beckett much too arrogant to feel that he bore any obligation toward anyone.

One can imagine that Beckett and Suzanne would have felt that they were imposing on the Sarrautes. Their acute embarrassment might well have given the appearance of aloofness and lack of politeness. On the other hand, they may simply have behaved rudely. For it is certainly true that Beckett could be distant and difficult when he did not like someone. And he was far from accommodating when he found himself in a situation that he disliked. Moreover, he seems to have found Nathalie Sarraute sharp and bitchy. On her side, an element of professional jealousy may have crept into her account of his behavior. Years later, she spoke with some asperity of his great admiration at the time for Simone de Beauvoir and clearly felt that he dismissed her own literary talent too airily. At the time she had published only *Tropismes* and this had received scant critical attention. Mme. Sarraute did, however, admit that Beckett got on extremely well with her husband and that he and Raymond used to go for long walks together.

Since there was little or no danger of their being arrested or denounced in the village, Beckett and Suzanne also used to go for walks in the countryside. But Paris was still too close for comfort. And it soon became clear that they would have to try to make their escape into the unoccupied zone. Beckett still had the mustache that he had grown in an attempt to disguise himself. Suzanne said that he looked even more like himself with the mustache than he did without it. And Nathalie Sarraute's husband settled matters once and for all when he said to Beckett: "Look, the first thing you must do is shave off that mustache! It makes you look like a typical English civil servant or a British officer!" Off came the mustache.

The Sarrautes then put Beckett and Suzanne in touch with their Russian friends Nahum and Sophie Liber, who were working with another Resistance group in Paris and who provided them with forged papers. So, at the beginning of October, just over six weeks after making their escape from the apartment in the rue des Favorites, they were taken over the line that separated the occupied from the unoccupied zone at Chalon-sur-Saône by a local *passeur* who was used to smuggling Resistance members into the free zone. It is likely that Beckett was escorted by one of the group of *passeurs* that had been set up by Chevallier and Jeannine Picabia's contact, André Jarrot, alias Dédé. The guides used a variety of routes: a poplar tree chopped down by Jarrot himself so that it lay across a large stream, or a route negotiated through long grass left deliberately uncut by farmers to allow people to pass more easily at night. Beckett said:

> I can remember waiting in a barn (there were ten of us) until it got dark, then being led by a *passeur* over streams; we could see a German sentinel in the moonlight. Then I remember passing a French post on the other side of the line. The Germans were on the road; so we went across the fields. Some of the girls were taken over in the boot of a car.[82]

13

Refuge in Roussillon

1942–45

1

SMALL BECKETT and Suzanne Deschevaux-Dumesnil eventually found a refuge from the Gestapo in the small village of Roussillon.[1] This village in the Vaucluse is often referred to as Roussillon d'Apt so as to distinguish it from the better-known large wine-growing area of Roussillon to the southwest. It stands high on a hill with imposing cliffs of red ocher that fall sharply away to its north side. Even the soil in the gardens is red. "But down there everything is red!" says Vladimir of a region where, in the French version of *Waiting for Godot*, he claims that he and Estragon had once been grape picking.[2] The village lies forty-eight kilometers from Avignon and eleven from Apt, both of which, although in Vichy France, were occupied by German troops soon after Beckett's arrival in Roussillon. Roussillon itself was not.

The reasons for this are several. The village was relatively inaccessible to heavy vehicles, since at the time there was only one reasonable road from Apt; there was also a shortage of adequate accommodation for German officers in the village, where only one house had a properly equipped bathroom; and there was no building sufficiently large to serve as a billet for their troops (some officers came to survey the school but found it too run-down and unsatisfactory for their purposes).[3] Roussillon remained therefore relatively safe throughout the war, although there was always the fear of a random German *rafle* to arrest either Jewish refugees who had fled there or those who, like Beckett, had Resistance connections.

Denunciation also never became a problem in Roussillon, but, inevitably, it lurked in the minds of those who had most reason to fear it. Stories of both denunciations and arrests were current in a number of local towns and villages in the region. Beckett and Suzanne took great care to frequent, in the main, only those local farmers whom they learned to trust or refugees who were in a similar position to themselves. However, Roussillon was, and still is, a very small community and at the time everyone knew that the strangers among them were seeking refuge from the war, although few knew exactly why. Beckett took care not to enlighten them.

Many villagers supposed that one or the other of the Beckett couple must be Jewish—the entire group of refugees was known collectively as "les Juifs"—

or that he (for she was obviously French) must be subject to the regulation of *résidence forcée*, according to which foreigners in Vichy France were obliged to live at a distance from the sea. Almost fifty years later, some members of the Resistance group with whom Beckett had gone out on sorties toward the end of hostilities did not know that he had been active earlier with another Resistance group in Paris or that, after the war, he had received the Croix de Guerre and the Médaille de la Reconnaissance for his contribution there. It did not do to talk too much of what one did or had done, even to apparent allies or friends. Beckett and Suzanne had already been betrayed once and did not want it to happen again.

But how did they learn of the comparative security to be found in Roussillon and how did they get there? This occurred through a friend of Suzanne named Roger Deleutre and his sister, Yvonne.[4] The Deleutre family owned a house and fairly large estate called Saint-Michel on the outskirts of the village; they had bought the place just before the war. The mother with her daughter, Yvonne, and her Jewish husband, Marcel Lob, accompanied by their two children, Henri and Denise, all moved there early in 1942. Her son, Roger, was to join them later.

Lob, a grammarian, had been dismissed from his university teaching post because he was Jewish; he was afraid of being arrested (as eventually he was) and deported. Throughout the war, he was obliged to hide his intellectual background and profession, claiming to be a simple *cultivateur* or farmer; his official papers cited this as his profession. His wife, who was an English teacher in the Lycée Impérial in Nice, found it difficult to teach there and opted for voluntary severance.

After the invasion of Paris by the Nazis, Roger Deleutre, a musician, was finding it extremely difficult to make a living and was thinking of joining his mother and sister in Roussillon. Since the early 1920s, when both of them were studying music, he had known Suzanne Deschevaux-Dumesnil. His sister, Yvonne, knew Suzanne too, for she sometimes used to go round to Suzanne's flat in Paris and sing to her accompaniment.

While she and Beckett were still in hiding in Paris, Suzanne contacted Roger to find out what the situation was in the remote Vaucluse village and whether they might find some degree of sanctuary there. Roger replied favorably but knew that, since Sam held a foreign passport, residence would need to be approved by the regional authority of the Vichy government, even though Ireland was a neutral country. So Marcel Lob, who knew the secretary general in Avignon, contacted this official to ask whether their Irish friend could come to live near his family. Of course, he revealed nothing of Sam's decidedly nonneutral actions so far during the war; indeed, he may have been quite unaware of these actions at the time. It was agreed informally at first that, if Beckett and Suzanne were willing to remain at Roussillon without seeking to travel elsewhere in France, residence there would in all likelihood be approved.

The last stages of their dangerous journey to Roussillon, however, proved far from simple. On September 29, 1942, they walked into Vichy, where they stayed for a couple of nights at the Hôtel Castelflor.[5] At first, they tried contacting the Irish representative in Vichy, who, according to Beckett, was extremely unsympathetic and unhelpful. They were told that they would have to report to police headquarters and, since they had no valid travel documents from Paris to Vichy, they decided that they would have to risk admitting that they had crossed the line clandestinely. From the Vichy police, they received a provisional safe-conduct pass which allowed them two days to travel by train to Avignon. There, they reported to the central police station; then, on the following day, to the Préfecture du Vaucluse. It was here that Lob's influence may well have helped Beckett and Suzanne. Finally, after six weeks on the run and a lot of help from their friends, they reached Roussillon, where they moved into a little room in the Hôtel de la Poste or, as it was known locally, the Hôtel Escoffier.

2

ON OCTOBER 6, Beckett and Suzanne walked up the steep, narrow cobbled path that separated the hotel from the little mairie (town hall) to put his name in the Register of Foreign Residents.[6] As he skimmed quickly over the page to see those who had registered there a few months before, he spotted, among Italians, Belgians, Lithuanians, and Russians, the names of two British residents, Dulcie Hope Woolland and Anna O'Meara Beamish. The latter attracted his attention, for not only did the lady in question bear the name of one of his favorite drinks (Beamish stout) but her recorded place of birth (Dublin) and her given names indicated her Irish origins.[7]

On their arrival, the two most pressing problems for Beckett and Suzanne, as for most refugees, were where they were to live and how they would manage to get enough to eat. Because of Ireland's position of neutrality in the war, they hoped to continue to receive through the ordinary mail the small annuity that was due to Beckett from his father's estate. But that could (and did) take many weeks to arrange. In the meantime, they stayed at the hotel, which was run by a widow, Mme. Adrienne Escoffier.[8]

Madame Escoffier was something of a character in the village. About forty years old at the time, she was a strong-minded but kindly woman who ran a small, profitable, old-style French village hotel with four or five guest rooms. She did the cooking herself, helped by her mother. Part of the hotel building, the Café Escoffier, was a meeting place for the villagers, who came there to drink, talk, and play cards. It also became an assembly point for members of the Resistance and, at midday and in the evening, those without radios of their own huddled together around an iron stove in the back kitchen to listen to the broadcasts of the BBC.[9] Miss Beamish had stayed at the hotel on her arrival in April, too, but by the time Beckett moved in, she was already renting a house on the eastern outskirts of the village that had belonged to Mme. Escoffier's parents. Beckett and Suzanne were soon to become her nearest neighbors.

It has been said that during the first few weeks spent at the Hôtel Escoffier, Beckett had a virtually complete mental breakdown.[10] I have found no evidence at all to support such a claim from those who knew him well in Roussillon. But it would certainly have been surprising if he and Suzanne had not been subject to feelings of deep depression. After all, they had just come through an extremely traumatic series of events since receiving the news of the arrest and imprisonment of their close friend Alfred Péron. They had little with them by way of personal possessions. They were living in cramped, fairly primitive conditions in an uncomfortable hotel that had fleas and mice. The primitive lavatory stood outside, at the edge of a cliff, and emptied down into what was called *le gouffre* ("the chasm"); so, when the wind blew fiercely, it whipped up soiled pieces of paper. They had to cross the road to get drinking water from a fountain in front of the hotel.[11] There were constant worries because of shortages of money, food, and clothing. They had no regular work to preoccupy them and, in such circumstances, writing must have seemed entirely out of the question for Beckett.

At first they knew almost no one in the village. There were even problems with those whom they did know, for Beckett found that he did not like or get on with the grammarian-become-farmer, Marcel Lob, in spite of feeling a great deal of sympathy for his situation. Generously, Mme. Lob has conceded that this fundamental disharmony resulted almost entirely from her husband's difficult character and antisocial nature.[12] But it meant that the atmosphere was often exceedingly strained and, as a result, Beckett and Suzanne went to the Lobs' house only rarely.

Gradually, as they lived for some weeks in the hotel, they began to learn who was who, and who was related to whom — a not uncomplicated matter in so small a rural village. There appeared to be innumerable Icards and several Blancs, for instance. Mme. Escoffier's sister-in-law, Agnès, taught in the village school, while Agnès's husband, Henri, acted as chauffeur to the village, running a small bus to Apt for the Saturday market and fetching the mail daily in a little Simca from a point on the *route nationale* in the valley below. When there was no petrol (as happened very often) Henri used a horse and cart to fetch whatever was needed. Bread and groceries were purchased from a small grocery store belonging to the Gulinis.

Other food was usually obtained from local farms. For this reason, there were never acute shortages in the village, but prices were pushed up by an active black market created by a few local suppliers. This led to those involved being extremely unpopular in the village; even today there are traces of real animosity toward them. For many people felt genuine anxiety as to where the money was coming from to buy their next meal or their next pair of shoes, and resented the profiteering that took place. Food was a constant preoccupation.

It was important for Beckett and Suzanne to find a way of obtaining provisions without depending on charity. So they were introduced by the Lob-Deleutres to two local farmers: the Bonnellys, whose vineyard lay south of Roussillon, and the Audes, tenant farmers who lived over four kilometers away in the tiny hamlet of Clavaillan. Since the farm and the vineyard of M. Bonnelly were nearer, Beckett first started doing day labor for him in exchange for produce, particularly wine. Potatoes seemed like gold dust at the time, and Beckett had what he later described as "two early triumphs." [13] First, although the fields were a sea of mud following the potato harvest, he and Suzanne were allowed to search in the ground, picking and keeping whatever had been overlooked by the farmworkers. Secondly, when Beckett found that the other farmer, Aude, whom he came to like and respect very much, owed grain to Marcel Lob, but did not want to give it to him personally, he went along to ask Aude if he could collect it, returning to Suzanne's great delight with a large sackful of grain balanced on his shoulders, which they then shared with her friends.

The other pressing problem was resolved when the Lobs put Suzanne in touch with a lawyer named Rousset, who owned a house in La Croix, a part of the village named after the large iron cross that stands close to the house. Beckett and Suzanne rented this house for the rest of the war. In advance of their move and through friends in Paris, Suzanne got in touch with the concierge of their apartment in the rue des Favorites. He found that the Gestapo, who had come to arrest Beckett, had fixed lead seals on the outer door. In spite of this, he contrived to get into the flat and send along some of the sheets and clothing that had been left behind in their hurried flight. [14]

The Roussillon house, looking today much as it did in 1942, is set quite high above the road from Roussillon to Apt. [15] There were several rooms that Beckett and Suzanne did not occupy. A small stove heated the dining room–sitting room, and this had a big chimney pipe that passed through the kitchen. Upstairs, the one large room that they used was unheated. So, when the temperatures fell during the first winter months of their stay and the mistral started to whistle noisily round the house, it was extremely difficult to keep warm. Beckett's own memories of the two years spent in Roussillon were of sharp extremes of winter cold and summer heat, as well as of the hard drudgery of the work that he did in the fields. A local landowner owned a grove of *chênes verts*, holm oaks, that he wanted uprooted. So Beckett agreed to do this in exchange for half the wood. Cutting down the trees, he found, was child's play compared with uprooting them, since he had to dig all around and cut the roots before they could be released. [16]

However unwelcoming the house seemed in the chill of January 1943, it was at least somewhere that he and Suzanne could temporarily call their own and, more important, be alone. It had a fairly large garden where, as spring came round, they could plant a few vegetables and store a large supply of logs. And it had a splendid view across the valley beyond Le Pont Julien toward the villages of Goult and Bonnieux. It had a degree of isolation but was less than ten minutes' walk from the center of the village. To the left and on the opposite side of the road was the house that was occupied for the next two years by Miss Beamish and her companion-secretary, Suzanne Allévy. They were introduced to Miss Beamish by Mme. Escoffier.

•   •

Soon Beckett established a routine of going to work on a more or less daily basis on the Audes' farm.[17] The farmer was generous with food, supplying Suzanne and Beckett with most of the provisions that they needed to live reasonably well: milk, eggs, meat, flour, root vegetables, and fruit in season. In exchange, Beckett worked without being paid in the fields, woods, and vineyard. Often accompanied by Suzanne, he would walk the four kilometers down to the farm, mostly taking a little-known path to avoid running into unexpected German patrols.

Beckett usually went out to work in the fields with Fernand Aude, the farmer's seventeen-year-old son and one of eight children, four of whom were still living at home. Fernand speaks admiringly of the gaunt Irishman's powers of endurance even under the fiercest summer sun and of his willingness to tackle most jobs, however unpleasant, on the farm. He remembers him making light of what seemed like a nasty cut on his hand, as he was pruning the vines, claiming that he had only his own carelessness to blame. Beckett helped, too, with harvesting the grain and with picking fruit: melons, cherries, and apples.[18]

It is likely that it was on the Audes' farm that Beckett acquired much of the precise knowledge of country life that surfaces from time to time in his writing, particularly in *Malone Meurt (Malone Dies)*. It was commonplace in Roussillon to see hens crossing the threshold of the farm kitchen and to hear at night the barking of the dogs answering each other across the valley, as they do in that novel. These sounds took Beckett back to his childhood in Foxrock.[19]

In one of the manuscript notebooks of *Watt*, much of which was written in Roussillon, Beckett copied out the following saying: "Et les caisses se touchent dans la vigne" ("And the crates are touching in the vines") followed by the name "Aude" and the date "Sept. 29, 1943."[20] This sentence, which sounds like a secret radio message intended for the ears of members of the Resistance, was actually used as an expression of misfortune by M. Aude, his son explained, when the ground was too sodden for the crates full of grapes to be dragged out from the vines by horse and sledge; they then had to be manhandled, "with the help of Sam."[21] Beckett extended in this way his range of French agricultural terminology and country sayings while he was working with the Audes and the Bonnellys.

When Suzanne accompanied Beckett to the Audes' farm, she would spend hours in the farmhouse with the mother and daughters, where, apparently, she talked a lot but did very little housework and no cooking. She seems to have tried to teach the youngest daughter some words of English, although later in Beckett's career she made no effort to learn it herself and had forgotten most of what she had picked up from him. She was not entirely idle, however, while in Roussillon, since, as well as trying to make their house comfortable, she gave music lessons to a niece of Elie Blanc, the village archivist, who lived up the road.[22] The girl came to her house and, since Suzanne had no piano, she taught her by using a system of colors that she had herself invented which stood for musical notes.

Quite often both she and Beckett would have lunch in the farmhouse kitchen with the Audes and, at least once a week, they would stay on for a large evening meal, returning across the field only after the cicadas had ceased their noisy exchanges. Although Sam and Suzanne appeared to have little in common with the Audes, they enjoyed the natural warmth and generosity of the family and admired their quiet dignity and charm. Visitors never went away empty-handed, it was said. Beckett became quite friendly with young Fernand, with whom he shared many a joke in the fields or over the dinner table, as they recapitulated the events of their day. Occasionally Beckett would teach the younger members of the family a new card game. More often he would sit silently sipping the wine that he had helped to produce.

But if Beckett made light of his manual work in the fields, it was not something to which he was accustomed and, in truth, he found it exhausting. However, it brought them a fairly plentiful supply of food and, in any case, he preferred the work, however hard, to the tedium of days spent merely waiting for the war to end. Like everyone else in Roussillon, he followed with keen interest BBC news reports on the progress of the fighting in North Africa, then in Italy and France, as the Allies invaded and began to drive back the German forces and make slow progress through the country.

3

BECKETT HAD, OF COURSE, almost no books with him during his stay in Roussillon. But Yvonne Lob, an *agrégée* in English, owned a fair number of late nineteenth- and early twentieth-century novels in English, which he borrowed from time to time. He seems to have read there stories and novels by Katherine Mansfield, Sinclair Lewis, and Aldous Huxley and he certainly read *Gone with the Wind*. It was in Roussillon, too, that he first read some of the novels and stories of Hugh Walpole, including the complete *Herries Chronicle*.[23] There is an echo of this experience in the novel *Watt*. Describing the "funambulistic stagger" of his central protagonist, Beckett has Lady McCann compare the movements of Watt's head and those of a bear. "Where had she read that even so, from side to side, bears turn their heads when baited?" she asks rhetorically, replying: "In Mr. Walpole, perhaps."[24] In Walpole's *Judith Paris*, Beckett had read a memorable account of an old bear being baited:

> Then the bear began quietly to realize that he was in the middle of his enemies. Carefully, with that same caution, he moved his head to look for his master, and when he saw him held with his coat torn and his brown breast baer he began to be angry. . . . But with his anger there rose also slowly his sadness and his bewilderment. He shuffled with his feet; his paw rose and fell again. He began to roll his head. Then he tried to break from his chain, and when he found that he could not, he jerked his head toward his master. Then again rubbed the drops of blood from his nose.[25]

The baited bear is a key image in Walpole's novel. It is an image of suffering, willfully inflicted on a vulnerable, old, captive creature. Reuben, the man who observes this scene, identifies totally with the wretched, lonely victim. But the bear is not just a victim. He raises his head to stare at the onlookers, distancing himself from them and becoming a symbol of dignity and suffering: "Something very grand entered into him, the grandeur of all captured and ill-treated things. He lifted his head and stared from under his jutting brows at the crowd, and was at once with that single movement, finer than all of them."[26]

Forty years later, a related image resurfaced when Beckett came to write *Catastrophe* in support of the Czech dissident writer Václav Havel. In *Catastrophe* the Protagonist, humiliated, reduced, "baited" throughout the play, "raises his head, fixes the audience," and reduces their applause to a stunned silence.[27]

4

THE INTEREST OF BECKETT'S LIFE in Roussillon increased considerably with the arrival of two further refugees from Nazism: the Polish-born French painter Henri Hayden, and his much younger French wife, Josette.[28] One day, Beckett was in the bar of the café with Miss Beamish. Accompanied by her two Airedales, she was waiting for the Haydens, who were coming to Roussillon via Apt from Mougins near Cannes. The picturesque nature of the Haydens' arrival in Henri Escoffier's crowded little bus amused Beckett: Josette climbed out of the bus itself, where she had been perched on some woman's knees with, on her own knees, a cat in a basket; Henri extricated himself with some difficulty from a small trailer and walked into the Café Escoffier carrying an old, battered suitcase.

Beckett had already learned from Miss Beamish why the Haydens needed refuge. Hayden, although baptized a Protestant, was of Jewish extraction. He and Josette had been leading something of a pillar-to-post existence since they had first left Paris during the exodus almost three years earlier. After a stay in the Auvergne, they moved with their painter friends Robert Delaunay and Sonia Delaunay-Terk to Mougins, where they got to know an English friend of Miss Beamish, Mme. D'Essones, the wife of an actor at the Comédie Française. When the Germans began to occupy the south, this lady contacted Miss Beamish, who reserved a room for the Haydens at the Hôtel Escoffier. As details of their journey from Mougins emerged, Beckett warmed to the quiet elderly painter with his more voluble, lively companion.

Josette recounted how they had come via Nice where they had friends, and had taken the Micheline train from Nice to Digne, which they found occupied by the Germans. The Micheline broke down so they arrived the first night at three o'clock in the morning. They were forced to check into a hotel for a second night, as the first bus to Apt did not leave until six in the morning. The night they spent there was a terrifying one. Hayden was sure that he was at last going to be arrested. For it was their bad luck to have chosen a hotel that was due to be used the next day by a visiting German general; at three o'clock in the morning, German soldiers started to check out the place. Hearing doors being opened and shut and voices speaking loudly in German, Henri hid inside a small cubbyhole, while Josette sat up in bed pretending to be sleepy and alone except for the cat huddled in her arms. Happily, the Germans did not bother to check too carefully the occupants of each room against the hotel register. So the ruse worked and the Haydens left the hotel for the morning bus, feeling that they had escaped by the skin of their teeth. And as, much later in the day, they were driven away from Apt to Roussillon in the crowded bus, at last they began to feel that they could breathe a little more easily.

The Haydens lived for some time in the hotel before Mme. Escoffier rented them the little house next door (which today forms part of a newsagent's shop), although they continued to take one meal a day in the café. Soon Beckett was meeting Hayden fairly regularly in the café for a drink and it was not long before the two men found that they shared a love of chess as well as of painting. So when Beckett walked into the village to buy bread or groceries from the Gulinis' shop, he used to call to play an evening game of chess with Hayden. This marked the beginning of a lifelong friendship.

The Haydens were soon added to the very small circle of Beckett's friends in Roussillon. Alone, Hayden and Beckett spoke little and played chess in almost total silence. When Josette was there, the conversation flowed more animatedly; she kept their glasses well filled. From time to time they planned what they would do if news came that the Germans were coming to Roussillon.[29] If it happened at Beckett's house, there was a sizable cave in the garden, hollowed out of the red rock, with piles of logs hiding the entrance; there they might lie low, undetected by a casual search. The cave still exists and can be entered through a wooden door complete with an air vent at the bottom. Hayden had also planned an escape route down the red cliffs that fell steeply away behind their little house. This path was so terrifying that a member of the local Maquis, Roger Louis, whose wife was staying in the Hôtel Escoffier, told Hayden that he would infinitely prefer to face the Gestapo.[30]

From time to time the two couples dined together, and on Christmas Day, 1943, Josette gave a dinner for Beckett and Suzanne, and Miss Beamish and her companion. She remembered Beckett and Miss Beamish, wineglasses in hand, singing a medley of old Irish songs.[31] After drinking too much of the Bonnellys' wine on such occasions, Beckett would satisfy a call of nature by using an old dustbinlike tube, originally used for wine production, that the Haydens kept behind their little house. By the side of it lay a bag of sawdust that was used to replenish what was soiled in the tube. The idea had evolved from what was provided for the cat. Beckett may have had this in the back of his mind when he placed his two old crones in *Endgame* in similar bins and had Nagg ask Nell whether Clov has yet changed her sawdust.[32]

Miss Beamish sometimes invited Beckett and Suzanne for afternoon tea or an evening meal with them at the house next door. She lived there with Suzanne Allévy, a younger, round, fair-haired French woman of Italian extraction.[33] It was tacitly accepted in the village that the women formed a lesbian couple. Although she was known simply as Miss Beamish, the small group of foreign or Jewish refugees were fully aware of the enormous pride that she took in the aristocratic ring of the name she used: Noel de Vic Beamish. This given name, spelled after the male fashion, was in fact a nom de plume, for her real name was a doubly impressive Anna O'Meara de Vic Beamish. She was noted in the village as something of an eccentric, for she dressed in men's clothes, wore trousers (often tweeds), a little Scottish-style bonnet, and boots, and used to smoke a pipe. When she wanted to read she put a monocle to her eye. She was a practicing Catholic and went to mass every morning in the little church of Saint-Michel. Miss Beamish also had a strong and, according to Beckett, a very likable personality and by introducing herself to everyone in the village, she made sure that she and Mlle. Allévy were known and well received.

Born in Dublin in 1883 of parents from Connaught, Miss Beamish was nearly sixty when Beckett first came to Roussillon. She had British nationality. She had moved from the coast for a period of *résidence forcée* as an alternative to the internment that, as a British subject, she would have experienced if she had stayed on in Cannes. She had lived for many years on the Côte d'Azur, teaching English at the Berlitz School of Languages in Cannes. Mlle. Allévy made a little money clipping and grooming dogs.

Miss Beamish was a novelist. By the time she met Samuel Beckett, she had already had six books published, including four novels with the delightful titles of *Smoke* (1927), *Tweet* (1934), *The King's Missal* (1934), and *Fair Fat Lady* (1937). She had also written two books about her dogs entitled with equal picturesqueness *Miss Perfection: The Story of an Airedale Terrier* (1931) and, with illustrations *Cocktail — Pup de Luxe* (1934). None of these was likely to become Samuel Beckett's bedtime reading, but they did testify to Miss Beamish's marked originality as a character.[34]

Miss Beamish made a great impression on Beckett, as she did on almost everyone whom she met in Roussillon. She established a friendly relationship with the farmer-vintner Bonnelly, and could buy wine more cheaply from him than any of the other refugees. So she often encouraged Beckett and Suzanne to accompany her to the Bonnellys' farm, sometimes with Mlle. Allévy, some-times with another Englishwoman named Miss Marshall, to buy red wine in oddly shaped bottles. Miss Marshall, who came to stay with Miss Beamish from time to time in Roussillon, has been described by some of the villagers as looking "like the caricature of an English woman," tall and angular, striding out in mannish fashion across the fields with Miss Beamish and her two Airedales.[35] Miss Beamish always had a male dog, while the more feminine Mlle. Allévy had a female. This naturally caused problems when the bitch was in heat, which they solved rather ingeniously by fastening pieces of linen around the bitch's hindquarters, to the great frustration of the male and the amusement of the villagers.[36]

Miss Beamish was the model for "old Miss McGlone" in *Krapp's Last Tape*, who "always sings at this hour."[37] In the second manuscript draft of that play,[38] the lady is named "old Miss Beamish" and, like Beckett's near neighbor, originates in Connaught. Whether the real Miss Beamish did actually sing regularly every evening is more debatable. Beckett did not remember this.[39] Yet it seems reasonable to suppose that the "songs of her girlhood," of Krapp's songstress,[40] might well in reality have floated across the road to the Beckett house. Wild rumors concerning Miss Beamish circulated in the village then, as they do now. It is believed by several people there today that she was involved with the British Secret Service and that she used to go out in the fields at night to broadcast clandestinely. No evidence has emerged to suggest that this was true.[41] It is more likely that she was merely exercising her dogs.

She gave regular English lessons to the painter Henri Hayden. During his youth in Warsaw, Hayden had had an English governess. So he decided to spend his time in Roussillon not only in painting but in improving his spoken English, to be ready, he hoped, for the inevitably successful outcome of the war. He would walk down the avenue de la Burlière several evenings a week to Miss Beamish's house, clutching his volume of Shakespeare's plays. Working through one of the plays seems to have been her preferred method of teaching the language. A mutual admiration for the works of Shakespeare would certainly have provided a further bond between Beckett and herself to add to that of their common profession and Irish origins.

5

THE WINTER OF 1943 was cold and dreary. The small village quickly came to feel claustrophobic, despite the relative security it offered. After all, Sam and Suzanne were virtual prisoners in Roussillon; they could go nowhere outside the immediate area without the risk of arrest. In the daytime, there were the numbing effects of manual work. On the weekends and when Beckett was not working in the fields, he and Suzanne used to go for very long walks, over small tracks that led across the fields toward Gordes or Saint-Saturnin-d'Apt, then return through the village in time perhaps to watch an evening game of *boules* close to the school in the place du Pasquier, called simply Le Pasquier, before dining — usually alone. At night, the clock on the church chimed the hours twice on the hour, a few minutes separating the two sets of chimes. In the summer months, mosquitoes sucked the blood of sleeping Jews and Aryans alike.

Diversions occurred from time to time. Often these were relatively ordinary events such as tea with Miss Beamish or a visit from Elie Blanc, the village historian.[42] One of the most pleasurable events for Suzanne was the visit of her mother from Troyes.[43] Mme. Dumesnil came by train, arriving eventually at the little wayside station of Notre-Dame-de-Lumière. As she was physically unable to walk the distance to Roussillon, she was met at the station by Beckett's farmer friend M. Aude, who went down to fetch her in their horse and carriage. When she got back to the farm where Suzanne and Beckett were waiting to greet her,

Aude recounted with amusement how she had squealed with laughter as the little cabriolet jolted them over the rough country tracks. Two weeks later she was able to relish the experience again as she was driven back to the station. Their last meal took place, just as their first one had, in the Audes' farmhouse kitchen.

For Beckett, since Henri Hayden's arrival, there was some contact at least with art. Almost every day the painter would go out on the paths and slopes around the village with his easel, paints, and brushes.[44] Often he would paint close to where Beckett was working, so that they could talk or share a picnic lunch of food and wine prepared by his young wife. At others in the evenings Beckett had the pleasure of seeing the canvas that Hayden had been working on throughout the day. The quality of the light and the varying colors of the rocks from dark red ocher to lighter shades of yellow thrilled Henri and he painted as fast as he could obtain canvases or make them himself out of old sheets.[45]

Another artist whom Beckett got to know in Roussillon owed his presence there to the Haydens. He was the interior decorator, potter, ceramicist, and painter Eugène Fidler; like everyone else, Beckett knew him at the time under the assumed non-Jewish name of Eugène Fournier.[46] Fidler was living there with his wife, Edith, with false papers that had been obtained for him by the mayor of Mougins, where he had earlier been living. It was in Mougins that he had come to know the Haydens. In Roussillon, the Fidlers lived at first with the Haydens in the little house next to the Hôtel Escoffier. Then, they rented an old mill on the top of a little hill outside the village; from where they could see if the Germans were coming and, if necessary, hide in the woods.[47]

Beckett met Fournier/Fidler with Hayden at the Café Escoffier, where both of them went to listen to the BBC. Fidler found Beckett shy and reserved but confessed a wish to improve his English. Hearing this, Beckett promptly offered to give him a few unpaid lessons. And, for some weeks, Beckett would walk to the Haydens', which lay halfway between their two houses, to give Fidler his English lesson; later, Fidler used to go to the house at La Croix. They spoke from time to time of painting, of Picasso, Kandinsky, and Kirchner, Beckett telling Fidler — who was inspired by Hayden to take his own painting seriously — that his friend Bram van Velde was among his favorite modern painters. Once when Beckett saw Fidler painting the surrounding countryside close to where he was working, he observed that for him it was a "paysage trop déclamatoire" ("too declamatory a countryside").[48]

6

HOWEVER MUCH the hard physical work in the fields occupied Beckett and anesthetized his body, as well as keeping the wolf from the door, it scarcely began to satisfy the needs of his mind. In the evening, therefore, he took up again the novel, *Watt*, that he had begun to write in Paris in February 1941. He had even written a small section of the novel while they were hiding out in Vanves. The heavy notebooks had then traveled with him as he and Suzanne made their escape south. He had tried to start the work again in November in the Hôtel Escoffier but managed to write only two lines. Now, newly settled into their house at La Croix, he began to write again on March 1, 1943.[49] He told no one in Roussillon about his writing, except Suzanne. He wrote, he said later, as a stylistic exercise and in order to stay sane, "in order to keep in touch." [50]

In *Watt*, he evoked settings from his childhood and his youth. He modeled Mr. Knott's house partly on his family home at Foxrock; he recreated his memories of traveling to school as a boy on the "Dublin Slow and Easy" railway and described Watt journeying first to and from a terminus based on Harcourt Street to an Irish village station based on Foxrock, with its nearby racecourse, in reality Leopardstown. Some of the characters in the book derived from his memories of local people: "the consumptive postman whistling *The Roses Are Blooming in Picardy*," who can be identified as Bill Shannon, one of Foxrock's postmen;[51] the porter at the railway terminus who frightened Beckett when he was a schoolboy; and the friendlier news agent who had his stall on the platform. "Cack-faced Miller," "Arsy Cox," and "Herring-gut Waller" sound like the nicknames that Beckett's father and uncle Gerald loved to attach to local Foxrock residents.[52] One of the novel's other Irish characters, Cream, was busy potting on the billiard table ("Cream's potting had been extraordinary, extraordinary, I remember, said Goff. I never saw anything like it. We were watching breathless, as he set himself for a long thin jenny, with the black of all balls." [53] Cream was a big old man who, during Beckett's childhood, used to live in the house at Killiney that was later occupied by his friend the Swift biographer Joe Hone.[54]

To these reminiscences, Beckett added in Roussillon a description of the unfortunate Lynch family; like Swift's own "A Modest Proposal," the passage offers a wonderful example of the grotesque in literature. He also indulged in various logical exercises or ways of passing time like imagining the various combinations of the song of the frogs heard in a ditch: "Krak, Krek, Krik." The hilarious meeting of the College Grants Committee (with, in the manuscript, its Provost in the chair, its Vice-Provost, its Treasurer, its Correspondent Secretary, and its Records Secretary—all based on polite but boringly long-winded meetings that Beckett had experienced at Trinity College) at which Louit produced Mr. Nackybal to display his prowess at square roots and cube roots was also written, doubtless to accompanying chuckles, in the long summer evenings in Roussillon. The manuscript is even more filled with memories of Ireland, and of Dublin in particular, than is the published novel.[55]

Beckett's personal recollections of Ireland are less important in *Watt*, however, than is his comic attack on rationality. The novel contains Watt's almost exhaustive efforts to conduct rational inquiry according to logical rules. He goes through, for example, all possible combinations of how the dog could be brought together with the leftovers from Mr. Knott's meal. There are always objections to any conclusions. Reason solves nothing. Watt, writes Rubin Rabinovitz, "proceeds as if he had memorized Descartes' *Rules for the Direction of the Mind* and resolved to follow its precepts literally."[56] As a young postgraduate, Beckett spent a lengthy period of time reading Descartes and later Cartesians like Geulincx and Malebranche. Yet if the "need to know" provides the impulse for most of the episodes of the book, "the difficulty and indeed impossibility of knowing"[57] are its conclusion.

This important aspect of the novel may have found its immediate inspiration in a personal and very radical divergence of view on the issue of reason and logic between Beckett and Marcel Lob. On several occasions, Beckett and Lob disagreed violently about rationalism, its power and its successes. Lob, a grammarian and a rationalist of the old school, who believed in the power of the mind and logic to resolve all problems, once stormed out at dinner after a disagreement on this subject with Beckett.[58] Beckett saw only the absurdity and pretentiousness of such claims. *Watt* is a practical demonstration of this.

At first reading *Watt* looks like a wild, extravagant novel — one that could have been written, it has been claimed, only by someone in a state of mental breakdown.[59] Yet it is a very funny book and there is a degree of conscious control that suggests the very opposite of a breakdown. Watt, the protagonist, may demonstrate some of the conventional symptoms of schizophrenia or obsessional neurosis. But the author seems perfectly well aware of what he is doing, as he makes Watt apply the causality of the rationalists to problems that lead eventually only to paradox.

7

A SMALL RESISTANCE GROUP operated from Roussillon[60] but was rarely involved in actual sabotage or fighting until near the end of the war. German patrols came to the village only three times in the course of the occupation. And this was precisely what the Resistance leaders in the region wanted. For the usefulness of Roussillon to the Resistance was not to draw too much attention to itself but to serve as a kind of supply depot for other more active groups in the Ventoux and Lubéron areas. The caves in the red ocher cliffs around the village provided useful and sizable hideaways for armaments and other supplies, and within the village itself there were a number of cellars, lofts, and other hiding places where arms (and sometimes men) could easily be hidden. Drops of supplies by parachute from the RAF were arranged from 1942 onward by a group at Apt that consisted of a number of former French air force personnel.

Local farmers, albeit reluctantly at times, provided a ready source of food for the *maquisards* from the mountains. They did not want to slaughter their sheep and cattle. They simply had little alternative: in such difficult times, if you were not for, you tended to be regarded as being against. But there was a lot of willing, practical support, too, for the Maquis groups from the villagers, including the shopkeepers. Hélène Albertini (née Gulini), then thirteen years old, remembers, for example, being told to carry out of the village baskets of food which she was to leave on the outskirts of a wood. She was told not to ask questions.[61]

Some farmers and landowners were themselves active in the Resistance. One of these was the leader of the Roussillon group, Aimé Bonhomme, who not only hid a large stock of explosives, grenades, rifles, and small arms in cellars under his house but had his own radio transmitter—Claude Blondel had a second one—hidden in a small suitcase.[62] He sheltered at least one British wireless operator in his house. And on a number of occasions, he ensured that the ordinary villagers, as well as members of the Resistance who had run out of food, were resupplied. Working throughout the night, he attached leads through an upstairs window of his house to the main electricity cable in the street outside so that he could secretly grind corn and thus avoid incriminating himself by registering an extra load on his meter.

The Vichy regime was actively anti-Semitic, anti-Masonic, and anti-Communist. So it is not surprising that, like so many of the groups in the south of France, the one based in Roussillon should originally have been Communist in inspiration. As it grew, however, the political opinions of its members tended to be far more diverse, as politics came to be subordinate to the main task of defeating the Nazis.

It was said earlier that no denunciations occurred in Roussillon. It would be more truthful to say that none ever reached the Vichy regime. Aimé Bonhomme arranged with the people in the village post office for any suspicious-looking letter—that is, one addressed to anyone in authority in Apt or Avignon—to be kept back and opened by him. Not a single one got through.[63] The local Resistance group could not control, however, what happened in other areas. And a denunciation by a Parisian woman who ran a flower shop in Apt touched Beckett and Suzanne very closely indeed.[64]

One day in March 1944, Yvonne Lob came to their house with the news that her husband, Marcel, had been denounced and arrested in Apt as a Jew. He was taken to the camp at Drancy near Paris, which served as the main sorting post and transit camp for Auschwitz. Roger Deleutre, Suzanne, and Beckett, under no illusions as to what his likely fate would be if Marcel were sent to a concentration camp, debated grimly as to what his wife could do to try to save him. There was a faint hope that if Mme. Lob could prove conclusively that Marcel was the husband of an Aryan, he might be taken out of Drancy and be given light duties elsewhere. She therefore contacted the bishop to obtain certificates of Roman Catholic baptism not only for herself and her brother but also for their parents. Eventually after much difficulty—her own certificate had disappeared—and enormous anxiety, she was successful in preventing her husband's immediate deportation, although he was still kept in detention as a Jew. He was put to work in a large warehouse sorting out the property of Jews whose homes had been systematically emptied: furniture, household utensils, books and papers—even a full shopping bag carried by a woman when she was arrested. All of these personal effects were grouped into categories and then dispatched to Germany.

Beckett followed with fascinated horror the workings of a bureaucracy that could spare or condemn a human being because he or she could or could not produce a certificate of baptism. It may well have been such a personal reminder of this kind of rationalistic barbarism that made him once again join the local Resistance group during the final months of the war. He shared Yvonne's renewed fears when, shortly before the liberation of Paris by the British, American, and Free French forces, Marcel was returned to Drancy and missed being sent to his death only by the heroic efforts of French railwaymen who held up the departure of the train for some days until the camp could be freed. Beckett found no consolation at all in the news that, with the liberation of the Vaucluse, Resistance fighters in Apt walked into the back room of the flower shop and put a handful of bullets into the florist's head.

In the absence of Marcel, Beckett frequently visited Yvonne and Roger at their smallholding to see what he could do to help them. Yvonne remembered him digging holes for her to plant *pois chiches* (chickpeas). She also recalled stopping work in May, asking him to listen to the beautiful song of the nightingale. "I'm not very fond of the nightingale," replied Beckett. "I much prefer the blackbird." The song of the nightingale (in spite of Keats) was too ostentatiously melodious for him.

For the first year or so of their stay in Roussillon, Beckett kept his distance from the Resistance fighters, feeling, probably with Suzanne's encouragement, that he had taken enough risks earlier in Paris. Beckett said that he couldn't see much point in rejoining the Forces Françaises de l'Intérieur before he did, which, as his volunteer's card shows, was in May 1944.[65] But Beckett had already been known for a long time to be a sympathizer, although he had given no inkling of his former Resistance activities. He was thought of in any case by the locals as an intellectual and, unlike many of the group who had been trained by Claude Blondel, a former *militaire*, in the use of guns, grenades, and explosives, consequently not a man of action. But, according to Aimé Bonhomme, Beckett helped him several times by hiding explosives in and around his own house. There is a story of Beckett leaving grenades visible, outside, by a geranium on the terrace, as, understandably enough, neither he nor Suzanne was happy to have them inside the house. But he had a number of other possible hiding places, including his garden hideaway and a space under the floorboards in an unoccupied room in the house, which he appears to have used.

Later, as the Americans were fighting their way up from the south, Beckett went out several times at night with the local *maquisards*, sometimes to fetch armaments from the caves, sometimes to pick up supplies parachuted in by the RAF. Because of his total inexperience with firearms, no pressure was exerted on him to become involved in actual sorties against the occupying forces. Indeed, some degree of concern was expressed when he proposed himself for lookout duties and volunteered to join a mission to control the *route nationale* toward the end of the fighting in that region. Bonhomme felt, however, that

Beckett should be allowed to assist if he wished and he was duly issued a gun. And so he underwent some basic training in the hills, firing a rifle and lobbing a few grenades. For several days he slept out in the open, while Suzanne moved in with the Haydens. One day while he was with the Maquis, his hair literally stood on end with horror as he watched his colleagues savagely clubbing a lamb to death. This revealed to Beckett how totally unsuited he was to this kind of life: "I was lily-livered," he said.[66] Josette Hayden could remember one occasion being with Beckett on the farm when the Audes discovered a rat and were about to kill it. Beckett rushed to intervene, picking the rat up and running across a field to let it run free into a ditch.[67]

In an attempt to ambush the retreating Germans, hideouts were dug out at the side of the road by members of the local Maquis. Almost fifty years later, Beckett could still recall "going out at night and lying in ambush with my gun. No Germans came. So, fortunately, I never had to use it."[68] But it was by accident rather than by design that Beckett was not there when the shooting really started—and ended almost as quickly. Early in August 1944, members of the local Resistance came out in numbers, armed to the teeth. They ranged themselves alongside the *Route Nationale 100* at Pont Julien with the idea of cutting the road and disrupting the retreat. They shot at the retreating German tanks with rifles and machine guns and attacked them with explosives. A very few tanks were damaged in the attack but, in the Germans' haste to escape from the advancing American forces, they mostly ignored the shots, as if they were gnat bites. The group from Roussillon and others of the region could have lost many men if they had provoked a real exchange of fire. But in the event, there were no casualties among the French.

Two days later, the Americans passed along the same road. Claude Blondel stopped one of their convoys and asked whether a small group of them would accompany members of the Resistance up the hill to Roussillon, as the villagers there were unaware of what was happening down in the valley below. So, with the French flag flying from the leading jeep, followed by a truck containing both Americans and men from the French Resistance, a small party of the liberating forces drove into the place Pasquier to the cheers of the Roussillonais.

Josette Hayden recounted how Mme. Escoffier rushed to get Hayden, pounding on their door, crying "Vite, vite, Monsieur Hayden, venez, les Américains sont arrivés" ("Monsieur Hayden, come quickly, the Americans are here") and inviting him to put his Shakespearean English to good use by acting as an interpreter. To his surprise he found that only the odd soldier originated in somewhere like Chicago. The rest were all either Polish or Yugoslavian. Still, his other East European languages came in useful as bottles of Mme. Escoffier's best vintage wine were hurriedly brought up from the cellars to fête the liberation and the imminence of an Allied victory.[69]

The Americans left the village soon afterward to rejoin their regiment. But that evening in Roussillon there was uninhibited joy, drinking, singing, and dancing. The Resistance group gathered together for a large party, while nearby, Beckett and Suzanne celebrated quietly with Henri and Josette Hayden, who had prepared a dinner for them. By the time Beckett left with Suzanne to join the Resistance celebrations, the festivities were already drawing to a close. Characteristically, they walked quietly out of the village to their rented house, wondering how long it would be before Paris was recaptured and they were able to return to their real home.

14
Aftermath of War
1945–46

1

BECKETT AND SUZANNE left Roussillon for Paris early in 1945.[1] Henri Hayden was too ill to travel with them, so he and Josette had to stay behind in the hilltop village for several months before they could return home later in the year.[2] Although Beckett's apartment in the rue des Favorites appeared to have been occupied in their absence, possibly even sublet by its owner, it had not been ransacked, as they feared. Nor had it been emptied of its contents. It had, according to Beckett, "miraculously survived," although the Gestapo had taken away some of his books and papers.[3] By contrast, he soon discovered that the Haydens' studio on the boulevard Raspail had been totally pillaged, all of Henri's paintings stolen and every item of furniture, household linen, and kitchen equipment removed. Suzanne grumbled, inappropriately in the circumstances, about a few bottles of oil and sun cream that were missing from their bathroom.[4] But, businesslike and practical as ever, she quickly set about cleaning, tidying, and restoring order in their little apartment. She liked order of a somewhat austere kind and wanted conditions in their rather cramped quarters to favor the resumption of Sam's writing career.

They returned, said Beckett, to a "grim Paris," where there was almost nothing to eat.[5] It was a special treat when Geer and Lisl van Velde, returning from the country,[6] brought two fowls, one for Beckett and one for Geer's brother, Bram. When told, after eating it, that his had been a cockerel, Beckett joked that they were so hungry that he had not looked at it closely enough to tell.[7] Once they had settled in, however, Beckett felt that he should travel to Ireland as soon as possible to see his mother and his brother, whom he had not seen for almost six years. He also wanted to find out what his financial position was likely to be when the war ended.

He was obliged to travel through England on his way to Dublin. So he thought that he might just as well check with Routledge in London as to whether any further royalties were due to him from the sales of *Murphy* and at the same time try to place his latest book with the firm. This led, however, to unexpected problems. The war was still raging in Germany, although it was to end only a few days later.[8] And when Beckett entered the country, the police and immigration controls were suspicious of someone traveling on an Irish passport who claimed to have been living in France throughout the war. There was still a deeply ingrained fear of pro-German fifth columnists.

Beckett was held up therefore for some days in London and, according to his own account, his passport and the bulky manuscript that he was carrying in his luggage were confiscated. In order to get the passport back, which was essential before he could continue his journey, he was obliged to appear at the War Office to account for his activities during the war. He told them about his work with the Resistance cell Gloria SMH, the arrest of some of its members and the consequent breakup of the group, and about his own escape from Paris and enforced residence in the Vaucluse.[9] As it happened, unknown to Beckett, two of the leading figures in the cell had already been independently debriefed by British intelligence almost two years before, and, if further checking was indeed carried out at that time, not only would the details of his account have been confirmed but the intelligence officer could have discovered a specific reference in one of the debriefings to an Irishman, "Sam Beckett," as an active member of the cell, which was under the control of the British SOE.[10]

Beckett walked through a heavily bomb-damaged London, where the fear of the huge V-2 rockets launched in the last few months was fresh in the minds of Londoners. Then a remarkable coincidence occurred. As he strolled along Oxford Street buying presents for his niece, Caroline, and his infant nephew, Edward, he bumped quite by chance into his Resistance colleague Jeannine Picabia, who, after the arrest of Jacques Legrand and Péron, had made her way to England through Spain in 1943 and was living in London.[11] From Jeannine, he would have learned that her mother, Gabrielle, had also reached safety in 1943. But she knew nothing of the fate of Péron, or of the dozens of others who had been arrested and deported to the concentration camps of Ravensbrück, Dachau, Buchenwald, or Mauthausen. It was not until the middle of June, while he was in Ireland, that Beckett learned that Péron had died "in Switzerland, on his way home, May 1st 1945."[12]

Knowing nothing of this and feeling a surge of unaccustomed optimism, he hoped to be back in Paris before very long, picking up his life as a writer where he had left it five years before. The war was almost over. Both he and Suzanne had survived, which had at one time seemed unlikely. But there was another reason for his optimism. The manuscript that he was carrying with him was his new novel, *Watt*, which he had finished in Roussillon on December 28, 1944 but tinkered with over the past few months. At least he had salvaged something from the dark days of war.

Once the manuscript had been released by the War Office, he was free to go round to see T. M. Ragg at Routledge's office on Carter Lane. They talked of his earlier novel, *Murphy*, Ragg promising to look into the sales figures. (A year later Beckett learned that the book had gone out of print during the war.[13] This meant not only that further income was unlikely,[14] but that he could not even purchase copies cheaply himself, as his contract would normally have allowed him to do.[15])

He also talked briefly to Ragg about his new novel, and, near the end of

May, after tidying up the manuscript, sent a copy from Ireland for Ragg and Read to consider.[16] The letter of rejection was not slow in coming. On June 6 Beckett received the following friendly but depressing reply from Ragg:

> Both Herbert Read and myself have read WATT, and both of us I am afraid have very mixed feelings about it and considerable bewilderment. To be quite frank, I am afraid it is too wild and unintelligible for the most part to stand any chance of successful publication over here at the present time, and that being so, we cannot see our way to allocating any of our very limited supply of paper to its production. I am sorry about this, and sorry indeed that we cannot feel the same whole-hearted enthusiasm for WATT as we did for MURPHY, but there it is![17]

In 1946, after leaving the book with James Greene of Curtis Brown,[18] who sent it on to Nicholson and Watson,[19] Beckett put it in the hands of Richard P. Watt of the London literary agency A. P. Watt and Son. He enjoyed the irony of having a Watt handling *Watt*. The agent sent it to numerous publishing houses, including, in March 1946, Beckett's original publisher, Chatto and Windus, where it received a baffled and hostile report.[20] Then it went on to Methuen and to Secker and Warburg, among others.[21] Earlier, Beckett's poet-diplomat friend, Denis Devlin, on leave from his diplomatic appointment to Washington, had taken another copy away with him to try it on the American market. Neither had any success. And the novel was destined to make the familiar rounds for several years, with, first, the A. P. Watt agency, then George Reavey handling it again. In turning it down in October 1946, Frederick Warburg wrote tantalizingly to R. P. Watt: "Puns would be too easy but the book itself is too difficult. It shows an immense mental vitality, an outrageous metaphysical skill, and a very fine talent for writing. It may be that in turning this book down we are turning down a potential James Joyce. What is it that this Dublin air does to these writers?"[22]

2

ON HIS RETURN to Foxrock, Beckett was appalled to see how much his mother had aged in the six years since he last saw her. She was seventy-four now. Her tall, upright figure had become stooped. She seemed frailer and more vulnerable and, most worryingly, her hands were beginning to shake slightly with the Parkinson's disease that progressed slowly but inexorably over the coming five years. He noticed that, as she put sugar in her tea or replaced the spoon in her saucer, it tinkled against the side of the cup. While he had been away, she had sold Cooldrinagh and had a little bungalow built on a plot of land across the road from the family home. So it was the first time that the prodigal son had seen her installed in her modest new house. When she reached the stage when her hand shook too much for her to write herself, her former housemaid, Lily

Condell, used to go in every week to write letters to Beckett for her.[23] Miss Condell summarized how May felt about "New Place" during her lengthy illness:

> She liked it when she was able to move around. She had a little rock garden. It's mostly all firs, like, but she had a little patch in there and she enjoyed herself. But then when she got she couldn't do anything, it was very sad, she used to stand with her hands leaning on the glass of the door and she used to say: "I'm like a prisoner here, Lily." Like she could see nothing except people going up and down the avenue. It was very lonely for her.[24]

Although upset at the changes in his mother, Beckett was relieved to find that his relationship with her was nothing like as tense as before the war, perhaps because of her greater frailty and vulnerability. They got on surprisingly well, helped by the fact that he was out so much, in demand among his relatives and friends. But it is clear from his correspondence that, on his annual visits after the war, he did all he could to please her, even escorting her (in spite of his firm agnosticism) to Tullow Church, where she had long been a regular worshipper, singing the hymns in his quavering voice but staying silent as the credo was recited.[25]

Frank had settled comfortably into his role of paterfamilias with a seven-year-old daughter and a two-year-old son to bring up. He worked extremely hard in his business and was regarded in the seaside village of Killiney and in the business world of Dublin as a man of high principle. He regularly attended his local church of the Holy Trinity at Ballybrack, where he was also a warden. He played golf, and one of the first things that Sam and he would have done, after lots of talk and a few games of chess, was to play a round of golf together at Carrickmines Golf Club.[26] There was a six-year gap in their relationship to be bridged. It is true that there was no longer very much in common between Sam and his older brother. But they shared half a lifetime of experience, and there was a bond of very real affection between them.

Beckett had arrived in Foxrock looking emaciated. Deirdre Hamilton, the youngest daughter of Boss and Cissie Sinclair, could remember having a meal with him at the beginning of his visit and noticing that it was the only time that she had ever seen him thoroughly clean his plate.[27] He was painfully aware of the contrast between the food shortages and deprivations that Suzanne and their friends were enduring in urban Paris and the relative luxury of rural, more affluent County Dublin. Consequently, he felt guilty at leading even a temporary life of ease. He enjoyed, of course, visiting Jack and Cottie Yeats again, and seeing his old friends Tom MacGreevy, Denis Devlin, and, briefly, Brian Coffey, who was over from a teaching post in a Jesuit school in Yorkshire.[28] But Paris was, he felt, his home. The balance had shifted permanently now. He worried about Suzanne, left on her own in Paris. He worried about the Haydens, returning without money to their empty, pillaged apartment. He worried about the van Veldes, who he knew had lost their home and had nowhere to live.[29]

And he worried a lot about Mania Péron, now a widow left to bring up twelve-year-old twins, Aléxis and Michel. He saw his bank manager and tried to sort out his finances. Then he visited his former dentist, Andrew Ganly, to have his teeth, badly neglected during the war, extracted or filled.[30] But he was very anxious to get back to Paris as soon as possible.

3

RETURNING TO FRANCE proved far more difficult than he had ever imagined. Seeking to have his papers put in order prior to his departure, he discovered that it was by no means certain that he would be allowed to return to the country at all. And in any case, as a foreigner he might not be allowed to keep his apartment in Paris. He also discovered that the transfer of sterling out of Ireland to France was rigorously restricted, except for commercial purposes.[31] And while the sums that he received from his father's will in 1933 remained the same, their value had diminished as the cost of living had shot up alarmingly. So it soon became clear that, even assuming he could get his money transferred regularly from his bank, he was going to be very badly off indeed unless the franc were to drop substantially in value. In the event, only the low rent of their apartment made it possible for him to live in France at all.[32]

Learning from his friend Alan Thompson, who was a physician at the Richmond Hospital, that the Irish Red Cross was about to set up a hospital in the Normandy town of St.-Lô, which had been devastated during the Allied D-Day invasions, he applied for and got the job of "Quartermaster/Interpreter" at the hospital, simply as a means of getting back into France and keeping his apartment legally.[33] Thompson had volunteered for one of the medical posts and, together with the director of the new hospital, Colonel Thomas McKinney, the three of them set off in an advance party on August 7, 1945,[34] going through London and spending a few days in Paris to confer with the French Red Cross. The sight that greeted them on their arrival in St.-Lô a few days later shocked Beckett:

> St[-]Lô is just a heap of rubble, la Capitale des Ruines as they call it in France. Of 2600 buildings 2000 completely wiped out, 400 badly damaged and 200 'only' slightly. It all happened in the night of the 5th to 6th June. It has been raining hard the last few days and the place is a sea of mud. What it will be like in winter is hard to imagine. No lodging of course of any kind. We stayed just with the chatelain of Tancry, about 4 miles out, in a huge castle with a 12th century half wing still standing. But since last Wednesday we have been with a local doctor in the town, quite near the hospital site, all 3 in one small room and Alan and I sharing a bed! We are chivvying the architect to get at least one hut ready, even without water or sanitary arrangements, so that we can occupy it.[35]

The only hospital in St.-Lô had been destroyed in the bombing. Although some wooden buildings had already sprung up in the town, people were still living in damp cellars or half-demolished rooms, sleeping on mattresses and coping with a lack of running water and primitive sanitation, as well as the cold, wind, rain, and mud. Inevitably, there was a lot of illness and many injuries. The Hôpital de la Croix-Rouge Irlandaise, to give it its full name, brought in necessary medical supplies, including blood serum and the new wonder drug penicillin, as well as providing a team of well-trained doctors and caring nurses. And, of course, vital to the entire project were the twenty-five wooden buildings that were soon erected on the outskirts of St.-Lô, including a much-needed aluminum-lined operating theater. Beckett gave his own account of what he used to do with the unit:

> I went over with Colonel McKinney and Dr. Alan Thompson to set things up. We went over in the boat with the first lot of stores. I can remember them all piled up on the quayside; a large amount of stores. Then we were joined by the rest of the group, Dr. Arthur Darley, and the surgeon, Mr. Freddie McKee, some others, and Tommy Dunne [who was Beckett's assistant quartermaster]. It was my job to store the supplies and do the driving. I used to do a lot of driving, drive the ambulances and the truck. It was a big concern. We had about six ambulances plus the trucks. I used to drive up to Dieppe to get supplies and bring back nurses. McKinney was the organizer.[36]

It was arduous work and far from straightforward. All kinds of problems cropped up at first, and Beckett's patience and linguistic skill were tested to the utmost in getting things done and smoothing over local suspicions and misapprehensions. Soon after their arrival in St.-Lô, he wrote gloomily:

> The hospital buildings are far from ready, and there is no question of getting the place running properly before middle of November, if we ever get it running at all. We have been quite misinformed by the French Red X and the whole thing is disappointing. It is complicated further by all kinds of obscure tensions between the local medical crowd and the Red X people in Paris. We have the impression that the locals would like the stuff, but don't want us (very reasonable attitude) and that the French Red X, for reasons not clear, insist on an Irish Staff. We hope soon to improvise a dispensary, laboratory and V.D. clinic, and have sent for a couple of doctors and technicians.[37]

At first, before the huts were built, the supplies were piled up in a huge granary on the second most important stud farm in France, which happened to be near to the hospital site.[38] The advance party camped out in primitive conditions. At the end of August they were joined by other members of the medical team. But it was not until Christmas 1945 that all the buildings were in use and the full complement of ten doctors and thirty-one nurses was in place and treating patients. The hospital was officially inaugurated on April 7, 1946.[39]

Beckett seems to have been liked and respected by most of the medical staff. The small, dapper, bespectacled Dr. Jim Gaffney, a pathologist who came with the second group, offered an unsolicited tribute to Beckett's conscientiousness and kindness in a letter concerning a trip that he made to Paris with Beckett and McKinney at the end of September:

> Saturday morning we did some of my business till lunch time and also Sam took me into Notre Dame which was magnificent. Sam has an assistant storekeeper [quartermaster] here named Tommy Dunne, a very decent little Dublin chap. Sam is a T.C.D. graduate, interested in writing and in letters generally; he has lived in Paris the last 6 years or 7. He is a most valuable asset to the unit — terribly conscientious about his work and enthusiastic about the future of the hospital, likes a game of bridge and in every way a most likeable chap, aged about 38–40, no religious persuasion; I should say a free thinker — but he pounced on a little rosary beads which was on a stall in Notre Dame to bring back as a little present to Tommy D. It was very thoughtful of him.[40]

Beckett liked his young, eager, fresh-faced Catholic assistant and always spoke of him with great affection.[41]

He was already a close friend of the urbane, likable Dr. Alan Thompson, whom he partnered at bridge and with whom he played innumerable games of chess. Another friend in the unit was the surgeon, Freddie McKee. McKee got to know a French student named Simone Lefèvre, who was much younger than himself, and used to visit her parents' home, which had been badly damaged but not destroyed in the bombardments. He told them about their writer/quartermaster/interpreter, Samuel Beckett, who spoke fluent French, and, at their invitation, brought his friend over for dinner. An old Pleyel piano had survived the bombing in a house where shells had literally passed through the building and, with enormous zest, Beckett used to play from memory some of the music that he knew by heart, mostly Chopin or Mozart.[42]

This marked the beginning of an enduring friendship between Beckett and the Lefèvres. Freddie McKee married Simone and they went back to Dublin, where he worked at the Richmond Hospital; every year when Beckett returned to see his mother he would spend some time in their company. And Simone's sister, Yvonne Lefèvre, who was the pharmacist at nearby Isigny-sur-Mer, also got to know him well while he was in St.-Lô. From 1946 on she used to send packages of butter from the country or bring them herself for Suzanne and him when she was in Paris. She also helped him to obtain a medicine called Parpanit for his mother. (It was an early treatment for Parkinson's disease.) Yvonne Lefèvre would send it to May Beckett by post, or he used to take it over to Ireland during his summer visits to Foxrock.[43]

Tall, slim, and handsome, with an aquiline nose, elegantly dressed in a striped three-piece suit, Dr. Arthur Darley also quickly became a close friend of Beckett.[44] Darley was a graduate in medicine from Trinity College, Dublin, and the son of a very famous Dublin violinist who toured internationally and helped to launch the career of the singer John MacCormack. Arthur Darley, Jr., was a talented violinist as well, who accompanied the singer Delia Murphy on records. He took his violin with him to St.-Lô and often used to entertain the hospital staff in the evening.

Darley was an interesting case study for a writer. Patients often expressed their thanks to him for their free treatment by offering him gifts of bottles of highly potent Calvados. Darley was very partial to this but, after a couple of drinks, his normally quiet, reserved personality would change completely. He quickly became wild in his behavior. He suffered acutely from the clash between two conflicting sides of his nature. For he was very pious, reading devotedly the lives of the saints, yet also very sensual. And he felt terrible remorse at the feelings of carnal desire that he tried hard but unsuccessfully to repress.

Most members of the Red Cross unit in St.-Lô were not constrained by such a sense of sin. Beckett told MacGreevy, who was considering at one time volunteering to work with the Irish hospital, that he would not like "the promiscuity" involved.[45] On Beckett's own admission, members of the Irish contingent used to while away their evenings less respectably than their days in the local *bordel*. An ambulance parked outside the brothel soon became a familiar sight in the town. Sometimes it was driven by Beckett, sometimes by one of the others. Quite a lot of drinking went on as well; according to Beckett, the director, Colonel McKinney, set a notable example.[46] The latter was virtually the only member of the group that Beckett did not take to.

But he really liked Darley, who appears several times by name in his later work. Sadly, this talented man and devoted physician, who worked in the tuberculosis ward in St.-Lô, himself suffered from the disease, probably contracted before he left Ireland, and died on December 30, 1948, at the early age of thirty-five. His death inspired Beckett to write a poem called "Mort de A.D." ("Death of A.D."). This touchingly evokes both Darley's physical appearance and the turbulence of his divided inner life.

> de moi de mon ami mort hier l'oeil luisant
> les dents longues haletant dans sa barbe dévorant
> la vie des saints une vie par jour de vie
> revivant dans la nuit ses noirs péchés

> ("my friend dead yesterday the brilliant eye
> the long teeth panting in his beard
> devouring the lives of the saints a
> life a day reviving in the night his black sins")[47]

Beckett worked incredibly hard in setting up the hospital. But it was not work that he relished. The interpreting came easily to him, although he found it difficult to talk to three or four people at the same time. But he found the inventory and administrative duties tedious and tiring. As for driving, his eyesight was so bad that some of the unfortunate nurses whom he drove back from

Cherbourg or Dieppe at great speed were terrified.[48] But he never seems to have had an accident, perhaps because there was so little traffic on the Normandy roads.

One apparently light-hearted but highly revealing story underlines why, in spite of his initial disadvantages, he proved to be so effective in his job.[49] He went with Arthur Darley, Tommy Dunne, and a young bacteriologist to a party that was being given by an American group in a small town twenty kilometers from St.-Lô. They drove over in the Red Cross van; when they were ready to leave, Beckett, who was driving, found that the van would not start. The Americans offered to put them up and drive them back to St.-Lô in the morning. But Beckett was going to leave early the following day and was taking Colonel McKinney with him to Paris. So although it was already one o'clock in the morning, he opted to walk back to the hospital. The two younger men agreed to accompany him. But, two miles before they reached the hospital, the two had to drop out, exhausted, by the roadside, while Beckett dragged himself determinedly on, seeing trees in the air as his eyes blurred with fatigue. He arrived at the hospital at six o'clock and had no time to go to bed, as they were leaving early for Paris.

Sheer obstinacy, an unwillingness to give up, was, he commented himself, a constant trait in his character. It was a trait that made him work indefatigably both at St.-Lô and, later, at his writing and directing. It is also an element in his characters that drives them on, encouraging them never to give up or fully surrender their human dignity. With humor, this is one of the positive forces in Beckett's work that saves it from being wholly pessimistic.

But by December 1945, with his contract coming to an end, he was very happy to quit his job, saying to MacGreevy: "If I don't feel myself quite free again soon, freedom will never again be any good to me."[50] He was very conscious that in April he would be forty years old. And he felt frustrated that his work at the hospital prevented him from getting on with his writing, which now assumed an even greater importance. Yet, added to his experiences during the war, this period at St.-Lô was probably vital in terms of the content of his postwar writing. It was in St.-Lô that he witnessed real devastation and misery: buildings — each one someone's home — reduced to rubble; possessions blown to pieces; a ward full of patients ill with tuberculosis, bringing back painful memories of Peggy and the Boss; people in desperate need of food and clothing, yet clinging desperately to life; a hospital created out of nothing on fields that became churned into a sea of mud. That his experiences in St.-Lô affected him very deeply is shown by the piece about "The Capital of Ruins" that he wrote for Radio Éireann in June 1946.[51] Working for the hospital also introduced him to a much wider cross section of the community than he had ever met in his daily life before the war.

Similarly, working first with the members of the Resistance in a common cause, then with the members of the Irish Red Cross unit brought him out of himself, distancing him from the arrogant, closed-in young man of the 1930s. It is significant that, in the letter to his sister quoted above, Dr. Gaffney did not mention Beckett's quiet, introspective manner, his sullenness, or his moods of depression, but rather his positive helpfulness, niceness, and thoughtfulness to others. Seeing someone like Darley, who was torn apart by inner conflicts, and observing, as well as participating in, the staffers' "promiscuity" revealed contradictions in human nature that brought him much closer to the realities of the human psyche than the bookish 1920s and 1930s had ever done. In 1935, his analysis had forced him to undertake a radical appraisal of himself. Now, ten years later, he was almost forced to step outside himself, not only in order to sympathize with others but to help them, as self-evidently much less fortunate than himself. And as the interpreter, he had to talk to people; otherwise nothing got done.

The war years as a whole had a profound effect on Beckett. It is difficult to imagine him writing the stories, novels, and plays that he produced in the creative maelstrom of the immediate postwar period without the experiences of those five years. It was one thing to appreciate fear, danger, anxiety, and deprivation intellectually. It was quite another to live them himself, as he had done at the time he was stabbed or when he was in hiding or on the run. Metaphysical angst, he had learned, could be profoundly disquieting and depressing. But it was seldom life-threatening, except for those few individuals who could not live with their awareness of the void and committed suicide. Many of the features of Beckett's later prose and plays arise directly from his experiences of radical uncertainty, disorientation, exile, hunger, and need. Acute awareness of the ambivalence that is part of charity also probably derives from this period in his life. Humor had proved, however, a strong lifeline many times before. And, in occupied Paris, in Roussillon, and in St.-Lô, it became — with an appreciation of life's simplest pleasures — one of the few things that made life at all tolerable.

4

BETWEEN THESE various crucial experiences in war-ravaged France, something else occurred while Beckett was staying in Foxrock with his mother that helped both to change him and to transform his approach to his own writing. The "revelation" that he had at that time has rightly been regarded as a pivotal moment in his entire career. And it has often been related to the "vision" that Krapp experiences in *Krapp's Last Tape* and has been located either in Dublin harbor or on the East Pier in Dún Laoghaire.[52] Krapp records his revelation in the following fragmented way:

> Spiritually a year of profound gloom and indigence until that memorable night in March, at the end of the jetty, in the howling wind, never to be forgotten, when suddenly I saw the whole thing. The vision at last. This I fancy is what I have chiefly to record this evening. . . . What I suddenly saw then was this, that the belief I had been going on all my life, namely [*Krapp switches off impatiently, winds tape*

forward, switches on again] — great granite rocks the foam flying up in the light of the lighthouse and the wind-gauge spinning like a propeller, clear to me at last that the dark I have always struggled to keep under is in reality my most [*Krapp curses, switches off, winds tape forward, switches on again*] — unshatterable association until my dissolution of storm and night with the light of the understanding and the fire.[53]

Krapp's "vision at last" has been widely regarded as a mirror reflection of Beckett's own revelation.[54] Yet it is different both in circumstance and kind. "Krapp's vision was on the pier at Dún Laoghaire; mine was in my mother's room. Make that clear once and for all," Beckett once exhorted me.[55] The wild, stormy night and the harbor setting of Krapp's fictional experience to some extent deliberately echo the Romantic mystical experience, with nature matching the excitement of an inner torment, revealing the truth to a man seeking to find his way. In speaking of his own revelation, Beckett tended to focus on the recognition of his own stupidity (*"Molloy* and the others came to me the day I became aware of my own folly. Only then did I begin to write the things I feel")[56] and on his concern with impotence and ignorance. He reformulated this for me, while attempting to define his debt to James Joyce: "I realised that Joyce had gone as far as one could in the direction of knowing more, [being] in control of one's material. He was always adding to it; you only have to look at his proofs to see that. I realised that my own way was in impoverishment, in lack of knowledge and in taking away, in subtracting rather than in adding."[57]

However, one element in particular of the Krapp passage relates it directly to Beckett's own experience: the darkness of an inner world was, indeed, an image that Beckett reproduced with friends to whom he spoke about his revelation. Beckett explained precisely what he meant by this part of Krapp's "vision." He wrote that the dark was " 'in reality my most—' Lost: [that is, when Krapp switches off the tape recorder and runs the tape forward] 'my most precious ally' etc. meaning his true element at last and key to the opus magnum." Light was therefore rejected in favor of darkness.[58] And this darkness can certainly be seen as extending to a whole zone of being that includes folly and failure, impotence and ignorance.

The second common element of major significance to Beckett's own future work was that he would draw henceforward on his own inner world for his subjects; outside reality would be refracted through the filter of his own imagination; inner desires and needs would be allowed a much greater freedom of expression; rational contradictions would be allowed in; and the imagination would be allowed to create alternative worlds to those of conventional reality. Beckett was rejecting the Joycean principle that knowing more was a way of creatively understanding the world and controlling it. But he was also turning his back on techniques of writing that flowed directly from this principle and that incorporated, as we have seen in the prose and poetry of the 1930s, quotations and learned allusions to build up intellectually complex patterns of ideas and images. In future, his work would focus on poverty, failure, exile, and loss — as he put it, on man as a "non-knower" and as a "non-can-er."[59]

The image of Beckett undergoing a conversion like "St. Paul on the road to Damascus" can too easily distort our view of his development as a writer. As critics have shown, some of his late themes were already deeply embedded in his earlier work, particularly his interest in Democritus' idea that "nothing is more real than nothing," and the quietistic impulse within his work. But the notion of "THE REVELATION" also hides several earlier and less sudden or dramatic revelations: the certainty that he had to dissociate himself at an early stage from Joyce's influence; the reassessment necessitated by almost two years of psychotherapy; the effect on him of being stabbed and in danger of dying; the freedom to discover himself as a writer that living away from Ireland, freed from his mother's sternly critical influence, offered him; the impact of the war years, when his friends were arrested and he was forced to escape and live in hiding; and the greater objectivity that working with others at St.-Lô allowed him to assume with respect to his own inner self. The ground had been well prepared.

5

BACK IN PARIS in 1946, the material conditions of life were appalling. Bread rationing cards, which had been abandoned with the wheat harvest and the autumn elections of 1945, were reintroduced on January 1, with an even lower bread allowance than before. This provoked demonstrations, and there were food riots in a number of towns, as people were simply going hungry. After the initial euphoria of the Liberation, the dominant mood became one of intense disappointment, disillusionment, and depression. On his own return to Paris, Richard Aldington wrote to his brother, Tony:

> Paris seems to be half-depopulated yet apartments are impossible to find. In almost every street you can see windows which are obviously closed permanently, and no effort seems to be made to find out why they are not in use. Moreover with the daily inflation of the franc, people prefer not to rent at present, because 10000 francs today may not be worth 100 in six months. And so on and so on. There are hideous scandals about wine and food rationing involving high government officials, and so on. A pretty world.[60]

Beckett's own position was that his allowance began to seem like a pittance in the face of the rising cost of living. Between the Liberation and January 1947, prices quadrupled. Salaries increased from between forty and fifty percent. But Beckett's money stayed the same, except for an initial increase caused by the devaluation of the franc in December 1945. It was one of the most miserable periods of his life. In the winter months, cold was the major problem. Even though the winter of 1945–46 was nothing like as severe as the previous icy one had been, it still snowed in March, and for the second year in a row the heating in their apartment block was not on.[61] Suzanne and he responded by piling on layer upon layer of clothing, but there were times when Beckett's fingers were blue with cold as he gripped his pen.

When he returned to Dublin in 1947, Beckett and the Haydens worked out a way of transferring money to Paris that evaded the exchange controls in force. How it worked was very simple: Beckett sent money (in May 1947, a sum of thirty pounds sterling, for example) to a Madame Béla in England for a friend of the Haydens, Paul Lévy, the owner of the review *Aux Ecoutes*, who held an account there; then Paul Lévy paid Beckett the equivalent sum in francs in Paris.[62] Yet, in spite of this ruse, funds remained desperately low. And as late as the beginning of 1948, he was writing to Tom MacGreevy:

> The news of France is very depressing, depresses me anyhow. All the wrong things, all the wrong way. It is hard sometimes to feel the France that one clung to, that I still cling to. I don't mean material conditions, which are appalling. It is quite impossible for me to live now with my pittance. I had hoped that my books would make up the difference. But there is little chance of their pleasing here more than elsewhere. The ten or fifteen thousand francs advance, when they are taken, last about a fortnight.[63]

Having been in Paris most of the time while Beckett was in St.-Lô, Suzanne had already struck up cordial relations with several local shopkeepers, and this helped in obtaining whatever food became available. At the time, they were eating mostly vegetarian food, so meat shortages did not worry them too much. But fresh vegetables to be used in the innumerable *purées* that Suzanne prepared were more of a problem.[64] Their meager rations were supplemented by the supplies of butter that Yvonne Lefèvre sent fairly often from Isigny-sur-Mer in Calvados; she became, in Beckett's own words, their good "angel."[65] They paid for this food and the postage on it, but were allowed to settle their bill at the end of the month whenever money was particularly tight.[66]

On his return to Paris, Henri Hayden was offered two warm overcoats. Since he needed only one, he offered the other to Beckett; Suzanne prevented it from looking too tramplike. Suzanne proved to be a great improviser, making a little go a very long way. Her talents as a dressmaker were invaluable at this time. With her Singer sewing machine, she could repair and restyle old clothes that they kept or were given: shirts had their cuffs and collars turned; frayed sheets were cut, turned, and rejoined in the middle ("sides to middle," as they were called at the time); sweaters with holes in them were reknitted; and two worn skirts could be combined by using bands from each separate one. She also earned them extra money with her skills. In fact, as late as January 1948, Beckett spelled out how much they depended on her efforts: "Suzanne earns a little money with her dressmaking. That is what we are living on at present. To crown everything my bank is having trouble with the department of finance over my account, I mean the bank in Dublin. I don't understand what it's all about. So it's a quiet and meagre life."[67]

"A quiet and meagre life" sums up fairly accurately Beckett's daily existence at that time. What it fails utterly to do is to convey the positive "frenzy of writing" in which he was engaged. The torrent of work that he produced in the four years immediately following the war never failed to surprise even Beckett himself. He wrote like a man freed from demons.

And he wrote in French.

15

"A Frenzy of Writing"
1946–53

1

THROUGHOUT THEIR TWO-YEAR STAY in Roussillon, Beckett had spoken little but French. Suzanne knew hardly any English. Consequently, he had used his native tongue only when he met Miss Beamish alone, for her companion, Suzanne Allévy, always spoke French. French was the language of his everyday life — working in the fields with Fernand Aude; talking in the farmhouse kitchen with the Aude family; discussing the progress of the war in Mme. Escoffier's café; and conversing, sparingly, between moves, during his regular games of chess with Henri Hayden. Apart from the few English books that he borrowed from Yvonne Lob, his reading had also inevitably been in French. Even in St.-Lô, after the war, his work had involved communicating in French with the authorities in Paris, Cherbourg, or Dieppe and contacting local people and services on behalf of the Irish Red Cross Hospital.

Beckett's decision to write his postwar prose fiction and, a little later, his first three plays in French was partly influenced, then, by circumstance. And the transition from writing poems in French and translating *Murphy* in 1938–40 to writing prose directly in French after the Second World War, although unusual for an English-language writer, was not too unnatural a switch for such an excellent linguist to make. *Watt*, a full-length novel, is something of an exception within this pattern of evolution. But the book had been started in English in Paris in February 1941, and, with a large part already written by the time they were forced to flee from the Gestapo, it had to be continued in the same language on the run and in Roussillon. In any case, *Watt* — which seems to have been an exercise for Beckett, written, he said, to keep himself sane — is such an extraordinary book that it stretches the very limits of language itself. One long section even contains a language that is scarcely English at all.

The change to French was not, however, entirely circumstantial. In retrospect, his experience of writing poems in French before the war looks like a deliberately chosen apprenticeship, during which he was learning to be a French writer in the same way that he had learned to write in English. Beckett claimed: "It was a different experience from writing in English. It was more exciting for me — writing in French." [1] On another occasion, he suggested that, for him, English was overloaded with associations and allusions; his work in

English throughout the 1930s bristled with erudite and literary allusions and what he called "Anglo-Irish exuberance and automatisms." [2] In this respect, the shift to writing in French may have been an important way of escaping from the influence of James Joyce. It was also easier, Beckett maintained, to write in French "without style." He did not mean by this that his French had no style, but that, by adopting another language, he gained a greater simplicity and objectivity. French offered him the freedom to concentrate on a more direct expression of the search for "being" and on an exploration of ignorance, impotence, and indigence. Using French also enabled him to "cut away the excess, to strip away the color" [3] and to concentrate more on the music of the language, its sounds and its rhythms.

His first published essay in French after the war was in a rather special category: a piece of art criticism rather than creative writing. He was invited by the editors of the journal *Cahiers d'art* to contribute an essay on the painting of his Dutch friends Geer and Bram van Velde, who were having separate individual exhibitions at the Galerie Maeght and the Galerie Mai respectively early in 1946. Exactly where and when the essay was written is not entirely clear. But it was probably early in 1945. [4]

He entitled the essay "La Peinture des van Velde ou le monde et le pantalon" ("The Painting of the van Veldes, or the World and the Pair of Trousers"). [5] The reference to the world and the pair of trousers alludes to the story of a tailor who takes many weeks to make a pair of trousers for a customer. The client objects that it took God only seven days to make the entire world. But, replies the tailor, "look at the world, and look at my trousers!"

Beckett's intellectually brilliant essay is a devastating attack on the pretentious, the phony, and the formulaic in art and art criticism. But it is also highly idiosyncratic. Kandinsky, Jack Yeats, and "that great unknown painter" [6] Karl Ballmer, all of whom he had met and whose work he admired, are singled out for special praise. And his friend Tom MacGreevy's book on Yeats, and the study of Kandinsky by Will Grohmann, who had been extremely kind to Beckett in Dresden, are commended as excellent examples of art criticism. [7] The essay is not always easy to follow. But it does raise fundamental issues concerning the relationship of the painter to the world. As in his later piece about the van Veldes, written for *Derrière le miroir* in 1948, Beckett is concerned in their painting primarily with "the visible thing, the pure object" [8] and with their approach to subject and object, reality and representation. Like his earlier comments on Paul Cézanne's and Jack Yeats's paintings, his essay tells us more about his own approach to art than it does about the van Veldes' painting.

2

A SHORT STORY, "Suite," later to be called "La Fin" ("The End"), was Beckett's earliest extended piece of prose fiction in French. It marked the beginning of an extraordinarily fertile period during which he produced four stories, four novels, and two plays, all written in French, not to mention a number of critical articles and poems: a "frenzy of writing," as Beckett himself described it.[9] Suzanne and he needed money very badly. And it is clear that part of the stimulus that compelled him to write as feverishly as he did at this time was the wish, even the obligation, to earn money by his pen.

It has always been thought that Beckett's first postwar story was written exclusively in French. But it was not. The manuscript shows that he started writing it in English on February 17, 1946, wrote twenty-nine pages, then, in mid-March, drew a line a third of the way down the page and wrote the remainder of the story in French.[10] Once he had embarked on the French version "Suite" was written fairly quickly. By the end of May 1946, he could write to George Reavey:

> I have finished my French story, about 45000 words I think. The first half is appearing in the July *Temps modernes* (Sartre's canard). . . . I hope to have the complete story published as a separate work. In France they don't bother counting words. Camus's *Etranger* is not any longer. Try and read it [Camus's novel], I think it is important.[11]

In view of the simpler, more direct kind of prose that Beckett was writing at this time and the concern with alienation from society that is an essential feature of his own stories, it is fascinating that Beckett should have been reading Camus's concise masterpiece of alienation with so much admiration.

It is hardly surprising that he should have thought of *Les Temps modernes* as an excellent outlet for his story. The review had been founded soon after the war by Jean-Paul Sartre, whom Beckett knew from prewar days through their mutual friend, Péron. Beckett never became a close friend of Sartre, but he believed that he and Simone de Beauvoir, whom he used to greet with a friendly nod in the cafés of Montparnasse, were likely to respond favorably to his writing. Although only ten issues old, *Les Temps modernes* had acquired a reputation for publishing avant-garde literature and thought.[12]

But Beckett was loath to negotiate with the editors of the review himself. So he used as an informal agent and intermediary the Dutch writer and translator Jacoba van Velde, Bram and Geer's sister, who was living in Paris and working under the name of Tony (or, as Beckett sometimes wrote it, Tonny) Clerx, the latter being her married name. Jacoba sent the first half of "Suite" separately to the review, before Beckett had revised the second part for publication.[13]

And this is how the trouble began. Beckett was led to understand through Tony Clerx that the second part of his story would appear in the autumn issue. But this was not to be. For Simone de Beauvoir seems genuinely to have believed that Beckett—who was, we should remember, almost totally unknown as a French writer at the time—had deliberately sought to mislead them into thinking that the first part of his story was the entire work. She was convinced that either he or his agent was trying to ensure publication in two consecutive issues instead of one, so that he could get a much longer story accepted than they originally thought they were buying. And Simone de Beauvoir, either more prudish or more cautious than Sartre, also appears to have thought that Beckett was attempting to deceive them by getting a commitment to a piece which contained, in the second half, too many references to itches in the privates and the arse and far too much pissing and farting to be compatible with the tone or, as Beckett put it later, "la bonne tenue" of the review. For those two reasons, she insisted on turning down part two.

Beckett was horrified. Tony Clerx talked to the contents editor, Paule Allard, and did all she could to woo the editorial committee. But Simone de Beauvoir refused to budge. Beckett responded to the rejection by sending her an injured letter in which he argued not so much about the misunderstandings that had occurred but about how, by her cruel decision, she had severed the life of his character.

> I wouldn't want you to misunderstand the purpose of this letter, which I write after much hesitation. I don't want to argue. I don't ask you to go back on what you have decided. But it is quite impossible for me to escape from the duty I have towards one of my creatures. Forgive these grand words. If I feared ridicule, I would stay silent. I have sufficient confidence in you to explain exactly what I feel. It is this. You allow me to speak only to cut me off before my voice has time to mean something. You halt an existence before it can have the least achievement. This is the stuff of nightmares. I find it difficult to believe that concerns of presentation could justify in your eyes such a mutilation.[14]

Although Beckett's heartfelt lament was ignored, his relations with the journal were not destroyed. He had not deliberately done what Simone de Beauvoir accused him of. But he had been naïve and certainly unprofessional in allowing an unfinished story to be sent on, without telling them that this was what it was. He would be more careful in the future. In an effort to rebuild fences, Paule Allard, who was favorably disposed toward him, published twelve poems which he had written in French before the war, only four issues later, in November of the same year.[15] It was a prompt as well as a welcome gesture of goodwill on the part of the editors. And it had the additional advantage of revealing Beckett to a literary public as a French poet as well as a prose writer.

3

BECKETT'S NEXT WORK was a first novel in French, entitled *Mercier et Camier*. He started this on July 5 and completed it on October 3, 1946.[16] He later regarded this book as an apprentice work and, after writing his later novel trilogy, was reluctant to see it published. One of the striking features of the novel is the delight that he takes in wordplay in French and in the unusual colloquialisms and quirks of a language in which writing prose creatively was for him a very new experience. Alfred Péron's adolescent son Aléxis remembered the author calling round at their apartment to see his mother after the war, and finding him very tickled at having just learned a French expression like "Le fond de l'air est frais." This colloquialism means, literally, "Deep down the air is cool," but its subtlety is really untranslatable.[17] Mercier and Camier undoubtedly echo some of Beckett and Suzanne's own conversations, as they trade different forms of the verb "s'asseoir" ("to sit down"), setting "s'assoyait" against "s'asseyait."[18] Discussion focuses on whether, as Mercier and Camier walk along without their umbrella, they will be soaked "comme des rats" ("like rats") or "comme des chiens" ("like dogs"). And Camier reveals Beckett's hypersensitive ear for the oddities of French syntax, when he comments on how strange the phrase "quelque humble que fût sa condition" ("however humble his condition may be") sounds.[19]

This feeling of strangeness in the language is not confined to French grammar and syntax but focuses on individual words as well: "les sas," an uncommon word for the locks of a canal or a river, is spelled out letter by letter "S-A-S." And, as certain words are highlighted by Mercier and Camier, Beckett's pleasure in adding to his own vocabulary emerges clearly. Having asked Camier to buy him a plum tart at the pâtisserie, for example, Mercier then confounds his companion by changing his request to "un massepain," a word for "marzipan" that Camier has seemingly never come across before. Although this bandying of words and phrases, arguing over definitions, and use of clichés, proverbs, and truisms recall Gustave Flaubert's Bouvard et Pécuchet (to which the title of the novel already suggests a debt), Mercier et Camier owes much of its vitality and sparkle to Beckett's own voyage of linguistic discovery. The book is an excellent illustration of his love of language, yet also of his critical attitude toward it. For even though he was now writing in French, he had not forgotten the radical critique of language as a whole by Fritz Mauthner that he had begun reading for Joyce (and himself) in the 1930s.

By this time, Beckett had been in France for over eight years and lived for more than seven of these with a Frenchwoman. His French was fluent and good, his range of vocabulary remarkable for a foreigner. Even so, it is hardly surprising that he wanted the accuracy and fluency of what he had written to be looked over by a native speaker before he was willing to send his first novel written in that language to a French publisher. While composing the first two drafts, he verified things with Suzanne as they came up. But discussions of detail were usually with Alfred Péron's widow, Mania.

Mania (Maya in the original language) was Russian by birth but had lived in France since she was five. Her French was therefore that of an educated Frenchwoman. She was also an agrégée d'anglais, who could spot an anglicism when she saw one. Before the war, Beckett had called round regularly at the Péron's to work on his translation of Murphy with Alfred. Now, after his friend's death, he continued to call on Mania, bringing sections of his typescripts with him. He either went over the text with her on the spot or left pages to be discussed later. He may have felt that Suzanne was too close to the material, or he may not have wanted to expose absolutely everything that he wrote to her judgment at an early stage. But he also clearly valued a fresh opinion when he was in the process of revising. Mania's queries and suggestions can occasionally be seen in her handwriting on an original typescript, although by this stage, her corrections are fairly rare.[20]

Although he continued to consult Mania even into the late 1950s, his little notes to her show him growing increasingly confident in his own judgment, arguing with her as to what could or could not be said in French. Soon she was consulting him as well, often having to give way on detail as he produced examples from his big Littré dictionary to prove his point. It may be that he continued to consult her for longer than he needed, out of habit or as a mark of friendship. When he translated articles for the review *transition*, he included her in the process and charged the editor for his consultations with her. But, particularly with respect to his early novels and stories, Mania had an important role to play as a sounding board. In addition, throughout the 1950s, hers was the "oeil de lynx" ("lynx's eye") to which Beckett submitted his proofs for correction.[21]

At the end of October 1946, Beckett was offered and accepted a contract by Pierre Bordas for a French edition of the translation of *Murphy* and a general contract for all future work in French and English (including translations).[22] "My affairs are now entirely in their hands," he commented with quiet satisfaction to George Reavey.[23] He also sent Bordas a copy of *Mercier et Camier*, finished at the beginning of October, and was given a further small advance of ten thousand francs in January 1947. At last it seemed that his troubles were over. But, alas, this was not to be. For *Murphy* sold badly, and Bordas seems to have decided that publishing Beckett was a waste of money.[24] It was some time, however, before Beckett learned that his search for a French publisher would have to be resumed again. Meanwhile, in the final months of 1946, he wrote three more stories also in French: "L'Expulsé" ("The Expelled") in October, "Premier amour" ("First Love") from October to November, and "Le Calmant" ("The Calmative") in December.

4

IN JANUARY 1947, Beckett turned to the theater, both for relief and for the sake of a challenge. His first full-length play was written fairly quickly, in French, from January to the end of February 1947. He called it *Eleutheria*, the Greek word for freedom. Throughout his lifetime, he adamantly refused to have this play either published or produced, although he allowed it to be shown at first to potential producers. Its publication was also announced in 1952. But he changed his mind very soon.

Why was Beckett so determined to block its publication and production? One reason may be that autobiographical tensions and reminiscences seemed insufficiently distanced or inadequately integrated into the play. These are of several different kinds. There are a few allusions to places and incidents in Beckett's own life. Some of them are fairly casual, although not always insignificant. For instance, the indolent "antihero" of the play, who, ironically, is named Victor Krap, lives, characteristically for a martyr to existence, in the little "impasse de l'Enfant-Jesus," which is close to the rue des Favorites and which Beckett passed on his walk along the rue de Vaugirard to Montparnasse. Madame Meck (*un mec* is a pimp, like the one who stabbed him) drives a Delage car, the same make that Peggy Guggenheim and Beckett himself used to drive before the war. This first layer of fairly trivial details is unlikely, however, to have bothered him too much.

More personal autobiographical memories may have worried him rather more. Victor's recurrent dream of his father on the diving board urging his son to plunge in after him, regardless of his fear of falling or of drowning, echoed Beckett's own experience as a child at the Forty-Foot. But the problem here was probably not the personal nature of the experience itself, but the fact that it was insufficiently woven into the dramatic fabric. After all, more than thirty years later, Beckett allowed a replay of the same incident with his father to stand in his prose work *Company*. The determined efforts of Madame Krap to prize her son out of his room and involve him by fair means or foul in the normal activities of gainful employment, love, marriage, doing and being, were very close to what his own mother had attempted to do with him in the 1930s. But he had drawn on this already in his novel *Murphy*. And there was nothing to upset anyone, even himself, in such harmless exorcism. More significantly, he may have felt uneasy about the way in which certain central issues, such as whether or not life is worth living and the validity or otherwise of suicide or euthanasia, emerge as deeply felt personal questions. In his more mature plays, Beckett's characters wear his heart on their sleeve with less evident signs of surgery than most of the characters in *Eleutheria* do.

Yet the main explanation for Beckett's refusal was the simple one that he found the play seriously flawed. He also recognized that his later writing had surpassed it and made it appear uncharacteristically clumsy and overexplicit. In addition, he acknowledged that, since he had written it, the theater itself had moved on with the plays of Eugène Ionesco, Jean Genet, and Arthur Adamov. He repeated all of these reasons to me only three years before he died, when we were discussing whether the play ought or ought not to be published. He still came out firmly against its publication.[25]

The real interest of the play is that it reveals Beckett's attitudes toward the theater of the past, as well as pointing forward to his own later, highly innovative drama. It parodies many features of traditional plays and experiments, not always happily, with more innovative techniques. In the first act, he mocks the traditions of boulevard comedy and melodrama, as the figures sit around in an Ibsen-style room discussing the absent main character; there are constant comings and goings; in the second act, the frenetic rhythms and frantic horseplay almost reach the point of knockabout farce, with a Glazier and his assistant fixing glass into a window and a whole range of people coming to extract Victor from his lair. At one point Victor even hides under the bed "as in Molière's day."[26] And, in the third act, a Spectator climbs onto the stage from a stage-box to comment on and attempt to resolve, after his own fashion, the vagaries of a dramatic situation with his notion of the clear-cut drama that he feels he ought to be watching. (Beckett was never again to use this Sheridan/Pirandello-like device; in the future, any representative of the audience was incorporated within the play itself.) As well as parodying dramatic genres, he also echoes Strindberg, Sophocles, Molière, Ibsen, W. B. Yeats, Hauptmann, and Shakespeare.[27] As parody, the play scintillates at times. But too often, at this and other levels, it fails to hold interest and falls into banality.

There are also problems with its dramatic innovations. Beckett's central idea was to create, in Victor, a main character who renounces the world of will and deliberately cultivates a Schopenhauerian willlessness. Victor is a faceless character who can impose his presence only through nonexistent characteristics. He does not listen; he does not even try to understand. Consequently he forgets what he is told from one moment to the next and is totally uninterested in the wishes, needs, or ideas of anyone else. He is both unwilling and unable to justify his voluntary exile from life. And the negative nature of his character means that he can function only with minimal dramatic success as a figure who is harassed by the pleas and demands of others and buffeted by the force of their reasoning. Even though the wish for some form of clarification, definition, even explanation of Victor's motives is mocked within the drama itself, it becomes, nonetheless, a very real factor in the failure of the play to hold dramatic interest. Since Victor is by choice a dead weight dramatically, much has to depend on the other characters, on the visual byplay, and on the quality of the writing. From all three points of view the play too often seems to fail, although the failure is neither uniform nor in itself without interest.[28]

The third act, for instance, is far more interesting than the rather obvious Pirandellian device of an intruding spectator might suggest. For once the Spectator has set foot on the stage, he himself experiences those pressures toward shapelessness, softness, and vagueness that have already been felt by others in the play. The phenomenon derives from the contagious nature of Victor's own lack of definition. "You are around like a sort of ooze," says the Glazier to Victor. "Take on a little contour, for the love of God."[29] Already, in the second act, the Glazier has exclaimed: "Don't you see that we are all busy focusing over and over on something that has no meaning? A meaning for it must be found, otherwise we might as well ring down the curtain."[30] At one point in the final act, the stage directions suggest that Beckett is trying to create the impression that the play as a whole is grinding to a halt of its own accord; this suggestion is a first tentative attempt at the threat of total collapse and stasis that was to become a chief ingredient in *Waiting for Godot*. Almost as interesting is the way in which the Spectator's attempts to explain why he has stayed in the theater at all lead to a comparison with a game of chess between two bad players (a passage that looks forward to the long-drawn-out quality of *Fin de partie* [*Endgame*], as well as its basic chessboard situation):

It's like watching a game of chess between two tenth rate players. Three quarters of an hour have gone by and neither of them has touched a piece. There they are like two half-wits gaping at the board; and there you are, even more half-wit than they, riveted to the spot, nauseated, bored to extinction, worn out, flabbergasted by such stupidity. Finally you can't stand it any longer. You say to them: "But for God's sake do this, do this, what are you waiting for, do this and it's finished, we can go off to bed." There's no excuse for you, it's against all the rules of good manners, you don't even know the blokes, but you can't help yourself, it's either that or hysterics.[31]

When the play was ready "for the road," as Beckett used to say of his work — this was as early as March or April 1947 — *Eleutheria* (or *L'Eleutheromane,* as he also thought of calling it), was handled, along with his French stories, novel, and poems, by Tony Clerx.[32] She circulated it to a number of theatrical producers. Grenier-Hussenot almost accepted it; then, early in 1948, Beckett could write that the open-minded experimental director Jean Vilar "is taken with the play and nibbling,"[33] But, although he wrote three months later that *"Eleutheria* is hithering-thithering and beginning to be spoken of a little, I think it will see the boards in time, even if only for a few nights,"[34] in the end no offer from Vilar materialized. However, as late as the summer of 1951, while the director Roger Blin was trying to find a theater and raise the money to present Beckett's next play, *En attendant Godot,* a friend of Adamov, Charles Bensoussan, was still interested in mounting a production of *Eleutheria.*[35] It was Beckett who finally decided to withdraw the play entirely.

Had Vilar accepted and directed *Eleutheria* early in 1948, when Beckett was eager to see it staged, it would certainly be talked of now, in spite of its limitations and flaws, as one of the plays that ushered in a new era in avant-garde French theater. For, of all the strikingly innovative postwar plays, only Jean Genet's *Les Bonnes (The Maids)* had as yet been put on in 1947 — and that with Jean Giraudoux's bland *L'Apollon de Bellac.* Ionesco's early dramatically startling plays had still to be written, let alone staged. Adamov was writing plays but nothing by him had yet been produced.[36] And the little theaters that had opened since the war with producers like Vilar, Blin, and Jean-Marie Serreau, who were on the lookout for new writing talent, had neither the space nor the funds to mount a play that called for a costly split-level stage and seventeen actors.

5

DURING THE POSTWAR YEARS, while Beckett was scribbling furiously away, the couple's financial position went from bad to worse, as inflation reduced the value of the little regular money that he was receiving from Ireland. Suzanne went on with her dressmaking, which earned them a little extra from time to time. Using her system based on colors,[37] she also gave piano lessons, some free to the children of friends, but others paid for by those who, although better off, were anxious not to seem to be extending charity too obviously to Beckett and herself. The Péron twins, Aléxis and Michel, were both subjected to classes before their mother concluded that, since neither of them had any desire to learn to play the piano, they were wasting their time and Suzanne's.[38]

Lack of money and an insufficient diet were responsible, perhaps, for Beckett's suffering a variety of minor but persistent ailments at this time. A year earlier, he had had a cyst lanced and drained by a specialist, a Dr. Givaudan;[39] more recently he had suffered from an abscess, as well as his usual troubles with his teeth. His whole system appeared to be run-down. So Suzanne persuaded him to see Dr. Roger Clarac, a homeopath on the rue des Petits-Champs, whom she used to consult regularly and in whom she fervently believed. Clarac proposed a complete change of air and large doses of sunshine.

They could not afford a proper holiday, so, after Beckett had spent the whole of May and June in 1947 with his mother in Foxrock, they jumped at the chance of living rent-free for a few months in the Villa Irlanda, 56 avenue Aristide Briand, in Garavan, close to Menton and the Italian border. This semi-isolated villa belonged to Ralph Cusack, who was married to one of the Sinclair sisters. It was in a dilapidated condition. Beckett and Suzanne slept on uncomfortable blow-up mattresses and cooked their food outside.[40] These were, in Beckett's own words, "difficult months." But the villa was close to the beach and they both loved the strong Mediterranean sun. Beckett went swimming regularly. It was here that he wrote the greater part of his next novel, *Molloy*, which he had begun on May 2, literally in "[his] mother's room" at New Place in Foxrock, although the very beginning of the novel seems to have been written last.

But their method of coping with the hot summer months from 1948 on was generally to rent a house or rooms in a village outside Paris. Before Menton, they had stayed in Avondant. After it, they stayed in a house called the Maison Barbier, in the little village of Ussy, which was situated on the river Marne some sixty kilometers east of Paris, not far from the bigger country town of La Ferté-sous-Jouarre. The house had one curious feature for a writer's country retreat: running at the foot of the small garden was the busy Paris-to-Strasbourg railway line. Conversation was therefore constantly interrupted by the noisy rattle of trains as they sped through. Passengers would wave to them in the garden as the train raced by. Visiting friends were astonished that Beckett and Suzanne could settle there, let alone work.[41] Yet Beckett, who adored silence and solitude, also had extraordinary powers of concentration, which were tested to the limit in the rented house. The crucial thing was, of course, that it was cheap. So they returned to the house, however unsuitable, for several years running. It was during those months that Beckett became so devoted to the Marne valley. And the village of Ussy-sur-Marne always seems to have been associated in his mind with creative success.

But, every year, Beckett returned faithfully to Foxrock to spend at least one month with his mother. Each year, he found her noticeable deterioration from Parkinson's disease heartbreaking: "I gaze into the eyes of my mother, never so blue, so stupefied, so heart-rending—the eyes of an issueless childhood, that of old age. . . . these are the first eyes I think I truly see. I do not need to see others; there is enough there to make one love and weep."[42]

Encouraged by Suzanne, he posted a lock of his mother's hair to Dr. Clarac so he could practice long-distance diagnosis and healing on her. In the light of Beckett's earlier attitude to the spiritualist Hester Dowden, it may seem surprising at first that he should have gone along with this. His skepticism had not disappeared. Yet for a long time he was swayed by Suzanne's faith in Clarac, partly because he was also so skeptical of what orthodox medicine could achieve and partly because of a wider sense that everything was so surprising that there might even be something in trying such a long shot. His love for his mother was so great that he would have done anything to make her better.

Dutifully, he escorted her to church on Sunday evenings, taking her as a treat to his father's church at Blackrock so that she could sit behind the very pillar where Bill used to hide his snooze during the sermon and his portly refusal to kneel during prayers. "Mr. Frost, loved and respected by us all, passed away yesterday morning, funeral rites tomorrow," intoned the vicar mournfully as his opening words.[43] More often, Beckett took her to her own church at Tullow, where they sat in the same pew in which she had worshipped thirty-five years before. After the service, a polite Beckett drove the old ladies of the parish back to their homes.[44]

But the weeks dragged painfully by. Receiving desperate letters from Suzanne, who was lonely and inconsolable during his absence, he was impatient to be back in Paris.[45] He went for long, exhausting walks in the surrounding hills, calling at little country bars on his way back for a Guinness. And he spent days playing golf by himself at Carrickmines Golf Club. In the clubhouse, he drank double whiskeys with his old golfing coach, James Barrett,[46] and smoked the Gauloises cigarettes that Suzanne used to send him, wrapped inside newspapers.[47] He saw old friends like Tom MacGreevy, Arland Ussher, and Con Leventhal and indulged in some serious drinking with one or two of them. In 1945, on his first visit after the war, he had found MacGreevy happy "doing the kind of work he likes, for the kind of people he likes."[48] Now, a few years later, he allowed what he really felt about the sort of thing MacGreevy was writing to show through, saying that he "found [himself] wishing again you were writing more for yourself and less for Ireland. I know you are doing what you want to do, in a sense. But it must leave you often with a starved feeling."[49] Beckett preferred by far the lighthearted, mischievous MacGreevy of the Ecole Normale days.

He saw quite a lot of Jack Yeats during his postwar stays in Ireland and bought another painting, *Regatta Evening*, from him. Yeats's wife, Cottie, died in May 1947, and Beckett went to her funeral.[50] The following summer, Maria Jolas wrote asking him to make inquiries about exhuming James Joyce's body from its Zurich grave and transporting it back to be reinterred in Ireland. "Seven years already," the undertaker told Beckett, putting on a troubled expression, like a doctor who is being consulted too late: "Do you think there will be anything to transport?"[51]

6

IN NOVEMBER 1947, in "spite of poverty," Beckett had declined an invitation to translate material for the "new" *transition;* Georges Duthuit was starting up the periodical again.[52] But financial pressures became particularly acute in the first few months of 1948, when even his regular allowance was not coming regularly through the banking system. To survive, Beckett was forced to try to make some money by giving English lessons and seeking translations.[53]

He applied to the United Nations Educational, Scientific and Cultural Organization in Paris for paid translating work and received a number of varied commissions.[54] In this he was helped by Jean Thomas, the former *secrétaire-général* at the Ecole Normale, who had now become an influential figure at UNESCO, and by Emile Delavenay, a former pupil at the Ecole.[55] But Beckett also swallowed his pride and offered his services to the review he had turned down only a few months before.

Transition was one of the new English-language "little" magazines that were founded after the war, like Sinbad Vail's *Points,* George Plimpton's *Paris Review,* Themistocles Hoetis's *Zero,* and Alexander Trocchi's *Merlin.*[56] Georges Duthuit took over the prewar *transition,* buying the title from Eugene Jolas and retaining him as an editorial adviser with, among others, Jean-Paul Sartre, Georges Bataille, Max-Pol Fouchet, and René Char, but changing the orientation of the review toward art and art criticism rather than literature. He also succeeded in making it intellectually more rigorous than the earlier magazine had ever been. The funds for payment to contributors tended to come through his wife, Marguerite. Her father, Henri Matisse, provided several cover illustrations gratis.

Georges Duthuit's letters, kept by his son, Claude, show that Beckett did far more translations than anyone has ever realized, for many of them appeared, at his own request, unsigned.[57] In addition, his work revising and vetting the work of other English translators for the review was extensive.[58] Independently of *transition,* Beckett also translated or revised other essays by Duthuit, including one, "Vuillard and the Poets of Decadence," at the end of which the translator is acknowledged, in the American *ArtNews;* he translated another essay of Duthuit on the American painter Sam Francis, "Sam Francis ou l'animateur du silence" ("Sam Francis, or the Animator of Silence"),[59] and he worked hard helping Ralph Mannheim translate Duthuit's book *The Fauvist Painters.*[60]

But Duthuit not only provided Beckett with a vital, additional source of income; he also became a personal friend. He was fifteen years older than Beckett. Tall, heavily built, with bright blue eyes, the extroverted Duthuit could fill a room with his laughter. He was a very cultured, extraordinarily brilliant man, with enormous charisma, who impressed Beckett with his wide knowledge of art and the exuberance and intelligence of his talk. He was a great animator himself and his friends included painters, writers, and critics. Since he was on a lecture tour of the United States at the outbreak of war, he stayed there for the duration, becoming very knowledgeable about English and American art and literature. On his return, his secretaries were at different times the talented young poet André du Bouchet and the critic Pierre Schneider. He was friendly with the Surrealists Eluard and Breton, and also among his friends were the French artists Nicolas de Staël, Pierre Tal Coat, and André Masson; the Swiss artist Alberto Giacometti; the Canadian painter Jean-Paul Riopelle; the American painters Sam Francis and Norman Blum; and many French writers, like Bataille, Char, and Sartre.

Some of these friends used to congregate at Duthuit's office at 96 rue de l'Université. The room had a big stove and they used to gather around it most days at half past five to smoke and talk. Then they would move across the road for drinks in the Café des Trois Maronniers.[61] Beckett only came occasionally to these early evening gatherings. More often, he used to lunch privately with Georges or call to go over the translations with him in the afternoon. Sometimes he dined with Duthuit and his writer friends. It was in this context, for instance, that he first met André Breton, whereas he had met Paul Eluard many years before with Edward Titus.

In the evening, he and Suzanne went over from time to time for dinner with Georges and Marguerite. But Suzanne so obviously disapproved of anything that smacked of self-indulgence that she made the Duthuits feel uncomfortable for offering them a decent three-course meal, even though they realized how much she and Sam needed one. "I hope," Georges Duthuit once said, "that we are not going to have to divide an egg into four because Suzanne is coming."[62] Suzanne probably felt embarrassed because they were in no position to reciprocate. For when they received Georges and Marguerite at the rue des Favorites, the food was always very simple and, perhaps because of their means, necessarily frugal. The Duthuits and Sam liked to laugh a lot and, as the others relaxed with a mixture of alcohol and friendly badinage, Suzanne tended to become less and less congenial—a familiar pattern when drinkers and principled nondrinkers mix. Consequently, when Beckett met Duthuit and his painter friends or introduced him to his own friends Bram and Geer van Velde, it was usually alone in Montparnasse for late-night drinks. It was at this period that Beckett started to meet Alberto Giacometti in late bars during their mutually insomniac early-morning hours, rarely talking of intellectual, or even artistic matters.

With Duthuit it was very different. Duthuit's own learned, subtle essays show that he was keenly intellectual and quite capable of following Beckett on some of his boldest, most challenging flights and of holding his own with him in debate. A personal sympathy developed between the two men that encouraged Beckett to talk very openly about his feelings as well as ideas to Duthuit, who, over the period from 1948 to 1952, seems to have taken on Tom MacGreevy's role as Beckett's main confidant.

Their private conversations led directly into their remarkable exchanges of ideas concerning art. The *Three Dialogues* on the work of Pierre Tal Coat, André Masson, and Bram van Velde, which were first published in *transition49*, represent only part of a debate that went on between them in private and by letter over many months. This allowed Beckett not only to develop his views on the split between the artist and the outside world but also to explore the consequences of a split that he saw in the self. In the dialogues, Beckett focused on his by now celebrated statement: "I speak of an art turning from it in disgust, weary of its puny exploits, weary of pretending to be able, of being able, of doing a little better the same old thing, of going a little further along a dreary road." In answer to Duthuit's "And preferring what?" Beckett replied memorably: "The expression that there is nothing to express, nothing with which to express, nothing from which to express, no power to express, no desire to express, together with the obligation to express." [63]

7

BECKETT'S CONTEMPORANEOUS WORK on his novel trilogy in French—*Molloy, Malone meurt (Malone Dies)*, and *L'Innommable (The Unnamable)*— stretched over an intensive period of a little more than two and a half years, from May 1947 until January 1950. These three novels, along with *En attendant Godot*, are the finest pieces of writing to emerge from this extraordinarily fertile, if financially impoverished, period. They are almost certainly the most enduring works that Beckett wrote. Together with the French stories, they illustrate very well how deeply the approach that Beckett dated from his "revelation" in his mother's house after the war affected his writing. And they reveal how his attitudes had changed with respect to the use of personal or erudite material since his prewar novels and poems.

These postwar works are, as Beckett said to Lawrence Harvey, a demonstration of how "work does not depend on experience—[it is] not a record of experience. Of course you use it." [64] It is not that personal experiences are absent from Beckett's writing at this time—quite the contrary. Sometimes such episodes stand out distinctly; sometimes they are hidden within themes that may seem distant from any such inspiration.

The French stories and novel trilogy draw heavily on Beckett's own memories, particularly of his childhood: "an oil lamp for choice, with a pink shade for preference" (that was in his childhood bedroom at Cooldrinagh) ("The End"); [65] the story of Joe Breem or Breen (which his father used to read to him as a child) ("The Calmative"); [66] the heavy "cylindrical ruler, you could have felled an ox with it" (that lay on his father's, then, later, his brother's desk at the Clare Street office) ("The Expelled"). [67] *Molloy* is full of such echoes of childhood: the

"Elsner sisters" (who taught Beckett in kindergarten), their cook, Hannah, and their dog, Zulu;[68] the stamps that Beckett and his brother collected in their albums and swapped as boys at home;[69] a description of the house based closely on Cooldrinagh;[70] his lyricism about his own green bicycle;[71] the teddy bear Baby Jack, Beckett's own bear. There are dozens of such examples.

Sometimes his use of past experience is much more complex and subtle than this. The passages on the "agent and the messenger" undoubtedly draw, for instance, on his acquaintance with the world of espionage. "Gaber [the messenger] was protected in numerous ways. He used a code incomprehensible to all but himself."[72] This evokes the Resistance practice of using codes, a practice with which Péron, Legrand, Picabia, and Beckett were familiar. But it is employed, obliquely, to suggest the ways of God, which surpass all human understanding, and of his angels and messengers. In its rudimentary plot, *Molloy* even borrows from the format of the detective novels that Beckett still read in order to relax. Molloy sets out on a psychological journey to find his mother; in the second part of the story, Moran is instructed to track down Molloy, only to kill someone at the end who resembles himself. But clues lead nowhere; plans appear aimless and go significantly awry; characters shade into one another, as in dreams; events lack importance, at least in terms of the plot; meetings are arbitrary and lead to no new developments. Sir Arthur Conan Doyle, whose stories Beckett loved as a boy, would have shuddered at a world so impervious to reason and deductive logic.

In *Malone meurt (Malone Dies)*, the entire section on the daily life of the Louis (in French) or the Lamberts (in English) — he surely had Balzac's Louis Lambert in mind here — and Saposcat (Sapo joins *Homo sapiens* with *skatos*, Greek for "of or concerning dung") is built upon the direct personal knowledge of country life Beckett gained through working on the Bonnellys' vineyard, on the Audes' farm, and on Marcel and Yvonne Lob's smallholding in Roussillon. The characters are no longer closely modeled on real-life people anymore (except perhaps on certain elements of Beckett himself), as they had been in his first novel, but their actions and activities derive from real-life sources: feeding the hens, killing the rabbits, burying the mule, slaughtering the pigs. These actions are used as part of a story that Malone tells himself, as he waits for his own ending.

These personal, autobiographical elements are not used referentially, either, in Beckett's postwar work; the memories seem to float up to the surface almost in spite of the author. Nor are details of locations used to specify or recreate place. Beckett echoes familiar walks with his father in the Dublin hills: "I saw the beacons, four in all, including a lightship. I knew them well, even as a child I had known them well. It was evening, I was with my father on a height, he held my hand. . . . He also taught me the names of the mountains."[73] And, in *Premier amour (First Love)*, the memory resurfaces of looking down from the mountainside on "the distant city lights, if I chose, and the other lights, the lighthouses and lightships my father had named for me, when I was small, and whose names I could find again in my memory, if I chose, that I knew."[74] In his

English poems and prose of the 1930s, he would have localized these places and things by giving their actual names. Now neither the mountains of Two Rock, Three Rock, Tibradden, Glendoo, and Killakee nor the beacons in Dublin Bay are named. Using them purely as undefined memories universalizes them, leaving feelings that are situated somewhere between ache and glow and evoking the closeness of the bond between father and son but not romanticizing it.

The "I" in "La Fin" ("The End") describes the disconcerting experience of finding that certain areas of a city once well known to him are now virtually unrecognizable:

> In the street I was lost. I had not set foot in this part of the city for a long time and it seemed greatly changed. Whole buildings had disappeared, the palings had changed position and on all sides I saw, in great letters, the names of tradesmen I had never seen before and would have been at a loss to pronounce. There were streets where I remembered none, some I did remember had vanished and others had completely changed their names. The general impression was the same as before.[75]

This passage could almost have come from one of Beckett's own letters and reflects the experience of his return to Dublin or Paris after the war. But it focuses on the experience of change and the feeling of estrangement that his protagonist feels, not on any specific localities. And so a fictional space is created that is related to the geographical space but has its own more universal validity.

More revealing still of the changes that occurred in Beckett's writing since the war is the way in which, instead of displaying his erudition as overtly as much of his prewar prose and poetry used to do, Beckett draws on it in passing, as a relic of a former wide-ranging education, or uses it in a comic parody of learning or as an invocation of ignorance, confusion, and bewilderment.

In his 1930s notes on ancient philosophy, for example, he had written of Heraclitus of Ephesus: "Primacy of flux in his cosmos. *All things flow.* For him it is not possible to step down twice into the same stream."[76] This finds its ironic echo in Molloy's "But it's a change of muck. And if all muck is the same muck that doesn't matter, it's good to have a change of muck, to move from one heap to another a little further on, from time to time."[77] In *Malone Dies*, Democritus' "Nihil est in intellectu, quod non fuerit in sensu" ("Nothing is in the intellect that will not first have been in the senses"),[78] which Beckett quoted in his 1930s notes in Italian and in his "Whoroscope" notebook in the Latin version used by Leibniz in his refutation of John Locke,[79] is taught to a parrot, to be repeated parrot fashion. Thinking of one of his earlier books—*Murphy*, in fact; "an old ship-wreck," he calls it—the narrator speaks of "those little phrases that seem so innocuous and, once you let them in pollute the whole of speech. *Nothing is more real than nothing.*"[80] Democritus' memorable phrase is allowed in only so that the narrator can say that he is "on [his] guard" against its dragging him down into its own dark. Similarly, Bernard de Mandeville's *Fable of the Bees* is evoked only so that, after seeking all the possible explanations for the bees' dance, the narrator can say "Here is something I can study all my life, and never understand."[81]

Philosophical and literary references abound in the trilogy: Leibniz's "preestablished harmony"; the Pythagorean music of the spheres;[82] Freud's "fatal pleasure principle";[83] echoes of *Hamlet* ("And had I had any tears to shed I should have shed them then in torrents, for hours"[84]); and the myth of Sisyphus ("But I do not think even Sisyphus is required to scratch himself, or to groan, or to rejoice, as the fashion is now, [an allusion to Albert Camus's 1942 *The Myth of Sisyphus*] always at the same appointed places"[85]). Homer's *Odyssey*, Dante's *Divina commedia*, and the Bible are all key sources. But none of them provides a key to the book itself.

Even Beckett's love of painting and sculpture glints through: "leaving me to go on my way alone, followed by a long rope trailing in the dust, like a burgess of Calais,"[86] recalling one figure in Rodin's group sculpture *The Burghers of Calais*; "and the cycle continues, joltingly, of flight and bivouac, in an Egypt without bounds, without infant, without mother,"[87] evoking the innumerable *Rest on the Flight to Egypt* pictures that Beckett had seen in European galleries. During his visit to Dresden in February 1937, Hans Posse, the director of the gallery, had "raved" to Beckett about the "Würzburger Residenz . . . with staircase frescoes by Tiepolo. I had heard of it," he wrote sarcastically in his diary.[88] And in *Malone Dies*, Beckett writes: "beside this window that sometimes looks as if it were painted on the wall, like Tiepolo's ceiling at Würzburg, what a tourist I must have been."[89]

Philosophical, literary, and artistic source material is used, however, in these enigmatic books in a way that is strikingly different from Beckett's earlier work. Scraps of erudition are almost submerged now in the flow of questions, hesitations, negations, and confusions. He deals in the novels with most of the philosophical problems of space, the self, and time. But he never relies on philosophical or (on the whole) psychological language. As the French literary critic Edouard Morot-Sir points out,[90] he deals with them as a poet and, I should stress, as a comic writer. The shadow of Cartesian man, the rationalist, reaching certainty through doubt, has been shown to loom over the trilogy. Descartes imagines, for instance, a man lost in a forest going in a straight line as the best method of escaping from it. But Molloy, on his crutches, goes around in circles, because he thinks that, with his particular disabilities, this is his best chance of approximating to movement in a straight line. So, in a scene of wild comedy, Molloy moves on toward his mother "blindly, in the dark," going on from doubt to even greater doubt. And Descartes's "discourse on method" proves to be just as valueless as any other philosophical system in discovering truth.[91] Mathematical reasoning too proves hollow in trying to understand or explain reality: Molloy rotating his sucking stones from his pockets to his mouth, or counting up the number of his daily farts—all lead back only to ignorance and, in Molloy's case, eventually to the possibility of the inner peace of the total skeptic (which he never manages to reach): "For to know nothing is nothing, not to want to know anything likewise, but to be beyond knowing anything, to know you are beyond knowing anything, that is when peace enters in, to the soul of the incurious seeker." [92]

But if philosophical themes are transformed into myths, so are psychological motifs. No longer does Beckett merely allude directly to psychological schools such as Gestalt or Külpe, as he did in *Murphy*. Jungian archetypes and Freudian themes have been so totally absorbed that they are used partially to structure the book and to supply comic detail in a world where neither depth psychology, nor any philosophical system, will ever manage to explain the inexplicable. But Beckett's integration of the ideas of Jung and Freud into his books —the ideas are hardly ever referred to explicitly but are echoed in many passages —is clearly important for both the narrative and the figures that Molloy and later Moran meet in their travels. Molloy's "basic problem is to find his mother —not the 'personal mother' but the mother within him, as primary variant of his anima," writes J. D. O'Hara in his essay "Jung and the 'Molloy' Narrative." [93] And O'Hara plausibly sees Moran, in the second part of the novel, as "a Freudian ego related to an id, a super-ego, and the external world." [94]

The three novels that Beckett wrote during this period of creative turmoil, particularly *L'Innommable*, are, perhaps in spite of their surface appearance, probably the most deeply personal books he ever wrote. Not in the obvious way that some of the early poems and prose were personal; rather, they reveal Beckett plunging deeply into his own psyche and dealing with the fragmentation he discovered in the self and with impulses and desires that are commonly repressed. What looks at first to be the product of the imagination alone often can be seen to come from a minute, scrupulous, and uncompromising analysis of a highly personal physical and mental world.

8

ON THE BASIS of the first year's sales figures for *Murphy*, Pierre Bordas was not interested in *Mercier et Camier* and, when he was offered Beckett's next two novels, declined to publish them. [95] Suzanne therefore set out to ensure that the novels were accepted somewhere else. Beckett summed up his debt to her a few months after her death:

> I owe everything to Suzanne. She hawked everything around trying to get someone to take all three books at the same time. That was a very pretentious thing for an unknown to want! She was the one who went to see the publishers while I used to sit in a café "twiddling my fingers" or whatever it is one twiddles. Sometimes she only got as far as leaving the manuscripts with the concierge; she didn't even see the publishers. It was the same with Roger Blin. She was the one who saw Blin and got him interested in *Godot* and *Eleutheria*. I kept out of the way. [96]

Suzanne's own faith in the value of Beckett's work and dogged determination to see it recognized by others were strengthened by the encouragement that they received from a number of literary figures. Tristan Tzara was one who read *Molloy* and admired it greatly.[97] An editor intermediary, Robert Carlier, was also very supportive, taking copies of *Molloy* and *Malone Dies* and trying to place them with many of the publishers whom he knew personally in Paris. But encouragement and praise were one thing, offers to publish quite another. And the books had passed through dozens of publishers' hands before Suzanne decided to make what Beckett has described as a "last ditch effort" with Jérôme Lindon.

As a twenty-one-year-old, Lindon had bought into the former Resistar publishing house of Vercors (Jean-Marcel Bruller), author of the famous nov *Le Silence de la mer*. In the two years since he had taken over as managin, director, he had published some exceptional books, including work by Maurice Blanchot, Georges Bataille, Pierre Klossowski. But they were mainly books passed on to him by Jean Paulhan, the chief secretary at Gallimard. Beckett's three novels were his own choice, and they initiated Lindon's career as a true publisher. Lindon explained his personal reactions to the first of the Beckett novels:

> I was going home to lunch. I saw a manuscript on Georges Lambrichs' [who worked with Lindon] desk. Doubtless Suzanne had just brought it in to him. [In fact the book had been delivered by Robert Carlier.][98] I said to him "What is that?" And he said "I believe it's very good," though he hadn't yet read it. I took it away, I took *Molloy* under my arm to go for lunch and in the Métro I started to read it. And as I changed trains at La Motte–Piquet Grenelle, in the lift I burst into hoots of laughter. And I thought "people are going to think I'm crazy"; then I thought "I risk dropping the manuscript" (which wasn't stapled or bound; it was in separate typed sheets). So I stopped reading, naturally, and stood with the manuscript behind my back . . . and people looked at me as I carried on laughing like a fool. They couldn't understand why I was laughing since I was clearly doing nothing. Then I came back to the office, finished reading the manuscript within the day and, that same evening, wrote to Suzanne to tell her "Yes, I'll take the book, there's no problem." And a few months later, I published *Molloy*.[99]

However, as soon as Lindon decided to publish *Molloy* and *Malone Dies* in 1950, Bordas became heavily proprietorial, invoking his general claim on Beckett's future work because of the original contract. Three years of acrimonious dispute followed before a settlement by which Bordas released Beckett (as he saw it) from his contract and Lindon purchased the remaining 2,750 unsold copies of the French *Murphy*.[100] Looking back on the correspondence, it seems as if Pierre Bordas, having seen that someone else wanted Beckett's work and then noting the initial critical reception that was accorded to *Molloy*, was determined to hang on to an author whom he felt he had spotted years before. In view of his unwillingness to publish Beckett's other books, there was little moral justification for his stance. And the real credit for discovering Beckett as a French writer must go to the young débutant publisher Jérôme Lindon.

9

EN ATTENDANT GODOT (Waiting for Godot) was written between October 1948 and January 1949. The dramatic situation is a simple one: Two men wait on two separate occasions by a skeletal tree for someone called Godot who, they hope, will come to save them. Two other men call and stay for a while. But the one for whom they are waiting does not arrive.

The visual conception of his new play was inspired, according to Beckett himself, by a painting by Caspar David Friedrich. This inspiration is at its most obvious in the two moonlight scenes that end each act, where the two figures of Estragon and Vladimir by the tree watching the moon rise are silhouetted against a night sky.[101] But it may be even more fundamental. The American theater scholar Ruby Cohn, a friend of Beckett, said that in 1975, while she was in Berlin for rehearsals of Waiting for Godot, she, together with Beckett, saw the Berlin Caspar David Friedrich paintings in the famous collection of German Romantics.[102] As they were looking at Friedrich's painting Mann und Frau den Mond betrachtend (Man and Woman Observing the Moon) of 1824, Beckett announced unequivocally: "This was the source of Waiting for Godot, you know." [103]

He may well have confused two paintings. For at other times, he drew the attention of friends to Zwei Männer betrachten den Mond (Two Men Contemplating the Moon) from 1819, in which two men dressed in cloaks and viewed from the rear are looking at a full moon framed by the black branches of a large, leafless tree. Although he had not seen this actual canvas since his visit to the Gemäldegalerie Neue Meister in Dresden in 1937, it is very well known through reproductions in books on Caspar David Friedrich. In any case, the Berlin painting is so similar in its composition to the Dresden picture that what he said could apply equally well to either.[104]

But there is rarely one simple, single source of inspiration for a literary creation. And the author will not necessarily be conscious of them all. The tramps gazing hand in hand at an alien world call to mind two powerful paintings by Jack B. Yeats: The Two Travellers, painted in 1942 and hanging in the Tate Gallery in London (Beckett probably saw it in the artist's studio on his return to Ireland in 1945), and Men of the Plain (which he could have seen in 1947 or 1948).[105]

Many other possible sources for the play have been suggested. A remark of St. Augustine, "Do not despair, one of the thieves was saved; do not presume, one of the thieves was damned," inspired the concern with the fifty-fifty chance of salvation that runs through the play. Beckett also referred one critic to *Murphy* for the origins of *Waiting for Godot* (perhaps its mind-body dualism) and the same critic went on to discuss how the play had grown out of Beckett's then unpublished novel *Mercier et Camier*.[106]

Simplistic expectations of biographical elements in *Waiting for Godot* have led to simplistic questions being put: Are Estragon and Vladimir Sam and Suzanne on their way south, contradicting each other simply to fill in the time? Are they Beckett and Henri Hayden doing the same, as they meet regularly for chess? Common sense suggests that snatches of dialogue did emerge from similar little "canters," particularly from conversations between its author and his companion. Beckett has conceded as much privately to friends. (Suzanne could be sharp and witty in her remarks, giving back as good as she got.) But where these passages occur in the play, and how significant they are, are more difficult to ascertain. And whatever real-life sources the dialogue may have, it probably owes far more to forms and rhythms borrowed from the music hall (cross-talk, recited monologues, songs, and a soliloquy) and to its philosophical sources (among which are Descartes, Geulincx, Kant, Schopenhauer, and Heidegger) than it does to any real-life conversations.

The play also springs out of Beckett's Irish background, and not simply in the sense that the English translation contains actual Irish phrases or sentence structures. Estragon, Vladimir, Pozzo, and Lucky have cosmopolitan names. But the world they inhabit — of sleeping in ditches, waiting by the roadside, eating scraps from chicken bones — the lineage of the tramps, and the less easily defined "feel" of the characters (even in French) is unmistakably Irish. As so often with Beckett, his inspiration is literary: the world of John Millington Synge's tinkers and beggars. Beckett admitted to feeling a great debt to Synge.

The basic situation of the play also owes a lot to Beckett's understanding of theater and perhaps to his own life. Waiting for someone to arrive or something to happen that might change events has frequently been a key feature of drama; Strindberg's *A Dream Play*, W. B. Yeats's *At the Hawk's Well*, and Maeterlinck's *Les Aveugles* are three such plays that were known to Beckett. Usually in the end, someone does come or something does happen to change the situation, although often it is not what the characters think or hope it will be. But Beckett used the fundamental fact that, in his own words to me, "all theatre is waiting" to create a central situation in which boredom and the avoidance of boredom are key elements in preserving dramatic tension of an unusual kind.

The originality of *Waiting for Godot* lies in the concrete reality of the silence that has somehow to be filled. So the tramp-clowns must talk, swap hats, eat carrots, play games so as "to hold the terrible silence at bay." The inspiration for such a use of silence could have come from an instinctive response to Strindberg's or Chekhov's theater, or from a philosophical meditation as to how Democritus' "nothing is more real than nothing" could be rendered in the theater. In *Eleutheria*, Beckett had already shown a character who aspired to nothing. What better in his next play than to make the absent figure of Mr.

Godot take on this property, leaving him open to assume any of the attributes his characters wish to confer on him? It is, after all, his crucial absence that the characters feel as they wait, and fend off the threatening incursions of silence.

The war years had revealed the concrete reality of waiting, as Beckett and Suzanne sat out the time in Roussillon. The war also revealed the importance of filling in the time, as they waited in what must have seemed like a painfully long dramatic pause for the nightmare to end and for their "real lives" to begin. It is not surprising that so many prisoners should have empathized with the situation of Beckett's tramps, longing for release or parole as well as understanding without any difficulty the painful business of time-filling with very limited resources.

The claustrophobic atmosphere, unreliable messengers, and unkept appointments may have derived, it has already been suggested, from Beckett's work for the Resistance and his escapades on the run.[107] He could hardly have written at that time about boots that pinch, about sleeping in a ditch but longing for a dry hayloft in which to spend the night, about wondering where the next meal was coming from—a pink radish or a carrot was indeed a treat—about appointments made and not kept, without drawing on his own experiences. He even allowed references to the Vaucluse, to M. Bonnelly's vineyard in Roussillon, and to the red soil there to stand at least for a short while, before cutting the more explicit of them. Closer to the postwar period, these allusions would have been inescapable.

One of the tramps was first given the Jewish name of Lévy. And Pozzo's treatment of Lucky reminded some of the earliest critics of a capo in a concentration camp brutalizing his victim with his whip. The years just before Beckett wrote Godot had seen unimaginable revelations and horrific film footage about the concentrations camps of Belsen, Dachau, and Auschwitz. Georges Loustaunau-Lacau, a survivor of Mauthausen, wrote two remarkable books describing life in the camp where Beckett's good friend Alfred Péron had been an inmate.[108] One was published shortly before Beckett wrote Godot.[109] Mania Péron knew these books, since they contained pitiful accounts of her husband's plight, and she probably lent them to Beckett.

The story is a moving one. Péron knew much of Baudelaire and some Verlaine by heart and, after a day picking up coal with his hands because, malnourished, he no longer had the strength to wield a shovel, he would recite their poems or his own love sonnets in the midst of nightmare scenes of starvation, sickness, and brutality; he even inspired enthusiasm in the most brutal of the capos, Otto, "who having rained down blows on him and harassed him with threats of the crematorium came humbly the night of this murderer's anniversary to beg him to recite: 'Wo ist der Dichter, der Franzose?' " ("Where is the poet, the Frenchman?").[110] The others, including Polo, a former tough mec du milieu (a pimp), protected the more delicate Péron ("Orpheus in hell, a lamb lost in a cage of wolves"),[111] keeping him alive for many months longer than he could ever have survived without the solidarity of such utterly dissimilar individuals.

Beckett would have read these accounts with a mixture of compulsion and horror. He knew that, if arrested, he would have been in that same camp, subject to the same daily brutalities. And he knew that he would never have survived such an ordeal. These are the kinds of human issues that inform the varied relationships between the characters in his play: one protecting the other fraternally, though irritated or angered by him; another treating a fellow human being as something worse than an animal, bellowing commands, cracking his whip, demanding total obedience, yet still charmed by hearing him recite. Even the victim, Lucky, kicks Estragon in his turn. And, in the interstices of the play, violence is taken for granted, as Estragon answers Vladimir's question "Beat me? Certainly they beat me." [112]

The violence in this play grows out of the experiences of its age. Yet, of course, even the Pozzo-Lucky relationship is not merely about man's inhumanity to man. In the master-slave duo, there is a mutual dependence that takes the relationship beyond mere exploitation or victimization. Very different kinds of biographical roots are buried deeply within this play, but they have been so successfully transcended that the personal, local, and particular have been transformed to a point at which they recede, almost disappearing from view.

10

IN THE EARLY SUMMER of 1950, Beckett's brother wrote to tell him that the Parkinson's disease against which his mother had been fighting for the past few years was gaining ground and that she was deteriorating rapidly. One day she fell, breaking her femur. On hearing this, Beckett rushed over immediately to Dublin, where he found her condition much worse than he had ever imagined. She had been taken into the Merrion Nursing Home at 21 Herbert Place, overlooking the Grand Canal and the Huband Bridge. Sam and Frank visited her there every day. Jean came in from Killiney whenever she could; she had two children to look after. And, as Frank still had to keep his quantity surveyor's business running, Beckett, feeling guilty at his prolonged absence, tried to assume the greater part of the burden of his mother's illness.

In the nursing home, May Beckett's leg was supported by a sling that proved to be most uncomfortable, as it forced her to lie on one side of her body only. But a broken leg was the least of her problems. For the dementia that had been brought on by Parkinson's disease worsened rapidly after her accident and, by July 24, Beckett could write that medical opinion confirmed that she was dying. No one, however, would, or perhaps could, say how long death would be in coming. "Most of the time her mind wanders and she lives in a world of nightmares and hallucinations," he wrote. [113]

He was profoundly affected by what he described as the "terrible moral and physical distress" that she clearly experienced whenever she surfaced from her state of profound lethargy. He sat watching over her for an entire week, leaving the nursing home only when it was absolutely necessary in order to eat or, when he could no longer bear to watch her suffer, to walk disconsolately alone along the towpath of the Grand Canal. Sitting by her bedside, he longed earnestly, yet compassionately that it would soon be "all over and done with, at last."[114] On those desolate walks, he thought with bitter irony of his own situation: an agnostic who desperately needed a God to blame for the unnecessary nature of his mother's suffering.

When eventually Beckett returned overwhelmed and exhausted to his mother's little bungalow in Foxrock, it was to express his emotion in some of the most beautiful lines found in any of his letters: "My mother's life continues its sad decline. It is like the decrescendo of a train I used to listen to in the night at Ussy, interminable, starting up again just when one thinks it is over and silence restored for ever."[115] And, as his mother declined into a state of unbroken coma, he wrote: "I don't stay with her any longer. It does no good. It is my brother who needs me more now. At least that makes me feel that I'm of some use to someone."[116]

By the end of the first week in August, Beckett too had to take to his bed with a high temperature and, to add to his troubles, a raging toothache. The doctor prescribed sulphamides, and Beckett decided that the next day, fever or no fever, he simply had to get treatment from his dentist. With a wit that was often his way of responding to adversity, he wrote to friends that, as far as he was concerned, the dentist could "extract whatever he wanted, except his balls" — adding "but why this restriction?"[117] However, he soon recovered and felt strong enough to cope alone with the visits to his mother, who by now could no longer open her eyes or speak. To everyone's astonishment, her phenomenally strong heart continued to "beat like that of a beginner."[118] Now that she was too weak to recognize them any longer and, he fervently hoped, too unaware to suffer any more, he sent Frank, Jean, and the children away for a short, much needed holiday.[119]

May Beckett died on August 25, 1950. Afterward her younger son was exhausted and distraught. He was unable to bring himself even to write to his two good friends Henri and Josette Hayden for over a week; then, when he did, having announced that at last it was over for his mother, he had to break off, saying that he could write no more.[120] The complex, highly emotional nature of his relationship with May made her death an even more traumatic experience for him. And the feelings of guilt that so often follow the death of a loved one were heightened in his case by the remorse he felt at not having been the dutiful son she wanted. But although it had been a dreadfully upsetting time for everyone, Beckett felt peculiarly alone in his sorrow. Frank had his wife, Jean, and his family to comfort him. Suzanne had never met May, who had refused to see her son's "mistress," and it would have been hypocritical and inappropriate for her to go over during his mother's final weeks. So he whose relationship with his mother had been the stormiest but also the closest felt that her loss left him suddenly alone. For although he had been unable to live with her, he had also been unable to sever their emotional ties.

The funeral service was held in the family church of Tullow. Beckett insisted on making the arrangements himself. He went to his old medical friend from St.-Lô days, Freddie McKee, who was now at the Richmond Hospital, and asked him to help him choose his mother's coffin.[121] May's body was driven in a cortège to the Protestant cemetery at Redford to be placed in the same grave as her beloved Bill. Beckett had been there so many times with her since 1933 — planting heather, watching her wash the headstone with a tiny sponge, changing the flowers in the pot — that it was hard to believe their visits were over. The little lane leading down to the rural cemetery, the short walk behind the coffin up the path to the grave on the left, the view looking down and across Greystones harbor to the house that May had occupied before the war brought back a flood of distressing memories. He wanted to get out immediately. But her things had to be sorted first, thrown out or given away, and New Place had to be put up for sale. He returned to Paris in September utterly distraught and went immediately to Ussy to recover, without seeing any of his friends.

It was one of the key features of Beckett's aesthetic that what he once described to me as "the cold eye" had to be brought to bear on a personal experience before it could be used in a work of art.[122] In this case, it was seven years before he had achieved enough control over his emotions to draw on elements of his mother's death in the short play *Krapp's Last Tape:* "Mother at rest at last," as Krapp noted in his indexed reminiscences; the phrase "drowned in dreams and burning to be gone," which transferred his own view of his mother to Krapp himself; and, most directly, the "house on the canal where mother lay a-dying, in the late autumn, after her long viduity," with the speaker waiting nearby on a "bench by the weir from where I could see her window." [123] The memories remained. But by then much of the pain had slowly ebbed away.

11

IN MAY 1949, ROGER BLIN directed a French translation of the play *The Moon in the Yellow River*, by the Irish writer Denis Johnston, at the little Théâtre de Gaîté-Montparnasse. This play had received its world première at the Abbey Theatre in Dublin in 1931, while Beckett was lecturing at Trinity College. Johnston, like Beckett, had been enamored of Ethna MacCarthy, and he was known personally to Beckett.[124] Since Beckett and Suzanne were on the lookout at the time for an appropriate director for his two plays, *Eleutheria* and *Godot*, it is highly unlikely, the artistic world of Montparnasse being as small as it is, that they would have failed to notice this seemingly auspicious combination of Irish playwright and French director. For *Godot* had been completed for several months, and was already circulating among directors, as *Eleutheria* had done. But, in spite of Suzanne's dedicated efforts, so far it had not found a taker.

In 1949, Roger Blin was better known in Paris as an actor than he was as a director. He had acted in more than thirty films during the 1930s and 1940s and appeared onstage alongside such illustrious names as Maria Casarès and Gérard Philippe.[125] He already knew of Beckett as an Irish poet who wrote in French, having read Péron's translation of the poem "Alba" on the radio.[126]

Beckett knew Blin, too, by sight from Montparnasse cafés and was aware that he was a close friend of the theater theorist Antonin Artaud, and of Arthur Adamov. But Blin was at the very beginning of his career as a director. It was not, as a letter to Georges Duthuit reveals, that Beckett was particularly impressed by him at first either as an actor or as a director.[127] What mattered most of all was that he appeared to have artistic courage, was known to be sympathetic to new, little-known, or unconventional plays, and, at least in theory, was in charge of a tiny Latin Quarter theater and able to choose what was put on there.

A year earlier, Blin had agreed to be, in name only, the legal owner of the Gaîté-Montparnasse. The real owners were his Greek friend the actress Christine Tsingos and her husband, but, since they were not French nationals, they could not obtain a license to run it. By agreeing to the use of his name for the license, Blin could participate in managerial decisions. And he hoped in this way to have at his disposal a theater in which he could direct the plays of his choice.[128]

For his second production at the theater, Blin chose Stindberg's *Ghost Sonata*, which he had always admired and which Beckett and Suzanne went to see — along with seventeen other spectators on the night that they went. Beckett returned to see it again. Suzanne then took both *Eleutheria* and *En attendant Godot* to Blin and, early in 1950, after the actor-director had read both plays, Beckett invited him over to their little apartment and was impressed by Blin's pleasant manner and his great love of theater.[129] Blin, who stammered badly when not onstage, talked about his deep interest in the Irish theater, and the two men discovered that they shared an admiration for the plays of Synge. He told Beckett that he wanted to put on *En attendant Godot*, but that *Eleutheria* had too many characters for his limited resources.

From the outset, however, Christine Tsingos did not like the play and refused to have it at the Gaîté-Montparnasse (possibly because there was no female role in it for her). So Blin had more copies typed and sent them around to the artistic directors of other little theaters. It was hoped then that *Godot* would be put on at the end of 1950 at the Théâtre des Noctambules, "as soon as Adamov's *Grande et Petite Manoeuvre* [in which Blin was playing] has exhausted its admirers."[130] But, in the event, Beckett had to wait two more years before Blin managed to put together a combination of money and a theater. With the help of Georges Neveux, a member of the grant-awarding commission, he was able to obtain a financial grant of five hundred thousand old francs from the Ministry of Education — section "Arts et Lettres" — as an aid toward the production of a first play.[131]

With this sum of money promised, an agreement was actually signed on July 23, 1952, with Mme. France Guy of the Théâtre de Poche for Blin to direct the play at her theater.[132] However, disagreement soon arose over the interpretation of the contract[133] and finally it passed to Jean-Marie Serreau at the two-hundred-and-thirty-seat Théâtre de Babylone. Serreau was deeply in debt and the theater was facing imminent closure, so he made the brave decision that since "he was going to shut up shop, why not finish in beauty?"[134] Blin decided to go with him. The money was enough to start paying the actors, who until then had been rehearsing for nothing, but the grant was still insufficient to fund a run. One or two private individuals, such as the young (later famous) French actress Delphine Seyrig, put money into the production to get it off the ground.[135] It helped that, on February 17, 1952, with the support of Maurice Nadeau, an abridged version of the play was performed in the studio of the Club d'Essai de la Radio and was broadcast on the radio. Jérôme Lindon also agreed to publish the play at Les Editions de Minuit in October. This promoted interest in the new work and gave it a certain cachet.

Blin responded immediately to the circus and music-hall features of Beckett's play. Shrewdly, he cast Lucien Raimbourg as Vladimir. Raimbourg, a cabaret singer and music-hall actor, who was with the Bouffes du Nord, was a tiny man with enormous blue eyes. After trying someone else, Blin chose a heavier, physically contrasting type, Pierre Latour, as Estragon. Blin himself rehearsed the part of Lucky. But there were problems with the actor playing Pozzo and, once he had withdrawn, Blin, who had been rehearsing the part for months and knew it by heart, reluctantly changed roles.

Slim and youthful for his age, Blin was not at all the physical type for Pozzo, and he disliked intensely playing this obese older bully, with a booming voice that he hated having to produce and an artificial belly that he had to strap on every night. It was at this point, some three weeks from the opening night on January 3, 1953, that Jean Martin was therefore brought in to play Pozzo's carrier or "knouk." Martin consulted a friend of his, Dr. Marthe Gautier, who later became a close friend of Suzanne and who told him about patients who trembled with Parkinson's disease. Martin incorporated this into his acting and astonishingly managed to sustain it, trembling from head to foot throughout the performance and dripping saliva from his mouth. It was a shocking image of human misery that disturbed many spectators and contributed powerfully to the impact of the play.[136] The large, battered case that he carried was found among the city's refuse by the husband of the theater dresser on his rounds as he worked clearing the dustbins.[137]

Beckett attended almost all the rehearsals. Suzanne often came with him or joined him there, and they both became friendly with Blin and Martin. Beckett was totally inexperienced in the theater at the time, so he rarely intervened and explained very little. He used to talk quietly to Blin before and afterward, making discreet suggestions and effecting some cuts, when he saw that a section of dialogue did not work onstage. Some of the lines were cut in the second French edition of the play.[138] Others have never been excised to this day.

Reactions to the first performances were very mixed. Josette Hayden remembered how at first numbers dropped off after the first night and how they felt they needed to drum up support for it among their friends. Josette and Henri went out to dinner with Sam and Suzanne to celebrate the thirtieth performance, but even then they did not foresee the extent of the success, which was gathering momentum. Most of the reviews were good and the play gained distinguished admirers, among them Jean Anouilh, Armand Salacrou, Jacques Audiberti, and Alain Robbe-Grillet. But its success was assured when it became controversial, for it surprised and shocked many conventional theatergoers. Beckett was told about an incident when the curtain had to be brought down after Lucky's monologue as twenty well-dressed, but disgruntled spectators whistled and hooted derisively.[139] During a stormy intermission, the most irate protesters came to blows with the play's supporters, then trooped back into the theater only to stomp noisily out again as the second act opened with the same two characters still waiting for Godot as they had been at the beginning of act one. Rumor had it that the entire episode had been organized by the theater as a publicity stunt, but it was perfectly genuine.[140] As *Godot* became the talk of theatrical Paris, the character of the audiences changed and it became the play that everyone simply had to see. People were regularly being turned away at the door, and new box-office records were set for the tiny Théâtre de Babylone.[141]

Exhausted by the long haul of getting the play into production, Beckett responded to all this excitement with amused detachment. But for all that, *Godot* changed everything for him. It marked both the end of his anonymity and the beginning of his theatrical and financial success. Soon offers to translate the play into different languages and present it in different countries began to flood into the Editions de Minuit office. But, above all, *Godot* forced people, as Kenneth Tynan put it later, to "re-examine the rules which have hitherto governed the drama; and, having done so, to pronounce them not elastic enough."[142]

16

Godot, Love, and Loss

1953–55

1

USING THE MONEY that his mother left him, Beckett had a two-room country house, with kitchen and bathroom, built in 1953 "on a remote elevated field beyond Meaux about 30 miles from Paris,"[1] near the village of Ussy-sur-Marne that he had grown to love. It was a simple little house with a gray slate roof and two narrow chimneys, one taller than the other, on its righthand slope; banal, austere, and aesthetically dull, it reflected his and Suzanne's total lack of interest in any kind of luxury or display.[2]

The two rooms, which opened into each other, were furnished with the same spartan simplicity as their Paris apartment: two single beds; a rectangular oak desk, at which Beckett worked, in a corner by the window; bookshelves above his desk, holding his dictionaries and his books on chess, and more bookshelves on the other side of the window; another rectangular table with a long, narrow drawer, placed at right angles to the desk; a round dining table; two wicker chairs with arms and cushions on the seat; a small wicker footstool; and a large wicker wastepaper basket. Nothing in the house was expensive. The most solid item was the oak desk at which Beckett wrote. The floor was laid with small red and white tiles arranged in large squares, like a chessboard. In a corner of the room off the entrance hall was a boiler with an ugly metal pipe running up the corner of the wall and along the ceiling. Radiators were installed under the low windows to heat the rooms when it was cold.

Outside the house to the right, by the edge of a small copse that did not belong to Beckett, was a surprisingly long, low outbuilding with a sloping roof. This was divided into two halves; to the right was a storage shed with a long narrow window and a door, in which his gardening tools were ranged meticulously in two long rows, with large tools — a scythe, rakes, forks, and spades — on the row above and small tools — a hand fork, garden shears, and trowels — on the row beneath. To the left was a covered but open area, where he and Suzanne used to sit out in the summer at a small table in bucket-style wickerwork chairs.

Beckett's life soon assumed two distinct rhythms: one, in Ussy, quiet, solitary, and contemplative; the other, in Paris, much more hectic, pressured, and exhausting. The pressure came from trying to keep up with rehearsals of his plays, working with his various translators, and coping with the dozens of people who wanted to meet him now that he was becoming famous, as well as seeing his many friends.[3] There were the painters: Henri Hayden, who with his wife, Josette, often dined with him at the Iles Marquises; Robert Pikelny, whom, for a time, he used to meet at the Sélect;[4] Geer and Lisl van Velde, whom he bumped into occasionally on the boulevard, but met less frequently for dinner now than in the late 1930s; Bram van Velde and Marthe Kuntz, whose abject poverty upset him. And there were his theater friends, Roger Blin and Jean Martin, with whom he sometimes went to the Bobino or the Cirque Médrano, on one occasion to see Buster Keaton play there.[5] Then there were the annual migrations to Paris of his Irish friends and relatives: Tom MacGreevy stopping off between Dublin and the art galleries of Italy or Germany;[6] Ralph Cusack calling on his way to Spéracédès in the Alpes-Maritimes, where he had purchased a large house for his huge family;[7] Ethna MacCarthy, Beckett's beloved Alba, staying in Paris to appeal against an adverse medical examination that threatened to prevent her from working as a doctor with the World Health Organization.[8]

When Con Leventhal was over in Paris, Beckett and he used to gamble together, playing Multicolor, a variant on roulette that was invented by Henri Poincaré.[9] There were three gambling clubs of that name, on the avenue de Wagram, the boulevard de Clichy, and the avenue de la République. Beckett frequented the one on the avenue de Wagram. Although he never became addicted, the game appealed to him and, ten years later, he still played occasionally at the Multicolor, mostly with Leventhal. On his nights out with friends, he often drank quite heavily, coming home late and sleeping in, as Suzanne busied herself disapprovingly around their little apartment. For more regular relaxation, he used to play billiards with the art critic Patrick Waldberg and, in the summer, fit in the occasional game of tennis with Mania Péron.

At the country cottage in Ussy, especially if he was there alone, he would get up late, work in the morning at his writing or self-translating, then do some manual work outside the house. Most days he went for a long walk before supper or cycled into La Ferté to buy food and drink. In the evening, he either wrote again or played games of chess against himself. He listened to a little Telefunken radio, tuning in to classical concerts or to plays like Racine's *Bérénice*, with Jean-Louis Barrault as Antiochus, which he enjoyed immensely.[10] He was an avid sports fan and listened to commentaries on the radio: international rugby on Saturday afternoons, especially when Ireland was playing France, and even boxing matches (about a fight between Turpin and Haurez, for instance, he wrote, "I thought they were going to kiss each other!")[11]

He read widely, books ranging from J. D. Salinger's *Catcher in the Rye* ("a very good novel . . . best thing I've read for years")[12] and Alexandre Dumas's *Le Sphynx rouge*[13] to Agatha Christie whodunits, which he devoured either in English or in French.[14] Early in 1954, he had a telephone installed at Ussy to help him to keep in touch with the business side of his work, but, in order to limit incoming calls, the number was given to only a few very close friends. With its stillness, silence, and solitude, the house at Ussy became a haven, intimately connected in his mind to the work that so often germinated there: "I seem to recuperate something in the silence and solitude," he wrote to Tom MacGreevy.[15]

2

IN THEIR FEBRUARY 1953 ISSUE, the newly reconstituted *Nouvelle revue française* published an extract entitled "Mahood" from his forthcoming prose work, *L'Innommable*, but with an entire section of the text removed. The excised passage, which spoke of the "tumefaction of the penis," contained an amusing account of a figure who has no hands with which to excite himself trying to provoke the imagined "flutter" of an erection by thinking about a horse's rump.

Jérôme Lindon wrote to Beckett warning him that a few sentences of the text had been deleted by the editors after the proofs had been corrected. Beckett was livid. He had not been consulted about the cut and no explanation for it had been offered either to him or to Lindon. When he saw a copy of the review, he went almost berserk. It was not, he wrote, merely a few sentences that were deleted but an entire half-page; nor was there any indication in the *Revue* that a cut had been made. A letter of protest was surely insufficient, he argued. Should they not take legal action? Or, at the very least, compel the editor, Jean Paulhan, under threat of legal proceedings, to publish the omitted passage in the next issue, together with an apology for the unauthorized omission? Would Lindon seek the advice of his brother-in-law, who was a lawyer, as to what they might do? The whole affair, Beckett concluded, was making him literally ill. His letters show that he was indeed acutely distressed.[16]

Lindon telephoned Paulhan, who explained that the matter had been decided during his own absence from the office with influenza. Wisely, Lindon advised Beckett to do nothing hasty. More letters were exchanged, Paulhan apologizing to Beckett not for the original omission but for not informing him at once that a cut was being made, as a result of a decision by the committee of management (André Malraux, Jean Schlumberger, and Roger Caillois). Legal advice had confirmed, he wrote, that they could be prosecuted and the review financially ruined if they had printed the offending passage, which might pass quite unnoticed (as it was soon to do) in the context of a book. This failed to placate Beckett who, under these circumstances, would have withdrawn his text altogether rather than see it published in mutilated form.

Beckett's murmurs of anger and resentment rumbled on for several months, even after an explanation and a brief apology were printed in the March issue of the review. It was not, he objected, the note that he and Lindon had asked for. Should not the facts of the sorry affair, he asked, be exposed now in another journal? Once again his young publisher proved a wise counselor, advising that, in such a report, the facts could be distorted and lent a meaning quite different from the one they had; indeed, might it not appear as if, in pressing the matter further, they were seeking the publicity that he knew Beckett loathed? These arguments convinced Beckett to abandon any further attempt to right what he saw as a blatant injustice.

His fierce reactions showed, however, just how strongly he felt about the freedom and integrity of the artist to write and publish his work without fear of change or censorship. So much so that when, a few weeks later, Barney Rosset of Grove Press in New York agreed to publish English translations of his novels and of *Waiting for Godot,* Beckett wrote:

> With regard to my work in general I hope you realize what you are letting yourself in for. I do not mean the heart of the matter, which is unlikely to disturb anybody, but certain obscenities of form which may not have struck you in French as they will in English and which frankly (it is better you should know this before we get going) I am not at all disposed to mitigate.[17]

Nor did he allow Rosset to defer or sidestep the issue, but insisted on dotting the i's, emphasizing that

> in raising the question of the obscenities I simply wished to make it clear from the outset that the only modifications of them that I am prepared to accept are of a kind with those which hold for the text as a whole, i.e. made necessary by the change from one language to another. The problem therefore is no more complicated than this: are you prepared to print the result? I am convinced you will agree with me that a clear understanding on this matter before we set to work is equally indispensable for you, the translator [Patrick Bowles, who was by then translating *Molloy*] and myself.[18]

A principle as sacred as that of artistic freedom and integrity, learned at the feet of the uncompromising James Joyce, was not to be easily sacrificed.

The success of *Godot,* first in Paris, then, within a few months, in many theaters throughout Germany, brought Beckett unaccustomed fame and more money than he had ever made before from his work.[19] Inevitably, it also increased the threats to his privacy. Requests for interviews from newspapers, literary reviews, and radio flooded into Jérôme Lindon's office. To one such request, Beckett replied: "As for the Radio, I'm sorry, but I simply can't do it. To all requests for interview, no matter where they come from, you can always, even more so now, answer 'no.' "[20] It was galling and sometimes downright embarrassing for Lindon to have to turn down some of these requests, particularly when they came from critics who had written well of Beckett's work and to whom both he and his author felt a genuine debt of gratitude.

When Maurice Nadeau, a member of the jury awarding the Prix Renaudot (an award for new novels), suggested that Beckett's *L'Innommable* should be submitted for the prize, Lindon wrote to Beckett saying that, contrary to what he had at first believed, the book appeared to have a good chance of being awarded the prize. Nadeau and Claude-Edmond Magny, another member of the jury, were among its leading supporters, and Lindon told him that a third juror, Georges Charensol, had telephoned to ask whether, if Beckett were to be awarded the prize, he would be willing to participate in the ensuing celebrations and give an interview to his own literary review, *Les Nouvelles littéraires*. The publicity value of such interviews and articles was obvious enough and would certainly have helped to sell far more copies of Beckett's books. Beckett gave an unequivocal no, however, to both queries, recognizing again that he was acting counter to his own publisher's interests. But he explained that it was not so much because he found such self-promotion and literary junketings offensive, but because they were simply impossible for him.[21] In the event, he failed to get the majority required to win the Prix Renaudot and, on this occasion at least, his resolutions were not put to the test. Time was to show that if they had been, he would have acted exactly as he described. As for Lindon, he always respected Beckett's wishes and consistently acted to protect his privacy, assuming responsibility over the years for answering many of the letters that a writer would normally deal with himself. Few publishers would have behaved with such a delicate regard for an author's finer feelings, especially when they seemed to work against their own commercial interests.

3

MOLLOY AND *MALONE MEURT* had appeared in 1951 to the acclaim of several leading Parisian critics.[22] And the success of *En attendant Godot* had focused a lot of attention on *L'Innommable*, which was published in July 1953 by Les Editions de Minuit.[23] Beckett's name was already beginning to mean something as a French writer. Meanwhile, however, his last English novel, *Watt*, still lay in a drawer, the leaves turning yellow. So when a group whom he referred to as "the Merlin juveniles here in Paris who are beginning a publishing business"[24] approached Beckett, he jumped at the chance of seeing his English book appear.

The "Merlin juveniles" were a group of young expatriate writers and translators who had moved to Paris and combined forces to bring out an English language magazine entitled *Merlin*. They had settled in Paris in the aftermath of the war, with images of Ernest Hemingway, Gertrude Stein, and Henry Miller in Paris in the 1920s still stirring at the back of their minds. They were seeking something of the intellectual openness, fervor, intensity of debate, and cultural tolerance and freedom for which Paris had earlier been renowned.

There was indeed something distinctly heady in the manifestations of the prevalent Existentialist ethos — with its animated café discussions on political as well as metaphysical issues — as well as in the dominant sense of angst and emphasis on choice and on what man does, as distinct from what he is. *Merlin* and George Plimpton's *Paris Review* (which made its first appearance in 1953, a year after *Merlin*) may have harked back to the era of the little literary magazines published in English in Paris during the late 1920s and early 1930s. But *Merlin* was strongly influenced by the thought of Sartre and by the writings of Albert

Camus, and its editors considered themselves deeply *engagés*. The second issue, for instance, contained a piece on Camus's *L'Homme révolté* by Richard Seaver. Seaver could remember meeting Jean-Paul Sartre to make an agreement allowing them to publish English translations of articles in *Les Temps modernes* without paying a fee.[25]

The prime movers in *Merlin* were Alexander Trocchi, a Scot of Italian parentage who held a degree in English from Glasgow University, and his petite nineteen-year-old American girlfriend, Alice Jane Lougee, whose name appeared on the title page of the review as its actual publisher.[26] Trocchi, a "tall, pale, boney young man with prominent cheekbones,"[27] a huge beak of a nose, and a vast supply of seemingly inexhaustible energy, supplied the confidence, some of the literary flair, and a good number of personal contacts. With a little help from her banker father in Limerick, Maine, Jane Lougee provided the initial funding, but after that, financing the review was always a struggle. Others involved were the South African writer Patrick Bowles (who was to translate *Molloy* into English, with Beckett's help), the English poets Christopher Logue and Austryn Wainhouse, and a Canadian writer called Henry Charles Hatcher.

The actual link with Samuel Beckett was established by another lively, earnest, influential member of the group, the American Richard Seaver, a graduate of the University of North Carolina, who had come over to Paris on an American Services Fellowship after serving with the Navy. He lived behind St.-Germain-des-Prés in an empty ground-floor banana-drying warehouse in the little rue du Sabot. Walking along the narrow, curving rue Bernard-Palissy on his way to the rue de Rennes and the cafés of St.-Germain, Seaver spotted the blue-on-white titles of Beckett's first two novels in the tiny display window of Les Editions de Minuit at number 7 and connected them with the Beckett who had been one of Joyce's friends and had written an essay on *Finnegans Wake*. He read the new novels with great fascination and enthused to his friends about them. Then he discovered *Murphy* in the French edition of Pierre Bordas, and the stories "Suite" and "L'Expulsé."

Seaver hoped to meet Beckett in February 1952 at a recording for the Club d'Essai of the French radio of the as yet unstaged *En attendant Godot*. But, although he sent a polite note that Roger Blin read out, Beckett himself did not turn up. So the meeting did not take place. Excited by his reading of the novels, Seaver decided to write an essay about them. He originally intended it for the review *Points*, but after he met the dynamic, voluble Trocchi, it appeared instead in the autumn 1952 issue of *Merlin*.[28] The first number of the new review had appeared a few months earlier. Seaver, now grandly named "Advisory Editor and Director," sent copies of the review to Beckett and Jérôme Lindon, from whom he learned that a novel written by Beckett in English was still unpublished. He next wrote to Beckett asking him if they could see a manuscript of the novel in question, with the aim of publishing an extract in their new magazine. At first, his letter was answered only by silence. Seaver then takes up the story:

We had all but given up when one rainy afternoon, at the rue du Sabot banana-drying *dépôt*, a knock came at the door and a tall, gaunt figure in a raincoat handed in a manuscript in a black imitation-leather binding, and left us almost without a word. That night half a dozen of us — Trocchi; Jane Lougee, *Merlin*'s publisher; English poet Christopher Logue and South African Patrick Bowles; a Canadian writer, Charles Hatcher; and I — sat up half the night and read *Watt* aloud, taking turns till our voices gave out. If it took many more hours than it should have, it was because we kept pausing to wait for the laughter to subside.[29]

The group quickly opted to include the passage that Beckett had chosen for them in their next volume. In this way, a link was forged between Beckett and the *Merlin* group, and other extracts and stories by him appeared in later issues. A decision had also been made to try to emulate earlier private press owners like Sylvia Beach and Edward Titus by publishing limited editions under the imprint "Editions Merlin." But there were serious financial problems in proceeding with the series on their own, as well as fears that Austryn Wainhouse's translation of the Marquis de Sade's *La Philosophie dans le boudoir*, which they wanted to publish, might affect their foreign-visitor status, if it should lead to a brush with the law. They also discovered that, under French business law, such a publishing house needed a French *gérant*, or manager.

Meanwhile, after a lengthy period of exhaustion — cured, he claimed, by a ten-day course of injections of a dubious cocktail of hormones — Maurice Girodias, the son of Jack Kahane, whose Obelisk Press had published early sections of *Finnegans Wake* and books by Henry Miller, was setting up a new little publishing house called Olympia Press. Girodias met Austryn Wainhouse, who told him about Editions Merlin's plans to publish the de Sade translation but also about some of the difficulties they were encountering and introduced him to the other members of the group. Girodias agreed to be their essential French associate and to publish the de Sade, together with a number of other "erotic novels" such as *Justine* and two Apollinaire translations done by members of the *Merlin* group. Soon, Trocchi, Logue, and another contributor, Philip Oxman, were writing their own "erotic fiction" and others were translating for the series, Girodias promising the writers and translators anonymity and guaranteeing that he would assume responsibility in the event of legal action. They were paid by the thousand words for their contributions.

One of the first books agreed upon for the collaboration in 1953 was for an edition of Beckett's *Watt*, along with Henry Miller's *Plexus* and, a few months later, a volume of Christopher Logue's poems, *Wand and Quadrat*. The Beckett and Miller books were publicized on the same publicity leaflet as the de Sade and the Apollinaire. As someone who in the end had declined to translate the Marquis de Sade for Maurice Girodias's father in the 1930s because he did not wish to be too closely associated with a predominantly pornographic publishing house, Beckett may have been a little uncomfortable with this. Yet he was happy to know that, at long last, *Watt* was being published, for, as he told Susan Manning, it had been turned down earlier by "a good score of London publishers."[30]

The publication itself had a difficult birth. Barney Rosset, who, for Grove Press, was keen to print from the Paris edition, was horrified by the lack of decent proofreading and by the "scrubby and ugly" typeface.[31] With the history of *Ulysses* in mind, Beckett must have feared the consequences of using a French printer to print a lengthy and difficult English text. Predictably, the printer's English proved to be nothing like as good as had been claimed. And as one set of errors was removed, yet another appeared. When the book was published in an edition of 1,125 copies[32] on the last day of August 1953, Beckett sighed with despair as he read his copy, just as he blanched at the sight of the "awful magenta cover from the Merlin Press"[33] with its frame of busy asterisks. His own copy (number 85 of the ordinary edition) shows that he found over eighty spelling and typographical errors, and that, on page nineteen, an entire sentence had been omitted.[34] All he could do was to restore the sentence and remove as many mistakes as possible for the American edition.

But the inaccuracies did not inspire him with confidence. And, a year later, Beckett became furious with the "Merlin juveniles" and with Trocchi in particular, not only for not paying him any royalties[35] but, primarily, for not allowing him to correct the proofs of the translation of "La Fin" ("The End"), that Richard Seaver had done in collaboration with Beckett. " 'The End,' " he wrote, "for want of proof correction, is full of ridiculous mistakes. Have written a stinker to Trocchi. Fed up with them."[36] The letter was indeed "a stinker"[37] and prompted an apologetic letter back from a hurt Trocchi,[38] who from one letter to the next had been demoted by Beckett from "My dear Trocchi" to "Dear Mr Trocchi." But the row soon blew over, and, by March 1955, Beckett also allowed Merlin to bring out the English translation of *Molloy*. In November of that year, he was merrily talking of taking "the Merlin lads" out to a meal at chez Marius.[39] But his relations with Girodias remained cooler and were soon to deteriorate further.

4

THE REMARKABLE SUCCESS of *En attendant Godot*, the publication of *L'Innommable*, and the belated appearance of *Watt* underlined for Beckett how long it had been since he had written anything new. In May 1953, he wrote: "Since 1950 [I] have only succeeded in writing a dozen very short abortive texts in French [the "Textes pour rien"] and there is nothing whatever in sight."[40] A few months later, he commented: "Inertia, literary, continues. Haven't the least desire to put pen to paper, prefer mixing mortar and stretching barbed wire, long may these dispositions continue."[41] This simulation of indifference or mock bravado disguised a deep dismay that crept into other letters at the impasse in which he had found himself since finishing *L'Innommable* three years earlier, just before his mother died.[42]

Perhaps in the hope that inspiration might conceivably return, he spent as much time as he could at Ussy, even though he often had to dash into Paris to look over contracts, re-rehearse *En attendant Godot*, meet visitors, and keep numerous dental appointments, as he suffered from prolonged toothache, then, after a series of extractions, a painful abcess in the mouth. Throughout the first year of their occupancy of their new cottage, he worked hard to enclose the large plot of land, get rid of the stones, and prepare the ground for sowing rye grass. Frank Beckett came over with his wife for a short stay in May and helped him to dig the holes for the first trees that were eventually planted: "2 negundos (look that up in your Webster), 1 prunus, 2 limes and a cedar that will begin to look like something, you'll see, fifty years after I'm dead, if it doesn't predecease me. . . . Poor trees, they'll avenge the Godot willow."[43] The house had been built on high ground so that he could have wonderful views across the Monts Moyens and the valley of the Marne. But, realizing that — with a road outside his gate — if he could see out, others could see in, and consequently see him, he quickly had a high wall of ugly gray blocks built around the property that entirely cut off his view.[44]

On his many return trips into Paris, Beckett busied himself by keeping a watchful eye on how *Godot* was faring. He was actively involved in re-rehearsing new actors for the *reprise* in Paris in late September, then followed their progress anxiously.[45] Blin too was keen to quit his role, since he had been complaining for months that the booming voice he needed to adopt to play Pozzo hurt and even displaced his testicles, playing havoc with his sex life.[46] The cast changes did not always work out satisfactorily. The day after the play returned to the stage of the Babylone, Beckett wrote:

> Last night over at last and safely. The first act went well, the second less well, the new Didi forgetting his lines all over the place, with me sweating in the back row. The audience didn't seem to mind. The lighting was bad too. It will be better next week. The new Pozzo gave it up finally as a bad job and Blin had to play.[47]

In the early days, Beckett slipped unobtrusively into the back row for quite a few performances of *En attendant Godot*. He also attended the German premiere in Berlin in September 1953.[48] But he found the experience of watching with an audience excruciatingly painful and soon decided not to inflict such an ordeal on himself again.[49]

Requests flowed into Lindon's office throughout 1953 for the acquisition of the English-language rights or for permission to translate or "adapt" *Godot* into English. After a couple of earlier options had expired,[50] an approach was made by a potential American backer, Harold Oram.[51] Worried by the very sound of the word "adaptation" and anxious about the quality of any resulting translation, Beckett decided to set about translating the play himself. He produced a first version fairly quickly for Oram.[52] Yet even though his translation was revised by the end of the year and ready for production and publication,[53] getting the play put on in English proved to be almost as big a nightmare as the French one had been.

5

THERE WAS ONE unexpected consequence for Beckett of his discussions concerning the English-language rights of *En attendant Godot*. On her way back from a vacation in Italy, a thirty-two-year-old American woman, Pamela Mitchell, came to Paris in mid-September 1953 on behalf of Harold Oram, Incorporated. She arranged to meet Beckett, Jérôme Lindon, and a man called Brandel, who hoped to work out a partnership deal with Oram.[54] At first, she spent only a week in Paris, but she returned there at the end of April 1954 to act as Oram's European account executive, renting a flat and staying for about nine months. The Oram organization was a fund-raising group that took an interest in worthwhile and rather unusual undertakings that needed substantial injections of cash. Most of these were humanitarian causes, like the Citizens' Committee for Displaced Persons and the International Rescue Committee, which worked with refugee groups raising money for people escaping to the United States, mainly from Eastern Europe. Few of the accounts that they served were theatrical in nature. But they had just managed to raise money to finance a Broadway production called *Take a Giant Step* that dealt, challengingly for the time, with the problems of a Negro boy living in suburban Hartford, Connecticut. This launched Louis Gossett's career as an actor. So when Thornton Wilder spoke to Harold Oram about an extraordinary play called *En attendant Godot* that was intriguing Paris, Oram decided to try to obtain the American rights and mount a production in New York. Pamela Mitchell went to Paris to clinch the rights, as well as to negotiate with Oram's prospective partner. The rights were duly obtained, but they were never taken up by Oram and his option lapsed.

In this case, Beckett certainly mixed business with pleasure. "Those were good evening[s] we had, for me," he wrote to Pamela Mitchell, "eating and drinking and drifting through the old streets. That's the way to do business. I'll often be thinking of them, that is of you."[55] An intelligent, highly resourceful woman, who had majored in American history at Vassar College, then worked in naval intelligence throughout the latter part of the war, Mitchell had (and still has) a delightfully dry sense of humor and a great personal warmth. Beckett was immediately attracted by this charming brunette with her lovely, winning smile.[56]

During the last few days of her visit, they spent every evening and part of each day together. Beckett showed Mitchell the sights, took her to a rehearsal of *En attendant Godot*, wined and dined her at the Iles Marquises, his favorite seafood restaurant, and at L'Escargot. If his "be fond of me, but not too fond, I'm not worth it, it'll make you unhappy, you don't know me,"[57] written immediately after her return to New York, conveys a fear of involvement, his later "ate a bouillabaisse the other evening at the Marquesas, with the inevitable Sancerre, and wished for you"[58] shows that he was not emotionally detached. In the next few months, Pamela was ill in New York, first with pneumonia, then with a severe attack of mumps. During that time, Beckett wrote her more than a dozen letters.

Then he learned that she was to come to live in Paris. Although he was outwardly enthusiastic, this made things far more difficult for him, since he was still living in a fairly small apartment with Suzanne and it was not easy to keep his meetings with the young American woman secret. Perhaps he did not even try.

Pamela stayed first at the Hôtel Montalembert. Then she rented an apartment at 4 *bis* rue de la Grande-Chaumière, opposite the hotel where Beckett had lived when he was stabbed in 1938. For a few weeks after her return to Paris, they met regularly. They wandered around the gardens and the parks, amused each other by playing little word games that he called "square words" and went to the Roland Garros tennis stadium together. They ate out a lot, sometimes at the Iles Marquises, sitting as far away as possible from the trout and lobster tank because it upset Beckett and under the photographs of boxers — including Georges Carpentier (whom he saw at the same restaurant one evening later in the year)[59] and Sugar Ray Robinson, whom Beckett referred to as "Ray Sugar." Sometimes they dined at the restaurant of Les Invalides air terminal, which served, he claimed, the best Beaujolais in Paris and where he used to love to eat ham with spinach. In later letters, he called Pamela by a pet name: Mouki. The affair, although brief, was intense, both romantic and sexual. But it was brusquely interrupted.[60]

6

AT ELEVEN O'CLOCK one night toward the end of May, Beckett suddenly received a telephone call from Jean with the devastating news that Frank had been diagnosed as having terminal lung cancer.[61] There had been indications of ill health for several months — worryingly low blood pressure and attacks of dizziness, followed by what was thought to be a debilitating attack of influenza — but no suggestion of anything as serious as cancer. Beckett was devastated. He rushed over to Killiney knowing only that Frank had not been told either the cause of his illness or that it was terminal. He stayed for three and a half months at Frank and Jean's house, Shottery. Nothing else mattered. It was one of the most terrible times of his life, comparable only with the deaths of his father and his mother.

Most of his time was spent helping Jean look after his brother or "pottering about cutting grass, cutting wood, clearing up, pushing a barrow, lighting bonfire."[62] The brothers used to sit outside on a paved area in the garden by the side of a lily pond that Beckett had helped his brother to dig;[63] Frank wore a floppy hat to protect him from the sun.[64] Beckett smoked French cigarettes and bought whiskey, gin, and beer to help him to cope. He also had health problems and had to have a painfully abscessed tooth extracted under general anesthesia.

He developed a routine for passing the days: shaving his brother after breakfast and sharing a late-morning whiskey with him; helping him dress for lunch or go outside in the early weeks of his illness; then, as his condition worsened, bringing him up his meals and chatting to him as normally as he could. Like his sister-in-law, he felt utterly desolate, yet both had to hide their desolation for the sake of his brother and the two children. He found that one of the worst things about the situation was "the atmosphere of duplicity and subterfuge"; he listened with an aching heart to his brother making plans for better days.[65] In a show of apparent normality, he wandered off to watch a cricket match and listened intently to stroke-by-stroke commentaries broadcast from the Wimbledon tennis championships: "Listened on the wireless to Drobny beating hell out of Hoad. Hope he does the same today to Patty."[66] Feigning normality again, he played the Bechstein piano and entertained the children when they came home from school, playing with their two "weird cats, Blacky and Whity."[67] But an occasional visit to the art gallery and a trip to the Gaiety Theatre proved to him how impossible it was to enjoy anything normal in such awful circumstances.[68]

Most evenings after dinner he walked alone along the seashore below the house overlooking beautiful Killiney Bay "with the tide coming in fast and a scatter of rain."[69] He sought solace in talking to his mother's old friend Susan Manning, of whom he was very fond, taking her out once for a drive in his brother's Rover 75 "by Glencullen and the Scalp and Enniskerry and Powers Court and old Connaught, lovely old names and places."[70] On one occasion, during a walk along the seashore with Susan's son, John:

> He hardly spoke at all. He would ask a few questions; he would turn and look at you with his fine brow and the eyes very like his mother. Astonishing. The brow and the eyes and the look. You could see him thinking and listening. . . . But I remember what impressed me actually was what he said. We were walking along the beach, he was hardly talking you know, and I think he knew his brother was dying then and he wasn't saying anything and he just stopped, he didn't look at me but he said: "It's like the tide going out."[71]

It was not until the middle of August, a month before Frank died, that Dr. Gilbert Wilson finally admitted to his patient that there was nothing more that could be done for him.[72] At night now, when Frank and Jean had gone to bed, Beckett used to sit alone in his room at his writing table "drinking a last beer before going to bed . . . and the sound of the sea on the shore, and my father's death, and my mother's, and the going on after them."[73] When eventually he went to bed, he would lie awake listening to "the old sea still telling the old story at the end of the garden."[74] To pass the time he read Robert Louis

Stevenson's letters written from the south of France and found them "very moving."[75] At less busy times during the day, he tried to work at a revision of Patrick Bowles's translation of *Molloy;* then, finding it easier to translate himself than to revise someone else's work, he started to translate *Malone meurt.*[76] But it was hard to concentrate on anything in such a state of morbid tension and intense unhappiness.

He poured out his misery in frequent letters to Pamela Mitchell, and, week by week, charted his brother's sad, slow deterioration. These letters reflect his shifting awareness of time throughout this dreadful experience. At first, the days passed by very quickly, perhaps because there was so much to be done; then they began to slow down to a painful crawl, as change seemed imperceptible and what change there was could only be for the worse: "And so soon it will have been another day and all the secret things inside a little worse than they were and nothing much been noticed," he wrote memorably.[77] Reading Beckett's own grim account of the slowing down of time in the light of an imminent ending that will not end, reflected in phrases like "things drag on, a little more awful every day, and with so many days yet probably to run what awfulness to look forward to"[78] or "Waiting [is] not so bad if you can fidget about. This is like waiting tied to a chair,"[79] is like being deeply immersed already in the world of *Fin de partie (Endgame)* where something slowly but inexorably is taking its course: "Finished, it's finished, nearly finished, it must be nearly finished."[80]

But, however slowly, the end finally came. His brother died on September 13, 1954. Beckett stayed on for two more weeks to help sort out the family's financial affairs. He saw the solicitors and McMillan, his brother's partner in the firm, and took the Rover back to Wilkinson's Garage on the canal in Leeson Street to sell it.[81] On his return to France, he spent only one night in the rue des Favorites, then took himself off to Ussy to recover, sometimes with Suzanne but more often alone, as she spent much of the time doing up their apartment in Paris. He stayed in the country for almost six weeks, waiting "until I am fit to be seen," in a state of acute grief and profound depression.[82] The past four months had been among the most traumatic of his life.

7

EARLY IN AUGUST, Beckett had written to Pamela Mitchell from Ireland: "Soon the leaves will be turning, it'll be winter before I'm home. And then? It'll have to be very easy whatever it is, I can't face any more difficulties, and I can't bear the thought of giving any more pain, make what sense you can of that, it's all old age and weakness, why will you not believe me?"[83] The message was clear: the sadness of his brother's illness and death had sharpened his awareness of the distress caused by deceit and emotional infidelity, and he had witnessed far too much pain to be willing to inflict any more. He was in no doubt from her letters that Pamela was very much in love with him. But the affair could not be allowed to continue. So, at the end of November, he took the decisive step to call it a day, arguing that, although he was very fond of her, he did not love anyone:

> For me things must go on as they are. I have not enough life left in me even to want to change them. They may change and leave me alone. I shall do nothing to try and stop that either.
>
> The notion of happiness has no meaning at all for me any more. All I want is to be in the silence. . . .
>
> Don't imagine I don't feel your unhappiness. I think of it every hour, with misery. For God's sake admit to yourself you know nothing of me and try and believe me when I tell you what I am. It is the only thing will help you. You will be happy one day and thank me for not involving you any deeper in my horrors.[84]

But this was not the last communication that passed between them. They saw each other several times during January, Beckett making it crystal clear to her that what mattered most of all to him was his work and that, largely for this reason, he was unwilling to change anything fundamental in his life. It is likely that his attachment and sense of loyalty to Suzanne were another important factor that he may not have wished to voice to Pamela. Suzanne was intimately associated in his mind with the peace and support that he needed for his work. But it was Pamela who made the decision that, since no more permanent relationship between herself and Beckett was possible, she should return to America.

In spite of her decision, during the last fortnight of her stay they achieved an exceptional closeness. He confided in her about ideas that were churning around in his head for a new play. As a going-away present, he gave her the three-volume Pléiade edition of Proust's *A la recherche du temps perdu*, Verlaine's *Oeuvres poétiques complètes*, and a subscription to the newspaper *Combat*. As her main "goodbye present," she gave him the "big, magnificent" *Vocabolario della lingua italiana*[85] (or *Vocabulary of the Italian Language*) by Nicola Zingarelli, which he consulted so as to "worm" his way back into reading Italian again,[86] and a beautiful edition of Baudelaire's poems.

He was left feeling terribly lonely, when she sailed back on the *Liberté* to New York. His letters after her departure are loving and tender: "Wish I could get up now and go to 4 bis [rue de la Grande-Chaumière] and lie down and never get up again. We'd play square words, between times, and every six hours you'd spoonfeed me with a hamburger and the pianist would die. No? Yes? You're right."[87] It is as if, given the safety of distance, he wants to restore, even reclaim their intimacy. They corresponded for the next seventeen years, although infrequently after 1956. But they saw each other whenever Pamela was in Paris and once, in 1964, when he went to New York. She described this later friendship as an "amitié amoureuse."[88]

8

BECKETT'S SIX WEEKS OF REST and recuperation at Ussy after his brother's death were disturbed by some news that threatened the peace and solitude that he was struggling to achieve there. Two years before, when he had purchased the land on which his cottage was built from the commune of Ussy, it had been unwilling to sell him a plot fifteen meters wide that lay at the foot of his property because it was needed for access to a small water supply station. Now, early in November 1954, he heard quite by chance that, following the death of the former mayor, the municipality had decided to sell the plot of land to a Monsieur Horviller who wanted to build a small hunting lodge there. Beckett was furious: It would spoil his view; it would ruin his peace; and knowing that it was to be used for hunting made the sale even more painful to him.

Once again he contacted Jérôme Lindon, who sought the help of a lawyer friend, Simon Nora.[89] Beckett wrote to the subprefect of Meaux, arguing that he had always wanted to buy the land and that it was grossly unfair that it should now be sold to anyone else. Nora also wrote to the subprefect about the proposed sale, emphasizing Beckett's importance in contemporary French literature and mentioning the decorations that he had received from the French Resistance for his patriotic achievements during the war.[90] He also mentioned the harm that could be done to someone of Beckett's delicate nervous disposition, if the land were to be sold to anyone else. In December, Beckett offered to make a gift of the plot of land to the municipality on his death. M. Horviller promptly countered with the same offer.[91]

Before Christmas, the municipal council "had a tempestuous meeting . . . and rained maledictions on my filthy foreign celibate sinful head, but nothing decided apparently."[92] Then, early in January, Beckett himself had to appear before the council,[93] which finally decided to allow Horviller to construct his small building, but set back "off the line" so as not to spoil the view from Beckett's cottage.[94] In spite of this concession, Beckett was so disgusted by the decision and resentful of how he had been treated by the commune that he vowed never to set foot in the village again. And even though, when he owned a car, he was allowed to use the building as a garage, he never did any shopping in Ussy and never again went to the local café-tabac for cigarettes or drink, preferring to cycle, "panting up the hills in bottom gear, refusing to give in, like my father,"[95] or later to drive over to the larger town of la Ferté-sous-Jouarre. When crossed, he could be difficult and unforgiving.

9

IT WAS NOT A DISPUTE about land, however, but continuing grief over his brother's death that made him feel "lousy and miserable and so nervous that the bawls are out of me, in the house and in the street, before I can stop them."[96] It was a strange time, since, while feeling in lousy form and worrying anxiously about "the old heart knocking hell out of me nightly and like an old stone in the day,"[97] Beckett paradoxically also felt a huge surge of creative energy coursing through his veins again as he wrote, fairly rapidly, a first version of *Fin de partie (Endgame)* with only two characters.

> It's queer to feel strong and on the brink at the same time and that's how I feel and I don't know which is wrong, probably neither. So much possible, and so little probable. The thing I always felt most, best, in Proust was his anxiety in the cab (Last volume) on his way home from the party. Often feel like that now, in all due humility, no, unhumbly. And sometimes I think I shall dribble on to 80.[98]

His letters to Pamela Mitchell show that he felt quite differently about the so far untitled play than about anything else that he had tried to write over the past five years. In February, he was totally caught up in the cruelly symbiotic relationship between two characters, A and B: "I have A out of his armchair flat on his face on the stage at the moment and B trying in vain to get him back. I know at least I'll go on to the end before using the waste-paper basket."[99] Then, a month later, he wrote: "Yes, I finished the play, but it's no good and I have to begin all over again."[100] Recognizing that it had to be totally reworked, he still felt that "A and B are not defunct, but sleeping, sleeping sound. One of these days I hope to kick them into better groans and howls than the ones you know."[101] His letters also show that, while he was writing this first version of *Fin de partie*, Beckett read the Book of Genesis and Baudelaire's poetry: "I've been reading in your grand Baudelaire and in the Holy Bible the story of the Flood and wishing the Almighty had never had a soft spot for Noah."[102] In the play's first draft, character B reads from the passage about the Flood in Genesis and character A even rephrases Beckett's own sardonic thought about Noah.[103] What makes these snippets of information about his reading so intriguing is that the reading leaves distinct traces even in the final published text. Ham(m) was a surviving son of Noah,[104] and the play is full of what have been called images of "discreation": an earth divided between land and water; Hamm's home, like an ark, a refuge from the outside world; a creation where, instead of being found good in the eyes of God, the light is dying; a land where the earth brings forth no grass and where Clov's seeds will "never sprout." A basic premise of the play is that it might be better if humanity were never to reconstitute itself again in this "old endgame lost of old."[105] Hamm also quotes and completes a passage from Baudelaire's sonnet "Recueillement," which Beckett had just been rereading in Pamela Mitchell's gift copy: "Tu réclamais le soir; il descend: le voici"[106] (in Beckett's English translation: "You cried for night; it falls: now cry in darkness"[107]). But these details also help to resolve a problem in scholarship. The important two-act first version of *Fin de partie* can be more precisely dated from Beckett's letters to Pamela Mitchell.[108]

Endgame is not, of course, autobiographical drama. Yet it followed hard

on the heels of Beckett's experience of the sickroom and of waiting for someone
to die, and is not only preoccupied with the slowness of an approaching end
but haunted by the tiny, practical details of caring for a dying patient: character
A calls for a catheter, wishes to be placed in the sunlight, asks if it is time for his
painkiller; character B comes when he is called, covers A with a rug, speaks of
getting him up and of putting him to bed, winds up the alarm clock, and takes
his temperature. There may be other equally precise personal associations
within the play. Beatrice Lady Glenavy, who knew the Beckett and Sinclair
families, suggests fairly plausibly in her memoirs that Hamm, the character
in the wheelchair, was modeled in certain respects on Beckett's aunt Cissie
Sinclair.

> When I read *Endgame* I recognised Cissie in Hamm. The play was
> full of allusions to things in her life, even the old telescope which
> Tom Casement had given me and I had passed on to her to amuse
> herself with by watching ships in Dublin Bay or sea-birds feeding on
> the sands when the tide was out. She used to make jokes about her
> tragic condition, she once asked me to "straighten up the statue" —
> she was leaning sideways in her chair and her arthritis had made her
> body heavy and hard and stiff like marble.[109]

More important, the play is full of images of death: in the early version, a
black box was present onstage and its cover opened to reveal a head staring
motionlessly out at the audience — an early glimpse of the presence of the two
other characters, who were to become Nagg and Nell; A and B often speak of
death and burial; "there are no more coffins"; the old doctor is dead; Mother
C's light has gone out. Some of these images were dropped when Beckett came
to rewrite the play a year later, moving it away from the personal. But many still
remain, residually, in the published text. The relationship between A and B
clearly owed little to Beckett's personal feelings for his brother, except perhaps
in that extraordinary way that, particularly in a sensitive creative writer, love or
grief can engender something that very much resembles its opposite. Yet the
play is profoundly marked by the death of his brother. Even its flintlike comedy
is sparked out of darkness and pain.

10

HIS LONG LATE-WINTER STAY in Ussy in the snow and bitter cold, and the
completion of the first *Fin de partie* in French brought the first real signs of
recuperation in Beckett in early March 1955. His trees were surviving after all,
"even the two apples showing shy signs of life. Shall soon have to buy a mechanical scyther-mower, never get round the grass otherwise. Visited by partridges
now daily, about midday. Queer birds. They hop, listen, hop, listen, never seem
to eat."[110] As for his own physical state, "the old carcass" was "up and down, one
day dying and the next lepping."[111] He even began to feel capable of meeting

people again. Soon, in a freak warm spell—the hottest last days of March since 1880—he found himself dashing from one appointment to another, meeting "old cronies from Ireland" including "directors of galleries and expiring gunmen all rusty bullets and Black and Tan scars. And cousins, there was never a man with so many cousins." [112]

Over this three-year period, a large number of Beckett's social commitments were undertaken for the sake of friendship. In the summer of 1953, he spent several sessions with Richard Ellmann, who was embarking on his monumental biography of Joyce. Beckett liked Ellmann "in spite of [his] incessant note-snatching," [113] and talked to him out of a sense of affectionate loyalty to Joyce. During the winter, he stayed several weeks in Paris because he could not leave Ethna MacCarthy to face her continued problems with the World Health Organization alone and he asked the Irish ambassador, Cornelius Cremin, if he could help her out. In February 1954, he forced himself to write a *hommage* to Jack Yeats for an exhibition of the Irish painter's work at the Wildenstein Gallery. He described writing it as "real torture," [114] but he also took the trouble to arrange with Maurice Nadeau to have a group of homages to Yeats printed in the April issue of *Les Lettres nouvelles* and to canvass critics he knew to write their own pieces for it. He was very disappointed when Georges Duthuit and Nadeau had a row that made Duthuit remove his contribution. In April 1955, he acted as best man at the wedding of Joyce's grandson, Stephen, although he loathed that kind of social occasion, which involved a lunch reception as well as the ceremony itself.

With his own financial position now much improved, he started to help more and more relatives and friends when they fell on hard times. [115] It was not just that Beckett was generous. He was simply unable to resist offering help. It was a deep compulsion. Many stories illustrate this mixture of vulnerability and generosity. One critic, Claude Jamet, witnessed an example in a Montparnasse café in the 1950s:

> I knew Beckett by sight. At two in the morning—the bars closed late, especially in Montparnasse—at a bar called the Rond-Point, which has disappeared now but used to be opposite the Dôme, Beckett was having a drink at the bar. There were a few lost intellectuals like Beckett and myself, and a few tramps. One of the tramps standing by Beckett said to him: "My word, that's a fine jacket you're wearing, a lovely jacket." And I saw Beckett take off his jacket and give it to the tramp. Without emptying the pockets either. [116]

Suzanne could be as generous as he was; her friends speak of how she would be ready to give away her last sou. Although her natural instincts were to protect Beckett, she did not act as a curb to his spontaneous generosity. On the contrary, their fellow feeling for those in need represented another bond between them.

On October 3, 1954, Beckett received two typed letters in French from Lüttringhausen prison near Wuppertal in Germany: one was from the Protestant pastor of the prison, Ludwig Manker; the other, a longer one, was simply signed "un Prisonnier." "You will be surprised," wrote the prisoner, "to be receiving a letter about your play 'Waiting for Godot,' from a prison where so many thieves, forgers, toughs, homos, crazy men and killers spend this bitch of a life waiting . . . and waiting . . . and waiting. Waiting for what? Godot? Perhaps." [117] The prisoner related how he had heard from a French friend about the play that was taking Paris by storm and had the first edition sent to him in prison; he had read it over again and again, then had translated it himself into German. Thanks to the intervention of Pastor Manker — and, we can add, the agreement and support of the prison director, a Dr. Engelhardt — he had obtained permission to put the play on in the prison, had cast it himself, rehearsed it and acted in it. The first night had been on November 29, 1953.

The effect on the prisoners was electric; the play was a triumph. "Your Godot was Our Godot," the prisoner wrote to Beckett. He explained that every inmate saw himself and his own predicament reflected in the characters who were waiting for something to come along to give their lives meaning. He then offered his own interpretation of the play, seeing in it a lesson of fraternity even in the worst of conditions: "We are all waiting for Godot and do not know that he is already here. Yes, here. Godot is my neighbour in the cell next to mine. Let us do something to help him then, change the shoes that are hurting him!" [118]

The prisoner added that the play had been performed fifteen times in the prison and that dramatists, theater directors, and critics had come to see it and write about it in the press.[119] Would Beckett do them the honor, he asked, of coming to see them perform? The prison pastor confirmed in his own letter how deeply the four hundred prisoners had been affected by the play. He himself kept the tree used in the production in the sacristy and said that for him this had become, in the quotation from the Book of Proverbs, "a tree of life." And he repeated that if the rumor that Beckett intended to come to the theater in Wuppertal to see the production of Godot were true, would he come on to the prison as his guest to see their version? It would mean so much to the prisoners, Pastor Manker concluded.[120]

Beckett was intensely moved by these letters and must have written to say that he hoped one day to come to meet with the prisoners.[121] For a month later, although weary by this time of the fuss about the play, he wrote to Con Leventhal: "I am hoping to go to the Rhineland, more precisely to the Lüttringhausen penitentiary to see a last performance of this fucking play by and for the prisoners, if permission can be obtained for them to do it again." [122]

Roger Blin told Deirdre Bair that a few months later a frozen figure, dressed in lightweight summer clothing, turned up at the theater in a freezing cold Paris, saying that, in a letter, Beckett had invited him to call if ever he were in the city. The penniless, half-starved prisoner had broken his parole to come to see him. Blin offered temporary shelter and provided him with warmer clothing. When Blin contacted Beckett, Suzanne was afraid that the prisoner might be violent. Beckett, on the other hand, was terrified not for his own safety, but of confronting the physical presence of the man. So he asked Blin to give the prisoner money but to tell him that Beckett was not in town and would not be back for some time. A few days later, Blin returned to find a note from the prisoner saying that Paris was too cold for him and that he was going south in search of warmth. The note made no mention of Beckett.

Some fascinating additional information can now be added to this story.[123] In 1956, under the name of the Spielschar der Landstrasse Wuppertal ("The Players' Troupe of the Open Road in Wuppertal"), the actors from the prison were allowed to present eight public performances of what they called *Man wartet auf Godot* in Frankfurt. The performances ran from August 8 to August 12 as part of the cultural program of the "Deutscher Evangelischer Kirchentag."[124] Beckett also went on receiving letters from the prisoner. In his notes on his meetings with Beckett, Patrick Bowles recorded how, on November 10, 1955, Beckett told him that the German prisoner was soon to be released from jail and wanted to tour the provinces and obscure villages of Germany with *Warten auf Godot*.

> "He will meet many difficulties, of course," Beckett said. Those of obtaining the rights, of acquiring money to pay for the production, other taxes and expenses, etc. "It would be a good idea," said Beckett, "I would like to do it, to write a play for him alone, and give it to him. And say, here you are, you need not worry about the rights."[125]

He did not write a play for the prisoner, but he did send him a small sum of money. In a July 1956 letter to his German agents, S. Fischer Verlag, Beckett asks for two hundred marks to be sent to the prisoner, which suggests that he was in all probability the recipient, Herr K. F. Lembke.[126]

The exchange of letters with the inmate and pastor of Lüttringhausen marked the beginning of Beckett's enduring links with prisons and prisoners. He had a natural sympathy for those who were incarcerated. He took a tremendous interest in productions of his plays performed by prisoners and was fascinated when he heard of the impact that *Godot* had in a number of prisons. On one occasion, when he was in Berlin, he asked if he could be taken around a jail to meet the inmates. And, later, perhaps partly out of a sense of guilt at not having met the German prisoner personally when he came to Paris, he gave a former prisoner from San Quentin financial and moral support over a period of many years.

11

THROUGHOUT HIS BROTHER'S illness and death and his involvement with Pamela Mitchell, negotiations were proceeding for the production of *Waiting for Godot* in England and the United States. In England, the producer Donald Albery requested a copy of the script. He asked several friends to read it, including the ballet dancer Margot Fonteyn and the young actress Dorothy Tutin, who had just had an overnight success in Peter Glenville's West End production of Graham Greene's *The Living Room*. Both of them encouraged Albery to try to mount a London production.[127] So Donald Albery and Peter Glenville eventually signed a contract for a United Kingdom production, with an option for the United States. One of the terms was that the play should be put on in London's West End within six months. This proved impossible to achieve because Glenville, who had just accepted a film contract, was not free to direct and because the producers wanted to include at least one, and preferably two, very well-known actors to add luster to the cast. A lot of time was, therefore, spent in trying to sign up Alec Guinness who, having read the play, was keen to play in it,[128] and Sir Ralph Richardson. The problem was juggling the heavy commitments of two such busy actors. Beckett saw this as "shilly-shally,"[129] wasting time star chasing. He wrote that he had "told them to get on with it with whatever people available and to hell with stars. If the play can't get over with ordinarily competent producing and playing, then it's not worth doing at all."[130] Albery and Glenville, on the other hand, believed that they were merely giving the play the best possible chance of succeeding in the West End. But, in spite of his understandable impatience, Beckett stayed committed to Donald Albery, largely because he liked him personally and because he believed he knew his business.

Finally, further not entirely unexpected problems[131] were encountered with the Lord Chamberlain, the official censor and licensee of plays for the theater. Beckett wrote to Rosset:

> We were all set for a London West End performance until the Lord Chamberlain got going. His incriminations are so preposterous that I'm afraid the whole thing is off. He listed 12 passages for omission! The things I had expected and which I was half prepared to amend (reluctantly), but also passages that are vital to the play (first 15 lines of Lucky's tirade and the passage [at the] end of Act II from "But you can't go barefoot" to "And they crucified quick") and impossible either to alter or suppress. However Albery (the theatre director) is trying to arrange things in London. I am to see him this week-end and all is not yet definitely lost.[132]

Albery arranged for a reading of the entire play in front of the Lord Chamberlain's officer by the cast of *I Am a Camera* in one of the larger dressing-rooms at the New Theatre; Dorothy Tutin read the part of the little boy.[133] All to no avail; cuts would have to be made, they were informed, or no license for public performance could be given. Eventually, the Lord Chamberlain's objections were circumvented by a first production at a private theater club. But for production in a public theater cuts still had to be made.[134]

Negotiations with Guinness and Richardson overlapped with these censorship problems. In October 1954, Beckett stopped off in London on his way back from Ireland after his brother's death to meet Albery and Glenville and to talk with Sir Ralph Richardson, who, wrote Beckett, wanted the low-down on Pozzo, his home address and curriculum vitae, and seemed to make the forthcoming of this and similar information the condition of his condescending to illustrate the part of Vladimir. Too tired to give satisfaction I told him that all I knew about Pozzo was in the text, that if I had known more I would have put it in the text, and that this was true also of the other characters. Which I trust puts an end to that star. . . . I also told Richardson that if by Godot I had meant God I would [have] said God, and not Godot. This seemed to disappoint him greatly.[135]

It has often been supposed on the basis of what Beckett said that Sir Ralph (to whom, incidentally, Beckett seems to have taken an instant dislike) rejected the part out of total lack of sympathy with the play and as a direct consequence of the unsatisfactory nature of Beckett's explanations. This does not appear to have been the case. In a letter to Jérôme Lindon at the end of July, Beckett wrote that Richardson had read and approved the play.[136] And as late as October 1954 — that is, *after* the meeting between Beckett and Richardson — Barney Rosset wrote to Beckett: "According to our latest communication from Donald Albery there is a good bit of life still left in SIR Ralph. Mr. Albery seems to think there is still a good chance for Richardson and Guinness to not only put on *Godot* in London, but to trot over here with it also."[137] The problem was rather one of Richardson's commitments with the Old Vic theater company. But it was to be a full two and a half years after the first production in France before the first English-language production opened in London and three years before the curtain finally went up in America.

One of the worst aspects of the delays in London was the knock-on effect on other productions. Several theater companies and individuals, including Sam Wanamaker, approached Beckett or Barney Rosset with requests to put on the play in New York. Most infuriatingly, the theater designer Leo Kerz wrote to Beckett from the New Repertory Theater asking for permission to mount a production of the play on Broadway with Buster Keaton as Vladimir and Marlon Brando as Estragon. But, because of a newly extended contract by which Donald Albery paid another £250 advance and received a further six months' option — with a clause again assigning him United States rights for six months after a London production — to his "extreme mortification"[138] Beckett had to say that such a production was out of the question. "It was bitter to have to say no," he wrote. "Imagine Keaton as Vladimir and Brando as Estragon!"[139] The timing of the first production in Ireland by Alan Simpson at the Pike Theatre Club in Dublin also hinged on the date at which the London production opened in a public theater. Although the rights acquired by Albery applied, strictly speaking, only to the British Commonwealth, of which Ireland was not a member, Beckett did not want the London production to be anticipated by the Pike Theatre. So Simpson was obliged to postpone several times the date of the Irish premiere.[140] Ironically, while preparations for a first production of the English text limped along in London, the play was being presented in Germany, Holland, Italy, and Spain, where its impact was still controversial.[141]

In England, Peter Glenville, the "star-haunted" director as Beckett unkindly dubbed him, decided, reluctantly, that he could not fit *Waiting for Godot* into his already overcrowded schedule. So Albery opted to produce the play on his own, seeking a replacement for Glenville as director. He chose a young director, Peter Hall, installed only a few months before as director at the Arts Theatre Club. And, since both Alec Guinness (despite a brief resurgence of hope in February that he might be free after all) and Ralph Richardson were now finally ruled out by other commitments, the way was open to use new and less well-known actors.

When he read the much-thumbed script, Peter Hall was impressed by "the enormous humanity and universality of the subject and by the extraordinary rhythms of the writing"[142] and immediately won his actors' hearts by announcing with modesty but eminent practicality at an early rehearsal: "[I] haven't really the foggiest idea what some of it means . . . but if we stop and discuss every line we'll never open. I think it may be dramatically effective but there's no way of finding out till the first night."[143]

Paul Daneman, who had just had a great success playing Justice Shallow in *Henry IV, Part II*, at the Old Vic, was asked to play Estragon to the Irishman Cyril Cusack's Vladimir. Cusack quickly withdrew. So Daneman was switched to play Vladimir. Donald Albery then signed up for eight pounds a week (but no money for rehearsals, except a few luncheon vouchers) an ebullient, talented twenty-three-year-old second-year student of biochemistry at Magdalene College, Peter Woodthorpe — fresh from playing King Lear in his first year at Cambridge — to play Estragon in what was his first professional engagement. With *Waiting for Godot*, Woodthorpe quit Cambridge, never to complete his degree.[144]

The early notion of Estragon and Vladimir as circus clowns evolved, according to Daneman, during rehearsals into a relationship that was more human and more domestic, like the affectionate bickering of a long-married couple. The "Beckett pause" also took up its residency for more or less the first time on an English stage. Silences were lengthened to the point of embarrassment before being broken. Peter Bull bellowed the "big, brutal bully," Pozzo, while Timothy Bateson played his "white-faced gibbering slave," Lucky.[145]

Bull vividly described the response of the first-night audience at the Arts Theatre Club on August 3, 1955:

> Waves of hostility came whirling over the footlights, and the mass exodus, which was to form such a feature of the run of the piece, started quite soon after the curtain had risen. The audible groans were also fairly disconcerting. . . . The curtain fell to mild applause, we took a scant three calls and a depression and sense of anti-climax descended on us all.[146]

Bull also described his feelings of panic when he realized that the rope whose other end was fixed around Lucky's neck, was caught up his sleeve and that he was therefore in great danger of throttling Timothy Bateson. What he does not say is that he also jumped eight pages ahead in the script, then — realizing after a few pages what he had done — went back to repeat the same lines all over again. Nobody noticed. People in the audience laughed ironically at the line "I've been better entertained," groaned at "And it's not over,"[147] and yawned as one of the tramps yawned in boredom at the long wait for Mr. Godot. At the intermission about half the stunned first-night audience left the theater. (Later on in the run and on tour, spectators shouted out comments like "This is why we lost the colonies!" and "Give him some rope," when Estragon asks Vladimir if he hasn't got a bit of rope with which to hang themselves.)

Rehearsals had been tough and everyone was tense and depressed about how things were going. The next day, the actors and directors were further depressed by the almost unanimously adverse criticism of reviewers in the daily newspapers: THE LEFT BANK CAN KEEP IT was the headline of Cecil Wilson's review, which added for good measure "This is tedious."[148] For Milton Shulman, it was "another of those plays that tries to lift superficiality to significance through obscurity."[149] Indeed obscurity, pretentious allegory, and boredom were the main charges leveled at the play. The actors faced tiny, hostile houses for the rest of the week. Little in the play itself was commended; only the acting and directing were praised. By comparison with the successes in France and Germany, the English production seemed conspicuously to have failed and to be doomed not even to finish its scheduled run.

Everything changed on Sunday, August 7, 1955, with Kenneth Tynan's and Harold Hobson's reviews in *The Observer* and *The Sunday Times*. Beckett was always grateful to the two reviewers for their support.[150] "I care little for its enormous success in Europe over the past three years," wrote Tynan, "but much for the way in which it pricked and stimulated my own nervous system. It summoned the music-hall and the parable to present a view of life which banished the sentimentality of the music-hall and the parable's fulsome uplift."[151] "Go and see *Waiting for Godot*," wrote Hobson. "At the worst you will discover a curiosity, a four-leaved clover, a black tulip; at the best something that will securely lodge in a corner of your mind for as long as you live."[152]

These were stirring words, and transformed the play, more or less overnight, into the rage of London. As a private theater club, the Arts Theatre was allowed a Sunday performance; by lunchtime that Sunday, Daneman, telephoning to book seats for some friends, got through eventually to a frantically busy box office only to find that the performance was sold out.[153] Woodthorpe commented: "The whole atmosphere changed then. Cheers, bravos, and laughter. It changed from morning to evening."[154] Daneman remembered only that "the silence instead of being antagonistic was more respectful!"[155] A transfer to the Criterion Theatre became inevitable. Business boomed, although, to Albery's anger and disgust, Daneman had earlier accepted a part in the *Punch Revue* and so had to be replaced, first by Hugh Burden, then later by several other Vladimirs. Woodthorpe's pay went up to forty pounds a week with their appearance in the West End; Peter Bull was the highest-paid member of the troupe, at forty-five pounds.[156]

Meanwhile, as the play continued, then went on tour, discussion raged on through February and March 1956 in the august pages of *The Times Literary Supplement*. G. S. Fraser (anonymously) described the play as "a modern morality play on permanent Christian themes";[157] no, wrote Katharine Wilson, on the contrary, it was a perfect example of an Existentialist play; it is neither, wrote John Walsh. A month later, on Beckett's birthday, a piece called "Puzzling about Godot" reviewed the lively, extensive correspondence that the play had provoked and concluded that its meaning remained an open question.[158] As for Beckett, a few days after receiving copies of the London reviews, he sighed that he was "tired of the whole thing and the endless misunderstanding. Why people have to complicate a thing so simple I can't make out."[159]

In the autumn of 1955, gentle pressure was exerted on Beckett to get him to travel to London to see the production of *Godot* following its transfer to the Criterion Theatre. It was hoped that Peter Hall would be able to direct the Broadway production and that he might be able to benefit from Beckett's reactions to what had been done. By this point, Albery had reached an agreement with a New York producer, Michael Myerberg, for a production that involved the well-known American comedians Bert Lahr and Tom Ewell. Since it quickly became apparent that Peter Hall would not be free after all, Myerberg signed up an American director, Alan Schneider. It seemed sensible, therefore, for Schneider to go over to Europe to see the London production and meet Beckett in Paris to talk about the play.

Beckett immediately took to the effervescent, highly voluble, and keenly intelligent Schneider. And since he was beginning to feel much more in control than he had done earlier in the year — he had just spent a week away in Zurich in October with Giorgio Joyce, visiting "the father's haunts and ways and where they ended in the woods above the town"[160] — he succumbed to Schneider's redoubtable powers of persuasion and accompanied him to London to see the production.

Beckett had a hectic time in London. He stayed at the expensive Regent Palace Hotel in Piccadilly near the Criterion Theatre. He dined with John, his cousin on the Beckett side, enjoying a favorite dish of mackerel,[161] and, over the first weekend, went to stay with Sheila Page, his cousin on the Roe side, in Surrey. Although during the week he developed yet another mouth infection, this did not prevent him from going to the theater every night for five nights. Schneider recalled that one of his fondest memories was of

> Beckett's clutching my arm from time to time and, in a clearly-heard stage whisper, saying: "It's ahl wrahng! He's doing it ahl wrahng!" about a particular bit of stage business or the interpretation of a certain

line. . . . Every night after the performance, we would retire to a pub
to compare what we had seen and heard with what he had intended,
try to analyze why or how certain points were being lost.[162]

Beckett disapproved of the use of music in the production, hated the cluttered
stage set ("it must be like a Salvator Rosa landscape," Beckett wrote before he
had even set eyes on it[163]) and disliked the "Anglican fervour" that was displayed
at the end of the play. But these objections have tended to obscure the fact that
Beckett thought Peter Hall capable of doing a good production, since he was
quite prepared to let him direct the play again in New York, had kind words for
the acting, and found Peter Woodthorpe's playing of Estragon, with his natural
Yorkshire accent, superb.[164] The first time Woodthorpe met Beckett was after
the show in his dressing-room. "Bloody marvellous!" said Beckett as he walked
over to embrace the young actor.

There was, Beckett wrote, "a great party in the theatre for its 100th there,
buckets of champagne and a powerful crowd. They were all very nice to me in
London, critics and journalists included, they left me alone."[165] Peter Woodthorpe remembered asking him one day in a taxi what the play was really about:
"It's all symbiosis, Peter; it's symbiosis," answered Beckett.[166]

17

Impasse and Depression

1956–58

1

THROUGHOUT THE LENGTHY NEGOTIATIONS over *Waiting for Godot*, Beckett felt a growing sense of frustration at his inability to write anything new. Suzanne recognized the by now familiar symptoms of creative impasse; the first version of *Fin de partie* had not worked out and, even a year later, he was still complaining of being deep in the "wastes and wilds of self-translation,"[1] translating *Malone meurt* and *L'Innommable* into English for Barney Rosset and, by then, *Fin de partie* for the actor and director George Devine. One day, however, an opportunity offered itself in the morning post. A few months before Beckett's London trip with Schneider, a young Sadlers Wells–trained dancer, Deryk Mendel, performed a clown number in a Paris cabaret called the Fontaine des Quatre Saisons. Asked to contribute to the next program another item featuring the same character (whom he called Frollo, after the character in Victor Hugo's *Hunchback of Notre Dame* who looked after Quasimodo), Mendel wrote to a number of authors — Ionesco, Schéhadé, Audiberti, Adamov, and Beckett — to ask if they would write a short scenario for him.[2] On receipt of his letter, Beckett promptly dispatched Suzanne to the cabaret to see the dancer perform. Impressed by Mendel and aware of the importance to Beckett of producing something new, she encouraged him to try to write a mime piece for Mendel.

A few weeks later, Beckett sent the dancer a script entitled *Acte sans paroles* (*Act Without Words*). This mime grew out of his youthful interest in the silent screen comedies of Buster Keaton, Ben Turpin, and Harry Langdon. But it has a bitter theme: the inevitable frustration and disappointment of life. The single character is constantly taunted by the appearance of an elusive carafe of water, which he tries but fails to reach by piling up various sizes of cubes. The mime also reflects Beckett's readings in behavioral psychology as a young man in the 1930s, when he looked at Wolfgang Köhler's book *The Mentality of Apes*, about the colony of apes in Tenerife, where experiments were conducted in which the apes also placed cubes one on top of another in order to reach a banana.[3] Even though the man in Beckett's mime shows even more ingenuity than the apes, he never attains his objective, for the carafe of thirst-quenching water is pulled up into the flies and disappears whenever he is about to grasp it. In retrospect, *Act Without Words* can be seen to look forward to the way in which mime becomes an integral part of several of Beckett's major plays. The second version of *Fin de partie* in particular, which followed the mime within a matter of months, developed the mimic elements of the play.

The piece was thought unsuitable for a cabaret, since to work properly it needed the wings and, above all, the flies of a theater. So, with Beckett's approval, Mendel decided to wait for a suitable theatrical occasion. But since, as a dancer, he preferred to work with music, and because Beckett wanted to help his young musician cousin John Beckett, it was agreed that John should come over to Paris to work on some music with Mendel. The musician and the dancer rehearsed intensively together for a week in a large rehearsal studio off the boulevard de Clichy in Montmartre, fitting the music to the approximate timings of the mime's movements. John Beckett modestly described his own musical contribution: "I did a little prelude — it only lasted about twenty minutes in all — just a kind of rumpus going on, and then the music which was all based on this kind of kaleidoscopic variation of a small number of ideas [played on the piano], with the ring of the xylophone and the harsher side drum. It was all very brittle sounds."[4] They had hoped to perform the mime that autumn in a musical evening at the Royal Court Theatre. But, by the time it was almost ready, it was too late to incorporate into the program and it had to wait more than a year for its first performance.

2

JANUARY 3, 1956, WAS THE OPENING NIGHT of the American premiere of *Waiting for Godot,* directed by Alan Schneider, at the Coconut Grove Playhouse in Miami. It was a fiasco. A combination of tense, ill-tempered rehearsals, an unduly complex set, an unsuitable venue, and some foolish preproduction hype of the play as the "laugh hit of two continents" almost guaranteed that it would flop. The audience left in droves at the intermission. And although the producer, Michael Myerberg, held Alan Schneider's inexperience in dealing with the famous comedian Bert Lahr (who played Estragon) partially responsible for the play's failure, he admitted later that he himself had blundered:

> I went too far in my effort to give the play a base for popular acceptance. I accented the wrong things in trying to illuminate corners of the text I felt were left in shadow in the London production. For instance, I cast the play too close to type. In casting Bert Lahr and Tom Ewell I created the wrong impression about the play. Both actors were too well known in specific types of performance. The audience thought they were going to see Lahr and Ewell cut loose in a lot of capers. They expected a farcical comedy, which *Waiting for Godot,* of course, is not.[5]

Beckett learned of the unfavorable reception given to the play in Miami in a cable from Alan Schneider, closely followed by letters from Schneider and

Barney Rosset: "I think this was to be expected and is not to be taken too much to heart," was his immediate reply to Rosset.[6] Then he wrote most sympathetically to the director:

> Success and failure on the public level never mattered much to me, in fact I feel much more at home with the latter, having breathed deep of its vivifying air all my writing life up to the last couple of years. And I cannot help feeling that the success of Godot has been very largely the result of a misunderstanding or of various misunderstandings, and that perhaps you have succeeded better than any one else in stating its true nature. Even with Blin I never talked so unrestrainedly and uncautiously as with you, probably because it was not possible at that stage. When in London the question arose of a new production, I told Albery and Hall that if they did it my way they would empty the theatre. I am not suggesting that you were unduly influenced by all I said or that your production was not primarily your own and nobody else's, but it is probably our conversations confirmed you in your aversion to half-measures and frills, i.e. to precisely those things that 90% of theatre-goers want.[7]

Schneider, so upset by the failure that he claimed he "wanted to shoot [himself] and blow up the Coconut Grove," recounts in his memoirs, *Entrances*, how moved he was by such extraordinary generosity of spirit on the part of an author.[8]

Beckett's calmness and apparent lack of concern stemmed not only from his easy familiarity with failure, nor from his indifference to the opinions of what he described as "the Miami swells and their live models,"[9] but from a conviction that his play was, in some mysterious way, special and would eventually find its public in the United States, as it had already done in France, Germany, and England. For a little later he wrote:

> There is something queer about the play, I don't exactly know what, that worms its way into people whether they like it or not. Even in Miami both audience and business have improved since the opening. And it is this that makes me feel that even now a Broadway production is not necessarily a mistake. In fact I think the man [Michael Myerberg] should have gone on with his original Boston-Washington-Philadelphia programme and that he would not have regretted it. But I am always wrong except, sometimes, where to be wrong is to be right.[10]

After some initial wavering, Myerberg decided to close the show in Miami, canceling both the planned tour and the intended New York opening. It was widely thought that the Miami failure worried him so much that he canceled the play because of the financial consequences, although, according to Rosset, Myerberg claimed it was "because the cast faded away. Pozzo got sick, Lucky was not able to go on at all, even at the first performance, and Ewell . . . was hysterical and impossible to control."[11]

There were then three months of total uncertainty as to whether the producer intended to honor the contract with Donald Albery for a Broadway production. Beckett could not avoid becoming, marginally at least, embroiled in some of the resulting machinations. For, afraid that Myerberg would fail to obtain a Broadway theater or, if he did, would simply turn the play into a vehicle for Bert Lahr to star in, both Rosset and Schneider pressed Beckett to intervene and secure Myerberg's agreement to an "off-Broadway" production. Their favored venue was the Théâtre-de-Lys, where the producer-directors Carmen Capalbo and Stanley Chase were keen to mount *Waiting for Godot* and where Brecht's and Kurt Weill's *The Threepenny Opera* had just played with outstanding success.

Beckett went so far as to inquire what the precise contractual position was in the United States, Albery confirming that Myerberg had every right to put on a Broadway production.[12] But Beckett became seriously concerned only when a rumor reached him that Myerberg was considering having changes made to his English translation. He promptly wrote to Albery to ensure that this did not happen. But he quickly tired of all the bickering, writing sharply at one point: "In presenting the play on Broadway, as he now seems resolved to do, Myerberg is simply carrying out his contract. You [Barney Rosset] and Alan Schneider say he is making a mistake. You may be right. On the other hand the event may prove him right. In any case what can we do about it? Nothing."[13]

In the end, Myerberg managed to set up a new production with Herbert Berghof as director and a new cast, with the exception of Bert Lahr. Recognizing his previous mistake, he adopted a totally different approach to the publicity, ironically advertising this time for "seventy thousand intellectuals" to make the venture pay. Berghof knew the play extremely well, having already directed it in an actors' studio production, in which he had played Estragon. He asked for a simple set, not stylized or complex as it had been in Miami. And his determination not to intellectualize the play (at least not with the actors) and his acceptance of comedy as an important though not an overriding element established a rapport with Bert Lahr that Alan Schneider had never managed to achieve. Berghof worked particularly hard at rebuilding Lahr's shattered confidence. But other actors have explained that he also succeeded in making the rehearsals into exciting journeys of discovery.[14]

The Broadway production opened in April at the John Golden Theatre and was a great success. Berghof was lavishly praised for his direction, and this time Bert Lahr triumphed as Estragon ("Without him, the Broadway production of Mr. Beckett's play would be admirable; with him, it is transfigured," wrote Kenneth Tynan in *Curtains*),[15] although Alan Schneider never accepted that Lahr had played any differently in New York than he had in Miami. Perhaps it was simply that the chemistry of the new cast worked better and that the expectations of the audience were now radically different.

Although, on the basis of some of the early reports and reviews, Beckett initially thought that Berghof's production sounded "very wrong and dreadful," [16] he gave a better balanced view after listening to the Columbia recording of the New York production:

> I find it quite good, as a record, especially Act I when Pozzo [played by Kurt Kasznar] is remarkable. The sound element (finger on c[h]ords of grand piano blown up through micro) is hardly disturbing, except perhaps at end of 1st act. Some changes and interpolations annoyed me mildly, especially at beginning of Act II. I thought Vladimir very wooden and did not at all agree with [Alvin] Epstein's remarkable technical performance in the tirade. The boy I thought very good. [17]

Beckett says nothing in praise of Bert Lahr. But he does not criticize him either. We should remember that he was writing here to Barney Rosset who, like Schneider, was hostile to what they saw as Lahr's tendency to play top banana. Although Alan Schneider said that Beckett always made him feel that what he had tried to accomplish in Miami was closer to what he had wanted, with characteristic politeness and an inherent sense of fair play, Beckett was not critical of Berghof's production.

The Broadway production ran for over a hundred performances and brought in five hundred dollars a week as Beckett's personal share of the box office. At the same time, according to Myerberg, it added substantially to that income by helping Grove Press sell almost three thousand copies of the cheap paperback at the theater alone. Suddenly, Beckett was making a fortune compared to anything he had earned before. The dollar checks were particularly welcome, because of the demands that he was making on his pocket by his own generosity, as well as by the increased expense of his new, if modest, house in the Marne valley. The money made everyday life much easier and guaranteed that the days of financial hardship were at last over. But neither he nor Suzanne lived very differently after this change in their circumstances. And money made almost no difference to Beckett's state of mind, which remained frustrated and depressed when he was not writing.

3

IN APRIL 1956, two visitors brought back painful, as well as poignant memories. His brother's daughter, Caroline, came over to Paris with "one of the Nursery Watson girls," [18] and throughout the week he and Suzanne devoted most of their time to finding things to interest the two eighteen-year-olds. They showed them the main tourist sights and took them out for meals; Suzanne took them shopping; and all four of them went to hear Suzanne's friend the concert pianist Monique Haas, play — disappointingly, in Beckett's opinion — Schumann's piano concerto. They also heard Pierre Dervaux conduct Henri Dutilleux's First Symphony. The "girls," as Beckett called them, were thrilled to accompany their uncle and Suzanne backstage to meet Monique Haas, whom they met in her dressing-room with her husband, the composer Marcel Mihalovici. They also got Dutilleux's autograph in the restaurant Chez Francis afterward. Often thinking about his late brother during the week, Beckett scanned Caroline's face "surreptitiously for traces of Frank, but in vain."[19] Neither he nor Suzanne had ever wanted children. Yet, although the sadness of his brother's death was constantly present, he enjoyed this renewed contact with his family and found the company of the girls briefly exhilarating if exhausting. It gave him a little of the feeling of having a grown-up family.

The visit to Paris of his old friend Nancy Cunard, who, after a break of more than twenty years, had written to tell him how much she had enjoyed the London production of *Waiting for Godot*, also took him back in time. She invited him to lunch with her on her way to her home in La Mothe Fénelon. Beckett felt an enormous debt of gratitude to Nancy as the first person to recognize his talent as a writer when she had published "Whoroscope." He had not forgotten, either, her kindness and generosity to him in 1930, when he was virtually penniless.

They chatted animatedly about mutual friends from the old days: Richard Aldington and Walter Lowenfels, for example, with whom Nancy had kept in touch. She talked of her recently completed book on George Moore and her current research into African ivories, to which Beckett, anxious to repay her generosity, offered to subscribe.[20] He asked her to send him a copy of her early poem "Parallax," which he remembered liking and wanted to read again. And he promised to sign some copies of "Whoroscope" that she said she could sell at a pound apiece.[21] Finally, with boyish enthusiasm, he spoke of his hope that a producer in America might stage *Waiting for Godot* with an all-black cast, a wish that he knew Nancy would be sure to share.

Meeting each other after so many years was a fascinating, but disquieting, experience. Nancy wrote to Solita Solano later that Beckett "looks like a magnificent Mexican sculpture now."[22] And, at sixty, her own skeletally thin body had lost its nymphlike charm; Beckett found her looking "very wraithy."[23] It was hard to connect the frail figure and lined face of the aging lady sitting opposite him at dinner to the sexually active, vibrant young woman who had whirled him around the Parisian nightspots with her black musician lover, Henry Crowder, in 1930. That, indeed, was another and a distant world.

These visits and those of good friends like Tom MacGreevy or other members of his family like Morris (and, by now, his wife, Mimi) Sinclair were a welcome break from the growing pressures of his life as a successful writer. Particularly in the wake of *Waiting for Godot*, he was interrupted more and more frequently by meetings in Paris that offered him less pleasure and made him tired and strained. During the summer he wrote: "We spend all the time we can in the country, but I have always to be dodging up to Paris to see this one or that one. Fortunately there is a good train up early in the morning and one back late in the evening, giving one a full day in Paris. But," he added plaintively, "there is not much peace anymore."[24]

Suzanne disliked his frequent absences. Yet she rarely accompanied him into Paris, since few of his visitors were ones with whom she felt at home, partly because so many of them inevitably excluded her from the conversation by speaking English. Many also belonged to Beckett's past life in Ireland. On days when she stayed behind in the country, the little cottage soon began to seem isolated; her future hostility to staying in Ussy at all was born during those lonely days. On his return from Paris Beckett complained, doubtless to her irritation, of how little time these trips to town left him for work. Yet rarely would he decline to go in to see his visitors, some of whom Suzanne felt he had no need to put himself out to meet at all. And, when he was in Ussy, he bewailed his failure to work on his new play and his inability to face translating *L'Innommable*, which Barney Rosset was waiting to publish. In March he wrote to Rosset: "I have not looked at the new play for some weeks now nor, I confess, pursued struggle with L'Inno. [the translation of *L'Innommable*]. But have dug fifty-six large holes in my "garden" for reception of various plantations, including 39 arbores vitae and a blue cypress." [25] What he called "pottering inertia" [26] was dangerously near setting in as he surveyed his "moribund plantations and [tried] to solve chess problems." [27] At such times of impasse, he was irritable and fractious, sometimes even insufferable.

His creative stagnation was relieved a little when, on a visit to Paris, Barney Rosset gave him what Beckett described as "a very handsome electrophone gramophone, with a pile of microgrooves." [28] When Suzanne was in Paris, she bought more records and took them back to Ussy, where they listened with intense pleasure to Schubert's *Winterreise* sung by Dietrich Fischer-Dieskau. Suzanne was, Beckett wrote, "crazy about *Iche grolle nicht* ["I Shall Not Chide You"] and *Iche habe im Traum geweint* ["I Wept in My Dream"]" in Schumann's *Dichterliebe*, settings of Heine's poems. [29] They were at their closest while they were sharing such moments of musical pleasure.

At this time also, more as therapy than out of boredom, Beckett set himself to read all of Racine's plays again, twenty-five years after he had lectured on them to students at Trinity College. He came to the conclusion that he approached *Andromaque* with far more understanding now than he had ever done before, "at least more understanding of the chances of the theatre today." [30] His readings of *Andromaque*, *Phèdre*, and *Bérénice* may have focused his mind on the theatrical possibilities of monologue and of what could be done with virtually immobile characters inhabiting a closed world in which little or nothing changes. [31] (*Bérénice* was, he thought, a wonderful example of just such a play.) This daily diet of Racinian claustrophobia forced Beckett to concentrate on the true essentials of theater: time, space, and speech. It pointed him in the direction that made a tightly focused, monologic play like *Happy Days* or *Play* possible. And eventually it was to lead him to write the short monologues of the 1970s.

Suzanne knew Beckett well enough to recognize that, for all his moaning and groaning, he would eventually return to what he regarded as "real work" at his desk. And, to her immense relief, he was soon working away feverishly at his new, so far untitled play, which he had begun the previous year. He finished a revised two-act version as early as the third week of February 1956, but, soon after his fiftieth birthday in April, he still maintained that the play was "crumbling to bits with the rest of my skull lumber."[32] At the beginning of May, he said that he hoped to be able to complete it in time for it to be put on with the mime at the Marseilles Festival of the Avant-Garde in August. On May 11, he wrote to Nancy Cunard that he had "taken on a big job which will keep me quiet and groaning for the next couple of months."[33] Most of the next few weeks were spent in remolding the entire play, changing it most radically from two acts to one but also working to shape it into an intricate musical patterning of themes and variations. The bulk of the work seems to have been done in May for, by the sixth of June, he could write to Nancy Cunard: "Have just succeeded in grinding out of my gritty old maw 'per lungo silenzio . . . fioco' [faint through long silence] the one-act howl for Marseille and am not a pretty sight as a result."[34] The play had given him more difficulty than anything he had written before.

In the end, either the organizers of the Marseilles Festival completed their arrangements too late or, from the festival's point of view, the play was finished too late to allow for what both Blin and Beckett regarded as adequate rehearsal time. At the beginning of July Beckett wrote to a new admirer of his work, Mary Hutchinson, a friend of Matisse and Georges Duthuit:

> In the programme of the Marseille festival, August 4th–August 14th, both mime and play are announced for performance. But it seems now very probable that we shall withdraw the play at least, and possibly the mime also, in view of our failure so far to obtain from the organisers either contracts or definite information about theatre, equipment and so on. The whole thing is hopelessly vague and it seems to me quite impossible to prepare the play properly in the time that remains, even if we got going on it under proper conditions tomorrow.[35]

The play was withdrawn and the search began for a theater in Paris in which the "new show," referred to at that time by Beckett simply as "HAAM," could be performed. It was not easy.[36] Beckett wrote to MacGreevy:

> Theatre directors expect you to arrive with your text under one arm and millions of franc notes under the other and this now seems to be established practice. With Godot after all we had a state grant of 750,000, and now nothing but a gloomy graceless act, a complicated mime and nos beaux yeux [our handsome eyes]. However, my publisher's energy and faith will I have no doubt do the trick in the end.[37]

Once again, it was to be a long wait. Meanwhile he was to be diverted into a new and creatively exciting direction.

4

BECKETT WROTE HIS FIRST PLAY for radio, *All That Fall*, during the summer of 1956 at the invitation of the BBC. His reputation was already known to the radio drama department through both the French and English productions of *Waiting for Godot*, for several members of the drama team (notably Barbara Bray, Donald McWhinnie, and Martin Esslin) kept in very close touch with developments in European theater. There had been animated discussions as early as 1953 as to whether the BBC should broadcast *Waiting for Godot*. Eventually, the idea had been rejected.[38] But the controller of the Third Programme, John Morris, was eager to broadcast something by Beckett, eager enough to follow up the approaches made in June on his behalf by the BBC representative in Paris, Cecilia Reeves,[39] and go over himself in mid-July to lunch with Beckett to discuss their proposal.[40] "I got the impression," wrote Morris after seeing Beckett, "that he has a very sound idea of the problems of writing for radio and that we can expect something pretty good."[41]

The BBC invitation prompted Beckett to think for the first time about the technique required for a medium of which sound and silence are the sole components. And it was probably through thinking about sound in general, as distinct from voice in particular, that he had the idea for a play in which sound effects would play a vital role. "Never thought about Radio play technique," he wrote to Nancy Cunard, "but in the dead of t'other night got a nice gruesome idea full of cartwheels and dragging feet and puffing and panting which may or may not lead to something."[42] As a letter to Aidan Higgins written the next day shows, he already thought of situating the play in his own bit of Ireland: "Have been asked to write a radio play for the 3rd [the BBC Third Programme] and am tempted, feet dragging and breath short and cartwheels and imprecations from the Brighton Rd to Foxrock station and back, insentient old mares in foal being welted by the cottagers and the Devil tottered in the ditch — boyhood memories."[43]

Boghill railway station, to which Mrs. Rooney tramps breathlessly to meet her husband, Dan, arriving on the city train, stands close to a racecourse, as Foxrock station did to Leopardstown ("the hills, the plain, the racecourse with its miles and miles of white rails and three red stands, the pretty little wayside station").[44] On her way, Mrs. Rooney encounters several villagers: Christy, his cart piled high with sty dung; Mr. Tyler, a retired bill-broker, on his bicycle; Mr. Slocum, the clerk of the local racecourse, in his limousine with its "new balloon tyres";[45] and, at the station itself, the stationmaster, Mr. Barrell, with his boy assistant, Tommy, and Miss Fitt, an ostentatiously devout member of the local Church of Ireland.

The names that Beckett uses are those of local people, sometimes slightly changed. The Becketts had a gardener called Christy; Beckett used to buy apples on his way home from school from a local market gardener named Tyler;

Foxrock's stationmaster, Mr. Joseph Farrell, was neatly transformed into Mr. Barrell; even the unusual name, Miss Fitt—which is chosen, as was Miss Carridge in *Murphy*, for its delightful pun—may have been a distant memory of a boy called E. G. Fitt with whom Beckett played cricket at Portora in 1923 or of a Rathgar lady resident[46]; and Slocum—another pun—was the maiden name of John Beckett's future wife, Vera, as well as that of James Joyce's bibliographer. If the main character, Mrs. Rooney (a common enough Irish name), owes her spirit to Beckett's formidable kindergarten teacher, Ida "Jack" Elsner, her fictional maiden name was Dunne, who was the local butcher on the Bray Road.[47] The play is partly brought to life by picturesque features of everyday life in Foxrock village. A horse and cart driven by one of the "cottagers"—non–property owners who lived in the Orchard Cottages close to the station—seeking to sell a load of dung from his pigsties for the gardens was a familiar sight there; Mr. Rooney thinks that he might "send Tommy for the cab,"[48] which in reality was kept near the station at Tracey's Garage; "Connolly's van," which raises a cloud of dust as it drives past, came from Connolly's Stores in nearby Cornelscourt village. And Mr. and Mrs. Rooney talk in the play about a preacher called Hardy who was, in reality, the Reverend E. Hardy, a near neighbor at Uplands on Kerrymount Avenue when Beckett was a child.[49]

These local details do more than supply local color. Evocative in themselves, they also fit dexterously into a complex kaleidoscope of images of sterility, decline and fall, suffering and death. Christy's cart is pulled, not by a mare as in the first manuscript, but by a hinny, the sterile offspring of a she-ass and a stallion. This allows Beckett to make a parallel with Christ riding into Jerusalem on a sterile beast of burden. Everything in the play is in decline or decay: Mr. Slocum's car engine, which "all morning went like a dream," dies away and refuses to start; bicycle tires go flat; rotting leaves pile up in the ditch; and even "the lovely laburnum," which Mrs. Rooney finds so moving, loses its tassels before the play is over. What had promised to be a "divine day for the meeting" is soon "shrouding, shrouding, the best of it is past." Everyone's relatives are in pain, and the different generations are united in a common lot of misfortune and sorrow: "your poor wife," "my poor blind Dan," "poor Pappy," "poor Maddy." All the characters contribute to the central theme of collapse, decline, dissolution, and death.[50]

But *All That Fall* is also full of echoes of Beckett's early Protestant upbringing and abandoned faith.[51] There are numerous allusions to the Bible and to well-known Protestant hymns: to the sparrows, in comparison with which men are said to be of more worth, and to the blind leading the blind—until both fall into the ditch. Mr. Rooney's "I dream of other roads, in other lands. Of another home, another—*(he hesitates)*—another home," and Mrs. Rooney's "never pause, till we come safe to haven"[52] are grounded in a Protestant outlook and terminology that recalls Charles Wesley's use of the word "home" and "haven" in his hymns.[53] The Christian hope of a Paradise where all will at last be well is echoed in a vague, nostalgic yearning for something essentially different from the painful, purposeless maelstrom of a purgatorial "here and now."

Invariably, the names of God and Christ are invoked in the radio play in a context of pain, frustration, or profound dissatisfaction. "Sigh out a something something tale of things, Done long ago and ill done," says Mrs. Rooney bitterly, applying Meleander's words from John Ford's *The Lovers Melancholy* to a sadly botched creation. Most explicitly, it is Mr. Tyler who announces that he is "merely cursing, under my breath, God and man, under my breath, and the wet Saturday afternoon of my conception."[54]

In spite of the apparent comic texture of the play, human misery and suffering emerge as so overwhelming that, when Psalm 145, verse 14 is quoted — "The Lord upholdeth all that fall, and raiseth up all those that be bowed down" — it is greeted by the lame, seventy-year-old Maddy Rooney and her blind husband, Dan, with wild laughter at its bitter irony.[55] At the end of the play, we are left with the clear possibility that Dan Rooney may have been responsible for the death of a child on the railway line. But, in the words of the critic Richard Coe, Mr. Rooney "did not invent death, nor did he first create in order to kill, nor did he prolong the suffering for his own pleasure, nor, finally, did he kill without a reason, as God does."[56]

The radio play clearly evolved out of Beckett's profound agnosticism. Yet an agnostic who attacks a God who does not exist for being cruel and unjust is practicing a particularly empty kind of rhetoric. The roots of Beckett's religious upbringing were very tenacious. But a much more personal turmoil probably accounts for the bitter tone of the attack in *All That Fall*. It was only two years since Beckett's brother, a firm believer and a faithful upholder of the Christian faith, had died in great suffering. Sam had been with Frank throughout his last months, had seen how little help his faith appeared to offer him at the end, and had felt acutely his own helplessness and distress. It is scarcely surprising, then, if when he returned to write in English and set the radio play in Foxrock, the bitterness and resentment that had built up inside him at the unjustified suffering of his brother should have found expression in a play that, for all its apparent dissimilarity, is the comic counterpart of *Fin de partie*.

Writing *All That Fall* detained Beckett in areas of recent experience too painful for his own good. In the last week of August 1956, he wrote to Barney Rosset that he was "in a whirl of depression at the moment,"[57] and a week later that he was "still deep in drain."[58] Early in September, most unusually, he canceled all his appointments in Paris for a week simply because he felt wholly incapable of facing people. Instead, satisfied at having created so much vitality and wit out of the pain and the silence, he completed the script of *All That Fall* and sent it to the BBC on September 27.[59]

5

BECKETT'S DEPRESSION was very slow to lift, as he began to experience renewed doubt about whether there was any way out of the impasse into which *The Unnamable* and *Fin de partie* had led him. The medium of radio, with the challenge of its technical constraints, offered one possible escape route. Indeed, Donald McWhinnie wrote: "My impression is that if he is to write at all in the near future it will be for radio, which has captured his imagination."⁶⁰ But McWhinnie was only partly right. For radio did not really solve the problem of where Beckett could go next in his prose and drama. Increasingly, he felt that he needed to see his last play staged as a possible way of discovering whether he could see any more permanent way forward: "I am panting to see the realisation," he wrote to Alan Schneider in mid-October, "and know if I am on some kind of road, and can stumble on, or in a swamp."⁶¹

So preliminary rehearsals of *Fin de partie* began with Roger Blin and Jean Martin. Since they had not yet secured a theater, they used to meet at Blin's flat in the rue Saint-Honoré near the Palais-Royal. Although it lay several kilometers from the rue des Favorites, Beckett preferred to walk there, trekking down to the river to cross the Pont Solférino so that he could go through the beautiful Jardin des Tuileries. Later, in November, they started to rehearse in the bar of the Théâtre de l'Oeuvre with whose director, Lucien Beer, they believed an agreement had been struck to put on the play and the mime in mid-January.

Beckett and Suzanne left Paris to spend their usual quiet Christmas holiday at Ussy. Neither of them really celebrated Christmas, however, and Beckett took a typically gloomy view of the prospects for the coming year: a "new turn of the old screw," as he often put it.⁶² He was anxious to see how the young trees that he had planted over the past three years were standing up to the winter cold. On their arrival, they made a tour of inspection of the prunus, the negundo (a kind of North American ash), the blue cypress, the arborvitae, and his most recent planting, a Lebanese cedar.⁶³ This interest even crept into a little play that he wrote in English in Ussy, dated "December 56" and called "The Gloaming."⁶⁴ One of the two players inquires of the other: "How are the trees doing?" The second replies: "It is difficult to say. We are in winter, you know. They are all black and bare, the evergreens included. One would have to cut into them with a knife. . . . Check trees for sap."⁶⁵ This piece of idiosyncratic, out-of-season gardening dialogue was severely pruned to become two laconic lines in the drastically rewritten, published text: "How are the trees doing?" / "Hard to say. It's winter, you know."⁶⁶ But Beckett was unhappy with the play, abandoned it unfinished, and, in this version at least, never released it.⁶⁷ It was probably thematically too close to *Fin de partie* and may well have seemed too personal and sentimental as well, the piece grinding to a halt with these lines: "Bring me back to the hot summer evening out in the Bay with my father in the little rowboat, fishing for mackerel with a spinner. To the time when it was still time. 'Do you remember what they look like?' 'Yes, father, all blue and silver.' "⁶⁸ The passage came, Beckett confided to me, from a vivid, personal memory of going as a child on a rare fishing trip with his father in a rowboat out in Dublin Bay. They had gone, he said, "fishing for mackerel with a spinner," using exactly the same phrase that he had used over thirty years before in his rejected play fragment.⁶⁹

While in Ussy, he learned that the premiere of *Fin de partie* with *Acte sans paroles*, due, or so he thought, to go on at the Théâtre de l'Oeuvre, had been postponed until the end of February.[70] He breathed a great sigh of relief, for this eased some of the immediate pressure that he was feeling. And he positively glowed with pleasure when he received news that the American all-black production of *Waiting for Godot* had at last materialized, beginning its life in Boston before moving on to Broadway. Pozzo, he learned, was played by Rex Ingram, the star of the film *The Green Pastures*, who weighed in at two hundred and sixty-five pounds, while two of the actors measured six feet three inches and six feet four and a half inches tall respectively. Lucky towered above them both at six feet eleven inches.[71] Barney Rosset reported: "The Boston production went off very well. To me the new Vladimir is incomparable — better than Marshall, and this greatly changes the whole play. The new Lucky [Earle Hyman] is absolutely different from the other one and the descriptions of the Boston critics, wherein they say he is 'astounding,' is about the best adjective available."[72] But only a little later Beckett was saddened to learn that this production with its "black giants"[73] had run for only five performances on Broadway before being taken off, a commercial though not an artistic disaster.[74]

6

BECKETT RETURNED TO PARIS to continue rehearsing *Fin de partie*. On January 13, 1957, he had the thrill of listening to the BBC Third Programme broadcast of his first play for radio. Exasperatingly, reception on his little radio was extremely poor and he could not catch everything. But he was able to form a good enough impression of the work for him to write the following appreciation to Donald McWhinnie, the producer:

> Bien travaillé [Good work]. Though the reception on Sunday was very poor I heard well enough to realize what a good job. I did not agree with it all, who ever does, and perhaps I should have if I had lost less of the detail. Things I liked particularly: the double walk sound in the second half, Dan's YES and their wild laugh (marvellous). O'Farrell [Mrs. Rooney] and Devlin [Mr. Rooney] I thought excellent most of the time, the latter a little perfunctory in parts (his long speeches), but this perhaps due to distortion. Miss Fitt [Sheila Ward] very good indeed. I didn't think the animals were right.[75]

The radio play was very warmly received and was chosen to be one of two BBC entries for the "Literary and Dramatic" category of the Prix Italia.[76]

Meanwhile, however, things were going sadly awry with the production of *Fin de partie*. After only four days of further rehearsal, Blin, Martin, and Beckett were devastated by the news that Lucien Beer was pulling out of his agreement with them, in favor, according to Blin, of a financially more attractive proposition from Robert Hossein.[77] Although detailed arrangements had been completed and John Beckett had made plans to come over to Paris to finish the music for the mime that was at last to accompany the play,[78] no formal, legally enforceable contract with an agreed production date had ever been signed. So, once again, they were left without a theater. Everyone was bitter and resentful and there was talk of bringing legal action against the director, a move with which Beckett wanted nothing to do.[79] Beer took a very different view, maintaining that he had merely deferred the production rather than canceled it and still had a financial stake in the play's future.

Meanwhile, George Devine, the director of the English Stage Company in London, had been in touch with Beckett to ask him if they could present *Acte sans paroles* with Ionesco's play *Les Chaises (The Chairs)* at the Royal Court Theatre. He had also asked if the company could be assigned the rights to produce Beckett's English translation of *Fin de partie* when it was finished. Devine had earlier considered putting the play on in French, and when he learned of the problems that Beckett and Blin were experiencing with the Théâtre de l'Oeuvre, he rushed over to Paris to see them. He wanted the French production to be put on at the Royal Court Theatre as part of a cultural and gastronomic event: a "French Fortnight" in London, organized by the Union Française des Industries Exportatrices.[80]

This explains how the world premiere of Beckett's second play in French came to be produced not in Paris, but in London at the Royal Court Theatre on April 3, 1957. The first-night gala performance was performed in front of the French ambassador, M. Chauvel, and his wife; Lord and Lady Harewood; Lord Bessborough; and fashionable first-nighters who turned up in their Daimlers and their Bentleys. This also explains why, among Roger Blin's papers, there is a brief, enigmatic telegram from Beckett in London to Blin, who was then on a flying visit to Paris, that reads "Palais décommandé,"[81] meaning that "Royalty" had decided (or been advised) not to attend the planned gala. Before Christmas, rehearsals had been with Roger Blin and Jean Martin alone, for Blin was having difficulty in finding two actors willing to play the couple confined to bins. Several old actors had said to Blin, plaintively, "The text is fine and I'd be happy to work with you. But this may well be my last appearance in Paris and for my last appearance to be in a dustbin—well, thank you, but no thank you."[82] Eventually, he found the excellent Georges Adet, who played Nagg in both the London and the Paris productions, and Christine Tsingos, his former associate at the Gaîté-Montparnasse, who was prepared to play the old woman, Nell, in London, but refused to appear in Paris in a role of such advanced senility.

Adet was quite old and played the role without his upper and lower dentures. He used to rehearse with his teeth in; then, once he was installed in the bin for the performance, take his dentures out and place them in a handkerchief. With the dentures removed, his face sank dramatically inward and his lower lip curled up in senile fashion into his mouth. Spectators often used to ask him afterward with admiration and amazement how he ever managed to achieve this remarkable effect, since for the curtain call he would resurface with his teeth back in place, deliberately flashing a big, toothy smile during the applause. Sneaking a sly wink at Blin or Martin, he never offered an explanation. (This is probably why he was so cross when, for the 1968 revival at the Théâtre 347, Blin lowered the safety curtain at the end of the play, insisting that the actors should not take a curtain call.[83])

Beckett came over to London for a fortnight to rehearse with the company. He stayed at first with Blin and Martin in a boardinghouse on Ebury Street convenient to the theater, but, growing tired of constantly having to feed sixpences into a gas meter in order to heat his room and becoming nervous and tense because he hardly ever found himself alone, he moved after three days into the nearby Royal Court Hotel.[84]

This was almost the first time that the actors had been able to rehearse on a proper stage (for until then they had only had a few afternoons on the Théâtre de l'Oeuvre stage among the furniture of the set for Fernand Crommelynck's *Chaud et froid*) and Blin and the cast appreciated the good technical facilities of the theater. George Devine, a great Francophile[85] and a fervent admirer of Beckett's work, was especially helpful and welcoming. On a couple of days, Beckett played the part of Hamm to allow Blin, who was directing as well as acting, to concentrate on Jean Martin's role as Clov. At other times he intervened far more actively than he had ever done at rehearsals of *En attendant Godot*. He cut several sections of the text,[86] and Blin himself suggested other changes. But there was far more disagreement between the writer and his director than there had ever been with *Godot*. For, by this stage, Beckett felt more confident of his own knowledge of the theater and was determined that his new play, which he rated more highly than *Godot*, should be played with the minimum of compromise and according to principles of which he approved. Sometimes exchanges between Blin and Martin and Beckett became overheated, although relations between the three men were good enough to prevent an out-and-out row from developing.

Before he had left Paris for London, Beckett had heard from Tom MacGreevy in Dublin that their mutual friend Jack B. Yeats was seriously ill and likely to die any day. In sending MacGreevy his address at the Royal Court Hotel, Beckett assured him that he would do his utmost to get over to Ireland, "if the end came."[87] Less than a week later, a morning phone call from Dublin confirmed the sad news that Yeats had died in the Portobello Nursing Home on March 28. The following day, Beckett sent MacGreevy a telegram: "Great sorrow Impossible attend Please arrange flowers Writing Sam."[88] On his return to Paris, he wrote to MacGreevy:

> I made a serious effort to get to Dublin for the funeral. Finally I had to accept that it was impossible. No seat on the Aer Lingus flight on the Friday afternoon. I should have had to travel by train and boat, which would have got me in in time. But I could get no assurance of a seat on the flight Dublin–London Saturday afternoon. I was very upset that I had to renounce, as I had always promised to myself I wd. go to Dublin again on that occasion.[89]

In the few quiet moments he had in London, Beckett often thought of his many visits to Jack Yeats's studio to see his magnificent paintings, of their companionable walks around Dublin, and of the tremendous inspiration that Yeats had been to him.

John Osborne's *The Entertainer* was being rehearsed at the Royal Court at the same time as *Fin de partie* and the French troupe bumped into Osborne, Laurence Olivier, Brenda de Banzie, and Dorothy Tutin from time to time in the theater or in restaurants or pubs around Sloane Square.[90] There were parties at Oscar Lewenstein's and two or three dinners at George Devine's house at Lower Mall in Hammersmith.[91] John Osborne could recall a dinner party when he sat listening to Devine and the designer Jocelyn Herbert chatting animatedly in French with Beckett and the French actors.[92] Beckett found himself meeting dozens of new people in London, including Sean O'Casey's seventeen-year-old daughter, Siobhan: "of a most moving beauty."[93] Many friends and members of the Beckett family also came from Dublin; his cousin Sheila Page and her husband, Donald, came up to London to see him. Among the numerous visitors due from Paris were Jérôme Lindon and his wife, Annette. This intensive round of rehearsals and social events was exhilarating but exhausting.

On the play's first night, Beckett was nowhere to be seen. It had been put out that he had left London a few days earlier. But he was characteristically lying low to avoid contact with the press.[94] In fact, he left on the afternoon of the gala premiere, meeting Con Leventhal and Ethna MacCarthy, who had just flown in for the show from Dublin, at Heathrow Airport. At Beckett's request, Con and Ethna waited with him until Suzanne arrived by plane from Paris. Leventhal and his wife then escorted her into central London to attend the first night, leaving Beckett to take the return flight home.[95] It seems a curious way for a couple to behave, but they had devised this strategy in order to protect Beckett's privacy, removing him from the first-night mêlée, while still allowing him to receive a report by telephone from Suzanne on how the performance had been received.

The presence of thirteen French theater critics in addition to the usual English ones made the first night into a tense affair. The evening began unusually for so solemn an occasion. Since theater performances in Britain at the time were always preceded by the national anthem, John Beckett had written some music based on "God Save the Queen" and the "Marseillaise" for piano, violin, bassoon, and clarinet. The music sounded like neither one nor the other and provoked some ill-contained mirth, even before *Fin de partie* began.

The actors were on edge, not only because they were playing in front of an English audience who might not follow the French too well, but also because so many friends, as well as the critics, had come over for the production from Paris. As a result, they felt that they did not succeed in finding the proper rhythm for the dialogue on the first couple of nights in London, although things improved considerably toward the end of the week.

During the brief run in London, Maurice Jacquemont, the director of a little Parisian theater called the Studio des Champs-Elysées, came over. Encouraged by the publicity that surrounded the London opening, as well as by what he saw, he felt that the play and mime would go extremely well in his own theater. He therefore agreed with Blin and Beckett that *Fin de partie* should open at the Studio on their return to Paris. Contracts were prepared for signature.[96] Since Lucien Beer had also been renewing his proposals to reinstate the production at his own theater, he was furious[97] when he heard that an agreement had indeed been concluded with Jacquemont and went on the offensive. He sought legal redress, then settled for arbitration on his own claims to produce the play.[98] As a result, two percent of the box-office takings on the first hundred performances at the Studio des Champs-Elysées had to be taken out of Beckett's own royalties and paid over to Beer.[99]

With the actors back in Paris, rehearsals of *Fin de partie* resumed, now at the Studio des Champs-Elysées. Since Christine Tsingos would not play the role in Paris, Germaine de France, the widow of the dramatist Lucien Nepoty, played Nell. This actress had played countless young leading ladies in plays of the "poetic boulevard" in the 1920s; although she was nearly seventy, she still had a pretty, girlish face with huge, childlike eyes that created an extraordinary effect as she emerged above the rim of her bin. She had a wonderful, old-style charm and was perfect for the part.

Beckett again attended rehearsals regularly. "Fin de partie at the Royal Court was rather an aberration," he wrote to Mary Manning, "but we are beginning now in the little Studio des Champs-Elysées, with better prospects. Playing before people who don't know the language has not much sense."[100] He believed that the play gained immeasurably from the smallness and the intimacy of the studio and thought that Blin had made enormous progress since London and now gave "a quite extraordinary performance."[101] He was always hypercritical, however, and, by the end of June, claimed that "the play [has] rattled very loose and wild"[102] and hoped that, after the summer recess, re-rehearsing it would pick things up in time for the reopening in September.

Beckett was still feeling extremely low. He found himself overwhelmed with minor chores and with checking some translations of his work, which depressed him still further.[103] "How sick and tired I am of translation," he wrote to MacGreevy, "and what a losing battle it is always. Wish I had the courage to wash my hands of it all, I mean leave it to others and try and get on with some work."[104] For the wearisome business of going over others' translations of his work was preventing him from making progress on the two major translations to which he had already committed himself: *Endgame* and *The Unnamable*.

Endgame was particularly pressing for, in order to clinch a deal with George Devine for its production at the Royal Court Theatre, he had to commit himself to supplying the English version by, at the very latest, mid-August 1957.[105] Peter du Sautoy of Faber and Faber, who had published *Waiting for Godot* and had a contract for the English rights of Beckett's plays, was also exerting pressure, through Jérôme Lindon, for the English translation.[106] Beckett fretted impatiently over his early efforts, feeling most of the time how much he was losing of the original: "I find it dreadful in English, all the sharpness gone, and the rhythms. If I were not bound by contract to the Royal Court Theatre I wouldn't allow it in English at all." [107] In May, he reported to Barney Rosset that he had done about a third of the first draft but only "with excruciating results" [108] and had finished the first draft by the middle of June. [109] But, after an exhausting final effort, the final text was eventually completed by August 12 and was dispatched to George Devine, Grove Press, and Faber and Faber.

As if all these various pressures were not enough, Beckett was bothered by a cyst that had been growing for some time in the roof of his mouth. The cyst had been discovered the previous year while he was in the middle of a painful course of "unending dental attention," [110] in which he had to have several teeth extracted and some bridges built. In June 1957, he wrote amusingly to Ethna MacCarthy:

> I am not so grand, though I spend most of my time in the quiet here [at Ussy], and expect shortly to have to undergo operation for removal of cyst shaped like Kelly's 3 balls in upper jaw and now thrusting hopefully, after I suppose 10 years surreptitious growth, against palate notably and sinuswards. My witch doctor is trying to reduce it by medical means, but I fear unsuccessfully. Ah well, I was always a great one for cysts. Bridges will be blown up in the process, and my surly gob more lopsided than ever. [111]

"Kelly's 3 balls" referred to the sign hanging outside Kelly's pawnbroker's shop in Dublin and the "witch doctor" who was treating the cyst nonsurgically was Suzanne's homeopath, Clarac. "Perhaps in this way," Beckett commented with dry humor later in the year, "I shall succeed in dying before an operation becomes necessary." [112] But, since X rays revealed that the cyst had come to a temporary standstill, he did not have the operation and allowed it to remain untreated for the time being. But, although he joked about it in letters and to some of his friends, privately he worried constantly about his health, wondering if, in the end, the growth might turn out to be malignant.

7

SEPTEMBER 1957 found Beckett swamped with visitors, both family and friends. But he and Suzanne managed to sneak away for a weekend break at Jérôme Lindon's large house in Etretat, where, although it rained much of the time, they took long walks along the cliffside paths. Beckett looked out for Les Golfs Hotel, where Joyce had stayed on a couple of occasions. He was reminded of this because he had brought with him, as his weekend reading, Stuart Gilbert's edition of the *Letters of James Joyce* in which he discovered two letters from Joyce written in that same hotel. [113]

He played golf by himself above the sea for the best part of the day, playing one ball after another just as he had done so many times at Carrickmines Golf Club thirty years before, and "with something of the old pleasure." [114] "Perhaps that's what one should do," he wrote to the Haydens, "go to live at Etretat and play golf every day until the limbs seize up. After all, I've seen one-legged golfers. It wouldn't perhaps be too bad a life." [115]

But a whole string of appointments awaited him on his return home. Not all of them lacked interest or pleasure. One or two were even great fun and, briefly, lifted his downcast spirits. Alan Schneider flew over in October to see *Fin de partie* and talk about the off-Broadway production that he was planning for the Cherry Lane Theater in January. Schneider gave his own account of their meetings:

> For four days, we met for lunch and later took long walks through Montparnasse, along the Seine, and through the Latin Quarter. We had dinner together too, talking about *Endgame* until all hours. One lovely sunny afternoon we polished off a pound of grapes while look-ing for a place in which we could play a game of Ping-Pong. Another time, I found a bookstore along the river that specialized in books on chess and presented Sam with one titled: "Five Hundred Endgames." I even got to meet Sam's "wife" Suzanne. [116]

Schneider was good for Beckett. After their stay in London the previous year, they felt relaxed in each other's company.

Small and bespectacled, Schneider wore a flat, peaked cap, which was to become his trademark. He was expansive and dynamic and had the kind of open, straightforward manner to which Beckett responded, and a well-developed sense of humor. He was not afraid to ask the kind of questions about the play that others might have avoided putting, and Beckett answered him in his turn as openly and honestly as he could. Beckett introduced him to Roger Blin and the French cast and took him twice to see the play.

When he left for home, Schneider felt that he knew *Endgame* "a hundred times more clearly than when I had arrived. I knew what Hamm should look like and sound like, knew how the ashcans should be placed and why, knew how carefully and exactly I would have to work on the play's rhythms and its tones. The mosaic of larger meanings was gradually falling into place, its total design still shadowy but at least perceivable." [117]

In November, Beckett spent a number of very pleasant, but "late and lubricated nights" with Donald McWhinnie, [118] who, after his great success with the BBC's *All That Fall*, was about to direct the Irish actor Patrick Magee in readings from *Molloy* and *From an Abandoned Work*, to be broadcast on the BBC Third Programme in December. "They record at the end of the month," wrote Beckett, "If I felt less shaky I'd go over, the 3rd [the BBC Third Pro-gramme] being untakable here." [119]

In Paris, he frequented the Dôme Café (mainly because it stayed open all night) where he met the painters Joan Mitchell and Jean-Paul Riopelle. He also went out sometimes with friends to La Palette restaurant, where, one night, he ran into a very friendly Jean-Paul Sartre, who—to Beckett's surprise, in view of his earlier dispute with Simone de Beauvoir—asked him if he would consider sending him something else for *Les Temps modernes*.[120]

Most of the time, however, Beckett found Paris increasingly difficult to cope with at this period of his life. Hell, he suggested, might well be an infinite series of enforced appointments.[121] He found speaking to people whom he did not know well more and more demanding, so he fortified himself regularly before every meeting with several whiskeys.[122] And, since almost everyone who passed through Paris brought him a bottle of his favorite Irish brand, he had plenty of the "hard stuff" on hand. After evenings such as those spent with McWhinnie, he walked home very unsteadily and surfaced very late in the morning.

He tried to get away to Ussy as often as possible and entered once again into the by now familiar downward spiral of depression and isolation. Already, by the end of 1957, Suzanne rarely stayed in their little cottage, and Beckett was often there alone. Arland Ussher suggested in a letter to Beckett that he thought one of the main problems of life was how to "convert loneliness (the worst of conditions) into aloneness (which is the best)."[123] Beckett replied: "What you say about loneliness and aloneness is very good (and true for some). From the former I suffered much as a boy, but not much in the last 30 years, bending over me in my old dying-bed where I found me early and the last words unending."[124] This distinction seemed clear-cut enough when etched in such resonant phrases, but, in reality, he found it harder to decide precisely where aloneness ended and loneliness began. Although he realized that he coped much better with solitude on a day-to-day basis than he could ever have done a few years before, too often, whenever his work was going badly, the distinction seemed a purely semantic one. And there was, of course, a vicious circle: the more he became accustomed to silence and solitude, the more he came to dread the intrusions of sound and company.

> I stay at this mournful address as much as possible, with occasional bouts in Paris trying to compress within a week a month's "business" from which I think it is time I retired and became as before I went into it, with all past instead of in store. It is like hanging from a ledge in a faint dream and a faint awareness of the three possibilities. Today since morning slow molten snow and the light hardly stronger than in the family vault. I am supposed to be translating *L'Innommable*, which is impossible. Not a sound all day and night but of the carts heaped high with the last mangels. No more heights, no more depths, the doldrums.[125]

The same day, he wrote to Mary Hutchinson that he felt "less like mercury than lead. Outside the peasants getting in the last mangels in the rain and inside an idiot shivering in his tuppenny-ha'penny havoc."[126] His mood was already depressed then when he received some shattering news that affected him very deeply.

8

ON DECEMBER 11, 1957, Beckett heard from Con Leventhal that his wife and Beckett's own former love, Ethna MacCarthy, was suffering from terminal cancer of the throat. He was utterly devastated. He wrote immediately to ask whether there was any specialist whom they could consult or any form of specialized treatment that they could obtain, either in Britain or America, adding: "I needn't tell you you may count on me financially up to the limit." [127] He was to repeat his offer on several subsequent occasions.

From December until Ethna's death eighteen months later, Beckett wrote her long, sometimes very beautiful letters, which can only be described as touching love letters written to someone for whom he had never lost his deep affection. Uncharacteristically, he deliberately padded his letters out with what he called "my silly news" [128] so as to interest and entertain her while she was ill at home or in hospital: "I suppose the best I have to do," he wrote to her, "is to open for you my little window on my little world." [129]

During the opening weeks of 1958, while he was in a mood of very deep depression, [130] he stayed alone at Ussy. Memories of Ethna when she was young and full of life and wit were juxtaposed with thoughts of her now, sick and dying. These memories helped to inspire the short, now famous play that he wrote fairly quickly in February 1958.

This play, which he eventually called *Krapp's Last Tape*, is unusual in Beckett's theatrical opus for its tender lyricism and for a poignancy that verges on sentimentality. Rehearsing many years later with the San Quentin Drama Workshop, Beckett commented: "A woman's tone goes through the entire play, returning always, a lyrical tone. . . . Krapp feels tenderness and frustration for the feminine beings." [131] And if the old man, Krapp, who listens to the tape recordings he made in his younger days, is fascinated by his recollections of the various women he has known in his life, he is obsessed by the eyes of one woman in particular. "The eyes she had! . . . Everything there, everything on this old muckball, all the light and dark and famine and feasting of . . . *(hesitates)* . . . the ages!" [132] The eyes of one woman are the touchstone for all the others, even for a woman whom Krapp encounters casually by the side of the canal, commenting admiringly: "The face she had! The eyes! Like . . . chrysolite!" [133]

When a biographical source has been suggested for the woman who inspired the yearning for what has long since past, Beckett's cousin Peggy Sinclair has been mentioned. Memories of visits to and farewells from Peggy are certainly evoked in the play. Peggy often wore green, and Krapp asks rhetorically: "What remains of all that misery? A girl in a shabby green coat, on a railway-station platform?" [134] Krapp reads again, "with tears again," [135] Theodor Fontane's novel *Effi Briest*, a book of which Beckett was very fond and over which Peggy often used to cry. But the play, like Beckett's own life up to that time, contains several different loves and there seems little doubt that the source for the girl with the haunting eyes is Ethna MacCarthy. For, as *Dream of Fair to Middling Women* had made clear a quarter of a century before, the "Alba," who on Beckett's own admission was closely modeled on Ethna,[136] had eyes like dark, deep pools.

The scene with the girl in the punt to which the middle-aged, then old man, Krapp, harks back in his recordings has also been related to an incident with Peggy Sinclair.[137] An incident in *Dream of Fair to Middling Women* off an Irish beach suggests such an affinity. Beckett himself did not remember the scene this way, however, denying that the girl in the boat in *Krapp's Last Tape* had anything at all to do with Peggy.[138] And the feelings expressed in this passage seem much closer to the tender yearning inspired by Ethna than to the emotion aroused by the more overtly physical Peggy. Small wonder that Beckett felt able to write to Ethna MacCarthy when the play was finished: "I've written in English a stage monologue for Pat Magee which I think you will like if no one else." [139]

If Ethna's terminal illness inspired Beckett by drawing him back in memory to the days of his youth in Ireland, other factors contributed to the composition of the play. George Devine wrote to Beckett in December 1957 saying that he wanted to present his translation of *Endgame* at the Royal Court Theatre in the Spring, not with the mime *Act Without Words* that had accompanied the earlier French production, but with N. F. Simpson's play *A Resounding Tinkle*. Beckett replied that he was not at all happy about this proposal and commented to Donald McWhinnie that he would rather they did not proceed until he could offer them "something else from my own muckheap more acceptable than the mime. This is not nosiness God knows and I have no doubt, having read Mr Tynan, that I would be in excellent company with Mr Simpson. I simply prefer right or wrong to be unrelieved." [140] Beckett was searching therefore at this time for an idea for a short play to accompany *Endgame* on the Royal Court program.

Also in December 1957, he heard Patrick Magee reading extracts from *Molloy* and *From an Abandoned Work* on the BBC Third Programme. In spite of the static through which he again strained to listen, first in Paris then, later in the month, in Ussy, when the readings were repeated, Beckett was impressed and moved by the cracked quality of Magee's distinctively Irish voice, which seemed to capture a sense of deep world-weariness, sadness, ruination, and regret. He had not yet met the actor, who had also been in *All That Fall*.[141] But he had heard enough through the interference to "thank my stars for Magee." [142] A few weeks later, he began to compose a dramatic monologue, which he first called the Magee Monologue, for a character who is described in the first draft as a "wearish old man" with a "wheezy ruined old voice with some characteristic accent." [143]

It has often been said (by Beckett among others) that he had no knowledge at all of tape recorders when he wrote a play that uses such a machine, sophisticated technology at the time, as its central device. However true this may at first have been in matters of detail, his correspondence shows that he had seen a tape recorder in operation when he went along in January 1958 to the BBC studio on the avenue Hoche in Paris, where Cecilia Reeves played for him the tapes of Magee's readings that had been sent over from London.[144] Staring at the reels that held his own words as they revolved on the tape deck and seeing, in a casual way at least, how the tape recorder worked helped him to imagine a play in which different moments of time could be captured, juxtaposed, and relived later. Beckett started to write the play on February 20; during the final stages of composition in March, when he needed detailed operating instructions, he wrote to ask Donald McWhinnie if he would send him a tape recorder manual.

Krapp's Last Tape contains many personal elements. Beckett's walks in the hills with his father and his favorite Kerry Blue terrier lie behind the memory of the younger Krapp tramping on a hazy Crohan mountain with the bitch, stopping to listen to the peal of the church bells. "At night, when I can't sleep," Beckett had written earlier to Susan Manning, "I do the old walks again and stand beside him again one Xmas morning in the fields near Glencullen, listening to the chapel bells."[145] Beckett had also experienced a lack of success resembling Krapp's "Seventeen copies sold . . . to free circulating libraries beyond the seas"[146] with the French *Murphy*, and had spent many an evening sitting alone at the "Wine-house" or village pub "before the fire with closed eyes, separating the grain from the husks."[147] Experiences of a very different order of importance to Beckett have lost their personal, purely local significance and have been more successfully integrated into the play's thematic structure. Even the most poignant memory of all, that of his mother's death some eight years before, has now been absorbed into a carefully structured pattern of images of black and white, sense and spirit, that Beckett later described in terms of Manichean dualism. Personal elements cannot simply be pinned down, then, to comfortable real-life equivalences. They convey more universal feelings of yearning or loss, nostalgia or regret, aspiration or failure.

Beckett always felt a great deal of affection for this play: "I feel as clucky and beady and one-legged and bare-footed about this little text as an old hen with her last chick," he wrote to Barney Rosset.[148] And, mocking himself, he wrote to Jacoba van Velde that the short play was "nicely sad and sentimental; it will be like the little heart of an artichoke served before the tripes with excrement of Hamm and Clov. People will say: good gracious, there is blood circulating in the man's veins after all, one would never have believed it; he must be getting old."[149]

He was fifty-two and, for his birthday, among presents from friends and well-wishers he received a couple of dozen handkerchiefs; to use them all, he said, he would need to start crying again. And there was plenty to cry about: "All of my friends are in hospital," he wrote. "I shall soon have to go on my rounds, closing their eyes."[150] For a few weeks before, he had heard that his oldest friend, Tom MacGreevy, had had a heart attack and that a relative, Ralph Cusack, suffering from high blood pressure, had recently had an operation and nearly died. But it was the terminally ill Ethna MacCarthy who occupied the tenderest center of his thoughts.

18

Censorship
and *How It Is*
1958–60

1

KRAPP'S LAST TAPE gave Beckett a very real sense of achievement. But he had mixed success with other pieces that he tried to write at this time, in both English and French. Before — not, as is widely thought, after — *Krapp's Last Tape*, he had tried to compose another radio play for Donald McWhinnie to direct, but had temporarily abandoned it.[1] (This was soon to become *Embers*. After some reworking, it was sent to the BBC in February 1959.[2] And, in spite of Beckett's own view that this was a "rather ragged" text,[3] it still won the RAI prize in the 1959 Prix Italia contest.)[4] But another play fragment, written this time in French after the Magee monologue, was conclusively aborted. And the Romanian-born composer Marcel Mihalovici, with whom he and Suzanne were very friendly, also asked Beckett if he would try to write the libretto for a half-hour opera for him. He wrote only one line: "Je n'ai pas envie de chanter ce soir" ("I have no desire to sing tonight")[5] before giving up. "There are two moments worthwhile in writing," he summed up to a friend, "the one when you start and the other when you throw it in the waste-paper basket."[6]

His own Sisyphean task was the translation into English of *L'Innommable*. He constantly grumbled at how difficult, even impossible it was. In January 1958, he wrote to Barney Rosset: "Since my failure to write another radio text I've been lashing away like mad at L'INNO and have now done a good three quarters of first draft. I'll never be able to settle down seriously to anything new till I get it out of the way."[7] Then, while writing *Krapp's Last Tape*, he reported: "Just to tell you I finished first draft of *L'Inno* this evening. A month to forget it, a fortnight to revise it, three weeks to retype it, you should have it sometime in the merry month."[8] He finished it at last on the first of June "and dispatched it with relief to NY today." As a consequence, he felt "flat and tired after the effort and dissatisfied with the result."[9] His tiredness is hardly surprising if one considers that, as well as translating the text, he also typed the entire manuscript himself on a Remington typewriter, using the customary fiddly, time-consuming carbon papers to make copies. In April, he wrote by hand to Donald McWhinnie: "Forgive filthy writing. I have my two middle fingers raw with typing."[10]

To finish off *The Unnamable*, he spent as much time as he could in Ussy.

Throughout the long winter months, he prowled from window to window, looking out onto the large expanse of frozen lawn that had become so pitted with molehills that he now sometimes quoted his address as "Ussy-sur-Moles" instead of "Ussy-sur-Marne." [11] Barney Rosset sent him a drum of molebane from the United States [12] that Beckett had to see through customs at the Gare des Batignolles and have sent on to the local railway station at La Ferté-sous-Jouarre. [13] A few days later, he started to apply it liberally to his clay soil. He loathed the idea of poisoning such harmless creatures. But he saw little alternative, short of accustoming himself to living in a lunar landscape.

2

DURING THE EARLY MONTHS of 1958, Beckett twice came into conflict with the forces of censorship in Ireland and England. These two incidents were fully covered in the national newspapers, although, typically, Beckett did not himself speak to any journalists. He had been asked by Brendan Smith for three mimes for Deryk Mendel to play [14] at the Dublin International Theatre Festival. At the same time, he had finally agreed to allow Alan Simpson to put on a straight reading of *All That Fall* at the Pike Theatre in Dublin and had given permission for him to produce *Endgame* there, once it had received its English premiere. But, before any of the productions could be set up, he heard that the festival's planned adaptation of Joyce's *Ulysses* and the new Sean O'Casey play, *The Drums of Father Ned; or a Mickrocosm of Ireland*, were not to be put on because the archbishop of Dublin, McQuaid, was opposed to them. Beckett's instinctive response was swift and decisive. Remembering his personal experiences of narrow-mindedness and bigotry as well as the banning of his own books in Ireland, he wrote to Alan Simpson:

> After the revolting boycott of Joyce and O'Casey I don't want to have anything to do with the Dublin Theatre "Festival" and am withdrawing both mimes and *All That Fall*. I have written to Brendan Smith to this effect. I am extremely sorry for any difficulties this may create for you. I know you will understand that it is quite impossible for me to do otherwise. [15]

Simpson was sympathetic to his stand. He was very anxious, however, to go ahead with the reading of *All That Fall*, which, he claimed, he would entirely dissociate from the festival. [16] But, while regretting the position he was putting him in, Beckett was too incensed to agree to his proposal and wrote:

> I am withdrawing altogether. As long as such conditions prevail in Ireland I do not wish my work to be performed there, either in festivals or outside them.
>
> If no protest is heard they will prevail for ever. This is the strongest I can make.

I have therefore to cancel the permission I gave you to present *All That Fall* and *Endgame*.
I hope you will forgive me.[17]

The ban on the performance of all Beckett's plays in Ireland—for this was the force of the diktat that he issued to his dramatic agent, Spencer Curtis Brown—was to last for some time.

He was also inevitably drawn into the disagreement between his English director, George Devine, and the British censor, Lord Scarborough, over the English-language production of *Endgame*. To be licensed, every play in England at the time (indeed, until 1968) had to be sent for approval to the Lord Chamberlain's office at St. James's Palace accompanied by a two-guinea reading fee and a five-shilling stamp charge. The play was then read by an anonymous reader called an Examiner, who pointed out everything that seemed dubious to him and recommended whether the play should or should not be licensed. The only way to circumvent this procedure was to present the play at a theater club or transform one's own theater into such a club to admit only members. (Tennessee Williams's *Cat on a Hot Tin Roof*, for instance, was playing at the time at the unlicensed Watergate Theatre Club.) Club regulations meant, however, that members had to register in advance before buying their tickets and sign in any guests who accompanied them. This was a cumbersome device that could adversely affect the box office takings.

The main problem the English censor had with *Endgame* lay in the "prayer scene," in which Hamm orders Clov and Nagg to pray to God. Hamm concludes, from the lack of response from the Godhead: "The bastard! He doesn't exist!"[18] The Lord Chamberlain found this scene blasphemous and refused to license the play unless a cut of twenty-one lines were made. Beckett agreed to change several words elsewhere in the play that were found objectionable—he got rid of "balls" and "arses," for example, and changed the line "I'd like to pee"—but he would not consent to the suppression or the mutilation of the prayer scene.[19] George Devine suggested to him that they stage the play as a club production or (in this he was half serious) have the actors deliver the shocking lines in French. Beckett replied:

> I am afraid I simply cannot accept omission or modification of the prayer passage which appears to me indispensable as it stands. And to play it in French would amount to an omission, for nine tenths of the audience. I think this does call for a firm stand. It is no more blasphemous than "My God, my God, why hast Thou forsaken me?[20]

He pondered several times on what Joyce would have done in similar circumstances and concluded that he too would have stood firm on such a matter of principle. Nor did he feel that he could or should shift his position for a projected production on the BBC Third Programme.[21]

Endgame was to remain a problem for many months to come. Already by February 10, 1958, it was announced in British newspapers that, after nearly two months of discussion, the Lord Chamberlain had still refused to grant the play a license.

> Devine tried to break the deadlock by gathering a small audience of writers and staging a rehearsed reading of the piece for the benefit of Lieutenant-Colonel Sir St Vincent Troubridge of the Lord Chamberlain's office. Besides reading Hamm, Devine was giving the stage directions *sotto voce*, and when he reached the offending passage he threw it away in the same undertone. However, the effort was wasted on Sir St Vincent who sat through the reading like a graven idol with his convictions unshaken. "It's because it's in English," Devine told [the playwright] Ann Jellicoe afterwards, "you can get away with much more in French. Think what you could get away with in Japanese!"[22]

It seemed ludicrous that a play, which had already been acted uncut in France, Germany, and the United States without representing any conspicuous threat to public order and morality, could not be presented in a public theater in Britain.

Needless to say, the British press homed in on this obvious absurdity. For an additional idiocy was that the Lord Chamberlain was banning a play that he had already allowed to be performed at the same theater in French only a year before.[23] The *Evening Standard* pertinently asked: "Does this mean that the Lord Chamberlain considers all people who understand French beyond hope — unredeemable atheists or agnostics who need not be protected from blasphemy? Or does he believe that knowledge of the French language bestows immunity from corruption?"[24] George Devine — who, ironically, received a "Commander of the Order of the British Empire" decoration from Buckingham Palace only two days after the ban was made public — commented that

> the same English version will soon be on sale here in book form, and the B.B.C. is talking of doing the play on the Third Programme. If it were filmed it could be shown with — if necessary — an "X" certificate. Anyone can offer it to the public except the poor old theatre. The only solution seems to be for the theatre to adopt the cinema's certificate system or for the Royal Court to by-pass the Lord Chamberlain as a theatre club. I have held out against that so far because I think the adult theatre public should be *treated* as adult. . . . Both Mr. Beckett and the Lord Chamberlain have been very nice about it, but so long as they both remain so firm I have no hope of putting on the play.[25]

Arguments dragged on long past the time when Devine had hoped to mount the production, until finally, as late as July, the Lord Chamberlain let it be understood that if a change were made to the word "bastard," a license might be granted. Beckett then made, as he put it, a "notable concession"[26] and offered them " 'SWINE' in a moment of gush and that's my last word on the matter."[27] His exasperation with the whole stupid business is revealed in a very tough letter to George Devine, in which he wrote that he was

> tired . . . of all this buggering around with guardsmen, riflemen, and hussars. There are no alternatives to "bastard" agreeable to me. Nevertheless I have offered them "swine" in its place. This is definitely and finally as far as I'll go. . . . If "swine" is not acceptable, then there is nothing left but to have a club production or else call the whole thing off. I simply refuse to play along any further with these licensing grocers.[28]

But his offer was accepted and, at long last, on August 6, the play was licensed for public performance. Beckett commented to Barney Rosset that he hoped God was pleased at being called a swine instead of a bastard,[29] adding to Ethna MacCarthy, "There's a nicety of blasphemy for you. I think I'd be rather less insulted by 'bastard' myself."[30]

Even then the Royal Court's troubles were not entirely over. For, incredibly, the "Lord Chamberpot," as Beckett used to refer to him, also found things to object to in *Krapp's Last Tape*. Donald McWhinnie recounted to me how, with George Devine, he went along to St. James's Palace and climbed up a poky staircase to the Lord Chamberlain's office to be told that part of the passage when Krapp talks of the moments that he spent with the girl in the punt was considered unacceptable.[31] When asked why, the officer explained with a sense of shock that the line "Let me in" on the recording clearly indicated that the man was, in his quaint terminology, "rogering" the girl and that this obvious obscenity could not be allowed to be described on stage. I once told Beckett that one of my postgraduate students insisted on interpreting this passage as a scene of sexual intercourse. "Tell her to read her texts more carefully," Beckett said with a chuckle. "She'll see that Krapp would need to have a penis at an angle of a hundred and eighty degrees to make coitus possible in the position he is in."[32] Such niceties of reading (or even human anatomy) cut no ice with the Lord Chamberlain and McWhinnie's explanation that Krapp was merely alluding to the girl's eyes was thought unconvincing. Eventually, such ludicrous objections to *Krapp* were dropped. But it was not until three weeks from its opening that the play was finally granted a license.

3

THE SPAT WITH the Lord Chamberlain and the consequent delays to the productions at the Royal Court Theatre meant that, in May 1958, instead of attending rehearsals in London as he thought he would be, Beckett was free to drive with Bram van Velde and Jacques and Andrée Putman to the opening of a big Bram van Velde exhibition at the Kunsthalle in Berne. He took great pleasure in seeing the painter's reputation growing so rapidly and felt that he should support his old friend. The four of them left Paris in Putman's car on May 7 for a four-day trip to Switzerland.

In Berne they received, in Beckett's words, the "unbelievable hospitality"[33] of Ida Chagall, daughter of Marc Chagall and wife of the gallery's director, Franz Meyer. Beckett was relieved to find that he had no difficulty in keeping off the subject of her father's paintings, which he disliked intensely. A fairly large group of writers, painters, and art critics had gathered in Berne to honor Bram: Michel Leiris, Michel Guy, Pierre Alechinsky, Georges Duthuit, Isabelle and Pierre Hebey, Michel Warren, and Jean Messagier, who gave a private party for the artist at his mill in Franche-Comté. The weather was fine and, once they got out of the "devilish Föhn,"[34] the wind that blew fiercely across Berne all the time they were there, the guests were able to loll in canvas chairs outside the mill, chatting animatedly. Beckett was dressed in a smart sports jacket and flannels. Helped by a plentiful supply of wine, he was in relaxed mood, far more at ease in such small groups than he ever was at large official receptions.

The opening of the exhibition itself surprised him by resurrecting the ghost of James Joyce. For, at the reception, he was introduced to Frau Carola Giedion-Welcker, the Zurich friend of the Joyces who had recommended the specialist who performed the final operation on Joyce. She was there in the company of a doctor "who said that Joyce died in his arms, that but for misdiagnosis or tardy diagnosis he could have been saved and even with that would have been saved today."[35] Misdiagnosis or not, nothing could bring Joyce back. And, as the doctor and Frau Giedion-Welcker went on talking casually, but with some hostility, of Joyce's son, Giorgio, Beckett found it impossible to escape from the haunting image of his dear friend dying in the arms of the man before him. Such bizarre tricks of life made him shudder.

The van Velde exhibition was a very fine one, with over a hundred paintings by Bram on display, including Beckett's *1937 Composition* and a gouache that he also owned; many were loaned by Jacques Putman or the Maeght Gallery. The artistic purpose of the visit continued with what Beckett described as "too many more or less forced visits to private collections, too many Klees,"[36] all packed into too short a time. But, in the Mueller private collection, one late self-portrait by Paul Cézanne made these visits worthwhile. Beckett, who admired Cézanne enormously, found the painting "overwhelmingly sad. A blind old broken man."[37] One nonartistic event was a visit to the city zoo where Beckett saw "the bears, two babies being bottle-fed by the keeper, their mother or I suppose mothers have tried to eat them, and a pair of adults, in a corner, in the shadows, yawning, initiating an absent-minded copulation that looked as if it must last 48 hours at least."[38] Zoos (like prisons) never did agree with Samuel Beckett.

Back in Paris, he spent an enormous amount of time alone working or out with his friends. Suzanne complained that he was never at home and, as a result, understandably enough, she started to frequent more and more her own circle of friends, which now included the writer Robert Pinget and the actor Jean Martin. She saw the pianist and music teacher Roger Deleutre and his wife, Denise, and a doctor involved in genetic research, Marthe Gautier, with whom she became very friendly. She was also friends with a Spanish painter, Manolo Fandos, and an Italian, Alberto Chiarini. She attended concerts avidly. Sometimes Beckett acompanied her, to a master class, for example, at the Salle Debussy given by the eighty-two-year-old Polish-born soprano, Marya Freund

> to a mere handful of girl students. They were doing Brahms. She sang very touchingly herself at the end Rain Lieder I hardly knew. I had not the cheek to pipe up and ask for Waldeinsamkeit or the Sapphische Ode. An American girl sang the Sally Gardens! Thinly, but Marya Freund was very pleased with it. She is an extraordinary old lady, told about the time she heard Brahms playing the piano at her parents' house in Poland.[39]

Music remained an abiding interest for Beckett. He often listened to classical concerts on France Musique, including a broadcast concert that Suzanne attended, which included Beethoven's Seventh Symphony, "the dearest of the nine."[40] Occasionally they went to the theater, mostly to support an author such as Marguerite Duras of whom he approved. He urged his friends to see her play *Le Square* at the tiny Théâtre de Poche in the rue Rochechouart, which Beckett also considered worth patronizing. The little play was, he thought, "infiniment émouvant" ("infinitely moving").[41]

He read eclectically, going back, out of sheer boredom he maintained, to an old favorite, the *Divina commedia*. He spent hours, just as he had as a student in Dublin, poring over Beatrice's explanations of the spots on the moon in the *Paradiso*, judging that he understood no more of it now than he had then.[42] But it was not long before he returned to the *Purgatorio* with his usual enthusiasm, fascinated by Botticelli's engraving of the indolent Belacqua, whom Beckett had used many years before as his representative antihero in *Dream of Fair to Middling Women* and *More Pricks Than Kicks*, sitting with his arms clasped around his knees, "holding his face between them downward bent."[43] This reimmersion in Dante may appear to have been casual enough, but less than a year later he was to copy Belacqua's fetal posture in the position adopted for sleep by the protagonist in his *Comment c'est (How It Is)*: "the sack under my head or clasped to my belly clasped to my belly the knees drawn up the back bent in a hoop the tiny head near the knees curled round the sack Belacqua fallen over on his side tired of waiting forgotten of the hearts where grace abides asleep."[44] It was probably rereading Dante also that launched him into the shorter prose pieces that he wrote in the 1960s, with their closed inner worlds of spheres and circles and bodies carefully positioned inside them.

Other books touched his personal life more closely: Hugh Kenner's *Dublin's Joyce*, "very brilliant and erudite but dementedly over-explicative it seems to me, though admittedly Joyce invites such herrdoktoring as much as any writer ever";[45] an essay by Claude Mauriac on his own writing that he found "quite good";[46] and Jean Genet's latest play, *Les Nègres (The Blacks)*, which Roger Blin was soon to direct and which Beckett found "very fine" from the extracts he had read.[47] In March, he was genuinely thrilled to receive from the bookseller Jake Schwartz, to whom he had already sent so many of his manuscripts, a copy of the 1911 edition of the *Encyclopaedia Britannica* with all but the last of the twenty-nine volumes intact. He took the set with him to Ussy, where he dipped into it constantly, using it as an invaluable reference whenever he wanted information relevant to his work, or reading it simply for the pleasure in erudition, which he had never lost.

On July 8, 1958, Beckett and Suzanne set out for a three-week holiday in Yugoslavia. One of their main aims was to spend the royalties that had been accruing for Beckett in Belgrade on the Serbo-Croatian translations of *Waiting for Godot* and *Molloy*. Since Yugoslavia was an Eastern bloc country, dinars could not be exported.[48] They stayed at the Hotel Moskva and met the picturesquely named Mme. Kaca Samardzic and her husband—she was reader for the publishing house Kosmos, which published Beckett in Belgrade—who offered them the use of their house in Rovinj.[49] But they preferred to go on to Zagreb, where they had arranged to meet their friend Jean Martin, then move to the little port of Lovran on the Fiume promontory, where they joined up with Roger Blin and Nicole at the Hotel Beograd.[50] Martin and Blin had come from giving two performances of *Fin de partie* during the Venice Biennale and they were only too delighted to be able to relax by the seaside as Beckett's guests.

For his part, Beckett was happy to pay for everyone's holiday in the local currency and to invite Barney Rosset to go there later in the year at his expense. Jean Martin stayed on with them after Blin and Nicole had returned to Paris, Suzanne and Beckett both enjoying his jovial company, his jokes, and his great gift for mimicry. The little seaside resort was very quiet and there was little for them to do. So Jean Martin, who was starting to write himself at the time, used to compose several pages every day in a notebook which, in the evening, Beckett would correct and revise as a means of entertaining himself, as well as of helping Martin.[51] The holiday was a resounding success. Beckett spent most of his days "diving off high rocks with as much relish as when I was ten,"[52] while Suzanne sunbathed on the quiet beaches. At fifty-two, Beckett experienced the same thrill he had felt when, as a child, he had dived from the Forty-Foot. To Suzanne's astonishment, he went back to repeat obsessionally the same dive again and again. Of the Yugoslavs with whom they came into contact, Beckett wrote: "I was left with the impression of a very sober, quiet, serious, likeable people, in great poverty,"[53] although he felt that they lived in fear of a Soviet intervention on the 1956 Hungarian model.[54] For once Beckett did not have his mail sent on from Paris, and they could find no Italian, French, or German newspaper less than a week old.[55] They returned to Paris via Vienna and Munich feeling refreshed and though "stupefied" by the sun and sea, bored with hotel life, and ready for home, also a little more prepared to face up to the problems ahead.

They needed to be. For, on his return, Beckett was met by a mountain of what he described as "50 letters and a cubic metre of parcel post,"[56] including the page proofs of *The Unnamable*. These he read and dispatched to New York within the first twenty-four hours. Mary Manning was visiting Paris from America with her second daughter and a friend, and he added them to the string of appointments that he had facing him in the first week. Suddenly life was back to normal.

4

IT TURNED OUT TO BE a hectic summer and autumn. Many late and heavily alcoholic nights were spent with friends from Dublin, London, and America. Donald McWhinnie and Patrick Magee, both heavy drinkers, were over and Beckett spent a lot of time going over the text of *Krapp's Last Tape* with Magee, working on differentiating the two voices of Krapp (the one younger, recorded on tape; the other, older, live) and on the rhythms of Krapp's recordings. Another afternoon, he discussed the forthcoming production of *Endgame* with George Devine, who hoped to persuade Alec Guinness to play the role of Hamm: "wot a ope," commented Beckett laconically.[57] By the time they met in September, having failed to get either Guinness or Charles Laughton, Devine had decided to act the part himself, with Jack MacGowran playing Clov. At the end of September, Beckett grumbled that he was dining with somebody different every evening, mostly at his favorite seafood restaurant, the Iles Marquises, visitors having flown in from London, Venice, Switzerland, and Constance.[58]

In the middle of this welter of appointments, he created a space for himself at Ussy, where he tried to write. He had imagined, he wrote to Rosset, "a good container for another short play (in French) but have only the vaguest of notions what to put in it. If I have the courage to stare long enough at the wood of my filthy old desk perhaps it will come."[59] But with too little time for his own work and too little peace and quiet, he lost interest in the piece, which he set aside to rework later and publish only in 1976. This "new short act in French"[60] became what is known in English either as *Theatre II* or *Rough for Theatre II*.

The play concerns two figures (A and B) seated at tables with an unspeaking third character (C) who stands silhouetted against the night sky, evidently waiting to commit suicide by throwing himself from the open window. The two speaking characters are there to investigate the temperament, character, and past life of this potential suicide, who never speaks. The play focuses, in fact, on a kind of bookkeeping, the books checked being those of the person about to kill himself, providing testimonies from others who knew him or "confidences" from the subject himself in an apparent attempt to help him to decide whether he should or should not take his own life. Taken with *Endgame* and the abandoned "The Gloaming," the macabre nature of this subject is revealing of Beckett's own mood at this period. Yet, in spite of this, the play has a surface lightness of tone and a delight in wordplay and stylistic parody that also bears witness to a kind of resilience, a need to apply humor to the underlying sadness.

Persistent bouts of insomnia had been plaguing Beckett ever since the July holiday; having so many social or business meetings, he found it impossible to catch up on lost sleep. So when he flew into London on October 21, he was already tired out. He felt he could face only the anonymity and impersonality of a hotel room and wanted to stay again at the Royal Court Hotel in Sloane Square, "a dreary family county hole, but handy to the place of entertainment."[61] But, since all the hotels in the area were fully booked, in the end he stayed with Patrick Magee in a seedy boardinghouse on the Cromwell Road.

He came to London chiefly to ensure that *Krapp's Last Tape* was properly done, and from the time of his arrival, he attended every rehearsal, working concentratedly with Donald McWhinnie and Magee. During lunchtime breaks from rehearsing, he used to go with the actors to a nearby pub, where his appearance was strikingly captured in an *Observer* profile:

> At midday, he sat in the pub nearby, not precisely holding court but somewhat frequented. He smoked French cigarettes and drank stout. He was thin, brown-faced, beaky, the pale blue eyes not deep-set but well lodged under frontal bone, a wide mouth stretched across the teeth, the hint of a dimple. His hair was not all grey and must have started fair. The voice was light and not without edge, but friendly, recognisably Irish. He would talk about anything else, not his work. He could be described as ascetic-looking. When he stands up, he is fairly tall, quick and neat in his movements.[62]

He had never intended to get involved with the production of *Endgame*. But what he saw at a run-through worried him a lot and he could not resist discussing it afterward with George Devine. Devine never really felt at ease in the role of Hamm. Circumstances were against him. He was directing as well as acting; though Blin had done this before him, the French actor-director had at least had the inestimable advantage of rehearsing with Beckett from the very beginning. In London, the author was able to supervise only the last few days of rehearsal and felt that there was little he could do at such a late stage.[63]

> Up to that point, Devine and MacGowran had been working on extracting the ghastly comedy from the Hamm-Clov relationship. Beckett did not approve what he saw and asked for stylistic corrections. Another director might have asserted his own authority, but Devine accepted Beckett's instructions, with the result that when the production opened the cast were still striving to achieve the "toneless voice" required by the author. One cannot say that the production would have been "better" without Beckett's assistance, though perhaps it might have been more popular.[64]

Devine wanted to please Beckett and cared far too much about both the part and the success of the play. As a result, there was a lot of nervous tension around, which overflowed into his own acting. John Osborne could remember Devine, "seated in his chair, fixed with fright, as he waited for the curtain to go up. Certainly the part had a special, personal appeal to the bleakest aspects of his nature."[65] Every night, Jocelyn Herbert, with whom Devine was living, "used to go and put the rug over him and the handkerchief over his eyes and he would be absolutely shaking like a jelly."[66]

Devine himself felt that he failed in the role of Hamm; in his own comments on the production, Beckett praised only MacGowran, who he felt could have been really good but never had enough direction.[67] However, the more sensitive critics were not quite as hostile as has sometimes been suggested. Philip Hope-Wallace even found *Endgame* "far subtler than the noisy French original as staged by Roger Blin,"[68] and Anthony Cookman sensed that Devine had

> done his best to bring the characters nearer to human sympathy. . . . And the paradoxical effect of the humanization of the characters is that it is easier for us to receive the play, not as a dogmatic statement containing the whole truth about life, but as a poem dramatizing a moment of despair which everybody perhaps knows at some time or other in their lives.[69]

But, for many reviewers — if they did not dismiss the play simply as "weird and wanton drivel"—the "message" was indeed one of unrelieved despair at the hopelessness and futility of life. Even Harold Hobson, Beckett's greatest supporter among the London critics, had serious reservations about this production, writing "There is nothing positively wrong . . . the cast simply have not that element that will radiate through the language, giving it body and soul."[70]

By contrast with the problems of *Endgame*, rehearsals of *Krapp's Last Tape* went incredibly smoothly: "Terrific performance by Magee," wrote Beckett to Mary Manning, "pitilessly directed by McWhinnie. Best experience in the theatre ever."[71] Yet the new shorter play was treated with only slightly more understanding than *Endgame* by the newspaper reviewers, although Magee's "brilliant tour de force"[72] performance was widely admired.

For once, Beckett stayed until after the first night, although he did not attend the performance itself. A post-premiere party at the Queens Restaurant, on the other hand, found him unusually affable and attentive to his many friends who had come along. Even more unusually, he spent several further days in a smog-filled London, meeting old friends and calling on the Cork Street gallery director Victor Waddington to help to arrange an exhibition for his friend Henri Hayden.

During his stay in London, he often met Barbara Bray, a thirty-four-year-old widow with two small daughters, who was at the time Donald McWhinnie's companion. She also worked as script editor in the drama department at the BBC. She was small and attractive, but, above all, keenly intelligent and well-read; Beckett seems to have been immediately attracted by her and she to him. Their encounter was highly significant for them both, for it represented the beginning of a relationship that was to last, in parallel with that with Suzanne, for the rest of his life.

The demanding work, heady excitement, and heavy drinking all took their toll on Beckett and, by the end of the week, he left for Paris feeling, to use a word from his own play, utterly "corpsed."[73] On his return home, he was so ill that, as he coughed his way through the rest of the month, he began to feel that his whole "way of life was in great need of a change."[74]

5

ONE OF THE FRIENDS whom he had met in London was Con Leventhal. Ethna MacCarthy's condition was now very serious. Beckett had described Con then as "like silk. Either he doesn't realize or the old mask is in great fettle. The latter probably."[75] Now, as he was recuperating in Paris, Beckett received a letter from Ethna, asking him if he would come over to see her for one last time. On November 21, he wrote that he was flying to Dublin "to see Ethna MacCarthy-Leventhal very ill. That should about finish me."[76]

The visit started on December 1 and turned out to be every bit as sad as he had imagined it would be. He stayed with his sister-in-law at the quiet Shottery in Killiney; in addition to his sadness at Ethna's condition, the house held distressing memories of his brother, both of his presence and of his death. There was still the furniture from the old family home, Cooldrinagh: the dining table with the burn inflicted by Frank with a red-hot poker; the folding inlaid card table in the sitting room, on which they used to play bridge; and, on the wall, the picture of yellow tulips that he remembered from their childhood. Outside in the garden, the lily pond was as Frank had planned it. Everything brought a lump to Beckett's throat. Afterward he wrote to Mary Manning: "Dublin was sad and grim and I seedier and seedier as the week went on. I never felt so cold in my life, except one afternoon in the Hamburg cemetery looking for Klopstock's tomb which isn't there."[77]

Traveling in to see Ethna in a flat in Lower Baggot Street was more harrowing still. Every evening, he went to see her and Con, returning to Killiney by the last train from Westland Row. Since she was finding eating more and more difficult, on the advice of the Pierre Curie Foundation Beckett brought her a little Cadillac food mixer so that lightly cooked meat, vegetables, eggs, and fruit could be liquefied to provide her with enough nutrition.[78] She seemed to have lost a lot of weight and, as Beckett looked into her tired, drawn eyes, he remembered what he had written of their great beauty only months before. Now Ethna spent most of the day crouching, silent, over the fire. He tried desperately hard to remain cheerful and positive for her sake and for Con's, encouraging her to go to London to see a Harley Street specialist. Yet all three of them knew that the end could not be long in coming. On his last visit, he walked away choked with sorrow.

He had intended to see virtually no one else and came close to achieving this ambition. He "sidled into the Arts Club with Con one evening for dinner, corn beef and cabbage I believe."[79] He went with his uncle Howard for a brief visit to Susan Manning, whom he found "grumbly and wandering."[80] Nothing could cheer him up. Even driving with Jean in the car over some of the back roads like the "dear old Ballyogan," mostly unspoiled and still with its share of tinkers, could only take him back in memory to happier times when he had walked those same back roads with his father. The nearest thing to pleasure was to find how much he liked his nephew, Edward, who was the "image of Frank at his age."[81] The sixteen-year-old was making excellent progress on the flute after only a year studying under the French flutist André Prieur. But this occasioned a family argument, for Edward wanted to continue to study music after leaving school and his mother wanted him to follow in his father's footsteps by going to Trinity College to study engineering. Beckett trod warily, for he saw only too clearly the affinities with the past—he going off to write against his mother's wishes, Frank joining his father's firm against his own wishes—and he wanted to avoid making things worse for his nephew. While he was at Shottery, he also helped Jean with her financial affairs, but soon discovered that she had the situation with Frank's estate well under control. He telephoned MacGreevy shortly after his arrival and they spoke of spending one evening together in Dublin but, finally, MacGreevy had to take the train to Killiney to see him off on his last day in Ireland. Beckett was in poor form, quiet, tired, sullen, and morose.

6

AT THE BEGINNING of January 1959, Beckett took himself off to Ussy, alone again, "with the snow and the crows and the exercise book that opens like a door and lets me far down into the now friendly dark."[82] Gazing out of his window at a stark white world, he saw his lawn pitted with little heaps of hard, solid, frozen clay and concluded that his year-long battle against the moles was as good as lost.[83] One morning, he woke to find that the barbed-wire fence separating his property from the small adjacent copse on its left-hand boundary had been broken down by wild boars. The animals had forced their way through the fence, bending in two the iron posts set in concrete. They had taken the same route out—being disappointed, Beckett surmised, at finding no potatoes or turnips growing there. They had left behind them six-inch deep holes in the lawn and clumps of their hair clinging to the barbs of the fence.[84] He had to obtain help from his handyman in La Ferté-sous-Jouarre to repair the fencing. But, he wrote to Aidan Higgins, "I spend most of my time in the country at Ussy, pottering and bloxing around paper and grass, battling with moles, dull sad life and nothing else for it, riding a bicycle and refusing to give in on the hills, puff and legs in Golden Shred [that is he had his "feet in marmalade" as in his early poem "Enueg II"]."[85] Occasionally Suzanne accompanied him to Ussy, but mostly he stayed there alone, swallowing "my fry of asparagus and spuds" and drinking half a liter of "gros bleu" before having a bath and going to bed.[86]

The exercise book he referred to contained a new prose text, first entitled "Pim," which he had started just before Christmas.[87] He had, he wrote, given up all thoughts of theater and radio for the time being and was "struggling to struggle on from where the Unnamable left me off, that is with the next next to nothing."[88] "Pim" was to become the three-part *Comment c'est (How It Is)*.

It was desperately hard going. *Comment c'est* proved to be one of the most difficult pieces he had ever written. He found that he could face working on it for only two or three hours a day at the most; a dozen lines a day were an achievement, half a page almost a triumph. There are five manuscript notebooks for the original version and, unusally, all of them were written at Ussy. For the text demanded an intensity of concentration that he could find only in his isolated country retreat; as one reads it, the silence with which he deliberately surrounded himself is almost tangible. For the next eighteen months, Beckett's writing life focused on this one major work. It was to take more than a year to write and a further six months to revise. And he wrote virtually nothing else.

Beckett outlined his new prose work in a letter to Donald McWhinnie:

> A "man" is lying panting in the mud and dark murmuring his "life" as he hears it obscurely uttered by a voice inside him. This utterance is described throughout the work as the fragmentary recollection of an extraneous voice once heard "quaqua on all sides." In the last pages he is obliged to take the onus of it on himself and of the lamentable tale of things it tells. The noise of his panting fills his ears and it is only when this abates that he can catch and murmur forth a fragment of what is being stated within. The work is in three parts, the first a solitary journey in the dark and mud terminating with discovery of a similar creature known as Pim, the second life with Pim both motionless in the dark and mud terminating with departure of Pim, the third solitude motionless in the dark and mud. It is in the third part that occur[s] the so-called voice "quaqua," its interiorisation and murmuring forth when the panting stops. That is to say the "I" is from the outset in the third part and the first and second, though stated as heard in the present, already over.[89]

Fragments of his "life" in the light are captured in the first part by the man who is lying in the mud and the dark. These fragments take on the form of images, related sometimes closely but rarely unambiguously to Beckett's own life. Some of these brief images derive from his childhood or his youth. Others appear to be wholly imaginary. The first "real-life" image is of a child, who sees another creature who may be himself seen as other, in a mirror for instance. The second is of a woman who sits watching the man (or boy) work at his table as she sews or embroiders, and takes fright at his immobility. The third is of a little child in a nightshirt kneeling at prayer. This image corresponds to the photograph of Beckett as a little boy posing on a cushion at his mother's knee on the veranda of Cooldrinagh:

> we are on a veranda smothered in verbena the scented sun dapples
> the red tiles yes I assure you
> the huge head hatted with birds and flowers is bowed down over my

> curls the eyes burn with severe love I offer her mine pale upcast to
> the sky . . . in a word bolt upright on a cushion on my knees whelmed
> in a nightshirt I pray according to her instructions.[90]

The photograph is much more likely to have been the source of this image than
the original experience in Beckett's childhood.

However strange and unreal the world created in *Comment c'est* may be,
other sections also evolve out of specific incidents in Beckett's own later life.
For example, he told Lawrence Harvey in 1962 that two pages of the second
part of the book were directly inspired by a visit ten years earlier to the hospital
of La Ferté-sous-Jouarre to bring flowers to a sick friend.[91] The sick woman and
the flowers reappear in the text: "The flowers on the night-table she couldn't
turn her head I see the flowers I held them at arm's length before her eyes the
things you see right hand left hand before her eyes that was my visit and she
forgiving marguerites from the latin pearl they were all I could find."[92] And
memories of the hill leading up to the Hôpital de Jouarre and the "Maison de
Retraite" are evoked in a description that is transformed by his imagination into
a winter landscape of black, white, and gray: "outside the road going down lined
with trees thousands all the same same species never knew which miles of hill
straight as a ribbon never saw that toil in winter to the top the frozen slush
the black boughs grey with hoar she at the end at the top dying forgiving all
white."[93]

"Paris has become nightmarish, privacy and quiet almost impossible," he
wrote in April 1959.[94] And his resentment of the constant intrusions at this time
even creeps into the strange, unpunctuated prose text that he was writing: "no
wish for callers hastening from all sides all sorts to talk to me about themselves
life too and death as though nothing had happened me perhaps too in the end
to help me last then goodbye till we meet again each back the way he came."[95]

But these autobiographical passages matter much less now than ever before. For what is most central is the exploration of "being" to which the text
devotes itself, asking the question what remains when everything superfluous is
taken away.

7

WHILE STRUGGLING WITH his recalcitrant text, he learned that Ethna MacCarthy
had moved from Dublin to East Ham Memorial Hospital in London to benefit
from the advice of a cancer specialist there. But only a few days later, he was
told that she could be given no further treatment for her throat cancer; all that
could be done now was to give her regular painkilling injections. "Your letter
leaves me in speechless sorrow,"[96] Beckett wrote to Con. He continued to write
to Ethna and send her magazines like *Paris-Match*. In March, he even picked a
few tiny flowers in the wood near his Ussy house and sent them to her with the

words: "This is just my heart to you and my hand in yours and a few wood violets I'd take from their haunt for no one else." [97]

Leventhal came over to Paris for a few days' break in April. Beckett tried to distract him by taking him out for an evening's gambling at the Multicolor club, just as they had done on earlier, happier occasions, for Con loved a flutter on the card tables almost as much as on the horses. But although they won, their hearts were not in the turn of the cards. They moved on for drinks at the Falstaff where, coincidentally, they met Beckett's cousin Morris Sinclair. In the end, it turned out to be a late and surprisingly convivial night. A stoic himself, Beckett was at his best when reassuring, advising, or consoling others.

On his return to London, Leventhal found his wife deteriorating fast. Barbara Bray wrote to Beckett telling him of her visits to the hospital, but, out of kindness, she said little of Ethna's worsening physical state. Their mutual friend and former pupil, Leslie "Yod" Daiken wrote simply saying that she was much, much worse. Ethna herself declared that she did not want to see Beckett again; they had said their last good-byes in Dublin. Beckett felt helpless, unable to do anything either for her or for her husband. In the last few weeks of April and early May, he found that he could no longer write to her, talking of what no longer mattered. Finally, toward the end of May, he wrote her a letter that arrived a day too late for her to read. For she had died on May 25. The letter was destroyed unopened. Afterward, Beckett wrote to Con: "May you find somehow somewhere a little comfort and peace and the blunting of all these dreadful days and the strength to go on." [98] For Beckett himself, the hurt went deep. From being a first love, Ethna had become a powerful inspiration for his work and, in later years, a very dear friend. [99]

Suzanne herself took ill for over a month in May with an "invincible feverish flu," [100] a hacking cough, and a temperature that flared up every evening. [101] Since she did not appear to be getting any better, Beckett worried greatly about her and, back in Paris, declined to attend a number of engagements, including a visit to the Dublin's Gate Theatre production of *St. Joan*, starring Siobhan McKenna, at the Théâtre des Nations, [102] so that he could look after her. He also worried constantly about his own health. He too had a bad attack of bronchial flu at the beginning of June. But, more significantly, the intraosseous cyst in his upper jaw was bothering him now more and more. He wanted to keep the surgeons away from it for as long as he could. [103] His concern over the cyst is hardly likely to have been lessened by his reading in the third volume of Freud's biography that the analyst had undergone thirty-three operations for cancer of the jaw in the last twelve or fifteen years of his life. [104] As usual, Beckett's anxieties increased at night, and, at Ussy, the nightingales in the wood singing under a full moon were a source of comfort: living creatures, awake like him. [105]

8

Two LETTERS, VERY DIFFERENT in tone, brought him again into touch with Dublin. The first, written in January, was from an old friend whom he always referred to as HO: H. O. White, an Emeritus Professor at Trinity College, Dublin. White wrote on behalf of the college to ask whether Beckett would be willing to accept the honorary degree of Doctor of Letters at the summer commencement ceremony on July 2. Beckett wrote to Con Leventhal:

> The first movement is to decline as usual, but I finally realize this is hardly possible and I have written to HO that I shall accept the honour if it is offered me. I don't underestimate it, nor pretend I am not greatly moved, but I have a holy horror of such things and it is not easy for me. If I were a scholar or a man of letters it might be different. But what in God's name have doctoracy and literature to do with work like mine? However there it is, right or wrong I'll go through with it if they ask me.[106]

Beckett decided to accept this particular doctorate, although he turned down dozens of others, not only because the honor came from his own alma mater, but also because he probably regarded it as a gesture of forgiveness for having walked out of his lectureship over twenty-five years before. And although both his parents, to whom the degree would have mattered most, were dead, the award may have seemed like a belated justification for a decision which at the time had so bitterly disappointed them. So he accepted the degree, while genuinely dreading what he described as the "Commencements farce."[107]

He fretted at the thought of dressing up for the dinner and of appearing in public to receive the degree in person; a sign of his extreme nervousness can be seen in the fuss that he made about what he could possibly wear ("I have no clothes but an old brown suit, if that's not good enough they can stick their *Litt. D.* up among their piles," he wrote),[108] until he discovered from his sister-in-law, Jean, that his brother's dinner jacket would more or less fit him.[109] He told only a few members of his family—his cousins Sheila and Molly, and, of course, Jean—and he spoke to only a few of his closest friends about the honor.

The second letter in March came from a distraught theater director, Alan Simpson. Simpson, who a year before had been prevented from putting on Beckett's plays at the Pike Theatre because of his ban on Irish performances, said that he was naturally astounded when he heard that *Krapp's Last Tape* and *Endgame* were being put on at the end of the month by a group of former university students called the Dublin University Players. He also enclosed a cutting from the *Evening Mail* in which Beckett was reported as having been "talked into" removing his self-imposed ban to allow these productions to take place.[110] Beckett wrote back immediately full of apologies:

If you are upset you are less so than I. I knew nothing about this company and this production and never had a word of a syllable of correspondence with anyone connected with it. . . . You know me well enough to realise I am incapable of playing such a low trick on you and that I am not to be "talked into" doing what I have decided against. As you see from enclosed I am trying to have the production stopped. I hardly think it will be possible at this stage without grave prejudice to these people, the thought of which is naturally distressing too. If I succeed it does not mean the rights revert immediately to you. But it means they will when I get tired of my stiff neck.[111]

"It is scandalously unfair to the Pike," he wrote to Leventhal, "and horribly embarrassing for me."[112] He explained what had happened. Kitty Black, who worked for his English dramatic agent, Curtis Brown, had married the previous summer and left the agency, and her successor had never been informed about the Irish ban. So, without any further consultation with him, permission had been given to the Dublin group and an advance payment accepted from them.

Beckett contacted the agent immediately in an attempt to have the production halted, but Spencer Curtis Brown himself wrote to tell Beckett that it was too late for anything to be done.[113] Even then the ban was not immediately lifted. In 1960, Cyril Cusack asked Beckett's permission to bring a production of *Krapp's Last Tape*, in which he would play Krapp to the Théâtre des Nations in Paris, with Shaw's *Arms and the Man*. Beckett gave him permission to give a couple of performances in Dublin before bringing the production to France. This prompted Alan Simpson to write another understandably aggrieved letter, asking whether his earlier ban had been lifted. It was as a result of this Cusack *Krapp's Last Tape* (which Beckett did not like at all)[114] that Beckett raised his "interdict" on his work in Dublin and also restated his wish that the Pike Theatre should continue to have an option on the first performance rights to all his plays in Ireland.[115]

9

THE COMPOSER MARCEL MIHALOVICI was still eager to write an opera based on a Beckett libretto. And, since there was nothing new, he asked if he could "make a chamber opera out of Krapp, for the RTF and for a theatre in Germany" (the Städtische Bühnen in Bielefeld).[116]

Mihalovici's personality was as large as his build. He was a warm, friendly man, full of enthusiasm and enormously generous. Beckett's liking for him was helped by his and Suzanne's great admiration for his wife's prodigious talent as a pianist. The Mihalovicis were perhaps the two people with whom, as a couple, he and Suzanne had most in common at this time. Being warmly disposed toward Marcel, Beckett took his latest proposal seriously. So, over dinner at the Mihalovicis' little flat at 15 rue du Dragon, they began to talk about how the new opera could be approached. It involved Beckett in coming to see the composer with Roger Blin, who acted the play several times in front of them. Mihalovici explains (in a quaintly dreadful translation of his original French published in *Beckett at Sixty*):

> In this way, I was able to absorb the cadence of the text, its rhythm and its length. And then I threw myself with lowered head into my audacious plan of composition. Beckett's help was, I can say, essential at that point. Because Beckett is a remarkable musician — did you know it? — he possesses an astonishing musical intuition, an intuition that I often used in my composition. . . . Beckett on occasion caused me to make changes in what I showed him in the score, he either approved or disapproved, made me modify certain stresses in the vocal line, while at the same time helping me to look for others.[117]

Mihalovici worked on his music for some fourteen months. When it was finished,[118] a play of a mere ten pages had been extended to nearly two hundred and sixty pages of musical score. He wrote the music using the French translation as his libretto. But his looseleaf spiral-bound working notebook shows how meticulously Beckett and his German translator, Elmar Tophoven, subsequently worked with Mihalovici. They sat at the piano, one on either side of the composer, adapting the text to the music or modifying the score to fit precisely the vocalization of the English and German versions. Beckett sometimes changed his original English text to provide extra "notes" or different rhythms; so "incomparable bosom" became "a bosom beyond compare" and, because of the need for an extra syllable to accommodate the music, "dunes" became "sand dunes."[119]

The play appealed to Mihalovici for its "various moods, lyrical, agressive, cynical or merely contemplative"[120] and offered him a tremendous challenge. The problems arose as a result of having a voice on the recorded tape accompanied by a live orchestra and from the vocally fascinating discontinuity between the voice of the younger Krapp on tape and that of the older Krapp singing live as he records.

This chamber opera grew directly from Beckett's friendship for Mihalovici. The music has sometimes been described as being too lush and Romantic for Beckett. And, late in his life, Beckett indeed suggested to me that he felt that this was probably true.[121] Yet, in the late 1950s, he certainly admired his friend as a musician and a composer ("some of his work is very fine I think," he wrote to MacGreevy)[122] and soon agreed to work with him again on another radio text with words and music, *Cascando*.

Beckett so often worked through friendship. In the course of his career, he wrote a number of dramatic pieces expressly for friends, and tried to write several more. And many of his social or cultural engagements in Paris around this date were undertaken to please his friends. He supported them by attending their concerts, performances, or exhibitions. He went to the Théâtre Antoine, for instance, on February 25 to see Albert Camus's adaptation of Dostoyevsky's *The Possessed*, mainly because Roger Blin was playing the part of Bishop Tikhon and Jean Martin had another minor role.[123] He met Eugène Ionesco from time to time in Montparnasse cafés and was invited by the dramatist to the first night of *Tueur sans gages (The Killer)*, which he found "rather diffuse."[124] He attended readings from Fernando Arrabal's plays at the Théâtre de Poche Montparnasse, for he also knew Arrabal personally and admired several of his plays.[125] At the time of *Fin de partie*, his friendship with the painter Avigdor Arikha deepened and became a lifelong rapport. In the 1960s, he gave Arikha financial support, which was mostly repaid later. But he also bought some of his paintings.

Even Beckett's reading owed a lot to his friendships. He read, for example, Robert Pinget's new novel and his play *La Manivelle*, which Beckett translated later in the year as *The Old Tune*;[126] he enjoyed the poems of Boris Pasternak, translated by his old friend George Reavey;[127] and Barney Rosset sent him Grove Press's edition of Roger Casement's *Black Diaries*, in which he became totally absorbed.[128] Fortunately, many of his friends were very talented, so the cultural experiences arising from these relationships offered him genuine pleasure.

It was not always plain sailing. Occasionally, Beckett's innate perfectionism and devotion to his work came into direct conflict with his friendship. One such conflict centered on the French premiere of *La Dernière bande* (Pierre Leyris's and Beckett's French translation of *Krapp's Last Tape*) at the Théâtre Récamier in the spring of 1960. Beckett was eager for Blin to initiate the role. But Blin had had enough of playing Beckett decrepits and, partly out of vanity and partly out of fatigue, cast R. J. Chauffard as Krapp. Beckett was never happy with this decision and sulked morosely. He judged that Chauffard's performance was unworthy of his play.[129] After this disagreement, to Blin's distress, Beckett cold-shouldered him for almost two years, until, most upset to learn that Blin had been suffering from heart trouble, he finally felt repentant and offered him the translation of his next major play.

10

BECKETT ARRIVED IN DUBLIN more than a week before the honorary doctorate was to be conferred on July 2, 1959. He wanted to allow himself plenty of time with his brother's family and hoped to see some of his oldest friends. He did not stay at Shottery this time, however, since a friend of Jean called Harriet Chance was occupying the guest room on the occasion of Caroline's twenty-first birthday party. Instead he checked in at a nearby hotel. He saw Con Leventhal on a number of occasions, including one evening when they dined with the writer-philosopher, Arland Ussher, whom they both liked well enough, but regarded with a certain wry humor. Beckett found that, as he aged, Arland — or Percy, as they still thought of him, for Ussher had changed his name since they first knew him — had come to resemble the older Irish dramatist Lennox Robinson. He also saw quite a lot of Tom MacGreevy, who had by now recovered from his heart attack but complained of being weighed down by countless administrative problems at the National Gallery of Ireland, of which he was director.

He begged to be excused from Caroline's birthday party, as about fifty to sixty guests were expected to congregate in a marquee in the garden and there was to be dancing; instead, he spent a convivial evening with MacGreevy in Dublin. Suzanne and Marthe Gautier flew in from Paris on the same day for a short holiday. Caroline met them at the airport and took them back to her mother's house. Since her mother knew even less French than Caroline, conversation faltered. For the next few days, Beckett took Suzanne and Marthe out into the country on some of the old drives: Pine Forest, the Military Road, Glendalough, and Annamoe. Suzanne found the countryside around Dublin enchanting.[130] But neither she nor Marthe seems to have attended either the ceremony or, in fact, the birthday party.[131]

Beckett had been dreading everything to do with the award of the honorary degree and the formal commencement dinner to which he had been invited by the Provost and Fellows. The event was, however, much pleasanter than he ever anticipated. He wore his brother's dinner jacket and a bow tie, which he had so much difficulty in tying that, in exasperation, he let it hang in a double knot.[132] Trinity College was looking lovely in the July evening sunlight and everyone was most friendly and welcoming. His sixty-five-year-old professor of Italian, Walter Starkie, came to the dinner, as did other good friends like H. O. White and Con Leventhal. To his great surprise, Beckett actually found himself enjoying himself.

The ceremony itself, with its Latin oration, in which, to his amusement, Beckett was referred to as a "modern Diogenes" and *Waiting for Godot* described as the modern equivalent of the Psalmist's *Expectans expectavi* [I waited patiently (for the Lord)], went smoothly and was soon over. Almost everyone he had ever known in Dublin seemed to be there to shake his hand. Even his mother's friend Susan Manning, who was "pretty shaky and wandering"[133] attended unbeknown to Beckett; he found out only later, when he called to take her out in the car for tea at the Salthill Hotel.

Suzanne and her friend flew directly back to Paris, but Beckett took a plane to England, where he stayed for a few days with his cousin Sheila and her husband, Donald Page, in their charming Sweetwater Cottage in Wormley, Surrey. Sheila's sister, Molly, was over from Princeton, where she had a job, and she wanted to see him. The days spent at Sweetwater were happy and peaceful. There was a large pond in the garden and Sam persuaded Donald that they should build "a boat out of an old door. And there was great fun unveiling this thing; we didn't know what it was going to be called. And we had a bottle of champagne and a flag. And it was called Eli."[134] Eli was the name Sam had given Sheila when they were both children at Cooldrinagh. The boat's flag was an old white shirt of Donald's. It was like being a little boy again playing with Frank, and they all had a wonderful time. When Sheila posted back to Paris a shirt that he had left in a drawer, Beckett wrote "Many thanks for shirt. You should have kept it for our next merry boat." [135] A photograph of Beckett on the pond shows that their handmade, rudimentary boat at least floated successfully.

Beckett also took the train to London, where he met up with a number of old Trinity College friends like Stuart MacGuinness and Geoffrey Thompson. Most of all, he saw the "BBC crowd" and listened to the recording of *Embers* at Broadcasting House, Portland Place. He did not think the production quite succeeded (although he was too polite to say so at the time), in spite of some good acting from Jack MacGowran and Kathleen Michael.[136] He dined with Donald McWhinnie and Jack MacGowran, rather more prosperous now.[137] He also saw a lot of Barbara Bray. After the initial attraction, when they mostly met in the company of Donald McWhinnie, their relationship had begun to evolve into a much more serious affair. She had been over to see him in Paris in April and was already corresponding with him on a regular basis. After his visit to London, she came over again for another week in mid-October.

A ceremony of a very different kind took place in Sorrento in September 1959. It was organized by Radiotelevisione Italiana to present the prizes in the Prix Italia, including the one awarded to the BBC for *Embers*. Beckett allowed himself to be coaxed into attending the ceremony with Donald McWhinnie and his new girlfriend, Pauline. They quickly regretted it. They were comfortably housed at the Royale Hotel with a wonderful view of Vesuvius and a pretty shingle beach nearby with strikingly clear water. But both he and McWhinnie found the ceremony itself "terrifying." [138] In addition, an excursion program had been laid on to allow everyone to see the Blue Grotto at Capri. But Beckett detested organized group outings. The trip was hot and crowded and the entire "awful jamboree" [139] was affected by a formality and a general atmosphere of sycophancy that Beckett loathed.[140] Beckett summed up the visit to one friend laconically: "Sorrento was horrible. . . . Sorry I went." [141] To another he wrote, "Nearly killed me. Never be the same again." [142]

11

WITH THE INCOME from a successful exhibition, earlier in the year, in London at the Waddington Gallery, Henri Hayden bought a secondhand Renault Dauphine, which he used to drive mainly in the country around La Ferté-sous-Jouarre when he went out painting. Beckett sometimes accompanied the Haydens into the Marne valley and, when he had anything heavy to transport, they made a very small detour to Ussy with him. Henri soon tired of driving, however, and, since neither Beckett nor Josette had a lot of confidence in his ability — his license dated from the days when he used to drive a taxi in Paris in the 1920s — Beckett opted to take the wheel himself. A few months later their skepticism was justified as Hayden smashed up the car, nearly dumping himself and his wife into the river Marne.

In this way, Beckett became accustomed to driving again on the small country roads. He saw that it would be much more convenient to own his own car rather than to trek back and forth to Ussy on the train.[143] So, in October, with the money from the Prix Italia, he emulated Hayden and purchased a little "uninspiring vehicle but useful,"[144] a Citroën Deux Chevaux. He complained constantly that he had never driven a duller car, an "ugly sluggish little beast"[145] "and queer with that."[146] With a strong wind blowing against him, he found that it was impossible to get into top gear.[147] He drove the car in Paris too, soon picking up a number of fines for illegal parking.

His life changed a lot at this time. Not only did he buy the car, but he and Suzanne decided that they needed to move into a roomier, more convenient apartment. They had occupied the same flat at 6 rue des Favorites for more than twenty years, except for the war years in Roussillon. "We simply must have our rooms where we can shut ourselves up, not possible at present," wrote Beckett.[148] This simple, straightforward remark conceals a massive buildup of tension. By this time, Beckett frequently met people in the evenings when he was in Paris, and Suzanne hated the fact that he used to come home in the early hours, often the worse for drink. She disturbed his sleep in the morning. And when he wanted to work, he badly missed the isolation, loneliness, and privacy of Ussy.

Problems also arose as a result of his relationships with other women. Several of Suzanne's friends have suggested that she was not at all indifferent to his liaisons, however discreetly they may have been conducted. But she was no fool and was well aware what was going on. There had been affairs in the past. But now, with the arrival on the scene of Barbara Bray, not yet resident in Paris, but visiting Beckett from time to time, there were unexplained absences. We cannot possibly know for sure whether he and Suzanne were still having sexual relations. It seems likely that they were not. Again, several friends have reported Suzanne as saying, that, if things were to carry on as they were, it would be much better if Sam simply took his things and moved out, since her situation had become ridiculous. It says much for the feelings of affection and loyalty that they had for each other that they should have remained together, particularly in the mid-1960s, when their relationship seems to have come under its greatest strain.

The layout of the newly built apartment allowed them both a much greater degree of freedom and independence. The seventh-floor flat at 38 boulevard Saint-Jacques did not consist, as has often been suggested, of two separate apartments, although there were two separate entrances. It was an apartment and a small studio combined. Suzanne had her own bedroom overlooking the tree-lined boulevard and, to the right, the Métro station of place Saint-Jacques. They shared a sitting room, also facing onto the boulevard, which contained a small piano. There was only one kitchen. Through the kitchen was a bedroom where Beckett slept in a somewhat monklike cell lined with low gray cupboards. Beyond that, facing the tiny, forbidding, barred windows of the cells in the Santé prison, was his study and a small independent bathroom. With this arrangement, it was possible for Beckett to come and go and for guests to call on him without disturbing Suzanne. On the other hand, it was not possible for anyone to stay the night with him without her knowing. Unless either of them was eating out, they took their meals together at a simple Formica table by the window in the sitting room. Although Beckett always worked in his study, he normally went through to Suzanne's room to say good-bye to her before going out alone for a meeting or a dinner. But they still went out from time to time as a couple. And, over the nexty twenty-five years, they almost invariably spent their holidays together.

They did not, then, lead separate lives. But the new arrangements allowed them to live *parts* of their lives independently—without one disturbing the other, if he or she did not want to be disturbed. Enough aspects of Beckett's life and facets of his character irritated Suzanne for the new living arrangements to suit her as well as Beckett. The balance in their relationship had now swung decisively in Beckett's direction; he no longer leaned on her as he had done ten, let alone twenty, years before. With Jérôme Lindon's active help, he was now managing his own affairs and making his own appointments with a host of friends, collaborators, or visitors. His work was sought after by publishers and editors in many countries. So Suzanne was no longer needed to hawk it around the publishing houses. Increasingly, she felt that she had been pushed out of the key role that she had occupied for so many years, and undoubtedly she resented this. But even though her role as devoted intermediary had been greatly reduced, she continued to be a constant support to Beckett in his work, taking a keen interest in everything he wrote, representing him at premieres of his plays in different countries and reporting back to him on how the play was being performed. Suzanne's deep admiration for Beckett's work never wavered. And, in his turn, he was profoundly grateful for all that she had done for him: "I owe everything to Suzanne," he told me only a few weeks before he died.[149] She remained by far the more practical partner, making sure that he was pestered as little as possible by unnecessary domestic chores and protecting him, as often as he allowed her to do so, from unwelcome intrusions.

More than this, however, she was very much her own woman, sharply critical of him when she thought it necessary, but supportive when he needed support. She had a strong, forceful personality and was not prepared to be put upon. But she offered him room to be himself and rarely allowed a clash of views to develop into a fierce conflict with someone who had a fiery temper and a will of iron. And, in crucial areas, such as political leanings or generosity of spirit, they were very alike. Only with such a common outlook could the relationship have survived the buffeting that Beckett so often gave it. It was not just his affairs or his drinking. His compulsive need to be alone, deeply immersed in the world of his own imagination, could not have made him an easy companion.

Many of those who knew Suzanne well spoke of her kindness and deep generosity. But they also spoke of her tendency to mock and criticize. She could be impatient, intolerant, and dismissive. It required very little for someone who was not in her inner circle of friends to be excluded entirely from her company —a casual slip of the tongue, a glance at a watch when someone was talking to her, too obvious a courting of or flirtation with her good-looking partner, and one quickly became persona non grata. And she could be totally unforgiving. At the end of the 1950s, with Beckett's literary reputation growing every year, it would hardly be surprising if she felt some jealousy as he was increasingly lionized and she was often ignored by those whom she regarded, sometimes rightly, as self-seeking sycophants. She had a dislike of fame that was the equal of Beckett's own. But it sometimes advertised itself too glaringly, so that it could sound like affectation or sour grapes. In most respects, she was the opposite of affected. She has sometimes been described as if she were very bourgeoise and rather *mondaine*. Yet although she dressed smartly, she never wore very costly clothes or shopped in expensive boutiques; indeed, she made many of her clothes herself or bought them cheaply (sometimes, even at this time, at the Marché aux Puces) and restyled them herself on her sewing machine. Her own rooms in the boulevard Saint-Jacques apartment were not in the least luxurious. If anything, they were more austere than Beckett's own: few ornaments; some stones from a beach; a number of paintings and drawings.[150] The furniture was basic and utilitarian: a simple divan single bed, an inexpensive upright piano and stool, a piece of furniture combining a bookcase and cupboards, a wicker-work footstool, an armchair, and a couple of cushions.

She and Beckett rarely ate in expensive restaurants and preferred to take the Métro rather than order a taxi. The days of having to consider where the next franc was coming from had undoubtedly marked them both. But, fundamentally, neither of them was interested in the least kind of acquisition or display. And the more money Beckett earned from his writing, the more it was soundly invested by a financial adviser, so that he did not have to bother about it. Much of it was given away.

19

Secret Wedding
and *Happy Days*
1960–63

1

On October 8, 1960, Beckett, staying quietly in Ussy, sat down at his oak desk, opened a cream, hardback notebook, and wrote: "Play. Female Solo 8. 10. 60 Ussy." After writing only four pages, he laid it aside, then started again in a pale green exercise book with graph paper. Some details of the play's setting were clear in his mind from the outset: "a grassy expanse rising gently front to a low mound, summit about 4' high";[1] the woman (first "W," then, "Mildred") is there, too, much as she is in the finished play, *Happy Days*, embedded in the mound up to her waist, with black bag and parasol, asleep with her head on her arms. Her male companion appears dressed in striped pajamas and seated at first on the lower ledge of the mound. But in the second notebook, he is hidden away behind it, so that the play can concentrate on the central image of the woman, partly buried in a cruel earth and exposed under a hellish sun.

This extraordinary image may have surfaced from the depths of Beckett's own imagination, since it had been anticipated in *The Unnamable*'s vision of Malone: "There are no days here, but I use the expression. I see him from the waist up, he stops at the waist."[2] But there may have been other sources of inspiration. Figures are buried in the ground in the final striking frames of Luis Buñuel's 1928 film, *Un Chien andalou*, the kind of avant-garde film that Beckett went to see during his Ecole Normale days. Buñuel and Dali's film script was printed in the same issue of the magazine *This Quarter* in which some of Beckett's own translations appeared.[3] Even closer to the woman in *Happy Days* is a photograph by Angus McBean of Frances Day, in the review *The Fleet's Lit Up*, in 1938. The actress, buried to her waist, is posed with a mirror held in another's hand. The image is one of those pastiches of à la mode Surrealism that McBean did for the *Daily Sketch*. We simply do not know whether Beckett had seen this photograph.

Over the next three months, he continued to work on his new play. But he was constantly interrupted by the need to make arrangements for the move into the new apartment in the boulevard Saint-Jacques. Even though the keys had been promised for the beginning of the year, they had still not moved by the early autumn. But by October 20, the carpets were laid, bookshelves were mounted on two walls of his study, and a few basic items of furniture, including a new gray metal desk, had been delivered. In mid-November, Beckett started to work there every day, driving round with one or two boxes of books on every trip. He even took time to classify his books alphabetically, working from top left to bottom right. Every night, he returned to the rue des Favorites to sleep. He looked forward eagerly to the additional freedom that the more spacious apartment would provide. Gazing down from his study window at the rear of the apartment building onto a private lane, lawns, and small, neatly kept gardens, he sensed that, once the noise made by the builders and carpenters had abated, he might find in this apartment the quiet that he needed to write again in Paris, as he had been unable to do in the cramped quarters of the rue des Favorites.[4] There was one negative feature: the gray Santé prison with its rows of barred cell windows, below to his right. The thought of men living in cages so close at hand filled him with real distress. "I'll learn to raise the eyes to Val de Grâce, Panthéon and the glimpse of Notre-Dame," he wrote to Tom MacGreevy.[5] But he had no regrets: "We leave [the rue des] Favorites and the abominable rue de Vaugirard without a pang—after 23 years there."[6] It was not until the new year of 1961 that he and Suzanne moved in completely, sleeping in their separate bedrooms.[7]

The first piece of work that Beckett tackled in the new apartment was a second draft of *Happy Days*. He removed a lot of extraneous material and gave Winnie and Willie their balancing names. Winnie's movements are so complicated that, at this stage, he must have acted out every single one in his study, using his own spectacles and toothbrush and borrowing one of Suzanne's bags, her lipstick, and her makeup mirror. Only in this way could he have ensured that Winnie's lines and movements work so smoothly together or interrupt each other so precisely as she takes her spectacles from her bag, puts them on, takes them off, polishes them, peers through them at her toothbrush, and so on. When Alan Schneider flew into Paris from New York early in February 1961, Beckett could not resist trying his "Rewrite" on him. Schneider responded with spontaneous delight to the daring nature of the concept—a woman buried up to her waist in the ground in act one and up to her neck in act two—and enthused about directing it himself soon in New York.

2

TOWARD THE END OF FEBRUARY, Beckett and Suzanne were in Bielefeld together for the first night of Marcel Mihalovici's opera of *Krapp's Last Tape* in the Städtische Bühnen. Beckett had heard the rehearsal of a concert version sung by "a good Swiss baritone,"[8] Deryk Olsen, at the Palais de Chaillot earlier in the month. But he looked forward with genuine enthusiasm to the fully staged production in Germany.[9] Suzanne traveled there with Marthe Gautier via Düsseldorf, while Beckett accompanied Mihalovici. The stage designer Matias Henrioud was with them. Most unusually, to please Mihalovici, Beckett agreed to attend a discussion of the opera arranged for the evening before the first night. He was asked to speak at the end. While the director of the Bielefeld opera, Dr. Joachim Klaiber, the general musical director, Bernhard Conz, and, finally, the composer, Mihalovici, were talking, Beckett started to shuffle uneasily in his seat. Then, when asked by Dr. Klaiber if he would give his own views on the opera and make a few remarks about his writing in general, he stood up, looked shyly, almost furtively around him, and, quietly but firmly, blurted out: "Actually I don't want to say anything at all about my work." He sat down abruptly, looking highly embarrassed, but feeling an enormous sense of relief at having escaped so lightly.

In a discussion with sixth-form pupils in a bookshop the following day, however, he either forgot his own shyness or managed to surmount it, responding willingly to the young people's enthusiastic questions. Some of his comments on this occasion were probably taken down in shorthand, as they appeared later, first in the *Mykenae Theaterkorrespondenz*, then in the theater magazine *Spectaculum*:

> For me, the theatre is not a moral institution in Schiller's sense. I want neither to instruct nor to improve nor to keep people from getting bored. I want to bring poetry into drama, a poetry which has been through the void and makes a new start in a new room-space. I think in new dimensions and basically am not very worried about whether I can be followed. I couldn't give the answers, which were hoped for. There are no easy solutions.[10]

The opera, superbly sung in German by the young American baritone William Dooley, was warmly received by a large audience. Beckett wrote:

> Bielefeld was a great success and the singer quite wonderful — golden voice and good actor withal. Chip [Mihalovici's nickname] was very pleased and so were we all. . . . The press on the whole was very warm, though there was a tendency to opine that the music had damaged the play — which I vigorously denied orally whenever occasion offered.[11]

After the performance, Beckett and Suzanne joined a group of friends at a party. Sitting at a long table with his friends, he was in jovial mood, switching easily from one language to another, politely answering questions, basking in Mihalovici's success and taking a keen interest in what the other guests, mainly musicians, were doing in their careers.[12] Suzanne, too, made an impact. Twenty-eight years later, the Kassel dramaturge Hans Joachim Schaefer retained a vivid impression of her:

> She seemed reserved, almost cool, but friendly; austere and inward-looking, but self-possessed. In her case too I was very struck by [her] eloquent eyes — I think they were of the same blue as Beckett's — but they were not so lively, radiant and open, rather sealed. In her measured sparse movements she made a rather "queenly" impression, a little unapproachable, as if stuck in her own world. She wore a severely

cut earth-brown suit that looked a little old-fashioned, a long skirt and a long hanging hand bag. It reminded me of pictures of Puritan women at the turn of the century. She looked English or Irish but not like a Frenchwoman. Involuntarily I thought of Quakers or rather of my image of Quakers.[13]

Beckett went on to Frankfurt to an evening celebration arranged in his honor by Dr. Siegfried Unseld, the head of the Suhrkamp publishing house.[14] It was another very public event, exactly the kind of occasion that Beckett loathed. The hall was crowded with Suhrkamp writers, numerous professors, publishers, booksellers, journalists, local dignitaries, and students. After an opening speech of welcome from Dr. Unseld, the philosopher Theodor Adorno, in his "inimitable glassy voice," gave a lengthy, profound disquisition on *Endgame*, speaking of loss of meaning, identity, decline, and decay.[15] Elmar Tophoven then read the whole of the as yet unpublished German translation of *From an Abandoned Work*. Finally, a by now trembling Samuel Beckett rose, went to the podium, and, in a shaky voice and as few words as he felt he could decently employ, thanked Unseld, Suhrkamp, Adorno, and his German translators, Elmar and Erika Tophoven.[16]

The same day, Unseld had entertained Beckett and Adorno (also one of his authors) to lunch. Describing the occasion later, he related:

> Adorno immediately developed his idea about the etymology and the philosophy and the meaning of the names in Beckett. And Adorno insisted that "Hamm" [in *Endgame*] derives from "Hamlet." He had a whole theory based on this. Beckett said "Sorry, Professor, but I never thought of Hamlet when I invented this name." But Adorno insisted. And Beckett became a little angry. . . . In the evening Adorno started his speech and, of course, pointed out the derivation of "Hamm" from "Hamlet" [adding that "Clov" was a crippled "clown"]. Beckett listened very patiently. But then he whispered into my ear — he said this in German but I will translate it into English — "This is the progress of science that professors can proceed with their errors!"[17]

Following a party at the Unselds' and some games of chess for which Beckett appears to have stayed on especially, he caught the train to Cologne, Suzanne and Marthe having already gone on to Hamburg with Matias.[18] At Cologne station, Beckett met up with the Tophovens, who had traveled on in advance to purchase their first car, a Volkswagen. They decided to make a lengthy detour to Amsterdam (calling for lunch in Straelen with Elmar Tophoven's mother) so that Beckett could meet Jacoba van Velde. Beckett drove the whole way. He took such pleasure in driving a car much faster than his own little Deux Chevaux that he exceeded the speed limit and was stopped in Holland by a police car. "Speak French to him, not German," counseled Elmar Tophoven, as they drew to a halt. "They don't like the Germans." Beckett murmured his abject apologies in French to the Dutch policeman and, after a few words of friendly caution, was allowed to drive on.[19]

They stayed on for a couple of days in Amsterdam, where Beckett visited the Rijksmuseum to look at the seventeenth-century Dutch paintings, including Rembrandt's famous *Self-Portrait as St. Paul*, the early portrait of *Saskia*, and the beautiful candle-lit *The Denial of St. Peter*, in which the source of light is hidden by the serving maid's right hand. The van Goyens and Ruisdaels were a joy. Beckett returned with the Tophovens by car via Delft (in honor of Vermeer's painting A *View of Delft*), then Straelen, to Paris. There he faced a major concern that had been dominating his thoughts over the past few months.

3

BECKETT KNEW that, if he were to die, Suzanne would not automatically inherit the rights to his work, since, under French law, there was no "common-law wife" legislation. Even a will can be contested. So, even though they had lived together for almost a quarter of a century, she would gain nothing from books whose publication she had single-handedly engineered. In addition, he had now become the owner of two properties and his work was at last making money.[20] So he determined to secure her future once and for all by marrying her.

There may have been additional reasons for doing so at this time. In a visit to Paris in January 1961, Barbara Bray had informed Beckett that she intended to move to Paris to live permanently with her two young daughters.[21] She had resigned from her job as script editor at the BBC, after being asked to go over to the production side, and was hoping to freelance in Paris as a translator and reviewer. Whether she made it clear that she was moving in order to be close to Beckett or not, it must have been obvious that he was an important part of her plans. In the past, Beckett had been able to see her whenever he went to London or whenever she came over to Paris for a short break. Now the imminence of her move changed the situation dramatically.

We do not know how aware Suzanne was of his particularly close liaison with Barbara, although there are signs in his work, notably in *Play*, that this may well have been the case. Beckett could have been in little doubt as to the extent of Barbara's love for and commitment to him. Yet, according to some of his friends, her arrival in Paris made him fear that his hand was about to be forced and led him to consider what he should do about it. As for Suzanne, she was now sixty-one and her situation as his longtime companion was beginning to seem increasingly vulnerable. She may have exercised some pressure on Beckett to marry her. Or he may simply have wanted to affirm where his true loyalty lay. Whatever the reason, the marriage to Suzanne made it clear—to Barbara, as well as to Suzanne—that he was unwilling and unlikely to leave the woman with whom he had already lived for more than twenty years.

The marriage must have been a shattering blow to Barbara. The wedding created a situation in which she had to choose between continuing the relationship or not (perhaps she even had to decide whether she should carry on with her plans to move to Paris). Yet it was also a purely practical step. It did not carry with it any vows of physical or emotional fidelity. Indeed, it allowed Beckett to carry on much as he had done before, his conscience clear at least as far as Suzanne's future material well-being was concerned. But, ironically, one way or another, further guilt was inevitable. He had already upset Suzanne by his infidelities. Now his decision to marry her inflicted pain on the "other woman." If he tried to end the relationship (as, according to one of his friends, at one stage he did) with Barbara, that too would bring even more pain, and consequently more guilt. It is likely, and quite in character, that he tried to keep everyone happy. And his play *Play*, started a year later, sharply parodies the stock responses of a man and two women intimately involved in an emotional triangle, including that of a man who wants the best of both worlds, domestic peace and extramarital spice. Yet the play still manages to express something of the torment of such a tangled web of emotions. It is no accident that it was Barbara Bray herself who, reviewing the world premiere of *Play* in Ulm, emphasized the very human side of this domestic drama set in purgatory, describing the three characters as "people in all their funny, disgraceful, pitiable fragility and all the touchingness, in spite of everything, of their efforts to love one another, and endure."[22]

Once he had made his decision to marry Suzanne, their main aim was to keep the projected "nuptials" from becoming public. This meant telling as few of their friends as they could and getting married in as much secrecy and with as much haste as possible. He had discussed his decision to marry with the Haydens and the Arikhas in Paris and with Tom MacGreevy, Con Leventhal, and Alan Schneider while they were visiting Paris. Now, he talked to the publisher of his prose writings in England, John Calder, as to how the plan could best be put into operation. Since he was of Irish nationality, Beckett needed to be married in England, not France, to establish Suzanne's inheritance. Joyce did the same for the same reason with Nora in July 1931, although, because Joyce's wedding took place in London, he did not entirely succeed in avoiding publicity. Getting married was easier in England than in France anyway. It was Calder's suggestion that Beckett should get married in the registry office of a quiet seaside town on the south coast of England. Folkestone fitted the bill admirably, since it was close to France and would allow them to return to Paris immediately after the wedding.[23]

A few days after his return from Amsterdam, Beckett set off in what he called his "two nags" (the Deux Chevaux) for Le Touquet. There he made the short hop across the Channel, using the Silver City Airways car ferry service to Ferryfield Airport at Lydd in Kent, only about fifteen miles across the reclaimed Romney marshland from Folkestone.[24] To be married in the registry office, he was first obliged to be in residence in Folkestone for a minimum of two weeks. So he checked into the seafront Hotel Bristol, which was demolished later in the 1960s, at numbers 3 and 4 on the high cliff road called the Leas, opposite the unusual 1885 Water Balance Lift.[25] A reservation had been made for him by John Calder.

The Bristol, a smallish hotel of only twenty-two rooms which cost from seven to nine guineas a week with full board, was chosen rather than a larger, better-known hotel like the Pavilion, the Grand, or the Metropole so as to lessen Beckett's chances of being recognized. The hotel was not particularly comfortable but it had a fully licensed bar. In registering, Beckett used his middle name, Barclay, to preserve his anonymity.[26] He feared that, if a local journalist were to get wind of his presence there and alert the national newspapers, a secret wedding would become impossible. Suzanne wanted no friends present as witnesses either. When he wrote to those other than the very small circle of intimates already in the know, he used innocuous phrases like "having a bit of rest here in Folkestone and environs." He signed a postcard to Avigdor Arikha in Paris simply "S," and wrote: "Sang coule plus calme dans la ville de Harvey" ("Blood flows more calmly in the town of Harvey"), for Folkestone was the birthplace of William Harvey, who discovered the circulation of the blood.[27]

The day after his arrival, Beckett called on the registrar of births, deaths, and marriages for the subdistrict of Folkestone in the offices at 29 Bouverie Square. The registrar, D. A. P. Cullen, was sympathetic and helpful and told Beckett that, as long as he retained his room at the Hotel Bristol, he could travel around the region as much as he liked. He avoided London like the plague. But he spent a few days with Sheila Page in Surrey. Being away on his own reminded him of the literary and artistic pilgrimages that he used to make in the mid 1930s. He visited Rye in East Sussex, taking a genteel afternoon tea in the half-timbered Ancient Vicarage where, tradition has it, the dramatist John Fletcher was born in 1579.[28]

Beckett also drove on to Brighton, where he spent a pleasant evening with the book collector and dealer Jake Schwartz, staying overnight at the former dentist's house. In a Brighton bookshop, he bought George Birkbeck Hill's six-volume edition of *Boswell's Life of Samuel Johnson* (1887), which he had worked on in the 1930s and had "been looking for in vain for years."[29] He did not breathe a word to Schwartz about his forthcoming marriage; to explain his presence in England, he simply said that he was resting after his recent trip to Bielefeld. This was to be a last occasion on which he felt trust for the dentist, whom he later used to call "the Great Extractor," for he soon learned through another dealer, Henry Wenning (who in future dealings shared the profits on sales far more generously with Beckett) that Schwartz had been paying him only a small percentage of the true value of his manuscripts.[30]

He took the car for numerous drives to Winchelsea and Canterbury, as well as Rye, Hastings, and Brighton,[31] and spotted on his map of the area the name "Borough Green," which he slipped into the second manuscript version of *Happy Days*—the nearby larger town of Sevenoaks supplied an alternative suggestion added by hand to typescript two[32]—and discovered the delightful names of Ash and Snodland in Kent, which he used a year later in *Play*.[33]

Mostly though, the dank days limped leadenly by, as he hung around the town "trying to be invisible."[34] He found the food in the hotel execrable, with "marvelous Dover sole reduced to consistency of paste,"[35] but sat on most nights in quiet country pubs relishing pints of draft Guinness. In the hotel, he tinkered with the manuscript of *Happy Days*, gazing out at the sea and the sky and the tips of a few fir trees rising from the wooded cliff. He also dealt with a huge pile of accumulated mail. But it was hard to concentrate and, feeling as he put it "half chlorophormed," [36] he regularly gave up and went to bed at half past nine.[37]

After a few days, something happened that put the entire wedding in doubt. Beckett received a message that his cousin John Beckett had been badly injured in a serious car accident in Ireland.[38] He thought he would be needed in Dublin and spoke of traveling over to be with John's mother and sister. But when he called his aunt Peggy, it was to learn that, although John, driving back home in a Mini from an evening playing Haydn string quartets with friends, had hit a wall about four A.M. in Little Bray, breaking his arms and badly injuring his hip and his ankle, his vital organs were undamaged and his life was not in danger.[39] Peggy assured Beckett that nothing could be gained by interrupting his stay and that a visit later on in the year would be far more welcome, since John was expected to have to remain in hospital for a minimum of three months, followed by a further three months of convalescence.[40] (In the end, John was hospitalized for a full five months.) Beckett had been prepared to abandon the wedding and start all over again. But, reassured by what he heard, he decided to stay put and to telephone John's future wife, Vera, and his aunt Peggy regularly in Ireland.

Suzanne did not need to reside in England to be married there, so she came over only three days before the wedding. Early on Saturday morning, March 25, 1961, the simple ceremony was conducted by Charles G. Mayled, the superintendent registrar, and registered by D. A. P. Cullen. So, in a marriage recorded as number 66, a fifty-four-year-old bachelor, Samuel Barclay Beckett, writer, was finally married to a sixty-one-year-old spinster, Suzanne Georgette Anna Deschevaux-Dumesnil, before two witnesses, E. Pugsley and J. Bond, who were either plucked off the street or worked in the registrar's office.[41] Two days later, back in Paris again, Beckett wrote to Con Leventhal: "It was good of you to wire and telephone. I wish you could have been with me, but Suzanne was determined on nobody. All went without a hitch, in absolute quiet. We returned to France the same morning and arrived in Paris Saturday in time for dinner after an easy drive from Le Touquet. Thank God it's done at last." [42]

There had been two minor scares about the secret getting out: the first when a case of champagne arrived at the hotel — it had been ordered by Barney Rosset from New York — and the second when, early on the morning of the wedding, a local reporter, a stringer for the *Daily Express*, telephoned John Calder at home to ask him whether a man getting married in Folkestone that day was his author Samuel Beckett. Thinking quickly, Calder said that this could not possibly be true since he had just received a postcard from the writer, who was on holiday in North Africa.[43]

4

ON HIS RETURN from the wedding, Beckett sat down to revise *Happy Days*. He was under a lot of pressure to finish it, having promised copies to several people who were planning productions and translations.[44] The difficulty was not only that he found "some damn thing always wrong each time I look at it,"[45] but that Paris was "chock full . . . of people to be seen"[46] and that he was constantly being interrupted. What he mentions in only a few letters is that he also became closely involved in helping Barbara Bray to settle down in Paris, asking Mania Péron and Edith Fournier (a former pupil of Mania) for advice as to where her two daughters, aged thirteen and nine, should go to school.[47] Their affair was far from over and, once Barbara had made up her mind to allow their relationship to continue, Beckett's marriage to Suzanne seems to have made very little difference to their closeness.

A final obstacle to completing his new play was being drawn into rehearsing an old one, *En attendant Godot*, at the prestigious Odéon Théâtre de France. Originally he had hoped to leave the direction almost entirely to Roger Blin, dropping in only occasionally. But the production was fraught with some hair-raising problems:[48] Two new actors, Etienne Bierry and Jean-Jacques Bourgois, had to be rehearsed as Estragon and Pozzo; Blin left after the first few weeks of rehearsal to direct Jean Genet's *The Blacks* at the Royal Court Theatre in London;[49] and Lucien Raimbourg, playing his old part of Vladimir, turned up, after making a film with Fernandel in the south of France, only a week before the production opened. Even the magnificent tree, sculpted especially by Alberto Giacometti, a friend of Blin as well as of Beckett, arrived late.[50] As a result, Beckett found himself helping Jean-Marie Serreau with everything, even playing Vladimir when Serreau, too, was not free. "Usual misery and confusion," he summed up with characteristic succinctness.[51] Although he had been "killed with rehearsing,"[52] in the end Beckett conceded that it was "an honourable production"[53] that did excellent business at the box office and received a splendid write-up in the press.[54] His spirits were lifted still further when he, along with Borges, was awarded the Prix International des Critiques or Prix Formentor. Its ten-thousand-dollar prize allowed him to help quite a few of his friends financially.[55]

Yet, with these various distractions, it was May before he could settle down properly to finish *Happy Days*.[56] Winnie's song at the end of the play was left until very late in the composition. After toying earlier with the more domestic "When Irish eyes are smiling,"[57] he finally wrote in by hand on the third typescript, the more poignant, less geographically specific, "I love you so" waltz duet from Franz Lehár's *Merry Widow*. He also modified the ending. When Kay Boyle asked him later in the year why Willie reaches up toward Winnie — to touch her or to grasp the revolver — he replied:

> The question as to which Willie is "after" — Winnie or the revolver — is like the question in *All That Fall* as to whether Mr Rooney threw the little girl out of the railway-carriage or not. And the answer is the same in both cases — we don't know, at least I don't. All that is necessary as far as I'm concerned — technically and otherwise — less too little, more too much — is the ambiguity of motive, established clearly I hope by Winnie, "Is it me you're after, Willie, or is it something else? Is it a kiss you're after, Willie, or is it something else?" and by the conspicuousness of revolver requested in stage-directions at beginning of Act II. To test the doubt was dramatically a chance not to be missed, not to be bungled either by resolving it. That's what I felt in any case. I know creatures are supposed to have no secrets for their authors, but I'm afraid mine for me have little else.[58]

Even though he was still not fully satisfied with the play before working on it in the theater,[59] he was immensely relieved to have the final typescript ready at last to be dispatched to Grove Press on June 7.

He was still intensely preoccupied with *Happy Days* throughout the summer — but now with future productions. He corresponded with Alan Schneider on almost every detail of its presentation,[60] even considering at one time going over to New York to lend him a hand.[61] One of his main reasons for wanting to be in England in the second half of June was to talk to McWhinnie about his directing the play at the Royal Court Theatre. Beckett's hope was that Joan Plowright, Laurence Olivier's wife, who was in the last few months of pregnancy, would be able to play Winnie after the birth of her first child. She was eager to act the part and he thought she was "worth waiting for."[62] Most of the discussion focused on where the world premiere of the new play should be held. Schneider offered to postpone his New York production if Beckett wanted the premiere in London. But since neither McWhinnie nor Plowright could be free for several months to come, the date of the first British production was bound to be uncertain. Beckett told Schneider therefore to proceed with his own plans for a mid-September world premiere at the Cherry Lane Theater in New York. In the meantime, he continued working with the Tophovens on their German translation in time for it to be played by Berta Drews at the Berlin Festival at the end of September.

5

THERE WERE OTHER nontheatrical reasons for Beckett's June 1961 trip to England. While in Folkestone for the wedding, he had spent a delightfully relaxed weekend with Sheila and Donald Page and learned that Sheila's sister, Molly, was going to be staying with them in June. And since Harold Hobson had invited him to see the test match at Lords Cricket Ground in London toward the end of June, he thought that, after the exhausting struggles with *Godot* and his efforts on the new play, the rest would do him good. A seasoned Silver City

Airways traveler by now, he took the car again from Le Touquet to Lydd and drove the slightly less than a hundred miles to Sweetwater cottage. He enjoyed the freedom of having the car to drive around the countryside of the southeast and was intrigued by the quiet, peaceful atmosphere of the middle-class English community. He met the Pages' friendly neighbors, Mick and Madge Bendon, whom he also used to see in Paris, and drove Sheila and Molly around the leafy country lanes. He also spent a lot of time sitting out on a deck chair in the garden reading. When Donald came home from the City, they played a few gentle games of croquet together on the Pages' beautifully kept lawns. Nothing could have been further from the bustle of Paris.

He spent the second week of his visit to England staying with John and Bettina Calder in their flat in Wimpole Street in London. There were a host of social and business appointments: a dinner invitation from Leslie and Lilian Daiken; an evening with Donald McWhinnie discussing the new play; and a visit to a late rehearsal of John Osborne's *Luther*, which he described as "unspeakable,"[63] but where he met George Devine, who confirmed that he very much wanted *Happy Days* for the Royal Court Theatre.

On June 26, 1961, McWhinnie's BBC television production of *Waiting for Godot* was being broadcast with Peter Woodthorpe as Estragon and Jack MacGowran as Vladimir. Beckett was invited to a party in Woodthorpe's basement flat in Chelsea to watch the film with Woodthorpe, McWhinnie, Mac-Gowran, and John and Bettina Calder. As they watched, Beckett displayed acute signs of irritation and unhappiness. He hated the entire experience. John Calder recounted what happened next:

> The whole thing came to an end. Long silence. Woodthorpe switched off his television set whereupon Sam put his head into his hands and said, "Thank you Donald, thank you for doing that for me. But, you know, it's not right on television. But thank you for doing that." Another long silence. Stupid me, to break the silence, said something, some remark to break this long silence which could have gone on for half an hour, you know, Sam with his head in his hands. Whereupon Donald McWhinnie with enormous relief turned round to me and said, "You stupid cretin publisher whatever you call yourself, what do you know about anything, what do you know about the theatre, what do you know about television, what do you know about dealing with these people that have got to fit into a certain style? You know nothing, stupid, ignorant . . ." and he went on at me like that. It was with great relief, you know, because he couldn't reply to Sam. Whereupon Sam blurted out, "Donald please don't. John didn't mean anything. Don't attack John. Please don't start so. I liked it very much, I really liked it very much. It was fine." Which it wasn't.[64]

But, in spite of the sudden outburst from McWhinnie, which arose from hurt pride, Beckett made two thought-provoking comments about how wrong he thought television was for *Waiting for Godot*. "My play," he said, "wasn't written for this box. My play was written for small men locked in a big space. Here you're all too big for the place." And he went on: "You see, you could write a very good play for television about a woman knitting. You'd go from the face to the knitting, from the knitting to the face."[65] Beckett must have smiled ruefully when he saw the words "Godot Well Adapted for Television" as the sub-heading of *The Times*'s review.

While he was in England, he accompanied the wheelchair-bound Harold Hobson to a crowded Lords Cricket Ground for the test match between England and Australia. It was a low-scoring game which ground slowly to an English defeat and Beckett felt that he let himself down by falling fast asleep during it, but he enjoyed the atmosphere and being there with Hobson, whom he liked. He was more upset than angry to read about the day that he had spent at Lords with Hobson in an article contributed by the critic pseudonymously to the *Sunday Times*. A week or so later, Hobson was in Paris, where his car broke down. Beckett took the opportunity to rap him gently over the knuckles about his article — but only after he had gone to enormous lengths to ensure that Hobson's car would be repaired in time for his departure.[66]

6

BECKETT'S RETURN TO FRANCE from England was marred by a most upsetting incident. He went to Ussy for "a few days' breather" only to find that:

> The place has been burgled, the iron shutters forced, a window broken and the whole place turned upside down. A number of things stolen, but nothing of value. A picture by Hayden overlooked and my books and papers merely scattered about the floor. Spent the day today clearing up the mess. The gendarmes told me there was an average of 12 such burglaries per week![67]

He was delighted not to have lost the Hayden painting, which he considered the only valuable item in his country house. But he was cross that the burglars, as well as enjoying all the food and drink they could find, had stolen his clothes, even his old underpants.

Clearing up took a little time. But it was not long before he embarked on the difficult task of translating *Comment c'est*. There were countless interruptions. Some were thankless chores; but others were pleasant occasions, as when Tom MacGreevy came over from Ireland to go to the Théâtre Sarah-Bernhardt with the Becketts to see the production of Mihalovici's opera in the Festival of the Théâtre des Nations that he had missed in Germany. A few days later, Beckett bumped into the American singer William Dooley in the street and learned with delight that, jointly with a bass from the Zagreb opera, Dooley had been awarded the prize of best singer in the festival and, on the strength of his Krapp, had received an offer from La Scala in Milan.[68] Beckett glowed with pleasure as he told friends about the singer's success.

He had intended going to Ireland at the same time as his London trip to see John Beckett, who was recovering slowly after further surgery on his hip. But he soon realized, with a deeply entrenched sense of guilt, that he was incapable of facing up to all that Ireland entailed by way of social commitments. Later in the year, he was able to be of direct, concrete help to another member of his family of whom he was extremely fond. His nephew, Edward, came over to Paris to take the examinations for entry to the famous Paris Conservatoire Supérieur de Musique. Beckett had been closely involved in discussions with the family that had run on for several years as to Edward's choice of career. Since his brother's death, he had acted as a combination of sounding board and unbiased adviser for his nephew. Jean, his mother, very much wanted her son to follow his father into engineering and to study for a degree at Trinity College, while, from an early stage, Edward was set on a career as a flutist. At that time in Dublin, relatively few boys studied music seriously — at the Municipal School of Music, for example, there were only two, a viola player and Edward — and it was regarded as a profession unlikely to enable a man to support himself. On a visit to Ireland, probably in December 1958 when he went over to visit Ethna MacCarthy, Beckett had accompanied his nephew to one of his flute lessons with his teacher, André Prieur, who had been a pupil of Marcel Moyse,[69] and later conferred with him as to the feasibility of Edward becoming a professional flutist.

In what seemed like a sensible compromise, Beckett persuaded Edward that he should enter Trinity in 1960 to do engineering. This would allow him, then, to have a choice of careers. He agreed and did the foundation year at TCD. But he spent far more time practicing the flute than working at his engineering. With André Prieur's encouragement, he determined to leave and go to Paris to study music, taking a sabbatical year with the promise that, if things did not work out in the Conservatoire's entrance exams, or even after his first year, he could still return to take up his palce in the engineering school.[70]

Edward came over to Paris in the last week in August and took the preliminary examinations in October and early November.[71] Beckett wrote with relief that

> Edward sailed through his prelim. Conservatoire exam. day before yesterday and we telephoned the good news to Jean that evening. Everyone with whom he has worked is impressed by his talent and I am pretty sure he will be successful again on November 6th (final test) and find himself received into that illustrious academy and a citizen of Paris for probably three years. He is a very lovable lad and an appealing mixture of maturity and boyishness.[72]

Indeed, Edward "sailed through" the final test as well.

Beckett and Suzanne took their duties in loco parentis very seriously and went out of their way to ensure that Edward had every opportunity to settle down well in Paris. They followed his progress at the Conservatoire with interest. But they also introduced him to several of their good friends (such as the actor

Jean Martin and the painter Manolo Fandos) asking them if they would look after their young nephew. The Becketts had a regular weekly dinner date with him, and Beckett sometimes took him to the cinema, or to the Falstaff in the rue du Montparnasse or the Rosebud bar in the rue Delambre. They played billiards together in the Trois Mousquetaires in the avenue du Maine. Beckett was extremely proud of his nephew and enjoyed the sense of relaxation that he felt in the young man's company. Suzanne mothered Edward to some extent, taking him to buy a tuxedo that he needed for concerts and inviting him occasionally to concerts with her husband and herself.

It was a year in which Beckett had been brought, partly by accident, partly by choice, to feel increasingly close to some members of his family. But this failed to bring him any closer to Ireland, except in his memories of the beautiful places that he could call to mind so vividly. Peter Lennon, an Irish exile who spent many evenings in Beckett's company at this time, has written well about the ambiguities in his attitude: "It was clear that recalling places in Ireland especially around the Dublin and Wicklow mountains gave him genuine plea-sure. The Featherbed? 'Lovely spot.' Luggala? 'Glorious.' And Killiney, of course, where the remnants of his family still lived within " 'strolling distance of the Bay.' "[73] Lennon rightly stressed that "the sense of Ireland was . . . strong in him; there was a subterranean emotional involvement and he had a weakness for those with a particular Irish desperation and vulnerability." But he was also right to stress that Beckett "despised the ethos of the place."[74]

7

IN THE AUTUMN OF 1961, Beckett added an American academic to his already large and growing group of friends. "Sam fait des copains comme un chien fait des chiots" ("Sam makes friends like a dog makes puppies"), Suzanne com-plained bitterly one day.[75] The latest addition to the throng was a tall, earnest Dartmouth professor of French and Italian, Lawrence Harvey, who was in Paris with his wife and family on a Guggenheim fellowship to write about Beckett's poetry and criticism. Many things in Harvey appealed to Beckett: his passionate love of French and Italian literature, particularly of French classical drama (Harvey had also written a book about Louise Labé's sonnets) and his knowledge of fourteenth- and fifteenth-century Florentine painting; his interest in French wines; and, above all, his keen interest in and intuitive understanding of Beck-ett's own work. But it was the man himself whom he liked. "I usually see as little as possible of such researchers," wrote Beckett to Tom MacGreevy, "but I took a liking to Harvey when I met him and have been giving him what help I can."[76] He recommended him to Con Leventhal, saying: "He is a very nice quiet gentle serious chap, more at home in the 17th than the 20th [century] and quite ignorant of Irish things. I wouldn't suggest your seeing him if I thought he would horripilate you. But I think you will like him too."[77]

Although passionately devoted to Beckett's work, Harvey used to argue vigorously with him about the profound differences that separated Beckett's views on life from his own. For Harvey was a devout Roman Catholic, like Tom MacGreevy, drawn to Beckett's work for what he saw as its deep undercurrents of spirituality. They began meeting for drinks and dinner at the beginning of November 1961, and Beckett soon met Harvey's intelligent wife, Sheila. He gave Harvey letters of introduction to Jérôme Lindon and to various friends in London and Dublin. Unusually for academic friends, the Harveys were also invited to visit Beckett at Ussy.

In Paris, at dinner and often until the early hours of the morning, Harvey used to ply Beckett with questions about his life and his ideas and, more searchingly, about his work, often about lines, words, or phrases that figured in his 1930s poems and novels. Beckett did not even object when Harvey started making notes on little cards that he took out of his jacket pocket as they talked over dinner. One night, in the early hours, Beckett wrote a message on a cocktail napkin: "Sheila, he is killing me with questions!"[78] Beckett knew what Harvey was writing and, when Harvey assured him that he would show him everything that he wrote and publish nothing to which he objected, he trusted him implicitly. Harvey lived up to that trust, removing all that Beckett objected to from his book, *Samuel Beckett, Poet and Critic*, when it was finished.

They talked a lot, of course, about everyday things in their lives. But, as the night wore on, Beckett also discussed with Harvey his feelings about his own writing. Writing was for him, he said, a question of "getting down below the surface" toward what he described as "the authentic weakness of being." This was associated with a strong sense of the inadequacy of words to explore the forms of being. "Whatever is said is so far from the experience"; "if you really get down to the disaster, the slightest eloquence becomes unbearable." In this he was far removed, he maintained, from the approach of James Joyce: "Joyce believed in words. All you had to do was rearrange them and they would express what you wanted."[79] Beckett never seems to have believed that this was achievable.

Toward the end of the Harveys' stay in Léveil-Brévannes, outside Paris, one of their children, John, was knocked down by a motorcar. He was not seriously injured, but the next day Beckett turned up for the first time at the château where the Harveys were staying to chat to their son. He also brought with him a large bundle of manuscripts, several of them unpublished, among which his 1932 novel, *Dream of Fair to Middling Women*, which he handed over with the minimum of fuss to Harvey as a gift.[80] It was a characteristic, almost reflex response to their upset.

8

AT THIS TIME, Beckett's publisher and long-standing friend, Jérôme Lindon, was confronting a worrying, indeed highly dangerous situation in his professional life. The story illuminates the stance that Beckett himself took on certain key political, moral, and humanitarian questions and reveals the constraint that was imposed on him by his position as a foreigner resident in France. When people have written about his lack of political involvement after the Second World War — for his engagement in the struggle against Nazism cannot be challenged — this very real constraint has been entirely forgotten.

France had been passing through a period of intense turmoil over the previous few years. General de Gaulle had been brought back as president in 1958 in an attempt to introduce a measure of stability. Apart from the country's severe economic problems, disagreements raged fiercely over the future of the French colony of Algeria. Toward the end of the 1950s, French society appeared to be tearing itself apart over this issue. One of the major problems came from the opposition of the increasingly strong National Liberation Front (FLN) independence movement in Algeria, which also operated in metropolitan France, and of the right-wing French Secret Army Organization, or OAS, which was dedicated to terrorist activities against those who, rightly or wrongly, it believed were supporting the Algerian cause.

Alongside the military struggle, which dates from November 1954, an intellectual battle was being waged in France, particularly from the spring of 1957, in which the methods used by the French military both in Algeria and in France itself were condemned. One of the key moments in this campaign was the publication in March 1957 of Pierre-Henri Simon's book *Contre la torture*, which claimed that torture had become institutionalized in the French army in its dealings with Algerians.

Jérôme Lindon's involvement in this battle for people's consciences came in two phases.[81] Along with Les Editions Maspero, he led the way by publishing at Les Editions de Minuit a series of *Documents* and books on torture committed by the French military in Algeria. The most important of the many books and brochures that he published was Henri Alleg's *La Question*, which appeared on February 18, 1958. Alleg, a member of the Algerian Communist Party and a former director of the review *Alger républicain*, described the torture that he had himself experienced at the hands of the French military. The publication of this *témoignage* had a tremendous impact in France, and two issues of newspapers containing articles about it *(France Observateur* and *L'Express)* were impounded. The book itself was seized, but only after five weeks, and by then sixty-five thousand copies had already been sold. As a result of this seizure, Lindon was backed by the League for the Rights of Man and supported by a number of leading French writers — Roger Martin du Gard, André Malraux, François Mauriac, and Jean-Paul Sartre — who signed a protest to the president of the Republic. Lindon followed the Alleg book with others on similar themes: *L'Affaire Audin* on the arrest, torture, and disappearance in Algiers of the Communist mathematician Maurice Audin; *La Gangrène*, the complaints of five Algerian students tortured in Paris; and Francis Jeanson's important *Notre Guerre*. Nine of the Editions de Minuit *Documents* concerning Algeria were seized.

The second phase of Lindon's involvement was in courageously publishing several books that encouraged disobedience and desertion by French military personnel in Algeria confronted with the evidence of such torture. This phase followed on the first simply because the issue of torture had never been resolved, or even properly addressed. The best-known example was a fictional work called *Le Déserteur*, published pseudonymously in March 1960 under a name that Lindon himself invented: Maurienne. This was an astute choice of name for the author, because it was the name of a region of France next to the Vercors and it was "Vercors" (another pseudonym) who had founded the Resistance press, Les Editions de Minuit. The real author of the novel was Jean-Louis Hurst. In this case not only was the book seized but proceedings were instituted against Lindon for "incitement to military disobedience."

The case achieved a high degree of international coverage. In the course of the proceedings two of his fellow publishers, Claude Gallimard and René Juillard, had pleaded for the sanctity of freedom of expression; more dramatically, former French soldiers had for the first time been able to present in public firsthand accounts of acts of torture that they had themselves witnessed in Algeria. *The Times* of London quoted a sergeant-major attached to a "psychological unit" as saying: "When a man of honour feels that the only way of escaping an order to torture is to desert, then I think he is right to do so."[82] On December 20, Lindon was fined two thousand new francs. But the revelations that emerged at the trial focused public attention even more sharply on the moral issues involved.

One result of the trial was to make Lindon himself into an OAS target. On the night of his court appearance, December 7, a bomb exploded outside his apartment in the boulevard Arago, blowing in a door and inflicting damage on the premises. Four days later, a Molotov cocktail was tossed through the small display window of the Editions de Minuit office in the rue Bernard-Palissy. Beckett anxiously summed up the situation of his friend to Aidan Higgins: "He [Lindon] goes in permanent personal danger."[83]

Torture was the kind of moral issue on which Beckett and Suzanne had very strong feelings, and both of them were intensely concerned about their friend in his troubles. Earlier, with the seizure of Henri Alleg's book, they had actively helped Lindon by encouraging friends like Marthe Gautier to secrete copies in their apartments so they could not be destroyed. At the time of the trial, Beckett once again showed himself willing to help directly by sending the text of a manifesto initiated by the novelist Claude Simon and supporting Lindon to John Calder (who had earlier published Alleg's book in English) and to Harold Hobson, intending that they should sign it;[84] in the end, the signatories were confined to those with French nationality. This was called the "Manifeste des 121," for Lindon halted the manifesto at 121 signatories by analogy with the more famous manifesto of the previous year,[85] although many more French publishers, writers, actors, and directors than that had signed the document supporting him. The act of signing the declaration was to have serious repercussions for two of the signatories, Roger Blin and Jean Martin, who found it impossible to obtain work for almost a year. Martin, who was performing at the state-funded Théâtre National Populaire, was kicked out of his job; he was forced to go to Helsinki to find theatrical work and, at one point, was reduced to asking Marthe Gautier whether she could find him some filing chores in the hospital where she worked.[86]

As is clear from all his actions, Beckett supported the manifesto but, like another Minuit author, Robert Pinget, who was Swiss, did not sign it because as a foreign resident dependent on a valid *carte de séjour* in order to stay in France, he would have laid himself open to the withdrawal of his residential permit and could have been deported. "He considered himself an Irishman who should not take up an official public position on what did not concern him directly," said Jean Martin.[87] For a foreigner, signing such declarations and petitions was, as Jérôme Lindon stressed, simply not worth the risk involved.[88] As it was, in addition to the moral support and the practical steps that he took to back Lindon, Beckett worried constantly about the personal safety of his friend and his family and about the difficult situation in which Roger Blin and Jean Martin found themselves. At one time, knowing that Jean Martin was trying to write during his enforced absence from the stage, Beckett gave him his own typewriter.[89] He probably also helped Roger Blin financially at this time, as he did on a number of other occasions.

9

IN THE AUTUMN OF 1961, Beckett was busy "plugging away grimly at translation of *Comment c'est*."[90] It was one of his most difficult, thankless tasks — he produced eight different versions — and took well over a year to complete. It could only be, he wrote to John Calder, "at the best, a most lamentable *à peu près* [approximation]."[91] As a relief, he returned to writing for radio. But his work took a new direction. Until that time, his plays for radio (*All That Fall* and *Embers*) had involved only voices and sound effects. Now music, which had always been important to him, was to play a key role. Avigdor Arikha wrote that

> listening to music was essential to him. It was part of our friendship (sharing passions). During the fifties we used to listen to music (mainly Beethoven chamber music, Schubert) during the day in my studio 10 Villa d'Alésia (where I lived 1955–1964). Later with Anne, always after dinner, at home. It was a ritual: he used to come at 8 pm, in later years a bit earlier, sometimes play the piano with Alba, chess with Noga [the Arikhas' daughters] (see my drawing 1980) et *à table*. After dinner we listened to music. Concerning pianists, his favourites were Yves Nat, Cortot, Schnabel, Solomon, Serkin, but not only [these]. He valued many pianists. Monique Haas and Mihalovici were on a more personal level. We had a period during which we listened to quite a bit of dodecaphonic music — Schoenberg, Berg, Webern (before 1959). But he always returned to romantic music — from Haydn

to Brahms. He disliked Wagner and also Mahler — actually antithetical to his sense of "less is more." [92]

Beckett's friendship with Mihalovici and Monique Haas brought him into close touch with modern music and musicians of the highest quality. Monique was particularly noted for her Debussy and Ravel recordings and, among modern composers, she played a lot of Hindemith, Bartók, Webern, and Stravinksy,[93] sometimes playing her latest concert piece for the Becketts when they went round for dinner. As with Hayden in painting, Beckett felt with Mihalovici that he was close to the creative process of a composer, as his friend talked about what he was engaged in.

But there were more precise reasons why Beckett introduced music into his radio plays. After the success of *Embers*, the BBC drama department made it clear that they would very much like another radio play from him. And Beckett wanted to provide a creative stimulus to his cousin John, who by the autumn was well on the way to recovery after his horrific accident. Independently, Marcel Mihalovici had received a request from the French radio station, RTF, for a composition that they could record and broadcast and he turned to Beckett for a radiophonic text. The resulting two plays, *Words and Music* and *Cascando*, were highly innovatory. The BBC producer, Michael Bakewell believed that they pioneered the role of music as an autonomous member of the cast of a play, quite different from its traditional role in radio drama as background or as creator of mood or atmosphere.

The actual idea of Words and Music figuring as separate dramatic characters may well have come to Beckett while sitting at the piano with Mihalovici and Blin in 1960. He listened as the composer played through the music of his opera *Krapp* while Blin read the words. He then worked hard with Mihalovici to adjust the words to the musical phrases and vice versa.[94] *Words and Music* bears the imprint of these struggles to bring the two different elements together. "Words" and "Music" are the two servants of an old man called Croak, who asks each of them for a contribution on the theme of love, inciting them at least to "be friends." On Croak's orders, and not very expertly either, Words attempts to sing his lines, following the musical phrases that are proposed to him by Music, very much as Blin did with Mihalovici in the latter's apartment.[95]

The two radio plays were written within a month of each other, *Words and Music* in November–December and *Cascando* in December 1961. John Beckett soon wrote his music for the first play, totally independently of Beckett.[96] But it was to be almost a year before Chip Mihalovici was able to compose the music for *Cascando*, since he was involved in writing the score for an opera buffa.[97] As a result of this and further delays, *Cascando* was not broadcast in French until October 13, 1963. Jean Martin played the part of La Voix, the Voice, while Roger Blin played L'Ouvreur, the Opener, an apt role for a man who may well have had a part to play in the genesis of the work.

10

BECKETT'S NEXT STAGE PLAY — called, with a nice irony, *Play* — was written only a few months after the two radio plays in which music played such an important role. So it is no coincidence that *Play* should have been so musically structured: a chorus for three voices, orchestrated like a musical score; a stage direction about the tempo, volume, and tone; and a repeat of the whole play da capo. Three figures, stuck up to their heads in funeral urns, respond to a shaft of light like orchestral players to the conductor's baton.

Yet, although the play tends toward the abstraction of music, Beckett knew perfectly well that this is unattainable in a text consisting of words. And even though some of the play's words may be missed the first time round, clichés are given new life by the context in which they are uttered and by characters who speak, though apparently dead. So a counterpoint is established between the banality of the narrative and the extraordinary nature of the setting. The "feel" of *Play* differs markedly from that of Beckett's earlier plays, except, at odd moments, *Happy Days*. It is steeped in a middle-class English "Home Counties" atmosphere rather than an Irish one. Beckett had been reminded of this world on the two visits that he made during the year to Sweetwater with the Pages and their neighbors. China cups of green tea sipped in the cool "morning room," the sound of an old hand mower ("some fool was cutting grass. A little rush, then another"),[98] a garden roller, a smoldering bonfire, and the chat about holidays on the Riviera or Grand Canary may be parodied features, but they have their roots in reality. Even the idiom is that of middle-class England: "peaked," "all heart to heart," "bygones bygones," "settle my hash," "not much stomach for her leavings," and so on. There are some literary antecedents for such a genteel world disrupted by powerful undercurrents of deep feeling: Katherine Mansfield is one, from whom Beckett may already have drawn some features of *Happy Days*. His startling idea with *Play* was to situate this replay of a middle-class adulterous affair in Limbo.

The initial holograph manuscripts of *Play* have not yet surfaced, so it is difficult to know exactly when he started to write it. His letters suggest that he wrote a first version sometime in April. At the beginning of the month, he wrote that he kept "pushing and pushing at the wall between me and new work, quite in vain, but recently a few gleams."[99] And, at the end of May, he told another American professor friend, Herbert Myron, that he hadn't "done a tap of work for months, but idea for a new act, one hour, three faces (mouths) and lights."[100] Between these two dates he seems to have written an early version of *Play*, in which the three characters are in boxes on stage, not urns. Lawrence Harvey has a note that he took down over dinner on April 30, 1962: "New play. *Must it.* 3 white boxes — no more than 3 feet high. 3 heads . . . Don't realize the others there. Play of light and dark. Must speak when light on (life) — (Must accept life). Histoire banale. Stage abolished."[101] At this early point, Beckett is clearly linking the idea of the three figures in white boxes to the theme added by Beethoven by hand to the late string quartet "Muss es sein" ("Must It Be"). This link was later dropped, although it is interesting that Beckett was seeing the mess of the triangular affair in the play as something that *must be* accepted as an unavoidable part of life. Interestingly, at the same dinner with Harvey, he referred to the end of Joyce's *Ulysses*, commenting that it was "saying yes to this atrocious affair of life." But the first version clearly did not work out and Beckett worked on the new play from May until August, struggling to mold it into shape.

He even took it away with him in August on a mountain holiday with Suzanne (who had a nasty bronchial cough). They went to Kitzbühel in Austria, from where he wrote to a friend that he had discovered the theme for the second part of his play: the presence or absence of a perceiving eye.[102] Finally, he decided that he was tinkering too much with his text and decided to leave it alone until he could return to his typewriter in Paris.[103]

Instead he worried about the prospects for the English premiere of *Happy Days*. It began to feel as if everything to do with the London premieres of his plays was fraught with problems. He and the producer, George Devine, had been waiting for almost a year for Joan Plowright to be free to play the demanding role of Winnie. Then, in May, Donald McWhinnie had to withdraw from directing the play. Devine agreed to take over, "with such help as I can give him," wrote Beckett.[104] But, during the Austrian holiday, Beckett heard that Joan Plowright was again pregnant and had been warned by her gynecologist that she must on no account attempt to act such a mammoth part in October.[105] "Perhaps we shd. decide to postpone production till she is past child-bearing — or the baronet beyond engendering," wrote Beckett with heavy sarcasm.[106] But neither he nor Devine wanted another lengthy postponement.

A search was quickly mounted for a suitable replacement. This proved to be far from easy. Beckett suggested bringing over the American actress Ruth White, who had played the part to almost universal acclaim in New York and had received an Obie award for her acting.[107] But this looked like an admission of defeat for Devine and, although in the event he did approach White, she was not available. Peggy Ashcroft was proposed but Devine did not consider her right for the part. At one stage, Beckett even contemplated withdrawing the option altogether from the Royal Court Theatre.

Meanwhile, every night, in their separate rooms, Beckett and Suzanne went to bed early. He snuggled down under the warmth of what he called his "édredon à cauchemars," "eiderdown for nightmares." For in Kitzbühel he dreamed more vividly than he had ever done before in his life. In one dream, "Joyce was dying," he wrote, "and was being carried at arms length like a quarter of beef," while in another, the rhinoceroses of Ionesco's play of that name, which he had seen the previous year, were rampaging in a little mountain chapel.[108]

During the day, *Happy Days* was constantly on Beckett's mind, and toward the latter part of their stay, he started to translate it into French. This proved to be very difficult. Even so, before he left, he managed to complete a rough draft of the whole of the first act, despite being interrupted periodically by what he described as "a crazy Irish setter" that used to wander into his room to lap up the water in the lavatory basin of his bathroom.[109] He had not the heart to close the door.

11

THE BECKETTS RETURNED to Paris on August 25, 1962, after staying in Innsbruck overnight on their way home, as they had done on the outgoing journey. On his return, there was much to do and many people to see. He could not get away to Ussy for over a week, because his nephew, Edward, was passing through Paris on his way to a music course in Cologne and because of other weekend engagements. Finally, he found a few days' peace in the country only to have to return for meetings with other visitors, among them his old friend from Dublin, Arland Ussher. Most satisfying of all, he had a surprise meeting at a concert with Stravinsky and his wife, with whom he had dined a year before in Amsterdam. Stravinsky embraced him like a long-lost friend, reminding him that he would be honored to compose the music for any opera that Beckett might wish to write. Before leaving for Russia, the composer sent a whole case of Sancerre over to Beckett's flat. Beckett was delighted, flattered, and moved and, as a gesture of thanks, sent several bottles of Jameson whiskey to Stravinsky's hotel. John and Edward Beckett, who were visiting Beckett at the time, came home with several bottles of the composer's wine.[110]

The problems with the casting of Winnie in *Happy Days* were finally resolved when, after some wavering, Joyce Redman turned down the part and, on the recommendation of the director John Dexter, at ten days' notice, Brenda Bruce was signed up. The production was put back by a couple of weeks, until November 1, and rehearsals began three weeks before that. As he had agreed with Devine, Beckett flew over to London to help.

At first, things seemed to go swimmingly and Beckett wrote enthusiastically to Avigdor Arikha:

> After two days rehearsal, I am very hopeful. . . . It didn't start any too well — voice and inflections wrong. But it's already much better. She is small, blonde, quite pretty, with a very fetching smile, a little too thin, 44 years old. . . . She has adopted a slight Scottish accent and it's amazing how well it works. She catches on very quickly and works very hard. Devine is very kind and there's an excellent working atmosphere. If she continues to progress at the same pace, it should result in something good.[111]

He and Brenda Bruce got on personally quite well. With Beckett towering above her, they trotted off together to spend "a jolly couple of hours buying the specs"[112] that Winnie was to wear. He inspected the hat that Jocelyn Herbert bought and modified for her, and the parasol, and he considered the color of her bodice, which should, he said, be pink, not yellow, since there was already so much of that color in the set.[113] Beckett irritated Brenda Bruce by saying softly, " 'Tis of no consequence," whenever she asked him what something meant. But, interestingly, over a meal one day, he confided to the actress how he came to write the play.

> He said, "Well I thought that the most dreadful thing that could happen to anybody, would be not to be allowed to sleep so that just as you're dropping off there'd be a "Dong" and you'd have to keep awake; you're sinking into the ground alive and it's full of ants; and the sun is shining endlessly day and night and there is not a tree. . . . There'd be no shade, nothing, and that bell wakes you up all the time and all you've got is a little parcel of things to see you through life." He was talking about a woman's life, let's face it. Then he said: "And I thought who would cope with that and go down singing, only a woman." [114]

But, for Beckett, things soon went wrong. Allowed by Devine more or less to take over as director, he became increasingly unhappy as Brenda Bruce struggled with a text that she had had far too little time to learn, let alone fully absorb, and with lines that Beckett tried to induce her to speak to a metronomically strict rhythm; at one stage he even brought a metronome into the theater and set it down on the floor, saying, "This is the rhythm I want." To the actress's astonishment, he then left it ticking relentlessly away. He also gave Brenda microscopically detailed notes. It was, as the theater critic Irving Wardle has put it, "as if someone battling with the scale of C major were suddenly placed under the baton of Karajan." [115] Brenda Bruce was, after all, still at the stage of sitting up until the middle of the night to learn her lines, then going through her part on the "Brighton Belle" train with Laurence Olivier to the consternation of commuting businessmen.[116] As they rehearsed, whenever she made a mistake, Beckett's head would sink into his hands and he would sigh with despair. However courteous and friendly he was in his personal relations with the actress, at rehearsal he totally undermined her self-confidence. A fortnight after his arrival, he wrote to friends that the production was heading for disaster and that he could do nothing to remedy the situation. In fact, the modest, insecure Brenda Bruce needed praise and encouragement, not criticism. And she was so shaken by Beckett's reactions and by her inability to get it right in his terms that she finally broke down in floods of tears.

Over the weekend, Beckett went away into the country with George Devine and Jocelyn Herbert and her children. On a walk with Sam and the children, Jocelyn suggested to him, gently but firmly, that Brenda Bruce couldn't cope with the pressure that he was putting on her. "Are you saying I ought not to go to rehearsals?" he asked. "I think you ought to stay away for a week," replied Jocelyn, "to give her time to get control of the text before you go back." Later, he told Bettina Calder bluntly: "I've been kicked out of rehearsals." He stayed away for most of the following week — seeing in the meantime a run-through of Jack MacGowran's one-man Beckett anthology, *End of Day*, at the New Arts

Theatre,[117] meeting his cousin John, staying a few days with his other cousin, Sheila Page, and going to a concert by Fischer-Dieskau of Hugo Wolf's Mörike lieder at the Festival Hall.[118] Then he returned to the Royal Court with an angelic smile and a big bunch of flowers for Brenda Bruce. But the damage had been done.

Beckett was never an actor's director. He seemed to be unable to put himself into an actor's skin and appreciate the problems that he or she was experiencing with the text or with what seemed too often like an alien way of working. For him, pace, tone, and, above all, rhythm were more important than sharpness of character delineation or emotional depth. But it was not only a musical approach to theatrical language that he was adopting. He also needed to find an acting style that suited his vision. He sought to achieve his effects minimally, taking out rather than putting in. For the actress this could be extremely disconcerting. Brenda Bruce asked: "So then, I mean, what about the part? Do you want some acting to go on? And I'm not sure that he really did, you see. He didn't really want me there. Not me — Brenda. I don't think he wanted any person doing it, in a way, it was all there in his head and if you made the slightest mistake . . ."[119]

In the end, Brenda Bruce gave an excellent performance. Reviewers praised her acting: "tour de force" was a much used phrase;[120] for *The Daily Telegraph's* W. A. Darlington, the performance was "Brenda Bruce at her finest"[121] and, with Maggie Smith, she was nominated for a BAFTA (British Academy Film and Television Awards) "Best Actress of the Year" award. Many of Beckett's friends reported back favorably to him on her performance.[122] "The Paris party were all very pleased with Brenda and the play," he wrote to Jocelyn Herbert. "Suzanne, who is hard to please, was quite enthusiastic. I was in no fit state, at the end, to judge anything."[123] This last sentence seems to represent the truth: obsessed by the way that he heard the text in his head, in this case he was past the point of judging the play or the performance at all objectively. However, he chuckled audibly when Brenda Bruce telephoned him in Paris during the run to tell him about "the man who stood up in the stalls and shouted at me until the house lights were put up and he was removed. I started again and the audience clapped. Then, five minutes later, he returned and walked to his seat, bowed to me and said 'Sorry, I forgot my raincoat.' "[124]

12

SOON AFTER *HAPPY DAYS* OPENED on November 1, 1962, Henri Hayden flew into London for an exhibition of his paintings at the Waddington Galleries. On the very day of the opening, he had a severe heart attack and was rushed into the French Hospital for treatment. His wife, Josette, checked into the Shaftesbury Hotel, where Beckett phoned regularly to find out about his friend's progress. He wrote to Hayden almost every other day, talking encouragingly about the success of the exhibition and discussing (as he had done with Ethna) little things to do with his own life that he would normally never have bothered writing about—dinners with John Calder and with his old Trinity College colleague Stuart Maguinness, problems with his heating, even the temperature in Ussy. He sent a little chess set back to London via John Calder to keep his friend amused.[125] And he pronounced himself ready to fly over at a moment's notice, if needed.

Earlier in the year, Beckett had helped the Haydens to move into a house at Reuil, only a few kilometers from his own cottage at Ussy. Now he went round there regularly to check that everything was in order. He awaited instructions as to what he should do about the Haydens' tax returns. Then he paid their taxes himself.[126] Back in Paris he called for their mail, paid the rent on their flat, and posted packets of Gauloises cigarettes to England for Josette.[127] When the Haydens returned home a month later, Beckett was waiting for them with his car at Orly airport in a temperature of minus ten to drive them home with uncustomary sedateness. Back in Paris he could not do enough to help.

But he had work to do. So, as soon as Hayden was settled in at home, he took himself off to Ussy. It was a winter of unremitting bitter cold that seemed to drag on for ever. On January 13, even the France-Scotland rugby match that he listened to on his radio lacked luster, as the French backs froze in the biting wind at the Colombes stadium.[128] For a few days, Beckett found himself snowbound and unable to get the car out to skid its icy way to La Ferté. So he lived on rice, bottles of wine, and tins of Heinz minestrone soup that he had stockpiled in the cupboard.[129]

As he was "struggling to liquidate" the translation of *Comment c'est*, "slow and obnoxious work,"[130] his mind was preoccupied with dark, disturbing thoughts. Illness, death, and controversy piled up like the snow-drifts around him: "My uncle Howard very bad with some circulatory trouble, but better I hear after operation, and my old T.C.D cricket crony down with cerebral haemorrage and just surviving alas I gather after operation."[131] At the end of February, he heard that Giorgio Joyce's wife, Helen Fleischman, had died near New York. Moreover, several quarrels had broken out between his friends and this always upset him dreadfully. John Calder and Barney Rosset had fallen out over the distribution of *Evergreen Review*, among other things, and his two publishers in Germany, Suhrkamp and Fischer, were at loggerheads over the allocation of the German rights (both publication and performance). Wearily, he wrote to Con Leventhal that he felt "tired and shaky and all these silly literary troubles have got me down."[132]

Quite unwittingly, he became embroiled in an unpleasant dispute about a film contract. In August 1962, on the advice of Lawrence Hammond, who worked for his London agent, Spencer Curtis Brown, he had signed a contract with Keep Films, Limited, for a film of *Waiting for Godot* with Peter O'Toole (and, they hoped, Peter Sellers). He did this, unusually, without consulting Jérôme Lindon, whose signature was required, since the play was written in French, to make such a contract legal. The deal had some bizarre features. Beckett was offered only three hundred pounds as an advance in the form of an option, together with a meager three and a half percent of takings, while, according to a report that appeared in *Ciné Revue*, the director John Huston, a friend of one of the principals of Keep Films, Jules Buck, was to be paid many times more than Beckett's advance merely for loaning the company his estate in Ireland for it to film there.

Lindon was concerned that Les Editions de Minuit had been excluded from these agreements. But he also felt very strongly that the contract neither protected Beckett's work sufficiently from unauthorized changes nor remunerated him adequately for the cinematographic rights. He reminded Curtis Brown that, if they had simply wanted to make a large amount of money from a film adaptation of *Godot*, they would have accepted the Hollywood offer from Bert Lahr and Paramount Pictures of twenty-five thousand dollars that they had turned down three years before. Beckett ate humble pie, writing what he described as a "miserere" to Lawrence Hammond, admitting his error and hoping that the matter could be amicably resolved. Lindon then proposed the annulment of the old contract and suggested a new one that would give Beckett an unambiguous right of veto over changes in the film adaptation and would bring him in more money. The affair dragged on throughout the whole of 1963 and it was March 1964 before Jules Buck finally "threw in the sponge" and accepted a check in repayment of any monies that Keep Films had already paid out. It was an ugly episode that upset Beckett and risked souring his relations with Jérôme Lindon. Instead it cemented them, encouraging them both to express their mutual affection and esteem, as well as bringing them together to seek a solution to a problem that Beckett alone had created by his unworldliness and lack of business acumen.

The trouble surrounding this helped to harden Beckett's opposition to any small- or large-screen adaptations of plays written for the stage or radio. The ones to which he had reluctantly given his consent — the 1961 BBC *Waiting for Godot*, for example, and the January 1963 RTF *Tous ceux qui tombent* (a television adaptation of Robert Pinget and Beckett's translation of *All That Fall*) [133] — confirmed him in his view that he was right to oppose such transpositions out of their original medium. So when, later in the year, Ingmar Bergman asked if he could stage the radio plays *All That Fall* and *Embers*, the answer was a firm no. [134]

As Beckett looked out on the snowy Ussy landscape, one pleasanter prospect at least peeped shyly over the horizon. Con Leventhal, alone in Dublin since Ethna's death, told him of his wish to quit his post at Trinity College and come to Paris to help lighten his administrative load. Beckett leaped at the opportunity. And, over the next few months, he spent a lot of time and effort, with the help of Josette Hayden, looking at flats in the Montparnasse area for Leventhal, finally arranging and paying the advance rental on a pleasant furnished apartment overlooking a courtyard at 144 boulevard du Montparnasse, just down the road from the Closerie des Lilas where they used to meet for drinks. Leventhal had a relaxed attitude to life and a delightfully puckish sense of humor, and, more crucially, was a friend from the old days, who could be trusted implicitly. Beckett looked forward very much to having him in Paris at the end of the academic session in July, for his convivial talk and companionship as much as for his practical help. When Leventhal finally arrived, a small group of Irishmen, including the poet John Montague and the journalist Peter Lennon, used to congregate in the Falstaff. They shared some riotous evenings with Beckett.[135]

13

ALTHOUGH HE FAILED to write a piece for Jack MacGowran—he called it, tentatively, "JM Mime," but abandoned it, as he put it himself, "in the absence of all inner need"[136]—he had more success with a second work that was also more or less written to order. Originally thought of as a television play, the "tempting offer" for a thirty-minute film was put to him personally by Barney Rosset on a visit to Paris in late February 1963.[137] It was to be part of an Evergreen Theater film project for which Rosset also commissioned scripts from Eugène Ionesco and Harold Pinter. When the contract was signed, Beckett received a fifteen-hundred-dollar advance, which he refrained from banking until he felt he had something worth offering. The first sketch was written in four days at Ussy at the beginning of April. He showed his outline to Alan Schneider on his visit to Paris at the end of May, then sent it on to Barney Rosset in New York on May 22.[138] Rosset, like Schneider, was intrigued by the strange, idiosyncratic nature of the script and began work to set up a production.

In June, Beckett made a hasty trip to Ulm with Alan Schneider to see two rehearsals of *Play*, the world premiere of which was being done in German. They had to travel overnight by train, since getting to Ulm by air was much too complicated. When Beckett arrived, he found the actors feeling rather lost with his text. Nancy Illig, who played Woman 2, recalled one incident arising out of this:

> The actor of the Man [Gerhard Winter] desperately threw this question out into the darkness of the auditorium: "Why am I dead?" The author seemed startled. He made various suggestions. Maybe because of a traffic accident? Or suicide? But mightn't he have died a natural death in bed? Obviously this question was not a relevant one for Beckett. When the actor insisted on knowing, Beckett said to [the director, Deryk] Mendel with a smirk: "The Absolute Camel." This referred to a joke both were familiar with which goes something like this: If an Englishman writes about a camel, he will use the title *The Camel*; a Frenchman will call it *The Camel and Love*; and a German, *The Absolute Camel*. The only thing important to Beckett was the situation: we were all three dead.[139]

Beckett was not overly impressed by what he saw of the rehearsals: "stock actors of little envergure" ("range"),[140] although he was to change his opinion of

Nancy Illig as he became better acquainted with her. But he concluded: "It will be a very careful and conscientious production, without more, but at least no director's improvements, which is a rare thing in Germany."[141] After seeing the play, Schneider went on to Berlin and Warsaw, while Beckett dashed back to Paris to be at the RTF studios for a further eight-hour recording session of his radio play *Cascando*. Although short, the trip had not been a waste of time, for it had succeeded in focusing Beckett's attention on a number of important problems to do with the shape of the urns, the repeat of the play, and, above all, the lighting of *Play*.

Back in Paris, rehearsals of *Cascando* continued in the "unbelievable confusion" of the "crazy Paris studios."[142] Beckett evoked the shambles very vividly:

> Different studio every time (i.e. different recording ambiance) and different technicians. A 4 hour session boiled down to 2 hours work, the other two devoted to finding tape, untwisting it, repairing apparatus, answering phone, etc. Disastrous. Mihalovici's music is fine, but the result most disappointing. Not rehearsed, not prepared, realized "Comme ça te pousse" ["as you go along"].[143]

But relief was at hand. As they had the previous year, he and Suzanne fled to the pure air and healthy living of the Austrian mountains, away from the petrol fumes of the city, and, above all, from the demands made by people. Suzanne no longer went away with him now to Ussy, so these holidays were the only times that they spent entirely alone. Their friends have pointed out how each of them tried to persuade the other to get away for the sake of his or her health. Paradoxically, in spite of the fact that they lived together in Paris, such a vacation was one of the rare occasions when Suzanne could actually influence what Beckett ate and drank.

They chose the Berghotel in Zell-am-See, two thousand meters above sea level. The food was delicious and copious (the chef coming to their table personally to see why they could not finish it). In spite of storms, they followed lovely mountain paths through the pine woods full of Alpine roses and yellow anemones. Beckett followed the same routine as the previous year in Kitzbühel: work in the morning; long, tiring walks in the afternoon; back to the hotel on the *téléphérique*; then dinner, followed by an hour of Austrian television and bed before ten. He played chess with himself, following the games in a book given to him by the Haydens. But, having difficulty now with his sight, he tediously had to take off his spectacles to see the book, then put them on again to see the chessboard. Still, it was a tranquil life and a sober one—which was perhaps one of the points of the exercise. The mineral water was, he wrote ironically, unforgettable.[144] But he managed to get through a lot of work, translating a few of the *Textes pour rien* into English and completing his English translation of *Cascando*.[145]

They returned from the Tyrol to the "Paris turmoil": "Estivating friends pouring through, leaving exhaustion in their wake and dreams of deserts. So it goes."[146] His niece, Caroline, and her girl friends passed through; the Irish novelist Aidan Higgins visited him; so did the English poet Nick Rawson[147] — both of them beneficiaries of Beckett's generosity. From July onward, Con Leventhal became a permanent feature of Beckett's life in Paris, which meant gambling at the Multicolor more often than usual. But it also meant at least that, in September, he had another pair of beady eyes to survey the second set of proofs of *How It Is*.[148]

14

BECKETT FINISHED his French translation of *Happy Days* in November 1962 and submitted it to Jérôme Lindon in December.[149] In a moment of inspiration, he borrowed the title, *Oh les beaux jours*, from Verlaine's poem "Colloque sentimental." Once again before completing it, he sent a copy of his typescript to Mania Péron for her views, accepting some minor revisions of the French.[150] Once he had a final text, he gave a copy to Roger Blin. After some reflection, an enthusiastic Blin handed it on to Madeleine Renaud, who immediately asked if she could premiere it in France. It took Beckett a little time to become accustomed to this somewhat surprising casting.[151]

Madeleine Renaud was known in France primarily as a classical actress, not conspicuously associated with avant-garde drama. She was indeed very much the grande dame of French theater: dresses by Yves Saint-Laurent, hair by Alexandre, shoes by Georgette, makeup by Elizabeth Arden. Nor was she, as Blin pointed out, really the right physical type for the part.[152] But she had a wonderful vocal range and an intensity that Blin thought would work in the role of Winnie. To Beckett's surprise, her husband, Jean-Louis Barrault, probably France's leading actor at the time, also expressed his keenness to play the tiny part of Willie himself.

There was no opportunity to present Beckett's play until the 1963 autumn season of the Théâtre de l'Odéon, especially reduced in size for the occasion. A few preliminary reading sessions on the text were arranged for early June before the Becketts went on holiday, when he found Madeleine Renaud "as quick as they make 'em and clearly resolved to put into it all she has."[153] Serious rehearsals started in August, Beckett meeting Blin, Barrault, and Renaud in the theater almost every afternoon. The opening was planned for the Teatro del Ridotto during the Venice Theater Festival at the end of September. At the outset, Beckett thought Madeleine was going to be "on the light side for this hardened sorrower,"[154] lacking in weight and gravity. But, after some splendid final rehearsals during which her performance became much more moving, he became convinced that "she will be very good," "a cross between Agnès and Madame Sans-Gêne."[155] Suzanne attended the Venice premiere with Marthe Gautier and Edward. After the first performance, Beckett learned on the telephone from Suzanne and Madeleine of the wildly enthusiastic reception the French actress had received from the Italian public.[156] (From this date on Suzanne and Madeleine were to become close friends, and Suzanne started to accompany the actress on her travels around Europe with the play to Belgrade, Prague, and Rome.) More rehearsals followed the Barraults' return to Paris and the play opened there at the end of October 1963.

The opening was frantically busy for Beckett, as even more friends than usual flooded into Paris: H. O. White came with the lecturer, R. B. D. French, overjoyed to see Beckett and Leventhal again, and Morris Sinclair traveled up from Geneva.[157] White was a frail, sick man and Beckett met him and French at the airport. He made a great fuss of "HO," helping him up the stairs of his hotel and inviting him with French to a "hooly" after the show with a group of friends at the Falstaff. Beckett could not recall the end of the party. White died only about three weeks after he left Paris, thrilled with his visit and with Beckett's warm hospitality. Instead of seeing how much pleasure he had given to a dying man, typically Beckett blamed the trip for White's demise: "I feel his Paris jaunt must have hastened his end," he wrote somberly to his cousin Morris Sinclair.[158]

The critics, whom Madeleine Renaud used to refer to as "les affreux" ("the terrible ones")[159] or "les fauves" ("the wild beasts"),[160] were divided about the play. Bernard Poirot-Delpech in *Le Monde* compared *Oh les beaux jours* to Aeschylus' *Prometheus* as a pure dramatization of solitude: "one syllable is enough to suggest all the doubts of the mind, one intonation all the terrors of the heart, one silence all the consolations of language."[161] To show Beckett that the world had not gone completely out of orbit, Jean-Jacques Gautier, who had always been antagonistic toward Beckett, attacked him even more fiercely than ever before in *Le Figaro*: the play was, he wrote, a repulsive "festival d'abjection" (a "celebration of abjection"), and he regretted that Madeleine Renaud was wasting her talents in this "apothéose du néant" ("apotheosis of nothingness"), while the novelist and translator Elsa Triolet (Louis Aragon's wife) was prompted to a strongly positive affirmation of life in the face of a play which she regarded as truly "atroce."[162]

Madeleine Renaud's performance was univerally praised. Much later Irving Wardle neatly summarized the difference between Renaud's incarnation of Winnie and the work of British actresses: "The woman she presents is not the bluff, earthy figure familiar from English productions of the play. She is an emblem of middle-class decorum, holding the sense of chaos and despair at bay by reliance upon a fixed code of good manners and regular habits."[163] Renaud's performance did not have the humor of Brenda Bruce or Ruth White or the Dublin Winnie, Marie Kean (in fact, the French translation may be less comic than the English original), but it had a fine lyricism and a beautiful musicality of gesture and voice. At times Renaud was almost unbearably moving. She captivated Beckett and became etched in his mind as the supreme embodiment of Winnie.[164]

20

"Theatre theatre theatre"
1964–67

1

BECKETT SPENT THE CHRISTMAS PERIOD of 1963 and the New Year in the seclusion of his country cottage. He lived on a monotonous diet of "Riz à la grecque and stewed prunes — day after day," washed down with dry white wine.[1] Several times a week, he chugged doggedly into La Ferté-sous-Jouarre in his aging Citroën, which he was to exchange in a couple of months for another of the same modest make but more recent vintage. Although he constantly bemoaned the Deux Chevaux's limitations, he felt great affection for the little car and never had the slightest desire to own a more comfortable, more powerful, or more luxurious model. He stocked up on food, wine, whiskey, and cigarettes and bought his newspaper. For much of the time over Christmas, he hobbled painfully around the house on a twisted ankle which, he wrote, at least "takes the old mind away from the other ills."[2] There was a growing number of such ills: He worried incessantly about the lump in the roof of his mouth, which had started to grow again, and was increasingly conscious that his eyesight was declining. In the course of the year, he also became aware of a stiffening in the tendons of his hand that was later diagnosed as Dupuytren's contracture.

As he looked ahead, the first half of 1964 appeared exciting, if daunting. His diary was full of promises already made: to help an inexperienced director in London with *Endgame*; to oversee a French revival of *Fin de partie*, before it set off on tour; to advise Barrault on the casting of a different production of the same play; to assist with two productions of *Play*, one in France and one in England; finally, and most worryingly of all for Beckett — since he had never ventured across the Atlantic before and had a picture of New York as a crazy, frenetic city — to fly to the United States to help with the shooting of *Film*. This looked like two or three promises too many. Apart from the danger of exhaustion and staleness, such a heavy dose of theater would make it impossible for him to escape to the country, where he could plunge into the solitude that was vital for his mental as well as physical well-being.

The first set of rehearsals to involve him closely was an *Endgame* rehearsed in London but performed in Paris at the Studio des Champs-Elysées. The newly formed company, originally called the Anglo-American Theatre — Paris, was commonly known as the English Theatre in Paris. Normally such a tiny company would never have had the money to hire actors of Jack MacGowran's and Patrick Magee's standing or to cover the expenses of a run in Paris. But this particular enterprise was funded primarily by two men: one, Victor Herbert, a passionate lover of theater who had retired to live in Paris, was the first man to sell a million dollars' worth of mutual funds for Bernard Cornfeld's Investors Overseas Services;[3] the other, John Dunn, had won a large first dividend in Vernon's Football Pools competition. Michael Blake, the young director of the company, in association with the producer, Philippe Staib, had approached Herbert and the pools winner to ask if they would finance a venture that would specialize in putting on English-language plays in Paris. They agreed, and the company went into production.

An ardent enthusiast of the plays of Beckett, Blake then wrote to the author asking if he would allow the company to perform *Endgame*. Remembering how dissatisfied Jack MacGowran had been with his own acting of Clov at the Royal Court Theatre six years before, yet how potentially outstanding he had thought he might be in the part, Beckett suggested that they invite MacGowran and Magee to play the leading roles of Clov and Hamm. Blake met Beckett and expressed delight at the prospect of working with two such talented Irish actors. As an added incentive, Beckett proposed that, if MacGowran and Magee were to be signed up, he would come over to England himself to lend a hand. This was how Beckett found himself in "Muttonfatville," as he often called London, from January 16 for just over a fortnight, rehearsing "with my darlings Jacky MacGowran and Pat Magee."[4]

He stayed off Hallam Street near Regents Park, having at first, in his own words, "a quiet weekend in front of the TV before the storm,"[5] watching the televised rugby. The storm turned out to be not the few minor squalls that quickly blew themselves out during rehearsal but the hurricane of sustained heavy drinking whistled up by the three Irishmen.

They started rehearsing in the cabaret room of a nightclub called The Establishment, transferred to a clubroom over a little pub-hotel off the Euston Road, and ended upstairs at the Royal Court Theatre. The American Clancy Sigal, who was writing about the production for *The Sunday Times* of London, gave a vivid description of an early rehearsal:

> They are working, downstairs, in the small well of a cabaret room, circumscribed on one side by the hammering of unseen carpenters, on the other by tables and chairs stacked up to the high ceiling. Beckett positions himself in front of the actors, a few feet away. The producer, Blake, his eyes bright and loving on the action, hunches over elaborate graphs, marks and notes at a nearby table.
>
> As the players run through their lines, Beckett pores over the text as though hearing it for the first time. He glares sharply, neutrally, at the action, infrequently prompting. "A little more pause there." A grainy, almost silent voice, a curious Irish lilt and lisp, with a repressed, lean bark. Leanness is the chief, the central characteristic of this man.[6]

Rehearsals were not without their problems. Both Pat Magee and Jack MacGowran, though at first polite in their skepticism, had little time for Blake's "ardent
commentaries,"[7] with Magee in particular showing a measure of contempt for
what he thought was the director's too-intellectual approach. The young man
would explain what he thought a particular line meant, at which point, Magee
would growl in his throaty County Armagh accent: "Yes, that's fine, man — but
how do you treat it?"

Beckett sat watching quietly and intently. At first, he rarely intervened.
Every so often one of the actors would turn toward him to ask how a difficult
line should be delivered. He always responded pragmatically, never discussing
the meaning of his play.

> "I only know what's on the page," he says with a friendly gesture. "Do
> it your way." . . . At the end of the day, Beckett says: "Don't look for
> symbols in my plays." Magee lights a cigarette and grins, *sotto voce*:
> "He means don't play it like symbols."[8]

Beckett helped the actors, however, to find the right tone for a particular speech
and encouraged them to adopt simple, concrete actions. Above all, he concentrated on establishing the interdependency of Hamm and Clov and "the love-
hate relationship" that exists between them throughout the play.[9] MacGowran
and Magee soon evolved into a formidable duo.

Things did not go anything like as well in the scenes between Nagg and
Nell. The latter, played by Nancy Cole, an inexperienced American latecomer
to theater, found the part hard going and, although Beckett was fond of her and
unwilling to sack her, the promoters had no such scruples, replacing her with
the more experienced Elvi Hale before the production opened in Paris.[10] Increasingly, Beckett took over at rehearsals and Blake faded more and more into
the background. An additional, unexpected pleasure was that Sean O'Casey
(whom Beckett never met personally) volunteered to lend them a skullcap,
delicately embroidered with a floral motif, for Magee to wear as Hamm. They
had a choice of red or black. Almost inevitably, Beckett opted for the black.

At lunch and after rehearsals, Magee and MacGowran consumed large
quantities of Guinness or Irish whiskey. Beckett worried because he was matching his friends drink for drink — as well he might worry, for they were awe-
inspiring drinkers. By the end of the month, he judged himself lucky to be "still
on my feet" and was fearful of leaving Magee and MacGowran alone.[11] In the
pub, some fascinating anecdotes were exchanged. Clancy Sigal told Beckett one
day how Doris Lessing, with whom he had lived in the late 1950s, had introduced him as an identifiable character, "Saul Green," a macho kind of American, into several of her books. He explained to Beckett what a disturbing
experience this had been. "Beckett shook his magnificent head. 'Identity is so
fragile — how did you ever survive?' He looked at me more closely, 'Or did
you?' "[12]

Beckett's social life in London was hectic. Drinks or meals with his dramatic agent, his publishers, and his cousin; invitations to see *Uncle Vanya* and Max Frisch's *Andorra* at the Old Vic, with a dinner party the following evening at John Calder's apartment with Max Frisch. He met Alan Schneider, who was over to direct Edward Albee's *Who's Afraid of Virginia Woolf?* at the Piccadilly Theatre. Albee was also in town for rehearsals and remembered going for drinks with Beckett, Harold Pinter, and Patrick Magee, who was about to play in Peter Brook's Royal Shakespeare production of Peter Weiss's play *Marat/Sade*, when they all sat around in the pub enthusiastically discussing the Marquis de Sade.[13] On February 4 Beckett fitted in a visit to a preview of Albee's play ("It was well received and should be a success," he wrote),[14] before flying back to Paris. For most of his stay in London, he was in a state of "even more than usual fatigue and confusion."[15] Even so, when the little "English Theatre" group came over to France for the premiere in mid-February, he turned up regularly to lend his support during the final stages of preparation. In retrospect, he wrote that "rehearsals of *Endgame* with Pat Magee and Jack MacGowran were exciting. They are both marvelous."[16] The play ran for a month, Beckett commenting with great satisfaction in March that they were now "Turnin 'em away" at the box office.[17]

2

BECKETT'S NEXT THEATER COMMITMENTS were even more taxing. Both centered on *Play*, not yet produced either in France or Britain. The French premiere was dogged from the outset by so many problems that it had to be postponed several times, finally taking place only on June 11, after nearly four months of rehearsals —for a play lasting just over twenty minutes.

One of the most intriguing things about the French production was the unusual context in which this astonishing play, a kind of "Feydeau from beyond the grave,"[18] was presented. The forty-nine-year-old director, Jean-Marie Serreau, small, stockily built, wearing small round spectacles, his hair closely cropped, was a human dynamo. Brimming over with new ideas, he persuaded François Mathey, the director of the Musée des Arts Décoratifs in Paris, to allow him, with the help of two architects, a designer, and an engineer, to transform a room that seated four hundred people into an excitingly innovative "lieu culturel" ("cultural space"). *Comédie (Play)* was only one item in a heterogenous mixture of theatre, poetry, opera, and marionettes that used multiple stages and experimental cinema and ran continuously at the Pavillon de Marsan from six-thirty until ten-thirty at night.[19]

The actors in *Comédie*—two future film stars, Delphine Seyrig and Michael Lonsdale, and Eléonore Hirt, rehearsed at first with Serreau, Danielle van Bercheycke, and Beckett in Delphine Seyrig's beautiful, spacious flat on the magnificent place des Vosges. They concentrated on acquiring what Beckett described as a "recto-tono," a tone not unlike that adopted by monks as they read from sacred texts at mealtimes.[20] When they finally got into the Pavillon de

Marsan, there was no stage, since it needed to be specially constructed for the occasion. During the preparation of the building, Serreau dashed here, there, and everywhere, trying to do a dozen or more things at once. So, to his irritation, Beckett was left to take the actors through the play himself, complaining that he "had to do it practically single-handed." [21]

The main technical problem was the spotlight, which had to fall very precisely and at great speed on each of the three heads in turn. For Beckett, the light was an all-important fourth player, an interrogator in this dark yet comic parody of a triangular domestic drama. Beckett felt strongly that the light should not pierce the darkness of the auditorium: "I don't mind if the spot hits from above, provided it does not involve auditorium space. Light, W1 [Woman 1] W2 [Woman 2] and M [Man] belong to the same separate world." [22] He also wanted a single mobile spot, not three separate spots. [23]

Serreau partially solved this problem in Paris by inventing an ingenious system with a mirror and some "butoirs" or "checks," stopping the switch so that the light focused on each speaker in turn. Since Danielle van Bercheycke operated the lights from a position below the actors in the prompt box, the impression was of the spotlight as a single interrogator or torturer. [24] But it took ages to prepare this device, [25] and, when it was ready, both the operator of the light and the actors needed more time to rehearse with it than the deadline allowed. Beckett was adamant that the play would not open until they were ready, and it was he who was responsible for the final postponement. [26] He could be very firm and tough when he felt that the integrity of his work was being compromised. Almost inevitably, then, some angry words ensued with the credited director. It has sometimes been said that, as a result of these disagreements, Beckett did not like or admire Jean-Marie Serreau. On the contrary, when Serreau died in 1973, it was Beckett, with checks of several thousand francs — a lot of money at the time — and the director Peter Brook, with royalties from one of his productions, who paid money into a trust fund to bring up the two young children of Jean-Marie's marriage (his second) to Danielle van Bercheycke. [27]

Rehearsing the French production helped Beckett to discover with Serreau a more satisfying variant for the "Repeat" of the play, when the three characters race through the same lines all over again. [28] They found that, if the level of the lighting was dimmed and the volume of the voices lowered, the reprise became dramatically far more effective. Beckett passed on his discovery to George Devine, who was directing the English original in London. [29]

Beckett was forced to dovetail his work on the French and English productions of *Play*. After several run-throughs of the French text, on March 14 he rushed over to London, where Billie Whitelaw, Robert Stephens, and Rosemary Harris were being put through their paces at the Old Vic Theatre for the National Theatre Company. "Pace" was the key word. The actors were astonished at the speed at which they were being urged to deliver their lines. From the outset, Devine stressed that the words did not convey thoughts or ideas but were simply "dramatic ammunition" [30] to be uttered. This naturally clashed with the actors' wish to "tell the story" and for it to be heard and understood.

On his arrival, Beckett argued that the lines should be delivered even faster. Kenneth Tynan, the literary manager of the National Theatre, and William Gaskill, backed up by Sir Laurence Olivier (who was away on tour for part of the dispute, but backed Tynan's stand) were horrified, interpreting this as a shameful neglect of intelligibility. They blamed Beckett almost entirely for what they saw as a debacle. Fierce arguments took place in the theater after rehearsals, with Devine and Beckett on one side and Tynan and Gaskill on the other. Tynan, who stammered badly when he was angry, became apoplectic with rage, and, turning purple, stormed noisily out of the theater.[31] John Beckett remembered meeting his cousin for lunch in a Lyons Corner House and finding him angrier after one such row than he had ever seen him before.[32]

The dispute became more acrimonious still when Tynan wrote Devine a formal letter saying that the production was being ruined by being played at such a breakneck speed and in an unintelligible monotone and that Beckett should be encouraged to leave as virtual codirector. Devine replied, also by letter:

> The presence of Beckett was of great help to me, and to the actors. . . . I assume you read the stage directions: "voices toneless except where indicated. Rapid movement throughout." It was always my intention to try and achieve this, as it is, in my opinion, the only way to perform the play as written. Any other interpretation is a distortion. . . . You'll have to have a bit more guts if you really want to do experimental works, which, nine times out of ten, only come off for a "minority" to begin with.[33]

Devine also made it clear that, if Beckett left, he left too, so there would be no production. Writing to a friend that, in general, there was an excellent working atmosphere, Beckett added dismissively: "Quelques jeunes cons pas d'accord" ("A few young fools not in agreement").[34] He stayed on, and Devine did exactly as he and the author wanted. The pace of the responses was so fast that, at the end, Beckett took a tape recording of the English version with him back to Paris to demonstrate to the French actors exactly how quickly he wanted the lines to go.[35]

In the script, Beckett had originally written of the three figures in the urns: "age and appearance indifferent." But after Suzanne had been to Berlin and seen how unlike each other the three actors appeared in Deryk Mendel's second production,[36] he changed the stage direction to "faces so lost to age and aspect as to appear almost part of the urns."[37] This "urnlike" appearance was achieved at the Old Vic by applying a mixture of porridge, egg white, and glue to the actors' faces. The pitted surface was then colored by a mixture of slimy brown, sludgy green, and white makeup to give an impression of encrustation brought about by age. Bits of debris used to fly off from around the actors' mouths as they spoke.[38] "It looked as though we were disintegrating in front of the audience," wrote Billie Whitelaw.[39] The urns were narrowed in shape, too, after the German production and were placed closer to each other, so as to bring the heads into closer proximity and preserve the shape of funeral urns rather than of almost circular tubs. A rod fixed inside the urns, linking one to another, offered the actors much needed support, providing them with a focal point onto which their tension could be directed.[40]

This period of intensive collaboration with directors of his plays was vital for Beckett. Above all, it made him appreciate that there were elements that he would never get right until he had staged the plays himself, and that, consequently, at some point in the future he needed to take sole responsibility for a production so as to identify the problem areas and ensure that at least one production conformed with his overall vision of the play. Serreau probably did Beckett an unwitting favor when he left him to get on with directing *Comédie*. For it was not to be long before Beckett took on and signed productions himself, starting by directing the actor Pierre Chabert, with whom he became friendly, in Robert Pinget's *L'Hypothèse*.[41] His detailed work on *Play* had also brought him into hands-on contact with the technology of theater, raising problems as to what lighting could or could not achieve. This contact, together with the fascination of watching his "talking heads" at close quarters, pouring out their torrents of sound, was probably a key factor in inspiring later plays like *Not I*, *That Time*, *Footfalls*, and *Catastrophe*, in which the theatrical spotlight plays such a crucial role.

The London production of *Play* was noteworthy for a more personal reason too: Beckett met Billie Whitelaw for the first time. He was bowled over by the rich vibrancy and musicality of her voice, her sensitive delivery of his lines and her remarkable flexibility as an actress. He was also captivated by her good looks and attracted by the warmth of her personality. This marked the beginning of a long working relationship and a close personal friendship that a few years later had, it seemed to many outsider observers, the hallmarks of romance, on his side at least. Beckett was very susceptible to physical beauty in a woman. But, in Billie Whitelaw, he saw something that he identified more closely with a beauty of the spirit. And he found this extremely moving.

Meanwhile, his romantic involvement with Barbara Bray continued. At this point in his life, she appears to have become more and more important to him, both intellectually and emotionally. They were frequently to be seen in each other's company, in London as well as in Paris. When he came over to England to attend rehearsals, she was often there as a calm, reassuring presence. Sometimes this was purely coincidental, since she was working at the time as a translator and as a critic on radio programs such as *The Critics* and *New Comment* on the BBC Third Programme.[42] Often, however, such meetings were prearranged. They behaved discreetly, not drawing attention to their liaison, for neither saw why it should be anyone else's business. But, for all its essentially private nature, many of those who knew Beckett well believe that this relationship represented a significant strand of stability in his life then and for many years to come.

However, there was no more commitment to sexual fidelity on his part in this extramarital relationship than in his marital one. He had many close friend-

ships with women. Some remained deep, yet platonic. Others developed, sometimes for a brief period only, into sexual relationships. He was very adept at
keeping such liaisons private.

One close female friend, with whom he may or may not have had an affair,
was the Dutch writer and translator Jacoba van Velde, an attractive, intelligent,
creative woman. She was three years older than Beckett. He had known both
her brothers well since the 1930s. And, as Tony or Tonny Clerx, she had acted
as his literary agent for some time after the war and been his regular translator
in Holland ever since *Waiting for Godot*. She was also a novelist herself, with
one highly successful novel to her credit, *De grote zaal (The Big Ward)* published in Holland in 1953. Although we have only Beckett's side of the correspondence from which to judge, it is clear that she shared with him the traumas,
disappointments, and lengthy fallow periods of the writing process, as well as its
satisfactions and rewards. In addition, Beckett was clearly a confidant as to the
state of her difficult relationship with her heavy-drinking companion, Fritz
Kuyper, with whom he sometimes saw her until they separated. He also helped
out financially on a number of occasions and was obviously very concerned for
her welfare. Several of their mutual friends were convinced that their relationship was more than friendship. If so, in a way that was characteristic of Beckett,
it evolved from and returned to a warm friendship; Beckett may well have
helped Jacoba at a time when she needed consolation and affection.

Whatever else was happening in his life, throughout this period Beckett
remained intensely involved with his immediate family. He worried a great deal
about Suzanne's health, particularly when her "old bronchial cold" recurred.
During the only break in what seemed like an interminable series of theatrical
commitments, a full week was taken up with the visit of his sister-in-law, Jean,
from Killiney for Edward's *concours* on June 6 at the Conservatoire. Although
Edward's talent as a flutist was such that they were hoping for a first prize, "he
got no award and remains with his 1st accessit of last year." "He has more
musicality than the rest of the class put together, and by far the finest tone,"
Beckett added proudly, "but for the gentlemen of the jury these qualities must
be of less account than mere mechanical accuracy."[43]

Even though this result meant a further year of study at the Conservatoire,
Edward took the setback extremely well. But his mother was upset, regretting
the degree in engineering that he would have been receiving from Trinity
College had he remained there as she had wanted. And so Beckett and Suzanne
spent several days consoling Jean and reassuring their nephew. Precisely a year
later, Edward gained the first prize.

After nine days of peace in Ussy, feeling stale with theater in general and
utterly bored with *Endgame*,[44] Beckett went over to London in June to help
Donald McWhinnie with the Royal Shakespeare Company's production, feeling fairly confident by now that he would soon be flying on directly to New
York in the middle of July for the shooting of *Film*. Again his equilibrium was
threatened by dozens of meetings, added to regular visits to Mooney's Pub with
the formidable drinking trio of MacGowran, Magee, and McWhinnie. He tried

to counterbalance the aftereffects by taking John Calder's dog for long walks around Mayfair and Hyde Park, looking for Murphy's old haunts, the Cockpit and the Round Pond, from thirty years before.

He relaxed by watching tennis on television and listening to music. For someone so interested in sports, he could hardly have chosen a more exciting or distracting week: The Wimbledon tennis championships were in full swing and England was playing (and losing to) Australia at cricket in the third test match. At night, he watched the tennis finals on BBC's "Match of the Day"—won by Roy Emerson and Maria Bueno—and at lunchtime in the pub, between rehearsals, a pint of draft Guinness in his hand, he sat thoroughly engrossed in the televised cricket.

3

THE MAJOR EVENT OF 1964 for Beckett was his long-awaited trip to New York. The weather throughout his stay was feverishly hot and humid, the work hectic and demanding. Yet Beckett seems to have savored every moment.[45] He flew into Idlewild (now J. F. Kennedy) Airport on July 10 and was met by Barney Rosset's friendly assistant, the petite Judith Schmidt, who escorted him to a tiny four-seater plane to fly to East Hampton on the tip of Long Island. Beckett's long legs barely fitted into the aircraft which Rosset had chartered for his use.

After a dramatic landing on a strip that was not fully illuminated for night landings, Beckett was met by Rosset and his young wife, Christine, who drove him to their remarkable house on Jericho Lane. It had been designed for Robert Motherwell by the French avant-garde architect Robert Charreau and resembled two Nissen or Quonset huts joined together. Downstairs there was a large open area; a balcony and smaller rooms extended off it on an upper floor. There were two smaller houses on the property, as well as a swimming pool and a tennis court. Beckett stayed there over the weekend with the director Alan Schneider, and the others who were working on the film. Beckett considered himself fortunate to have the services of a first-rate cinematographer in Boris Kaufman, who had done brilliant work for Jean Vigo on *Atalante* and *Zéro de conduite*. They swam and he played a few games of tennis against Rosset, then Seaver. To his disgust, he missed the ball at times on account of his deteriorating sight. "I'll never play again," he announced in exasperation, although it was obvious that he had once played fairly well.

Most of the time, they talked almost non-stop about the film. Unbeknownst to Beckett, the discussion was being recorded by a tape recorder underneath the table; a transcript of the conversation has been published.[46] This reveals that Beckett was intensely concerned with introducing detailed echoes and parallels from one shot of the film to another, with the camera positions and with what he termed "the angle of immunity." The plot of the film is very simple. As Alan Schneider explained: "It's a movie about the perceiving eye, about the perceived and the perceiver—two aspects of the same man. The perceiver desires like mad to perceive, and the perceived tries desperately to hide. Then, in the end, one wins."[47] In the film, the protagonist is split into an object (O) and an observing eye (E), "the former in flight, the latter in pursuit,"[48] and certain of the shots were envisaged so as to contrast two "absolutely different visual problems." Beckett spent a lot of time discussing with Boris Kaufman and the cameraman, Joe Coffey, how best they could distinguish between these two different ways of perceiving. The script was modified over the first weekend; by Tuesday, when Judith Schmidt retyped it, it had evolved into a very precise shooting script.

Beckett and Schneider stayed the rest of the week in rooms at the top of Barney Rosset's New York house on Houston Street, making detailed plans for the actual filming, which was to begin the following Monday. Sometimes Beckett was driven around the city in a picturesque old English sports car, a Morgan, owned by Coffey. Sometimes they walked around choosing locations. Beckett liked the look of a huge, crudely cemented old wall in Lower Manhattan that was scheduled for demolition and an apartment building (more like a large uninhabited warehouse) that lay in the shadow of the Brooklyn Bridge. They decided to film the opening exterior scene there rather than on Commerce Street or Minetta Lane, which had been selected earlier. The vestibule and staircase were another location that had been chosen in advance. This was approved by Beckett. But the room interior was built especially for the film as a studio set, so that every nail hole, section of chipped plaster, and piece of torn wallpaper could be made to conform to Beckett's succinct request in his "Notes for Film" that there should be a "Memorable Wall."[49]

Buster Keaton had been hired by Rosset and Schneider to play the central protagonist, after approaches had been made to Charlie Chaplin, Zero Mostel, and Jack MacGowran. Beckett was sad that MacGowran was not available to play the part because of another film engagement in July, the only time when Alan Schneider was free. But to meet Keaton and work with him in New York was an unexpected pleasure, for he had never forgotten his early passion for Keaton's films. It had been his suggestion that Keaton be asked to play the part. Yet the first meeting between the two men was awkward and embarrassing. Alan Schneider, who introduced them in Keaton's hotel suite, recounts:

> When Sam and I arrived, Keaton was drinking a can of beer and watching a baseball game on TV; his wife was in the other room. The greetings were mild, slightly awkward somehow, without meaning to be. The two exchanged a few general words, most of them coming from Sam, then proceeded to sit there in silence while Keaton kept watching the game. I don't even think he offered us a beer. Not out of ill will; he just didn't think of it. Or else maybe he thought that a man like Beckett didn't drink beer.
>
> Now and then, Sam — or I — would try to say something to show some interest in Keaton, or just to keep the non-existent conversation going. It was no use. Keaton would answer in monosyllables and get right back to the Yankees — or was it the Mets? . . .

It was harrowing. And hopeless. The silence became an interminable seventh-inning stretch.[50]

Beckett's respect for Keaton survived this unfortunate meeting. He ended up admiring the sheer professionalism of the actor as, dressed in overcoat, boots, and his old flattened Stetson hat, with a handkerchief hanging down inside it, he did take after take in the sweltering New York heat. But Buster Keaton and he were too different and their worlds too far apart for them ever to become friends. (Before Beckett left, however, he started to read Keaton's autobiography, *My Wonderful World of Slapstick*.)

The actual shooting was characterized by worry, even panic. When the rushes of the first frenetic day's outdoor filming were viewed, it was clear that it had been an almost total disaster. There were light problems, traffic problems, actor problems, and camera problems—caused by a wobbling dolly on a rough roadbed—but, above all, a strobe effect, as Schneider, making his début as a movie director, panned the extras up and down the street, unaware that this constituted a problem. The sequence was unwatchable. Yet the budget did not allow the scenes to be reshot. As the atmosphere turned sour and bickering began, Beckett proposed that they should eliminate the entire scene, although he had wanted it there to establish from the beginning the distinction between the two different ways of seeing, so that the same object "is perceived in quick succession, first by O and then by E."[51] Yet he was flexible enough to suggest that they retain only the better-quality images of Keaton running along the wall and sidling into the apartment building.

Everything went much better once they got to work in the interior room set. Keaton was on his own then and, in a slapstick scene with a cat and a dog, absolutely in his element, in spite of problems with a shy, uncooperative Chihuahua. Beckett

> was always there, and always watching from above the set, unobtrusive but dominant, always eager to answer or to look through the camera, or help with a move. I used to look up at him as he sat there for hours, motionless and intent, his elbows akimbo on the light rail, staring down at us through his spectacles like some wise old owl contemplating with interested but detached equanimity a bunch of frantic beavers building some nonsensical mud-stick dam.[52]

Some thrilling discoveries had been made even before Beckett left Paris. One, the photograph of the head with large eye sockets that is pinned to the wall, suggested to him by Avigdor Arikha, was a reproduction of a Sumerian head of the god Abu in the museum in Baghdad.[53] Others were made during the shooting:

> The rocker we were using happened to have two holes in the headrest, which began to glare at us. Sam was delighted and encouraged us to include the headrest.[54] The folder from which photographs were taken

had two eyelets, well proportioned. Another pair of "eyes" for O to avoid. We wound up combing the set for more: walls, props, wherever.[55]

The scene with Keaton in the room slowly covering the mirror, the parrot's cage, and the goldfish bowl; removing the print of the severe staring image of God from the wall; and tearing up photographs of his own life has its own atmosphere and slow, compelling pace and, Schneider believed, "a strange special snow-soft texture of its own."[56] Hours were spent getting the exact close-ups that they required of Buster Keaton's "creased, reptilian" eye to replace the abandoned outdoor scene with the extras. Finally came the startling moment when O in the rocking chair is finally confronted by E, a discovery that provokes a look of horror when he discovers that, in Beckett's words, "the pursuing perceiver is not extraneous, but self."[57]

In addition to such intensely absorbing work on the film, Beckett's life in New York gyrated like a whirlwind in the intense heat. He met Edward Albee and Alain Resnais, dined with Kay Boyle, and spent an evening with the Reaveys, Jean having prepared a dinner that consisted of some of the foods mentioned in his writing, ending with *banane à la Krapp*.[58] He enjoyed one evening with his former love Pamela Mitchell, who came to New York especially to see him.

Most of his time was spent in the convivial company of "the Grove Press crowd" (Rosset and Schneider, Dick Seaver, Fred Jordan, and Judith Schmidt) and the producer of the film, Milton Perlman, rushing from the studio room set to the screening room of a film laboratory, then on to a variety of restaurants in Greenwich Village—the Brittany, the Brevoort, the Granada—and an Irish bar, the Emerald Isle. He even accompanied his friends to a pre-opening showing of *The Pawnbroker* and may well have seen Vigo's *L'Atalante*.[59] Judith Schmidt and Dick Seaver took particular care of him. One of the high spots was a visit with Seaver to a baseball game on July 31. It was a double-header, the Mets playing at Shea Stadium. The Mets, surprisingly for a young expansion team, won both games, Beckett remarking that he should come to see them more often. Seaver explained the rules and commented from time to time on what was happening. Soon no explanations were required, as Beckett followed the game with unfeigned interest and understanding. In the middle of the second game, Seaver turned to him and asked: "Would you like to go now?" "Is the game over then?" queried Beckett. "Not yet," replied Seaver. "We don't want to go then before its finished," said Beckett, settling back into his seat for the remainder of the long evening.[60]

During the visit, Beckett struck up a close friendship with the film's editor, Sidney Meyers. This evolved out of their common interests in music and painting as well as their detailed technical discussions about the film. Born in the same year as Beckett, the balding Meyers was something of a Renaissance man, who wore his culture lightly, lacked pretension, and had a light and ready wit.[61] Meyers was very knowledgeable about painting, particularly modern painting, and toward the end of Beckett's stay, accompanied him to the Museum of Modern Art, as well as the Metropolitan Museum, where Beckett looked with an expert's eye at the wonderful seventeenth-century Dutch collection.[62] At the end of the filming, Beckett was captivated by all the technical details, as he helped Meyers and Schneider to edit a first rough cut of the film on the Moviola. Almost thirty years after writing to the famous Eisenstein to ask if he could work with him in any capacity, however humble, there he was in New York involved in editing his very own film.

By now, however, he was fretting to return home. So an early morning flight was booked for him on August 6. Barney and Christine Rosset set their alarm clock for an early hour so that they could drive him to Idlewild Airport. The Rossets woke late, horrified to find that they had overslept. As they rushed out of their bedroom, they saw Beckett fast asleep on a chair outside their door, his bags packed, and wearing an overcoat—in early August. He had been much too polite to wake them up! Since the morning flight had already left, Rosset made a late-afternoon reservation for him, and Judith Schmidt cabled Suzanne to say that he would not be arriving after all in Paris until early the following day.[63] Rosset, Christine, and Beckett then spent the rest of the day at the World's Fair in Flushing Meadow. They wandered around the exhibits until Rosset suddenly turned to his wife and asked: "Where is Sam?" They had lost him in the crowd. After retracing their steps, they found him fast asleep again, sitting bolt upright on a bench in the shade. Before leaving the fair, he bought two knitted Greek bags, one for Christine and one for Suzanne. Sweaty and tired, all three of them sought refuge in an air-conditioned bar at Idlewild, where Christine, who looked much younger than her years and did not have her driver's license with her, was refused a drink by the barman.[64]

> "This is somehow not the right country for me," Mr Rosset reported Beckett saying in the bar, "the people are too strange." Then with a "God bless," he got on the plane, and was gone, never to return again.[65]

4

ON HIS RETURN TO FRANCE, Beckett spent as long as he could in Ussy, working determinedly on a new prose text that for a long time refused to assume any sort of satisfactory shape.[66] He tried composing it in both French and English, but was not happy with the results in either language. The eventual outcome was an overcomplex text in English called *All Strange Away*, which remained unpublished for more than ten years, and four short passages, which he entitled "Faux départs" ("False Starts"), three in French and one in English. A year later, these fragments appeared in the German literary magazine *Kursbuch*.

The theater would not, however, let him go. He resisted the blandishments of Peter Brook, the director, and of Jeremy Brooks, the literary manager of the

Royal Shakespeare Company, to adapt Calderón's *Life Is a Dream*.[67] Beckett told them that he would refresh his memory of the play and think it over, but, by the end of the year, he declined the offer. He found it impossible, however, to say no to close friends. So, when the director Anthony Page came to Paris with George Devine's proposal that Beckett should fly to London to help Page with a revival of *Waiting for Godot* at the Royal Court Theatre, with Nicol Williamson and Alfred Lynch playing Vladimir and Estragon, Beckett wrote to his agent: "I feel dubious about it but want to please George. I suggested MacGowran and Magee for Lucky and Pozzo but I doubt if they will be free, or if Jacky would accept any role but Vladimir. However they must be asked."[68] In the event, MacGowran accepted the alternative part of Lucky. Magee was not free to act Pozzo, so the role was played, outstandingly in Beckett's opinion, by Paul Curran. Nicol Williamson had a stunning success. Beckett stayed for the third time that year with John and Bettina Calder on Wimpole Street; according to Calder, he

> came home one evening and said, "You know, there's a touch of genius in that man [Nicol Williamson] somewhere." . . . It was a wonderful production. Nick was extraordinary. I have never heard anybody do Vladimir's speech so that it ended up as a trumpet call, you know, the "I can't go on, what have I said." The "I can't go on" was screamed at the audience with a trumpet voice.[69]

However tired of the play Beckett claimed to be, *Waiting for Godot* still held a special place in his affections. When the manuscript and rare-book dealer Henry Wenning asked if he could sell the original French manuscript for him, Beckett replied: "Rightly or wrongly have decided not to let *Godot* go yet. Neither sentimental nor financial, probably peak of market now and never such an offer. Can't explain."[70]

5

RETURNING TO PARIS on New Year's Eve after "the devilish hard work"[71] of the Royal Court production with "a young director and young actors I did not know,"[72] but satisfied with the result, an exhausted Beckett vowed solemnly that there would be "no more theatre for me now for many a long day."[73] Yet, at the beginning of February 1965, he responded to a desperate appeal from the Schiller-Theater dramaturge, Albert Bessler, to come to Berlin to bail out yet another production of *Waiting for Godot*. Things were going appallingly. The production was due to open on February 25. Yet the actors, who had been rehearsing since early January, still did not know their lines. More crucially, personal animosities had built up between the director, Deryk Mendel, and the cast, and between various members of the company. According to the actors Horst Bollmann and Klaus Herm, one problem was that too much emphasis had been put by Mendel on the supposed metaphysical meaning of the play. Mendel admitted:

> There was constant friction between myself and the actors, and the actors between themselves. It practically came to a standstill. Then we sent for Sam. I went to see the director [of the Schiller-Theater] and he said, "We'll telephone Sam and ask him to come, then we shall see." Sam didn't want to and they beseeched him to come. So he did. He came and stayed right till the end.[74]

Beckett knew Mendel well, liked him, and had worked with him already at the Royal Court Theatre and the Studio des Champs-Elysées. So, he felt that he could hardly say no again to such an urgent plea for help: "If I had refused to go the 3rd time they asked," he commented, "they wouldn't have put it on at all, with sad results for the director, so I had to."[75] He flew into Berlin on February 5 and was comfortably housed at the pleasant Akademie der Künste (Academy of Arts). It was a pleasant environment that, over the years, he grew fond of, with a pond, many different kinds of trees, small cobbled walkways, and, above all, plenty of open space.[76] In the freezing cold, Beckett set off for long walks in the Tiergarten, dressed warmly in heavy lace-up shoes, a loose sweater, a sports jacket, trousers with large cuffs, a scarf, and an overcoat. He revisited his favorite seventeenth-century Dutch paintings in the West Berlin galleries. And, in deference to his recent work with Buster Keaton, he went to see Keaton again in his 1927 film *The General*, finding it, however, disappointing.[77]

With the author there to give advice and pour oil on turbulent waters, rehearsals improved, but were still difficult. The atmosphere in the theater was icier than the weather outside. The acrimony that had grown up between Bernhard Minetti, playing Pozzo, and Horst Bollmann and Stefan Wigger, playing Vladimir and Estragon, persisted throughout.[78] Having Beckett there seems to have calmed the actors. He himself found the entire experience painful and depressing; "grim" and "pénible" were the words that he used to friends.[79] His only ambition was, he wrote, "empêcher le pire" ("to prevent the worst").[80] One of the problems was that Vladimir and Estragon had in his view been wrongly cast. One rehearsal session of four hours a day was also, he felt, "pure madness."[81] The famous Bernhard Minetti was, he added, "quite undirectable" and gave the worst performance that he had ever seen from any actor.[82] On the other hand, he thought highly of Klaus Herm, who played Lucky. And he thought that Bollmann and Wigger could be good if they exchanged roles. Although Beckett worked tactfully through the director, the production was gradually brought closer to his own vision of the play. Contrary to what had been happening earlier, he worked pragmatically, concentrating on the concrete and totally ignoring the metaphysical. For he was only too aware of how much had still to be done at a practical level to salvage the production in a very short time.[83]

Beckett had to leave Berlin to fly to London a week before the first night for the long weekend of February 18–21, having promised Jack MacGowran that he would help him work on the text for the recording of his one-man show, *Beginning to End*, for the BBC television program *Monitor*.[84] He wandered along to an exhibition of Jack B. Yeats's paintings at the new Waddington Gallery at 25 Cork Street, forgetting that, on a Saturday afternoon in England, the gallery would be closed.[85] Intensely disappointed, he came back with only a catalogue.[86] The Schiller-Theater paid his return fare from Berlin to London to ensure that he would come back for the final few crucial days of rehearsal of *Warten auf Godot*. In the end, to his astonishment, the production was surprisingly well received by both the public and the critics alike, and the close collaboration between Mendel and Beckett was pronounced a resounding success.[87] At the first-night party, however, Beckett, not really satisfied, spoke of coming back himself perhaps one day to do his own production. Ten years later he did.

Beckett took a morning flight to Paris on February 25. After unpacking his bags, he began to open his mail. Among a huge pile of letters and packages, he found two letters and a telegram from Italy. One with a Trieste postmark was already two weeks old. It was from an Italian actress, Clara Colosimo.[88] He skimmed it quickly, scarcely able to believe what he was reading. A second letter from the president of a regional Italian National Union of Writers, Guido Sambo, confirmed his worst fears: He was in the middle of an international incident with potentially serious consequences. An enclosed press cutting from the *Corriere della Sera* of February 21 showed that the incident had already reached the public sphere.[89]

"Sciopero della fame di una attrice" ("Hunger strike of an actress") read the newspaper headline, in bold type. Clara Colosimo explained in her letter that, since Beckett's agents in Italy would not give her permission to play Winnie in *Happy Days* at the Teatro della Piccola Commenda in Milan, she had embarked on a hunger strike. Beckett's eye ran quickly down the page of badly typed French with Italianate spellings, noting that she had been allowed to play the part of Winnie already in Trieste, Udine, Mestre, Verona, and Muggia and that she was now asking him to intervene on her behalf to allow her to play it in Milan. But worse was to come. A telegram dated February 22, again in Italianate French, read: "TROISIEME JOURS DE GREVE ATTENDS VOSTRE AIDE COLOSIMO." ("THIRD DAYS OF HUNGER STRIKE AWAIT YOUR HELP. COLOSIMO.")[90] The newspaper article explained that Signora Colosimo had appealed to the Italian minister of arts as well as to numerous personalities of the worlds of theater and literature, and, it was claimed, had even written to Beckett himself but all to no avail. That morning, the article went on, a doctor had tried to dissuade Clara Colosimo from her hunger strike but she remained immovable. The letter from Guido Sambo was more recent and spoke worryingly of how, on the fifth day of her hunger strike, Signora Colosimo's health was giving cause for concern: "We beg you to intervene," he pleaded.[91]

Beckett picked up the telephone to discuss with Jérôme Lindon what he could possibly do. He immediately dispatched a telegram to the president of the

Union of Writers: "Beg you to intervene with Colosimo to stop this hunger strike. Letter follows. Beckett."[92] Then, in a letter drafted on the back of Sambo's own, Beckett wrote, in French, that he knew nothing of the circumstances of the dispute, had no personal objection to her acting the part, and deplored

> the violent means that she has chosen to put pressure on her opponents — and doubtless on me too — and renew here the terms of my telegram in which I beg you to ensure that her strike is brought to an end. It may be fairly easy for me, once I know what the dispute is about, to secure agreement from those involved and accede to Madame Colosimo's request. But she must first break off this unjustifiable action. Then perhaps the true factors in the case can be communicated calmly either to myself or to my publisher.[93]

As a result of this letter and the intervention of Signor Sambo, Clara Colosimo eventually gave up her hunger strike after ten days and, under medical guidance, gradually began to take nourishment again.

The dispute over the rights to play Winnie was complex and had to do with the regions in which Signora Colosimo was allowed to play; another, better-known Italian actress, Laura Adani, had been granted wider rights. In the end, both Beckett and his publisher refused to overrule the authorized agent, Connie Ricono, and it was left to Dr. Ricono to sort out the disagreement. They must both have breathed a huge sigh of relief when they did not need to get more deeply involved. However, two years later, Beckett did intervene on Clara Colosimo's behalf, asking the same agent to authorize a series of performances of *Giorni felici (Happy Days)* at the Teatro Goldoni in Rome.[94] He was treading carefully on this occasion, not wanting to risk any repetition of the earlier incident.

6

AT THE END OF JANUARY 1965, Beckett wrote to Tom MacGreevy: "In November I had a long overdue operation on my jaw ('benignant' tumour). Successful, and nothing to worry about, but another will probably be necessary, less dramatic, to close the wound which though quite healthy cannot heal spontaneously. But not for some months."[95] By March, the hole that the operation had created in the roof of his mouth showed no real signs of healing by itself and Beckett was told that surgery would definitely be needed to close it. Although he described it as uncomfortable rather than painful, he found that the plate he was forced to wear was a nuisance and the prospect of "going to the grave" with it filled him with little enthusiasm, since it made eating an arduous, unpleasant exercise. Drinking was a strange experience since any liquid went into his nose.[96] He also found it difficult to inhale his cigarette smoke.[97] In letters to friends he made light of the prospect of another operation involving what the surgeons called a "plastic" or a "graft with palate tissue."[98] But he worried a lot about it in private.

"The most wretched Spring within memory of daffodils"[99] then brought him yet another dental abscess, which pulled him down even further and prevented him from spending as much time as he wanted in the country.[100]

He managed to do some writing, especially early in 1965, while waiting for the tissues of his palate to be ready, "dancing and singing" as he put it,[101] to be operated on. Before the Berlin crisis, he worked on two separate pieces: a prose text in French, *Imagination morte imaginez*, and a short play in English, *Come and Go*. The texts are so different from one another that it is strange to think of him working on them more or less in tandem. Yet the same processes of cutting, reducing, simplifying, and refining are apparent in both.

The prose piece developed one of the themes of *All Strange Away*, concentrating on a skull-like white rotunda in which two white bodies are placed back to back (recalling Dante's damned, placed "arsy-versy," "watering their bottoms with their tears" as Beckett had put it in an earlier notebook),[102] paring it down to leave only a few pages of stark prose. Heat and cold, white and black — with a brief intermediate gray — stillness and silence characterize the little world that is summoned up here by an imagination that is determined not to expire utterly.

The strange vision that is first discovered, then explored bears little apparent relation to any real world and seems to owe far more to a purely formalist structure. Yet residual echoes of this world are still there, even in such an enigmatic, pared-down text, but transformed by the imagination and precisely structured and organized. The rotunda springs from an eighteen-inch-high wall like a tiny mausoleum; in *All Strange Away* Beckett spoke of it in terms of the Pantheon or certain beehive tombs.[103] It is a "vault," inspired, Avigdor Arikha said, by the view from Beckett's study window of the church of the Val-de-Grâce[104] but miniaturized, converted from real experience to "imaginative experience."[105] The vault has a ring of bone about it, like a human skull. The left eyes of the two bodies open alternately and remain open without blinking for lengthy periods; they are a "piercing pale blue." Both bodies have the physical characteristics of human beings — feet, knees, arse, hair, eyes, and breath. But, in their stillness, they almost attain the inanimate.

The fascination of this text comes from the way in which the imagination shifts its own position in relation to these various elements, going in, moving out, ascending, examining, descending, and returning inside the rotunda like some versatile, miniature camera eye. Inside this little created world, the two figures are like embryos waiting either for birth or for extinction. *Imagination morte imaginez* is an extraordinary creation, compelling or rebarbative according to the responses of the reader. It gave its creator more trouble than anything he had written since *Fin de partie* or *Comment c'est*. Beckett wrote to Lawrence Harvey at the end of January 1965 that he had "started again for the 20th time, this time in French again, on what will not be written. Imagination morte imaginez."[106] In March, he confessed to Avigdor Arikha: "J'ai bouclé la rotonde. Pour en être délivré. 1000 mots. 6 mois de ratures" ("I have finished with the rotunda. To be rid of it. 1000 words. Six months of erasures").[107]

However elliptical the French prose text may be, it is very dense and demanding. By comparison, the little play that he wrote at this time is extremely simple. Pain lies much closer to its transparent surface. On January 21, 1965, Beckett wrote: "I have finished a playlet (one and a half pages, 3 to 4 minutes playing time) promised to John Calder for the opening of his new theatre in Soho. The MS will amuse you: about 25 pages to arrive at that!"[108]

The play, which Beckett entitled *Come and Go*, can for once be easily summarized. Three female characters, Flo, Vi, and Ru, "ages indeterminable," sit side by side on an almost invisible bench in a zone of soft light at the center of the stage. Each woman in turn makes a single exit, moving silently away into the surrounding darkness before returning once more into the light. During her absence, the other two express first concern, then horror at her present condition and her future fate. The essential item of information about the absent one — that she is doomed — is not stated aloud, but is whispered, unheard by the audience, into the ear of a horrified companion. "They are 'condemned' all three," Beckett wrote to Jacoba van Velde.[109]

"Flo" and "Vi" are shortened forms of common women's names, Florence, Flora, or Florrie; and Violet, or Viola. "Ru" is more unusual and has been associated with Ophelia's madness scene with Laertes in *Hamlet*. But Beckett's aunt on the Roe side, who was married to his mother's brother Edward Price Roe, was named Rubina. And the Roe girls, his cousins and Rubina's daughters, attended Miss Wade's school, alluded to in the play. "I imagine a stone lion in the playground of the school," Beckett wrote to his Dutch translator. "They used to sit on it together side by side."[110] Yet however local these allusions may appear, the play as a whole attains a much more universal level. This is achieved by the common appearance of the three women, by the evocation of their common plight, by the diaphanous, almost dreamlike nature and symmetry of their movements as they drift away and return, and by the uniform patterning of their crossed hands. When directed like a subtle piece of delicate chamber music and hauntingly choreographed and acted, this little play has a stark visual beauty and a musical quality that make it as compelling as anything that Beckett ever wrote.

7

HIS HEALTH PREOCCUPIED HIM at this time far more than he would have wished, and while he was incapacitated and unable to eat or speak properly, it became difficult for him to see all but his closest friends. Before the operation, however, he led a more or less normal life, going out to Ussy as often as seemed feasible, meeting people over in Paris for business or pleasure. At the end of March, Lawrence Harvey was in Paris from Florence. Walking down the boulevard from the Closerie des Lilas one night after spending some ten hours with his American friend, Beckett spoke to Harvey of how Paris was full of memories: "Every building, every bench, has memories for me. That one there is new; that is one of the few unchanged. I sat on that bench with Ethna [MacCarthy] waiting for a friend." "You'll think it's senility," he added with a grin.[111]

A copy of *Film* was sent over to Paris from Grove Press and, at the end of March, he showed the almost finished film to two small groups of friends, including Lindon, Leventhal, and the Arikhas. After this testing of the water, he wrote enthusiastically, "Big success — even allowing for partiality,"[112] but still could not resist adding a few final suggestions. Some months later, he wrote to Judith Schmidt: "Please no music or other sound than the 'hssh!' which as I told Alan I would like in but wd. prefer out if it involves an audible sound track. This sounds nonsense but he'll know what I mean."[113] The film was shown at the Venice Film Festival in the first week of September.

Three years earlier, Beckett had commented on how unsatisfactory television seemed as a medium for *Waiting for Godot* with its "small figures in a big space," and how successful he thought a play based on close-up could be on the small screen. Now, with his experience of editing *Film* on a Moviola with Sidney Meyers and Alan Schneider fresh in his mind, he began to conceive of a TV play in which the camera could gradually be moved (dollied) in more and more tightly to focus on a single male figure in a room, with a voice inside the head as its sole accompaniment. He also wanted to write something for Jack MacGowran; he wrote to him, for instance, on July 4, 1963: "I haven't a gleam for the new work for you at the moment and feel sometimes that I've come to an end. It's a comfort to know you understand and won't press me."[114]

Significantly, it was on his own fifty-ninth birthday that Beckett started to compose a text for a female voice that was to echo in the head of a male protagonist, also in his late fifties. He first called the figure Jack, which was then changed to Joe in the middle of the first draft.[115] The first manuscript was written quickly, within a fortnight. Anniversaries prompted Beckett, as they had Joyce before him, to think back to his family and his homeland, while feeling an overwhelming sense of guilt for what he had done or failed to do. The woman's voice is an accusing voice of conscience, a Jungian anima or inner self.[116] As she speaks to the man, she alludes to other voices that have returned in the past to haunt "that penny farthing hell you call your mind."[117] These voices include those of his father and his mother, which he has already managed to "throttle" in his head. He cannot avoid listening intently to this voice, even though at the same time he tries to strangle it and reduce it to silence. The play is full of verbs conveying what Joe's voice describes as "mental thuggee": "throttle," "muzzle," "spike," "squeeze," "tighten," "silence," "garotte," "finish," "mum," "strangle," "stamp out," "exterminate," "still," "kill," "lay," "choke." "It is his passion to kill the voices which he cannot kill," said Beckett.[118] Joe is tormented by this low, torturing voice, which reminds him of his broken promises and of his present loveless plight. Reluctantly, he is forced into a kind of living hell as he struggles to avoid a full confrontation with what he has done. Like Krapp, Joe has opted for selfish detachment and now pays the consequences. The play is full of a vivid sense of remorse for hurt done to dear ones and regret for love spurned or love unrequited.

Beckett had written *Eh Joe* with Jack MacGowran's doleful, haunted eyes and expressive face in mind. But, once it was finished, he wrote tactfully to his Irish friend: "I hope I did not seem to assume that you would necessarily want to do it because it comes from me. I assure you I don't. I do hope you will take it but if on reading it again and thinking it over you decide it is not for you no one will better understand than I." [119]

The television play was not written as a specific commission and it was Margaret MacLaren of the Curtis Brown agency who proposed sending it to the BBC. So Beckett posted a copy to Michael Bakewell, the head of plays, who had already directed *Words and Music*. [120] After some discussion, the BBC agreed to pay Beckett a fee of two hundred and fifty pounds. [121] The corporation was snail-like in fixing dates both for the recording and the broadcast, and Beckett found it frustrating to be kept in doubt for months as to when he might be needed. In the end, a German version, translated by Elmar and Erika Tophoven and directed by Beckett himself, was broadcast by Süddeutscher Rundfunk almost three months before the BBC one, although the recording at the BBC preceded it. [122]

In June 1965, Suzanne and he decided that in view of his low state of health and with the surgical graft arranged for soon after their return, he was in desperate need of a holiday before the operation. They went via Turin to stay for three weeks at the Hotel Moderno, Courmayeur, in the quiet Valle d'Aosta, breathing again with relief the pure mountain air. While he was there, he translated *Eh Joe* very quickly into French[123] and also managed to translate *Imagination morte imaginez* into English. [124] But too soon they had to return to Paris, Beckett dreading the forthcoming operation, but hoping that the graft would be successful.

The operation was performed early on Monday morning, July 19,[125] by a surgeon named Dr. René Bataille, who advised Beckett to eat only soups or liquefied food and talk as little as possible. He was allowed to smoke only a few cigarettes a day. This, he was told, would give the graft the best possible chance of healing. [126] But already, by the end of July, when the stitches were removed, he knew that the operation had not been one hundred percent successful and would have to be repeated in a few months' time. Meanwhile, he had to see his dentist for all kinds of "dental devilry," [127] including several extractions and a new plate that he needed to help him to eat properly. It was the summer of 1966 before the operation was successfully performed.

On the last day of October 1965, in his Paris study, he started to write, in a soft-covered notebook with a color picture of a jaguar on its cover, one of his strangest, most enigmatic works. After lying unfinished in his desk drawer for five years, this text became *Le Dépeupleur (The Lost Ones)*.

Moving on from the miniature rotunda of *Imagination Dead Imagine*, Beckett now imagined a much larger, flattened cylinder inhabited by two hundred people[128] — an entire society or miniature Leviathan compared with his earlier pieces. The enclosed world of the lost ones grows out of his imagination but is nurtured by his renewed immersion in Dante's *Divina commedia*. Searchers seek a way out by climbing ladders to niches and tunnels in the walls of the cylinder or stretch their arms out to touch the ceiling; others dream "of a trapdoor hidden in the hub of the ceiling giving access to a flue at the end of which the sun and other stars would still be shining" — the closing words of Dante's *Inferno*.[129] The nonsearchers sit "for the most part against the wall in the attitude which wrung from Dante one of his rare wan smiles"[130] — Beckett had written out on a small card the occasions when Dante smiles in the *Divina commedia*.[131] But the text echoes other books that he had read and absorbed: Robert Burton's *Anatomy of Melancholy*; possibly the quincunx from Sir Thomas Browne's *The Garden of Cyrus*;[132] and the "secret passages" or "private galleries" of Dr. Johnson's *Rasselas* — "a grand book," according to Beckett.[133] It has recently been suggested that patterns of behavior in the cylinder are borrowed from Platonic or neo-Platonic thinking.[134]

Le Dépeupleur and some of the other short prose texts of the 1960s owe a lot to his recent work in film and television. A determined effort is made to "see" the entire structure and organization of the cylinder and to describe the workings of the "abode" as precisely as the "eye of the mind" (or the lens of a camera) will allow. Beckett's obsession with vision and with problems associated with vision — an obsession only partly influenced by his own declining sight — also affects the "seeing" and the describing. He referred himself to one section in an early manuscript as "une grande myopie" ("a great myopia"),[135] and deterioration of vision in the cylinder is still stressed in the published version. The whole text could be defined as "myopic."

Critics have argued fiercely as to whether *Le Dépeupleur* is a purely formalist work, a self-contained world that does not reach out beyond itself, or whether it is a piece of rhetorical fiction or an allegory. If it is an allegory, the fictional world, regarded as an allegory of the nonfictional so-called real world, would be a place in which everyone is looking for his or her "lost one," climbing ladders to no avail, indulging in more acts of violence than of fraternity. It has been pointed out, however, that only the final fifteenth section, added four years later, confers allegorical significance on a text which otherwise resists the efforts of those looking for a meaning beyond the fictional world itself.[136]

While working on this recalcitrant text, Beckett followed with a dismay born of familiarity the illness of his friend, the actor-director George Devine. After his performance as the drag queen Baron von Epp in John Osborne's *A Patriot for Me*, George had a severe heart attack in August and was rushed off to St. George's Hospital. Eleven days later, a blood clot paralyzed the left side of his body.

> In mid-October, two months after his admission, the hospital discharged him and he went home to the Flood Street flat with Jocelyn [Herbert]. His speech had returned almost to normal, but he remained paralysed in the arm and leg and confined to a wheelchair. . . . He was, and clearly saw himself, in the situation of a Beckett character: a perfectly functioning intelligence trapped in a ruined body and watch-

ing the process of its own extinction. He could not accept life on those terms.[137]

Beckett wrote to George in hospital, enclosing a glowing article about him from *Combat*.[138] Then, after Devine left hospital, he wrote: "I am sure being home again will help enormously, physically and every way. I am hoping to be in London this month or next for the TV play, if I can screw a date out of the BBC. It will be great then to see you together again in the place where you have given me so many happy hours."[139]

Sadly, on the morning of January 20, 1966, George had another massive coronary thrombosis and died. So, when Beckett finally came to London five days later for *Eh Joe*, his visit coincided with the funeral at Golders Green Crematorium. He took a taxi with William Gaskill and his friend, Keith Johnstone. But neither they nor the driver knew where the crematorium was. "Hoop Lane," said Beckett knowingly. It was pouring with rain, and friends stood around at first under streaming umbrellas, then in a dreadful little waiting room until they were summoned inside by Laurence Olivier.

> It was a cold, awkward occasion. It brought together people from all parts of Devine's life, but failed to unite them. They came in uncomfortably in their wet coats, not sure where to stand, and there was nothing in the ceremony — as agnostic as Devine could have wished — to release the weight of private feeling. A short reading and a passage from Britten's *War Requiem*, and then out into the rain again.[140]

8

MICHAEL BAKEWELL related how, a month before Devine's death, he went over to meet Samuel Beckett in Paris to discuss the forthcoming production by Alan Gibson of *Eh Joe*: "I met Beckett to talk the play over in a bar somewhere off the Avenue Montaigne. On the back of an old envelope he drew the set, the exact placing of the furniture (what little there was), the movements of the actor and the tracking line of the camera. These were presented not as absolutes but as the only way in which the play could work."[141]

Siân Phillips, who had been cast as the woman's voice — Beckett had wanted Billie Whitelaw, but she was not free — could not record the woman's voice in the evenings when the studio set was available, since she was acting in Shaw's *Man and Superman*. So the voice text had to be rehearsed and recorded separately during the day in a BBC sound studio. After tea at MacGowran's Hampstead home and after hearing her first reading, Beckett went over the text meticulously with Phillips. She recounted:

> It was explained to me that every punctuation mark had a precise value and I began metronoming my way through the text, reading

appallingly but gradually remembering that a full stop is not a colon is not a hyphen is not an exclamation mark is not a semicolon. We worked like machines, beating time with our fingers and, after some hours, the relentless rhythm and the beautiful, but equally relentless, blue eyes were making me feel ill, so I suggested that I should go home and continue working on my own.[142]

The next day at a rehearsal in the studio, Beckett first read through the entire text himself, then went through it with Phillips, repeating it slowly, almost mesmerically, word for word, emphasizing above all the musical rhythms of the piece. Although Welsh herself, she found herself unconsciously adopting Beckett's Irish accent, rhythms, and intonations. It took several sessions to get it right and she asked for an additional take. The vocal colorlessness at which Beckett was aiming was achieved by placing a microphone right up against her lips; her voice was recorded with both high and low frequencies filtered out.[143]

Apart from his shuffling around the room, to check that no one is there to perceive him, MacGowran as Joe had only to react to the woman's voice replayed to him in the studio. Yet he described the experience as

the most gruelling 22 minutes I have ever had in my life, because as you know the figure is silent, listening to this voice in his head which he is trying to strangle the memory of. It's really photographing the mind. It's the nearest perfect play for television that you could come across, because the television camera photographs the mind better than anything else. The words are having an effect on him as he attempts to strangle the voice in his head, which he finally does. It's a little victory that he has at the end in dismissing the voice; he finally crushes it.[144]

As Beckett's appointment diary shows, his few days in London were frantic: meetings with Harold Pinter, Mary Hutchinson, John Calder, and Beckett's nephew Edward, as well as with a bereft Jocelyn Herbert, George's companion. He even fitted in two visits to the Pierre Bonnard exhibition at the Royal Academy.[145] On January 27, he went to Broadcasting House for a recording of a selection of his poems read by MacGowran and Denys Hawthorne, produced by Martin Esslin.[146]

On February 4, with MacGowran, he met John and Edward Beckett, who were to provide the music for MacGowran's readings from Beckett's work for Claddagh Records.[147] He turned up at the Pye Studios on Edgware Road in a loose-fitting sports jacket and flannels, with his hair standing almost on end and looking even more disheveled than usual.[148] Beckett's favorite theme from the slow movement of Schubert's "Death and the Maiden" Quartet 14 in D Minor was used to introduce and conclude the readings. Edward played the first violin part on his flute and John Beckett played the second violin, the viola, and the cello parts on an old, groaning pedal harmonium that was brought in by a supplier of unusual theatrical items, Impossibles Limited. It was a highly unusual combination of instruments. Beckett himself played a simple pedestal dinner gong on the record to separate one extract from another, giving exactly the right weight to each stroke. As far as we know, this is Beckett's only recorded musical performance. Coached in his detailed phrasing and rhythms by Beckett, MacGowran was in splendid form and produced an exceptionally fine recording.

9

IN MARCH, before going to Stuttgart to direct *Eh Joe* in German, Beckett took a short spring holiday with Suzanne in Santa Margherita Ligure, east of Genoa. They lived quietly at the Hotel Lido, Beckett restricting his drinking to half a liter of Chianti every day, writing to a friend, only half jokingly, that this "was not before time!" Determined to secure plenty of rest, Beckett indulged in what he described as some gentle "far niente."[149]

He had arranged to fly alone directly to Stuttgart from Milan on March 25. Dr. Müller-Freienfels of Süddeutscher Rundfunk had promised him first-rate technical facilities in the television studios. It was Beckett's first solo experience of directing for television, but he had derived enormous confidence from his work in London at the BBC and from the earlier *Film* in New York.[150] In addition, he was working with two actors whom he knew already: Deryk Mendel and Nancy Illig. Illig, who had played Woman I in Mendel's production of *Play* in Ulm, was a revelation to Beckett in Stuttgart both as an actress and as a person. They got on famously, spending several nights until dawn, mostly with Mendel, talking together. They stayed friends, corresponding for the next twenty-three years.

During rehearsals Beckett concentrated most of his effort on the rhythms and tones of Nancy Illig's whispered, accusatory phrasing. She recounts how, after she had worked hard to make the whispered words come to life by shading, characterizing, and letting emotion creep in: "Beckett came in one morning and said "Now we'll make it all dead,' and this is how by progressive reduction we ended up with the hammering staccato of a ghost's voice."[151] Even with the voice of a ghost, Nancy Illig still managed to be incredibly moving and reduced Mendel to tears: "She was fantastic, fantastic," he said.[152]

A week after his return from Stuttgart on April 1, Jocelyn Herbert came over to Paris to see Beckett and have a holiday. Over the next few days, he was a superbly hospitable host, escorting the tall, good-looking Jocelyn around Paris. She went to see the triple bill of Beckett, Ionesco, and Pinget plays at the Odéon Théâtre de France, and, after the performance, Beckett took her out to dinner with Madeleine Renaud, Jean-Louis Barrault, and the stage designer Matias. Beckett had always liked and admired Jocelyn. Now their relationship became much warmer and more loving.

Several times while playing billiards with Jocelyn in a café, Beckett commented on how much his eyesight was failing, even though he played so well that it scarcely seemed to make any difference to his game.[153] One direct result of her visit was that she managed to persuade him to make an appointment with an oculist. After Jocelyn's return, he had planned to come over to England for ten days in May to stay with Sheila Page and to spend the following weekend with Jocelyn at Andrews Farm. But, after listening to the report on the state of his eyes, he was so upset that he promptly canceled the visit.

> I saw the oculist. Double cataract (entre nous). One eye far advanced and nothing to be done about. The other less and possibility of preventing it getting worse. Been given rather complicated treatment local and general. Not only eyes but all feels pretty dim. 4 months treatment then back for another examination. No op. if the right eye can be stabilised. Not hopeful personally, but when was I ever about anything! Very disappointed but really no choice. To go would be just kicking myself on. So shall stay here till we go to Italy in June if we do.[154]

He was prescribed eye drops, suppositories, and homeopathic granules, which he was instructed to take for twenty days a month over a period of four months. He was also told to keep the glasses that he had for reading and was given a stronger pair for what he termed "navigation." But he "made the interesting discovery that by wearing both pairs together I can see perfectly for driving. By day, not by night."[155] It was only later in the year that he was told how unwise, even irresponsible this was. "These are plugs that were my eyes," he wrote — deliberately reworking Shakespeare's (and T. S. Eliot's) "Those are pearls that were his eyes" from *The Tempest*[156] — adding, "but it's nice to feel they can always remove the crystallines."[157] Nonetheless, an operation for cataract was not always successful and no one contemplated one, let alone two, such operations without great anxiety at a time when laser surgery had yet to be developed. Thinking of his declining sight resurrected all the old specters of blindness and dependence. It was a depressing prospect and, in the short term, it complicated further treatment of his other medical problems. "Done nothing about jaw [i.e., the second operation], don't see how the two can be dealt with at the same time (conflicting medicine)," he wrote. "For a 60th year it's a 60th year. What my uncle Gerald with his wooden leg would have called a good innings. If few runs."[158]

He spent May 1966 in the country working hard, feeling that he must write as much as he could while his eyesight held out. He was so deeply embroiled in the complications of a second *Le Dépeupleur* manuscript that, unusually, he was working at his desk by six-thirty in the morning. In the afternoon, he "poked around out of doors" or sprawled naked in a deck chair in the sun.

> There have been marvellous days. Dinner with the Haydens [who were living nearby at Reuil] a few times. Played chess once. Had him crucified for 20 moves then made a mistake that led to a draw. Have the Hayden [Haydn] sonatas but no sign of a piano. Better get one quick. Perhaps could hire one from the blind tuner at La Ferté. En attendant le Bechstein [While waiting for the Bechstein].[159]

Such apparently inconsequential remarks reveal his concern with blindness and with making the most of the time that remained while he still had his sight.

The previous year, Suzanne and he had left some things in the Hotel Moderno in Courmayeur with the intention of returning. They stayed in the hotel this time for almost the whole of June, taking enormous walks, with Mont Blanc visible in the distance, along little paths and shortcuts in a region of the Italian mountains that they now knew almost by heart. Beckett had felt shaky, "poorly" even, when he left Paris, perhaps from a combination of worries about his health, too much alcohol, and too many cigarettes. Now, under Suzanne's watchful eye, he settled down to a more sensible regime: less tobacco, more oxygen, and no whiskey. Most days he read the newspaper *La Stampa*.

In the evenings he tried to keep in touch with his own "work in regress with usual vanishing point in view."[160] In the first week, he managed to write only ten lines. It was hard to concentrate on this text, *Le Dépeupleur*, which had become complex and intractable. One of the problems was that, on holiday, it was impossible to hold in his mind all the details of what he had written earlier in his notebooks.[161] The eight versions that have been preserved make it clear how difficult this must have been. Shortly after returning home, he laid the text aside in favor of a shorter, simpler prose piece that, in his own words, could be regarded as the "result or miniaturization of *Le Dépeupleur*."[162]

To add to worries concerning his own health, bad news reached them on holiday. Josette Hayden's father was in his final illness and, after innumerable blood transfusions, he finally died.[163] Closer to Beckett, his brother's widow, Jean, fell seriously ill and, after Suzanne and he had returned to France, she was hospitalized in Dublin. At the same time, Suzanne's mother was admitted to the Hôpital Cochin "not far from where we live, and recovering — to be what, a vegetable, indefinitely."[164]

The simpler text in French to which he turned in July and August was provisionally called "Blanc," then, finally, *Bing*. He worked steadily on it until, by August 18, he could write to a friend from Ussy, "I succeed in hanging on here trying to squeeze a last wheeze from the old bag and pipes. Seem to have got something suitably brief and outrageous all whiteness and silence and finishedness. Hardly publishable which matters not at all."[165] "All the verbs have perished," he wrote.[166] And, from the debris of the earlier text, he commented that "months of misguided work have boiled down to 1000 words."[167] The published work has a telegrammatic briskness about it. But it is not just that so many of the verbs have perished. In a text that begins confidently with the words "all known," the little that can be known comes in "traces blurs signs no meaning."[168] The cylinder has become a small white cube; the two hundred inhabitants have been reduced to one, with a hint or hope of a possible other ("perhaps not alone"); the lexical units have themselves been reduced in number. If there is stylistic richness (and there is) it is achieved through conjunction and combination, and enigma lies at the very heart of the seeing as well as the describing.

Edward and Caroline's mother died suddenly on August 28. Beckett received the news by telephone at Ussy and dashed over to Dublin to be with his relatives at the funeral. It seemed that nowadays he only visited Ireland on melancholy missions — to see someone before he or she died or to follow a coffin into a familiar graveyard. He stayed in Killiney nearly a week, seeing "some phantoms human and natural. Most of the old haunts scarcely recognizable. Up in the mountains no change. Went round Carrickmines links, unchanged, with Edward now a good player. Trinity little change." [169]

These returns from exile were disturbingly macabre. Even his meetings with his old friends, Tom MacGreevy and Arland Ussher, brought him little real pleasure: MacGreevy was visibly failing after his recent heart trouble, and Arland Ussher seemed a stranger. Death, always at the still (or absent) center of Beckett's work, loomed once again in the forefront of his mind: "Giacometti dead. George Devine dead," he wrote. "Yes, take me off to the Père Lachaise [cemetery], tearing through the red traffic-lights." [170]

10

HE WAS FURIOUSLY BUSY in September. Because of its brevity, the proofs of *Bing* in French took only a short time to correct. But he had promised Calder and Rosset that he would send them translations of the three novellas — one of "Le Calmant," by himself, and the two others done in the 1950s by Dick Seaver — as well as English versions of his new texts *Assez (Enough)* and *Bing (Ping)*. He also found himself "trapped" yet again in "theatre, theatre, theatre," [171] unable to escape from this awful treadmill on this occasion because Jean-Marie Serreau had taken himself off yet again, this time to Dallas and New York. Although the plays that were in rehearsal had been done earlier in the year, there were two new actors now and a new person operating the light in *Comédie*. Pierre Chabert was again playing in Robert Pinget's *L'Hypothèse*, and Pinget came to watch a couple of run-throughs. After rehearsing, Beckett, Chabert, Pinget, and Matias trooped merrily off to play billiards in the rue de la Gaîté. But, by this time, Beckett, renewing the cliché as was his wont, was "fed up to the plates with theatre," [172] and longing to get away from such stressful commitments.

In addition, so many friends were now seeking his company that life was a whirl of meetings: an evening with Dick Seaver, over from New York; dinner with Jacoba van Velde and her companion, Fritz; a drink with a new friend, Arié Dzierlatka, a composer from Geneva; help for Jean-Louis Barrault with a French text of Shakespeare's *Henry VI*: " 'The pretty vaulting sea refused to drown me.' French me that," he commented. [173] He ended the month utterly drained. Suzanne, too, was exhausted from coping with her sick mother. They succeeded in finding a pleasant apartment for the old lady in Passy, and someone to look after her. But all this had taken its toll. Suzanne consequently felt that they both needed a third spell away from the pressures of Paris. The ophthalmologist, who optimistically detected a ten percent improvement in the better eye and no further deterioration in the worse one, also underlined yet again the need for Beckett to smoke and drink less, as well as to continue with the medication that she had prescribed. So they agreed to seek the sun, fit in some late-summer swimming, and try to carve out another spell of peace, quiet, and sobriety.

After some hesitation, they chose Greece and the Greek islands as their destination. Christine Tsingos was acting in *Happy Days* in both French and Greek in Athens later in the month, and Suzanne promised her that she would try to see the play on their way back home. Beckett did almost no work. Instead they had the "best laze for years," [174] first at Vougliament on the coast not far from Athens, then at the Hôtel des Roses in Rhodes. Luxuriating in a sea temperature of seventy-two degrees, Beckett did what he described as some "copious" swimming and dived with renewed relish. They came back from what had been a real holiday refreshed, with Beckett determined to spend a large part of the winter working at Ussy. For once this proved possible. During November and early December he launched "5 weeks of fierce assault" [175] on the English translation of the *Textes pour rien (Texts for Nothing)* — fifteen years after he had written them — for publication in John Calder's forthcoming book of collected short pieces that Beckett picturesquely entitled *No's Knife*. It was not what he wanted to be writing. But at least it was an escape from theater.

21

Accident, Illness, and "Catastrophe"
1967–69

1

THE CLOSING YEARS of the 1960s found Beckett in a low state both physically and emotionally, although to the outside world he may have appeared "at the crest . . . of the wave — or thereabouts," as Krapp had put it.[1] He had been nominated several times already for the Nobel Prize for Literature. His work had been translated into many languages and was studied in universities throughout the world; his plays were being put on in dozens of theaters in many countries; and countless academics, many of them known to him personally, were creating a positive avalanche of books and articles on his prose and his plays.

Numerous requests were also being made to adapt his work for film or television. Mostly Beckett gave a firm no to such requests for adaptations. Only occasionally did he give them his seal of approval. His decisions were based on what he regarded as the suitability or otherwise of the work for that medium, never on the amount of money that was involved. Sometimes, however, he agreed to a proposal out of friendship, or because he felt sympathy for the person making the request. Erwin Leiser, head of the Deutsche Film-und-Fernsehakademie (the German Film and Television Academy) in Berlin, for instance, asked Beckett if he could present his two mimes on German television with Ladislav Fialka, an excellent mime artist from Prague. And Beckett agreed to this small adaptation.[2] On the other hand, Keep Films had come back with a renewed offer for a film of *Waiting for Godot*, in which Peter O'Toole, one of the firm's principals, was anxious to play a part: "I do not want a film of *Godot*," Beckett wrote tersely.[3]

In his own terms, however, all this success was an infallible recipe for disaster. It increased the gulf between him and Suzanne, who hated all the trappings of fame. It also made it far more difficult for him to retain the privacy that he cherished more than anything else except his work. The number of people trying to see him had increased steadily and, although Jérôme Lindon spared him many meetings by constantly reiterating that he never gave interviews or that he was away from Paris, Beckett, courteous to a fault, found it impossible not to see those whom he already knew and who wrote to him directly. Some of his friends were heavy drinkers, and Beckett could still enjoy escaping from time to time into an alcoholic haze. This was anathema to Suzanne, who was, after all, the one who had to witness the depressing after-effects and listen to his complaints, regrets, and recriminations the following day.

The persistent demands put on him in Paris made it harder for him to get away to his country cottage to find the peace and quiet he needed for creative work. But when he did manage to get away, he faced a completely different set of problems. For ever since Suzanne had decided a few years before that she would never set foot in the place again, Beckett mostly went there alone. When writing was going well, time passed quickly enough. But when, as happened only too often, he found himself trapped in a creative impasse, the little house could be a desperately lonely place. He drank alone most heavily when things were going badly for him creatively. Experience had shown that whiskey provided a much stronger anesthetic than wine and, some time before, the grocer in the marketplace at La Ferté-sous-Jouarre had started to put in a special order for his favorite "J.J." (that is, John Jameson) Irish whiskey. Every day, rain or shine, he went out for long walks and from time to time, would call in his car on the Haydens when they were staying at their country house in nearby Reuil. Still, too often, there were vast tracts of time to be filled.

When he could neither work nor face serious reading, he borrowed *série noire* thrillers from the Haydens, which he consumed voraciously, or he listened to classical music on his little radio. But, in February 1967, he "bought a little German piano [a Schimmel] for the country and take it out on Haydn and Schubert. My nose so close to the score that the keyboard feels behind my back. Get it by heart in the end and lean back."[4] He also studied the chess columns in *Le Monde* regularly and spent hours playing chess against himself, reenacting some of the famous games described in the "best games" books by Alexander Alekhin, Mikhail Tal, José Raúl Capablanca y Graupera, and the current champion, Tigran Vartanovich Petrosian.[5] He had recently been given Irving Chernev's *The Most Instructive Games of Chess Ever Played: 62 Masterpieces of Modern Chess Strategy*, which he studied avidly.[6] And, a few years later, a friend added Spassky's and Fischer's best games[7] to his growing collection of chess books, which he divided between his Paris apartment and Ussy.

2

EARLY IN 1967, he was deep in another impasse. Jack MacGowran had asked him to write another play for him. But not a flicker of inspiration came to penetrate the gloom. Madeleine Renaud, too, had made it clear after the phenomenal success of *Oh les beaux jours* that she would dearly love him to write a new play for her to perform; but although he made a start early in February, it soon ground to an abrupt and permanent halt.[8] This was only partly the result of the intractability of the material or of a failure of the creative imagination. There were other, more tangible reasons.

He was staying at Ussy at the time and worrying a lot about his eyesight. Since February he had been on a three-month course of treatment for his eyes. And this was resumed during the summer: "Still doing treatment for eyes. Silly drops, suppositories and homeopathic pellets. Like a poultice on a wooden leg. Don't know when op."[9] He still managed to drive his Deux Chevaux between the villages around the Monts Moyens, as there was little traffic on the winding country roads and he knew every corner and crossing by heart. But now, whenever he had to travel into Paris, he left the car at the railway station in La Ferté-sous-Jouarre, for he no longer felt safe driving in the capital.

Back in February the mornings were bitterly cold and he had great difficulty in starting his car. One particularly frosty day, after the engine had at last spluttered reluctantly into life, he drove down the hill to the little garage in Ussy to ask the owner to check over the spark plugs and battery for him and, if necessary, look at the starter. The amiable *garagiste* told him that this would not take very long and that he would attend to the car straightaway, if Monsieur would care to wait. Grateful for such prompt attention, Beckett said that he would go for a short walk. As he turned to leave, he took a few steps forward and fell straight into the deep garage pit. The inadequacy of his lateral vision, more than any lack of attention, had prevented him from noticing the large, gaping hole in the concrete floor.

He climbed painfully out of the pit. Stoically, if foolishly, he claimed that there was no need for a hospital checkup and was driven back to his house by the *garagiste*. However, he soon found that the pains in his side were becoming acute. So, swallowing his pride, he contacted the Haydens, who drove him to their house, where a local doctor urged him to have an X ray of his ribs. The radiologist at La Ferté-sous-Jouarre discovered two cracked ribs to add to a colorful collection of large and painful bruises.[10]

Beckett stayed with the Haydens in Reuil for almost a week. Every morning, his breakfast was brought up to him in bed by Josette Hayden before he ventured downstairs to sit, painfully erect, in an armchair, dressed like some gaunt Father Christmas in Josette's red dressing-gown, in front of a log fire that he had especially asked them to light.[11] On his return to Paris, it was a long time before he could cough or sneeze without pain. Even breathing was uncomfortable at first.[12] It was not until after his birthday in mid-April that, back in Ussy again, he could speak with any real conviction of feeling better: "Ribs seem to have healed, no difficulty any more with breathing, laughing and sneezing. Even clearing the throat was a problem at the beginning! But must have got some hefty bruises into the bargain and all soreness not yet gone. Back mowing the grass anyway and other mild activities."[13]

But it was Beckett's confidence as much as his body that was shaken by the fall. He felt increasingly fearful of the damage that he might do himself in future, if his sight continued its recent decline. He was obsessed by the very real fear that he was starting to go blind; to close friends he dwelt morbidly on James Joyce's progress toward blindness, which he had witnessed through most of the 1930s, when he used to read to his friend. It was a prospect that filled him with horror. And since his eyes were clearly not responding to treatment, he became more and more aware of the need to seek out specialist medical advice.

So began a three-year-long sequence of medical consultations. First, he visited a doctor who referred him to another Parisian ophthalmologist. She confirmed the previous diagnosis, namely that cataracts were forming on both his eyes. One of them, she told him, was indeed already significantly worse than the other and might require surgery fairly soon. Then his German publisher, Dr. Siegfried Unseld, suggested that he might see a Berne specialist, a Professor Goldmann.[14]

Depressing thoughts about the state of his eyes were reinforced by news of the illness and death of one of his oldest friends, Tom MacGreevy. This did not come as a complete surprise, since he had last met Tom "looking wretched" in the autumn of 1966, when he was in Dublin for his sister-in-law's funeral.[15] He wrote sadly to tell George Reavey how it had happened: "They had to (?) operate poor Tom for a dangerous hernia recurrence. Immediately after op he had another coronary and there was no hope. He dragged on for about a week and died in hospital. His doctor, an old friend of mine, wrote that he did not 'suffer too much.' On sait ce que ça veut dire. [One knows what that means]."[16]

Beckett found Tom's death devastating. For many weeks his thoughts returned constantly to "dear Tom," to whom he had once been so close, with whom he had shared so many private thoughts, and who, for almost forty years, had been his faithful correspondent, confidant, and friend.[17] Deliberately, he took himself off to Ussy, so that he could be totally alone; he was feeling very confused and in need of a large dose of silence.[18]

After these worries and upsets, it was with a great sense of relief that he flew off on June 22 to Sardinia with Suzanne for an early summer holiday. For the first of their two visits to the island that year, they chose the Hotel Las Tronas, only ten minutes' walk from the town of Alghero. The weather was unfailingly kind. The hotel was quiet and peaceful, and their rooms had fine views overlooking the sea. The beach was beautiful, part fine sand, part tiny pebbles. Even the local white wine was surprisingly drinkable. They lunched regularly together in a little bistro by the beach and spent almost every day from midday until six sunbathing on the warm sand. It was a wonderful spot in which to do nothing but walk, swim, and rest.[19] Best of all for Beckett, he was never embarrassed by being recognized.

On their return, Beckett stayed in Paris just long enough to deal with his mail and see a few friends before leaving for Ussy to prepare for his trip to Berlin, where he was due to direct *Endspiel (Endgame)*, for the first time himself. Since Ludovic and Agnès Janvier were spending a large part of the summer not far away from him in the Marne valley, he took the opportunity to work with them on the French translation of *Watt*, on which they had begun collaborating a year earlier.[20] Their customary working practice in Paris was for one or the other of them to walk over with their suggestions to Beckett's flat on the boulevard Saint-Jacques, where they usually spent several hours going over the text in meticulous detail. During the summer, they drove over to his cottage. They relate how Beckett used to lapse into long periods of silence as he weighed up several different ways of rendering the English, opting for particular words or phrases as much for their sounds and rhythms as for their meaning; he sometimes even counted out the syllables on his fingers. He used his big French dictionary (*Littré*) and the *Petit Robert* that Ludovic Janvier had bought him. But he had a remarkably retentive memory and could remember over twenty definitions of a word, once he had read them in the *Littré*. They made splendid progress and a draft version was completed by the middle of August 1967.[21]

3

FOR HIS COMING PRODUCTION of *Endspiel*, he gradually learned the whole of the revised German text by heart. He prepared a detailed notebook in which he noted down all the repetitions and echoes and made various cuts and changes.[22] So, by the middle of August, he was at last ready to come to grips with his first solo production at the Schiller-Theater. Although nervous at the prospect of directing in German, he felt confident that he had prepared as thoroughly as he could, even more arduously than if he had been directing the play in English or French.

He flew into Berlin on August 16. The following day, he and Matias went along to the theater with Matias's model of the stage set, partly to show it to the actors but also to instruct the Schiller-Theater technical crew, who were to build it in the designer's absence. Matias was to return to Berlin in the final week or so of rehearsals to make final adjustments to the set and the costumes. Otherwise, except for an excellent German assistant, Michael Haerdter, Beckett was to be working on his own.

At the theater, he was quiet and reserved, for he was feeling, he admitted, more than a little apprehensive at working with established German theater stars of the stature of Ernst Schroeder (Hamm), who would undoubtedly have their own acting style. According to Beckett, Minetti had been "clamouring for the role" of Hamm, "but I worked with him (Pozzo) in *Godot* and never again."[23] Nor did he know Gudrun Genest and Werner Stock, who were to play the old couple, Nagg and Nell, confined to garbage cans and to whom he jokingly referred in letters as "les poubellards" or "the trashcanners."[24] Horst Bollmann (Clov), who already knew the author, reassured the others that, although professionally exacting, Beckett was very amiable and considerate to work with.

Rehearsals took place in a friendly atmosphere. Schroeder and Bollmann were eager for Beckett's help and took readily to his direction, Schroeder with more difficulty than Bollmann. At first, it was hard for him not to see Pat Magee and Jack MacGowran in the parts of Hamm and Clov and hear their Irish voices echoing in his head. But soon he was describing Ernst Schroeder as "having something of Pat Magee but more gelatinous. At every moment he seems to be on the point of exploding."[25] On the whole, he found the German actors too emotional for his taste and had to calm them down and ensure that they maintained the aggression between Hamm and Clov, while at the same time containing it.[26] "Hold back" became one of his commonest pieces of advice. He offered them a main image on which to cling: "Imagine," he said, "their relationship is like flames and ashes. The flames are blazing and then they sink into ashes. But there is always the danger that the flames will blaze again."[27]

Frau Genest and Werner Stock (who had acted the part of Nagg in the German premiere ten years earlier) played the geriatric but tender exchanges of Nagg and Nell tonelessly, as Beckett wanted. From the beginning, he found these two actors excellent, adding a "Dieu merci" ("thank God") to this judgment.

In directing *Endgame* in German, Beckett aimed above all to simplify the play: "Keep it simple, everything simple," he said on the opening day of rehearsal.[28] In this way, he focused attention on certain dramatic essentials such as the tense nature of the relationships, the play's structural patterning, the fact that little or nothing changes, and the protracted nature of the ending depicted there. "The play is full of echoes; they all answer each other," he said at one rehearsal.[29] Horst Bollmann summed up Beckett's directing in musical terms: "what is important for him is the rhythm, choreography and shape of the whole production."[30]

He stayed a second time in the Akademie der Künste's residential block, this time in an enormous, sparsely furnished studio on the third floor. With autumn drawing in, it was quite cold and he took to wearing two polo-necked sweaters in the evening. His two-floor atelier was so spacious that, filching an image from *Endgame*, he wrote to a friend: "I feel like a little bit of grit in the middle of the steppe."[31] A gallery served as his bedroom and was reached by a stone staircase; below were a big table, a writing desk, and a smaller table that offered him plenty of work space. The studio overlooked the tops of trees (with "a poplar that murmurs to me")[32] and Bellevue Park with its alleys full of squirrels and baby rabbits. A casual breakfast was served on the ground floor of the same building. For several days on end, he saw the German dramatist Rolf Hochhuth, who was in Berlin for rehearsals of his controversial play *Soldaten*, in which Hochhuth accuses Winston Churchill of instigating the bombing of Dresden and other civilian targets, as well as being implicated in the death of the Polish general Sikorsky. But he exchanged only a few words with him in passing, for Beckett usually sat down at the table alone, absorbed in a newspaper. He ate his other meals in a restaurant close to the theater or near the Akademie. The ones that he preferred and at which he met visitors whenever possible were, in the morning, the Café Ziegler (now the Café Hardenberg) in Hardenberg-strasse and, in the evening, the Börsenstuben. But, more and more often, especially on later visits to the Akademie, he ate alone at the nearby Restaurant Giraffe, where he was served by an Italian waiter who spoke to him in French. He never consumed large quantities of food but was discriminating, even slightly fastidious in his tastes. He preferred good-quality fish dishes like sole and liked his white wines very dry indeed; "German white wines are really awful," he wrote after washing down six Dutch oysters with a Mosel that he felt at best should accompany the strawberries.[33] As for whiskey, he could find no Jameson in Berlin and at first had to make do with a twelve-year-old Ballantyne, then with a Johnnie Walker Black Label, which he concluded he might even end up liking.[34]

Outside the theater, he established a regular routine. "As always in Berlin I walk a great deal. I've discovered a beautiful walk by the river Spree that I do every day after rehearsals, taking a long detour."[35] He smoked far too many strong Gauloises and wondered whether these might be responsible for a recurring dream that he was having; in it, he was holed up in the middle of piles of bricks and rubble with lorries coming and going to and fro—perhaps a memory of the ruined town of Saint-Lô after the war. He resolved to try to get used to smoking cigarillos for the sake of his health as well as of his dreams.[36]

His failing eyesight made him hesitate to wander in parts of Berlin that he did not already know well. But although the theater was only too happy to send a car, he preferred his daily half-hour walk, varying the route slightly sometimes for the sheer pleasure of walking down Joseph Haydn Strasse with the melodies of a Haydn sonata, Klavierstücke, or Variations in F minor, played recently on his Schimmel, running through his head.[37]

Sadder things preoccupied him on these morning walks after he read in his mail that his uncle Jim, who was a well-known anesthetist in Dublin and of whom he was fond, had returned home after having had both his legs amputated and had surely only a short time to live. His response was characteristically positive and practical: he offered financial help to the family to allow them to keep their father at home. He thought, too, about the support that he had pledged to the Spanish playwright Fernando Arrabal. As a favor to Arrabal, who had been imprisoned on charges of blasphemy and treason against the Franco government, he had not only written a letter of protest, but, unusually, had agreed to appear himself in front of the tribunal at what he described as this "ridiculous trial."[38] He dreaded the self-exposure and press coverage that would be involved and joked that his appearance would only add to Arrabal's sentence if the writer were found guilty. He felt a moral obligation to help, but could hardly suppress a sigh of relief when he found that he was unable to appear, as the date of the trial coincided with the first night at the Schiller-Theater. Although he had been pessimistic about Arrabal's chances, in the end the writer was acquitted, thanks partly to a European-wide press campaign but also to letters of support from Beckett and other prominent writers.

Rehearsals at the Schiller-Theater took place either in the morning or in the evening. This allowed him time to work on his revision of the French translation of Watt. Some days he worked for three or four hours at a time. He made good progress and hoped to have at least half the project finished before leaving Berlin. He dined with new friends, like Erwin Leiser, or with older ones, like the Schiller-Theater's chief dramaturge, Albert Bessler, and the lively, humorous intendant general, Boleslaw Barlog, in whose home he sat sipping wine in a large, blue, winged armchair, surrounded by original paintings by

Kirchner, Schmidt-Rottluff, Dix, and Kokoschka and listening to records of Schubert and Beethoven chamber music.[39] On September 12, he spent a highly convivial evening—much assisted by alcohol, according to Beckett—with the actors at Ernst Schroeder's lovely house on the Wannsee, finishing the evening in more relaxed mood with Horst Bollmann and his wife.[40] To relax after rehearsals or long stints of translation, he read thrillers by Agatha Christie, Edgar Wallace, Erle Stanley Gardner, and Rex Stout in his room at the Akademie.[41]

The impression given by his letters to friends is of a constant diet of lonely walks and dinners alone. But this is not entirely true. For Beckett was not without female companionship in Berlin. Some time early in September, he met a young woman from Tel Aviv who was also staying in the same residential block as a guest of the Academy of Cinema and Television. Mira Averech wrote film scripts and occasional journalism, precisely the kind of occupation that would normally have made Beckett bolt for cover. But he responded to a woman's charm and good looks. And Ms. Averech was distinctly attractive.

The affair—although she does not actually describe it as such in her article about Beckett[42]—began with Beckett offering her his ticket for the premiere of *Endspiel*, then appearing outside her door one night with a bottle of Johnnie Walker and two imitation Waterford crystal glasses. From this developed a relationship which lasted for the remainder of his stay in Berlin. Although they tried to keep it secret, it was known to the Academy staff. They corresponded afterward for about five years. Beckett's walks in the park and nightcaps were not always then taken alone in the last ten days of his stay. Like several other casual relationships with women in the past, this one, although warm and affectionate, was not deeply significant. But at least it had the effect of sending him home full of vitality, brimming over with enthusiasm for his delightful stay in friendly Berlin where he had had such "a pleasant and exciting time."[43]

In mid-September, while this brief liaison was going on, Suzanne flew into Berlin for a few days. Conveniently, she was booked into the central Hotel Kempinski on the Kurfürstendamm. On the first evening of her arrival, she attended a rehearsal of *Endspiel* and responded with such spontaneous delight that she gave the actors and Beckett himself a much needed lift. Beckett found time to escort her to a concert by the Berlin Philharmonic Orchestra. Barbara Bray also came to Berlin to see the play. This must have led to some interesting scheduling. Fortunately, since by this time Beckett was beginning to feel drained, Matias flew in a couple of days later to offer invaluable help on the final technical details of the production as the September 26 premiere approached. Beckett always dreaded the last few days of rehearsal, not only because they meant minute, necessary, but boring modifications to lighting, props, and costumes, together with tedious photo calls, but also because, as he put it, "it's the start of all the dinners. The peace is over!"[44]

The last few days were as hectic as he feared. Some weeks earlier, the first night had been put off from the twenty-fifth to the twenty-sixth to avoid clashing with the first night of Madeleine Renaud and Jean-Louis Barrault, who were appearing in *Oh les beaux jours*. But this meant that Beckett had to entertain his French friends, help them with their final preparations, then turn up once again to congratulate them after the performance, as well as put the finishing touches to his own production. Eventually, Madeleine Renaud had a fantastic success and *Endspiel*, too, received glowing reviews from the main German newspapers. The production had been a fascinating learning experience for Beckett as a director. But, more than that, he had set up very friendly relations with the Schiller-Theater actors and staff that were to last for many years to come and lead to five more productions with the company over the coming decade.

4

A FORTNIGHT AFTER HIS RETURN to Paris, Suzanne and he returned to Alghero in Sardinia, staying at the same hotel, even in the same rooms as before. As it was the end of the season, the only meal being served at the almost empty hotel was breakfast. But they discovered good restaurants in town, and the October weather was still warm enough for Beckett to swim regularly. The idea behind the three-week holiday was to restore Beckett's energies after his exhausting stay in Berlin and build him up for the possible results of investigations on his eyes. For while they were in Sardinia Siegfried Unseld let him know that an appointment had been arranged with Dr. Goldmann at the Salem-Spital in Berne. So, only a few days after coming back from holiday, Beckett flew off again, staying the nights of November 3 and 4 at the Hôtel Bellevue-Palais in Berne. Although the diagnosis of double cataracts was confirmed and he was told that the cataracts were developing, though very slowly, he was reassured to learn that the back of his eye was normal and that a later operation on both eyes would have every chance of success.[45] He could have no idea at this stage that he would have to cope for almost three more years with increasingly restricted vision.

The New Year of 1968 found him working hard in his country house, still trying to finish the French translation of *Watt*. Revising the text on his own was tedious and time-consuming.[46] He did not enjoy himself at all. "Up to eyes in French translation of *Watt*," he wrote. "Wearisome thankless chore and I fear pernicious";[47] "Can't think of anything else till it's out of the way which can hardly be before May or June."[48] As a creative counterbalance to this daily slog, he had the first glimmerings of an idea for another television play for his old friend Jack MacGowran. On January 7, Beckett wrote to MacGowran saying that it would be "perhaps the old idea of a man waiting in a room seen first at normal remove then investigated in detail."[49] Josette Hayden noted down Beckett's thoughts as he poured them out excitedly to Henri and herself on the very day that he wrote to MacGowran. Her note is probably all that remains of the original sketch: "A man is waiting, reading a newspaper, looking out of the window, etc., seen first at a distance, then again in close-up, and the close-up forces a very intense kind of intimacy. His face, gestures, little sounds. Tired of waiting he ends up getting into bed. The close-up enters into the bed. No words or very few. Perhaps just a few murmurs."[50] The fragment anticipates in some respects both the "tryst" theme and the transition from distance shot to tighter close-up employed by Beckett later in the television play *Ghost Trio*. But the idea had to wait eight years before it came to fruition in a modified form.

The period of seclusion at Ussy was not allowed to last for very long. Among other things, he needed to return to Paris to talk to Madeleine Renaud and Jean-Louis Barrault about an ORTF (Office de Radio-Télévision Française) production of *Dis Joe (Eh Joe)* for French television. Far more disturbing was a journey he had to make to Dublin. John Beckett's mother, Peggy, of whom he was very fond, died on March 17, 1968,[51] and Beckett hurried to his travel agent to arrange to go over the next day for her funeral.[52] He spent all his time in Greystones and Killiney, almost exclusively with members of his family, especially Peggy's children, the twins, John and Ann, and his niece, Caroline. He stayed at the Grand Hotel in Greystones, which for some odd reason, he noticed, seemed to smell of hay.[53] As he looked out at the sea over the low stone balustrade of the hotel terrace, memories flooded back of the holidays spent in the little harbor village with his mother, father, and brother—all dead now. He stayed only a few days, then flew back to Paris and rushed off to the country, once more depressed and in urgent need of a little quiet.[54] His plans for the summer were to spend a few weeks in May in Ussy, most of June in Sardinia, then part of July in England with Sheila and Donald Page.[55] But events decided otherwise.

5

IN THE CLOSING DAYS of April, he began to feel discomfort, then sharp pains in his chest. He coughed badly and at times had difficulty in getting his breath. He also seemed extremely unwell in himself and, worryingly, started to lose weight. Suzanne called in her homeopathist and herbalist, Dr. Clarac, who treated Beckett with mild herbs, prescribing frequent drinks of carrot juice to build up his strength. "Treating Sam with carrot-juice" became a phrase often used by Beckett's friends to stigmatize the treatment that he was offered at this time: Josette and Henri Hayden, Jérôme and Annette Lindon, Avigdor and Anne Arikha were all horrified at his deterioration and appalled at what they saw as the little or nothing that was being done for him medically. Not for the first time, there were strong differences of view between Suzanne, who believed wholeheartedly in Clarac's approach, and less credulous friends who recognized that her husband was becoming more and more seriously ill.

The first clear indication that something was desperately wrong occurred at the beginning of May at a major retrospective of Henri Hayden's paintings opened by André Malraux at the Musée National d'Art Moderne.[56] Even though he was feeling dreadful, Beckett did not want to disappoint Henri and Josette. So, sporting a smart new gray suit, a white shirt, and an elegant tie under a well-cut, expensive-looking raincoat, he dragged himself along to the opening of the exhibition in the morning, and, with an increasingly raging fever, turned up at a private party in the evening on the second floor of the Falstaff restaurant to honor Henri. Several members of Beckett's family, who all knew the Haydens, had arrived in Paris from Dublin, Geneva, and London for this important exhibition; among them were Morris and Mimi Sinclair and John and Vera Beckett. All of them were invited to the party; Beckett's close friends Avigdor and Anne Arikha, and Con Leventhal and his companion, Marion Leigh, were also there.[57]

Mimi Sinclair arrived at the party with a small cut on her leg caused by a stone, as she and her husband had become caught up in reprisals against a student demonstration. For May 3 was also the first day that the students' revolt during the *événements* of May could really be said to have taken off. The Falstaff is situated only a few yards away from the boulevard Montparnasse, and "all that evening police and demonstrators ebbed and flowed up and down the boulevards of the Latin Quarter, dancers in a grotesque ballet. The students lit fires on the roads, melting the tar and loosening the cobble-stones which they hurled at their enemies."[58] At the party, there was talk of the students' grievances, of the strong-arm tactics of the CRS (riot police), and of the ill-timed departure the previous day of the prime minister, Georges Pompidou, with his foreign minister, Couve de Murville, for Tehran. Beckett sat listening, huddled silently over a drink, coughing feverishly and so clearly ill that his friends insisted that he should be escorted home and put to bed. Even then he was reluctant to leave and stayed on quite late.

The next day, a high temperature forced him to call in more orthodox medical opinion. Fortunately for him, a doctor with whom he was on friendly terms had his consulting room in a nearby apartment. The doctor was a picturesque, long-haired, bearded figure, an enthusiast for Ireland and all things Irish, who, after his initial training in medicine, had become a psychotherapist. Beckett said that this neighbor probably saved his life.[59]

The doctor examined him thoroughly with a stethoscope and, tapping his chest, found that, instead of hearing the hollow echo that should emanate from a healthy lung, he detected a firm, full sound caused by some sort of growth. In light of the previous injury to Beckett's lung and the potential seriousness of his present condition, the doctor made an immediate appointment for him to see a specialist at the Hôpital Cochin. There, he underwent a lengthy series of exploratory X rays, blood tests, and, most urgently, a bronchoscopy. This last and most important of all the tests presented unusual problems in Beckett's case. For he had been drinking heavily for some time and it was considered ill-advised for him to have an anesthetic. And so his doctor friend drove him to the hospital and stayed to use with him a technique of *"rêves éveillés dirigés"* ("guided waking dreams") that is close to hypnosis. In his mind, Beckett was led back to the childhood walks that he used to take with his father in the Dublin mountains. In this way, the specialist managed to insert the necessary tube into his lung and obtain the sample needed for the biopsy.

Beckett, not unnaturally, assumed that he must have lung cancer, since Frank had died from that disease. But it was soon established that he had a severe abscess on the lung. This was serious, he was told, but could be treated successfully at home over an extended period of time with regular doses of antibiotics and a strict regime that included a total ban on smoking and drinking. Although he had earlier declared himself "quite incapable of following any reasonable regime,"[60] the disastrous consequences of ignoring medical advice this time were explained to him by the specialist: he was told very bluntly that, if he failed to do as they advised, the abscess would fail to heal and would probably kill him.

Beckett was confined to his flat for weeks on end; he stopped answering the phone;[61] he smoked no cigarettes; he drank no alcohol. Outside, in the streets of Paris, chaos reigned as the demonstrations continued and spread to include workers; street battles between students and the riot police raged ever more fiercely. Beckett followed events closely in the newspapers and on the radio: the "Night of the Barricades," May 10–11, that began just up the boulevard in the place Denfert-Rochereau; the student occupation on May 15 of the Odéon Théâtre de France, of which his friend, Jean-Louis Barrault, was the director; and the forced closure of the Musée National d'Art Moderne, bringing Henri Hayden's exhibition to an abrupt and premature end.

Inevitably, however, his own illness was the main focus of his concern. Writing to relatives and close friends anxious for news of his condition, he tried to make light of the infection. Yet he felt obliged to warn them that a complete cure would take a very long time.

Throughout the early part of the summer — during which demonstrations were banned, elections were called by de Gaulle, and order was eventually restored in Paris — Beckett was to remain like a prisoner in his own flat. When Jack MacGowran came over to Paris, he was not well enough to see him.[62] All he felt capable of doing was prowling catlike from study to bedroom and back, or walking through the small kitchen into Suzanne's flat for a cursory chat.[63] He would stand or sit for ages at his study window, looking across at the barred windows of La Santé prison and feeling almost as cooped up as its inmates.

By July, he was allowed to go out for short walks around the block whenever the weather was good. Apart from the grocer opposite or the garage proprietor nearby, to whom he would raise a frail hand in greeting or murmur a barely audible "Bonjour" as he left the apartment block, for weeks on end, he saw no one except Suzanne, on whom he depended for all his practical needs. Even Jérôme Lindon, who normally used to stop by regularly, was asked not to visit for some weeks. Beckett was simply not up to the strain of receiving visitors and did not want his friends to see him in such a weakened state. He was sixty-two. But he felt as if he were eighty.

Another bronchoscopy and further tests showed that, although there had been some progress, the abscess was far from healed. He was warned that he would have to go on taking great precautions and doing very little. It sometimes seemed that it would be difficult for anyone to do less. Having asked if he could be allowed an occasional evening glass of whiskey, he was told firmly that this would harm him but that he could drink a single glass of champagne before dinner. Learning this, the Haydens contacted a wine merchant who delivered first one, then a second case of miniature bottles of champagne to 38 boulevard Saint-Jacques.[64] Beckett greeted this relaxation of his regime with relief, drinking the champagne with much relish. He soon had enough of the little bottles to last him for weeks. He thanked the Haydens "de tout gosier" ("with all my gullet").[65]

It was August before his lung started to respond well to treatment, but he was advised to adhere very strictly to the regime that the doctors had given him. At the end of the month, he walked as far as the offices of the Society of Dramatic Authors and Composers, on the rue Ballu, to pick up a check and deposit it in the bank. Every sortie was like a minor triumph. When Con Leventhal eventually managed to get in to see him, he was shocked at how thin Beckett was and how depressed he had become. This expressed itself in irritation and impatience but, above all, in the loss of his usually ready sense of humor.

By the second week in September, Beckett could write: "I am not yet 'cured,' but much better."[66] Later that month, he was able to go out far more frequently, even when it was raining, boasting with restored humor that he was now the proud owner of the first umbrella of his life.[67] He had put on a few kilos, begun to see a few close friends again (though not yet for dinner) and dared to speak of going away to seek the sun, perhaps to the Canary Islands.[68] By the end of October, he was answering the phone again but was still only drinking a little white wine in the evening and going out rarely into the cool, autumnal air.[69] "Really much better," he wrote to Con Leventhal, "but tired of and by abstinence, precautions and antibiotics."[70]

His heart sank when he received the typescript of part of the Tophovens' German translation of Watt and proofs of the same book in French[71] from Les Editions de Minuit, arriving as both did hard on the heels of the American proofs of Cascando and Other Dramatic Pieces.[72] He arranged several meetings in his study with "Top," as Beckett called his German translator, to discuss any difficulties with the translation for Suhrkamp Verlag.[73] And, although he found none of this easy to cope with, he reassured himself with the thought that, only a few months before, he would have been quite incapable of doing it at all.

"I have to get out of France for the worst of the winter," he wrote in November, "and we are leaving in search of sun and dryness early December and expect to be away about 2 months."[74] And so, in desperate need of sunshine, fresh air, and walks by the sea after his seven-month-long illness, Beckett and Suzanne were eventually able to leave on December 2 for what turned out to be a three-month holiday. In the end, they chose not the Canaries but the Portuguese islands of Madeira and Porto Santo. Right up to their departure, Beckett was still taking antibiotics, a form of medicine that Suzanne hoped he would soon suspend. For, as a fervent believer in homeopathic medicine, she volubly castigated all strong artificial drugs.

6

As THEIR PLANE BANKED STEEPLY to land on the short stretch of runway perched precariously on the edge of the rock — pilots have described landing on Madeira as like setting a plane down on the deck of an aircraft carrier — the terrain of mountains surrounded by a wide expanse of choppy sea looked promising enough to two people seeking only peace and quiet. The airport had the friendly relaxed air of a very small island; Beckett described local immigration controls as "all a big joke."[75] But, on closer inspection, the town of Funchal was a great disappointment. He wrote: "It's noisier than Paris. I've never seen so many taxis per square metre; they're even on the pavements. There's a pathetic harbour and the town is very dense, built on different levels and squashed between the mountains and the sea. There are no walks and no beaches."[76] The weather, raining and chilly at first, was hardly what they had been led to expect, either. However, Beckett promptly stopped taking his antibiotics and soon began to feel much better.[77]

The address from which they wrote while they were in Funchal was the Quinta da Ribeira hotel. But Suzanne had made the arrangements for their visit in Paris and had expressed the wish that they stay in Madeira anonymously. So the travel agent arranged for them to stay in reality at a small residence called the Vila Marina, close to the Estrada Monumental. Some surprise was expressed at their request to have separate bedrooms prepared, but Suzanne offered her customary explanation that her husband wrote mainly at night and that, consequently, he needed the freedom of his own room.

Beckett and Suzanne were interested in the island's flora, of which there are said to be two thousand species. They soon found that walks were possible after all between the banana plantations, along the "levadas" or irrigation canals built to carry the rainfall of the northern part of the island to the lower slopes of the south. They visited the Jardim Botânico, where Suzanne was thrilled by the profusion of orchids, camellias, bougainvillea, and gardenias, but most of all by the anthuriums, shaped like red arum lilies, and the famous *Strelitzia* or bird-of-paradise flowers.[78] Beckett took his usual interest in the wines and liked the menu with its emphasis on fish dishes. The Madeiran specialty, "espada" or black scabbard fish, did not compare for delicacy with his favorite Dover sole, but it was still palatable. With her keen interest in dressmaking, Suzanne watched fascinated as the island women worked concentratedly at their delicate lace tablecloths, napkins, and blouses.

French currency controls prevented them from bringing large sums of money out of the country but, before leaving Paris, they had arranged with Barney Rosset to send two thousand dollars in royalties, which had been accruing at Grove Press in New York, to a bank in Funchal.[79] For her part, Suzanne had arranged with the travel agency, Davo Voyages in Paris, that they could pay the remainder of the money owing to a local agent, Carlos Jardim, who knew of

Beckett's reputation as a writer, once the money had arrived from New York.[80] The local agent (to whom later Beckett asked Lindon to send complimentary copies of his books) also helped them when they decided to change their plans and move on to Porto Santo. For the crowded nature of Funchal and the prospect of even greater animation — people were due to flock in for the New Year celebrations — made them happy to leave for the smaller island on December 12, after a stay in Funchal of only ten days.[81]

Porto Santo was much more to their taste. There were only two planes a week; their hotel looked onto a wide expanse of sandy beach, which separated it from the village; there were almost no other vacationers; and they could walk every day either along the seashore or into the island's picturesque interior. The only disadvantage was the hotel's construction; it was prefabricated, so everyone could hear everything through the walls. But from the middle of January, they were the only remaining guests in a one-hundred-forty-bed hotel,[82] so this scarcely mattered.

Atlantic storms of enormous ferocity strike the islands from time to time and, after a good deal of tempestuous weather, Beckett began to wonder whether they had chosen the wrong ocean in the wrong hemisphere.[83] Late in their stay, Porto Santo was completely cut off by sea from Madeira, and food supplies began to run uncomfortably low. Even bread was in short supply as a boat with flour on board was unable to disembark its much-needed cargo on account of the size of the waves.[84] But, in the middle of January, there was a brief spell of sunny weather, which allowed them to sit on the beach. Beckett did not yet dare swim, for the sake of his lung. But they both adored the peace, silence, and solitude of the little island.

The aridity of the interior, the primitive huts, and the oxen or donkeys that pulled the old plows all fascinated Beckett. He was enchanted by the simple little old windmills built on the hillsides, and the walls made of loose stones piled one on top of the other reminded him of Ireland.[85] He had no desire to work, and in truth there was little to do other than read, rest, and walk. Jérôme Lindon had taken out a subscription to *Le Monde* for them, and copies used to arrive in batches, bringing news of a remote outside world. Typically for a linguist, Beckett entertained himself by teaching himself Portuguese, "an easy language but unpronounceable," he concluded.[86] He made enough headway to read an Agatha Christie novel in Portuguese.[87] But he also spent some time reading the poems of the Portuguese poet Fernando Pessoa, finding from time to time (although not quite often enough to satisfy Beckett) some wonderful passages.[88]

Intermittently he thought about his coming production of *Krapp's Last Tape* in Berlin[89] and dashed off some notes to Alan Schneider with his suggestions for a proposed television version of the play, with Jack MacGowran playing Krapp.[90] He looked in desultory fashion at his postwar story *Premier amour* (*First Love*), which Jérôme Lindon had asked if he could bring out in a limited edition.[91] From time to time he thought of how, over the past year, he had been forced to neglect his little cottage at Ussy; he wrote wittily to a friend that his Schimmel piano — Schimmel being not only the manufacturer's name but also the name of a white horse and, in German, a word meaning mold — must after all this time be growing more hair in its mane.[92]

But most of the time in Porto Santo he merely rested, aware that his body needed a prolonged period of rehabilitation to allow "the cavity in [his] lung" to fill up.[93] One day Suzanne and he were delighted to see in a copy of Le Figaro that they found in the hotel a photograph of Josette's husband, Henri, with their dog, Fal (named after the Montparnasse bar-restaurant the Falstaff, where they had bought it).[94] The photograph had been taken to honor Hayden on his birthday; for, since his abbreviated May retrospective at the Musée National d'Art Moderne in Paris, Hayden was becoming increasingly recognized in France as a major painter.

Beckett also heard from Josette Hayden and from Elmar Tophoven that a German television crew from Radio-Television Bremen had visited Paris to shoot a program about Beckett and his work, including interviews with many of his friends.[95] The television crew had even gone to Ussy to shoot footage of Beckett's cottage. In their letters, Tophoven and Josette Hayden, who escorted them there, explained to Beckett how they had managed to draw the cameraman farther and farther away down the road in order to render the pictures of his house less readily identifiable.[96]

Beckett wrote to his friends from Porto Santo saying that he should have realized that the documentary would inevitably disintegrate into a circus.[97] Yet, while feeling guilty that others should have been disturbed on his behalf, he could scarcely suppress a chuckle at the thought that at least on this remote island he and Suzanne were safe from these intrusions into their privacy.

But even out there in the Atlantic, he still could not escape news of the Grim Reaper. He learned that Gastone Novelli, a young, talented Italian painter with whom he had corresponded, had died suddenly in Milan of a heart attack.[98] Closer to home, he also heard from Morris Sinclair that Morris's sister, Beckett's cousin Nancy Cusack, had committed suicide.[99]

The Becketts did not return to Paris until the beginning of March, spending two final weeks at the Hotel Citadella in Cascais near Lisbon.[100] Their stay in Portugal was far from trouble-free: they were both unwell, with flu-like symptoms; besides late in February, an unusual earthquake struck the Lisbon area, close to where they were living.[101] Earthquake or no, they were still delighted to have escaped the worst of the damp, cold Parisian winter and to have been out of "the petrol chamber" of the city.[102]

7

SHORTLY AFTER THEIR RETURN HOME, Beckett went along to the Hôpital Cochin for further X rays and blood tests. He was told that his blood could be in better shape, but X rays confirmed that the cavity in his lung was healing well: "Soon I shall be coughing and spitting again without misgiving," he wrote.[103] He was given permission to start smoking cigarettes again, if he wished, once the damp weather had relented but, cautiously, waited until the end of the year before he resumed, meanwhile confining himself to a few small cigarillos a day.

He was anxious to find out whether he could still cope by himself at Ussy, where he had not stayed for almost a year. In spite of finding "everything sopping wet under a black sky. Worst possible place for me," [104] he discovered that he could manage reasonably well, although there was, he commented, "not much fun here, but at least silence." [105] He saw this as very much *his* silence, necessary to his work, and simmered with anger and resentment at the prospect of its being disturbed by a motorway which was to be built through the valley. He wrote to Kay Boyle: "The autoroute de l'Est will pass close by and spoil all the country round. Its course has been laid down and the lands expropriated, but no sign of it yet and we may be spared the few years more." [106]

He planned to concentrate for a spell on writing and reading. He read Leymarie's book on Vincent van Gogh with much enjoyment and Maurice Nadeau's new book on Flaubert[107] with some disappointment. He played the piano a lot, working on the Haydn Variations that the young composer Melanie Daiken, daughter of his former pupil Leslie Daiken, had given him.[108] His only company while in Ussy was the Haydens, who came to stay in their country house nearby. A renewed series of games of chess with Henri lifted his flagging spirits and he planned to return to his "refuge" as often as possible during the summer, when Hayden would be in the valley to paint.

8

WORK, HOWEVER, did not go at all well. "Fear I've shot my bolt on me and the work both shadowier than ever. At least you'll have a long hank of near-néant [near nothing] fornenst [in front of] you," he wrote to Lawrence Harvey, who was looking forward to dining with him.[109] Out of many weeks of concentrated work eventually emerged a short piece of prose, which Beckett entitled *Sans*. He called the text *Lessness* in English and wrote part of the blurb himself for the Calder and Boyars Signature book cover, describing it as having "to do with the collapse of some such refuge as that last attempted in *Ping* and with the ensuing situation of the refugee. Ruin, exposure, wilderness, mindlessness, past and future denied and affirmed, are the categories, formally distinguishable, through which the writing winds, first in one disorder, then in another." [110] Two sentences in the opening paragraph of the new piece convey something of the contrast between, on the one hand, eternity and fixity and, on the other, the feeble, if still resilient, flicker of being: "All sides endlessness earth sky as one no sound no stir" surrounds the "Grey face two pale blue little body heart beating only upright." [111]

Biography can help little to illuminate this beautiful, spare text, which owes so much to the imagination and to Beckett's interest in mathematical permutations.[112] Yet it is not at all difficult to imagine it being created in the silence of Ussy, the gray skies counterbalancing life stirring in and around the "little body ash grey locked rigid heart beating face to endlessness. On him will rain again as in the blessed days of blue the passing cloud."[113]

9

TWO THEATRICAL PRODUCTIONS of his own work during 1969 aroused Beckett's fury. The first would have made any writer angry. During the time he was acting as literary manager at the National Theatre in London, Kenneth Tynan had asked Beckett if they could adapt his radio play *All That Fall* for a stage production or make a film of it. Sir Laurence Olivier and Joan Plowright were keen on the idea and even visited Beckett in Paris to discuss the possibility of their carrying it out. Beckett told them squarely that the play was written specifically to "come out of the dark" and that he was sure it would not work in any other medium. He disliked turning people down (especially someone like Tynan, who had been one of the earliest defenders of *Waiting for Godot* in England). Tynan, who was then living in Paris, on leave from the National Theatre to write about French drama for the *New Yorker*, asked Beckett if he had a short piece that could be used in an erotic revue called *Oh! Calcutta!*, which he was devising for production first in New York, then in London. Not wishing to be thought uncooperative or standoffish, Beckett sent him a brief piece called *Breath*, which he described in the following way:

> My contribution to the Tynan circus is a forty second piece entitled BREATH. . . . It is simply light coming up and going down on a stage littered with miscellaneous unidentifiable muck, synchronised with sound of breath, once in and out, the whole (ha!) begun and ended by same tiny vagitus-rattle. I realized when too late to repent that it is not unconnected with

> *On entre, on crie*
> *Et c'est la vie.*
> *On crie, on sort,*
> *Et c'est la mort.*

> ["One enters and cries/And that's life./
> One cries and exits/And that's death."]

> If this fails to titillate I hand in my aprob [approbation].[114]

It is clear from this final remark that Beckett intended his sketch to be an ironic comment on what was to follow in the show. As an opening sketch in an erotic revue, it would, of course, have been funny simply because of its deliberate failure to live up to the audience's expectations. However, someone— whether Tynan himself or, according to him,[115] someone else connected with the production—tampered with Beckett's text, adding the phrase "including naked people" to the clutter of "miscellaneous unidentifiable muck." When the illustrated book was published by Beckett's own publishers, Grove Press, not only was this addition retained but, even though a list of contributors preceded the contents page, Beckett was the only one to whom a sketch had been attributed, although the agreement had been that it should be anonymous. And the photograph facing his script clearly displayed the naked parts of bodies that he had first heard about in the New York reviews sent on to him by Alan Schneider and others.

Beckett was, predictably, livid at this travestied version of his work and tried to extricate himself from the contract which he had signed in March with the producer Michael White.[116] Deirdre Bair reports that in a letter to her Beckett admitted calling Tynan a "liar" and a "cheat,"[117] and this was certainly one of the few occasions when he allowed his anger to become public. He quickly contacted his publishers and agents in Britain and the United States, commenting to John Calder: "Herewith *Breath* piece. Extricate me from that and God will reward you."[118] In the event it was Curtis Brown who extricated him from the "wasps' nest" as he called it,[119] but only after its New York run, stopping all further productions that did not strictly adhere to the text as it had been submitted.[120] Beckett felt badly let down by Tynan and, not surprisingly in view of what had occurred, withdrew the sketch entirely from the London production of *Oh! Calcutta!*

If the new man at Curtis Brown who was representing Beckett had an early success with the *Breath* contract, he plunged rapidly down from glory with an Abbey Theatre production of *Waiting for Godot* that Beckett never wanted to take place. Beckett wrote angrily to John Calder: "John Barrett of Curtis Brown has issued without my consent a licence to the Abbey Theatre to present *Godot* in a super production with Peter O'Toole "leading" the cast. I have wired him to put a stop to this immediately. I ask you to support me in this and ensure compliance with my wishes. The decision is absolutely final."[121]

Beckett's objections to this production were various. He had not entirely forgiven his native country for the censorship perpetrated eleven years before, when he had withdrawn his mimes from the Dublin spring festival. And he also appears to have felt a personal aversion to Peter O'Toole appearing in his play, perhaps after an incident at the Falstaff when O'Toole had been going to throw Peter Lennon down the stairs before Beckett intervened.[122] And he also seems to have hesitated to entrust *Godot* to the Abbey, never, even at this late stage, having quite forgiven Simpson for changing the opening line in his early production at the Pike Theatre, "beginning, instead of 'Nothing to be done,' 'Nothing doing.' "[123] Now Beckett was furious when he heard that the Abbey had been given a license. He described the dispute as a "sickening business" and grumbled sourly to Con Leventhal:

Licence granted by Curtis Brown without my permission. Tried to stop it but faced with fait accompli with rehearsals in full swing. Succeeded only in limiting run to 1 month and preventing TV and other subsidiary exploitation as well as inscription in rep. The next bright offer was for *Godot* in London in the Round House with Spike Milligan(?) and some other slapstick TV knockabout rednose.[124]

And, after hearing news of the Abbey run, he adopted an I-told-you-so attitude, reporting to his friend:

> Mary Manning-Howe wrote that Abbey *Godot* was appalling and O'Toole-ridden beyond redemption. I presume the "production" was his into the bargain. It is a relief that it [is] over and done with for bad and all. O'Toole's agent offered a large sum for TV rights which I refused. And it doesn't go into the Abbey rep. Cursed Brown have gone to the dogs since Spencer left.[125]

10

AT THE END OF AUGUST, Beckett flew into Berlin to direct *Krapp's Last Tape* in German at the Schiller-Theater Werkstatt. It was to be performed by a well-known sixty-year-old German actor, Martin Held. Beckett thought Held too large and lumbering to be ideal for the part. But he soon discovered that the actor was also extremely gifted, only too willing to accept directorial help and, as Beckett put it to a German friend, "sehr fleissig" ("a very hard worker"). In the end, the production was one of Beckett's greatest successes as a director of his own plays and received enthusiastic notices in Germany and elsewhere when it toured Europe.

Once more he stayed at the Akademie der Künste. On the first morning, he was awakened early by a sharp tap-tap-tap on his window. Getting out of bed and going over to the window he found perched on the window ledge and pecking at the glass an almost tame jackdaw — a regular inhabitant of the Akademie he later learned. Would it were Edgar Allan Poe's raven, he commented; instead, it recalled for him the death image in *Krapp's Last Tape:* "the vidua or weaver-bird . . . Black plumage of male . . . The vidua-bird." [126] He did not like his room in the Akademie as much as the one that he had occupied during his last stay. With time on his hands, he began to work in his room on the English translation of *Sans (Lessness)* and fulfilled a number of social obligations, even remembering to dispatch his customary good-wishes telegram to Madeleine Renaud on the first night of *Oh les beaux jours* in London.[127]

Martin Held lent him an anthology of German poems into which he dipped many times. This included Goethe's "Prometheus," a poem that he had known well in the 1930s,[128] when he had made his pilgrimage to Goethe's house in Weimar. At dinner now with friends in Berlin, he quoted with relish in German some of the rebellious, accusatory lines of the poem:

Cover your skies, Zeus, with vaporous clouds and try out
Like a boy knocking the heads off thistles
Your strength against oak trees and mountain tops.
....

Here I sit making men in my own image
A race that shall resemble me
A race that shall suffer and weep
And know joy and delight
And be heedless of you, as I am.[129]

"Und Dein nicht zu achten, wie ich" ("And be heedless of you, as I am"): Beckett intoned the line slowly in German.[130] For he knew the poem by heart, having shared its sentiments for much of his life. Indeed, it is not at all surprising that Beckett should have been reminded of Goethe's poem at this time, since, in *Lessness*, composed in French only a few months before, he had written that the sole upright figure of his text with "little body grey face" "will curse God again as in the blessed days face to the open sky the passing deluge."[131]

In spite of the poor state of his eyes, Beckett visited the Charlottenburg Palace again to see Frederick the Great's fine collection of Watteau paintings. He remarked that, like most of the others, the famous *L'Enseigne de Gersaint* was being kept in a dreadful condition.[132] He also went back to Dahlem to see the "magnificent Giorgione between two Antonellos": "what a great wall they make!" he wrote.[133] He visited the recently completed Neue Nationalgalerie and admired Ludwig Mies van der Rohe's design of steel and glass but thought that too many bad modern German paintings were on show.[134]

One evening, he attended a superb concert by the Berlin Philharmonic in what the Berliners called Karajan's Circus because of the tentlike shape of the concrete roof. Herbert von Karajan conducted Bartók's "Music for Strings, Percussion, and Celesta" and Beethoven's Eroica symphony.[135] But, returning to his seat after the intermission he found himself utterly lost in the two-thousand-seat hall, unable to read the seat numbers on account of his failing eyesight. Incidents like this perturbed him greatly and convinced him that only operations on both of his cataracts could now help him to lead a normal life.

One day, he went to the Wannsee to look for the memorial to Heinrich von Kleist. He was intrigued by the story of the suicide pact that Kleist had made in 1811 with a friend, Henriette Vogel. On a first visit there alone he failed to find the tomb which stands on the smaller Wannsee, at the exact spot where they both shot themselves. So later he asked a friend to accompany him. Even before his visit, Beckett could recite by heart the line from *Prinz Friedrich von Homburg* that is engraved on the Kleist memorial: "O Unsterblichkeit — nun bist du ganz mein": "Oh immortality, now you are all mine." Now he thought of its young author blowing his brains out, and turned quickly away.

Suicide represented for him an unacceptable kind of surrender: a surprising attitude, perhaps, in one who held such a somber view of human existence, but an attitude as integral to him as this dark assessment itself. This need to see life stoically through—whether it be tragedy or farce—to a natural end derived partly from his Protestant legacy. But it also came from a firm personal determination to go on, refusing stubbornly to give in.

11

AFTER PHONING SUZANNE in Paris, he booked a flight for the morning after the opening night, October 5. He arranged to fly directly to Tunis, merely changing planes in Frankfurt without returning home. Suzanne was to meet him in Tunis bringing him some lighter-weight clothing and they planned to spend a week at the Hôtel des Orangers in Hammamet, then travel farther south. They intended to return to Paris about the middle of November. However, their plans were blown completely off course, and not only by the freak storms that hit Tunisia.

Torrential rain had been falling since the end of September and the south of the country suffered especially severe flooding, with reports of 352 deaths and thirty-four-thousand homes destroyed.[136] Because of the floods, the hotel at Hammamet was thronged with "stampeding," "baffled hordes" of tourists;[137] it was, Beckett wrote, "Pigalle-on-Sea."[138] They therefore merely picked up their mail at the hotel and left a few days later for Nabeul, the "little capital of Cap Bon about 40 miles south of Tunis."[139]

It was in the Hôtel Riadh on the afternoon of October 23 that Beckett was horrified to receive the following telegram from Jérôme Lindon: "Chers Sam et Suzanne. Malgré tout ils t'ont donné le Prix Nobel—je vous conseille de vous cacher. Je vous embrasse"[140] ("Dear Sam and Suzanne. In spite of everything, they have given you the Nobel Prize—I advise you to go into hiding. With affection.") That morning, Lindon had received a telegram addressed to Beckett from Karl Ragnar Gierow, permanent secretary of the Swedish Academy, informing him in English:

> At its session today the Swedish Academy decided to award you the 1969 Nobel Prize for Literature and hoping that it would be possible for you to be present in Stockholm on Nobel Day December 10 to receive the prize from the hands of his Majesty the King. I want to wish you and Mrs Beckett welcome and to convey my warmest congratulations.[141]

The next day, a second telegram was sent from Gierow asking Lindon to inform Beckett that his presence in Stockholm, although eminently desirable, was by no means a condition of his acceptance of the Nobel Prize. In the meantime an announcement of the identity of the new Nobel laureate had been made in Stockholm to the agencies of the world's press. Lindon telephoned the Nabeul hotel and spoke first to a distressed Suzanne, who genuinely regarded the award as a "catastrophe." Beckett was no less perturbed. He saw only too clearly how much his long-term future would be disrupted by the celebrity, in addition to his present peace being shattered. These appalled reactions even became public, with words like "catastrophe" and "distressed" finding their way into press reports.[142]

Beckett's reflex response was to go into hiding for as long as it took for the hubbub to die down. Jérôme Lindon spoke vaguely of the laureate having taken a prolonged holiday, even having gone on a cruise somewhere, he knew not where. Once it became clear, however, that Beckett's hideaway was known to the press, Lindon in Paris and the hotel manager in Nabeul spoke of the Nobel Prize winner having left on an excursion. Next it was rumored that he had checked into another hotel under a false name. Inevitably, the elusiveness of their quarry served only to make the journalists more and more determined to track him down. Almost every large hotel in the area was telephoned to see if a Mr. Beckett or someone resembling him — "bespectacled and wiry-haired" were the key words — had registered there. For the first few days, Beckett remained cooped up in his room, where his meals were brought up discreetly to him. But, with dozens of journalists milling around the foyer of the hotel seeking information or clamoring for an interview, it soon became obvious that something had to be done. Jérôme Lindon flew into Tunis to help. Astutely, he negotiated a gentlemen's agreement with the press that they should be allowed a few minutes to take photographs, provided that his publicity-shy author was allowed to remain totally silent. Three days after the award, then, Beckett made an appearance in the drawing room of a different hotel, smoking a cigar, with his hair cut very short. He was looking very suntanned. In his light sports jacket, turtleneck sweater, and casual trousers, he sat down, looking ill at ease, said nothing, and puffed away at his cigar. The cameras whirred and, before the cigar even had time to burn down a single centimeter, he was whisked away and back to his room.

The first ten days were the worst. Early in November, although they had been refused an interview, a Swedish television crew turned up in the town; after avoiding them for two days, Beckett eventually issued them a photograph — this time, he commented ironically, in color. To escape for a swim, he used to creep furtively down a service staircase and out of a back exit to find a deserted stretch of beach well away from the hotel. He relied constantly on the cooperation, goodwill, and friendly evasiveness of the hotel staff.[143] There was just one more or less public engagement: the governor invited ten couples to a reception in his honor that he felt it would have been very rude to refuse to attend.[144]

The weather soon improved and, later in November, with the departure of journalists and tourists alike, he was able to swim every day and live quietly, almost alone now in the hotel, answering all the letters and telegrams of congratulations himself, "pounding on the heels of mail like tiny Achilles after giant tortoise,"[145] as he put it. One day, he was tickled to receive a card from an authentic M. Georges Godot who lived in Paris; Mr. Godot told him how sorry he was to have kept him waiting. Not at all, said Beckett in his reply, thanking him, on the contrary, for revealing himself so promptly.[146] Suzanne returned twice to Paris to deal with domestic and business matters. But Beckett stayed firmly put, recognizing that Paris would still be a torment to him.

With a tailing off of his mail, he began to work a little more on the English translation of *Sans*. But once he had finished off the last bottle of Johnnie Walker Black Label in Nabeul and found himself reduced to drinking VAT 69 and reading, faute de mieux, Jacques Bainville's book on Napoleon, which he described as being "like sawdust. One page and you feel as if you are choking,"[147] he decided in mid-December that it was high time to start moving slowly north. They spent a month in Cascais before returning, with very mixed feelings, to Paris.

In the meantime, someone had to accept the Nobel Prize on December 10 in his place, since Beckett had made it clear from the outset that he would not attend to make a speech. "Lindon," he wrote Con Leventhal, "is very kindly facing the turnips in my stead on that Nobloodybeldamday."[148] Beckett telegraphed Stockholm on October 27 that he was honored by the award but that he hoped His Majesty would forgive him for not attending the ceremony. He felt bad at inflicting such a formal occasion on his friend, particularly when, later, he learned that Lindon had gone to Stockholm with an influenzalike infection that laid him low for a fortnight on his return.[149] Fever notwithstanding, Lindon fulfilled his obligations, receiving the diploma and the gold medal on Beckett's behalf from the eighty-seven-year-old king in Stockholm Concert Hall and attending the official dinner with the Irish Ambassador to Sweden. If there was some acrimony because the prize was not collected by the ambassador of the country concerned, as normally happened when a laureate was absent, none of it reached Beckett, who regarded it as only appropriate that he should be represented by the man who had made all this possible by publishing his books. The acceptance by Lindon was not intended as a snub to Ireland but as an acknowledgment of the great debt that he felt toward his friend. All he regretted was that his acceptance of the prize had caused Lindon so much trouble.[150]

Why did Beckett accept the Nobel Prize at all? Certainly not for the money, since he gave the sum of 375,000 kronor (worth at the time £30,000, or about $45,000) away very quickly. He arranged, for instance, for various payments to be made even before the money was transferred to France. One of the chief beneficiaries was the library of Trinity College, Dublin; this gift was a riposte, surely, to those who accused him of insulting his native country. Many individual writers, directors, and painters also benefited financially from the prize, the money arriving anonymously, although recipients could not fail to be aware of the source. One very real reason for Beckett accepting the Nobel Prize was that he did not wish to be publicly discourteous (Sartre had earlier caused something of a public scandal by turning it down). Another was that he wanted the publishers who had shown faith in his work, especially in the early days, to be rewarded with an increase in the sales of his books. To turn the prize down would also have seemed unfair, and again discourteous, to those who, since

Maurice Nadeau and others had put his name forward twelve years before, had regularly proposed him for the prize. But there had always been an unusual mixture of perfectly genuine humility and concealed pride in Beckett. He had, after all, invested almost everything in his work, knew what it had cost him in terms of effort and sacrifice, and could not lightly reject an acknowledgment of his achievement at such a high level.

22

Vision Restored

1970–74

1

"Up to the cataracts" was a favorite expression of Beckett.[1] It should by rights have been reserved exclusively for the period after the Nobel Prize, when the stress was at its most intense and his cataracts were slowly but surely worsening. He and Suzanne finally arrived home in late January 1970, having been away for almost four months. The first two weeks were spent attacking the accumulated piles of mail, dealing with business matters by post or on the telephone, and meeting the hordes of well-wishers who were eager to congratulate him personally. He also had to fit in hours of traction and massage for his back, which he had ricked while hoisting a heavy suitcase onto a trolley at Orly air terminal.[2] He even had to write letters standing up, his "3rd lumbar vertebra objecting to the 'seated station.' "[3]

Innumerable requests for newspaper and magazine interviews were promptly turned down on his behalf by Jérôme Lindon. But, understandably, his English and American publishers, as well as Lindon himself, were pressing Beckett for new texts to publish. The problem of a publication in French was easily, though not painlessly, resolved. He fished two prose works, *Mercier et Camier* and the novella *Premier amour*, written in French soon after the Second World War, out of what he referred to as "his trunk" in the cellar. He was unhappy at the prospect of releasing work over twenty years old that he no longer liked. But he saw the logic of having something new to offer the French public so soon after the Nobel Prize. As far as English texts were concerned, he had nothing, either old or new, that he thought worth publishing. So he promised Barney Rosset and John Calder that he would start to translate *Mercier et Camier* as soon as possible. But his heart sank at the thought of the effort involved. "For the sake of dubious peace,"[4] and as an immediate concession, he agreed that his early stories, *More Pricks Than Kicks,* could be reprinted.[5]

Jean-Louis Barrault and Madeleine Renaud were making their comeback at this time as a cultural force in the French theater. In 1968, Barrault had been sacked from his post at the government-subsidized Théâtre de l'Odéon for fraternizing with the students who occupied the theater during the upheaval of the *événements* of May. Now, after a European tour of his spectacular, mammoth adaptation of Rabelais, he was back in Paris with an ambitious three-month-long cycle of Beckett's plays at the newly reopened Théâtre Récamier. Roger Blin was the codirector of the cycle.[6]

In view of what had happened, Beckett badly wanted to help Barrault to reestablish himself. So, as well as dashing round to the Récamier theater to see the final run-throughs of *Happy Days*[7] and helping Blin direct *Godot* yet again, Beckett was soon advising on a Greek *Happy Days*, in which Christine Tsingos, who had played Nell in the original *Fin de partie* and whom Beckett liked personally, was to give four performances in Greek at the Théâtre Récamier before going on to play again in Athens.[8] He was also asked by Barrault to direct their friend Jean Martin in *La Dernière bande (Krapp's Last Tape)*. At one stage, he thought that the operations planned on his eyes would make this impossible.[9] But he was disappointed to learn that, since the cataracts were not quite ripe enough, the surgeon was unwilling to operate until the summer at the very earliest. This left him with no good reason for refusing Barrault and Martin. So, in early April, he started rehearsing, mostly transferring what he had learned in Berlin to the French production. His return home was every bit as frenzied as he had feared. And it was far from over.

Jack MacGowran flew into Paris on the first of April 1970. Beckett was enormously fond of the Irish actor, but worried intensely about his physical health and state of mind. There were three weeks to go before the opening night of MacGowran's one-man show, *Beginning to End*, an anthology of Beckett's writing, at the Théâtre Edouard VII; Beckett spent as much time as he could spare from rehearsing Martin in *Krapp's Last Tape* with Jack, mostly encouraging and reassuring him. For the actor lived on his nerves and seemed exhausted most of the time. Although he had stopped drinking, he slept badly and took countless pills to enable him to cope. Jack's wife, Gloria, had come along with her daughter, Tara, to lend him her moral support and ensure that he got to appointments and to the theater on time. Remarkably, though, MacGowran was able to draw on hidden reserves of strength and his great talent as an actor enabled him to come brilliantly alive in performance.

The first night was one of those glittering Parisian social occasions which Beckett normally avoided like the plague. The women were dressed in the height of fashion, although, by official request, the men did not wear tuxedos. All Paris was there: a deputation of Rothschilds; Salvador Dali; the Irish ambassador, an old schoolfellow of Jack MacGowran, with most of the members of the Irish embassy; and Irish, French, English, German, and American writers, directors, and actors.

As usual, Beckett did not attend the performance itself. Instead, he waited patiently for MacGowran in his dressing room to congratulate him immediately after the show. And, out of affection for his friend, he stayed on to chat convivially with guests at a reception in the theater bar. He met there the film star James Mason, who had been at the Irish premiere of *Beginning to End* and who had recently been filming Burgess Meredith's film *The Yin and Yang of Mr. Go* in Hong Kong with MacGowran. Beckett even posed for the photographers, although the flash bulbs hurt his sore eyes.

Resuming rehearsals of *Krapp's Last Tape*, Beckett and Jean Martin worked at a feverish pace as time ran out. Beckett knew Jean Martin very well. And as they rehearsed together, he confided in him about the autobiographical nature of parts of the play. He spoke with emotion of the death of his own mother at the root of the "mother at rest at last" passage and of the revelation that he had experienced in his mother's house after the war, which is echoed in Krapp's "vision at last." And he spoke, briefly but movingly, of the woman with the hauntingly beautiful eyes, linking her with Ethna MacCarthy, whom he had loved when he was a young man and who had died of cancer more than ten years before.[10] But whatever emotional depths are plumbed in this play, as a director Beckett worked hard at avoiding sentimentality. For reasons of immediacy and truth, Martin asked if he could operate the tape recorder himself; it is usually controlled from the wings by a stage-manager. This seemed unnecessarily risky to Beckett.[11] But, with a duplicate tape recorder ready to cut in if anything should go drastically wrong, he agreed. Nothing serious ever did.[12]

Although performances went smoothly enough and were well received by the Parisian critics, Beckett believed that preparations for the production had been too rushed; he described it as "approximate theatre."[13] And he breathed a huge sigh of relief that this frenetic period in his life semed to be drawing to a close. He now had to concentrate on improving his health in preparation for his first eye operation, which he thought was likely to take place in mid-June. So he took a month's break with Suzanne in Sardinia.[14]

2

THEY LEFT PARIS on May 4 to stay again at the Hotel Las Tronas in Alghero. Beckett took along the French text of *Mercier et Camier* with him to translate but, in the event, did little except rest — and grieve. For just over a week after their arrival in Sardinia, they heard that one of his closest friends, Henri Hayden, had died in Paris on May 12. Henri was in his eighty-seventh year and had been ill for some time, so the news was not entirely unexpected.

Only a few weeks before, the Haydens had moved from their old flat on the boulevard Raspail into a new studio with an elevator at 25 rue du Montparnasse. Beckett knew that Josette would be desolated by Henri's death and utterly lost in her new surroundings. He telephoned her immediately from the hotel, then wrote worrying where it would be best for her to stay, suggesting that she might be better in the Haydens' country cottage at Reuil, provided that she did not go there alone. "But perhaps," he thought, "places have nothing to do with it at all and it is in one's head that one must carry on the struggle."[15] He found her "very broken. But brave."[16] He admired her courage in venturing to see Jean Martin in *Krapp's Last Tape*[17] and in traveling to Bourges to represent her late husband at an exhibition of his paintings at the Maison de la Culture.[18] But, from bitter personal experience, he knew that ultimately grief must be borne alone.

The weather picked up in late May, allowing him to swim at last. But the death of his old friend cast a huge shadow over a holiday from which he had hoped for so much. He received and corrected the proofs of *Le Dépeupleur* early during their stay in Sardinia, and, a little later, found in his mail copies of the French editions of *Premier amour* and *Mercier et Camier*. He regretted, he said at the time, that he had ever agreed to their publication at all.[19]

Suzanne returned to Paris before him. He stayed on in Alghero until June 8, returning in time for a crucial appointment the following afternoon with the eye consultant surgeon, Professor Guy Offret of the Hôtel-Dieu hospital near Notre Dame. To his great dismay, the surgeon found "no 'progress' in the condition"[20] and decided not to operate then but to defer surgery yet again, until the autumn. Beckett was upset. But, instead of feeling too sorry for himself, he tried to focus on offering help to someone who needed it far more, lunching with Josette Hayden and finding her "very low and lost."[21]

3

"I AM DISTURBED AT EVERY TURN—from without and from within," he wrote early in July.[22] Out of a sense of duty, he forced himself to translate some of *Mercier et Camier*. But he made little progress and soon abandoned the work for a period of months. Deliberately, he took himself off alone to Ussy for the whole of August in an attempt to restore himself by one of his customary immersions in solitude. In the country he began to write again: "Trying to write on from *Lessness*—in that same scape only dust instead of sand."[23] "The work has started again," he wrote to Jocelyn Herbert, "and I am fighting to keep it going and to bring it to something more than the abandoned shorts of these past years."[24] In this respect, he did not succeed. For what he wrote became yet another "short" in French. It was published by Georges Visat in a deluxe illustrated edition early the following year.

The painter Geneviève Asse related how this text came to be published and why it was called "Abandonné." She had met Beckett several years before and telephoned him one day to ask if he had a text that she could illustrate.[25] He called her back later to say that all he had available was this short piece of residua. He took the text around to her studio in the impasse Ricaut. He stood for ages, with his spectacles pushed back on his head, looking intently at her subtle blue and gray light-filled studies. They talked a little of their mutual friends Bram and Geer van Velde. But the silence was mostly unbroken. He came to visit her several times as she worked on the engravings for the book.

The text did not have a title until she had finished her work. One day, he suggested "Abandonné" and asked specifically that it should be printed as if the letters were carved out of stone. On his walk from the boulevard Saint-Jacques to her studio, halfway up the boulevard Auguste-Blanqui, he used to pass a monument to Ernest Rousselle, the president of the French commission for children who are abandoned and in need.[26] At its foot is a bronze statue of a curly-haired, young child with no shoes, reclining with his eyes closed and his head on a traveling bag. Beneath the statue, a single word, "Abandonné!" is cut out of the stone. This fragment later became the first section of a text that he did not complete for a further five years, entitling it eventually *Pour finir encore* (*For to End Yet Again*). Signs of the transition from sand to dust about which Beckett wrote still show in the published text: "Grey cloudless sky grey sand as far as eye can see long desert to begin. Sand pale as dust ah but dust indeed deep to engulf the haughtiest monuments which too it once was here and there." [27]

It had been a long time since he had last stayed in his little cottage and he did not find it easy to cope on his own with his blurred tunnel vision. He badly wanted his cataracts removed now, saying that it was "not so much a question of seeing for seeing, but to be able to get about without [a] helping hand." [28] He had too many memories of James Joyce in the late 1930s, dependent on friends and helpers like Beckett himself for reading, note-taking, and dictation, not to feel deep concern at his growing incapacity. Foolishly, he still drove his little Citroën around the quiet country roads, terrifying his friends.

His stay in Ussy was disturbed by a deluge of minor irritations and demands on his time and his purse. [29] His mail was now colossal. But, more seriously, he found that he was in yet another creative impasse that lasted for more than a year. He blamed the Nobel Prize.

4

ONCE THE DATE for his first operation was fixed, his principal concern was to ensure that his relatives and close friends knew what was happening, without worrying them too much and without either the fact or the place of his operation becoming public knowledge. His recent brushes with the world press in Tunisia had shown him how disturbing its intrusions could be. So he did not mention the surgery in letters until the very last moment and then was deliberately vague as to precisely where the clinic was. To his cousin Sheila Page, he wrote that the first operation was to take place "in a nursing home quite near here. Shall be in about a week. I feel fine and am not worrying so don't you either" [30] and to Mary Hutchinson that "the kindest thing my friends can do is to take no notice of me during that time." [31]

The nursing home was a little clinic, "a quaint dirty old place," [32] on the boulevard Arago called the Clinic of the Sainte Marie de la Famille, run by sisters of the order. It was just around the corner from his flat in the boulevard Saint-Jacques, so Suzanne could easily visit him. The operation on his left eye took place on October 14. A few days later, Beckett was able to stumble out into the pale autumn sunlight for a little stroll around the garden. The surgeon was delighted with his progress and he was able to leave the clinic after the minimum period of a week. On his return home, he wrote that there was "not much vision yet, only great brig[h]tness" [33] and that, though he was "limp as weak jelly" and the "world just one big bright blur," he understood that "forms will soon emerge."[34] Less than a month later, he could write: "The eye is healing well and it seems that vision will be excellent far and near. But getting about is still difficult, also reading and writing. It is a very slow tedious business. My next appointment with surgeon is in a month from now. I hope then to get final glasses, and fix date for second operation probably late Jan[uary]."[35]

Although he still walked around with some difficulty, Beckett began to see a few of his close friends again in November. He met John and Bettina Calder, but on separate evenings, since they had separated, prior to seeking a divorce.[36] Barney and Christine Rosset telegrammed him that they were coming to Paris,[37] and on December 1, he was well enough to have dinner with them. They told him about Jack MacGowran's triumph in *Beginning to End* at Joseph Papp's Newman Theater in New York. He was delighted for Jack. Only a month before, playing the title role on Broadway in a play called *Gandhi*, the actor had been devastated because it closed after only one performance: having read the reviews, the backers had withdrawn their support.[38] By contrast, MacGowran's playing of Beckett's derelict won him an Obie and a gold plaque from the New York Drama Critics' Circle.[39]

On the same day as his dinner with the Rossets, Beckett put on his overcoat and scarf against the morning cold and went to the official opening of a major Bram van Velde retrospective of ninety paintings at the Palais de Tokyo, the west wing of the Musée National d'Art Moderne.[40] Bram's brother, Geer, and many of his old friends, some of whom were also friends of Beckett, had turned up to honor the artist: Roger Blin, Avigdor Arikha, Jacques Putman, and Pierre Tal Coat. Beckett wandered around the exhibition in the company of Avigdor Arikha, looking intently at the paintings through his thick tinted "cataract glasses." Even so, he was relieved to see that he could appreciate Bram's canvases in a way that only a few weeks before would have been impossible.

He had a quiet few moments chatting with Bram, whom he found as silent and uncommunicative as ever. For once, though, the painter was suavely dressed in an elegant dark suit with a striped tie, and he looked fit and well.[41] His well-groomed, urbane appearance contrasted with the "50 years of suffering"[42] and poverty that Beckett knew he had experienced. Bram's present celebrity was further confirmed by the opening of another exhibition of his recent work at the Galerie Knoedler in Paris on the same evening as the museum retrospective. Beckett went to see the second exhibition later in the week.

Over Christmas and the New Year, he felt hopeful that, with the improvement already noticeable in the condition of his first eye and with an operation planned in February he would soon be able to work more comfortably, perhaps even normally again. So he arranged that, provided the next operation was as successful as the first, he would go to Berlin to direct *Happy Days* in German at the Schiller-Theater for the August Festival. It felt good to start planning once more. He even started to work again, although at first he had to take writing very gingerly indeed. Jérôme Lindon had asked him for a French translation of the script of *Film*, which had been published by Grove Press in 1969, and he soon set about the work. At the same time he tackled a few more pages of the English translation of *Mercier et Camier*.[43] He was able to complete the *Film* translation and give it to Jérôme Lindon before going into the nursing home for his second eye operation.[44] But his heart was still not in *Mercier et Camier*, and he made little progress.

The operation on the right eye was performed, again by Professor Offret, on February 17 in the same clinic as the first. Beckett found everything less forbidding this time, and was able to leave the nursing home in what was regarded as lightning time. To his delight, the result was again extremely successful.[45] Only a fortnight after surgery, he wrote to Jack MacGowran: "Second cataract operation successfully over. Eyes still dim but prospects bright."[46] At first, he ventured tentatively out into the boulevard Saint-Jacques and the adjacent streets. But, with the arrival of spring and feeling his confidence burgeoning, he walked down the avenue de l'Observatoire into the Jardin du Luxembourg, where he took pleasure in seeing things that had previously lain outside his range of vision, like the time on the Palace clock, which he could make out now from the Petit-Luxembourg.[47] One of the remaining problems was that the two eyes had to learn to synchronize one with the other: "Both eyes done now and getting on," he wrote. "Homologous lobes still disconcerted. Hope they learn in time."[48] Eventually, both his far and his near vision improved quite dramatically, as the recovery of his near vision was helped by a strong preexisting myopia.

In March, he received a sad letter from Ireland telling him that his uncle, the anesthetist Dr. James Beckett, had died. This hardly came as a surprise, as it was almost four years since his uncle Jim had had both legs amputated. But he will still depressed by the news. For he could remember Jim Beckett when he had cut an impressive figure, brimming over with life, confidence, and good humor, a fine athlete and a powerful swimmer. Recently he had tended to think of him as "a stump of a man," the equivalent of Bill Lynch in his own parodied genealogy of the Lynch family in *Watt*.[49] But he remembered, too, the bravery with which his uncle had faced up to so many illnesses and operations and thought of the sadness of Jim's children. He wrote letters of condolence to his daughters, Margo and Olga, and telephoned to explain that, on doctor's orders, he would be unable to attend the funeral.

Pleased at his own progress, however, Beckett began to feel positive and energetic. He even accepted proposals that he would have rejected in the past. In April, Alan Schneider flew to Paris to discuss an American television version of *Krapp's Last Tape* that he would direct, with Jack MacGowran playing Krapp. At dinner, Beckett and he mulled over some of the technical problems involved, Beckett picking up his suggestions sent from Porto Santo and passing on to Schneider ideas that he had put forward when West-Deutscher Rundfunk had recorded the play for television with Martin Held in 1969.[50] What Beckett would never have approved of when the film was made was the generally busy nature of the production, as well as what must frankly be described as some dreadful overacting from Jack MacGowran. It is one of MacGowran and Schneider's least successful pieces of work.

But, at the end of April, just as his eyes were continuing to improve, Beckett caught a nasty bout of flu, which gave him intermittent fevers and forced him to postpone for over a week seeing the oculist for the final prescription for his spectacles. The flu affected his morale, making him feel low and depressed and in need, he wrote, of "a few weeks of sun and briny."[51] Suzanne hoped that a total change of scene early in June, with plenty of Mediterranean sunlight, sea air, and country walks would dramatically improve his health and lift his spirits before he had to go to Berlin to direct *Happy Days* in German. They paid a return visit to Santa Margherita de Ligure where they had spent some fairly happy, or at least contented days of their own five years earlier. This time they stayed at the Imperial Palace Hotel rather than the Lido. But, at the end of June, Beckett reported from the coastal resort that their stay was "not very successful so far and benefit to carcass nil to put it mildly. Weather on the whole grey and cold, but looking up now. Bathing out of the question — beaches and seas a nightmare."[52] In another letter, he described the seawater as "Ligurian soup."[53] While on holiday, he received a letter from the Society of Dramatic Authors in Paris pointing out that, since he was now sixty-five years old, arrangements needed to be made for the liquidation of his pension. He hardly needed to be reminded of this. He complained that he was feeling too tired to go anywhere, "except twice to Rapallo round the corner. Sit about the little harbour and try to think about *Happy Days* in German. Wish to God I hadn't taken it on."[54] Fame, too, brought its familiar problems. The Nobel Prize was still fairly recent and the Italian press, having discovered that Beckett was staying in the hotel, was pressing for an interview with him.[55] As usual, it was Suzanne who dealt incisively with the matter, although the staff of the Imperial Palace earned their eternal gratitude by helping to keep the journalists at bay.

Beckett had brought his copy of Dante with him, and one day he set out on a personal pilgrimage to discover the stream that Dante had described in the *Divina commedia* as dividing Chiavari from Sestri Levante. To his intense disappointment he found that the "limpid waters" of Dante's *fiumana bella* were only "a ditch now."[56]

5

RETURNING TO PARIS on July 8, he prepared meticulously for his production of *Happy Days*.[57] He met a few times with Matias, who had designed the set for Roger Blin's Paris production eight years earlier and went over some ideas with him suggesting that they move Winnie from the "exact centre of the mound" to a little off center. This made the set asymmetrical and gave a little more prominence to her companion, Willie. Beckett had sketched out one set of detailed notes in a large tan notebook before leaving for Italy and had continued working on it in Santa Margherita. Now, in a smaller, red notebook, he started to analyze the play in even more minute detail.[58] He made changes to the German text and introduced a number of cuts.[59]

He stressed the "agedness" and "endingness" of the objects that Winnie takes out of her bag. He noted the pitch, volume, and duration of the bell that wakes her and marks out her day. He sketched Willie's invisible crawl into his hole and his crawl up the mound toward Winnie, and described his morning-suited appearance. He then listed all of Winnie's smiles, happy expressions, and signs of sadness and counted all her repeated refrains and gestures, dividing both the words and the gestures into interrupted and uninterrupted ones. His aim was to establish patterns, echoes, and contrasts of movements and gestures. Finally, he traced and recorded the sources of all the quotations from the "classics" that she uses, setting out the English original texts and the German translations on facing pages.

On August 9, 1971, happy with the improvement in his eyesight and satisfied that he was as well prepared as he could possibly be, he flew into Berlin to direct *Happy Days* himself for the first time. He stayed in the same large studio as he had for *Endgame* and was welcomed by many of the same friendly people. But during most of his stay, he was in constant pain from his shoulders, arms, and neck; the condition was diagnosed as periarthritis, inflammation of the tissues surrounding the joints. The pain was so bad that, in Paris, he had not been able to drive; now, in Berlin, he found writing painful. He tried massage; then, for a whole week, he had plaster compresses applied to his shoulder. They had little or no effect. So he went back to sessions of twice-weekly massage from a formidably strong Prussian masseuse who, he maintained, had "une poigne d'acier" ("a grip of steel"). One small consolation was that he discovered that he could, after all, obtain a favorite Irish whiskey, Tullamore Dew. So he kept several bottles in his room at the Academy of Arts for the remainder of his stay.[60]

Although the atmosphere was good and everyone at the theater was cooperative, there were a lot of difficulties with this production. Werner Stock, who was going to play Willie, had been hospitalized and was forced to withdraw; a replacement proved unsatisfactory and the third actor they found, Rudi Schmitt, had only a fortnight in which to rehearse before the opening night. Beckett found the actress who had been chosen beforehand to play Winnie, Eva-Katharina Schultz, lost at first in a text as demanding as *Happy Days*. She was understandably nervous at working for the first time with Beckett. The main problem, however, was that because of the repertory system operating at the Schiller-Theater, amazingly, she was acting *five* other roles while rehearsing *Happy Days*.[61]

Beckett concentrated on specific features of Schultz's performance, such as the rhythm, pace, pitch, and volume of her voice and the rhythm and timing of her movements. He was anxious to ensure that all Winnie's movements should be as crisp, precise, and economical as possible. Quoting Kleist's essay on the marionette theater to reinforce his argument, he argued that precision and economy would produce the maximum of grace. His aim was to achieve a musicality of gesture as striking as that of voice.[62] Questions of meaning rarely cropped up. When they did, Beckett tried hard to answer them without confusing the actors but also without being condescending. With the introduction of the dazzling front of house spots, Schultz, staring out unblinkingly for as long as she was able, was almost blinded by the light and needed eyedrops.

The problems in Berlin were not confined to *Happy Days*. Earlier in the year, arrangements had been made to bring Jack MacGowran's *Beginning to End* to Berlin as part of the festival. A few weeks before the opening, Beckett suddenly heard that, since MacGowran had applied for American citizenship, he no longer possessed a valid Irish passport. But he had not yet acquired an American one either. This meant that he was unable to travel — "He suddenly discovers this," commented Beckett sarcastically.[63] With the help of the Schiller-Theater's dramaturge, Albert Bessler, and the Intendant General, Boleslaw Barlog, plus some letters from Beckett, the difficulty was resolved, though not before Beckett had become caught up in the general anxiety.

But it was not all anxiety. One day, with Ruby Cohn, his American theater-scholar friend, who had come to Berlin to attend rehearsals and write about the production, Beckett went to a late lunch to sample, for the first time in his life, a chow mein in an open-air restaurant close to the theater.[64] Beckett was amused when a smiling young woman came over to his table as she was leaving the restaurant and introduced herself as Denise Coffey, who was with the Young Vic company on tour with *The Taming of the Shrew*. She reminded him that she had played Winnie herself earlier that year in *Happy Days* with the Young Vic and invited him to a performance of the *Shrew* that evening. Since he had a rehearsal, he had to decline. Next day, he was touched when four red roses arrived at the theater, sent from the airport by Denise Coffey on behalf of herself and the Young Vic.[65]

One evening, he was invited to see the famous clown Charlie Rivel, on his farewell tour.[66] By this time, Rivel was seventy-five years old. Beckett described him as having "a bulging stomach" — shown off to disadvantage by the long red shift that he used to wear as his costume — and "dragging a foot behind him"[67] as he shuffled around in exaggeratedly long, flat, black shoes. Rivel used to do an amusing parody of Charlie Chaplin as an acrobat — a number that United Artists unsuccessfully tried to forbid as representing a copy — and another of Maria Callas with a false bust and a huge hat decorated with ornate ostrich feathers.[68] Funny moments in Rivel's act took Beckett back to his youth at the circus and music hall in Dublin and reminded him of his meeting with Karl Valentin in Munich in 1937.

There were a number of social engagements. One evening, he had dinner with Stefan Wigger and Horst Bollmann, who had played Estragon and Vladimir in the earlier *Waiting for Godot*[69] and who were eager to see Beckett return to direct his own production of the play.[70] On September 7, he dined with a German couple from Kassel, Gottfried and Renate Büttner, both of whom were doctors. They had just returned from a visit to Russia and interested Beckett in some photographs of the work of a Russian sculptor, Vadim Sidur, who was experiencing difficulties with the authorities because of the individualistic style of his work. The Büttners presented Beckett with Christian Morgenstern's poems before they left; but Beckett was equally appreciative of the bottle of Weleda massage oil that they had brought him for the pain in his shoulders. Thanks to the improvement in his sight, he was able to visit the art galleries in West Berlin again, although he was afraid now of being recognized. He bought dozens of picture postcards — Caspar David Friedrich, Courbet, Daumier, Monet, van Gogh, Max Liebermann — and sent them off to friends.

Beckett cheered up immeasurably a week from opening night. His neck pain had eased and he was sleeping better. More important, he found Eva-Katharina Schultz much improved; the second act, he commented, was already not at all bad.[71] A few days later, it had become "very good indeed" and his young German Winnie was, he said, now excellent at times; he even conceded that he had never heard Winnie's dolly story better delivered. Willie, too, though he had had only a few rehearsals, was improving steadily.[72] Although visitors were flying in almost every day, putting him under extra strain, Beckett felt that, in spite of his earlier fears, the production now stood a good chance of success.

At the dress rehearsal, as is customary in Germany, the auditorium was fairly full. Beckett sat apart in a small side balcony watching intently, frowning slightly but no longer taking notes. He had a few words of advice to say to the actors afterward but was more intent on encouraging than on criticizing. Rehearsals had been difficult, and it had been touch and go. But they had not only avoided the disaster Beckett feared but, thanks to hard work and some good acting from Eva-Katharina Schultz, the end result was very satisfying. At the first-night party, Beckett turned up resplendent in a dark suit, white shirt, and tie, to relax and joke with his friends. But he still could not fly back to Paris, as he wanted to do. Jack MacGowran had to be met at Tempelhof Airport, then rehearsed in *Beginning to End*. So Beckett stayed on a few extra days in Berlin to help. Everything went without a hitch and, with packed houses for both performances, MacGowran, too, was showered with praise.

6

BECKETT RETURNED TO PARIS on September 22 with the idea of embarking immediately on the translation of *Le Dépeupleur*. But the stresses and strains of Berlin had left him exhausted. Suzanne's immediate response was to suggest another trip to the sun; in this they followed an established pattern that was to continue well into the 1980s. They used to leave, mostly for North Africa, two or three times a year. They went away partly for health reasons: Suzanne suffered increasingly from bronchitis during the winter months and needed a dry climate, while Beckett was bothered intermittently by lumbago and wanted "to try and get a little warmth into the old bones and joints."[73] But these trips were also an escape. Ussy was too close to Paris, making Beckett feel that he should return to town whenever visiting friends asked to meet him. He was almost a martyr to friendship, making promises like "but, of course, I'd come in like a shot if you were to be in Paris" in his correspondence. Suzanne regularly used to pave the way for their holidays by visiting the resort, usually with Marthe Gautier, and staying in the hotel where they were planning to go. After she had vetted a place, Beckett knew that all would be well. In this respect, he still relied on her.

He and Suzanne left Paris for Malta on October 8 and returned on November 14, 1971. They stayed at the impressive Selmun Palace Hotel, a converted eighteenth-century fortress set high on a promontory in the northern part of the island close to Melleiha. There were magnificent views from the hotel over St. Paul's Bay to the south and the islands of Comino and Gozo to the north. Except for one or two late-season vacationers, the small, select hotel was exceptionally empty and quiet. After three peaceful weeks, Beckett could write: "Swimming, driving and enjoying sun, quiet, emptiness. Best antidote to Paris so far and certainly to be revisited. Aches no better but somehow more tolerable."[74] He found the local wine drinkable and his joy was complete when, as in Berlin, he discovered that he could get Tullamore Dew whiskey in the nearby village.[75] Beckett often walked alone down the little winding road toward the ruined Campbell Fort, enjoying the "great quiet and stoney vacuity in this part of the island."[76] The silence had an extraordinary intensity, which encouraged him at last to make progress with his translation of Le Dépeupleur.

He was relieved to find that, following the eye operations, he could manage things that he had thought he would never do again. They rented a little Ford Escort and he drove confidently around the island. They visited the vast dome of St. Mary's Church in Mosta and the Cathedral of St. Peter and St. Paul in the beautiful, honey-colored, walled "silent city" of Mdina, where he was asked to leave the church for being improperly dressed in shorts—a reminder, he noted, of the fact that St. Paul was "wrecked on these shores and set about getting them the way they are."[77] A little later, they took the recently introduced car ferry to the smaller, tranquil island of Gozo, known as Malta's Eye.[78] They saw the megalithic temples, the oldest free-standing structures in the world, at Ggantija and drove across the little island to see "what passes for Calypso's Cave,"[79] where, captivated, Odysseus was reputed to have been detained for seven years by the nymph Calypso. Beckett described the cave as a "gloomy hole,"[80] but conceded that the attribution had been upheld by some serious scholars.[81]

Most important of all to Beckett, however, the restoration of his sight allowed him to see the famous signed Caravaggio painting, the Beheading of St. John the Baptist, in the Oratory of St. John's Co-Cathedral in Valletta, which he described as "a great painting, really tremendous."[82] He sat for more than an hour in front of the painting, allowing it to work on his imagination. Had he seen nothing else on the island, this alone would have made the trip to Malta worthwhile. For it provided him with inspiration for his next piece of creative writing, Not I, begun on March 20, 1972. In this play, one of the most strikingly innovative pieces of modern theater, an illuminated mouth, set high in the darkness to stage left, spews out words at an astonishing pace, telling of a sad, lonely, silent life. She—for the voice is female—is watched by an unspeaking "Auditor" figure, who stands to stage right, clad in a djellaba, and raises and lowers his arms in "a gesture of helpless compassion."[83] Beckett told his painter friend Avigdor Arikha, and, independently, wrote to me: "Image of *Not I* in part suggested by Caravaggio's *Decollation of St John the Baptist.*"[84]

The second source of inspiration for *Not I* was discovered in the course of their next holiday in Morocco. They flew into Tangiers in the first week of February 1972 and traveled on to Tarudant south of the Atlas Mountains, where they stayed in the comfortable Gazelle d'Or. The day after their arrival, Beckett wandered into the rather ugly town to buy whiskey and cigars. He watched with great curiosity as, with not a solitary camel in sight, whole families were hoisted onto the backs of little donkeys; individual Arabs squatted for hours in the shade of huge eucalyptus trees.

As he wandered through the orange groves, his senses were sharpened by the strangeness of his surroundings and by the quality of the light and the silence, which was broken intermittently by the wailing chant of the pickers of olives and oranges. He watched fascinated as an elongated wild cat dragged itself slowly along the ground, its emaciated belly rubbing in the dust, and as flocks of beautiful white birds like small storks congregated on the branches of the trees.[85] In the distance, the summits of the Atlas Mountains (a "vast crystaline land-mass," as his guidebook put it) were covered with snow. One night, an upside-down crescent moon astonished him so much that he sketched it in a letter to Jérôme Lindon.[86]

For the final part of their five-week visit, they traveled north to an old town, El Jadida, founded by the Portuguese, on the coast a hundred kilometers south of Casablanca. During their visit, the "feast of the throne" took place and the streets were festooned with colorful flags and lanterns. But the weather was very disappointing; it rained a lot and Beckett was hardly ever able to swim in the very cold sea. However, he hired a Simca 1100 in Marrakesh, so they were able to see a lot of the countryside. Suzanne adored the North African sunsets, and the landscape stretching away into the vast distance reminded her of her youth in Tunisia.

Their stay in El Jadida was wonderfully restful and invigorating. Sitting in a café, Beckett observed "a solitary figure, completely covered in a djellaba, leaning against a wall. It seemed to him that the figure was in a position of intense listening. . . . Only later did Beckett learn that this figure . . . was an Arab woman waiting there for her child who attended a nearby school."[87] The concept of *Not I* was, therefore," wrote Enoch Brater, "initially sparked by Beckett's preoccupation with the isolated listener, the unidentified auditor on stage." The source for this link between the Auditor and Beckett's Moroccan experience was Beckett himself. What probably happened is that the image of the djellaba-clad figure coalesced with his sharp memories of the Caravaggio painting. For perhaps even more striking than the partially disembodied head of John the Baptist in the Caravaggio are the watching figures. Most powerful of all is an old woman standing to Salome's left. She observes the decapitation with horror, covering her ears rather than her eyes. This old woman emerges as the figure in Caravaggio's masterpiece whose role comes closest to the Auditor in Beckett's play, reacting compassionately to what he/she hears.[88]

As a result of these two holiday experiences, Beckett could at last see how the idea of a disembodied head or mouth, which he had had many years before,[89] might be made to work in the theater. "Can you stage a mouth? Just a moving mouth with the rest of the stage in darkness?" he had asked Ruby Cohn.[90] Now he had his answer: with the Auditor, Mouth has acquired her silent witness; and the spectator has his or her surrogate representative on stage.

He already had the visuals of his play in mind, then, when he started to write *Not I* a week after his return from Morocco. Words were pressing to come out. So he simply opened the floodgates and let them flow. The story that Mouth recounts of a life that she will not acknowledge as her own came from a variety of other sources. Beckett said: "I knew that woman in Ireland. I knew who she was — not 'she' specifically, one single woman, but there were so many of those old crones, stumbling down the lanes, in the ditches, beside the hedgerows. Ireland is full of them. And I heard 'her' saying what I wrote in *Not I*. I actually heard it."[91]

Although there is only one specific local geographic allusion in the play itself,[92] the entire monologue has the feel of old Ireland, evoking the life of an Irish "bag lady," brought up, it would seem, in a Protestant home for waifs, then living alone, totally shut in on herself, speaking to no one — until something happens that releases a stream of sound, so that words flow out of her like water gushing from the mouth of a stone lion in a fountain.

Yet Beckett's "she" belongs to his own world far more than she does to that of any visible Irish reality, past or present. The being evoked by Mouth is isolated, fragmented, absent, and distressed, a "lost soul" in more than the everyday sense. Asked further about the sources of *Not I*, Beckett referred questioners back to his own novel *The Unnamable*.[93] There we already find the voice, the source of which is indeterminable: "It issues from me, it fills me, it clamours against my walls, it is not mine, I can't stop it, I can't prevent it, from tearing me, racking me, assailing me. It is not mine, I have none, I have no voice and must speak, that is all I know."[94] There is also the flood of sound where "the words swarm and jostle like ants, hasty, indifferent, bringing nothing, taking nothing away, too light to leave a mark"[95] and the concern with avoiding the first-person pronoun, which is expressed in *The Unnamable* as "I shall not say I again, ever again, it's too farcical, I shall put it in its place, whenever I hear it, the third person, if I think of it"[96] and in *Not I* by Mouth, asserting vehemently "What? . . . Who? . . . No! . . . She!"[97]

As so often with Beckett's work, this stark, anguished drama evolved organically out of his own intellectual preoccupations and his personal experience. He had never really lost, for example, the fascination for the unusual, the macabre, or the mentally disturbed that had emerged so clearly in *Murphy* and *Watt*. So this particular "lost soul," mute for so long, then unstoppable in her verbal discharge, takes her place in a long line of split personalities, psychotics, or obsessional neurotics, who assume, nonetheless, more universal significance.[98]

7

BECKETT WANTED THE WORLD PREMIERE of his new play to be one on which he himself could work. He was genuinely doubtful about it, anxious to "find out if the new piece is theatre in spite of all or can be coaxed into it."[99] He sent off a copy of the script to Oscar Lewenstein at the Royal Court Theatre in London, offering the Court first refusal.[100] But, in the end, again more out of friendship than because of any delays in London, he allowed Alan Schneider the opportunity to present it first. Schneider was looking for another success after having experienced a rather lean time recently on Broadway.[101] He teamed up with the American actor-director Hume Cronyn to do a short season of Beckett plays starring Cronyn himself and his wife, Jessica Tandy, with the lanky Henderson Forsythe.

Cronyn's own interest in Beckett went back over ten years to the time at which he had sought an option on the rights of *Happy Days* for Jessica Tandy to play with the English-Speaking Theatre in Rome.[102] Now the plan was for Jessica to perform *Happy Days* and for Hume himself to act *Krapp's Last Tape* and the mime *Act Without Words I* at Lincoln Center in New York. More than anything else, what they needed was a new play from Beckett that would attract more publicity and could be put on the program with *Krapp's Last Tape*.

During the summer of 1972, at Barney Rosset's suggestion, the earnest trio of Schneider, Tandy, and Rosset flew over to Paris to meet Beckett. Schneider had asked Beckett in advance whether he might have anything new for them. They arranged to meet for dinner; at the beginning of the evening, Beckett took a few typewritten pages from his inside jacket pocket. As they passed the pages around, he talked about his latest play, explaining very precisely how the play should look and dwelling particularly on the image of the Mouth. Jessica Tandy explained: "I wanted anything I could get from him. And what I got was that Mouth had no control over her words. They were just pouring out. This was a wonderful thing to keep in my head. What it meant was, I found, you must not think what you are saying. It just has to come out."[103]

Before they left, a tired, jet-lagged Jessica Tandy irritated Beckett slightly by putting what he considered some rather silly questions. "What had happened to the woman in the field," for instance; "had she been raped?" But he had heard fine things about Tandy's acting from Alan Schneider and was charmed by her warm friendliness and modesty. On their return to the United States, an agreement was duly signed between Beckett and Hume Cronyn,[104] and the world premiere took place in New York on November 22, with Jessica Tandy as Mouth and Henderson Forsythe as Auditor. *Happy Days* with Jessica Tandy and *Act Without Words I* with Hume Cronyn played on different evenings.

Jessica Tandy found the experience of acting *Not I* terrifying. But, for her, the problem was not one of forgetting the text. "I don't know whether Beckett ever knew this, but I made it possible for me not to have to think by being in this contraption in which I was wheeled on. . . . I had a TelePrompTer right in front of me. So I didn't have to think at all. I only had to know the excruciating panic. I was free — and I had his dots there in front of me!"[105] She had to be wheeled on in a sort of black box because the plays were being done almost in the round. In this contraption, she stood holding on to two iron bars on either side of the box. The main problems found in any production of this play revolve around succeeding in blacking out everything except for the illuminated mouth and ensuring that the actress playing Mouth does not move her mouth even a few centimeters out of a very tightly focused spotlight. In the New York production, the first problem was solved by dressing Tandy entirely in black, with a black cloth mask or shroud on her head. At first her head was held during rehearsals by a tight strap; she found it unbearable and unnecessary, so it was subsequently abandoned. The second was answered by having an operator hidden in front of the box to reset the focus on the mouth if it should move even slightly out of the light. "I didn't ever find it fun to do. . . ." confessed Tandy, summing up the experience. "I found the challenge exhilarating. But the nature of the piece was such, the panic so dreadful, that I didn't enjoy it."[106]

8

AT THE END OF DECEMBER 1971, a dynamic, likable Milanese gallery owner, Luigi Majno, had asked Beckett for a new text for a mutual friend, Stanley William Hayter, the founder of Atelier 17, to illustrate in a deluxe art edition.[107] Beckett replied that he had no new text available for the moment.[108] But he wanted to oblige Bill Hayter, whom he had known since the 1930s and respected greatly, both as an engraver and as an authority on modern print techniques. Hayter was the man who taught Picasso, Miró, Masson, and Tanguy.[109] So, after the feeling of release that followed the writing of *Not I*, in June 1972 he started work on a short, calm piece of prose which, eventually, he called *Still*. It was finished by the end of July.[110] Majno came up to Paris especially to meet Beckett at the Closerie des Lilas, where they sat at the table at which Proust used to sit. Beckett first told Majno that he would have to talk to his agent to acquire the rights to publish *Still*; then, after a few Irish coffees and some moments of indecision, with his head buried in his hands, he blurted out: "Here's the manuscript. Do whatever you want!"[111]

Still explores how a mind, situating itself outside the body, investigates the most minute aspects of its consciousness, the minuscule movements and sense impressions that deny complete stillness. A figure sits bolt upright in a chair, unmoving it appears at first, at a window, watching the sun set. Yet, on closer inspection, the body is seen to be trembling all over. *Still* is not, then, still at all. The text is both intensely personal and coolly dispassionate. The "small upright wicker chair with armrests"[112] in which the figure sits is Beckett's own "narrow chair" at Ussy, and the "valley window" looks out across the valley of the Marne, which Henri Hayden painted so many times. The Ussy cottage has windows that allow one to see in several different directions. From one of these windows, Beckett could indeed "turn head now and see it the sun low in the southwest sinking." The pose of the seated figure, his head in his hand, was one often adopted by Beckett.

"Legs side by side broken right angles at the knees as in that old statue some old god twanged at sunrise and again at sunset" contains a memory of the colossal statue at Thebes named Memnon by the Greeks — actually the Egyptian king Amenophis — which emitted a musical sound at dawn. But it also presents the figure pictorially in terms of the angles of its legs, followed later by the angles of its arms; Beckett was deliberately providing Hayter with strong visual material with which to construct his three etchings. There is a lot of hypersensitive observation in *Still*. But the text is not only descriptive. It is, as the title additionally suggests, itself *almost* a still-life. It is "quite dark," "quite quiet," "quite still."

Still seems in fact to have evolved out of Beckett's love of painting and his friendship with various painters. He was becoming quite accustomed, for instance, to seeing himself through the eyes of Avigdor Arikha, who had been drawing or etching his head for several years. Several of the silverpoints or goldpoints of the previous year show Beckett with his hand to his head or to his mouth.[113] In *Still*, we move from one visual image to another, focusing on *near* stasis. Beckett's fascination with frozen gestures in painting — Vermeer's *The Geographer* and *The Astronomer* are good examples — may lie behind this beautiful text. It shows Beckett's obsession with vision. The gesture of raising the hand from the armrest to the head is taken frame by frame, frozen almost second by second. In this way a text written with potential illustration in mind itself takes on an almost hypnotic, visual quality. But the viewpoint constantly shifts and readjusts itself. In this way, *Still* challenges the relationship of the reader to the text just as, only a few weeks before, *Not I* had challenged that of the spectator to the play.

Beckett's eyes were now stabilized, and he found that his vision had improved dramatically since the two operations. He had to use five or six different pairs of spectacles, with different pairs for typing, driving, playing chess, or playing the piano. This complicated life, but selecting the correct pair was well worth the trouble. However, he had virtually lost all lateral vision, so that, when driving, he had to "turn head ninety degrees at every intersection"[114] to see if it was safe to move on. The figure in *Still* similarly has to "normally turn head now ninety degrees to watch sun." The "normally" is, of course, not normal at all, except for Beckett after his operations. As a direct consequence of this absence of lateral vision, he began to drive less regularly in Paris. The restriction could also be very embarrassing for him in public. One day, as he entered an elevator with Ruby Cohn, he bumped into the large bust of a woman standing at the side, whom he simply could not see. The woman was annoyed and complained, thinking that he must have done so deliberately.[115]

But there were compensating rewards. He was able to look at paintings again with almost literally fresh eyes. He continued to visit the Arikhas' apartment regularly to look at new work. And he also made prearranged visits to the studio of the fifty-year-old Buenos Aires–born French painter Sergio de Castro, in the rue du St. Gothard on his way to the Parc de Montsouris, where he loved to walk.[116] Several of the new friends that he made in the 1970s were associated with painting and sculpture: the American sculptor Helaine Blum, for example, whom he saw every year for the next sixteen years, when she came to stay with friends in Paris. With his newly sharpened vision, Beckett also resumed going to public galleries like the Musée d'Art Moderne, although he hated to be recognized, as happened now more and more frequently.[117]

9

THE SUMMER OF 1972 was virtually given over to visitors and family: Deirdre Bair, writing Beckett's biography; the novelist Kay Boyle and the playwright Israel Horowitz, over from the United States; his nephew, the flutist, Edward, on his way through to Nice to work with Rampal; John Beckett conducting two concerts with his ensemble, Musica Reservata, in the Sainte Chapelle; John Calder and Martin Esslin over in Paris together to discuss Patrick Magee's forthcoming BBC reading of The Lost Ones; Nick Rawson; Ruby Cohn. He liked all of these people. Even so, he still felt that "being in Paris is mostly siege fever."[118]

He invented strategies for coping with less pleasurable pressures. He answered the telephone, for instance, only between eleven o'clock and noon and had an on-off switch that enabled him to use it otherwise only for outgoing calls. Friends knew when they could reach him. Sometimes he did not even switch the phone on: "I haven't been opening the phone regularly for some time," he wrote to Mary Hutchinson.[119] All his other meetings were arranged by letter. Nonpersonal letters were dealt with by a quick comment added to the letter itself or by a system of signs for Les Editions de Minuit to answer for him with standard replies: "Mr. Beckett does not give interviews"; "Mr. Beckett is away in the country"; "Mr. Beckett does not read theses and manuscripts on his work"; and so on. This was the only way to carve out any time for writing.

In Paris he had developed his own routine. Work in the mornings, dealing with his personal correspondence virtually every other day; an afternoon walk in the Jardin du Luxembourg or the Parc de Montsouris; drinks or dinners at the Closerie or the Iles Marquises. Most days, he stopped by Barbara Bray's quiet apartment in the rue Séguier at the end of the afternoon. Sometimes he played Schubert, Haydn, or Beethoven on her piano. She had an extra telephone line especially installed so that he could call her. Occasionally she joined him at Ussy. But usually he stayed there alone. Even in nearby Reuil, he saw less and less of Josette Hayden now that Henri was dead, although he never failed to send her postcards whenever he and Suzanne were away.

On September 3, Suzanne and he were off again to the "bare old rock" of Malta, staying for a second year at the Selmun Palace Hotel and "tootling around in a Triumph [car] from beach to beach."[120] Among the many pleasant effects of the island was "that of making me wonder how I ever wrote a line and if it is conceivable I'll ever write another," he wrote.[121] Every evening he played chess with a little magnetized chess set that the Arikhas had given him, and read Kurt Vonnegut, Jr.'s, novel *Slaughterhouse-Five*. He was fascinated by the book. His new play was still very much on his mind. He heard from Oscar Lewenstein about arrangements for the coming double bill of *Not I* and *Krapp's Last Tape* at the Royal Court Theatre. Albert Finney had been signed up to play Krapp but they did not yet have anyone cast for Mouth. Beckett asked for Billie Whitelaw. He had long ago decided that if he were well enough, he would go over for rehearsals, for this would offer him the chance to get the new play right.

In the meantime, on his return from Malta, he "entered a dark night of the teeth *(nuit dentaire),*" as he put it.[122] Starting on November 7, he had eight teeth extracted in forty-eight hours and, a week later, imprints taken for dental plates. It took him ages to become accustomed to eating, especially in public, with what he called his new "buccal crockery."[123] But there was a feeling of relief at being rid of what, in retrospect, seemed like sixty-six years of toothache. A month later, in mid-December, he felt well enough to fly to England for rehearsals of his astounding new play.

10

IN LONDON, he stayed at the huge, rather grand, "old-style" Hyde Park Hotel, ten minutes' walk from the Royal Court Theatre down Sloane Street. Rehearsals were strenuous and, at times, very tense. Anthony Page, assisted by Beckett, directed both plays. The staging of *Not I* was as new and as difficult for Beckett as it was to everyone else. *Krapp's Last Tape*, on the other hand, was so familiar to him that boredom set in even before rehearsals began. He never believed in Albert Finney as Krapp. And Finney became acutely conscious that he was not satisfying the playwright. It was difficult for both actor and author. The chemistry simply did not work. Beckett fell asleep at one rehearsal[124] and left one of the recording sessions in despair, saying afterward that he had disgraced himself.[125] Finney tried too hard to compensate, drawing in vain on his entire palette of colors as an actor. The result was disastrous. "Finney miscast,"[126] Beckett soon concluded. The main problem for him was the delivery of the lines: "You hear it a certain way in your head and Albert can't do it," he said dismissively. One day, with uncharacteristic aggression and immodesty, he held up his little finger, announcing that there was more poetry in his fingertip than there was in Finney's whole body.[127]

With *Not I*, things were very different, although sometimes equally tense. Billie Whitelaw played the part of Mouth. Rehearsals strengthened his admiration for the actress, with whom he had worked nine years before on *Play*, and deepened their friendship. It was as if the traumas associated with creating this extraordinary role cemented their bond. The part itself was demanding enough. But the physical discomfort involved in presenting the stage image made it into an even more demanding, tougher assignment.

At first, Billie Whitelaw wanted to stand high on a dais. But she found that this did not work for her. So she sat ten feet high on a tall podium in a chair on what is called an "artist's rest," a device on which a film actor wearing armor rests because he cannot sit down. The chair looked disquietingly like an electric chair; in late rehearsals, it seemed as if Whitelaw were being prepared for some medieval torture. Her entire body was draped in black so that it was not discernible in the darkness, and only her mouth was illuminated by two spots from below, hidden by a screen from the audience; her body was strapped into the chair with a belt around her waist; her head was clamped firmly between two pieces of sponge rubber, so that her mouth could not move out of the spotlight, and the top part of her face was covered with black gauze, with a black transparent strip for her eyes. And, as in *Play*, a bar was fixed to which the actress could cling and on to which she could direct her tension.[128] Unlike Jessica Tandy who did not accept these rigorous constraints and made the technology fit her needs as a person, Billie Whitelaw accepted the imposed immobility and total blackout in the theater so that Beckett's play would have its greatest possible impact.

In the course of rehearsals, Billie Whitelaw's son, Matthew, was very ill and Whitelaw was up during the night looking after him. A few years before, he had been desperately ill with meningitis, so she was naturally distraught now that something was seriously wrong with him again. As a result of her sleepness nights, she became exhausted. One day at rehearsal, she lost her bearings completely; she felt as if she were losing her balance.

> Yes, for the first couple of rehearsal performances, when the blindfold went on and I was stuck half-way up the stage, I think I had sensory deprivation. The very first time I did it, I went to pieces. I felt I had no body; I could not relate to where I was; and, going at that speed, I was becoming very dizzy and felt like an astronaut tumbling into space. . . . I swore to God I was falling, falling. . . .[129]

On January 2, she "broke down" into floods of tears. Holding her hands, the distressed Beckett blamed himself and what he had written for putting her through this dreadful ordeal. But, although worried about their slow progress on the play, he was a main provider of sympathy and concern. He had been aware from the beginning of the difficulties with her son's illness and suggested canceling rehearsals until the situation at home had improved. Very professionally, Whitelaw quickly pulled herself together; the following day, once Beckett had established that she had had a better night with her son and felt up to continuing, it was as if nothing had happened.[130]

The problems, of course, remained: "For instance, there is no time to breathe," said Billie Whitelaw.[131] She therefore went into training, practicing verbal sprints and time trials (sometimes using the time clock at athletics meetings on television) until she could build up the required speed, enabling herself to cram so many words into such a brief time span. "I've been practising saying words at a tenth of a second. . . . No one can possibly follow the text at that speed but Beckett insists that I speak it precisely. It's like music, a piece of Schoenberg in his head," she said.[132]

It was not easy for Anthony Page to work on the new play with Beckett in such close attendance, nor for Beckett to work through Page. They disagreed at first as to the pace at which the play should go, and there was quite a lot of tension in the arrangement. After consultations with Oscar Lewenstein, it was finally decided that it would be best if Page, although still remaining nominally as the director, were to leave the way more or less clear for Beckett to direct *Not I*, while Beckett opted out of *Krapp's Last Tape*.[133]

There was a strong backup team. The designer, Jocelyn Herbert, and the assistant director, Anton Gill, constantly supported Billie Whitelaw. And, since the actress chose to memorize the text rather than use any method of prompting that involved a printed script, she needed someone disciplined and reliable as her prompt. With an earpiece as a safety device — it was wired to the stage manager, Robbie Hendry — she felt much more secure. Two other practicalities reassured her. Hendry held a microphone in his hand and, since Whitelaw had a visual memory and could imagine the pages in her mind's eye, he let her hear the sound of each page turning; they also had an agreed warning system that she could use when she was in trouble: a repetition of the phrase (always only a few words) that she had just said was a sign that she needed a prompt.[134]

Those who saw the first production on which Beckett worked are unlikely ever to forget its astonishing impact. Critics spoke of the hypnotic, almost hallucinatory effect of watching Mouth and of the dramatic force of the strange, standing, listening figure. The text came through with searing power as a harsh shriek of anguish, all the more potent because it demanded total concentration for the spectator to catch the words. For Beckett, it was an exciting time, seeing his vision realized. It was also exciting for him to work so closely with Billie Whitelaw again. She still never asked him about the meaning of his lines, simply how to deliver them.

His affections must have been somewhat divided on this occasion, since he was surrounded by close women friends: Jocelyn Herbert, of whom he was also extremely fond, was often there, and Barbara Bray also came over for a few days to visit him and see the production. It must have seemed at times like a profusion of riches for a sixty-six-year-old who had virtually reached Shakespeare's "sans teeth" stage.

Being in London for the first time in six years inevitably meant a host of social demands which, added to the strain of rehearsals, he found extremely wearing. Staying in a sumptuous, rather anonymous hotel at least gave him a bolt-hole into which he could retire when he was tired. But he dealt with all of this pressure much better than he had ever expected he would, buoyed up by working on his new play with this "marvellous actress"[135] and "marvellous person."[136]

11

TIRED BUT EXHILARATED, Beckett returned home on January 18, two days after the press night. Knowing that he had committed himself to produce two English translations and a French one over the next few months, he took his usual course of action and beat a hasty retreat to Ussy before Paris could overwhelm him. He revised and, by February 11, completed the translation of *Premier Amour.*[137] He had a much harder time with "that old ghost,"[138] *Mercier et Camier*, restarting and abandoning several times a translation that he had started three years before and no longer liked. On the first of March, he decided to make an attempt to translate *Not I* into French but broke down, twelve days later, after only five pages. Fragmenting the syntax and transposing the verbal ambiguities presented more daunting problems. As a relief he played his little Schimmel piano so often that, by August, five of the strings had broken so that "Field's *Nocturnes* now its last straw."[139]

Throughout 1973, he seemed to be constantly receiving bad news. Jack MacGowran died at the end of January. Beckett sent his deep condolences to Gloria and their daughter, Tara, and he received a telegram from Billie Whitelaw telling him that her performances would be dedicated to Jack's memory. He was saddened by the death of his old friend — "another one gone," as he was wont to say — and did all he could over the years to help the MacGowran family financially.[140] Then, within a few days of hearing of Jack's death, he also learned that the actress Christine Tsingos, a good friend of both Suzanne and himself, had been found dead on the terrace from an attack of asthma, her inhaler clutched in her hand, after playing *Happy Days* in Athens.[141] The deaths were a grim *memento mori*, but Beckett responded with typical complexity and ambiguity. "Time," he wrote to Kay Boyle, "gets like a last oozing, so precious and worthless together."[142] And, if he genuinely sorrowed for his friends, in a mood of weary stoicism, he could also happily doggerelize a Chamfort maxim as:

> The trouble with tragedy is the fuss it makes
> Over life and death and other tuppenny aches.[143]

Characteristically, he turned to work as a consolation, applying himself with a heavy heart but determination to the recalcitrant *Mercier et Camier*. It was to be midsummer before, at long last, on August 12, he completed the rough draft. Three months later, he started to revise and retype it, "cutting out the worst," he wrote.[144] The English text is indeed far more compact than the French.[145] To someone who had just written the spare prose of *Still*, the unfocused diffuseness and volubility of *Mercier et Camier* must have seemed irritating and tedious.

After writing *Not I*, Beckett felt dismay at his failure to write anything that he considered significant. The few pages of *Still*, the short related "Sounds," "Still3," and "As the Story Was Told" (written as a memorial for the German writer Günther Eich), however beautifully crafted they are, did not add up, in Beckett's own eyes, to very much over a two year period. In February 1973, he wrote to Mania Péron that his work was not advancing at all.[146] Since his mood, health, and nervous stability depended so much on the satisfaction or otherwise that he obtained from his writing, he often felt at a very low ebb. When Bettina Jonic dined with him in Paris in August, for example, she found him nervous, depressed, and not at all well.[147] In a letter to Barney Rosset six months later, he summed up the time since *Not I*: "It has been a dull period for me and continues so with persistent sense of deterioration and too slack and stupid to set about the adventure of getting that [the sense of deterioration] into writing, the only remaining one."[148]

12

THIS SENSE OF DULLNESS was soon to change. Although for the first few months of 1974 he appeared to be ambling along in familiar, well-trodden tracks ("the usual old plod")[149] with regular stays in Ussy, two further trips to Morocco, plus, as a novelty, a three-day break in Le Touquet at the end of June,[150] the second half of the year was saved by a sudden burst of creative energy akin to that which had produced *Not I*.

On June 8, in Paris, he began to imagine a play he called *That Time*, referring to it later as a "brother to *Not I*."[151] In it he returned to the image of a human head illuminated in the darkness—this time a whole head, not just a mouth: "Old man (sitting) in dark. Facing front, a little off centre. Face alone lit faintly. Very white, long white hair standing on end." In the margin, he asked, "Head on white pillow?"[152] The inspiration was probably pictorial again, perhaps William Blake's engravings of Job or God the Father. But Man Ray's photograph (now in the Museum of Modern Art in New York) *Femme aux longs cheveux (Woman with Long Hair)* of 1929 anticipates Beckett's image, with its long hair spread out fanlike above the head.[153]

The powerful single visual image of the old man's head is contrasted with a three-part text spoken by the same voice but emanating from three different sources to his left, to his right, and above his head. Any movements are drastically reduced; the old man does not open his mouth to speak but merely opens and closes his eyes four times. At the end, he breaks into an enigmatic grin, "toothless for preference."[154] If the image of the old man (even without its white pillow) resembles a death scene, the triptych of sound, experienced by the spectator as three discrete, but interrelated, recorded texts, reveals Beckett's long-standing preoccupation with musical structure.

From the very outset, he was fascinated by the possibilities of permutating the different texts and themes and establishing formally where the silences, which resemble pauses in the movements of a sonata, are to be situated. But the different stories of A, B, and C, which were intended at first to correspond roughly to three aspects of life—the factual, the mental, and the affective—soon evolved into the stories of three distinct periods of a man's life. ("The B story has to do with the young man, the C story is the story of the old man and the A story that of the man in middle age," Beckett explained).[155] There is a lot of biographical reminiscence, especially in the play's earliest versions. Places such as Barrington's Tower, which became Foley's Folly, or the walk up from the wharf to the high street to catch a Number 11 bus, the trams having disappeared, or the "Doric terminus of the Great Southern and Eastern"[156]—the boarded-up Harcourt street railway terminus, to which Beckett traveled daily as a boy—situate A's story in and around Dublin. Somewhat less precisely, the Portrait Gallery, Library, and Post Office identify London (or at least another big city) as the venue for C's story. The setting of B's story is, by comparison with these two cityscapes, rural—wood, canal towpath, and sandy beach—and is given an Impressionist landscape of sunlight, blue sky, and "wheat turning yellow."[157] Yet the geographical is less important than the feelings of confusion, solitude, desolation, and death that flood in as the protagonist ranges widely over his past life.

While Beckett cannot be equated with the protagonist of *That Time*, there are still many points of contact. There is an absence of nostalgia as A searches for the place where he hid as a child, ending up in even greater solitude; vows of love and idealized togetherness in B's story end in a solitary acceptance of the void, "a great shroud billowing in all over you";[158] the old man's memories in C's story end with the dust of Macbeth's "dusty death." For over the entire play looms the shadow of Beckett's lengthy meditation on the powers of that "cancer Time." Time not only deforms ("We are not merely more weary because of yesterday, we are other,"[159] he had written in his early study of Proust) but sweeps man along on a tide which makes the past appear remote, uncertain, even illusory, and sees the individual human life as the fleeting disturbance of a still, silent, indifferent world, a diminutive ripple on the surface of infinite Time. It is in this deeper sense that the play evolves out of Beckett's life, as, at sixty-eight, he gazes back on its many different moods and phases.[160] The play also echoes some of Beckett's most cherished themes: an absence of an identifiable self; man forced to live a kind of surrogate existence, trying to "make up" his life by creating fictions or voices to which he listens; a world scurrying about its business, ignoring the signs of decay, disintegration, and death with which it is surrounded. Yet if all this sounds deeply somber, even pessimistic, there remains a strongly positive impulse to confer form on such concerns. Form (and here poetry) has become a central bulwark, perhaps even providing a reason for the need to express, the sources of which Beckett genuinely never seems to have understood.

He worked on *That Time* intensively over June, July, and August 1974, both in Ussy and in Paris. The manuscripts and typescripts chart its steady progress; the letters reveal its gradual evolution from July to late September.[161] Again, Beckett was very conscious that, as with *Not I*, he had written a play that was "on the very edge of what was possible in the theatre."[162] In a manuscript note, he wrote: "To the objection visual component too small, out of all proportion with aural, answer: make it smaller on the principle that less is more."[163] Again he wanted to be involved in the first production to see how successfully the problems could be resolved.

Throughout the summer, while deeply involved in the intricacies of this beautiful meditation on time, he brought himself back regularly, sometimes too abruptly to everyday reality in order to keep in touch with members of his family and his friends. Edward Beckett was the soloist in one of Mozart's flute concertos with the New Irish Chamber Orchestra in the chapel of the Sorbonne, and Beckett went along to applaud.[164] His cousin Sonny Sinclair and Sonny's wife, Mimi, came up to Paris for these concerts, and they all met up with Con Leventhal and Marion at Josette Hayden's house in Reuil.[165] Earlier, Beckett had received a sad letter from his cousin John, telling him of the sudden death by a heart attack of John's brother, Peter. Could he help in any way financially? he asked immediately. With medical expenses? With a car for the widow? Or in any other way?[166] There were numerous other instances of his generosity: contributions, at Alec Reid's request, to the Interaid charity, for example,[167] as well as a check to help with the medical expenses of an operation for the son of an acquaintance.[168] Few writers have distributed their cash with as much liberality as Beckett.

13

THROUGHOUT THE SUMMER, then in Tangier in September, Beckett reshaped *Happy Days* and *Waiting for Godot* for new productions in London and Berlin. In London, Dame Peggy Ashcroft was to play Winnie at the National Theatre, directed by Peter Hall. And Beckett had promised to come over to help. Rehearsing at the Old Vic in October, he proposed sizable cuts to the text. One major one proved highly unpopular with Peggy Ashcroft and with Peter Hall, who wrote in his diary:

> The primary one [cut] concerned the parasol that burst into flames. This he said had never worked. The parasol is supposed to burn away because of the force of the unremitting sun. Sam has had trouble about that all over the world, with fire authorities and theatre technicians. He now asks that the parasol merely smokes and the material melts away like some kind of plastic under heat. He also, surprisingly, wants to cut an entire page of dialogue relating to the parasol. This disturbed Peggy because it is good and she has learnt it. And it also disturbed me because I think he's only cutting it out of a memory of all the difficulties of the past. I shall bide my time.[169]

In the end, actress and director agreed among themselves that the most drastic cut would never really be made and, according to Dame Peggy, when Beckett returned to Paris, quite a lot of the text was restored.[170] The dramatic bursting into flames of the parasol was preserved too — precisely because it was so dramatic.

During preliminary talks, then actual rehearsals, Beckett guided Dame Peggy and the director through Winnie's intricate physical movements, relating them with minute precision to the text. He was a splendid guide. Peter Hall writes in his diary: "Afternoon of *Happy Days*. Sam continuing to talk us through it, giving meticulous physical and verbal instructions. The text sounds beautiful, balanced, rhythmic, incantatory, in Sam's gentle Anglo-Irish brogue."[171] After listening to Beckett's delivery of the text, Peggy Ashcroft came to rehearsal the next day with the suggestion that the role was crying out to be played in an Anglo-Irish accent. With Hall's and (more reluctantly) Beckett's agreement, she adopted a brogue modeled on that of her good friend the poet laureate, Cecil Day-Lewis, with whom she had often done poetry readings with the Apollo Society and who had died shortly before.

There were plenty of disagreements. Sir Peter Hall offers hints in his diary as to the nature of the difficulties encountered: "Sam looks no different to twenty years ago: still the aesthetic visionary face, the nervous energy. He walked round the room anxiously searching for his glasses while he held them in his hand. He is gentle, arrogant, not wanting to discuss but to assert. Yet never wanting to quarrel. The problem of the pacifist in a hostile world."[172] There was, in fact, a clash of personalities between Beckett and Dame Peggy. Beckett was ready to quit rehearsals well before he actually did, fretting and impatient, tired of working through an intermediary and irritated by Dame Peggy's reluctance to give herself up to an emotion-free reading of the part. From her point of view, she was unwilling to give way on this because she felt she needed to find the "absolute reality" of the character.[173] Like Brenda Bruce, she also found Beckett either unwilling or unable to appreciate the problems of an actress trying to come to terms with memorizing and interpreting his text.[174] Although he admired her, Beckett never felt that Peggy Ashcroft was really suited to this role. And, however finely tuned a performance she gave, he may well have been right.

While in London for rehearsals from October 13 to November 4, as well as meeting numerous friends, Beckett surprised BBC Radio's head of drama, Martin Esslin, by popping in unannounced to Studio B16 at Portland Place, where Patrick Magee was recording all his *Texts for Nothing* under Esslin's direction. Esslin relates how

Beckett sat in the back and said to me: "He's still doing it too emphatically, it should be no more than a murmur." So I stopped it and Pat came in and he told him too: "More of a murmur," until finally the engineer said: "If it becomes any more of a murmur, there's nothing there." In order to explain it to Pat, Sam said: "You see this is a man who is sitting at an open window on the ground floor of a flat. He is looking out into the street and people are passing a few yards away from him but to him it is as if it were ten thousand miles away." So it was a description of schizophrenic withdrawal symptoms.

Esslin then told them about one of the BBC producers who had been out sick for six months. Normally one of the sanest of men, one day he was in the bank cashing a check and the next thing he knew, he was sitting in a corner crying. Later he described the experience as being as if the whole world had disappeared and as if he was entirely divorced from reality. "He had even written a little pamphlet about this when he got cured. . . . And Sam became fascinated and said: 'This is fascinating. Can you give me the title of this pamphlet? This is exactly what I was about.' "[175]

23

Shades

1975–77

1

On December 26, 1974, Beckett flew into Berlin with the stage designer Matias Henrioud, to direct *Warten auf Godot*, which he had been rethinking in his mind and reshaping in his notebooks over the past few months. "If this doesn't purge them," he wrote to a friend, "nothing will."[1] Hans Lietzau, the new Intendant of the Schiller-Theater company, had assembled the actors whom Beckett had specifically asked for: Stefan Wigger, Horst Bollmann, Martin Held, and Klaus Herm. At Beckett's request, he had also commissioned Matias to design the set and the costumes. Although the set was very simple, much thought had gone into its conception. It was acted on a plain, raked stage with a stone and a skeletal tree as its sole distinguishing features. Costumes were governed by the interdependence of the play's characters, a principle that Beckett had discussed previously with Matias in Paris. So Vladimir wore his own striped trousers, as from an old morning suit that has seen better days, with Estragon's too-small black jacket, while Estragon wore his own black trousers with Vladimir's too-large striped jacket. Lucky's checked waistcoat was of the same material as Pozzo's trousers, and his shoes picked up the color of Pozzo's hat, while his trousers were of the same cloth as Pozzo's gray jacket. All the colors were dark or autumnal in tone.

Repetition and contrast were the hallmarks of Beckett's own first production of his best-known play: repetition of word, theme, gesture, and movement. The contrasting heights of Estragon and Vladimir reflected their contrasting natures; Pozzo's hectoring voice and dominant manner were set against Lucky's submissiveness and silence. The production was not naturalistic. Beckett explained: "It is a game, everything is a game. When all four of them are lying on the ground, that cannot be handled naturalistically. That has got to be done artificially, balletically. Otherwise everything becomes an imitation, an imitation of reality. . . . It should become clear and transparent, not dry. It is a game in order to survive."[2]

A trifle stooped at the age of sixty-eight, with his gray, spiky hair standing almost on end some days, Beckett used to turn up to rehearsals in a light polo-neck sweater or, when it was cold, a thicker, rib-knit cream pullover or tweed jacket, with dark flannels and soft, comfortable leather shoes. Sometimes he wore dark glasses to protect his eyes from the fierce spotlights, as he stood on stage demonstrating moves or gestures to the actors. He often worked with a small cheroot in his hand, gesturing expressively with it. Although he spoke fluent German, he was assisted by a talented, conscientious young assistant director, Walter Asmus, whose English was excellent.

Rehearsals were friendly but concentrated affairs. Although everyone got on well, Beckett's perfectionism and the actors' great desire to please him meant that an underlying tension was inevitable. In view of the tremendous success of this production, it is easy to forget what a great effort it represented for Beckett and how strained and depressed he so often was about the way rehearsals were proceeding. "Je suis crevé," he wrote to Jacoba van Velde, "avec cafard à couper au couteau" ("I am exhausted, with a depression you could cut with a knife").[3] Mostly he managed not to communicate his despondency to the actors, of whom he became very fond. But his frustration came out after rehearsals, with friends and in his personal letters. "I'm sick and tired of theatre and of *Godot* in particular," he wrote, for instance, to Alan Schneider. "To have to listen to these words day after day has become torture."[4] After three weeks of rehearsals, he felt so low that he wrote to Jocelyn Herbert: "I have decided I must stop this theatre activity. The way I have to go about it means I can think of nothing else. And the result is quite out of proportion with the efforts I make, so unfitted am I to direct actors."[5] His despondency resulted in part from his tendency to blame himself whenever difficulties arose or progress was slow. But the basic problem was the same as before: he had a clear picture of the play in his head and, however well everyone performed, reality could hardly ever live up to this mental vision. And *Godot*, a big production on the main stage of the Schiller-Theater, made greater demands on him as a director than any of his other plays had done.

Since the other actors were involved in another production, he worked first with Klaus Herm on Lucky's monologue. Herm plied him with questions, showing his keenness by the research he had already done into the names quoted by Lucky. Walter Asmus reported the conversation:

> Herm: "Peterman exists."
> "I haven't thought of that," says Beckett. "And Steinweg, the name means nothing."
> Herm: "Belcher, that one was a navigator. . . ."
> Beckett interrupts him excited and with delight: "No, Belcher, that is the opposite of Fartov, English to fart. And Belcher, to belch." With one blow the mysticism about Beckettian names is destroyed.[6]

Tall, thin Stefan Wigger and short, portly Horst Bollmann took a while to adapt to Beckett's stylized patterns of movement, but each then developed his own idiosyncrasies of movement, gesture, and expression. Only Martin Held appeared to be having difficulty in learning his lines. This was explained when, on January 13, he quit the production, turning up at the theater with a medical certificate to say that he was not well enough to take part. Beckett knew from his 1969 Schiller production with Held that the actor suffered from debilitating attacks of migraine. But on this occasion he would not accept that anything was seriously wrong with Held, except for a lack of motivation. Words like "pretext" occur in his letters[7] and, privately, he exclaimed, "Mon oeil!" ("My eye!"),[8] as he spoke about Held's protestations of illness. Feeling that the man with whom he had worked so successfully six years before had let him down, Beckett never really forgave what he saw as a lack of loyalty.

Fortunately, the only available actor who could possibly play the "heavy," Pozzo, was Karl Raddatz, who turned out to be keen, talented, and very convincing in the role. According to Beckett, he was "very good but slow at learning the lines."[9] But two weeks had been lost and it meant returning to square one for the scenes involving all four actors. In spite of this false start, Beckett could write by the third week in February that he was "feeling less depressed with rehearsals" and claim that it was a blessing in disguise that they had lost Held,[10] even though first one and then another of the quartet had been forced to take a few days off with flu, the infection skipping only himself and the boy.[11] All four actors were eventually to give consummate performances in a breathtakingly beautiful production. Beckett came to admire Wigger and Bollmann very much as actors and judged Klaus Herm to be "a remarkable Lucky. Most moving."[12]

At rehearsal, Beckett followed the patterns of moves that he had worked out meticulously in advance, adjusting them if they did not work in the stage space available. Many of the visual gags were developed on the spot in close collaboration with the actors. Asmus insists that, contrary to what many people seem to believe, Beckett was remarkably open to suggestions from himself and the cast.[13] Nonetheless, it is astonishing how far the actual performance mirrored Beckett's conception of the play as he had set it down in his red notebook — complete with diagrams and arrows — before he ever arrived in Berlin.

Certain features of what he was consciously doing as a director are hardly discernible, however, from his notes. One is the way in which Estragon's and Vladimir's style of acting transformed vaudeville movements into something almost balletic. He also adapted many music-hall gags and rhythms: the "three hats for two heads" routine from the Marx Brothers film *Duck Soup*; a parodied verbal "shoot-out at the O.K. Corral" scene; and the comic repetition of names, "Bozzo . . . Bozzo," "Pozzo . . . Pozzo," each speaker intercutting his line with that of the other. Another element at which his notebook barely hints is how electric the still, silent, waiting tableaux became, as Estragon and Vladimir tried to conjure up other ways of cheating the threatening silence.

Beckett's approach as a director was strongly influenced by his knowledge and love of painting. The most obvious example was the moonlight scene at the end of each act, where the skeletal tree and the two figures of Estragon and Vladimir watching the moon rise are silhouetted against a night sky, emulating the Caspar David Friedrich painting that had originally inspired Beckett.[14] Some of the static tableaux were shaped by paintings in a much less obvious way than these two moonlight scenes. Two in particular recall paintings by Pieter Bruegel the Elder: *The Blind Leading the Blind*, recreated in the second act (with reduced numbers in Beckett's play) by Pozzo following his guide, Lucky, on a shorter lead than in the first act. Lucky is a grotesque who could have existed relatively unremarkably in the world of Bosch, Bruegel, or one of Beckett's favorite painters, Brouwer.[15] When, in the second act, all four figures sprawl horizontally on the ground, the scene, as organized by Beckett, again calls to mind a Bruegel painting: *The Land of Cockaigne*, where three figures are lying, one of them with his legs outstretched like Estragon's, gazing up at "the zenith."[16]

When Pozzo is raised from the ground and slumps between the two tramps, the scene, again as directed by Beckett, reflects his knowledge of paintings of the Crucifixion or the Descent from the Cross. The trio may call to mind Giovanni Bellini's *The Dead Christ with Angels*, or a late-sixteenth-century Giulio Procaccini picture on the same theme, or again the "Prodigal Son"'s studio picture (circa 1550) of *The Dead Christ*, which Beckett had seen many times in the National Gallery of London. These echoes may well not be conscious ones, since Beckett had so totally absorbed this pictorial iconography that his imagination could draw on it quite naturally.

While he was in Berlin, he lived again in Atelier 1 on the third floor of the Akademie der Künste.[17] On his return late in the afternoon, he used to watch the bare branches of the trees outside his window fill up regularly with cawing crows, reminding him of the birds that flocked so noisily into his own trees at Ussy every evening at sunset. He had been lent a pair of binoculars and he trained them on the ducks, magpies, doves, even seagulls that he could identify in or among the trees.[18] He loved being able to see the birds and the animals so sharply again.

He was a creature of habit and, before and after rehearsals, in the bright, cold weather, he would walk, feet splayed out a little comically, for hours on the icy paths of the familiar Bellevue Park and in the Tiergarten. As the end of February approached, he calculated that he must have trudged some two hundred and fifty kilometers since his arrival.[19] Most evenings, wrapped up warmly in a scarf and thick overcoat, he headed briskly down the Bartningallee across Altonaer Strasse and Händelallee to the welcoming, light wood–paneled dining room of the Restaurant Giraffe in Klopstockstrasse, with its emblem of a large giraffe on the wall behind the bar and an old-fashioned clock with a brass surround. He sat at his favorite table, dining either alone or with friends, whom he usually invited to share a whiskey with him first in his room at the Akademie.

He met his German publisher, Siegfried Unseld, who came over from Frankfurt to see him, and had appointments with the former intendant of the Schiller-Theater, Boleslaw Barlog, and its dramaturge, Albert Bessler, of whom he had grown extremely fond.[20] Barlog's successor, Hans Lietzau, returned home from London on crutches, his thigh having been broken by a car on Shaftesbury Avenue as he stepped out of a taxi on the wrong side of the road, as if he were in Germany,[21] and Beckett went round to see him at his home on Trabener Strasse one day.[22] Beckett was always exceptionally sociable in Berlin. He invited Ruby Cohn over to his studio for tea several times, serving her little pieces of bread with cheese but no butter. He had more time available and scarcely ever refused to see people who asked to meet him, even when he hardly knew them.[23]

2

A NEW AND SURPRISING FRIENDSHIP evolved in Berlin. The beginnings of the story went back over twenty years to 1955. In a Los Angeles courtroom, a twenty-one-year-old man, Douglas — known as Rick — Cluchey, was condemned to life imprisonment without the possibility of parole for kidnapping, robbing, and shooting Robert Spencer, a middle-aged hotel executive. Cluchey and his codefendant robbed Spencer of eight hundred dollars and a diamond ring worth a thousand dollars. The crime, which took place in Spencer's own car, was aggravated in the eyes of the law by the fact that the victim was wounded in the course of the robbery. (The wounded man, however, said that if Cluchey had really intended to shoot him, he would have shot him in his head or shoulders and not loosed off the gun into the backseat.) The two robbers also drove the man over a state boundary, which made the offense even more serious. Under California law, only two sentences were available for someone found guilty of such a crime: death in the gas chamber or life imprisonment. The presiding judge, named Lynch, expressed his personal opinion that either sentence was too harsh for a first felony, but Cluchey served twelve years in San Quentin until, on the recommendation of the judge, his sentence was commuted by the governor to one allowing for the possibility of parole.[24]

While he was in San Quentin, several things happened to Cluchey: he began to read widely; he became secretary to the prison chaplain, so that he could have privacy and use of a typewriter; and, most unusually, he started to write, act, and direct. On November 19, 1957, early in his sentence, what turned out to be one of the most important events of his life occurred: the San Francisco Actors Workshop, directed by Herbert Blau, came to San Quentin to play Samuel Beckett's *Waiting for Godot*. Cluchey was in the audience and was bowled over by the play, as many of the convicts were. Cluchey himself then explains how he came to be involved in Beckett's plays:

> I began first to act in Beckett's plays in 1961 while serving a life sentence at San Quentin in California. Although many other of my fellow convicts had a similar interest, as early as 1958, we were all, none the less, required to be patient and wait until the Warden of that day decided to allow us the special sanction of an experimental workshop, where such plays might be performed. So, in 1961, with the advent of our own small theatre, we began to produce a Beckett trilogy, as the first works to emerge from this little workshop. Thus our first effort was, Godot, then, Endgame and lastly, Krapp's Last Tape. In all we gave no less than seven productions of Beckett's circle of

plays during a three year period. All of the plays were acted and directed by convicts for a convict audience.[25]

Cluchey played Vladimir in *Waiting for Godot* in two San Quentin productions and directed *Endgame* in 1962 in the former gallows room, which had been made into a sixty-five-seat theater. The following year he acted Krapp. A member of the San Francisco Actors Workshop, Alan Mandell, who has acted many times with Cluchey since his release and had a distinguished career in the theater and in films, used to drive over to the prison to provide regular acting classes for the inmates. Mandell did a lot to encourage and support Cluchey's work in theater.

Another person who played a key role in Cluchey's career outside prison and was partly responsible for his meeting Beckett was the head of radio drama at the BBC in London, Martin Esslin. Esslin, informed about the Actors Workshop's visit to the prison by Blau, gave an account of this production and its impact on the prisoners in his well-known book *The Theatre of the Absurd*. A few years later, while he was again visiting California, he received a call from the warden of San Quentin. The prisoners, flattered to have figured so prominently in Esslin's book, wanted him to come to talk to them. After his lecture and a performance of John Mortimer's *Dock Brief* — in which the murderer was played by a real murderer — Esslin was shown around the prison by Cluchey, who told him how impressed he had been by *Waiting for Godot* and how it had inspired him to write his own play, *The Cage*. Some years later, Esslin received a call from Cluchey, now out on parole and touring prisons with his play with the support of the United States Information Service, asking if he could help him to obtain a venue in London. This was arranged for them at the Open Space, and while he was in London acting, Cluchey did a BBC broadcast about his story. Esslin gave him Beckett's address and spoke to the Nobel Prize winner about him.[26]

In 1974, Cluchey came over to Europe with the group, the San Quentin Drama Workshop, which he had organized outside prison. He contacted Beckett in February, sending him details of the workshop productions, asking permission for the company to do *Endgame* again without paying royalties, and proposing that any income would be devoted to training former prisoners in theater. In reply, Beckett gave his authorization and, characteristically, waived all fees.[27] Later in the year, Cluchey sent Beckett photographs and a tape of their *Endgame* and told him that on August 24, Teresita, who had been playing Nell in their production, had given birth to a son whom they had named Louis Beckett Cluchey.[28] In December, the San Quentin Drama Workshop arranged to give two performances of *Endgame* at the American Center in Paris, hoping that Beckett would be able to see what they were doing. It was then that Cluchey met Beckett for the first time and learned that he was going to direct *Waiting for Godot* in Berlin a month later. Since Cluchey was invited to direct Jean Genet's one-act prison drama *Deathwatch* at the Forum Theater in Berlin at the same time, Beckett suggested that he might also wish to attend their rehearsals of

Godot and perhaps help him with the production. So Cluchey became his second production assistant.

In this way, Beckett soon became the ex-prisoner's patron, helping him later by directing the workshop group, taking a great interest in his welfare and that of his family, and helping him with gifts of money, sometimes for substantial amounts. Many checks were sent, a few of which Cluchey never cashed. And when Beckett was awarded the Common Wealth Award in Dramatic Arts in 1987, with a money prize of eleven thousand dollars, he arranged through Barney Rosset that this money was passed on to Cluchey.[29] Late in Beckett's life, when Cluchey and his family were having a desperately hard time, he set up a trust fund administered by the University of Maryland to ensure that Cluchey was paid a regular monthly allowance.

This might suggest that Beckett's position was simply that of financial benefactor. It was not. Over the years, he became extremely fond of Rick, worrying about him as if he were his adopted son. He grumbled and became exasperated with him at times, as one would about a wayward child. But Beckett's fondness and sense of responsibility for Cluchey remained until the very end of his life. In making his financial gifts, he knew perfectly well what he was doing.

Berlin cemented their friendship. They made an oddly assorted couple in bars and restaurants: Beckett, tall, almost skeletally thin, with his spectacles pushed back onto his spiky hair, as he listened to Cluchey recounting tales of life in the notorious penitentiary; Cluchey, shorter, stockier, with bushier hair, sideburns, and a small mustache, the tattoos down both his arms visible on his wrists. Beckett was fascinated by what he heard and by Cluchey himself. Prison was a world that he did not know at all but one that made him shudder because of his fear of enclosure and claustration, his hatred of violence and degradation, and his horror at a penal system in which for so many there was no hope of either rehabilitation or release. The man sitting next to him at rehearsals and at dinner or, later, acting Krapp, Hamm, or Pozzo under his direction or supervision, had come through all that and survived. No wonder he wanted to help him to carry on.

3

Rehearsals of *Warten auf Godot* took place from eleven in the morning until three in the afternoon, leaving a large slice of the day for Beckett to reconsider the problems that emerged at rehearsal, answer his mail, meet friends, and write or translate. He corrected a set of proofs sent on by Con Leventhal from Paris and, on January 6, began to write a new piece for a commemorative volume, to be published by Fata Morgana, with a "garland" of texts for Bram van Velde's eightieth birthday in October. The text Beckett produced started its life as a prose piece of seven pages in length. It was finally reduced to a mere half page. The manuscripts show that he worked on it for two days early in January, then returned to revise it, still in Berlin, on March 2.

Between these two dates, other images, along with those from the *Godot* production, were revolving in his head. As he sat alone in the extraordinary quiet of his Akademie studio, in his imagination he heard reverberating the pacing tread of another lost soul walking up and down in a strip of light. We do not know where this auditory image came from. It could have been his own experience of pacing in his leather-soled slippers on the hard tiles at Ussy or, it has been suggested,[30] a distant memory of his mother, unable to sleep, pacing in the bedroom at Cooldrinagh. But it could equally well have come from more recent reality: the actors dragging their feet as they paced out the patterns of their moves on the floor of the wooden stage, or shuffling footsteps heard in a quiet art gallery. (Ruby Cohn remembered Beckett stopping at this time in the Neue Nationalgalerie in Berlin and asking her to listen to the sounds of the footsteps on the hard, polished floor.[31] But we do not know whether this happened before or after the image captured his interest.) He was hypersensitive to sounds. His cousins John and Ann, Aunt Peggy's children, recalled him coming to the family home, Field Place in Greystones, for the wake after their mother's funeral, and sitting with his head down at the kitchen table, their mother's wall clock ticking noisily away behind him. He seemed dreadfully disturbed, then finally blurted out: "Look, I can't go on another minute with this clock. You'll have to stop it ticking!"[32]

If the inspiration for what he sometimes referred to as his "pacing play," *Footfalls*, which he began in the Akademie on March 2, was an auditory one, the movements in it are envisaged from the outset as precisely as those that he had devised for the Schiller-Theater actors. The diagrams in the first manuscript resemble those in his Schiller-Theater notebook. The young woman — Mary in the first version, May in a later one — paces in a steady rhythm, seven steps across the forestage in a strip of light, revolving "it all . . . in [her] poor mind."[33]

The first scene — called later by Beckett the "dying mother" scene — takes the form of a dialogue between May and her mother. The mother is not physically present on stage, but her voice emanates eerily from the darkness. Beckett's deep memories of nursing his mother and his brother surface as May, anxious to relieve her mother's pain, asks a series of compassionate questions, including "Would you like me to inject you again?"[34] A second section, written at the same time in Berlin, differs markedly from the finished version. Here, Mother's voice evokes the strange, loveless life of a maiden "fooled into this world" by a general practitioner named Haddon. (Haddon, who makes another appearance in *Company*, was, according to Beckett, a real-life doctor who practiced in the Stillorgan area during his childhood.)[35] The woman has, the voice tells us, not been out for thirty years, but has paced here relentlessly, in the old home, "back and forth, back and forth, with tread more measured than at sentry-go."[36] This monologue was to be entirely rewritten in October, when Beckett added a third section for May, who, like Mouth in *Not I*, relates (improvises, according to

Beckett) a tale of herself in the third person, as a spectral figure haunting the church where she used to pace at nightfall. May then tells of a parallel couple, a mother who may have glimpsed a trace of the ghost of May at Evensong, and her daughter, originally called Emily, later Amy, a "dreadfully unhappy" girl, who shares May's periods of absence, as well as her obsessive "revolving it all."

When Beckett looked for a family name for the mother in the narration, that of "Mrs. Winter" sprang naturally to mind because he already knew a woman of that name, who was for many years the housekeeper of his cousin Sheila Page. When he met the real Mrs. Winter's daughter, Betty Dimond, in 1978, one of the first things he said was "You know, you and your mother are in one of my plays."[37] Yet the name was probably adopted only because it had the right degree of coldness for his own "winter's tale," just as he changed the "south door" of the church in the manuscript to the "north door" at a late stage for the same reason.

Footfalls grew out of Beckett's long-standing interest in abnormal psychology. May's solitary pacing seems like the externalization of some inner anguish. For the enigmatic "it all" which she constantly revolves in her "poor mind" is linked to her own life in particular, to the point when "it" began, and to life in general. Beckett himself experienced the world consistently enough as an alien place and had met or read of others who expressed their distress in ways every bit as strange as that of May: years ago in the mental hospital in Beckenham, or when he was visiting Lucia Joyce in the hospital at Ivry in 1939. The woman in *Footfalls* was specifically linked by Beckett with a young female patient of Jung, of whom Beckett heard him speak in 1935. The patient had "never really been born," Beckett explained to Charlotte Joeres, who played Mother in the 1976 Schiller-Theater Werkstatt production. May in *Footfalls* is Beckett's own poignant recreation of the girl who had never really been born, isolated and permanently absent, distant, and totally encapsulated within herself.

If we think of May for a moment purely as a clinical case, her symptoms are of a total distancing of herself from the outside world, a radical agoraphobia, and a chronic neurosis which finds its outlet in her obsessional pacing. Beckett had studied both Freud and his disciples with a keenness bred of his own personal neuroses. And only two years before writing *Footfalls*, he had also met the daughter of an old friend, who described to him graphically her own depression, distress, and extreme agoraphobia, telling him how, unable to face the world, she used to pace relentlessly up and down in her apartment. She was being treated at the time with lithium, which Beckett also took from time to time for depression. It is possible, then, that there may be an association between the distressed figure in *Footfalls* and yet another real-life person.[38]

But May's eternal pacing reflects more than a psychologically disturbed personality. It assumes almost mythic status, harking back to Ixion on his wheel, Tantalus tortured by hunger and thirst, or Sisyphus pushing his stone forever uphill. May's own eternal chore, however, is an inner compulsion rather than a preordained punishment. Yet, ordained or self-imposed, the end result is the same: her pacing is inexorable, and her distress is inescapable.

Some doubt has been expressed as to whether Beckett wrote *Footfalls* for his favorite actress, Billie Whitelaw. Ruby Cohn said that when he spoke to her about his idea for a new play in Berlin at the beginning of March, he made no mention of any such association. On the other hand, a few months later, he wrote to Cohn saying that he was "working on pacing play for Billie."[39] He discussed the play with me as early as April 1975, then, in September, wrote me that he was "no forrarder with Billie ideas."[40] To Whitelaw herself, he wrote on November 3: "I have a little play for you that I would like to put in your fair hand."[41] and again, in a letter dated December 29, "There seems to have been some confusion about the play I have written for you."[42] Although, then, it may be true that he had no one in the forefront of his mind when he first put pen to paper in Berlin, he almost immediately envisaged Whitelaw as the one for whom it was intended.

4

BECKETT RETURNED FROM BERLIN on March 9, 1975, exhausted, but elated by the tremendous success of his production of *Warten auf Godot*. After only a day's rest, he had to face another intensive month of directing, this time in French. Months earlier, he had agreed to direct Madeleine Renaud in *Pas moi (Not I)* with "yet another"[43] — his third — production of *La Dernière bande (Krapp's Last Tape)*, this time in the smaller auditorium of the Théâtre d'Orsay. "Nevermore," he wrote, all in one word, when the productions were finished — with Verlaine's poem, Poe's Raven, or Gauguin's painting of the same name in mind.[44] Yet, tired as he was, he gave the work his all, finding a number of fascinating new production ideas for Pierre Chabert in *La Dernière bande* — the shadow of Krapp seen drinking on the wall of his den, and the overhead lamp that started to swing as Chabert, originally by accident, caught it with his head as he stood up, all of which he retained. He did what he could to get Madeleine Renaud to approximate to the frenetic speed and tonelessness of Mouth in *Pas moi*. He never found it easy to imagine Madeleine in this role;[45] when it was done, the best he could say was that Madeleine was "pleased. She has made a great effort," whereas, in the same letter, he wrote, "I like Chabert's *Krapp*."[46] Technical difficulties with the figure of the Auditor meant that, particularly in view of the doubts that he had already expressed about its viability — perhaps it was an error of the creative imagination, he once said to me[47] — Beckett abandoned the image altogether, leaving only the illuminated Mouth to spew out its words at the audience.

Eventually he managed to flee to Ussy for the first time since the previous November: "Larks and cuckoos satisfactory," he wrote, "swallows few. Nightingales in the copse behind the house."[48] All was far from idyllic, however. For he found that his privacy was under even more serious threat from a housing development than from the Paris-to-Strasbourg motorway (to which, in spite of his earlier panic, he was already reconciled even before it was opened: "Too far

from my shack to be a nuisance. Perhaps even company, nights, the lights"[49]).
But dozens of other people with cars living close to his country retreat were a
different matter altogether. An application, he learned, had been lodged to build
twenty houses on a single plot in the field immediately across the road from his
house. He was horrified at the prospect, signed a local petition against it, and
saw the end of his seclusion there as imminent. In any case, in his seventieth
year, he began to envisage the likelihood that he might not always be able to
cope there alone.[50] A couple of weeks later, he breathed an enormous sigh of
relief when he heard that the municipality had turned the housing project
down.[51] The scare had revealed, however, how fragile his peace in the country
might be.

So, back at his oak desk, seated in his wicker chair, he made the most of
what peace he still had, working on *That Time*, advancing it another stage, yet
still feeling that there was room for improvement. In June, he and Suzanne took
themselves off again to Tangier for a six-week break, staying at the by now
familiar Hôtel les Almohades. To avoid the fatigue of driving, this time he
deliberately did not rent a car. Instead, he relaxed, strolling around the streets,
with their sharply defined contrasts of bright sunlight and deep shade, in tan
shorts, an open-necked shirt, and sunglasses, with a bag slung over his right
shoulder, in which he carried his student edition of Dante. Every day, he swam
in the sea and "reread the *Inferno* between bouts of sand and sea."[52]

"The long Tangier sloth"[53]—during which, he joked to Kay Boyle, "the
head yawned itself off and has not been heard of since"[54]—restored his spirits.
So he took yet another look at the *That Time* manuscript, deciding that his
previous misgivings were unwarranted and that, with some slight reorganization
of the three voices the play might conceivably work.[55] After this, in September,
while waiting for the old creative voice to start its low murmuring again, he
translated some "ancient bits and scraps of radio and theatre" for his English
publisher, Faber and Faber. The "scraps" consisted of two aborted fragments of
theater from the late 1950s and early 1960s and two short pieces for radio from
roughly the same period. A month later, inspiration returned and he switched
his attention to his "pacing play," rewriting the mother's monologue and adding
the "Sequel" with its parallel mother-and-daughter relationship.

On October 27, at Ussy, Beckett started "beating myself (feebly) against
another impossible—but not theatre."[56] This was a prose piece beginning with
the sentence "Long observation of the ray." It remained unfinished. The literary
critic Steven Connor wrote perceptively of it: "It forms a link between two
important preoccupations in Beckett's work, the preoccupation with cylinders
and enclosed spaces to be found in *The Lost Ones*, *Ping*, *All Strange Away* and
"Closed Space," and the preoccupation with the dynamics of looking which
runs from *Play* and *Film* through to *Ill Seen Ill Said*."[57]

This unpublished piece is probably one of Beckett's driest and least emotional texts. But it illustrates rather well some of his obsessions at that time: his
attempt to explore all observable features of an imagined world; his concern
with permutations of a number of different elements as in the prose piece

Lessness or, in more emotional form, in his play *That Time*; and his determination to pursue further the relationship between eye and mind.

5

BECKETT WAS TO BE SEVENTY on April 13, 1976. Everyone except himself seemed eager to celebrate this special landmark. Academic tributes were being organized in several countries, and his plays were to be staged almost worldwide.

He was caught up most closely in the events happening in London. The Royal Court Theatre planned an ambitious season of his plays, with a visit from the Schiller-Theater *Warten auf Godot*, as well as several homegrown products. He felt honored and flattered but genuinely dismayed at the thought of all the fuss that this would entail. In prospect, it looked every bit as bad in terms of disturbance as the post–Nobel Prize year had been. *That Time*, with Patrick Magee, was intended to be the star attraction on a triple bill of "shorts" with *Play* and, originally, *Come and Go*. But then, as late as February 1976, Beckett added the completed *Footfalls*, starring Billie Whitelaw, to the program, replacing the last play.

The BBC was eager to share in the celebrations. It had plenty of radio material recorded earlier that it could recycle: *Embers*, *All That Fall*, and the late Jack MacGowran's two separate readings of Beckett's poems. But Martin Esslin wanted something brand-new. So he was thrilled when Beckett agreed to let him record the first-ever production of the second of his newly translated radio plays, *Rough for Radio II*, with Beckett's three friends Harold Pinter, Billie Whitelaw, and Patrick Magee in the speaking parts; another, silent character, Dick—Alfred Péron's Resistance name—wields a bullwhip, creating the sounds of heavy blows on human flesh.

Television presented a bigger problem. The BBC had only a ten-year-old black-and-white recording of *Eh Joe* and a 1972 color film of *Krapp's Last Tape* in their archives. So the television producers, too, were on the lookout for new material. At its London premiere, *Not I* had caused great excitement at the BBC. And, surprisingly, Beckett had consented, as early as February 1973, to a film being made of Billie Whitelaw's performance, after the end of her run. This was not done at the time for a number of reasons.[58] But, then it was agreed that a "test recording" should be made, which would be subject to both Whitelaw's and Beckett's veto: any objection from either of them and it would be promptly killed off. So, on February 13, 1975, the producer, Tristram Powell, had the camera set up in front of Billie Whitelaw's mouth—the Auditor having been discarded—and Mouth appeared on the screen in powerful close-up. The film had to be shot with an extra-large reel of film to avoid breaks in the take. Approved by Billie Whitelaw at a private showing, the film of *Not I* lay waiting for Beckett's final approval.[59] Tristram Powell wrote to Beckett: "There's no doubt that the close-up of the mouth, held uncut for the length of the play, makes an extraordinary impression. Every word comes over with complete clarity and although it is totally different from the theatre experience, it makes its own hallucinatory effect on film." [60] For once, a transfer to another medium had worked brilliantly in its own terms.

After Beckett had given his approval, the problem switched to finding suitable accompanying material. Beckett suggested "Eh Joe would be the best. If they still have the film. Jackie [MacGowran] is very good and Billie wd. [would] be pleased. And about one hour's worth of jolly time would be had by all. We have had enough of *Krapp* for a generation — modeste inquit." [61] But, apart from the issue of black-and-white, the editor of the BBC *Second House* series did not want to use another single-performer piece with *Not I*. So Beckett was asked if Donald McWhinnie could make a selection from his nontelevision writings. He did not favor this idea within the time available. Then he set the pulses racing at the BBC by suggesting that "this programme should be postponed and that I try to write a new piece for TV to be directed by Donald. If this agreeable to BBC I need to know what length is required. If I don't succeed we can then consider in tranquillity the adaptation of existing material." [62] The prospect of a new play being written especially for the BBC proved so attractive that the program including *Not I* was postponed until the autumn of 1976, missing the birthday but landing a much bigger prize.

Beckett would have been unlikely to commit himself to writing a new television play without having some idea of how this might work. Indeed, he had already envisaged his central theme of a man waiting in a room for someone to arrive many years before. Ruby Cohn also remembered visiting him at the Akademie der Künste in Berlin at the beginning of 1975: "I remember once he had a huge sheet of music, and he was working something out, and I said 'What are you working out?' And he said: 'Oh, just playing with an idea.' " [63] The "playing" seems to have evolved into a television play involving musical quotations, which he first called *Tryst*, then renamed *Ghost Trio*. This suggests that some preliminary work was being done nearly a year before the play was actually written.

While staying with Suzanne in Tangiers again in 1976, he wrote to Con Leventhal that he had "got down first corpse of TV piece. All the old ghosts. *Godot* and *Eh Joe* over infinity. Only remains to bring it to life." [64] Tramping along the North African coastline, suffering from a heavy, persistent cold [65] and feeling "strangely weary," he hummed over a few bars from the largo of Beethoven's Fifth Piano Trio, Opus 70, Number 1, visualizing a strange "tryst": a man waiting in the "familiar chamber" for a visit from a woman (departed lover? reluctant muse? or death herself?). Intermittently, the man listens to fragments of a recording of a theme from the largo, until a boy arrives, like the messenger from Mr. Godot, to tell him not with words but with a negative shake of the head that she will not be coming — not that night at least.

As well as harking back to *Godot* and *Eh Joe*, *Ghost Trio* grew naturally out of Beckett's other recent writing. It shared in the ghostliness and mystery of *Footfalls*, but moved even further into the realm of "shades." The male figure drifts silently around the room; the woman's voice we hear is flat and unearthly;

there is no visible source for the light; the boy is enigmatic, more of a messenger from another world than the boy in *Godot*; and the music itself, commonly known as "the Ghost," has specific ghostly associations. On the first typescript of *Tryst*, Beckett wrote in by hand the word "Macbeth." When I asked him directly what he meant by this note, he explained that the record sleeve of his own recording (the version made by Daniel Barenboim) linked this piano trio with Beethoven's music for an opera based on *Macbeth*. Notes on my own recording communicate the same information and help to explain why the largo from this trio should have played such an integral part in his television play:

> The most original movement of the trio turns out to be the Largo assai espressivo which plunges into the spirit world of the night. The fact that sketches for this D minor movement are on the same sheet as those for an opera planned on the basis of Shakespeare's *Macbeth* (including a witches' chorus in D minor) is certainly more than mere chance. The nickname "Ghost Trio" sometimes applied to this work is in no way inappropriate, if only because of this D minor movement. Outlines become blurred, softly flickering expanses of sound, piano tremolos, and descending chromatic scales conjure up an uncanny, oppressively deathly mood.[66]

"The Ghost" retained for Beckett something of *Macbeth*'s doom-laden atmosphere and involvement in the spirit world.

Ghost Trio, like *Footfalls*, has the form of a complex set of variations on appearance and reality. Nothing is quite what it seems. The room is described as if it were simple and unproblematic, like the interior of a house in a child's drawing: wall, door, window, pallet. Yet the images that we see are all nonnaturalistic, a series of rectangular shapes, almost abstract, barely functional. Even the male figure ("Sole sign of life a seated figure")[67] was made to look like an abstract shape in a production that Beckett later directed for Süddeutscher Rundfunk. The female voice appears to be instructing the camera what it should reveal. Yet it moves independently of her commentary as well. The voice also seems to predict the patterns of the man's movements, at times even to be prompting them; yet she is capable of getting them wrong. By comparison with the earthy, substantial figure of Joe, haunted by the voices in his head and suffering physical torment as he struggles to strangle them, the figure in *Ghost Trio*, drifting soundlessly "through space with no visible propulsion,"[68] resembles an ethereal presence, situated somewhere midway between the real world and a world of spirit.

6

SEEING HIS THREE NEW PLAYS onto the stage and the television screen took up most of Beckett's time and sapped his energy in 1976. He agreed to help Donald McWhinnie with the first production of *That Time* and to cast an eye over the revival of *Play* in the Royal Court Theatre season. But, partly because Billie Whitelaw was to play May in *Footfalls* and because he longed to work with her again, he also volunteered to direct the world premiere of his latest play.

He flew into Heathrow on April 16 to be met by Jocelyn Herbert, who was again designing the plays. She drove him to her country home, Andrews Farm, a sixteenth-century farmhouse at Long Sutton near Basingstoke that she had bought years before with George Devine. They relaxed, went for long country walks, drank whiskey, and talked whenever they felt like it, sometimes about the staging of *Footfalls*. For Beckett was totally at ease with this dear friend. Three days later, he moved into his usual rather grand fifth-floor room overlooking the park at the Hyde Park Hotel to start rehearsals. Although there were "more people to see than [he could] manage,"[69] for once he enjoyed his five-week stay in the "Great Wen" immensely, still meeting dozens of friends, including, as he put it, "beaucoup de fantômes de ma promotion" ("a lot of ghosts from my year [at Trinity College]").[70] With one of these, his old Portora Royal School and TCD friend Geoffrey Thompson, he reminisced affectionately about when they used to read Keats together in the fields around the school ("Take into the air my quiet breath," murmured Beckett) and of the day in February 1926 when, as regular visitors to the Abbey Theatre, they witnessed the riots at the Thursday evening performance of Sean O'Casey's controversial play *The Plough and the Stars*.

The Royal Court Theatre had managed to bring over the Schiller-Theater's *Warten auf Godot*. After the first night, Beckett attended a noisy party in the theater basement. He was in a highly convivial mood for such a crowded gathering, enjoying introducing the German actors to his English, French, and Irish friends. He glided easily again from one language into another, positively beaming with bonhomie and delighted at the ecstatic reception that the German company had been given.

In the theater proper, too, he was working with friends: McWhinnie, Jocelyn Herbert, Billie Whitelaw, and Patrick Magee, above all, but supported by Robbie Hendry, the efficient stage manager of *Not I*; Jack Raby, a lighting director whom he respected; and Duncan Scott, a lighting operator for *Play*, whose company he very much enjoyed. He relaxed in the bar, joking and smiling readily. "We had a great atmosphere at the theatre," he wrote, "and the work went well."[71]

Working with Billie Whitelaw was a constant delight for Beckett. His eyes used to light up whenever he talked about her. For her part, she never treated him, or even regarded him, as an old man. With his face like an Aztec eagle, only slightly stooped bearing, and proud, aloof demeanor, counterbalanced by the twinkle in his eye, he still cut an impressive, even handsome figure. Billie Whitelaw tuned in to his plays instinctively, connecting with them musically as well as emotionally. They would sit facing one another at the theater or in her apartment in Camden Square, reciting the text phrase by phrase, Whitelaw capturing Beckett's every inflection. Watching them work together, one noticed that she hardly ever missed the slightest nuance. She would sometimes herself suggest ways of saying things, dropping her voice to a ghostly whisper, for instance, in the "Sequel" of *Footfalls*.[72] She said: "When we rehearsed eyeball to eyeball, he opened up in me whatever there was to open up. . . . I can still hear him saying 'Too much colour, Billie, too much colour.' That was his way of saying 'Don't act.' He wanted the essence of what was in you to come out."[73]

On stage, theirs was an intense collaborative effort, conducted in half whispers or silence. The shapes, movements, sounds mattered to Beckett as much as the words. In order that each step should be heard as May paced, sandpaper was attached to the soles of Whitelaw's soft ballet slippers. Jocelyn Herbert took an old gray dress that she had bought on the Portobello Road, added bits of lace curtain to it, then dyed and shredded the material, tearing rather than cutting it to give it raw edges, adding or taking away until Beckett, Whitelaw, and she were totally satisfied with its ghostly appearance.

Much time was spent on getting May's posture exactly right as she paced up and down; she was a stooping, twisted figure, her hands clutching her upper arms across her body. As the lights fade from section to section, so the figure stoops lower and lower; "she is in the process of disappearing," said Billie Whitelaw. "Everything is frost and night," commented Beckett as she was about to speak the "Sequel"; "make this bit ghostly," he interjected.[74] With Rose Hill, who played the Mother, he used musical terms to convey how he wanted her lines to be spoken. With both actresses every syllable was lent its own importance, every pause given its due weight.

One of the striking features of *Footfalls* and also of *That Time*, which he worked on with Donald McWhinnie, was its pictorial — even, in the case of *Footfalls*, sculptural — quality. Again memories of paintings, drawings, or engravings may have helped him to confer their final form on the stage images. Billie Whitelaw said that she felt

> like a moving, musical, Edvard Munch painting — one felt like all three — and in fact when Beckett was directing *Footfalls*, he was not only using me to play the notes, but I almost felt that he did have the paintbrush out and was painting, and, of course, what he always has in the other pocket is the rubber, because as fast as he draws a line in, he gets out that enormous india-rubber and rubs it all out until it is only faintly there.[75]

The attention that Beckett devoted to every element of visual detail of his plays was as minute and painstaking as one of the seventeenth-century Dutch masters that he so much admired. But if some of his images may have been inspired by paintings of Rembrandt, Caravaggio, Giorgione, Antonello da Messina, or Blake, they still appear strikingly modern and post-Expressionist. This is because of their boldness, their strange, haunting quality, and what one might call their rawness. It is also because Beckett distorts them radically by isolating the head or mouth from the rest of a body (as in *Not I* and *That Time*) or reduces the substantiality of the figure (as in *Footfalls* and *Ghost Trio*). He plays off sight against sound, introduces ambiguity into our perceptions and challenges what we think we are seeing: a real person, for instance, or a ghost? He spent ages adjusting the position of Billie Whitelaw's hands on her upper arms, creating, whether he recognized it or not, a striking parallel with the picture of *The Virgin of the Annunciation* by Antonello da Messina, which had impressed him in the Alte Pinakotek in Munich forty years before. Yet while the face of the Virgin is calm and serene, Beckett's image is transformed into a tortured soul, her hands clawlike, her face full of pain and distress.

7

EXHILARATED BY THE ADRENALINE coursing through his veins at the London rehearsals, Beckett found his return to Paris like an icy bath of reality. Suzanne, now seventy-six years old, was ill, and they were unable to go away to Morocco as they had intended. Minor frustrations and irritations accumulated, as well as some major upsets. The Tophovens' translations of *Footfalls* and *That Time*, needed for a Schiller-Theater production he was to do himself in September, were not, Beckett felt, up to their usual high standard,[76] and he had to hold up their publication with Suhrkamp until they could work on them together. Meanwhile, his own efforts to translate *That Time* into French met with little or no success.

There had been worries during his stay in London that Magee was turning up at the theater the worse for drink; on several occasions, as he played the Listener in *That Time*, he started to sway out of the spotlight. Now Beckett heard with dismay from the Royal Court that Magee had finally been sacked for being drunk onstage in *Endgame* and that the understudy had taken over as Hamm for the last few performances. It upset Beckett to think that his old friend would be out of work, and he welcomed the suggestion that Magee should read his *For to End Yet Again* on the BBC, adding dryly: "in a sober moment if possible."[77]

But these concerns seemed utterly trivial in the light of the news that he received in July and August. He was devastated to learn that Geoffrey Thompson, who had been in such excellent form at dinner only a few weeks before and looking forward to another five years of private practice as a psychoanalyst, had suddenly died of a massive heart attack. "He was very dear to me," Beckett wrote to a mutual friend.[78] Then, in the middle of the long, sweltering summer of 1976, his former agent, the poet and Russian translator George Reavey, a year younger than Beckett, also died in New York.

> *Adieu George,*
> *to whom I owed so much, with whom shared*
> *so much, for whom cared so much*

was his simple, moving valediction.[79] There were too many letters of sympathy to write to grieving widows. The decimation of his generation was not confined to the men either. Peggy Sinclair's sister, Sally, Beckett's cousin, died of a heart attack in August during one of her visits to Dublin. In his reply to the aunt who conveyed the sad news, he went back again to his own father's death: "I think of Gerald, June 1933, in the porch at Cooldrinagh, to the scent of the verbena mother so loved, saying to her, Well, May, he's got it over. What is it all about, in the end, for us all, from the cry go, but get it over?"[80] Life had always seemed in a very real sense a vale of tears to Beckett, and death was a constant theme in his work. But now, although he was saddened by feelings of loss as one after another of his friends or relatives was culled, a growing sense of resignation crept into his later writing: "I can't grieve for the dead," he wrote in a weary mood.[81] He was almost obsessed at this time by Matthias Claudius's poem "Death and the Maiden," in which Death is seen as a comforter, welcoming the maiden into its arms. Even before the most recent summer cull, alone at Ussy, he had played over again the records of Schubert's somber *Winterreise* song cycle on what he called his "electrophone" — "shivering through the grim journey again."[82]

Even so, in old age, humor remained his almost automatic reflex response to adversity. It was a constant lifeline. This did not mean that he took blows lightly. The things he laughed at were very often those that worried him most of all. Duncan Scott recalled his response to old age, for example:

> During dinner . . . he started to complain about old age: how his mental faculties were impaired, his memory faulty, his body ill-coordinated; about how frequently he needed to piss when drinking. At his third exit from the table, he growled: "My bloody old bladder!" For any expression of impatience or anger was followed at once either by a self-deprecatory remark or by a witticism, and his whole face would become suddenly so impishly, sharply, alive and bright, that you would swear afterwards that even his hair stood on end.[83]

"Impish" was a good word for him, even at seventy, when his wit could be just as spontaneous and inventive as when he was thirty. Scott recounted how

> I came across him looking confused on the staircase leading from the upper circle bar to the Theatre Upstairs. "Where are you trying to get to?" He explained that he was looking for the main auditorium. At the Royal Court this is situated below street level. When he was reminded of this fact, [he commented:] "Oh dear. I seem to have lost my sense of altitude!"[84]

But life was determined to test his resilience, as well as his humor. He wrote to his aunt on August 22:

> No sooner back from Brest, [where he and Suzanne had gone for a short break] than I hear my little house at Ussy has been broken into and what little of value was there removed: a television set, electrophone, 2 typewriters, etc. Going out tomorrow for a quick look and clean up. Second burglary there. First time through steel shutters and

window. This time merely kicked the front door down. In the middle of the afternoon.[85]

When he arrived to check on the damage and loss, he found that, although the burglars had made less of a mess than on the previous occasion, they had stolen his "dear old chess set" — a Staunton with traditional figures weighted in their base for stability[86] — which, because it had been handed on from his father, was of great sentimental value. This incident upset him enormously. But he already had his Lufthansa ticket to fly to Berlin on August 29, so there was little time to do anything about replacing his property. The typewriters were indispensable, but the chess set was irreplaceable; and he never did get around to replacing the "electrophone," which Barney Rosset had given him.

8

REHEARSALS OF *FOOTFALLS* AND *THAT TIME* at the Schiller-Theater Werkstatt were much harder going than at the Royal Court. Beckett wrote:

> Here the odd ups and familiar downs. Interesting young actress for *Footfalls* but erratic and given to despond not always without tears. She may be quite good finally. No difficulties with Herm (Lucky) in *That Time* save a curious shortness of breath unnoticeable in recording thanks to excellent sound engineer. Great technical keenness and efficiency all round.[87]

Hildegard Schmahl, who played May, was in her mid-thirties, "rather introverted, sensitive, meditative and serious."[88] She had already played several major roles at the Schiller-Theater and had turned increasingly toward politically motivated theater. Above all, she wanted to understand her role. So she sought explanations. Beckett always seemed embarrassed and uncomfortable explaining, having done this minimally with Billie Whitelaw. But now he revealed more than ever before, recalling the Jung lecture from 1935, and describing what the nub of the play was for him ("If [it] is full of repetitions, then it is because of these life-long stretches of walking. That is the centre of the play, everything else is secondary"[89]), and stressing the importance of the "parallelisms" between the mother and daughter.

There were, as he suggested, some tears and, for a couple of days, Beckett left Frau Schmahl to work alone. While he was away, she went to a psychiatric clinic to talk to a doctor about patients suffering from obsessional neuroses and try to develop some understanding of the part. It must have been hard for Beckett, with Billie Whitelaw's achievement so freshly imprinted on his mind. It was probably even harder for the German actress to follow Whitelaw, for the author did not attempt to hide his enthusiasm and admiration for the earlier performance. Nonetheless, the adjectives that he applied to Hildegard Schmahl changed as rehearsals progressed, "very interesting" evolving into "excellent." *That Time* was much more straightforward and was carried off with few hitches.

Everyone seemed to be in Berlin while Beckett was there. Even in his seventies, he was still shy at meeting new people and nervous beforehand. First meetings with him could be excruciatingly embarrassing. His friend Ruby Cohn introduced him, for example, to the Nobel Prize winner in medicine, Max Delbrück, who had been honored in the same year as Beckett. An ardent admirer of Beckett's work, Delbrück had been dismayed when Beckett did not turn up for the award ceremony in Stockholm. Aware that Delbrück, whom she knew in San Francisco, was in Berlin at this time, she asked Beckett if he would like to meet him.

> Beckett said, "Oh Ruby, you know I can't meet people: I never know what to say." I said, "Well, he's a nonstop talker, he'll do all the talking. And I didn't tell him that I would introduce you, or anything like that, so if you really don't want to do it, don't. But I've never asked you to meet anybody, and I think you might even find him interesting. He's a very brilliant and cultured man." And Beckett said, "Well, on a Sunday, when I'm not rehearsing. But I don't usually shave on a Sunday." Well, he did shave. And Max's wife and Max and I and Sam had a drink at the Giraffe, out of doors, and Max, who is a nonstop talker, was so overwhelmed by meeting Beckett that he was completely tongue-tied. And of course Sam, pathologically shy, wasn't saying anything either. . . . So there they were two Nobel Prize winners, with virtually nothing to say to each other.[90]

The New York avant-garde theatrical group Mabou Mines was also performing its adaptations of *Cascando* and *The Lost Ones* with Lee Breuer's piece *The B-Beaver Animation* in the Nationalgalerie. One day, a note was slipped under Beckett's door in the Akademie der Künste, inviting him to meet members of the group and see what was being done with his pieces.[91] He already knew two members of the company, Fred Neumann and David Warrilow, although not well at this stage. But he had received glowing reports — from Alan Schneider among others — of Lee Breuer's and Thom Cathcart's adaptation of *The Lost Ones*, and about David Warrilow's astonishing performance.

Cathcart had conceived the brilliant idea of seating the live audience in a cylindrical rubber space that, like a vertical amphitheater, mirrored the cylinder of the text. The spectators were asked to remove their shoes before they entered this dark foam-rubber environment. Some eighty lighting cues from start to finish, including nine blackouts, echoed the environmental fluctuations in the text. Philip Glass had composed fifty minutes of music to convey the sound referred to in Beckett's text as a "faint stridulence as of insects." Another inspired idea was to miniaturize the cylindrical world, representing it as a cross section of a cylinder that was about eighteen inches high, and to transform the 205 people who live inside it into so many tiny German dolls about half an inch high. So Warrilow was able not only to narrate the text but also to move the figures, who are set down in a small circle of light onto tiny ladders or into "niches or alcoves" in the cylinder wall.

David Warrilow described Beckett's visit to the company:

> He asked to see the set of *The Lost Ones*, to examine the figures, the ladders and so on, he asked a lot of questions, including the big one, "did you cut the text?", which I was dreading. I was just dreading that one, but it was fine; I said yes we had and he just nodded. He said to me privately, "I'm sorry but I won't be able to see a performance because I have a phobia of public situations.[92]

Beckett was also shown the set of *Cascando*, which was playing at the time. Faced by this, he is quoted as saying: "My, you have adapted it, haven't you?"[93] Although privately he described this particular adaptation as "by all accounts regrettable,"[94] he stayed characteristically polite to the cast and became good friends with several of them, especially Neumann and Warrilow.

The Lost Ones was an altogether different kettle of fish. Although he was irritated at first by the stage adaptation and by the fact that he had never authorized it, except as a reading-demonstration, or even been consulted on what was being done, he came to accept that Lee Breuer's adaptation worked outstandingly well in its own terms. After learning about it, he told his agents that they should go on refusing all adaptations as a matter of course without even consulting him, but stressed that Mabou Mines productions were exceptions to the rule.[95] It may be, however, that it was the success of this version (together with his friendship for certain directors or actors and a growing mellowness — or weariness, depending upon how one sees it) that prompted him over the last twelve years of his life to allow various prose texts to be adapted, mostly by people whose work he already knew. When he agreed to a proposal (sometimes, it should be said, against his better judgment), he often chose to have an input into the adaptation and sometimes became genuinely interested in solving the problems posed by a particular adaptation for the stage.

Around noon on September 20, Morton Feldman, the American composer and professor of music at the State University of New York at Buffalo, came to meet Beckett during a rehearsal in the small Werkstatt theater. Feldman, who wore thick horn-rimmed glasses because his eyesight was so poor, described their meeting: "I was led from daylight into a dark theater, on stage, where I was presented to an invisible Beckett. He shook hands with my thumb and I fell softly down a huge black curtain to the ground. The boy [who had escorted him] giggled. There were murmurs. I was led down steps and to a seat in the front aisles."[96] After this unpropitious start, Feldman invited Beckett to lunch at a nearby restaurant, where Beckett only drank a beer.

> He [Beckett] was very embarrassed — he said to me, after a while: "Mr. Feldman, I don't like opera." I said to him, "I don't blame you!" Then he said to me "I don't like my words being set to music," and I said, "I'm in complete agreement. In fact it's very seldom that I've used

words. I've written a lot of pieces with voice, and they're wordless." Then he looked at me again and said, "But what do you want?" And I said "I have no idea!" He also asked me why I didn't use existing material. . . . I said that I had read them all, that they were pregnable, they didn't need music. I said that I was looking for the quintessence, something that just hovered.[97]

Feldman then showed Beckett the score of some music that he had written on some lines from Beckett's script for *Film*. Showing keen interest in the score, Beckett said that there was only one theme in his life. Then he spelled out this theme.

"May I write it down?" [asked Feldman]. (Beckett himself takes Feldman's music paper and writes down the theme. . . . It reads "To and fro in shadow, from outer shadow to inner shadow. To and fro, between unattainable self and unattainable non-self.") . . ."It would need a bit of work, wouldn't it? Well, if I get any further ideas on it, I'll send them on to you."[98]

At the end of the month, still in Berlin, Beckett mailed to Morton Feldman in Buffalo a card with a note: "Dear Morton Feldman. Verso the piece I promised. It was good meeting you. Best. Samuel Beckett."[99] On the back of the card was the handwritten text (Beckett never called it a poem) entitled "Neither," beginning "to and fro in shadow / from inner to outer shadow / from impenetrable self to impenetrable unself / by way of neither." The text compares the self and the unself to "two lit refuges whose doors once neared gently close" and owes one striking image to the play on which he was working so intently: "unheard footfalls only sound."

When he wrote this text for Feldman, Beckett did not know the composer's work at all. But, by a strange coincidence, only a few days after posting "Neither," and in London by this time, he was listening to Patrick Magee reading his own *For to End Yet Again* on BBC Radio 3 when he noticed that, in the second part of the "Musica Nova" concert that followed the reading, there was an orchestral piece by Morton Feldman. He listened to it and found he liked it very much.[100]

9

FROM BERLIN, Beckett flew directly to London on October 2 without returning home. The rehearsal and shooting dates for *Ghost Trio* at the Ealing film studios had been booked months ahead. Ronald Pickup, who had been in *Play* at the Royal Court Theatre, acted the figure in the room and the voice was that of Billie Whitelaw. Donald McWhinnie directed. Beckett stood alone at times on the studio floor, in his familiar turtleneck sweater, arms folded, looking at the gray set through tinted glasses and watching Pickup's movements as he rehearsed. At times he almost lost patience with the delays caused by the statutory tea breaks and the noisy chat of technicians. It was, he whispered, not like that at all in Germany; there, you felt that everyone was personally involved.[101]

Intensely practical as always, he felt the need, nonetheless, to bring up one fascinating theoretical point to illustrate what he said about the relations between economy and the grace and harmony that he wanted to see in the movements of the protagonist of *Ghost Trio*. Beckett referred first Ronald Pickup, then myself, to Heinrich Kleist's essay "Über das Marionettentheater" ("On the Marionette Theater"). For the speaker in Kleist's essay, puppets possess a mobility, symmetry, harmony, and grace greater than any human dancer (or a fortiori any actor) can possibly achieve, because they lack the self-consciousness that puts human beings permanently off balance.

At lunchtime, over a glass of Guinness in a public house close to the film studio, Beckett recounted Kleist's other remarkable tale of the fencing bear on the same theme. This concerns an expert fencer who, having beaten a young man, is taken on to fight a bear:

> "Thrust, thrust," Baron G said, "and try to strike him." After I had recovered from my astonishment, I lunged at him with the rapier, and the bear, making a short movement with his paw, parried the pass. I tried to deceive him by feints, the bear did not move. I attacked him afresh with skill momentarily inspired. I would have surely struck a man's breast. The bear made only a short movement with his paw and parried the pass. I was now almost in the same situation as the young Baron G [his former opponent]. The bear's seriousness intervened to upset my composure. I made alternate passes and feints. I dripped with sweat. In vain; the bear not only parried all my passes like the first fighter of the world, he did not accept my feints; no fighter on earth could have done that. Eye to eye, as if he could read my mind, he stood raising his paw ready for battle, and when my passes were not really meant he did not move.[102]

The bear represents, symbolically, the creature without awareness of self, who, as a result, is able to respond naturally and unselfconsciously to the thrusts of the fencer and not be deceived by what are only false passes. Further, in parrying the actual thrusts, the bear does what he has to do with the strictest economy and the maximum of grace.

Beckett applied Kleist's two examples to the figure in *Ghost Trio* as he moves to the window or the door, or looks up from the pallet to the mirror. From the two different kinds of movement in the play, one sustained, economical, and flowing, the other abrupt and jerky as F "thinks he hears her," it is as if Beckett's figure is poised midway between two worlds. For his "man in a room" is still, in spite of everything, a creature bound to a world of matter, not quite the still-life figure that at moments he appears to be. Nor is he totally free of self-consciousness, as his look in the mirror indicates, or wholly indifferent to the world of the nonself, as his responses to stimuli from outside or from within his own mind suggest. We are brought then to question the substantiality of the figure present, in miniature anyway, on our television screen. In the end, this disarmingly simple little play turns out to be a complex work reflecting Beckett's interest in the consciousness of self, his intense concern with visual shape (it is, wrote the *Guardian*'s Michael Billington, "a mesmeric piece of painting for TV"),[103] and his challenging use of a medium that, in spite of *Eh Joe*, was still relatively new to him.

While he was in London, with McWhinnie and the three actors involved, he viewed the film shot by the BBC of the Royal Court Theatre's *Play*. He was so unhappy with the poor quality of the film that, while staying in "a hotel slap on the sea at Le Touquet," where there was, he said, "Great beach . . . — and forest,"[104] he began to write a replacement television piece to accompany *Not I* and *Ghost Trio*.[105]

The idea did not come to him easily. Soon after his departure from London, he wrote to Jocelyn Herbert: "Thoughts [were] jostling in my head for something to replace *Play*. Rejected one after another as too complicated for Ealing [that is, for the film studios there]. Hope to find something simple in the end."[106] He had reread some of W. B. Yeats's poems, including "The Tower," before leaving Paris (perhaps taking his copy with him on the week's holiday) and built part of his new play around the closing lines of this poem. The play contained some of the same elements as *Ghost Trio*: a solitary figure returning to his "little sanctum"; a voice commenting on the action — this time the protagonist's own voice, in the first person singular, describing the actions of the man we see on screen; and the situation of someone longing for a woman (or perhaps a ghost) to appear to him. The play, *. . . but the clouds . . .*, as he eventually entitled it after provisionally calling it "Poetry only love," has indeed something of the "same mood as G.T. [*Ghost Trio*]."[107] It also evidences Beckett's characteristic preoccupation with light and dark oppositions and with permutations and patterns of movement. Although the man tells how, like a character from a John Millington Synge play, he used to walk (or "stravague," to use a word Beckett liked) the roads from break of day, what matters, above all, is that "she" should appear to him at night.

The fleeting image of the woman's face — Billie Whitelaw's in the BBC film, and probably so already in Beckett's head, for he asked Jocelyn Herbert to obtain copies of John Haynes's photographs of the two of them together at rehearsal — is associated with W. B. Yeats's words "But the clouds of the sky / When the horizon fades / Or a bird's sleepy cry / Among the deepening shades." This suggests that the new play may have grown out of Beckett's thinking about those gone "among the deepening shades," combined with an attempt to materialize a beautiful face that seemed to him to incarnate spirit. It is an interesting coincidence at the very least that, only four days before writing *. . . but the clouds . . .*, his cousin John sent him a family group photograph — the one reproduced earlier in this book — with the faces of all the Beckett forebears, long since dead. "Thanks for your letter with moving photograph," Beckett wrote. "How wan they look, how resigned, apart from progenitor."[108]

The face of Cissie, young, fresh, and rather lovely, must have struck him as particularly moving, as he remembered pushing her, crippled with arthritis, in her wheelchair. Back at 38 boulevard Saint-Jacques, he went on reworking the short television play, although for several weeks he felt groggy from an attack of influenza. Suzanne was even iller with the same virus, and her health was a matter of concern to him, as it so often was at this time.

The new play was dispatched to the BBC on November 18,[109] and Beckett arranged to come over again to London before Christmas to record it at Ealing with the same team that had worked on *Ghost Trio:* Tristram Powell producing, Donald McWhinnie directing, and Ronald Pickup and Billie Whitelaw acting. Once again he stood on the studio floor, looking through the camera lens. But McWhinnie, Pickup, and Beckett worked out the moves on the spot far more than they had ever done in *Ghost Trio.* "It was more like making a real film," commented Pickup.[110] Beckett agreed, exceptionally, that he would allow a camera to film a few moments of him at work in the studio, provided that nothing of what he was saying was recorded. (Once processed, the film turned out to be blurred and quite unusable. It was a few days before Christmas; perhaps the technicians had been imbibing heavily before they processed it, or perhaps someone had decided that a film of Beckett would never be made.) On Christmas Eve, he flew back to Paris, satisfied to know that, with his most recent television play now filmed, he had salvaged the program, to which he gave the collective title *Shades.*

24

Politics and *Company*
1977–79

1

WHEN BECKETT'S TWO NEW TELEVISION PLAYS were eventually shown, with the filmed version of *Not I* on BBC2 in April 1977, they were mostly greeted with puzzled acclaim. According to an enthusiastic Michael Billington, they made one "wonder why naturalism is still television drama's dominant mode."[1] Ironically, it was Dennis Potter, the playwright who did most in recent years to challenge naturalism on British television, who attacked the plays in his *Sunday Times* review with a series of sour questions: "Would Solzhenitsyn have understood? Would the Jews on the way to the gas chamber? Question: Is this the art which is the response to the despair and pity of our age, or is it made of the kind of futility which helped such desecrations of the spirit, such filth of ideologies come into being?"[2] Beckett read the English Sunday newspapers regularly and, as someone who had joined the battle against fascism as a Resistance agent precisely because of what the Nazis were doing to the Jews, he must have been deeply wounded by such a poisoned barb.

In fact, two other major cases of a radical, systematic abuse of human rights preoccupied him very much at this period of his life. Sickened by the policy of apartheid in South Africa, he had long refused to allow his plays to be performed in any theater there that insisted on racial segregation. "Please refuse permission for production of *Endgame* by this Pretoria theatre and all other future proposals from S. Africa to present my work before segregated audiences," he wrote firmly in 1972, restating unequivocally an attitude that his dramatic agent had already been honoring at his request for many years.[3] Because of South African law, this meant that his drama was excluded from the majority of theaters, with the exception of a few in universities where a nonracial educational policy was practiced. All attempts to persuade him or his agents to make an exception to this rule were consistently refused. Even Patrick Magee's tour in 1975 with a program of readings from Beckett's work was forced to exclude South Africa; Beckett's London agent wrote: "Mr Beckett has never allowed his plays to be performed in South Africa and this programme of excerpts must be subject to the same embargo."[4] Friendship in this case had to take second place to principle.

But, in 1976, Beckett was led to reassess, although not alter his position.

While he was in London in April to May of that year for rehearsals at the Royal Court Theatre, his agent there, Warren Brown, received a letter from a young man named Mannie Manim, the artistic director of a Johannesburg professional theater group called the Company, asking if they could perform *Waiting for Godot* in their first season.[5] Manim had come to see Brown the previous winter to explain that they were creating a new theater complex in what used to be the Indian Fruit Market in Johannesburg—hence the complex's name, the Market Theatre.[6]

The proposal had much to recommend it to Beckett: Mannie Manim was, according to Brown, of mixed race himself; the director chosen to direct the play was a black South African, Benjy Francis, who had studied at the Drama Centre in London and directed Athol Fugard's *Boesman and Lena*; the cast of *Waiting for Godot* was intended to be multiracial (in the end it turned out to be entirely black); and, most crucially, there was a guarantee that the company would perform only in front of nonsegregated audiences. Brown wrote to Beckett that "to deny them the opportunity to do *Godot* is almost playing into the hands of the apartheid movement."[7] In view of this and after discussing the matter face to face with his agent, Beckett decided to permit the performance. The license, which was issued on May 18, 1976, contained a specific clause "requiring that tickets of admission [be] sold on a multi-racial, non-discriminatory basis."[8]

It was a summer of deep political unrest in South Africa, which Beckett followed in the newspapers and on French television. Demonstrations, riots, and violence were followed by ever harsher police crackdowns. The director and actors in *Waiting for Godot*, who were unable to live in Johannesburg itself because of the Group Areas Act, often had to travel to the theater in difficult circumstances and at considerable personal risk to themselves and their families. The audience, white or black, were even less prepared to leave their homes in such troubled, dangerous times. So the season was a near financial disaster for the company, even though the play itself was well received by local critics. Manim reported that although blacks still made up only a small part of the audience, their numbers were growing gradually and that the quiet nonracial policy of Manim's theater had so far not been challenged by the authorities.[9]

At the beginning of August 1976, another theater group, this one in Cape Town called the Space, run by Brian Astbury, was granted a license by Curtis Brown to present *Endgame*. This agreement, too, contained a nondiscrimination clause.[10] The Space was naturally functioning without official permission, which created problems in paying royalties through official banking channels,[11] but which represented a substantial plus as far as Beckett was concerned. After these two productions, Beckett's agents were vigilant, making sure that any South African company that wanted to do Beckett's plays should be a professional one "so that specific, contractual undertakings could be written into the licence regarding fully integrated audiences."[12] If either the agents or Beckett was in any doubt, the license was simply refused.

While Beckett was in London later in October for the recording of *Ghost Trio*, two outstanding black actors, John Kani and Winston Ntshona, were arrested after performing Athol Fugard's *Sizwe Bansi Is Dead* in Butterworth town hall in the Transkei. (The Transkei was soon to acquire debatable independence as, the antiapartheid movement asserted, a dumping ground for all South Africa's dispossessed nonwhites.) Fugard's play about the South African pass laws insulted the Transkei homeland and was "inflammatory, vulgar and abusive," said the minister of justice.[13] There was a demonstration outside the South African embassy in London; photographs of actors (including Albert Finney, Robert Morley, Sheila Hancock, and Kenneth Williams) with antiapartheid banners were splashed across the London newspapers, and a letter to *The Times* signed by British actors condemned the imprisonment, saying that it was appalling that the actors, both of whom were Equity members, should be "arraigned for expressing dramatic truths."[14] British Equity sent a telegram to John Vorster, the South African prime minister, asking him to order the actors' immediate release.

It comes as no surprise, then, to find that, later on, Beckett allowed one of the most famous mixed-race productions of *Godot* to be performed at the Baxter Theatre in the University of Cape Town, where it was directed by Donald Howarth and featured the same two actors, John Kani and Winston Ntshona, playing Didi and Gogo. Pozzo, dressed in checked shirt and gumboots reminiscent of an Afrikaaner landlord, and Lucky ("a shanty town piece of white trash")[15] were played by two white actors, Bill Flynn and Peter Piccolo. The production traveled to the Long Wharf Theater in New Haven, Connecticut, then played at the Old Vic in London, to mostly sympathetic, if mixed reviews. The Baxter Theatre version has often been portrayed as if it were an explicitly political production; in fact, this aspect received relatively little stress. What such a reaction showed, however, was that, although the play can in no way be taken as political allegory, there are elements that are relevant to any local situation in which one man is being exploited or oppressed by another.

A second instance of political repression affected Beckett more closely. While he was in Berlin in September for the Schiller-Theater productions of *That Time* and *Footfalls*, he received a letter from a young Polish writer and translator, Antoni Libera. Libera confined himself at first to queries concerning the texts of the two plays for his translations into Polish. He then wrote to ask if he might be officially invited to see Beckett's Schiller-Theater productions, since only with such an invitation did he stand any chance at all of obtaining his passport and the right to travel from Warsaw to West Berlin. At Beckett's request, the Schiller-Theater forwarded a formal invitation. And Beckett also sent Libera a personal letter of invitation, having assured the Polish translator in an earlier note that he would be happy to contribute to the expenses of his visit to Berlin.[16] He contacted the Akademie der Künste to arrange for a room to be given to Libera which Beckett said he would pay for. Then he waited for news of Libera's visit.

On December 18, Libera wrote to Beckett that, sadly, he had been unable to see the play because his passport had been withheld. He then described in graphic detail the political situation that resulted in such a curtailment of individual freedom. This letter, sent with a book of poems, the *Sonnets de Crimée* by Adam Mickiewicz, never arrived in Paris. It had been confiscated by the postal censor in Warsaw. Instead, some months later, learning of its nonarrival, Libera arranged for the same letter to be posted again, this time in France, by a friend.[17]

When Beckett eventually read this remarkable account of what was happening in Poland, it touched him very deeply. Libera started with his own case, explaining that he personally was not well thought of for a variety of reasons: he had displayed too much sympathy for Polish writers and musicians abroad; he was a friend of and secretary to the writer Jerzy Andrzejewski (a leading dissident, author of *Ashes and Diamonds, The Inquisitors,* and *The Gates of Paradise,* and a close friend of Czesław Miłosz); and he had been involved in supporting those who had rallied to the defense of the workers. Recent attacks on those demonstrating against rises in food prices, Libera went on, had been harsh. There had been a number of deaths, and hundreds of ordinary people had been arrested, beaten up, or tortured. A Committee for the Defense of Workers had been set up, part of whose function was to offer money to families who had been left without means as a result of the arrest of the breadwinner; to give legal advice to those accused by the police; and to try to persuade the authorities to pursue police officers who were guilty of criminal acts. Instead, members of the committee were themselves being cruelly victimized: they were prevented from traveling; were unable to publish; were subject to harassment, search, and arrest without trial. A distinguished Polish actress, Halina Mikołajska, the first Polish Winnie in *Happy Days* and a member of the Committee for the Defense of Workers, was being prevented from appearing on the stage or in films; her car had been vandalized and her apartment broken into by an anonymous group that terrorized her family. A Committee of Solidarity with Polish Workers had been set up in Paris, wrote Libera; Beckett's friend Maurice Nadeau was a member.[18]

Beckett read this personal account with a shudder of horror and recognition. It reminded him only too vividly of the repressive measures adopted by the Nazis in Germany in the mid-1930s against those who were not of pure "Aryan" stock or were hostile to the regime. But the personal examples of actors unable to find employment also recalled events of only a decade ago, when his French friends had been ostracized for signing a manifesto against torture in Algeria. On such matters as the abuse of human rights, censorship, and attacks on individuals by a repressive political regime, his instinctive reponse was to ask what he could do to help. Mostly this involved making contributions (sometimes quite large ones) to fund-raising organizations and in giving regular support to Amnesty International.[19]

In this case, however, he went even further. He instructed his literary and dramatic agents that all the Polish royalties on his work should be paid to Antoni Libera to be distributed as he thought fit. These were used, at first, to support underground publishing houses; money was also given to writers who were in financial difficulty or had been imprisoned by the regime. When times became even more difficult in Poland, Beckett signed an appeal — a very rare event for him — against the proclamation of martial law at the end of 1981. On a more personal level, he ordered food parcels to be sent to Libera on three separate occasions.

Throughout the period from 1976 until his death thirteen years later, Beckett took a keen interest in all that was happening in Eastern Europe. He would do almost anything for those who had managed to get out of these countries or who had stayed behind only to be persecuted by the regime for their ideas or their writings. It did not matter to him whether the regime perpetrating the oppression was left-wing (like the Communists in Eastern Europe) or right-wing (like the Fascists in Spain or the National Party in South Africa). It was enough that they were behaving barbarously and unjustly.

Where individuals were concerned, Beckett seems to have responded instinctively to their need, often without looking very deeply into the rights or wrongs of their case. An example of this came to my attention in an unusual way one day in 1977. In my own mail one morning, there was a copy of a book called *Loi de Dieu* by Jack Thieuloy. It was inscribed to me, in the words of the author, "at the suggestion of Samuel Beckett." In a footnote to the prologue, there was an intriguing note: "Merci, *old Sam the great* (et quelques autres, Michel Leiris, Claude Mauriac, Daniel Guérin, Pierre-Jean Remy) pour votre chèque de soutien à mes procès. . . ." ("Thanks, old Sam the great . . . for your check in support of my trial expenses. . . .").[20] I wrote to Beckett to ask him what this was about. He replied "Jack Thieuloy. He was in the Santé prison for some months for some little arson misdemeanour and was awarded the Anti-Goncourt while there. Very gifted I think but the kind of writing I haven't the courage for."[21]

What had happened, according to Thieuloy,[22] was that, as a member of a left-wing anarchist group, he was accused of involvement in placing a Molotov cocktail outside the apartment of Françoise Mallet-Joris, the secretary of the Goncourt committee. He was arrested and then released, but later rearrested for being implicated in another fire-bombing by a group of anarchists. Despite his firm denials of guilt in this later attack, he was condemned to four months in the Santé prison. Beckett, who had met Thieuloy earlier, gave money to a Comité de Soutien (a Committee of Support) to assist him with his legal costs. It was not that Beckett condoned these incendiary attacks. He merely wanted to ensure that someone who might be unjustly accused and condemned should have the chance to be properly defended and that a system of justice often unfairly weighted against the poor, the underprivileged, or the politically undesirable should not have everything its own way.

Beckett's attitudes were basically left-wing and antiestablishment. He was also totally opposed to capital punishment; his horror at executions dates back to the first story, "Dante and the Lobster," in *More Pricks Than Kicks*. His heart went out to all prisoners, whose treatment he considered as equivalent to the cruel caging of animals. He hated to hear the wailing and clamoring of the prisoners in the cells of the nearby Santé prison. It is said that he used to communicate by mirror messages sent in Morse code with at least one prisoner in the Santé, who was housed in a cell clearly visible from Beckett's study window. On one occasion, as the door to his apartment was standing ajar, Elmar Tophoven walked in to find Beckett standing at the open window, clearly signaling to someone. Beckett promptly raised and lowered his arms to indicate to the prisoner across the way that the exchange would have to be interrupted because someone had just called to see him. He explained to Tophoven: "They have so little to entertain them, you know." [23]

His responses were motivated by spontaneous feelings of sympathy for the underdog: the failure, the invalid, the prisoner (political or otherwise), the beggar, the tramp, even the rogue. The actor-writer Jack Emery remembered meeting him in the Coupole in April 1975 when an invalid ex-soldier hobbled in selling sentimental postcards. Beckett bought all the cards the man was carrying, although they were not of a kind that he would ever have dreamed of sending to anyone.[24] He developed a reputation as a soft touch. This he undoubtedly was. He had an almost total inability to filter out pain and distress, no matter who was experiencing it, combined with an extremely rare capacity for listening and empathizing. As a result, people poured out their troubles to him as if he were a father confessor. He responded in the only way possible for him: by offering sympathy and, where appropriate, help. His empathy was a remarkable gift. But it must often have seemed like a burden as well, as troubles were showered upon him.

It also made him vulnerable and open to exploitation. Many of his friends felt protective of him, seeing him as an innocent at home and abroad, who was unaware that he was being exploited or even, very occasionally, well and truly conned. There is one sense in which Beckett was indeed an innocent: he always tended to believe the best of someone, unless and until events proved the contrary. And because of his own remarkable integrity, few people let him down. When one or two did — by selling collections of his private letters, books, manuscripts, or paintings that he had given them, or by changing what had been agreed between them in order to benefit themselves — he was very upset for a time but soon found plausible excuses for their behavior: they had fallen on bad times and needed the money; the pressures they were under were to blame, not themselves; there were doubtless good reasons unknown to him; or it was a matter of little importance anyway. Mostly he forgave his friends for their human weaknesses.

His attitude was complicated by the fact that he also rather liked rogues. One of the reasons for this was that he found their company a lot more fun than that of dour, respectable citizens, who quickly bored the pants off him. He had after all run away from the milieu of respectable, middle-class Protestant Foxrock, first to the less genteel, more relaxed atmosphere of the Dublin bars, then to Paris where the cult of *laissez-aller* prevailed in artistic milieus at least, where one's sexual preferences and conduct were a matter of more or less total indifference and where nobody worried if one drank too heavily. So a number of likable rogues figured with the needy and the indigent among his acquaintances. But Beckett was usually well aware of when he was being "done," as opposed to being "done in the eye," to borrow a phrase from his own German diaries.[25] And he derived a certain amusement from it.

But although long-suffering, he was capable of outrage, particularly against those who took liberties with his work. What annoyed him most of all was when he was presented with a fait accompli, someone having done something without asking his permission, and then, belatedly, asking for his approval. And when his patience snapped and he decided that action had to be taken, he could be very forthright and damning.

2

THE DAYS OF OUR YEARS are threescore years and ten; and if by reason of strength they be fourscore years, yet is their strength labour and sorrow; for it is soon cut off, and we fly away.[26]

Following his seventieth birthday, Beckett decided to take the words of the Psalmist seriously. So he did everything he could, while continuing to live in a busy city, to create a seclusion in which he could write for the short time that he thought remained. He had always believed that, in old age, things would be simplified and one would be free to concentrate on essentials; he associated old age with the idea of light, of illumination. And he often spoke of how writers like Goethe and Yeats had produced their best work when they were old men.

His efforts to achieve a kind of monastic calm in Paris were, of course, doomed to failure. He still could not bring himself to say no to old friends who were keen to see him. He was sent packages by registered mail, which necessitated his going to the post office and queuing to extricate material that he mostly did not want. Business matters could not always be resolved by his literary or dramatic agents without consulting him. And his work created a wash that threatened to become a tidal wave swamping all future writing.

He still accepted the odd invitation to direct a television or stage play that he had not yet directed so that at least one production would exist very much as he envisioned it. But he refused virtually all other invitations. It was not simply that he had a phobia about appearing in public situations or could not bear intrusions into his private life. Privacy and peace had become necessities for his writing. "Damned to fame," he wrote in a personal notebook at this time, quoting Pope's The Dunciad,[27] as he took steps to avoid what he considered the worst of fame's trappings.

Since he set so much store by his work, the frustration was very great when the writing led nowhere. And at times he fumed against people and circumstances, when the problem lay in an absence of inspiration. Early in 1977, he wrote: "Attempts to get going on new work [are] fruitless"[28] and "writing [is] in the doldrums";[29] "With me endless interruptions, endless mail, no possibility of work. Submerged. See no way out."[30] The cry was a familiar one. But the sense that time was rapidly running out made it more desperate than ever before. In Paris and Ussy, he still suffered from his old nocturnal panics — only in Tangier, for some reason, did the attacks abate[31] — and he was often profoundly depressed. When this depression was at its most acute, he dosed himself with lithium, particularly when he was staying alone in Ussy. The "friendly dark," so often a friend to his work, also menaced his mental equilibrium.

His mail regularly contained sad news. In recent years he had lost touch to some extent with his old friend the painter Geer van Velde, but he was very upset when he learned that Geer had died in March 1977.[32] A month later, Dame Peggy Ashcroft wrote that Mary Hutchinson, whom he had seen regularly in Paris or London over the past fifteen years, had died in the hospital[33] — ironically, while watching *Ghost Trio* on television. "Heartening thought," he quipped bitterly.[34]

But even more depressing news lay in store. The health of his oldest and dearest friend, A. J. Leventhal, began to deteriorate disquietingly and he was diagnosed as suffering from cancer of the liver. At the end of 1978, Leventhal went over to London for surgery; while he was hospitalized or recuperating prior to traveling back, Beckett wrote or telephoned regularly for news. Then the summer of 1979 became one of the saddest for many years, as Con's condition declined swiftly. In the end, the only consolation was that he did not suffer severe pain. He died on October 3. Beckett wrote to Jocelyn Herbert: "Sad days here. My old friend Con Leventhal died here of cancer early this month. A friendship of over 50 years through thick and thin. Now ashes in urn No 21501 in the basement of Père Lachaise Columbariesca."[35]

For the moment, his own health appeared to be on an "even keel in the crooked last straight, there's metaphors for you."[36] Yet he worried incessantly about his physical deterioration; he had an enlargement of the prostate, for instance, and, although tests showed that the condition was benign, the deaths of his friends inevitably focused his attention on the grim truth of Psalm 90.

His sadness spilled over into numerous little poems called "Mirlitonnades," which he wrote mostly in 1977 and 1978. He described them himself as "gloomy French doggerel," even gloomier than his translations of Chamfort. But some of them are beautifully crafted. These "rimailles," "rhymeries," or "versicules," as he first labeled them, were jotted down at odd moments in Ussy, in a hotel room or in a bar in Paris, Stuttgart, or Tangier on any handy scrap of paper — envelope, beer mat, or, in one case, a Johnnie Walker Black Label whisky label. They were then often carefully reworked, before being copied into a tiny leather-bound *sottisier* or commonplace book that he carried around in his jacket pocket.

Some of the poems arose out of particular moments or incidents in his life. "Ne manquez pas à Tanger / le cimetière Saint-André" ("Do not miss in Tangier / the Saint-André cemetery") with its bench dedicated "to the memory of Arthur Keyser" was composed on the first of May in Tangier, following a visit to the cemetery there. On a second visit to the same cemetery in August, he spotted the tombstone of a perpetual optimist: "Caroline Hay Taylor" ("one who never turned her back but / marched breast forward," read the headstone) who had died in Ireland forty-five years before in August 1932. A parallel "mirliton-nade," "Ne manquez pas à Stuttgart / la longue Rue Neckar," along which Beckett tramped so often and where he sometimes ate in a small Italian restaurant, was written in Stuttgart on the day he began to direct . . . *but the clouds . . .* , the second television play in the Süddeutscher Rundfunk program, *Schatten (Shades).* This poem is heavily ironic, for the long Neckarstrasse in Stuttgart is the kind of dreary, uninspiring city road that, in Klaus Herm's words, "makes one feel positively homesick." [37]

Other little poems were prompted by lines or phrases that had stuck in his mind during his reading: lines from Voltaire's poem about the Lisbon earth-quake of November 1 (All Saints Day), 1755, for instance, or Pascal's "I seek only to know my own nothingness." Another adopts the phrasing of La Fon-taine's sombre fable "Le Lièvre et les Grenouilles" ("The Hare and the Frogs") — he had first read La Fontaine at Trinity College, Dublin — taking its paren-thetical line "Que faire en un gîte à moins que l'on ne songe" ("What can one do in a den but dream") and making it the focus of a quatrain about a buck hare ("un bouquin") that leaves its "gîte."

In March and April 1977, he thought of perhaps writing a play about the Fates: "Attempts to get going on something new in vain. Just a few rhymes in French. Wish I could do an Atropos all in black, with her scissors." [38] Instead, these thoughts inspired two of the Mirlitonnades. In the first, one of the Fates spins out life's thread on her spindle; in the second, the "noire soeur qui es aux enfers" ("black sister who art in hell"), waits to cut it; "qu'est-ce que tu attends" ("what are you waiting for"), he asks in his final line. [39] The apparent slightness and playfulness of form of these late 1970s "poèmes courts" (or "miniature poems") should not disguise the seriousness and, to use Beckett's own word, "gloom" of their themes. Although they have been largely ignored by critics writing about Beckett's work, they offer startling insights into the darkness of his private moods at this time.

3

ALTHOUGH OFTEN DEPRESSED, he continued to commit himself well into the future. Planning ahead helped to keep him going. He accepted commitments to direct the two television plays with Süddeutscher Rundfunk and *Spiel (Play)* with the Schiller-Theater, and also thought of directing the French translation of *Footfalls* in Paris with the enchanting Delphine Seyrig as May. He even contemplated with pleasure a future prospect of directing Billie Whitelaw in *Happy Days;* "no harm looking forward," was his muted comment. [40]

Beckett went to Stuttgart to direct his two new television plays in May

1977.[41] He stayed at the Park Hotel at 21 Villastrasse, in room 422. "The hotel is not bad," he wrote, "but the room tiny. Outside the studios I see no-one. In London the hotel was a sanctuary. It's not the same here. So I drag myself around the parks."[42] In fact, he became good friends with the American camera-man Jim Lewis, as well as the producer Dr. Müller-Freienfels. And he had known Klaus Herm, the actor in *Ghost Trio* and . . . *but the clouds* . . . , for twelve years, having already worked with him on the two Schiller-Theater *Godot* productions. As in Berlin, he visited the Staatsgalerie at quiet moments, buying postcards such as Rembrandt's painting of the Apostle Paul, or a Salomon van Ruysdael, to send to Avigdor Arikha and Jocelyn Herbert. But he also wrote three little poems in the Park Hotel, including one of seventeen lines, dated "S [Stuttgart] 26. 6. 77," which he gave to Jim Lewis. This begins:

> *one dead of night*
> *in the dead still*
> *he looked up*
> *from his book.*[43]

The poem looks forward to two of his works from the 1980s, one in theater and one in prose: *Ohio Impromptu* and *Stirrings Still*.

Beckett's appointment books for this period show how often he telephoned Suzanne whenever he was away, checking as to how she was and fretting when-ever he found her unwell. But if, at one level, the bond between them remained extremely close, at another, that of sexual and emotional fidelity, it continued much as it had done over the past two decades. Very often, when he was away, Barbara Bray used to come to stay for about a week, and he would set aside certain evenings or keep an entire weekend free to be with her. But he had many women friends and often continued to see them whether or not there had been or still was a romantic involvement. Sex was not always an essential ingredient in the intimacy. Beckett had an extraordinary gift for making the person he was seeing feel the center of his attention. In this respect, he was the same with male friends, whom he often kept separate one from another. Some of these were not necessarily even on speaking terms with each other, separated as they were by widely differing attitudes to politics, literature, or art. One had taken a very different path from Beckett during World War II, yet he still saw him. Others adopted totally opposing positions on, for example, the Arab-Israeli conflict, yet he saw them both. French friends rarely knew his English or Irish friends well, if at all. And his friends and acquaintances ranged widely from writers, painters, musicians, and actors to academics, publishers, and critics. Sometimes the only factor these people had in common was their friendship with Beckett.

4

ONE OF HIS FRIENDSHIPS led him to direct yet another production of *Krapp's Last Tape*. It was the last thing he wanted to do. He wrote to me in June 1977:

> What has messed me up is my having agreed to direct Rick Cluchey in *Krapp* in Berlin (Akademie Theatre) in September. He was offered 10 performances on condition I direct and I haven't the heart to refuse. Michael Haerdter will assist. They came here [to Stuttgart, where Beckett was directing the two television plays] the other day for preliminary work. It will be heavy going.[44]

But although difficult, it was anything but heavy. Rehearsal conditions at the Akademie der Künste were far from ideal: "limited access to stage, inadequate technical equipment, little help from Academy staff, etc."[45] So for the first few days and whenever the stage was not available, they rehearsed in Beckett's own studio. In spite of this and other problems, he wrote: "The team has done a good job none the less and Rick is an impressive Krapp, in spite of having to play the part, in this very strict and stylised production, clearly against his temperament."[46] It was the friendly family atmosphere that Beckett relished most of all, for Rick had his wife, Teri, and three-year-old son, Louis Beckett Cluchey, staying with him in Berlin. At rehearsals, it was like working with a bigger family.

When he returned to direct *Play* at the Schiller-Theater in September 1978, the San Quentin company was also in Berlin, and Beckett rehearsed *Endgame* with the Clucheys, Bud Thorpe, and Lawrence Held. The same atmosphere prevailed. Held commented:

> I think Sam liked being with us because we were relaxed with him. We didn't put any pressure on him. We weren't continually canonising him or challenging him. He didn't have to continually prove who he was to us. We knew that apart from winning the Nobel Prize for literature and having written some of the most important plays of the twentieth century, he was a guy who liked to drink scotch, smoke funny little cigars, talk, laugh and tell stories.[47]

There were some hilarious incidents. Rehearsals took place, for instance, in the restored Matthäuskirche, after, with Beckett's backing, they insisted on moving out of a circus tent, where they found they could not rehearse properly:

> I think it really started one night, in the middle of rehearsal, and Rick said, "Can we have a break?" And Sam goes, "Well, yes of course — does anybody mind if I smoke?" Now, this is in the church, remember: Sam looks around reverently and somebody says, "We've got a can over here," and he goes, "Oh good, well I'll put my ashes in the can," and Rick goes, "That's right, we also got a bottle of wine." And Sam

goes, "Where'd you get the bottle of wine?" Rick says, "Well you know, it's the communion wine from the back." Rick had broken into the stash in the back and brought out the communion wine. Later he had to replace it because the government didn't like what he had done. So we had a little wine and Sam thought this was hysterical.[48]

This was followed by the arrival of Dr. Walter Georgi, a Berlin psychiatrist known to Beckett and to the San Quentin group, who walked in carrying a bottle of Bell's whisky.

Even though he was rushed off his feet, Beckett started to trust the group and realize that he could relax with them. In Thorpe's words: "we weren't there to do anything to hurt him, but, at the same time too, as we could not work in an incredibly austere situation, we had to have fun. And when he realized we had to have fun, he relaxed and he could have fun."[49] And for Beckett, what great fun it was to be twenty-five again — until he realized how exhausted he was as he collapsed into bed at the Akademie after a day spent rehearsing two different companies.

5

IN AUGUST 1977, the actor David Warrilow, who had had such a resounding success with the adaptation of *The Lost Ones*, wrote to Beckett asking him if he would write a solo piece for him to perform. Asked what he had in mind, Warrilow wrote back saying that he "had an image of a man standing on stage lit from above. He's standing there in a sort of cone of light. You couldn't see his face and he's talking about death."[50] Beckett's reply began:

"My birth was my death."
But I could never manage 40 min. (5000 words) on that old chestnut.
Not with it now within reach. I think the best wd. [would] be for you
to make your own selection from existing texts. You have my carte
blanchâtre [i.e. whitish] and blessing in advance. And no lack there
of the mood you have in mind.[51]

Even so, the very next day, after his Sunday morning walk along the quiet, tree-lined boulevard Saint-Jacques,[52] he sat down at his desk and wrote out again: "My birth was my death." This became the opening sentence of a new text that he decided after all to try to write for Warrilow. At first he called it "Gone." He began writing it in the first person singular and drew on memories of his own childhood: his father teaching him how to strike a match on his buttocks; the various operations involved in lighting an old-style oil lamp — removing the white glass globe, then the smoke-blackened inner glass chimney, and, finally, lighting the wick with a match or a spill; what his mother had told him about how he was born just as the sun was sinking behind the larches "new needles turning green"[53]; a gleam of light catching the large brass bedstead that had stood in his parents' bedroom at Cooldrinagh.

But he also drew on more recent experiences and feelings. He returned to the calculations that he had written out on a "Rendez-vous" slip in February as to the number of days that he had lived, writing in his new text: "Twenty five thousand five hundred and fifty dawns."[54] He drew on memories of going "from funeral to funeral . . . I almost said of loved ones."[55] That he was thinking here almost inevitably of the little Protestant cemetery at Greystones, where his mother and father and uncle Gerald were buried with other relatives, is suggested by a scene in the monologue where all the photographs that were once pinned to the wall are taken down, torn to pieces, and scattered on the floor with the dust and the cobwebs. "There was father. That grey void. There mother. That other. There together. Smiling. Wedding day. There all three."[56]

The mood of "clearing the decks," with the idea either of sparing himself further distress or of tidying up in preparation for his own end, seems to have spilled over into Beckett's life for, only a few days after writing these lines, he wrote to a friend from his cottage at Ussy that he was "enjoying [himself] throwing everything out, books and other rubbish, not absolutely indispensable. All pictures out of sight including big Geer v. [van] Velde, behind the piano."[57] During his absence in Germany in September for the San Quentin *Krapp's Last Tape*, his whole house was painted inside and out by a local young man and since the walls, painted "grey, like the proprietor,"[58] were now bare and uncluttered, he chose to leave them that way. Life here emulated art, or at least echoed the mood that inspired it. There is a strong if underplayed emotional charge in the evocation of the main theme of his play about death which is reflected in the "Thirty thousand nights of ghosts beyond. Beyond that black beyond. Ghost light. Ghost nights. Ghost rooms. Ghost graves. Ghost . . . he all but said ghost loved ones."[59]

Beckett worked on "Gone," first in Paris then in Ussy, throughout the rest of the summer. But, by November, he had to admit that the new text was "becalmed in deep water and likely to founder . . . He [Warrilow] does not know I am — was — trying."[60] It was to remain unfinished for over a year. Then, in January 1979, Martin Esslin wrote to ask Beckett if he had an unpublished piece that could appear in *The Kenyon Review*. Beckett replied from Stuttgart, where he was directing Heinz Bennent in a new Süddeutscher Rundfunk production of *Eh Joe*, telling him of the piece that he had attempted to write for Warrilow:

> It broke down as usual after a few thousand groans, but is not perhaps definitely down the drain. Just text, no stage directions, but I could manage one or two to give it an air. It could be entitled *From an abandoned (interrupted) soliloquy*. I'll dig it up and clean it up, or the best of it, when I get back to Paris end of this week, and send it on. To give you a little pleasure wd. [would] give me much.[61]

On his return to Paris, a bronchial infection, for which he sought the help of an acupuncturist, Dr. Yen, held up his work on the play. But, after retyping it, revising it fairly drastically, and adding a set of stage directions, on his seventy-third birthday he sent a copy to Esslin. The same day, he dispatched a second copy to David Warrilow with this accompanying note: "I send you as to its instigator this unsatisfactory abandoned monologue. I do not expect you to use it. But on the off-chance of your wishing to I have checked with Barney Rosset and you wd. [would] have his blessing. It was written some years ago on the spur of your suggestion and put aside till now."[62] The piece was eventually entitled A *Piece of Monologue* and was performed by Warrilow at La Mama Theater Club in December 1979. This was one of two pieces — one "very limited in scope and ambition"[63] — that Beckett spoke or wrote about to friends at this time.

6

THE SECOND PIECE was far more ambitious. In January 1977, he jotted down some notes, then wrote the opening pages of a piece initially called "Verbatim" or the "Voice."[64] Soon he came to think of this text not just affectionately as a text to "keep [him] going (company),"[65] but as a major piece of writing that was vital to his continuing as a writer. "Tried to get going again in English to see me through, say for company, but broke down. But must somehow . . ." he wrote plaintively to Ruby Cohn at the beginning of May 1977.[66]

Company comes closer to autobiography than anything Beckett had written since *Dream of Fair to Middling Women* in 1931–32. Yet the autobiographical features are far from straightforward. Some of the "life scenes" are familiar from Beckett's childhood: his mother's long labor and his father's absence at his birth; being taught to swim by his father at the Forty-Foot;[67] throwing himself from the top of a fir tree in the garden to land on its lower branches.

Some incidents, like the one of the little boy walking with his mother and pestering her with questions about the sky, had been used in earlier work, but with different replies from the mother. There is thus considerable doubt as to which version might represent an authentic memory.[68] The scene with his father chuckling as he read *Punch* was another moving personal reminiscence for Beckett, although he told me that, by placing it in the summerhouse, he was deliberately fictionalizing the incident. It did not happen there at all, he said. He also claimed that the other scene in the summerhouse, with the young woman, was fictional, although it seems likely to have been a conflation of several moments of intimacy — probably, in view of the description of the woman's body, with his first actual love, his cousin Peggy Sinclair.

The incidents are selected like scenes in a novel to highlight certain themes, especially those of solitude and lovelessness. While revealing what seem to be personal, often intimate moments, the book counters certain major premises of confessional autobiography, one of which is that the present self can be explained by referring back to earlier experiences in one's own life. Traditional autobiography relies on a linear notion of time and on a causal view of human development. And Beckett breaks this mold by not presenting the memories chronologically and by deliberately ignoring any significant impact that they may or may not have had on a later self.

The irony of writing the biography of someone who holds so firmly and so convincingly to the elusiveness of the past escaped neither Beckett nor myself, as we talked about the memories trawled up in *Company*. At one moment, we laughed uproariously at the idea of reaching "truth" in so shifty an area as a human life. Beckett did go so far, however, as to concede that he had earlier spent almost an hour correcting any number of factual errors that had already been disseminated about his relatives, his upbringing, and his early life. And, as he spoke about some of the scenes and the characters in *Company*, he fleshed them out in more detail. The woman who believed she could fly was, he thought, one of the Elvery family, with whom his mother had been on friendly terms. Mrs. Coote was, he was certain, married to the philatelist neighbor from whom Frank used to obtain his stamps and to whom his mother had been very kind when her husband died.[69] Yet it was clear, throughout our discussion, not only that real-life incidents had been shaped and transformed to fit the fiction but that the skepticism that, as a young man, he had brought to his criticism of the role of memory (involuntary as well as voluntary) in Proust had been reinforced by the distance that separated him from his own past. Memory emerges here as very much like invention.[70]

In any case, memories of "life scenes" form a relatively small part of *Company*, fifteen paragraphs, compared with the forty-two that explore the situation of the figure lying on his back in the dark. And the rest of the work — Beckett's first piece of extended prose fiction in seventeen years — is a complex play on uncertainties. Where are the memories coming from in the first place? Whose voice is speaking when "he" hears, "You first saw the light on such and such a day"? Who is this "he" anyway? A fictional construct created by the writer (a figure devised by the deviser for company), or Beckett himself? Is what the voice is saying intended for him or for someone else? Is anyone else there? Questions like these are essential to Beckett's own "remembrance of time past." Moreover, the end brings the explicit reminder that what has been recounted to the "he" who is lying on his back in the dark, as well as to the reader, is mere fable:

> "The fable of one with you in the dark. The fable of one fabling of one with you in the dark. And how better in the end labour lost and silence. And you as you always were.
> "Alone."[71]

7

"LABOUR LOST," OF COURSE, echoes Shakespeare, as do several other words and phrases in *Company* (for example, the "bourneless dark," the "girdle" around the earth, "the place beneath"). And the book reflects Beckett's reading as much as it does his personal memories. "So sat waiting to be purged the old lutist cause of Dante's first quarter smile and now perhaps singing praises with some section of the blest at last"[72] evokes Dante's Belacqua in the *Purgatorio*; the "half blind," "the shadowy light," the "darkness visible" are borrowed from Milton; "unmoved mover" is an Aristotelean term. Beckett spent comparatively little of his time now reading modern literature but regularly went back to what he called the "old chestnuts": Chaucer, Pascal, Schopenhauer, Shakespeare, Dante, La Fontaine, Pope, Swift, Kierkegaard, Goethe, Heine, and Mallarmé. Quotations from all these authors appear in his personal notebook at this date, just as others had been copied out in his 1930s notebooks. But he has so naturally absorbed and reworked these and other memorable phrases, that they sometimes creep into his writing so unobtrusively that they are no longer easily detected. Nor are they used in an ostentatiously clever way, as they sometimes were in 1932. Beckett still read widely. Early in 1978, for leisure, he was reading Samuel Pepys's diary,[73] and, while rehearsing *Play* in Berlin, he reread Fontane's *Irrungen, Wirrungen (Mistakes, Confusions)* "a good title for rehearsal time," he commented.[74]

Among his close friends, he had always had rather fewer writers than painters and musicians. This remained true at the end of the 1970s. He kept in touch, now mostly by telephone, with Robert Pinget, who was a member of the small circle of Suzanne's close friends. For some years, he had met, occasionally for dinner, the Romanian-born philosopher Emil Cioran, but was finding that he had less in common with Cioran in terms of outlook than he had at first thought. Of American writer friends, he also had the occasional drink with the dramatist Israel Horovitz, and he saw Edward Albee occasionally. He met the younger New York writer Paul Auster, who admired Beckett's work and sent him copies of his own writing, including his translations of some poems of André du Bouchet, which Beckett enjoyed.[75] He saw the novelist Raymond Federman.

Beckett admired several contemporary writers. One was his friend Harold Pinter, whom he saw when in London or when Pinter came over to Paris. Pinter used to send Beckett copies of his plays in typescript and Beckett had considerable respect for the English playwright's work.[76] Pinget was one writer whom he felt had been generally undervalued. He also admired the American novelist Saul Bellow, who was awarded the Nobel Prize for Literature in 1976.[77] Beckett read Bellow's *Humboldt's Gift* in May 1978 "and found it remarkable."[78] Soon after reading the book, he saw the New York publisher, writer, and collector of Beckett first editions, Bill Targ, and his literary agent wife, Roslyn, on one of their annual visits to Paris. He told them how much he admired the novel and how he would like to meet Bellow. Targ knew Bellow from his own days as a Chicago bookseller, so that the next time they were in Paris, when Bellow was also there, he arranged a meeting between the two writers at the Hôtel Montalembert. Both were shy and awkward, Bellow perhaps even more than Beckett. Neither of them wanted to talk about his own work. Roslyn Targ found herself forced to chat animatedly to fill in the silences.[79] It was like a replay of the encounter with Max Delbrück.

Music and musicians still played an important part in what remained a richly varied cultural life. Music had always been for Beckett the art form that came closest to pure spirit. He often listened to music at Avigdor and Anne Arikha's apartment in the square du Port-Royal, and he tuned in to concerts and talks about music on *France Culture* as often as possible. He hardly ever went, however, to concerts anymore, dreading being recognized or accosted by strangers. In spite of the growing difficulties that the muscular contracture in his hand created when he stretched the tendons to span a full octave, he still played his little Schimmel piano — Chopin waltzes and sonatas, Schubert's "Impromptus" and sonatas, Haydn's sonatas, Beethoven's "Variations for Piano," and, perhaps more surprisingly, Béla Bartók's "Microkosmos" and Erik Satie's "Entertainment." [80] Privately, he met many musicians. When the concert pianist Andor Foldes was in Paris, usually accompanied by his wife, Lili, Beckett used to spend time with them, talking about Foldes's concert repertoire and tours and congratulating him when he heard of his success in many countries. Their friendship, which was based on mutual admiration (Beckett quite often signed copies of his own work for Foldes) went back to 1967, when he and Suzanne first heard the pianist play all of Beethoven's piano concertos on two evenings in Paris: "a great feat," was Beckett's comment.[81] Since then, Foldes had sent them several of his recordings, including Beethoven's "Emperor" Concerto.[82]

What is striking at this period of Beckett's life is how often his work was set to music or directly inspired pieces of music — an indication not just of the challenge that his writing set composers but also of its essential musicality. He was as conscious as any modern composer of the importance of precisely timed silence. At rehearsals when he was directing his own plays, musical terms like "piano," "fortissimo," "andante," "allegro," "da capo," "cadenza" tripped lightly off his tongue. Between 1976 and 1977, at least six different musical settings or operas were approved by Beckett's agents, sometimes only after Beckett had given them his personal blessing. At the end of August 1976, while directing in Berlin, he met the Heidelberg-based composer Professor Wolfgang Fortner, who wanted to set *That Time* to music (and saw him again a year later once the problems had been solved and the work finished).[83] During the same visit to Berlin, his meeting with Morton Feldman occurred. And at about the same date, after some initial misgivings, he authorized Heinz Holliger to set *Not I* and *Come and Go* to music.[84] Indeed, his attitude to musicians who wanted to adapt his work was much freer than it was to stage or film directors wishing to do the same thing.

Although he rarely visited public art galleries in Paris now, he never lost his love of painting. He supported artists whom he knew and admired, like Avigdor Arikha. He preferred not to attend private views but would slip in, discreetly and mostly alone, once the crowds had melted away. Once, he escorted Josette Hayden to an exhibition of about fifty of Henri's landscapes of the Marne, some drawings and gouaches ("very fine and well presented," he commented).[85] There were new artist friends to meet, too. He was the first morning visitor (so as to miss anyone else) at a fine exhibition in November

1979 of Louis Le Brocquy's paintings at the Galerie Jeanne Bucher. Le Brocquy and his wife, Anne Madden, also a painter, had been introduced to Beckett the previous year by their mutual friend, Con Leventhal.[86] The three were to remain on warm, friendly terms until Beckett's death; Louis did studies of his head and designed two productions of *Waiting for Godot* at the Gate Theatre. Yet another painter whom Beckett occasionally met when he came to Paris was Jean-Michel Folon. The Canadian sculptor Sorel Etrog, who had just finished work on a remarkable illustrated edition of *Imagination Dead Imagine* for John Calder,[87] also made appointments to see Beckett when he was over in Paris. In the mid-seventies Beckett met the American painter Jasper Johns, to discuss with him a collaboration on a fine volume of *Foirades / Fizzles*, prose fragments that were illustrated by Johns's remarkable etchings. Although he respected Johns's work Beckett did not warm to the man; as a result, no further collaboration took place.

From the autumn of 1975, he went out less and less often to dine in restaurants. Instead, he started meeting his visitors at the Petit Café of the PLM Hôtel Saint-Jacques on the other side of the boulevard. Many people felt that this was a strange café for Beckett to adopt as his preferred meeting place. It took over in the final years of the 1970s from the Closerie des Lilas, which he felt was becoming much too modish and where he began to feel as if he were on display. The PLM had a number of distinct advantages: it was close to his apartment; as a tourist hotel it was anonymous; and the waiters were discreet and friendly without being familiar. Beckett was able to have a quiet, mostly undisturbed drink with a friend and in just over an hour's time be back at his desk or checking that Suzanne was all right. He used to meet close friends like Con Leventhal and Avigdor Arikha there, as well as more casual visitors. Quite often in the last few years of their lives, he and Suzanne would walk down the road to have a meal together in the PLM restaurant.

8

FOR SOMEONE who, years before, had constantly announced to friends that his directing days were over, the closing years of the 1970s were crammed full of intense theatrical activity. Apart from supervising the San Quentin Drama Workshop (twice) and directing all his television plays with Süddeutscher Rundfunk, he also worked with two of his favorite actresses: Delphine Seyrig in *Pas (Footfalls)* in March 1978 and Billie Whitelaw in *Happy Days* in June 1979.

He prepared in Tangier for his coming project with Delphine Seyrig in February, working on the French text and thinking about the "dynamics" of *Pas*. On his return to Paris, he plunged almost immediately into rehearsals. He loved the modern, independent, free spirit in Delphine Seyrig, and he spoke affectionately of how she used to arrive at the theater, with her hair tousled and windswept from a motorscooter ride across the city, then quickly transform herself into the strange, timeless "girl who had never really been born." He had great respect for her sensitivity as an actress. He also admired what she had done with the role and told me two days after the premiere that he had loved working with her.[88] Seyrig, on the other hand, never really felt at ease with Beckett. She was too overawed by his reputation as a great writer, and his taciturn manner disturbed her. She never felt that her delivery was musically precise enough for him, or that she ever achieved what she could have done with the part of May, if she had not been intimidated by him.[89]

Directing *Happy Days* with Billie Whitelaw a year later should have been unadulterated joy. It was not. Beckett had been looking forward to it ever since his work with her on *Footfalls* and had made some fruitless efforts to have the new production put on earlier. At long last he traveled to London on April 22, 1979, for six weeks of rehearsals, having prepared for the production for months on end and rethought his entire approach to Winnie.

Beckett had hoped that Ronald Pickup would play the part of Willie. But Pickup was not available. So eight potential actors were selected by the assistant director, Roger Michell, and asked to audition at the Irish Club in Eaton Square. Beckett hated this kind of occasion, finding it embarrassing and painful to turn anyone down. One of the actors, Leonard Fenton, read an extract from Beckett's novel *Molloy*, which he had done in an earlier program arranged by John Calder. Two days later, the choice was narrowed down to two. Fenton knew from Calder that Beckett was passionately fond of Schubert and, partly to fill an embarrassing silence, told him that he sang *Winterreise*. Beckett's face lit up: "Ah," he enthused, "that is his masterwork. Do you sing it in English or in German?" "In German," replied Fenton. Beckett turned with a smile to Michell, saying: "That's it. I've decided," and Fenton was offered the part. One day, arriving at rehearsal unusually late for him after a sleepless night, Beckett turned to Fenton and said "Sing 'An die Musik' for me, please." Fenton sang, unaccompanied. At the end, a restored Beckett said: "That's better. Now we can rehearse!"[90]

Knowing from past experience how meticulous Beckett was, Billie Whitelaw had learned her lines before rehearsals began. Unfortunately, Beckett then made many small changes in the script, adding to its recurrent verbal patterns: "And now" for "What now," "talk" for "speak," and so on. He had also made some substantial cuts in the first act. Because the textual changes were so minute and were introduced at such a late stage, Whitelaw inevitably made mistakes, as her brain found it difficult to override what it had already absorbed. Rehearsals became very tense affairs, since Beckett could not prevent himself from putting his head into his hands whenever she got the text wrong. Not surprisingly, this disturbed Whitelaw, who felt under tremendous pressure. Beckett was very aware that he was upsetting Billie by his irritated behavior but seemed incapable of doing anything about it. Stuart Burge, the artistic director of the Royal Court at the time, takes up the story:

> After three and a half weeks Billie came to me and confessed that in spite of their very close and congenial relationship she could no longer

endure the strain of Sam's obsession with the pronunciation, tone and emphasis of each syllable of every word in the long text. She needed the freedom to find her own way into the character but I did not relish the prospect of "letting the director go." I consulted Jocelyn Herbert, the Designer, who was a great friend of Sam's and invited them to dinner together [on May 17] with another mutual friend, Donald McWhinnie, the Director. It was a stimulating evening and far from being an embarrassment, the proposition that he should absent himself from rehearsal for a while turned out to be entirely acceptable.[91]

During the time Beckett was away, Whitelaw regained her confidence and her composure and, with the pressure blissfully removed, worked with Robbie Hendry, the stage manager. Beckett filled his own schedule with innumerable meetings, dinners, and drinks. Barbara Bray was in London and doubtless helped him to adopt a sensible attitude toward what had happened.

On his return to the theater a week later, the storm had passed. Apologies were exchanged; there were embraces all round; calm was restored and friendship renewed. Some tremendous work had, in fact, been done on which a more relaxed Billie Whitelaw could draw. Beckett's earlier rethinking of the part conferred a quality of strangeness, tension, and discontinuity on Winnie's thoughts and actions. "One of the clues of the play is interruption. Something begins; something else begins. She begins, but doesn't carry through with it. She's constantly being interrupted or interrupting herself. She's an interrupted being. She's a bit mad. Manic is not wrong, but too big. . . . A child-woman with a short span of concentration — sure one minute, unsure the next."[92] "She's like a bird," he told me before rehearsals began, adding to Martha Fehsenfeld: "Like a bird with oil on its feathers."[93]

It was a powerful as well as subtle performance of a part that was perhaps not ideally suited to Billie Whitelaw. And, in view of the rocky straits that she had negotiated, it was a great triumph for the actress. As they sat side by side on a sofa at a first-night party in Bettina Jonic's South Kensington apartment, with Billie looking resplendent in a stunning white dress, Beckett must have been delighted with the acclaim he was receiving from the dozens of guests. But, as he deflected any praise addressed to him to the actress by his side, he was self-critical enough to recognize that he had got there by the skin of his teeth.

25

"Fail better"
1979–82

1

"Physically I am more or less all right — but the mind in [a] bad mess," Beckett wrote to Walter Asmus at the beginning of the 1980s.[1] He often made light of his physical problems. The muscular contracture in his hand was getting steadily worse. He used to perform hand exercises, gripping a chestnut in his palm, for example, and working the tendons to keep his fingers flexible.[2] But during the 1980s, his restricted grip made practical tasks increasingly difficult. He consulted a number of doctors, none of whom was able to help him very much.

His prostate trouble had worsened, too. But, following X rays and blood tests, he was assured that the trouble was benign and, since it caused him no actual pain, he regarded it as a minor inconvenience, to be joked about with good friends. He was able to sympathize, however, with Alan Schneider who had surgery in May 1982, saying that so far he had managed to "keep the plumbers at bay."[3]

In the last few years of his life, Beckett became frailer and thinner. His hands were now noticeably distorted and he swung his right leg a little more stiffly than before as he walked. Greeting him with a fond embrace, you noticed how prominent his shoulder blades felt, even through a heavy wool sweater, and how thin his wrists and forearms had become.

He dressed at this time in an odd mixture of old and new, smart and shabby, mostly the result of accident rather than design. Relatives and friends gave him new scarves, socks, shirts, and sweaters as Christmas or birthday presents. But, although he never looked seedy, he took no real interest in clothes. For preference, he donned a comfortable, much-washed knitted sweater, usually in cream, gray, or beige, which he wore under an old sheepskin coat. When it was cold, he pulled an old beret down — squarely, not rakishly — over his large, protruding ears. The canvas bag that he carried across his body was beginning to look worn. One day in a London taxi, Schneider noticed that Beckett had on a pair of thick tweed trousers that he had not seen him wearing before. "I like the pants, Sam," said Schneider. "Where did you buy them?" "From the charity [thrift] shop," answered Beckett with a cheeky grin.[4]

He ate little and, more often than not, only in the evening. When dining out with friends, he would eat frugally: fish, preferably sole, with French fries, which he sometimes used to eat with his fingers. It has been suggested that his frugality came from a wish to retain his trim, athletic appearance. It was more likely the result of a lack of real interest in food. He still drank regularly: a beer at lunchtime, and one or two whiskeys at the end of the afternoon or just before dinner, at which he often drank white Beaujolais. (Visitors brought him Irish whiskey as a gift, and he soon had far more bottles of the "hard stuff" stacked away in his cupboard than he could ever consume.) He rarely imbibed the kind of quantities that he used to do in his younger and middle years — but enough to sway precariously at times as he weaved his way through the heavy traffic of the busy boulevard Montparnasse after an evening meal.

In the late 1980s, he ate out much less frequently. Suzanne had never been a cook, and while she was responsible for what they ate at home, the food was frugal as well as simple: salads bought in a shop in the rue de la Santé; carrots purchased already grated; cheese, rice, and eggs. Increasingly over the last few years of their lives, as his wife became frailer, Beckett did most of the shopping himself, crossing the bridge over the Métro line to the little North African grocery on the other side of the boulevard to buy a few things for their table.

Although he still saw Barbara Bray regularly, relying on her for practical help and talking to her about his work (only she can say how intimate they remained at this time, for he never talked about their relationship), he worried more and more about Suzanne. After her eightieth year, she suffered frequently from respiratory problems. Earlier, she had had a cyst gradually cut away from the side of her temple. Now, more worryingly, she had a growth by her eye for which she refused to have an operation, being of the view that nature should take its own course.

2

BECKETT NEVER ACCEPTED actual commissions for plays. But he could sometimes be prompted or persuaded to write for a particular actor or a specific occasion. In January 1978, Alan Schneider had introduced him to Daniel Labeille, a professor of theater studies and director at the Cayuga County Community College of the State University of New York (SUNY).[5] Labeille, who was given leave to produce some arts programs for television, wrote to Beckett on October 1, 1979, with a proposal that Schneider and Lee Breuer should be invited to the Buffalo campus of SUNY to rehearse two of Beckett's shorter plays with professional actors and that a film would be made of the entire creative process by the well-known documentary filmmakers, Donn Pennebaker and his wife, Chris Hegedus.[6] Beckett gave the project his immediate blessing, largely because Schneider was involved. After some discussions as to which plays should be used,[7] Labeille wrote to Beckett at the beginning of March 1980 asking if he could possibly write something especially for the occasion, which had now become a mini-festival to honor his seventy-fifth birthday. Beckett replied succinctly: "A new piece for the occasion if I possibly can. I doubt it."[8] Yet, in spite of his doubts, by the beginning of August, a very beautiful short play, *Rockaby*, had emerged.

A woman, dressed in a black, high-necked evening gown, rocks rhythmically to and fro in a rocking chair. She sits totally still, and the rocking seems to occur independently of her. But the movements are carefully synchronized with the rhythms of her recorded voice reciting the words of a poem. Intermittently, she joins in three of the lines: "time she stopped," "living soul," and "rock her off."[9] Both voice and rocking halt temporarily until the woman's call for "more" starts them off again. When the chair finally comes to rest and the voice stops, the woman's head inclines forward. Like the woman whose life is evoked in the poem, she has apparently died.

In creating this unusual stage image, Beckett drew on a store of personal memories. There was the frail figure of his maternal grandmother, "little Granny," Annie Roe, dressed in "her best black," sitting in a rocking chair at the window of Cooldrinagh, where she lived out the final years of her life. The woman in the play gazes out at other windows for "another living soul," as Beckett himself sat, often for hours on end, staring at the rows of Santé prison cell windows. One biographical starting point shades almost imperceptibly into another, as the creative imagination shapes, develops, and transforms its sources.

But there are also glimpses of paintings that Beckett knew: Whistler's *Study in Gray and Black*, known as *Whistler's Mother*; Madame Roulin in van Gogh's *La Berceuse*;[10] Rembrandt's *Margaretha Trip (de Geer)*.[11] The flashes of light and color from the jet sequins sewn onto the rocking woman's dress may echo the magnificent Giorgione self-portrait that had so captivated him in Brunswick in 1936. Jack Yeats's painting of an old woman sitting by the window with her head drooping low onto her chest has something of the ambiguity of *Rockaby*'s closing moments. The picture, reproduced in the Yeats exhibition catalogue, which was in Beckett's library, is entitled *Sleep*, but the woman could be asleep for ever. The woman in *Rockaby* is rocked from cradle to grave as the poem moves through overlapping cycles of need and disillusionment into a final dismissal of life — "Fuck life," says the woman's voice with startling crudeness — and an acceptance of death.

In a letter in 1982 to American Equity, Beckett wrote that this play had been written for Billie Whitelaw.[12] But he was writing at a point when he and Schneider were trying to find good reasons to persuade Equity to allow the British actress to perform the play again in New York, and the statement was not strictly true. In his original letter asking Beckett for the play, Labeille had directly associated the name of Irene Worth (an earlier Winnie in *Happy Days*)[13] with the project. And, sending him the new play, Beckett had written "Herewith for yr. Festival if you think it worth while. For Alan Schneider and Irene Worth if they think it worth while."[14] So it would be truer to say that he wrote the play *for the occasion*, believing at the time that Irene Worth was going to play it.[15]

In the event, Worth did not play the part, as she was suddenly offered a leading role in a film and the *Rockaby* project could not be deferred to suit her plans.[16] Beckett wrote firmly to Labeille: "*Rockaby* was written for yr. Project and must have its first performance on this occasion. If Irene Worth is not available another actress should be found."[17] So Billie Whitelaw was signed up to play "W. Woman in chair." And Beckett, who had been consulted about the change of casting, declared himself "very pleased with switch to Billie."[18]

After this, Beckett remained closely involved with the project. He explained several key details of the play to Labeille in Paris.[19] He telephoned Billie Whitelaw several times, reading the entire play over to her on the phone and answering all her questions about it.[20] Finally, he also spent the evening of March 24 with Schneider, going over the production in minute detail before rehearsals started in London, prior to the play's being staged in Buffalo.[21] After rehearsing in Whitelaw's Camden Square apartment and recording the voice in a Soho studio,[22] Schneider, Whitelaw, and the film crew arrived in Buffalo on April 4, with only four clear days to get everything technically right for the opening. The premiere, on April 8, 1981, was ecstatically received.[23]

Later, Whitelaw's musically subtle performance was revived at the Cottesloe Theatre in London by Alan Schneider, using the original recording. Beckett came over for a few rehearsals. So, at last, at the beginning of December 1982, he was able to see for himself what Schneider and Whitelaw had done with his play. Long before that, however, he had listened with enjoyment to a tape of Billie's voice.[24] While he was in London, Labeille took him in a taxi to a studio at the BBC to watch Pennebaker's lively yet moving film. Afterward, Beckett commented quietly, "I liked the film."[25] At the Cottesloe Theatre, he made discreet suggestions as to the timing and lighting levels. There were, he conceded, a few minor things on the tape that he heard a little differently in his head.[26] But he found the play beautifully realized and thought Whitelaw's performance so compelling that he came to regard the play as her own. The production was, he put it succinctly to Schneider, "Great."[27]

3

A SECOND SHORT PLAY was provoked in the same way by S. E. Gontarski, an Associate Professor of English at Ohio State University, who asked if Beckett would write a dramatic piece for an international symposium planned for May 1981 in Columbus, to honor him on his seventy-fifth birthday. Back came his stock response: "You know how unfitted I am to write to request." But he added, "I shall of course bear yours in mind and do my best to let you have something for your 1981 Symposium."[28]

The play, *Ohio Impromptu*, was not written until late in 1980. But Beckett made a number of false starts at the end of March and in the first week of April, while staying in Ussy: "I thought I was on to something," he wrote to Gontarski in June, "but it has petered out. I'll try again."[29] The fragments that "petered out" — one focuses on a ghost returning from the underworld to speak at such a conference, the other on a figure trying and failing to thread a needle — were drily witty, teasing, and whimsical. But both were abandoned, perhaps because the first piece seemed too trite and the second too personal.[30]

On the surface at least, the finished play appears much more impersonal than the earlier sketches and differs completely from them. It is, wrote Michael Billington, "brilliant minimalist theatre proving that Beckett uses the stage like a painter to create images that will haunt you to the grave."[31] The setting of this "meticulously sculpted tableau"[32] resembles the interior of a seventeenth-century Dutch painting, and the two male figures, a Reader and a Listener, seated at the table, with their long hair and "long black coats," could have been borrowed from Rembrandt or, if we take away the painter's color, Vermeer.[33]

On the table in front of the two figures is a large, black, wide-brimmed "old world Latin Quarter hat"[34] such as James Joyce used to wear so jauntily. Reader reads from a book about a man who moves away from where he had lived "so long alone together" with a companion, who has clearly left him, perhaps even died; the first man goes to live in a single room on the far bank of the river. From time to time, the man is visited by a stranger who is sent by his former love to comfort him. On each visit, the comforter spends the night reading the "sad tale" to the man. Habitually he leaves at dawn. But, at the end of the spoken text, the visitor is said to stay on so that they sit together "as though turned to stone." The stage image converges with the narrative, as the two "raise their heads and look at each other." The image of the river (the Seine) with its two arms flowing into one another after they have divided to flow around the island (the Allée des Cygnes or Isle of Swans, where Beckett and Joyce used to walk together) is a clue to the meaning of the play. For at its emotional center lie sadness, loss, and solitude, contrasted with a memory of togetherness.

This feeling of loss suggests that the figure in the narrative who has been left to live alone is deeply rooted in Beckett's personal and imaginative life. Several of his friends who saw Beckett and Suzanne in the last ten years of their lives, when they were often sharp or irritable with each other, were surprised by a dinner conversation that I had in 1981 with Beckett about *Ohio Impromptu*. We spoke first of the link with Joyce: "Of course," he commented of the hat and the Isle of Swans. I then told him that I had heard the "dear face" who is evoked by the Reader referred to as if it were the face of Joyce. "It is a woman, isn't it?" I asked. "It's Suzanne," he replied. "I've imagined her dead so many times. I've even imagined myself trudging out to her grave."[35] When he wrote *Ohio Impromptu*, Suzanne was eighty years old. Together they had shared hardship, war, and finally the burdens of celebrity. Although they had, in many ways, gradually come to lead very independent lives (at one time Suzanne had commented bitterly to a friend, "Notre mariage, c'est un mariage de célibataires" ["Our marriage is a marriage of bachelors"]) they had nonetheless remained a couple for over forty years. Whatever other emotional attachments Beckett had had during that time, there had never been any question of his leaving her. And both the sharing and the life he had sought to live alone appear to be evoked in this play: "Could he not now turn back? Acknowledge his error and return to where they were once so long alone together. Alone together so much shared. No. What he had done alone could not be undone. Nothing he had ever done alone could ever be undone. By him alone."[36]

This is probably as deeply personal as anything that Beckett had written since *Krapp's Last Tape*. For although he needed to be alone, the thought of Suzanne dying was intolerable to him. It was probably made even more devastating because of the guilt with which he knew he would be burdened. Indeed, ten days after his wife died, Beckett sighed to me: "So much regret, so much regret." This regret is already presaged obliquely in *Ohio Impromptu*. The success of the play, however, is that, through its visual and verbal imagery, it manages to transcend any purely personal inspiration.

David Warrilow was chosen by Alan Schneider, Gontarski, and Beckett to play the Reader, Beckett advising him to make his delivery "calm, steady, designed to soothe. Bedtime story."[37] The world premiere was an exciting occasion for the hundreds of intrigued academics who had gathered for the Ohio conference. Having created the part, Warrilow went on to play the Reader in English in New York, Edinburgh, and London, and in French in Paris. The play provoked great interest and controversy. When it was brought to the Edinburgh Festival in 1984, B. A. Young of the *Financial Times* confessed that he could make nothing of it at all. Others wrote more enthusiastically, Michael Billington emphasizing "Beckett's ability to combine a potent, Rembrandtesque puritan image with language that is concrete and allusive at the same time."[38]

Warrilow, tall and lean, flamboyantly dressed, favoring the bow tie and the floral waistcoat, visited Beckett whenever he was in Paris and became a regular correspondent. As well as having a great personal liking for the actor, Beckett was impressed by his ability to perform in French as well as in English[39] and came to regard him, with Billie Whitelaw, as one of the leading performers of his work. Warrilow, for his part, felt passionately about Beckett's writing and became a devoted friend, as fond of the man as he was of his plays.

So often Beckett's new friendships evolved out of his work. In 1980, he met Joe Chaikin, the brilliant American actor-director and founder of the Open Theater, who was in Paris with a Manhattan Theatre Club production of *Endgame* at the American Center and was eager to create a one-man show based on *Texts for Nothing* and *How It Is*.[40] Fred Neumann of Mabou Mines was also in Paris with Chaikin, understudying Hamm; he met Beckett for drinks, asking about how he thought the short prose text *From an Abandoned Work* could be staged. Although Beckett did not himself see these actors perform, he had tape recordings of Warrilow and Chaikin and offered them his reactions and his advice[41] and a whole network of friends kept him closely informed about productions of his plays right up to his death.

4

ON MAY 7, 1980, Beckett took the plane to London to direct *Endgame* with Rick Cluchey and the San Quentin Drama Workshop. He was bored with the play and did not want to do it again. But the BBC had turned down a new production of *Eh Joe* with Cluchey and Billie Whitelaw, so Beckett felt even more strongly committed to making *Endgame* work for a disappointed Cluchey. He fell into his old routines, staying in his usual room at the Hyde Park Hotel, walking in the park, telephoning Suzanne regularly, and meeting close friends, including Barbara Bray, who came over and introduced her friend Irene Worth to Beckett, and a fleeting overnight visit to his cousin Sheila Page during the weekend.

This London visit differed from the previous ones. The play, which was to be put on at the Peacock Theatre in Dublin, was being rehearsed at the Riverside Studios in Hammersmith, since Beckett was adamant that he would not return to Dublin. It was too far to walk to rehearsals, so he shared a taxi with the three male members of the cast, Bud Thorpe, Rick Cluchey, and Alan Mandell. Teri Cluchey came over to join the company later from South America. Beckett allowed so many friends and visitors to attend rehearsals that the theater sometimes seemed like a bear-garden:

> Among those who came to watch were Billie Whitelaw, Irene Worth, Nicol Williamson, Alan Schneider, Israel Horovitz, Siobhan O'Casey (Sean's daughter), three writers with Beckett books in progress, two editors who'd published him and one who wanted to, and an impressive collection of madmen and Beckett freaks who had learned of his presence via the grapevine. One lady, in her early twenties, came to ask if Beckett minded that she'd named her dog after him (Beckett: "Don't worry about me. What about the dog?").[42]

The man who wrote this account was a lively American writer, Lawrence Shainberg, author of a book on brain surgery, who was also in London to meet Beckett. It was the first time that they had met, although, the previous year, Beckett had been fascinated to read his book. Now, he questioned Shainberg closely about neurosurgery, "asking, for example, exactly how close I had stood to the brain while observing surgery, or how much pain a craniotomy entailed, or, one day during lunch at rehearsals: 'How is the skull removed?' and 'Where do they put the skull bone while they're working inside?' "[43] Beckett never lost his long-standing curiosity about medical matters. Anything abnormal, unusual, or macabre fascinated him.

On this visit, he was much more open with journalists and photographers than usual, entirely to publicize the San Quentin Drama Workshop. Maeve Binchy of *The Irish Times* came to watch but was asked not to do an actual interview. Polite to a fault, however, Beckett joined her in a break, during which he chatted about the recent changes in Dublin and gave his recollections of the personalities on the old *Irish Times* — Bertie Smyllie, the editor, for instance.[44] But when Binchy's article appeared containing a cameo portrait of Beckett with spiky, Brylcreemed hair and long, narrow fingers, he exploded with anger, shaking the paper and saying, "What does this have to do with it? This is why I don't like to do these things."[45] The article itself was not in the least offensive. Beckett simply regarded it as trite, personal, and irrelevant to what was happening on stage, which was what really mattered.

With friends, he was in a more genial mood, enjoying rehearsing at the Riverside Studios. Lunch was a chat over a glass of draft Guinness and a cheroot smoked at the bar or at a local pub-restaurant. Since Teri had not yet arrived from Puerto Rico to play Nell, Beckett sometimes read in the part himself: "He put his head onto his left shoulder, and sat there and put his hands up as though they were on the edge of the bin, saying: 'Nell is a whisper of life. Just a whisper of life.' "[46] Then he launched into a quaking rendition of Nell's lines that those who were present have never forgotten.

"Conducting" is a more appropriate word for what he was doing as a director. Sitting behind him, the scholar-actress Rosemary Pountney noticed, as the actors spoke their lines, that his left hand was beating out the rhythms like Karajan's.[47] "It was all rhythm and music," said Thorpe, who played Clov. "He said to us, 'Now I am going to fill my silences with sounds.' And added 'For every silence there will be sounds, be they the shuffling of feet, steps, dropping of things, and so on.' "[48] On May 22, he flew back to Paris, exhausted with the strain of meeting so many people, but happy that he had again set the actors on the right musical road.

5

THIS SURFEIT OF THEATER and television did not prevent Beckett from doing what he regarded as more essential work with pen and paper. Ever since October 1979, he had been working on a remarkable new prose piece in French, which became *Mal vu mal dit (Ill Seen Ill Said)*. This meticulously woven tapestry of words is best read as an exquisite prose poem. A narrator recounts the fable of a woman, dressed in black, who lives alone in a cabin in a zone of stones. She is surrounded by an enigmatic group of twelve indistinct figures, a number which recalls the Apostles or the signs of the zodiac, but whose significance is never explained. One of the major events is a regular visit that she makes to a white tombstone. The woman herself may be a ghost, a memory, a fiction, or a mixture of all three.

This text seems as remote as anything could possibly be from Beckett's life. It has often been seen as a wholly imagined construct. Yet even in a book as mysterious as this, there are recognizable elements: Standing stones echoing the cromlechs in the countryside near Foxrock;[49] visits to the tomb by this "old so dying woman," recalling the dedicated care that his mother lavished on his father's grave; familiar objects from Beckett's childhood, such as the buttonhook hanging from a nail; a groove in the flagstone at the woman's front door, like the one worn by Beckett's wheelbarrow in the step of his shed at Ussy.

Notes in a 1977–82 commonplace book show that Beckett was rereading the Book of Job and *King Lear* around this date.[50] Both are evoked when the old woman's eye is described, like Gloucester's, as "vile jelly,"[51] and "the eye of flesh"[52] echoes Job's "Hast thou eyes of flesh, / Or seest thou as man seest?" There are many echoes of Racine and Milton. But, as before, Dante casts his immense shadow over the entire book. The emphasis on the position of the sun, the marble-white rock, the snow-whitened pastures, and the flock of lambs all draw on the *Divina commedia*, which Beckett by now knew almost word for word.[53]

Beckett's knowledge of the Scriptures transforms the everyday and the familiar into something much more evocative. Most obviously, the figure of the woman also recalls either the mother of Christ or Mary Magdalene visiting his tomb. The buttonhook worn through much use is "of silver pisciform," the fish being an early symbol for Christ. It hangs by its hook from a nail, the narrator commenting: "the nail. Unimpaired. All set to serve again. Like unto its glorious ancestors. At the place of the skull. One April afternoon. Deposition done."[54] Golgotha, the place of the skull, seems to extend its domain every year: "Of striking effect in the light of the moon these millions of little sepulchres."[55] The lamb that follows the woman ("reared for slaughter like the others it left them to follow her")[56] picks up another familiar symbolic representation of Christ. But the woman proceeds on her way alone. Such religious allusions or associations create a haunting, desolate world in which mystery and ambiguity are dominant.

Scholars disagree as to whether a biographical dimension is more deeply embedded in this text. "What . . . is the significance," asks Lawrence Graver, "of the fact that the narrator's struggle to express depends on bringing a dead woman back to life, on obsessively charting the last days of her suffering, and reproducing her death?"[57] And is this woman a ghostly shade of Beckett's own mother? Beckett would have been aware of Melanie Klein's theory of artistic creation, according to which the writer is driven by the "desire to rediscover the mother of the early days, whom [he] has lost actually or in [his] feelings."[58] Is his text, then, an attempt to reconstitute, even to repossess and perhaps exorcise the mother figure by seeing and saying—or "ill seeing" and "ill saying," for, in spite of the astonishing succinctness and purity of Beckett's prose, words inevitably betray—the "old so dying woman," her physical being, and her actions? There is, some critics insist, no specific evidence in the text to link the dark lady with the person of mother, let alone *the* mother. Nor, they say, can we be certain that she is a widow, although her dark dress and ritual visits to the tomb suggest bereavement and mourning.[59]

In the final months of his life, Beckett's feelings of love for his mother and remorse at having, as he saw it, let her down so frequently, struck me as still intense, almost volcanic. It was virtually the only "no-go" area in our conversations. Whenever the subject arose, it was clear that it was too painful, even unbearable, for him to discuss. But whether he would and did face such strong emotions and try to come to terms with them when alone with his writing is quite a different matter. There are some indications that this might be happening in *Ill Seen Ill Said*, where the "dark lady" is endowed with a quiet dignity and a nobility that manages to survive imminent disintegration and decay.

To the "trembling fingers" and obsessional concern with the grave already mentioned can be added the feeling that part of the text represents a highly charged attempt to say farewell to a loved one who has been haunting the narrator: "No more tear itself away from the remains of trace. Of what was never. Quick say it suddenly can and farewell say say farewell. If only to the face. Of her tenacious trace."[60] The position is, of course, complicated by the fact that we know that Beckett was at this time imagining *himself* bereaved—even, as he put it to me, going out to visit an imagined tomb. So a fascinating possible conjunction emerges: the author, haunted by the recurring image of his mother, creates this dark female figure who reflects that "ghost" but also expresses his own sense of real and imagined loss—real loss of his mother, imagined loss of his wife. At such depths of the psyche, how can there after all be any real certainty?

As almost always happened with Beckett, the deep feelings that lie at the roots of his work are either depersonalized or displaced onto more neutral ground, in this case, partly on to landscape, where "everywhere stone is gaining."[61] The widely acknowledged power of much of his writing, particularly in the late work, comes from the fact that emotions are strictly contained but never totally abandoned. A phrase from *Footfalls*, "as one frozen by some shudder of the mind,"[62] or another from *Ill Seen Ill Said*, "Silence at the eye of the scream,"[63] illustrate his startling ability to encapsulate emotion and express it memorably. So, as you read late Beckett, you may find yourself suddenly and unaccountably moved to tears.

Beckett sent the original French version of *Mal vu mal dit* to Jérôme Lindon at the beginning of December 1980 and preparations were begun for its publication in May 1981.[64] In the meantime, on December 10, in Paris, he started to translate the text into English, finishing a first forty-four-page draft by January 10. A few days later, he took himself off to Ussy "for a welcome spell to revise and retype *Ill Seen Ill Said*. . . . Never had such difficulty with a translation. Or I forget. I forget."[65]

6

AT THE BEGINNING OF 1981, his seventy-fifth year, Beckett wrote to Jocelyn Herbert: "I dread the year now upon us and all the fuss in store for me here, as if it were my centenary. I'll make myself scarce while it lasts, where I don't know. Perhaps the Great Wall of China, crouch behind it till the coast is clear."[66]

The festivities in the United States represented no real threat to his privacy.

Once the plays were written and he had given advice about them, they were far enough away to require only his customary goodwill telegram and the odd telephone inquiry. He rarely read newspaper reviews now or, if he did, he skimmed through quickly for an overview. But he relished Billie Whitelaw's chatty phone calls and Alan Schneider's lengthy typed letters, bubbling over with detailed information. Even so, he sighed at all the fuss that was being made, writing to me, "If only they'd stop," and repeating his notebook entry: " 'Damned to fame' like in the *Dunciad*."[67]

But "they" would not stop. The huge Festival d'Automne in Paris in October looked an intimidating prospect to someone who felt that "Solitude is paradise."[68] Tom Bishop and Michel Guy put together an impressive program of events, spread over six theaters, consisting of thirteen Beckett works in French and English: plays, adaptations, readings, and discussions.[69] And Bishop assembled twenty-five television and film recordings from all over the world and invited scholars to give academic papers at the Centre Pompidou in Beaubourg.

The thought of hundreds of his friends and well-wishers as well as dozens of performers (most of them known to him) congregating on his doorstep at the same time, as well as the media coverage that would inevitably focus on such an event, was enough to induce nervous hysteria and frighten him into finding a convenient, comfortable, and, above all, distant bolt-hole. "The Autumn Festival celebrations will take place without me," he wrote to Jocelyn Herbert in May.[70] But, courteous to a fault, he wrote to Michel Guy, "If I go away, it is only out of nervousness. I am conscious of the great honour being paid to my work and warmly thank all those who have contributed to it."[71] It is an indication of just how warmly he felt about Billie Whitelaw and Delphine Seyrig that the only contribution he even considered making to the Festival d'Automne was "to refresh Billie or Delphine in *Footfalls* if they are available. . . . Then vanish."[72] In the end, neither actress could participate in the festival. And Beckett certainly vanished, hiding away in the Hôtel les Almohades in sun-drenched though windy Tangier.

During the same year he still took on demanding commitments. He spent the days around his birthday in April in a television studio of Süddeutscher Rundfunk in Stuttgart trying to work out what he had described as a "crazy invention for TV."[73] In fact, *Quadrat I and II* (originally *Quad*) was a startlingly original piece for a septuagenarian to have dreamed up. It harked back some seventeen years to the "J. M. Mime," which he had tried unsuccessfully to write for Jack MacGowran.[74] But this nonverbal piece for four dancers also developed naturally out of Beckett's interest in choreographing movement and from his radical mistrust of language. He spoke to the SDR cameraman, Jim Lewis, about the difficulty that he now had in writing down any words without having the intense feeling that they would inevitably be lies.[75] His fascination with the visual image and his interest in musical structure took over from dramatic writing that depended primarily on language. The image had always been important in Beckett's plays. Now, in his last few pieces for stage and television, it was paramount.

Quad is based on a geometrical figure and on permutations of regular movements. First one, then two, then three, then four figures—dancers or mime artists—dressed in white, yellow, blue, and red djellabas appear one after another to scurry along the sides and across the diagonals of a square, shuffling in strict rhythm to a rapid percussion beat. The figures then depart one by one in the order in which they appeared, leaving another to recommence the sequence. Each of them traces out half of the quadrangle, moving first along the side, then across the diagonal. Strikingly, all of them avoid the center, which is clearly visible in the middle of the square. In Beckett's typescript, the center of the quadrangle is "supposed a danger zone."[76] As the figures hurtle toward one another, they look as if a collision must be inevitable. But by making a sudden, consistent deviation to the left as they approach the center, they skirt this "danger zone" and avoid colliding.

Comic at first, their mobility comes to seem almost manic because of the speed and repetitiveness of the movements. Whether the piece reminds the viewer of busy traffic on the place de la Concorde, rodents in a maze, human beings scurrying frenziedly about their business, or prisoners exercising desperately in a courtyard, there is something eminently Dantesque about its imagery, with the figures resembling Gustave Doré's engravings of Dante and Virgil in Hell.[77] The "dancers" always turn to the left. In a letter to his Polish translator, about *Company*, Beckett explained that "Dante and Virgil in Hell always go to the left (the damned direction), and in Purgatory always to the right."[78]

Dr. Müller-Freienfels jumped at the chance of presenting this bold piece of television. Beckett visited Stuttgart for five days in April for discussions and preliminary rehearsals of a piece he saw as "bristling with problems."[79] The initial work did not go well and, on his return to Paris, he suggested calling the whole thing off. "The few days in Stuttgart were not very satisfactory," he wrote to a friend. "I'm quite lost in TV technicalities and shall never write again for that medium"[80]—another promise to himself which he went on to break within a few months. But after a "kind and irresistible" letter from Dr. Müller-Freienfels,[81] Beckett returned as originally planned on May 31 for a twelve-day stint supervising the production.

After numerous practical trials in the SDR studio, Beckett made several important changes to his original script, some forced upon him, others adopted voluntarily. Differentiating color was restricted to the costumes rather than to the lighting. The movements were faster than he had at first imagined. One instruction that was successfully preserved was that each player had a distinctive percussion sound which began when he or she—for the mime artists were two men and two women—came in and started the series of movements. They wore headphones under their hoods so that they could hear the percussion beats, for any error in their steps would destroy the rhythmic timing and require a further reshoot.[82]

But the most important change came when Müller-Freienfels took Beckett back home for dinner after the completion of the shooting and told him how impressive the piece looked in black-and-white on the monochrome monitor in the production box. A friend then proposed that they show the color version first, then the black-and-white version. Beckett was fascinated by this idea and asked if they might record another version the next day at a slower speed and in black-and-white. The fast percussion beats were also removed, so the only sounds that were heard were the slower, shuffling steps of the weary figures and, almost inaudible, the tick of a metronome. Beckett was delighted when he saw this stunning effect, commenting that the second version (or *Quadrat II*, as he called it) took place "ten thousand years later."[83]

7

BACK IN PARIS for the summer, after meeting his German publisher, Dr. Siegfried Unseld, for coffee in the PLM hotel on Sunday morning, August 9, 1981,[84] Beckett returned to his desk to write three brief paragraphs of a new piece of prose in English. After starting with his 1960s concern with imagining "a body" and "a place" where there was neither, he wrote: "All before. Nothing else ever. Ever tried. Ever failed. No matter. Try again. Fail again. Fail better."[85] The will to "fail better" provided this text with its initial impetus. And, in order to fail better, the strategy Beckett adopted was to strive for the worst.

He took his cue from Edgar's speech in *King Lear*. He copied out quotations from three different points in the speech into his little commonplace book: "The lamentable change is from the best, / The worst returns to laughter"; "Who is't can say, I am at the worst"; and "The worst is not so long as one can say, This is the worst."[86] For some time, when he alluded to his new text in letters, he entitled it "Better worse." Later on, he called the book *Worstward Ho*, playing on the title of Webster and Dekker's play *Westward Hoe* (1607) and Charles Kingsley's better known novel *Westward Ho!* (1855). At one level, the text, like *Ill Seen Ill Said*, is concerned with the failure of language: when anything is said, it must inevitably be missaid. So language is deliberately pared down, reduced to a few lexical items assembled in a variety of combinations, so that it reaches out toward an "unworsenable worse." It is part of the strategy to be rid of Romantic accretions. So images evoking human memories or literary allusions are excised. That at least is how it first appears.

Yet certain things happen that are not in the least accidental. The words in *Worstward Ho* resurrect themselves, particularly powerfully when read aloud. They do this in a variety of ways. The most obvious of these is how words or new combinations of words are coined around the notion of "worse" and "worst": "unworsenable," "unmoreable," "unlessenable," "evermost," "meremost," "dimmost," "unleastening," "unnullable least." Nouns are used as verbs, verbs as nouns, adverbs as adjectives. More startling is the capacity of a reduced skeletal language of "worsening words" to sing a litany of what we might in our turn coin as "last-ditchness." A word like "preying" has multiple associations of sound; "throw up" means both "give up" and "vomit"; "secretes" means "oozes" and "hides away"; "still" is used in several senses. But, even more significantly, the remaining words combine alliteratively to chisel a hard, spare, yet still moving poetic prose: "Where in the narrow vast? Say only vasts apart. In that narrow void vasts of void apart." [87] Or again Beckett, the lover of word games, crossword puzzles, rude limericks, and tongue twisters, makes alliteration test the most agile of tongues: "thenceless thitherless there" [88] and, better (or worse) still, "To last unlessenable least how loath to leasten." [89]

That Beckett's highly ambivalent attitude toward words had not left him is clear enough from the following passage, where his love of even impoverished, inadequate words comes through: "No mind and words? Even such words. So enough still. Just enough still to joy. Joy! Just enough still to joy that only they. Only!" [90] The literary critic Enoch Brater writes: "That quality of being less has now degenerated into that quality of being worse. And yet there is still no occasion to despair. Quite the contrary: the language is almost heroic in its mad determination to go on. The void cannot be conquered, but it can still be described, especially when part of the description is the writer's inability to describe it." [91]

Where the seeing and the saying are almost impossibly difficult, images still manage to burn their way searingly through: "Clenched eyes. Staring eyes. Clenched staring eyes"; "Head sunk on crippled hands"; "There in the sunken head the sunken head." Even the apparent literary and culturally barren waste-land proves to be a myth. "Time to lose. Gain time to lose. As the soul once. The world once" [92] is a vestigial trace of the biblical "What shall it profit a man, if he gain the whole world, and lose his soul," [93] just as the word "pox," as in "a pox on bad," and the phrase "a watch of night at last to come" still recall Shakespeare.

Actual biographical traces are rare in such dire straits of the mind. Yet, however dimly perceived or imagined, a startling image is created that Beckett admitted to me was one of the most "obsessional" (his word) of his childhood memories: that of an old man walking hand in hand with a child. We come closer here to human feeling than at any other point in the book, as Beckett introduces yet another key obsession with the "holding hand":

> Hand in hand with equal plod they go. In the free hands — no. Free empty hands. Backs turned both bowed with equal plod they go. The child hand raised to reach the holding hand. Hold the old holding hand. Hold and be held. Plod on and never recede. Slowly with never a pause plod on and never recede. Backs turned. Both bowed. Joined by held holding hands. Plod on as one. One shade. Another shade. [94]

Although more autonomous than this image of enduring inseparability, the description of the third figure to survive the "worsening," the old woman, has a similar resonance: "Nothing and yet a woman. Old and yet old. On unseen knees. Stooped as loving memory some old gravestones stoop. In that old grave-yard. Names gone and when to when. Stoop mute over the graves of none." [95] However distant from real-life people these almost unrecognizable, insubstantial figures may be, the emotional power of the scenes in which they appear stems partly from their continued capacity to relate backward to the "shades" of Beckett's past life and — inevitably if we have lost loved ones — our own lives, as well as to project forward, in the case of the second scene, into a future when even the names on our tombstones will have been effaced. We are light-years away from simple autobiographical connections. Yet the reality of these emotional traces, as well as the sheer courage of such a bold encounter with language, infinity, and the void, prevent the text from being arid and utterly inhuman. The imagination, however ruined, is still alive. In spite of its almost manic use of wordplay, the text is far too tortured and tormented to be judged a mere linguistic exercise. And there *is* a human subtext after all, in spite of the narrator's tactics of reducing, shedding, and omitting as he strives to "worsen."[96]

Beckett took seven months to write even the first draft of *Worstward Ho*. At times during the winter of 1981–82, it sickened him. "Struggling with impossible prose. English. With loathing," he wrote to Alan Schneider in February.[97] Yet he was driven on by the compulsion to express that had always seemed more important than anything else in his life. The text that was published a year later in England and the United States is difficult and uncompromising. Yet it justifies perseverance and, with *Ill Seen Ill Said*, may come to be judged as one of his greatest works.

8

EARLY IN 1982, Beckett was busy translating his three latest short plays. *Rockaby* and *Ohio Impromptu* went into French relatively easily. But A *Piece of Monologue* presented what Beckett described as "insoluble problems," and was eventually "reduced to a free version, shorter, entitled *Solo*."[98] The main problem centered on the word "birth," described by the speaker in the English original by the position and movements of tongue and lips. No similar word is vocalized in this way in French. So Beckett omitted whole passages from the French version, which he called an "adaptation" rather than a translation. Even so, it was finished by the end of February and delivered to Les Editions de Minuit by March 2.[99]

While struggling with this intractable translation, he was also writing a new play in French. *Catastrophe* was dedicated to the Czech dissident writer Václav Havel, the spokesman of Charter 77 and cofounder of VONS, the acronym of the Czech Committee for the Defense of the Unjustly Persecuted. Havel, who had been under house arrest, was finally imprisoned for four and a half years for subversion at a trial with other Chartists in October 1979. That same year, Amnesty International adopted the jailed dissidents in Czechoslovakia as prisoners of conscience.

It has sometimes been suggested that Beckett's dedication of the play to Václav Havel was coincidental or an afterthought. But he was expressly invited to write such a piece by the AIDA (the French acronym of the International Association for the Defense of Artists). The writers approached (including Arthur

Miller, André Benedetto, Victor Haim, and Elie Wiesel) knew in advance that their work would be played at the Avignon Festival in July as part of "Une Nuit pour Václav Havel" ("A Night for Václav Havel"), by which collective support was to be demonstrated for the imprisoned playwright.[100] Beckett certainly considered this a "group gesture."[101]

He took an avid interest in what was happening to intellectuals, writers, and artists in Eastern Europe. His concern was aroused by press reports of arrests and imprisonments. His help took, we have seen, several different forms: contributions to Amnesty International and support for the "Index on Censorship"; signing the Declaration against Martial Law in Poland; donating his Polish royalties to the families of imprisoned writers. But his sympathy focused particularly on individuals. His help to Antoni Libera, his Polish translator, extended beyond food parcels. In June 1982, Beckett wrote to Stan Gontarski and talked with me about helping Libera to get out of Poland altogether: "If you can set something in motion my name and full support are at yr. disposal," he wrote.[102] (Money, I was told, was no problem.) We took steps to make this possible, although Libera finally decided not to leave his native country.

Beckett was appalled to learn that, as part of the punishment for his courageous stand against abuses of human rights, Václav Havel had been forbidden to write. This seemed the ultimate oppression. Standing on a ledge outside Beckett's study window was a small sculpture—a gift from the Russian sculptor Vadim Sidur[103]—as a permanent reminder of the struggle for artistic freedom in a totalitarian regime.

Beckett sometimes expressed regret that, because of his essentially nondidactic approach to writing, he was unable (and had certainly been unwilling) to write anything that dealt overtly with politics.[104] Now he had the opportunity to write a play that would demonstrate his solidarity with a victimized, imprisoned fellow writer but could express his own themes and be written in his own manner. He wasted no time. He was asked for a contribution early in the year and, although the first manuscript carries no date, the second is dated "20 February 1982."[105]

A Protagonist stands on a podium, while, with the help of a female Assistant, a Director prepares him for a theatrical spectacle, which appears to consist of nothing more or less than the figure's own physical appearance. He is treated like an object or an anatomical specimen, not a human being. His body is gradually exposed and molded into a pose, as if made out of modeling clay. His own will is totally disregarded and he is treated from the outset as a victim to be reduced and humiliated. The assumption is that he has no feelings. Each successive uncovering and reifying gesture increases the horror that this play-within-a-play provokes.

But the end is startling. The figure has been inspected, adjusted, and modified to the will of the Director, whose final act is to get the unseen lighting engineer to light his head for the conclusion or "catastrophe."[106] At the Assistant's suggestion that the Protagonist might conceivably "raise his head . . . an instant . . . show his face . . . just an instant," the Director sneers: "For God's sake! What next? Raise his head? Where do you think we are? In Patagonia? Raise his head! For God's sake! . . . Good. There's our catastrophe. In the bag."[107] Yet, as the light focuses on the head of the Protagonist alone, in a powerful, dramatic moment, the trembling figure does just that, stilling the recorded "storm of applause" with his look, as he raises his head in a gesture of defiance and independent will. The Director's reifying of the Protagonist can be seen as an attempt to reduce a living human being to the status of icon of impotent suffering.[108] But, at the end of the play, the Protagonist resists this status, as, refusing total domination, he reasserts his humanity and his individuality in a single, vestigial, yet compelling movement.

There have been disagreements as to how exclusively political this play is. The Protagonist has been identified with the beleaguered artist whose privacy is being progressively invaded as he is subjected to increased public exposure. The play has also been related to Beckett's own horror at self-exposure, and linked to the essentially exhibitionistic nature of theater. It has been seen as demonstrating the impossibility for an artist to shape his work in such a way that it reveals what he intends it to reveal; art in the end escapes him. And it has been suggested that the theatrical metaphor carries far less political import than the dedication to Havel might suggest. But while accepting the play's richly suggestive, multi-layered nature, we must also take seriously its political reverberations.

On or just below the surface prowl so many haunting, horrifying memories. The Protagonist, dressed in old gray pajamas and reduced to an anatomical exhibit, a victim of the Director's wish to "whiten" the flesh to that of a corpse, recalls images of the concentration camp or Holocaust victim. Beckett deliberately uses anatomical words: "cranium," "sinciput," "tibia."[109] The theatrical metaphor may dull, distance, or domesticate the horror, but it never completely abandons it, even though the hands of the Protagonist may be "claw-like" through "fibrous degeneration," a natural disease rather than from starvation or ill-treatment. (In French, Beckett borrowed his own condition, Dupuytren's contracture, from an earlier, abandoned *Ohio Impromptu* draft, doubtless feeling that he could use it here because it was sufficiently depersonalized.) "In my mind," he wrote to me, "was Dupuytren's contracture (from which I suffer) which reduces hands to claws."[110]

While the play is no simple, straightforward political parable, its final political message is unambiguously presented in the image of the Protagonist's raising of his head. Beckett told me that in referring to what one might describe as the "grand finale," a reviewer had claimed that it was "ambiguous." "There's no ambiguity there at all," he said angrily. "He's saying: You bastards, you haven't finished me yet!"[111]

The play can be interpreted at both a political and a metaphysical level; a program note for the Haymarket, Leicester, production, for example, suggests that "it can be seen as either examining the suppression of the individual by a totalitarian state or as an attempt by the devil to strip man of his own soul." At both levels the attempt conspicuously fails. The human spirit asserts itself, in spite of everything. It is often forgotten that Beckett's work is as much about persisting and continuing as it is about ending.

Catastrophe was presented in Avignon on July 20, 1982. Beckett saw a brief extract from the production on television and was horrified to see the Protagonist bound from his shoulders down to his knees. "It was literally massacred at Avignon by all accounts," he wrote.[112] He was all the more concerned therefore that, when it was directed in America by Alan Schneider and, later, in Paris by Pierre Chabert, it should be done as he wanted it. Yet the mere presence of Beckett's play in Avignon had a profound impact on the man to whom it was dedicated. In 1983, Beckett was deeply moved to receive a letter from Václav Havel after his release from prison in which he spoke of his first contact with Beckett's work: "During the dark fifties when I was 16 or 18 of age, in a country where there were virtually no cultural or other contacts with the outside world, luckily I had the opportunity to read *Waiting for Godot*. . . . I have been immensely influenced by you as a human being, and in a way as a writer, too." He went on to describe the emotion he felt on hearing of *Catastrophe*:

> I mention all this to make clearer to you the shock I experienced during my time in prison when on the occasion of one of her one-hour visits allowed four times a year, my wife told me in the presence of an obtuse warder that at Avignon there took place a night of solidarity with me, and that you took the opportunity to write and to make public for the first time, your play *Catastrophe*. For a long time afterwards there accompanied me in the prison a great joy and emotion and helped to live on amidst all the dirt and baseness . . . you are not one of those who give themselves away in small change — so that your participation in the Avignon event is even more valuable.
>
> Thank you very much indeed. You not only helped me in a beautiful way during my prison days, but by doing what you did you demonstrated your deep understanding for the meaning of affliction which those who are not indifferent to the run of things have to take upon themselves occasionally, at the present time just as well as they had to do it in the past.[113]

After his release from prison, Havel wrote a play in response, which he dedicated in his turn to Beckett. It was called *The Mistake*. "The two plays together added to each other and were supportive of each other," Havel told the American civil libertarian Martin Garbus, adding modestly, "I hope by saying that, I am not suggesting that I am equal as a playwright to Samuel Beckett."[114]

9

IN APRIL 1982, Beckett wrote to Dr. Müller-Freienfels at the Süddeutscher Rundfunk television studio in Stuttgart that two German filmmakers Alfred

Behrens and Michael Kuball wanted to make a film of *Murphy*. Müller-Freienfels was unenthusiastic about this idea, but repeated his hope that Beckett might soon write something else new for them. Beckett replied: "I often think of you all and wish I could look forward to being with you again. But I fear there is not much invention left in me, crazy or otherwise. Though I keep trying." [115]

Suzanne was ill at this time and they were unable to go away as they had planned to the Valle d'Aosta. (It was the middle of August before they could escape to the Hotel Moderno in Courmayeur, where Beckett spent much of his time reading Kafka and kept up his Italian by reading *La Stampa*. [116]) Nor could Beckett leave Suzanne alone to go to Ussy, where burglars had again tried to break into his cottage, this time unsuccessfully: "merely smashed glass," he wrote. [117] So he was stuck in Paris thinking about Müller-Freienfels's invitation. Invention soon returned in the shape of another haunting nonverbal piece that he first called the *Nachtstück*, [118] then *Nacht und Träume*.

In *Nacht und Träume* a figure called the "dreamer" is sitting, "head bowed, grey hair, hands resting on table." A male voice first hums, then, when the evening light fades, sings the last few bars of Schubert's beautiful late lied "Nacht und Träume," which sets to music a slightly modified text by the Austrian poet Heinrich Josef von Collin. "Kehre wieder, heil'ge Nacht / Holde Träume, kehret wieder," sings the voice ("Return, holy night / Return, O you sweet dreams"). The head of the dreamer falls to rest on his hands and, as he sleeps, he dreams of his "dreamt self." An image in the top righthand corner of the screen is of the same figure at a table in the same posture. From outside the small circle of "kinder light" appears a disembodied left hand, which rests gently on his head. As the hand is withdrawn, B (the "dreamt self") slowly raises his head and a right hand emerges offering a chalice, which it brings to B's lips, then a cloth with which it wipes his brow. The figure raises his head further to gaze up at the invisible face, then raises his own right hand to meet the one coming from outside the circle. B then rests his own left hand on the joined hands and together they sink to the table, B's head then resting on them. Finally, the disembodied left hand rests gently on B's head. After a return to the original image of the dreamer and a repeat of the Schubert lied, the dream returns to follow the same sequence but in close-up and slower motion, until, finally, both dream and dreamer fade out.

If the Schubert lied, a favorite of Beckett, was a main source of inspiration, painting provided him with his imagery. Directed by the author, the dark, empty room, with its rectangle of light and its black-coated figure hunched over the table, resembled a schematized seventeenth-century Dutch painting even more explicitly than does *Ohio Impromptu*.

In religious paintings, a vision often appears in a top corner of the canvas —normally the Virgin Mary, Christ ascended in his glory, or a ministering angel. The chalice, cloth, and comforting hand are, similarly, images commonly found in religious paintings. Beckett's cameraman, Jim Lewis, said that "at the moment when the drops of perspiration are wiped from the brow of the character, Beckett simply said that the cloth alluded to the veil that Veronica used to wipe the brow of Jesus on the Way of the Cross. The imprint of Christ's face remains on the cloth."[119]

"What a help that would be in the dark! To close the eyes and see that hand!" the narrator had said in *Company*. The "helping hand" is an image of consolation. Hands in painting had always fascinated Beckett. As a young man, he had a reproduction of Dürer's wonderful etching of praying hands hanging on the wall of his room at Cooldrinagh.[120] Beckett insisted to Dr. Müller-Freienfels that "the sex of the hands must remain uncertain. One of our numerous teasers."[121] To me, he said that these "sexless hands" "might perhaps be a boy's hands." But in the end he concluded: "I think no choice but female for the helping hands. Large but female. As more conceivably male than male conceivably female."[122]

After a brief visit for preliminary discussions at the end of September, Beckett returned to Stuttgart on October 24 to rehearse and record. The piece was performed by a mime artist, Helfrid Foron, who had been in *Quad*, for Beckett decided that the part simply did not "need an actor of [Klaus] Herm's importance for a part that requires no acting, but simply a minimum of controlled movement such as a trained mime seems best qualified to provide."[123]

The play could have been sentimental, even maudlin. The mysterious quality of the action, the beauty of the singing of Schubert's lied, and the specificity of the repeated, almost ritualistic patterns avoid this. What on the printed page seems a very slight piece acquires on the screen a strange, haunting beauty. It evokes, more clearly perhaps than any other of Beckett's plays, that "purity of the spirit" that had long been important in his life as well as in his work. When it was eventually broadcast at the beginning of June 1983, it attracted an audience of two million viewers.[124]

26

Winter Journey

1983–89

1

ON DECEMBER 21, 1982, Beckett took himself off into the Marne mists and the silence of Ussy to spend Christmas and the New Year alone. He ached to start writing again. But, in his letters, he could speak only of feeling "such inertia and void as never before. I remember an entry in Kafka's diary. 'Gardening. No hope for the future.' At least he could garden. There must be words for it. I don't expect ever to find them."[1] He had lived so long with the constant fear that inspiration would at last completely dry up. Now it seemed to have happened.

His frustration was not made any more bearable by the persistence of his belief that old age ought to be a time when it would be simpler to pin down "being." He wrote to George Tabori the Hungarian-born director, "The long crooked straight is laborious but not without excitement. While still 'young' I began to seek consolation in the thought that then if ever, i. e. now, the true words at last, from the mind in ruins. To this illusion I continue to cling."[2] But it began to seem as if he were clinging to a piece of flotsam that was finally breaking apart in the waves. In May 1983, he wrote that it "[is] a very barren patch for me. The wall won't recede and I have no reverse gears. Can't turn either."[3]

He did not exaggerate. The little that he contrived to write seemed to take him forever and left him dissatisfied and unfulfilled. His efforts to translate *Worstward Ho* into French soon ground to a halt. How, he asked me, do you translate even the first words of the book: "On. Say on" without losing its force?[4] Although his friend Edith Fournier had discussed the book with him and he had chosen her title, *Cap au pire*, from among several that she suggested, it was not until after his death that she translated the book.

In the summer of the previous year, he had been invited to write a new stage play for the 1983 Steirischer Herbst or Autumn Festival in Graz in Austria. He tried unsuccessfully for months but threw everything into the wastepaper basket until February and March 1983, when a sudden breakthrough occurred. He managed to write in French a short, enigmatic, yet strangely compelling piece, which he entitled *Quoi où* (*What Where*). Music (and the biography of a musician) again supplied him with a crucial part of his inspiration.

Beckett adored Franz Schubert's song cycle *Winterreise*, or *Winter Journey*, based on twenty-four melancholic poems by Schubert's contemporary Wilhelm

Müller. He used to listen spellbound to Dietrich Fischer-Dieskau's stunning recording of the songs, marveling at Gerald Moore's sensitive accompaniment. He listened first alone or with Suzanne, later with the Arikhas. He also knew about Schubert's connections with the town of Graz.[5] What, then, could be more appropriate than to link his own contribution for the Graz festival to this song cycle, partly written there?

In the Schubert lieder, the traveler in the opening poem, "Gute Nacht" ("Good Night") has lost his love and journeys disconsolately on from May into snowy winter. In the spine-chilling "Der Wegweiser" ("The Signpost") the signpost points to "one road that I must follow / From which no one e'er returned." The cycle of the seasons provided Beckett with the formal structure of his play, moving from spring to the final "It is winter. / Without journey,"[6] suggesting death but also alluding quite explicitly to Schubert's title, *Winterreise*.

A closely related source of inspiration for *What Where* links two poems with Beckett's own life. In his production notes for a later television version of the play, Beckett wrote "For PA [playing area] the light of other days."[7] And he admitted that he expressly associated this play with Thomas Moore's poignant poem, "The Light of Other Days" which includes the lines "Sad Memory brings the light / Of other days around me." The second stanza is particularly relevant to Beckett's somber mood when he wrote *What Where*.

> When I remember all
>   The friends, so linked together,
> I've seen around me fall,
>   Like leaves in wintry weather;
> I feel like one
> Who treads alone
> Some banquet-hall deserted,
>   Whose lights are fled,
>   Whose garlands dead,
> And all but he departed!
> Thus, in the stilly night,
>   Ere slumber's chain has bound me
> Sad Memory brings the light
> Of other days around me.[8]

Beckett often spoke of feeling like "one / Who treads alone / Some banquet hall deserted," with so many of his friends and relatives recently "departed": Tom MacGreevy; Con Leventhal; Geoffrey Thompson; Geer and Bram van Velde; his cousin, Jack "Velvet Bunny" Roe; and, only three months before he wrote this play, an old friend from Trinity College, the classical scholar Stuart Maguinness.[9] In a letter to Mary Manning at the beginning of 1984, he wrote: "Even for space gazing no zest left. It's Holy Ghost I'll be soon. No less than all the dear departed. Without their advantages."[10] In *What Where*, the Voice of Bam, which, Beckett commented, could be thought of as coming from "beyond the grave," summons up the shades of four figures, dressed, in the stage version at least, in identical long gray gowns, to give evidence. The play begins with "We are the last five. / In the present as were we still." But it ends with the Voice of Bam alone again in the winter of life saying: "I am alone. / In the present as were I still."[11]

With his play Beckett also associated "Voyelles," a sonnet of Arthur Rimbaud that Joyce used to recite by heart in French and that Beckett knew well. In the notebook that he prepared for the Stuttgart television version, he considered using colors for the robes of the different figures: "As alike as possible. Differentiated by colour."[12] The figures in the play are Bam, Bem, Bim, and Bom, and they are distinguished by Rimbaud's

> Black A, white E, red I, green U, blue O — vowels
> Some day I will open your silent pregnancies.[13]

There would, however, be "no green," affirmed Beckett.[14] If there had been, the name of the first missing shade — if that person is not already the "Voice of Bam" — would have been "Bum," a joke centered on an absence that would have amused Beckett.

What is more surprising than these characteristically evocative links with literature and music is that, once the figures have been summoned up (from the dead?), each of them is subjected in turn to a puzzling sequence of persistent, brusque questions. The following extract gives the feel of the repetitious, staccato dialogue:

> BAM: He didn't say anything?
> BOM: No.
> BAM: You gave him the works?
> BOM: Yes.
> BOM: And he didn't say anything?
> BOM: No.
> BAM: He wept?
> BOM: Yes.
> BAM: Screamed?
> BOM: Yes.
> BAM: Begged for mercy?
> BOM: Yes.
> BAM: But didn't say anything?
> BOM: No.[15]

On Bam's orders, Bom is then taken away by Bim to make him confess that the first to be interrogated, who is not named, has indeed confessed that he "said it to him." The process is then repeated with Bim and Bem, the item of missing information becoming "where" rather than "what."[16]

Reviewers in both the United States and Britain tended to concentrate almost exclusively on the play's possible political resonance.[17] Alan Schneider, commenting on this, wrote to Beckett: "What Where most people keep wanting to interpret on the literal political level — I think it may suffer from coming after

Catastrophe."[18] It was certainly appreciated less than the other recent plays. "For once Beckett's constant themes of mortality and time and his more recent preoccupation with political brutality don't find an image of matching resonance," wrote Michael Billington in *The Guardian*, once the production had been imported to British soil.[19] Beckett himself was dissatisfied with it almost from the outset[20] and set about rethinking it completely when the opportunity arose to film it for German television.

The enigma at the heart of *What Where* is never resolved. Indeed, Alan Schneider may well be right that its hidden theme is that of "the impossibility of understanding human existence."[21] So, if someone is responsible for an unnamed crime, that crime appears likely to be Calderón's "original sin of being born," which Beckett had evoked at the beginning of his career in his essay, *Proust*. Consequently, the overall perpetrator is unlikely ever to be known, let alone apprehended. Bam's closing words, "Time passes. / That is all. / Make sense who may. / I switch off"[22] echo, then, more widely than within the play itself. Aptly, these words turned out to be the last four lines that Beckett ever wrote for the stage.

2

HIS FAILURE TO WRITE anything substantial was a constant source of frustration and annoyance to him. But at least it gave him time to focus intently on some of the productions of his plays. The main excitement revolved around three of his new plays, two of which, *Catastrophe* and *What Where*, were being staged by Alan Schneider in New York for the first time in English, together with a reprise of *Ohio Impromptu*. *What Where* was put on at extremely short notice.[23] Although a continent away, Beckett was consulted about some of the most intricate production details.[24] He met Schneider as usual first in Paris, then, after the director had returned to New York, started telephoning him for reports on how rehearsals were going. He had hardly ever done this before. Once the plays were under way in the sweltering heat of a New York summer at the Harold Clurman Theater on Theater Row on West Forty-second Street, he followed the saga of cast changes necessitated by David Warrilow's absence through illness.[25]

When the three plays opened on June 15, 1983, the American reviews were glowing. "Samuel Beckett's new plays tantalize the mind as well as the eye. . . . We are transfixed by the intensity of the artistic vision" (Mel Gussow in *The New York Times*); "[the plays are] implosions of theatrical genius! These productions, directed by Alan Schneider, are definitive for our time. You have to accept a gift of genius!" (Clive Barnes); and "the greatest living playwright continues to redefine drama" (Alisa Solomon in *The Village Voice*). It had been a long time since headlines such as "The Left Bank Can Keep It" or "And It's Only Fit for the Dustbin" were more normal. The odd carping critic was now the odd one out. Times had indeed changed.

More flattering still, in February 1984, the Writers and Directors Theater, next door to the Harold Clurman, was renamed the Samuel Beckett Theatre. Billie Whitelaw was chosen to inaugurate the theater with *Footfalls* and *Rockaby*. To contrast with these two character parts, she read *Enough* first out of costume, as herself. Schneider wrote to Beckett shortly afterward:

> The main thing is that Billie was just splendid, like a piece of exquisite music, and the evening is a total triumph for her—and you. . . . The combination of *Footfalls* and *Rockaby* really works, building to a tremendous intensity, not a squeak in the audience throughout. And I must confess that they seem to enjoy the contrast with her reading of *Enough*, which she is doing very simply.[26]

It was "exquisite music" to Beckett's ears to learn of the triumph of a favorite actress. At the beginning of March, he was surprised, as well as flattered, to learn from Schneider that

> the *Rockaby* evening is the most sought-after theatre event of the season. All hell is breaking loose. We are selling out at the Samuel Beckett Theatre (!), turning away hundreds on weekends. We are the talk of the town, and Billie has been absolutely besieged by newspaper and TV people; she has had hardly a moment to herself. . . . [She] has found depths and intensity—in that tiny theatre—which leave an unforgettable image.[27]

Sandwiched between these two productions a season of Beckett plays was directed by Pierre Chabert at Jean-Louis Barrault's and Madeleine Renaud's new theater in Paris, the Théâtre du Rond-Point. Beckett was keen for Delphine Seyrig to inaugurate *Rockaby* in French. He had been very disappointed with Madeleine Renaud's *Pas moi (Not I)* and felt that, as with the earlier play, the new work needed a younger woman to play it.

His decision created considerable ill-will with Madeleine's husband: "The Barrault indignant that *Berceuse [Rockaby]* not for Madeleine," wrote Beckett.[28] He loathed situations like this. Yet he was unwilling to compromise on what he thought best for his work. When he and Chabert discovered that Delphine Seyrig was otherwise committed, it was Catherine Sellers, not Madeleine Renaud, who was contacted and offered the role. After watching Sellers in a dress rehearsal, Beckett pronounced her "excellente."[29]

Beckett met Pierre Chabert several times to talk over the complications with Barrault and offer his advice at some late rehearsals. Michael Lonsdale, famous by now for his Hollywood films as well as his stage appearances, played the Reader in *L'Impromptu d'Ohio (Ohio Impromptu)* and the Director in *Catastrophe* in the September 1983 production at the Rond-Point. The triple bill included this time *Berceuse*, not *Quoi où (What Where)*. And, to the astonishment of French reviewers, the legendary Barrault played the two totally silent parts, Listener in the *Impromptu* and the Protagonist in *Catastrophe*. Although he was praised for a beautifully expressive mime in the latter, he was not happy in these roles. And, sadly, he seems never to have forgiven Beckett for, in his eyes, deserting Madeleine Renaud. Equally sadly, Beckett does not appear to have made much of an effort to repair the rift.

3

IN THESE PRODUCTIONS, Beckett listened, advised, worried, placated, and reassured when things were going badly. But he had no personal responsibility for them. In the San Quentin Drama Workshop's 1984 *Waiting for Godot,* on the other hand, he was a key player. He had enjoyed working with the group in the past but, feeling too old now, low in spirits, and weary of directing, he was desperately eager not to be involved.[30] Cluchey made it clear, however, that their funding, which came from an Australian arts festival, entirely depended on his active participation.[31] And Beckett simply could not refuse Rick,[32] whom he worried about now even more than before. The Workshop was dispersed to the four corners of the globe and Cluchey was out of work in Chicago. "Rick at the old loose end again and wondering how he'll make it," wrote Beckett with concern to Alan Mandell in March 1983. Letters to Cluchey during the year included several generous checks for the Cluchey children.[33] But, aware of how much hinged on this production for the Adelaide Festival, Beckett agreed to "survey" or "oversee" it, if it were to be directed by Walter Asmus. Asmus started rehearsing in Chicago, then was helped by Beckett at the Riverside Studios in London.

Beckett came to London on February 19, 1984, to start work the very next morning,[34] insisting on paying his own flight expenses and hotel bill rather than feel indebted to the Australian producers.[35] He had already agreed with Rick Cluchey that "[his] royalties [should go] to your gallant company as always."[36] His preparations for the forthcoming production had none of his old, obsessive meticulousness and concentration.[37] Mentally and physically, he simply did not feel up to the task.[38] Since the actors had been rehearsing for several weeks already and were accustomed to acting a certain way, he was reluctant at first to interfere, anxious to upset neither the cast nor his director friend. He thought of flying back immediately to Paris, giving Suzanne's health as his excuse. After I assured him, at the actor's request, that they wanted nothing more than for him to help, difficulties were smoothed over and, in the next ten days, he managed to shape the production in the direction he wanted.

At the point at which he had to leave — a little earlier than was originally intended because of his own fatigue and a scare (whether true or exaggerated) about Suzanne — the production had developed a quiet, melancholic beauty; "a moonlight production" he called it. Humor was there but it was subdued. Again Beckett worked musically. But it was a warm, human production as well. Vladimir and Estragon held hands touchingly as they stood together by the tree, silhouetted sharply against the sky, seeking comfort from each other for their long vigil. Whenever he spoke about it, Beckett insisted that the production was directed by Walter Asmus, only "in collaboration with the author." [39] But he seemed fairly happy with the end result, writing "I agree that the production, generally speaking, is now very presentable." [40]

He returned to Paris with some treasured moments. Lucky, for example, was to be played for some performances by a small, bald-headed actor named J. Pat Miller. While the others were going through their paces, Miller used to sit on the floor silent and distant in a corner of the studio, his feet drawn up underneath him and his arms clasped around his knees, in fetal posture. When his turn came to launch himself into Lucky's long monologue, it was astounding. He built the speech into so overwhelming and searing a performance that Beckett, hearing him for the first time, sat totally transfixed, tears welling up in his eyes. [41] After the rehearsal, he told Miller that he was the best Lucky he had ever seen. He was glad that he had praised him so fulsomely for, a few months later, he heard that J. Pat Miller had died of AIDS.

4

IN THE LAST FEW YEARS of his life, Beckett gained something of a reputation for objecting to productions of his play that deviated radically, at least as he and his friends saw it, from what he had written. He was often represented as a tyrannical figure, an arch-controller of his work, ready to unleash fiery thunderbolts onto the head of any bold, innovative director unwilling to follow his text and stage directions to the last counted dot and precisely timed pause. This reputation resulted from almost saturation coverage in the international press of two or three cases. Yet the truth of his position was more complex and certainly far more interesting than this caricature suggests.

The American Repertory Theater Company's production of *Endgame*, directed by JoAnne Akalaitis, in Cambridge, Massachusetts, in December 1984 was one of the most celebrated of these cases. The objections of Beckett and his agents in the United States were to the theater set—a subway depot with a derelict subway car extending across the stage; a rear metallic wall with various levels of narrow iron ladders reaching up to the top and small alcoves behind the walls; large puddles of water on the stage floor; seven large oil cans; the use of music by Philip Glass as an overture and occasionally as "incidental music"; and the "purposeful" casting of two black actors in the roles of Hamm and Nagg, which added a "dimension to the play that Beckett had not put there." [42] A compromise was reached at the last moment to avoid a legal action reaching court. In an agreed program insert, Beckett insisted that the play as it was being staged was no longer his play, while Robert Brustein, the artistic director of the American Repertory Theater, explained his position and defended the right of a director to offer his or her interpretation of a play.

Brustein legitimately asked why legal action was being threatened against the ART production when no action had been taken in other, more blatant cases of violation of Beckett's text and stage directions. [43] He alluded to André

Gregory's controversial production in 1973, when American colloquialisms were substituted for some of Beckett's actual words and to a 1983 Brussels production (by Marcel Delval), which was set in a former warehouse that was flooded with water covering eight thousand square feet. Why, he asked, had no action been taken then?

Beckett certainly believed that the text of the author should be respected by a director and that this fidelity should extend to the stage directions, when they are carefully planned as his were. Most living playwrights would take a similar view. Beckett believed that this still left the director with plenty of freedom to maneuver. But whether any action was taken in a particular case depended on some very human factors. As a result, Beckett could appear, and indeed was, inconsistent.

Deryk Mendel, David Warrilow, Fred Neumann, Lee Breuer, and, later, Pierre Chabert, Barry McGovern and Michael Colgan, Katharine Worth, and S. E. Gontarski were allowed to do things with his work that Beckett would have refused outright if the proposals had emanated from anyone else. Only a few months before the ART case, he gave David Warrilow his permission for a film to be made of *The Lost Ones* — already adapted for the theater, of course, by the same group of which JoAnne Akalaitis was herself a founding member. In agreeing, Beckett wrote: "OK for *Lost Ones* film with the stipulations you indicate. No such request from you will ever be refused by me."[44] For one very human factor was that he did not like to disappoint a friend. Later the same month, he even agreed to a proposal from Fred Neumann of Mabou Mines, to adapt *Worstward Ho* for the stage.[45] And, a year before, he had personally authorized Neumann to stage an adaptation of *Company*, with music by Philip Glass.[46]

It made a tremendous difference if he liked and respected the persons involved or if he had been able to listen to their reasons for wanting to attempt something highly innovative or even slightly different. The evidence suggests that he did not even know at first that JoAnne Akalaitis was directing the Boston *Endgame*. In this case, it seems unlikely that he would have felt any less hostile to the set designs or the music, even if Akalaitis had flown the Atlantic to discuss the production with him. But he may well have accepted a fairly bold compromise. He would, for example, in view of his known antiracist opinions, almost certainly have agreed happily to the multiracial casting if the reasons for it had been explained to him: that two first-rate black actors were already members of the ART company and that the director wanted to extend the universality of the play by giving major roles to black actors.

Whether Beckett permitted a given production also depended on who drew his attention to it and the terms in which that person described it. In his younger days, he could go almost berserk over anything that appeared to be compromising the integrity of his work. As an old man, he was much mellower. But his anger could still be ignited. Like a bonfire on a wet day, however, it needed a little tinder and a certain amount of priming and fanning. If certain close friends whose judgment he trusted communicated their feelings of shock, horror, or dismay graphically enough, he could be stimulated to anger and, occasionally, action. After hearing part of Fred Jordan's report on the Boston production, Beckett was, according to Rosset, "the angriest I had ever heard Beckett in the more than thirty years I have known him."[47] And once he was angry, he could be very obstinate, determined, and unforgiving.

Mostly, of course, word never reached him about productions that would have struck him as outrageous until it was too late for anything to be done about it. Or if it did, he usually ignored them. In his own good discussion of the issue, Jonathan Kalb selects among many possible examples an Italian television production of *Happy Days*, directed by Roberto Ciulli, "in which there was no mound, and Winnie (Veronica Bayer) walked around the theater calling to Willie (Rudolf Brand) who lurked in the wings and worked the stage machinery."[48] A "conceptual" production like that of George Tabori at the Münchner Kammerspiele, which was presented as a rehearsal, prompted the following remark from Beckett: "I heard about Tabori's *Godot* and squirmed. Since then there has been one 'für Kinder' [for children]. A version for the mentally deficient no doubt in preparation."[49] Yet the Tabori production was authorized by Beckett; more surprisingly, aware by then of the director's approach, he even agreed to a film of it being made.[50] Nor did he prevent Tabori, whom he knew personally, from doing other productions of his plays in the future. For, when confronted with such an issue, even with adaptations or styles of production that were total anathema to him, *far more often than not* he urged compromise and conciliation rather than legal action and condemnation. His reactions to André Gregory's 1973 Manhattan Project production of *Endgame* were calm, lucid, and, in view of what he had heard and read about it, remarkably mild, tolerant, and fair:

> I simply do not feel justified at this distance, with nothing more to go on, not having myself seen a performance, in asking that steps be taken to have it stopped. . . .
>
> Even in the hypothesis of a personal request from me to Gregory have we not to consider the amount of work, however misguided, that has gone into this production and the situation of the actors? This kind of massacre and abuse of directorial function is happening the whole time all over the place. . . .
>
> The best I can suggest is that we ensure a strictly limited series of performances at NYU [New York University] at the conclusion of which the rights revert to us and this production lapses. Any more drastic procedure seems to me unadvisable.[51]

Only rarely did Beckett or his agents resort to stopping or attempting to stop a contracted performance. There are good reasons for this. Censorship of any kind was abhorrent to him. So he was reluctant to institute legal proceedings and to take late actions that would harm a particular director, actor, or company financially. It was also, of course, a risky thing to do, in view of the huge potential costs of legal action.

On one issue, he was less inconsistent than others. He felt very strongly that the characters in his plays were either male or female and that their sex was not interchangeable. There were many requests, sometimes fervent personal appeals made directly to him, for women to be allowed to play the male characters in Waiting for Godot. Beckett (or his agents) always turned them down, though he himself showed signs of wilting several times under the intense emotional pressure that was brought to bear on him.[52]

In the 1980s, several women's acting companies put on the play either without any permission or without his dramatic agent being fully informed about what was happening.[53] "Women don't have prostates," said Beckett,[54] an allusion to the fact that Vladimir in Waiting for Godot frequently has to leave the stage to urinate, on account of his enlarged prostate. This explanation was merely an indication of a deep conviction that the characters in Waiting for Godot are distinctively male. Beckett sometimes made comparisons between different musical instruments; he clearly saw the roles in terms of their vocal qualities as well as their physical sexual difference.[55]

The most public airing of this argument concerning gender came for Beckett almost four years later with his decision to refuse a Dutch theater company, De Haarlemse Toneelschuur, the rights to play Waiting for Godot in Haarlem with women acting all the roles. The company persisted, and this time legal action was not only threatened but taken. The case was brought to court in April 1988 with a Dutch lawyer, J. M. van Veggel, representing the French Société des Auteurs et Compositeurs Français, who were acting on Beckett's behalf.[56] The lawyer argued that the integrity of the text was being violated by substituting women actresses (impersonating men, for this was what was happening) for the male ones asked for in the text. The lawyer reflected Beckett's own feelings about vocal quality by arguing that replacing men with women was rather like substituting violins for trumpets and that this violated the integrity of the play. Beckett, it was also claimed, had been misled because he had never been informed of the gender change beforehand.

The judge in the Haarlem court listened intently to the arguments on both sides, read the play, then saw a performance of the female Godot. He ruled that, since the performance remained very close to the actual dialogue and also followed the stage directions, the integrity of the play had not in fact been violated. And he evoked the argument used by Robert Brustein in the ART program and by Actors Equity to support mixed-race casting: since the play was about the human condition in general, he maintained that it could be played by either men or women. Nor, he ruled, was there any desire for sensation or scandal or for preaching any feminist message in the Dutch production.[57] Beckett had lost his case. But the issue of gender seemed to him to be so vital a distinction for a playwright to make that he reacted angrily, instituting a ban on all productions of his plays in the Netherlands.

As a result of such disputes, Beckett contracts in several countries were tightened up to state specifically that no additions, omissions, or alterations should be made to the text of the play or the stage directions and that no music, special effects, or other supplements should be added without prior consent. Whether this could result in turning Beckett's theater into a wax-works is another question. If it is applied too rigorously, there is a great danger that it might. Beckett's plays resemble pieces of music in which actors can play the notes differently — vary the tempo, the phrasing, and the tonal quality — and produce startlingly different performances. But they can too easily be made to sound cacophonous. There have been painful examples of productions that ignore the stage directions or distort the text. The failure of these productions mostly comes, however, from weaknesses in the directorial conception or insensitivities on the part of the director or actor to the plays' music. Some of the more imaginatively successful adaptations or freer productions suggest that, if outstanding directors were to be dissuaded from tackling Beckett's plays because of a fear of legal action being taken if they should deviate from the straight and narrow, we would risk losing a rich and vital source of renewal. A Beckett style that is not Beckett's own but that still works is probably discoverable. But it will need to be one that does not ignore the musical structures and precise timing on which the plays are based.

5

ONE OF THE REASONS for Beckett's low spirits in the mid-1980s was that, on January 20, 1984, Roger Blin, a friend who went back to the early fifties, had died. Although they had seen much less of each other in the past few years, Beckett still felt an enormous debt of gratitude to Blin. Both he and Suzanne, who also knew Roger well, were deeply upset by the news of his death. They went to his funeral at the crematorium of the Père Lachaise cemetery. It was an appalling experience.

The day was cold and miserable. Everyone filed quietly into the crematorium and sat down in silence. The room was soon filled to overflowing with Blin's friends, for he was a popular figure in French theater. There was no priest, no ritual, no music. Nothing. Utter silence. After a time of quiet contemplation, the coffin slid slowly away. Everyone sat on for over an hour, as the body was cremated. The cracking of the bones in the heat of the incinerator could be heard in the crowded, silent room. Beckett broke down completely at this point, sobbing bitterly. After leaving the crematorium, he stood for a few moments alone, leaning against a pillar in his beige sheepskin coat and dark beret.[58] He looked a broken man. Suzanne walked over to comfort him. The ashes were brought out, still warm, for the Blin family, as friends shook hands with each other, then drifted away in silent despair. These terrible moments were to haunt him for the years to come.[59]

Since December 1983, Beckett had been planning to go to Stuttgart to direct the German translation of *Quoi où* for television. His plans were to fly to Stuttgart for two days of preliminary discussions on April 25, then to return in mid-May for the actual shooting of the film. However, in mid-April, close to his seventy-eighth birthday, he was taken ill with a viral infection that confined him to bed, then kept him from going out. Any visit to Germany was out of the question and, since the Los Angeles Olympic Games were soon to be filling the summer television schedules,[60] it was agreed that the production should be postponed for another year. Suzanne was also ill.

Although he remained weak and tired for many weeks to come, Beckett's health gradually began to pick up. But he was still feeling low when he received yet another sudden, unexpected blow. At the beginning of May, he heard that Alan Schneider, who was in London to direct a play at the Hampstead Theatre Club, had been crossing the road at Swiss Cottage to post a letter to Beckett when he was knocked down by a motorcyclist. Accustomed to the New York traffic, he had looked the wrong way before crossing. He was unconscious in intensive care at the Royal Free Hospital for about forty-eight hours before he died, irremediably brain-damaged. Billie Whitelaw stayed by his bedside all the first night, until his wife, Jean, and their son, David, and a friend, Sheila Webber, arrived from across the Atlantic to be with him at the end. As she watched and waited for Jean to arrive, Billie Whitelaw looked up and saw over the head of Schneider's bed the name of the doctor in charge. It was Dr. Beckett.[61]

Soon after Alan's death, Jean Schneider telephoned Beckett from London. He said all he could to console her. Billie Whitelaw also telephoned him. What could one say? Just over three months before, Alan had himself written to Beckett about the death of Roger Blin: "I know what he meant to you and how you must feel. Nothing I can say will be of the slightest solace. But I want you to know that I am thinking of you and hoping you will summon the strength, as you always have, to go on."[62] Now Alan himself was dead.

Beckett was invited to write something about his American friend for *The New York Times*.[63] He declined. It was a public gesture which throughout his life he had never been able to make. Even if he had attempted to put pen to paper, his heart would have been too full to express his grief. It had been a terrible year. Two more old friends had left "the banquet hall."

6

IN APRIL 1984, during his recovery from his viral infection, Beckett had written to Avigdor and Anne Arikha: "My old head nothing but sighs (of relief?) of expiring cells. A last chance at last, I'll try. 'From where he sat with his head in his hands he saw himself rise and disappear.' Ineffable departure. Nothing left but try—eff it."[64]

The theme of a man seeing himself rise and disappear was developed, intermittently, over the next few years in several short manuscript fragments. At first, Beckett did not seem to have known whether to write his text in French or English or whether to use the present or the past tense. Manuscripts show him attempting both. The shortness of the fragments (a page, a half page or even a quarter of a page at a time), numerous erasures, additions made at many different

dates, and notes to himself, suggest that he found writing harder than ever
before. Even though he told David Warrilow in November that his pen [was]
"beginning to hover again over the *vierge papier*,"[65] by the end of 1984 he was
summing up his achievement as "not a written word worth having since
Worstward Ho a year ago. But I can't call it a day."[66] It was to take him three
whole years to complete the collection of fragments that were eventually published in 1988 as *Stirrings Still* under rather unusual circumstances.

The man in the first fragment is like Verlaine in his prison cell, writing his
poem "Le ciel est, par-dessus le toit, / Si bleu, si calme" ("The sky over the roof /
So blue, so calm"). Standing in a room with a small high window, looking out
at the cloudless sky, the ghostly Beckett figure hears persistent cries, as well as
the strokes of the clock marking the passing hours. A second fragment, written
later, reads in part: "To this end for want of a stone on which to sit like Walther
and cross his legs the best he could do was stop dead and stand stock still which
after a moment of hesitation he did and of course sink his head as one deep in
meditation which after another moment of hesitation he did also."[67] The reference is to the German Minnesinger poet Walther von der Vogelweide, (ca.
1168–ca. 1228) and his famous poem "Ich sass auf einem Steine" ("I sat on a
stone"). "Walther" had inspired several of Beckett's early poems, particularly
"Da Tagte Es."[68]

But, even at this stage, there are vestiges of Beckett's past life. His doctor
friend from St.-Lô days, Arthur Darley, of whom Beckett had earlier written the
poem "Mort de A.D.," is alluded to in the piece: "The same place and table as
when Darly [*sic*] for example died and left him," and, later, "A clock afar struck
the hours and half-hours. The same as when among others Darly once died and
left him."[69] The death of friends and the need for comfort that partly inspired
Nacht und Träume and *What Where* still haunted Beckett.[70] In a first draft in
French, again a human hand appears just out of reach as in *Nacht und Träume*.[71]
The death of Arthur Darley (he died of pulmonary tuberculosis on December
30, 1948),[72] was already very remote. But it is emblematic of those more recent
—"among others"—whose death it would be too painful (and indelicate) to
evoke.

The death of friends is in any case only one of the themes in this complex,
haunting piece about a spectral doppelgänger, who comes and goes, surviving
minimally in the imagination, which still, in spite of everything, manages to
strike sparks of life from language. Frank Kermode wrote of Beckett's "last
mantras" that "they are inescapably paradoxical: representing the last possible
act of imagination, they also suggest that even this quasi-Berkeleyan man, existing as perceived but almost not perceiving, cannot be represented without the
payment of a tribute, however reluctant, to a specifically human power, not
extinguished as long as one can speak of such things."[73]

In April 1986, Beckett's American publisher, Barney Rosset, was dismissed
as chief editor at Grove Press by Ann Getty and Lord Weidenfeld, to whom
Rosset had recently sold the company. Beckett was deeply shocked to learn of
his friend's dismissal and immediately tried to think of ways in which he could

help him to make some money and reestablish himself as a publisher. He considered allowing Rosset to publish the still unpublished 1931–32 novel *Dream of Fair to Middling Women*, but thought it too awful.[74] Then he thought of translating his early play in French, *Eleutheria*, concluding that it also was too dreadful to be published, saying to me that he could not do it, "not even for Barney." (He nevertheless gave the copy of the French typescript to his American publisher friend and, with this simple act of generosity or indifference, laid the foundation for a bitter controversy after his death as to whether he ever intended the play to be published, either in French or in English.)

He then began to rework the two previously written fragments of prose and to add a third fragment to produce the text that became *Stirrings Still*. In July 1986, he added the phrase "For Barney Rosset" to the earlier manuscripts, as he rewrote and then typed them. But, in December of the same year, he still had to write to Rosset that "No sign of 3rd so far and fear little hope the way I am now."[75] It was not until late 1987 that he was able to send on the final fragment to complete the text, which was published in a signed, deluxe, limited edition with illustrations by Louis Le Brocquy in 1988. It had been a long uphill struggle.

7

BECKETT'S HEALTH had started to decline as early as 1986, with what he referred to as "respiratory troubles." In fact, this was the beginning of emphysema. By the spring of the following year, he was using an oxygenator to help him breathe more easily. He used it intermittently at first, then on a more regular basis. Soon he was unable to go even as far as Ussy because of his need to have access to oxygen.

In April 1987, he fell heavily while crossing the bridge over the boulevard Saint-Jacques, scorning the handrail: "His face was scratched, his palms and arms in scabs,"[76] and he had some painful bruises. Afterward he still used to meet friends and visiting scholars at the PLM hotel but walked down the boulevard more gingerly than before. He continued to lose his balance, however, from time to time, falling again in the park. Suzanne's health, too, was a constant source of anxiety. She had had two cataract operations with implants in April and December 1986, which had lifted her spirits. But she was very frail now and unable to do much in the apartment. More upsettingly, in her final years, she became a shadow of her former self, egoistical and hostile toward him. This upset Beckett dreadfully.

At the end of July 1988, he fell yet again, this time in his own kitchen, cracking his head against the shelf over a radiator and knocking himself out. Suzanne found him lying unconscious on the floor. He was taken first to the hospital at Courbevoie to see if he had damaged his skull or had any internal bleeding. Then he was transferred to the Hôpital Pasteur for tests to determine the cause of his constant falls. Although the results were inconclusive, it was thought that, like his mother at the end of her life, he was suffering from Parkinson's disease, although he did not display the classic symptom of a trembling of the hands. He moved for general nursing care and regular physiotherapy into a "hôtel et maison de retraite médicalisée" (a "hotel and medical retirement home") called Le Tiers Temps ("The Third Age"). His last original work, a poem, "Comment dire" ("What Is the Word"), was written in French in the hospital after regaining full consciousness, then finished in the home. The spidery handwriting is very moving, precisely because Beckett is rediscovering words again. The first word is "folie" ("folly").

Le Tiers Temps was a modest establishment down the long rue Rémy-Dumoncel, between the avenue du Général-Leclerc and the avenue René Coty, the former avenue du Parc-de-Montsouris. Number 26, a large extended house, had been a former maternity home: "Light of day. Now light of night," Beckett wrote to Kay Boyle.[77] The home was not too far from his apartment in the boulevard Saint-Jacques, close enough for Suzanne to visit him in the first few months of his stay, helped by his nephew Edward.

He had his own drab room with a small adjoining bathroom, in an annex at the back of the house. The room was spartanly furnished with a bed, a small bedside table, a chest of drawers, some shelves on which he kept his current reading (biographies of Oscar Wilde and Nora Joyce, with some Kafka), and a small brown fridge that he bought himself. By the window stood a small writing table, at which he sat to answer his mail. In the center of the room hung an imitation chandelier with three electric light bulbs. He borrowed a portable television set from time to time, reserving it mostly for Saturday afternoons when major rugby internationals were being televised; as in the past, he never made appointments to clash with these matches. On one occasion, he watched a program about Bram van Velde, noting with emotion that, as he was being interviewed in a garden, Bram was carrying a copy of Beckett's book *Compagnie*.[78] He had a telephone on which he used to call Suzanne and his friends in Paris, but he could not telephone abroad.

Outside his room was a small open garden area with a solitary tree, where he used to walk, even when he was very unsteady on his legs. A strip of green nonslip matting was laid alongside the wall, and when he did not feel well enough to venture out, he used to say, "I could only walk along the Gaza Strip today";[79] it is referred to jokingly in the residence as the Champs-Elysées. Beckett used to feed the pigeons regularly outside his door. One visitor said: "He kept *biscottes* in his dressing-gown pocket to give to the pigeons. What was noticeable was that he could easily have thrown the crumbs to them while standing up. But, unsteady on his feet as he was, he had to risk falling over by bending down to feed them almost out of his hand."[80]

Many of Beckett's friends were horrified to see how simply he was living and felt that he could and should enjoy more comfort and more luxury. By this time productions of his plays throughout the world had made him a rich man, and he could certainly have afforded the most expensive nursing home or private nursing care. But the room reflected the austerity with which he had always lived. And it was by no means sordid. He was comfortable there. He had no need for luxury, he protested. The staff were very kind, looking after his welfare and carrying his meals through to his room because he found it too depressing to eat with the other old people. He had daily visits from a physiotherapist who tried to get his legs working again. His homeopathic doctor, Dr. Coulamy, lived farther up the same street and used to call to see him most days, bringing in his newspaper, *Libération*. The *directrice* was a kind, intelligent lady who loved music and with whom he spoke about Schubert. There were nurses on duty, among them one called Nadja whom he grew to like.

One of the problems was that, while he was in hospital, it was discovered that he was seriously undernourished. He had been eating so little with Suzanne that he had to be given vitamins to build up his strength again. The trouble did not lie, however, only in his "old legs" or the problems that the suspected Parkinson's disease posed. Emphysema meant that his brain was slowly being starved of oxygen. He needed regular sessions now with an oxygen mask from the canisters by his bedside. He was perfectly well aware that smoking had contributed to the lack of elasticity in his lungs, but felt that to stop now would have no discernible impact on his health. He was probably right.[81] And, except for one spell of two weeks early in September 1989, when he was receiving a course of intensive vitamin injections into the muscles every day and was forced to abstain on the consultant's orders, he also kept on having a regular couple of glasses of whiskey at the end of every afternoon. He was acutely conscious of every aspect of his physical decline, observing it almost as if his body belonged to someone else. But he still joked about it: "Hold on a minute, getting up isn't as easy as that," as he said to me, and his legs were, he wrote, "as tired of carrying me, as of me being carried."[82]

He had quite a number of regular callers. Edward came over from England several times to visit him, first at the Hôpital Pasteur, then in the Tiers Temps. At his request, a close friend, Edith Fournier, whom he had seen regularly for over thirty years and of whom he was extremely fond, looked after Suzanne during her illness and also came round to the Tiers Temps to help him, bringing his mail, doing errands, and buying anything that he wanted. Alberto Chiarini, a close friend of the Becketts', dropped in frequently, bringing him little treats like fruit. Jérôme Lindon, his publisher, called on a weekly basis, just as he had in his apartment.

Although he told many of his correspondents that he did not want to see people in the home, he still received a lot of occasional visitors. Roger Blin's former lover, Hermine Karagheuz, either telephoned or called to see him. And when the actor David Warrilow was in Paris he too was a regular caller. The San Quentin actors were over in 1988 videotaping recreations of his own productions, so the director, Walter Asmus, came to discuss details with him, and the actors Rick Cluchey, Bud Thorpe, Alan Mandell, and Lawrence Held came round to try to cheer him up with their old warmth and geniality. He had regular meetings with me to talk about his life. He kept to a set routine, going for a walk whenever he was well enough and making appointments mostly at the end of the afternoon, when he would take a whiskey with his visitor.

In the first few months of his stay at Le Tiers Temps, he made some progress with his walking, as his strength gradually returned thanks to a better balanced diet and sustained physiotherapy. At first he used to go back to his apartment in the boulevard Saint-Jacques. But, with Suzanne now irritable and bad-tempered, his visits were no longer enjoyable and it soon became too far for him to walk. One day, he was driven to Ussy by his doctor, a visit that upset him dreadfully, as he realized that he would be unlikely ever to return. Edith Fournier also took him out for a drive in a rental car. For some months, he walked gingerly around the quiet streets when it was fine and the pavements were dry, passing the house in the rue Hallé that used to belong to Mary Reynolds, where he and Suzanne had spent the first night after the arrest of Alfred Péron. This brought a sharp pang of nostalgia.

Writing was physically difficult for him now. Nonetheless, he persisted in translating *Stirrings Still* into French and, finally, did an English version of *What Is the Word*, which Barbara Bray typed on her computer and printed out for him. He signed a copy in dedication to Joe Chaikin.

Suzanne had been declining rapidly in the last few months; on July 17, she died. A few friends attended her funeral in the Cimetière de Montparnasse. Beckett was well enough to attend, helped by his friends and relations. Afterward, during our weekly meetings, I found him sad and filled with remorse. He did not live for many months after her.

On Wednesday, December 6, he was discovered by the nurse unconscious in his bathroom. After coming round, he was taken by ambulance to the hospital out at Massy, where the *directrice* of the Tiers Temps could be sure of finding him a room. He spent forty-eight hours in the cardiology department. Initial tests to see whether his loss of consciousness was caused by a heart attack proved negative, and he was transferred on December 8 to the neurological unit of the Hôpital Saint-Anne, where he had been a month before, for examination by a consultant neurologist.

On hearing of Beckett's collapse, his nephew Edward rushed over from England; as the seriousness of his condition became clear, his niece came from Killiney. A doctor friend, Eoin O'Brien, also came over from Dublin. For some days, Beckett was in a state of confusion, having at first periods of total absence (in French "des syncopes") then lapsing into unconsciousness, from which he emerged from time to time. For a while he was even well enough to sit in a chair and talk briefly to Jérôme Lindon about a proposed Pléiade edition of his complete work, except for *Eleutheria*, which he still wanted withheld. By December 11, he was very weak and in a coma, not at first seemingly in pain, but then, over the next few days, in a state of growing distress for which he was sedated. Edith Fournier, who stayed with him toward the end, told him that Václav Havel had become president of Czechoslavakia. A smile flickered across his lips.

During his last forty-eight hours, Beckett was much calmer. He died peacefully at one P.M. on Friday, December 22, 1989. It was the Christmas weekend and the family decided to keep the funeral both private and secret. This decision was made to avoid a large public funeral, which Beckett would never have wanted. If it had been announced in advance, both French and Irish governments would have wanted to be represented. Instead, he was buried quietly beside Suzanne in the Cimetière de Montparnasse, which is what he had agreed himself some months earlier, after at least considering the possibility of being buried at Ussy. Born on Good Friday, he was buried at 8:30 A.M. on the day after Christmas. A handful of relatives and friends attended the interment. Other friends were upset because they did not know when the funeral was or could not get there because of the holiday. Hundreds would have wished to be there, for Beckett was loved by many people. For weeks afterward, his grave was strewn not only with flowers but also with little messages written in dozens of languages, including Chinese and Japanese: lines of thanks or tributes scribbled on any available scrap of paper, even a page torn from a student's exercise book. One message was crammed onto a Métro ticket. It was a characteristically low-key departure for this quiet Dubliner, to whom the world came to pay homage.

Notes and Sources

ABBREVIATIONS USED IN NOTES

All interviews are conducted by James Knowlson (JK) unless otherwise stated.
"GD" refers to Beckett's unpublished German diaries.

NAMES OF PERSONS

AA = Avigdor and Anne Arikha
SB = Samuel Beckett
LH = Lawrence Harvey
HH = Henri and Josette Hayden
JH = Jocelyn Herbert
MH = Mary Hutchinson
JK = James Knowlson
AJL = A. J. Leventhal
JL = Jérôme Lindon
TM = Tom MacGreevy
MM = Mary Manning Howe (Mrs. Adams)
PM = Pamela Mitchell
BR = Barney Rosset
GR = George Reavey
SP = Sheila Page (née Roe)
JS = Judith Schmidt (now Judith Douw)
AS = Alan Schneider

Beckett's letters to the following friends were written in French and I have supplied my own translations:
Avigdor and Anne Arikha (AA), Henri and Josette Hayden (HH), Georges Duthuit, Jérôme Lindon (JL), Jacoba van Velde, and, in the case of a few letters, Morris Sinclair.

LIBRARIES AND ARCHIVES

BBC = British Broadcasting Corporation Written Archives, Caversham
Bloomington = Lilly Library, Indiana University, Bloomington
Boston = Boston College
Boston Univ. = Boston University
CW, Reading = Chatto and Windus Archive, University of Reading
Dartmouth = Lawrence Harvey Papers, Dartmouth College

Delaware = Emily Holmes Coleman Papers, University of Delaware Library
De Paul = De Paul University, Chicago
Imec = Institut des Mémoires de l'Edition Contemporaine, Paris
Kent State = Kent State University
McMaster = Mills Memorial Library, McMaster University
Minuit = Archive of Les Editions de Minuit, Paris
Princeton = Princeton University Library
Reading = Archive of the Beckett International Foundation, University of Reading
Routledge, Reading = Routledge Archive, University of Reading
SIU, Carbondale = Morris Library, Southern Illinois University at Carbondale
St. Louis = Washington University, St. Louis
Syracuse = Syracuse University Library
TCD: Trinity College Dublin Library
Texas = Harry Ransom Humanities Research Center, University of Texas at Austin
Tulsa = McFarlin Library, University of Tulsa

MANUSCRIPT AND LETTER SOURCES

I have consulted manuscripts and letters of Samuel Beckett at or from all of the institutions abbreviated above and, in addition, have had access to similar material at the Beinecke Rare Book and Manuscript Library, Yale University; the Bibliothèque Jacques Doucet; the Bibliothèque Nationale; the Bibliothèque Polonaise, Paris; the University of California, San Diego; Ohio State University, Columbus, Ohio; the Harvard College Library; the University of Kansas Libraries, Lawrence, Kansas; the National Library of Ireland, Dublin; the State University of New York at Buffalo Library; the New York Public Library; University College, London, Library. Beckett's friends allowed me to have copies of their letters from him. Those from which I have quoted are attributed in the notes; others, which are not quoted, have still supplied me with much background information.

Most works are cited in the notes by author and title; fuller information may be found in the bibliography.
    References to works by Beckett are to English-language editions unless otherwise stated.

1: IMAGES OF CHILDHOOD, 1906–15

1. The myth was treated seriously by Deirdre Bair in *Samuel Beckett* (New York: Harcourt Brace Jovanovich; London: Jonathan Cape, 1978), pp. 3–4. It has been repeated in countless books and essays ever since.
2. SB, comment to Alec Reid, 10 Feb. 1966 (Reid Notebooks in private hands). I am most grateful to Professor Terence Brown for allowing me to consult and quote from the late Alec Reid's notebooks and correspondence.
3. SB, *Collected Poems in English and French* (London: John Calder, 1977), p. 17.
4. Interview with SB, 12 Nov. 1989.
5. SB, *Collected Poems in English and French*, p. 17.
6. SB, *Company*, John Calder (London: John Calder, 1980), p. 16.
7. Interview with Samuel Roe's granddaughter, Sheila Page, née Roe (called henceforward in the text, Sheila Page and, in the notes, SP), 19 Jan. 1990.
8. There are many Roes recorded in the registers of St. Mary's Church, Leixlip, from 1675 onward. An inscription on a monument in the church refers to the death of Walter

Roe on May 26, 1749. I am grateful to Mrs. Suzanne Pegley for her invaluable archival work in the parish registers of St. Mary's, Leixlip, and St. Andrew's, Lucan, and to the Reverend Bruce Pierse for his help.

9. Beckett's maternal grandfather, Samuel Robinson Roe, was an active member of Leixlip Parish Church, first as a churchwarden, then as the treasurer. In 1870 he presented "two handsome collecting plates" to the church (entry in St. Mary's Vestry Book).

10. Interview with SB, 9 July 1989. SP added: "They had a big house in those days and my grandfather was rich. I remember going to see the house, biggish, with steps up to the front door. A big gentleman's country house. They had the Liffey running at the end of their property. And the salmon leap was there; I remember that. And the boys were all great fishermen. And shots" (interview with SP, 20 April 1990).

11. Eoin O'Brien, *The Beckett Country, Samuel Beckett's Ireland* (Dublin: The Black Cat Press, 1986), p. 347, n. 6.

12. Samuel Robinson Roe seems to have owned or rented several other properties in the area. His name is linked either as owner or tenant with several houses in Leixlip and Celbridge, including Bridge Lodge at the Mill, the Toll House on Leixlip Bridge, and Black Castle on Mill Lane in Leixlip. I thank the present occupant, John Colgan, for information about the Toll House.

13. Anne Belas was born on December 28, 1839, and baptized in February 1840.

14. Interview with SP, 20 April 1990.

15. Interview with SB, 9 July 1989.

16. Marriage Register 1863, Book 16, Representative Church Body Library. Married 9 July 1863.

17. The name of Belas appears in parish registers as Belas, Bellas, and Beyliss.

18. I am grateful to Suzanne Pegley and Susan Schreibman for their excellent work in tracing the birth certificates of the Roe and Beckett families for me.

19. SP described the Roes as "a large family of two or three girls and three or four boys." One of her uncles lived in Vancouver and an aunt, Esther, lived in Honolulu (interview with SP, 20 April 1990).

20. Edward Price Roe was a student at Trinity College, where, after his father's death, he was obliged to support himself in order to complete his studies. He worked part-time in Johnsons, a prestigious jewelry shop in Dublin and, since he possessed a very fine voice, sang in a Dublin choir. But he never had enough money to join Trinity College's sports clubs, although he was an excellent athlete and won cups for tennis in Nyasaland, where he later went to work. A small replica of the "Nyasaland Tennis Championship Lawn Tennis Challenge Cup" shows that Edward Price Roe won the Challenge Cup from 1903 to 1906, 1908 and 1909, and held it again from 1911 to 1918. The original is now played for as the Roe Cup (interview with SP, 19 Jan. 1990).

21. Bair, *Samuel Beckett*, p. 8.

22. Interview with SB, 9 July 1989.

23. Interview with SP, 19 Jan. 1992.

24. Interview with SB, 9 July 1989. There is no trace of her presence in the records of the Adelaide hospital staff, however, at that time.

25. Bair, *Samuel Beckett*, p. 7.

26. Interview with May Beckett's parlormaid, Lily Condell, 10 Aug. 1992.

27. Interview with Lily Condell, 4 Aug. 1992.

28. This portrait of May Beckett comes from interviews with SB, SP, Mary Manning Howe (Mrs. Adams), James Guilford, and Lily Condell, between 1989 and 1992.

29. Harry was born on July 22, 1880, and died in February 1929 of tuberculosis. His only son, William George, was actually called John and was known in the family as "South Africa John" to distinguish him from his musician cousin, John, the son of Gerald (John [i.e., William George] Beckett to JK, 29 Aug. 1992).

30. Interview with SB, 9 July 1989.

31. Information about R. Atkinson and Co., Poplin Manufacturers, comes from an advertisement for the company sent to me by Horner Beckett, to whom I am most grateful for his help.

32. Horner Beckett has an oil portrait of James Beckett and a silver teapot with the inscription "Presented to James Beckett by the Members of the Liberal Friendly Brothers Society in testimony of his Integrity Ability & Zeal as their Secretary for upwards of 10 years. Dublin October 1857" (Horner Beckett to JK, 8 Sept. 1992).

33. The contract for the building of a portion of the hospital was dated 1870 (Horner Beckett to JK, 8 Sept. 1992).

34. This was a prestigious contract for the Beckett brothers to secure and, at a very grand social occasion, the first stones were laid by the Prince of Wales, later King Edward VII, on April 10, 1885. The two fine buildings which flank Leinster House were completed for about £200,000 each in 1890 (brochure, "The National Library of Ireland and Science and Art 1877–1977," p. 3).

35. It is some indication of the size and prestige of the building firm that, after the brothers split up, James Beckett, Ltd., had workshops at the South Dock Works in Ringsend that covered some 100,000 square feet. James went on to construct large commercial and industrial buildings in Dublin, such as the W. and R. Jacobs Biscuits complex on Bishop Street and several Provincial Banks throughout Ireland.

36. Horner Beckett to JK, 8 Sept. 1992. Beckett's grandfather also did work such as rebuilding the premises at 33 Dawson Street adjoining the Royal Irish Automobile Club so as to add to the club's facilities (Royal Irish Automobile Club, Report 1909, p. 5).

37. This musical setting has been preserved. "Crossing the Bar," words by Lord Tennyson, music by Fannie Beckett, no. 1 in C, no. 2 in E (Dublin: Pigott and Co., n.d.).

38. Deirdre Hamilton to JK, 4 Sept. 1992.

39. Interview with John Beckett, 27 Aug. 1991.

40. Interview with Cissie's son Morris Sinclair, 22 May 1991.

41. Beatrice Lady Glenavy, Today We Will Only Gossip (London: Constable, 1964), pp. 31–32.

42. Interview with Gerald's daughter, Ann Beckett, 3 Aug. 1992.

43. Ibid.

44. James's son, Desmond Beckett, to JK, 27 Sept. 1992.

45. He was chosen to play water polo for Ireland at the age of sixteen and captained the Irish team in the 1924 Olympic Games in Paris (Desmond Beckett to JK, 27 Sept. 1992).

46. John Heuston to JK, 2 Nov. 1994.

47. However, toward the end of his life, Jim had to have both his legs amputated and Beckett helped him financially to stay on at home: "Jim would have ended up in a public ward in a long-term geriatric hospital except for Sam," commented his niece (interview with Ann Beckett, 3 Aug. 1992).

48. Interview with SB, 9 July 1989.

49. Interview with SB, 12 Aug. 1989.

50. Interview with SB, 9 July 1989.

51. Edward Beckett has a cup won by his grandfather with the inscription "Dublin Swimming Club. 440 Yards Sealed Handicap Won by W. Beckett (Scratch)."

52. Interview with SP, 19 Jan. 1990. Beckett plays hilariously with the idea of a "man's man" and a "woman's woman" in Watt (Paris: Olympia Press, 1958), pp. 152–53.

53. Interview with James Guilford, 5 Aug. 1992.

54. Ibid.

55. Interview with SB, 9 July 1989.

56. SB, Dream of Fair to Middling Women (New York: Arcade Publishing, in association with Riverrun, 1992), pp. 53–54.

57. Beckett's father was a member of the RIAC from February 1906 until November 1908. He resumed his membership in April 1921 and Mrs. May Beckett became a member in July 1926 (Members' Register of the Royal Irish Automobile Club, abstract

1901–32). I am grateful to Cornelius F. Smith, Lt. Col. D. J. Healy, and Mr. W. Fitzsimmons for their help.

58. Interview with SB, 22 Aug. 1989.

59. Geoffrey Perrin to JK, 3 Feb. 1993. See David Bowles, Carmel Callaghan, and Tony Cauldwell, *Foxrock Golf Club 1893–1993*, n.d., p. 208.

60. Interview with SB, 22 Aug. 1989.

61. SB, *All That Fall*, in *Collected Shorter Plays* (London: Faber and Faber, 1984), p. 25.

62. Interview with SP, 19 Jan. 1990.

63. SB, *Worstward Ho* (London: John Calder, 1983), p. 13.

64. Interview with Mary Manning Howe (Mrs. Adams), 12 March 1992.

65. I am grateful to Mary Manning for her generosity in making available the relevant pages of her autobiography and for allowing me to quote from it. A slightly fuller version is recounted in Bair, *Samuel Beckett*, p. 7.

66. SB to Ann Beckett, 14 Jan. 1983, and interview with SP, 19 Jan. 1990.

67. "Sam's mother was mad on donkeys" (interview with SP, 19 Jan. 1990).

68. Ibid.

69. SB, *A Piece of Monologue*, in *Collected Shorter Plays*, p. 265.

70. SB, *More Pricks Than Kicks* (London: Calder and Boyars, 1970), p. 110.

71. Interview with SB, 9 July 1989.

72. SB, *Watt*, p. 52.

73. *Thom's Official Directory*, 1901, p. 1306.

74. Belacqua in *Dream of Fair to Middling Women*, for instance, "was heartily glad to get back to his parents' comfortable private residence, ineffably detached and situated and so on, and his first act, once spent the passion of greeting after so long and bitter a separation, was to plunge his prodigal head into the bush of verbena that clustered about the old porch . . . and longly to swim and swoon on the rich bosom of its fragrance, a fragrance in which the least of his childish joys and sorrows were and would for ever be embalmed" (*Dream of Fair to Middling Women*, p. 145). Even allowing for the fact that by the time he wrote these lines, Beckett had published a study of memory and habit in Proust and was quite capable of parodying the role played by the madeleine in that vast novel, the verbena probably did quite genuinely evoke Cooldrinagh for him.

75. Interviews with Lily Condell, 10 Aug. 1992, and with SP, 19 Jan. 1990.

76. Interview with Lily Condell, 10 Aug. 1992.

77. SB, *Company*, pp. 15–16.

78. Interview with SB, 9 July 1989.

79. SB to TM, 4 Aug. 1932 (TCD).

80. SB, *No's Knife, Collected Shorter Prose 1947–1966* (London: Calder and Boyars, 1967), p. 82.

81. These personal recollections are taken from LH's undated interview with SB (Dartmouth).

82. SB, *More Pricks Than Kicks*, pp. 12, 17.

83. SB to Herbert Myron, 22 Jan. 1962 (Boston Univ.).

84. Interview with SP, 20 April 1990.

85. SB, *Collected Poems in English and French*, p. 24.

86. SB, *Dream of Fair to Middling Women*, p. 8.

87. This photograph was especially posed on the porch of Cooldrinagh in the early evening light, so that Dorothy Elvery, the sister of Beatrice Lady Glenavy, could base a painting that she was preparing for the Taylor Art Scholarship, a double image called *Twins*, on the little nightgowned figure of the two-year-old Samuel. The picture is reproduced in Dorothy Kay [Elvery], *The Elvery Family: A Memory*, edited by Marjorie Reynolds (Cape Town: The Carrefour Press, 1991), p. 37. Dorothy Elvery based a later painting, *Child at Prayer*, on the same photographic image of Sam Beckett. This later painting, executed circa 1918, is reproduced in Marjorie Reynolds, *Everything You Do Is*

a Portrait of Yourself; Dorothy Kay: A Biography. Privately published by Alec Marjorie Reynolds, South Africa, 1989, p. 14.

88. Both of these stories come from an undated interview of LH with SB (Dartmouth).

89. Interview with SP, 19 Jan. 1990.

90. SB, *Molloy*, in *Molloy Malone Dies The Unnamable* (London: Calder and Boyars, 1959), p. 123.

91. SB, *Malone Dies*, in *Molloy Malone Dies The Unnamable*, p. 206.

92. Ibid.

93. Interview with James Guilford, 5 Aug. 1992.

94. The distant memory of Bill Shannon lay behind "the consumptive postman whistling 'The Roses are Blooming in Picardy' " in SB, *Watt*, p. 52, and *Dream of Fair to Middling Women*, p. 146. See O'Brien, *The Beckett Country*, pp. 18–19.

95. Richard Walmesley-Cotham to JK, 12 May 1989.

96. SB, *Company*, p. 28. The identification was made by Beckett in an interview on August 12, 1989.

97. Interview with SB, 9 July 1989.

98. Frank specialized in Irish and Trinidad and Tobago stamps and built up a fine collection of British stamps, overprinted with the imprint (in Irish) "Provisional Government of Ireland, 1922," then "Irish Free State, 1922." When he died in 1954, his collection was sold as one of the leading stamp collections in Dublin.

99. SB, *Molloy*, in *Molloy Malone Dies The Unnamable*, p. 109.

100. "The Togo 1 mark carmine, issued in 1900, is one of a series of stamps issued by the German authorities when Togo was one of their colonies. The 'pretty boat' was a well-known design featuring Kaiser Wilhelm's yacht" (philatelist Robin Holley to JK, 1992).

101. SB, *Molloy*, in *Molloy Malone Dies The Unnamable*, p. 121. Information concerning the stamps in *Molloy* is from an article by Philip Baker, "The Stamp of the Father in *Molloy*," *Journal of Beckett Studies*, vol. 5, no. 1 (spring 1996), and from philatelist Robin Holley to JK, 1992.

102. This story was recounted by SB to LH, undated interview (Dartmouth).

103. SB, *Company*, p. 28.

104. Interview with SP, 19 Jan. 1990.

105. Bair, *Samuel Beckett*, p. 15.

106. Interview with Lily Condell, 4 Aug. 1992.

107. Interview with Lily Condell, 10 Aug. 1992.

108. Interview with SP, 19 Jan. 1990.

109. Ibid.

110. SB to Mrs. Read, 4 Sept. 1967 (Ellmann Papers, 003 [Tulsa]).

111. SB, *Dream of Fair to Middling Women*, pp. 135–36.

112. Interview with SP, 20 April 1990. In a typescript of *Fin de partie*, Beckett has written "Quand ce n'était pas du beurre c'était de la margarine" ("When it was not butter, it was margarine") (typescript 1, p. 42 [Ohio]).

113. SB to TM, 6 Oct. 1937: "I am what her savage loving has made me" (TCD).

114. Interview with SB, 22 Aug. 1989.

115. SB, *From an Abandoned Work* in *No's Knife*, p. 148.

116. SB, *For to End Yet Again* (London: John Calder, 1976), pp. 40–41.

117. SB, *Company*, p. 41.

118. SB, *Dream of Fair to Middling Women*, p. 1.

119. Interview with Mrs. Sheila Brazil, who took over from her mother as postmistress in Foxrock in 1925, 14 July 1991.

120. SB, *Company*, p. 12.

121. SB, *All That Fall*, in *Collected Shorter Plays*, p. 15.

122. Interview with SB, 12 Aug. 1989.

123. Alec Reid (Reid Notebooks) and "The Reluctant Prizeman," *Musight* (Dublin), November 1969, pp. 63–69.

124. Interview with Lily Condell, 4 Aug. 1992.

125. Interview with SB, 12 Aug. 1989.

126. In 1906, the year of Beckett's birth, Mrs. Elise Elsner is recorded as being at Taunus with Miss Ida Elsner, "teacher of languages and music," and Miss P. W. Elsner.

127. Interview with SB, 22 Aug. 1989.

128. The story was related by Garret Gill to Alec Reid (Reid Notebooks).

129. Information given by that one pupil, Garret Gill, to Alec Reid (Reid Notebooks).

130. LH, undated interview with SB (Dartmouth).

131. SB, *Molloy*, in *Molloy Malone Dies The Unnamable*, pp. 105–106. In an early version of *Fin de partie*, too, written early in 1955, character A tells character B that the dog that he has just given him reminds him very much of (in French) "Zoulou" (ms. 1660 [Reading]).

132. *Thom's Official Directory*, 1913. Their father, a good cellist, immigrated to Ireland from Germany in 1851.

133. LH, undated interview with SB (Dartmouth).

134. Interview with Mrs. Sheila Brazil, 14 June 1991, and an undated note of LH on a meeting with a man called McCann, a taxi driver in Foxrock, who remembered picking Miss Elsner up and hearing her pithy language (Dartmouth).

135. SB, *All That Fall*, in *Collected Shorter Plays*, p. 14.

136. "Was the ruin still there where none ever came where you hid as a child slip off when no one was looking and hide there all day long on a stone among the nettles with your picture-book" (SB, *That Time*, in *Collected Shorter Plays*, p. 229).

137. LH, undated interview with SB (Dartmouth).

138. Rubina White Roe died on October 31, 1913, at the age of forty-six and is buried in Redford cemetery near Greystones in the same grave as her young son, Price, who died, aged eight, in 1907.

139. Interview with SP, 19 Jan. 1990.

140. SB, *Come and Go*, in *Collected Shorter Plays*, p. 194.

141. Mary Manning, unpublished autobiography.

142. Interview with SP, 20 Nov. 1992.

143. Geoffrey Perrin to JK, 3 Feb. 1993.

144. The copy of Diabelli's "Piano Duet in D" has an inscription in Beckett's hand (when he was eight years old): "The celebrated Duet in D for two performers on the Pianoforte composed by A. Diabelli Bought a[t] Piggots [sic] and Co." The sheet music was in Beckett's country cottage at Ussy when he died.

145. Interview with SP, 19 Jan. 1990.

146. This record of Beckett's attachment to stones is taken from an account by Gottfried Büttner of a dinner with Beckett in Berlin on September 9, 1967. Beckett went on to link this with Freud's idea. I am grateful to Dr. Büttner for allowing me to use his account.

147. SB, *Malone Dies*, in *Molloy Malone Dies The Unnamable*, p. 182.

148. SB, *Waiting for Godot* (London: Faber and Faber, 1965), pp. 44–45.

149. Ibid., p. 64.

2: SCHOOL DAYS, 1915–23

1. SB, "Texts for Nothing VII," in *No's Knife*, p. 105.

2. SB, *Watt*, p. 26.

3. Ibid., p. 27.

4. SB, "Texts for Nothing VII," in *No's Knife*, p. 104.

5. A. E. Le Peton, who had previously been a French master at Strangeways School on St. Stephen's Green, started his own school, Earlsfort House, in about 1908.

6. Interview with SB, 22 Aug. 1989. Mr. Exshaw is evoked in one of the manuscript drafts of an unpublished prose text beginning "Long Observation of the Ray" written in 1976 (ms. 2909 [Reading]).

7. Andrée Sheehy Skeffington, Skeff, A Life of Owen Sheehy Skeffington, 1909–1970 (Dublin: The Lilliput Press, 1991), p. 28.

8. Andrew Ganly, in a program on Radio Telefís Éireann compiled for Beckett's seventieth birthday and first broadcast in April 1976.

9. Interview with SB, 22 Aug. 1989. Whether Beckett's allegation was true or not is, of course, now quite impossible to determine. Although this proves nothing, Le Peton was married and had two sons. Later in life, he was reduced for some reason to becoming a butler near Oxford (interview with Professor John O. Wisdom, a contemporary of Beckett at Earlsfort House, 5 Aug. 1992).

10. Interview with SB, 22 Aug. 1989.

11. Visit to Cooldrinagh and talk with the owner, Mr. Arthur Finegan, 10 Aug. 1992.

12. Geoffrey Perrin to JK, 3 Feb. 1993.

13. Interviews with John Manning, 19 June 1990, and Mary Manning, 12 March 1992.

14. James Barrett was the professional at Carrickmines Golf Club from 1906 until 1950. James Barrett (the professional's son, who also played golf with Beckett) to JK, 2 Aug. 1992.

15. LH, undated interview with SB (Dartmouth).

16. Interview with SB, 22 Aug. 1989.

17. Interview with Richard O'Sullivan, 10 Aug. 1992.

18. Ibid.

19. LH, undated interview with SB (Dartmouth).

20. Ibid.

21. Ibid. I have found no independent confirmation of Beckett's identification of Lister as this particular unfortunate.

22. Ibid.

23. Interview with John O. Wisdom, 5 Aug. 1992. See Andrée Sheehy Skeffington, Skeff, pp. 30–31.

24. Interviews with Richard O'Sullivan, 10 Aug. 1992, and John O. Wisdom, 5 Aug. 1992.

25. LH, undated interview with SB (Dartmouth).

26. Ibid.

27. Ibid.

28. Ibid.

29. Vivian Mercier, "The Old School Tie," The Bell, XI, no. 6, March 1946, reprinted in Michael Quane, Portora Royal School (1618–1968) (Monaghan: Cumann Seanchais Chlochair, 1968), p. 56. I am most grateful to Keith Haines of Campbell College for sending me a copy of this history of Portora.

30. LH, undated interview with SB (Dartmouth).

31. General Sir Charles Jones to Richard Neill, 12 Nov. 1969 (Portora Archive), reproduced in a document from Portora Royal School, ms. 1227/1/2/4 (Reading).

32. Bair found such a consensus among those like General Sir Charles Jones and Dr. J. A. Wallace, now long since dead (Samuel Beckett, p. 28 and note 62). Dr. Cyril Harris wrote to me that "Sam Beckett was somewhat different from any of the boys that I had been associated with. He was not particularly odd but he gave the impression of being a solitary withdrawn person" (letter to JK, 26 Oct. 1992).

33. The Impartial Reporter and Farmer's Journal, 4 Jan. 1990.

34. LH, undated interview with SB (Dartmouth).

35. A judgment of Thompson reported by Beckett to LH (Dartmouth).

36. Tom Cox and Douglas Graham, both contemporaries of Beckett, spoke of his winning the Seale Prize on two occasions in the first of four Radio Telefís Éireann programs, directed by Andy Mahoney and first broadcast in April 1976.

37. John Beckett (Beckett's cousin in South Africa), to JK, 14 Sept. 1992.

38. H. S. Corscadden to JK, 1 Dec. 1992.

39. Quane, *Portora Royal School (1618–1968)*, p. 56.

40. Colonel George Graham to JK, 15 Oct. 1992. In a note on his copy of *The Beckett Country*, Beckett's contemporary, Douglas Graham, who later became the headmaster of Portora, corrected Eoin O'Brien, who had written that Tetley was the swimming coach. "He was *cricket* coach . . . and always as an umpire wore the cricket-cap of St. Catherine's College, Cambridge." Other former pupils agree that Breul, not Tetley, supervised swimming. O'Brien seems to be correct, however, in identifying Tetley as the "little bullet-headed bristle-cropped / red-faced rat of a pure mathematician" referred to in Beckett's poem "For Future Reference" (*The Beckett Country*, p. 116). The remark may have been an isolated one that stung Beckett, or merely poetic license, with the poet getting his revenge on someone he disliked intensely. I am most grateful to the Reverend Graham's son, John, for allowing me to use these notes and to Lois Overbeck for first putting me in touch with him.

41. H. S. Corscadden to JK, 1 Dec. 1992.

42. A photograph of Tetley from *Portora*, vol. XIX, no. 3 (1925), p. 1, is reproduced in O'Brien, *The Beckett Country*, p. 118.

43. Research tape of an interview with Geoffrey Thompson for the Telefís Éireann radio program, April 1976, kindly supplied to me by his widow and daughter.

44. In his final year at Portora, only three of his subjects were quite good — arithmetic, geometry, and English — and his French lay at the midway point of the marks (200 out of the 400 possible) (Bair, *Samuel Beckett*, p. 30). Dr. Bair was advised by Dr. J. A. Wallace, who, with the benefit of the mark books, could write in 1969, "He [Beckett] was in a class of outstanding academic excellence, and, to those junior, he did not seem to be of more than good average ability, and this was backed up by the exam results" (J. A. Wallace to Richard Neill, 21 Nov. 1969, reproduced in the document from Portora Royal School, ms. 1227/1/2/4 [Reading]).

45. H. S. Corscadden to JK, 1 Dec. 1992.

46. Notes of Reverend Douglas Graham on O'Brien's *The Beckett Country*, confirmed by a letter from H. S. Corscadden to JK, 1 Dec. 1992.

47. Dr. Cyril Harris to JK, 26 Oct. 1992.

48. John Beckett (Beckett's cousin in South Africa) to JK, 14 Sept. 1992.

49. H. S. Corscadden to JK, 1 Dec. 1992.

50. Douglas Graham claims in a note on O'Brien's *The Beckett Country* that Breul taught Beckett German and not English. Here, Graham is wrong and O'Brien is correct, for Beckett was adamant that he never studied German either at school or at university. German was hardly ever taught at that time, although Greek was, mainly to those destined for the Church (Colonel George Graham to JK, 15 Oct. 1992).

51. Research tape for Radio Telefís Éireann radio program, April 1976.

52. As seen, for instance, in Stephen Leacock's *Nonsense Novels*. John Lane (London and New York: The Bodley Head, 1911).

53. Ibid., p. 73.

54. Research tape for Radio Telefís Éireann radio program, April 1976.

55. SB, *More Pricks Than Kicks*, p. 21.

56. The story is related by his roommate at Trinity College, Gerald Pakenham Stewart, in his memoirs (typescript, p. 15), now published as *The Rough and the Smooth* (New Zealand: Heritage Press, 1995.)

57. The later captain of boxing, Douglas L. Graham, pointed out: "What we at Portora called 'light heavy-weight' was probably about welter-weight, i.e. 10 stones plus" (notes of Douglas Graham on O'Brien's *The Beckett Country*). A boy two years older than

Beckett wrote: "I shall never forget the way he dealt with me in a school boxing tournament. I met him in a semi-final bout and he quickly knocked me through the side ropes and out of the ring. That was the end of my boxing career." (Cyril Harris to JK, 26 Oct. 1992).

58. SB comment to JK, James Knowlson, *Samuel Beckett: An Exhibition* (London: Turret Books, 1971), p. 21.

59. *Portora*, 1923, XVII, no. 3, p. 12. Beckett played rugby and cricket for the school under the captaincy of the all-round sportsman, and later Irish international rugby football star, A. M. Buchanan. Beckett played for the First XV rugby club as scrum half and, in his final year, acted as honorary secretary to both cricket and rugby clubs.

60. O'Brien, *The Beckett Country*, p. 117.

61. Results in the school magazine, *Portora*, in 1921, show that he also won the Junior Sprint Race. His name is engraved on a cup which is believed to be the Junior Champion Swimming Cup. In his last year at the school, he tied for second place in the sprint with his friend Charles Jones, but, characteristically it would seem, had to abandon the Senior Long Race because of "lack of training." (*Portora*, 1923, XVII, no. 3, p. 19).

62. General Sir Charles Jones in the document from Portora Royal School (ms. 1227/1/2/4 [Reading]).

63. Interview with SB, 22 Aug. 1989.

64. General Sir Charles Jones in the document from Portora Royal School (ms. 1227/1/2/4 [Reading]).

65. O'Brien, *The Beckett Country*, p. 358, n. 11.

66. There are contradictory views as to whether Beckett did or did not contribute to *Portora* magazine. One of his classmates and friends, Tom Cox, said with some degree of conviction that he wrote light humorous articles (Radio Telefís Éireann program, first broadcast in April 1976); Herbert Gamble, who knew him almost as well, said that he believed that he did not (document from Portora Royal School, ms. 1227/1/2/4 [Reading]). See also Bair, *Samuel Beckett*, p. 31. Beckett himself told Vivian Mercier that he did not remember ever writing for *Portora* magazine (answers to questionnaire of Vivian Mercier, 17 Oct. 1976). My own view is, that if he did, the most likely contribution, under the pseudonym of "John Peel," was a sonnet entitled "To the Toy Symphony" in commemoration of the school orchestra's performance of Haydn's "Toy Symphony" in 1922, in which Beckett played "some sort of bird call." See O'Brien, *The Beckett Country*, p. 119.

67. Gerald Pakenham Stewart, a contemporary of Beckett at Portora and later a friend at Trinity College, knew the lines by heart, as did the Irish actor Patrick Magee. Both Magee and Beckett recited these lines to me on separate occasions in the 1970s, Beckett rather proudly.

68. General Sir Charles Jones in the document from Portora Royal School (ms. 1227/1/2/4 [Reading]).

69. Thomas B. Tackaberry's name is on the Board of Honour of those who obtained a Junior Exhibition Scholarship in 1892.

70. The story is taken from Douglas Graham's account of what happened, preserved among his papers. It is reproduced by kind permission of his son, John Graham. His father recounted it on the first of the Radio Telefís Éireann programs commemorating Beckett's seventieth birthday in April 1976.

71. Interview with SB, 22 Aug. 1989. This is corroborated by Herbert Gamble, the boy in whose bed he finished the story: "I remember that he sometimes used to tell me stories in what was known as the blue dormitory after lights out and that on one occasion this got us into trouble with the then Headmaster, the Rev. E. G. Seale. I wish I could remember what the stories were, but unfortunately I can't. That would have been in 1921 when Beckett was 15 and I was 14" (Sir Herbert Gamble, ms. 1227/1/2/4 [Reading].)

72. Quane, *Portora Royal School*, p. 56.

3: THE GROWTH OF A MIND, 1923–26

1. Interview with Eileen Williams, née Adamson, 22 May 1992.

2. LH, undated interview with SB (Dartmouth).

3. SB to Roger Little, 18 May 1983 (Little).

4. Interview with SB, 5 July 1989.

5. T. B. Rudmose-Brown, unpublished memoirs, quoted in Roger Little, "Beckett's Mentor, Rudmose-Brown: Sketch for a Portrait," *Irish University Review*, vol. 14, no. 1 (spring 1984), p. 36. I owe a great debt to Professor Little for his writing about Rudmose-Brown and for invaluable help with my own research.

6. Rudmose-Brown published a volume of essays on French poets, *French Literary Studies*; two prose anthologies, *French Short Stories* (Oxford: Clarendon Press, 1925) and *French Town and Country* (London: Nelson, 1928); and educational editions of Racine's *Andromaque* (Oxford: Clarendon Press, 1917), a play on which Beckett himself lectured a few years later and which he always admired, and Marivaux's *Les fausses confidences* (London: Fisher Unwin, n.d. [1928]).

7. Interview with Professor David Webb, 12 Aug. 1992.

8. LH, undated interview with SB (Dartmouth).

9. A. J. Leventhal was introducing extracts from Rudmose-Brown's unpublished memoirs in *Dublin Magazine*, XXI (Jan.–Mar. 1956), pp. 30–51. Quoted in Roger Little, "Beckett's Mentor, Rudmose-Brown: Sketch for a Portrait," pp. 34–35.

10. LH, undated interview with SB (Dartmouth).

11. Ibid.

12. Interview with SB, 5 July 1989.

13. LH, undated interview with SB (Dartmouth).

14. Interview with SB, 5 July 1989.

15. Leconte de Lisle's *Poèmes antiques*, *Poèmes barbares*, and *Poèmes tragiques* and Henri de Régnier's collections, *Histoires incertaines*, *Le Plateau de laque*, *La Cité des eaux*, *La Sandale ailée*, and *Esquisses vénitiennes* were all on the 1926 and 1927 undergraduate syllabuses at Trinity College.

16. The anthology was published as *A Book of French Verse from Hugo to Larbaud* (London: Oxford University Press, 1928). Verlaine's *Fêtes galantes* and *Sagesse* were both on the undergraduate syllabus in 1926, as was a *Choix de poésies* in 1927.

17. SB, *Dream of Fair to Middling Women*, p. 165.

18. Beckett's copy of *Délie* with annotations in his hand still exists (Avigdor Arikha).

19. Proust's *Du côté de chez Swann* ("Combray"), Gide's *Isabella* and *La Porte étroite*, Jammes's *Choix de poésies*, and Le Cardonnel's *De l'une à l'autre aurore* were all on the undergraduate French program for Beckett's final year, as was R. de la Vaissière's anthology of twentieth-century poetry. Rudmose-Brown also supervised a number of postgraduate theses on modern poetry, including an interesting Ph.D. by Phyllis Ackroyd, entitled *Louis Le Cardonnel*, introduction by Rudmose-Brown.

20. See Roger Little, "Echanges de lettrés: l'amitié franco-irlandaise de Valery Larbaud et T. B. Rudmose-Brown," *Contrasts* (Dublin), no. 21 (spring 1982), pp. 25–27, and "Valery Larbaud et les lettres irlandaises: connaissance de Rudmose-Brown," *Revue de littérature comparée*, no. 1 (1983), pp. 101–111.

21. The myth has arisen that, when Beckett first went to live in Paris, through Rudmose-Brown's French connections, he became a personal friend of Francis Jammes, Vielé-Griffin, Léon-Paul Fargue, Paul Valery, and Valery Larbaud. This is scarcely true at all. Beckett denied knowing either Jammes or Vielé-Griffin. He came to know Fargue and Valéry slightly, but the intermediary was James Joyce. More surprisingly, since he was sent abroad with a fulsome letter of introduction to Valery Larbaud from Rudmose-Brown and the French writer was a friend of James Joyce, he hardly knew Larbaud until June 1940 (interview with SB, 5 July 1989).

22. Thomas Brown Rudmose-Brown, *Walled Gardens* (Dublin: Talbot Press; London: Fisher Unwin, 1918).

23. "Extracts from the unpublished memoirs of T. B. Rudmose-Brown," *Dublin Magazine*, vol. XXI, no. 1 (Jan.–Mar. 1956), p. 33.

24. Ibid., p. 31.

25. In his book *The Irish Beckett* (Syracuse, New York: Syracuse University Press, 1991), John P. Harrington is probably right to see Beckett's contributions in the context of a wider opposition to the tendencies to isolate the newly autonomous, predominantly Catholic state from corruption by outside influences. And he is certainly right to see Beckett as extremely knowledgeable and closely involved with such issues of local concern.

26. Valery Larbaud Archive, Bibliothèque Municipale, Vichy, letter R554. Quoted in Little, "Beckett's Mentor, Rudmose-Brown: Sketch for a Portrait," p. 37.

27. Again quoted in Roger Little, "Beckett's Mentor," p. 41.

28. SB, *More Pricks Than Kicks*, p. 61.

29. Ibid.

30. SB, *Dream of Fair to Middling Women*, p. 146.

31. Interview with SB, 5 July 1989.

32. SB's student notes on Machiavelli, the "Italian Renaissance Purists" (Bembo, Speroni, Castiglione), Carducci, Ariosto, and, in much greater detail, Dante have been preserved. There are also several drafts of his student essays in Italian and English on Carducci and D'Annunzio, for example, in one of which he concludes "Carducci is an excellent university professor but an excessively bad poet."

33. In *Thom's Official Directory*, 1921, Miss Ida Elsner and Miss W. Pauline Elsner are listed as being at 21 Ely Place.

34. SB's student notes make it clear that there were explanations in Dante that he found extremely hard to follow. For instance, after paraphrasing Beatrice's explanation of the movement of the angelic choirs in Canto XXVIII of the *Paradiso*, he writes, "Don't understand a word of this."

35. Interview with SB, 5 July 1989. Beckett also wrote, "No, he [Rudmose-Brown] had no part in the Dante revelation. This I seem to have managed on my own, with the help of my Italian teacher, Bianca Esposito" (SB to Roger Little, 18 May 1983).

36. The card was donated by SB to the archive of the Beckett International Foundation at the University of Reading in 1989. The Dante edition itself is now in private hands.

37. Interview with SB, 5 July 1989. His real-life Italian teacher looked after her father, the musician Signor Michele Esposito, in Ranelagh. (After 1922, when the title was conferred upon him, he became "Commendatore" Esposito.) During Beckett's youth, Esposito was professor of piano at the Royal Irish Academy of Music and a conductor and pianist of great renown in Ireland. Beckett remembered attending a series of concerts in which Esposito played all of Beethoven's piano sonatas. Beckett judged Esposito to have been "a good, though not a great pianist," and said that he used to play too many wrong notes (interview with SB, 8 Aug. 1989). But he admired Esposito's editing of nineteen sonatas of Domenico Scarlatti, whom Beckett rated highly as a composer (Morris Sinclair to JK, 3 April 1992). Bianca's father may have been the model for the Italian music teacher in his radio play *Embers*, for his teaching methods were notorious in Dublin musical circles (see Enid Starkie, *A Lady's Child*, p. 238.)

38. SB, *More Pricks Than Kicks*, p. 20.

39. In a letter to TM, written in 1931, Beckett gave him the name and the address of his former pensione in Florence (TCD).

40. SB, *Krapp's Last Tape*, in *Collected Shorter Plays*, p. 58.

41. SB, *More Pricks Than Kicks*, p. 16.

42. Ibid., p. 20.

43. The Muniment books at Trinity College contain Beckett's detailed marks in all the various subjects. In 1924, his Latin was quite good and his mathematics very average.

44. I am grateful to Professor Frederik Smith of the University of North Carolina at Charlotte for generously sharing his research on the English courses at Trinity College with me.

45. SB attended Trench's lectures on *Henry V* and *A Midsummer Night's Dream; Julius Caesar* and *Coriolanus; As You Like It* and *Twelfth Night; The Merchant of Venice* and *The Tempest; Richard III* and *Romeo and Juliet;* and *Macbeth* and *Hamlet.*

46. SB, *More Pricks Than Kicks,* "Fingal," p. 30. The *Hamlet* allusion is to act I, scene ii.

47. SB, *More Pricks Than Kicks,* "Draff," p. 198. The *Romeo and Juliet* allusion is to act V, scene iii.

48. Philip Howard Solomon, "Lousse and Molloy: Beckett's Bower of Bliss," *Australian Journal of French Studies,* vol. 6, no. 1 (1969), pp. 65–81. One of Rudmose-Brown's examination questions on the *Faerie Queene* was on the overthrow of the "Bowre of blisse."

49. Several quotations from Chaucer, including the epigraph to *Dream of Fair to Middling Women,* were copied out a little later by SB in a 1931–32 notebook.

50. Interview with SB, 12 Aug. 1989. See *No's Knife,* p. 143.

51. Quoting from John Donne's second Elegy, Beckett said of Thelma in the story "What a Misfortune" that "she had at least the anagram of a good face" (*More Pricks Than Kicks,* p. 128).

52. I draw here on my own conversations over twenty years with Beckett, and specifically on a conversation with Barbara Bray, 13 June 1992.

53. William York Tindall, *Samuel Beckett,* p. 37.

54. Interview with SB, 13 Sept. 1989.

55. SB checked off the productions that he could remember seeing at the Abbey Theatre between 1923 and 1927 on a letter from John McCormick to JK, October 7, 1970 (ms. 1227/1/2/16 [Reading]).

56. Bill Cunningham in Radio Telefís Éireann program, first broadcast April 1976.

57. W. H. Lyons (one of Beckett's students at TCD), "Backtracking Beckett," in *Literature and Society: Studies in Nineteenth and Twentieth Century French Literature. Presented to R. J. North,* Birmingham, England: 1980, p. 214.

58. SB, *Endgame* (London: Faber and Faber, 1958), 1964 repr., p. 12.

59. SB to JK, 11 April 1972 (Knowlson).

60. This debt is more fully discussed in James Knowlson and John Pilling, "Beckett and John Millington Synge," in *Frescoes of the Skull: The Later Prose and Drama of Samuel Beckett* (London: John Calder, 1979; and New York: Grove Press, 1980), "Beckett and John Millington Synge," pp. 259–74.

61. *The Times,* London, 31 Dec. 1964.

62. James Agee, *Agee on Film,* quoted in Tom Dardis, *Keaton: The Man Who Wouldn't Lie Down,* p. 69.

63. Dardis, *Keaton,* pp. 120, 131.

64. Interview with Eileen Williams, 22 May 1992.

65. A front-row rugby forward, Jem Higgins by name, tries to arrange a rendezvous with a beautiful woman called the Alba at this café, whose name Beckett deliberately misspelled as "Bon Bouche" (SB, *Dream of Fair to Middling Women,* p. 154).

66. Interview with Eileen Williams, 22 May 1992.

67. SB, "A Wet Night," *More Pricks Than Kicks,* pp. 57–59, and "Sanies I," *Collected Poems in English and French,* p. 18.

68. Ethna MacCarthy, letter (posted from East Ham Memorial Hospital) to Denis Johnston, 21 May 1959 (ms. 10066\170, 203 [TCD]). She died only three days later.

69. Denis Johnston, ms. 10066/288/324 (TCD).

70. Interview with SB, 13 Sept. 1989.

71. Interview with Eileen Williams, 22 May 1992 and Denis Johnston's "Nine Rivers," a talk for the BBC, in which Ethna is the ninth river, "Euterpe" (ms. 1006/30–32 [TCD]).

72. LH, undated interview with SB (Dartmouth).

73. Interview with Georges Belmont, 3 Aug. 1991.

74. SB, *Collected Poems in English and French*, p. 17.

75. LH, undated interview with SB (Dartmouth).

76. Geoffrey Perrin to JK, 3 Feb. 1993.

77. Joseph Maunsell Hone, "A Note on My Acquaintance with Sam Beckett" (Texas).

78. LH, undated interview with SB (Dartmouth).

79. Beckett joined the Historical Society, which held debates once a week but had the advantage of having a billiards table and a quiet room where he could go to read or write between classes. He did not speak in debates.

80. Interview with SB, 11 July 1989.

81. The trial went from Donnybrook to Stillorgan, Dundrum, Stepaside, Glencullen, Pine Forest, Glencree, and Sally Gap, to the Glenview Hotel, then up the "Waterfall of Bricks" through Delgany and via the watersplash to Kilmacanogue, Goat's Pass, Enniskerry, Kilmalin, Devil's Elbow, and through some of the same little villages back to Donnybrook (*Irish Cyclist & Motor Cyclist*, 11 March 1925, p. 18).

82. Interview with John Manning, 19 June 1990.

83. Gerald Pakenham Stewart, memoirs (typescript, p. 14), now published as *The Rough and the Smooth*.

84. Tom Cox in the first Radio Telefís Éireann program, broadcast in April 1976. Nat Gould is referred to by Beckett in his 1929 essay on James Joyce, "Dante . . . Bruno. Vico . . Joyce," SB, *Disjecta: Miscellaneous Writings and a Dramatic Fragment*, ed. Ruby Cohn (London: John Calder, 1983), p. 28.

85. "I have had the old internal combustion heart and head a couple of nights, in the bed where I had it the first time almost exactly 11 years ago, but as little anxiety as then" (SB to TM, 26 April 1937 [TCD]).

86. He was soon to use Ronsard's bringing together of Love and Death in the *Sonnets pour Hélène* to conclude his story "Love and Lethe" (SB, *More Pricks Than Kicks*, p. 105).

87. His copy still exists. Henry Debraye's *En Touraine et sur les bords de la Loire (châteaux et paysages)* was given by Alan Thompson to Eoin O'Brien. It is signed "S. B. Beckett. Tours. August 1926."

88. Henry Debraye, *Touraine and Its Châteaux* (London and Boston: The Medici Society, 1926), p. 11.

89. The exercise book in which, on his return to Trinity College, Beckett took notes on the remainder of Dante's *Paradiso* has on the first page "Bought at Tours: Sept. 3rd 1926."

90. The account of the meeting between Beckett and Charles L. Clarke is based on an undated interview with Beckett by Lawrence Harvey (Dartmouth). Lois Overbeck also kindly provided me with copies of letters from Mrs. Constance Clarke, Charles's widow, and generously shared the results of her research on Clarke with me.

91. Gerald Pakenham Stewart to JK, 14 May 1992.

92. Geoffrey Thompson in the first Radio Telefís Éireann program, broadcast in April 1976.

93. Gerald Pakenham Stewart to JK, 14 May 1992.

94. Interview with Marysette Mayoux, 21 Sept. 1990.

95. Interview with SB, 13 Sept. 1989.

96. SB, "Ding-Dong," *More Pricks Than Kicks*, p. 42.

97. Ibid., pp. 42–43.

98. Gerald Pakenham Stewart, memoirs (typescript, p. 15), now published as *The Rough and The Smooth*.

99. LH, undated interview with SB (Dartmouth).

100. SB, *Endgame*, p. 37.

101. Gerald Pakenham Stewart, memoirs (typescript, p. 15), now published as *The Rough and The Smooth*.

4: ACADEMIC SUCCESS AND LOVE, 1927–28

1. A. A. Luce to JK, 24 Sept. 1970.
2. Interview with SB, 13 Sept. 1989.
3. The Board of Trinity College recommended "Samuel Barclay Beckett (Scholar) as Lecturer in English at the Ecole Normale" on March 22, 1927 (Register of the Minutes of the Board of Trinity College, Dublin [cited in future references as Minutes], vol. 23).
4. My attention was first drawn to the row involving Beckett by Thomas MacGreevy's biographer, Susan Schreibman, who kindly offered me information from the Minutes of the Board of Trinity College that was confirmed by correspondence in the MacGreevy papers.
5. The appointment was sanctioned by the Board of Trinity College at a meeting on January 22, 1927. It was on a temporary basis (Minutes, vol. 23).
6. MacGreevy's written French remained inaccurate, even in the mid-1930s, as his letters to his French friend Jean Coulomb show.
7. Copy of letter from William McCausland Stewart to Dr. Louis Purser (MacGreevy Papers, ms. 8141 [TCD]).
8. Dr. Louis Purser to TM, May 13, 1927 (MacGreevy Papers, ms. 8141 [TCD]).
9. The letter in which Beckett was offered the Besançon post was from the National Office of the French Universities and Schools and was dated July 6, 1927. An application had to be made before July 14 (It is referred to in Minutes, vol. 23, at the meeting of Oct. 1, 1927).
10. Formal agreement to Beckett's appointment was only given through the French Consul-General and recorded in the Minutes of the Board at a meeting on April 28, 1928 (Minutes, vol. 24).
11. Interview with SB, 5 July 1989.
12. Telephone interview with Vida Ashworth's daughter, Janet Barcroft, 11 Aug. 1992.
13. Interview with SB, 5 July 1989.
14. Ibid. Vera Esposito said of her mother: "I took after my mother, who was not Italian but Russian, from St. Petersburg, which she had left, with her father, in 1867, never to return. They settled near Naples, (she was then sixteen) where she later met my father and they were married quite young. She had brown hair, blue-grey eyes, and a pink-and-white complexion" (letter to Richard Ellmann, 18 June 1955, Ellmann Papers, 011, Dockrell file [Tulsa]).
15. Interview with SB, 5 July 1989.
16. Vera Esposito Dockrell, letter to Richard Ellmann, 14 April 1955, Ellmann Papers, 011, Dockrell file (Tulsa).
17. SB, interview with Richard Ellmann, 21 June 1954, Ellmann Papers, 003, Beckett file (Tulsa). The actual phrase in Dante, *Purgatorio*, Canto 25, 1. 123, is "caler non meno."
18. Vera Esposito wrote of Beckett at this time: "He was then a total abstainer, detesting drink and drunkenness, keeping away from the athletic circles in the University for this reason. His parents were very strict with him and they belonged to one of the most rigid Protestant sects. They were wealthy people and so he has not known poverty. He wished to get out of Ireland at all costs, and did so" (letter to Richard Ellmann, 14 April 1955, Ellmann Papers, 011, Dockrell file [Tulsa]).
19. These two Joyce stories were recounted by Richard Ellmann in his biography *James Joyce* (Oxford: Oxford University Press, new and revised edition, 1983), pp. 155, 160–61. Beckett was Ellmann's 1954 source for Esposito's compliment to Joyce on his singing, while it was Vera Esposito who told Ellmann about the drunken incident.
20. Mario Esposito was the author of a number of studies of Latin manuscripts and treatises published from 1912 to 1921 either in the *Proceedings of the Royal Irish Academy* in Dublin or the *Revue des bibliothèques* in Paris. He also published privately a book entitled *Mélanges philologiques, textes et études de littérature ancienne et médiévale* (Florence, 1921).

21. This is recounted in Ulick O'Connor, *Oliver St. John Gogarty* (London: New English Library, 1967), p. 156.

22. It was this holiday that provided the source for one of the few moments of near lyricism that are found in Beckett's 1956 play, *Endgame:* Nell, one of the old crones consigned to dustbins, remembers being out on the water of Lake Como in a rowing boat, from which she could see "down to the bottom. So white. So clean" (*Endgame,* p. 21).

23. Mario Esposito to Richard Ellmann, 15 Dec. 1968 (Ellmann Papers, 011, Dockrell file [Tulsa]).

24. SB, *Dream of Fair to Middling Women*, pp. 129–30.

25. Ibid., p. 130.

26. Mario Esposito to Richard Ellmann, 15 Dec. 1968 (Ellmann Papers, 011, Dockrell file [Tulsa]).

27. SB, *Dream of Fair to Middling Women*, p. 130. The allusions are to Dante's *Paradiso,* canto III.

28. SB, *More Pricks Than Kicks*, pp. 54–55.

29. Beckett's copy still exists in private hands. Vasari is referred to in *Dream of Fair to Middling Women*, p. 77.

30. In one of his stories, he referred to Tommaso Masaccio as "sweaty Big Tom": "she looked, with that strange limey hobnailed texture of complexion, so frescosa, from the waist up, my dear, with that distempered cobalt modesty-piece, a positive gem of ravished Quattrocento, a positive jewel, my dear, of sweaty Big Tom" (*More Pricks Than Kicks,* p. 67). The particular Masaccio being referred to here is, however, not in Florence but is the central panel of the *Madonna and Child* in the National Gallery of London (O'Brien, *The Beckett Country*, p. 362, n. 28).

31. Bianca Esposito's talent for question spotting is reflected in "Dante and the Lobster," when the Signorina suggests to Belacqua that he should work at " 'Dante's rare movements of compassion in Hell. That used to be' her past tenses were always sorrowful 'a favourite question' " (SB, *More Pricks Than Kicks*, p. 18).

32. A. A. Luce to JK, 24 Sept. 1970.

33. Interview with SB, 20 Sept. 1989.

34. These poems were published in a volume entitled *Tragiques suivis du voyage sentimental* (Paris: Stock etc., 1922).

35. Rudmose-Brown printed one of Chennevière's poems, "Coule le temps," in *A Book of French Verse from Hugo to Larbaud.*

36. The Register of Chambers, 1911–1960 (Trinity College Dublin, MUN/V/39a/3, p. 419) shows that Beckett did not vacate his rooms in Trinity until January 9, 1928, when he went to teach at Campbell College, Belfast.

37. Jules Romains, *Bertrand de Ganges*, ed. A. G. Lehmann (London: Harrap, 1961) p. 8.

38. Arthur Hillis, a classics student who knew Beckett, said that *Les Copains* was a very fashionable book at the time among Trinity arts students and one of his own favorite French novels.

39. LH, undated interview with SB (Dartmouth).

40. Interview with SB, 20 Sept. 1989.

41. Bair wrote that, while in Paris, Beckett "did next to nothing for his essay on Jouve" (*Samuel Beckett,* p. 90) and Enoch Brater states that he offered his monograph on Proust in place of the Jouve essay (*Why Beckett* [London: Thames & Hudson, 1989], p. 26). Other critics have also regarded this as true. For example: "Samuel Beckett arrived in Paris in 1928 with the intention of writing a scholarly work on the French poet Pierre-Jean Jouve" (Thomas Cousineau, *Waiting for Godot: Form in Movement*, p. 1).

42. LH, undated interview with SB (Dartmouth). John Fletcher also has Beckett submitting the research essay on the Unanimists as a condition of the award required (*The Novels of Samuel Beckett*, p. 13).

43. LH, undated interview with SB (Dartmouth).

44. Interview with Miles Delap, 31 Jan. 1992.

45. Interview with SB, 13 Sept. 1989.

46. *The Campbellian*, vol. VI (July 1928), p. 412.

47. Batting at number five, Beckett notched up the highest score of 21 runs, then went on to bowl out one of the school's opening batsmen.

48. The son of Sir William Duff Gibbon, a tea planter in Ceylon, Gibbon had volunteered to fight in the army as a private in the 1900–1901 Boer War and had become a lieutenant colonel in the First World War. He was a distinguished rugby player at school and at Oxford, but because of a serious shoulder injury, for many years he had been unable to play at first-class level. So he had confined himself to coaching and writing highly cogent manuals of the game: *First Steps to Rugby Football* and *Rugby Football in Theory and Practice*. (Information about William Duff Gibbon comes from A.C.L. Hall, the librarian and archivist of Dulwich College, where Gibbon was a master, and from Dulwich College's school magazine.)

49. Keith Haines to JK, 10 Jan. 1992.

50. LH, undated interview with SB (Dartmouth).

51. Ibid.

52. It is rumored that this story is apocryphal. However, Beckett himself recounted it to me — with great relish — late in life when I asked him how he had got on at the school.

53. SB to TM, undated (but, from internal evidence, 14 July 1932 [TCD]).

54. Chrimes himself quit teaching school soon afterward to become an engineer with Sir Alexander Binney Son and Deacon; then, following his marriage in 1938, he went abroad to work in Ceylon. After the war, he moved to Singapore, where eventually he became managing director of the Singapore Slipway and Engineering Company and chairman and general manager of the Penang Harbour Board. The information about Chrimes's career comes from the *Register of Graduates of Keble College, Oxford*, and from details lodged at the Institution of Mechanical Engineers.

55. SB, *More Pricks Than Kicks*, p. 116.

56. LH, undated interview with SB (Dartmouth).

57. Interview with Deirdre Hamilton (née Sinclair), Peggy's sister, 20 June 1991, and Morris Sinclair to JK, 7 June 1992.

58. Interview with Deirdre Hamilton, 20 June 1991.

59. Constance Clarke to Lois Overbeck and Martha Fehsenfeld, 14 March 1992.

60. Interview with SB, 13 Sept. 1989.

61. SB, *Dream of Fair to Middling Women*, p. 114.

62. Ibid., p. 113.

63. Interview with SB, 13 Sept. 1989.

64. SB, *Dream of Fair to Middling Women*, p. 14.

65. Morris Sinclair to JK, 27 May 1991.

66. The portrait of Peggy Sinclair is owned by Drs. Gottfried and Renate Büttner. I am most grateful to them for welcoming me into their home, showing me around Kassel, and supplying me with documents.

67. SB, *Dream of Fair to Middling Women*, p. 4.

68. SB, *Krapp's Last Tape*, in *Collected Shorter Plays*, p. 58.

69. Morris Sinclair to JK, 27 May 1991.

70. SB, *Dream of Fair to Middling Women*, p. 114.

71. Gerald Pakenham Stewart to JK, 14 May 1992.

72. Marcel Proust, *A l'Ombre des jeunes filles en fleurs*, vol. II (Paris: Gallimard, NRF, 1919), 119th printing, p. 99. Beckett's copy, with the passage about the pain of separation underlined and the marginal autobiographical note, was given by him to the Beckett International Foundation in the University of Reading. I am grateful to Adam Piette for drawing my attention to the significance of this entry.

73. Beckett's stay in Laxenburg is proved by the presence of his name as guest number

451 in the *Fremden-protokoll der Marktgemeinde Laxenburg*, 1927–1933, no. 3, band 9. His date of arrival there is given as October 4 and his departure (to Paris) as October 31. He stayed in the Blauer Hof. His date of birth and status as a student are also given. I owe a great debt to Monika Seidl, who performed research for me in Laxenburg and provided most of the detailed information that I have used on the "Hellerau-Laxenburg" school.

74. Interview with Morris Sinclair, 22 May 1991, and Morris Sinclair to JK, 7 June 1992.
75. SB, *Dream of Fair to Middling Women*, pp. 13–14.
76. Ibid.
77. "Prospectus of Summer Courses of the Hellerau-Laxenburg School in Rhythmical, Musical and Physical Education (Gymnastics) and Dance," 1931.
78. SB, *Dream of Fair to Middling Women*, p. 13.
79. Johann Voigt, interview with Monika Seidl, Sept. 1992.
80. SB, *Dream of Fair to Middling Women*, p. 15.
81. Ibid.
82. Ibid., p. 19.
83. Ibid.
84. Ibid., p. 31.

5: The Paris Years, 1928–30

1. Information on conditions at the Ecole Normale Supérieure at the end of the 1920s comes from interviews with *normaliens* who were contemporaries of Beckett (Emile Delavenay, Georges Pelorson, and Claude Jamet), from numerous letters to me from former *normaliens*, and from letters to Thomas MacGreevy from William McCausland Stewart (in Trinity College, Dublin, Library).
2. SB, *Dream of Fair to Middling Women*, p. 52.
3. Every year, twenty-eight students were admitted to the Ecole Normale in letters and the same number enrolled to read the sciences. These were spread thinly over a wide range of academic subjects.
4. Emile Delavenay to Richard Ellmann, 17 March 1982 (copy from Emile Delavenay).
5. Interview with Emile Delavenay, 17 May 1991 and letter from Delavenay to Richard Ellmann, 17 March 1982 (copy from Emile Delavenay).
6. SB, undated (1930) letter to TM (TCD).
7. By the time Beckett was in residence, a number of cold showers had been installed downstairs in the basement, but few of the students were hardy enough to use them (interview with Emile Delavenay, 17 May 1991).
8. Interview with Georges Belmont (Pelorson), 3 Aug. 1991. After the war, Georges Pelorson changed his name to Georges Belmont; he is referred to henceforward as Belmont.
9. Tom MacGreevy described his room in this way in a third-person autobiographical sketch, ms. 10381/204 (TCD).
10. Ibid.
11. William Stewart, like Beckett and MacGreevy a former student at Trinity College, Dublin, became a distinguished professor of French at the University of Bristol in England.
12. Information from an enclosure with a letter of William Stewart to TM, 4 Feb. 1927 (ms. 8141, 14 [TCD]).
13. My description of Tom MacGreevy is based on interviews with Samuel Beckett; with Jean Coulomb, who was one of MacGreevy's best friends at the Ecole Normale and, later, director of the Centre National de la Recherche Scientifique; with Emile Delavenay, who studied under MacGreevy; with Georges Belmont; and with other *normaliens* who kindly sent me their detailed written memories of the two *lecteurs*.
14. See Susan Schreibman's introduction to The *Collected Poems of Thomas MacGreevy*

(Dún Laoghaire: Anna Livia Press; Washington, D.C.: The Catholic University of America Press, 1991) and Patricia Boylan, *All Cultivated People: A History of the United Arts Club Dublin*, (Gerrards Cross, Bucks.: Colin Smythe, 1988), *passim*.

15. Interview with Georges Belmont, 3 Aug. 1991.

16. LH, undated interview with SB (Dartmouth).

17. MacGreevy reviewed books, as well as ballet and opera, for example, for a number of journals during a two-year stay in London after he graduated. After acting as assistant editor of *The Connoisseur*, a journal of the visual arts, and working as an occasional lecturer at the National Gallery in London, he had become extremely knowledgeable about painting. He was a fervent admirer of Italian art. His translation of Paul Valéry's *Introduction to the Method of Leonardo da Vinci* was published by the poet, translator, and publisher John Rodker, a friend of James Joyce. In addition, he was a published poet and, before Beckett's arrival, was touting a small collection of his poems around the publishers.

18. The Cochon de Lait (which indeed used to serve excellent suckling pig) still exists but is now called the Restaurant Bastide-Odéon.

19. The Mahieu was the regular haunt of the poet and critic André Thérive. Beckett was with Alfred Péron and the sole first-year student of English at the Ecole, Georges Pelorson (Belmont), when he met Thérive in the company of Louis Le Cardonnel, a French poet known to his former professor Rudmose-Brown (SB to TM, undated 1930 [TCD]).

20. Emile Delavenay to Richard Ellmann, 17 March 1982 (copy from Emile Delavenay).

21. Alan Duncan was the son of Ellie Duncan, one of the main founders of the Dublin Arts Club and founder of the Municipal Gallery in Dublin (see Boylan, *All Cultivated People, passim.*).

22. Interview with SB, 23 Oct. 1989.

23. See Noel Riley Fitch, *Sylvia Beach and the Lost Generation*, (New York, London: W. W. Norton, & Co., 1983), pp. 277–78.

24. SB, *Dream of Fair to Middling Women*, p. 37. James Joyce regularly mixed these two drinks together, although one was a strong apéritif and one a digestif, and invited his friends to mix this fairly lethal cocktail. Interview with Georges Belmont, 4 Aug. 1991.

25. SB to TM, undated (from internal evidence, summer 1930 [TCD]).

26. Beckett recounted how he used to scale the front railings in this way, adding that the height of the railings had been raised since then, making them virtually impossible to scale (interview with SB, Sept. 1989).

27. Roger Bernard to JK, 23 April 1991. Also interview with Georges Belmont, 3 Aug. 1991.

28. Camille Marcoux to JK, 15 April 1991.

29. Ibid.

30. Ulysse Nicollet to JK, 23 April 1991.

31. Richard Aldington, *Life for Life's Sake*, p. 319.

32. Interview with SB, 20 Sept. 1989.

33. Tom MacGreevy, unpublished autobiographical fragment, ms. 8054 (TCD).

34. Lucien Roubaud, undated letter to JK.

35. For example, SB to TM (undated, but probably late July 1930 [TCD]), where he writes of going to the opera *Louise* with his uncle Harry Sinclair. He also went to the opera with the Joyces.

36. Georges Belmont, "Remembering Sam," *Beckett in Dublin*, S. E. Wilmer, ed. (Dublin: The Lilliput Press, 1992), p. 111.

37. Interview with SB, 10 Nov. 1989.

38. SB to TM (undated, but probably late July 1930 [TCD]).

39. Interview with SB, April 1989.

40. Tom MacGreevy, unpublished memoirs (TCD) and Richard Ellmann, interview with SB, 1953 (Ellmann Papers, 003 [Tulsa]).

41. Mario Esposito to Richard Ellmann, 15 Dec. 1958 (Ellmann Papers, 011, Dockrell file [Tulsa]).

42. Vera Esposito Dockrell to Richard Ellmann, 14 April 1955 (Ellmann Papers, 011, Dockrell file [Tulsa]).

43. Interview with Bill Cunningham, 11 Aug. 1992.

44. A comment made by Joyce on Dante's *Purgatory*, which they both loved, impressed Beckett: "What runs through the whole of Dante," Joyce once said to Beckett, "is less the longing for Paradise than the nostalgia for being. Everyone in the poem says 'Io fui' — I was, I was" (Richard Ellmann, interview with SB, 28 July 1953, Ellmann Papers 003, [Tulsa]). In *Rough for Radio II*, the Animator points out that, in the *Purgatorio*, "There all sigh, I was, I was. It's like a knell." *Collected Shorter Plays*, p. 118. Several of Beckett's own later characters echo this thought — "Be again, be again," intones Krapp. But there is an ambiguity about living life all over again that is characteristically Beckett's own. So even Krapp concludes with yearning "All that old misery . . . Once wasn't enough for you" (*Krapp's Last Tape*, in *Collected Shorter Plays*, p. 63).

45. This is Beckett's own word for his meeting with Joyce (LH, interview with SB [Dartmouth]). The meeting must have happened during the first few days of his stay in Paris, for Beckett could remember staying on for dinner and finding Joyce exceptionally worried about the state of his wife's health. Nora's first exploratory operation for cancer was on November 8, and this was followed by a period of radium treatment, then by a hysterectomy at the end of February 1929.

46. Interview with SB, 20 Sept. 1989.

47. Interview with SB, 23 Oct. 1989.

48. Ellmann, *James Joyce*, p. 648.

49. Beckett's extensive notes on "Cow" contain such items of information as that there were 25,000 licensed bulls annually in the Irish Free State and 1.5 million milch cows. There are also manuscript and typescript pages of notes on the *Trueborn Jackeen*.

50. See, for a résumé of the different opinions, Barbara Reich Gluck, *Beckett and Joyce: Friendship and Fiction* (Lewisburg: Bucknell University Press, 1979), p. 175, n. 59.

51. James Joyce, *Finnegans Wake* (London: Faber and Faber, 1964), p. 467. This section, without "ill-starred punster," was published in *transition*, 13, Summer 1928.

52. Interview with SB, 20 Sept. 1989.

53. *Our Exagmination Round His Factification for Incamination of Work in Progress* (Paris: Shakespeare and Company, 1929; reprint, London: Faber and Faber, 1959), pp. 6, 14, 21, 14.

54. James Joyce to Harriet Shaw Weaver, 18 March 1930: "The revision of this last fragment has been a frightful job, extending over two months day and night sometimes till one in the morning, with seven different people helping me to do seven different parts of the labour. . . ." *The Letters of James Joyce*, vol. I, Stuart Gilbert, ed., (London: Faber and Faber, 1957), p. 290.

55. LH, undated interview with SB (Dartmouth).

56. SB, *Ohio Impromptu* in *Collected Shorter Plays*, pp. 285–86.

57. Interview with SB, 20 Sept. 1989.

58. Richard Ellmann, interview with Nino Frank, 20 Aug. 1953 (Ellmann Papers, 046 [Tulsa]).

59. Interview with SB, 20 Sept. 1989.

60. Richard Ellmann, interview with SB, 28 July 1953 (Ellmann Papers, 003 [Tulsa]).

61. Ibid.

62. Richard Ellmann, interview with Lucie Léon Noel, 19 July 1953 (Ellmann Papers, 153 [Tulsa]).

63. Richard Ellmann, interview with Maria Jolas, 22 July 1953 (Ellmann Papers, 054 [Tulsa]).

64. Richard Ellmann, interview with Lucie Léon Noel, 31 Aug. 1953 (Ellmann Papers, 153 [Tulsa]).

65. Interview with SB, 20 Sept. 1989.

66. James Joyce to Valery Larbaud, 30 July 1929, *Selected Letters of James Joyce*, Richard Ellmann, ed. (London: Faber and Faber, 1975), p. 344.

67. Undated interview with SB, April(?) 1989.

68. Beckett regularly brought the mail when Joyce was staying in the Neuilly clinic with Nora at the time that she had her hysterectomy (Brenda Maddox, *Nora, A Biography of Nora Joyce*. London: Hamish Hamilton, 1988, p. 327).

69. Bozena Berta Delimata, "Reminiscences of a Joyce Niece," *James Joyce Quarterly*, vol. 19, no. 1 (fall 1981), p. 55.

70. Albert Hubbell, undated script to Richard Ellmann (Ellmann Papers, 052 [Tulsa]).

71. Delimata, "Reminiscences of a Joyce Niece," p. 55.

72. Ibid., p. 50.

73. James Joyce to Harriet Shaw Weaver, 19 Oct. 1929, *The Letters of James Joyce*, vol. 1, p. 285.

74. Richard Ellmann, interview with SB, 21 June 1954 (Ellmann Papers, 011 [Tulsa]).

75. Interview with SB, 23 Oct. 1989.

76. Albert Hubbell, undated script to Richard Ellmann (Ellmann Papers, 052 [Tulsa]). Stuart Gilbert speculated otherwise to Richard Ellmann, saying that "Beckett may have slept with Lucia. At that time [he was] a heavy drinker. He had some interest in her, perhaps to the point of copulation." (interview with Richard Ellmann, 7 Aug. 1953 [Ellmann Papers, 048 {Tulsa}]).

77. Maddox, *Nora*, p. 337.

78. Interview with SB, 27 Oct. 1989.

79. SB to Mr. Bushrui, 29 Sept. 1980 (Ellmann Papers [Tulsa]).

80. SB, *Dream of Fair to Middling Women*, p. 37.

81. From Samuel Putnam, *Paris Was Our Mistress, Memoirs of a Lost and Found Generation*. (London: Plantin Publications, Plantin Paperbacks, 1987). (First edition 1947.)

82. *Bérénice* was presented at the Odéon Théâtre de France on December 2, 1929. This was the Odéon production in which Rome was symbolized not by any kind of grandiose or even schematic kind of set but by a few moments of sound. See Paul Blanchart, *Firmin Gémier* (Paris: L'Arche, 1954), p. 302. Beckett commented on having seen "Racine at Odéon, when the set didn't matter" (German diaries, henceforward GD, notebook 4, 21 Jan. 1937).

83. Kay Boyle recounts how Beckett enthused to her about Machiavelli's play when they first met: "He wanted to make me understand that it was the most powerful play in the Italian language, the language with which he was so much in love." (Kay Boyle, "All Mankind Is Us," in Ruby Cohn, *Samuel Beckett: A Collection of Criticism*, p. 16.) Beckett was still "boosting" *Mandragola* to a German director, Eggers-Kastner, in Munich in 1937 (GD, notebook 6, 19 March 1937). The play was presented by Madame Valsamaki's company. I thank Prue Winnett for her help in tracing these plays.

84. Beckett's translations of Montale, Franchi, and Comisso were published in *This Quarter*, vol. II (April, May, and June 1930), pp. 630, 672, 675–683.

85. SB, *Dream of Fair to Middling Women*, p. 40.

86. Ibid., p. 38.

87. Ibid., p. 41.

88. Ibid., p. 42.

89. Morris Sinclair to JK, 27 May 1991.

90. SB to TM, undated (probably June 1930 [TCD]).

91. Morris Sinclair to JK, 22 Nov. 1992.

92. Rubin Rabinovitz, *The Development of Samuel Beckett's Fiction* (Urbana and Chicago: University of Illinois Press, 1984), p. 17.

93. SB, "Assumption," *transition*, vol. 16–17 (June 1929), p. 271.

94. Rubin Rabinovitz, *The Development of Samuel Beckett's Fiction*, p. 18.

95. In her biography of Nancy Cunard, Anne Chisholm writes that over one hundred

poems had been submitted before the final week. Anne Chisholm, *Nancy Cunard* (Harmondsworth: Penguin Books, 1981), p. 206. But Nancy Cunard herself remembered the number as being almost seventy. "The Hours Press," *Book Collector*, vol. 13, no. 4 (winter 1964), pp. 188–96.

96. One of the books that he had been studying more thoroughly than the others was Adrien Baillet's *La Vie de Descartes* (*The Life of Descartes*). Another, now convincingly shown to have been heavily used in writing "Whoroscope," was J. P. Mahaffy's *Descartes* (1901). (The picturesque Mahaffy was a philosopher at Trinity College, Dublin.) See Francis Doherty, "Mahaffy's Whoroscope," *Journal of Beckett Studies*, n.s., vol. 2, no. 1 (1992), pp. 27–46. Mahaffy's *Descartes* was published in the series "Philosophical Classics for English Readers" (Edinburgh and London: William Blackwood, 1901).

97. SB to Nancy Cunard, Jan. 26, 1959 (Texas). "Them were the days" is a quotation from "Whoroscope" as well as a play on the obvious cliché.

98. It is probably on account of the ostentatious cleverness and display of esoteric knowledge in the poem that, in a late dedication written in his friend Con Leventhal's copy, Beckett wrote that "Whoroscope" was "un mauvais poème" ("a bad poem") and dedicated it to "celui qui comprend que les mauvais poèmes ne sont pas précisément les derniers" ("one who understands that bad poems are not exactly the last ones").

99. Nancy Cunard, *These Were the Hours* (Carbondale: Southern Illinois University Press, 1969), p. 111.

100. Chisholm, *Nancy Cunard*, p. 207. Ten pounds was a substantial sum at the time and corresponded to half of the advance on royalties that Beckett received from Chatto and Windus for *Proust*.

101. "Good indeed about The Dolphin Books, to which all success! MacGreevy has started on his essay [on T. S. Eliot] and suggests an essay on Proust by one Samuel Beckett, at the Ecole Normale, whom I do not know personally, but to whom I have allotted the Nancy Cunard 10 pound prize for a poem on Time. The essay will probably be good" (Richard Aldington to Charles Prentice, 18 June 1930 [CW, Reading]).

102. Charles Prentice to Richard Aldington, 20 June 1930 (CW, Reading). The reason for this aversion to commissioning the Dolphin books is clear from Aldington's letter: "I've urged MacGreevy to go ahead on his essay about the Hero ["Death of a Hero," part of MacGreevy's 1931 essay, *Richard Aldington*] etc., but warned him that the essay cannot be commissioned. I think it is essential that you should not commission *anything* for the Dolphin Books, since it is important to have good and appropriate stuff only" (Richard Aldington to Charles Prentice, 18 June 1930 [CW, Reading]).

103. Only sixteen Dolphin books appeared in all, including Aldous Huxley, *Vulgarity in Literature*; T. F. Powys, *The Only Penitent*; Norman Douglas, *London Street Games*; Lennox Robinson, *The Far-Off Hills*; Sylvia Townsend Warner, *Opus 7*; and Richard Aldington, famous since the success of his First World War novel, *Death of a Hero*, provided *Stepping Heavenward*.

104. All the design work was done, for six guineas, by the famous designer Edward Bawden, of Holbein Studios, but it was carefully supervised and vetted by Charles Prentice himself.

105. Charles Prentice to SB, 10 Oct. 1930 (CW, Reading).

106. SB to Charles Prentice, 14 Oct. 1930 (CW, Reading).

107. Prentice turned down, albeit reluctantly, *Dream of Fair to Middling Women*, which both he and his partner, Harold Raymond, considered uncommercial and which was not published until after Beckett's death. However, they went on to accept his later *More Pricks Than Kicks*, which largely grew out of *Dream*. Sales of these stories were then very poor. So when, two years later, they were offered and turned down *Murphy*, it was a marginal decision in which Prentice participated as an outside reader but did not himself make, as he had left Chatto and Windus several years before.

108. Charles Prentice to Richard Aldington, 10 March 1930 (CW, Reading).

109. In spite of all efforts to trace it, the latter part of Beckett's correspondence with

Prentice after Prentice left Chatto and Windus in 1934 has not yet come to light. It is clear from Beckett's German diaries of 1936–37 that he was still corresponding regularly with him at that time.

110. Undated interview with SB, (April?) 1989.

111. Richard Aldington, *Pinorman: Personal Recollections of Norman Douglas, Pino Orioli, and Charles Prentice* (London: Heinemann, 1954), pp. 87–88, and *Life for Life's Sake,* p. 354.

112. In *An Innkeeper's Diary,* quoted in Oliver Warner, *Chatto and Windus, A Brief Account of the Firm's Origin, History and Development* (London: Chatto and Windus, 1973), pp. 19–20.

113. Warner, *Chatto and Windus,* pp. 19–20.

114. "We (Péron) are galloping through A.L.P. [Anna Livia Plurabelle]. It has become comic now. I suppose that is the only attitude" (SB to TM, undated [from internal evidence, late summer 1930] [TCD]).

115. SB to TM, undated (ca. 18 July 1930 [TCD]).

116. See Arlen J. Hansen, *Expatriate Paris: A Cultural and Literary Guide to Paris of the 1920s* (New York: Arcade Publishing, 1990), p. 202.

117. SB to TM, undated (ca. 18 July 1930 [TCD]).

118. SB to TM, undated (probably June 1930 [TCD]).

119. This was in keeping with the uncluttered nature of the Dolphin series, as well as Beckett's own impatience with scholarly apparatus. His main sources were: Ernst Robert Curtius, *Marcel Proust* (acknowledged); Léon-Pierre Quint, *Marcel Proust: sa vie, son oeuvre* (Paris: Editions du Sagittaire, 1925; unacknowledged); Arnaud Dandieu, *Marcel Proust: sa révélation psychologique* (Paris: Firmin-Didot, 1930; unacknowledged) and, perhaps, Jacques Gabriel Benoît-Méchin, *La musique et l'immortalité dans l'oeuvre de Marcel Proust* (Paris: Simon Kra, 1926).

120. SB to TM, undated (probably summer 1930)(TCD). Keats's memorable line from the "Ode to a Nightingale" is used toward the end of Beckett's story "Dante and the Lobster" (*More Pricks Than Kicks,* p. 21).

121. SB to TM, July 7 (this may be an error for August), 1930 (TCD).

122. SB, *Proust. Three Dialogues. Samuel Beckett & Georges Duthuit* (London: Calder and Boyars, 1970 repr.) pp. 90–91.

123. SB to TM, 7 July 1930 (TCD). The passage quoted by Beckett comes from D'Annunzio's novel *Il Fuoco* (Milan: Fratelli Treves, 1904), p. 92, which Beckett had clearly been reading. English translation by Kassandra Vivaria, *The Flame of Life* (London: Heinemann, 1915), p. 63. I am grateful to Professor John Pilling for this reference.

124. SB, *Proust,* p. 91. Beckett made this less uniformly antagonistic by congratulating D'Annunzio on his fine description of the *Concert,* which he quoted in Italian — although he could not resist attacking the "horrible pomegranates" of D'Annunzio's novel *Il Fuoco (Flame of Life)* as "bursting and bleeding, dripping the red ooze of their seed, putrid on the putrid water" (p. 91), even though the example seems less relevant than the others to his argument.

125. SB to TM, undated (July 1930).

126. A study that reveals this pessimistic reading of Proust is Nicholas Zurbrugg, *Beckett and Proust.* (Gerrards Cross, Bucks.: Colin Smythe, 1988).

127. SB to TM, undated (probably 19 Sept. 1930).

128. Ibid.

129. Ibid.

6: ACADEME: RETURN AND FLIGHT, 1930–31

1. SB to TM, from Cooldrinagh, undated (late Sept.)(TCD).

2. Ibid.

3. SB to TM, 5 Oct. 1930 (TCD).

4. SB to TM, 14 Nov. (1930)(TCD).

5. SB to TM, 5 Oct. 1930 (TCD).

6. SB to TM, 14 Nov. (1930)(TCD).

7. This talk is ms. 1396/4/15 (Reading).

8. Beckett uses the same adjective of Marseille in a letter to TM, 20 Dec. 1931 (TCD).

9. SB to TM, undated (TCD).

10. SB, *Le Concentrisme*, translated by John Pilling on Mencard 118, The Menard Press, 1990.

11. Undated conversation with SB.

12. Georges Belmont, undated reply to letter from JK, 5 March 1991. Georges Belmont (Pelorson) went over a draft of the present chapter, giving his detailed memories of the play.

13. *T.C.D.: A College Miscellany*, 26 Feb. 1931, p. 116.

14. Ibid.

15. "This *vitaccia* is terne [dull] beyond all belief. Thursday, Friday and Sat. we gave 3 plays at the Peacock — *La Quema, Souriante Mme Beudet* and *Le Kid* (Corneille and Bergson)" (SB to TM, 24 Feb. 1931 [TCD]).

16. *The Irish Times*, 20 Feb. 1931.

17. "We had a nice Cartesian Infanta in the *Kid*, inarticulate and stupefied, crossing the stage to Ravel's *Pavane*" (SB to TM, 24 Feb. 1931 [TCD]). Cf. SB, *More Pricks Than Kicks*, p. 101.

18. *The Irish Times*, 20 Feb. 1931.

19. In an interview, 14 Oct. 1989, Georges Belmont corrected the information given in Bair, *Samuel Beckett*, pp. 127–28, where it is said that he played the role of the silent figure who manipulated the hands of the clock.

20. *The Irish Times*, 20 Feb. 1931.

21. Bair, *Samuel Beckett*, pp. 127–28.

22. Interview with Georges Belmont, 14 Oct. 1989.

23. Georges Belmont to JK, March 1991.

24. SB to TM, 24 Feb. 1931 (TCD).

25. *T.C.D.: A College Miscellany*, 26 Feb. 1931, p. 116.

26. Interview with Georges Belmont, 14 Oct. 1989.

27. Georges Belmont to JK, March 1991.

28. Seamus O'Sullivan asked him to review Tom MacGreevy's study of T. S. Eliot for the *Dublin Magazine*, along with Eliot's translation of St. John Perse's "richly decorative and sometimes gaudy 'prose-poem,' " *Anabase* (Peter Ackroyd, *T. S. Eliot*, p. 189). In the end, he produced reviews of neither book for he thought that MacGreevy was known too widely to be his personal friend and he did not like the St. John Perse poem, which he thought of as "bad Claudel; with abominable colour" (SB to TM, 11 March 1931 [TCD]), although, interestingly enough, he said that he liked the translation whenever Eliot forgot about being faithful to the original.

29. SB to TM, 25 Jan. 1931 (TCD).

30. SB to Charles Prentice, 27 Oct. 1930 (CW, Reading).

31. SB to TM, 14 Nov. (1930)(TCD).

32. SB to TM, 11 March 1931 (TCD).

33. Ibid.

34. LH, undated conversation with SB (Dartmouth).

35. "I long to be away and of course can't bear the idea of going and can't understand why Hamburg, where it won't be warm and where I will be probably frightened. That's the latest cardiac feather. Fear — followed by no genitive" (SB to TM, 11 March 1931 [TCD]).

36. James Joyce to Harriet Shaw Weaver, 4 March 1931, *Letters of James Joyce*, vol. I, p. 302.

37. "Forgive this scramble. I only knew I was going this morning" (SB to Charles Prentice, 23 March 1931 [CW, Reading]).

38. SB to Charles Prentice, 25 March 1931 (CW, Reading). Beckett writes that he is unable to meet Prentice the next day as he is taking the nine o'clock boat train to Paris.

39. Leon Edel, "A Paris Letter," *Canadian Forum*, April 1931, and "The Genius and the Injustice Collector," *American Scholar* (autumn 1980).

40. Robert McAlmon and Kay Boyle, *Being Geniuses Together* (London: Hogarth Press, 1984), p. 279.

41. Soupault's account was published as the introduction to the French "Anna Livie Plurabelle" in the *Nouvelle revue française*, no. 212 (1 May 1931), pp. 633–36.

42. James Joyce, *Haveth Childers Everywhere* (London: Faber and Faber, May 1931).

43. SB to TM, 29 May 1931 (TCD). Almost sixty years later, he still felt slighted by the way in which his version had been underestimated and discarded (interview with SB, 20 Sept. 1989).

44. This version, passed over by Beckett scholars, forms six separate items in the Beinecke Rare Book and Manuscript Library at Yale University, Ms. Box 6 F 3-8, Joyce, Anna Livia Plurabelle. A letter from Beckett to Philippe Soupault accompanying the typescript, dated July 5, 1930, expressed some misgivings as to what they had done, and it could well be that Beckett's own lack of conviction, or perhaps his modesty, affected the outcome. However, the Beckett-Péron translation got to a heavily corrected proof stage for the literary review *Bifur* before Joyce intervened and suggested a revision. The heavily corrected first proof for *Bifur* is catalogued as F 5.

45. In a 1980 interview with (and a letter to) Noel Riley Fitch, Beckett remembered that it was Soupault and not Adrienne Monnier who read the "Anna Livia Plurabelle" translation (*Sylvia Beach and the Lost Generation*, p. 314, and note on p. 430). Contemporary accounts like that of Edel are, however, surely more reliable. In Joyce's letter to Sylvia Beach of May 10, 1931, he writes: "I think Miss Monnier should record the reading of A. L. P. for Coppola and sell the discs" (*The Letters of James Joyce*, vol. I, p. 304), which is more likely to apply if she had read it rather than Soupault.

46. McAlmon and Boyle, *Being Geniuses Together*, pp. 279–80.

47. *The European Caravan: An Anthology of the New Spirit in European Literature*, compiled and edited by Samuel Putnam, Maida Castelhun Darnton, George Reavey, and J. Bronowski. *Part I: France, Spain, England and Ireland* (New York: Brewer, Warren & Putnam, 1931).

48. SB to TM, 29 May 1931 (TCD).

49. Ibid.

50. This account of the row is based on a letter from TM to Charles Prentice, received July 15, 1931 (CW, Reading) in which MacGreevy writes: "His mother saw some of his manuscripts and turned him out of the house a fortnight before he left Dublin. His father and brother are, of course, very fond of him always. But I fear he is very unhappy"; and on the reply from Prentice to TM, also July 15, 1931 (CW, Reading).

51. Most of the entries in this 1931–32 notebook are, as in the later "Whoroscope" notebook, striking quotations from a wide range of books that Beckett was reading. They are often single words or phrases. A substantial number of these quotations are checked off as having been used later, mostly in *Dream of Fair to Middling Women* or in the poems written in the early 1930s.

52. SB to TM, (27) Aug. 1932 (TCD).

53. SB to TM, 12 Dec. 1932 (TCD).

54. SB to Charles Prentice, 30 June 1931 (CW, Reading).

55. SB to TM, undated, but early August 1931 (TCD).

56. VLADIMIR: But you were there yourself, in the Macon country.

ESTRAGON: No, I was never in the Macon country. I've puked my puke of a life away here, I tell you! Here! In the Cackon country! (*Waiting for Godot*, pp. 61–62).

57. SB, *More Pricks Than Kicks*, p. 26.
58. TM to Charles Prentice, received 15 July 1931 (CW, Reading).
59. SB to TM, undated (early Aug. 1931)(TCD).
60. Ibid.
61. Ibid.
62. Ibid.
63. Ellmann, *James Joyce*, pp. 639–40.
64. SB to TM, undated (early Aug. 1931)(TCD).
65. Ibid.
66. SB to TM, undated (probably late Aug. 1931)(TCD).
67. SB to TM, 8 Nov. 1931 (TCD).
68. SB to TM, 9 Oct. 1931 (TCD).
69. SB to TM, undated (probably late Aug.) 1931 (TCD). Interestingly, the words used here are almost identical with the picture of the little Belacqua pedaling away on his bicycle at the beginning of *Dream of Fair to Middling Women*.
70. SB to TM, undated (ca. 9 Sept. 1931)(TCD).
71. "All of the images are my own," commented Beckett with pride to LH of "Yoke of Liberty" (undated note, ca. 1962 [Dartmouth]).
72. SB to TM, 9 Oct. 1931 (TCD).
73. LH, undated interview with SB (Dartmouth).
74. SB, "Yoke of Liberty," in *The European Caravan*, p. 480.
75. SB, *Collected Poems in English and French*, p. 13.
76. Interview with Georges Belmont, 3 Aug. 1991.
77. SB to MM, 22 May 1937 (Texas).
78. SB to TM, undated 1931 (TCD).
79. SB, *Dream of Fair to Middling Women*, p. 44.
80. SB to TM, 8 Nov. 1931 (TCD).
81. Ibid.
82. Ibid.
83. LH, undated interview with SB (Dartmouth).
84. Some of these features are explored in detail by Eoin O'Brien in *The Beckett Country*, pp. 200–208.
85. SB, *Collected Poems in English and French*, p. 12. A fuller discussion of these features of the poem is to be found in Lawrence Harvey, *Samuel Beckett: Poet and Critic* (Princeton, N.J.: Princeton University Press, 1970), pp. 127–38.
86. SB to TM, 8 Nov. 1931 (TCD).
87. SB to TM, undated (end of September 1931)(TCD).
88. Thomas MacGreevy, *Richard Aldington* (London: Chatto and Windus, 1931), p.17.
89. Samuel Putnam gives a good account of the lively, fashionable opening of the Sphinx brothel in *Paris Was Our Mistress*, pp. 90–93.
90. LH, undated interview with SB (Dartmouth).
91. The 1931–32 notebook contains all Beckett's notes on several of these fairy tales, including the stories of Cinderella, Blue-Bird, Rominagrobis, Belle-Belle, or the Fortunate Knight, and Tom-Thumb, the last evoked in *Dream of Fair to Middling Women*, "that would be like working out how many pebbles in Tom Thumb's pocket," p. 216; the notebook asks, "How many pebbles in Tom Thumb's pocket?" — an interesting allusion in the light of the later permutation of pebbles in different pockets in *Molloy*.
92. LH, undated interview with SB (Dartmouth).
93. SB to TM, 9 Oct. 1931 (TCD).
94. SB, *Collected Poems in English and French*, p. 20.
95. SB to TM, 20 Dec. 1931 (TCD). A footnote in *More Pricks Than Kicks* expressed the same irritation at the way the Perugino painting was displayed in the gallery: "This figure [he is referring to the figure of Mary Magdalene], owing to the glittering vitrine behind which the canvas cowers, can only be apprehended in sections. Patience, how-

ever, and a retentive memory have been known to elicit a total statement approximating to the intention of the painter" ("Love and Lethe," p. 93).

96. SB to TM, 20 Dec. 1931 (TCD).

97. See Pietro Scarpellini, *Perugino* (Electra Editrice, 1984), p. 102, and *Tutta La Pittura del Perugino* (Milan: Rizzoli Editore, 1959), p. 104, for the history of the *Pietà*. The coats of arms were finally all but removed during a further 1947 restoration.

98. SB, *More Pricks Than Kicks*, p. 93.

99. "Another of Orpen's friends was William Sinclair, the man whom Cissie Beckett, Sam Beckett's aunt, had married." Glenavy, *Today We Will Only Gossip* (London: Constable, 1964), p. 36. See also William Orpen, *Stories of Old Ireland and Myself* (London: Williams and Norgate, 1924), pp. 43–44, and Bair, *Samuel Beckett*, p. 58.

100. SB to TM, 20 Dec. 1931 (TCD). The Keating referred to here was almost certainly Seán Keating (1889–1978).

101. SB to TM, undated 1931 (TCD).

102. SB to TM, undated (summer) 1930 (TCD).

103. Interview with SB, 9 July 1989.

104. Some of these feelings surface much later on in Beckett's radio play, *Embers*; see SB, *Collected Shorter Plays*, p. 96.

105. SB to TM, 20 Dec. 1931 (TCD).

106. SB, *More Pricks Than Kicks*, p. 96.

107. LH, undated interview with SB, 14 May (Dartmouth).

7: *DREAM OF FAIR TO MIDDLING WOMEN,* 1932–33

1. Beckett had earlier considered going "as far as Cologne anyway" (SB to TM, 20 Dec. 1931 [TCD]).

2. These two letters no longer exist. Beckett told me about writing them. Interview with SB, Oct. 1989.

3. Bair, *Samuel Beckett*, p. 137.

4. LH, undated interview with SB (Dartmouth). Beckett insisted to me that he *never* lived with the Sinclairs at any time for months on end (interview with SB, Oct. 1989). Deirdre Hamilton (Sinclair) also did not think that Beckett ever stayed for six months in Kassel (letter to JK, 26 Nov. 1992).

5. Charles Prentice to SB, 8 Feb. 1932 (CW, Reading).

6. Richard Aldington to TM, 25 Feb., 27 April, 17 May, 15 June, all 1932 (TCD). On February 25, Aldington asked MacGreevy to "thank Sam for his charming letter" (TCD).

7. Beckett translated nearly twenty articles for *Negro Anthology Made by Nancy Cunard 1931–1933*. For an excellent account of this extraordinary creation, see Anne Chisholm, *Nancy Cunard*, pp. 255–95.

8. The idea, expressed in the foreword to the first Irish edition of *Dream of Fair to Middling Women* (Dublin: The Black Cat Press, 1992, p. vii), that this was written very quickly in a few weeks during the summer of 1932 is mistaken. Beckett's letter to Charles Prentice (15 Aug. 1931) makes quite clear that the "Sedendo et Quiescendo" section of *Dream*, and probably the next section, called at that stage "They go out for the evening," were already written in Ireland by, at the latest, the end of July 1931 (CW, Reading). An earlier letter to TM in which Beckett alludes to the "German comedy" that he is writing "in a ragged kind of way, on and off" is also probably a reference to the Kassel section of *Dream* (SB to TM, 29 May 1931 [TCD]).

9. A letter from Charles Prentice to Samuel Beckett dated June 29, 1932, acknowledging receipt of the typescript of *Dream of Fair to Middling Women* effectively dates the completion of the novel, including the typing, as, at the very latest, the final week of June (CW, Reading).

10. Quoted in *Collected Poems of Thomas MacGreevy*, introduction by Susan Schreibman, p. xxx.

11. SB, *Dream of Fair to Middling Women*, p. 133.
12. Ibid., p. 120.
13. Gerry Dukes, "How It Is with Bouncing Bel," *The Irish Times*, 31 Oct. 1992.
14. Rubin Rabinovitz, *The Development of Samuel Beckett's Fiction*, pp. 25–27.
15. SB, *Dream of Fair to Middling Women*, p. 49.
16. Interview with SB, 20 Sept. 1989.
17. SB, *Dream of Fair to Middling Women*, p. 5.
18. Ibid., p. 15. The painter was Andrea del Sarto.
19. Ibid., pp. 68–69.
20. Ibid., p. 75.
21. Ibid., p. 101.
22. Ibid., p. 103.
23. "Walther is racked, in a distinctly medieval way, by the conflicting claims of eros and agapé, piety and pity, matter and spirit. . . . Love, especially sexual love, is seen to be subject to the rigours of decay from the moment day dawns, and its eternal aspect seems constantly threatened by the random and meaningless intrusion of death" (John Pilling, *Samuel Beckett*. London, Henley and Boston: Routledge and Kegan Paul, 1976, p. 135).
24. SB, *Dream of Fair to Middling Women*, pp. 23–24. See *Purgatorio* IV and VI.
25. Ibid., p. 15.
26. Terence Killeen, "Play It Again Sam!" *The Irish Times*, 5 Nov. 1992.
27. SB, *Dream of Fair to Middling Women*, p. 33.
28. Ibid., p. 50.
29. Ibid., pp. 50, 33.
30. Richard Ellmann, interview with SB, 21 June 1954 (Ellmann Papers, 011 [Tulsa]).
31. Undated conversation with SB.
32. SB, *Dream of Fair to Middling Women*, p. 51.
33. Beckett's student Dante is now in private hands. I thank the owner for confirming all the details as being those of the edition described in *Dream*.
34. Two of his notebooks on Dante from 1925–26 have been preserved. They contain very detailed notes, which are mostly confined to a summary of what happens in each canto, with only the occasional personal comment.
35. SB, *Dream of Fair to Middling Women*, p. 49.
36. Ibid., p. 151.
37. Ibid., pp. 190–91.
38. Ibid., pp. 54–55.
39. Ibid., p. 164.
40. Ibid., p. 177.
41. SB to TM, 11 March 1931 (TCD).
42. This identification of Beaufret as the model for the character Lucien has been independently confirmed by Georges Belmont, who was a friend of both Beckett and Beaufret at the Ecole Normale.
43. SB, *Dream of Fair to Middling Women*, p. 22.
44. Ibid., pp. 116–17.
45. Ibid., p. 47.
46. Ibid. Beckett's good friend Alfred Péron was, to use a phrase from *Dream*, a "bosom butty" of Sartre (having shared a *turne* [or study] with him at the Ecole Normale) and continued to see him throughout the 1930s. So the gestures may have been Beaufret's and the repulsion Sartre's. Or disgust at the "otherness" of the body may simply have been in the (largely Teutonic) philosophical air that Sartre, Beaufret, and Beckett were breathing at the time.
47. SB, *Dream of Fair to Middling Women*, p. 37.
48. Ibid.
49. Ibid., pp. 48–49.

50. Henri Evrard knew all *Les Nuits* of Alfred de Musset by heart and could recite them from memory (interview with Georges Belmont, 3 Aug. 1991).

51. Madame Renée Evrard to JK, 17 May 1991.

52. SB, *Dream of Fair to Middling Women*, pp. 144–45.

53. The *Oxford English Dictionary* defines "fricatrice" as "a lewd woman"; for example, Ben Jonson, *Volpone*, act IV, scene ii: "To a lewd harlot, a base fricatrice." Beckett had used the word "fricatrix" in a 1931 letter to Tom MacGreevy (TCD).

54. "Geoffrey is up to his eyes and of course parked with the Fricas" (SB to TM, 18 Aug. 1934 [TCD]).

55. SB, *Dream of Fair to Middling Women*, p. 169.

56. Ibid., p. 76.

57. Morris Sinclair to JK, 15 Nov. 1992.

58. All these specific allusions are discussed, often with accompanying photographs, in O'Brien, *The Beckett Country*.

59. LH, undated interview with SB (Dartmouth).

60. Lucia's later letters to her second guardian, Jane Lidderdale, suggest that she never accepted in her mind that her relationship with Beckett was over. See, for example, Lucia Joyce's letter, 20 Oct. 1973 (University College London Library). However, this may simply have been an effect of her illness; many schizophrenics seem to lack any sense of the passage of time.

61. Ellmann, *James Joyce*, p. 650.

62. Interview with SB, 5 July 1989.

63. Paul Léon to Harriet Shaw Weaver, quoting Joyce, 19 July 1935. Cited in Ellmann, *James Joyce*, p. 650.

64. James Joyce to Harriet Shaw Weaver, 17 Jan. 1932 (*Letters of James Joyce*, vol. 1, p. 312).

65. Beckett told me of Joyce's remorse and of how, later in the 1930s, James Joyce would ask him (as he also did Maria Jolas and Paul Léon) to go out into the street and give a hundred-franc note to the first down-and-out that he came across in memory of Joyce's father. Interview with SB, 20 Sept. 1989.

66. Interview with SB, 20 Sept. 1989. The lines of the poem as printed are: Of the dark past / A boy is born / With joy and grief / My heart is torn // Calm in his cradle / The living lies. / May love and mercy / Unclose his eyes! // Young life is breathed / On the glass; / The world that was not / Comes to pass. // A child is sleeping: / An old man gone. / O, father forsaken, / Forgive your son! (see Ellmann, *James Joyce*, p. 646).

67. Harriet Shaw Weaver went along to see Geoffrey Faber to establish what the attitude of the Faber publishers' board would be to bringing out *Ulysses*. "Harriet was left with the impression that he and the firm had been rather shaken by a recent successful prosecution of a young man sent to Wormwood Scrubs for six months merely for asking a printer whether he would print an obscene manuscript for private circulation only" (Jane Lidderdale and Mary Nicholson, *Dear Miss Weaver*. New York: The Viking Press, 1970, p. 315).

68. Harold Raymond to TM, 15 March 1932 (CW, Reading).

69. Richard Aldington to TM, 17 Feb. 1932 (TCD).

70. Cited in Ellmann, *James Joyce*, p. 653.

71. SB to Charles Prentice, 15 Aug. 1932 (CW, Reading).

72. SB to Samuel Putnam, 28 June 1932 (Princeton).

73. Charles Prentice to SB, 5 July 1932 (CW, Reading).

74. This account of the circumstances in which "Drunken Boat" was written is based on an interview with SB prior to the publication by Whiteknights Press of a facsimile edition of the poem edited by Felix Leakey and James Knowlson in 1976.

75. The date of SB's departure from Paris is established by a letter to TM, 14 July 1932 (TCD).

76. SB to TM, 14 (July 1932)(TCD). In this letter Beckett described his journey from Paris, his lodging in London, and his activities since his arrival there.

77. He obtained letters of introduction and testimonials from Gibbon (the headmaster of Campbell College, Belfast), Rudmose-Brown, and Jean Thomas (SB to Tom McGreevy, 14 [July 1932] [TCD]).

78. In early February, Beckett proposed that he should write a study of André Gide for the Dolphin series, but, for commercial reasons, Prentice turned it down (Charles Prentice to SB, 8 Feb. 1932 [CW, Reading]).

79. *Dream of Fair to Middling Women* was posted to Prentice at the end of June (Prentice to SB, 29 June 1932 [CW, Reading]).

80. Among these were "There Is a Happy Land," an early title for "Sanies II," and a long, unpublished poem entitled "Spring Song," a typescript of which was discovered among A. J. Leventhal's papers; this is now in Texas. Another copy is in private hands. Both "Spring Song" and "There Is a Happy Land" were rejected by Charles Prentice (Prentice to SB, 27 July 1932 [CW, Reading]).

81. Charles Prentice to SB, 19 July 1932 (CW, Reading).

82. SB to GR, 8 Oct. 1932 (Texas).

83. He had earlier written to MacCarthy and had a copy of his study of Proust sent to him (Charles Prentice to SB, 21 July 1932 [CW, Reading]). MacCarthy promised to write a letter of recommendation to the publisher Grayson, mentioning that Beckett might write studies of Alfieri or Vico for him.

84. SB to TM, 14 (July 1932) and 4 Aug. 1932 (TCD).

85. Charles Prentice sent SB an introduction to the director of the British Museum Reading Room on July 21, 1932 (CW, Reading). Beckett wrote: "I couldn't stand the British Museum any more. Plato and Aristotle and the Gnostics finished me" (SB to TM, 4 Aug. 1932 [TCD]). For his reading of Aretino and Aristotle on Thales, see LH, undated interview with SB about "Serena I" (Dartmouth).

86. SB to TM, 4 Aug. 1932 (TCD).

87. LH, undated interview with SB (Dartmouth).

88. Alexander Pope, *Moral Essays*, Epistle III, 11. 339–40. Beckett used Pope's term for the Monument in a poem written a little later: "and afar off at all speed screw me up Wren's giant bully," ("Serena I," *Collected Poems in English and French*, p. 22).

89. LH, undated interview with SB (Dartmouth).

90. SB to TM, 13 (Sept. 1932) and (for its completion) SB to TM, 8 Oct. 1932 (TCD). With the October letter is a copy of the poem which is also in TCD library, in a different form from its published version. Beckett described the poem in a letter to GR, also 8 Oct. 1932 (Texas).

91. Harvey, *Samuel Beckett: Poet and Critic*, p. 87. Beckett himself did not think too well of his poem: "I'm enclosing the only bit of writing that has happened to me since Paris and that does me no particular credit as far as I can judge" (SB to TM, 8 Oct. 1932 [TCD]).

92. SB to TM, 4 Aug. 1932 (TCD).

93. Ibid.

94. Ibid.

95. SB to TM, 18 (Aug. 1932)(TCD).

96. Ibid.

97. SB to TM, 4 Aug. 1932 (TCD).

98. Quoted in Michael S. Howard, *Jonathan Cape, Publisher*, p. 137.

99. SB to TM, 18 (Aug. 1932)(TCD).

100. Ibid., and SB to GR, 8 Oct. 1932 (Texas).

101. LH, interview with SB, March 1962 (Dartmouth).

102. SB to TM, 30 Aug. 1932 (TCD).

103. SB to TM, 1 Feb. (1933)(TCD).

104. SB to TM, undated (1933). He also bought Scarlatti's sonatas but, as they were

intended for the harpsichord, he found them "Much too skin and bones for a piano" (SB to TM, also undated [1933] [TCD]).

105. SB to TM, Aug. 1932; also 23 (April) 1933 (TCD).

106. "I went to the Gallery yesterday and looked at the Spanish Room and the Poussins. The El Greco St. Francis looks very flashy when you can turn your head and see the Rubens version in the next room. The Poussin Entombment is extraordinary, I never saw such blue and purple, such lyrical colour. They say now that the small Spanish head in the corner is a Velasquez. I don't believe it" (SB to TM, Aug. 1932 [TCD]).

107. SB to TM, 13 (Sept. 1932)(TCD).

108. SB to TM, 5 Jan. (1933)(TCD). While a student at Trinity College, he had played cricket many times in country matches for a team that Hone had organized and knew him as a friend of Percy Ussher and the painter, Jack Yeats.

109. This became *Swift or the Egotist* (London: Victor Gollancz, 1934). Hone had earlier written a study of Bishop Berkeley with Rossi: *Bishop Berkeley: His Life, Writings and Philosophy* (London: Faber and Faber, 1931).

110. SB to TM, 3 Feb. 1931 (TCD).

111. Interview with SB, 10 Nov. 1989.

112. Ibid.

113. SB to TM, 15 May 1935 (TCD).

114. SB to TM, Aug. 1932 (TCD).

115. Ibid.

116. "I made a desperate effort to get something started on Gide but failed again" (SB to TM, 13 [Sept. 1932] [TCD]).

117. *Joseph Andrews* enchanted him: "Such a thing never to have read!" (SB to TM, 8 Oct. 1932 [TCD]).

118. "He was not a bad-looking young fellow, a kind of cretinous Tom Jones" (SB, *More Pricks Than Kicks*, p. 111).

119. SB to TM, 8 Oct. 1932 (TCD).

120. He had read *Gulliver's Travels* as a child. Now he read it again (SB to TM, 1 Feb. [1933] [TCD]).

121. SB to TM, 12 (Dec. 1932)(TCD). The quotation is taken from Rahel Sanzara, *The Lost Child (Das verlorene Kind)*, translated by Winifred Katzin (London: Victor Gollancz, 1930).

122. SB to TM, 5 Dec. (1932)(TCD).

123. Ibid.

124. SB to TM, 12 (Dec. 1932)(TCD).

125. "We saw St Nicholas's which is charming and where they say Cristoforo C. [Christopher Columbus] had a dish of mass before committing his indiscretion" (i.e., discovering America)(SB to TM, 8 Oct. 1932 [TCD]) becomes in "What a Misfortune": "on the usual wings to Galway, Gate of Connaught and dream of stone, and more precisely to the Church of Saint Nicholas whither Belacqua projected, if it were not closed when they arrived, to repair without delay and kneel, with her on his right hand at last for a pleasant change, and invoke, in pursuance of a vow of long standing, the spirits of Crusoe and Columbus, who had knelt there before him" (SB, *More Pricks Than Kicks*, pp. 135–36).

126. SB to TM, 5 Jan. (1933)(TCD). Beckett relates the anecdote about Dean Swift and Stella in this letter.

127. SB to TM, 23 (April 1933)(TCD). Beckett felt that this poem was not a great success, since, in a letter with the poem, he wrote: "I find it more and more difficult to write and I think I write worse and worse in consequence" (SB to TM, 13 May [1933] [TCD]).

128. SB to TM, 12 (Dec. 1932) and 5 Jan. (1933)(TCD).

129. SB to TM, 12 (Dec. 1932)(TCD).

130. SB to TM, 23 (April 1933)(TCD).

131. Ibid.
132. SB to TM, undated (1933)(TCD).
133. SB to TM, 13 May (1933) (TCD).
134. Ibid.
135. SB to TM, 22 June (1933)(TCD).
136. SB to TM, undated (1933)(TCD).
137. SB to TM, 23 (April 1933)(TCD).
138. SB to TM, 22 June (1933)(TCD).
139. SB to TM, 2 July 1933 (TCD).

8: THE LONDON YEARS, 1933–35

1. SB to TM, 2 July 1933 (TCD).
2. Ibid.
3. SB, *More Pricks Than Kicks*, pp. 195–96.
4. SB, "Malacoda," *Collected Poems in English and French*, p. 26. Another pictorial image, that of a painting of a butterfly poised on a spray of flowers by the Dutch flower painter Jan van Huysum ("lay this Huysum on the box / mind the imago it is he"), suggests that the memory of his father will live on in the son's memory, as indeed it did until Beckett's own death. Harvey gives an excellent discussion of this poem in *Samuel Beckett, Poet and Critic*, pp. 108–112.
5. SB to TM, 25 (July 1933) (TCD).
6. SB to TM, 2 July 1933 (TCD).
7. SB to TM, 25 (July 1933) (TCD). He even felt the need to open his evening bottle of Guinness, he said, "very piano and reverent" and was allowed to play only one tune on the piano, "Crossing the Bar," which had been set, or rather, in his own words, "upset to music by my paternal grandmother."
8. SB to TM, 25 (July 1933) (TCD).
9. Interview with SB, 10 Nov. 1989.
10. SB to TM, 1 Nov. 1933 (TCD). This attitude resurfaced over thirty years later in the radio play *Embers*, where the sea makes an obsessive, sucking sound from which the main character, Henry, is unable to escape: "Listen to it! *(Pause.)* Lips and claws! *(Pause.)* Get away from it! Where it couldn't get at me! The Pampas! . . . And I live on the brink of it! Why?" (SB, *Embers*, in *Collected Shorter Plays*, p. 98.)
11. SB to TM, 9 Oct. and 1 Nov. 1933 (TCD).
12. Charles Prentice to SB, 25 Sept. 1933 (CW, Reading).
13. SB to TM, 6 Dec. 1933 (TCD). "Echo's Bones," the story, remains unpublished as I write. A typescript is at Dartmouth College, Hanover, New Hampshire.
14. Charles Prentice to SB, 13 Nov. 1933 (CW, Reading).
15. SB to TM, 6 Dec. 1933 (TCD).
16. Deirdre Bair wrote that Beckett came to London *before* Christmas 1933 in order to make contact with a psychoanalyst (*Samuel Beckett*, p. 176). The evidence reveals this as highly unlikely. A letter to TM (January 8) implying that he was making a *return* visit to London in January 1934 was wrongly dated and was actually written in January 1935, as was Beckett's next letter, of January 29. Both letters were written from Gertrude Street, where Beckett moved only in September 1934. Also, Charles Prentice, who was living and working in London at the time, was writing to Beckett at 6 Clare Street, Dublin, throughout the whole of December 1933 about the proofs of his book of stories, *More Pricks Than Kicks*. There are letters from Prentice to Beckett on December 4, 7, 11, 18, and 20, all addressed to Dublin (CW, Reading). Prentice would not, of course, have done this, if Beckett had already been resident in London.
17. John Fletcher, *The Novels of Samuel Beckett*, p. 38, and interview with SB, 10 Nov. 1989.

18. TM to Jean Coulomb (in French), 4 Aug. 1935 (Jean Coulomb).

19. SB to Morris Sinclair (in French), 27 Jan. 1934 (Sinclair).

20. SB to AJL, 7 May 1934 (Texas), and to Nuala Costello, 27 Feb. 1934 (Costello).

21. Edward Dowden (1843–1913) was the author of *Shakespere, A Critical Study of His Mind and Art* (London: H. S. King, 1875) and *The Life of Percy Bysshe Shelley* (London: Kegan Paul and Trench, 1886).

22. David Piper, *The Companion Guide to London*, p. 195.

23. Interview with SB, 10 Nov. 1989.

24. TM to Jean Coulomb, 4 Aug. 1935 (Coulomb).

25. SB to TM, 28 Aug. 1934 (TCD). See also his letters to TM, 18 Sept. 1934 and (sending his "spinsterian pound") 20 Feb. 1935 (TCD).

26. SB to TM, 18 Aug. 1934. (TCD)

27. Wilfred Bion was nine years older than Beckett. He was born in Muttra in the United Provinces of India in 1897. He died in November 1979.

28. According to a survey done in 1935, while Beckett was a patient, 44 percent of the patients treated at the Tavistock were suffering from "anxiety states" (H. V. Dicks, *Fifty Years of the Tavistock Clinic*, pp. 69–70).

29. This description of his symptoms is based on SB to TM, 1 Jan. and 10 Mar. 1935 (TCD).

30. SB to Morris Sinclair (in French), 27 Jan. 1934.

31. Interview with SB, 10 Nov. 1989.

32. In February 1935, Beckett wrote to MacGreevy: "On Monday I go [to Bion] for the 133rd time" (SB to TM, 8 Feb. [1935] [TCD]). There were a few breaks in treatment during which he returned to Ireland or went on a short holiday to France with his brother.

33. Bion captained the school rugby and swimming teams. (Photographs of W. R. Bion in the water polo and football teams are in his autobiography, *The Long Week-End, 1897–1919; Part of a Life* [Abingdon: Fleetwood Press, 1982].) Later, at Queen's College, Oxford, where he read for a degree in modern history, he became captain of swimming. He played rugby at university until an injury prevented him from obtaining his "blue." He also played for the famous Harlequins.

34. Gérard Bléandonu, *Wilfred R. Bion*, and talks with Bion's second wife, Francesca (1990 and 1995).

35. SB to TM, 8 Sept. (16 Sept.) 1934, and 31 Aug. (1935) (TCD).

36. SB to TM, 8 Oct. 1935 (TCD). During the First World War, Bion served in the Royal Tank Regiment, winning the DSO at Cambrai. He recounts some of his traumatic wartime experiences with humor as well as horror in *The Long Week-End.*

37. These lectures are printed in C. G. Jung, *The Collected Works*, vol. 18, *The Symbolic Life: Miscellaneous Writings*, ed. Sir Herbert Read, Michael Fordham, and Gerhard Adler; trans. R. F. C. Hull (London: Routledge and Kegan Paul, 1977). The lecture that Beckett attended is printed with the discussion on pp. 70–101.

38. Dicks, *Fifty Years of the Tavistock Clinic*, pp. 36–37.

39. I owe a great debt of gratitude to Miss Pearl King for advice on W. R. Bion and the Tavistock Clinic. She directed my initial reading and, at the "Biography and Psychoanalysis" conference introduced me to a number of psychoanalysts who knew Bion or others who worked at the Tavistock. I am also grateful for advice from Dr. Malcolm Pines and Dr. Robert Hinshelwood. Mrs. Francesca Bion kindly gave me copies of some of her husband's books as well as much information.

40. Dicks, *Fifty Years of the Tavistock Clinic*, p. 67.

41. Interview with SB, 10 Nov. 1989. The personal notes that he refers to here have not yet been discovered.

42. SB to TM, 1 Jan. 1935 (TCD). In an unpublished two-page story (a draft for the Lyons teashop scene in *Murphy*), entitled "Lightning Calculation," written at 34 Ger-

trude Street, Beckett wrote, "The first thing he [the main character, called Quigley] did was consult the notes on dreams made at various stages of the night" (ms. 2902 [Reading]).

43. SB to Morris Sinclair (in French), 27 Jan. 1934 (Sinclair).

44. Robert S. Woodworth, *The Contemporary Schools of Psychology* (New York: The Ronald Press, 1931).

45. In the opening chapter of *Murphy*, Neary speaks like a Gestalt psychologist: "Murphy, all life is figure and ground" (SB, *Murphy*. London: Calder and Boyars, 1963, [1st ed. London: Routledge, 1938] p. 7). Later in the book, Beckett makes a Gestalt joke: "No sooner had Miss Dwyer . . . made Neary as happy as a man could desire, than she became one with the ground against which she had figured so prettily. Neary wrote to Herr Kurt Koffka demanding an immediate explanation. He had not yet received an answer" (*Murphy*, p. 37). Koffka (1886–1940) was one of the founders of Gestalt psychology, which Beckett had just read about in Woodworth's book. Beckett copied out from Woodworth: *"Figure and Ground in Gestalt Psychology.* The figure stands out from the ground in virtue of the fundamental distinction between them. . . . This distinction is of the first importance for Gestaltists and a fundamental principle of their conception of experience and behaviour." Hence the joke.

46. SB, *Murphy*, p. 58.

47. Jean-Michel Rabaté has an interesting discussion of Beckett's use of the Külpe school (and Gestalt psychology) in his *Beckett avant Beckett* (Paris: P.E.N.S., 1984), pp. 139–145, although he leans on a less likely source book, Gardner Murphy's *Historical Introduction to Modern Psychology* (London: Kegan Paul, 1929). We cannot assert, of course, that Beckett had not read Murphy, merely that we now know that he *had* read the Woodworth.

48. We know, almost to the day, when Beckett was reading Adler. He writes, "I have finished with Adler. Another one trackmind [sic]. Only the dogmatist seems able to put it across" (SB to TM, 8 Feb. 1935 [TCD]). His notes on all these books still exist.

49. Beckett took detailed notes on the following books: Alfred Adler, *The Neurotic Constitution*; Otto Rank, *The Trauma of Birth*; Karin Stephens, *The Wish to Fall Ill*; and Wilhelm Stekel, *Psychoanalysis and Suggestion Therapy*, as well as on Jones and Freud.

50. These quotations are taken from Beckett's own typewritten notes.

51. Only Beckett's personal notes on his sessions, if they still exist, or W. R. Bion's case notes, if they have been preserved, would be able to take much of this beyond mere speculation.

52. Geoffrey Thompson, 1976 Radio Telefís Éireann broadcast for Beckett's seventieth birthday.

53. SB to TM, 26 April (1935) (TCD).

54. SB to TM, 10 March (1935) (TCD).

55. Ibid.

56. SB to TM, 6 Oct. 1937 (TCD).

57. SB to TM, 10 March 1935 (TCD).

58. Wilfred R. Bion, *The Long Week-End*, and *All My Sins Remembered*, with *The Other Side of Genius. Family Letters* (Abingdon: Fleetwood Press, 1985).

59. The quotations are from SB, "A Case in a Thousand," *The Bookman*, Aug. 1934, pp. 241–42.

60. SB to AJL, 7 May 1934 (Texas).

61. The original contract with Chatto and Windus for Beckett's book of short stories, entitled at that stage *Draff*, was dated October 3, 1933 (CW, Reading).

62. Charles Prentice to SB, 11 Dec. 1933 (CW, Reading).

63. Charles Prentice to B. W. Huebsch of Viking Press, 23 Jan. 1934; to Stanley Rinehart, 1 Feb. 1934; and to SB about Harrison Smith and Haas having turned the book down, 3 May 1934. B. W. Huebsch wrote, rejecting it: "The book is rather mad, a bit incoherent, and is written in the allusive style that makes strong demands on the reader,"

but, he added, "the author strikes me as being a very good bet for the future" (B. W. Huebsch to Charles Prentice, 31 Jan. 1934 [All letters CW, Reading]).

64. Harold Raymond to S. B. Gundy of Doubleday Doran and Gundy, Ltd., 16 May 1934 (CW, Reading).

65. SB to Morris Sinclair, 13 July 1934 (Sinclair).

66. Interview with SB, 20 Sept. 1989.

67. SB to TM, undated (8 Aug. 1934) (TCD).

68. SB to TM, 18 Aug. 1934 (TCD).

69. SB to TM, 31 Dec. 1935 (TCD).

70. SB to TM, 18 Aug. 1934 (TCD).

71. Arthur Calder-Marshall in *The Spectator*, 1 June 1934. But when Beckett was reading (or rereading) *Tristram Shandy* in August 1938 it "irritated [him] in spite of its qualities" (SB to TM, undated [5 Aug. 1938] [TCD]).

72. Francis Watson in *The Bookman*, vol. LXXXVI, no. 514 (July 1934), pp. 219–20.

73. Edwin Muir, "New Short Stories," *The Listener*, 4 July 1934.

74. *The Times Literary Supplement*, 26 July 1934.

75. *The Morning Herald*, 13 July 1934.

76. *The Morning Post*, 22 May 1934.

77. *John O'London's Weekly*, 9 June 1934.

78. Richard Sunne in *Time and Tide*, 26 May 1934: "too clever a book to be first-rate."

79. Ibid.

80. *The Times Literary Supplement*, 26 July 1934.

81. Charles Prentice to Richard Aldington, 6 June 1934 (CW, Reading).

82. Charles Prentice to SB, 8 Nov. 1934 (CW, Reading). Beckett's own letter is not in the Chatto and Windus file.

83. SB to TM, undated (8 Aug. 1934)(TCD).

84. Ibid.

85. SB to TM, 18 Aug. 1934 (TCD).

86. SB to TM, undated (3 and 8 Aug.) 1934 (TCD).

87. SB to TM, undated (8 Aug. 1934) (TCD).

88. Ibid.

89. "He [his brother, Frank] tells me Mother is exceeding her income, mainly on the head of my treatment. This is very troubling" (SB to TM, 1 Jan. 1935 [TCD]).

90. SB to TM, 26 April (1935) (TCD).

91. SB to TM, 1 Jan. 1935 (TCD).

92. Ibid.

93. Patrick O'Dwyer to JK, 21 June 1993, reporting what Nuala Costello had told him.

94. SB to TM, 6 Dec. 1933 (TCD).

95. I am grateful to Ms. Valerie Costello for sending me copies of Beckett's letters to Nuala and to Patrick O'Dwyer for information and for his piece on Nuala's letters from Paris in the *Tuam Annual*.

96. SB to TM, 8 Feb. (1935) (TCD).

97. SB to TM, 8 Sept. (1935) (TCD).

98. Interview with SB, 10 Nov. 1989.

99. Nuala Costello's main claim to fame now is that Beckett entrusted her with a copy of his translation of Rimbaud's "Le Bateau ivre" ("The Drunken Boat"). She was responsible for this translation being preserved. Beckett also gave her a copy of the spoof lecture that he had given four years before at Trinity College on "Le Concentrisme." She died on March 11, 1984, leaving the Rimbaud translation and the TCD lecture in her will to the Beckett Archive at the University of Reading.

100. SB to TM, 10 March (1935) (TCD).

101. SB to AJL, 7 May 1934 (Texas).

102. *The Spectator*, 23 March and 23 June 1934 (reviews of Eduard Mörike's *Mozart on the Way to Prague* and Albert Feuillerat's *Comment Proust a composé son roman*); *The*

Bookman, vol. LXXXVII (Christmas 1934), pp. 10, 14, 111 (reviews of Ezra Pound, *Make It New*; Giovanni Papini, *Dante Vivo*; and Sean O'Casey, *Windfalls*); and *The Criterion*, vol. XIII (July 1934), pp. 705–707 (a review of J. B. Leishman's translation of Rainer Maria Rilke's *Poems*).

103. SB, *Disjecta: Miscellaneous Writings and a Dramatic Fragment*, p. 70.

104. Beckett described MacGreevy's recently published *Poems* as "probably the most important contribution to post-War Irish poetry" (SB, *Disjecta*, p. 74).

105. Ibid., p. 75.

106. Ibid., p. 70.

107. Ibid.

108. Harrington, *The Irish Beckett*, p. 30.

109. SB to TM, undated (8 Aug. 1934) (TCD).

110. John Harrington, *The Irish Beckett*, p. 33.

111. SB to TM, undated (8 Aug. 1934) (TCD).

112. SB to TM, 18 Aug. 1934 (TCD).

113. This essay, entitled "Censorship in the Saorstat," was finished before August 27, 1934, the date on the envelope of the letter to MacGreevy. The letter itself is dated August 28, 1934 (TCD). There is an error in the notes (p. 174) in *Disjecta*, where it is claimed that the piece was written in 1935. This is assumed because Beckett's *More Pricks Than Kicks* was not placed on the Register of Prohibited Publications until March 31, 1935 — and Beckett quotes his number at the end of the piece — and because it cites the register of banned books as of September 30, 1935. But these changes were made when Beckett revised the article for intended publication in Paris in 1936 by Eugene Jolas.

114. SB, "Censorship in the Saorstat," *Disjecta*, p. 84.

115. Ibid., p. 85.

116. Ibid., p. 87.

117. "Looking through my essuie-cul de réserve [my reserve toilet-paper] I find an article of about 2000 words on the censorship in Ireland, commissioned about this time 2 years ago by the Bookman and still inédit [unpublished]" (SB to GR, 6 May 1936 [Texas]). A postcard from Maria Jolas to Reavey for sale on a "Waiting for Godot Books" catalogue, p. 62, item 599, thanks him for sending the article by Beckett, but regrets that it reached her too late to be included. See also his letter to TM, 7 May 1936 (TCD).

118. The piece of music that he and Hester regularly used to practice together was Ravel's "Pavane pour une Infante défunte" "with special reference to the obeisances in the dance" (SB to TM, 10 March 1935 [TCD]).

119. SB to TM, 8 Feb. 1935 (TCD).

120. This was not the better-known artist, book illustrator, and frequent contributor to *Punch*, Leonard Raven-Hill (1867–1942).

121. SB to TM, 8 Feb. (1935) (TCD).

122. SB to TM, 10 March (1935) (TCD).

123. Wilhelm Furtwängler was in Britain with the Berlin Philharmonic Orchestra for its annual tour in January 1934. Beckett bought a ticket for one of their concerts at the Queen's Hall. The main part of the program consisted of Schumann's Fourth Symphony and Beethoven's Seventh Symphony.

124. The English newspapers were expressing grave anxiety at this time about the Nazis' recent treatment of the Jews, with the boycott of Jewish businesses in the preceding April and the introduction of the "Aryan paragraph" of the Civil Service Act of July 1, 1933, which meant that men of the stature of Einstein, Max Reinhardt, and the conductor Bruno Walter were removed from their posts. The question of Furtwängler's relations with National Socialism are discussed in *The New Grove Dictionary of Music and Musicians*, Stanley Sadie, ed., vol. 7, 1980, p. 38, and in C. Reiss, *Wilhelm Furtwängler: A Biography*.

125. Telephone conversation with John Beckett, 17 Feb. 1992.

126. Interview with Bettina Jonic, 14 Oct. 1994.

127. Beckett thought that the Allegro of the Third String Quartet, the last piece Beethoven wrote, had an incomparable beauty. On hearing it again, he was struck by the preceding Cavatina, "a movement which in calm finality and intensity goes beyond anything that I have ever heard by the venerable Ludwig and of which I wouldn't have thought him capable" (SB to Morris Sinclair [in French], 4 March 1934 [Sinclair]).

128. Ibid.

129. Chris Ackerley, "Beckett's 'Malacoda': or, Dante's Devil Plays Beethoven," *Journal of Beckett Studies,* n.s., vol. 3, no. 1 (1993), pp. 59–64. "Malacoda" is printed in SB, *Collected Poems in English and French,* p. 26.

130. SB, *Dream of Fair to Middling Women,* p. 18. Cf. (Schubert): "They sit up to all hours playing the gramophone, An die Musik is a great favourite with them both"; (Mozart): "The little Hexenmeister of Don Giovanni"; (Chopin): "[he] suffered the shakes and grace-note strangulations and enthrottlements of the Winkelmusik of Szopen or Pichon or Chopinek or Chopinetto" (SB, *More Pricks Than Kicks,* pp. 121, 184, 190).

131. E.g., Schubert's melancholic "Death and the Maiden" quartet, used at the beginning of *All That Fall;* the songs and tunes in *Waiting for Godot* and *Happy Days;* and, more crucially, Beethoven's Fifth Piano Trio, known as "The Ghost," quoted in his television play *Ghost Trio* and Schubert Lieder used in *Nacht und Träume* and alluded to in *What Where.*

132. Only now, after so much has been written about Beckett, has a book charting the significance of music in his work been prepared, by Mary Bryden.

133. SB to Morris Sinclair, 13 July 1934 (Sinclair).

134. Arthur Hillis advised me on Beckett's musical activities in London, as well as giving me information on Beckett's student days at Trinity College, Dublin. I am extremely grateful to him.

135. SB to TM, undated (23 Sept. 1935) (TCD).

136. SB to Morris Sinclair (in French), undated (but, from internal evidence, July 1934).

137. For an understanding of Beckett's feelings about opera, I have benefited greatly from interviews with Arthur Hillis (3 Feb. 1992), and Bettina Jonic (14 Oct. 1994).

138. The trip was, he wrote "very hot and unexciting, except [for] the pictures at Chantilly" (SB to Morris Sinclair, 13 July 1934 [Sinclair]). Of Beckett's notes, only the entries on the Louvre (17 June 1934) and Chantilly (18 June 1934) are dated. From their position in relation to each other in the notebook, however, it appears that he visited Hampton Court before June 1934 and the Wallace Collection on his return to London after the summer break. But this is inconclusive, since the undated entries might have been compiled from catalogues.

139. SB to TM, 18 Aug. 1934 (TCD).

140. My biggest single debt in this part of my book is to the fine painter Avigdor Arikha, who first drew my attention to Beckett's intimate knowledge of the Old Masters. Everything else in this part of the chapter and elsewhere derives from that initial insight.

141. Beckett bought the following catalogues at this time: *National Gallery Trafalgar Square Catalogue,* 1929, 86th edition; *National Gallery Illustrations to the Catalogues:* vol. I, Italian Schools, Trafalgar Square, 1930; Sir Charles Holmes, *National Gallery Illustrated Guide,* 1931; C. H. Collins Baker, *Catalogue of the Pictures at Hampton Court* (Glasgow: Maclehose and Co., 1929); Trenchard Cox, *A General Guide to the Wallace Collection* (London: HMSO, 1933); *A Descriptive and Historic Catalogue of the Pictures in the Gallery of Alleyn's College of God's Gift at Dulwich,* 1926. All these catalogues, together with others from Ireland, France, Germany, and Italy, were later given to Avigdor Arikha.

142. SB, *Dream of Fair to Middling Women,* p. 174.

143. SB, *Murphy,* p. 172. Beckett saw the powerful painting *The Circumcision* (at the time attributed to Bellini; now thought to be from Bellini's studio) in the National Gallery in London just before he started to write *Murphy.* Several other paintings that

he also saw there are alluded to in the same novel: Claude's *Landscape: Narcissus* and Tintoretto's *The Origin of the Milky Way* (referred to, respectively, on pp. 155 and 98). Watt's bloody appearance in *Watt* is compared with Hieronymus Bosch's painting *Christ Mocked (The Crowning with Thorns)*, also in the National Gallery (SB, *Watt*, p. 174).

144. In whichever European gallery he found himself in the 1930s, Beckett used to look out for the "exquisite" paintings of Elsheimer, a German painter (1578–1610) who spent many years living and painting in Rome.

145. Spotlight painting was inspired by the subtle lighting effects created by emulating moonlight, candlelight, torchlight, or the light of a bonfire. Beckett's letters from London and his personal notes reveal that he was fascinated by the history and development of "spotlight painting" as a genre. "It is very hard," he wrote, "to see the Elsheimers [Adam Elsheimer was a leading "spotlight" painter] in the German room [at the National Gallery of London], but the *Tobias and the Angel* seems exquisite. Rubens let off a lot of obituary steam for him, deplored his "indolence"! The Geertgen *Adoration* [or *The Nativity, at Night* by Geertgen tot Sint Jans, which also hangs in the National Gallery] must be one of the earliest spotlight paintings." "Surely," he added knowledgeably, "it is only half the story to date them from Raphael's *Liberation of St. Peter*. I never saw the Oxford Uccello mentioned in this connection either" (SB to TM, 20 Feb. [1935] [TCD]). Beckett knew van Honthorst's and Elsheimer's work well enough to add his own comments to his notes on R. H. Wilenski's *An Introduction to Dutch Art*.

146. SB to TM, 8 Sept. 1934 (TCD).

147. Ibid.

148. Ibid.

149. SB to TM, undated (16 Sept. 1934) (TCD).

9: *MURPHY,* 1934–36

1. SB to TM, 8 Sept. 1934 (TCD).
2. Ibid.
3. SB, *Murphy*, p. 50.
4. SB, *Play*, in *Collected Shorter Plays*, p. 154.
5. SB to TM, 8 Sept. 1934 (TCD).
6. Ibid.
7. SB, *Murphy*, p. 47.
8. SB to TM, 8 Oct. 1935 (TCD).
9. SB to TM, 8 Sept. 1934 (TCD).
10. SB to TM, 29 Jan. 1935 (TCD).
11. SB to TM, 14 Feb. (1935) and 10 March (1935) (TCD).
12. SB to TM, 20 Feb. (1935) (TCD).
13. SB to TM, 8 Feb. (1935) (TCD).
14. SB to TM, 26 April (1935) (TCD).
15. Ibid.
16. SB to TM, 1 Jan. 1935 (TCD).
17. SB to TM, 5 May 1935 (TCD). In Charlemont House, a painting by Jean Lurçat (the same artist on whose studio floor Beckett had slept three years before) had just been attacked by an irate spectator who had put a large hole through the middle sky. Beckett was taken to the "casualty wards" or back room of the gallery to see the extent of the damage to *Decorative Landscape* and talked to the custodian about the motive and circumstances (SB to TM, 15 May 1935).
18. This account of Beckett's tour of rural England is based on his letters to TM and AJL in July and August 1935, on an undated interview with Beckett, and on my own retracing of his footsteps.
19. SB to TM, 25 (July 1935) (TCD).

20. This list of places, together with Droitwich, Cheddar, Bideford, Westward Ho!, the Doone Valley, and Elstree is given in SB to AJL, 7 Aug. (1935) (Texas).

21. SB to TM, 25 (July 1935) (TCD).

22. The Glen Lyn Hotel, partly destroyed by fire soon after Beckett and his mother stayed there, and now used as guest cottages and flats, is set in twenty-five acres of beautiful gardens with an exciting (and dangerous) river gorge and ravine. I thank Richard J. Soutter of the Tourist Information Centre in Lynton most warmly for giving me information about the hotel where the Becketts stayed and the surrounding area.

23. SB to TM, 25 (July 1935) (TCD).

24. SB to TM, 25 (July 1935) (TCD).

25. When Beckett came to confer the title of *Worstward Ho*, with its play on "worst word," on his own 1983 prose text, it was with the memory of this mostly happy tour with his mother, as well as of Kingsley's novel, in mind.

26. SB to TM, 14 Feb. (1935) (TCD). A week later he wrote: "I like Jane's manner, in the sense that there is material that can be situated most conveniently in the crochet mode, and somehow Elinor Dashwood [in *Sense and Sensibility*] is realised as concubine no less desirable than Fielding's Sophie [in *Tom Jones*]" (SB to TM, 20 Feb. [1935] [TCD]).

27. SB to TM, 25 (July 1935) (TCD).

28. I thank Dr. Graham Nicholls, the curator of Dr. Johnson's Birthplace Museum in Lichfield, for his advice and for the efforts he made to find evidence of Beckett's visit in the 1935 visitors' book.

29. SB to TM, 31 Aug. (1935) (TCD).

30. Ibid.

31. Ibid.

32. *Murphy* is one of the few remaining major manuscripts of Beckett in private hands and is not available for consultation by scholars. I briefly saw the six holograph manuscript notebooks, consisting of eight hundred pages in all, in a bank vault in London in 1976 and noted down then the title and the initial date. There are five red notebooks and one blue notebook. The manuscript differs radically from the finished text at many points.

33. "I have been working hard at the book and it goes very slowly, but I do not think there is any doubt now that it will be finished sooner or later. The feeling that I must jettison the whole thing has passed, only the labour of writing the remainder is left" (SB to TM, 8 Oct. 1935 [TCD]). By this date he had written about twenty thousand words.

34. SB to TM, undated (22 Sept. 1935) (TCD).

35. Even so, he sent a postcard to Con Leventhal to check whether Neary really could bash his head against the buttocks of the statue of Cuchulain (A. J. Leventhal, "The Thirties," in *Beckett at Sixty* [London: Calder and Boyars, 1966], pp. 11–12).

36. SB to Morris Sinclair, July 1934 (Sinclair).

37. SB, *Murphy*, p. 54.

38. These statues are referred to in *Murphy* on pp. 188, 106, and 68 respectively. The *Rima* was Jacob Epstein's stone relief statue, erected in 1925 as a tribute to the naturalist W. H. Hudson. It was so controversial at the time that it had twice been tarred and feathered before Beckett came to London.

39. SB, *Murphy*, p. 13.

40. Ibid., p. 14.

41. In preliminary notes made for *Murphy*, Beckett wrote: "Purgatorial atmosphere sustained throughout" ("Whoroscope" notebook, Ms. 3000 [Reading]). The Purgatorial entries in the notebook are discussed by John Pilling in "From a (W)horoscope to *Murphy*," *The Ideal Core of the Onion: Reading Beckett Archives*, Reading, 1992, pp. 9–10.

42. SB, *Murphy*, p. 47.

43. Ibid., p. 5.

44. Ibid., p. 74.

45. SB to Morris Sinclair, 5 May 1934 (Sinclair) and to AJL, 26 July 1934 (Texas).

46. "Sheep were grazed in the park as a means of maintaining the grass until 1959 and would certainly have been present in the thirties" (Mrs. J. Adams, superintendent of the Central Royal Parks, letter to JK, 16 March 1993).

47. Linda Ben-Zvi, *Samuel Beckett* (Boston: Twayne, 1986), p. 45.

48. SB to TM, 8 Sept. (1935) (TCD).

49. SB, *Murphy*, p. 101.

50. The "Hindu polyhistor of dubious caste," who has been writing a fine-art monograph (*The Pathetic Fallacy from Avercamp to Kampendonck*), commits suicide after complaining "My fut . . . 'ave gut smaller than the end of the needle" (SB, *Murphy*, p. 134). This comes from the actual suicide of an insane Chinese man on Gower Street, who had made the same bizarre claim before he killed himself (SB to AJL, 26 July 1934 [Texas]).

51. SB to TM, 8 Sept. (1935) (TCD).

52. Ibid.

53. SB to TM, undated (23 Sept. 1935) (TCD).

54. SB to TM, 8 Oct. 1935 (TCD).

55. SB, *Murphy*, p. 19.

56. "Whoroscope" notebook (ms. 3000 [Reading]).

57. SB, *Murphy*, p. 22.

58. "Racinian lighting, darkness devoured" ("Whoroscope" notebook, [ms. 3000 {Reading}]).

59. The dates on which certain events occurred, and the colors associated with different characters or places — shades of Flaubert's *Madame Bovary* — are governed either by the solar spectrum ("violet, indigo, blue, green, yellow, orange, red: in that order") or by their links with the planets. Beckett did research on the star signs in books about astrology. But he probably obtained most of his information about the year in which the novel is set from an almanac, *Whitaker's*, or even, as the novel implies, *Old Moore's* (" 'But this is *Old Moore*,' said Miss Counihan, 'not the *Weekly Irish Times*.' " [*Murphy*, p. 147]).

60. This post was normally held for six months, but Dr. Thompson was granted an extension and remained in the post until the end of October (Patricia H. Allderidge, archivist and curator of the Bethlem Royal Hospital, to JK, 12 Feb. 1993). I am very grateful to Ms. Allderidge for her generous help with my questions about the building, the staff, and the regime at the Bethlem Royal Hospital in 1935.

61. Bair, *Samuel Beckett*, p. 219.

62. SB to TM, undated (23 Sept. 1935) (TCD). Geoffrey Thompson did not take Beckett around the actual hospital wards at Bethlem until mid-September 1935, although he had welcomed him several times at the hospital before then for chats and games of chess.

63. SB, *Murphy*, pp. 116–17.

64. LH interview with SB, 2 Feb. 1962 (Dartmouth).

65. SB, *Murphy*, publisher's blurb on back cover of paperback edition (Jupiter Books, Calder and Boyars, 1969 reprint).

66. "Whoroscope" notebook (ms. 3000 [Reading]).

67. Fletcher, *The Novels of Samuel Beckett*, p. 45.

68. SB, *Murphy*, p. 109.

69. Ibid., p. 115.

70. Ibid., pp. 114–15.

71. Patricia H. Allderidge to JK, 12 Feb. 1993.

72. Ibid.

73. SB, *Murphy*, p. 176.

74. Tom MacGreevy's and Charles Prentice's good friend Richard Aldington had used the names of "Bim" and "Bom" in "Enter Bim and Bom," the epilogue to his 1931 novel

The Colonel's Daughter. The names may have appealed to Beckett and remained in his mind until he used them himself in his last play, *What Where.*

75. Patricia H. Allderidge to JK, 12 Feb. 1993.

76. SB, *Murphy*, p. 164.

77. For an excellent analysis of the chess game in *Murphy*, see Bair, *Samuel Beckett*, pp. 220–21 and 224–25.

78. SB, *Murphy*, p. 168.

79. Ruby Cohn, *Back to Beckett* (Princeton, New Jersey: Princeton University Press, 1973), p. 34.

80. SB, *Murphy*, p. 86.

81. Ibid., p. 152.

82. An identification suggested in James Mays's article "Young Beckett's Irish Roots," *Irish University Review*, vol. XIV, no. 1 (1984), p. 23. For Macran, see Walter Starkie, *Scholars and Gypsies* (London: John Murray, 1963), pp. 4–5, 113–15, and 119–20. When he became a young lecturer, Beckett would have dined on Commons with this colorful, formidably erudite don. John O. Wisdom, a contemporary of Beckett at Trinity College (and fellow pupil earlier at Earlsfort House School), wrote about Macran's treatment of Hegel: "Macran's Treatment of the History of Modern Philosophy," *Hermathena*, vol. LXV (1945), pp. 20–33, and vol. LXVI (1945), pp. 40–54.

83. Beckett wrote out in his "Whoroscope" notebook: "Whether more torment to love a lady & never enjoy her, or always to enjoy a lady whom you cannot choose but hate (Dilemma of Agripyne in Old Fortunatus. Give to Neary)." The quotation is not given in these exact words in *Murphy* but the idea conveys the nub of the dilemma that Neary faces with Miss Counihan and Miss Dwyer.

84. James Mays, "Mythologized Presences: *Murphy* in Its Time," in *Myth and Reality in Irish Literature,* Joseph Ronsley, ed. (Waterloo, Ont.: Wilfred Laurier University Press, 1977), p. 210.

85. Beckett told me that, in real life, while writing *Murphy*, he punned, also in French, on the name of Nuala Costello as "nu(e) à la côte à l'eau" or "naked on the seashore" — wishful thinking with Nuala in mind. After the pun on Celia's name, Mr. Kelly comments: "To be punning her name consoled him a little, a very little" (SB, *Murphy*, p. 82).

86. Celia Kelly owes part of her ambivalent status as a reformed prostitute to the character of Bellafront in Thomas Dekker's play *The Honest Whore,* which Beckett had read and from which he quotes in his "Whoroscope" notebook. Associated with the flesh, Celia reflects that side of Murphy which he himself claims to hate, and Dekker's condemnatory yet comic attitude to woman as fleshly temptress fits snugly into Murphy's dream of escaping from the contingent world.

87. See Mary Bryden, *Women in Samuel Beckett's Prose and Drama* (London: Macmillan Educational, 1993), p. 36.

88. SB, *Murphy*, p. 73.

89. The biography of Hester Dowden by Edmund Bentley gives several transcripts of psychic sittings in which she used a Ouija board. *Far Horizon, A Biography of Hester Dowden Medium and Psychic Investigator* (London: Rider and Company, 1951), pp. 50–58.

90. Ibid., "The Coming of Johannes," pp. 80–88.

91. SB, *Murphy*, p. 70.

92. Ibid., p. 73.

93. Ibid., p. 63.

94. " 'Call me Austin' said Ticklepenny, 'or even Augustin' " (SB, *Murphy*, p. 67).

95. Ibid., p. 133.

96. Ibid., p. 63.

97. See Gregory A. Schirmer, *The Poetry of Austin Clarke*, pp. 23–43.

98. Beckett had derived little or no pleasure from reading Clarke's poems for his *Bookman* piece and he was anticipating Clarke's hostility after he had situated the poet among those he called the Antiquarians. Denis Devlin told Tom MacGreevy that Clarke would pursue Beckett to his grave for the *Bookman* piece (Devlin to TM, 31 Aug. 1934 [TCD]). But a later letter from SB to TM suggests that MacGreevy had been tactful enough not to pass this on to Beckett: "Austin Clarke was at Cissie's one evening I was there, together with Salkeld and ffffffffrench-Mullen. . . . Clarke was full of hate but didn't seem to bear me any ill will for the *Bookman* article, if he ever saw it. He is really pathetic and sympathetic. Or is it that one clutches at any kind of literary contact?" (SB to TM, dated 5 June 1936, but really 1937 [TCD]). This letter shows, however, that Beckett had been expecting an adverse response. In an undated letter of 1935 to GR, probably November 1935, he spoke of sending a copy of *Echo's Bones* to Humbert Wolfe at the *Observer*, "lest it should fall into the black claws of Austin Clarke" (Texas).

99. SB to Percy (Arland) Ussher, 27 March 1938 (Texas).

100. For a gingerly handled account of this episode, see Susan Halpern, *Austin Clarke: His Life and Works*, Dublin: The Dolmen Press, 1974, pp. 36–37.

101. The identification of Ticklepenny with Austin Clarke is discussed in Mays's excellent article, "Mythologized Presences: *Murphy* in Its Time," pp. 199–201. Although Beckett's correspondence has allowed me to add to this argument, I am indebted to Professor Mays for his illuminating discussion and for communicating a letter to him on the subject from Austin Clarke himself.

102. James Mays, letter to JK, 27 Jan. 1993.

103. SB, *Murphy*, p. 6. Beckett had, of course, just seen the ballet *Petrushka*.

104. Ibid., pp. 96–97.

105. SB to TM, 7 July 1936 (TCD). This letter is reprinted in SB, *Disjecta*, pp. 102, 175, but with the wrong date of July 17.

106. SB to TM, 14 Feb. (1935) (TCD).

107. For a study of Beckett's debt to these authors, I refer the reader to a book by Frederik Smith, entitled "Beckett and the Eighteenth Century" (forthcoming). I am grateful to Professor Smith for letting me read certain chapters.

108. SB to AJL, 7 May 1934 (Texas) and to Nuala Costello, 10 May 1934 (Costello).

109. "Whoroscope" notebook (ms. 3000 [Reading]).

110. SB to TM, undated (16 Sept. 1934) (TCD). This letter contains a remarkable critique of Rousseau "as a champion of the right to be alone and as an authentically tragic figure . . ."

111. SB to AJL, 7 May 1934 (Texas). "There's a good passage in *Buddenbrooks* where Mann speaks of happiness, success etc., as analogous with light from a star, its foyer abolished when it most bright, and that brightness its own knell. So please God it is with unhappiness, if it can be bright, and with the bells rung in the distant heart. Or do I offend you? It's a basis for quietism anyhow, if basis be needed."

112. SB to TM, 8 Feb. (1935) (TCD).

113. SB to TM, 14 Feb. (1935) (TCD).

114. Beckett made extensive notes on both Gooch and Sorel.

115. SB, *Murphy*, p. 160.

116. Ibid.

117. In his notes, Beckett quotes other lines from *David and Fair Bethsabe* to illustrate the statement that "Peele important not as a dramatist, but as a lyricist." "Now comes my lover tripping like the roe, / And brings my longing tangled in her hair."

118. SB to TM, 29 Jan. (1935; Beckett dated this wrongly 1934) (TCD). "They are doing *The Alchemist* at the Embassy next week and I hope to go. What an admirable dramatic unity of place the besieged house provides and how much he makes of it. The feverish, obsidional atmosphere of *Nourri dans le Sérail* etc." (SB to TM, 10 Mar. [1935] [TCD]).

119. SB, *Murphy*, p. 18.

120. Ibid., pp. 8, 37.

121. SB to TM, undated (23 Sept. 1935) (TCD).

122. Herbert Read to T. M. Ragg, 1 Feb. 1938 (Routledge [Reading]).

123. SB, *Murphy*, p. 76.

124. Jung, *The Collected Works*, vol. 18, *The Symbolic Life*, p. 74.

125. SB, *Murphy*, p. 80.

126. Ibid. Michael Mooney has produced an important study of Murphy and the pre-Socratics: "Presocratic Scepticism: Samuel Beckett's *Murphy* Reconsidered," *ELH: A Journal of English Literary History*, vol. 49, pp. 214–34.

127. SB to TM, 26 July, 19 Aug., and 19 Sept. 1936 (TCD). "I cannot see anyone throwing much light on Spinoza except Spinoza," he remarked almost two years later to Arland Ussher (SB to Arland Ussher, 6 April 1938 [Texas]).

128. SB to TM, 16 Jan. (1936) (TCD).

129. SB to TM, 5 Mar. 1936 (TCD).

130. SB to TM, 8 Oct. 1935 (TCD).

131. Interview with Ursula Thompson, June 1990.

132. Ibid.

133. Bair, *Samuel Beckett*, p. 185.

134. "George Reavey and Samuel Beckett's Early Writing," interview with George Reavey by James Knowlson, *Journal of Beckett Studies*, no. 2 (summer 1977), p. 10.

135. SB, letter to GR, 15 Mar. 1935 (Texas).

136. Some of this revising had been done prior to sending the poems to Wishart for consideration in August 1932. Beckett then wrote to MacGreevy: "Typing out the poems yet again and fiddling about with them I felt more than ever that all the early ones — all the Caravan ones — were fake and that nothing could be done with them and that it was only à partir de *Whoroscope* [from "Whoroscope" on] that they began to be worth anything" (SB to TM, [27] Aug. 1932 [TCD]).

137. The poems were posted to *Poetry* magazine on Nov. 1, 1934 from 34 Gertrude Street, into which he had moved early in September. Someone there, probably an assistant editor, wrote on the envelope: "The long one ["Enueg I"] seems pure Joycean but might be worth taking," and someone else, probably the editor, Professor Morton Dauwen Zabel, added: "maybe. I feel lukewarmish" and he rejected them. I thank Lois Friedberg-Dobry for her help on the Zabel papers.

138. Con Leventhal had copies of both these poems in his files until his death. Beckett gave another copy of "Spring Song" to Georges Belmont. That the unpublished poem "Spring Song" may have been revised after August 1935 is shown by the lines taken from an incident when Beckett was rebuked in a swimming pool: "Ub to d'navel mister ub to d'navel" clearly alludes to an incident in the public baths at Paddington. "I found a sign from SOS [Seán O'Sullivan]. We bathed together but not alone at Paddington, where my Jantzen Pantchen [i.e., his latest swimming costume] falling far short of cavernous navel and aborted mammae earned me an official rebuke" (SB to AJL, 7 Aug. [1935] [Texas]). The two versions of this poem that exist (in Leventhal and Belmont's copies) are very different indeed.

139. SB to TM, 18 Oct. (1932) (TCD).

140. "The Undertaker's Man is the hardest to mitigate. It never was a poem and the best I can do now is to cut my losses. Yet it has something that will not let me leave it out altogether" (SB to TM, 8 Sept. [1935] [TCD]). In October, he wrote that it was "well changed" (SB to TM, 8 Oct. 1935 [TCD]).

141. Pilling, *Samuel Beckett*, p. 159.

142. LH, undated interview with SB (Dartmouth).

143. SB to TM, 31 Dec. (1935) (TCD).

144. Ibid.

145. SB to TM, 16 Jan. (1936) (TCD).

146. Ibid.

147. "The new stuff, some of it [Jack Yeats's recent painting], is superb. One small picture especially, *Morning*, almost a skyscape, wide street leading into Sligo looking west as usual, with boy on a horse, 30 pounds. If I had ten I would beard him with an easy payments proposition. But I have not. I let fall hints here that were understood but not implemented. But I have not given up hope of raising it. Do you think he would be amenable to instalments[?] It's a long time since I saw a picture I wanted so much" (SB to TM, 29 Jan. 1936 [TCD]; Beckett dated it in error 1935). At the beginning of May, he bought the picture by putting ten (borrowed) pounds down and paying the remaining twenty later (SB to TM, 7 May 1936 [TCD]).

148. SB to TM, 31 Dec. (1935) (TCD).

149. SB to TM, 7 May 1936 (TCD).

150. "Ethna MacCarthy has got the job of doing his Provençal lectures and I have been helping her out of the Tresor dou Felibrige. Aubanel seems the best of them. They have Mistral's *Mireio* and *Memori et Raconte*" (SB to TM, 29 Jan. 1936; Beckett dated this in error 1935). Beckett's thirteen pages of typed notes on Mistral and the Félibrige writers (Joseph Roumanville and Théodore Aubanel) still exist. Twelve pages consist of notes on Mistral in Gaston Paris's book, *Penseurs et poètes*.

151. Some serious problems arise at this period with Bair's previous biography of Beckett. A major long letter to Tom MacGreevy, dated wrongly by Beckett June 5, 1936, is actually from June 1937. This places some of his socializing and a job application *after* his trip to Germany, not before. References to the libel action and a message from a painter in Munich within the letter clinch this redating.

152. SB to TM, 29 Jan. 1936 (Beckett dated this in error 1935) (TCD).

153. Interview with Mary Manning, 13 March 1992.

154. SB to TM, 25 March 1936 (TCD).

155. "Said O'Brien, pointing to a plane of light: 'That's a lovely waterfall.' Yeats had the answer pat: 'If waterfalls looked like nothing but waterfalls and planes of light like nothing but planes of light, etc.' Tonks was beautiful, decrepit and pleasant, very willowy and Honeish [Joe Hone, whom Beckett knew, had written a book about Henry Tonks], full of George Moore, Rowlandson and Sickert" (SB to TM, 27 June 1936 [TCD]).

156. SB to TM, 9 Sept. 1936 (TCD).

157. Ibid.

158. SB to TM, 6 Feb. (1936) (TCD).

159. SB to TM, 7 May 1936 (TCD).

160. SB to TM, 27 June 1936 (TCD).

161. SB to TM, 25 March 1936 (TCD).

162. SB to TM, 6 Feb. (1936) (TCD).

163. SB to TM, 26 July (1936) (TCD).

164. SB to TM, 22 June (1933) and "started the Spanish again" (SB to TM, 7 Sept. [1933] [TCD]). Even at the end of 1935, Beckett had not totally discounted the idea of going away to Spain (see SB to TM, 8 Oct. 1935 [TCD]).

165. Testimonial of T. B. Rudmose-Brown, 7 July 1932. This earlier testimonial was included with other later ones when Beckett applied for the lectureship in Italian at the University of Cape Town on July 19, 1937. I am most grateful to Ms. Clare Stableford of the university's Appointments Office for making copies of the testimonials available to me, and to the novelist and lecturer in English J. M. Coetzee for first bringing their existence to my attention.

166. Beckett's various notes on Goethe and his typescript of the poem have been preserved.

167. SB to TM, 25 March 1936 (TCD).

168. "I have been working at German and reading Faust. Finished Part 1 last night. It leaves me with an impression of something very fragmentary, often irrelevant and too concrete, that perhaps Part 2 will correct. Auerbach's Cellar, the Witches kitchen and Walpurgisnacht, for example, — little more than sites and atmospheres, swamping the

corresponding mental conditions. All the *on and up* is so tiresome also, the determined optimism à la Beethoven, the unconscionable time a-coming" (SB to TM, undated [19 Aug. 1936] [TCD]). My thanks are due to Professor Wolfgang van Emden for his help.
169. Elizabeth Stockton to JK, 11 April 1992.
170. Ibid.
171. SB, *Collected Poems in English and French*, p. 30.
172. Interview with Mary Manning, 13 March 1992.
173. SB to TM, 19 Sept. 1936 (TCD).

10: GERMANY: THE UNKNOWN DIARIES, 1936–37

1. SB to TM, 9 Oct. 1936 (TCD).
2. In *Murphy*, Miss Counihan gives Neary "a forenoon appointment at the grave of Father Prout (F. S. Mahony) in Shandon Churchyard, the one place in Cork she knew of where fresh air, privacy and immunity from assault were reconciled" (*Murphy*, p. 38). Beckett had either been to the churchyard before on one of his earlier trips from Cork to Hamburg or wrote this into the manuscript of the novel at a late stage. The first seems more likely.
3. SB, unpublished German diaries, notebook 1, 28 Sept. 1936. (I refer to these diaries from now on as "GD".) I am greatly indebted to Edward Beckett for drawing my attention to the existence of these six voluminous diaries, which he discovered in an old trunk in Beckett's cellar at 38 boulevard Saint-Jacques. I thank him most warmly for his generosity in passing them on to me and giving me exclusive use of them.
4. SB, GD, notebook 1, 29 Sept. 1936.
5. SB, GD, notebook 1, 30 Sept. 1936.
6. SB, GD, notebook 1, 1 Oct. 1936.
7. Ibid.
8. SB, GD, notebook 1, 5 Oct. 1936.
9. Bair, *Samuel Beckett*, p. 242.
10. SB, GD, notebook 1, undated entry (but either 3 or 4 Oct. 1936). Also SB to TM, 9 Oct. 1936 (TCD).
11. SB, GD, notebook 2, 13 Nov. 1936.
12. SB, GD, notebook 1, 7 Oct. 1936, where John 11:26 is quoted in German and is referred to wrongly as verse 36. Beckett quoted the lines in English in a letter to TM, 9 Oct. 1936 (TCD).
13. SB, GD, notebook 1, 19 Oct. 1936.
14. SB, GD, notebook 1, 9 Oct. 1936.
15. Ibid.
16. SB, GD, notebook 1, undated entry (but either 3 or 4 Oct. 1936).
17. SB, GD, notebook 1, 18 Oct. 1936.
18. SB, GD, notebook 3, 31 Dec. 1936.
19. SB, GD, notebook 1, 9 Oct. 1936.
20. SB, GD, notebook 1, 11 Oct. 1936.
21. Among the books lent to Beckett by Fräulein Schön were Rudolf Binding, *Die Waffenbrüder* (Frankfurt am Main: Rütten and Loening, 1935) and *Sankt Georgs Stellvertreter* (Frankfurt am Main, Rütten and Loening, 1934); Hans Leip, *Herz im Wind: Geschichten von der Wasserkante* (Jena: E. Diederichs, 1934); Henry von Heiseler, *Wawas Ende ein Dokument* (Munich: A. Langen and G. Müller, 1933); Wilhelm Schäfer, *Die Anekdoten* (Munich: A. Langen and G. Müller, 1928 or 1929 edition); a collection of lyrical poetry, *Das kleine Gedichtbuch — Lyrik von Heute*; Ernst Wiechert, *Hirtennovellen* (Munich: A. Langen and G. Müller, 1934); and Rainer Rilke's *Die ausgewählten Gedichte* (Leipzig: Insel-Bücherei, 1935).
22. SB, GD, notebook 1, 12 Oct. 1936.
23. SB, GD, notebook 1, 20 Oct. 1936.

24. A manuscript version of this translation into German, dated August 18 (1936), is preserved in one of SB's exercise books. All but one of the changes suggested by Klaudia Ascher and referred to in an entry in Beckett's diary (GD, notebook 1, 2 Nov. 1936), were incorporated into his manuscript.

25. Fräulein Ascher lent Beckett several novels by Ernst Wiechert with which he had little sympathy—e.g., *Die Magd des Jürgen Doskocil* (Munich: Langen and Müller, 1934; translated as *The Girl and the Ferryman*, [London: Pilot Press, 1947]) and what was probably *Das Spiel vom deutschen Bettelmann* (Munich: Langen and Müller, 1934). Beckett bought for himself Ernst Wiechert's *Der Todeskandidat* (Munich: Langen and Müller, 1934).

26. SB, GD, notebook 1, 24 Oct. 1936.

27. SB, GD, notebook 2, 20 Nov. 1936.

28. SB to TM, 9 Oct. 1936 (TCD).

29. The gallery owned, he wrote, "a lot of superb van Goyens, a landscape given to Brouwer that might be a potboiler, a van Uden-Teniers not so good as Dublin's, two Everdingens, an Elsheimer, a Dirck Hals"; he greatly admired Elsheimer's *Predigt Johannis des Täufers*, an "exquisite" Philips Wouwerman *(Reiter an der Düne)*, and an Aert Van der Neer *(Mondscheinlandschaft)*. (SB, GD, notebook 1, 8 Oct. and 18 Oct. 1936. Also SB to TM, 9 Oct. 1936 [TCD].) On his October 18 visit, he referred to there being a good Roymerswaele *(Berufung des Apostels Matthäus)*, an excellent Hinrich Funhof *(Maria in Ährenkleid)*, and a good Hans Burgkmair *(Christus am Ölberg)* and spoke of how lovely the Van der Heyden ivy pavilion was *(Pavillon beim Huis ten Bosch* by Jan Van der Heyden).

30. SB, GD, notebook 1, 21 Oct. 1936.

31. Ibid.

32. SB, GD, notebook 2, 19 Nov. 1936. This painting is now in the Museum of Modern Art in New York.

33. Ibid.

34. SB, GD, notebook 2, 22 Nov. 1936.

35. SB, GD, notebook 5, 15 Feb. 1937.

36. SB, GD, notebook 1, 25 Oct. 1936. The professor was Benno Diederich, born in 1870. His biographies were *Emile Zola* (Leipzig: 1898) and *Alphonse Daudet* (Hamburg: 1901).

37. SB to TM, 18 Jan. 1937 (TCD).

38. SB, GD, notebook 2, 13 Nov. 1936.

39. SB, GD, notebook 2, 10 Nov. 1936.

40. SB, GD, notebook 2, 16 Nov. 1936.

41. SB to TM, 18 Jan. 1937 (TCD).

42. SB, GD, notebook 2, 23 Nov. 1936.

43. Ibid.

44. The fullest account of Rosa Schapire, her publications, and her private collection is given in Gerhard Wietek's article on her in the *Jahrbuch der Hamburger Kunstsammlungen*, vol. 9 (1964), pp. 114–62.

45. SB, GD, notebook 2, 22 Nov. 1936.

46. SB, GD, notebook 2, 14 Nov. 1936.

47. SB to TM, 18 Jan. 1937 (TCD).

48. SB, GD, notebook 2, 15 Nov. 1936.

49. Ibid.

50. SB, GD, notebook 3, 20 Dec. 1936.

51. "All the lavatory men say Heil Hitler" (SB to MM, 14 Nov. 1936 [Texas]). The diaries show Beckett's impatience or irritation on a number of occasions.

52. SB, GD, notebook 4, 11 Jan. 1937.

53. For example, Beckett wrote: "The modern rooms of the Kronprinzenpalais are closed, i.e. modern German painting from Nolde on. I got a permit in Hamburg to visit

the various works no longer accessible to German public, and shall try it on director of Kronprinzenpalais here, though it is only valid for Hamburg. On the ground floor are wonderful Munchs and Van Goghs" (SB to TM, 22 Dec. 1936 [TCD]).

54. I am most grateful to Dr. Helmut Leppien, the director of the Hamburger Kunsthalle, for his guidance as to what happened at this time in Germany with respect to modern art, as well as for the great kindness that he extended to me when I visited Hamburg and the Kunsthalle.

55. SB to TM, 18 Jan. 1937 (TCD).

56. SB, GD, notebook 2, 24 Nov. 1936.

57. SB, GD, notebook 2, 26 Nov. 1936.

58. SB, GD, notebook 2, 15 Nov. 1936.

59. SB, GD, notebook 2, 25 Nov. 1936.

60. SB, GD, notebook 2, 26 Nov. 1936. A book on Bargheer shows some of the work that Beckett might well have seen in his studio: Wolfgang Hesse, *Eduard Bargheer: Leben und Werk* (Campione d'Italia: Galleria Hesse, 1979).

61. SB, GD, notebook 2, 26 Nov. 1936.

62. Ibid.

63. SB, GD, notebook 2, 25 Nov. 1936.

64. SB, *Disjecta*, p. 118.

65. SB, GD, notebook 2, 26 Nov. 1936.

66. *Der Maler Willem Grimm 1904–1986* (Hamburg: Hans Christians Verlag, 1989).

67. SB, GD, notebook 1, 26 Oct. 1936, where an entry refers to photographs of Bremen's "crooked spire" in *The Irish Times* sent by his mother as "designed to stimulate me into feuilletons."

68. SB, GD, notebook 1, 25 Oct. 1936.

69. SB, *First Love* (London: Calder and Boyars, 1973), pp. 12–13.

70. SB, GD, notebook 2, 27 Nov. 1936.

71. In the Hanover gallery, he looked admiringly at the Master of the Golden Table, at Master Bertram's great *Passion Altar*, and, with less enthusiasm, at their Flemish and Dutch collections.

72. SB, GD, notebook 2, 6 Dec. 1936.

73. SB, GD, notebook 2, 9 Dec. 1936.

74. SB, GD, notebook 3, 18 Dec. 1936.

75. SB, GD, notebook 2, 9 Dec. 1936.

76. For example, *That Time, Rockaby,* and *What Where.* I am especially grateful to Dr. Reinhold Wex, the director of the Herzog-Anton-Ulrich gallery in Brunswick, for making it possible for me to have an extended private viewing of the Giorgione and other pictures in the collection.

77. SB, GD, notebook 2, 6 Dec. 1936.

78. SB, GD, notebook 2, 9 Dec. 1936.

79. I am grateful to Pastor Henning Kühner, of the Andreaskirche, for allowing me to replicate Beckett's climb and for escorting me personally up the tower.

80. SB, GD, notebook 2, 9 Dec. 1936.

81. SB, GD, notebook 2, 8 Dec. 1936.

82. SB to TM, 18 Jan. 1937 (TCD).

83. SB to MM, 13 Dec. 1936 (Texas).

84. SB to MM, 18 Jan. 1937 (Texas).

85. SB, GD, notebook 4, 14 Jan. 1937.

86. SB, GD, notebook 4, 15 Jan. 1937.

87. Karl Scheffler, *Deütsche Maler und Zeichner im neunzehnten Jahrhundert* (Leipzig: Insel Verlag, 1911), although Beckett probably bought a later printing.

88. SB, GD, notebook 2, 16 Dec. 1936.

89. Ibid.

90. SB, GD, notebook 3, 20 Dec. 1936.

91. Ibid.

92. SB, GD, notebook 3, 18 Dec. 1936.

93. Ibid.

94. He often picks out tiny details, as, for instance, in Veneziano's *Adoration of the Kings*: "Joseph, Virgin, toe kissing immensely prostrate adorer, camel — ass chord of dignity and impotence, colossal rump of Schimmel, flowers, birds (storks in air and peacock on shed), water, big cypress, figure dangling from gallows in far background — all wonderful" (GD, notebook 3, 20 Dec. 1936). I am grateful to Dr. Henning Bock, the director of the Gemäldegalerie at Dahlem in Berlin, for receiving me so warmly during a visit to Berlin, and for his advice and that of Frau Dina Panneck of the Nationalgalerie and of Dr. Magdelena Moeller of the Brücke Museum.

95. SB, GD, notebook 4, 15 Jan. 1937.

96. Ibid.

97. Ibid.

98. SB, GD, notebook 3, 26 Dec. 1936.

99. SB, GD, notebook 4, 13 Jan. 1937. In Beckett's copy of the catalogue of the Kaiser-Friedrich-Museum and Deutschen Museum, which he gave to Avigdor Arikha, he has added to no. 1631, Geertgen tot Sint Jans's *Johannes der Täufer*, the note "cp. Hermit in Indian miniature." And, in the *Indische Miniaturen* catalogue of the Staatliche Museen in Berlin (n.d.), which he bought, there is an illustration of precisely this miniature, *Besuch beim Eremiten* (volume 1, p. 42).

100. SB, GD, notebook 4, 12 Jan. 1937.

101. Ibid. In a letter to TM (18 Jan. 1937 [TCD]), Beckett wrote: "Voltaire's room is altogether charming and comic, complete Princesse de Babylone, with fantastic birds and flowers all over the walls and ceiling and La Fontaine on the chair covers, and yet somehow full of exile and loneliness." The birds and flowers are still on the walls but the chair covers are no longer in the Voltaire room.

102. SB, GD, notebook 4, 12 Jan. 1937. "Real pornography, that would make Fragonard look like Fra Angelico" (SB to TM, 18 Jan. 1937 [TCD]).

103. SB, GD, notebook 4, 12 Jan. 1937.

104. Ibid.

105. SB to MM, 18 Jan. 1937 (Texas).

106. Friedrich Hebbel, *Gyges und sein Ring, Eine tragödie in fünf Acten* (Vienna: Verlag von Tendler und Comp., 1856).

107. SB, GD, notebook 4, 12 Jan. 1937.

108. SB to MM, 18 Jan. 1937 (Texas).

109. SB, GD, notebook 4, 12 Jan. 1937.

110. Walther Bauer, *Die notwendige Reise.* (Berlin: B. Cassirer, 1932).

111. SB, GD, notebook 4, 18 Jan. 1937.

112. Ibid. The same day, Beckett wrote to Mary Manning that "provoked by belated romantic German novels I find new planes of justification for the bondage in the chair that were not present to me at the time. Or rather for the figure of the bondage in the chair. If I am not careful I shall become clear as to what I have written" (SB to MM, 18 Jan. 1937 [Texas]).

113. SB to TM, 9 Oct. 1936 (TCD).

114. SB to GR, 13 Nov. 1936 (Texas).

115. SB to MM, 14 Nov. 1936 (Texas).

116. SB to MM, 13 Dec. 1936 (Texas).

117. SB to GR, 20 Dec. 1936 (Texas).

118. SB, GD, notebook 5, 19 Feb. 1937.

119. Josef Eichheim also played in Bertolt Brecht's *Leben Eduards des Zweiten von England* in Munich in March 1924 and played Stromer in Billinger's *Rauhnacht*, also in Munich, in October 1931. See Günther Rühle, *Theater für die Republik 1917–1933*

(FAM, 1967), pp. 508, 511, 1089. He was in many films. I am most grateful to John Wieczorek and John Sandford for their help in tracing this actor.

120. SB to MM, 18 Jan. 1937 (Texas).
121. SB to TM, 16 Feb. 1937 (TCD).
122. SB, GD, notebook 4, 23 Jan. 1937.
123. SB, GD, notebook 4, 26 Jan. 1937.
124. SB, postcard to TM, 25 Jan. 1937 (TCD).
125. SB, GD, notebook 4, 28 Jan. 1937.
126. SB to TM, 16 Feb. 1937 (TCD).
127. SB, GD, notebook 4, 27 Jan. 1937.
128. SB, GD, notebook 4, 29 Jan. 1937.
129. SB to GR, 30 Jan. 1937 (Texas).
130. SB to TM, 22 Dec. 1936 (TCD).
131. SB, GD, notebook 4, 2 Feb. 1937.
132. SB, GD, notebook 4, 5 Feb. 1937.
133. SB to TM, 16 Feb. 1937 (TCD).
134. SB, GD, notebook 5, 15 Feb. 1937.
135. SB, GD, notebook 4, 7 Feb. 1937.
136. Frau Bienert had a fantastically rich treasure trove of modern art and Beckett appreciated how privileged he was to be allowed a lengthy private view. "She opens drawer within drawer in the study with the Mondrians and Kandinsky and produces work wrapped up in brown paper and gives it up on condition that I show it to nobody in Germany" (GD, notebook 5, 15 Feb. 1937). They lived in dangerous times, and Frau Bienert admitted that she no longer normally showed her paintings to anyone. Grohmann did an illustrated catalogue of the collection, which Beckett was given by Ida Bienert: Will Grohmann, *Die Sammlung Ida Bienert Dresden* (Potsdam: Muller and I. Kiepenheuer, [1933]). The catalogue was given by Beckett to Avigdor Arikha.
137. SB, GD, notebook 5, 15 Feb. 1937.
138. SB, GD, notebook 4, 10 Feb. 1937.
139. SB, GD, notebook 4, 2 Feb. 1937.
140. Ibid.
141. SB, GD, notebook 4, 3 Feb. 1937.
142. SB to TM, 16 Feb. 1937 (TCD).
143. SB, GD, notebook 4, 12 Feb. 1937.
144. Herr Höfer, the proprietor of the pension where Beckett stayed at 15 Bürgerwiese, had interestingly done drawings of the Zwinger before the heavy restoration work that had to be done on the building. Beckett saw Höfer's drawings, which he admired, in the print room of the Zwinger Gallery.
145. SB to TM, 16 Feb. 1937 (TCD).
146. SB to Georges Duthuit, 27 July 1948 (Duthuit), referring to what Duthuit had said about the Italians' use of space. Beckett remembered Antonello da Messina's *Sebastian* as being "formidable, formidable. C'était dans la première salle, j'en étais bloqué chaque fois" ("wonderful, wonderful. It was in the first room. I had to stop there every time").
147. He enthused about many of the Brouwers that he saw in Germany, including one in the Zwinger: "an early bright [painting], almost in the manner of Dirck Hals or Duyster, Peasants making music, what they didn't do long in the world that he found" (GD, notebook 4, 5 Feb. 1937).
148. SB, GD, notebook 5, 14 Feb. 1937.
149. He consistently preferred Romanesque to Gothic and Rococo to Baroque. He would sometimes spend as long in front of a sculpture or carving as in front of a picture. He could be very forthright in his views, as in his remark about the famous Adam Kraft ciborium in St. Lawrence's church in Nuremberg: "a frightful machine, more gothic than the gothic, a miracle of laborious statics, a skyscrapery in dingy limestone with the

pinnacle bent to follow the curve of the vaulting, showing that he could have gone on had not space forbidden" (SB to TM, 7 March 1937 [TCD]).

150. SB, GD, notebook 5, 23 Feb. 1937.
151. SB, GD, notebook 5, 2 March 1937.
152. SB, GD, notebook 6, 17 March 1937.
153. Ibid.
154. SB to TM, 7 March 1937 (TCD).
155. Beckett had two catalogues in his library; one was the 1928 Munich catalogue, *Old Pinakothek Munich*, with 200 illustrations, given to him by his cousin; the other was the *Katalog der Älteren Pinakothek München* (München: Amtlicher Katalog, 1936). This copy was bought in Munich and contains Beckett's few marginal notes.
156. SB to TM, 9 Jan. 1936 (wrongly dated by Beckett 1935) (TCD).
157. SB, GD, notebook 5, 13 March 1937.
158. SB, GD, notebook 5, 8 March 1937.
159. SB to TM, 25 March 1937 (TCD).
160. SB, GD, notebook 5, 9 March 1937.
161. Ibid.
162. SB, GD, notebook 5, 11 March 1937.
163. SB, GD, notebook 5, 15 March 1937.
164. SB, GD, notebook 6, 17 March 1937.
165. SB to TM, 25 March 1937 (TCD).
166. He thought Ende's painting was "the very worst, dream, myth, idea painting. . . . Not a trace of direct optical experience" (GD, notebook 6, 19 March 1937). Fortunately, Edgar Ende talked more interestingly and they soon embarked on a discussion yet again of language. The painter has, wrote Beckett, "a pleasant figure of the feeling he has of imprisoning people in conversation, of putting bars all round them with questions and allusions, against each a bar of prejudice springs up. Doesn't agree that communication is impossible. I say in the end one is either a solipsist or one is not" (GD, notebook 6, 31 March 1937). Josef Mader had studied under Ahlers-Hestermann in Köln, which was condemnation enough in Beckett's eyes: "Tigers, lions, birds, horses, male and female nudes in lurid landscapes. Pitifully bad, drawing, colour, composition, conception, all. I find fingers to admire! And this is among the best! Part of what is too good for the Nazis! And personally so pathetic, humble and sincere" (GD, notebook 6, 23 March 1937).
167. SB, GD, notebook 6, 26 March 1937.
168. Ibid.
169. Trying to convey to Eggers the insights that he thought he had gained about Ballmer's painting from reading a Rudolf Steiner–inspired pamphlet, "Aber Herr Heidegger," written by Ballmer, he wrote: "Try and explain in what sense 'Aber Herr Heidegger' was a clarification of Ballmer's painting and get rather tied up" (GD, notebook 6, 26 March 1937).
170. SB, GD, notebook 5, 11 March 1937.
171. SB, GD, notebook 2, 17 Nov. 1936.
172. SB, GD, notebook 3, 25 Dec. 1936.
173. SB, GD, notebook 3, 25 Dec. 1936.
174. Beckett found him a "sturdy little man with strong face and the Pfeiferstube voice, rather distressing at first, like most appalling catarrh, as though each word a labour of Hercules. Talks about the Pfeiferstube. I pay convincing compliments" (GD, notebook 6, 30 March 1937).
175. SB, GD, notebook 6, 31 March 1937.
176. SB, GD, notebook 6, 14 March 1937.
177. SB, GD, notebook 6, 1 April 1937.
178. SB, letter to Peter Gidal, 12 Sept. 1972 (Gidal).
179. I owe the Karl Valentin part of this suggestion to Peter Gidal (letter to JK, 19 July [1990]).

180. SB to TM, 25 March 1937 (TCD).
181. SB, GD, notebook 5, 13 March 1937.
182. SB, GD, notebook 6, 26 March 1937.
183. SB, GD, notebook 6, 25 March 1937.
184. SB, GD, notebook 1, 6 Oct. 1936.

11: A PERMANENT HOME, 1937–39

1. SB to TM, 26 April 1937 (TCD).
2. Ibid.
3. SB to Joe Hone, 3 July 1937 (Texas).
4. His reasons were that he did not want another university teaching post; his interests lay in Europe and in European culture; and, finally, he had also learned that Mary Manning was due to move soon to Buffalo with her husband and living in such close proximity to her after their affair did not seem like a good idea (SB to TM, 7 July [1937] [TCD]). He was, however, still hesitating about it at the beginning of August (SB to TM, 4 Aug. 1937 [TCD]).
5. In spite of his hesitation, Beckett went ahead with an application that included a brief curriculum vitae. He wrote about this in letters to TM (7 July and 4 Aug. 1937 [TCD]). In his résumé he listed, perhaps for reasons of tact, *More Pricks Than Kicks* as *Short Stories* and *Echo's Bones* as *Poems.* His application included testimonials from Rudmose-Brown (one dated June 5, 1937, the other July 7, 1932), Walter Starkie, R. W. Tate, and Jean Thomas; his referees were Thomas Ross, Solicitor; Captain Reverend A. A. Luce, and Dr. Geoffrey Thompson. (See also Chapter 9, note 165.)
6. SB to TM, 7 July (1937)(TCD) and MM, 11 July 1937 (Texas). He was recommended for this translation by Axel Kaun, whom he had met in Berlin and corresponded with in 1937.
7. SB to TM, 4 Aug. 1937 (TCD).
8. SB to TM, 26 April 1937 (TCD).
9. May Beckett's maid, Lily Condell, spoke of Beckett's and his mother's strong attachment to Wolf, the older of the two Kerry Blues. She related a delightful story of how "if Mrs. Beckett was going for the bus she would leave her out at the bus-stop and she used to have a pink scarf around her, and she was black, and she would leave her case beside her and if the bus had come the busman knew her and they'd wait if she [Mrs. Beckett] hadn't come" (interview with Lily Condell, 4 Aug. 1992).
10. Bair interprets his mother's act in having the dog put down in his absence and her subsequent grief ("feigned or real," she wonders), as part of "a pattern of behavior deliberately designed to provoke him" (*Samuel Beckett,* p. 251). I find this psychologically less convincing than that she took responsibility for the dog being put down as an act of kindness.
11. SB to TM, 7 Aug. 1936 (TCD).
12. SB to TM, 14 May 1937 (TCD).
13. SB to MM, 22 May 1937 (Texas).
14. Morris Sinclair to JK, 11 Oct. 1993. I am most grateful to Morris Sinclair for all the information and advice he gave me about his family and Samuel Beckett at this time.
15. SB to TM, 7 July (1937)(TCD).
16. Interview with Lily Condell, 4 Aug. 1992.
17. SB to TM, 23 Aug. 1937 (TCD).
18. SB to TM, 7 July (1937)(TCD).
19. SB to TM, 14 Aug. 1937 (TCD).
20. SB to TM, 23 Aug. 1937 (TCD).
21. Interview with Mervyn Wall, 11 Aug. 1992.
22. SB to TM, 23 Aug. 1937 (TCD).
23. SB to TM, 7 July (1937) (TCD).

24. SB to Arland Ussher, 15 June 1937 (TCD).

25. Two of the paintings that Beckett mentioned seeing were In Memory of Boucicault and Bianconi (now in the National Gallery of Ireland), and The Little Waves of Breffny (now in a private Dublin collection). He also mentions Yeats's Low Tide and Boy and Horse, of which he had photographic reproductions.

26. One of the reasons for the invitation was that Yeats had expressed a wish to see the donkey that his mother stabled in one of the outhouses. Beckett was delighted to find that his mother got on so well with Yeats (SB to TM, 5 June 1937, wrongly dated by Beckett as 1936 [TCD]). There is real affection for his mother in this letter. Later that summer, he took her and his aunt Cissie to Yeats's studio to see some of the recent landscapes painted in his "largest and freeest manner" (SB to TM, 7 July 1937 [TCD]).

27. SB to TM, 14 Aug. 1937 (TCD). At an earlier time in private conversation, Beckett had clearly suggested to MacGreevy an affinity between Yeats and Constable (SB to TM, 4 Aug. 1937 [TCD]). Now he concentrates on what he sees as their differences: "There is nothing of the kind in Constable, the landscape shelters or threatens or serves or destroys, his nature is really infected with 'spirit,' ultimately as humanised and romantic as Turner's was and Claude's was not and Cézanne's was not. God knows it doesn't take much sensitiveness to feel that in Ireland[,] a nature almost as inhumanly inorganic as a stage set. And perhaps that is the final quale of Jack Yeats's painting, a sense of the ultimate *inorganism* of everything. Watteau stressed it with busts and urns, his people are *mineral* in the end. A painting of pure inorganic juxtapositions, where nothing can be taken or given and there is no possibility of change or exchange" (SB to TM, 14 Aug. 1937 [TCD]).

28. SB to TM, 14 Aug. 1937 (TCD). The painting that Beckett refers to here "is named 'A Storm,' painted in 1936. When last I heard of it it was in the possession of the Waddington Galleries, London" (Hilary Pyle, letter to JK, 26 Oct. 1993).

29. SB to Georges Duthuit, 2 March 1954 (Duthuit).

30. SB, *Proust. Three Dialogues. Samuel Beckett & Georges Duthuit*, p. 66.

31. SB to TM, 21 Sept. (1937)(TCD).

32. He described himself to Mary Manning, for instance, as "willless in a grey tumult of *idées oiseuses* [idle notions]" (SB to MM, 30 Aug. 1937 [Texas]).

33. SB to MM, 30 Aug. 1937 (Texas).

34. SB to MM, 22 May 1937 (Texas).

35. Beckett had read some Johnson at college. Notes on *Rasselas*, Johnson's lives of Ascham and Dryden, Boswell's *Life of Johnson* and *The Journal of a Tour to the Hebrides* in his personal "Whoroscope" notebook probably date them between 1934 and 1936 (Reading). Another private notebook, bought in Dublin in July 1936, shows him reading Johnson in August of that year, preparing for his forthcoming trip to Germany by either translating Johnson's famous letter to Lord Chesterfield into German or copying out an existing German translation. The letter from Dr. Johnson to Lord Chesterfield is in a lined exercise book inscribed on the front cover "6, Clare Street, Dublin, IFS, 13/7/36." The preceding entries, written in the same pen, are dated August 1936. This suggests that the Johnson material, even though it is in German, dates from the months preceding his departure for Hamburg, although, as a few entries at the rear of the book show, he also took this exercise book with him to Germany.

36. A letter from Beckett to Tom MacGreevy dated June 5, 1936 (TCD), in which he discusses his progress on his Johnson project, was wrongly dated by Beckett and from internal evidence was clearly written on June 5, 1937.

37. SB to MM, 13 Dec. 1936 (Texas).

38. Ibid.

39. These notebooks were generously given by Ruby Cohn with the other Johnson material to the Beckett Archive in Reading, after Beckett had given them to her. As well as taking copious notes on Dr. Johnson and Mrs. Thrale, Beckett also noted down information and anecdotes concerning Arthur Murphy, who introduced Johnson to the

Thrales; Fanny Burney; Frank Barber (Johnson's black servant); Dr. Robert Levett; Polly Carmichael; Mrs. Elizabeth Desmoulins; and Johnson's blind friend Mrs. Anna Williams. He had his own copy of Boswell's famous *Life of Johnson* in Birkbeck Hill's edition of 1887, which, though he gave so many of his books away, he kept in his library until his death. He also read an extensive list of other works relating to Dr. Johnson and to Mrs. Thrale.

40. Ruby Cohn, *Just Play*, p. 149. Professor Cohn here gives an excellent account of the contents of the manuscript notebooks.

41. Proved by the date of purchase of his Johnson notebooks and by the fact that his German diaries contain no references at all to work on Dr. Johnson. The first volume was bought in Munich along with the final volume of his German diaries. Beckett referred to this volume as "its brother." It has black, soft, shiny covers and is identical with the sixth volume of his diary. The two notebooks have the name of the stationer (Fritz Führer) on a small sticker in the bottom right-hand corner of the inside back cover. (Purchase of notebooks referred to in a diary entry of March 17, 1937, GD, notebook 6). The second and third volumes containing notes on Johnson, which follow sequentially, were purchased from Browne and Nolan's in Dublin.

42. At the end of April, Beckett was writing with excitement of the consequences of his theory of impotence: "It becomes more interesting—the fake rage to cover his retreat from her [Mrs. Thrale], then the real rage when he realises that no retreat was necessary, and beneath both the despair of the lover with nothing to love with" (SB to TM, 26 April 1937 [TCD]). But, by the beginning of July, his letters show that the focus has shifted and a more tragic Johnson is emerging in Beckett's mind.

43. SB to MM, 11 July 1937 (Texas).

44. SB to TM, 4 Aug. 1937 (TCD).

45. "And if the play is about him [Dr. Johnson] and not about her [Mrs. Thrale]," he wrote, "it does not mean that he was in the right, or any nonsense like that, but simply that he being spiritually self conscious was a tragic figure, i.e. worth putting down as part of the whole of which oneself is a part, and that she, being never physically self conscious is less interesting to me personally" (SB to TM, 4 Aug. 1937 [TCD]).

46. Frederik Smith explores what Beckett called his "Johnson fantasy" in a forthcoming book, *Beckett and the Eighteenth Century*. I am most grateful to Professor Smith for his help in this area of Beckett's work.

47. SB to MM, undated (Dec.) 1937 (Texas).

48. SB to TM, 6 Dec. 1933 (TCD).

49. Linda Ben-Zvi, *Samuel Beckett*, p. 55. This, together with Cohn, *Just Play*, pp. 161–62, provides the best discussion of the links between the Johnson fragment and Beckett's later drama.

50. SB to TM, 4 Sept. (1937)(TCD).

51. SB to TM, 21 Sept. (1937)(TCD).

52. SB to TM, 28 Sept. 1937 (TCD).

53. Morris Sinclair, letter to JK, 11 Oct. 1993.

54. SB to TM, 6 Oct. 1937 (TCD).

55. The idea was suggested by Bair, *Samuel Beckett*, p. 263.

56. Morris Sinclair, letter to JK, 11 Oct. 1993.

57. SB to TM, 10 Dec. 1937 (TCD).

58. SB to TM, 1 Nov. (1937) and 10 Dec. 1937 (TCD).

59. Interview with SB, 23 Oct. 1989.

60. Interview with Elisabeth van Velde, 12 Sept. 1990. Beckett owned two Geer van Velde paintings from this period and in this style. One is called *Silvester 1937–8*. It was given by Beckett to the Beckett Archive in Reading in April 1973. The other, dated November 1937, was found in Beckett's cellar after his death.

61. In Joyce's *Ulysses*, Bloom "crossed at Nassau street corner and stood before the window of Yeates and Son, pricing the field glasses. Or will I drop into old Harris's and

have a chat with young Sinclair? Wellmannered fellow. Probably at his lunch" (James Joyce, *Ulysses*, Corrected Text, edited by Hans Walter Gabler with Wolfhard Steppe and Claus Melchior. London: Penguin Books, 1986, p. 136).

62. There had been a divorce petition against Morris Harris in 1906, when his second wife had alleged that he had been having an affair with his housekeeper and sister-in-law, Sarah White. "James Joyce, being acquainted with the grandchildren, followed the suit closely; in it, Morris Harris had been charged with as many sins as are levelled against Leopold Bloom in *Ulysses* and against Humphrey Chimpden Earwicker in *Finnegans Wake*" (Louis Hyman, *The Jews of Ireland*. Dublin: Irish University Press, 1972, p. 148).

63. My account of the Sinclair-Gogarty libel action is based on documents in the National Archives in Dublin, High Court 1937, 300/P, which include Beckett's own affidavit and F. R. Higgins's evidence given on Commission (that is, by sworn statement in his absence) *(The Irish Reports)* and on press reports in the Irish and English newspapers *(The Irish Times*, 23, 24, 25, and 28 Nov.; *The Irish Independent*, 23, 24, and 25 Nov.; and *The* [London] *Times*, 23, 24, and 30 Nov.). I also owe a debt to Ulick O'Connor's excellent chapter in his biography of Oliver St. John Gogarty. Although a few mistakes have crept in, O'Connor gives a full and lively account of the case as a whole. I have concentrated on the part that Beckett played in the case and on the impact that it had on him. I am indebted to the Dublin solicitor Ernest Keegan, to Mary Gaynor of the Law Society in Dublin, and to Susan Schreibman for obtaining various photocopies for me.

64. Oliver St. John Gogarty, *As I Was Going Down Sackville Street* (London: Rich and Cowan, 1937), pp. 70–71. The book was the *Evening Standard* choice and the Book Society Recommendation for April 1937.

65. That the word "genuinely" was italicized in the American edition of Gogarty's book was one of the points that was discussed during the actual trial.

66. St. John Gogarty, *As I Was Going Down Sackville Street*, p. 71.

67. Morris Sinclair to JK, 27 May 1991.

68. Ibid.

69. Interview with SB, 9 July 1989.

70. For example, by Ulick O'Connor, *Oliver St. John Gogarty*, and Bair, *Samuel Beckett*.

71. SB to TM, 14 May 1937 (TCD).

72. It was on May 11, a week after Boss Sinclair died, that Harry issued a "plenary originating summons" claiming damages for libel. On May 22, the motion was served on Dr. Gogarty asking for an interlocutory injunction that would restrain further publication of the book pending the trial of the action for libel. This motion was considered by Judge Hanna on June 4 and was heard on appeal in the Supreme Court on June 18. (Details of the preliminary application for an interlocutory injunction and the Supreme Court appeal are based on the report in *The Irish Reports*, 1937, pp. 377–85.)

73. No affidavit was submitted at this stage of the motion by Gogarty; the publishers, Rich and Cowan, who were resident outside the jurisdiction of the Irish court, did not appear upon the motion. Later, the trial libel action against the publishers was not proceeded with for the same reason.

74. *The Irish Reports*, 1937, pp. 378, 380.

75. SB to TM, 14 May 1937 (TCD).

76. O'Connor, *Oliver St. John Gogarty*, p. 249.

77. *The Irish Times*, 23 Nov. 1937.

78. A document among the court papers (300/P) shows that Beckett's *More Pricks Than Kicks* and *Whoroscope* were among the Defendant's Proofs that were put in on November 22, 1937.

79. SB, *More Pricks Than Kicks*, p. 61.

80. Beckett could have pointed out that in the story "A Wet Night" (yet another suggestive title) the Jesuit priest is given some of the best lines and comes out of the argument

more impressively than the more extreme and vituperative Polar Bear. But witnesses are not, of course, allowed this degree of latitude.

81. *The Irish Times*, 24 Nov. 1937.

82. Ibid.

83. *The Irish Independent*, 24 Nov. 1937.

84. LH, undated interview with SB (Dartmouth). The incident of the attack on Beckett was recounted by Brian Coffey in a letter to George Reavey of January 9, 1938 (Texas). When Coffey wrote to Reavey, he had just been told exactly what happened by the Duncans themselves, the people most likely to know. I therefore base my narrative mostly on this almost first-hand statement. I also include the personal account that Beckett gave me. The only major discrepancy concerns the time at which the attack occurred: 8:30 P.M. according to Coffey, one A.M. according to Beckett; the latter is more likely to be true. Other details are added from letters by SB to TM, GR, and Arland Ussher; from Frank Beckett to TM; from Renée Evrard to JK; and from interviews with Ann Beckett, John Beckett, Georges Belmont (Pelorson), and Elisabeth van Velde.

85. Interview with SB, 23 Oct. 1989.

86. Beckett's registration details at the Hôpital Broussais still exist: "no. 123 — surgery." Entry: 7 January 1938; discharge, 22 January 1938; residence: 9 rue de la Gde [Grande] Chaumière — 6e. Although his place of birth was given as Dublin, Ireland, his nationality was mistakenly written down as French. The nature of his illness was a "Hémothorax gauche" (bleeding of the left thorax) and he was taken to the Salle Follin (Follin Ward) of the hospital (Extract from files, 3 Nov. 1993). I thank Mme. Valérie Poinsotte, the archivist of the Assistance Publique Hôpitaux de Paris for kindly answering my queries.

87. Interview with SB, 23 Oct. 1989.

88. SB to GR, 13 Jan. 1938 (Texas).

89. Telephone interview with Ann Beckett, 20 Oct. 1993. She and her twin brother, John, were making their way to the Gaiety Theatre for an annual visit to the pantomime when their father, Dr. Gerald Beckett, heard the newsboys' cries and bought an *Evening Herald* to see who had been stabbed.

90. SB to TM, 21 Jan. 1938 (TCD).

91. SB to TM, 27 Jan. 1938 (TCD).

92. SB to TM, 12 Jan. 1938 (TCD).

93. Interview with Elisabeth van Velde, 13 Sept. 1990. Nino Frank remembered making two visits to Beckett with Joyce. He said that they stayed on each occasion about fifteen minutes, in the course of which Joyce and Beckett exchanged only about three sentences but seemed very devoted to each other. Richard Ellmann, interview with Nino Frank, 20 Aug. 1953 (Ellmann Papers, Box 046 [Tulsa]). On Beckett's discharge from hospital, he returned to the Hôtel Libéria to find an "immense bunch of Parma violets" waiting for him from Joyce and Nora (SB to TM, 27 Jan. 1938 [TCD]).

94. Renée Evrard, letter to JK, 17 May 1991. Mme. Evrard wrote, however, of how Beckett's distinct originality had created a sense of amused sympathy among the nursing staff.

95. SB to TM, 21 Jan. 1938 (TCD).

96. SB to TM, 11 Feb. 1938 (TCD).

97. Ibid.

98. LH, undated interview with SB (Dartmouth).

99. SB to Arland Ussher, 27 March 1938 (Texas).

100. SB to Arland Ussher, 6 April 1938 (Texas).

101. Peggy Guggenheim, *Out of This Century* (London: André Deutsch, 1980), p. 164.

102. SB, *Collected Poems in English and French*, p. 39.

103. Adrienne James Bethell, née Hope, had married John Lionel Bethell in April 1933 (*Irish Times*, 1 May 1933) and ran an antique shop at 24 Lower George's Street, Dún Laoghaire. According to a Dublin *Evening Press* note (10 Nov. 1969), Beckett autographed a copy of *Whoroscope* for her and wrote her personal letters; she also owned

a Geer van Velde painting. I thank Martha Fehsenfeld and Lois Overbeck for this information.

104. In her memoirs, Peggy Guggenheim speaks of how on "the tenth day of our amours Beckett was untrue to me. He allowed a friend of his from Dublin to creep into his bed. I don't know how I found out but he admitted it saying that he simply had not put her out when she came to him" (*Out of This Century*, p. 164). The only Irishwoman whom Beckett speaks of seeing at this date was Mrs. Adrienne Bethell: "a Mrs Bethell from Dublin [was here] whom I know quite well" (SB to TM, 5 Jan. 1938, [TCD]). The "know quite well" is probably a hint to MacGreevy.

105. "Peggy Guggenheim has been here and I have seen quite a lot of her. She is starting a gallery in Cork Street, opens on 22nd inst. [i.e., January] with Cocteau drawings and furniture. Then there will be Kandinsky, Arp, Brancusi, Benno, etc., and in May a Geer van Velde one man" (SB to TM, 5 Jan. 1938 [TCD]).

106. Guggenheim, *Out of This Century*, p. 162.

107. Interview with Elisabeth van Velde, 13 Sept. 1990.

108. Guggenheim, *Out of This Century*, p. 167.

109. "We went to Marseille in Delage. He drives like John and dives like John and gets more and more like him. In September I hope to drag him to Dalmatia" (Peggy Guggenheim, letter to Emily Coleman, undated but postmarked 4 July 1938 [Delaware]).

110. Guggenheim, *Out of This Century*, pp. 167–68.

111. Interview with Elisabeth van Velde, 13 Sept. 1990.

112. Ibid. Beckett's love of "Voltigeurs" is referred to in his unpublished story "Echo's Bones" (Dartmouth).

113. Guggenheim, *Out of This Century*, p. 176.

114. Beckett tired of being in the middle of their discussions about money, van Velde pressing Peggy for 250 guineas rather than 250 pounds (SB to TM, 26 May [1938] [TCD]).

115. Interview with Elisabeth van Velde, 13 Sept. 1990.

116. Ibid.

117. Peggy Guggenheim to Emily Coleman, undated but postmarked 4 July 1938 (Delaware) and *Out of This Century*, p. 179.

118. Peggy Guggenheim to Emily Coleman, undated but postmarked 4 July 1938 (Delaware).

119. "So I spent my evenings with Beckett, when he was in Paris. Just like Hoare he likes me, when I belong to some one else [although her heart was, she claimed, still with Beckett, she was having an affair in the late summer with Yves Tanguy, even staying in Beckett's flat with him while Beckett was away]. . . . My only wise crack in months was to S.B. 'I offered to lend you the car to go to Brittany because I forgot I was no longer in love with you.' " (Peggy Guggenheim, letter to Emily Coleman, undated but postmarked 23 Sept. 1938 [Delaware]).

120. SB to Gwynned Vernon Reavey, 14 April 1938 (Texas).

121. SB to TM, 22 April (1938)(TCD).

122. Interview with John Beckett, 27 Aug. 1991.

123. SB to GR, 22 April 1938 (Texas).

124. Desmond O'Grady, "Beckett in Paris," *Poetry Ireland Review*, no. 37 (winter 1992–93), p. 130.

125. Interview with Avigdor Arikha, 23 Feb. 1992.

126. SB to TM, 26 May (1938)(TCD).

127. It was a mixture of old and new friends. He dined with Nancy Cunard in February on her way back from Madrid, finding her unable to discuss anything but Spanish revolutionary politics. And, shortly afterwards, he met Jimmy Stern, to whom the poet Laz Aaronson had introduced him at Christmas. Beckett took to Stern, an Irishman who had a novel coming out with Secker in the autumn (SB to TM, 8 March 1938 [TCD] and SB to GR, 8 March 1938 [Texas]).

128. Adler lent Beckett three pictures when the painter went to join the van Veldes in Cagnes, visited him in his apartment, and sold Beckett a painting (SB to TM, 18 April 1939 [TCD]).

129. In January 1939, at Beckett's request, Hayter engraved an inscription on a piece of limestone for Joyce's birthday.

130. SB to GR, 28 Feb. and 5 March 1939 (Texas).

131. SB to TM, 18 April 1939 (TCD).

132. Undated interview with SB.

133. SB to GR, 6 Dec. 1939 (Texas).

134. SB to TM, 3 April 1938 (TCD).

135. Noël Arnaud, "Etranges Volontés," *Temps mêlés / Documents Queneau*, no. 150, 33–36 (July 1987), pp. 297–315.

136. Péron's translation, which Beckett described as "not one of his best efforts," was published in *Soutes*, vol. 9 (1938), p. 41 (SB to TM, 3 April 1938 [TCD]).

137. SB to TM, 22 Dec. 1937 (TCD).

138. SB to TM, 5 Jan. 1938 (TCD).

139. "Norah [*sic*] was in a frightful state, would not go out at all New Year's Eve, after I had sat listening for 2 hours to Shem [Joyce] trying to persuade her, with result that he would not go out either and I spent the last hour of the old year alone with Helen and Giorgio. I hope to get the parents out to see Modern Times this evening" (SB to TM, 5 Jan. 1938 [TCD]).

140. SB to TM, 3 and 22 April (1938)(TCD).

141. At the beginning of October 1938, a scholar of Eastern myth and Buddhist thinking named Heinrich Zimmer sent Joyce a dedication copy of his book *Maya der indische Mythos* (Berlin: Deutsche Verlags-Anstalt, 1936). Joyce asked Beckett if he would read it and take brief notes on it for him. These notes were handed over with the book when Beckett returned it, and were preserved between its pages. This volume is in James Joyce's library, in the State University of New York at Buffalo library. The three pages of notes clearly written in Beckett's hand are described in *The Personal Library of James Joyce, University of Buffalo Studies*, pp. 42–47. Scholars have often speculated as to how Beckett could have acquired a knowledge of Eastern thinking. Here is one book at least which would have provided him with such detailed information. (I am grateful to Robert Bertholf, curator of the Poetry/Rare Books Collection in Buffalo, and to Michael Basinski for their kind help and advice.)

142. Fritz Mauthner, *Beiträge zu einer Kritik der Sprache*. 3rd ed., 3 vols., Leipzig: F. Meiner, 1923. Beckett remembered reading Mauthner much earlier to Joyce (see Linda Ben-Zvi, "Fritz Mauthner for Company," *Journal of Beckett Studies*, no. 9 [1984], pp. 65–88). But he may have been mistaken. His own notes are certainly of this later period or, again, he may be taking up an old interest.

143. SB to Ian Parsons accompanying the typescript of *Murphy*, 29 June 1936 (CW, Reading).

144. Warner wrote that it was "really amusing, and is written with such individuality that if the firm were prepared to lose money, it would be a good thing to lose it on." He concluded, however, that the novel would have no commercial success (Oliver Warner, reader's report dated 2 July 1936 [Reports, 1937, CW, Reading]). Ian Parsons added to the report: "Yes, this is good, but in parts only, rather than as a whole, I think. And I'm quite sure it would be un-sellable. Beckett is a brilliant young man, but I doubt if he'll ever have more than an extremely limited public. And it isn't as if this book were so 'good' in any absolute sense — its more of a good joke. Reluctantly, I think we ought to let it go." The typescript was returned to Beckett on July 15, 1936.

145. Richard Church, letter to Harold Raymond, 11 Jan. 1937 (CW, Reading). Reavey sent a letter from Richard Church to himself, saying nice things about the novel, to Beckett (Bair, *Samuel Beckett*, pp. 247–48).

146. Harold Raymond, letter to Richard Church, 19 Jan. 1937 (CW, Reading).

147. Jack B. Yeats, letter to T. M. Ragg, 22 Nov. 1937 (Routledge, Reading). Martha Fehsenfeld was the person who discovered this letter and told Beckett about it in the mid-1980s. He had completely forgotten that Jack Yeats had recommended the book.

148. T. M. Ragg, letter to Jack B. Yeats, 8 Dec. 1937 (Routledge, Reading).

149. He was sent a copy of the proofs by Ragg, who wrote: "Do read it soon. It gave me great joy. And if you can do anything when the time comes to get it noticed in the press, I should be very publication [error for "pleased"]. Publication date has not yet been fixed but it will probably be sometime towards the end of next month" (T. M. Ragg to Herbert Read, 15 Jan. 1938 [Routledge, Reading]).

150. Herbert Read, letter to T. M. Ragg, 1 Feb. 1938 (Routledge, Reading).

151. SB letter, written in pencil from his hospital bed, to GR (17 Jan. 1938)(Texas).

152. Ibid.

153. Ibid.

154. SB to GR, 13 Jan. 1938 (Texas).

155. SB to GR, 20 Feb. 1938 (Texas).

156. SB to TM, 21 Feb. 1938 (TCD).

157. Although at one time, contrary to what has been thought, he did accept Kahane's offer, saying: "I have accepted the Sade translation at 150 francs per 1000. He wants to postpone for 3 or 4 months. I have written saying that I can't guarantee being of the same mind then or having the time to spare" (SB to GR, 8 March 1938 [Texas]). But he finally changed his mind and withdrew.

158. SB to TM, 21 Feb. 1938 (TCD).

159. On April 22 (1938), Beckett wrote to MacGreevy of having only written two poems in French since he arrived in Paris; then, on June 15, he spoke of enclosing "the last few poems in French" (TCD).

160. SB to TM, 3 April 1938 (TCD). In fact, he wrote more in French during these years than has ever been recognized. Not only did he translate *Murphy* into French with Alfred Péron, but also a letter to George Reavey in the autumn of 1938 shows that he was in the middle of translating his own story "Love and Lethe," from *More Pricks Than Kicks*, into French. In this he was probably helped again by Péron. When this was finished early in 1939, it was sent on to Jean Paulhan by Jean-Paul Sartre. And he began to write an article in French on Joyce's forthcoming *Finnegans Wake* for the *Nouvelle revue française*.

161. These range from place names, like the all too familiar "Rue de Vaugirard" (the title of Poem X) and the "Arènes de Lutèce," the Roman amphitheater off the rue Navarre and the rue Monge, with its unusual statue of the French anthropologist Gabriel de Mortillet (Poem XII), to the words of a traditional French song, "mon père m'a donné un mari" (Poem II), to a voice commenting on a football match heard on the radio next door, and to a fly observed minutely on Beckett's window pane. "Ascension" (Poem IV) brings together the ascension of Christ to the Father with the death of the tubercular "green-eyed" Peggy, who died in May, the month in which Ascension Thursday occurs. "Ainsi a-t-on beau" (Poem VIII) sets the recent death of his own father (and the indistinctness of his father's appearance in his memory) side by side with the vast eons of time, the time of the mammoth, the ice age, the Lisbon earthquake, and Kant, whom Beckett had been reading enthusiastically in German since his copies had arrived from Germany at the beginning of January.

162. They were found in Beckett's copy of Kant when the volumes were given to Avigdor Arikha. Beckett subsequently confirmed that they, too, were a gift.

163. These poems were discovered recently among the papers of Bram van Velde left with Jacques Putman. Written on them in Bram's hand are the words "Poèmes à [not *de*] Beckett." So there has to be at least a small measure of doubt as to the authorship, in spite of the common subject.

164. SB to TM, 18 April 1939 (TCD).

165. SB to GR, 16 June 1939 (Texas).

166. LH, undated interview with SB (Dartmouth).

167. SB to TM, 26 May (1938) (TCD).

168. SB to TM (5 Aug. 1938)(TCD). Later, however, he wrote to William York Tindall that he had a great admiration for Sterne and particularly for *Tristram Shandy* (letter, 15 Jan. 1963, is quoted on a "Waiting for Godot Books" catalogue, p. 64, item 570).

169. SB to TM, 11 Feb. 1938 (TCD). Beckett told me that he liked the book.

170. SB to TM, 26 May (1938)(TCD).

171. SB to TM, 18 April 1939 (TCD).

172. Interview with Mita and Edmund Tuby, close friends of Suzanne before she met Beckett, 24 Nov. 1994. Mita also studied at the Ecole Normale de Musique in the 1920s. I am most indebted to them both for information about Suzanne when she was younger.

173. For example, another pianist, Roger Deleutre, his sister, Yvonne, and Mita and Edmund Tuby.

174. SB, *Dream of Fair to Middling Women*, p. 188.

12: Exodus, Occupation, and Resistance, 1940–42

1. SB to GR, 27 Sept. 1938 (Texas).

2. SB, letter in French to Arland Ussher, 6 April 1938 (Texas).

3. SB to GR, 27 Sept. 1938 (Texas).

4. SB to TM, 18 April 1939 (TCD).

5. LH, undated interview with SB (Dartmouth).

6. For an excellent account of what he calls "The Overrunning of the West," see B. H. Liddell Hart, *History of the Second World War* (London: Cassell and Co., 1970; Book Club Associates edition, 1973), pp. 65–86.

7. SB to GR, 21 May 1940 (Texas).

8. Richard Ellmann relates how Maria Jolas called Joyce on June 13 to tell him that no one could leave Paris by train, as the Gare de Lyon was closed. Joyce replied that this could not be true as Samuel Beckett had just come to Vichy from Paris (Ellmann, *James Joyce*, p. 732).

9. Interview with SB, 11 July 1989. It has been said that Valery Larbaud merely cashed an Irish check (the latest allowance due from his father's estate) for Beckett on his French bank (Ellmann, *James Joyce*, p. 732, and Bair, *Samuel Beckett*, p. 306). He may well have done so. However, speaking to me, Beckett was adamant that Larbaud had been far more generous than this, providing an actual loan.

10. This account of Beckett's and Suzanne's journey from Vichy to (in the end) Arcachon on the Atlantic coast is based on Beckett's own words to Lawrence Harvey in an undated interview (Dartmouth) and to me on July 11, 1989.

11. That Beckett's papers applied for in September 1939 had still not been sorted out a matter of days before their hasty departure is shown by a letter to George Reavey dated May 21, 1940 (Texas).

12. LH, undated interview with SB (Dartmouth).

13. SB to Stuart Maguinness, 21 Aug. 1958 (Reading).

14. See Guggenheim, *Out of This Century*, p. 208.

15. Jean Bourdier (owner of the Villa Saint-Georges), letter to JK, 7 July 1992.

16. I am most grateful to Jean Bourdier for kindly replying to my inquiries and for sending me a photograph of the Villa Saint-Georges, where Beckett and Suzanne stayed.

17. LH, undated interview with SB (Dartmouth).

18. Interview with George Reavey by JK, 6 Aug. 1971, *Journal of Beckett Studies*, no. 2 (summer 1977), p. 13.

19. LH, undated interview with SB (Dartmouth).

20. Letter to SB from the Irish Legation, 28 Nov. 1940 (Lindon).

21. Some of these details of everyday life in Paris are borrowed from Henri Amouroux, *La Grande histoire des Français sous l'Occupation*, Vol. 2, *Quarante millions de*

Pétainistes: juin 1940–juin 1941, pp. 157–204. I am also grateful to Anise Postel-Vinay, Germaine Tillion, Emma Lévin-Lechanois, and Josette Hayden for talking to me about daily life in France during the early years of the Occupation.

22. "V: Would you like a radish? / E: Is that all there is? / V: There are radishes and turnips. / E: Are there no carrots? / V: No. Anyway you overdo it with your carrots" (SB, *Waiting for Godot*, p. 68).

23. LH, undated interview with SB (Dartmouth).

24. Ellmann, *James Joyce*, pp. 734–41.

25. For information used here, I am deeply grateful to members of Gloria SMH: Violette Rougier-Lecoq (who kindly responded to my advertisement in *Voix et Visages*, the bulletin of the Association Nationale des Anciennes Déportées et Internées de la Résistance); to a close friend of Alfred Péron, Pierre Weydert; and to Henri Boussel, the leader of the allied railway cell, Rail. I am most grateful to Germaine Tillion for her full account of the events that led up to the betrayal of the Resistance cell; to Anise Postel-Vinay (née Girard) for her invaluable help; to Andrée Jacob for vital information that put me on the track of other members of the Resistance group; to Jean Laroque, the former Conseiller of the Cour de Cassation, for information about Jacques Legrand and other matters; and to the senator and former minister André Jarrot, for information on Resistance activities in Chalon-sur-Saône. I also owe a great debt to the SOE adviser, Gervase Cowell, who answered my questions and supplied me with the debriefing documents of two of the leaders of Beckett's Resistance cell, Jeannine Picabia and her mother, Gabrielle Buffet-Picabia. I am most grateful to Mark Seaman of the Imperial War Museum in London for first setting me on my path with invaluable guidance. This chapter is based especially on my own interviews with Samuel Beckett. Credit should be paid, however, to Deirdre Bair, whose excellent chapter in her biography of Beckett, based primarily on interviews with Jeannine and Gabrielle Buffet-Picabia, first revealed the nature of Beckett's active involvement with the Resistance.

26. Notes of Alec Reid on a conversation with Beckett of 10 Feb. 1966 (Reid; in private hands).

27. See Marrus and Paxton, *Vichy France and the Jews*.

28. SB, comment to Alec Reid, Paris, 10 Feb. 1966 (Reid, in private hands).

29. Interview with SB, 18 Oct. 1989. Paul Léon's son, Alexis, confirmed that he was indeed taking the first part of his *baccalauréat* at that time. Interview with Alexis Léon, 24 July 1992.

30. Lucie Léon Noel to JK, 12 Jan. 1971. They were cruelly deceived by a woman who claimed that, for money, she could get these rations through to Léon. This deceit continued even after he had died.

31. A document of the 6th Bureau of the Ministry of the Armed Forces, dated March 7, 1955, confirms that Beckett had been an agent P.1 (which counted as active military service) in Gloria SMH from September 1, 1941 (Lindon). This was not a particularly late entry into the cell. One of the most active members, Suzanne Roussel, joined only in June 1941 and quite a few of the other members were not recruited until several months after this. (This information comes from the official liquidation papers of the cell drawn up by Suzanne Roussel and kindly lent to me by Madame Violette Rougier-Lecoq, who joined the cell in March 1941.)

32. Gervase Cowell, SOE Adviser, to JK, 20 May 1992.

33. Information from Gervase Cowell, 19 June 1992. See also Nigel West, *MI6, British Secret Intelligence Service Operations 1909–45* (London: Weidenfeld and Nicolson, 1983), pp. 141–45.

34. Gabrielle Bailly-Cowell-Picabia's attestation saying that Jean Laroque, a friend of Jacques Legrand, had belonged to this cell from November 1940, if accurate, seems to suggest that the late summer or early autumn may be considered as a starting date for the cell proper. Attestation read to Jean Laroque by JK, 26 Feb. 1994, and confirmed by him.

35. Etoile and its offshoot, Interallié, which was run by "Armand," one of the aliases of

the Polish intelligence officer Captain Roman Garby Czerniawski (see Roman Garby Czerniawski, *The Big Network* [London: Ronald, 1961]) and Rail (a railway network run at La Chapelle depot in Paris by Henri Boussel), as well as Gloria SMH and another cell called F2, were overseen by Michel Brault, a French international lawyer and member of the French Deuxième Bureau (see Henri Noguères, *Histoire de la Résistance en France de 1940 à 1945* [Paris: Robert Laffont] vol. I, pp. 191–94, 406–407; for Gloria SMH and Interallié, vol. II, pp. 216–22). Interallié operated in all three areas of Resistance activity: information, escape, and sabotage. But, as early as the summer of 1941, it was betrayed by Mathilde Carré, who was known as Victoire, Micheline, or (as she has become notorious in histories of the Resistance and in a film in which she was played by Françoise Arnoul) La Chatte (The Cat). As a result of this betrayal, Gloria SMH became even more important to the Allies as a supplier of information in the latter part of 1941 and 1942.

36. Interview with Jean Laroque, a close friend of Jacques Legrand, 26 Feb. 1994.

37. Descriptions of Suzanne Roussel and Simone Lahaye are based on an interview with Anise Postel-Vinay, 24 Feb. 1994.

38. Like many members of Gloria SMH, Simone Lahaye was deported and interned in Ravensbrück. She wrote two books about her experiences: *Un Homme libre parmi les morts* (Paris: G. Durassié, 1954) and *Les Rachetés: portraits et récits de bagne, 1942–45* (Paris: G. Durassié, 1963).

39. Aléxis Péron remembered Suzanne Roussel as being merely a *surveillante* at the Lycée Buffon, but Pierre Weydert thinks that she was an English teacher there and that she passed the *agrégation* after the war.

40. See Liddell Hart, *History of the Second World War*, p. 377. It is clear that Gloria SMH agents were among many cells, including those organized by Gilbert Renault ("Colonel Rémy"), who were watching the ships during the blockade, bombing, repair, and eventual escape of the three warships.

41. Interview with Anise Postel-Vinay, 24 Feb. 1994; the debriefing of Jeannine Picabia at SOE headquarters in London on 14 March 1943; and interviews with Pierre Weydert, Violette Rougier-Lecoq, and Henri Boussel, 28 Nov. 1990.

42. Interview with Anise Postel-Vinay, 24 Feb. 1994.

43. Gervase Cowell to JK, 25 June 1992.

44. Interview with SB, 17 Nov. 1989.

45. M. R. D. Foot, *Resistance: An Analysis of European Resistance to Nazism 1940–1945* (London: Eyre Methuen, 1976), p. 99.

46. Debriefing of Jeannine Picabia at SOE headquarters in London, 14 March 1943 (SOE files, London).

47. SB, letter to an unnamed official, 14 Oct. 1945 (Lindon).

48. Bair, *Samuel Beckett*, p. 311.

49. Pierre Weydert to JK, 16 May 1992.

50. Interview with Aléxis Péron, 14 June 1992. Lazaro was a neighbor of Mania Péron and her twin sons after the war.

51. Deirdre Bair reports Jeannine Picabia as remembering that a man called Jimmy Reed acted as the courier for, not the photographer of, Beckett's typed material (Bair, *Samuel Beckett*, p. 311). This name, which was the only one Picabia was familiar with, sounds very much like that of Beckett's Greek. It is possible that, several decades after the events concerned, confusion entered into one or the other set of memories, although Beckett is very unlikely to have forgotten who his main contact was. "Reed" could be someone's mishearing of "the Greek."

52. Foot, *Resistance: An Analysis of European Resistance to Nazism 1940–1945*, p. 15.

53. According to Jeannine Picabia's debriefing with SOE, it was Beckett, whom she had known before the war, who had first introduced her to Péron. "I wanted to organize something in Nantes and Lorient," she said, "and through Sam Beckett, an Irishman

whom I knew before the war, I met Alfred Péron in Paris who had para-militaires groups, and a woman called Suzanne Roussel, whose working name was Hélène" (debriefing of Jeannine Picabia at SOE headquarters in London, 14 March 1943 [SOE]). Although Péron brought Beckett into the Resistance, therefore, he seems to have first met the Picabias through Beckett.

54. Born in November 1881, she had spent two years studying music in Berlin and had also lived in Dresden. Usefully, then, she spoke fluent German. Her marriage to the painter Francis Picabia had been dissolved in 1925, although they had remained friends. Since then, she had carried on her journalistic work and her lecturing. She was intelligent and cultured, well read in several literatures, and fascinated by painting.

55. The account of Gabrielle Picabia's hugely varied Resistance activities is taken from her debriefing with British SOE in 1943 (SOE).

56. Debriefing of Gabrielle Buffet-Picabia (SOE).

57. Debriefing of Jeannine Picabia (SOE).

58. Eugène Condette, *Les Chemins d'une destinée, Histoire d'un Compagnon de la Libération* (Mâcon: X Perroux, 1966), p. 54. The book is about André Jarrot's courageous work with the Resistance.

59. Interview with André Jarrot, 23 Feb. 1994.

60. Interview with SB, 17 Nov. 1989.

61. This account of Robert Alesch's betrayal of the group is based on extended interviews with Germaine Tillion, June 23–26, 1993, and on documents and newspaper reports of the trial.

62. Germaine Tillion, *Ravensbrück* (Paris: Editions du Seuil, 1973), p. 15.

63. Interview with Germaine Tillion, 24 June 1993.

64. Report of Allesch's trial at the Palais de Justice in *France-Soir*, 22 May 1948.

65. Interview with Jean Laroque, 26 Feb. 1994.

66. Interview with Germaine Tillion, 24 June 1993.

67. It has been claimed by other members of the cell from their memories of the trial that, because of his position and the fluency of his French and German, Alesch had already contrived to get himself appointed as visiting chaplain to the prison and could establish contact with the Resistance prisoners there, including the de Vomécourt brothers. Germaine Tillion, however, maintained that the appointment to the chaplaincy occurred later, when Alesch is said to have learned things in the confessional that he immediately passed on to the Abwehr.

68. Interview with Jean Laroque, 25 Feb. 1994. The Banque Worms still exists but is part of UAP, Union d'Assurances de Paris.

69. The information concerning the sums involved comes from an interview with Germaine Tillion and from Robert Alesch's own testimony to the *juge d'instruction*, Maître Donsimoni, at the time of his trial. Alesch also claimed there that he paid fifty thousand francs to intermediaries and kept the rest for further expenses until he handed them over to another "Jeannine," who, if she ever existed except in Alesch's fertile imagination, is believed to have been a member of the Valenty organization betrayed by Victoire (or Micheline, "La Chatte"). Gervase Cowell to JK, 20 May 1992.

70. Only three days before I contacted him, Jean Laroque had torn up a letter from the Banque Worms in 1950 asking for information about the payment, which had not up to that date been reimbursed.

71. Debriefing of Jeannine Picabia (SOE).

72. Debriefing of Gabrielle Buffet-Picabia (SOE).

73. I am most grateful to Violette Rougier-Lecoq for providing me with sheets of detailed documentation relating to members of Gloria SMH and their arrests. These papers were part of the material assembled by Suzanne Roussel during the liquidation of the cell.

74. LH, undated interview with SB (Dartmouth).

75. Ibid.

76. Ibid.

77. Interview with SB, 17 Nov. 1989.

78. SB, letter to an unnamed official, 14 Oct. 1945 (Lindon).

79. One of Kay Boyle's novels, *Avalanche*, published by Simon and Schuster in New York in 1944, was based on the Resistance activities of Mary Reynolds and Marcel Duchamp. They are the "Monsieur et Madame Rose Sélavy" to whom the book is dedicated, and Kay Boyle shared the profits from its sales with them. See Sandra Whipple Spanier, *Kay Boyle: Artist and Activist* (New York: Paragon House, 1988), pp. 160–63 and n. 36, p. 237. "Rrose [*sic*] Sélavy" was one of Duchamp's several pseudonyms (Arturo Schwartz, "Rrose Sélavy alias Marchand de Sel alias Belle Hélène, *Marcel Duchamp* [Paris: L'Arc, Librairie Duponchelle, 1990], pp. 29–35).

80. Interview with SB, 27 July 1989.

81. This account of Beckett's stay comes from a long interview with Nathalie Sarraute, 25 March 1991.

82. LH, undated interview with SB (Dartmouth). Bair states in *Samuel Beckett*, p. 318, that they did not use a *passeur* to cross from the occupied to the free zone but openly took the train from Chalons to Lyon. This is contradicted by Beckett's own description of the manner of their crossing. They may well, of course, have taken the train from Paris to Chalons or after they had arrived in the "free" zone.

13: REFUGE IN ROUSSILLON, 1942–45

1. This chapter is based on interviews with Samuel Beckett, Fernand Aude, Claude Blondel, Mme. Bonnelly, Josette Hayden, Paulette Icard (née Aude), Yvonne Lob (OBE), Eugène Fidler, Elie Blanc, Aimé Bonhomme, Elie Icard, Hélène Albertini (née Gulini), Juliette Ferrier, Roger and Bernadette Louis, Jean David, M. and Mme. Vitter, and André Lagier. I thank all those from Roussillon for their kindness to my wife and myself during our visit to the village. I am also grateful to John Reilly for giving me copies of his interviews in Roussillon, prepared for his film on Beckett made for "Global Village."

2. *Waiting for Godot*, p. 62. In the French text, the names of Roussillon and the farmer, Bonnelly, for whom Beckett and Suzanne actually did pick grapes, are given. In English, these names are omitted and the grape-picking is moved farther north so as to have "Cackon country" echo "Macon country," whereas in French "Merdecluse" had picked up "Vaucluse" and in German "Breisgau" rhymes with "Scheissgau."

3. Interview with Hélène Albertini, July 1990.

4. Interview with Yvonne Lob-Deleutre, July 1990.

5. The information about Beckett and Suzanne's short stay in Vichy and their meetings with officials there are taken from a Vichy police document: a safe-conduct pass from Vichy to Avignon, dated September 29, 1942, which has been preserved (Lindon).

6. The register of the "visas d'arrivée délivrés aux étrangers" (arrival visas issued to foreigners) who were resident in the commune of Roussillon with Beckett's entry is still preserved in the Mairie in the village. His date of birth is given as April 13, 1906, in Dublin, his nationality as Irish, his present address as the Hôtel Escoffier, and his previous place of residence as Paris; it is noted that he has no profession. His identity card number was CI 40. HH 99.530.

7. Anna O'Meara Beamish's date of birth was given as April 30, 1883, and her place of birth as Dublin. But her nationality was still noted as being British. She was recorded in the register as a teacher of English.

8. Details of the hotel and of its proprietress, Adrienne Escoffier, are taken from interviews with Jean David, the present owner of what is now the Restaurant David, and with Hélène Albertini, Juliette Ferrier, Claude Blondel, and Fernand Aude, July 1990. I am grateful to M. David, who was also the mayor of Roussillon, for giving me some old photographs of the hotel.

9. Interview with Josette Hayden, April 1989.

10. Bair, *Samuel Beckett*, pp. 327–31.

11. Interview with Josette Hayden, 12 Sept. 1990.

12. Interview with Yvonne Lob, July 1990, and her letter to JK, 9 Aug. 1990.

13. LH, undated interview with SB (Dartmouth).

14. Ibid.

15. Interview with the owners, M. and Mme. Vitter, July 1990, who took over the rental of the house twenty-five years earlier, in 1965, when little had been changed since the war. The kitchen stove and the pipe were no longer there. But the upstairs room was clearly exactly as it was when Beckett was there.

16. LH, interview with SB, 7 Nov. 1961 (Dartmouth).

17. Details of Beckett's work in the fields and visits to the Audes' farm are taken from an interview with Fernand Aude, 18 July 1990.

18. Interview with Fernand Aude, 18 July 1990.

19. SB, *Malone Dies*, in *Molloy Malone Dies The Unnamable*, pp. 204–206.

20. SB, ms. notebooks of *Watt*, notebook 3, p. 190 (Texas).

21. Fernand Aude to JK, undated but received 10 July 1992.

22. John Reilly, interview with Elie Blanc, July 1989.

23. Interview with Yvonne Lob, July 1990, and her letter to JK, 9 Aug. 1990. Beckett read Hugh Walpole's novels in four volumes of the Albatross Modern Continental Library edition (Hamburg, Paris, Bologna, 1932–34). The actual volumes are now in the archive of the Beckett International Foundation, donated by Yvonne Lob.

24. SB, *Watt*, pp. 33–34.

25. Hugh Walpole, *Judith Paris* (Hamburg: The Albatross Verlag, 1932), pp. 54–55.

26. Ibid., p. 55.

27. SB, *Catastrophe*, in *Collected Shorter Plays*, p. 301. The play was dedicated to the then imprisoned Václav Havel.

28. The account of the Haydens' arrival in Roussillon is based on three lengthy interviews with Josette Hayden in April 1989, February 1990, and September 1990. Josette Hayden is adamant that Bair's account is here seriously mistaken and that, contrary to what Bair says, Beckett and Suzanne had already been in Roussillon for a year before they arrived there. Mme. Hayden kindly went over this section of my own chapter line by line to ensure its accuracy. I am most grateful to her.

29. Interviews with Josette Hayden, April 1989 and February 1990.

30. Interview with Roger Louis, 19 Sept. 1990.

31. Interview with Josette Hayden, April 1989.

32. Interview with Josette Hayden, 12 Sept. 1990.

33. Details concerning Miss Beamish and her companion, Suzanne Allévy, are taken from interviews with Hélène Albertini and Paulette Icard, July 1990; Josette Hayden, April 1989 and February 1990; and SB, November 1989.

34. After the war, with John Farquharson acting as her literary agent, she went on to write another twenty popular histories or historical novels, the last appearing (she was eighty-seven) in 1971, the year that she probably died. Suzanne Allévy became her executrix and continued living in the house in Cannes that they had shared after the war, until her own death in 1985 (Denise Verrando, in Cannes, to JK, 9 Aug. 1990).

35. Interviews with Mme. Bonnelly and Hélène Albertini, July 1990.

36. Interview with Edith Fidler, 21 May 1991.

37. SB, *Krapp's Last Tape*, in *Collected Shorter Plays*, p. 58.

38. This manuscript draft "Crapp's Last Tape" is in the Humanities Research Center in the University of Texas at Austin. See Lake, *No Symbols Where None Intended*, Austin, Texas, 1984, p. 105, note 227.

39. Interview with SB, July 1989.

40. SB, *Krapp's Last Tape*, in *Collected Shorter Plays*, p. 58.

41. This was suggested by Mme. Bonnelly and by Elie Icard. But others, like Aimé Bonhomme, the Resistance leader in Roussillon, and Claude Blondel, another prominent member of the Resistance there, knew nothing of such intelligence activities on Miss Beamish's part.

42. Elie Blanc visited Beckett and Suzanne several times at their house just down the road from his (John Reilly, interview with Elie Blanc, July 1989).

43. The account of Madame Dumesnil's visit is taken from interviews with Paulette Icard and Fernand Aude, July 1990.

44. Interviews with Josette Hayden, April 1989 and February 1990, and with Yvonne Lob, July 1990.

45. Interview with Josette Hayden, 12 Sept. 1990.

46. John Reilly, interview with Eugène Fidler, July 1989. JK, interview with Eugène Fidler, July 1990.

47. Interview with Josette Hayden, 12 Sept. 1990.

48. JK, interview with Eugène Fidler, July 1990.

49. All of these dates can be seen in the manuscript notebooks of Watt, preserved at the Harry Ransom Humanities Research Center in the University of Texas at Austin.

50. LH, undated interview with SB (Dartmouth).

51. SB, Watt, p. 52. He is identified by Mrs. Sheila Brazil in O'Brien, The Beckett Country, p. 18, and p. 348, n. 22.

52. Interview with SB, August 1989. Beckett did not specifically remember his father using the nickname Cack-faced Miller but quoted to me other such nicknames — Wall-eyed Watt, for instance.

53. SB, Watt, p. 15.

54. SB to MH, 31 July 1957 (Texas).

55. In the manuscript, for example, he wrote that "£50 had been shamefully frittered away, in Mr Tisler's stew on the northern bank of the Canal between the Leeson St. and Portobello Bridges, on stout and whiskey" (SB, holograph manuscript of Watt, notebook 4, written at Roussillon, p. 81 [Texas]).

56. Rabinovitz, The Development of Samuel Beckett's Fiction, p. 125.

57. The phrase is taken from Harvey, Samuel Beckett, Poet and Critic, p. 352.

58. Interview with Yvonne Lob, July 1990.

59. Bair, Samuel Beckett, pp. 327–31.

60. The section on the activities of the Resistance group in Roussillon and Beckett's involvement is based on a number of interviews with members of that group. The interviews are with Aimé Bonhomme (by John Reilly in July 1989 and by JK in July 1990) and with Claude Blondel, Elie Icard, and Roger Louis (by JK in September 1990). Some details were also provided by Josette Hayden in an interview in February 1990. The book La Résistance au pays d'Apt de la Durance au Ventoux (Cavaillon, 1982, no author is given) has a list of members of the Roussillon group, which includes the name of Samuel Beckett.

61. Interview with Hélène Albertini, July 1990.

62. This radio transmitter is the one now displayed in the Musée de la Résistance in Fontaine de Vaucluse.

63. The same thing happened immediately after the war with any letter accusing local people of any form of mild collaboration or black-market practice. Interview with Aimé Bonhomme, July 1990, and discussions with his son, André, who showed me one such letter of postwar denunciation.

64. The account of Marcel Lob's arrest and imprisonment in Drancy comes from an interview with his wife, Yvonne Lob, July 1990.

65. LH, undated interview with SB (Dartmouth). Beckett's membership card of the Roussillon Resistance cell has been preserved (Lindon).

66. LH, undated interview with SB (Dartmouth).

67. Interview with Josette Hayden, 12 Sept. 1990.
68. Interview with SB, July 1989.
69. Details provided by Josette Hayden, interview, Feb. 1990.

14: AFTERMATH OF WAR, 1945–46

1. Doubt has been cast on whether he went to, or even through, Paris at all at this time (Bair, *Samuel Beckett*, p. 335). Beckett told Harvey that they returned together and stayed on in Paris for a few months, before he left alone for Ireland around Easter (LH, undated interview with SB [Dartmouth]).
2. Interview with Josette Hayden, 3 April 1993.
3. LH, undated interview with SB (Dartmouth).
4. Interview with Josette Hayden, 3 April 1993.
5. LH, undated interview with SB (Dartmouth).
6. Bair stated that Geer and Lisl van Velde were living in Beckett's apartment when Suzanne returned alone from Roussillon (*Samuel Beckett*, p. 686, n. 38). However, Lisl van Velde denied that she and Geer ever lived at 6 rue des Favorites, although, while they were living in a little hotel, they met both Suzanne and Beckett in Paris (telephone interview with Lisl van Velde, 7 March 1995).
7. Telephone interview with Lisl van Velde, 7 March 1995.
8. The formal end to the war in Europe was May 8, 1945.
9. This account of the difficulties that Beckett encountered in London is based almost verbatim on LH's undated notes on what Beckett told him (Dartmouth).
10. Debriefing of Jeannine Picabia, "Organisation of the Service," 14 March 1943, p. 1. Gabrielle Buffet-Picabia's debriefing took place in August 1943 (SOE).
11. Bair, *Samuel Beckett*, p. 336.
12. SB to GR, 20 June 1945 (Texas).
13. The accounts situation was unclear at the time of Beckett's visit to Routledge. A year later, on asking Routledge for six copies of the novel, he was exasperated to learn that it "went out of print" in 1942. Three decades later, Beckett told Deirdre Bair that the information that Norman Franklin of Routledge had given to Beckett's bibliographers in the 1960s was incorrect and that it had been remaindered *before* the war (Bair, *Samuel Beckett*, p. 686, n. 33). But he was mistaken. In fact, Franklin was much closer to the truth than Beckett was. The sales figures were almost as he listed them, although he omitted one crucial piece of information: the book had gone out of print in March 1943 and the Beckett account with the European Literary Bureau had been closed. Routledge's royalty statements for *Murphy* show that, in 1942–43, 750 unbound copies of the 1,500 copies printed were sold to a buyer, who has not so far been traced. (These copies may have been destroyed in enemy bombing.) But royalties were paid on these copies to the European Literary Bureau in March 1943, when the account was closed. (I thank Gilian Furlong, archivist at University College, London's Watson Library for her help, and Michael Bott, archivist at the University of Reading, for his help and advice.)
14. Strangely enough, five years later, he did receive a small check for the final royalty payments that had been paid by Routledge to the European Literary Bureau (SB to GR, 11 Dec. 1950 [Texas]).
15. SB to GR, 1 Sept. 1946 (Texas).
16. SB to "Mr. Ragg," 25 May 1945, telling him he is "sending [him] by registered post the manuscript that I mentioned to you while in London last month" (Routledge, Reading).
17. T. M. Ragg, letter to SB, 6 June 1945 (Routledge, Reading). SB wrote to GR: "My book *Watt* has been turned down by Routledge. Mr Ragg and Mr Read agreed that it was 'wild and unintelligible' and felt very sorry for the author of *Murphy*. I have forgotten the name of the agents who took over from you, and don't know if they exist still. If you

know of any agent, preferably young, with even half the tenacity you displayed in handling *Murphy* I should be glad to know his name" (SB to GR, 20 June 1945 [Texas]).

18. This information about Greene, who was Brian Coffey's brother-in-law, is found in Bair, *Samuel Beckett*, p. 340.

19. "I dumped *Watt* with a fellow on the way through last August and understand that Nicholson and Watson are nibbling" (SB to GR, 31 Oct. 1945 [Texas]). This publisher finally did not nibble after all. Beckett got his own back by using their names, together like this, in a list of names (with Jackson, Johnson, and Wilson) as "all whore-sons" (SB, *Malone Dies*, in *Molloy Malone Dies The Unnamable*, p. 218).

20. Report no. 6038, with the note that it was returned to A. P. Watt with a formal letter on April 8, 1946 (CW, Reading).

21. A typescript of *Watt* went to Methuen in June 1946 and to Secker and Warburg in September 1946. SB to GR re: Methuen, 19 June (1946) (Texas); a letter from R. P. Watt to Secker and Warburg, 3 Sept. 1946 and a letter of rejection from Frederick Warburg to R. P. Watt, 9 Oct. 1946 (Secker and Warburg, Reading).

22. Frederick Warburg, letter to R. P. Watt, 9 Oct. 1946 (Secker and Warburg, Reading).

23. "Usually mother dictates her letters to a girl who comes in, but the last was in her own hand, four whole pages" (SB to TM, 26 Sept. [1948] [TCD]).

24. Interview with Lily Condell, 10 Aug. 1992.

25. SB to Georges Duthuit, 2 and 22 Aug. 1948 (Duthuit).

26. Telephone interview with Edward Beckett, 7 March 1995.

27. Interview with Deirdre Hamilton, 20 June 1991.

28. SB to Gwynned Reavey, 10 May 1945, and to GR, 20 June 1945 (Texas).

29. SB to GR, 31 Oct. 1945 (Texas).

30. Bair, *Samuel Beckett*, p. 341.

31. SB to Gwynned Reavey, 20 June 1945 (Texas).

32. SB to TM, 24 Nov. 1947 (TCD).

33. SB to Gwynned Reavey, 20 June 1945 (Texas).

34. SB to TM, 6 Aug. (1945) (TCD).

35. SB to TM, 19 Aug. 1945 (TCD).

36. Interview with SB, 10 Nov. 1989. One hundred and seventy-four tons of equipment, including six ambulances, a lorry, and a utility wagon, were sent over on the cargo ship *Menapia* in the middle of August from Dublin docks to Cherbourg. Using his excellent French, Beckett arranged for this material to be transported by road or rail from the docks to the future hospital. At St.-Lô, he made out stock cards for this material, as well as liaising with the French Red Cross in Paris and with local medical services. (For an excellent account of the details of the Irish Red Cross venture in St.-Lô, see O'Brien, *The Beckett Country*, pp. 315–42).

37. SB to TM, 19 Aug. 1945 (TCD).

38. SB, "The Capital of Ruins," talk for Radio Éireann, June 1946. The text was printed in O'Brien, *The Beckett Country*, pp. 333–37.

39. O'Brien, *The Beckett Country*, p. 328.

40. Dr. Jim Gaffney, letter to his sister, Nora, 2 Oct. 1945, quoted in O'Brien, *The Beckett Country*, pp. 326–27.

41. Interview with SB, 10 Nov. 1989.

42. Interview with Simone McKee, 26 June 1993; Yvonne Lefèvre to JK, 22 March 1995 (Lefèvre).

43. There are three letters from Beckett to Yvonne Lefèvre in which he alludes to buying Parpanit from her for his mother. Two, on June 23 and August 22, do not have the year, which is probably, however, 1948; the other one is dated April 26, 1949 (Lefèvre). My information about the supply of Parpanit comes from a letter from Yvonne Lefèvre to JK, 22 March 1995 (Lefèvre).

44. My account of Dr. Arthur Darley is based upon interviews with SB, with Darley's friend and executor, Ernest Keegan, and with Simone McKee, as well as on the memo-

ries of Mary Crowley, the matron of the Irish Hospital at St.-Lô, as transcribed in O'Brien, *The Beckett Country*, p. 339.

45. SB to TM, 21 Dec. 1945 (TCD).

46. Interview with SB, 10 Nov. 1989.

47. SB, *Collected Poems in English and French*, p. 54. The translation is by Darley's friend and executor, Ernest Keegan.

48. Interview with Simone McKee, 26 June 1993.

49. LH, undated interview with SB (Dartmouth).

50. SB to TM, 21 Dec. 1945 (TCD), written when he had agreed to leave.

51. See O'Brien, *The Beckett Country*, pp. 333–37. The talk does not appear ever to have been broadcast.

52. Bair relates Krapp's vision as that of Beckett himself: "On one of his late-night prowls, when he [Beckett] had been drinking just enough to make his thought processes churn, he found himself out on the end of a jetty in Dublin harbor, buffeted by a winter storm. Suddenly the vision occurred which was to result in the voluminous production . . . that has come to be defined as 'Beckettian' " (Bair, *Samuel Beckett*, p. 350). Many other critics have repeated this identification (e.g., Lake, *No Symbols Where None Intended*, p. 49). O'Brien corrects the location of Krapp's revelation as being not Dublin harbor but Dún Laoghaire's pier, because of the recognizable features of the lighthouse on the East Pier and of the anemometer (or, as in the final published text, the "wind gauge"). But then he writes: "The piers of Dún Laoghaire have acquired a place of immense significance in literary history: it was on the east pier, one fateful night, that Beckett [not Krapp] saw the course he would pursue in his literature." O'Brien continues: "This revelation, for such is the word that Beckett applies, however reticently, to the event, is portrayed vividly and poignantly in the play, *Krapp's Last Tape*" (O'Brien, *The Beckett Country*, pp. 81–83).

53. SB, *Krapp's Last Tape*, in *Collected Shorter Plays*, p. 60.

54. For example, in *As No Other Dare Fail* (London: John Calder, 1986), pp. 8, 12.

55. Undated interview with Samuel Beckett (ca. 1987). Beckett wrote to Richard Ellmann: "All the jetty and howling wind are imaginary. It happened to me, summer 1945, in my mother's little house, named New Place, across the road from Cooldrinagh" (SB to Richard Ellmann, 27 Jan. 1986, Ellmann Papers [Tulsa]).

56. Gabriel d'Aubarède, *Nouvelles littéraires*, 16 Feb. 1961, quoted in Graver and Federman, eds., *Samuel Beckett: The Critical Heritage* (London, Henley, and Boston: Routledge and Kegan Paul, 1979), p. 217.

57. Interview with SB, 27 Oct. 1989. This more or less echoes what he said to Israel Shenker: "The more Joyce knew the more he could. He's tending towards omniscience and omnipotence as an artist. I'm working with impotence, ignorance. There seems to be a kind of esthetic axiom that expression is achievement — must be an achievement. My little exploration is that whole zone of being that has always been set aside by artists as something unusable — as something by definition incompatible with art." Israel Shenker, interview with Beckett, *The New York Times*, 5 May 1956, quoted in Graver and Federman, eds., *Samuel Beckett: The Critical Heritage*, p. 148.

58. Notes sent in 1987 to JK, who at the time was preparing an edition of Beckett's theatrical notebook of *Krapp's Last Tape*.

59. Shenker, interview with SB, *The New York Times*, 5 May 1956, quoted in Graver and Federman, *Samuel Beckett: The Critical Heritage*, p. 148.

60. Richard Aldington, letter to P. A. G. Aldington, 8 Oct. 1946 (SIU, Carbondale).

61. SB to TM, 24 Nov. 1947 (TCD).

62. SB to HH, 29 April 1947 (Hayden) and undated interview with Josette Hayden, who kindly explained to me how this ruse worked.

63. SB to TM, 4 Jan. 1948 (TCD). The sum of ten thousand francs is not plucked from the air. This was the sum that Beckett was paid by Bordas for the translation of *Murphy*.

64. Yvonne Lefèvre (who dined with Beckett and Suzanne in Paris), 22 March 1995 (Lefèvre).

65. SB to Yvonne Lefèvre, undated (1947) (Lefèvre). Several other letters or cards have been preserved from 1947–48 in which Beckett thanks Yvonne Lefèvre for the "colis" (or packages) just received.

66. SB to Yvonne Lefèvre, 5 April 1948 (Lefèvre).

67. SB to TM, 4 Jan. 1948 (TCD).

15: "A FRENZY OF WRITING," 1946–53

1. Shenker, interview with SB, *The New York Times*, 5 May 1956, quoted in Graver and Federman, *Samuel Beckett: The Critical Heritage*, p. 148.

2. Quoted in Lake, *No Symbols Where None Intended*, p. 49.

3. Ibid., p. 50.

4. Beckett himself told his bibliographers that he wrote it early in 1945, but went on to say that this was *after* the Bram and Geer exhibitions, which was a slip of the memory. Certainly it was written before the autumn of 1945. Yet, in St.-Lô, he was remote from the world of art galleries, paintings, museums, and libraries, even away from his own books, and tired to the point of exhaustion. It must then have been written either before he left Paris in April 1945 or while he was in Ireland from May until August — slightly less likely but certainly not impossible.

5. This essay was reprinted in French in SB, *Disjecta*, pp. 118–32.

6. Ibid., p. 118 ("[le]grand peintre inconnu qu'est Ballmer").

7. Many of the paintings that Beckett chooses as his examples were ones that he had himself seen before the war (Giorgione's *Venus*, for example, in Dresden, or Mantegna's *Triumph of Caesar* at Hampton Court) or other famous paintings that he knew in reproduction (such as Vermeer's *View of Delft* in The Hague).

8. SB, *Disjecta*, p. 126.

9. LH, undated interview with SB (Dartmouth).

10. The manuscript of "Suite" is in Boston College Library, Calvin Israel Collection. The first twenty-nine pages in English are dated quite regularly from February 17 to March 13. The French section, by contrast, is not dated.

11. SB to GR, 27 May 1946 (Texas).

12. *Les Temps modernes* had already published essays by de Beauvoir, Sartre, and Maurice Merleau-Ponty, Boris Vian's "Les Fourmis" ("The Ants"), Nathalie Sarraute's "Portrait d'un inconnu" ("Portrait of a Man Unknown"), and Maurice Blanchot's "Le Paradoxe d'Aytré" ("The Paradox of Aytré"); extracts from Jean Genet's "Pompes funèbres" ("Funeral Rites") had also appeared there, and Genet's startling "Journal du Voleur" ("Diary of a Thief") was accepted for publication in the same issue as Beckett's own first story.

13. SB to Tony Clerx (Jacoba van Velde) 15 May 1946, in which Beckett congratulates her on placing "Suite," but expresses concern that it might also have been accepted, according to Tristan Tzara, by the review *Fontaine*. His letter to Jacoba of June 30, 1946, makes it clear that the second part of the story was unfinished when she sent the first (Bibliothèque Nationale).

14. My translation of Beckett's letter in French to Simone de Beauvoir, which was printed in Lake, *No Symbols Where None Intended*, p. 82.

15. The poems were sent in again by Tony Clerx (SB to Tony Clerx [Jacoba van Velde], undated [ca. Sept. 1946] [Bibliothèque Nationale]).

16. Richard Admussen's description of the manuscripts in *The Samuel Beckett Manuscripts, A Study* (Boston: G. K. Hall, 1979), pp. 66–67, is not accurate here, having wrong dates. Lake, *No Symbols Where None Intended*, pp. 151–52, corrects these errors and is reliable.

17. Interview with Aléxis Péron, July 1989. The phrase in question turns up later in *En attendant Godot*.

18. SB, *Mercier et Camier* (Paris: Les Editions de Minuit, 1970), p. 15.

19. Ibid., p. 21.

20. Aléxis Péron has a typescript of *Molloy*, for example, which has both Beckett's and his mother's amendments. A comparison with the Editions de Minuit printed text (*Molloy* (Paris: Les Editions de Minuit, 1951), pp. 205–208, shows that Beckett sometimes accepted but quite often overruled Mania Péron's suggestions. A substantial portion of this typescript was in the end omitted from the published book.

21. SB to Mania Péron, 12 Feb. 1953, undated (26 March 1953), and 5 April 1953 (Aléxis Péron).

22. Pierre Bordas to SB, 29 Oct. 1946 (Minuit).

23. SB to GR, 15 Dec. 1946 (Texas).

24. Beckett's comment to MacGreevy that it had sold only six copies in the first few months (letter of 18 March 1948 [TCD]) has misled slightly. When Beckett asked for a royalty statement in May 1951, Bordas found that it had sold 285 copies (statement in Les Editions de Minuit files).

25. After Beckett's death, there was a bitter dispute between his former American publisher, Barney Rosset, and the Beckett estate. Finally it was agreed that the play should be published in 1995 in French and Rosset was reluctantly allowed to publish it in an English translation.

26. SB, *Eleutheria* (Paris: Les Editions de Minuit, 1995), p. 74; *Eleuthéria*, Michael Brodsky, trans. (New York: Foxrock Inc., 1995), pp. 68–69. The title of the French edition is written without an accent, the American title with one. Future references are to the American edition, unless otherwise stated. A new English translation by Barbara Wright is to be published by Faber and Faber in London in 1996.

27. These allusions are very fully discussed by Dougald McMillan and Martha Fehsenfeld in *Beckett in the Theatre*, pp. 30–45.

28. I have tried to explore in greater detail elsewhere why this play seems to me to fail. See James Knowlson and John Pilling, *Frescoes of the Skull: The Later Prose and Drama of Samuel Beckett*, pp. 23–38.

29. SB, *Eleuthéria*, p. 81.

30. Ibid., pp. 117–18.

31. SB, *Eleuthéria*. I infinitely prefer this translation by John Spurling in John Fletcher and John Spurling, *Beckett: A Study of His Plays*, p. 50, to the translation by Michael Brodsky in *Eleuthéria*, pp. 143–144.

32. SB to GR, 14 May 1947 (Texas).

33. SB to TM, 4 Jan. 1948 (TCD).

34. SB to TM, 18 March 1948 (TCD).

35. JL to Suzanne Dumesnil, 22 May 1951. In her reply, Suzanne says that "About *Eleutheria* Beckett is more and more anxious about this work. But he thinks there might perhaps be a way of reworking it" (letter in French to JL, 25 May 1951). Charles Bensoussan wrote to Lindon on July 1, 1951, saying that he had requested a meeting with Beckett. It was at this point that Beckett presumably expressed his serious reservations about the play. (All these letters are in the Editions de Minuit files.)

36. On the "New Theatre" in Paris after the war, see David Bradby, *Modern French Drama 1940–1980*, pp. 53–86. I am grateful to Professor Bradby for his advice.

37. This information is based on conversations with Edward Beckett (who showed me the system), Irène Lindon, and Aléxis Péron.

38. Interview with Aléxis Péron, July 1989.

39. SB to HH, (19) May 1947 (Hayden), recommending Givaudan to perform a similar small operation for Hayden.

40. Morris Sinclair to JK, 27 May 1991.

41. Interview with JL, July 1989.

42. SB to Georges Duthuit, in French, 2 Aug. (1948) (Duthuit).

43. Ibid.

44. SB to Georges Duthuit, in French, 22 Aug. 1948 (Duthuit).

45. SB to Georges Duthuit, in French, 27 July 1948, Aug. 1948, and undated (Aug. 1948) (Duthuit).

46. SB to Georges Duthuit, undated (from internal evidence, 12 Aug. 1948) (Duthuit).

47. SB to Georges Duthuit, 27 July 1948 (Duthuit).

48. SB to GR, 10 May 1945 (Texas).

49. SB to TM, 18 March 1948 (TCD).

50. SB to HH, (19) May 1947 (Hayden).

51. SB to Georges Duthuit, in French, 22 Aug. 1948 (Duthuit). Beckett did not approve of the Joyce committee's plans and soon dropped out of any involvement in the project. "Mother sent me *Irish Times* with account of Yeats reburial. I suppose the intention was to do him proud. And to think there are people who want that kind of thing for Joyce!" (SB to TM, 26 Sept. [1948] [TCD]).

52. SB to TM, 24 Nov. 1947 (TCD).

53. SB to TM, 18 March 1948 (TCD).

54. SB to TM, 4 Jan. 1948 (TCD). He was commissioned to translate an anthology of Spanish poetry (which was not published until 1958). Emile Delavenay recounts how Beckett was also called in to rewrite a talk, "The Cultural Essence of Chinese Literature," given by a Chinese professor from Berkeley, Chen Shih Hsiang. Emile Delavenay, *Témoignage: d'un village savoyard au village mondial 1905–1991* (La Calade, Aix-en-Provence: Diffusion Edisud, 1992), pp. 352–53. This unknown translation by Beckett of Chen Shih Hsiang's lecture was published in *Interrelations of Cultures: Their Contribution to International Understanding* (Paris: UNESCO, 1953).

55. A note in the Beckett bibliography concerning translations in a volume of homage by UNESCO to Goethe indicates that there are likely to be others on which Beckett worked. Raymond Federman and John Fletcher, *Samuel Beckett: His Works and His Critics* (Berkeley, Los Angeles and London: University of California Press, 1970), pp. 98–99.

56. The creation of these new magazines and the period in general is well evoked in James Campbell, *Paris Interzone* (London: Secker and Warburg, 1994).

57. Beckett wrote to Georges Duthuit about his translations "Je ne tiens pas à signer" ("I don't particularly want to sign") (SB to Georges Duthuit, 17 July 1948 [Duthuit]).

58. Once the detailed scholarly work interrelating the references in the letters with the various translations has been done a substantial new body of translations by Beckett will emerge. A swift check suggests that Beckett translated Henri Michaux, "To Right Nor Left" (*transition 48*, no. 4, pp. 14–18); Paul Eluard's seven poems on Picasso (*transition 49*, no. 5, pp. 6–13); René Char's poem "Courbet: Les Casseurs de Caillou" ("Courbet: The Stone-Breakers") (*transition 49*, no. 5, pp. 48–49). (Tina Jolas, who was married to René Char, told Rémi Labrusse that Beckett had translated Char.) He was also responsible for the translation of Jacques Prévert's "Picasso Goes for a Walk" (*transition 49*, no. 5, pp. 50–53) (which he did not like); Alfred Jarry's "The Painting Machine" (*transition 49*, no. 5, pp. 38–42); André Du Bouchet's "Félix Fénéon or the Mute Critic" (*transition 49*, no. 5, pp. 76–79); Francis Ponge, "Braque, or Modern Art as Event and Pleasure" (*transition 49*, no. 5, pp 43–47; "C'est dégoûtant," commented Beckett in a letter to Georges Duthuit, 1 March 1949 [Duthuit]); a long essay on Apollinaire by his old Resistance colleague Gabrielle Buffet-Picabia (*transition 50*, no. 6, pp. 110–25); probably two of Duthuit's own pieces called "Sartre's Last Class" in numbers 3 and 4; and his important article "Matisse and Byzantine Space" (*transition 49*, no. 5, pp. 20–37). The pieces that he vetted are too numerous to list here. Rémi Labrusse, who wrote an excellent piece on Beckett and Duthuit ("Beckett et la peinture: le témoignage d'une correspondance inédite," *Critique*, Aug.–Sept. 1990, nos. 519–520, pp. 670–680), generously provided some of the information on which these links are made. I am grateful to

Martha Fehsenfeld and Lois Overbeck for sending me photocopies of *transition* essays and poems.

59. The rough translation of this piece by Georges Duthuit on Sam Francis is in the Beckett Archive, ms. 2926 (Reading).

60. Georges Duthuit, *Les Fauves* (Geneva: Les Trois Collines, 1949); translated into English by Ralph Mannheim as *The Fauvist Painters* (New York: Wittenborn, Schultz, 1950) in the collection "The Documents of Modern Art." According to Rémi Labrusse, Mannheim wrote offering to have Beckett sign this translation but Duthuit replied negatively, explaining that Beckett had done it as a favor to him and did not wish to be acknowledged (Duthuit to Mannheim, 21 Jan. 1950).

61. My portrait of Georges Duthuit is based on interviews with Claude Duthuit, Pierre Schneider, and Josette Hayden.

62. Interview with Claude Duthuit, 26 Nov. 1990.

63. SB, *Disjecta*, p. 139. In this connection Beckett saw Bram van Velde as not being concerned with expression at all. "I suggest that van Velde is the first whose painting is bereft, rid if you prefer, of occasion in every shape and form, ideal as well as material, and the first whose hands have not been tied by the certitude that expression is an impossible act" (SB, *Disjecta*, p. 143). A letter to Duthuit shows that he recognized that this was very much his own interpretation of what van Velde was doing and was perhaps closer to his own feelings than to Bram's (SB to Georges Duthuit, 2 Feb. 1949 [Duthuit]).

64. LH, undated interview with SB (Dartmouth).

65. SB, "The End," in *No's Knife: Collected Shorter Prose 1947–1966*, p. 48.

66. "The son of a lighthouse keeper, a strong muscular lad of fifteen, those were the words, who swam for miles in the night, a knife between his teeth, after a shark, I forget why, out of sheer heroism" (SB, "The Calmative," in *No's Knife: Collected Shorter Prose, 1947–1966*, p. 28). Beckett confirmed to me that his father used to read to him this particular story at night. I do not yet know where it was published.

67. SB, "The Expelled," in *No's Knife: Collected Shorter Prose, 1947–1966*, p. 18. In a letter of June 23 1992 to Philip Baker, Ian McMillan, who joined Frank Beckett in the quantity surveying business of Beckett and Medcalf in 1944, described such a heavy "cylindrical ruler," used in the old days by quantity surveyors, which had been in the Beckett office for as long as he could remember. The police sergeant in *Molloy* threatens Molloy with such a "cylindrical ruler," and the lawyer who gives him money plays with such a ruler. It also occurs in other works, for instance the radio play *Embers*. I am grateful to Philip Baker for passing on this information to me and giving me permission to quote it.

68. SB, *Molloy*, in *Molloy Malone Dies The Unnamable*, pp. 105–106.

69. Ibid., p. 121.

70. "The roof's serrated ridge, the single chimney-stack with its four flues, stood out faintly against the sky spattered with a few dim stars. I offered my face to the black mass of fragrant vegetation that was mine": Ibid., p. 128.

71. "Dear bicycle, I shall not call you bike, you were green, like so many of your generation, I don't know why": Ibid., p. 16.

72. Ibid., p. 106.

73. SB, "The End," in *No's Knife: Collected Shorter Prose 1947–1966*, p. 66.

74. SB, *First Love*, p. 59.

75. SB, "The End," in *No's Knife: Collected Shorter Prose 1947–1966*, pp. 46–47.

76. SB, philosophical notes.

77. SB, *Molloy*, in *Molloy Malone Dies The Unnamable*, p. 41.

78. SB, *Malone Dies*, in *Molloy Malone Dies The Unnamable*, p. 218.

79. G. W. Leibniz, *Les nouveaux essais sur l'entendement humain*. Book II, chapter I in *Opera philosophica* (Berlin, 1840), p. 223.

80. SB, *Malone Dies* in *Molloy Malone Dies The Unnamable*, p. 193.

81. SB, *Molloy*, in *Molloy Malone Dies The Unnamable*, p. 170.

82. Ibid., p. 62.

83. Ibid., p. 99.

84. Ibid., p. 121.

85. Ibid., p. 133.

86. Ibid., p. 129.

87. Ibid., p. 66.

88. SB, GD, notebook 4, 6 Feb. 1937.

89. SB, *Malone Dies*, in *Molloy Malone Dies The Unnamable*, p. 236.

90. Edouard Morot-Sir, "Grammatical Insincerity in *The Unnamable.*" In Harold Bloom, ed., *Samuel Beckett's Molloy, Malone Dies, The Unnamable*, ed. Harold Bloom (New York: Chelsea House, Modern Critical Interpretations, 1988), pp. 131–44.

91. I am indebted to a good essay by Michael Mooney, "*Molloy*, Part I: Beckett's "Discourse on Method," *Journal of Beckett Studies*, 3 (summer 1978), pp. 40–55.

92. SB, *Molloy*, in *Molloy Malone Dies The Unnamable*, p. 64.

93. J. D. O'Hara, "Jung and the 'Molloy' narrative," in S. E. Gontarski, ed., *The Beckett Studies Reader* (Gainesville: University Press of Florida, 1993), p. 131. O'Hara has also written a much fuller study of Beckett's novel trilogy in the light of Jung and Freud and I thank him for allowing me to read the manuscript and for many fruitful conversations on this subject.

94. J. D. O'Hara, "Freud and the narrative of 'Moran,' " *Journal of Beckett Studies*, Second Series, vol. 2, no. 1, Autumn 1992, p. 48.

95. In a letter of January 13, 1948, Pierre Bordas told Tony Clerx that she could dispose elsewhere of the manuscript of *Molloy*, "which it was not possible for him to publish immediately" (Minuit).

96. Interview with SB, 27 Oct. 1989.

97. See Maurice Nadeau, *Grâces leur soient rendues*, mémoires litteraires (Paris: Albin Michel, 1990), pp. 363–64. Others to encourage Beckett were the editor A. C. Gervais, who sent Suzanne Dumesnil a copy of his letter to Max-Pol Fouchet, 21 Oct. 1949, and Max-Pol Fouchet himself, who described Beckett as one of the most important writers of the time (copy of letter of Max-Pol Fouchet to A. C. Gervais, 23 Oct. 1949, from which Gervais quoted to Suzanne Dumesnil [Minuit]).

98. A letter to Georges Lambrichs from Suzanne Dumesnil dated October 5, 1950, makes this order of events clear (Minuit). At about the same time, Lambrichs arranged to print an extract from *Malone meurt (Malone Dies)* in the review 84, published by Les Editions de Minuit, which he edited with Jean Paulhan: "Malone s'en conte," 84, no. 16 (Dec. 1950), pp. 45–58. Georges Lambrichs to Suzanne Dumesnil, 16 Oct. 1950 (Minuit).

99. Interview with JL, 13 July 1989.

100. Pierre Bordas to JL, 1 Dec. 1953 (Minuit).

101. At this point in a notebook prepared by Beckett for his own production of the play in Berlin in 1975, he alluded specifically to "K. D. Friedrich"—that is, the German Romantic painter Caspar David Friedrich (reproduced in *The Theatrical Notebooks of Samuel Beckett*, Vol. I: *Waiting for Godot*, Dougald McMillan and James Knowlson, eds., [London: Faber and Faber, and New York: Grove Press, 1994], p. 236).

102. These paintings were hanging at the time in Mies van der Rohe's Neue Nationalgalerie. They were moved in the autumn of 1986 to the Knobelsdorff Wing of the Charlottenburg Palace.

103. Ruby Cohn to JK, confirmed on 9 August 1994.

104. In manuscript notebook four of *Watt*, written in Roussillon in 1943, however, there is a reference among "images of images" to "Kaspar David Friedrich's Men and Moon" (fourth manuscript notebook of *Watt*, the first page of which is headed, "Roussillon October 4th 1943" [Texas]). And since Beckett had not returned to Berlin before writing *Waiting for Godot*, it was in all likelihood the Dresden picture of the two men observing the moon that he had in mind when he wrote the play. Cf. also SB, *Malone Dies*, in

Molloy Malone Dies The Unnamable, p. 198. I am grateful to Mary Bryden for the *Watt* notebook reference.

105. This was suggested earlier in Marilyn Gaddis Rose, *Jack B. Yeats: Painter and Poet*, (Berne and Frankfurt: Herbert Lang), 1972, p. 45.

106. Colin Duckworth, introduction to *En attendant Godot* (London: Harrap, 1966), pp. xlv–lxxv.

107. Hugh Kenner, *A Reader's Guide to Samuel Beckett*, pp. 30–31.

108. The first was Georges Loustaunau-Lacau, *Chiens maudits: souvenirs d'un rescapé des bagnes hitlériens*, section on Alfred Péron, pp. 89–95.

109. Georges Loustaunau-Lacau, *Mémoires d'un Français rebelle 1914–48*, pp. 313–14.

110. Ibid., p. 314 (my translation).

111. Ibid., p. 313 (my translation).

112. SB, *Waiting for Godot*, p. 9.

113. SB to HH, 24 July 1950 (Hayden).

114. SB, *Krapp's Last Tape*, in *Collected Shorter Plays*, p. 60.

115. SB to HH, 31 July 1950 (Hayden).

116. Ibid.

117. SB to HH, 9 Aug. 1950 (Hayden).

118. Ibid.

119. SB to HH, 19 Aug. 1950 (Hayden).

120. SB to HH, 31 Aug. 1950 (Hayden).

121. Interview with Simone McKee, 26 June 1993.

122. Undated personal conversation with SB, ca. 1980.

123. Quotations from SB, *Krapp's Last Tape*, in *Collected Shorter Plays*, pp. 57, 62, 59.

124. Denis Johnston refers to his love affair with Ethna MacCarthy, whom he names Euterpe, in a piece called *Nine Rivers*, ms. 10066/30–32 (TCD). But this love affair would have been known to Beckett when he was a student with Ethna.

125. Blin had been directed by such well-known *cinéastes* as Jean Renoir, Marcel Carné, Marc Allégret, and Abel Gance. For a list of his roles and of plays that he directed, see Lynda Bellity Peskine, ed., *Roger Blin. Souvenirs et propos recueillis par Lynda Bellity Peskine* (Paris: Gallimard, 1986).

126. Ibid., p. 80.

127. SB to Georges Duthuit (undated, but March 1950) (Duthuit).

128. This account of how Blin came to be manager-director at the Gaîté-Montparnasse is taken from Peskine, *Roger Blin. Souvenirs et propos*, pp. 65–66, and an interview with Blin's friend (the original Lucky in *En attendant Godot*) Jean Martin, September 1989.

129. SB to Georges Duthuit (undated, but March 1950) (Duthuit).

130. SB to GR, 11 Dec. 1950 (Texas).

131. Peskine, *Roger Blin. Souvenirs et propos*, pp. 83–84.

132. Original agreement with the Théâtre de Poche, three signed copies, 23 July 1952 (Minuit).

133. There are numerous letters about this disagreement: e.g., JL to France Guy, 12 Nov. 1952; France Guy, letters to Roger Blin and to JL, 16 Nov. 1952; Roger Blin to J. Joujard at the Ministry, 22 Nov. 1952 (Minuit).

134. Peskine, *Roger Blin. Souvenirs et propos*, p. 83 (my translation).

135. Delphine Seyrig was a former pupil of Roger Blin. She read the play while she was on tour and thought it compelling and very beautiful. On her return to Paris, she proposed to Serreau that he should use the money that an uncle had left her with which to travel (interview with Delphine Seyrig, 29 Jan. 1990).

136. Jean Martin described how the shattering effect that his acting had on the theater dresser, who was horrified and felt like vomiting, determined them to retain this startling way of playing Lucky (interview with Jean Martin, Sept. 1989).

137. Ibid.

138. Some of these changes are recorded in the notes of *En attendant Godot*, ed. Colin Duckworth.
139. One of the protesters wrote a vituperative letter dated February 2, 1953, to *Le Monde*.
140. Beckett was told about the "bagarre" in a letter from JL, February 4, 1953 (Minuit), and a few days later he thanked Mania Péron for "les détails succulents" which she added (SB to Mania Péron, 12 Feb. 1953) (Péron).
141. JL to SB, 4 Feb. 1953 (Minuit).
142. Kenneth Tynan in *The Observer*, 7 Aug. 1955; reprinted in Graver and Federman, eds., *Samuel Beckett: The Critical Heritage*, p. 97.

16: *Godot*, Love, and Loss, 1953–55

1. SB to GR, 12 May 1953 (Texas).
2. Beckett authorized me to make two visits to his Ussy house during the last few months of his life. My description is based on dozens of photographs taken then, on accounts of friends who had visited Beckett there, and on photographs of the exterior and interior in the 1950s and 1960s from the Lawrence Harvey collection (Dartmouth) and from Sheila Page.
3. Beckett became closely involved from early March 1953 with the German translation of the play, going over it in great detail with a young German, Elmar Tophoven, a former *Lektor* at the Sorbonne, who had already translated plays by Arthur Adamov. His translation was sent to Beckett at Ussy by Lindon on 16 Feb. 1953 (letters of JL to SB, 16 Feb. 1953, and of SB to JL, 19 Feb. 1953 [Minuit]). At the same time, he was helping Patrick Bowles of the *Merlin* group with his English translation of *Molloy*. Some months later, he found the Spanish translation of *Godot* "bad, full of mistakes and omissions and unjustifiable liberties" (SB to AJL, 21 Jan. 1954 [Texas]) but could not face improving it, commenting that he was "sick of all this old vomit and despair more and more of ever being able to puke again" (SB to BR, 22 Jan. 1954 [Syracuse]).
4. Robert Pikelny, born at Łódź in Poland in 1904, had lived in France since he was seventeen years old and knew Pascin and Soutine. Beckett knew him through Henri Hayden. Pikelny mainly painted scenes of the circus, dance, and horse racing. He had a large exhibition in 1952 and exhibited at the Revel Gallery in Burlington Arcade in London in October–December 1953, when Beckett wrote to Herbert Read on his behalf (SB, letters to HH, 17 Sept. 1953 [Hayden] and to TM, 30 Oct. 1953 and 14 Dec. 1953 [TCD]).
5. SB to PM, 12 Jan. 1954 (Mitchell).
6. SB to GR, 29 Sept. 1953 (Texas).
7. SB to Susan Manning, 6 April 1954 (Texas).
8. SB to AJL, 17 Nov. 1953 (Texas), and to TM, 14 Dec. 1953 (TCD).
9. SB to PM, 13 March 1955 (Mitchell).
10. SB to TM, 27 Sept. 1953 (TCD).
11. SB to JL, undated (1953) (Minuit).
12. SB to PM, 25 Nov. 1953 (Mitchell). Patrick Bowles lent him the book "and I liked it very much indeed, more than anything for a long time" (SB to Loly Rosset, 20 Nov. 1953 [Syracuse]).
13. SB to PM, 13 March 1954 (Mitchell).
14. SB to PM, 17 Feb. 1955 (Mitchell).
15. SB to TM, 11 Aug. 1955 (TCD).
16. SB to JL, 11 Feb. 1953. My account of the dispute with the NRF is based primarily on the exchange of letters between Beckett and Jérôme Lindon between February and April 1953 (Minuit).
17. SB to BR, 25 June 1953 (Syracuse).

18. SB to BR, 18 July 1953 (Syracuse).

19. "Have made a good deal of money with it already (more in a couple of months than with all my other writings put together) and hope to make a good bit more" (SB to Susan Manning, 16 April 1953 [Texas]).

20. SB to JL, 8 Jan. 1953 (Minuit).

21. SB to JL, 1 Dec. 1953 (Minuit).

22. Maurice Nadeau wrote several perceptive essays on Beckett's novels: "Samuel Beckett, l'humour et le néant," *Mercure de France*, vol. CCCXII (Aug. 1951), pp. 423–25, and "Samuel Beckett ou le droit au silence," *Les Temps modernes*. vol. VII (Jan. 1952), pp. 1273–82. Georges Bataille also wrote "Le silence de Molloy" in *Critique*, vol. VII (May 1951), pp. 387–96.

23. *L'Innommable* was delivered to Jérôme Lindon by Suzanne at the beginning of February 1953 (SB to JL, 5 Feb. 1953 [Minuit]).

24. SB to GR, 8 May 1953 (Texas).

25. Telephone conversation with Richard Seaver, 26 Jan. 1994.

26. My account of the founding of *Merlin* and of the publication of *Watt* by Merlin and the Olympia Press in the "Collection Merlin" is based on the following main sources: Richard Seaver's introduction to his *I Can't Go On, I'll Go On*; an interview with Richard Seaver, 1 Dec. 1993; an interview with Jane Lougee Bryant; and *Les Jardins d'Eros*, the second volume of Maurice Girodias's autobiography, *Une Journée sur la terre*.

27. PM to JK, 20 March 1994.

28. Richard Seaver, "Samuel Beckett: An Introduction," *Merlin*, no. I (autumn 1952), pp. 73–79. Reprinted in Graver and Federman, eds., *Samuel Beckett: The Critical Heritage*, pp. 79–87.

29. Richard Seaver, ed., *I Can't Go On, I'll Go On*, p. xv.

30. SB to Susan Manning, 16 April 1953 (Texas).

31. BR to SB, 4 Aug. 1953 (Syracuse).

32. Maurice Girodias is quoted by Bair (*Samuel Beckett*, p. 433) as saying that they printed two thousand copies, but this was a mistake.

33. SB to GR, 29 Sept. 1953 (Texas). The twenty-five special copies on fine paper that were signed by Beckett and sold at treble the price of the ordinary edition do not have this magenta cover with its somewhat lurid frame of asterisks, but are of a more subdued beige and have no asterisks.

34. Beckett's own corrected copy is in the Beckett Archive (Reading).

35. Alexander Trocchi set out what Merlin owed Beckett in a letter dated May 29, 1954, and the dates on which they intended to pay him. In a letter to Beckett, July 31, 1954, Trocchi explained that the payments had not been made because of Beckett's absence in Ireland. Beckett answered, politely still at this stage, on August 3, 1954 (McMaster).

36. SB to PM, 27 Aug. 1954 (Mitchell).

37. The letter in question is SB to Alexander Trocchi, 27 Aug. 1954 (McMaster).

38. Alexander Trocchi to SB, 30 Aug. 1954. The draft letter is in McMaster but is also reproduced in Andrew Murray Scott, ed., *Invisible Insurrection of a Million Minds: A Trocchi Reader*, pp. 115–16.

39. SB to AJL, 22 Nov. 1955 (Texas).

40. SB to GR, 12 May 1953 (Texas).

41. SB to AJL, 6 Aug. 1953 (Texas).

42. The manuscript of *L'Innommable* was completed at Ussy in January 1950. See Lake, *No Symbols Where None Intended*, p. 58.

43. SB to PM, 27 Oct. 1953 (Mitchell).

44. Interview with JL, July 1989. Photographs of Beckett with his brother in May 1953 show that the wall was by then already mostly built.

45. In a letter of September 16, 1953, Beckett told Mania Péron they were re-rehearsing every day (Péron). Raimbourg, cast in a new play by Armand Salacrou (SB to TM, 27 Sept. 1953), had to be replaced as Vladimir by Pierre Asso and a new actor rehearsed for

Pozzo (SB to PM, 26 Sept. 1953, and 1 Nov. 1953—"Have to go down now to that bloody theatre and encourage the new Pozzo" [Mitchell]).

46. SB to JL, 19 Feb. 1953, and interview with a friend of Roger Blin.

47. SB to PM, 26 Sept. 1953 (Mitchell).

48. "I came back from Berlin on Saturday [the premiere was September 8, 1953]. It was badly played there, above all badly directed, but well received. I should have preferred the opposite. Everyone was very kind" (SB to HH, 17 Sept. 1953).

49. Speaking of another of his visits to the Babylone revival, Beckett wrote: "Last time I went I ended up under the seat, moaning. The trousers didn't come down at end. Technical accident. That finished me" (SB to PM, 12 Jan. 1954 [Mitchell]).

50. The situation was a complex one. A Raymond W. Anderson proposed translating, publishing, and putting on the play in the United States of America, if given an option (JL to SB, 8 April 1953 [Minuit]) and, until April, the U.S. rights were under offer to the literary agent Marion Saunders. The English rights had been under offer to a Madame Strassova (JL to Denise Tual, 18 May 1953 [Minuit]).

51. The American director and producer Garson Kanin, probably with Thornton Wilder, sought the rights of adaptation for England and the United States in May 1953 (Denise Tual [a friend of Garson Kanin] to SB, 6 May 1953 [Minuit]) and this approach may have been linked with that of Harold Oram, since Thornton Wilder knew Oram well and had certainly talked to him about *Waiting for Godot* (JL to SB, 5 May 1953 [Minuit] and PM to JK, 20 March 1994).

52. The first translation was sent to the United States by the end of June 1953 for Oram and Barney Rosset. Harold Oram, Inc., had taken out an option to mount a production of *Godot*, which expired at the end of October 1953.

53. SB to BR, 29 Dec. 1953 (Syracuse).

54. Some notes made by Pamela Mitchell at the time show that she discussed relative proportions of both investment and percentage of profit, if Brandel and Oram were to form a partnership to mount a production of *Waiting for Godot* (Mitchell).

55. SB to PM, 26 Sept. 1953 (Mitchell).

56. The meeting with Beckett was arranged through Alexander Trocchi and the *Merlin* group, who already knew Oram. Notes made by Pamela Mitchell at the time show that she had meetings with Trocchi, Brandel, and Jérôme Lindon as well as Beckett during her week's stay September 14–21, 1953 (Mitchell). She is fairly certain that Beckett had met Oram earlier, probably at Trocchi's apartment, and that they had liked each other.

57. SB to PM, 5 Oct. 1953 (Mitchell).

58. SB to PM, 27 Oct. 1953 (Mitchell).

59. SB to PM, 13 March 1955 (Mitchell).

60. The account of the relationship with Pamela Mitchell is based on two long interviews with Miss Mitchell and on the sixty-one letters that Beckett wrote to her over a period of seventeen years. She has also kindly read my chapter to remove inaccuracies.

61. SB to Susan Manning, 21 May 1955 (Texas), referring back to the events of a year before.

62. SB to PM, 30 June 1954 (Mitchell).

63. The photograph of Samuel Beckett in a small boat printed in Bair, *Samuel Beckett*, facing p. 115, and described as the pond at Shottery, is not of the tiny lily pond there but of the larger one at Sweetwater Cottage, Sheila Page's cottage in Surrey.

64. Interview with Caroline Beckett Murphy, 19 June 1991. A photograph of such an occasion is published in O'Brien, *The Beckett Country*, p. 343 and in this book.

65. SB to PM, 23 June 1954 (Mitchell).

66. SB to PM, 30 June 1954 (Mitchell). Drobny beat B. Patty in the semifinals of the Wimbledon championships (June 30, 1954) and went on to beat the Australian Ken Rosewall in the final on July 2, 1954, by three sets to one. It was Drobny's third final. "Drobny Does It at Last," *The Times* (London), 3 July 1954.

67. SB to PM, undated letter (probably mid-June), 1954 (Mitchell).

68. He went to see Cyril Cusack's production of Synge's *Playboy of the Western World* at the Gaiety Theatre. "Didn't much enjoy myself, in spite of alternate stout and whiskey. Then driving home at 1 a.m. against the stream of drunken bona fides returning to town" (SB to PM, 12 July 1954 [Mitchell]).

69. SB to PM, 10 June 1954 (Mitchell).

70. SB to Susan Manning, 18 Oct. 1954 (Texas). He also called on Susan's sister, Louie Bennett, the founder of the first women's trade union in Ireland. She lived in a little bungalow in Killiney just down the hill from Frank's house.

71. Interview with John Manning, 19 June 1990.

72. Frank's general practitioner was Dr. Brian Mayne, who brought in for his advice T. G. Wilson, an ear, nose, and throat specialist who lived on the Brighton Road at Foxrock. Gilbert Wilson was also the godfather of Frank's son, Edward (Edward Beckett to JK, 8 May 1994).

73. SB to PM, 5 June 1954 (Mitchell).

74. SB to PM, 19 Aug. 1954 (Mitchell). Along with his earlier experience of living briefly by the sea with his mother at Greystones, this probably laid the foundations for his radio play *Embers*, which evokes the sucking sound of the sea and is full of feelings of guilt and remorse.

75. SB to PM, 6 Aug. 1954 (Mitchell). The edition of *The Letters of Robert Louis Stevenson* that Beckett read at Shottery was the fifth. It was in four volumes, published by Methuen in London in 1922 (letter from Edward Beckett to JK, 18 April 1994).

76. SB to JL, 12 July 1954 (Minuit), to BR, 12 July 1954 (Syracuse), and to Elmar Tophoven, 13 Aug. 1954 (Tophoven). He translated only the opening ten pages or so in Killiney.

77. SB to PM, undated letter (probably mid-June), 1954 (Mitchell).

78. SB to PM, 27 Aug. 1954 (Mitchell).

79. SB to PM, 22 July 1954 (Mitchell).

80. SB, *Endgame*, p. 12. These letters reveal that this sad personal experience may well be an unnoticed source of inspiration for a play of which he wrote a first, two-act version only a few months after his brother's death.

81. Interview with Edward Beckett, 31 March 1994.

82. SB to PM, 17 Sept. 1954 (Mitchell).

83. SB to PM, 6 Aug. 1954 (Mitchell).

84. SB to PM, undated (27 Nov. 1954) (Mitchell).

85. Nicola Zingarelli's *Vocabolario della Lingua Italiana*, in an edition printed in Bologna in 1954, was among the books remaining in Beckett's library after his death.

86. "Have been reading in your big magnificent Zingarelli with much satisfaction and wishing he was more explicit about the difference between the s's of cosa and rosa and the zz's of mezzo and pazzo. Seem to have forgotten more Italian than I thought" (SB to PM, 17 Feb. 1955 [Mitchell]). Confirmed as her main "good-bye present" to him (PM to JK, 20 March 1994). Later Beckett started buying the Italian weekly illustrated *Oggi* to restore some of his old fluency in Italian (SB to PM, 18 Aug. 1955 [Mitchell]).

87. SB to PM, 26 March 1955 (Mitchell).

88. Interview with PM, 5 Dec. 1993.

89. JL to Simon Nora, 9 Dec. 1954 (Minuit).

90. Among the Beckett papers at Les Editions de Minuit, there is a "Note concernant un terrain vendu par la commune de Ussy sur Marne à Monsieur Samuel Beckett," which is based on JL's letter to Nora of December 9, 1954.

91. Frantz Gaignerot, the sub-prefect of Meaux, to the mayor of Ussy, 28 Dec. 1954 (Minuit).

92. SB to PM, 27 Dec. 1954 (Mitchell).

93. SB to PM, undated (Jan. 1955) (Mitchell).

94. "In the country the new neighbour has built his horrible garage-cum-summer hovel but as agreed well off the line. In the autumn I'll shut it off with a curtain of the densest

conifers to be obtained. But it will never be the same" (SB to PM, 18 April 1955 [Mitchell]).

95. SB to PM, 23 Feb. 1955 (Mitchell).

96. SB to PM, 17 Feb. 1955 (Mitchell).

97. SB to PM, 13 March 1955 (Mitchell).

98. SB to PM, 23 Feb. 1955 (Mitchell).

99. SB to PM, 17 Feb. 1955 (Mitchell).

100. SB to PM, 13 March 1955 (Mitchell).

101. SB to PM, 18 April 1955 (Mitchell).

102. SB to PM, 7 Feb. 1955 (Mitchell).

103. "Ah Noé, Noé, toi aussi il fallait se repentir de t'avoir fait" ("Ah Noah, Noah, it repenteth me that you also were created") (typescript, ms. 1660, p. 43 [Reading]). This passage survived in manuscript and typescript versions written a year later, but was then dropped and did not find its way into the final script.

104. Enoch Brater discusses some allusions to the story of Noah in *Endgame* and the much later *Not I* in "Noah, *Not I*, and Beckett's 'Incomprehensibly Sublime' " *Comparative Drama*, vol. 8, no. 3 (Fall 1974), pp. 254–63.

105. SB, *Endgame*, p. 51.

106. SB, *Fin de partie* (Paris: Les Editions de Minuit, 1957), p. 111.

107. SB, *Endgame*, p. 52.

108. See Gontarski, *The Intent of Undoing in Samuel Beckett's Dramatic Texts*, pp. 42–54. A number of references to sections of the play show that Gontarski's "stage 3," the two-act typescript in ms. 1660 (Reading), is the typescript of a manuscript likely to have been written as early as January–February 1955.

109. Glenavy, *Today We Will Only Gossip*, p. 178. In a letter to Mary Hutchinson, June 6, 1958, the former Beatrice Elvery describes many other details of Cissie's final years that she sees as related to *Endgame* (Texas). Beckett saw Cissie in an old people's home while he was staying in Killiney and used to take her out in her wheelchair.

110. SB to PM, 13 March 1955 (Mitchell).

111. SB to PM, 26 March 1955 (Mitchell).

112. Ibid.

113. SB to AJL, 6 Aug. 1953 (Texas).

114. SB to TM, 1 March 1954 (TCD). Beckett was bowled over by Yeats's paintings, going to the February 1954 exhibition himself five or six times and encouraging all his friends and correspondents to go to see it.

115. At this stage, his gifts were often quite small sums (the price of a meal or a hotel room) but sometimes they were far more substantial. Early in 1955, for instance, with Françoise Porte and Georges Duthuit, he contributed to the purchase of a large, light-filled studio for Bram van Velde in the boulevard de la Gare (Claire Stoullig, ed., *Bram van Velde*, p. 184). Letters to Bram and to Pamela Mitchell suggest that he ran himself short of money so as to do this (SB to Bram van Velde, 8 April 1955, reproduced in the above catalogue, p. 185, and to PM, 18 April 1955 [Mitchell]).

116. Interview with Claude Jamet, 3 July 1991.

117. Letter from the Lüttringhausen prisoner to SB, 1 Oct. 1954 (Minuit) (my translation).

118. Ibid.

119. This was no idle boast, as the *Illustrierte Woche* had published a photographic feature about the production: "Das Drama vom Warten auf Gott," *Illustrierte Woche*, no. 30 (24 July 1954), pp. 812–13. (The prisoner who translated, directed, and acted in the play is on the right in the photograph with Vladimir, Pozzo, and Estragon [Frau Helga Manker to JK, 22 March 1994]). There was also a long article about the production entitled "Sie warten hinter Gittern" in the evangelical magazine *Der Weg*, no. 16/17 (1954).

120. Ludwig Manker to SB, 3 Oct. 1954 (Minuit).

121. The widow of Pastor Manker assured me that there were no letters from Beckett among her husband's papers after his death in April 1985 (Frau Helga Manker to JK, 22 Mar. 1994).

122. SB to AJL, 5 Nov. 1955 (Texas).

123. I am most grateful to the present pastor of Lüttringhausen, Hans Freitag, for his research on my behalf on this whole episode and to Frau Hämer, the widow of an Evangelical Carer at the prison, for her letter to Pastor Hans Freitag, February 13, 1994, which was sent on to me.

124. Documents from Pastor Freitag, including the program of cultural events and letters from Hans Freitag to the German Evangelical Synod in February 1988.

125. Patrick Bowles, "How to Fail: Notes on Talks with Samuel Beckett," *PN Review*, no. 96, vol. 20, no. 4 (March–April 1994), p. 28.

126. SB to S. Fischer Verlag, 14 July 1956, and from S. Fischer Verlag to SB, 19 July 1956, informing him that the money had been paid over to Herr Lembke (S. Fischer Verlag).

127. Telephone interview with Dorothy Tutin, 3 Feb. 1994.

128. Telephone conversation with Sir Alec Guinness, 18 Jan. 1994.

129. SB to BR, 21 Aug. 1954 (Syracuse).

130. SB to PM, 25 July 1954 (Mitchell).

131. Beckett wrote: "There is talk [of playing it] in New York, but in my opinion it could not be played unexpurgated either in England or America, and I refuse to expurgate it" (SB to Susan Manning, 16 April 1953 [Texas]).

132. SB to BR, 21 April 1954 (Syracuse).

133. Telephone interview with Dorothy Tutin, 3 Feb. 1994.

134. The script belonging to Paul Daneman, who played Vladimir in the first Arts Theatre production, shows that Vladimir's line "Hmm. It would give us an erection" was added in pencil for the private club production, after being omitted following the earlier brushes with the Lord Chamberlain (Daneman).

135. SB to BR, 18 Oct. 1954 (Syracuse).

136. SB to JL, 29 July 1954 (Minuit).

137. BR to SB, 28 Oct. 1954 (Syracuse).

138. SB to Howard Turner at Grove Press, 2 Aug. 1955 (Syracuse).

139. SB to PM, 17 Feb. 1955 (Mitchell).

140. The story is related by Carolyn Swift in *Stage by Stage* (Co. Dublin: Poolbeg Press, Swords, 1985), pp. 176–201. Many letters have been preserved both from her husband, Alan Simpson, to Beckett and from Beckett to Simpson. They date from throughout 1954 and 1955 and are now in Trinity College Dublin Library. Simpson would have liked to proceed on Cyril Cusack's suggestion that it would be fitting if the first production in English were to be in Dublin. But Beckett replied tartly: "As to the propriety of first production in English being in Dublin, I'm afraid I have no feeling about that at all" (SB to Alan Simpson, 9 April 1954 [Swift]).

141. Beckett received news from Roger Blin that his play had been "violently attacked by the Roman Catholic press in Holland and that the municipality of Arnhem got the wind up and were on the point of banning the production saying it was a homosexual work because Gogo says to Didi, 'Tu vois, tu pisses mieux quand je ne suis pas là'! ['You see you piss better when I'm not around.'] But they seem to have been calmed by the threat of the players' director to resign if the play was banned and rehearsals continued" (SB to PM, 7 Feb. 1955 [Mitchell]). In fact, the entire cast seems to have offered its resignation. Similar problems were encountered with the Catholic Church in Madrid, where announcements of the performance were not allowed in the press and where no kind of publicity at all was permitted. Even then a performance was given to some acclaim in the Faculty of Philosophy and Letters of the University.

142. Extract from an interview on the BBC Third Programme, 14 April 1961. See also Peter Hall's autobiography, *Making an Exhibition of Myself* (London: Sinclair Stevenson, 1993), pp. 102–108.

143. Quoted in Peter Bull, *I Know the Face But . . .* , reprinted in Ruby Cohn, ed., *Casebook on "Waiting for Godot"* (New York: Grove Press, 1967), p. 39.

144. Interview with Peter Woodthorpe, 18 Feb. 1994.

145. The adjectives are borrowed from Harold Hobson's crucial *Sunday Times* (London) review, Aug. 7, 1955.

146. Peter Bull, *I Know the Face But . . .* , quoted in Ruby Cohn, ed., *Casebook on "Waiting for Godot,"* pp. 41–42.

147. SB, *Waiting for Godot*, pp. 38, 34.

148. Cecil Wilson, *The Daily Mail*, 4 Aug. 1955.

149. Milton Shulman, "Duet for Two Symbols," *The Evening Standard*, 4 Aug. 1955.

150. Sir Harold Hobson remained a good friend of Beckett for the rest of his life and they saw each other fairly regularly in Paris and London (Harold Hobson, *An Indirect Journey: An Autobiography* [London: Weidenfeld and Nicolson, 1978], pp. 233–34).

151. Kenneth Tynan, *The Observer*, 7 Aug. 1955.

152. Harold Hobson, *The Sunday Times* (London), 7 Aug. 1955.

153. Interview with Paul Daneman, 14 Feb. 1994.

154. Interview with Peter Woodthorpe, 18 Feb. 1994.

155. Paul Daneman, telephone interview, 5 April 1994.

156. Peter Woodthorpe, telephone interview, 5 April 1994.

157. [G. S. Fraser] *The Times Literary Supplement*, 10 Feb. 1956, p. 84.

158. The letters or articles mentioned in *The Times Literary Supplement*, in addition to the G. S. Fraser article, are Katharine M. Wilson, March 2, 1956, p. 133; J. S. Walsh, March 9, 1956, p. 149; and "Puzzling about Godot," April 13, 1956, p. 221. There were other letters on Feb 24, March 23, March 30, and April 6, 1956.

159. SB to TM, 11 Aug. 1955 (TCD).

160. SB to TM, 6 Nov. 1955 (TCD). As a card from Zurich to the Haydens shows, he was there on October 8 for a few days (Hayden).

161. Telephone interview with John Beckett, 5 Feb. 1994.

162. Alan Schneider, *Entrances, An American Director's Journey* (New York: Viking Penguin Inc., 1986), p. 225.

163. SB to JL, 24 Sept. 1955 (Minuit). He saw photographs of the production early in November and thought it "all wrong" (SB to BR, 10 Nov. 1955 [Syracuse]).

164. SB to BR, 2 Feb. 1956. "The Gogo was by far the best I had seen."

165. SB to PM, 16 Dec. 1955 (Mitchell).

166. Interview with Peter Woodthorpe, 18 Feb. 1994. He told Woodthorpe that he regretted calling the absent character Godot, because of all the theories involving God to which this had given rise. Beckett escorted Woodthorpe, to whom he took a liking, to hear a cellist playing at his cousin John Beckett's house in Chiswick. In the taxi, he told the young actor that he would like to see him playing Dr. Johnson in a play that he dreamed of writing. It would, he said, be a monologue with Dr. Johnson and his cat, Hodge, as the only characters; other cats might enter, he added, but no other human being! Clearly the idea of a play about Dr. Johnson, first imagined and indeed begun in a different form eighteen years before, had still not been entirely abandoned. When Woodthorpe wrote to him later reminding him of his proposal, Beckett replied that he had given up on the idea.

17: IMPASSE AND DEPRESSION, 1956–58

1. SB to AS, 30 April 1957 (Boston).

2. My account of the origins of *Act Without Words I* is based on an interview with Deryk Mendel (3 March 1993), a further telephone interview with him (5 Feb. 1994), and an interview with John Beckett (8 July 1992).

3. Wolfgang Köhler, *The Mentality of Apes* (London: Kegan Paul, Trench, Trubner & Co., New York: Harcourt Brace & Co., 1925). Photographs in this book show one of the

apes succeeding in doing what Beckett's mime character cannot do because he is thwarted by life. This book was on Beckett's psychological reading list in 1934–35.

4. Interview with John Beckett, 8 July 1992.

5. Michael Myerberg, quoted in John Lahr, *Notes on a Cowardly Lion: A Biography of Bert Lahr* (New York: Limelight Editions, 1984), p. 262.

6. SB to BR, 6 Jan. 1956 (dated by Beckett in error 1955) (Syracuse).

7. SB to AS, 11 Jan. 1956 (Boston).

8. Schneider, *Entrances*, p. 236.

9. SB to AS, 11 Jan. 1956 (Boston).

10. SB to BR, 17 Jan. 1956 (Syracuse).

11. BR to SB, 23 Jan. 1956 (Syracuse).

12. If Myerberg did not proceed with a New York production, Albery would have liked to "export" the British one. Rosset and Beckett also spoke again about the possibility of bringing over the English director, Peter Hall, to direct an American cast. For Beckett felt that, after the discussions that they had had in London, Hall was in a position to do a much sharper, less cluttered production. (SB to BR, 15 March 1956 [Syracuse]).

13. SB to BR, 2 Feb. 1956 (Syracuse).

14. For example, Alvin Epstein, who played Lucky, quoted in Lahr, *Notes on a Cowardly Lion*, p. 277.

15. Tynan's praise is quoted in Lahr, *Notes on a Cowardly Lion*, p. 282. Brooks Atkinson wrote: "But Bert Lahr is the actor who gives Mr. Beckett's drama its size, pathos and humanity. . . . For years we have all laughed at Mr. Lahr's dim-witted buffooneries. In 'Waiting for Godot' we can still laugh at a good many of them. But we also have to admire the versatility of his craftsmanship, the magnetism of his personality and the truth of his characterization" (*The New York Times*, 20 April 1956).

16. SB to BR, 2 May 1956 (Syracuse).

17. SB to BR, 30 Aug. (1956) (Syracuse).

18. SB to TM, 9 April 1956 (TCD).

19. Ibid.

20. She had, she told Beckett, been visiting collections of African ivories in Switzerland, Holland, and Germany and was just returning from three months spent in London working at the British Museum, in Liverpool and at the Pitt-Rivers Museum in Dorset (for details, see Anne Chisholm, *Nancy Cunard*, pp. 398–99).

21. SB to BR, 2 May 1956 (Syracuse). In May, Beckett returned seven copies of *Whoroscope*, duly signed (SB to Nancy Cunard, 11 May 1956 [Texas]).

22. Anne Chisholm, *Nancy Cunard*, p. 400.

23. SB to AJL, 24 April 1956 (Texas).

24. SB to TM, 30 July 1956 (TCD).

25. SB to BR, 15 March 1956 (Syracuse).

26. SB to TM, 4 June 1956 (TCD).

27. SB to BR, 19 April 1956 (Syracuse).

28. SB to TM, 30 July 1956 (TCD).

29. Ibid. The Schumann pieces were from Opus 48, No. 7 and Opus 48, No. 13 (1840).

30. SB to TM, 4 June 1956 (TCD).

31. This was suggested by Vivian Mercier in *Beckett / Beckett*, pp. 78–83.

32. SB to BR, 19 April 1956 (Syracuse).

33. SB to Nancy Cunard, 11 May 1956 (Texas).

34. SB to Nancy Cunard, 6 June 1956 (Texas). The Italian quotation is from Dante's *Divina commedia*, *Inferno*, Canto I.

35. SB to MH, 4 July 1956 (Texas).

36. It was offered first to Jacques Hébertot, in whose theater *En attendant Godot* had just been successfully revived. But, although a booking by Hébertot in November seemed at one time likely, this failed to materialize and, in spite of the great avant-garde European success of *En attendant Godot*, Beckett, Lindon, and Blin found themselves still

on the lookout for another pocket-size theater run by an administrative director with the courage to put on *Fin de partie*.

37. SB to TM, 18 Oct. 1956 (TCD).

38. E. J. King Bull reported initially for the BBC with great enthusiasm on the French script (report dated 15 April 1953 [BBC]). But the same consultant was not so impressed by Beckett's English translation, and since the head of radio drama, Val Gielgud, was hostile to the play, the project was scrapped, to the great disgust of several other members of the radio drama department.

39. Cecilia Reeves to Head of Drama (Sound), 21 June 1956 (BBC).

40. John Morris to Samuel Beckett, 11 July 1956, and SB to John Morris, 12 July 1956 (BBC). The invitation was also associated with the Third Programme's interest in obtaining the rights to broadcast the English translation of Beckett's new play, *Fin de partie*, and with the wish of Michael Barry, the head of BBC television drama, to see his first mime piece, then referred to as *Soif* (or *Thirst*), televised.

41. John Morris to Head of Drama (Sound), 18 July 1956 (BBC).

42. SB to Nancy Cunard, 5 July 1956 (Texas).

43. SB to Aidan Higgins, 6 July 1956 (Texas).

44. SB, *All That Fall* in *Collected Shorter Plays*, p. 25. Beckett would have heard the phrase "Nice day for the races," which occurs in the play and which he once thought of using as its title, as a regular greeting on race days at Leopardstown.

45. Ibid., p. 17.

46. The sole entry under the name of Fitt in *Thom's Official Directory* during Beckett's childhood was a Rathgar resident, Miss Marian Fitt. With his liking for funny names, Beckett's father would have been unlikely to miss this and may have pointed it out to his sons.

47. In an early manuscript, Mrs. Rooney's name was Kennedy. A Mr. and Mrs. George Kennedy lived at a house in Foxrock called The Ark, not far from the Beckett home.

48. SB, *All That Fall* in *Collected Shorter Plays*, p. 29.

49. Again, just as in the play, Hardy was only an occasional visiting preacher, not "the incumbent" of the local Tullow church, who was the Reverend G. W. Newport Clarke. Another Reverend Edward John Hardy (not the same one, as Mrs. Rooney makes clear) really had written a book called *How to Be Happy Though Married* (London: T. Fisher Unwin, 1885) and *Still Happy Though Married* (London: T. Fisher Unwin, 1914). See R. E. R. Madelaine, "Happy-Though-Married Hardy," *Notes and Queries*, new series, vol. 29, no. 4 (Aug. 1982), pp. 348–9.

50. SB, *All That Fall* in *Collected Shorter Plays*. pp. 12–36.

51. Even when he was a very old man, Beckett used to say good-bye to his friends using as his parting words the common Irish farewell "God bless," although he was an unbeliever.

52. SB, *All That Fall* in *Collected Shorter Plays*, pp. 32, 34.

53. E.g., Charles Wesley's "Swift to our heavenly country move / Our everlasting home above" and "To the haven of Thy breast / O Son of Man, I fly."

54. SB, *All That Fall* in *Collected Shorter Plays*, pp. 14, 15.

55. When another, more fervent churchgoer, Miss Fitt, evokes Christ's role as a guide and comforter to mankind by humming the tune of Cardinal Newman's well-known hymn "Lead, Kindly Light," Mrs. Rooney joins in with the words, inquiring with feigned innocence (and an irony reminiscent of Voltaire at his most bitter), whether it was this hymn or "Rock of Ages" (sung so movingly by Bessie in Sean O'Casey's *The Plough and the Stars*) that had been sung by the drowning passengers aboard the sinking *Lusitania* or *Titanic*.

56. Richard N. Coe, "God and Samuel Beckett," *Meanjin Quarterly*, vol. 24, no. 1 (1965), p. 71.

57. SB to BR, 23 Aug. 1956 (Syracuse).

58. SB to BR, 30 Aug. (1956) (Syracuse).

59. SB to John Morris, 27 Sept. 1956 (BBC).

60. Donald McWhinnie, internal memo, 21 Feb. 1957 (BBC).

61. SB to AS, 15 Oct. 1956 (Boston).

62. SB to BR, 17 Dec. 1957 (Syracuse).

63. SB to Jacoba van Velde, 27 Dec. 1956 (Bibliothèque Nationale).

64. The original manuscript draft has been preserved as ms. 1396/4/6 in the Beckett Archive (Reading).

65. "The Gloaming," ms. 1396/4/6 (Reading).

66. SB, *Rough for Theatre I* in *Collected Shorter Plays*, p. 68. See note 67.

67. Two later versions of "The Gloaming" in French and English were written in the 1970s. The English version was published only much later in *Ends and Odds*, under the title of *Theatre I*. This play fragment is sometimes called *Rough for Theatre I*.

68. "The Gloaming," ms. 1396/4/6 (Reading).

69. Interview with SB, 9 July 1989.

70. SB to Jacoba van Velde, 27 Dec. 1956 (Bibliothèque Nationale).

71. Ibid.

72. BR to SB, 14 Jan. 1957 (Syracuse).

73. SB to Jacoba van Velde, 27 Dec. 1956 (Bibliothèque Nationale).

74. Beckett was told of this closure in a letter from Judith Schmidt of Grove Press, January 30, 1957 (Syracuse).

75. SB to Donald McWhinnie, 14 Jan. 1957 (dated by Beckett in error 14 Dec. 1956 but stamped by the BBC 17 Jan. 1957) (BBC). The explanation for the final remark is that Beckett disapproved of having the animal noises that Mrs. Rooney hears made by a human impersonator. He expressed his perplexity before the recording and was never happy with the sounds that were recorded afterward (SB to Donald McWhinnie, 18 Dec. 1956 [BBC], and Donald McWhinnie to SB, 1 Jan. 1957 [BBC], offering his explanation).

76. Laurence Gilliam, head of features, to SB, 15 July 1957 (BBC).

77. Peskine, Lynda Bellity, ed., *Roger Blin: Souvenirs et propos*, p. 111.

78. SB to TM, 30 Jan. 1957 (TCD).

79. Ibid.

80. SB to Elmar Tophoven, 23 Feb. 1957 (Tophoven), and SB to Aidan Higgins, 4 March 1957 (Texas).

81. SB, telegram to Roger Blin, 28 Feb. 1957 (IMEC, Paris).

82. Peskine, Lynda Bellity, ed., *Roger Blin: Souvenirs et propos*, p. 119 (my translation).

83. Ibid., pp. 121–22.

84. Interview with Jean Martin, 17 Sept. 1990.

85. The playwright John Osborne had a running joke with George Devine about the latter's Francophile bias and used to tease him about his "French Fortnights" (John Osborne to JK, 23 Oct. 1991).

86. The cuts included a whole page and a half toward the end of the play when Clov talks of seeing the advancing figure of a child through his telescope.

87. SB to TM, 23 March 1957 (TCD).

88. SB, telegram to TM, 29 March 1957 (TCD).

89. SB to TM, 5 April 1957 (TCD).

90. Interview with Jean Martin, 17 Sept. 1990.

91. Ibid.

92. John Osborne to JK, 23 Oct. 1991.

93. SB to MM, 28 April 1957 (Texas).

94. Interview with Jean Martin, 17 Sept. 1990. At least one journalist, Edward Goring of the *Daily Mail*, tracked down Beckett in the Royal Court Hotel and tried but failed to get an interview with him.

95. Bair, *Samuel Beckett*, p. 484, except that Beckett did not leave "several days before the opening."

96. Beckett signed the contracts and returned them to Jérôme Lindon on April 19 (SB to JL, 19 April 1957 [Minuit]).

97. Jérôme Lindon, anxious to find a Parisian home for the play as soon as possible, especially since it was already being performed in London, had resumed negotiations with the Théâtre de l'Oeuvre. He was able to write to Beckett at the Royal Court Theatre with some fresh proposals from Beer (JL to SB, 22 Mar. 1957 [Minuit]. He also wrote on the same day with the same news to Deryk Mendel). Beckett briefly believed that it was likely that they would be returning to Paris to play at the Oeuvre (SB to HH, 24 March 1957 [dated 14 March in error] [Hayden]). But Roger Blin, cross at how they had been treated by Beer and learning almost certainly too late of these renewed overtures, wrote a mocking letter to Beer.

98. Lynda Bellity Peskine, ed., *Roger Blin: Souvenirs et propos*, p. 119.

99. JL to M. Mauge, in the Service Juridique of the Société des Auteurs Dramatiques, 16 May 1957 (Minuit).

100. SB to MM, 28 April 1957 (Texas).

101. SB to AJL, 28 April 1957 (Texas).

102. SB to MH, 30 June 1957 (Texas).

103. Jacques Putman pressed him for a translation of his 1949 piece on Bram van Velde, who was preparing an important exhibition at the Galerie Michel Warren which ran from May 7 until June 1, 1957. In January, he met the writer Robert Pinget on a number of occasions to revise his French translation of *All That Fall* and went over the German translation of *Fin de partie* with his German translator, Elmar Tophoven. Later in the spring, he vetted the German *Malone meurt* and translations of his poems into German. Then, in late June, he checked the Italian translation of *Molloy* which he found "excellent on the whole, but with a good few mistakes" (SB to TM, 3 July 1957 [TCD]).

104. SB to TM, 30 Jan. 1957 (TCD).

105. "I have had to undertake to produce an English version of *Fin de partie* for Devine within six months. That seems to me impossible too, but it was the only way of clinching the deal" (SB to Aidan Higgins, 4 March 1957 [Texas]).

106. Peter du Sautoy to JL, 28 Feb. 1957 (Minuit).

107. SB to TM, 3 July 1957 (TCD).

108. SB to BR, 18 May 1957 (Syracuse).

109. SB to MH, 13 June 1957 (Texas).

110. "I shall probably have to have an operation on my upper jaw where a cyst is looped somewhere above the palate. Minor, but ticklish I imagine, and an infernal nuisance. My mouth is in a sorry state, in spite of unending dental attention. Have 'em all out will soon I'm afraid be the only solution" (SB to TM, 30 Jan. 1957 [TCD]).

111. SB to Ethna MacCarthy, 13 June 1957 (Texas).

112. SB to Ethna MacCarthy, 22 Nov. 1957 (Texas).

113. SB to TM, 25 Oct. 1957 (TCD).

114. SB to MH, undated (late Sept.) 1957 (Texas).

115. SB to HH, 24 Sept. 1957 (Hayden).

116. Schneider, *Entrances*, p. 249. The book in question is Henri Rinck's *150 Endspielstudien* (Leipzig: Viet and Co., 1909). The copy remaining in Beckett's library after his death is inscribed by Alan (Schneider), 1958.

117. Schneider, *Entrances*, p. 250.

118. SB to BR, 21 Nov. 1957 (Syracuse).

119. Ibid.

120. SB to TM, 27 Nov. 1957 (TCD).

121. SB to HH, 17 Sept. 1957 (Hayden).

122. "What I find more and more difficult to cope with is Paris, and people, and speech. I can't do it without drink, and alone I am quite content with a few glasses of wine at dinner" (SB to TM, 27 Nov. 1957 [TCD]).

123. Arland Ussher to SB, 28 Feb. 1957 (TCD).

124. SB to Arland Ussher, 14 April 1957 (TCD).

125. SB to Ethna MacCarthy, 22 Nov. 1957 (Texas).

126. SB to MH, 22 Nov. 1957 (Texas).

127. SB to AJL, 11 Dec. 1957 (Texas).

128. SB to Ethna MacCarthy, 14 Aug. 1958 (Texas).

129. SB to Ethna MacCarthy, 27 Sept. 1958 (Texas).

130. Interview with Avigdor Arikha, 23 Feb. 1994.

131. James Knowlson, ed., *Samuel Beckett: Krapp's Last Tape*, Theatre Workbook 1, (London: Brutus Books Ltd., 1980), p. 130.

132. SB, *Krapp's Last Tape* in *Collected Shorter Plays*, p. 62.

133. Ibid., p. 60.

134. Ibid., p. 58.

135. Ibid., p. 62.

136. Interview with SB, 13 Sept. 1989.

137. Bair, *Samuel Beckett*, p. 87.

138. Interview with SB, 17 Nov. 1989.

139. SB to Ethna MacCarthy, 2 June 1958 (Texas).

140. SB to Donald McWhinnie, 23 Dec. 1957 (McWhinnie). Beckett had written to George Devine on December 14, 1957, objecting to his proposal (Herbert).

141. Bair claims that Beckett had been over in London for the recording of *All That Fall* the previous year when he had met Patrick Magee (*Samuel Beckett*, p. 489). But according to Barbara Bray and Michael Bakewell, although he had intended to come, he had been either unable or unwilling to travel (interviews with Barbara Bray, July 1991, and with Michael Bakewell, 21 Mar. 1994). It is also clear from letters to Donald McWhinnie that Beckett had still not yet met Magee in April 1958 (SB to Donald McWhinnie, 27 April 1958 [McWhinnie]).

142. SB to MH, 21 Dec. 1957 (Texas).

143. The first draft is in a notebook entitled "Eté 56." The manuscript is dated 20.2.58. Ms.1227/7/7/1 (Reading).

144. "I heard the tapes with the keenest enjoyment and appreciation. Magee's performance is unforgettable. I hope it may be possible for me to acquire them, or have copies made, for my personal use" (SB to Donald McWhinnie, 28 Jan. 1958 [McWhinnie]).

145. SB to Susan Manning, 21 May 1955 (Texas).

146. SB, *Krapp's Last Tape* in *Collected Shorter Plays*, p. 62.

147. Ibid., p. 57.

148. SB to BR, 1 April 1958 (Syracuse). A few days later he also wrote to Rosset: "I feel — to a disturbing degree — the strangest of solicitudes for this little work" (SB to BR, 10 April 1958 [Syracuse]).

149. SB to Jacoba van Velde, 12 April 1958 (Bibliothèque Nationale).

150. Ibid.

18: CENSORSHIP AND *How It Is*, 1958–60

1. Beckett was working on this radio play in the middle of December 1957 (SB to Jacoba van Velde, 18 Dec. 1957 [Bibliothèque Nationale]). In mid-February, he wrote to McWhinnie that when he had finished translating *L'Innommable*, he would "return to the radio text and see if there is anything to be saved from that wreck" (SB to Donald McWhinnie, 15 Feb. 1958 [Reading]).

2. He dispatched the script in February to the BBC drama department under the provisional title of "Ebb"; then, a few weeks later, he changed the title to the one under which it was broadcast and published, *Embers* (BBC).

3. SB to MM, 23 Jan. 1959, and to Ethna MacCarthy, 4 Feb. 1959 (Texas).

4. It has been widely reported that *Embers* won the Prix Italia but, as Clas Zilliacus has

pointed out, it did not (Clas Zilliacus, *Beckett and Broadcasting*, Åbo Akademi, [Åbo: 1976], p. 97). The RAI (Radiotelevisione Italiana) prize represented half the monetary value of the actual Prix Italia, which was awarded in 1959 to the play *Beach of Strangers* by the Canadian John Reeves.

5. SB, letters to BR, 10 April (Syracuse); Jacoba van Velde, 12 April (Bibliothèque Nationale); TM, 21 April 1958 (TCD); and Ethna MacCarthy, 2 June 1958 (Texas).

6. SB to Jacoba van Velde, 12 April 1958 (Bibliothèque Nationale).

7. SB to BR, 27 Jan. 1958 (Syracuse).

8. SB to BR, 23 Feb. 1958 (Syracuse).

9. SB to TM, 2 June 1958 (TCD).

10. SB to Donald McWhinnie, 27 April 1958 (Reading).

11. SB to BR, 27 Jan. 1958 (Syracuse).

12. BR to SB, 11 Dec. 1957 and SB to BR, 17 Dec. 1957 (Syracuse).

13. SB to BR, 20 and 27 Jan. 1958 (Syracuse).

14. SB to Alan Simpson, 15 Jan. 1958 (Swift).

15. SB to Alan Simpson, 17 Feb. 1958 (Swift).

16. Carolyn Swift to SB, 22 Feb. 1958 (Swift).

17. SB to Carolyn Swift, 27 Feb. 1958 (Swift).

18. SB, *Endgame*, p. 38.

19. In a letter to Rosset dated January 20, 1958, Beckett wrote: "I had lunch a week ago with Devine and confirmed to him that I could not allow the prayer passage to be either suppressed or mutilated by the Lord Chamberlain. He was very understanding and did not press me. He went back to London very warlike. He may present the play at the Arts" (Syracuse).

20. SB to George Devine, 26 Dec. 1957 (Texas) quoted in Lake, *No Symbols Where None Intended*, p. 98.

21. There is a lot of correspondence in the BBC files about this possibility in the light of the Lord Chamberlain's attitude in the theater. E.g., SB to Donald McWhinnie, 13 Jan. 1958; report by R. D'A Marriott, 29 Jan. 1958; Donald McWhinnie to SB, 1 April 1958 (BBC).

22. Irving Wardle, *The Theatres of George Devine* (London: Jonathan Cape, 1978), p. 205.

23. There had been a few complaints earlier about the sex slang. "The Lord Chamberlain suggested Beckett substitute '*bêtises*' for '*conneries*.' Beckett countered with '*âneries*.' The Lord Chamberlain agreed." Lake, *No Symbols Where None Intended*, p. 98.

24. "Censor's Whim," *The Evening Standard*, 11 Feb. 1958, p. 4.

25. Cecil Wilson, "The Play London Saw in French Is Banned in English," *Daily Mail*, 10 Feb. 1958.

26. SB to Aidan Higgins, 7 Aug. 1958 (Texas).

27. SB to BR, 29 July 1958 (Syracuse).

28. SB to George Devine, 28 July 1958 (Texas), quoted in Lake, *No Symbols Where None Intended*, p. 99.

29. SB to BR, 18 Aug. 1958 (Syracuse).

30. SB to Ethna MacCarthy, 14 Aug. 1958 (Texas).

31. Donald McWhinnie, conversation with JK, April 1972.

32. SB, undated conversation with JK, ca. 1982.

33. SB to TM, 2 June 1958 (TCD).

34. SB to Ethna MacCarthy, 2 June 1958 (Texas).

35. SB to TM, 2 June 1958 (Texas).

36. Ibid.

37. Ibid.

38. SB to Ethna MacCarthy, 2 June 1958 (Texas).

39. SB to TM, 18 Feb. 1958 (TCD). The "Rain Lieder" is probably Brahms's song

"Regenlied"; the "Waldeinsamkeit" ("Sylvan Solitude") is probably Brahms's "Feldein-samkeit," Opus 86, No. 2; and the "Sapphische Ode" is Opus 94, No. 4. I am grateful to Professor John Pilling for help with musical identifications.

40. SB to TM, 19 Oct. 1958 (TCD).

41. SB to AA, undated (6 May 1958) (Arikha).

42. SB to MH, 9 April 1958 (Texas), and to Jacoba van Velde, 12 April 1958 (Biblio-thèque Nationale). Cf. one of his earliest stories, "Dante and the Lobster," in *More Pricks Than Kicks*, p. 9.

43. Dante Alighieri, *Hell, Purgatory, and Paradise*, Canto IV, trans. by H. F. Cary, London, 1869, p. 79.

44. SB, *How It Is* (London: John Calder Ltd., 1964), p. 26. The last phrase is a direct allusion to Belacqua's need for prayers to counter his delayed repentance: "Because I, to the end, repentant sighs / Delay'd; if prayer do not aid me first, / That riseth up from heart which lives in grace." Dante, *Purgatory*, Canto IV, H. F. Cary trans., p. 79.

45. SB to MM, 13 Aug. 1958 (Texas).

46. SB to BR, 5 March 1958 (Syracuse).

47. Ibid.

48. SB to Donald McWhinnie, 5 July 1958 (Reading), and to BR, 3 July and 29 July 1958 (Syracuse).

49. SB to Jacoba van Velde, 15 July 1958 (Bibliothèque Nationale).

50. Ibid. and interview with Jean Martin, September 1990.

51. Interview with Jean Martin, September 1989.

52. SB to Ethna MacCarthy, 14 Aug. 1958 (Texas).

53. SB to BR, 29 July 1958 (Syracuse).

54. SB to Ethna MacCarthy, 14 Aug. 1958 (Texas).

55. Ibid. and postcard to HH, 17 July 1958 (Hayden).

56. SB to BR, 29 July 1958 (Syracuse), and to HH, 30 July 1958 (Hayden).

57. SB to BR, 18 Aug. 1958 (Syracuse).

58. SB to HH, 23 Sept. 1958 (Hayden).

59. SB to BR, 21 Aug. 1958 (Syracuse).

60. SB to Ethna MacCarthy, 27 Sept. 1958 (Texas). The original manuscript with the date "Ussy 15.8.58" is in Trinity College, Dublin (ms. 4661).

61. SB to TM, 19 Oct. 1958 (TCD).

62. "Messenger of Gloom," The Observer Profile, *The Observer*, 9 Nov. 1958.

63. Wardle says that Beckett was there for two weeks' rehearsal (*The Theatres of George Devine*, p. 206) and Bair suggests a fairly lengthy period of rehearsal (*Samuel Beckett*, pp. 499–500). But he did not leave Paris until October 21 and the first night was on October 28.

64. Wardle, *The Theatres of George Devine*, p. 206.

65. John Osborne to JK, 23 Oct. 1991.

66. Interview with Jocelyn Herbert, 3 July 1992.

67. SB to MM, 21 Nov. 1958 (Texas).

68. Philip Hope-Wallace, "Subtler 'Endgame,'" *Manchester Guardian*, 30 Oct. 1958.

69. Anthony Cookman, "When Boredom Is Fun," *The Tatler and Bystander*, 12 Nov. 1958.

70. Harold Hobson, *The Sunday Times* (London), 9 Nov. 1958.

71. SB to MM, 21 Nov. 1958 (Texas).

72. *The Times* (London), 29 Oct. 1958.

73. SB, *Endgame*, p. 25. Beckett uses the word in a letter to Ethna MacCarthy, 18 Nov. 1958 (Texas).

74. SB to Ethna MacCarthy, 18 Nov. 1958 (Texas).

75. SB to MM, 21 Nov. 1958 (Texas).

76. Ibid. His visit was announced in a letter from Beckett to Ethna MacCarthy, 18 Nov. 1958 (Texas). Many letters to friends refer to the great sadness he felt.

77. SB to MM, 2 Jan. 1959 (Texas). In fact, as his German diaries show, he misremembered here, since he had found Klopstock's tomb.

78. Interview with Edward Beckett, 31 March 1994.

79. SB to Aidan Higgins, 24 March 1959 (Texas).

80. SB to MM, 2 Jan. 1959 (Texas).

81. Ibid.

82. SB to Ethna MacCarthy, 10 Jan. 1959 (Texas).

83. SB to Ethna MacCarthy, 4 Feb. 1959 (Texas).

84. SB to BR, 17 May 1959 (Syracuse).

85. SB to Aidan Higgins, 24 March 1959 (Texas).

86. SB to Ethna MacCarthy, 22 April 1959 (Texas).

87. 'Pim' was started in a soft exercise book of forty-eight sheets of graph paper on December 17, 1958, at Ussy.

88. SB to AJL, 3 Feb. 1959 (Texas).

89. SB to Donald McWhinnie, 6 April 1960 (Reading).

90. SB, How It Is, pp. 16–17.

91. LH, interview with SB, 2 Feb. 1962 (Dartmouth).

92. SB, How It Is, p. 85.

93. Ibid.

94. SB to TM, 10 April 1959 (TCD).

95. SB, How It Is, p. 13.

96. SB to AJL, 10 Jan. 1959 (Texas).

97. SB to Ethna MacCarthy, 24 March 1959 (Texas).

98. SB to AJL, 27 May 1959 (Texas).

99. Ethna was not the only old friend to die in May. Joe Hone, the Swift biographer and Beckett's old cricketing companion, also died that same month in Ireland. Arland Ussher sent the obituary that he had written for The Irish Times. Although Beckett had lost touch with Hone many years before, "ça me fait quelque chose" ("it does something to me") and "there was something lovable about him and I was very sorry," he wrote to MacGreevy (SB to TM, 10 April and 17 May 1959 [TCD]). Some months later, he learned from a young Irishman called O'Grady, who had been working in Rome, that his good friend from the 1930s, Denis Devlin, the poet and Irish ambassador there, had died; "it really knocked me all of a heap. . . . [I] had much fondness for him," he said (SB to TM, 21 Sept. 1959 [TCD]).

100. SB to TM, 17 May 1959 (TCD).

101. SB to AJL, 26 May 1959 (Texas).

102. SB to TM, 17 May 1959 (TCD).

103. SB to Ethna MacCarthy, 22 April 1959 (Texas).

104. SB to TM, 19 July 1959 (TCD).

105. SB to Ethna MacCarthy, 22 April 1959 (Texas).

106. SB to AJL, 3 Feb. 1959 (Texas).

107. SB to AJL, 2 April 1959 (Texas).

108. Ibid.

109. SB to AJL, 26 May 1959 (Texas).

110. Alan Simpson to SB, 19 March 1959 (Swift).

111. SB to Alan Simpson, 24 March 1959 (Swift).

112. SB to AJL, 2 April 1959 (Texas); also letter to BR, 8 April 1959 (Syracuse).

113. Spencer Curtis Brown to SB, 25 March 1959 (Curtis Brown).

114. "Cusack's KRAPP was very disappointing, no feeling for the thing or the wrong feeling, under-acted out of existence, recording inaudible, synchronisation unspeakable, direction execrable when there was any. All the more disappointing as he is a remarkable

actor with great presence and properly handled could have been excellent" (SB to AS, 4 Aug. 1960 [Boston]).

115. SB to Alan Simpson, 24 Mar. 1959 (Swift), to AJL, 2 April 1959 (Texas), and to TM, 10 April 1959 (TCD).

116. SB to BR, 20 March 1959, and to Judith Schmidt, 5 Jan. 1960, reserving the U.S. and Canadian performance rights for Mihalovici (Syracuse).

117. Marcel Mihalovici, "My Collaboration with Samuel Beckett," in *Beckett at Sixty*, pp. 20–21.

118. "Mihalovici has finished his opera" (SB to JS, 20 July 1960 [Douw]; also SB to AS, 4 Aug. 1960 [Boston]).

119. Mihalovici's original notebook with his French version and music written in blue ink, Tophoven's German in pencil, and Beckett's English text in red ink is in the Beckett Archive at Reading University, ms. 1227/7/10/2 (Reading).

120. Marcel Mihalovici, "My Collaboration with Samuel Beckett," *in Beckett at Sixty*, p. 21.

121. JK, undated conversation with Samuel Beckett.

122. SB to TM, 10 April 1959 (TCD); also Beckett to BR, 20 March 1959 (Syracuse).

123. SB to AA, 25 Feb. 1959 (Arikha).

124. SB to BR, 20 March 1959 (Syracuse).

125. He especially admired *Les Deux Bourreaux (The Two Executioners)* and *Le Cimetière des Voitures (The Vehicle Graveyard)* (SB to BR, 20 March 1959 [Syracuse]).

126. SB to BR, 20 March 1959 (Syracuse).

127. SB to GR, 20 Nov. 1959 (Texas).

128. SB to BR, 5 May 1959 (Syracuse), and SB to TM, 17 May 1959 (TCD). He also read David Greene's and Edward Stephens's *J. M. Synge 1871–1909* (New York: MacMillan, 1959), which he considered "very dull and cautious" (SB to TM, 19 July 1959 [TCD]). He found Aldous Huxley's book on mescaline impossible to read, since he always thought Huxley "so unremittingly smart. 'The divine Not-Self of Flannel Bags!!' " (SB to TM, 19 July 1959 [TCD]).

129. "Very disappointed by French KRAPP. Slovenly production (ten days rehearsal, final tape three days before couturière [dress rehearsal]) and very unsatisfactory performance by Chauffard, simply unfitted, vocally and every other way, for the part" (SB to Donald McWhinnie, 6 April 1960 [Reading]). He says the same in a letter to AJL, 8 May 1960 (Texas).

130. SB to MM, 21 July 1959 (Texas).

131. In an interview on August 3, 1992, Caroline (Beckett) Murphy contradicted almost all the details of the birthday party and Suzanne's arrival that were given in Bair's account (*Samuel Beckett*, p. 510) of the occasion: the statement that Beckett was staying at the Shottery, the number of guests given, and the statement that Suzanne and a friend arrived unannounced in the middle of the party. That friend, Marthe Gautier, and Edward Beckett also confirmed these as errors (interviews with Edward Beckett, 31 March 1994, and with Marthe Gautier, 8 June 1994).

132. Interview with Edward Beckett, 31 March 1994.

133. SB to MM, 21 July 1959 (Texas).

134. Interview with Sheila Page, 20 April 1990.

135. SB to SP, 25 July 1959 (Page).

136. SB to MM, 21 July 1959 (Texas).

137. "Jack in the big money now, musicals etc." (SB to MM, 21 July 1959 [Texas]).

138. Interview with Pauline McWhinnie, 28 Nov. 1991.

139. SB to SP, 29 Sept. 1959 (Page).

140. Only the additional presence of two pleasant Irish visitors—Robert Farren, the controller of programs at Radio Éireann, and his wife—made an occasion in which he had to meet so many unknown people at all bearable. On his return to Ireland, Farren

proposed staging the radio play *Embers* at the Abbey Theatre in Dublin (Robert Farren to SB, 4 Jan. 1960). Beckett declined the offer.

141. SB to AJL, 28 Oct. 1959 (Texas).

142. SB to MH, 21 Sept. 1959 (Texas).

143. SB to Ethna MacCarthy, 4 Feb. 1959 (Texas), where he writes of getting up in the dark at six A.M. to go into town to have lunch with Harold Hobson.

144. SB to AJL, 28 Oct. 1959 (Texas).

145. SB to MM, 22 Dec. 1959 (Texas).

146. SB to SP, 13 Nov. 1959 (Page).

147. SB to JS, 26 Oct. 1960 (Douw).

148. SB to MM, 22 Dec. 1959 (Texas).

149. Interview with SB, Oct. 1989.

150. On her walls were a Jankel Adler from 1938, paintings by her friend Manolo Fandos, and some small van Veldes, to which in the late 1970s were added a couple of Henri Haydens (a predominantly red still life and an orange landscape of the valley of the Marne) and several unidentified drawings, one by Roger Blin.

19: Secret Wedding and *Happy Days*, 1960–63

1. SB, notebook, "Eté 1956," ms. 1227/7/7/1 (Reading).

2. SB, *The Unnamable*, in *Molloy Malone Dies The Unnamable*, p. 295.

3. Enoch Brater, *Why Beckett*, p. 100, where a photograph is reproduced of the two figures buried in the earth in *Un Chien andalou*.

4. SB to JS, 18 Jan. 1961 (Syracuse).

5. SB to TM, 7 Feb. 1960 (TCD). He could have added the white rotunda of the nearby Observatoire, the tall, dark gray — almost black — spire of the church of the nuns of the order of St. Joseph de Cluny, and, misleadingly tiny in the far distance, the domes of the Sacré-Coeur. Beckett became very upset later on when a large building was constructed that blocked his view of the Panthéon.

6. SB to TM, 22 Sept. 1960 (TCD).

7. SB to JS, 7 Jan. 1961: "Sleeping here now — or trying to" (Syracuse).

8. SB to JS, 12 Feb. 1961 (Syracuse).

9. SB to JS, 14 Feb. 1961 (Syracuse).

10. Dr. Hans Joachim Schaefer, "Memories of a Meeting with Beckett and His Wife," document to Dr. Gottfried Büttner, 16 Nov. 1989. Beckett's words were also printed in *Spectaculum*, vol. 6, 1963, p. 319. I am most grateful to Dr. Büttner for sending me this information.

11. SB to TM, 10 Mar. 1961 (TCD). Beckett did all he could to help Mihalovici — for example, sending the score of the opera to Goddard Lieberson, the president of Columbia Records, whom he knew personally (SB to JS, 9 Mar. 1961 [Douw]).

12. Interview with Marthe Gautier, 8 June 1994.

13. Dr. Hans Joachim Schaefer, "Memories of a Meeting with Beckett and His Wife," document to Dr. Gottfried Büttner, 16 Nov. 1989.

14. The "Seventh Suhrkamp Publishing House Evening" ("Hommage à Samuel Beckett in Anwesenheit des Autors" ["Homage to Samuel Beckett in the Presence of the Author"]) was held at the Cantate-Saal in Frankfurt on February 27, 1961, at eight P.M. It was reviewed in the *Frankfurter Allgemeine Zeitung*, March 1, 1961.

15. Everything, Adorno claimed, is reduced in the play to the tag ends or detritus of existence — talk, names, reactions, feelings, even language: "This loss of meaning, it must be understood, undermines the dramatic form down to the innermost structure of its language." (Theodor W. Adorno, "Towards an Understanding of *Endgame*," in Bell Gale Chevigny, *Twentieth Century Interpretations of Endgame*, p. 83; the essay was originally printed in *Noten zur Literatur II* [Frankfurt am Main: Suhrkamp, 1961]).

Theodor Adorno presented Beckett with a dedication copy of his talk on *Endgame*, dated February 27, 1961, which Beckett then gave to Avigdor Arikha (AA, fax to JK, 20 May 1994).

16. Interview with Erika Tophoven, 25 Jan. 1990, and report in the *Frankfurter Allgemeine Zeitung*, 1 March 1961.

17. Siegfried Unseld, in an address to the Second International Beckett Symposium in The Hague, 8 April 1992. Adorno preserved the link with Hamlet in the published version of his essay on *Endgame*.

18. Interview with Marthe Gautier, 8 June 1994, and telephone interview with Matias, 13 June 1994.

19. Interview with Erika Tophoven, 25 Jan. 1990.

20. By now, for example, three productions of *Krapp's Last Tape* were running concurrently in New York, Los Angeles, and San Fancisco, bringing him in about five hundred dollars a month from that one play alone. A revival of *En attendant Godot*, which had been bringing in money regularly for eight years, was scheduled for the Théâtre de l'Odéon in Paris at the beginning of May.

21. "Barbara has been and just gone. She will be coming to live in Paris with her daughters this year" (SB to AJL, 21 Jan. 1961 [Texas]).

22. Barbara Bray, "The New Beckett," *The Observer*, 16 June 1963.

23. Telephone interview with John Calder, 20 May 1994.

24. The Silver City Airline inaugurated this route in 1948, although the first commercial flights only began in July 1954. It was a route that John Calder had already used several times and that Beckett was to take on several later occasions when he wished to bring his car over to England. The Bristol Superfreighters with their Hercules engines carried three cars and up to fourteen passengers across the Channel in only twenty minutes; in 1961, it cost three pounds for a small car out of season and three pounds for an adult passenger.

25. My information about Beckett's stay in Folkestone comes from his correspondence with friends and from my own stay there in May 1994. My thanks are extended to Christine Labrosciano in the town's information office, to Keith Rosenz for information on hotels, and to Pauline Davey and Robert Paine in the local archives of the Folkestone Library for their invaluable help.

26. SB to TM, 10 March 1961 (TCD).

27. SB to AA, 9 March 1961. (William Harvey was born in Folkestone on April 1, 1578, and his statue stands looking out to sea up the road from where Beckett's hotel used to be.) Beckett used the same "S" signature on a postcard to AJL (23 March 1961). In a letter also to AJL (February 9), Beckett had spoken of perhaps dealing with "nuptials early March" (Texas).

28. SB to JS, 3 March (error for April) 1961 (Douw). He undoubtedly also saw (although he does not mention this in his letters to friends) Lamb House in West Street, where Henry James lived from 1898 until his death and wrote *The Wings of the Dove*, *The Ambassadors*, and *The Golden Bowl*.

29. SB to AJL, 27 March 1961 (Texas).

30. See Bair (who was able to talk to Henry Wenning), *Samuel Beckett*, pp. 534–35.

31. SB to JS, 3 March (error for April) 1961 (Douw).

32. These manuscripts and typescripts are preserved in the Ohio State University Library at Columbus, Ohio.

33. He may even have driven through Ash on his return journey from Canterbury to the coast, since it lies on the A257 going east to Sandwich.

34. SB to TM, 27 March 1961 (TCD).

35. SB to Herbert Myron, 9 March 1961 (Boston Univ.).

36. SB to BR, 17 March 1961 (Syracuse).

37. SB to HH, 17 March 1961 (Hayden).

38. Exactly how Beckett heard this news is unclear. It certainly could not have been as

a result of "a telegram from Gerald Beckett," as Bair claims (*Samuel Beckett*, p. 531) since Beckett's uncle had been dead for eleven years. According to Ann Beckett, John's sister, he probably heard from his aunt Peggy or from Vera, John's future wife — but via Suzanne in Paris, as the family was unaware that he was in Folkestone.

39. Telephone interviews with John Beckett and Ann Beckett, 19 May 1994, and SB to HH, 14 March and 17 March 1961 (Hayden).

40. SB to HH, 17 March 1961 (Hayden).

41. Marriage certificate supplied by Folkestone Registration Office for Births, Deaths and Marriages, May 1994. I am grateful to the staff in Folkestone for their help and advice.

42. SB to AJL, 27 March 1961 (Texas).

43. Telephone interview with John Calder, 20 May 1994.

44. Dr. Albert Bessler from the Schiller-Theater was eager to include the play in the Berlin Festival at the end of September, so Elmar and Erika Tophoven needed it to start translating it as soon as possible; Jacoba van Velde wanted it for translation into Dutch; and Beckett had suggested to Schneider and Rosset that they would have it in June "*at latest* for better or worse" (SB to JS, 14 March 1961 [Douw]).

45. SB to Leslie Daiken, 27 May 1961 (Daiken).

46. SB to JS, 17 April 1961 (Douw).

47. SB to Mania Péron, 6 July 1961 (Péron).

48. My account of these problems is based on a telephone interview with Jean Martin, 27 May 1994, and an interview with Etienne Bierry, 9 June 1994.

49. Jean Genet's *The Blacks*, translated by Bernard Frechtman and directed by Roger Blin, who spoke no English, opened at the Royal Court Theatre in London on May 30, 1961.

50. Beckett and Giacometti stood for hours on either side of the tree contemplating how the plaster leaves that Giacometti had also sculpted could best be fixed on for the beginning of the second act. After the production, Giacometti is said to have presented one of the leaves to Beckett (telephone interview with Jean Martin, 27 May 1994, and interview with Etienne Bierry, 9 June 1994). "Giacometti did a fine tree for Godot," wrote Beckett. "But at the Générale [he] left at the interval because he couldn't bear it any longer! His tree, he said, perhaps he meant something else" (SB to AJL, 18 May 1961 [Texas]). Both tree and leaf have disappeared.

51. SB to JS, 3 March (error for April) 1961 (Douw).

52. SB to JS, 2 May 1961 (Douw).

53. SB to AJL, 18 May 1961 (Texas).

54. SB to Henry Wenning, 18 May 1961 (St. Louis), and to JS, 18 May 1961 (Syracuse).

55. He paid the airfares and hotel expenses, for example, of Leslie and Lilian Daiken to enable them to come to Paris (SB to Leslie Daiken, 2 May and 10 May 1961 [Daiken]), offered Con Leventhal a year's subscription to the literary review *Arts* (SB to AJL, 13 Jan. 1961 [Texas]), and gave occasional gifts of money to, among others, his Dutch translator, Jacoba van Velde, and the English poet Nick Rawson.

56. The second act was rewritten in two days on May 13 and 14.

57. "When Irish eyes are smiling" was added by hand to the first typescript of Act II (Ohio).

58. SB to Kay Boyle, 7 Oct. 1961 (Texas).

59. SB to Henry Wenning, 2 June 1961 (St. Louis) and to Jacoba van Velde, 2 June 1961 (Bibliothèque Nationale).

60. Beckett's letters to AS (17 Aug., 25 Aug., and 3 Sept. 1961) give his answers to Schneider's questions, much information on how he sees his play, and the sources of Winnie's quotations. They are invaluable and are being published by Boston College, edited by Maurice Harmon.

61. SB to John Calder, 31 July 1961 (Bloomington), and to MH, 3 Aug. 1961 (Texas).

62. SB to SP, 20 Oct. 1961 (Page).

63. SB to TM, 17 July 1961 (TCD). *Luther* opened at the Theatre Royal in Nottingham on June 26, 1961.

64. Interview with John Calder, 7 July 1990.

65. Interview with Peter Woodthorpe, 18 Feb. 1994.

66. See Bair, *Samuel Beckett*, pp. 537–38; however, Hobson's piece, under the pseudonym Atticus, was published in the *Sunday Times* and not the London *Times*. "Oh My Hobson and My Beckett," *Sunday Times* (London), 2 July 1961, p. 13.

67. SB to SP, 8 July 1961 (Page).

68. SB to TM, 17 July 1961 (TCD) and to SP, 8 July 1961 (Page).

69. Interview with Edward Beckett, 31 March 1994.

70. Ibid.

71. As part of the initial testing process, each candidate had to have a lesson with the professor of his instrument. So Beckett accompanied Edward to the Conservatoire for a flute lesson with Professor Crunelle, whom Beckett characteristically nicknamed Crusty Crunelle (interview with Edward Beckett, 31 Mar. 1994).

72. SB to SP, 20 Oct. 1961 (Page).

73. Peter Lennon. *Foreign Correspondent. Paris in the Sixties* (London: Picador, 1994), p. 70.

74. Ibid., p. 74.

75. AA, fax to JK, 8 April 1994.

76. SB to TM, 31 March 1962 (TCD).

77. SB to AJL, 4 April 1962 (Texas).

78. Interview with Sheila Harvey, 13 March 1990.

79. All of these quotations are taken from Lawrence Harvey's notes on his discussions with Beckett in the Harvey papers at Dartmouth College.

80. Interview with Sheila Harvey, 13 March 1990.

81. A good account of the involvement of Jérôme Lindon and Les Editions de Minuit in the intellectual debate about Algeria is to be found in Anne Simonin's essay "Les Editions de Minuit et les Editions du Seuil: deux stratégies éditoriales face à la guerre d'Algérie," in *La Guerre d'Algérie et les intellectuels français* (Paris: Editions Complexe, 1991), pp. 219–45.

82. *The Times* (London), 8 Dec. 1961, p. 13c.

83. SB to Aidan Higgins, 18 Dec. 1961 (Texas). Two months later, another friend of Beckett, the professor of English Jean-Jacques Mayoux, also became a target of the bombers. On the Wednesday, Beckett told Avigdor Arikha, he had listened to Mayoux talking for two hours about the painter Constable; then on the Thursday Mayoux was "plasticated" (SB to AA, 17 Feb. 1962 [Arikha]). This "infamous violence" was also referred to by Beckett in a letter to Jean Reavey, 17 Feb. 1962 (Texas).

84. SB to John Calder, ca. 17 Dec. (received 18 Dec.) 1961 (Bloomington).

85. The earlier manifesto is discussed in Bernard Droz and Evelyne Lever, *Histoire de la guerre d'Algérie 1954–1962* (Paris: Editions du Seuil, 1982), pp. 282–85.

86. Interview with Marthe Gautier, 8 June 1994.

87. Telephone interview with Jean Martin, 15 June 1994.

88. Interview with Jérôme Lindon, 7 June 1994.

89. Telephone interview with Jean Martin, 15 June 1994.

90. SB to BR, 22 Sept. 1961 (Syracuse).

91. SB to John Calder, 22 Jan. 1962 (Bloomington).

92. AA, fax to JK, 8 April 1994.

93. Beckett wrote: "She [Monique] had a triumph at the Lucerne Festival and I heard her over [the radio] play superbly Stravinsky's *Capriccio* at the Festival of Holland with its Gebouw Orchestra conducted by Rosbaud" (SB to TM, 30 Sept. 1962 [TCD]).

94. The dates on the manuscripts of the two radio plays suggest that *Words and Music* and *Cascando* were written in the last two months of 1961. However, the fact that the

"text-music tandem" that he wanted to share with John Beckett—before the latter's accident put him hors de combat—was conceived many months before, at least by the beginning of February (letter to JS, 12 Feb. 1961 [Syracuse]) and in all likelihood well before then, brings this much closer in time to Beckett's active participation in the Mihalovici opera.

95. The two radio plays had deep roots in interests, tensions, and longings in Beckett's life that are different both in time and character from these explanations. *Words and Music* echoes Beckett's perennial interest in the themes of medieval romance, the love of Dante for Beatrice, and the love poems of the troubadours, above all the Provençal and German Minnesinger poets (See Clas Zilliacus, *Beckett and Broadcasting*, pp. 105–108). The play is dominated by an obsession with the haunting face of a woman that is glimpsed in the ashes and by the eyes of a woman, like those evoked earlier by Krapp. Those eyes started out their life, at least, as Ethna MacCarthy's.

96. Interview with John Beckett, 8 July 1992.

97. The opera buffa was *Les Jumeaux*, about Plautus. It had words by Claude Rostand.

98. SB, *Play*, in *Collected Shorter Plays*, p. 151.

99. SB to AJL, 4 April 1962 (Texas).

100. SB to Herbert Myron, 31 May 1962 (dated 1961 in error) (Boston Univ.).

101. LH, card with notes, 30 April 1962 (Dartmouth).

102. SB to HH, 16 Aug. 1962 (Hayden). A typescript numbered "4" (with the manuscript note "Corrections Ehrenbachhöhe [the hotel in Kitzbühel] August 1962") shows that it was there that he elaborated on the presence or absence of an eye to perceive, perhaps even to judge the three figures who are immured in urns, adding the speech: "Are you listening to me? (-) Is there anybody listening to me? (-) Is there anybody looking at me? (-) Is there anybody bothering about me at all?" (Original in St. Louis; photocopy in Reading, ms. 1528/5).

103. SB to HH, 16 Aug. 1962 (Hayden).

104. SB to MH, 11 June 1962 (Texas).

105. SB to MH, 16 Aug. 1962 (Texas), and to HH, 22 Aug. 1962 (Hayden).

106. SB to MH, 16 Aug. 1962 (Texas).

107. SB to JS, 15 May 1962 (Douw).

108. SB to HH, 16 Aug. 1962 (Hayden).

109. SB to HH, 22 Aug. 1962 (Hayden).

110. Interviews with Edward Beckett, 14 Dec. 1990 and 31 March 1994.

111. SB to AA and Anne Arikha, 9 Oct. 1962 (Arikha). He wrote in similarly enthusiastic terms to HH, letter of 9 Oct. 1962 (Hayden).

112. Interview with Brenda Bruce, 7 April 1994.

113. SB to George Devine, 4 Sept. 1962 (Herbert) and interview with Jocelyn Herbert, 13 April 1994.

114. Interview with Brenda Bruce, 7 April 1994.

115. Wardle, *The Theatres of George Devine*, p. 207.

116. Interview with Brenda Bruce, 7 April 1994.

117. Beckett described Jack MacGowran's late-night Beckett show at the New Arts Theatre as "a monstrous salad with good moments to judge from the bad rehearsal I saw" (SB to HH, 20 Oct. 1962 [Hayden]). But the one-man show was at an early stage and, later, after working with MacGowran on both the selection of passages and the performance, he was much more complimentary.

118. Fischer-Dieskau's concert of Wolf's songs was on October 26, 1962.

119. Interview with Brenda Bruce, 7 April 1962.

120. E.g. Philip Hope-Wallace, *The Manchester Guardian*, 2 Nov. 1962, and Bernard Levin, *The Daily Mail*, 2 Nov. 1962.

121. W. A. Darlington, *The Daily Telegraph*, 2 Nov. 1962. *The Times's* reviewer, Harold Hobson in *The Sunday Times*, 4 Nov. 1962, and Kenneth Tynan in *The Observer*, 4 Nov. 1962, were a little more critical.

122. For instance, Beckett's friend Avigdor Arikha telephoned him from London enthusiastically, and Josette Hayden reported later on how impressed she had been.

123. SB to JH, 8 Nov. 1962 (Herbert).

124. Brenda Bruce to JK, 18 Sept. 1970; interview, 7 April 1994; and telephone conversation, 15 April 1994.

125. SB to HH, ca. 8 Dec. 1962 (Hayden).

126. SB to HH, 3 Dec. 1962 (Hayden).

127. SB to HH, ca. 8 Dec. 1962 (Hayden).

128. The French team, captained by P. Lacroix, was defeated in the last minute by a Scottish XV, captained by K. J. F. Scotland, 11–6. This was the first Scottish win for six years. Ten tons of straw, part of which had ultimately to be burnt away, had been spread over the ground in order to keep it playable.

129. SB to AJL, 15 Jan. 1963 (Texas).

130. SB to AJL, 1 Feb. 1963 (Texas).

131. SB to MH, 26 Feb. 1963 (Texas).

132. SB to AJL, 15 Jan. 1963 (Texas).

133. *Tous ceux qui tombent* was broadcast on French television on January 25, 1963. Beckett wrote to John Barber of Curtis Brown (2 June 1963), "In a weak moment I let French TV do *All That Fall*, with disastrous results" (Curtis Brown).

134. John Barber of Curtis Brown to SB, 29 May 1963, and SB's reply, 2 June 1963 (Curtis Brown).

135. Interview with John Montague, 6 Aug. 1992.

136. SB to MH, 26 Feb. 1963 (Texas).

137. SB to AJL, 27 Feb. 1963 (Texas).

138. For a full account of early versions of *Film* see Gontarski, *The Intent of Undoing in Samuel Beckett's Dramatic Texts*, pp. 105–111.

139. Nancy Illig, in Ben-Zvi, ed., *Women in Beckett: Performance and Critical Perspectives*, p. 24.

140. SB to AJL, 11 June 1963 (Texas).

141. SB to Henry Wenning, 10 June 1963 (St Louis).

142. SB to John Calder, 4 June 1963 (Bloomington), and to Herbert Myron, 2 June 1963 (Boston Univ.).

143. SB to LH, 2 July 1963 (Dartmouth).

144. My account of the Becketts' stay in Zell-am-See is based on letters to Henri and Josette Hayden, 19 and 22 June, and 1, 7, and 11 July 1963 (Hayden); to Sheila Page, 21 June 1963 (Page); to Mary Hutchinson, 20 June 1963 (Texas); to John Calder, 20 June 1963 (Bloomington); and to Lawrence Harvey, 2 July 1963 (Dartmouth).

145. He posted the revised translation to Faber and Faber for publication in its *Play and Two Short Pieces for Radio*, on July 11, 1963 (SB to HH, 11 July 1963 [Hayden]).

146. SB to Henry Wenning, 31 July 1963 (St. Louis).

147. SB to MH, 31 July 1963 (Texas).

148. SB to HH, 2 Sept. 1963 (Hayden). These proofs needed very special attention, since Beckett had decided that each page should always end with a broken line. He was even prepared to make small textual changes if necessary to ensure that this could happen (SB to Declan Barber of John Calder's publishing house, 20 Oct. 1963 [Bloomington]). Many letters were exchanged between him and the small staff of John Calder until he was fully satisfied with the layout. The entire proofreading and correcting process took up to six months. As a result, the 1964 Calder edition of *How It Is* is the finest of them all.

149. SB to HH, 3 Dec. 1962 (Hayden).

150. SB to Mania Péron, undated (1962) (Péron).

151. SB to MH, 28 Dec. 1962 (Texas).

152. Linda Bellity Peskine, ed., *Roger Blin: Souvenirs et propos*, pp. 162–63.

153. SB to AJL, 11 June 1963 (Texas).

154. SB to Herbert Myron, 9 Sept. 1963 (Boston Univ.).
155. SB to Herbert Myron, 28 Sept. (1963) (Boston Univ.).
156. SB to Jacoba van Velde, 28 Sept. 1963 (Bibliothèque Nationale).
157. SB to Arland Ussher, 9 Nov. 1963 (TCD).
158. SB to Morris Sinclair, 20 Dec. 1963 (Sinclair).
159. SB to LH, 28 Oct. 1963 (Dartmouth).
160. Madeleine Renaud to JL, 23 Oct. 1963 (Minuit).
161. Bernard Poirot-Delpech, *Le Monde*, 31 Oct. 1963.
162. Jean-Jacques Gautier, *Le Figaro*, 30 Oct. 1963, and Elsa Triolet, *Les Lettres françaises*, 7–13 Nov. 1963.
163. Irving Wardle, *The Times* (London), 27 Sept. 1969.
164. SB to Jacoba van Velde, 8 Nov. 1963 (Bibliothèque Nationale), and to Arland Ussher, 9 Nov. 1963 (TCD).

20: "THEATRE THEATRE THEATRE," 1964–67

1. SB to Herbert Myron, 4 Jan. 1964 (Boston Univ.).
2. Ibid.
3. Interview with John Calder, 7 July 1990.
4. SB to Herbert Myron, 4 Jan. 1964 (Boston Univ.).
5. SB to HH, 21 Jan. 1964 (Hayden).
6. Clancy Sigal, "Is This the Person to Murder Me?" *The Sunday Times* (London) *Colour Magazine*, 1 March 1964, p. 17.
7. Ibid., p. 22.
8. Ibid., pp. 17–19.
9. "MacGowran on Beckett," interview by Richard Toscan, in S. E. Gontarski, ed., *On Beckett: Essays and Criticism*, p. 218.
10. SB to MM, 12 April 1964 (Texas).
11. SB to HH, 31 Jan. 1964 (Hayden).
12. Clancy Sigal: " 'You can't do it!' I shouted. 'Oh, can't I?' she shouted back." *The New York Times Book Review*, 12 April 1992, pp. 13–14.
13. Interview with Edward Albee, 13 Dec. 1993.
14. SB to JS, 7 Feb. 1964 (Syracuse).
15. SB to JS, 24 Jan. 1964 (Syracuse).
16. SB to JS, 7 Feb. 1964 (Syracuse).
17. SB to JS, 7 March 1964 (Syracuse). The English Theatre in Paris production laid the groundwork for the much better known *Endgame* staged a few months later by the Royal Shakespeare Company, in which Magee and MacGowran again acted Hamm and Clov, with Nagg and Nell (Brian Pringle and Patsy Byrne) drawn from Peter Hall's own company. Donald McWhinnie directed.
18. Gilles Sandier, *Arts*, 10 June 1964 (my translation).
19. Elisabeth Auclaire-Tamaroff and Barthélémy, *Jean-Marie Serreau découvreur de théâtres*, pp. 76–80. (On the same program were recitations from Borgès's *Bibliothèque de Babel* and Luciano Berio's opera, *Circles*, sung by Berio's wife, Cathy Berberian; *Double Music* by John Cage; the marionettes of Yves Joly; and a visually thrilling production by the talented young Spanish director Victor Garcia, of *La Rosa de Papel* of Valle Inclan and Lorca's *El Retablillo de Don Cristobal*.)
20. Interview with Michael Lonsdale, 2 April 1993.
21. SB to TM, 9 June 1964 (TCD).
22. SB to AS, 26 Nov. 1963 (Boston).
23. SB to Siegfried Unseld, 1 July 1963 (Suhrkamp).
24. I am most grateful to Danielle van Bercheycke for her patience in explaining how this device worked and to Delphine Seyrig, Michael Lonsdale, and Eléonore Hirt for their accounts of this production.

25. Interview with Eléonore Hirt, 19 Sept. 1990, and letter from Eléonore Hirt to JK, 31 July 1990; interview with Michael Lonsdale, 2 April 1993.

26. "We were to have opened last week, but I refused" (SB to TM, 9 June 1964 [TCD]).

27. Interviews with Michael Lonsdale, 2 April 1993, and with Danielle van Bercheycke, 3 April 1993.

28. Repeating the play at all proved to be a difficulty in some productions. Alan Schneider explains in his autobiography (*Entrances*, pp. 341–43) how he was forced by his producers to ask Beckett's permission — a permission granted reluctantly — to abandon the repeat for the American premiere. Beckett wondered himself at first whether the da capo might have been an error. The idea, he explained, was that, with the speeches going so fast and being so disjointed, intelligibility would at first be only partial and things would be understood the second time around that were missed the first time (SB to Siegfried Unseld, 1 July 1963 [Suhrkamp]). Beckett is right: the repeat works only if the speed of both parts is sufficiently fast; otherwise it appears pointless or self-indulgent.

29. SB to George Devine, 9 March 1964, quoted in James Knowlson, *Samuel Beckett: An Exhibition*, p. 92.

30. Notes by George Devine on *Play* (Reading). These notes were used more or less in this form in the National Theatre program, where it becomes clear that "dramatic ammunition" was Beckett's own phrase, used presumably in discussions with Devine.

31. Interview with Billie Whitelaw, 4 May 1993. The actress gives a lively, interesting account of her memories of rehearsals with Beckett present and of the quarrel about pace and intelligibility in her autobiography, *Billie Whitelaw . . . Who He?* (London: Hodder and Stoughton, 1995), pp. 76–82.

32. Interview with John Beckett, 8 July 1992.

33. George Devine to Kenneth Tynan, undated, reproduced in Wardle, *The Theatres of George Devine*, p. 208.

34. SB to HH, 29 March 1964 (Hayden).

35. Interview with Delphine Seyrig, 29 Jan. 1990.

36. "Suzanne found the faces excessively made up and characterized: ageing missus and exciting mistress, etc. This would be completely wrong. There [They] are all in the same dinghy at last and should be as little differentiated as possible. Three grey disks" (SB to AS, 26 Nov. 1963 [Boston]).

37. SB to Siegfried Unseld, 1 July 1963 (Suhrkamp).

38. Interviews with Jocelyn Herbert, 28 July 1992, and Billie Whitelaw, 4 May 1993.

39. Whitelaw, *Billie Whitelaw . . . Who He?*, p. 80.

40. Interviews with Jocelyn Herbert, 28 July 1992, and Billie Whitelaw, 4 May 1993.

41. For an interview with Pierre Chabert about being directed by Beckett in *L'Hypothèse*, see McMillan and Fehsenfeld, *Beckett in the Theatre*, pp. 314–17.

42. She appeared on *The Critics* eleven times in 1964, had a translation-cum-adaptation of Stendhal's *The Charterhouse of Parma* in four episodes broadcast as the "Sunday Play" in June and July, and interviewed Jack MacGowran and Patrick Magee about their work with Beckett on *Endgame* on *New Comment*, BBC Third Programme, 2 June 1964.

43. SB to TM, 9 June 1964 (TCD). SB to HH, 7 June 1964, added the information that Edward received one vote for a first prize, then failed by only one to receive the second prize (Hayden).

44. "J'en ai ma claque de cette sacrée pièce" ("I'm fed up to the back teeth with this blessed play") (SB to HH, 6 July 1964 [Hayden]).

45. "I enjoyed N.Y. Heat and humidity desperate. Had to stop every few yards and hold on to things, chiefly pillar boxes" (SB to MM, 25 Dec. 1965 [Texas]).

46. For an account of the composition of *Film* and a transcription of the recording, see Gontarski, *The Intent of Undoing in Samuel Beckett's Dramatic Texts*, pp. 101–111, 187–92.

47. "Beckett," *The New Yorker*, 8 Aug. 1964, pp. 22–23.

48. SB, *Film*, p. 11.

49. Manuscript "Notes for Film," begun at Ussy, 5 April 1963, ms. 1227/7/6/1, p. 11 (Reading).

50. SB, *Film*, pp. 71–72. My quotations in this section are taken from the original Grove Press text rather than from Alan Schneider's biography, *Entrances*, published after Schneider's death, because the reprint has not always been improved by the editors.

51. "Beckett on *Film*," in Gontarski, *The Intent of Undoing in Samuel Beckett's Dramatic Texts*, p. 188.

52. SB, *Film*, p. 85.

53. Interview with Avigdor Arikha, 23 Feb. 1994.

54. In his manuscript notes Beckett had not envisaged these "eye" holes but had written: "Make chair back memorable" and foresaw an "upright back, intersecting wooden bars or lozenges" ("Notes for Film," ms. 1227/7/6/1, p. 15 [Reading]).

55. SB, *Film*, p. 85.

56. Ibid., p. 90.

57. Ibid., p. 11.

58. Bair, *Samuel Beckett*, p. 574.

59. I am most grateful for Judith Douw, née Schmidt, for kindly copying for me the entries in her appointment book relating to Beckett's visit to New York in July–August 1964. I have also had access to Beckett's own appointment books for this period and thank Edward Beckett most warmly.

60. Interviews with Dick Seaver, 26 May 1993, and Judith Schmidt, 25 May 1993.

61. After attending the City College, Meyers had become a professional violinist, playing with the Cincinnati Symphony Orchestra under Fritz Reiner before turning to film directing and editing. He had won a Venice Film Festival Award fifteen years earlier for *The Quiet One*, a documentary about a Harlem boy rescued from family neglect by the Wiltwyck School.

62. Information on Sidney Meyers and on the Beckett-Meyers friendship (for they corresponded until Meyers died five years later) comes from an interview with his widow, Edna Meyers (2 Dec. 1993), from documents on her husband given to me by Mrs. Meyers, and from Beckett's own letters to Meyers.

63. Interview with Judith Schmidt, 25 May 1993.

64. Interview with Barney Rosset, 23 May 1993.

65. Patsy Southgate, "Rosset Remembers Beckett," *Summer Book Supplement to the East Hampton Star and the Sag Harbor Herald*, 24 May 1990.

66. By the third week in August, he was able to write from the country that he was "taking things easy here, but forcing myself to write in the mornings. Scant success so far." In October, he wrote: "Work has not yet broken down again, but only about 4000 words." Two weeks later, still at Ussy, he admitted: "Bitter cold here. Work trembling on edge of ashcan. Author also" (SB to JS, 17 August, 23 Oct., and 6 Nov. 1964 [Syracuse]).

67. Jeremy Brooks to SB, 20 Nov. 1964. Peter Brook also wrote temptingly to Beckett on November 24, 1964: "As you are the only person in the world who could recreate this play from its core, I wonder if such a work might appeal to you."

68. SB to Suzanne Finlay of Curtis Brown (draft), Nov. 1964.

69. Interview with John Calder, 7 July 1990.

70. SB to Henry Wenning, 8 Sept. 1964 (St. Louis).

71. SB to Henry Wenning, 1 Jan. 1965 (St. Louis).

72. SB to Henry Wenning, 21 Jan. 1965 (St. Louis).

73. SB to Henry Wenning, 1 Jan. 1965 (St. Louis).

74. Interview with Deryk Mendel, 3 March 1993.

75. SB to JS, 1 March 1965 (Douw).

76. The buildings in the area had been individually designed by Werner Düttmann in 1957 as a riposte to the dull, uniform Stalinist blocks of East Berlin. So a variety of building materials was used, with brick, stone pillars, panels of small stones, and a copper roof for the Academy theater, which was opened in 1960. I am most grateful to the

administrator of the Akademie der Künste and to Frau Lübold for receiving me as their guest.

77. SB to JS, 1 March 1965 (Douw).

78. Interview with Deryk Mendel, 3 March 1993.

79. A word used by SB to AJL, 10 Feb. 1965; to Jack MacGowran, 1 March 1965; to MH, 1 March 1965 (all in Texas); and to JS, 14 Feb. 1965 (Douw). "Pénibles répétitions" appears in a letter to Jacoba van Velde, 28 Feb. 1965 (Bibliothèque Nationale), and in an undated letter to JL (Minuit).

80. SB to JL, undated (Feb. 1965) (Minuit).

81. SB to AJL, 10 Feb. 1965 (Texas).

82. SB to MH, 1 March 1965, and to Jack MacGowran, 1 March 1965 (Texas). "Un Pozzo à s'arracher yeux et oreilles" ("a Pozzo to make you tear your hair out") (SB to AA, 17 Feb. 1965 [Arikha]).

83. My account of the difficulties at the Schiller-Theater rehearsals is based on interviews with Deryk Mendel (3 March 1993), Klaus Herm (9 Nov. 1994), Boleslaw Barlog (9 Nov. 1994), and Horst Bollmann (13 Nov. 1994).

84. SB to JS, 14 Feb. and 1 March 1965 (Douw). The program was broadcast under the title *Beginning to End: A Television Exploration of the World of Samuel Beckett*, on Tuesday, February 23, 1965, on BBC I.

85. The Jack Yeats exhibition of oil paintings mainly from 1935 until 1955 ran at the Waddington Gallery from mid-February until March 13. Many of the paintings were drawn from the private collection of the late Richard McGonigal.

86. SB to TM, 8 March 1965 (TCD).

87. Klaus Völker, *Beckett in Berlin* (Berlin: Edition Hentrich, Frölich & Kaufmann, 1986), pp. 70–75.

88. Clara Colosimo to SB, 12 Feb. 1965 (Minuit).

89. *Corriere della Sera*, 21 Feb. 1965 (Minuit).

90. Telegram from Trieste, 11:15 A.M., 21 Feb. (1965) (Minuit) (my translation).

91. Guido Sambo to SB, 24 Feb. 1965 (Minuit) (my translation).

92. Draft of telegram from SB to the Unione Nazionale Scrittori Guiliani e Dalmati, 28 Feb. 1965 (Minuit) (my translation).

93. SB, undated draft of letter and the typescript of the letter sent from Les Editions de Minuit dated 28 Feb. 1965 to the Unione Nazionale Scrittori Guiliani e Dalmati (Minuit) (my translation).

94. SB to Dr. Connie Ricono, 3 July 1967 (Ricono). I am most grateful to Dr. Ricono for her help in clarifying matters relating to the Italian rights of *Giorni felici (Happy Days)* and for information to do with Beckett's plays in Italy in general.

95. SB to TM, 30 Jan. 1965 (TCD).

96. SB to JS, 7 Jan. 1965 (Douw).

97. Interview with John Calder, 7 July 1990.

98. SB to JS, 1 March 1965 (Douw).

99. SB to JS, 27 April 1965 (Douw).

100. SB to MH, 10 April 1965 (Texas).

101. SB to JS, 7 Jan. 1965 (Douw).

102. "Été 56" manuscript notebook, ms. 1227/7/7/1 (Reading). The allusion is to Dante's *Inferno*, Canto XX.

103. Samuel Beckett, *All Strange Away* (London: John Calder, 1979), p. 28.

104. Interview with Avigdor Arikha, 23 Feb. 1994.

105. LH, undated interview with SB (Dartmouth).

106. SB to LH, 30 Jan. 1965 (Dartmouth).

107. SB to AA, undated (14 March 1965) (Arikha).

108. SB to Henry Wenning, 21 Jan. 1965 (St. Louis). The "dream theatre," as Beckett termed it — John Calder's hope for a small theater center in the heart of London's Soho

—never materialized, but the play was still dedicated to his publisher (SB to MH, 5 April 1965, and to Aidan Higgins, 12 May 1965 [Texas]).

109. SB to Jacoba van Velde, 3 Dec. 1965 (Bibliothèque Nationale).

110. Ibid.

111. LH, interview with SB, 29–30 March 1965 (Dartmouth).

112. SB to JS, 29 March 1965 (Syracuse).

113. SB to JS, 16 Aug. 1965 (Douw).

114. SB to Jack MacGowran, 4 July 1963 (Texas).

115. The original holograph manuscript is dated on the first otherwise blank page 13/4/65 and at the end of the draft 1/5/1965 (original in St. Louis; photocopy in Reading, ms. 1537/1).

116. An interesting interpretation in the light of the Jungian anima and Erick Neumann's book *The Great Mother: an Analysis of the Archetype* (Princeton, N.J.: Princeton University Press, 1972) is found in Rosette Lamont's essay "Beckett's *Eh Joe*: Lending an Ear to the Anima," in Ben-Zvi, ed., *Women in Beckett: Performance and Critical Perspectives*, pp. 228–34.

117. SB, *Eh Joe* in *Collected Shorter Plays*, p. 202.

118. Dialogue with Siegfried Melchinger, "Regie Samuel Beckett: Der Autor im Umgang mit der Technik," *Theater heute*, May 1966, p. 15 (my translation).

119. SB to Jack MacGowran, 15 May 1965 (Texas).

120. Interview with Michael Bakewell, 21 March 1994.

121. The negotiations are recorded in detail in the BBC Written Archives at Caversham (e.g., Margaret McLaren to Edward Caffery at the BBC copyright department, 1 July 1965, turning down an initial offer of £125 and asking for £600. Curtis Brown settled for £250 as a compromise fee at the end of July).

122. The Süddeutscher Rundfunk recording was broadcast on April 13, 1966, Beckett's birthday, and the BBC version on BBC TV2 went out on July 4, 1966.

123. "Work fitfully at French version of *Eh Joe*" (SB to John Calder, 30 June 1965 [Bloomington]) followed by letters to AA, 4 July 1965 [Arikha] and HH, 5 July 1965 [Hayden] when he says the translation is finished).

124. SB to John Calder, 14 July 1965 (Bloomington).

125. SB to John Calder, 30 June 1965 (Bloomington).

126. SB to HH, 22 July 1965 (Hayden).

127. SB to John Calder, 30 June 1965 (Bloomington).

128. SB to JH, 7 Dec. 1965 (Herbert).

129. SB, *The Lost Ones*, p. 18. The Dante allusion is to the *Inferno*, Canto XXXIV.

130. Ibid., p. 14. The Dante allusion is to the *Purgatorio*, Canto IV.

131. This handwritten card is preserved in the Beckett Archive (Reading).

132. Peter Murphy, "The Nature of Allegory in 'The Lost Ones,' or the Quincunx Realistically Considered," *Journal of Beckett Studies*, no. 7 (spring 1982), pp. 71–88.

133. Patrick Bowles, "How to Fail: Notes on Talks with Samuel Beckett," *PN Review*, 96, vol. 20, no. 4, (March–April 1994), p. 26. Bowles's note is dated September 30, 1953.

134. Eyal Amiran, *Wandering and Home: Beckett's Metaphysical Narrative*, pp. 166–71. Now that we know the extent of Beckett's knowledge of Plato and Socrates from his early 1930s notes, this idea has to be taken seriously.

135. Samuel Beckett, untitled first manuscript of *Le Dépeupleur* (original in St. Louis; photocopy in Reading, ms. 1536/2).

136. Peter Murphy, "The Nature of Allegory in 'The Lost Ones,' " *Journal of Beckett Studies*, no. 7 (spring 1982), pp. 71–88.

137. Wardle, *The Theatres of George Devine*, p. 278.

138. SB to JH (Herbert) and to MH (Texas), both 30 Aug. 1965.

139. SB to JH, 15 Oct. 1965 (Herbert).

140. Wardle, *The Theatres of George Devine*, p. 280. The occasion is also described in

William Gaskill's *A Sense of Direction* (London: Faber and Faber, 1988), pp. 71–72, and by John Osborne in *Almost a Gentleman: An Autobiography*, vol. II, 1955–1966 (London: Faber and Faber, 1991), p. 267.

141. Michael Bakewell, "Working with Beckett," *Adam International Review*, vol. XXV, 337–39, p. 72.

142. Interview with Siân Phillips, 7 April 1994.

143. Clas Zilliacus, *Beckett and Broadcasting*, p. 198, and interview with Michael Bakewell, 21 March 1994.

144. "MacGowran on Beckett," *Theatre Quarterly*, vol. 3, no. 2 (July–Sept. 1973), p. 20.

145. "The high points are incomparable, but too many low ones. Over 300 works. The ambition seems to have been to show all they could lay their hands on, indiscriminately" (SB to TM, 16 Feb. 1966 [TCD]). The huge Pierre Bonnard exhibition had opened at the Royal Academy on January 6 and was to last until March. It received huge publicity. Beckett bought the catalogue, but did not like Denys Sutton's introduction.

146. On the same occasion, realising that some of the poems that he had suggested in a letter to Jack MacGowran some weeks before were not being read (SB to Jack MacGowran, 6 Jan. 1966 [Texas]), he wrote down his own selection, which included "The Vulture" and "Echo's Bones," "Serena I" and "Serena III," and two of the poems from *Watt*, "Who may tell the tale" and "Watt will not." On February 9, 1966, the day of Beckett's return to Paris, this second program was recorded by the same two readers with an introduction also by Professor John Fletcher. The first program was broadcast on March 8, 1966, and the second on November 24, 1966. My thanks go to John Fletcher for information (telephone interview, 13 March 1994).

147. Interviews with John and Edward Beckett, 14 March 1994.

148. See photograph on the record sleeve of Claddagh Records's *MacGowran Speaking Beckett*.

149. SB to HH, 16 March 1966 (Hayden).

150. Ibid.

151. Nancy Illig, "Acting Beckett's Women," Ben-Zvi, ed., *Women in Beckett: Performance and Critical Perspectives*, p. 26.

152. Interview with Deryk Mendel, 3 March 1993.

153. Telephone interview with Jocelyn Herbert, 8 March 1994.

154. SB to JH, 6 May 1966 (Herbert).

155. SB to JH, 16 May 1966 (Herbert).

156. William Shakespeare, *The Tempest*, Ariel's song, Act I, scene ii; and T. S. Eliot, *The Waste Land*, I, "The Burial of the Dead," 1. 48.

157. SB to JH, 2 June 1966 (Herbert).

158. Ibid.

159. SB to JH, 16 May 1966 (Herbert).

160. SB to JH, 16 June 1966 (Herbert).

161. SB to AA, 21 June 1966 (Arikha).

162. SB, autograph note with the manuscripts of *Le Dépeupleur* and *Bing* (St. Louis). Reproduced in R. Admussen, *The Samuel Beckett Manuscripts*. p. 22.

163. SB to MH, 24 June 1966 (Texas), and to JH (announcing the death), 8 July 1966 (Herbert).

164. SB to JH, 18 Aug. 1966 (Herbert).

165. Ibid.

166. SB to JL, 19 Aug. 1966 (Minuit).

167. SB to JS, 25 Aug. 1966 (Douw).

168. Samuel Beckett, "Ping" in *No's Knife: Collected Shorter Prose: 1945–1946*, p. 165.

169. SB to LH, 25 Sept. 1966 (Dartmouth).

170. "Giacometti mort. George Devine mort. Oui, conduis-moi au Père Lachaise, en brûlant les feux rouges" (SB to Jacoba van Velde, undated 1966 [Bibliothèque Nationale]).

171. SB to JS, 25 Sept. 1966 (Douw).
172. SB to JH, 3 Oct. 1966 (Herbert).
173. Ibid.
174. SB to MH, 21 Oct. 1966 (Texas).
175. SB to JH, 27 Dec. 1966 (Herbert).

21: Accident, Illness, and "Catastrophe," 1967–69

1. SB, *Krapp's Last Tape* in *Collected Shorter Plays*, p. 57.
2. Erwin Leiser to SB, 2 Jan. 1967 (Minuit). SB wrote giving his permission, subject to Jérôme Lindon's agreement, on the back of Leiser's letter.
3. SB to JL, 18 April 1967. Denise Sée, acting for Keep Films, had written to Jérôme Lindon on April 12, 1967, asking if the film rights of *Godot* were still available and whether they were prepared to negotiate. The following day, Lindon asked SB what his position was in principle, informing him that Peter O'Toole would like to adapt *Godot* for the cinema (Minuit).
4. SB to AS, 24 April 1967 (Boston).
5. Among the chess books in SB's library at Ussy on his death were Alexander Alekhin, *My Best Games of Chess 1924–1937* (London: G. Bell, 1939); P. H. Clarke, *Mikhail Tal's Best Games of Chess* (London: G. Bell, 1961); P. H. Clarke, *Petrosian's Best Games of Chess* (London: G. Bell, 1964); Dr. E. Wildhagen, *Weltgeschichte des Schachs* (Hamburg, 1963).
6. Irving Chernev's book was published by Faber and Faber, London, in 1965. Beckett also had in his Paris study: Ruben Fine, *The Ideas Behind the Chess Openings: Chess Marches On. A Vivid Record of Leading Chess Centres of the World*, 1945, 2nd printing 1964; Heinz Machatscheck, *Sowjetische Meisterpartien*, 1956; and Henri Rinck, *150 Endspielstudien 150 Fins de partie*, Leipzig: Veit & Co. 1909.
7. Bernard Cafferty, *Spassky's 100 Best Games* (London: B. T. Batsford, 1972) and Robert G. Wade and Kevin J. O'Connell, *The Games of Robert J. Fischer* (London: B. T. Batsford, 1972). Among his chess books, Beckett also had C. H. O'D. Alexander, *Fischer v. Spassky, Reykjavik 1972: An Account of the Struggle for the World Chess Championship, with Illustrated Biographies of the Players* (Harmondsworth: Penguin Books, 1972).
8. SB confided this failure to Alan Schneider: "Had an idea for a 40 min. play for the *Petit Odéon* (105 seats) and I suppose I could find it again if I looked, but haven't been able to write it. Only the wish to oblige Madeleine in any case, no heart in theatre now" (SB to AS, 8 Feb. 1967 [Boston]). The manuscript of this draft and a partial typescript are now in the Beckett Archive, ms. 2927 and ms. 1227/7/16/3 (Reading).
9. SB to AS, 15 July 1967 (Boston).
10. "I just strolled into a garage pit with my head back to front as usual. Couldn't have broken anything better" (SB to John Calder, 15 March 1967 [Bloomington]).
11. This account of Beckett's fall in the garage at Ussy is based on an interview with Josette Hayden, November 1989, and another telephone conversation with her, December 1990. Bair reported that the accident occurred in the garage next door to his apartment building in Paris (*Samuel Beckett*, p. 597). But Josette Hayden looked after Beckett for some days after the fall and is adamant that the accident happened in Ussy. This is further confirmed by a letter from SB to Nick Rawson, 3 March 1967 (TCD). See n. 12, this chapter.
12. "I had a fall in the country a week ago and broke 2 ribs. Got back here yesterday and all will be well. A bit uncomfortable for a few more weeks" (SB to Nick Rawson, 3 March 1967 [TCD]).
13. SB to SP, 18 April 1967 (Page).
14. Professor Dr. Goldmann, the specialist in Berne, was suggested (along with the name of Professor Thiel of Frankfurt) by Siegfried Unseld in a letter to SB from Suhrkamp Verlag of February 8, 1967 (Suhrkamp), Beckett replying that his banal cataracts

were unworthy of a great specialist. During the year, however, he was convinced by Dr. Unseld that it would be wise to seek Goldmann's advice.

15. SB to GR, 22 Dec. 1967 (Texas).

16. SB to GR, 12 April 1967 (Texas).

17. He wrote "very sad about Tom McG. Friends since 28" (SB to MH, 24 March 1967 [Texas]).

18. SB to MH, 5 April 1967 (Texas).

19. SB to HH, 7 June (1967) (Hayden).

20. This was not the first attempt to translate *Watt* into French. In a letter to Aidan Higgins of November 28, 1961, SB spoke of a woman (unnamed, but she was Edith Fournier) who "has written on *Comment c'est* and is gallantly translating *Watt* in spite of my refusal to have it appear in French" (Texas).

21. A fascinating account of the Janviers' translating sessions with Beckett is in Ludovic Janvier and Agnès Vaquin-Janvier, "Traduire avec Beckett: *Watt*," *Revue d'esthétique*, "Samuel Beckett," special issue (1986), pp. 57–64. Reprinted in 1990.

22. The notebook prepared by SB for the Schiller-Theater has been published as Volume 2 in S. E. Gontarski, ed., *The Theatrical Notebooks of Samuel Beckett*.

23. SB to AS, 24 April 1967 (Boston).

24. SB to HH, undated (10 Sept. 1967) (Hayden).

25. SB to HH, 5 Sept. 1967 (Hayden).

26. SB to HH, 24 Aug. 1967 (Hayden) and account by Dr. Gottfried Büttner of a dinner with SB, 9 Sept. 1967.

27. Interview with Horst Bollmann, 13 Nov. 1994. I thank Walter Asmus for his invaluable help in Berlin.

28. Michael Haerdter, "A Rehearsal Diary," in McMillan and Fehsenfeld, *Beckett in the Theatre*, p. 204.

29. Ibid., pp. 208 and 212.

30. Interview with Horst Bollmann, 13 Nov. 1994.

31. SB to HH, 20 Aug. 1967 (Hayden).

32. Ibid.

33. SB to HH, undated (10 Sept. 1967) (Hayden).

34. SB to HH, 14 Sept. 1967 (Hayden).

35. SB to HH, 24 Aug. 1967 (Hayden).

36. SB to HH, undated (but certainly early September) 1967 (Hayden).

37. These pieces of music by Haydn were found at Ussy after Beckett's death.

38. SB to HH, undated (but, from internal evidence, 10 Sept. 1967) (Hayden).

39. Interview with Boleslaw Barlog, 9 Nov. 1994.

40. Interview with Horst Bollmann, 13 Nov. 1994.

41. Mira Averech, "Beckett," *Globe*, no. 44 (February 1990), p. 58.

42. Ibid. The version of events recounted here derives partly from this article, partly from two subsequent telephone conversations with Mira Averech, and partly from a friend of Beckett to whom he spoke about having had a brief liaison while he was in Berlin.

43. SB to Jack MacGowran, 30 Sept. 1967 (Texas).

44. SB to HH, 20 Sept. 1967 (Hayden).

45. SB to Siegfried Unseld, 4 Nov. 1967 (Suhrkamp).

46. On February 7, 1968, SB wrote to JL that he would finish the third part of *Watt* that day, and on March 4, that there remained only what he called an "untranslatable poem" in it (the poem "To Nelly") to translate (Minuit).

47. SB to Nick Rawson, 14 Jan. 1968 (TCD).

48. SB to Jack MacGowran, 7 Jan. 1968 (Texas).

49. Ibid.

50. This note, written in French in Josette Hayden's hand and translated by myself, is dated January 7, 1968 (Hayden).

51. The funeral was not in August (see Bair, *Samuel Beckett*, p. 600), when Beckett was ill with the abscess on his lung and would have been unable to travel.

52. SB to JS, 18 March 1968 (Syracuse).

53. Interview with John Beckett, 8 July 1992.

54. SB to MH, 29 March 1968 (Texas).

55. SB to JS, 27 April 1968 (Syracuse).

56. The opening of Hayden's major retrospective was on May 3, the same day as the revival of Roger Blin's production of *Fin de partie* and the first night of really serious street fighting in the Latin Quarter.

57. This account of SB's appearance and the state of his health at the Hayden exhibition and the evening celebration comes from interviews with Josette Hayden and Avigdor Arikha, November 1990. There are also photographs by P. L. Buer of Beckett alone and with Hayden at the Musée d'Art Moderne (Hayden).

58. Patrick Seale and Maureen McConville, *French Revolution 1968* (Harmondsworth and London: Penguin Books and Heinemann, 1968), p. 70. See David Caute, *Sixty-eight: The Year of the Barricades* (London: Hamish Hamilton, 1988), Chapter 11.

59. Edward Beckett, telephone conversation, Nov. 1990.

60. SB to George and Jean Reavey, 14 Jan. 1968 (Texas).

61. SB to AJL, 4 May 1968 (Texas).

62. SB to Jack MacGowran, 16 July 1968 (Texas).

63. "I get up, dress and sit around, drinkless and tobaccoless. It seems a long time since I answered the phone or saw anyone" (SB to Dick Seaver, 21 June 1968 [Syracuse]).

64. SB to HH, 23 Aug. 1968 (Hayden) and interview with Josette Hayden, 19 Nov. 1989.

65. SB to HH, 28 Aug. 1968 (Hayden).

66. SB to MH, 11 Sept. 1968 (Texas).

67. SB to HH, 16 Sept. 1968 (Hayden).

68. SB to HH, 16 Sept. 1968 (Hayden) and (for his meeting with the Haydens and the plans for a holiday in the Canaries) to MH, 26 Sept. 1968 (Texas).

69. SB to MH, 27 Oct. 1968 (Texas).

70. SB to AJL, 29 Oct. 1968 (Texas).

71. Ibid.

72. The corrected galley proofs of *Cascando* were acknowledged by Judith Schmidt in a letter of September 24, 1968 (Syracuse).

73. SB to Elmar Tophoven, 11 Sept. 1968 (Tophoven).

74. SB to Jean Reavey, 7 Nov. 1968 (Texas).

75. SB to HH, dated 5 Nov. (error; in reality Dec.) 1968 (Hayden).

76. Ibid. SB wrote in precisely these terms to JL too (letter, correctly dated this time, 5 Dec. 1968) (Minuit).

77. In a letter to JL dated January 14, 1969, SB wrote: "In Paris I should be shut up in the house, still stuffing myself full of antibiotics. It's already more than a month now since I stopped taking them" (Minuit).

78. This account of their brief, rather unsatisfactory stay in Funchal is based on a personal visit to the island, a private conversation with SB about it, and his letters to friends from Madeira.

79. Beckett wrote to Barney Rosset acknowledging the transfer and telling him of their decision to move to the smaller island of Porto Santo in a letter dated December 5, 1968 (Syracuse).

80. Letter to JK from the travel agent in Funchal, Carlos Jardim, May 2, 1990. These facilities for paying locally were also referred to by SB in a letter to JL, dated December 5, 1968 (Minuit).

81. SB to JL, 5 Dec. 1968 (Minuit) and to BR, 5 Dec. 1968 (Syracuse).

82. SB to Elmar and Erika Tophoven, 17 Jan. 1969 (Tophoven).

83. SB to HH, 7 Jan. 1969 (Hayden).

84. SB to HH, 11 Feb. 1969 (Hayden).

85. SB to HH, 25 Dec. 1968 (Hayden).

86. Ibid.

87. SB to HH, 11 Jan. 1969 (Hayden).

88. SB to HH, 11 Feb. 1969 (Hayden).

89. SB to HH, 31 Dec. 1968 (Hayden).

90. SB to HH, 4 Feb. 1969 (Hayden) and to AS, 15 Feb. 1969 (Boston).

91. JL sent him a copy of the story "Premier amour" ("First Love"), the typescript of which had to be retrieved from the United States, on December 16, 1968, asking if he could publish limited editions of this text and of Mercier et Camier.

92. SB to HH, 25 Jan. 1969 (Hayden). SB's exact expression was "Le Schimmel a dû reprendre du poil de la crinière."

93. SB to BR, 5 Dec. 1968 (Syracuse).

94. SB to HH, 31 Dec. 1968 (Hayden).

95. Details of the Radio Bremen crew's visit and SB's reaction to it are taken from his letter to Henri and Josette Hayden, February 11, 1969 (Hayden), from interviews with Josette Hayden and Erika Tophoven, who were both in the documentary, and from the film itself, which has been preserved.

96. Interview with Josette Hayden, Nov. 1990.

97. SB to HH, 11 Feb. 1969 (Hayden).

98. SB to HH, 31 Dec. 1968 (Hayden).

99. SB to HH, 11 Feb. 1969 (Hayden).

100. Misleadingly, they collected their mail at the Estalagem Albatroz but were, according to SB, let down by this hotel and did not stay there (SB to HH, 16 Feb. 1969) (Hayden).

101. "Earth quook when we were in Cascais. But to scant effect" (SB to MH, 5 April 1969 [Texas], and letters to JH, 5 March 1969 [dated April in error by Beckett] [Herbert], and John Kobler, 10 March 1969 [Texas]).

102. SB to Jack MacGowran, 17 Jan. 1969 (Texas).

103. SB to John Kobler, 10 March 1969 (Texas).

104. SB to MH, 18 March 1969 (Texas).

105. SB to JH, 22 April 1969 (Herbert).

106. SB to Kay Boyle, 2 June 1969 (Texas).

107. Maurice Nadeau, Gustave Flaubert écrivain (Paris: Denoël, 1969).

108. SB to Melanie Daiken, 22 April 1969 (Daiken).

109. SB to LH, 26 March 1969 (Dartmouth).

110. SB, Lessness (London: Calder and Boyars, Signature Series 9, 1970), back cover blurb.

111. Ibid., p. 7.

112. Slightly different views are expressed on how randomly or otherwise the different sets of images are combined in Ruby Cohn's Back to Beckett, p. 265, and in Edith Fournier's "Samuel Beckett, mathématicien et poète," Critique, Aug.–Sept. 1990, vol. xlvi, nos. 519–20, pp. 660–69.

113. SB, Lessness, pp. 8–9.

114. SB to John Kobler, 21 April 1969 (Texas).

115. Bair reports a telephone conversation in 1974 with Tynan in which he disowned responsibility for the tampering (Samuel Beckett, p. 603, n. 41). The dispute is simply not dealt with in Kathleen Tynan's The Life of Kenneth Tynan (London: Weidenfeld & Nicolson, 1987).

116. Warren Brown to SB, 10 March 1969 (Curtis Brown), in which Brown wrongly called the sketch a mime. In his reply, Beckett corrected this and stressed that "the only right involved is that granted by me to Kenneth Tynan to include the piece in a revue — Oh Calcutta, presumably — he was putting on in New York" (SB to Warren Brown, 11 March 1969 [Curtis Brown]).

117. Bair, *Samuel Beckett*, p. 603.

118. SB to John Calder, 27 Aug. 1969 (Bloomington).

119. SB, letter (in French) to AA, 21 Sept. 1969 (Arikha).

120. While SB was directing *Krapp's Last Tape* in Berlin, he heard from John Barrett of Curtis Brown on September 8 that he could withdraw the sketch; a few days later, John Calder wrote to him: "I hope to let you have news that Michael White and Tynan have accepted the withdrawal of *Breath* without difficulty. You have in any case a legal right to withdraw" (John Calder to SB, 15 Sept. 1969 [Bloomington]).

121. SB to John Calder, 13 Nov. 1969 (Bloomington).

122. Lennon, *Foreign Correspondent*, pp. 179–81.

123. SB to MM, 7 Jan. 1969 (Texas). The changed line was "It's no good."

124. SB to AJL, 26 Nov. 1969 (Texas).

125. SB to AJL, 6 Jan. 1970 (Texas).

126. SB to HH, 14 Sept. 1969 (Hayden). The quotation is from SB, *Krapp's Last Tape*, in *Collected Shorter Plays*, p. 59.

127. SB to HH, 25 Sept. 1969 (Hayden).

128. He copied out the entire poem by hand in one of his notebooks before visiting Germany in the autumn of 1936.

129. *Poems of Goethe*. A Selection with Introduction and Notes by Ronald Gray (Cambidge: Cambidge University Press, 1966), pp. 47–48.

130. Account by Gottfried Büttner of a dinner in Berlin with SB and Büttner's wife, Renate. I am most grateful to Dr. Büttner for supplying me with this information.

131. SB, *Lessness*, p. 8.

132. SB to HH, 25 Sept. 1969 (Hayden).

133. SB to HH, 30 Sept. 1969 (Hayden). The Giorgione in question was the *Portrait of a Young Man* in the State Museum at Dahlem, a postcard of which SB sent to Avigdor and Anne Arikha on September 3, 1969.

134. SB to HH, 9 Sept. 1969 (Hayden).

135. SB to HH, 25 Sept. 1969 (Hayden).

136. *The Times* [London], 2 Oct. 1969, p. 7. By October 25, the number of the dead had climbed to seven hundred and Tunis was said to be isolated from the south (*The Times* [London], 25 Oct. 1969, p. 4: "the disaster has set the country's economy back by years").

137. SB, letters to Kay Boyle, 5 Nov. 1969 (Texas) and to JH, 18 Nov. 1969 (Herbert).

138. SB to HH, 10 Oct. 1969 (Hayden).

139. SB to AJL, 19 Oct. 1969 (Texas).

140. Document in pencil and capital letters in Les Editions de Minuit with a note of the date and time (13:05 [1:05 P.M.]) at which the telegram was sent.

141. Telegram from Karl Ragnar Gierow of the Swedish Academy, 23 Oct. 1969 (Minuit).

142. For example, in *The Evening Herald* of Dublin, 24 Oct. 1969, and *The Times* in London, 25 Oct. 1969.

143. E.g.: "Our hideout here is as good as any and better than most. The Arabs are a great bulwark, but it's hard going much of the time. Often cooped up in room for days on end, but manage the odd swim" (SB to SP, 1 Nov. 1969 [Page]), and "Still manage the odd swim by stealth and miles of beach. Arabs marvellous and very helpful" (SB to Henry Wenning, 2 Nov. 1969 [St Louis]).

144. SB to JL, 6 Nov. 1969 (Minuit).

145. SB to AJL, 26 Nov. 1969 (Texas).

146. SB to AA, 21 Nov. 1969 (Arikha).

147. SB to AA, 7 Dec. 1969 (Arikha).

148. SB to AJL, 26 Nov. 1969 (Texas).

149. JL to SB, 22 Dec. 1969 (Minuit). SB replied: "Sans moi et ce sacré voyage tu

n'aurais pas été malade" ("Without me and that damned journey you would not have been ill") (SB to JL, 29 Dec. 1969 [Minuit]).
150. See SB to JL, 6 Nov. 1969 (Minuit).

22: VISION RESTORED, 1970–74

1. SB to Nick Rawson, 1 March 1970 (TCD) and to Alec Reid, 18 April 1970 (Reid papers, in private hands).
2. SB to Aidan Higgins, 30 Jan. 1970 (Texas).
3. SB to John Kobler, 29 Jan. 1970 (Texas).
4. SB to John Kobler, 5 Feb. 1970 (Texas).
5. These stories had not been issued except in a limited edition "for scholars" since 1934.
6. As Barrault made clear, Blin's codirectorship was an honorary one. The Compagnie Renaud-Barrault and Blin were not linked by any contract except that of friendship (Colette Godard, "Cycle Beckett au Récamier," Le Monde, 10 Feb. 1970).
7. Madeleine Renaud had toured with this production earlier. She had performed at the Royal Court Theatre, London, for instance, September 25–October 4 1969, alternating Beckett's Oh les beaux jours with Marguerite Duras's L'Amante anglaise.
8. SB to MH, 1 March 1970 (Texas). Beckett had written that he thought that Christine Tsingos would be remarkable as Winnie, "very different from Madeleine" (SB to Josette Hayden, 1 June 1970 [Hayden]).
9. SB to Roger Blin, 21 Dec. 1969 (IMEC).
10. Interview with Jean Martin, 17 Sept. 1990.
11. Beckett shuddered with horror when Alan Schneider told him how the Canadian actor Donald Davis, who also operated the recorder himself, kept splicing equipment in the drawer of Krapp's table in case the tape should become entangled or break. Interviews with Alan Schneider and Donald Davis, in Knowlson, ed., Samuel Beckett: Krapp's Last Tape, Theatre Workbook No. 1, pp. 52–64.
12. Interview with Jean Martin, 17 Sept. 1990.
13. SB to MH, 18 May 1970 (Texas).
14. "Still up to eyes in 2 theatres. Till end of month. Then great sigh of relief and jet haste to Sardinia for a month" (SB to SP, 18 April 1970 [Page]).
15. SB to Josette Hayden, 1 June 1970 (Hayden).
16. SB to MH, 18 May 1970 (Texas).
17. SB to Josette Hayden, 1 June 1970 (Hayden).
18. SB to MH, 18 May 1970 (Texas).
19. SB to Josette Hayden, 1 June 1970 (Hayden).
20. SB to MH, 16 June 1970 (Texas).
21. Ibid.
22. SB to MH, 2 July 1970 (Texas).
23. SB to Kay Boyle, 6 Sept. 1970 (Texas).
24. SB to JH, 9 August 1970 (Herbert).
25. The information relating to the publication of Abandonné comes from an interview with the artist, Geneviève Asse, March 2, 1993.
26. The inscription under the bronze bust, labeled "Ernest Rousselle 1836–1896" is "Président du Conseil Municipal de Paris du Conseil Général de la Seine de la Commission des enfants assistés et moralement abandonnés."
27. SB, For to End Yet Again and Other Fizzles, p. 11. For a discussion of this text, see John Pilling, "Ends and Odds in Prose," in Knowlson and Pilling, Frescoes of the Skull, pp. 186–90.
28. SB to JH, 9 Aug. 1970 (Herbert).
29. Beckett sent Jack MacGowran a check to save him from having to sell the Jack Yeats painting he had given him. He also arranged payment of an outstanding debt to a

publicity agent relating to MacGowran's show, *Beginning to End* (SB to Jack and Gloria MacGowran, 9 July 1970). He helped out the writer Jean Demélier, enabling him to travel to England, and supported Nick Rawson's successful attempt to get into Keble College, Oxford. He declared himself honored by a proposal for a large exhibition devoted to his work to be held at the University of Reading in England (SB to JK, 26 July 1970 [Knowlson]).

30. SB to SP, 10 Oct. 1970 (Page).

31. SB to MH, 10 Oct. 1970 (Texas).

32. SB to Nick Rawson, 19 Nov. 1970 (TCD).

33. SB to John Calder and Marion Boyars, 23 Oct. 1970 (Bloomington). He wrote the same message (in French) on the same day to Jacoba van Velde (Bibliothèque Nationale) adding that he would be getting his first "verre d'attente" (provisional lens) soon.

34. SB to JH, 23 Oct. 1970 (Herbert).

35. SB to MH, 10 Nov. 1970 (Texas).

36. Calder came over to his flat on November 8 for a drink, as Beckett was still unfit to dine out. Beckett wrote with a thick felt pen: "Fear no question of my dining out for some time. Suggest you come to me for a drink Sunday Nov 8" (SB to John Calder, 10 Nov. 1970 [Bloomington]). But, by the end of the month, he was able to dine at the Closerie des Lilas with Bettina.

37. Telegrams from the Rossets to Beckett, dated November 20 and 23, about their visit, and from Beckett to the Rossets, dated November 21, making the dinner appointment, are at Syracuse University.

38. The first and only night of *Gandhi*, written by Gurnay Campbell, was October 1, 1970. After this débâcle (for which the play itself and not the actor was blamed), Mac-Gowran, who had shaved his head for the title role, could not face acting in the Beckett one-man show in New York for at least a month.

39. Later in December, as writing got progressively easier for him, Beckett wrote offering warm congratulations to his Irish actor friend: "The news of your marvellous success in N.Y. is the best for many a long day. Bravo, bravissimo. . . . I imagine you'll be getting fat offers right left and centre after this and probably be staying on in the States for a time" (SB to Jack MacGowran, 24 Dec. 1970 [Texas]).

40. SB to GR, 1 Dec. 1970 (Texas).

41. Photographs of this opening showing, among others, the friends of Bram mentioned are reproduced in Claire Stoullig, *Bram van Velde*, pp. 223–24.

42. SB to GR, 1 Dec. 1970 (Texas).

43. SB to MH, 20 Jan. 1971 (Texas). Beckett had started the draft translation when he and Suzanne were in Alghero, Sardinia, on May 6, 1970. He resumed it on December 15 but added only a few pages then, working in a set of Giramondo brand notebooks (with photographs of Ireland on the pictorial covers) that he had bought in Italy (ms. 1396/14/17 [Reading]). He reached only the first page of the second section of *Mercier and Camier*.

44. SB to MH, 16 March 1971 (Texas).

45. The dates of the operation and of his release from the nursing home are confirmed by a telegram from Beckett to Barney Rosset dated 24 Feb. 1971 (Syracuse).

46. SB to Jack MacGowran, 1 March 1971 (Texas).

47. "Both eyes castrated now and doing as well as can be expected. Corresponding lobes not pleased but no doubt they'll learn to take it. From the little Luxembourg I can read the time on the Palace clock and God knows one shd. [should] be grateful for that" (SB to GR, 15 April 1971 [Texas]).

48. SB to Nick Rawson, 16 April 1971 (TCD).

49. JK, conversation with SB, 1970.

50. Two cameras were to be used, for instance, with quite different functions. One camera would observe the general situation and Krapp's exits to his cubbyhole at the back of the stage, while still being able to move forward and back or to the left and the

right; the second would have much more freedom to investigate "from all angles and often from above, detail of table situation, hands, face, machine ledger, boxes and tapes" (SB, "Suggestions for TV *Krapp*," in Clas Zilliacus, *Beckett and Broadcasting*, p. 204).

51. SB to BR, 3 May 1971 (Syracuse).
52. SB, postcard to MH, 28 June 1971 (Texas).
53. SB to MH, 9 July 1971 (Texas).
54. SB, postcard to MH, 28 June 1971 (Texas).
55. SB to JL, 24 June 1971 (Minuit).
56. SB to MH, 9 July 1971 (Texas). Beckett's search was for "that stream / That 'twixt Chiaveri and Siestri draws / His limpid waters through the lowly glen" (said to be the Lavagno River). Dante, *The Vision of Hell, Purgatory and Paradise, Purgatory*, Canto XIX, H. F. Cary trans., p. 105.
57. This account of Beckett's work preparing for his production of *Glückliche Tage* draws on the afterword and notes of James Knowlson, *Happy Days / Oh les beaux jours* (bilingual ed.; London: Faber and Faber, 1978) and on Ruby Cohn, *Just Play*, pp. 251–53.
58. These two notebooks and an annotated copy of the play with Beckett's cuts and changes are preserved in the Beckett Archive, ms.1227/7/8/1, ms. 1396/4/10, and ms. 1480/1 (Reading).
59. Beckett later marked up his cuts and changes for me in a German text. I am also grateful to Eva-Katharina Schultz for sending me her acting script.
60. These various details are taken from letters from SB to Josette Hayden, 25 Aug. and 1 Sept. 1971 (Hayden).
61. Interview with Eva-Katharina Schultz, 14 Nov. 1994.
62. Ibid.
63. SB to AJL, 25 Aug. 1971 (Texas).
64. Interview with Ruby Cohn, 23 Aug. 1991.
65. Interview with Denise Coffey, 3 July 1990. The meeting with the Young Vic company is also alluded to in a letter from SB to MH, 19 Sept. 1971 (Texas).
66. SB to Josette Hayden, 15 Sept. 1971. (Hayden).
67. Ibid.
68. See Charlie Rivel with J. C. Lauritzen, *Poor Clown* (London: Michael Joseph, 1973).
69. SB to Josette Hayden, 15 Sept. 1971 (Hayden).
70. He had been asked by Boleslaw Barlog whether he would come back to Berlin the following spring to direct *Waiting for Godot*. And although he had said that this was impossible at such short notice, the possibility of directing the play during a later season was left open.
71. SB to Josette Hayden, 10 Sept. 1971 (Hayden).
72. SB to Josette Hayden, 15 Sept. 1971 (Hayden).
73. SB to Ruth Davis, 7 March 1974 (John Beckett).
74. SB, postcard (of Caravaggio's *Beheading of St. John the Baptist* in St. John's Cathedral, Valletta), to MH, 26 Oct. 1971 (Texas).
75. SB to AA, 25 Oct. 1971 (Arikha).
76. SB to GR, 20 Oct. 1971 (Texas).
77. SB to AJL, 25 Oct. 1971 (Texas).
78. Ibid. and postcard to MH, 26 Oct. 1971 (Texas).
79. SB to MH, 26 Oct. 1971 (Texas).
80. SB to AJL, 25 Oct. 1971 (Texas).
81. SB, postcards to AA, 25 Oct. (Arikha), to Elmar and Erika Tophoven, also 25 Oct. (Tophoven), and to MH, 26 Oct. 1971 (Texas).
82. SB to Josette Hayden, undated (Hayden). "Vu cette formidable peinture à Valletta (la cathédrale de St. Jean)" ("saw this wonderful painting in Valletta [the Cathedral of St. John]") (SB to AA, 25 Oct. 1971 [Arikha]). On the same day Beckett sent a postcard of the Oratory of the Cathedral, with the Caravaggio prominent on the back wall, to

Elmar and Erika Tophoven with the comment "C'est un Caravaggio et des meilleurs" ("It is a Caravaggio and one of the best") (Tophoven).

83. SB, *Not I*, in *Collected Shorter Plays*, p. 215.

84. SB to JK, 28 April 1973 (Knowlson).

85. SB to Josette Hayden, 16 Feb. 1972 and ca. 18 Feb. 1972 (Hayden).

86. SB to JL, 18 Feb. 1972 (Minuit).

87. Enoch Brater, 'Dada, Surrealism, and the Genesis of *Not I*,' *Modern Drama*, vol. XVIII (March 1975), p. 50.

88. It may be no accident that, when Beckett restored the figure of the Auditor to the April 1978 Paris production that he directed — having removed it three years before for technical reasons — the gesture of Auditor at the end of the play was not only "a simple straightforward raising of arms from sides and their falling back, in a gesture of helpless compassion" (SB, *Not I*, in *Collected Shorter Plays*, p. 215) but an actual covering of the ears with the hands, as if the figure were unable to bear any longer the flood of sound issuing from Mouth. What has never been remarked on is that a painting by Mattia Pregi and his studio hanging on the lefthand wall of the Oratory depicts the blessed Adrian Fortesque holding his hands out in precisely the position of Auditor's gestures. Could it be that Beckett absorbed, perhaps even unconsciously, this raising of the arms as he gazed at the Caravaggio painting?

89. The idea of putting a head onstage without any accompanying body has been traced back in Beckett's work some nine years before *Not I* to the unpublished theater fragments called "Kilcool": "Woman's face alone in constant light. Nothing but fixed lit face and speech." (For a good discussion of the "Kilcool" fragments, which are in Trinity College, Dublin, Library, see Gontarski, *The Intent of Undoing in Samuel Beckett's Dramatic Texts*, pp. 134–42.)

90. Quoted in Gontarski, *The Intent of Undoing in Samuel Beckett's Dramatic Texts*, p. 132; confirmed by Ruby Cohn, 8 July 1994.

91. SB to Deirdre Bair and others, quoted in Bair, *Samuel Beckett*, p. 622.

92. The allusion is to Croker's Acres, the "Gallops" that belonged to Richard Webster Croker, who trained his horses on the meadows close to Leopardstown Race Course, only fifteen minutes' walk from Beckett's family home up the Ballyogan Road. See O'Brien, *The Beckett Country*, pp. 45–51.

93. JK, conversation with SB at rehearsals of the play in the Royal Court Theatre, London, January 1973.

94. SB, *The Unnamable*, in *Molloy Malone Dies The Unnamable*, p. 309.

95. Ibid., p. 358.

96. Ibid.

97. SB, *Not I*, in *Collected Shorter Plays*, p. 217 and *passim*.

98. Scholars have focused on the possible Jungian parallels both in Mouth (whose disconnected psychological state is related to a failure to achieve a coherent sense of an individual self) and in Auditor (who has been regarded as the "shadow" or alter ego of Mouth). Beckett had sufficient grounding in psychology and psychoanalytical theory to make such parallels perfectly justifiable.

99. SB to Kay Boyle, 3 Nov. 1972 (Texas).

100. SB to JH, 12 June 1972 (Herbert).

101. SB to JS, 29 May 1972 (Douw).

102. Interview with Hume Cronyn, 26 April 1994.

103. Interview with Jessica Tandy, 26 April 1994.

104. Two copies of this August 23, 1972, agreement, one signed by Barney Rosset for Beckett and Hume Cronyn and a second, amended one signed by Beckett, are in Boston College Library. The production was to be in either the Vivian Beaumont or the Forum Theater of the Lincoln Center.

105. Interview with Jessica Tandy, 26 April 1994.

106. Ibid.

107. Majno asked a number of Nobel Prize winners, including Neruda and Asturias, for texts to be illustrated by distinguished artists. Interview with Luigi Majno, 1 June 1994.

108. SB to Luigi Majno, 9 Jan. 1972 (Majno).

109. See S. W. Hayter, *About Prints* (London, New York, Toronto: Oxford University Press, 1962).

110. SB to Luigi Majno, 3 July and 27 July 1972 (Majno).

111. Interview with Luigi Majno, 1 June 1994.

112. All quotations from "Still" are taken from SB, *For to End Yet Again and Other Fizzles*, pp. 19–21.

113. As in *Samuel Beckett with Hand on Head* of January 1971 and *Samuel Beckett, Double Profile* of a month later. These heads are reproduced in Duncan Thomson, *Arikha*, pp. 61, 63.

114. SB to JH, 12 June 1972 (Herbert).

115. JK, conversation with Ruby Cohn, 22 July 1994.

116. It was in the airy St. Gothard studio and apartment that he spent hours looking at some of de Castro's most recent landscapes (1967–71), which had been painted in Tunisia. After his recent visits to North Africa, Beckett found them compelling and "very beautiful" (SB to JH, 16 June 1972 [Herbert]). He urged friends in London on no account to miss seeing them in an exhibition called "Landscapes of Light" that Denys Sutton mounted at the Wildenstein Gallery at the end of June. "Pass the word round" (SB to MH, 15 June 1972 [Texas]) and to John Calder (16 June 1972 [Bloomington]). Beckett also admired two large new, very powerful paintings of books that de Castro painted at Whitsun 1972.

117. Interview with Sergio de Castro, 2 March 1993.

118. SB to JH, 12 June 1972 (Herbert).

119. SB to MH, 24 Aug. 1972 (Texas).

120. SB to MH, 15 Sept. 1972 (Texas).

121. SB to Martin Segal, 14 Sept. 1972 (Segal).

122. SB to JK, 18 Oct. 1972 (Knowlson).

123. SB to John Kobler, 28 Jan. 1973 (Texas).

124. SB to AJL, 2 Jan. 1973 (Texas).

125. JK, conversation with SB at a rehearsal of *Not I*, 3 Jan. 1973.

126. SB to John Kobler, 28 Jan. 1973 (Texas).

127. JK, conversation with SB at a rehearsal of *Not I*, Jan. 1973.

128. I am most grateful to three of the participants in this production for their help: Billie Whitelaw; Jocelyn Herbert; and, for invaluable information, the stage manager, Robbie Hendry. Billie Whitelaw has written her own vivid account in *Billie Whitelaw . . . Who He?*, pp. 116–32.

129. Interview with Billie Whitelaw for the University of London Audio-Visual Centre, 1 Feb. 1977. *Journal of Beckett Studies*, no. 3 (summer 1978), p. 87.

130. I was with Beckett and Whitelaw at the very beginning of this particular rehearsal and can vouch for both the sympathy expressed and the professionalism of both actress and author-director.

131. Interview with Billie Whitelaw, 1 Feb. 1977, *Journal of Beckett Studies*, no. 3 (summer 1978), p. 86.

132. Billie Whitelaw, *The Sunday Times* (London), 14 Jan. 1973.

133. Interview with Jocelyn Herbert, 21 July 1994.

134. Interview with Robbie Hendry, 21 July 1994.

135. SB to Kay Boyle, 22 Jan. 1973 (Texas).

136. SB to Nick Rawson, 16 Feb. 1973 (TCD).

137. SB to JL, 11 Feb. 1973 (Minuit). He had sketched a version of this translation in April–May of the previous year. The first manuscript is dated 24 April 1972–18 May 1972; ms. 1227/7/14/1 (Reading).

138. SB to JH, 20 Aug. 1973 (Herbert).

139. Ibid.

140. "Happy to waive performance royalties any time any where for benefit of Gloria [MacGowran's wife] if it can be arranged" (SB to John Kobler, 11 April 1973 [Texas]). He did this with *Beginning to End.*

141. SB to Mania Péron, 8 Feb. 1973 (Péron).

142. SB to Kay Boyle, 22 Aug. 1973 (Texas).

143. Quoted in ibid.

144. SB to JK, 8 Nov. 1973 (Knowlson).

145. In 1987, Kickshaws in Paris published *MAC*, the "Passages from *Mercier et Camier* by Samuel Beckett excluded from the English edition, now gleaned, translated and printed, for private circulation only, by John Crombie . . . in a trial run of forty copies."

146. SB to Mania Péron, 8 Feb. 1973 (Péron).

147. Bettina Calder to BR, 31 Aug. 1973 (Boston).

148. SB to BR, 10 Feb. 1974 (Boston).

149. SB to John Kobler, 3 June 1974 (Texas).

150. SB to Morris Sinclair, 2 July 1974 (Sinclair).

151. SB to JK, 24 Sept. 1974 (Knowlson). In a letter to Ruby Cohn of July 23, 1974, he also referred to *That Time* as "*Not I's* little brother."

152. Ms. of *That Time*, dated 8 June 1974; ms. 1477/1 (Reading).

153. We simply do not know whether Beckett knew this photograph, although Ray had taken other photographs of James Joyce, Kay Boyle, Tristan Tzara, Marcel Duchamp, and Francis Picabia, all of whom were known to Beckett.

154. SB, *That Time*, in *Collected Shorter Plays*, p. 235.

155. W. D. Asmus, "Rehearsal Notes for the German Première of Beckett's *That Time* and *Footfalls* at the Schiller-Theater Werkstatt, Berlin (Directed by Beckett)," *Journal of Beckett Studies*, no. 2 (summer 1977), p. 92.

156. SB, *That Time*, in *Collected Shorter Plays*, p. 231.

157. Ibid., p. 228.

158. Ibid., p. 234.

159. SB, *Proust and Three Dialogues with Georges Duthuit*, p. 13.

160. How Beckett's close knowledge of the Bible is revealed in *That Time* is discussed in Knowlson and Pilling, *Frescoes of the Skull: The Later Prose and Drama of Samuel Beckett*, pp. 213–16.

161. By the beginning of July, it was "advancing slowly"; by August 22, it was "perhaps finished"; by September 1, it still "needs revision"; but by September 24, it was "nearly ready for the road" (SB to BR, 3 July [Boston], to Nick Rawson, 22 Aug. [TCD], to GR, 1 Sept. [Texas] and to JK, 24 Sept. 1974 [Knowlson], respectively).

162. JK, conversation with SB, prior to the production of *That Time* in May 1976.

163. Ms. 1639 (Reading).

164. SB to SP, 11 Aug. 1974 (Page).

165. SB to John Beckett, 11 Aug. 1974 (John Beckett).

166. SB to John Beckett, 18 Feb. 1974 (John Beckett).

167. SB to Alec Reid, 4 July 1974 (Reid papers, in private hands).

168. SB to JL, 21 Sept. 1973 (Minuit).

169. John Goodwin, ed., *Peter Hall's Diaries, The Story of a Dramatic Battle* (London: Hamish Hamilton, 1983), pp. 123–24.

170. Undated interview with Peggy Ashcroft, ca. spring 1976.

171. Goodwin, ed., *Peter Hall's Diaries*, p. 124.

172. Ibid., p. 123.

173. For Peggy Ashcroft's thoughts on how she approached this "absolute reality" in Beckett, see Michael Billington, *Peggy Ashcroft* (London: John Murray, 1988), p. 238.

174. Undated interview with Peggy Ashcroft, ca. spring 1976.

175. Interview with Martin Esslin, 7 May 1992, confirmed by telephone 2 Aug. 1994.

23: SHADES, 1975–77

1. SB to GR, 8 Jan. 1975 (Texas).
2. Quoted in Walter Asmus, "Beckett Directs *Godot*," *Theatre Quarterly*, vol. 5, no. 19 (1975), pp. 23–24.
3. SB to Jacoba van Velde, 14 Feb. 1975 (Bibliothèque Nationale).
4. SB to AS, 11 Feb. 1975 (Boston).
5. SB to JH, 19 Jan. 1975 (Herbert).
6. Walter Asmus, "Beckett Directs *Godot*," *Theatre Quarterly*, vol. 5, no. 19 (1975), p. 22.
7. SB to Matias, 14 Jan. 1975 (Matias), to JH, 19 Jan. 1975 (Herbert), to Elmar and Erika Tophoven, 25 Jan. 1975 (Tophoven), and to AS, 11 Feb. 1975 (Boston).
8. SB to Elmar Tophoven, 21 Jan. 1975 (Tophoven).
9. SB to JH, 19 Jan. 1975 (Herbert).
10. SB to AJL, 17 Feb. 1975 (Texas).
11. SB to Josette Hayden, 7 Feb. 1975 (Hayden).
12. SB to AS, 11 Feb. 1975 (Boston).
13. Walter Asmus, "Beckett Directs *Godot*," *Theatre Quarterly*, vol. 5, no. 19 (1975), p. 20. Klaus Herm said something similar in an excellent interview with Jonathan Kalb in *Beckett in Performance* (Cambridge: Cambridge University Press, 1989), pp. 197–205.
14. Dougald McMillan and James Knowlson, eds., *The Theatrical Notebooks of Samuel Beckett*. Vol. I: *Waiting for Godot* (London: Faber and Faber, and New York: Grove Press, 1993), p. 236.
15. The third figure from the left in Brueghel's *The Parable of the Blind* might indeed be Lucky, although in the play Pozzo is the one who has gone blind. The latter resembles the figure who has fallen down at the right side of the painting.
16. Coincidentally, the American director Herbert Berghof, who directed the New York production with Bert Lahr and E. G. Marshall, had some of these same pictures in mind as he rehearsed: "I studied Bosch and Brueghel in detail," he said. "I used certain attitudes in the paintings for the visualization of the images in the play. I'd never tell the actors that. But in Brueghel and Bosch you have actions pertinent to Beckett" (John Lahr, *Notes on a Cowardly Lion, The Biography of Bert Lahr*, p. 276).
17. Interviews with Frau Ingeborg Lübold and Dr. Wolfgang Trautwein, and visit to Beckett's atelier at the Akademie der Künste, 23 Aug. 1993.
18. Interview with Ruby Cohn, 23 Aug. 1991, and SB to Josette Hayden, 7 Feb. 1975 (Hayden).
19. SB to Josette Hayden, 25 Feb. 1975 (Hayden).
20. SB to Elmar and Erika Tophoven, 25 Jan. 1975 (Tophoven).
21. SB to AJL, 27 Jan. 1975 (Texas) and to AS, 11 Feb. 1975 (Boston).
22. SB to Josette Hayden, 7 Feb. 1975 (Hayden).
23. Interview with Ruby Cohn, 23 Aug. 1991.
24. Details of Cluchey's criminal offense and trial are taken from Los Angeles newspaper accounts reprinted in Rick Cluchey, *The Cage*, Künstlerhaus Bethanien, Frankfurt am Main, 1977.
25. Rick Cluchey, "My Years with Beckett," *Beckett. Krapp's Last Tape*, San Quentin Drama Workshop with *Endgame*, Künstlerhaus Bethanien, 1977.
26. Interview with Martin Esslin, 7 May 1992.
27. SB to Rick Cluchey, 25 Feb. 1974 (De Paul).
28. Rick Cluchey to SB, 11 Sept. 1974 (De Paul).
29. Peter Zeisler to SB, 18 Feb. 1987, and SB to Peter Zeisler, 26 Feb. 1987, asking for Barney Rosset to accept the money on his behalf "so that through him I may dispose of this sum in the US," and to BR (26 Feb. 1987), instructing him: "please give the total sum to Rick Cluchey with my love" (Boston).

30. Bair, *Samuel Beckett*, pp. 10–11.

31. Ruby Cohn, seminar at the University of Reading, 11 June 1994.

32. Interviews with John Beckett, 8 July 1992, and Ann Beckett, 3 Aug. 1992.

33. SB, *Footfalls*, in *Collected Shorter Plays*, p. 240.

34. Ibid.

35. SB to Antoni Libera, 11 Dec. 1980 (Libera). Beckett is replying to questions from Libera in a letter to him of October 29, 1980.

36. Original manuscript of *Footfalls*, ms. 1552/1 (Reading).

37. Interview with Mrs. Winter's daughter, Betty Dimond, 1 July 1994.

38. This friend wishes to remain anonymous.

39. SB to Ruby Cohn, 15 May 1975 (Cohn).

40. SB to JK, 19 Sept. 1975 (Knowlson). There are several references in other letters later in the year to having "finished a short play for Billie Whitelaw" (SB to MH, 23 Dec. 1975 [Texas]) and to "Billie's new piece [being] finished" (SB to JH, 23 Nov. 1975 [Herbert]).

41. SB to Billie Whitelaw, 3 Nov. 1975 (Whitelaw).

42. SB to Billie Whitelaw, 29 Dec. 1975 (Whitelaw).

43. SB to GR, 23 March 1975 (Texas).

44. SB to Nick Rawson, 15 April 1975 (TCD).

45. SB to Josette Hayden, 25 Feb. 1975 (Hayden).

46. SB to MH, 15 April 1975 (Texas).

47. JK, undated conversation with SB, ca. 1975.

48. SB to John Beckett, 11 May 1975 (John Beckett).

49. SB to Kay Boyle, 7 March 1976 (Texas).

50. SB to JH, 30 May 1975 (Herbert).

51. SB to JH, 30 June 1975 (Herbert).

52. SB to MH, 1 Aug. 1975 (Texas).

53. SB to John Kobler, 25 July 1975 (Texas).

54. SB to Kay Boyle, 8 Aug. 1975 (Texas).

55. Beckett wrote to Alan Schneider that his misgivings had been over the "disproportion between image (listening face) and speech and much time lost in trying to devise ways of amplifying former. I have now come to accept its remoteness and stillness — apart from certain precise eye movements, breath just audible in silences and final smile — as essential to the piece and dramatically of value" (SB to AS, 8 Aug. 1975 [Boston]).

56. SB to JH, 23 Nov. 1975 (Herbert).

57. Steven Connor, "Between Theatre and Theory: *Long Observation of the Ray*," in John Pilling and Mary Bryden, eds., *The Ideal Core of the Onion*, 1992, p. 79.

58. Nothing could be transmitted while the existing contracts gave the Royal Court Theatre exclusivity, and for some time the Royal Court thought of presenting the play again, perhaps in conjunction with *Happy Days*. Billie Whitelaw was also in another play and was feeling jaded. In the meantime, Beckett expressed renewed doubt as to the desirability of doing a television version.

59. The provisional film was then edited and shown in June 1975 in a four-seat viewing room to Billie Whitelaw, Jocelyn Herbert, Richard Odgers, and Warren Brown (the two last from Beckett's agent, Curtis Brown). Whitelaw and Herbert were delighted with the result and Whitelaw agreed that, as far as she was concerned, it might go ahead, as long as Beckett was in agreement and a suitable program could be arranged around it.

60. Copy of Tristram Powell's letter to SB, 16 Oct. 1975 (Curtis Brown).

61. SB to Warren Brown, 15 Sept. 1975 (Curtis Brown).

62. Warren Brown, letter to Tristram Powell quoting SB, 22 Dec. 1975 (Curtis Brown).

63. Interview with Ruby Cohn, 23 Aug. 1991.

64. SB to AJL, 15 Jan. 1976 (Texas); he had earlier written about a play for television (BBC) to accompany *Not I* in a letter to AA, 13 Jan. 1976 (Arikha).

65. SB to Josette Hayden, 14 Jan. and 26 Jan. 1976 (Hayden).

66. Notes by Hans Christoph Worbs to the Phillips recording by the Beaux Arts Trio of Beethoven's piano trios.

67. SB, *Ghost Trio*, in *Collected Shorter Plays*, p. 249.

68. Beckett's manuscript notes for *Ghost Trio*, ms. 1519/1 (Reading).

69. SB to GR, 9 May 1976 (Texas).

70. SB to Jacoba van Velde, 2 June 1976 (Bibliothèque Nationale).

71. SB to SP, 10 July 1976 (Page).

72. From my notes on the rehearsals of *Footfalls*, attended at Beckett's invitation in May 1976.

73. Barbara Lovenheim, interview with Billie Whitelaw, "A Canvas Who Has Lost Her Paintbrush," *The New York Times*, 2 Sept. 1990, p. 20. Billie Whitelaw develops this idea in her autobiography, *Billie Whitelaw . . . Who He?*, pp. 144–46.

74. Details from a discussion with Billie Whitelaw and Jocelyn Herbert at an Annenberg Fellowship seminar at the University of Reading, 11 June 1994.

75. Interview with Billie Whitelaw, *Journal of Beckett Studies*, no. 3 (summer 1978), p. 89.

76. SB to JH, 28 July 1976 (Herbert).

77. SB to Martin Esslin, 4 Aug. 1976 (Esslin).

78. SB to Robert Steen, 14 Nov. 1976 (Steen).

79. SB, "In Memoriam: George Reavey," *Journal of Beckett Studies*, no. 2 (summer 1977), p. 1.

80. SB to his aunt, Peggy Beckett, the widow of James Beckett, 22 Aug. 1976 (John Beckett).

81. Ibid.

82. SB to John Beckett, 11 May 1975 (John Beckett).

83. Duncan Scott, letter and notes to JK, 22 March 1993.

84. Duncan Scott, letter to JK, 22 March 1993.

85. SB to Peggy Beckett, 22 Aug. 1976 (John Beckett).

86. Interview with Edward Beckett, 29 Sept. 1994.

87. SB to AJL, 14 Sept. 1976 (Texas).

88. W. D. Asmus, "Rehearsal Notes for the German premiere of Beckett's 'That Time' and 'Footfalls' at the Schiller-Theater Workstatt," *Journal of Beckett Studies*, no. 2 (summer 1977), p. 83.

89. Ibid., p. 85.

90. Interview with Ruby Cohn, 23 Aug. 1991.

91. Interview with Fred Neumann, 29 April 1994.

92. David Warrilow, interview with Jonathan Kalb, *Beckett in Performance*, p. 221.

93. Interview with Fred Neumann, 29 April 1994.

94. SB to AJL, 14 Sept. 1976 (Texas).

95. SB to JL, 22 Sept. 1976 (Minuit).

96. John Dwyer, "In the Shadows with Feldman and Beckett," "Lively Arts" section, *Buffalo* (New York) *News*, 27 Nov. 1976.

97. Howard Skempton, interview with Morton Feldman in *Music and Musicians*, May 1977, p. 5.

98. John Dwyer, "In the Shadows with Feldman and Beckett," "Lively Arts" section, *Buffalo* (New York) *News*, 27 Nov. 1976.

99. SB to Morton Feldman, 31 Sept. (must be an error for 1 Oct.) 1976 sent by Feldman with an explanatory letter to JK, 6 Sept. 1977. Ms. 3033 (Reading).

100. SB to John Beckett, 18 Oct. 1976 (John Beckett).

101. JK, conversation with Beckett at rehearsal, Dec. 1976.

102. Heinrich von Kleist, "About the Marionette Theatre," Cherna Murray, trans., *Life and Letters Today*, vol. 16, no. 8 (summer 1937), pp. 104–105.

103. Michael Billington, *The Guardian*, 19 April 1976.

104. SB to John Beckett, 18 Oct. 1976 (John Beckett).

105. The first manuscript of the television play is dated "Le Touquet 21.10.1976," and a second handwritten version is dated "Le T. 25.10."

106. SB to JH, 18 Oct. 1976 (Herbert).

107. SB to JH, 14 Nov. 1976 (Herbert).

108. SB to John Beckett, 18 Oct. 1976 (John Beckett).

109. SB to Tristram Powell, 18 Nov. 1976 (Powell).

110. Telephone interview with Ronald Pickup, 23 Sept. 1994.

24: POLITICS AND *COMPANY,* 1977–79

1. Michael Billington, "Beckett," *The Guardian,* 18 April 1977.

2. Dennis Potter, *The Sunday Times* (London), 24 April 1977.

3. SB to Jennifer Sheridan, 28 Feb. 1972 (Curtis Brown).

4. Warren Brown to Robert Youdelman, 4 June 1975 (Curtis Brown).

5. Mannie Manim to Warren Brown, 11 May 1976 (Curtis Brown).

6. Warren Brown to SB, 17 May 1976 (Curtis Brown).

7. Ibid.

8. Memorandum of Agreement, 18 May 1976 (Curtis Brown).

9. Mannie Manim to Warren Brown, 30 Aug. 1976 (Curtis Brown).

10. Memorandum of Agreement with the Astbury Space Theatre, 6 Aug. 1976 (Curtis Brown).

11. Brian Astbury to Sue Freathy, 9 May 1978 (Curtis Brown).

12. Warren Brown, letter to Jo Dunstan of The Centre at St. George's Cathedral, Cape Town, 29 June 1976 (Curtis Brown).

13. *The Times* (London), 16 Oct. 1976, p. 5.

14. *The Times* (London), 14 Oct. 1976, p. 15.

15. Irving Wardle, *The Times* (London), 19 Feb. 1981.

16. SB to Antoni Libera, 6 Nov. 1976 (Libera).

17. Antoni Libera to SB, 2 June 1977 (Libera).

18. Antoni Libera to SB, 18 Dec. 1976 (Libera), received by Beckett only in June 1977.

19. SB to Kay Boyle, 11 Dec. 1977 (Texas).

20. Jack Thieuloy, *Loi de Dieu* (Paris l'Athanor, 1977), p. 8.

21. SB to JK, undated, but with a 11 Nov. 1977 postmark (Knowlson).

22. Interview with Jack Thieuloy, 13 June 1992.

23. JK, undated conversation with Elmar Tophoven.

24. Jack Emery, telephone interview, 8 Sept. 1994.

25. SB, GD, notebook 5, 2 March 1937. See Chapter 10, "Germany: The Unknown Diaries," p. 237.

26. Psalms 90:10.

27. Notebook, ms. 2901 (Reading).

28. SB to Ruby Cohn, 6 Feb. 1977 (Cohn).

29. SB to MH, 6 Feb. 1977 (Texas).

30. SB to JH, 15 May 1977 (Herbert).

31. SB to JL, 15 Dec. 1978 (Minuit).

32. SB to JK, 12 March 1977 (Knowlson).

33. SB to Josette Hayden, 27 April 1977 (Hayden).

34. SB to Tristram Powell (who had sent him Mary Hutchinson's obituary), 3 May 1977 (Powell).

35. SB to JH, 21 Oct. 1979 (Herbert).

36. SB to John Kobler, 21 March 1977 (Texas).

37. Interview with Klaus Herm, 9 Nov. 1994.

38. SB to AS, 18 April 1977 (Boston). Beckett had made the following notes in his notebook: "ministers of Pluto, sitting at foot of his throne." "Clotho (youngest—birth—

distaff," "Lachesis — life — spindle," "Atropos — death — scissors dressed in black," "a clew of thread (yarn)," and "Proserpine."

39. This quatrain was dated "T [Tangier] 21.4.1977." The notes concerning the Fates just quoted appear on the next page of Beckett's notebook. Ms. 2901 (Reading).

40. SB to JK, 19 June 1977 (Knowlson).

41. I am most grateful to Edward Beckett for lending me Beckett's appointment books for the period 1964–1986. One of the years covered in this chapter, 1978, is, unfortunately, missing.

42. SB to Josette Hayden, 4 June 1977 (Hayden).

43. Ms. 2901 (Reading).

44. SB to JK, 19 June 1977 (Knowlson).

45. SB to AS, 24 Sept. 1977 (Boston).

46. Ibid.

47. Lawrence Held, fax to JK, 12 May 1995.

48. Interview with Bud Thorpe, 2 Dec. 1993.

49. Ibid.

50. Interview with David Warrilow by Eric Prince, *Journal of Beckett Studies*, 2nd series, vol. 1, nos. 1 and 2 (1992), p. 120. "I just play to make the space mine," said Warrilow (p. 128).

51. SB to David Warrilow, 1 Oct. 1977 (Reading).

52. SB to JH, 15 May 1977 (Herbert).

53. SB, *A Piece of Monologue*, in *Collected Shorter Plays*, p. 265.

54. First manuscript draft of "Gone," ms. 2068 (Reading).

55. Ibid.

56. SB, *A Piece of Monologue*, in *Collected Shorter Plays*, p. 266.

57. SB to JH, 2 Nov. 1977 (Herbert).

58. Ibid.

59. SB, *A Piece of Monologue*, in *Collected Shorter Plays*, p. 269.

60. SB to JK, 10 Nov. 1977 (Knowlson).

61. SB to Martin Esslin, 14 Jan. 1979 (Esslin).

62. SB to David Warrilow, 13 April 1979 (Reading).

63. SB to JH, 2 Nov. 1977 (Herbert).

64. The notes that describe the characteristics of the voice are jotted down in Beckett's 1977–82 notebook, ms. 2901 (Reading). The date at the beginning of these notes is "16.1.76," but this is almost certainly an error for 1977. The related text called "The Voice" is dated "Paris Jan 77."

65. SB to JH, 2 Nov. 1977 (Herbert).

66. SB to Ruby Cohn, 3 May 1977 (Cohn).

67. SB, *Company*, p. 23.

68. SB, *Malone Dies* in *Molloy Malone Dies The Unnamable*, p. 270, and "The End" in *No's Knife: Collected Shorter Prose 1947–1966*, p. 46.

69. Interview with SB, 12 Aug. 1989.

70. Christopher Ricks expresses serious reservations on this issue in his interesting book, *Beckett's Dying Words*, especially pp. 149–50.

71. SB, *Company*, p. 89.

72. Ibid., p. 84.

73. SB to AJL, 23 Feb. 1978 (Texas).

74. SB to AJL, 24 Sept. 1978 (Texas).

75. SB to Paul Auster, 13 May 1977, thanking him for his translation of du Bouchet's poems with its introduction, which he found "very sensitive and enlightening" (New York Public Library).

76. Beckett had dedication copies of eleven of Harold Pinter's books and a typescript of *Mountain Language* from 1961 to 1988 in his library when he died.

77. In a letter to Beckett following the announcement, I somewhat rashly commented

in a postscript: "another Nobel prize-winning pessimist." Beckett replied promptly and aptly: "Where did you get the idea I was a pessimist?" (SB to JK, 28 Oct. 1976 [Knowlson]).

78. SB to Dr. Gottfried Büttner, 9 May 1978.

79. Interview with William Targ, 29 Nov. 1993.

80. All these pieces of music were found on a cupboard shelf near the piano at Ussy after Beckett's death.

81. Lili Foldes to JK, 10 April 1993.

82. SB to Andor and Lili Foldes, 18 March 1967 (Lili Foldes).

83. Beckett's appointment books for 1976 and 1977 show that he met Wolfgang Fortner twice, in Berlin on August 30, 1976, and in Paris on November 16, 1977.

84. "Feel obliged finally to authorize Heinz Holliger and his publisher Schott-Mainz to use texts of Not I and Come and Go for his musical settings of these works" (SB to Warren Brown, 24 Nov. 1976 [Curtis Brown]). Gerald Barry was given permission to set to music an excerpt from Waiting for Godot beginning "All the dead voices." And, since Mihalovici had already composed his opera, Krapp, SB allowed, on what he called the "lamb-sheep principle," Ahti Aho of Finland to compose a chamber opera based on the same play (authorizations sent to Gerald Barry on 1 April 1976 and to Ahti Aho on 10 April 1977 [Curtis Brown]).

85. SB to MH, 6 Feb. 1977 (Texas). The exhibition was at the Musée d'Art Moderne de la Ville de Paris. He went there on February 3, 1977.

86. Anne Madden le Brocquy writes interestingly of their meetings with Beckett over the period 1978–89 in her biography of her husband, Louis Le Brocquy: A Painter Seeing His Way.

87. SB, Imagination Dead Imagine, with illustrations by Sorel Etrog (London: John Calder, 1979). A note reads "Designed and illustrated by Sorel Etrog between 1969 and 1977."

88. JK, conversation with SB, 13 April 1978.

89. Interview with Delphine Seyrig, 29 Jan. 1990.

90. Interview with Leonard Fenton, 10 June 1994.

91. Stuart Burge to JK, 23 March 1993. Billie Whitelaw explains the difficulties in Billie Whitelaw . . . Who He?, pp. 151–53.

92. Notes made by Martha Fehsenfeld at rehearsals at the Royal Court Theatre (ms. 2102 [Reading]).

93. Ibid.

25: "FAIL BETTER," 1979–82

1. SB to Walter Asmus, 8 Sept. 1981 (Asmus).

2. Interview (June 1994) with Claude Thomas, barman at the Closerie des Lilas since 1966, who watched Beckett doing this many times with a "marron d'Inde" (horse chestnut) gripped tightly in his hand.

3. SB to AS, 20 June 1982 (Boston).

4. Interview with Daniel Labeille, 8 Jan. 1995.

5. I am most grateful to Daniel Labeille for his great kindness in supplying me with copies of his letters to Beckett as well as Beckett's to him and for checking the accuracy of my account. I am also grateful to Irene Worth and Billie Whitelaw for additional details.

6. "Penne," as he was called, was already well-known for his films, Monterey Pop and Don't Look Back, in which he covered Bob Dylan's 1966 British tour, and for his pioneering work with Richard Leacock in harnessing synchronous sound to a hand-held camera.

7. Beckett favored Come and Go and Footfalls. But the two fragments, Theatre I and Theatre II, were also considered: "For me they are abortions," Beckett commented. "But

I suppose what is not? More or less" (SB to AS, 1 Dec. 1980—but probably an error for 1 Jan. 1980, for Christmas was clearly over when he wrote [Boston]).

8. SB to Daniel Labeille, 17 March 1980 (Labeille).

9. These and subsequent quotations are from SB, *Rockaby*, in *Collected Shorter Plays*, pp. 275–82.

10. The suggestions of affinities with the Whistler and van Gogh paintings were made in Enoch Brater's *Beyond Minimalism: Beckett's Late Style in the Theater* (New York and Oxford: Oxford University Press, 1987), pp. 168, 175–76. I am indebted to Brater's chapter "Play as Performance Poem."

11. Rembrandt's *Margaretha de Geer*, her white ruff contrasting with the simple, dark plainness of her gown (National Gallery, London) was often seen by Beckett.

12. A copy of Beckett's letter to Equity dated February 9, 1982, is enclosed with one to AS of the same date (Boston).

13. Irene Worth had played Winnie the previous year in Andrei Serban's production. Barbara Bray had given Beckett a glowing report of her acting (interview with Irene Worth, 16 May 1994) and Schneider had written to him: "She is a marvelous actress, and does some fine things. Quite different, I gather from Billie's (and Ruth White's) [Winnie]" (AS to SB, 23 June 1979 [Boston]).

14. SB to Daniel Labeille, 5 Aug. 1980 (Labeille).

15. To David Gothard, 11 Dec. 1983, SB wrote: "*Rockaby* was not written with Irene Worth in mind" (Gothard).

16. Interview with Irene Worth, 16 May 1994.

17. SB to Daniel Labeille, 9 Oct. 1980 (Labeille).

18. SB to Daniel Labeille, 18 Feb. 1981 (Labeille).

19. E.g.: "The woman in no way initiates the rock. The memory initiates the rock"; the eyes should be "more closed than open as [the] piece progresses"; the "rocker is mother's —no richness, no ornateness, but plain"; but the headdress "must glitter . . . perhaps feathers." These and other details were given by Daniel Labeille in a talk at a conference on Beckett, March 24, 1984, at the University of Texas at Austin and are in Brater's *Beyond Minimalism: Beckett's Late Style in the Theater*, pp. 173–74.

20. He phoned Whitelaw on February 22 and March 8, commenting politely to Schneider, "Hope you don't mind this encroachment" (SB to AS, 24 Feb. 1981 [Boston]).

21. SB to AS, 24 Feb. 1981 (Boston) and an entry in his 1981 appointment book.

22. AS to SB, (18) April 1981 (Boston).

23. Although only four performances were given at the Center Theater in Buffalo, the production was also seen in New York at the La Mama theater, then at the SUNY–Purchase campus in Westchester County.

24. SB to Daniel Labeille, 16 June 1981 (Labeille).

25. Interview with Daniel Labeille, 6 Jan. 1995.

26. JK, conversation with SB, immediately after a rehearsal, Dec. 1982.

27. SB to AS, 27 May 1981 (Boston).

28. SB to S. E. Gontarski, 2 Mar. 1980 (Gontarski). I owe a debt to Stan Gontarski for his help with this part of my narrative.

29. SB to S. E. Gontarski, 20 June 1980 (Gontarski).

30. The difficulty that the protagonist has in threading the needle comes from two of Beckett's own major impediments, his defective eyesight and his Dupuytren's contracture of the hand. Beckett writes: "Parkinson's—Dupuytren—seldom united. Either one has P. or D. Seldom both" (ms. 2930 [Reading]).

31. Michael Billington, *The Guardian*, 15 Aug. 1984.

32. Kalb, *Beckett in Performance*, p. 49.

33. I not only think of the appearance of the figures in *The Geographer* or *The Astronomer* but also of the stark, almost frozen nature of their gestures.

34. This and subsequent short quotations are from SB, *Ohio Impromptu*, in *Collected Shorter Plays*, pp. 285–88.

35. JK, conversation with SB, 1981.

36. SB, *Ohio Impromptu*, in *Collected Shorter Plays*, p. 286.

37. SB to David Warrilow, 19 Feb. 1981 (Reading).

38. Michael Billington, *The Guardian*, 15 Aug. 1984.

39. This resulted from his degree in French from the University of Reading and his work for several years as an editor on the magazine *Réalités* in Paris.

40. This was praised for its sharply comic qualities and the high standard of its acting by the theater critic of *Le Monde*, 22 Feb. 1980.

41. Of *A Piece of Monologue* he wrote to Warrilow: "My initial impression was of over-slowness. But as it went on I was won over. Breath dramatisation of speechlessness very effective" (SB to David Warrilow, 15 Feb. 1980 [Reading]). To Joe Chaikin, he wrote of his tape of extracts from *How It Is:* "I listened to it with much interest. I thought the utterance too brisk and lively, especially end of *How It Is*, for such consternation and extremity. But you know what authors are." Beckett gave Chaikin *"carte blanche* to use the *Texts* as you please + end of *How It Is*," but asked later: "How stage that bodilessness? That groping *vox inanis* (soulless voice)" (SB to Joe Chaikin, 29 Jan. 1981 and 17 March 1981 [Kent State]).

42. Lawrence Shainberg, "Exorcising Beckett," *The Paris Review*, no. 104, vol. 29 (Fall 1987), pp. 100–101.

43. Ibid., p. 102.

44. Maeve Binchy, "Beckett Finally Gets Down to Work — as the Actors Take a Break." *The Irish Times*, 14 May 1980.

45. Interview with Bud Thorpe, 2 Dec. 1993.

46. Ibid.

47. Interview with Rosemary Pountney, 10 Dec. 1994.

48. Interview with Bud Thorpe, 2 Dec. 1993.

49. For further details on the Cromlechs, see O'Brien, *The Beckett Country*, pp. 20, 23, 27, 29, 349 n. 36, 353 n. 15.

50. Beckett Archive, ms. 2901 (Reading).

51. SB, *Ill Seen Ill Said*, (London: John Calder, 1982), p. 52.

52. Ibid., p. 17.

53. Dante makes his customary appearance in both French and English versions: "The eye will return to the scene of its betrayals. On centennial leave from where tears freeze" (SB, *Ill Seen Ill Said*, p. 27). This is expressly linked with *Purgatorio*, Canto XXXII, verse 47 in an early manuscript note (ms. 2205 [Reading]). My attention was drawn to Beckett's marginal note in the French manuscript by the Japanese scholar Naoya Mori.

54. SB, *Ill Seen Ill Said*, pp. 56–57.

55. Ibid., p. 26.

56. Ibid., p. 36.

57. Lawrence Graver, "Homage to the Dark Lady: *Ill Seen Ill Said*," in Ben-Zvi, ed., *Women in Beckett: Performance and Critical Perspectives*, p. 148.

58. Melanie Klein, "Love, Guilt, and Reparation," quoted in ibid., p. 148.

59. See Bryden, *Women in Samuel Beckett's Prose and Drama*, pp. 154–58.

60. SB, *Ill Seen Ill Said*, pp. 58–59.

61. Ibid., p. 26.

62. SB, *Footfalls*, in *Collected Shorter Plays*, p. 242.

63. SB, *Ill Seen Ill Said*, p. 29.

64. JL to SB, 9 Dec. (1980) (Minuit).

65. SB to Ruby Cohn, 25 Jan. 1981 (Cohn).

66. SB to JH, 11 Jan. 1981 (Herbert).

67. SB to JK, 20 May 1981 (Knowlson).

68. SB to Lawrence Shainberg, undated (but probably late March) (Shainberg).

69. The plays included Rick Cluchey's *Krapp's Last Tape* in English, the Mabou Mines company's *Come and Go*, Madeleine Renaud in *Oh les beaux jours*, and a new produc-

tion of *Fin de partie*. Both English and French adaptations of *Texts for Nothing* by Joe Chaikin and by Jean-Claude Fall were on view. David Warrilow acted in *Ohio Impromptu, A Piece of Monologue,* and *The Lost Ones,* as well as directing a new production of *Rockaby* with Helen Bishop and acting in an adaptation of *Eh Joe* directed by Alan Schneider.

70. SB to JH, 1 May 1981 (Herbert).

71. SB to Michel Guy (in French) quoted in Colette Godard, "Beckett et David Warrilow au Festival d'automne," *Le Monde,* 6 Oct. 1981.

72. SB to Rick Cluchey, 9 March 1981 (De Paul).

73. SB to Dr. Müller-Freienfels, 30 Jan. 1980 (Süddeutscher Rundfunk). This was written at the end of 1979 or January 1980, a little earlier than has been thought to be the case. He proposed a production date well over a year later, presumably concluding that it would require a lot of thought and discussion.

74. Gontarski, *The Intent of Undoing in Samuel Beckett's Dramatic Texts,* pp. 179–181.

75. Jim Lewis, "Beckett et la caméra," *Revue d'esthétique,* hors série (1990), pp. 376–77.

76. Beckett Archive, ms. 2199 (Reading).

77. The long gowns make them look like Gustave Doré figures, although, unlike those of Doré's Dante and Virgil, the heads of the players in *Quadrat* as well as their bodies are covered.

78. SB to Antoni Libera (in French), 11 Dec. 1980 (Libera).

79. Some of the same people were involved with it as in previous Süddeutscher Rundfunk productions: his friend Jim Lewis was again the cameraman, and the set design and costumes were again executed by Wolfgang Wahl; but Bruno Voges replaced Walter Asmus as Beckett's assistant. Beckett was offered DM 15,000 to direct the play with daily expenses of DM 31 (Dr. Müller-Freienfels to SB, 3,14, and 28 April 1981 [Süddeutscher Rundfunk]).

80. SB to AS, 22 April 1981 (Boston).

81. SB to Dr. Müller-Freienfels, 30 April 1981 (Süddeutscher Rundfunk).

82. Martha Fehsenfeld, "Beckett's Late Works: An Appraisal," *Modern Drama,* vol. 25, no. 3 (September 1982), pp. 360–61.

83. Interview with Dr. Müller-Freienfels, April 3, 1996.

84. SB's appointment book, 1981.

85. Beckett Archive, ms. 2602 (Reading).

86. Beckett Archive, ms. 2901 (Reading).

87. SB, *Worstward Ho,* p. 28.

88. Ibid., p. 12.

89. Ibid., p. 33.

90. Ibid., p. 29.

91. Enoch Brater, "Voyelles, Cromlechs and the Special (W)rites of *Worstward Ho*," in James Acheson and Kateryna Arthur, eds., *Beckett's Later Fiction and Drama* (Basingstoke and London: Macmillan, 1987), p. 172.

92. SB, *Worstward Ho,* p. 20.

93. Mark 8:36.

94. SB, *Worstward Ho,* p. 13.

95. Ibid., p. 45.

96. There is a good discussion of this aspect of *Worstward Ho* in Paul Davies, *The Ideal Real: Beckett's Fiction and Imagination* (Toronto and London: Associated University Presses, 1994), pp. 213–25.

97. SB to AS, 4 Feb. 1982 (Boston).

98. SB to David Warrilow, 12 March 1982 (Reading).

99. On March 3, 1982, JL wrote to SB, "Lu une première fois *Solo*. Magnifique" ("Gave *Solo* a first reading. Magnificent") (Minuit).

100. A copy of *Catastrophe* was with Jérôme Lindon by March 11 and was sent on by Lindon to the Association internationale de défense des artistes on April 5 (JL to SB, 11

March 1982, and to the AIDA, 5 April 1982 [Minuit]). Beckett sent me "confidentially" a copy of the typescript of *Catastrophe*, saying that it was "the piece for *La Nuit de A.I.D.A.*) (*Une Nuit pour V.H.*), Avignon, July 21" (SB to JK, 13 April 1982 [Knowlson]).

101. SB to AS, 4 April 1982: "Wrote a short act in French (*Catastrophe*) for a group gesture toward Vaclan [Václav] Havel, for next Avignon Festival. Not yet translated."

102. SB to S. E. Gontarski, 5 June 1982 (Gontarski).

103. Sidur had turned from creating heroic social-realist statuary to follow a freer path as an artist and was penalized as a consequence. Drs. Gottfried and Renate Büttner had first interested Beckett in his fate in 1971 and more recently had sent him a major book about Sidur with a photo of the sculpture that Beckett had been given on its dust cover. These two works on Sidur, *Skulturen Graphiken* (Constance, West Germany: Universitätsverlag Konstanz, eingeleitet von K. Eimermacher, 1978), and a catalogue of an exhibition in 1980 with the same title as this book, were still in Beckett's library at his death (letters from Gottfried Büttner and telephone interview with him, 17 Dec. 1994).

104. JK, undated conversation with Avigdor Arikha.

105. The manuscripts are in the Beckett Archive, ms. 2457 (Reading).

106. The word is used "in its more technical, theatrical sense, derived from its Greek roots, *kata* (down), *strophein* (turn), to allude to the scene of classical tragedy depicting the downward turn of the protagonist's fortunes" (Dougald McMillan, "Human Reality and Dramatic Method: *Catastrophe*, *Not I* and the Unpublished Plays," in Acheson and Arthur, eds., *Beckett's Later Fiction and Drama*, p. 98).

107. SB, *Catastrophe*, in *Collected Shorter Plays*, p. 300.

108. Painting may again have helped to inspire Beckett. The flesh of the Protagonist is whitened to approximate stone or white marble, and his hands are together, raised to his chest, like the praying, stonelike figures in a Mantegna painting. Behind Beckett's image, even if only obliquely evoked, lie centuries of iconography of the martyred Christ and martyred saints.

109. In the French original, "sinciput" is used instead of "tête" or even "crâne," "tibia" instead of "jambe."

110. SB to JK, 20 June 1983 (Knowlson).

111. JK, undated conversation with SB, ca. Oct. 1984.

112. SB to Ruby Cohn, 31 July 1982 (Cohn).

113. Václav Havel to SB, 17 April 1983 (Minuit). "Beautiful letter in English from Havel, sent from Stockholm. He still in Prague" (SB to JK, 21 May 1983 [Knowlson]).

114. Martin Garbus, "Godot Is Here," *The Nation*, 29 Jan. 1990, p. 12.

115. SB to Dr. Müller-Freienfels, 15 May 1982 (Süddeutscher Rundfunk).

116. SB to AA, 28 Aug. 1982 (Arikha).

117. SB to Kay Boyle, 6 April 1982 (Texas).

118. He sent this "further aberration" to the German producer on June 15 (SB to Dr. Müller-Freienfels, 15 June 1982 [Süddeutscher Rundfunk]). Müller-Freienfels received the piece enthusiastically, saying they would be very glad to produce it for German TV (Müller-Freienfels to SB, 5 July 1982 [Süddeutscher Rundfunk]).

119. Jim Lewis, "Beckett et la caméra," p. 379.

120. Morris Sinclair to JK, 11 Oct. 1993.

121. SB to Dr. Müller-Freienfels, 30 July 1982 (Süddeutscher Rundfunk).

122. SB to Dr. Müller-Freienfels, 5 Aug. 1982 (Süddeutscher Rundfunk).

123. Ibid.

124. Dr. Müller-Freienfels to SB, 3 June 1983 (Süddeutscher Rundfunk).

26: WINTER JOURNEY, 1983–89

1. SB to Lawrence Shainberg, 7 Jan. 1983 (Shainberg).

2. SB to George Tabori, 23 July 1983 (Tabori).

3. SB to JK, 21 May 1983 (Knowlson). On May 9, 1983, he wrote to Alan Mandell, "I languish in sterility" (Mandell).

4. "I find I cannot translate *Worstward Ho.* Or with such loss that I cannot bear the thought" (SB to Antoni Libera, 1 Aug. 1983 [Libera]). On December 16, 1983, on his own and Beckett's behalf, Jérôme Lindon wrote to the Beckett scholar Jean-Jacques Mayoux, professor of English at the Sorbonne, to ask whether he would undertake such an onerous task. In the end, Mayoux did not translate it.

5. In his Paris library, Beckett had Otto Erich Deutsch's *Schubert, die Dokumente seines Lebens* (Kassel and New York: Bärenreiter, 1964), which contains several letters relating to Schubert's stay in Graz. Among his books at Ussy was Gerald Moore's *The Schubert Song Cycle and Thoughts on Performance* (London: Hamish Hamilton, 1975).

6. SB, *What Where*, in *Collected Shorter Plays*, p. 316.

7. Samuel Beckett's manuscript production notes prepared before and during the filming of *Was Wo* in Stuttgart, June 1985, ms. 3097 (Reading).

8. Thomas Moore, *Complete Poetical Works* (New York: Thomas Y. Crowell, 1895), p. 224. But Beckett may well have read these lines in slightly abbreviated form in his father's old copy of John Bartlett's *Familiar Quotations* (Boston: Little, Brown, 1885), which he had on the shelves in his study.

9. Beckett learned of the death of Stuart Maguinness from Arthur Hillis while he was in London at the beginning of December 1982. "I mourn the loss of a dear friend and send to you and Juliet my deep sympathy" (SB to Olive Maguinness, 15 Dec. 1982 [Reading]).

10. SB to MM, 9 Jan. 1984 (Texas).

11. SB, *What Where* in *Collected Shorter Plays*, pp. 310 and 316.

12. Beckett's manuscript production notes, ms. 3097 (Reading). Beckett also sent his cameraman, Jim Lewis, a postcard reproduction of the cowled, robed statue of John Donne, which he had seen at St. Patrick's Cathedral in Westminster, with the suggestion that the costumes for the figures in *Was Wo* might be modeled on this.

13. *Arthur Rimbaud: Complete Works*, Paul Schmidt, trans. (New York: Harper and Row, 1975), p. 123.

14. Martha Fehsenfeld, "Everything Out but the Faces: Beckett's Reshaping of *What Where* for Television," *Modern Drama*, vol. 29, no. 2 (June 1986), p. 233.

15. SB, *What Where* in *Collected Shorter Plays*, p. 312.

16. Beckett had already employed the idea of an interrogation many years before in *Rough for Radio II*, where Fox, the figure of the tormented, creative artist, is tortured to produce a sequence of words that will satisfy his interrogators. In the new play the repeated, cyclical nature of the interrogation changes the form but not the point of the torture.

17. "What is new, in two of the three pieces, is the overt expression of his [Beckett's] political consciousness" (Mel Gussow, *The New York Times*, 16 June 1983) and "an opaque, sometimes comedic, picture of inquisition and perhaps torture" (William A. Raidy, *The* [Newark, N.J.] *Star-Ledger*, 15 June 1983).

18. AS to SB, 19 June 1983 (Boston).

19. Michael Billington, *The Guardian*, 15 Aug. 1984.

20. "Just finished a short piece — theatre — for the Graz autumn Festival, to my dissatisfaction" (SB to Kay Boyle, 20 March 1983 [Texas]).

21. Diana Barth, "Schneider Directs Beckett," *Showbill*, Dec. 1983, p. 3.

22. SB, *What Where*, in *Collected Shorter Plays*, p. 316.

23. On May 20, 1983, Beckett wrote to tell Alan Schneider that Graz had no objection to an American premiere. He sent Schneider the translated script on May 25; Schneider received it only on June 1, with an opening on June 15 (Boston).

24. Schneider's letters to Beckett at this date give an indication of the details they were discussing on the telephone — e.g., AS to SB, wrongly dated May 9, 1983. It was clearly June 9, since, as noted above, the script of *What Where* did not arrive in New York until June 1 (Boston).

25. The main concern was the serious mental depression and physical health of one of the stars, David Warrilow, who had roles in all three plays. Eventually, Warrilow, suffering from an alcohol addiction, became too ill to act and his understudy took over until Alvin Epstein replaced him. Once Warrilow was better and able to return to the production, he and Epstein alternated the roles of Director and Protagonist in *Catastrophe* (AS to SB, letters between 16 July and 20 Nov. 1983 [Boston]).

26. AS to SB, 17 Feb. 1984 (Boston College).

27. AS to SB, 2 March 1984 (Boston College).

28. SB to David Warrilow, 11 July 1982 (Reading). For several months in the summer of 1982, Barrault (in what can only be regarded as a fit of pique) would not reply to Pierre Chabert's inquiries as to whether the theater would or would not be available for a Beckett season. With Beckett's agreement, Jérôme Lindon then became involved, writing to Barrault twice, on October 20 and November 8, 1982. Finally, after a delay of almost five months, Barrault telephoned Lindon suggesting that Chabert should call to see him. Agreement for a Beckett season the following autumn was confirmed on November 19, 1982 (Minuit).

29. SB to AA, 14 Sept. 1983 (Arikha).

30. "How I dread the prospect" (SB to JK, 24 Jan. 1984 [Knowlson]).

31. Rick Cluchey, letter to SB, 27 June 1983 (De Paul).

32. "I have told Rick I could give them one week in London between conclusion of their rehearsals in Chicago and departure for Adelaide. This mainly to ratify the festival's insistence that I should 'survey' (as Rick puts it) the production. That is the most I can do" (SB to Walter Asmus, 18 Oct. 1983 [Asmus]).

33. E.g., SB to Rick Cluchey, 8 Feb., 31 May, and 23 Sept. 1983 (De Paul).

34. SB to JK, 24 Jan. 1984 (Knowlson) and appointments diary entry for 20 Feb. 1984.

35. "I prefer to meet myself my travel and hotel expenses. I'll take care of booking at Hyde Park or elsewhere. Please thank Adelaide for their kind offer and decline" (SB to Rick Cluchey, 2 Nov. 1983 [De Paul]).

36. SB to Rick Cluchey, 23 Sept. 1983 (De Paul). A copy of this letter was sent to Sue Freathy at Curtis Brown.

37. Some months before the production, Beckett had asked me to send him a photocopy of his own 1975 Schiller-Theater production notebook, since, in the meantime, he had given it to the Beckett Archive (Reading). And he marked up two copies of the text. But, on his arrival in London, he still did not know it by heart and this always bothered him at rehearsals.

38. JK, conversation with SB, 20 Feb. 1984.

39. E.g., SB to David Gothard, 5 April 1984 (Gothard) and to Joe Chaikin, 9 April 1984 (Kent State).

40. SB to JK, 6 March 1984 (Knowlson). "On the whole pleased with result. . . . Cable from Rick from Adelaide: 'Smash success all three'!!" (SB to Alan Mandell, 21 March 1984 [Mandell]).

41. Interview with Walter Asmus (who was sitting beside Beckett in the theater), 13 Nov. 1994.

42. The objections are taken from Fred Jordan's report on the ART production to Barney Rosset (Boston).

43. The ART claimed, almost correctly, that the text itself was delivered as written. (The "almost" must be added because some lines were repeated and others were delivered from a loudspeaker and not from the actors onstage).

44. SB to David Warrilow, 5 Aug. 1984 (Reading).

45. This was staged in New York in 1986.

46. *Company* was presented (in a joint production by Mabou Mines and the New York Shakespeare Festival) at Joseph Papp's Public Theater in New York in January 1983, conceived and directed by Frederick Neumann and Honora Fergusson. Neumann was the main performer.

47. Statement by Barney Rosset, 11 Dec. 1984, quoted in several press reports (Boston).

48. Kalb, *Beckett in Performance*, p. 87.

49. SB to Klaus Herm, 9 Aug. 1984 (Herm).

50. SB to Dr. Krista Jussenhoven (of S. Fisher Verlag), 23 July 1983.

51. SB to BR, 13 Feb. 1973 (Boston).

52. In May 1982, Beckett received a moving personal plea from a Frau Osterkamp regarding a female *Waiting for Godot* in Regensburg, which she wanted to take on to the Berlin Festival. It is clear that, although this was finally not authorized by S. Fischer Verlag, Beckett was not unmoved by this letter, agreeing that it might perhaps go to Berlin on two conditions: "1) That this production go no further. 2) That my position be made clear, i.e. one of total disapproval" (SB to Dr. Krista Jussenhoven, 3 June 1982 [S. Fischer]).

53. For example, the Denver Center Theater Company (contracted before it was known that they intended to use women) was obliged to display a disclaimer poster in the lobby of the Space Theater: "Samuel Beckett wrote *Waiting for Godot* for five male characters and has never approved otherwise." (Correspondence about this particular production is at Boston College.) In Germany, confronted in May 1982 with the prospect of a female Hamm playing in *Endgame*, Beckett wrote: "The thought of Hamm played by an actress is intolerable" (SB to Helmar Fischer, 27 May 1982. See also SB to Dr. Krista Jussenhoven, 2 July 1982 [S. Fischer]).

54. Ben-Zvi, ed., *Women in Beckett: Performance and Critical Perspectives*, p. x.

55. Edward Albee took a similar line on sexual difference in August 1984, when he threatened legal action against a production of *Who's Afraid of Virginia Woolf* by four male actors. In this case, the director gave way and canceled the production. It was reported that the leasing contracts of Albee's plays stipulated things that might not be changed. "Specifically, actors must be of the same sex as the characters," confirmed Albee. "There is a fine line between interpretation and distortion. There are certain stage directions that are meant to be followed" (Richard Lacayo, "Directors Fiddle, Authors Burn," *Time*, 21 Jan. 1985, p. 74).

56. The case is discussed, in English, in Cobi Bordewijk, "The Integrity of the Playtext: Disputed Performances of *Waiting for Godot*," Buning, Marius, Houppermans, et. al., eds; *Samuel Beckett Today/Aujourd'hui*, (Amsterdam, Atlanta: Rodopi, 1992), pp. 147–52; and, in Dutch, in Lucia van Heteren, *Laten we gaan*, TheaterCahiers 3 (Amsterdam: Nederlands Theater Instituut, Uitgeverij International Theatre and Film Books, 1992), pp. 94–98.

57. Sentence no. 148, Arrondissementrechtbank te Haarlem, 29 April 1988, quoted in Cobi Bordewijk, "The Integrity of the Playtext," p. 152.

58. A photograph of him with his back to the camera was reproduced in Mira Averech, "Quelques jours dans la vie de Samuel Beckett," *Globe*, no. 44 (Feb. 1990), p. 59.

59. My account of Roger Blin's cremation is based upon interviews with Michèle Meunier (17 Sept. 1990) and with Blin's companion, Hermine Karagheuz (26 Feb. 1994).

60. Dr. Müller-Freienfels, letter to SB, 28 Dec. 1983 (Süddeutscher Rundfunk).

61. Telephone interview with Billie Whitelaw, 25 Jan. 1995.

62. AS to SB, 29 Jan. 1984 (Boston).

63. JL to SB, 4 May 1984 (Minuit).

64. SB to AA, 27 April 1984.

65. SB to David Warrilow, 23 Nov. 1984 (Reading).

66. SB to MM, 16 Dec. 1984 (Texas).

67. First nonlimited publication, *The Guardian*, 3 March 1989.

68. Beckett had Walther von der Vogelweide's *Gedichte Alt und Neudeutsch* (Berlin and Leipzig: n.d.) in his personal library.

69. First nonlimited publication, *The Guardian*, 3 March 1989.

70. In his drafts or notes there are several allusions to Beckett's childhood: "The voice of his nanny telling him when he refused his bread and milk that he would follow a crow

for a crust," probably recorded with the idea either of introducing the phrase "a crow for a crust" or the image of a "crow flapping slow and low with a big crust in its beak," in all probability a death image (ms. 2935/1/3 [Reading]).

71. Ms. 2933/2 (Reading).

72. Death certificate of Arthur Darley, district of Rathmines 2, recorded 10 Jan. 1949. Darley was only thirty-five years old when he died. I am most grateful to Darley's executor and cousin, Ernest Keegan, for information on Arthur Darley's life and death.

73. Frank Kermode, "A Miserable Splendour," *The Guardian*, 3 March 1989.

74. He telephoned me to ask if the archivist at the University of Reading would send him a copy of the typescript, which was held in the Beckett Archive. The copy was duly dispatched and Beckett telephoned again, saying that *Dream* was too awful for him to contemplate its being published, and asking for a copy of his unpublished play, *Eleutheria*.

75. SB to BR, 19 Dec. 1986 (Boston). On May 21, 1987, he wrote to Alan Mandell: "Third 3rd (Fragment 3) for Barney begun but far from completion. Very thin and dumb these days" (Mandell).

76. Note by the recipient on letter from SB to Marek Kedzierski, 23 April 1987.

77. SB to Kay Boyle, 5 June 1989 (Texas).

78. I interviewed him the next day and spoke to him about the program. He was very moved by it.

79. Interview with Edith Fournier, 3 May 1995.

80. Interview with Hermine Karagheuz, 26 Feb. 1994.

81. He enjoyed the odd Davidoff or Diplomate cigarillo (he had earlier smoked Panthères) and kept on smoking until his final illness.

82. SB to BR, 19 Nov. 1988 (Boston).

Bibliography

PUBLICATIONS BY SAMUEL BECKETT

PRINCIPAL WORKS IN FRENCH AND ENGLISH IN CHRONOLOGICAL ORDER OF PUBLICATION

Note: Details of the first edition in England are given here. When the first edition is in French, this is followed by details of the first edition of the translation published in England. Details of editions published by Grove Press Inc. (now Grove/Atlantic Inc.) are also supplied.

"Dante . . . Bruno. Vico . . Joyce." In *Our Exagmination Round His Factification for Incamination of Work in Progress*. Paris: Shakespeare and Company, 1929.

Whoroscope. Paris: The Hours Press, 1930. Reprinted in *Poems in English*. London: John Calder, 1961. New York: Grove Press, 1963.

Proust. London: Chatto and Windus, 1931. New York: Grove Press [1957]. Reprinted with *Three Dialogues: Samuel Beckett and Georges Duthuit*. London: John Calder, 1965.

More Pricks Than Kicks. London: Chatto and Windus, 1934. Reprinted London: John Calder, 1970. New York: Grove Press, 1972.

Echo's Bones and Other Precipitates. Paris: Europa Press, 1935. Reprinted in *Poems in English*. London: John Calder, 1961 and in *Collected Poems in English and French*, London: John Calder, 1977. New York: Grove Press, 1963.

Murphy. London: Routledge and Sons, 1938. Reprinted London: John Calder, 1963. New York: Grove Press [1957].

Molloy. Paris: Les Editions de Minuit, 1951.

Molloy. English translation by Patrick Bowles in collaboration with Samuel Beckett. Paris: Olympia Press, 1955. New York: Grove Press, 1955.

Malone meurt. Paris: Les Editions de Minuit, 1951.

Malone Dies. London: John Calder, 1958. New York: Grove Press, 1956.

En attendant Godot. Paris: Les Editions de Minuit, 1952.

Waiting for Godot. London: Faber and Faber, 1956. New York: Grove Press, 1954.

L'Innommable. Paris: Les Editions de Minuit, 1953.

The Unnamable. In *Molloy Malone Dies The Unnamable*. London: John Calder, 1959 (1960). New York: Grove Press, 1958.

Watt. Paris: Collection Merlin, Olympia Press, 1953. New York: Grove Press, 1959.

Nouvelles et textes pour rien. Paris: Les Editions de Minuit, 1955.

Translations of the stories and *Texts for Nothing* in *No's Knife*. London: Calder and Boyars, 1967. *Stories and Texts for Nothing*. New York: Grove Press, 1967.

"From an Abandoned Work," *Trinity News*, vol. III, no. 4 (1956). Reprinted London: Faber and Faber, 1958 and in *No's Knife*. London: Calder and Boyars, 1967. Also in *The Complete Short Prose 1929–1989*. New York: Grove Press, 1995.

All That Fall. London: Faber and Faber, 1957. New York: Grove Press, 1957.

Fin de partie, suivi de Acte sans paroles. Paris: Les Editions de Minuit, 1957.

Endgame, A Play in One Act, Followed by Act Without Words, a Mime for One Player. London: Faber and Faber, 1958. New York: Grove Press, 1958.

Acte sans paroles. In *Fin de partie suivi de Acte sans paroles.* Paris: Les Editions de Minuit, 1957.

Act Without Words. In *Endgame, A Play in One Act, Followed by Act Without Words, a Mime for One Player.* London: Faber and Faber, 1958. New York: Grove Press, 1958.

Anthology of Mexican Poetry. Translated by Samuel Beckett. Compiled by Octavio Paz. Bloomington, Ind.: Indiana University Press (UNESCO Collection of Representative Works: Latin American Series), 1958.

Krapp's Last Tape. In *Krapp's Last Tape and Embers.* London: Faber and Faber, 1959. New York: Grove Press, 1960.

Embers. In *Krapp's Last Tape and Embers.* London: Faber and Faber, 1959. New York: Grove Press, 1960.

Poems in English. London: Calder and Boyars, 1961. New York: Grove Press, 1963.

Comment c'est. Paris: Les Editions de Minuit, 1961.

How It Is. London: John Calder, 1964. New York: Grove Press, 1964.

Happy Days. London: Faber and Faber, 1962. New York: Grove Press, 1961.

Acte sans paroles II. First published in French in *Dramatische Dichtungen,* Band I. Frankfurt: Suhrkamp Verlag, 1963. Reprinted in *Comédie et actes divers.* Paris: Les Editions de Minuit, 1966. *Act Without Words II.* In *Eh Joe and Other Writings.* London: Faber and Faber, 1967. Also in *Krapp's Last Tape and Other Dramatic Pieces.* New York: Grove Press, 1960.

Cascando. First published in *Dramatische Dichtungen,* Band I. Frankfurt: Suhrkamp Verlag, 1963. Reprinted in *Comédie et actes divers.* Paris: Les Editions de Minuit, 1966.

Cascando, in *Play and Two Short Pieces for Radio.* London: Faber and Faber, 1964. Also in *Cascando and Other Short Dramatic Pieces.* New York: Grove Press, 1967.

Words and Music. In *Evergreen Review,* vol. VI (1962). Reprinted in *Play and Two Short Pieces for Radio.* London: Faber and Faber, 1964. Also in *Cascando and Other Short Dramatic Pieces.* New York: Grove Press, 1967.

Play in *Play and Two Short Pieces for Radio.* London: Faber and Faber, 1964. Also in *Cascando and Other Short Dramatic Pieces.* New York: Grove Press, 1967.

Imagination morte imaginez. Paris: Les Editions de Minuit, 1965. Reprinted in *Têtes-mortes.* Paris: Les Editions de Minuit, 1967.

Imagination Dead Imagine. London: Calder and Boyars, 1965. Reprinted in *No's Knife.* London: Calder and Boyars, 1967. Also in *The Complete Short Prose 1929–1989.* New York: Grove Press, 1995.

Assez. Paris: Les Editions de Minuit, 1966. Reprinted in *Têtes-mortes.* Paris: Les Editions de Minuit, 1967.

Enough. In *No's Knife.* London: Calder and Boyars, 1967. Also in *The Complete Short Prose 1929–1989.* New York: Grove Press, 1995.

Bing. Paris: Les Editions de Minuit, 1966. Reprinted in *Têtes-mortes.* Paris: Les Editions de Minuit, 1967.

Ping in *No's Knife.* London: Calder and Boyars, 1967. Also in *The Complete Short Prose 1929–1989.* New York: Grove Press, 1995.

Come and Go. London: Calder and Boyars, 1967. Also in *Cascando and Other Short Dramatic Pieces.* New York: Grove Press, 1967.

Eh Joe. In *Eh Joe and Other Writings.* London: Faber and Faber, 1967. Also in *Cascando and Other Short Dramatic Pieces.* New York: Grove Press, 1967.

Film. In *Eh Joe and Other Writings.* London: Faber and Faber, 1967. New York: Grove Press, 1969.

No's Knife: Collected Shorter Prose 1945–1966. London: Calder and Boyars, 1967.

Poèmes. Paris: Les Editions de Minuit, 1968.

Sans. Paris: Les Editions de Minuit, 1969.

Lessness. London: Calder and Boyars, 1970. Also in *The Complete Short Prose 1929–1989.* New York: Grove Press, 1995.

Mercier et Camier. Paris: Les Editions de Minuit, 1970.

Mercier and Camier. London: Calder and Boyars, 1974. New York: Grove Press, 1974.

Le Dépeupleur. Paris: Les Editions de Minuit, 1970.

The Lost Ones. London: Calder and Boyars, 1972. New York: Grove Press, 1972.

Premier amour. Paris: Les Editions de Minuit, 1970.

First Love. London: Calder and Boyars, 1973. *First Love and Other Shorts.* New York: Grove Press, 1974.

Breath. In *Gambit,* vol. 4, no. 15 (1969). Reprinted in *Breath and Other Short Plays.* London: Faber and Faber, 1972. Also in *First Love and Other Shorts.* New York: Grove Press, 1974.

Not I. London: Faber and Faber, 1973. Also in *First Love and Other Shorts.* New York: Grove Press, 1974.

Au loin un oiseau, with etchings by Avigdor Arikha. New York: Double Elephant Press, 1973.

"Afar a Bird" in *For to End Yet Again and Other Fizzles.* London: John Calder, 1976. Also in *Fizzles.* New York: Grove Press, 1976.

Still, with etchings by William Hayter. Milan: M'Arte Edizione, 1974.

Still. London: Calder and Boyars, 1975. Reprinted in *For to End Yet Again and Other Fizzles.* London, John Calder, 1976. Also in *Fizzles.* New York: Grove Press, 1976.

As the Story Was Told. In *Günter Eich zum Gedächtnis.* Frankfurt: Suhrkamp Verlag, 1975. Reprinted in *As the Story was Told: Uncollected and Late Prose.* London: John Calder, 1990. Also in *The Complete Short Prose 1929–1989.* New York: Grove Press, 1995.

Drunken Boat, a translation by Samuel Beckett of Arthur Rimbaud's poem *Le Bateau ivre.* Reading, England: Whiteknights Press, 1976.

Theatre I and *Theatre II.* In *Ends and Odds.* London: Faber and Faber, 1977 and New York: Grove Press, 1976.

Rough for Radio I. First published in English as "Sketch for Radio Play" in *Stereo Headphones,* no. 7 (spring 1976). Reprinted as *Radio I* in *Ends and Odds.* London: Faber and Faber, 1977 and New York: Grove Press, 1976.

Rough for Radio II. New York: Grove Press, 1976. In *Ends and Odds.* London: Faber and Faber, 1977 and New York: Grove Press, 1976.

Pour finir encore et autres foirades. Paris: Les Editions de Minuit, 1976.

Fizzles, with etchings by Jasper Johns. London: Petersburg Press, 1976.

For to End Yet Again and Other Fizzles. London: John Calder, 1976. *Fizzles.* New York: Grove Press, 1976.

All Strange Away. New York: Gotham Book Mart, 1976.

All Strange Away. London: John Calder, 1979. Also in *The Complete Short Prose 1929–1989.* New York: Grove Press, 1995.

That Time. New York: Faber and Faber, 1976. Reprinted in *Ends and Odds.* London: Faber and Faber, 1977 and New York: Grove Press, 1976.

Footfalls. London: Faber and Faber, 1976. Reprinted in *Ends and Odds.* London: Faber and Faber, 1977 and New York: Grove Press, 1976.

Ghost Trio. In *Journal of Beckett Studies,* No. 1, winter 1976. Reprinted in *Ends and Odds.* London: Faber and Faber, 1977 and New York: Grove Press, 1976.

Ends and Odds. London: Faber and Faber, 1977. *Ends* includes *Not I* (1973), *That Time* (1974), *Footfalls* (1975), *Ghost Trio* (1976), *. . . but the clouds . . .* (1976); *Odds* includes *Theatre I* (ca. 1960), *Theatre II* (ca. 1960), *Radio I* (ca. 1960), and *Radio II* (ca. 1960) and (without *. . . but the clouds . . .*). New York: Grove Press, 1976.

Collected Poems in English and French. London: John Calder, 1977.

Poèmes suivi de Mirlitonnades. Paris: Les Editions de Minuit, 1978.

Company. London: John Calder, 1979. New York: Grove Press, 1980.

Mal vu mal dit. Paris: Les Editions de Minuit, 1981.

Ill Seen Ill Said. London: John Calder, 1982. New York: Grove Press, 1981.

A Piece of Monologue. The Kenyon Review, New Series, vol. I, no. 3 (summer 1979). Reprinted in *Rockaby and Other Short Pieces.* New York: Grove Press, 1981. Also in *Three Occasional Pieces.* London: Faber and Faber, 1982.

Rockaby in *Rockaby and Other Short Pieces.* New York: Grove Press, 1981. Also in *Three Occasional Pieces.* London: Faber and Faber, 1982.

Ohio Impromptu in *Rockaby and Other Short Pieces.* New York: Grove Press, 1981. Also in *Three Occasional Pieces.* London: Faber and Faber, 1982.

Catastrophe. In *Catastrophe et autres dramaticules.* Paris: Les Editions de Minuit, 1982.

Catastrophe. London: Faber and Faber, 1984. Also in *Ohio Impromptu, Catastrophe, What Where.* New York: Grove Press, 1983.

Worstward Ho. London: John Calder, 1983.

Disjecta: Miscellaneous Writings and a Dramatic Fragment. Ruby Cohn, ed. London: John Calder, 1983 and New York: Grove Press, 1983.

What Where. In *Ohio Impromptu, Catastrophe, What Where.* New York: Grove Press, 1983. Also in *Collected Shorter Plays.* London: Faber and Faber, 1984.

Nacht und Träume. In *Collected Shorter Plays.* London: Faber and Faber, 1984 and New York: Grove Press, 1984.

Quad. In *Collected Shorter Plays.* London: Faber and Faber, 1984 and New York: Grove Press, 1984.

Collected Shorter Plays. London: Faber and Faber, 1984 and New York: Grove Press, 1984.

Collected Poems 1930–1978. London: John Calder, 1984.

Stirrings Still. Illustrations by Louis le Brocquy. New York: Blue Moon Books and London: John Calder, 1988.

Collected Shorter Prose 1945–1980. London: John Calder, 1988.

Comment dire. Paris: Les Editions de Minuit, 1989.

Nohow On (Company, Ill Seen Ill Said, Worstward Ho). London: John Calder, 1989 and New York: Grove Press, 1995.

As the Story Was Told: Uncollected and Late Prose. London: John Calder, 1990

Dream of Fair to Middling Women (published posthumously). New York, London, and Paris: Arcade Publishing in association with Riverrun Press and Calder Publications, 1992.

Eleutheria. Published posthumously. Paris: Les Editions de Minuit, 1995.

Eleuthéria. New York: Foxrock, Inc., 1995 and, in a different translation, London: Faber and Faber, 1996.

The Complete Short Prose 1929–1989. New York: Grove Press, 1995.

Biographies and Memoirs of Samuel Beckett

Bair, Deirdre. *Samuel Beckett: A Biography.* London: Jonathan Cape, 1978.

Bernold, André. *L'amitié de Beckett 1979–1989.* Paris: Hermann, 1992.

Brater, Enoch. *Why Beckett.* London: Thames and Hudson, 1989.

Juliet, Charles. *Rencontre avec Samuel Beckett.* Paris: Editions Fata Morgana, 1986.

Works of Criticism

Abbott, H. Porter. *The Fiction of Samuel Beckett: Form and Effect.* Berkeley, Cal.: University of California Press, 1973.

Acheson, James, and Kateryna Arthur, eds. *Beckett's Later Fiction and Drama: Texts for Company.* Basingstoke and London: Macmillan, 1987.

Admussen, Richard. *The Samuel Beckett Manuscripts: A Study.* Boston: G. K. Hall, 1979.

Amiran, Eyal. *Wandering and Home: Beckett's Metaphysical Narrative.* University Park, Penna.: Pennsylvania State University Press, 1993.

Andonian, Cathleen Culotta. *Samuel Beckett: A Reference Guide.* Boston: G. K. Hall, 1989.

Armstrong, Gordon S. *Samuel Beckett, W. B. Yeats and Jack Yeats: Images and Words.* Lewisburg, Penna.: Bucknell University Press; London and Toronto: Associated University Presses, 1990.

Baldwin, Hélène L. *Samuel Beckett's Real Silence.* University Park, Penna.: Pennsylvania State University Press, 1981.

Barnard, G. C. *Samuel Beckett: A New Approach.* London: Dent, 1970.

Beja, Morris, S. E. Gontarski, and Pierre Astier, eds. *Samuel Beckett: Humanistic Perspectives.* Columbus, Ohio: Ohio State University Press, 1983.

Ben-Zvi, Linda. *Samuel Beckett.* Boston: Twayne, 1986.

———, ed. *Women in Beckett: Performance and Critical Perspectives.* Urbana and Chicago: University of Illinois Press, 1990.

Bishop, Tom, and Raymond Federman. *Beckett.* L'Herne, no. 31, Paris, 1976.

Bloom, Harold, ed. *Samuel Beckett's Molloy, Malone Dies, The Unnamable: Modern Critical Interpretations.* New York: Chelsea House, 1987.

Brater, Enoch, ed. *Beckett at 80: Beckett in Context.* New York and Oxford: Oxford University Press, 1986.

———. *Beyond Minimalism: Beckett's Late Style in the Theater.* New York and Oxford: Oxford University Press, 1987.

Breuer, Rolf. *Die Kunst der Paradoxie, Sinnsuche und Scheitern bei Samuel Beckett.* Munich: Wilhelm Fink, 1976.

Brienza, Susan D. *Samuel Beckett's New Worlds: Style in Metafiction.* Norman, Okla., and London: University of Oklahoma Press, 1987.

Bryden, Mary. *Women in Samuel Beckett's Prose and Drama.* Basingstoke and London: Macmillan, 1993.

Buning, Marius, and Lois Oppenheim, eds. *Beckett in the 1990s.* Amsterdam and Atlanta: Rodopi, 1993.

Burkman, Katherine, ed. *Myth and Ritual in the Plays of Samuel Beckett.* London and Toronto: Associated University Presses, 1987.

Butler, Lance St. John, and Robin J. Davis, eds. *Rethinking Beckett: A Collection of Critical Essays.* Basingstoke and London: Macmillan, 1990.

Calder, John, ed. *Beckett at Sixty: A Festschrift.* London: Calder and Boyars, 1967.

Carey, Phyllis, and Ed Jewinski, eds. *Re: Joyc'n Beckett.* New York: Fordham University Press, 1992.

Chabert, Pierre, ed. *Revue d'esthétique.* Numéro spécial Beckett (hors série). Toulouse: Editions Privat, 1986.

Chevigny, Bell Gale, ed. *Twentieth Century Interpretations of Endgame.* Englewood Cliffs, New Jersey: Prentice-Hall, 1969. 2nd rev. ed., 1990.

Coe, Richard. *Beckett.* Edinburgh and London: Oliver and Boyd, 1964.

Cohn, Ruby, *Back to Beckett.* Princeton, N.J.: Princeton University Press, 1973.

———, ed., *Casebook on Waiting for Godot.* New York: Grove Press, 1967.

———, ed., *Casebook on Waiting for Godot.* London: Macmillan, 1987.

———. *The Comic Gamut.* New Brunswick, N.J.: Rutgers University Press, 1962.

———. *Just Play: Beckett's Theater.* Princeton, N.J.: Princeton University Press, 1980.

———, ed. *Samuel Beckett: A Collection of Criticism.* New York: McGraw Hill, 1962.

Connor, Steven. *Samuel Beckett: Repetition, Theory and Text.* Oxford: Blackwell, 1988.

Cousineau, Thomas. *Waiting for Godot: Form in Movement.* Boston: Twayne, 1991.

Croussy, Guy. *Beckett.* Paris: Hachette, 1971.

Davies, Paul. *The Ideal Real: Beckett's Fiction and Imagination.* London and Toronto: Associated University Presses, 1994.

Davis, Robin J., and Lance St. John Butler, eds. *"Make Sense Who May": Essays on Samuel Beckett's Later Work.* Gerrards Cross, England: Colin Smythe, 1989.

Dearlove, Judith. *Samuel Beckett's Nonrelational Art.* Durham, N.C.: Duke University Press, 1982.

Doll, Mary A. *Beckett and Myth: An Archetypal Approach.* Syracuse, N.Y.: Syracuse University Press, 1988.

Duckworth, Colin, ed. *Samuel Beckett: En attendant Godot.* London: Harrap, 1966.

Esslin, Martin, ed. *Samuel Beckett: A Collection of Critical Essays.* Englewood Cliffs, N.J.: Prentice Hall, 1965.

———. *Mediations: Essays on Brecht, Beckett and the Media.* London: Eyre Methuen; Baton Rouge: Louisiana State University Press, 1980.

———. *The Theatre of the Absurd.* Harmondsworth: Penguin Books, 1968.

Federman, Raymond. *Journey to Chaos: Samuel Beckett's Early Fiction.* Berkeley and Los Angeles: University of California Press, 1965.

——— and John Fletcher. *Samuel Beckett: His Works and His Critics.* Berkeley, Los Angeles, and London: University of California Press, 1970.

Finney, Brian. *Since "How It Is": A Study of Beckett's Later Fiction.* London: Covent Garden Press, 1972.

Fitch, Brian T. *Beckett and Babel: An Investigation into the Status of the Bilingual Work.* Toronto, Buffalo, and London: University of Toronto Press, 1988.

Fletcher, John. *The Novels of Samuel Beckett.* London: Chatto and Windus, 1964.

———. *Samuel Beckett's Art.* London: Chatto and Windus, 1967.

——— and John Spurling. *Beckett: A Study of His Plays.* London: Eyre Methuen, 1972.

Fletcher, Beryl, John Fletcher, Barry Smith, and Walter Bachem, eds. *A Student's Guide to the Plays of Samuel Beckett.* London and Boston: Faber and Faber, 1978.

Foster, Paul. *Beckett and Zen.* London: Wisdom Publications, 1989.

Friedman, Alan, Charles Rossman, and Dina Scherzer, eds. *Beckett Translating: Translating Beckett.* University Park, Penna.: Pennsylvania State University Press, 1987.

Friedman, Melvin J. *Samuel Beckett Now.* Chicago and London: University of Chicago Press, 1970.

Gidal, Peter. *Understanding Beckett.* Basingstoke and London: Macmillan, 1986.

Gluck, Barbara Reich. *Beckett and Joyce: Friendship and Fiction.* Lewisburg, Penna.: Bucknell University Press; London: Associated University Presses, 1979.

Gontarski, S. E. *The Intent of Undoing in Samuel Beckett's Dramatic Texts.* Bloomington: Indiana University Press, 1985.

———, ed. *The Beckett Studies Reader.* Gainesville: University Press of Florida, 1993.

———, ed. *On Beckett: Essays and Criticism.* New York: Grove Press, 1986.

Graver, Lawrence, and Raymond Federman, eds. *Samuel Beckett: The Critical Heritage.* London, Henley, and Boston: Routledge and Kegan Paul, 1979.

Hale, Jane A. *The Broken Window: Beckett's Dramatic Perspective.* West Lafayette, Ind.: Purdue University Press, 1987.

Hamilton, Kenneth, and Alice Hamilton. *Condemned to Life: The World of Samuel Beckett.* Grand Rapids, Mich.: W. B. Eerdmans, 1976.

Harrington, John P. *The Irish Beckett.* Syracuse, N.Y.: Syracuse University Press, 1991.

Harvey, Lawrence E. *Samuel Beckett, Poet and Critic.* Princeton, N.J.: Princeton University Press, 1970.

Hesla, David. *The Shape of Chaos: An Interpretation of the Art of Samuel Beckett.* Minneapolis: University of Minnesota Press, 1971.

Hill, Leslie. *Beckett's Fiction: In Different Words.* Cambridge, England: Cambridge University Press, 1989.

Janvier, Ludovic. *Pour Samuel Beckett.* Paris: Les Editions de Minuit, 1966.

Kalb, Jonathan. *Beckett in Performance.* Cambridge, England: Cambridge University Press, 1989.

Kennedy, Andrew. *Samuel Beckett*. Cambridge, England: Cambridge University Press, 1989.

Kenner, Hugh. *A Reader's Guide to Samuel Beckett*. London: Thames and Hudson, 1973.

————. *Samuel Beckett: A Critical Study*. Berkeley: University of California Press, 1968.

Kern, Edith. *Existential Thought and Fictional Technique: Kierkegaard, Sartre and Beckett*. New Haven: Yale University Press, 1970.

Knowlson, James, ed. *Happy Days: Samuel Beckett's Production Notebook*. London and Boston: Faber and Faber, 1985.

————. *Samuel Beckett: An Exhibition*. London: Turret Books, 1971.

————, ed. *Samuel Beckett: Krapp's Last Tape*, Theatre Workbook no. I. London: Brutus Books, 1980.

————, ed. *The Theatrical Notebooks of Samuel Beckett*, III, *Krapp's Last Tape*. London: Faber and Faber, 1994.

———— and John Pilling. *Frescoes of the Skull: The Recent Prose and Drama of Samuel Beckett*. London: John Calder, 1979.

————, ed. Samuel Beckett, *Happy Days / Oh les beaux jours*. London: Faber and Faber, 1978.

Lake, Carlton, ed. *No Symbols Where None Intended*. Austin: Harry Ransom Humanities Research Center, University of Texas at Austin, 1984.

Levy, Eric P. *Beckett and the Voice of Species: A Study of the Prose Fiction*. New York: Barnes & Noble, 1980.

Levy, Shimon. *Samuel Beckett's Self-Referential Drama: The Three I's*. Basingstoke and London: Macmillan, 1990.

Locatelli, Carla. *Unwording the Word: Samuel Beckett's Prose Works After the Nobel Prize*. Philadelphia: University of Pennsylvania Press, 1990.

Lyons, Charles. *Samuel Beckett*. Basingstoke and London: Macmillan, 1983.

McCarthy, Patrick A., ed. *Critical Essays on Samuel Beckett*. Boston: G. K. Hall, 1986.

McMillan, Dougald and Martha Fehsenfeld. *Beckett in the Theatre*. London: John Calder, 1988.

McMillan Dougald, and James Knowlson, eds. *The Theatrical Notebooks of Samuel Beckett*, vol. I, *Waiting for Godot*. London: Faber and Faber, 1994.

McMullan, Anna. *Theatre on Trial: Samuel Beckett's Later Drama*. New York and London: Routledge, 1993.

Megged, Matti. *Dialogue in the Void: Beckett and Giacometti*. New York: Lumen Books, 1985.

Mercier, Vivian. *Beckett / Beckett*. New York: Oxford University Press, 1977.

————. *Modern Irish Literature: Sources and Founders*. Oxford, New York, Toronto: Oxford University Press, 1994.

Morot-Sir, Edouard, H. Harper, and Dougald McMillan, eds. *Samuel Beckett: The Art of Rhetoric*. Chapel Hill: North Carolina Department of Romance Languages, 1976.

Morrison, Kristin. *Canters and Chronicles: The Use of Narrative in the Plays of Samuel Beckett and Harold Pinter*. Chicago: University of Chicago Press, 1983.

Murphy, P. J. *Reconstructing Beckett: Language for Being in Samuel Beckett's Fiction*. Toronto: University of Toronto Press, 1990.

————, Werner Huber, Rolf Breuer, and Konrad Schoell. *Critique of Beckett Criticism: A Guide to Research in English, French and German*. Columbia, S.C.: Camden House, 1994.

O'Brien, Eoin. *The Beckett Country: Samuel Beckett's Ireland*. Dublin: Black Cat Press, 1986.

Onimus, Jean. *Beckett*. Paris and Bruges: Desclée de Brouwer, 1968.

Oppenheim, Lois. *Directing Beckett*. Ann Arbor: University of Michigan Press, 1994.

Peter, John. *Vladimir's Carrot: Modern Drama and the Modern Imagination*. London: André Deutsch, 1987.

Pilling, John. *Samuel Beckett*. London, Henley and Boston: Routledge and Kegan Paul, 1976.

———, ed. *The Cambridge Companion to Beckett*. Cambridge, England: Cambridge University Press, 1994.

——— and Mary Bryden. *The Ideal Core of the Onion: Reading Beckett Archives*. Reading, England: Beckett International Foundation, University of Reading, 1992.

Pountney, Rosemary. *Theatre of Shadows: Samuel Beckett's Drama 1956–76*. Gerrards Cross, England: Colin Smythe, 1988.

Rabaté, Jean-Michel. *Beckett avant Beckett*. Paris: P. E. N. S., 1984.

Rabinovitz, Rubin. *The Development of Samuel Beckett's Fiction*. Urbana and Chicago: University of Illinois Press, 1984.

Reid, Alec. *All I Can Manage More Than I Could*. Dublin: Dolmen Press, 1968.

Ricks, Christopher. *Beckett's Dying Words*. Oxford: Clarendon Press, 1993.

Robinson, Michael. *The Long Sonata of the Dead: A Study of Samuel Beckett*. London: Rupert Hart-Davis, 1969.

Rojtman, Betty. *Forme et signification dans le théâtre de Beckett*. Paris: Nizet, 1976.

Rosen, Steven. *Samuel Beckett and the Pessimistic Tradition*. New Brunswick, N.J.: Rutgers University Press, 1976.

Scherzer, Dina. *Structure de la trilogie de Beckett: Molloy, Malone meurt, L'Innommable*. The Hague and Paris: Mouton, 1976.

Seaver, Richard, ed. *I Can't Go On, I'll Go On: A Samuel Beckett Reader*. New York: Grove Weidenfeld, 1976.

Simon, Alfred. *Beckett*. Paris: Pierre Belfond, 1983.

Smith, Joseph H., ed. *The World of Samuel Beckett, Psychiatry and the Humanities*, vol. 12. Baltimore and London: The Johns Hopkins University Press, 1991.

States, Bert O. *The Shape of Paradox: An Essay on Waiting for Godot*. Berkeley, Cal.: University of California Press, 1978.

Tagliaferri, Aldo. *Beckett et la surdétermination littéraire*. Paris: Payot, 1977.

Tindall, William York. *Samuel Beckett*. New York and London: Columbia University Press, 1964.

Völker, Klaus. *Beckett in Berlin*. West Berlin: Edition Hentrich, Frölich and Kaufmann, 1986.

Watson, David. *Paradox and Desire in Samuel Beckett's Fiction*. Basingstoke and London: Macmillan, 1990.

Webb, Eugene. *The Plays of Samuel Beckett*. Seattle: University of Washington Press, 1972.

———. *Samuel Beckett: A Study of His Novels*. London: Peter Owen, 1972.

Wilmer, S. E., ed. *Beckett in Dublin*. Dublin: The Lilliput Press, 1992.

Worth, Katharine, ed. *Beckett the Shape Changer*. London: Routledge and Kegan Paul, 1975.

Zilliacus, Clas. *Beckett and Broadcasting: A Study of the Works of Samuel Beckett for and in Radio and Television*. Åbo, Finland: Åbo Akademi, 1976.

Zurbrugg, Nicholas. *Beckett and Proust*. Gerrards Cross, England: Colin Smythe, 1988.

Other Works

Ackroyd, Peter. *T. S. Eliot*. London: Cardinal, Sphere Books, 1988.

Ackroyd, Phyllis. *Louis Le Cardonnel*. London: Dent; Dublin: Hodges, Figgis and Co., 1927.

Alfred Adler. *The Neurotic Constitution*. London: Kegan Paul and Co., 1921.

Aldington, Richard. *The Colonel's Daughter*. London: Chatto & Windus, 1931.

———. *Life for Life's Sake*. London: Cassell, 1968.

———. *Pinorman: Personal Recollections of Norman Douglas, Pino Orioli, and Charles Prentice*. London: Heinemann, 1954.

Amouroux, Henri. *La Grande histoire des Français sous l'Occupation*. Vol. 2: *Quarante millions de Pétainistes, juin 1940–juin 1941*. Paris: Robert Laffont, 1977.

———. *La Vie des Français sous l'Occupation*. Paris: Fayard, 1961.

Anzieu, Didier. *Beckett et le psychanalyste*. Paris: Mentha/Archimbaud, 1992.

Aslan, Odette. *Roger Blin: Qui êtes-vous?* Paris: La Manufacture, 1990.

Atik, Anne. *Offshore*. London: Enitharmon Press, 1991.

Auclaire-Tamaroff, Elisabeth, and Barthélémy. *Jean-Marie Serreau découvreur de théâtres*. Paris: L'Arbre Verdoyant, 1986.

Augustine. *The Confessions of St. Augustine*. New York: Airmont, 1969.

Auster, Paul. *Groundwork: Selected Poems and Essays 1970–1979*. London and Boston: Faber and Faber, 1990.

Azéma, Jean-Pierre, and François Bédarida. *La France des années noires*. Vol. I: *De la défaite à Vichy*. Vol. II: *De l'Occupation à la Libération*. Paris: Les Editions du Seuil, 1993.

Baillet, Adrien. *La Vie de Monsieur Descartes*. Paris: Daniel Horthemels, l691.

Bartlett, John. *Familiar Quotations*. Boston: Little Brown and Co., 1885 (SB's copy).

Baudelaire, Charles. *Les Fleurs du mal*. Introduction by Paul Valéry. With twenty drawings by Charles Baudelaire. Paris: Payot, 1928 (SB's copy; a gift from Pamela Mitchell).

Bauer, Walther. *Die notwentige Reise*. Berlin: Cassirer, 1932.

The Samuel Beckett Collection: A Catalogue. Reading, England: The Library, University of Reading, 1978, and typescript supplements (various dates).

Beevor, Anthony, and Artemis Cooper. *Paris After the Liberation, 1944–1949*. London: Hamish Hamilton, 1994.

Beja, Morris. *James Joyce: A Literary Life*. Basingstoke and London: Macmillan, 1992.

Benstock, Shari. *Women of the Left Bank: Paris 1900–1940*. London: Virago, 1987.

Bentley, Edmund. *Far Horizon: A Biography of Hester Dowden, Medium and Psychic Investigator*. London: Rider and Co., 1951.

Berkeley, George. *Berkeley's Commonplace Book*. G. A. Johnston, ed. London: Faber, 1930 (SB's copy).

———. *A New Theory of Vision*. A. D. Lindsay, ed. London: J. M. Dent and Sons, 1926 (SB's copy).

Beschreibendes Verzeichnis der Gemälde im Kaiser-Friedrich Museum und Deutschen Museum. 9th printing. Berlin: 1931.

Billington, Michael. *Peggy Ashcroft*. London: John Murray, 1988.

Bion, Wilfred R. *All My Sins Remembered: Another Part of a Life* and *The Other Side of Genius: Family Letters*. Abingdon, England: Fleetwood Press, 1985.

———. *The Long Week-End, 1897–1919: Part of a Life*. Abingdon, England: Fleetwood Press, 1982.

[Bion, Wilfred R.], *Revue française de psychanalyse*, no. 5, *Bion*, vol. LIII, Sept.–Oct., 1989.

Bléandonu, Gérard. *Wilfred R. Bion: La vie et l'oeuvre, 1897–1979*. Paris: Dunod Bordas, 1990.

Boswell, James. *Boswell's Life of Johnson, Including Boswell's Journal of a Tour to the Hebrides and Johnson's Diary of a Journey to North Wales*. 6 vols. George Birkbeck Hill, ed. Oxford: Clarendon Press, 1887 (SB's copy).

Bowles, David, Carmel Callaghan, and Tony Cauldwell. *Foxrock Golf Club 1893–1993*, n.d.

Boyle, Kay. *Avalanche*. New York: Simon and Schuster, 1944.

Boylan, Patricia. *All Cultivated People: A History of the United Arts Club Dublin*, Gerrards Cross, England: Colin Smythe, 1988.

Bradby, David. *Modern French Drama, 1940–80.* Cambridge, England: Cambridge University Press, 1984.

Breton, André. *Manifestes du surréalisme.* Paris: Gallimard, 1979.

Brown, Terence. *Ireland: A Social and Cultural History 1922–1985.* London: Fontana, 1985.

Brunschvicg, Léon. *Spinoza et ses contemporains.* Paris: Félix Alcan, 1923 (SB's copy).

Bull, Peter. *I Know the Face But . . .* London: Peter Davies, 1959.

Burton, Robert. *The Anatomy of Melancholy.* 3 vols. N. K. Kiessling, T. C. Faulkner, R. L. Blair, ed. Oxford: Clarendon Press, 1994.

Campbell, James. *Paris Interzone.* London: Secker and Warburg, 1994.

Catalogue of Paintings, 13th–18th Century. 2nd revised ed. Linda B. Parshall, trans. Berlin-Dahlem: Staatliche Museen Preussischer Kulturbesitz, 1978.

Catalogue of Pictures and other works of Art in the National Gallery of Ireland and the National Portrait Gallery. Dublin: The National Gallery, 1928 (SB's copy).

Caute, David. *Sixty-eight: The Year of the Barricades.* London: Hamish Hamilton, 1988.

Chaikin, Joe. *The Presence of the Actor.* New York: Atheneum, 1972.

Channin, Richard, Samuel Beckett, et al. *Arikha.* Paris: Hermann, 1985.

Chisholm, Anne. *Nancy Cunard.* Harmondsworth: Penguin Books, 1981.

Claudius, Mathias. *Sämtliche Werke.* Berlin and Darmstadt: Temple Verlag, 1774 (SB's copy, containing an engraving of the "Freund Hain" skeleton and a card inserted at the "Death and the Maiden" poem).

The Comprehensive Teacher's Bible. London: S. Bagster and Sons; New York: James Pott and Co., n. d. (SB's copy. Genesis 10: 5, 20, 31, and 32 are marked with lines in the margin; the verses relate to the sons of Ham, Shem, and Noah).

Condette, Eugène. *Les Chemins d'une destinée: histoire d'un compagnon de la Libération* (on the Resistance work of André Jarrot). Mâcon: Perroux, 1966.

Courtney, Cathy. *Jocelyn Herbert: A Theatre Workbook.* London: Art Books International, 1993.

Cunard, Nancy, ed. *Negro Anthology. Made by Nancy Cunard 1931–1933.* London: Wishart and Co., 1934.

———. *Parallax.* London: Hogarth Press, 1925 (SB's copy, dedicated to him by Cunard).

———. *These Were the Hours.* Carbondale, Ill.: Southern Illinois University Press, 1969.

Dante Alighieri. *The Vision; or Hell, Purgatory, and Paradise [The Divine Comedy].* Rev. Henry Francis Cary, trans. London: Bell and Daldy, 1869 (SB's copy).

Dante Alighieri. *La Divina commedia.* Commento di C. T. Dragone. Alba, Italy: Edizioni Paoline, 1960 (SB's copy).

Dardis, Tom. *Keaton: The Man Who Wouldn't Lie Down.* London: Virgin Books, 1989.

Davies, Martin. *Early Netherlandish School.* London: National Gallery Catalogues, 1955.

Debraye, Henri. *En Touraine et sur les bords de la Loire (châteaux et paysages).* Grenoble: Editions J. Rey, 1926.

Delavenay, Emile. *Témoignage: d'un village savoyard au village mondial 1905–1991.* La Calade, Aix-en-Provence: Diffusion Edisud, 1992.

Democritus. *Démocrite: doctrines philosophiques et réflexions morales.* Translated and introduced by Maurice Solovine. Paris: Félix Alcan, 1928 (SB's copy).

Descartes, René. *Choix de textes.* L. Debricon, ed. Paris: Louis Michaud, n. d. (Jean Beaufret's copy, in SB's library).

———. *Oeuvres philosophiques.* 3 vols., F. Alquié, ed. Paris: Garnier, 1973.

Dicks, H. V. *Fifty Years of the Tavistock Clinic.* London: Routledge and Kegan Paul, n. d..

Doyle, Richard. *Richard Aldington: A Biography.* Basingstoke and London: Macmillan, 1989.

Droz, Bernard, and Evelyne Lever. *Histoire de la guerre d'Algérie 1954–1962.* Paris: Les Editions du Seuil, 1982.

Eadie, John. *A New and Complete Concordance to the Holy Scriptures on the Basis of Cruden.* John Eadie, D.D., LL.D., ed. London: Charles Griffin and Co., 1875 (SB's copy).

Elborn, Geoffrey. *Francis Stuart: A Life.* Dublin: Raven Arts Press, 1990.

Eliot, T. S. *The Waste Land and Other Poems.* London and Boston: Faber and Faber, 1985.

Ellmann, Richard. *a long the riverrun: Selected Essays.* London: Hamish Hamilton, 1988.

———. *James Joyce.* New and revised ed. London: Oxford University Press, 1983.

———, ed. *Selected Letters of James Joyce.* London: Faber and Faber, 1975.

Fahy, Catherine. *The James Joyce–Paul Léon Papers in the National Library of Ireland: A Catalogue.* Dublin: National Library of Ireland, 1992.

Fernand, Jean. *J'y étais: récits inédits sur la Résistance au pays d'Apt.* Association des Médaillés de la Résistance de Vaucluse, 1987.

Ferrers Howell, A. G. *Dante, His Life and Work.* Revised ed., London and Edinburgh: T. C. and E. C. Jack and T. Nelson and Sons, 1920 (SB's copy, dated Dublin, September 1927).

Fielding, Henry. *The Adventures of Joseph Andrews.* London: Michael Barstow, 1889.

———. *The History of Amelia.* 2 vols. London: Hutchinson, 1905.

———. *The History of Tom Jones.* R. P. C. Mutter, ed. Harmondsworth: Penguin Classics, 1986.

Findlater, Richard, ed. *At the Royal Court: 25 Years of the English Stage Company.* Ambergate, England: Amber Lane Press, 1981.

Fitch, Noel Riley. *Sylvia Beach and the Lost Generation: A History of Literary Paris in the Twenties and Thirties.* New York and London: W. W. Norton and Co., 1983.

Fontane, Theodor. *Effi Briest: Roman.* Berlin: F. Fontane, 1896 (SB's copy).

Foot, M. R. D. *Resistance: An Analysis of European Resistance to Nazism 1940–1945.* London: Eyre Methuen, 1976.

———. *S.O.E. in France: An Account of the Work of the British Special Operations Executive in France, 1940–44.* London: Her Majesty's Stationery Office, 1966.

Ford, Hugh D. *Published in Paris: American and British Writers, Painters, and Publishers in Paris, 1920–1939.* New York: Macmillan, 1975.

Fox, Richard M. *Louie Bennett: Her Life and Times.* Dublin: Talbot Press, 1958.

Freud, Sigmund. *Collected Papers.* London: Hogarth Press, International Psychoanalytical Press, and the Institute of Psychoanalysis, 1924–1950.

Gaskill, William. *A Sense of Direction: Life at the Royal Court.* London: Faber and Faber, 1988.

Galerie der Romantik, Nationalgalerie. Berlin: Staatliche Museen Preussischer Kulturbesitz, 1977.

Gilbert, Stuart, ed. *The Letters of James Joyce.* London: Faber and Faber, 1957.

Girodias, Maurice. *Une Journée sur la terre.* Vol II: *Les Jardins d'Eros.* Paris: Editions de la Différence, 1990.

Glenavy, Beatrice Lady. *Today We Will Only Gossip.* London: Constable, 1964.

Goethe, Johann Wolfgang von. *Faust.* German text with Gérard de Nerval's French translation. Paris: Gibert, n.d. (1947).

———. *Poems of Goethe: A Selection.* With introduction and notes by Ronald Gray. Cambridge, England: Cambridge University Press, 1966.

Gogarty, Oliver St. John. *As I Was Going Down Sackville Street.* London: Rich and Cowan, 1937.

Gooch, G. P. *Germany and the French Revolution.* London: Longmans, Green and Co., 1927.

Goodwin, John, ed. *Peter Hall's Diaries: The Story of a Dramatic Battle.* London: Hamish Hamilton, 1983.

Greene, David, and Edward M. Stephens. *J. M. Synge, 1871–1909.* New York: Macmillan, 1959 (SB's copy).

Grimm, Jacob, and Wilhelm Grimm. *Die Märchen der Brüder Grimm*. 2 vols. Leipzig: Insel Verlag, 1918 (SB's copy).

Grohmann, Will. *Die Sammlung Ida Bienert Dresden*. Potsdam: Müller and Kiepen-heuer, n.d. (1933).

Guggenheim, Peggy. *Out of this Century*. London: André Deutsch, 1980.

Haines, Keith. *Neither Rogues nor Fools: A History of Campbell College and Campbelli-ans*. Belfast: Campbell College, 1993.

Hall, Sir Peter. *Making an Exhibition of Myself*. London: Sinclair Stevenson, 1993.

Halpern, Susan. *Austin Clarke: His Life and Works*. Dublin: The Dolmen Press, 1974.

Hebbel, Friedrich. *Gyges und sein Ring: eine Tragödie in fünf Acten*. Vienna: Von Ten-dler, 1856.

Hess, Hans. *Lyonel Feininger*. New York: Harry N. Abrams, 1961.

Hesse, Hermann. *Demian: die Geschichte einer Jugend*. Berlin: S. Fischer, 1919. *Demian*. W. J. Strachan, trans. London: Picador, 1995.

Hesse, Wolfgang. *Eduard Bargheer: Leben und Werk*. Galleria Hesse, Campione d'Italia, 1979.

Hobson, Harold. *An Indirect Journey: An Autobiography*. London: Weidenfeld and Nicol-son, 1978.

Hölderlin, Friedrich. *Sämtliche Werke*. Leipzig: Insel Verlag, n.d. (SB's copy, dated "24/ 12/37").

Howard, Michael S. *Jonathan Cape, Publisher*. London: Jonathan Cape, 1971.

Hyman, Louis. *The Jews of Ireland*. Dublin: Irish University Press, 1972.

Illustrated General Catalogue, National Gallery, London. 2nd revised ed. London: Na-tional Gallery, 1986.

Johnson, Samuel. *A Dictionary of the English Language . . . to Which Is Prefixed a History of the Language and an English Grammar*. 8th. ed. 2 vols. London: J. Johnson, 1799 (SB's copy).

———. *Johnsonian Miscellanies*, George Birkbeck Hill, ed. 2 vols. 1897; reprinted Lon-don: Constable and Co., 1966 (SB's copy).

———. *Rasselas: A Tale*. In *The Works of Samuel Johnson, LL.D.* 2 vols. London: Jones and Co., 1825.

Jones, Ernest. *Papers on Psychoanalysis*. London: Baillière, Tindall and Cox, 1920.

———. *Sigmund Freud: Life and Work*. 3 vols. London: The Hogarth Press, 1953–57 (SB's copy).

Jonson, Ben. *The Complete Plays of Ben Jonson*. G. A. Wilkes, ed. Oxford: Clarendon Press, 1981–82.

Joyce, James. *Dubliners*. London: Jonathan Cape, 1914; reprinted 1946.

———. *Finnegans Wake*. London: Faber and Faber, 1964.

———. *Haveth Childers Everywhere*. London: Faber and Faber, 1931.

———. *A Portrait of the Artist as a Young Man*. London: The Egoist Ltd., 1917.

———. *Ulysses: The Corrected Text*. Hans Walter Gabler with Wolfhard Steppe and Claus Melchior, eds. London: Penguin Books in association with The Bodley Head, 1986.

Juliet, Charles. *Rencontres avec Bram van Velde*. Paris: Editions Fata Morgana, 1978.

Jung, C. G. *The Collected Works*. Vol. XVIII: *The Symbolic Life: Miscellaneous Writings*. R. F. C. Hull, trans. London and Henley: Routledge and Kegan Paul, 1977.

Kant, Immanuel. *Immanuel Kant's Critique of Pure Reason*. Norman Kemp Smith, trans. London: Macmillan, 1929.

Katalog der Alten Meister, Kunsthalle zu Hamburg. 3rd printing, Hamburg: Lütcke and Wulff, 1930.

Katalog der Älteren Pinakothek München. Munich: Amtlicher Katalog München, 1936.

Katalog der Neueren Meister, Kunsthalle zu Hamburg. 2nd printing. Hamburg: Lütcke and Wulff, 1927.

Kay [Elvery], Dorothy. *The Elvery Family: A Memory*. Marjorie Reynolds, ed. Cape Town: The Carrefour Press, 1991.

Keats, John. *The Complete Poems*. Harmondsworth: Penguin Classics, 1988.

Kirchner, Ernst L. *Kirchner — Zeichnungen*. Introduction by Willi Grohmann. Dresden: E. Arnold, 1925.

Kober, Jacques. *Bram van Velde et ses loups*. La Bartavelle, Gap, France, 1989.

Köhler, Wolfgang. *Gestalt Psychology*. London: G. Bell and Sons, 1930.

———. *The Mentality of Apes*. London: Kegan Paul, Trench, Trubner and Co., 1925.

Lahaye, Simone. *Un Homme libre parmi les morts*. Paris: G. Durassié, 1954.

———. *Les Rachetés: portraits et récits de bagne, 1942–45*. Paris: G. Durassié, 1963.

Lahr, John. *Notes on a Cowardly Lion: The Biography of Bert Lahr*. New York: Limelight Editions, 1984.

Laing, R. D. *The Divided Self*. Harmondsworth: Penguin Books, 1969.

———. *The Self and Others: Further Studies in Sanity and Madness*. London: Tavistock Publications, 1961.

Lalande, André. *Vocabulaire technique et critique de la philosophie*. 3 vols. Paris: Félix Alcan, 1932 (SB's copy).

Leacock, Stephen. *Nonsense Novels*. London and New York: John Lane, The Bodley Head, 1911.

Leibniz, G. W. *The Monadology and Other Philosophical Writings*. Robert Latta, trans. Oxford: Clarendon Press, 1898.

———. *Opera philosophica*. Berlin: Sumtibus G. Eichleri, 1840.

Lennon, Peter. *Foreign Correspondent: Paris in the Sixties*. London: Picador, 1994.

Lewenstein, Oscar. *Kicking Against the Pricks: A Theatre Producer Looks Back*. London: Nick Hern Books, 1994.

Liddell Hart, B. H. *History of the Second World War*. London: Cassell and Co., 1970. Reprinted. London: Book Club Associates, 1973.

Lidderdale, Jane, and Mary Nicholson. *Dear Miss Weaver*. New York: The Viking Press, 1970.

Loustaunau-Lacau, Georges. *Chiens maudits: souvenirs d'un rescapé des bagnes hitlériens*. Paris: Editions du Réseau Alliance, 1945.

———. *Mémoires d'un français rebelle 1914–48*. Paris: Robert Laffont, 1948.

McAlmon, Robert, and Kay Boyle. *Being Geniuses Together*. London: Hogarth Press, 1984.

McCormack, W. J. *From Burke to Beckett: Ascendancy, Tradition and Betrayal in Literary History*. Cork: Cork University Press, 1994.

McDougall, Richard, ed. *The Very Rich Hours of Adrienne Monnier: An Intimate Portrait of the Literary and Artistic Life in Paris Between the Wars*. London: Millington Books, 1976.

McMillan, Dougald. *transition 1927–1938: The History of a Literary Era*. London: John Calder, 1976.

MacGreevy, Thomas. *Collected Poems of Thomas MacGreevy*. Schreibman, Susan, ed. Dún Laoghaire, Ireland: Anna Livia Press, 1991.

———. *Richard Aldington: An Englishman*. London: Chatto & Windus, 1931.

Madden Le Brocquy, Anne. *Louis Le Brocquy: A Painter Seeing His Way*. Dublin: Gill and Macmillan, 1994.

Maddox, Brenda. *Nora: A Biography of Nora Joyce*. London: Hamish Hamilton, 1988.

Maeterlinck, Maurice. *Théâtre*. Vol. I: *La Princesse Maleine, L'Intruse, Les Aveugles*. Paris: Fasquelle, [n.d.] (SB's copy).

Magee Bryan. *The Philosophy of Schopenhauer*. New York: Oxford University Press, 1989.

Mahaffy, J. P. *Descartes*. Edinburgh and London: William Blackwood, 1901.

Der Maler Willem Grimm 1904–1986. Hamburg: Hans Christians, 1989.

Marrus, Michael R. and Robert O. Paxton. *Vichy France and the Jews.* New York: Basic Books, 1981.

Mauthner, Fritz. *Beiträge zu einer Kritik der Sprache.* 3rd. ed. 3 vols. Leipzig: F. Meiner, 1923 (SB's copy).

Milton, John. *Paradise Lost.* London: The Temple Classics, 1904 (SB's copy).

Molière, J. B. Poquelin. *Théâtre complet.* Paris: Hachette, n.d. (SB's copy, dated July 1926).

Monnier, Adrienne. *Rue de l'Odéon.* Paris: Albin Michel, 1989.

Morlino, Bernard. *Philippe Soupault: Qui êtes-vous?* Paris: La Manufacture, 1987.

Murphy, Gardner. *Historical Introduction to Modern Psychology.* London: Routledge and Kegan Paul, 1928.

Nadeau, Maurice. *Grâces leur soient rendues: mémoires littéraires.* Paris: Albin Michel, 1990.

———. *Gustave Flaubert écrivain.* Paris: Denoël, 1969.

National Gallery Trafalgar Square Catalogue. London: The Trustees of the National Gallery, 1929.

Noguères, Henri. *Histoire de la Résistance en France de 1940 à 1945.* Paris: Robert Laffont. Vol. I, 1967; vol. II, 1969.

O'Connor, Garry. *Sean O'Casey.* London: Hodder and Stoughton, 1988.

O'Connor, Ulick. *Oliver St. John Gogarty.* London: New English Library, 1967.

Orpen, William. *Stories of Old Ireland and Myself.* London: Williams and Norgate, 1924.

Osborne, John. *Almost a Gentleman: An Autobiography.* Vol. II: 1955–1966. London: Faber and Faber, 1991.

Paine, Lauran. *Mathilde Carré, Double Agent.* London: Robert Hale, 1976.

Paris, Gaston. *Penseurs et poètes: James Darmesteter, F. Mistral, Sully Prudhomme, A. Bida, Ernest Renan, A. Sorel.* Paris: C. Lévy, 1896.

Pascal, Blaise. *Pensées.* Paris: Flammarion, n.d. (SB's copy).

Passerini, G. L. *Le vite di Dante: Scritte da Villani, Boccaccio, Manetti.* Florence: Sansoni, 1917 (SB's copy, dated 1936).

Pergamon and Bode Museum: The Ancient World on Museum Island, Berlin. Mainz: Philipp von Zabern, 1991.

Peskine, Lynda Bellity, ed. *Roger Blin: souvenirs et propos recueillis par Lynda Bellity Peskine.* Paris: Gallimard, 1986.

Piper, David. *The Companion Guide to London.* London: Collins, 1964.

Plautus, *Works.* Paul Nixon, trans. London: Heinemann, 1916 (SB's copy).

Pope, Alexander. *The Poetical Works of Alexander Pope.* Edinburgh: Gall and Inglis, 1881 (SB's copy, dated 3/36).

Proust, Marcel. *A la recherche du temps perdu.* 107th ed. 16 vols. Paris: Gallimard, NRF, 1919 (SB's copy; one volume missing).

Putnam, Samuel. *Paris Was Our Mistress: Memoirs of a Lost and Found Generation.* London: Plantin Publications, 1987 (first published 1947).

Pyle, Hilary. *Jack B. Yeats: A Catalogue Raisonné of the Oil Paintings.* 3 vols. London: Deutsch, 1994.

———. *Jack B. Yeats: A Biography.* London: Routledge and Kegan Paul, 1970.

Quane, Michael. *Portora Royal School (1618–1968).* Monaghan, Ireland: Cumann Seanchais Chlochair, 1968.

Rabelais, François. *Oeuvres complètes.* Paris: Bibliothèque de la Pléiade, Gallimard, 1994.

Racine, Jean. *Théâtre complet.* Félix Lemaistre, ed. Introduction by L.-S. Auger. Paris: Garnier, n.d. (SB's copy).

Rank, Otto. *The Trauma of Birth.* London: Kegan Paul and Co., 1929.

Reiss, C. *Wilhelm Furtwängler: A Biography.* London: Frederick Muller, 1955.

La Résistance au pays d'Apt de la Durance au Ventoux. Cavaillon, 1982.

La Résistance en Vaucluse: documents et témoignages. Service éducatif des archives départementales de Vaucluse, Centre départemental de documentation pédagogique, Recueil no. 8, 1980.

Reynolds, Marjorie. *"Everything You Do Is a Portrait of Yourself"*: Dorothy Kay: A Biography. Rosebank, South Africa: privately published by Alec Marjorie Reynolds, 1989.

Ribier, Maurice. *Les Semailles de Corot.* Privately published, n.d. (on Henri Hayden).

Rivel, Charlie, with J. C. Lauritzen. *Charlie Rivel: Poor Clown.* London: Michael Joseph, 1973.

Romains, Jules. *Bertrand de Ganges.* A. G. Lehmann, ed. London: Harrap, 1961.

Rose, Marilyn Gaddis. *Jack B. Yeats, Painter and Poet.* Berne and Frankfurt: Herbert Lang, 1972.

Rudmose-Brown, Thomas Brown. *French Literary Studies.* Dublin: Talbot Press; London: Fisher Unwin, 1917.

———. *Walled Gardens.* Dublin: Talbot Press; London: Fisher Unwin, 1918.

La Sainte Bible qui contient le vieux et le nouveau testament. New York: Société Biblique Américaine, 1874 (SB's copy. Genesis 11: 14–21 is marked in the margin).

Sauerlandt, Max. *Die Kunst der letzen 30 Jahre.* Berlin: Rembrandt, [c. 1935].

Schirmer, Gregory A. *The Poetry of Austin Clarke.* University of Notre Dame Press and Dublin: The Dolmen Press, 1983.

Schneider, Alan. *Entrances: An American Director's Journey.* New York: Viking Penguin, 1986.

Schopenhauer, Arthur. *Essays and Aphorisms,* R. J. Hollingdale, trans. Harmondsworth: Penguin Books, 1970.

———. *Sämtliche Werke.* 5 vols. Leipzig: Insel Verlag, 1922–23 (SB's copy).

———. *The World as Will and Idea.* R. B. Haldane and J. Kemp, trans. 3 vols. Kegan Paul, Trench, Trübner and Co., 1896.

Scott, Andrew Murray. *Alexander Trocchi: The Making of the Monster.* Edinburgh: Polygon, 1991.

———, ed. *Invisible Insurrection of a Million Minds: A Trocchi Reader.* Edinburgh: Polygon, 1991.

Seale, Patrick, and Maureen McConville. *French Revolution 1968.* Harmondsworth: Penguin Books; London: Heinemann, 1968.

Simms, G. O. *Tullow's Story: A Portrait of a County Dublin Parish.* Carrickmines, Ireland: The Select Vestry of Tullow Parish, 1983.

Skeffington, Andrée Sheehy. *Skeff: A Life of Owen Sheehy Skeffington, 1909–1970.* Dublin: The Lilliput Press, 1991.

Sorel, Albert. *L'Europe et la révolution française.* 8 vols. Paris: Plon, n.d.

Spanier, Sandra. *Kay Boyle, Artist and Activist.* New York: Paragon House, 1988.

Starkie, Enid. *A Lady's Child.* London: Faber and Faber, 1941.

Starkie, Walter. *The Waveless Plain.* London: John Murray, 1938.

Stekel, Wilhelm. *Psychoanalysis and Suggestion Therapy.* London: Kegan Paul and Co., 1923.

Stendhal (Henri Beyle). *Le Rouge et le noir.* Paris: Garnier, n.d. (SB's copy, dated "Dublin November 1926").

Sterne, Laurence. *The Works of Laurence Sterne.* 5th ed. 7 vols. Dublin: D. Chamberlaine, 1780 (SB owned Volume 4 of this edition, which includes *A Sentimental Journey Through France and Italy*).

———. *The Works of Laurence Sterne.* London: Oxford University Press, 1910 (SB's copy, which includes *Tristram Shandy*).

Stoullig, Claire. *Bram van Velde.* (Catalogue of the Musée National d'Art Moderne). Paris: Centre Georges Pompidou, 1989.

Swift, Carolyn. *Stage by Stage.* Swords Co. Dublin: Poolbeg, 1985.

Swift, Jonathan. *Gulliver's Travels.* The World's Classics Series. John Hayward, 1955; reprinted London: Oxford University Press, 1963 (SB's copy).

————. *The Prose Works of Jonathan Swift, D.D.* Vol. 6: *The Drapier's Letters*. London: G. Bell and Sons, 1922 (SB's copy).

Tapping, G. Craig. *Austin Clarke: A Study of His Writings*. Dublin: The Academy Press, 1981.

Thieuloy, Jack. *Loi de Dieu*. Paris: L'Athanor, 1977.

Thomson, Duncan. *Arikha*. London: Phaidon, 1994.

Thompson, Alexander Hamilton. *A History of English Literature and of the Chief English Writers*. London: Murray, 1914 (SB's copy, dated Feb. 1923).

Thrale, Hester Lynch. *Dr. Johnson: "The Anecdotes" of Mrs. Piozzi in Their Original Form*. Richard Ingrams, ed. London: Chatto & Windus, 1984 (SB's copy).

Tillion, Germaine. *Ravensbrück*. Paris: Les Editions du Seuil, 1973 and 1988.

Tynan, Kathleen. *The Life of Kenneth Tynan*. London: Weidenfeld and Nicolson, 1987.

Tynan, Kenneth. *Oh! Calcutta: An Entertainment with Music*. New York: Grove Press, 1969.

Verzeichnis der ausgestellten Gemälde in der Niedersächsischen Landesgalerie Hannover. Hannover: Niedersächsisches Landesmuseum, 1989.

Verzeichnis der Gemälde und Skulpturen des 19. Jahrhunderts, Nationalgalerie, Berlin. East Berlin: Staatliche Museen Preussischer Kulturbesitz, 1976.

Viatte, Germain. *Geer van Velde*. Paris: Editions "Cahiers d'Art," Louis Carré, 1989.

Vogelaar, Christiaan. *Netherlandish Fifteenth- and Sixteenth-Century Paintings in the National Gallery of Ireland: A Complete Catalogue*. Dublin: The National Gallery of Ireland, 1987.

Walpole, Hugh. *Judith Paris* in *The Herries Chronicle*. Hamburg: The Albatross Verlag, 1932.

Wardle, Irving. *The Theatres of George Devine*. London: Jonathan Cape, 1978.

Warner, Oliver. *Chatto and Windus. A Brief Account of the Firm's Origin, History and Development*. London: Chatto and Windus, 1973.

West, Nigel. *MI6: British Secret Intelligence Service Operations 1909–45*. London: Weidenfeld and Nicolson, 1983.

West, Trevor. *The Bold Collegians: The Development of Sport in Trinity College, Dublin*. Dublin: The Lilliput Press, 1991.

Whitelaw, Billie. *Billie Whitelaw . ... Who He?* London: Hodder and Stoughton, 1995.

Wilenski, R. H. *An Introduction to Dutch Art*. London: Faber and Faber, 1929.

Woodworth, Robert S. *The Contemporary Schools of Psychology*. New York: The Ronald Press, 1931.

Wyatt, A. J., and W. H. Low. *Intermediate Text-book of English Literature*. 2 vols. Part I. London: University Tutorial Press, 1920 (SB's copy, dated "Michaelmas Term, 1923").

Wylie, Laurence. *Village in the Vaucluse*, 3rd ed. Cambridge, Mass.: Harvard University Press, 1974.

Yeats, Jack B. *The Amaranthers*. London and Toronto: William Heinemann, 1936.

————. *The Charmed Life*. London: Routledge and Kegan Paul, 1938.

————. *The Late Paintings*. Bristol: Arnolfini; London: Whitechapel Art Gallery, The Hague: Haags Gemeentemuseum, 1991.

Yeats, W. B. *The Collected Poems of W. B. Yeats*. London: Macmillan, 1933.

Young, Jordan R. *The Beckett Actor: Jack MacGowran, Beginning to End*. Beverley Hills, Calif.: Moonstone, 1987.

Zingarelli, Nicola. *Vocabolario della lingua italiana*. Bologna: N. Zanichelli, 1954 (SB's copy — a gift from Pamela Mitchell).

Index

obs against the pale grass. Sean circled the camp and two of his sentries awake and attentive. He had Mbejane on the north side and now he went there. ards in front of him he picked up the shape of the bush beside which he had left Mbejane. Suddenly smiled and sank down onto his hands and knees, he d his rifle across the crooks of his elbows and began alk. Moving flat along the ground silently, slowly he in on the bush. Ten paces from it he stopped and his head, careful to keep the movement inchingly He stared, trying to find the shape of the Zulu among craggy branches and bunches of leaves. The point of a ing spear pricked him below the ear in the soft of his behind the jaw bone. Sean froze but his eyes rolled ways and in the starlight he saw Mbejane kneeling over holding the spear.

Does the Nkosi seek me?' asked Mbejane solemnly, but e was laughter deep down in his voice. Sean sat up and ed the place where the spear had stung him.

Only a night ape sees in the dark,' Sean protested.

'And only a fresh caught catfish flops on its belly,' uckled Mbejane.

'You are Zulu,' Sean stated, recognizing the arrogance, hough he had known immediately from the man's face d body that he was not one of the bastard Natal tribes o spoke the Zulu language but were no more Zulu than a by-cat is a leopard.

'Of Chaka's blood,' agreed Mbejane, reverence in his ice as he said the old king's name.

'And now you carry the spear against Cetewayo, your ng?'

'My king?' The laughter was gone from Mbejane's voice. y king?' he repeated scornfully.

There was silence and Sean waited. Out in the darkness

Immediately concerned, Garrick turned to her. 'I'm terribly sorry, my dear. How thoughtless of me.' He touched the horses with the whip and they went down the slope towards the homestead.

The lawns of Theunis Kraal were green and there were cannas in bloom, red and pink and yellow.

It's beautiful, thought Anna, *and it's mine. I'm not poor any more.* She looked at the gabled roof and the heavy yellow wood shutters on the windows as the carriage rolled up the drive.

There was a man standing in the shade of the veranda. Anna and Garrick saw him at the same time. He was tall with shoulders as wide and square as the crosstree of a gallows. He stepped out of the shadow and came down the front steps into the sunlight. He was smiling with white teeth in a brown burnt face; it was the old irresistible smile.

'Sean,' whispered Anna.

– 26 –

Sean really noticed him for the first time when they stopped to water the horses. They had left Chelmsford's Column the previous noon to scout towards the north-east. It was a tiny patrol – four mounted white men and a half-a-dozen Nongaai, the loyal Native troops from Natal.

He took the reins from Sean's hands. 'I will hold your horse while you drink.' His voice had a resonance to it and Sean's interest quickened. He looked at the man's face and liked it immediately. The whites of the eyes had no yellow in them and the nose was more Arabic than negroid. His colour was dark amber and his skin shone with oil.

Sean nodded. There is no word in the Zulu language for 'thank you', just as there are no words for 'I am sorry'.

Sean knelt beside the stream and drank. The water tasted sweet for he was thirsty; when he stood again there were damp patches on his knees and water dripping from his chin.

He looked at the man who was holding his horse. He wore only a small kilt of civet-cat tails: no rattles nor cloak, no head-dress. His shield was black rawhide and he carried two short stabbing spears.

'How are you called?' Sean asked, noticing the breadth of the man's chest and the way his belly muscles stood out like the static ripples on a windswept beach.

'Mbejane.' Rhinoceros.

'For your horn?' The man chuckled with delight, his masculine vanity tickled.

'How are you called, Nkosi?'

'Sean Courtney.'

Mbejane's lips formed the name silently and then he shook his head.

'It is a difficult name.' He never said Sean's name – not once in all the years that were to follow.

'Mount up,' called Steff Erasmus. 'Let's get moving.'

They swung up onto the horses, gathered the reins and loosened the rifles in the scabbards. The Nongaai who had been stretched out resting on the bank stood up.

'Come on,' said Steff. He splashed through the stream. His horse gathered itself and bounded up the far bank and they followed him. They moved in line abreast across the grassland, sitting loose and relaxed in their saddles, the horses trippling smoothly.

At Sean's right stirrup ran the big Zulu, his long extended stride easily pacing Sean's horse. Once in a while Sean dropped his eyes from the horizon and looked down at Mbejane; it was a strangely comforting feeling to have him there.

They camped that night in a shallow valley of grass.

There were no cooking fires; they [...] the black strips of dried salt meat, a[...] cold water.

'We're wasting our time. There [...] Zulu in two days' riding,' grumbled [...] troopers.

'I say we should turn back and rejo[...] getting farther and farther away from [...] we're going to miss the fun when it star[...]

Steff Erasmus wrapped his blanket [...] shoulders: the night's first chill was on t[...]

'Fun, is it?' He spat expertly into the [...] have the fun, if we find the cattle.'

'Don't you mind missing the fighting?'[...]

'Look, you, I've hunted bushmen in t[...] Kalahari, I've fought Xhosas and Fingo[...] river, I went into the mountains after [...] Basutos. Matabele, Zulu, Bechuana – I've [...] of them. Now four or five hundred head of [...] be payment enough for any fun we miss.' S[...] adjusted his saddle behind his head. 'Any[...] you think there won't be guards on the her[...] them. You'll get your fun – I promise you.'

'How do you know they've got the c[...] insisted Sean.

'They're here,' said Steff, 'and we'll find th[...] his head towards Sean. 'You've got the fir[...] your eyes open.' He tilted his top hat forwar[...] groped with his right hand to make sure his [...] him and then spoke from under the hat, 'G[...] others settled down into their blankets: fully [...] on, guns at hand. Sean moved out into th[...] check the Nongaai pickets.

There was no moon, but the stars were fa[...] earth; they lit the land so that the four grazi[...]

a jackal barked twice and one of the horses whickered softly.

'There was another who should have been king, but he died with a sharpened stick thrust up into the secret opening of his body, until it pierced his gut and touched his heart. That man was my father,' said Mbejane. He stood up and went back into the shelter of the bush and Sean followed him. They squatted side by side, silent but watchful. The jackal cried again up above the camp and Mbejane's head turned towards the sound.

'Some jackals have two legs,' he whispered thoughtfully. Sean felt the tingle along his forearms.

'Zulus?' he asked. Mbejane shrugged, a small movement in the darkness.

'Even if it is, they will not come for us in the night. In the dawn, yes, but never in the night.' Mbejane shifted the spear in his lap. 'The old one with the tall hat and grey beard understands this. Years have made him wise, that's why he sleeps so sweetly now but mounts up and moves in the darkness before each dawn.'

Sean relaxed slightly. He glanced sideways at Mbejane.

'The old one thinks that some of the herds are hidden near here.'

'Years have made him wise,' repeated Mbejane. 'Tomorrow we will find the land more broken, there are hills and thick thorn bush. The cattle will be hidden among them.'

'Do you think we'll find them?'

'Cattle are difficult to hide from a man who knows where to look.'

'Will there be many guards with the herds?'

'I hope so,' answered Mbejane, his voice a purr. His hand crept to the shaft of his assegai and caressed it. 'I hope there will be very many.'

'You would kill your own people, your brothers, your cousins?' asked Sean.

'I would kill them as they killed my father.' Mbejane's voice was savage now. 'They are not my people. I have no people. I have no brothers – I have nothing.'

Silence settled between them again, but slowly the ugliness of Mbejane's mood evaporated and in its place came a sense of companionship. Each of them felt comforted by the other's presence. They sat on into the night.

– 27 –

Mbejane reminded Sean of Tinker working a bird, he had the same half-crouched gait and the same air of complete absorption. The white men sat their horses in silence watching him. The sun was well up already and Sean unbuttoned his sheepskin coat and pulled it off. He strapped it onto the blanket roll behind him.

Mbejane had moved out about fifty yards from them and now he was working slowly back towards them. He stopped and minutely inspected a wet pat of cow dung.

'*Hierdie Kaffir verstaan wat hy doen,*' opined Steff Erasmus approvingly, but no one else spoke. Bester Klein fidgeted with the hammer of his carbine; his red face was already sweaty in the rising heat.

Mbejane had proved right, they were in hilly country. Not the smoothly rounded hills of Natal but hills with rocky crests, deeply gullied and ravined between. There was thorn forest and euphorbia covering the sides of the hills with a lattice work of reptile grey trunks, and the grass was coarse and tall.

'I could use a drink,' said Frikkie Van Essen and wiped his knuckles across his lips.

'Chee peep, chee peep,' a barbet called stridently in the

branches of the kaffir boom tree under which they waited. Sean looked up; the bird was brown and red among the scarlet flowers which covered the tree.

'How many?' asked Steff and Mbejane came to stand at his horse's head.

'Fifty – no more,' he answered.

'When?'

'Yesterday, after the heat of the day they moved slowly down the valley. They were grazing. They cannot be more than half an hour's ride ahead of us.'

Steff nodded. Fifty head only, but there would be more.

'How many men with them?'

Mbejane clucked his tongue disgustedly. 'Two *umfaans*.' He pointed with his spear at a dusty place where the print of a half grown boy's bare foot showed clearly. 'There are no men.'

'Good,' said Steff. 'Follow them.'

'They told us that if we found anything we must go back and report,' protested Bester Klein quickly. 'They said we shouldn't start anything on our own.'

Steff turned in his saddle. 'Are you frightened of two *umfaans*?' he asked coldly.

'I'm not frightened of anything, it's just what they told us.' Klein flushed redder in his already red face.

'I know what they told us, thank you,' said Steff. 'I'm not going to start anything, we're just going to have a look.'

'I know you,' burst out Klein. 'If you see cattle you'll go mad for them. All of you, you're greedy for cattle like some men are for drink. Once you see them you won't stop.' Klein was a railway ganger.

Steff turned away from him. 'Come on, let's go.'

They rode out of the shade of the kaffir boom tree into the sunlight, Klein muttering softly to himself and Mbejane leading them down the valley.

The floor of the valley sloped gradually and on each side

of them the ground rose steep and rocky. They travelled quickly with Mbejane and the other Nongaai thrown out as a screen and the horsemen cantering in a line with their stirrups almost touching.

Sean levered open the breech of his rifle and drew out the cartridge. He changed it for another from the bandolier across his chest.

'Fifty head is only ten apiece,' complained Frikkie.

'That's a hundred quid – as much as you earn in six months.' Sean laughed with excitement and Frikkie laughed with him.

'You two keep your mouths shut and your eyes open.' Steff's voice was phlegmatic, but he couldn't stop the excitement from sparkling in his eyes.

'I knew you were going to raid,' sulked Klein. 'I knew it, sure as fate.'

'You shut up also,' said Steff and grinned at Sean.

They rode for ten minutes; then Steff called softly to the Nongaai and the patrol halted. No one spoke and every man stood with his head alert and his ears straining.

'Nothing,' said Steff at last. 'How close are we?'

'Very close,' Mbejane answered. 'We should have heard them from here.'

Mbejane's exquisitely muscled body was shiny with sweat and the pride of his stance set him apart from the other Nongaai. There was a restrained eagerness about him, for the excitement was infectious.

'All right, follow them,' said Steff. Mbejane settled the rawhide shield securely on his shoulder and started forward again.

Twice more they stopped to listen and each time Sean and Frikkie were more restless and impatient.

'Sit still,' snapped Steff. 'How can we hear anything with you moving about?'

Sean opened his mouth, but before he could answer they

142

all heard an ox low mournfully ahead of them among the trees.

'That's it!'

'We've got them!'

'Come on!'

'No, wait!' Steff ordered. 'Sean, take my farlookers and climb up that tree. Tell me what you can see.'

'We're wasting time,' argued Sean. 'We should—'

'We should learn to do as we're damn well told,' said Steff. 'Get up that tree.'

With the binoculars slung around his neck, Sean clambered upwards until he sat high in a crotch of two branches. He reached out and broke off a twig which obscured his vision, then exclaimed immediately, 'There they are, right ahead of us!'

'How many?' Steff called up to him.

'A small herd – two herdboys with them.'

'Are they among the trees?'

'No,' said Sean, 'they're in the open. Looks like a patch of swamp.'

'Make sure there aren't any other Zulus with them.'

'No—' Sean started to answer but Steff cut him short.

'Use the glasses, dammit. They'll be hiding if they're there.'

Sean brought up the glasses and focused them. The cattle were fat and sleek skinned, big horned and bodies dappled black on white. A cloud of white tick-birds hovered over them. The two herdboys were completely naked, youngsters with the thin legs and the disproportionately large genitals of the Africans. Sean turned the glasses slowly back and forth searching the patch of swamp and the surrounding bush. At last he lowered them.

'Only the two herdboys,' he said.

'Come down then,' Steff told him.

The herdboys fled as soon as the patrol rode out into the

143

open. They disappeared among the fever trees on the far side of the swamp.

'Let them go,' laughed Steff. 'The poor little buggers are going to be in enough trouble as it is.'

He spurred his horse forward into the vivid green patch of swamp grass. It was lush: thick and tall enough to reach his saddle.

The others followed him in with the mud squelching and sucking at the hooves of the horses. They could see the backs of the cattle showing above the grass a hundred yards ahead of them. The tick-birds circled squawking.

'Sean, you and Frikkie cut around to the left—' Steff spoke over his shoulder and before he could finish the grass around them was full of Zulus, at least a hundred of them in full war dress.

'Ambush!' yelled Steff. 'Don't try and fight, too many of them. Get out!' and they dragged him off his horse.

Horses panicked in the mud, whinnying as they reared. The bang of Klein's rifle was almost drowned in the triumphant roar of the warriors. Mbejane jumped to catch the bridle of Sean's horse; he dragged its head around.

'Ride, Nkosi, quickly. Do not wait.'

Klein was dead, an assegai in his throat and the blood bursting brightly from the corners of his mouth as he fell backwards.

'Hold on to my stirrup leather.' Sean felt surprisingly calm. A Zulu came at him from the side; Sean held his rifle across his lap and fired with the muzzle almost in the man's face. It cut the top off his head. Sean ejected the cartridge case and reloaded.

'Ride, Nkosi!' Mbejane shouted again. He had made no effort to obey Sean: his shield held high he barged into two of the attackers and knocked them down into the mud. His assegai rose and fell, rose and fell.

'*Ngi Dhla*,' howled Mbejane. 'I have eaten.' Fighting

madness on him, he jumped over the bodies and charged. A man stood to meet him and Mbejane hooked the edge of his shield under his and jerked it aside, exposing the man's left flank to his blade.

'*Ngi Dhla*,' Mbejane howled again.

He had torn an opening in the ring of attackers and Sean rode for it, his horse churning heavily through the mud. A Zulu caught at his reins and Sean fired with his muzzle touching the man's chest. The Zulu screamed.

'Mbejane,' shouted Sean. 'Take my stirrup!'

Frikkie Van Essen was finished; his horse was down and Zulus swarmed over him with red spears.

Leaning out of the saddle Sean circled Mbejane's waist with his arm and plucked him out of the mud. He struggled wildly but Sean held him. The ground firmed under his horse's hooves, they were moving faster. Another Zulu stood in their way with his assegai ready. With Mbejane kicking indignantly under one arm and his empty rifle in his other hand Sean was helpless to defend himself. He shouted an obscenity at the Zulu as he rode down on him. The Zulu dodged to one side and darted in again. Sean felt the sting of the blade across his shin and then the shock as it went on into his horse's chest. They were through, out of the swamp and into the trees.

Sean's horse carried him another mile before it fell. The assegai had gone in deep. It fell heavily but Sean was able to kick his feet out of the irons and jump clear. He and Mbejane stood looking down at the carcass – both of them were panting.

'Can you run in those boots?' asked Mbejane urgently.

'Yes.' They were light *veldschoen*.

'Those breeches will hold your legs.' Mbejane knelt swiftly and with his assegai cut away the cloth until Sean's legs were bare from the thighs down. He stood up again and listened for the first sounds of pursuit. Nothing.

'Leave your rifle, it is too heavy. Leave your hat and your bandolier.'

'I must take my rifle,' protested Sean.

'Take it then,' Mbejane flashed impatiently. 'Take it and die. If you carry that they'll catch you before noon.'

Sean hesitated a second longer and then he changed his grip, holding the rifle by the barrel like an axe. He swung it against the trunk of the nearest tree. The butt shattered and he threw it from him.

'Now we must go,' said Mbejane.

Sean glanced quickly across at his dead horse, the leather thongs held his sheepskin coat onto the saddle. All Anna's hard work wasted, he thought wryly. Then following Mbejane he started to run.

The first hour was bad; Sean had difficulty matching his step to that of Mbejane. He ran with his body tensed and soon had a stabbing stitch in his side. Mbejane saw his pain and they stopped for a few minutes while Mbejane showed him how to relax it away. Then they went on with Sean running smoothly. Another hour went by and Sean had found his second wind.

'How long will it take us to get back to the main army?' grunted Sean.

'Two days perhaps . . . don't talk,' answered Mbejane.

The land changed slowly about them as they ran. The hills not so steep and jagged, the forest thinned and again they were into the rolling grassland.

'It seems we are not being followed.' It was half an hour since Sean had last spoken.

'Perhaps,' Mbejane was non-committal. 'It is too soon yet to tell.'

They ran on side by side, in step so their feet slapped in unison on the hard-baked earth.

'Christ, I'm thirsty,' said Sean.

'No water,' said Mbejane, 'but we'll stop to rest a while at the top of the next rise.'

They looked back from the crest. Sean's shirt was soaked with sweat and he was breathing deeply but easily.

'No one following us,' Sean's voice was relieved. 'We can slow down a bit now.'

Mbejane did not answer. He also was sweating heavily but the way he moved and held his head showed he was not yet beginning to tire. He carried his shield on his shoulder and the blade of the assegai in his other hand was caked with black, dry blood. He stared out along the way they had come for fully five minutes before he growled angrily and pointed with his assegai.

'There! Close to that clump of trees. Can you see them?'

'Oh, hell!' Sean saw them: about four miles behind, on the edge of the forest where it thinned out, a black pencil line drawn on the brown parchment of grassland. But the line was moving.

'How many of them?' asked Sean.

'Fifty,' hazarded Mbejane. 'Too many.'

'I wish I had brought my rifle,' muttered Sean.

'If you had they would be much closer now – and one gun against fifty—' Mbejane left it unfinished.

'All right, let's get going again,' said Sean.

'We must rest a little longer. This is the last time we can stop before nightfall.'

Their breathing had slowed. Sean took stock of himself: he was aching a little in the legs, but it would be hours yet before he was really tired. He hawked a glob of the thick gummy saliva out of his throat and spat it into the grass. He wanted a drink but knew that would be fatal folly.

'Ah!' exclaimed Mbejane. 'They have seen us.'

'How do you know?' asked Sean.

'Look, they are sending out their chasers.' From the head

147

of the line a trio of specks had detached themselves and were drawing ahead.

'What do you mean?' Sean scratched the side of his nose uneasily. For the first time he was feeling the fear of the hunted – vulnerable, unarmed, with the pack closing in.

'They are sending their best runners ahead to force us beyond our strength. They know that if they push us hard enough – even though they break their own wind while they do it – we will fall easily to the others that follow.'

'Good God.' Sean was now truly alarmed. 'What are we going to do about it?'

'For every trick, there is a trick,' said Mbejane. 'But now we have rested enough, let us go.'

Sean took off down the hill like a startled duiker, but Mbejane pulled him up sharply.

'That is what they want. Run as before.' And once again they fell into the steady lope, swinging long-legged and relaxed.

'They're closer,' said Sean when they reached the top of the next hill. Three specks were now well ahead of the others.

'Yes.' Mbejane's voice was expressionless. They went over the crest and down the other side, the slap-slap-slap of their feet together and their breathing an unaltering rhythm: suck blow, suck blow.

There was a tiny stream in the bottom of the valley, clean water rippling over white sand. Sean jumped it with only a single longing glance and they started up the far slope. They were just short of the crest when behind them they heard a thin distant shout. He and Mbejane looked round. On the top of the hill they had just left, only a half a mile away, were the three Zulu runners, and as Sean watched they plunged down the slope towards him with their tall feather head-dresses bobbing and their leopard-tail kilts swirling about their legs. They had thrown aside their shields, but each man carried an assegai.

'Look at their legs,' exulted Mbejane. Sean saw that they ran with the slack, blundering steps of exhaustion.

'They are finished, they have run too hard.' Mbejane laughed. 'Now we must show them how afraid we are: we must run like the wind, run as though a hundred Tokoloshe* breathe on our necks.'

It was only twenty paces to the crest of the slope and they pelted panic-stricken up and over the top. But the instant they were out of sight Mbejane caught Sean's arm and held him.

'Get down,' he whispered. They sank into the grass and then crawled back on their stomachs until they lay just below the crest.

Mbejane held his assegai pointed forward, his legs were gathered up under him and his lips were drawn back in a half grin.

Sean searched in the grass and found a rock the size of an orange. It fitted neatly into his right hand.

They heard the Zulus coming, their horny bare feet pounding up the hill and then their breathing, hoarse hissing gasps, closer and closer until suddenly they came up over the crest. Their momentum carried them down to where Sean and Mbejane stood up out of the grass to meet them. Their fatigue-grey faces crumbled into expressions of complete disbelief; they had expected to find their quarry half a mile ahead of them. Mbejane killed one with his assegai, the man did not even lift his arms to parry the thrust; the point came out between his shoulders.

Sean hurled the rock into the face of another. It made a sound like a ripe pumpkin dropped on a stone floor; he fell backwards with his assegai spinning from his hand.

* A chimera of Zulu mythology.

The third man turned to run and Mbejane landed heavily on his back, bore him down and then sat astride his chest, pushed his chin back and cut his throat.

Sean looked down at the man he had hit; he had lost his head-dress and his face had changed shape. His jaw hung lopsided, he was still moving feebly.

I have killed three men today, thought Sean, *and it was so easy.*

Without emotion he watched Mbejane come across to his victim. Mbejane stooped over him and the man made a small gasping sound then lay still. Mbejane straightened up and looked at Sean.

'Now they cannot catch us before dark.'

'And only a night ape can see in the dark,' said Sean. Remembering the joke, Mbejane smiled; the smile made his face younger. He picked up a bunch of dry grass and wiped his hands on it.

The night came only just in time to save them. Sean had run all day and at last his body was stiffening in protest; his breathing wheezed painfully and he had no moisture left to sweat with.

'A little longer, just a little longer.' Mbejane whispered encouragement beside him.

The pack was spread out, the stronger runners pressing a scant mile behind them and the others dwindling back into the distance.

'The sun is going; soon you can rest.' Mbejane reached out and touched his shoulder; strangely, Sean drew strength from that brief physical contact. His legs steadied slightly and he stumbled less frequently as they went down the next slope. Swollen and red, the sun lowered itself below the land and the valleys were full of shadow.

'Soon now, very soon.' Mbejane's voice was almost crooning. He looked back: the figures of the nearest Zulu were indistinct. Sean's ankle twisted under him and he fell heavily; he felt the earth graze the skin from his cheek and he lay on his chest with his head down.

'Get up,' Mbejane's voice was desperate. Sean vomited painfully, a cupful of bitter bile.

'Get up.' Mbejane's hands were on him, dragging him to his knees.

'Stand up or die here,' threatened Mbejane. He took a handful of Sean's hair and twisted it mercilessly. Tears of pain ran into Sean's eyes and he swore and lashed out at Mbejane.

'Get up,' goaded Mbejane and Sean heaved to his feet.

'Run,' said Mbejane, half-pushing him and Sean's legs began to move mechanically under him. Mbejane looked back once more. The nearest Zulu was very close but almost merged into the fading twilight. They ran on, Mbejane steadying Sean when he staggered, Sean grunting in his throat with each step, his mouth hanging open, sucking air across a swollen tongue.

Then quickly, in the sudden African transition from day to night, all colour was gone from the land and the darkness shut down in a close circle about them. Mbejane's eyes flicked restlessly back and forth, picking up shapes in the gloom, judging the intensity of the light. Sean reeled unseeing beside him.

'We will try now,' decided Mbejane aloud. He checked Sean's run and turned him right at an acute angle on their original track, now they were heading back towards the hunters at a tangent that would take them close past them but out of sight in the darkness.

They slowed to a walk, Mbejane holding Sean's arm across his shoulders to steady him, carrying his assegai ready in his other hand. Sean walked dully, his head hanging.

They heard the leading pursuers passing fifty paces away in the darkness and a voice called in Zulu, 'Can you see them?'

'*Aibo!*' Negative answered another.

'Spread out, they may try to turn in the dark.'

'*Yeh-bo!*' Affirmative.

Then the voices were passed and silence and night closed about them once more. Mbejane made Sean keep walking. A little bit of moon came up and gave them light and they kept going with Mbejane gradually working back onto a course towards the southeast. They came to a stream at last with trees along its bank. Sean drank with difficulty, for his throat was swollen and sore. Afterwards they curled together for warmth on the carpet of leaves beneath the trees and they slept.

– 28 –

They found Chelmsford's last camp on the following afternoon: the neat lines of black camp fires and the flattened areas where the tents had stood, the stakes which had held the horse pickets and the piles of empty bully-beef tins and five-pound biscuit tins.

'They left two days ago,' said Mbejane.

Sean nodded, not doubting the correctness of this. 'Which way did they go?'

'Back towards the main camp at Isandhlwana.'

Sean looked puzzled.

'I wonder why they did that.'

Mbejane shrugged. 'They went in haste – the horsemen galloped ahead of the infantry.'

'We'll follow them,' said Sean.

The spoor was a wide road for a thousand men had passed along it and the wagons and gun carriages had left deep ruts.

They slept hungry and cold beside the spoor and the

next morning there was frost in the low places when they started out.

A little before noon they saw the granite dome of Isandhlwana standing out against the sky and unconsciously they quickened their pace. Isandhlwana, the Hill of the Little Hand. Sean was limping for his boot had rubbed the skin from one heel. His hair was thick and matted with sweat and his face was plastered with dust.

'Even army bully beef is going to taste good,' said Sean in English, and Mbejane did not answer for he did not understand, but he was looking ahead with a vaguely worried frown on his face.

'Nkosi, we have seen no one for two days' march. It comes to me that we should have met patrols from the camp before now.'

'We might have missed them,' said Sean without much interest, but Mbejane shook his head. In silence they went on. The hill was closer now so they could make out the detail of ledge and fissure that covered the dome in a lacework pattern.

'No smoke from the camp,' said Mbejane. He lifted his eyes and started visibly.

'What is it?' Sean felt the first tingle of alarm.

'N'yoni,' said Mbejane softly and Sean saw them. A dark pall, turning like a wheel slowly, high above the hill of Isandhlwana, still so far off that they could not distinguish the individual birds: only a shadow, a thin dark shadow in the sky. Watching it Sean was suddenly cold in the hot noonday sun. He started to run.

There was movement below them on the plain. The torn canvas of an overturned wagon flapped like a wounded bird, the scurry and scuffle of the jackals and higher up the slope of the kopje the hunch-shouldered trot of a hyena.

'Oh, my God!' whispered Sean. Mbejane leaned on his

153

spear; his face was calm and withdrawn but his eyes moved slowly over the field.

'Are they dead? Are they all dead?' The question required no answer. He could see the dead men in the grass, thick about the wagons and then scattered more thinly back up the slope. They looked very small and inconsequential. Mbejane stood quietly waiting. A big black kolbes vulture planed across their front, the feathers in its wing-tips flated like the fingers of a spread hand. Its legs dropped, touched and it hopped heavily to rest among the dead, a swift transformation from beautiful flight to obscene crouching repose. It bobbed its head, ruffled its feathers and waddled to dip its beak over a corpse that wore the green Hunting Tartan of the Gordons.

'Where is Chelmsford? Was he caught here also?'

Mbejane shook his head. 'He came too late.'

Mbejane pointed with his spear at the wide spoor that skirted the battlefield and crossed the shoulder of Isandhlwana towards the Tugela. 'He has gone back to the river. He has not stopped even to bury his dead.'

Sean and Mbejane walked down towards the field. On the outskirts they picked their way through the debris of Zulu weapons and shields; there was rust forming on the blades of the assegais. The grass was flattened and stained where the dead had lain, but the Zulu dead were gone – sure sign of victory.

They came to the English lines. Sean gagged when he saw what had been done to them. They lay piled upon each other, faces already black, and each one of them had been disembowelled. The flies crawled in their empty stomach cavities.

'Why do they do that?' he asked. 'Why do they have to hack them up like that?'

He walked on heavily past the wagons. Cases of food and drink had been smashed open and scattered in the grass, clothing and paper and cartridge cases lay strewn around the dead, but the rifles were gone. The smell of putrefaction was so thick that it coated his throat and tongue like castor oil.

'I must find Pa,' Sean spoke quietly in almost a conversational tone. Mbejane walked a dozen paces behind him. They came to the lines where the Volunteers had camped. The tents had been slashed to tatters and trampled into the dust. The horses had been stabbed while still tethered to their picket lines; they were massively bloated. Sean recognized Gypsy, his father's mare. He crossed to her.

'Hello, girl,' he said. The birds had taken her eyes out; she lay on her side, her stomach so swollen that it was as high as Sean's waist. He walked around her. The first of the Ladyburg men lay just beyond. He recognized all fifteen of them although the birds had been at them also. They lay in a rough circle, facing outwards. Then he found a sparse trail of corpses leading up towards the shoulder of the mountain. He followed the attempt that the Volunteers had made to fight their way back towards the Tugela and it was like following a paper chase. Along the trail, thick on each side of it, were the marks where the Zulus had fallen.

'At least twenty of them for every one of us,' whispered Sean, with a tiny flicker of pride. He climbed on up and at the top of the shoulder, close under the sheer rock cliff of Isandhlwana, he found his father.

There were four of them, the last four: Waite Courtney, Tim Hope-Brown, Hans and Nile Erasmus. They lay close together. Waite was on his back with his arms spread open, the birds had taken his face away down to the bone, but they had left his beard and it stirred gently on his chest as the wind touched it. The flies, big metallic green flies, crawled thick as swarming bees in the open pit of his belly.

Sean sat down beside his father. He picked up a discarded felt hat that lay beside him and covered his terribly mutilated face. There was a green-and-yellow silk cockade on the hat, strangely gay in the presence of so much death. The flies buzzed sullenly and some came to settle on Sean's face and lips. He brushed them away.

'You know this man?' asked Mbejane.

'My father,' said Sean, without looking up.

'You too.' Compassion and understanding in his voice, Mbejane turned away and left them alone.

'I have nothing,' Mbejane had said. Now Sean also had nothing. There was hollowness: no anger, no sorrow, no ache, no reality even. Staring down at this broken thing, Sean could not make himself believe that this was a man. Meat only; the man had gone.

Later Mbejane came back. He had cut a sheet of canvas from one of the unburned wagons and they wrapped Waite in it. They dug his grave. It was hard work for the soil was thick with rock and shale. They laid Waite in the grave, with his arms still widespread in *rigor mortis* beneath the canvas for Sean could not bring himself to break them. They covered him gently and piled rocks upon the place. They stood together at the head of the grave.

'Well, Pa – ' Sean's voice sounded unnatural. He could not make himself believe he was talking to his father.

'Well, Pa – ' he started again, mumbling self-consciously. 'I'd like to say thanks for everything you've done for me.' He stopped and cleared his throat. 'I reckon you know I'll look after Ma and the farm as best I can – and Garry also.' His voice trailed away once more and he turned to Mbejane.

'There is nothing to say.' Sean's voice was surprised, hurt almost.

'No,' agreed Mbejane. 'There is nothing to say.'

For a few minutes longer Sean stood struggling to grapple with the enormity of death, trying to grasp the utter finality of it, then he turned away and started walking towards the

Tugela. Mbejane walked a little to one side and a pace behind him. *It will be dark before we reach the river*, thought Sean. He was very tired and he limped from his blistered heel.

– 29 –

'Not much farther,' said Dennis Petersen.

'No,' Sean grunted. He was irritated at the statement of the obvious; when you come out of Mahoba's Kloof and have the Baboon Stroom next to the road on your left hand, then it is five miles to Ladyburg. As Dennis had said: not much farther.

Dennis coughed in the dust. 'That first beer is going to turn to steam in my throat.'

'I think we can ride ahead now.' Sean wiped at his face, smearing the dust. 'Mbejane and the other servants can bring them in the rest of the way.'

'I was going to suggest it.' Dennis was obviously relieved. They had almost a thousand head of cattle crowding the road ahead of them and raising dust for them to breathe. It had been two days' drive from Rorke's Drift where the Commando had disbanded.

'We'll hold them in the sale pens tonight and send them out tomorrow morning – I'll tell Mbejane.'

Sean clapped his heels into his horse and swung across to where the big Zulu trotted at the heels of the herd. A few minutes' talk and then Sean signalled to Dennis. They circled out on each side of the herd and met again on the road ahead of it.

'They've lost a bit of condition,' grumbled Dennis looking back.

'Bound to,' said Sean. 'We've pushed them hard for two days.'

A thousand head of cattle, five men's share of Cetewayo's herds – Dennis and his father, Waite, Sean and Garrick – for even dead men drew a full share.

'How far ahead of the others do you reckon we are?' asked Dennis.

'Dunno,' said Sean. It wasn't important and any answer would be only a guess: pointless question is just as irritating as obvious statement. It suddenly occurred to Sean that but a few months previously a question like that would have started a discussion and argument that might have lasted half an hour. What did that mean? It meant that he had changed. Having answered his own question, Sean grinned sardonically.

'What're you laughing at?' asked Dennis.

'I was just thinking that a lot has changed in the last few months.'

'Ja,' said Dennis and then silence except for the broken beat of their hooves. 'It's going to seem funny without Pa,' Dennis said wistfully. Mr Petersen had been at Isandhlwana. 'It's going to seem funny being just Ma, the girls and me on the farm.'

They didn't speak again for a while. They were thinking back across the brief months and the events that had changed their lives.

Neither of them yet twenty years of age, but already head of his family, a holder of land and cattle, initiated into grief and a killer of men. Sean was older now with new lines in his face, and the beard he wore was square and spade-shaped. They had ridden with the Commandos who had burned and plundered to avenge Isandhlwana. At Ulundi they had sat their horses behind the ranks of Chelmsford's infantry in the hot sun, quietly waiting as Cetewayo massed his impis and sent them across open ground to overwhelm the frail square of men. They had waited through the din of the regular, unhurried volleys and watched the great black bull of Zulu tearing itself to shreds against the square. Then at the end the ranks of infantry had opened and they had ridden out, two thousand horsemen strong, to smash for ever the power of the Zulu empire. They had chased and hunted until the darkness had stopped them and they had not kept score of the kill.

'There's the church steeple,' said Dennis.

Sean came back slowly out of the past. They were at Ladyburg.

'Is your stepmother out at Theunis Kraal?' asked Dennis.

'No, she's moved into town – the cottage on Protea Street.'

'I suppose she doesn't want to be in the way now that Anna and Garry are married,' said Dennis.

Sean frowned quickly.

'How do you like old Garry getting Anna?' Dennis chuckled and shook his head. 'I reckon you could have got twenty-to-one odds he didn't have a chance.'

Sean's frown became a scowl. Garry had made him look such a damn fool – Sean hadn't finished with Anna.

'Have you heard from them yet? When are they coming home?'

'The last time we heard was from Pietermaritzburg; they sent a wire to Ma just to say they were married. She got it a couple of days before I arrived home from Isandhlwana. That was two months ago; as far as I know we haven't heard since.'

'I suppose Garry's so firmly settled on the nest they'll have to prise him off with a crowbar.' Dennis chuckled again, lewdly. Sean had a sudden and shockingly vivid mental picture of Garry on top of Anna; her knees were up high, her head was thrown back and her eyes were closed; she was making that little mewing sound.

'Shut up, you dirty bastard,' snarled Sean.

Dennis blinked. 'Sorry, I was only joking.'

159

'Don't joke about my family, he's my brother.'

'And she was your girl, hey?' murmured Dennis.

'Do you want a punch?'

'Cool down, man, I was joking.'

'I don't like that kind of joke, see?'

'All right. All right. Cool down.'

'It's dirty, that's dirty talk.' Sean was trying desperately to shut out the picture of Anna; she was in wild orgasm, her hands pleading at the small of Garrick's back.

'Jesus, since when have you become a saint?' asked Dennis and, urging his horse into a gallop, drew ahead of Sean; he kept going along the main street towards the hotel. Sean considered calling him back, but finally let him go.

Sean turned right into a shady side street. The cottage was the third house down. Waite had purchased it three years before as an investment. It was a charming little place, set among trees in a small green garden with flowers: thatched, whitewashed and surrounded by a wooden picket fence. Sean hitched his horse at the gate and went up the path.

There were two women in the sitting-room when he pushed the door open. They both stood up, surprise instantly becoming delight as they recognized him. It warmed him inside to see it – it's good to be welcome.

'Oh Sean, we weren't expecting you.' Ada came quickly to him. He kissed her and saw that sorrow had left its marks on her. He felt vaguely guilty that Waite's death had not wrought so obvious a change in him. He held her away at arm's length.

'You're beautiful,' he said. She was thin. Her eyes were too big for her face and the grief was in them like shadows in the forest, but she smiled and laughed at him.

'We thought you'd be back on Friday. I'm so glad you've come earlier.'

Sean looked past Ada.

'Hello, Strawberry Pie.' She was hovering impatiently for his attention.

'Hello, Sean.' She flushed a little with his eyes on her, but she did not drop hers.

'You look older,' she said, hardly noticing the dust that caked his skin, powdered his hair and eyelashes, and reddened his eyes.

'You've just forgotten what I look like,' he said, turning back to Ada.

'No, I'd never do that,' whispered Audrey so softly that neither of them heard her. She felt swollen up inside her chest.

'Sit down, Sean.' Ada led him to the big armchair across from the fireplace. There was a daguerreotype of Waite on the mantel.

'I'll get you a cup of tea.'

'How about a beer, Ma?' Sean sank into the chair.

'Of course – I'll get it.'

'No.' Audrey flew across the room towards the kitchen. 'I'll get it.'

'They're in the pantry, Audrey,' Ada called after her, and then to Sean, 'She's such a sweet child.'

'Look again,' Sean smiled. 'She's no child.'

'I wish Garry—' Ada cut herself short.

'What do you wish?' Sean prompted her. She was quiet for a moment, wishing that Garrick could have found a girl like Audrey instead of –

'Nothing,' she said to Sean and came to sit near him.

'Have you heard from Garry again?' asked Sean.

'No. Not yet, but Mr Pye says he had a cheque come through the bank – cashed in Capetown.'

'Capetown?' Sean raised a dusty eyebrow. 'Our boy's living life to the hilt.'

'Yes,' said Ada, remembering the size of that cheque. 'He is.'

161

Audrey came back into the room: she had a large bottle and a glass on a tray. She crossed to Sean's chair. Sean touched the bottle; it was cold.

'Quickly, wench,' Sean encouraged her. 'I'm dying of thirst.'

The first glass emptied in three swallows. Audrey poured again and, with the replenished glass in his fist, Sean settled back comfortably in the chair.

'Now,' said Ada, 'tell us all about it.'

In the warmth of their welcome – his muscles aching pleasantly, the glass in his hand – it was good to talk. He had not realized that there was so much to tell. At the first hint of slackening in his flow of speech either Ada or Audrey was ready with a question to keep him going.

'Oh, my goodness,' gasped Audrey at last. 'It's nearly dark outside, I must go.'

'Sean,' Ada stood up. 'Will you see that she gets home safely?'

They walked side by side in the half darkness, under the flamboyants. They walked in silence until Audrey spoke.

'Sean, were you in love with Anna?' She blurted out the question and Sean experienced his standard reaction: quick anger. He opened his mouth to blast her, then checked. It was a nice question. Had he been in love with Anna? He thought about it now for the first time, phrasing the question with care that he might answer it with truth. He felt a sudden rush of relief and he was smiling when he told her.

'No, Strawberry Pie, no, I was never in love with Anna.' The tone of his voice was right, he wasn't lying. She walked on happily beside him.

'Don't bother to come up to the house.' She noticed for the first time his stained and dirty clothing that might embarrass him in front of her parents. She wanted it to be right from the start.

162

'I'll watch you till you get to the door,' said Sean.

'I suppose you'll be going out to Theunis Kraal tomorrow?' she asked.

'First thing in the morning,' Sean assured her. 'There's a hell of a lot of work to do.'

'But you'll be coming to the store?'

'Yes,' said Sean and the way he looked at her made her blush and hate her redhead's skin which betrayed her so easily. She went quickly up the path and then stopped and looked back.

'Sean, please don't call me Strawberry Pie any more.'

Sean chuckled. 'All right, Audrey, I'll try to remember.'

– 30 –

Six weeks had gone since his return from the Zulu Campaign, Sean reflected, six weeks that had passed in a blur of speed. He sipped coffee from a mug the size of a German beer *stein*, sitting in the centre of his bed with his nightshirt hitched up to his waist and his legs crossed in comfortable Buddha fashion. The coffee was hot; he sipped noisily and then exhaled steam from his mouth.

The last six weeks had been full – too full for brooding grief or regret, although in the evenings, when he sat in the study with Waite's memory all about him, the ache was still there.

The days seemed to pass before they had fairly begun. There were three farms now: Theunis Kraal and the other two rented from old man Pye. He had stocked them with the looted cattle and the purchases he had made since his return. The price of prime beef had dropped to a new low, with nearly a hundred thousand cattle brought back from Zululand and Sean could afford to be selective in his buying. He could also afford to wait while the price climbed up again.

Sean swung his legs off the bed and walked across the room to the washstand. He poured water from the jug into the basin and tested it tentatively with one finger. It was so cold it stung. He stood hesitating in his ridiculously feminine nightshirt, with dark chest hairs curling out above the elaborately embroidered front. Then he mustered his courage and plunged his face into the basin; he scooped water with both hands and poured it over the back of his neck, massaged it into his hair with hooked fingers and emerged at last blowing heavily with water dripping down onto his nightshirt. He towelled, stripped off the damp garment and stood naked peering out of the window. It had lightened enough for him to make out the smoky swirl of drizzle and mist beyond the pane.

'A hell of a day,' he grumbled aloud, but his tone was deceptive. He felt excitement for this day; he was fresh and sharp-edged, hungry for breakfast, ready to go for there was work to do.

He dressed, hopping on one leg as he got into his breeches, stuffing in the tails of his shirt and then sitting on the bed to pull on his boots. Now he was thinking about Audrey – he must try and get into town tomorrow to see her.

Sean had decided on matrimony. He had three good reasons. He had found that it was easier to get into the Bank of England's vaults than to get under Audrey's petticoats without marrying her. When Sean wanted something no price was too high to pay.

Living at Theunis Kraal with Garry and Anna, Sean had decided that it would be pleasant to have his own woman to cook for him, mend his clothes and listen to his stories, for Sean was feeling a little left out.

The third consideration, by no means the least significant, was Audrey's connections with the local bank. She was one of the very few weaknesses in old man Pye's armour. He might even weigh in with Mahoba's Kloof Farm as a wedding present, though even the optimist in Sean realized that this hope was extravagant. Pye and his money were not easily parted.

Yes, Sean decided, he would have to find time to get into town and tell Audrey – in Sean's mind it wasn't a question of asking her. Sean brushed his hair, combed his beard, winked at himself in the mirror and went out into the passage. He could smell breakfast cooking and his mouth started to water.

Anna was in the kitchen. Her face was flushed from the heat of the stove.

'What's for breakfast, little sister?'

She turned to him, quickly brushing the hair off her forehead with the back of her hand.

'I'm not your sister,' she said. 'I wish you wouldn't call me that.'

'Where's Garry?' Sean asked as though he had not heard her protest.

'He's not up yet.'

'The poor boy's exhausted, no doubt.' Sean grinned at her and she turned away in confusion. Sean looked at her bottom without desire. Strange that Anna being Garry's wife should kill his appetite for her. Even the memory of what they had done before was vaguely obscene, incestuous.

'You're getting fat,' he said noticing the new heaviness of her body. She ducked her head but did not answer and Sean went on, 'I'll have four eggs, please, and tell Joseph not to dry them out completely.'

Sean went through into the dining-room and Garry came in through the side door at the same moment. His face was still vacant from sleep. Sean got a whiff of his breath; it smelled of stale liquor.

'Good morning, Romeo,' said Sean and Garry grinned sheepishly. His eyes were bloodshot and he hadn't shaved.

'Hello, Sean. How did you sleep?'

'Beautifully, thank you. I take it that you did also.' Sean sat down and spooned porridge from the tureen.

'Have some?' he asked Garry.

'Thanks.' Sean passed him the plate. He noticed how Garry's hand shook. *I'll have to talk to him about letting up on the bottle a trifle.*

'Hell, I'm hungry.' They talked the jerky, disconnected conversation of the breakfast table. Anna came through and joined them. Joseph brought the coffee.

'Have you told Sean yet, Garry?' Anna spoke suddenly, clearly and with decision.

'No.' Garry was taken by surprise, he spluttered his coffee.

'Told me what?' Sean asked. They were silent and Garrick fluttered his hand nervously. This was the moment he had been dreading – what if Sean guessed, what if he knew it was his baby and took them away, Anna and the baby, took them away and left Garry with nothing. Haunted by wild unreasonable fears, Garrick stared fixedly across the table at his brother.

'Tell him, Garry,' commanded Anna.

'Anna's going to have a baby,' he said. He watched Sean's face, saw the surprise change slowly to delight, felt Sean's arm close round his shoulders in a painful hug, almost crushing him.

'That's great,' Sean exulted, 'that's wonderful. We'll have the house full of kids in no time if you keep that up, Garry. I'm proud of you.'

Grinning stupidly with relief Garrick watched Sean hug Anna more gently and kiss her forehead.

'Well done, Anna, make sure it's a boy. We need cheap labour around here.'

He hasn't guessed, thought Garrick, *he doesn't know and it will be mine. No one can take it away from me now.*

That day they worked in the south section. They stayed together, Garry laughing in happy confusion at Sean's banter. It was delightful to have Sean give him so much attention. They finished early; for once Sean was in no mood for work.

'My reproductive brother, every barrel loaded with buck-shot.' Sean leaned across and punched Garry's shoulder. 'Let's knock it off and go into town. We can have a few quick ones to celebrate at the hotel and then go and tell Ada.'

Sean stood up in the stirrup and yelled above the moo and mill of the herd.

'Mbejane, bring those ten sick ones up to the house and don't forget that tomorrow we are going to fetch cattle from the sale pens.'

Mbejane waved in acknowledgement and Sean turned back to Garrick.

'Come on, let's get the hell out of here.'

They rode side by side, globules of moisture covering their oilskins and shining on Sean's beard. It was still cold and the escarpment was hidden in the wet mist.

'It's real brandy-drinking weather,' said Sean and Garrick did not answer. He was frightened again. He didn't want to tell Ada. She would guess. She guessed everything, she would know it was Sean's child. You couldn't lie to her.

The horses' hooves plopped wetly in the mud. They reached the spot where the road forked and climbed over the ridge to Ladyburg.

'Ada's going to love being a grandma,' chuckled Sean, and at that moment his horse stumbled slightly, broke its gait and started favouring its near fore. Sean dismounted, lifted the hoof and saw the splinter driven deep into the frog.

'Damn it to hell,' he swore. He bent his head, gripped the hilt of the splinter with his teeth and drew it out.

'Well, we can't go into Ladyburg now, that leg will be sore for days.' Garry was relieved; it put off the time when he must tell Ada.

'Your horse isn't lame. Off you go, man, give her my love.' Sean looked up at him.

'We can tell her some other time. Let's get back home,' Garry demurred.

'Go on, Garry, it's your baby. Go and tell her.'

Garrick argued until he saw Sean's temper rising, then with a sigh of resignation he went and Sean led his own horse back to Theunis Kraal. Now that he was walking the oilskin was uncomfortably hot and heavy, Sean took it off and slung it over the saddle.

Anna was standing on the *stoep* as he came up to the homestead.

'Where's Garry?' she called.

'Don't worry. He's gone into town to see Ada. He'll be back by supper-time.'

One of the stable boys came to take Sean's horse. They talked together and then Sean stooped to lift the injured hoof. His breeches tightened across his buttocks and enhanced the long moulded taper of his legs. Anna looked at him. He straightened up and his shoulders were wide beneath the damp white linen of his shirt. He smiled at her as he came up the steps of the *stoep*. The rain had made his beard curl and he looked like a mischievous pirate.

'You must take better care of yourself now.' He put his hand on her upper arm to lead her inside. 'You can't stand around in the cold any more.' They went in through the glass doors. Anna looked up at him, the top of her head on a level with his shoulder.

'You're a damn fine woman, Anna, and I'm sure you're going to make a fine baby.' It was a mistake, for as he said it his eyes softened and his face turned down towards her. He let his arm drop around her shoulders.

'Sean!' She said his name as though it were an exclamation of pain. She moved quickly, fiercely within the circle of his arm, her body flattened itself against his and her hands went up to catch in the thick hair at the back of his head. She pulled his face down and her mouth opened warm and wet across his lips, her back arched and thrust her thighs against his legs. She moaned softly as she kissed him. For startled seconds Sean stood imprisoned in her embrace, then he tore his face away.

'Are you mad?' He tried to push her from him, but she fought her way back through his fending hands. She locked her arms around him and pressed her face against his chest.

'I love you. Please, please. I love you. Just let me hold you, that's all. I just want to hold you.' Her voice was muffled by the damp cloth of his shirt. She was shivering.

'Get away from me.' Roughly Sean broke her hold and almost threw her backwards onto the couch beside the fireplace.

'You're Garry's wife now, and you'll soon be the mother of his child. Keep your hot little body for him.' Sean stood back from her with his anger starting to mount.

'But I love you, Sean. Oh, my God, if I could only make you understand how I've suffered, living here with you and not being able to touch you even.'

Sean strode across to where she sat. 'Listen to me.' His voice was harsh. 'I don't want you. I never loved you, but now I could no more touch you than I could go with my own mother.' She could see the revulsion in his face. 'You're Garry's wife; if ever again you look at another man I'll kill you.'

He lifted his hands, holding them with the fingers crooked ready. 'I'll kill you with my bare hands.'

His face was close to hers. She could not bear the

expression in his eyes: she lashed out at him. He pulled back in time to save his eyes, but her nails gouged bloody lines across his cheek and down the side of his nose. He caught her wrists and held her while a thin trickle of blood dribbled down into his beard. She twisted in his hands, jerking her body from side to side, and she screamed at him.

'You swine, you dirty, dirty swine. Garry's wife, you say. Garry's baby, you say.' She threw her head back and laughed wildly through her screaming. 'Now I'll tell you the truth. What I have within me you gave me. It's yours! Not Garry's!' Sean let go her wrists and backed away from her.

'It can't be,' he whispered, 'you must be lying.' She followed him.

'Don't you remember how you said goodbye to me before you went to war? Don't you remember that night in the wagon? Don't you remember – don't you? Don't you?' She was talking quietly now, using her words to wound him.

'That was months ago. It can't be true,' Sean stammered, still moving away from her.

'Three and a half months,' she told him. 'Your brother's baby will be a little early, don't you think? But lots of people have premature babies—' Her voice droned on steadily, she was shivering uncontrollably now and her face was ghostly pale. Sean could stand it no longer.

'Leave me, leave me alone. I've got to think. I didn't know.' He brushed past her and went out into the passage. She heard the door of Waite's study slam shut and she stood still in the centre of the floor. Gradually her panting came under control and the storm surf of her anger abated to expose the black reefs of hatred beneath. She crossed the floor, went down the passage and into her own bedroom. She stood in front of the mirror and looked at herself.

'I hate him.' Her lips formed the words in the mirror. Her face was still pale. 'There's one thing I can take from him. Garry's mine now, not his.'

170

She pulled the pins from her hair and let them drop onto the floor; her hair fell down her back. She shook it onto her shoulders then lifted her hands and tangled it into confusion. Her teeth closed on her own lips, she bit until she tasted blood.

'Oh, God, I hate him, I hate him,' she whispered through the pain. Her hands came down onto the front of her dress. She tore it open, then in the mirror looked without interest at the round bosses of her nipples that were already darkening with the promise of fruition. She kicked off her shoes.

'I hate him.' She stooped and her hands went up under her skirts into the petticoats. She loosened her pantaloons and stepped out of them; she held them across her chest to tear them, then threw them next to the bed. She swept her arm across the top of her dressing-table: one of the bowls hit the floor and burst with a splash of face-powder and there was the sudden pungent reek of spilled perfume. She crossed to the bed and dropped onto it. She lifted her knees and her petticoats fell back like the petals of a flower: her white legs and lower body were the stamen.

Just before nightfall there was a shy knock on her door.

'What is it?' she asked.

'The Nkosikazi has not told me what I should cook for dinner.' Old Joseph's voice was raised respectfully.

'There will be no dinner tonight. You and all the servants may go.'

'Very well, Nkosikazi.'

Garrick came home in the dark. He had been drinking; she heard him stagger as he crossed the *stoep*, and his voice slur as he called.

'Hallo. Where's everybody? Anna! Anna! I'm back.' Silence for a while as he lit one of the lamps and then the hurried thump, thump of his peg along the passage and his voice again edged with alarm.

171

'Anna, Anna, where are you?'

He pushed the door open and stood with the lamp in his hand. Anna rolled away from the light, pressing her face into the pillow and hunching her shoulders. She heard him set the lamp down on the dressing-table, felt his hands pulling down her skirts to cover her nakedness, then gently turn her to face him. She looked into his face and saw the uncomprehending horror in it.

'My darling, oh Anna, my darling, what's happened?' He started at her broken lips and her breasts. Bewildered he turned his head and looked at the bottles on the floor, at her torn pantaloons. His face hardened and came back to her.

'Are you hurt?' She shook her head.

'Who? Tell me who did it.' She turned away from him again, hiding her face.

'My darling, my poor darling. Who was it – one of the servants?'

'No,' her voice stifled with shame.

'Please tell me, Anna. What happened?'

She sat up quickly and threw her arms about him, holding him hard so her lips were near his ear. 'You know, Garry. You know who did it.'

'No, I swear I don't, please tell me.'

Anna drew her breath in deep, held it a second then breathed it out. 'Sean!'

Garrick's body convulsed in her arms, she heard him grunt as though he had been hit. Then he spoke. 'This too. Now this too.'

He loosened her hands from his neck and pushed her gently down onto the pillows. He crossed to the cupboard, opened one of the drawers and took out Waite's service pistol.

He's going to kill Sean, she thought. Garrick went out of the room without looking at her again. She waited with

172

her hands clenched at her sides and her whole body stretched tightly. When the shot came at last it was surprisingly muted and unwarlike. Her body relaxed, her hands opened and she began to cry softly.

– 31 –

Garry limped down the passage. The pistol was heavy and the checkered grip rough in his hand. There was light showing under the study door at the end of the passage. It was unlocked. Garrick went in.

Sean sat with his elbows on the desk and his face in his hands but he looked up as Garrick came in through the door. The scratches had already dried black across his cheek, but the flesh around them was red and inflamed. He looked at the pistol in Garrick's hand.

'She has told you.' There was no question or expression in his voice.

'Yes.'

'I hoped that she wouldn't,' said Sean. 'I wanted her to spare you that at least.'

'Spare me?' Garrick asked. 'What about her? Did you think of her?'

Sean did not answer, instead he shrugged and laid back tiredly in his chair.

'I never realized before what a merciless swine you are,' choked Garrick. 'I have come to kill you.'

'Yes.' Sean watched the pistol come up. Garrick was holding it with both hands, his sandy hair hung forward onto his forehead.

'My poor Garry,' Sean said softly and immediately the pistol started to shake. It sank until Garrick held it, still with both hands between his knees. He crouched over it, blubbering – chewing at his lips to stop himself. Sean

173

started out of his chair to go to him, but Garrick recoiled against the door-jamb.

'Keep away from me,' he yelled, 'don't touch me.' He threw the pistol, the sharp edge of the hammer cut across Sean's forehead, jerking his head back. The pistol glanced off and hit the wall behind him. It fired and the bullet splintered the panelled woodwork.

'We're finished,' Garrick screamed. 'We're finished for ever.' He groped wildly for the door and stumbled out into the passage, through the kitchens into the rain. He fell many times as the grass caught his peg, but each time he scrambled up and kept running. He sobbed with each step in the utter darkness of the night.

At last the growl of the rain-engorged Baboon Stroom blocked his way. He stood on the bank with the drizzle blowing into his face.

'Why me, why always me?' He screamed his agony into the darkness. Then with a rush of relief as strong as the torrent in the river-bed below him he felt the moth flutter its wings behind his eyes. The warmth and the greyness closed about him and he sank down onto his knees in the mud.

– 32 –

Sean took very little with him: his bedroll, a rifle and a spare horse. Twice in the darkness he lost the path to Mbejane's kraal but each time his horse found it again. Mbejane had built his big grass beehive hut well away from the quarters of the other servants, for he was Zulu of royal blood. When at last Sean came to it there were a few minutes of sleepy stirring and muttering within before Mbejane, with a blanket draped around his shoulders and an old paraffin lamp in his hand, came out to Sean's shouts.

'What is it, Nkosi?'

'I am going, Mbejane.'

'Where to?'

'Wherever the roads lead. Will you follow?'

'I will get my spears,' said Mbejane.

Old man Pye was still in his office behind the bank when they reached Ladyburg. He was counting the sovereigns and stacking them in neat golden piles and his hands were as gentle on them as a man's hands on the body of the woman he loves, but he reached quickly for the open drawer at his side as Sean shouldered the door open.

'You don't need that,' said Sean and Pye lifted his hand guiltily off the pistol.

'Good gracious! I didn't recognize you, my boy.'

'How much have I got credited to my account?' Sean cut through the pleasantries.

'This isn't banking hours, you know.'

'Look here, Mr Pye, I'm in a hurry. How much have I got?'

Pye climbed out of his chair and crossed to the big iron safe. Shielding it with his body he tumbled the combination and swung open the door. He brought the ledger across to the desk.

'Carter – Cloete – Courtney,' he muttered as he turned the pages. 'Ah – Ada – Garrick – Sean. Here we are. Twelve hundred and ninety-six pounds eight and eight pence; of course, there are last month's accounts at the store still unpaid.'

'Call it twelve hundred then,' said Sean. 'I want it now and while you are counting it you can give me pen and paper.'

'Help yourself, there on the desk.'

Sean sat at the desk, pushed the piles of gold out of his way, dipped the pen and wrote. When he had finished he looked up at old Pye.

175

'Witness that, please.'

Pye took the paper and read it through. His face went limp with surprise.

'You're giving your half share of Theunis Kraal and all the cattle to your brother's first born!' he exploded.

'That's right, please witness it.'

'You must be mad,' protested Pye. 'That's a fortune you're giving away. Think what you're doing – think of your future. I had hoped that you and Audrey—' He stopped himself and went on. 'Don't be a fool, man.'

'Please witness it, Mr Pye,' said Sean and, muttering under his breath, Pye signed quickly.

'Thank you.' Sean folded the document, slipped it into an envelope and sealed it. He put it away inside his coat.

'Where's the money?' he asked.

Pye pushed a canvas bag across to him. His expression was one of disgust; he wanted no truck with fools.

'Count it,' he said.

'I'll take your word for it,' said Sean and signed the receipt.

Sean rode out past the sale-pens and up the escarpment along the road to Pietermaritzburg. Mbejane trotted at his stirrup leading the spare horse. They stopped at the top of the escarpment. The wind had blown the clouds open and the starlight came through. They could see the town below them with here and there a lighted window.

I should have said goodbye to Ada, Sean thought. He looked down the valley towards Theunis Kraal. He could see no light. He touched the letter in the inside pocket of his coat.

'I'll post it to Garry from Pietermaritzburg,' he spoke aloud.

'Nkosi?' asked Mbejane.

'I said, "It's a long road, let us begin."'

'Yes,' agreed Mbejane. 'Let us begin.'

176

– II –

Witwatersrand

– 1 –

They turned north from Pietermaritzburg and climbed steadily up across bleak grassland towards the mountains. On the third day they saw the Drakensberg, jagged and black as the teeth of an ancient shark along the skyline.

It was cold; wrapped in his kaross Mbejane trailed far behind Sean. They had exchanged perhaps two dozen words since they left Pietermaritzburg for Sean had his thoughts and they were evil company. Mbejane was keeping discreetly out of his way. Mbejane felt no resentment, for a man who had just left his home and his cattle was entitled to brood. Mbejane was with sadness himself – he had left a fat woman in his bed to follow Sean.

Mbejane unplugged his small gourd snuff-box, picked a pinch and sniffed it delicately. He looked up at the mountains. The snows upon them were turning pink in the sunset and in a little while now they would make camp, and then again perhaps they would not. It made no difference.

Sean rode on after dark. The road crossed another fold in the veld and they saw the lights in the valley below.

'Dundee,' Sean thought without interest. He made no effort to hasten his horse but let it amble down towards the town. Now he could smell the smoke from the coal mine, tarry and thick in the back of his throat. They entered the main street. The town seemed deserted in the cold. Sean did not intend stopping – he would camp on the far side;

but when he reached the hotel he hesitated. There was warmth in there and laughter and the sound of men's voices and he was suddenly aware that his fingers were stiff with cold.

'Mbejane, take my horse. Find a place to camp beyond the town and make a fire so I won't miss you in the dark.'

Sean climbed down and walked into the bar. The room was full, miners most of them – he could see the grey coal dust etched into their skins. They looked at him incuriously as he crossed to the counter and ordered a brandy. He drank it slowly, making no attempt to join the loud talk around him.

The drunk was a short man but built like Table Mountain, low, square and solid. He had to stand on tiptoe to put his arm around Sean's neck.

'Have a drink with me, *Boetie*.' His breath smelt sour and old.

'No thanks.' Sean was in no mood for drunks.

'Come on, come on,' the drunk insisted; he staggered and Sean's drink slopped onto the counter.

'Leave me alone.' Sean shrugged the arm away.

'You've got something against me?'

'No. I just feel like drinking alone.'

'You don't like my face, maybe?' The drunk held it close to Sean's. Sean didn't like it.

'Push off, there's a good fellow.'

The drunk slapped the counter.

'Charlie, give this big ape a drink. Make it a double. If he don't drink it, I ram it down his throat.'

Sean ignored the proffered glass. He swallowed what remained in his own and turned for the door. The drunk threw the brandy in his face. The spirit burned his eyes and he hit the man in the stomach. As his head came down Sean hit him again – in the face. The drunk spun sideways, fell and lay bleeding from his nose.

'What you hit him for?' Another miner was helping the drunk into a sitting position.

'It wouldn't cost you nothing to have a drink with him.' Sean felt the hostility in the room; he was the outsider.

'This boy is looking for trouble.'

'He's a tough monkey. We know how to handle tough monkeys.'

'Come on, let's sort this bastard out.'

Sean had hit the man as a reflex action. He was sorry now, but his guilt evaporated as he saw them gathering against him. Gone too was his mood of depression and in its place was a sense of relief. This was what he needed.

There were six of them moving in on him in a pack. Six was a fairly well-rounded number. One of them had a bottle in his hand and Sean started to smile. They were talking loudly, spreading courage and waiting for one of their fellows to start it.

Sean saw movement out of the side of his eye and jumped back to cover it with his hands ready.

'Steady on there,' a very English voice soothed him. 'I have come to offer my services. It seems to me you have adversaries and to spare.' The speaker had stood up from one of the tables behind Sean. He was tall, with a gauntly ravaged face and an immaculate grey suit.

'I want them all,' said Sean.

'Damned unsporting.' The newcomer shook his head. 'I'll buy the three gentlemen on the left if your price is reasonable.'

'Take two as a gift and consider yourself lucky.' Sean grinned at him and the man grinned back. They had almost forgotten the impending action in the pleasure of meeting.

'Very decent of you. May I introduce myself – Dufford Charleywood.' He shifted the light cane into his left hand and extended his right to Sean.

'Sean Courtney.' Sean accepted the hand.

'Are you bastards going to fight or what?' protested one of the miners impatiently.

'We are, dear boy, we are,' said Duff and moved lightly as a dancer towards him, swinging the cane. Thin as it was it made a noise like a well-hit baseball along the man's head.

'Then there were five,' said Duff. He flicked the cane and, weighted with lead, it made a most satisfactory swish. Like a swordsman he lunged into the throat of the second miner. The man lay on the floor and made a strangling noise.

'The rest are yours, Mr Courtney,' said Duff regretfully.

Sean dived in low, spreading his arms to scoop up all four pairs of legs at once. He sat up in the pile of bodies and started punching and kicking.

'Messy, very messy,' murmured Duff disapprovingly. The yelps and thuds gradually petered into silence and Sean stood up. His lip was bleeding and the lapel was torn off his jacket.

'Drink?' asked Duff.

'Brandy, please.' Sean smiled at the elegant figure against the bar. 'I won't refuse another drink this evening.'

They took the glasses to Duff's table, stepping over the bodies as they went.

'Mud in your eye!'

'Down the old red lane!'

Then they studied each other with frank interest, ignoring the clearing up operations being conducted around them.

'You are travelling?' asked Duff.

'Yes, are you?'

'No such luck. I am in the permanent employ of Dundee Collieries Ltd.'

'You work here?' Sean looked incredulous for Duff was a peacock among pigeons.

'Assistant Engineer,' nodded Duff. 'But not for long; the taste of coal-dust sticks in my craw.'

'May I suggest something to wash it out?'

'A splendid idea,' agreed Duff.

Sean brought the drinks to the table.

'Where are you headed?' asked Duff.

'I was facing north when I started,' shrugged Sean, 'I just kept going that way.'

'Where did you start from?'

'South.' Sean answered abruptly.

'Sorry, I didn't mean to pry.' Duff smiled. 'Yours is brandy, isn't it?'

The barman came round from behind the counter and crossed to their table.

'Hello, Charlie,' Duff greeted him. 'I take it you require compensation for the damage to your fittings and furniture?'

'Don't worry about it, Mr Charleywood. Not often we have a good barney like that. We don't mind the odd table and chair as long as it's worth watching. Have it on the house.'

'That's extremely good of you.'

'That's not what I came across for, Mr Charleywood. I've got something I'd like you to take a look at, you being a mining chap and all. Could you spare a minute, sir?'

'Come on, Sean. Let's see what Charlie's got for us. My guess is it's a beautiful woman.'

'It's not actually, sir,' said Charlie seriously and led the way through into the back room. Charlie reached up and took a lump of rock down from one of the shelves. He held it out to Duff. 'What do you make of that?'

Duff took it and weighed it in his hand, then peered closely at it. It was glassy grey, blotched with white and dark-red and divided by a broad black stripe.

'Some sort of conglomerate.' Duff spoke without enthusiasm. 'What's the mystery?'

'Friend of mine brought it down from Kruger's Republic on the other side of the mountains. He says it's gold bearing. They've made a big strike at a place called Witwatersrand just outside Pretoria. Of course, I don't put much store by these rumours 'cos you hear them all the time: diamonds and gold, gold and diamonds.'

Charlie laughed and wiped his hands on his apron.

'Anyway my friend says the Boers are selling mining licences to them as want to dig for the stuff. Thought I'd just get you to have a look.'

'I'll take this with me, Charlie, and pan it in the morning. Right now my friend and I are drinking.'

– 2 –

Sean opened his eyes the next morning to find the sun burning in through the window above his bed. He closed them again hurriedly and tried to remember where he was. There was a pain in his head that distracted him and a noise. The noise was a regular croaking rattle; it sounded as though someone was dying. Sean opened his eyes and turned his head slowly. Someone was in the bed across the room. Sean groped for a boot and threw it; there was a snort and Duff's head came up. For a second he regarded Sean through eyes as red as a winter sunset and then he subsided gently back into the blankets.

'Keep it down to a bellow,' whispered Sean. 'You are in the presence of grave illness.'

A long time later a servant brought coffee.

'Send word to my office that I am sick,' commanded Duff.

'I have done so.' The servant clearly understood his master. He went on, 'There is one outside who seeks the other Nkosi.' He glanced at Sean. 'He is greatly worried.'

'Mbejane. Tell him to wait,' said Sean.

They drank coffee in silence, sitting on the edge of their beds.

'How did I get here?' asked Sean.

'Laddie, if you don't know, then nobody does.' Duff stood up and crossed the room to find fresh clothing. He was naked and Sean saw that although he was slim as a boy his body was finely muscled.

'My God, what does Charlie put in his liquor?' complained Duff as he picked up his jacket.

He found the lump of rock in the pocket, brought it out and tossed it onto the packing-case that served as a table. He regarded it sourly as he finished dressing, then he went to the great pile of bachelor debris that filled one corner of the room. He scratched around and came out with a steel pestle-and-mortar and a battered black gold pan.

'I feel very old this morning,' he said as he started to crush the rock to powder in the mortar. He poured the powder into the pan, carried it out to the corrugated iron water tank beside the front door and filled the pan from the tap.

Sean followed him and they sat together on the front step. Duff worked the pan, using a practised dip and swing that set the contents spinning like a whirlpool and slopped a little over the front lip with each turn. He filled it again with clean water.

Suddenly Sean felt Duff stiffen beside him. He glanced at his face and saw that his hangover had gone; his lips were shut in a thin line and his bloodshot eyes were fastened on the pan.

Sean looked down and saw the gleam through the water, like the flash of a trout's belly as it turns to take the fly. He felt the excitement prickle up his arms and lift the hair on his neck.

Quickly Duff splashed fresh water into the pan; three

more turns and he flicked it out again. They sat still, not speaking, staring at the golden tail curved round the bottom of the pan.

'How much money have you got?' Duff asked without looking up.

'Little over a thousand.'

'As much as that. Excellent! I can raise about five hundred but I'll throw in my mining experience. Equal partners – do you agree?'

'Yes.'

'Then why are we sitting here? I'm going down to the bank. Meet me on the edge of town in half an hour.'

'What about your job?' Sean asked.

'I hate the smell of coal – the hell with my job.'

'What about Charlie?'

'Charlie is a poisoner – the hell with Charlie.'

– 3 –

They camped that night in the mouth of the pass with the mountains standing up before them. They had pushed the pace all that afternoon and the horses were tired – they turned their tails to the wind and cropped at the dry winter grass.

Mbejane built a fire in the shelter of a red stone outcrop and they huddled beside it brewing coffee, trying to keep out of the snow-cold wind, but it came down off the mountains and blew a plume of sparks from the fire. They ate; then Mbejane curled up beside the fire, pulled his kaross over his head and did not move again until morning.

'How far is it to this place?' Sean asked.

'I don't know,' Duff admitted. 'We'll go up through the pass tomorrow – fifty or sixty miles through the mountains

– and then we'll be out into the high veld. Perhaps another week's riding after that.'

'Are we chasing rainbows?' Sean poured more coffee into the mugs.

'I'll tell you when we get there.' Duff picked up his mug and cupped his hands around it. 'One thing's certain – that sample was stinking with gold. If there's much of that stuff around somebody's going to get rich.'

'Us, perhaps?'

'I've been on gold stampedes before. The first ones in make the killings. We might find the ground for fifty miles around as thick with claim pegs as quills on a porcupine's back.' Duff sipped noisily at his coffee. 'But we've got money – that's our ace in the hole. If we peg a proposition we've got capital to work it. If we're too late we can buy claims from the brokers. If we can't, well, there're other ways of getting gold than grubbing for it – a store, a saloon, a transport business, take your pick.'

Duff flicked the coffee grounds out of his mug. 'With money in your pocket you're somebody; without it anyone can kick you in the teeth.' He took a long black cheroot out of his top pocket and offered it to Sean. Sean shook his head and Duff bit the tip from the cheroot and spat it into the fire. He picked up a burning twig and lit it, sucking with content.

'Where did you learn mining, Duff?'

'Canada.' The wind whipped the smoke away from his mouth as Duff exhaled.

'You've been around?'

'I have, laddie. It's too damn cold to sleep; we'll talk instead. For a guinea I'll tell you the story of my life.'

'Tell me first, I'll see if it's worth it!' Sean pulled the blanket up around his shoulders and waited.

'Your credit is good,' agreed Duff. He paused dramatically.

'I was born thirty-one years ago, fourth and youngest son to the sixteenth Baron Roxby – that is, not counting the others who never made it to puberty.'

'Blue blood,' said Sean.

'Of course, just look at my nose. But please don't interrupt. Very early in the game my father, the sixteenth Baron, dispelled with a horsewhip any natural affection we may have owed him. Like Henry the Eighth he preferred children in the abstract. We kept out of his way and that suited everybody admirably. A sort of armed truce.

'Dear father had two great passions in life: horses and women. During his sixty-two glorious years he acquired a fine collection of both. My fifteen-year-old cousin, a comely wench as I recall, was his last and unattained ambition. He took her riding every day and fingered her most outrageously as he helped her in and out of the saddle. She told me about it with giggles.

'However father's horse, a commendably moral creature, cut short the pursuit by kicking father on the head, presumably in the middle of one of these touching scenes. Poor father was never the same again. In fact so much was he altered by this experience that two days later, to the doleful clangour of bells and a collective sigh of relief from his sons and his neighbours who owned daughters, they buried him.'

Dufford leaned forward and prodded the fire.

'It was all very sad. I or any of my brothers could have told father that not only was my cousin comely but she had the family sporting instincts developed to a remarkable degree. After all who should know better than we? We were her cousins and you know how cousins will be cousins. Anyway father never found out and to this day I feel guilty – I should have told him. He would have died happier . . . Do I bore you?'

'No, go on. I've had half a guinea's worth already,' Sean laughed.

'Father's untimely decease made no miraculous changes in my life. The seventeenth Baron, brother Tom, once he had the title was every bit as tight-fisted and unpleasant as father had been. There I was at nineteen on an allowance too small to enable me to pursue the family hobbies, gathering mould in a grim old castle forty miles from London, with the development of my sensitive soul being inhibited by the undiluted company of my barbaric brothers.

'I left with three months' advance allowance clutched in my sweaty palm and the farewells of my brothers ringing in my ears. The most sentimental of these was "don't bother to write".

'Everybody was going to Canada: it seemed like a good idea so I went too. I made money and spent it. I made women and spent them also, but the cold got to me in the end.'

Duff's cheroot had died; he re-lit it and looked at Sean.

'It was so cold you couldn't urinate without getting frostbite on your equipment, so I began to think of lands tropical, of white beaches and sun, of exotic fruits and even more exotic maidens. The peculiar circumstances that finally decided me to leave are painful to recall and we will not dwell upon them. I left, to say the least, under a cloud. So here you see me freezing slowly to death, with a bearded ruffian for company and not an exotic maiden within a day's ride.'

'A stirring tale – well told,' applauded Sean.

'One story deserves another – let's hear your tale of woe.'

Sean's smile slid off his face. 'Born and bred here in Natal. Left home a week or so ago, also in painful circumstances.'

189

'A woman?' asked Duff with deep compassion.

'A woman,' agreed Sean.

'The sweet bitches,' sighed Duff. 'How I love them.'

– 4 –

The pass ran like a twisted gut through the Drakensberg. The mountains stood up sheer and black on each side of them, so they rode in shadow and saw the sun only for a few hours in the middle of the day. Then the mountains dropped away and they were out into the open.

Open was the word for the high veld. It stretched away flat and empty, grass and brown grass dwindling to a distant meeting with the pale empty sky. But the loneliness could not blunt the edge of their excitement: each mile covered, each successive camp along the ribbon road ground it sharper until at last they saw the name in writing for the first time. Forlorn as a scarecrow in a ploughed land the signpost pointed right and said, 'Pretoria', pointed left and said, 'Witwatersrand'.

'The Ridge of White Waters,' whispered Sean. It had a ring to it that name – a ring like a hundred millions in gold.

'We're not the first,' muttered Duff. The left-hand fork of the road was deeply scored by the passage of many wagons.

'No time to worry about that.' Sean had the gold sickness on him now. 'There's a little speed left in these mokes – let's use it.'

It came up on the horizon as a low line above the emptiness, a ridge of hills like a hundred others they had crossed. They went up it and from the top looked down.

Two ridges ran side by side, north and south, four miles or so apart. In the shallow valley between they could see the flash of the sun off the swamp pools that gave the hills their name.

'Look at them,' groaned Sean.

The tents and wagons were scattered along the length of the valley and in between them the prospect trenches were raw wounds through the grass. The trenches were concentrated along a line down the centre of the valley.

'That's the strike of the reef,' said Duff, 'and we're too late – it's all pegged!'

'How do you know?' protested Sean.

'Use your eyes, laddie. It's all gone.'

'There might be some they've overlooked.'

'These boys overlook nothing. Let's go down and I'll show you.' Duff prodded his horse and they started down. He spoke over his shoulder to Sean. 'Look up there near that stream – they aren't wasting time. They've got a mill going already. It's a four-stamp rig by the looks of it.'

They rode into one of the larger encampments of tents and wagons; there were women at work around the fires and the smell of food brought saliva jetting from under Sean's tongue. There were men also, sitting among the wagons waiting for their suppers.

'I'm going to ask some of these characters what's going on here,' said Sean. He climbed down off his horse and tossed the reins to Mbejane. Duff watched him with a wry grin as he tried in succession to engage three different men in conversation. Each time Sean's victim avoided his eyes, mumbled vaguely and withdrew. Sean finally gave up and came back to the horses.

'What's wrong with me?' he asked plaintively. 'Have I got a contagious clap?'

Duff chuckled. 'They've got gold sickness,' he said.

'You're a potential rival. You could die of thirst and not one of them would spit on you, lest it gave you strength to crawl out and peg something they hadn't noticed.'

He sobered. 'We're wasting time. There's an hour left before dark, let's go and have a look for ourselves.'

They trotted out towards the area of mauled earth. Men were working pick and shovel in the trenches, some of them lean and tough-looking with a dozen natives working beside them; others fat from an office stool, sweating and gritting teeth against the pain of blistered palms, their faces and arms burnt angry red by the sun. All of them greeted Sean and Duff with the same suspicious hostility.

They rode slowly towards the north and every hundred yards with sickening regularity they came across a claim peg with a cairn of stones around its foot and the scrap of canvas nailed to it. Printed in crude capitals on the canvas was the owner's name and his licence number.

Many of the claims were as yet untouched and on these Duff dismounted and searched in the grass, picking up pieces of rock and peering at them before discarding them again. Then once more they moved on with sinking spirits and increasing exhaustion. They camped after dark on the open windy ridge and while the coffee brewed they talked.

'We're too late.' Sean scowled into the fire.

'We've got money, laddie, just remember that. Most of these gentlemen are broke – they are living on hope, not beef and potatoes. Look at their faces and you'll see despair starting to show. It takes capital to work reef gold: you need machinery and money for wages, you have to pipe in water and pile rock, you need wagons and time.'

'Money's no good without a claim to work,' brooded Sean.

'Stay with me, laddie. Have you noticed how many of these claims haven't been touched yet? They belong to speculators and my guess is that they are for sale. In the next few weeks you'll see the men sorted out from the boys—'

'I feel like packing up. This isn't what I expected.'

'You're tired. Sleep well tonight and tomorrow we'll see how far this reef runs – then we'll start some scheming.'

Duff lit one of his cheroots and sucked on it: in the firelight his face was as gaunt as a Red Indian's. They sat on in silence for a while, then Sean spoke.

'What's that noise?' It was a dull tom-tom beat in the darkness.

'You'll get used to that if you stay around here much longer,' said Duff. 'It's the stamps on that mill we saw from the high ground. It's a mile or so farther up the valley; we'll pass it in the morning.'

They were on the move again before the sun was up and they came to the mill in the morning's uncertain light. The mill crouched black and ugly on the smooth curve of the ridge, defiant as a quixotic monster. Its jaws thumped sullenly as it chewed the rock; it snorted steam and screeched metallically.

'I didn't realize it was so big,' said Sean.

'It's big all right,' agreed Duff, 'and they cost money, they don't give them away. Not many men around here can afford a set-up like that.'

There were men moving around the mill, tending its needs, feeding it rock and fussing about the copper tables over which its gold-laden faeces poured. One of the men came forward to offer them the usual hospitality. 'This is private ground. We don't want sightseers around here – keep on going.'

He was a dapper little man with a round brown face and a derby hat pulled down to his ears. His moustache bristled like the whiskers of a fox terrier.

'Listen, Francois, you miserable bloody earthworm, if you talk to me like that I'll push your face around the back of your head,' Duff told him, and the dapper one blinked uncertainly and came closer, peering up at them.

'Who are you? Do I know you?'

Duff pushed his hat back so the man could see his face.

'Duff!' crowed the little man delightedly. 'It's old Duff.' He bounced forward to take Duff's hand as he dismounted. Sean watched the orgy of reunion with amusement. It lasted until Duff managed to bring it under control and lead the little Afrikander across to make the introduction.

'Sean, this is Francois du Toit. He's an old friend of mine from the Kimberley diamond fields.'

Francois greeted Sean and then relapsed once more into the excited chorus of '*Gott*, it's good to see you, old Duff.' He pounded Duff's back despite the nimble footwork that Duff was using to spoil his aim. Another few minutes of this passed before Francois composed himself to make his first coherent statement.

'Listen, old Duff, I'm just in the middle of cleaning the amalgam tables. You and your friend go down to my tent. I'll be with you in half an hour, tell my servant to make you some breakfast. I won't be long, man. *Gott*, man, it's good to see you.'

'An old lover of yours?' asked Sean when they were alone.

Duff laughed. 'We were on the diamond fields together. I did him a favour once – pulled him out of a caving drive when the rock fall had broken his legs. He's a good little guy and meeting him here is the proverbial answer to a prayer. What he can't tell us about this goldfield no one else can.'

Francois came bustling into the tent well under the promised half hour and during breakfast Sean was an outsider in a conversation where every exchange began, 'Do you remember – ?' or 'What happened to old so and so?'

Then, when the plates were empty and the coffee mugs

filled, Duff asked, 'So, what are you doing here, Franz? Is this your own outfit?'

'No, I'm still with the Company.'

'Not that whoreson Hradsky?' Duff registered mock alarm. 'Tha – tha that's ta – ta – terrible,' he imitated a stutter.

'Cut it out, Duff.' Francois looked nervous. 'Don't do that, you want me to lose my job?'

Duff turned to Sean with an explanation. 'Norman Hradsky and God are equals, but in this part of the world God takes his orders from Hradsky.'

'Cut it out, Duff.' Francois was deeply shocked but Duff went on imperturbably.

'The organization through which Hradsky exercises his divine powers is referred to with reverently bated breath as "The Company". In actual fact its full and resounding title is The South African Mining and Lands Company. Do you get the picture?'

Sean nodded smiling and Duff added as an afterthought, 'Hradsky is a bastard and he stutters.'

It was too much for Francois. He leaned across and caught Duff's arm. 'Please, man. My servant understands English, cut it out, Duff.'

'So the Company has started on these fields, hey? Well, well, it must be pretty big,' mused Duff and Francois followed with relief onto safer ground.

'It is! You just wait and see, it's going to make the diamond fields look like a church bazaar!'

'Tell me about it,' said Duff.

'They call it the Rotten Reef or the Banket or the Heidelberg Reef – but in fact there are three reefs, not one. They run side by side like layers in a sandwich cake.'

'All three have pay gold?' Duff shot the question and Francois shook his head. There was a light in his eyes; he was happy talking gold and mining.

'No – you can forget about the outer reef, just traces there. Then there's the Main Reef. That's a bit better, it's as much as six feet thick in places and giving good values, but it's patchy.'

Francois leaned eagerly across the table; in his excitement his thick Afrikaans accent was very noticeable.

'The bottom reef is the winner, we call it the Leader Reef. It's only a few inches thick and some places it fades out altogether, but it's rich. There's gold in it like plums in a pudding. It's rich, Duff, I'm telling you that you won't believe it until you see it!'

'I'll believe you,' said Duff. 'Now tell me where I can get some of this Leader Reef for myself.'

Francois sobered instantly, a shutter dropped over his eyes and hid the light that had shone there a moment before.

'It's gone. It's all gone,' he said defensively. 'It's all been pegged, you've come too late.'

'Well, that's that,' said Duff and a big silence settled on the gathering. Francois fidgeted on his stool, chewing at the ends of his moustache and scowling into his mug. Duff and Sean waited quietly; it was obvious that Francois was wrestling with himself, two loyalties tearing him down the middle. Once he opened his mouth and then closed it again; he blew on his coffee to cool it and the heat came off it in steam.

'Have you got any money?' He fired the question with startling violence.

'Yes,' said Duff.

'Mr Hradsky has gone down to Capetown to raise money. He has a list of a hundred and forty claims that he will buy when he gets back.' Francois paused guiltily. 'I'm only telling you this because of what I owe you.'

'Yes, I know.' Duff spoke softly. Francois took an audible breath and went on.

'On the top of Mr Hradsky's list is a block of claims that belongs to a woman. She is willing to sell and they are the most likely-looking propositions on the whole field.'.

'Yes?' Duff encouraged him.

'This woman has started an eating-house about two miles from here on the banks of the Natal Spruit. Her name is Mrs Rautenbach, she serves good food. You could go and have a meal there.'

'Thanks, Francois.'

'I owed it to you,' Francois said gruffly, then his mood changed quickly and he chuckled. 'You'll like her, Duff, she's a lot of woman.'

Sean and Duff went to eat lunch at Mrs Rautenbach's. It was an unpainted corrugated-iron building on a wooden frame and the sign above the veranda said in letters of red and gold 'Candy's Hotel. High-class cuisine. Free toilet facilities. No drunks or horses admitted. Proprietor Mrs Candella Rautenbach.'

They washed off the dust in the enamel basin which stood on the veranda, dried themselves on the free towel and combed in the free mirror on the wall.

'How do I look?' asked Duff.

'Ravishing,' said Sean, 'but you don't smell so good. When did you last bath?'

They went into the dining-room and found it almost full, but there was an empty table against the far wall. The room was hot and thick with pipe smoke and the smell of cabbage. Dusty, bearded men laughed and shouted or ate silently and hungrily. They crossed the room to the table and a coloured waitress came to them.

'Yes?' she asked. Her dress was damp at the armpits.

'May we have the menu?'

The girl looked at Duff with faint amusement. 'Today we got steak and mashed potatoes with pudding afterwards.'

'We'll have it,' Duff agreed.

'You sure as hell won't get nothing else,' the girl assured him and trotted back to the kitchen.

'The service is good,' Duff enthused. 'We can only hope that the food and the proprietress are of the same high standard.'

The meat was tough but well flavoured and the coffee was strong and sweet. They ate with appreciation until Sean, who was facing the kitchen, stopped his fork on its way to his mouth. A hush was on the room.

'Here she is,' he said.

Candy Rautenbach was a tall and bright, shiny blonde and her skin was Nordic flawlessness as yet unspoiled by the sun. She filled the front of her blouse and the back of her skirt with a pleasant abundance. She was well aware of and yet not disconcerted by the fact that every eye in the room was on one of those areas. She carried a ladle which she twitched threateningly at the first hand that reached out to pinch her rump, the hand withdrew and Candy smiled sweetly and moved on among the tables. She stopped occasionally to chat with her customers and it was clear that many of these lonely men came here not only to eat. They watched her avidly, grinning with pleasure when she spoke to them. She reached their table and Sean and Duff stood up. Candy blinked with surprise.

'Sit down, please.' The small courtesy had touched her. 'You are new here?'

'We got in yesterday,' Duff smiled at her. 'And the way you cook a steak makes me feel as though I were home again.'

'Where are you from?' Candy looked at the two of them with perhaps just a shade more than professional interest.

'We've come up from Natal to have a look around. This is Mr Courtney – he is interested in new investments and he thought that these goldfields might provide an outlet for some of his capital.'

Sean just managed to stop his jaw dropping open and then quickly assumed the slightly superior air of a big financier as Duff went on.

'My name is Charleywood. I am Mr Courtney's mining adviser.'

'Pleased to meet you. I am Candy Rautenbach.' She was impressed.

'Won't you join us for a few minutes, Mrs Rautenbach?' Duff drew back a chair for her and Candy hesitated.

'I have to check up in the kitchen – perhaps later.'

'Do you always lie so smoothly?' Sean spoke with admiration when Candy had gone.

'I spoke no untruths,' Duff defended himself.

'No, but the way you tell the truth! How the hell am I going to play up to the role you have created for me?'

'You'll learn to live with it, don't worry. Just look wise and keep your mouth shut,' Duff advised. 'What do you think of her anyway?'

'Toothsome,' said Sean.

'Decidedly palatable,' agreed Duff.

When Candy came back Duff kept the conversation light and general for a while, but when Candy started asking some sharp questions it was immediately apparent that her knowledge of geology and mining was well above average and Duff remarked on it.

'Yes, my husband was in the game. I picked it up from him.' She reached into one of the pockets of her blue and white checked skirt and brought out a small handful of rock samples. She put them down in front of Duff. 'Can you name those?' she asked. It was the direct test, she was asking him to prove himself.

'Kimberlite. Serpentine. Feldspar.' Duff reeled them off and Candy relaxed visibly.

'As it happens I have a number of claims pegged along the Heidelberg Reef. Perhaps Mr Courtney would care to have a look at them. Actually, I am negotiating at the moment with The South African Mining and Lands Company who are very interested.'

Sean made his solitary but valuable contribution to the conversation. 'Ah yes,' he nodded sagely. 'Good old Norman.'

Candy was shaken – not many men used Hradsky's Christian name. 'Will tomorrow morning be convenient?' she asked.

– 5 –

That afternoon they bought a tent from a disillusioned hopeful who had thrown up his job on the Natal Railways to make the pilgrimage to Witwatersrand and now needed money to get home. They pitched it near the Hotel and went down to the Natal Spruit to take a long overdue bath. That night they held a mild celebration on the half bottle of brandy that Duff produced from his saddlebag and the next morning Candy took them out to the claims. She had twenty of them pegged right along the Banket. She led them to a spot where the reef outcropped.

'I'll leave you two to look around. If you're interested we can talk about it when you come to the Hotel. I've got to get back now, there'll be hungry mouths to feed.'

Duff escorted Candy to her horse, giving her his arm across the rough ground and helping her into the saddle in a manner he must have learned from his father. He watched her ride away then came back to Sean. He was elated.

'Tread lightly, Mr Courtney, walk with reverence for beneath your feet lies our fortune.'

They went over the ground, Sean like a friendly bloodhound and Duff cruising with the restless circling of a tiger shark. They inspected the claim notices, paced out the boundaries and filled their pockets with chips of rock, then they rode back to their tent and Duff brought out his pestle, mortar and pan. They took them down to the bank of the Natal Spruit and all afternoon crushed the rock and worked the pan. When they had tested the last sample Duff gave his judgement.

'Well, there's gold – and I'd say it's payable gold. It's not nearly as rich as the one we panned at Dundee but that must have been a selected piece of the Leader Reef!' He paused and looked seriously at Sean. 'I think it's worth a try. If the Leader Reef is there we'll find it and in the meantime we won't lose money by working the main reef.'

Sean picked up a pebble and tossed it into the stream in front of him. He was learning for the first time the alternate thrill and depression of gold sickness when one minute you rode the lightning and the next you dropped abruptly into the depths. The yellow tails in the pan had looked pathetically thin and undernourished to him.

'Supposing you're right and supposing we talk Candy into selling her claims, how do we go about it? That four-stamp mill looked a devilishly complicated and expensive bit of machinery to me, not the kind of thing you can buy over the counter in every general dealer's store.'

Duff punched his shoulder and smiled lopsidedly at him. 'You've got your Uncle Duff looking after you. Candy will sell her claims – she trembles when I touch her, a day or two more and she'll be eating out of my hand. As for the mill . . . When I came out to this country I fell in with a rich Cape farmer whose lifelong ambition had been to have his own gold mine. He selected a ridge which in his undisputed wisdom as a grower of grapes he considered to be an ideal place for his mine. He hired me to run it for him, purchased a mill of the latest and most expensive vintage and prepared himself to flood the market with gold.

201

After six months when we had processed vast quantities of assorted quartz, schist and earth and recovered sufficient gold to fit into a mouse's ear without touching the sides, my patron's enthusiasm was somewhat dampened and he dispensed with my invaluable services and closed the circus down. I left for the diamond fields and as far as I know the machinery is still lying there waiting for the first buyer with a couple of hundred pounds to come and pick it up.' Duff stood up and they walked back towards the tent. 'However, first things first. Do you agree that I should continue the negotiations with Mrs Rautenbach?'

'I suppose so.' Sean was feeling more cheerful again. 'But are you sure your interest in Mrs Rautenbach is strictly line of duty?'

Duff was shocked. 'Don't think for a minute that my intentions are anything but to further the interests of our partnership. You can't believe that my animal appetite plays any part in what I intend doing?'

'No, of course not,' Sean assured him. 'I hope you can force yourself to go through with it.'

Duff laughed. 'While we are on the subject I think this is as good a time as any for you to develop a stomach ailment and retire to your lonely bed. From now on until we've got the agreement signed your boyish charm will be of no great value in the proceedings. I'll tell Candy that you've given me authority to act on your behalf.'

Duff combed his curls, put on the clothes that Mbejane had washed for him and disappeared in the direction of Candy's Hotel. Time passed slowly for Sean; he sat and chatted with Mbejane, drank a little coffee and when the sun went down retired to his tent. He read one of Duff's books by the light of the hurricane lamp but could not concentrate on it; his mind kept straying to thoughts of blonde hair. When someone scratched on the canvas door he leapt up with a confused hope that Candy had decided to come and deal with him direct. It was the coloured girl from the Hotel, her crinkly black hair at odds with what he had been thinking.

'Madame says she's sorry to hear about your sickness and to tell you to have two spoons of this,' she told him and offered Sean the bottle of castor oil.

'Tell your mistress, thank you very much.'

Sean accepted the medicine and started to close the tent flap again.

'Madame told me to stay and make sure that you took two full spoons – I have to take the bottle back and show her how much you've had.'

Sean's stomach cringed. He looked at the coloured girl standing resolute in the doorway, determined to carry out her instructions. He thought of poor Duff doing his duty like a man – he could do no less. He swallowed down the thick clinging oil with his eyes closed then went back to his book. He slept uneasily, starting up occasionally to look at the empty bed across the tent. The medicine drove him out into the cold at half past two in the morning. Mbejane was curled up next to the fire and Sean scowled at him. His regular contented snoring seemed a calculated mockery. A jackal yelped miserably up on the ridge, expressing Sean's feelings exactly, and the night wind fanned his bare buttocks.

Duff came home in the dawning. Sean was wide awake.

'Well, what happened?' he demanded.

Duff yawned. 'At one stage I began to doubt whether I was man enough. However, it worked out to the satisfaction of all concerned. What a woman!' He pulled off his shirt and Sean saw the scratches across his back.

'Did she give you any castor oil?' Sean asked bitterly.

'I'm sorry about that.' Duff smiled at him sympathetically. 'I tried to dissuade her – truly I did. She's a very motherly person. Most concerned about your stomach.'

203

'You still haven't answered my question. Did you make any progress with the claims?'

'Oh that—' Duff pulled the blankets up under his chin. 'We disposed of that early on in the proceedings. She'll take a down payment of ten pounds each on them and give us an option to buy the lot at any time during the next two years for ten thousand. We arranged that over dinner. The rest of the time was devoted, in a manner of speaking, to shaking hands over the deal. Tomorrow afternoon – or rather this afternoon – you and I'll ride across to Pretoria and get a lawyer to write up an agreement for her to sign. But right now I need some sleep. Wake me at lunch time. Goodnight, laddie.'

Duff and Sean brought the agreement back from Pretoria the following evening. It was an impressive four-page document full of 'in so much as' and 'party of the first part'. Candy led them to her bedroom and they sat around anxiously while she read it through twice.

She looked up at last and said, 'That seems all right – but there is just one other thing.' Sean's heart sank and even Duff's smile was strained. It had all been too easy so far.

Candy hesitated and Sean saw with faint surprise that she was blushing. It was a pleasant thing to see the peach of her cheeks turning to ripe apple and they watched it with interest, their tension lessening perceptibly. 'I want the mine named after me.'

They nearly shouted with relief.

'An excellent idea! How about the Rautenbach Reef Mine?'

Candy shook her head. 'I'd rather not be reminded of him – we'll leave him out of it.'

'Very well – let's call it the Candy Deep. A little premature, I suppose, as we are still at ground level, but pessimism never pays,' suggested Duff.

'Yes, that's lovely,' Candy enthused, flushing again but this time with pleasure. She scrawled her name across the bottom of the document while Sean fired out the cork of the champagne which Duff had bought in Pretoria. They clinked glasses and Duff gave the toast 'To Candy and the Candy Deep – may one grow sweeter and the other deeper with each passing day.'

– 6 –

'We'll need labour, about ten natives to start with. That'll be your problem,' Duff told Sean. It was the following morning and they were eating breakfast in front of the tent. Sean nodded but didn't try to answer until he had swallowed his mouthful of bacon.

'I'll get Mbejane onto that right away. He'll be able to get us Zulus, even if he has to drive them here with a spear at their backs.'

'Good – in the meantime you and I'll ride back to Pretoria again to buy the basic equipment. Picks, shovels, dynamite and the like.' Duff wiped his mouth and filled his coffee cup. 'I'll show you how to start moving the overburden and stacking the ore in a dump. We'll pick a site for the mill and then I'll leave you to get on with it while I head south for the Cape to see my farmer friend. God and the weather permitting ours will be the second mill working on these fields.'

They brought their purchases back from Pretoria in a small ox wagon. Mbejane had done his work well. There were a dozen Zulus lined up for Sean's approval next to the tent with Mbejane standing guard over them like a cheerful sheepdog. Sean walked down the line, stopping to ask each man his name and joke with him in his own language. He came to the last in the line. 'How are you called?'

'My name is Hlubi, Nkosi.'

Sean pointed at the man's well-rounded paunch bulging out above his loincloth.

'If you come to work for me, we'll soon have you delivered of your child.'

They burst out in delighted laughter and Sean smiled at them affectionately: proud simple people, tall and big-muscled, completely defenceless against a well-timed jest. Through his mind flashed the picture of a hill in Zululand, a battlefield below it and the flies crawling in the pit of an empty stomach. He shut the picture out quickly and shouted above their laughter.

'So be it then – sixpence a day and all the food you can eat. Will you sign on to work for me?'

They chorused their assent and climbed up onto the back of the wagon. Sean and Duff took them out to the Candy Deep and they laughed and chattered like children going on a picnic.

It took another week for Duff to instruct Sean in the use of dynamite, to explain how he wanted the first trenches dug and to mark out the site for the mill and the dump. They moved the tent up to the mine and worked twelve hours every day. At night they rode down to Candy's Hotel to eat a full meal and then Sean rode home alone. He was so tired by evening that he hardly envied Duff the comfort of Candy's bedroom; instead he found himself admiring Duff's stamina. Each morning he looked for signs of fatigue in his partner but, although his face was lean and gaunt as ever, his eyes were just as clear and his lopsided smile just as cheerful.

'How you do it beats me,' Sean told him the day they finished marking out the mill site.

Duff winked at him. 'Years of practice, laddie, but between you and me the ride down to the Cape will be a welcome rest.'

'When are you going?' Sean asked.

'Quite frankly I think that every day I stay on here increases the risk of someone else getting in before us. Mining machinery is going to be at a premium from now on. You have got things well in hand now . . . What do you say?'

'I was starting to think along the same lines,' Sean agreed. They walked back to the tent and sat down in the camp chairs, from where they could look down the length of the valley. The week before about two dozen wagons had been outspanned around Candy's Hotel, but now there were at least two hundred and from where they sat they could count another eight or nine encampments, some even larger than the one around Candy's place. Wood and iron buildings were beginning to replace the canvas tents and the whole veld was criss-crossed with rough roads along which mounted men and wagons moved without apparent purpose.

The restless movement, the dust clouds raised by the passage of men and beasts, and the occasional deep crump, crump of dynamite firing in the workings along the Banket – all heightened the air of excitement, of almost breathless expectancy that hung over the whole goldfield.

'I'll leave at first light tomorrow,' Duff decided. 'Ten days' riding to the railhead at Colesberg and another four days by train will get me there. With luck I'll be back in under two months.' He wriggled round in his chair and looked directly at Sean. 'After paying Candy her two hundred pounds and with what I spent in Pretoria I've only got about a hundred and fifty left. Once I get to Paarl I'll have to pay out three or four hundred for the mill, then I'll need to hire twenty or thirty wagons to bring it up here – say eight hundred pounds altogether to be on the safe side.'

Sean looked at him. He had known this man a few short weeks. Eight hundred was the average man's earnings for three years. Africa was a big land, a man could disappear easily. Sean loosened his belt and dropped it onto the table; he unbuttoned the money pouch.

'Give me a hand to count it out,' he told Duff.

'Thanks,' said Duff and he was not talking about the money. With trust asked for so simply and given so spontaneously the last reservations in their friendship shrivelled and died.

– 7 –

When Duff had gone Sean drove himself and his men without mercy. They stripped the overburden off the Reef and exposed it across the whole length of the Candy claims, then they broke it up and started stacking it next to the mill site. The dump grew bigger with every twelve-hour day worked. There was still no trace of the Leader Reef but Sean found little time to worry about that. At night he climbed into bed and slept away his fatigue until another morning called him back to the workings. On Sundays he rode across to Francois's tent and they talked mining and medicines. Francois had an enormous chest of patent medicines and a book titled *The Home Physician*. His health was his hobby and he was treating himself for three major ailments simultaneously. Although he was occasionally unfaithful, his true love was sugar diabetes. The page in *The Home Physician* which covered this subject was limp and grubby from the touch of his fingers. He could recite the symptoms from memory and he had all of them. His other favourite was tuberculosis of the bone; this moved around his body with alarming rapidity taking only a week to leave his hip and reach his wrist. Despite his failing health, however, he was an expert on mining and Sean picked his brain shamelessly. Francois's sugar diabetes did not prevent him from sharing a bottle of brandy with Sean on Sunday evenings. Sean kept away from Candy's Hotel – that shiny blonde hair and peach skin would have been too much temptation. He couldn't trust himself not to wreck his new friendship with Duff by another importunate affair, so instead he sweated away his energy in the trenches of the Candy Deep.

Every morning he set his Zulus a task for the day, always just a little more than the day before. They sang as they worked and it was very seldom that the task was not complete by nightfall. The days blurred into each other and turned to weeks which quadrupled like breeding amoebae and became months. Sean began to imagine Duff giving the Capetown girls a whirl with his eight hundred pounds. One evening he rode south for miles along the Cape road, stopping to question every traveller he met and when he finally gave up and returned to the goldfields he went straight to one of the canteens to look for a fight. He found a big, yellow-haired German miner to oblige him. They went outside and for an hour they battered each other beneath a crisp Transvaal night sky surrounded by a ring of delighted spectators. Then he and the German went back into the canteen, shook each other's bleeding hands, drank a vow of friendship together and Sean returned to the Candy Deep with his devil exorcized for the time being.

The next afternoon Sean was working near the north boundary of the claims; at this point they had burrowed down about fifteen feet to keep contact with the reef. Sean had just finished marking the shot holes for the next blast and the Zulus were standing around him taking snuff and spitting on their hands before attacking the rock once more.

'Mush, you shag-eared villains. What's going on here, a trade union meeting?' The familiar voice came from above their heads. Duff was looking down at them. Sean scrambled straight up the side of the trench and seized him in a bear hug. Duff was thinner, his jowls covered with a pale stubble and his curly hair white with dust. When the fury of greeting had subsided a little Sean demanded, 'Well, where's the present you went to fetch me?'

Duff laughed. 'Not far behind, all twenty-five wagons full of it.'

'You got it then?' Sean roared.

'You're damn right I did! Come with me and I'll show you.'

Duff's convoy was strung out four miles across the veld, most of the wagons double-teamed against the enormous weight of the machinery. Duff pointed to a rust-streaked cylinder that completely filled one of the leading wagons.

'That is my particular cross, seven tons of the most spiteful, stubborn and evil boiler in the world. If it's broken the wagon axle once it's broken it a dozen times since we left Colesberg, not to mention the two occasions on which it capsized itself – once right in the middle of a river.'

They rode along the line of wagons.

'Good God! I didn't realize there'd be so much.' Sean shook his head dubiously. 'Are you sure you know how it all fits together?'

'Leave it to your Uncle Duff. Of course, it's going to need a bit of work done on it, after all it's been lying out in the open for a couple of years. Some of it was rusted up solid, but the judicious use of grease, new paint and the Charleywood brain will see the Candy Deep plant breaking rock and spitting out gold within a month.' Duff broke off and waved to a horseman coming towards them. 'This is the transport contractor. Frikkie Malan – Mr Courtney, my partner.'

The contractor pulled up next to them and acknowledged the introduction. He wiped the dust off his face with the sleeve of his shirt.

'*Gott*, man, Mr Charleywood, I don't mind telling you

that this is the hardest money I've ever worked for. Nothing personal – but I'll be *vragtig* glad to see the last of this load.'

– 8 –

D uff was wrong; it took much longer than a month. The rust had eaten deep into parts of the machinery and each bolt they twisted open was red with the scaly cancer. They worked the usual twelve-hour day chipping and scraping, filing and greasing, knuckles knocked raw against steel and palms wet and red where the blisters had burst. Then one day suddenly and miraculously they were finished. Along the ridge of the Candy Deep, neat and sweet smelling in its new paint, thick with yellow grease and waiting only to be fitted together, lay the dismembered mill.

'How long has it taken us so far?' Duff asked.

'It seems like a hundred years.'

'Is that all?' Duff feigned surprise. 'Then I declare a holiday – two days of meditation.'

'You meditate, brother – I'm going to do some carousing.'

'That's an excellent alternative – let's go!'

They started at Candy's place but she threw them out after the third fight so they moved on. There were a dozen places to drink at and they tried them all. Others were celebrating, because the day before old Kruger, the President of the Republic, had given official recognition to the goldfields. This had the sole effect of diverting the payments for mining licences from the pockets of the farmers who owned the land into the Government coffers. No one worried about that, except possibly the farmers. Rather it was an excuse for a party. The canteens were packed with swearing, sweating men. Duff and Sean drank with them.

211

The Crown and Anchor boards were doing a steady business in every bar and the men who crowded around them were the new population of the goldfields. Diggers bare to the waist and caked with dirt, salesmen with loud clothes and louder voices selling everything from dynamite to dysentery cure, an evangelist peddling salvation, gamblers mining pockets, gentlemen trying to keep the tobacco juice off their boots, boys new-flown from home and wishing themselves back, Boers bearded and drab-suited, drinking little but watching with inscrutable eyes the invaders of their land. Then there were the others, the clerks and farmers, the rogues and contractors listening greedily to the talk of gold.

The coloured girl, Martha, came to find Sean and Duff on the afternoon of the second day. They were in a mud-brick and thatch hut called The Tavern of the Bright Angels. Duff was doing a solo exhibition of the Dashing White Sergeant partnered by a chair; Sean and the fifty or so other customers were beating the rhythm on the bar counter with glasses and empty bottles.

Martha skittered across to Sean, slapping at the hands that tried to dive up her skirts and squealing sharply every time her bottom was pinched. She arrived at Sean's side flushed and breathless.

'Madame says you must come quickly – there's big trouble,' she gasped and started to run the gauntlet back to the door. Someone flipped up her dress behind and a concerted masculine roar approved the fact that she wore nothing under the petticoats.

Duff was so engrossed in his dancing that Sean had to carry him bodily out of the bar and dip his head in the horse trough outside before he could gain his attention.

'What the hell did you do that for?' spluttered Duff and swung a round-arm punch at Sean's head. Sean ducked

212

under it and caught him about the body to save him falling on his back.

'Candy wants us – she says there's big trouble.'

Duff thought about that for a few seconds, frowning with concentration, then he threw back his head and sang to the tune of 'London's Burning',

> 'Candy wants us – Candy wants us
> We don't want Candy, we want brandy.'

He broke out of Sean's grip and headed back for the bar. Sean caught him again and pointed him in the direction of the Hotel. Candy was in her bedroom. She looked at the two of them as they swayed arm-in-arm in the doorway.

'Did you enjoy your debauch?' she asked sweetly. Duff mumbled and tried to straighten his coat. Sean tried to steady him as his feet danced an involuntary sideways jig.

'What happened to your eye?' she asked Sean and he fingered it tenderly; it was puffed and blue. Candy didn't wait for an answer but went on, still sweetly:

'Well, if you two beauties want to own a mine by tomorrow you'd better sober up.'

They stared at her and Sean spoke deliberately but nevertheless indistinctly.

'Why, what's the matter?'

'They're going to jump the claims, that's the matter. This new proclamation of a State goldfield has given the drifters the excuse they've been waiting for. About a hundred of them have formed a syndicate. They claim that the old titles aren't legal any more; they are going to pull out the pegs and put in their own.'

Duff walked without a stagger across to the washbasin beside Candy's bed; he splashed his face, towelled it vigorously then stooped and kissed her. 'Thanks, my sweet.'

213

'Duff, please be careful,' Candy called after them.

'Let's see if we can't hire a few mercenaries,' Sean suggested.

'Good idea, we'll try and find a few sober characters – there should be some in Candy's dining-room.'

They made a short detour on their way back to the mine and stopped at Francois's tent; it was dark by then and Francois came out in a freshly ironed nightshirt. He raised an eyebrow when he saw the five heavily armed men with Sean and Duff.

'You going hunting?' he asked.

Duff told him quickly and Francois was hopping with agitation before he had finished.

'Steal my claims, the thunders, the stinking thunders!' He rushed into his tent and came out again with a double-barrelled shotgun.

'We'll see, man, we'll see how they look full of buckshot.'

'Francois, listen to me,' Sean shouted him down. 'We don't know which claims they'll go to first. Get your men ready and if you hear shooting our way come and give us a hand – we'll do the same for you.'

'Ja, ja, we'll come all right – the dirty thunders.' His nightshirt flapping around his legs Francois trotted off to call his men.

Mbejane and the other Zulus were cooking dinner, squatting round the three-legged pot. Sean rode up to them.

'Get your spears,' he told them. They ran for their huts and almost immediately came crowding back.

'Nkosi, where's the fight?' they pleaded, food forgotten.

'Come on, I'll show you.'

They placed the hired gunmen amongst the mill machinery from where they could cover the track which led up to the mine. The Zulus they hid in one of the prospect trenches. If it developed into a hand-to-hand fight the syndicate was in for a surprise. Duff and Sean walked a little way down the slope to make sure their defenders were all concealed.

'How much dynamite have we got?' Sean asked thoughtfully. Duff stared at him a second, then he grinned.

'Sufficient, I'd say. You're full of bright ideas this evening.' He led the way back to the shed which they used as a storeroom.

In the middle of the track a few hundred yards down the slope they buried a full case of explosive and placed an old tin can on top of it to mark the spot. They went back to the shed and spent an hour making grenades out of bundles of dynamite sticks, each with a detonator and a very short fuse. Then they settled down huddled into their sheepskin coats, rifles in their laps and waited.

They could see the lights of the encampments straggled down the valley and hear an occasional faint burst of singing from the canteens, but the moonlit road up to the mine remained deserted. Sean and Duff sat side by side with their backs against the newly painted boiler.

'How did Candy find out about this, I wonder?' Sean asked.

'She knows everything. That hotel of hers is the centre of this goldfield and she keeps her ears open.'

They relapsed into silence again while Sean formed his next question.

'She's quite a girl – our Candy.'

'Yes,' agreed Duff.

'Are you going to marry her, Duff?'

'Good God!' Duff straightened up as though someone had stuck a knife into him. 'You going mad, laddie, or else that was a joke in the worst possible taste.'

'She dotes on you and from what I've seen you're fairly well disposed towards her.' Sean was relieved at Duff's quick rejection of the idea. He was jealous, but not of the woman.

'Yes, we've got a common interest, that I won't deny –

but marriage!' Duff shivered slightly, not altogether from the cold. 'Only a fool makes the same mistake twice.'

Sean turned to him with surprise. 'You've been married before?' he asked.

'With a vengeance. She was half Spanish and the rest Norwegian, a smoking bubbly mixture of cold fire and hot ice.' Duff's voice went dreamy. 'The memory has cooled sufficiently for me to think of it with a tinge of regret.'

'What happened?'

'I left her.'

'Why?'

'We only did two things well together and one of them was fight. If I close my eyes I can still see the way she used to pout with those lovely lips and bring them close to my ear before she hissed out a particularly foul word, then – hey ho! back to bed for the reconciliation.'

'Perhaps you made the wrong choice. You look around, you'll see millions of happily married people.'

'Name me one,' challenged Duff and the silence lengthened as Sean thought.

Then Duff went on, 'There's only one good reason for marriage, and that's children.'

'And companionship – that's another good reason.'

'Companionship from a woman?' Duff cut in incredulously. 'Like perfume from garlic. They're incapable of it. I suppose it's the training they get from their mothers, who are after all women themselves, but how can you be friends with someone who suspicions every little move you make, who takes your every action and weighs it on the balance of he loves me, he loves me not?' Duff shook his head unhappily. 'How long can a friendship last when it needs an hourly declaration of love to nourish it? The catechism of matrimony, "Do you love me, darling?" "Yes, darling, of course I do, my sweet." It's got to sound convincing every time otherwise tears.'

Sean chuckled.

'All right, it's funny – it's hilarious until you have to live with it,' Duff mourned. 'Have you ever tried to talk to a woman about anything other than love? The same things that interest you leave them cold. It comes as a shock the first time you try talking sense to them and suddenly you realize that their attention is not with you – they get a slightly fixed look in their eyes and you know they are thinking about that new dress or whether to invite Mrs Van der Hum to the party, so you stop talking and that's another mistake. That's a sign; marriage is full of signs that only a wife can read.'

'I hold no brief for matrimony, Duff, but aren't you being a little unfair, judging everything by your own unfortunate experience?'

'Select any woman, slap a ring on her third finger and she becomes a wife. First she takes you into her warm, soft body, which is pleasant, and then she tries to take you into her warm, soft mind, which is not so pleasant. She does not share, she possesses – she clings and she smothers. The relation of man to woman is uninteresting in that it conforms to an inescapable pattern, nature has made it so for the very good reason that it requires us to reproduce; but in order to obtain that result every love, Romeo and Juliet, Bonaparte and Josephine not excepted, must lead up to the co-performance of a simple biological function. It's such a small thing – such a short-lived, trivial little experience. Apart from that man and woman think differently, feel differently and are interested in different things. Would you call that companionship?'

'No, but is that a true picture? Is that all there is between them?' Sean asked.

'You'll find out one day. Nature in her preoccupation with reproduction has planted in the mind of man a barricade; it has sealed him off from the advice and experience of his fellowmen, inoculated him against it. When your time comes you'll go to the gallows with a song on your lips.'

'You frighten me.'

'It's the sameness of it all that depresses me – the goddamn monotony of it.' Duff shifted his seat restlessly then settled back against the boiler. The interesting relationships are those in which sex the leveller takes no hand – brothers, enemies, master and servant, father and son, man and man.'

'Homosexuals?'

'No, that's merely sex out of step and you're back to the original trouble. When a man takes a friend he does it not from an uncontrollable compulsion but in his own free choice. Every friendship is different, ends differently or goes on for ever. No chains bind it, no ritual or written contract. There is no question of forsaking all others, no obligation to talk about it – mouth it up and gloat on it the whole time.' Duff stood up stiffly. 'It's one of the good things in life. How late is it?'

Sean pulled out his watch and tilted its face to catch the moonlight. 'After midnight – it doesn't look as if they're coming.'

'They'll come – there's gold here, another uncontrollable compulsion. They'll come. The question is when.'

The lights along the valley faded out one by one, the deep singsong voices of the Zulus in the prospect trench stilled and a small cold wind came up and moved the grass along the ridge of the Candy Deep. Sitting together, sometimes drowsing, sometimes talking quietly, they waited the night away. The sky paled, then pinked prettily. A dog barked over near Hospital Hill and another joined it. Sean stood up and stretched, he glanced down the valley towards Ferrieras Camp and saw them. A black moving blot of horsemen, overflowing the road, lifting no dust from the dew-damp earth, spreading out to cross the Natal Spruit then bunching together on the near bank before coming on.

'Mr Charleywood, we have company.'

Duff jumped up.

'They might miss us and go on to the Jack and Whistle first.'

'We'll see which road they take when they come to the fork. In the meantime let's get ready. Mbejane,' shouted Sean and the black head popped out of the trench.

'Nkosi?'

'Are you awake? They are coming.'

The blackness parted in a white smile. 'We are awake.'

'Then get down and stay down until I give the word.'

The five mercenaries were lying belly down in the grass, each with a newly-opened packet of cartridges at his elbow. Sean hurried back to Duff and they crouched behind the boiler.

'The tin can shows up clearly from here. Do you think you can hit it?'

'With my eyes closed,' said Sean.

The horsemen reached the fork and turned without hesitation towards the Candy Deep, quickening their paces as they came up the ridge. Sean rested his rifle across the top of the boiler and picked up the speck of silver in his sights.

'What's the legal position, Duff?' he asked out of the corner of his mouth.

'They've just crossed our boundary – they are now officially trespassers,' Duff pronounced solemnly.

One of the leading horses kicked over the tin can and Sean fired at the spot on which it had stood. The shot was indecently loud in the quiet morning and every head in the syndicate lifted with alarm towards the ridge, then the ground beneath them jumped up in a brown cloud to meet the sky. When the dust cleared there was a struggling tangle of downed horses and men. The screams carried clearly up to the crest of the ridge.

'My God,' breathed Sean, appalled at the destruction.

'Shall we let them have it, boss?' called one of the hired men.

'No,' Duff answered him quickly. 'They've had enough.'

The flight started, riderless horses, mounted men and others on foot were scattering back down the valley. Sean was relieved to see that they left only half a dozen men and a few horses lying in the road.

'Well, that's the easiest fiver you've ever earned,' Duff told one of the mercenaries. 'I think you can go home now and have some breakfast.'

'Wait, Duff.' Sean pointed. The survivors of the explosion had reached the road junction again and there they were being stopped by two men on horseback.

'Those two are trying to rally them.'

'Let's change their minds, they're still within rifle range.'

'They are not on our property any more,' disagreed Sean. 'Do you want to wear a rope?'

They watched while those of the syndicate who had had enough fighting for one day disappeared down the road to the camps and the rest coagulated into a solid mass at the crossroad.

'We should have shot them up properly while we had the chance,' grumbled one of the mercenaries uneasily. 'Now they'll come back – look at that bastard talking to them like a Dutch uncle.'

They left their horses and spread out, then they started moving cautiously back up the slope. They hesitated just below the line of boundary pegs then ran forward, tearing up the pegs as they came.

'All together, gentlemen, if you please,' called Duff

politely and the seven rifles fired. The range was long and the thirty or so attackers ran doubled up and dodging. The bullets had little effect at first, but as the distance shortened men started falling. There was a shallow donga running diagonally down the slope and as each of the attackers reached it he jumped down into it and from its safety started a heated reply to the fire of Sean's men. Bullets spanged off the machinery, leaving bright scars where they struck.

Mbejane's Zulus were adding their voices to the confusion.

'Let us go down to them now, Nkosi.'

'They are close – let us go.'

'Quiet down, you madmen, you'd not go a hundred paces against those rifles,' Sean snarled impatiently.

'Sean, cover me,' whispered Duff. 'I'm going to sneak round the back of the ridge, rush them from the side and lob a few sticks of dynamite into that donga.'

Sean caught his arm, his fingers dug into it so that Duff winced.

'You take one step and I'll break a rifle butt over your head – you're as bad as those Blacks. Now keep shooting and let me think.' Sean peered over the top of the boiler but ducked again as a bullet rang loudly against it, inches from his ear. He stared at the new paint in front of his nose, put his shoulder against it; the boiler rocked slightly. He looked up and Duff was watching him.

'We'll walk down together and lob that dynamite,' Sean told him. 'Mbejane and his bloodthirsty heathens will roll the boiler in front of us. These other gentlemen will cover us, we'll do this thing in style.'

Sean called the Zulus out of the trench and explained to them. They chorused their approval of the scheme and jostled each other to find a place to push against the boiler.

Sean and Duff filled the front of their shirts with the dynamite grenades and lit a short length of tarred rope each.

Sean nodded to Mbejane.

'Where are the children of Zulu?' sang Mbejane, shrilling his voice in the ancient rhetorical question.

'Here,' answered his warriors braced ready against the boiler.

'Where are the spears of Zulu?'

'Here.'

'How bright are the spears of Zulu?'

'Brighter than the Sun.'

'How hungry are the spears of Zulu?'

'Hungrier than the locust.'

'Then let us take them to the feeding.'

'*Yeh-bo.*' Explosive assent and the boiler revolved slowly to the thrust of black shoulders.

'*Yeh-bo.*' Another reluctant revolution.

'*Yeh-bo.*' It moved more readily.

'*Yeh-bo.*' Gravity caught it. Ponderously it bumped down the slope and they ran behind it. The fire from the donga doubled its volume, rattling like hail against the huge metal cylinder. The singing of the Zulus changed its tone also; the deep-voiced chanting quickened, climbed excitedly, and became the blood trill. That insane, horrible squealing made Sean's skin crawl, tickled his spine with the ghost fingers of memory, but it inflamed him also. His mouth opened and he squealed with them. He touched the first grenade with the burning rope then flung it in a high spluttering sparking arc. It burst in the air above the donga. He threw again. Crump, crump. Duff was using his explosive as well. The boiler crashed over the lip of the donga and came to rest in a cloud of dust; the Zulus followed it in, spreading out, still shrieking, and now their assegais were

222

busy. The white men broke, clawed frantically out of the ravine and fled, the Zulus hacking at them as they ran.

When Francois arrived with fifty armed diggers following him the fight was over.

'Take your boys down to the camps. Comb them out carefully. We want every one of those that got away,' Duff told him. 'It's about time we had a little law and order on this field.'

'How will we pick out the ones that were in on it?' asked Francois.

'By their white faces and the sweat on their shirts you will know them,' Duff answered.

Francois and his men went, leaving Sean and Duff to clean up the battlefield. It was a messy job – the stabbing spears had made it so. They destroyed those horses that the blast had left still half alive and they gleaned more than a dozen corpses from the donga and the slope below it. Two of them were Zulus. The wounded, and there were many, they packed into a wagon and took them down to Candy's Hotel.

It was early afternoon by the time they arrived. They threaded the wagon through the crowd and stopped it in front of the Hotel. It seemed the entire population of the goldfield was there, packed around the small open space in which Francois was holding his prisoners.

Francois was almost hysterical with excitement. He was sweeping the shotgun around in dangerous circles as he harangued the crowd. Then he darted back to prod one of the prisoners with the twin muzzles.

'You thunders,' he screamed. 'Steal our claims – hey – steal our claims.'

At that moment he caught sight of Duff and Sean bringing the wagon through the press.

'Duff, Duff. We got them. We got the whole lot of

them.' The crowd backed respectfully away from the menace of that circling shotgun and Sean flinched as it pointed directly at him for a second.

'So I see, Francois,' Duff assured him. 'In fact, I have seldom seen anyone more completely had.'

Francois's prisoners were swathed in ropes; they could move only their heads and as additional security a digger with a loaded rifle stood over each of them. Duff climbed down off the wagon.

'Don't you think you should slacken those ropes a little?' Duff asked dubiously.

'And have them escape?' Francois was indignant.

'Do you think they'd get very far?'

'No, I don't suppose so.'

'Well, another half hour and they'll all have gangrene – look at that one's hand already, a beautiful shade of blue.'

Reluctantly Francois conceded and told his men to untie them.

Duff pushed his way through the crowd and climbed the steps of the Hotel. From there he held up his hands for silence.

'There have been a lot of men killed today – we don't want it to happen again. One way we can prevent it is to make sure that this lot get what they deserve.' Cheers were led by Francois.

'But we must do it properly. I suggest we elect a committee to deal with this affair and with any other problems that crop up on these fields. Say ten members and a chairman.'

More cheers.

'Call it the Diggers' Committee,' shouted someone and the crowd took up the name enthusiastically.

'All right, the Diggers' Committee it is. Now we want a chairman, any suggestions?'

'Mr Charleywood,' shouted Francois.

'Yes, Duff – he'll do.'

'Yes, Duff Charleywood.'

'Any other suggestions?'

'No,' roared the crowd.

'Thank you, gentlemen.' Duff smiled at them. 'I am sensible of the honour. Now, ten members.'

'Jock and Trevor Heyns.'

'Karl Lochtkamper.'

'Francois du Toit.'

'Sean Courtney.'

There were fifty nominations. Duff baulked at counting votes so the committee was elected by applause. He called the names one at a time and judged the strength of the response to each. Sean and Francois were among those elected. Chairs and a table were brought out onto the veranda and Duff took his seat. With a water-jug he hammered for silence, declared the first session of the Diggers' Committee open and then immediately fined three members of the crowd ten pounds each for discharging firearms during a meeting – gross contempt of Committee. The fines were paid and a proper air of solemnity achieved.

'I'll ask Mr Courtney to open the case for the prosecution.'

Sean stood up and gave a brief description of the morning's battle, ending, 'You were there, Your Honour, so you know all about it anyway.'

'So I was,' agreed Duff. 'Thank you, Mr Courtney. I think that was a very fair picture you presented. Now,' he looked at the prisoners, 'who speaks for you?'

There was a minute of shuffling and whispering, then one of them was pushed forward. He pulled off his hat and blushed purple.

'Your Worship,' he began, then stopped, wriggling with embarrassment.

'Your Worship.'

225

'You've said that already.'

'I don't rightly know where to begin, Mr Charleywood – I mean Your Honour, sir.'

Duff looked at the prisoners again.

'Perhaps you'd like to reconsider your choice.'

Their first champion was withdrawn in disgrace and a fresh one sent forward to face the Committee. He had more fire.

'You bastards got no right to do this to us,' he started and Duff promptly fined him ten pounds. His next attempt was more polite.

'Your Honour, you can't do this to us. We had our rights, you know, that new proclamation and all, I mean, them old titles wasn't legal no more now, was they? We just came along as peaceful as you please, the old titles not being legal, we got a right to do what we done. Then you bastards, I mean Your Honour, dynamited us and like we had a right to protect ourselves, I mean after all, didn't we, sir?'

'A brilliant defence most ably conducted. Your fellows should be grateful to you,' Duff complimented him, then turned to his Committee. 'Well now, how say you merry gentlemen. Guilty or not guilty?'

'Guilty.' They spoke together and Francois added for emphasis, 'The dirty thunders.'

'We will now consider sentence.'

'String them up,' shouted someone and instantly the mood changed. The mob growled: an ugly sound.

'I'm a carpenter, I'll whip you up a handsome set of gallows in no time at all.'

'Don't waste good wood on them. Use a tree.'

'Get the ropes.'

'String them up.'

The crowd surged in, lynch mad. Sean snatched Francois's shotgun and jumped up onto the table.

'So help me God, I'll shoot the first one of you that

touches them before this court says so.' They checked and Sean pressed his advantage. 'At this range I can't miss. Come on, try me – there's two loads of buckshot in here. Someone will get cut in half.' They fell back still muttering.

'Perhaps you've forgotten, but there's a police force in this country and there's a law against killing. Hang them today and it'll be your turn tomorrow.'

'You're right, Mr Courtney, it'll be cruel, heartless murder. That it will,' wailed the spokesman.

'Shut up, you bloody fool,' Duff snarled at him and someone in the crowd laughed. The laughter caught on and Duff sighed silently with relief. That had been very close.

'Give them the old tar and feathers.'

Duff grinned. 'Now you're talking sense. Who's got a few barrels of tar for sale?' He looked round. 'What, no offers? Then we'll have to think of something else.'

'I've got ten drums of red paint – thirty shillings each, good imported brand.' Duff recognized the speaker as a trader who had opened a general dealer's store down at Ferrieras Camp.

'Mr Tarry suggests paint. What about it?'

'No, it comes off too easily – that's no good.'

'I'll let you have it cheap – twenty-five shillings a drum.'

'No – stick your ruddy paint,' the crowd booed him.

'Give them a twist on Satan's Roulette Wheel,' shouted another voice, and the crowd clamoured agreement.

'That's it – give them the wheel.'

'Round and round and round she goes – where she stops nobody knows,' roared a black-bearded digger from the roof of the shanty across the road. The crowd howled.

Sean watched Duff's expression – the smile had gone. He was weighing it up. If he stopped them again they might lose all patience and risk the shotgun. He couldn't chance it.

'All right. If that's what you want.' He faced the terrified cluster of prisoners. 'The sentence of this court is that you play roulette with the devil for one hour and that you then leave this goldfield – if we catch you back here again you'll get another hour of it. The wounded are excused the first half of the sentence. I think they've had enough. Mr du Toit will supervise the punishment.'

'We'd prefer the paint, Mr Charleywood,' pleaded the spokesman again.

'I bet you would,' said Duff softly, but the crowd was carrying them away already, out towards the open veld beyond the Hotel. Most of them had staked claims of their own and they didn't like claim jumpers. Sean climbed down off the table.

'Let's go and have a drink,' Duff said to him.

'Aren't you going to watch?' asked Sean.

'I've seen it done once before down in the Cape. That was enough.'

'What do they do?'

'Go and have a look, I'll be waiting for you at the Bright Angels. I'll be surprised if you stay the full hour.'

By the time Sean joined the crowd most of the wagons had been gathered from the camps and drawn up in a line. Men swarmed round them fitting jacks under the axles to lift the big back wheels clear of the ground. Then the prisoners were hustled forward – one to each wheel. Eager hands lifted them and held them while their wrists and ankles were lashed to the rim of the wheel with the hub in the middle of their backs and their arms and legs spread-eagled like stranded starfish. Francois hurried along the line checking the ropes and placing four diggers at each wheel, two to start it and another two to take over when those were tired. He reached the end, came back to the centre again, pulled his watch from his pocket, checked the time, then shouted.

'All right – turn them, *kerels*.'

228

The wheels started moving, slowly at first then faster as they built up momentum. The bodies strapped to them blurred with the speed.

'Round and round and round she goes – round and round and round she goes,' chanted the crowd gleefully.

Within minutes there was a burst of laughter from the end of the line of wagons. Someone had started vomiting, it sprayed from him like yellow sparks from a catherine wheel. Then another and another joined in. Sean could hear them retching and gasping as the centrifugal force flung the vomit up against the back of their throats and out of their noses. He waited a few more minutes but when their bowels started to empty he turned away gagging and headed for the Bright Angel.

'Did you enjoy it?' asked Duff.

'Give me a brandy,' answered Sean.

– 9 –

With the Diggers' Committee dispensing rough justice a semblance of order came to the camps. President Kruger wanted no part in policing the nest of ruffians and cut-throats which was growing up just outside his Capital and he contented himself with placing his spies among them and leaving them to work out their own salvation. After all, the field was far from proved and the chances were that in another year the veld would again be as deserted as it had been nine months before. He could afford to wait; in the meantime the Diggers' Committee had his tacit sanction.

While the ants worked, cutting down into the reef with pick and with dynamite, the grasshoppers waited in the bars and shanties. So far only the Jack and Whistle mill was turning out gold, and only Hradsky and Francois du Toit knew how much gold was coming out of it. Hradsky was still in Capetown crusading for capital and Francois spoke to no one, not even to Duff, about the mill's productivity.

The rumours flew like sand in a whirlwind. One day it seemed that the reef had pinched out fifty feet below the surface, and the next the canteens buzzed with the news that the Heyns brothers had gone down a hundred feet and were pulling out nuggets the size of musket balls. Nobody knew but everybody was prepared to guess.

Up at the Candy Deep, Duff and Sean worked on relentlessly. The mill took shape on its concrete platform, its jaws open for the first bite at the rock. The boiler was swung up onto its cradle by twenty sweating, singing Zulus. The copper tables were fitted up ready to be smeared with quicksilver. There was no time to worry about the reef nor the dwindling store of money in Sean's cash belt. They worked and they slept – there was nothing else. Duff took to sharing Sean's tent up on the ridge and Candy had her featherbed to herself again.

On the twentieth of November they fired the boiler for the first time. Tired and horny-handed, their bodies lean and tempered hard with toil, they stood together and watched the needle creek up round the pressure gauge until it touched the red line at the top.

Duff grunted. 'Well, at least we've got power now.' Then he punched Sean's shoulder. 'What the hell are you standing here for – do you think this is a Sunday School picnic? There's work to do, laddie.'

On the second of December they fed the mill its first meal and watched the powdered rock flow across the amalgam tables. Sean threw his arm round Duff's neck in an affectionate half-Nelson, Duff hit him in the stomach and pulled his hat down over his eyes, they drank a glass of brandy each at supper and laughed a little but that was all. They were too tired to celebrate. From now on one of them must be in constant attendance on that iron monster. Duff took the first night shift and when Sean went up to the mill next morning he found him weaving on his feet, his eyes sunk deep in dark sockets.

'By my reckoning we've run ten tons of rock through her. Time to clean the tables and see just how much gold we've picked up.'

'You go and get some sleep,' said Sean and Duff ignored him.

'Mbejane, bring a couple of your savages here, we're going to change the tables.'

'Listen, Duff, it can wait an hour or two. Go and get your head down.'

'Please stop drivelling – you're as bad as a wife.'

Sean shrugged. 'Have it your own way, show me how you do it then.'

They switched the flow of powdered rock onto the second table that was standing ready; then with a broad bladed spatula Duff scraped the mercury off the copper top of the first table, collecting it in a ball the size of a coconut.

'The mercury picks up the tiny particles of gold,' he explained to Sean as he worked, 'and lets the grains of rock wash across the table and fall off into the dump. Of course it doesn't collect it all, some of it goes to waste.'

'How do you get the gold out again?'

'You put the whole lot in a retort and boil off the mercury – the gold stays behind.'

'Hell of a waste of mercury, isn't it?'

'No, you catch it as it condenses and use it again. Come on, I'll show you.'

Duff carried the ball of amalgam down to the shed, placed it in the retort and lit the blow-lamp. With the heat on it the ball dissolved and started to bubble. Silently they stared at it. The level in the retort fell.

'Where's the gold?' Sean asked at last.

231

'Oh, shut up,' Duff snapped impatiently, and then, repentant, 'Sorry, laddie, I feel a bit jaded this morning.'

The last of the mercury steamed off and there it was, glowing bright, molten yellow. A drop of gold the size of a pea. Duff shut off the blow-lamp and neither of them spoke for a while. Then Sean asked, 'Is that all?'

'That, my friend, is all,' agreed Duff wearily. 'What do you want to do with it – fill a tooth?'

He turned towards the door with a droop to his whole body.

'Keep the mill running, we might as well go down with our colours flying.'

– 10 –

It was a miserable Christmas dinner. They ate it at Candy's Hotel. They had credit there. She gave Duff a gold signet ring and Sean a box of cigars. Sean had never smoked before but now the sting of it in his lungs gave him a certain masochistic pleasure. The dining-room roared with men's voices and cutlery clatter, the air was thick with the smell of food and tobacco smoke while in one corner – marooned on a little island of gloom – sat Sean, Duff and Candy.

Once Sean lifted his glass at Duff and spoke like an undertaker's clerk. 'Happy Christmas.'

Duff's lips twitched back in a dead man's grin. 'And the same to you.'

They drank. Then Duff roused himself to speak. 'Tell me again – how much have we got left? I like to hear you say it; you have a beautiful voice, you should have played Shakespeare.'

'Three pounds and sixteen shillings.'

'Yes, yes, you got it just right that time – three pounds

and sixteen shillings – now to really make me feel Christmassy, tell me how much we owe.'

'Have another drink.' Sean changed the subject.

'Yes, I think I will, thank you.'

'Oh please, you two, let's just forget about it for today,' pleaded Candy. 'I planned for it to be such a nice party – look, there's Francois! Hey, Francois – over here!'

The dapper du Toit bustled across to their table.

'Happy Christmas, kerels, let me buy you a drink.'

'It's nice to see you.' Candy gave him a kiss. 'How are you? You're looking fine.'

Francois sobered instantly. 'It's funny you should say that, Candy. As a matter of fact I'm a bit worried.' He tapped his chest and sank down into an empty chair. 'My heart, you know, I've been waiting for it to happen, and then yesterday I was up at the mill, just standing there, you understand, when suddenly it was as though a vice was squeezing my chest. I couldn't breathe – well, not very well anyway. Naturally I hurried back to my tent and looked it up. Page eighty-three. Under "Diseases of the Heart".' He shook his head sadly. 'It's very worrying. You know I wasn't a well man before, but now this.'

'Oh, no,' wailed Candy. 'I can't stand it – not you too.'

'I'm sorry, have I said something wrong?'

'Just in keeping with the festive spirit at this table.' She pointed at Duff and Sean. 'Look at their happy faces – if you'll excuse me I'm going to check up in the kitchen.' She went.

'What's wrong, old Duff?'

Duff flashed his death's head grin across the table at Sean.

'The man wants to know what's wrong – tell him.'

'Three pounds sixteen shillings,' said Sean and Francois looked puzzled.

'I don't understand.'

'He means we're broke – flat broke.'

'*Gott*, I'm sorry to hear that, Duff, I thought you were going good. I've heard the mill running all this month, I thought you'd be rich by now.'

'The mill's been running all right and we've recovered enough gold to block a flea's backside.'

'But why, man? You are working the Leader Reef, aren't you?'

'I'm beginning to think this Leader Reef of yours is a bedtime story.'

Francois peered into his glass thoughtfully.

'How deep are you?'

'We've got one incline shaft down about fifty feet.'

'No sign of the Leader?' Duff shook his head and Francois went on.

'You know when I first spoke to you a lot of what I said was just guessing.'

Duff nodded.

'Well, I know a bit more about it now. What I am going to tell you is for you alone – I'll lose my job if it gets out, you understand?'

Duff nodded again.

'So far the Leader Reef has only been found at two places. We've got it on the Jack and Whistle and I know the Heyns brothers have struck it on the Cousin Jock Mine. Let me draw it for you.' He picked up a knife and drew in the gravy on the bottom of Sean's plate. 'This is the Main Reef running fairly straight. Here I am, here is the Cousin Jock and here you are in between us. Both of us have found the Leader and you haven't. My guess is it's there all right – you just don't know where to look.

'At the far end of the Jack and Whistle claims the Main Reef and the Leader are running side by side two feet apart but by the time they reach the boundary nearest to the Candy Deep they've opened up to seventy feet apart. Now on the boundary of the Cousin Jock they're back to fifty feet apart. To me it seems that the two reefs form the shape of a long bow, like this.' He drew it in. 'The Main Reef is the string and the Leader Reef is the wood. I'm telling you, Duff, if you cut a trench at right-angles to the Main Reef you'll find it – and when you do you can buy me a drink.'

They listened gravely and when Francois finished Duff leaned back in his chair. 'If we'd known this a month ago! Now how are we going to raise the money to cut this new trench and still keep the mill running?'

'We could sell some of our equipment,' suggested Sean.

'We need it, every scrap of it, and besides if we sold one spade the creditors would be on us like a pack of wolves, howling for their money.'

'I'd make you a loan if I had it – but with what Mr Hradsky pays me—' Francois shrugged. 'You'll need about two hundred pounds. I haven't got it.'

Candy came back to the table in time to hear Francois's last remark.

'What's this all about?'

'Can I tell her, Francois?'

'If you think it will do any good.'

Candy listened, then thought for a moment. 'Well, I've just bought ten plots of ground in Johannesburg, this new Government village down the valley, so I'm short myself. But I could let you have fifty pounds if that would help.'

'I've never borrowed money from a lady before – it'll be a new experience. Candy, I love you.'

'I wish you meant that,' said Candy, but luckily for Duff his hearing failed him completely just as Candy spoke. He went on hurriedly.

'We'll need another hundred and fifty or so – let's hear your suggestions, gentlemen.'

There was a long silence, then Duff started to smile and he was looking at Sean.

'Don't tell me, let me guess.' Sean forestalled him. 'You're going to put me out to stud?'

'Close – but not quite right. How are you feeling, laddie?'

'Thank you, I'm all right.'

'Strong?'

'Yes.'

'Brave?'

'Come on, Duff, let's have it. I don't like that look in your eye.'

Duff pulled a notebook out of his pocket and wrote in it with a stump of pencil. Then he tore out the page and handed it to Sean. 'We'll have posters like this put up in every canteen on the goldfields.'

Sean read it:

ON NEW YEAR'S DAY MR SEAN COURTNEY HEAVY-WEIGHT CHAMPION OF THE TRANSVAAL REPUBLIC WILL STAND TO MEET ALL COMERS IN FRONT OF CANDY'S HOTEL FOR
    A PURSE OF FIFTY POUNDS ASIDE.
    Spectators' Fee, 2s. All Welcome.

Candy was reading it over his shoulder. She squeaked.

'That's wonderful. I'll have to hire extra waiters to serve drinks and I'll run a buffet luncheon. I suppose I could charge two shillings a head?'

'I'll fix the posters,' Francois was not to be outdone, 'and I'll send a couple of my chaps down to put up a ring.'

'We'll close the mill down until New Year – Sean will have to get a lot of rest. We'll put him on light training only. No drinking, of course, and plenty of sleep,' said Duff.

'It's all arranged then, is it?' asked Sean. 'All I've got to do is go in there and get beaten to a pulp?'

'We're doing this for you, laddie, so that you can be rich and famous.'

'Thank you, thank you very much.'

'You like to fight, don't you?'

'When I'm in the mood.'

'Don't worry, I'll think up some dirty names to call you – get you worked up in no time.'

– 11 –

'How are you feeling?' Duff asked for the sixth time that morning.

'No change since five minutes ago,' Sean reassured him.

Duff pulled out his watch, stared at it, held it to his ear and looked surprised that it was still ticking.

'We've got the challengers lined up on the veranda. I've told Candy to serve them free drinks – as much as they want. Every minute we can wait here gives them a little longer to take on a load of alcohol. Francois is collecting the gate money in my valise; as you win each bout the stakes will go into it as well. I've got Mbejane stationed at the mouth of the alley beside the Hotel. If there's a riot one of us will throw the bag to him and he'll head for the long grass.'

Sean was stretched out on Candy's bed with his hands behind his head. He laughed. 'I can find no fault with your planning. Now for pity's sake calm down, man. You're making me nervous.'

The door burst open and Duff leapt out of his chair at the crash. It was Francois, he stood in the doorway holding his chest.

'My heart,' he panted. 'This is doing my heart no good.'

'What's happening outside?' Duff demanded.

'We've collected over fifty pounds gate money already.

There's a mob up on the roof that haven't paid, but every time I go near them they throw bottles at me.'

Francois cocked his head on one side. 'Listen to them.' The noise of the crowd was barely softened by the flimsy walls of the Hotel. 'They won't wait much longer – you'd better come out before they start looking for you.'

Sean stood up. 'I'm ready.'

Francois hesitated.

'Duff, you remember Fernandes, that Portuguese from Kimberley?'

'Oh no!' Duff anticipated him. 'Don't tell me he's here.'

Francois nodded. 'I didn't want to alarm you but some of the local boys clubbed in and telegraphed south for him. He arrived on the express coach half an hour ago. I had hoped he wasn't going to make it in time, but—' He shrugged.

Duff looked at Sean sadly.

'Bad luck, laddie.'

Francois tried to soften the blow. 'I told him it was first come first served. He's sixth in the line so Sean will be able to make a couple of hundred quid anyway – then we can always say he's had enough and close the contest.'

Sean was listening with interest. 'This Fernandes is dangerous?'

'They were thinking of him when they invented that word,' Duff told him.

'Let's go and have a look at him.'

Sean led the way out of Candy's room and down the passage.

'Did you get hold of a scale to weigh them with?' Duff asked Francois as they hurried after Sean.

'No, there's not one on the fields that goes over a hundred and fifty pounds – but I have Gideon Barnard outside.'

'How does that help us?'

'He's a cattle dealer – all his life he's been judging animals on the hoof. He'll give us the weights to within a few pounds.'

Duff chuckled. 'That'll have to do then. Besides I doubt we'll be claiming any world titles.'

Then they were out on the veranda blinking in the brightness of the sun and the thunder of the crowd.

'Which is the Portuguese?' whispered Sean – he needn't have asked. The man stood out like a gorilla in a cage of monkeys. A shaggy coating of hair began on his shoulders and continued down his back and chest, completely hiding his nipples and exaggerating the bulge of his enormous belly.

The crowd opened a path for Sean and Duff and they walked along it to the ring. Hands slapped Sean's back but the well-wishes were drowned in the churning sea of sound. Jock Heyns was the referee – he helped Sean through the ropes and ran his hands over his pockets.

'Just checking,' he apologized. 'We don't want any scrap iron in the ring.' Then he beckoned to a tall, brown-faced fellow who was leaning on the ropes chewing tobacco.

'This is Mr Barnard our weighing steward. Well, what do you say, Gideon?'

The steward hosed a little juice from the side of his mouth.

'Two hundred and ten.'

'Thank you.' Jock held up his hands and after a few minutes was rewarded with a comparative silence.

'Ladies and Gentlemen.'

'Who you talking to, Guvnor?'

'We are privileged to have with us today – Mr Sean Courtney.'

'Wake up, *Boet*, he's been with us for months.'

239

'The heavyweight champion of the Republic.'

'Why not make it the world, cock, he's got just as much right to that title.'

'Who will fight six bouts—'

'If it lasts that long.'

' – for his title and a purse of fifty pounds each.'

Sustained cheering.

'The first challenger – at two hundred and ten pounds – Mr Anthony—'

'Hold on,' Sean shouted, 'who says he's first?'

Jock Heyns had taken a deep breath to bellow the name. He let it escape with a hiss. 'It was arranged by Mr du Toit.'

'If I fight them, then I pick them – I want the Port . . .'

Duff's hand whipped over Sean's mouth and his whisper was desperate. 'Don't be a bloody fool – take the easy ones first. Use your head – we aren't doing this for fun, we're trying to finance a mine, remember?'

Sean clawed Duff's hand off his mouth. 'I want the Portuguese,' he shouted.

'He's joking,' Duff assured the crowd, then turned on Sean fiercely. 'Are you mad? That dago's a man-eater, we're fifty pounds poorer before you start.'

'I want the Portuguese,' repeated Sean with all the logic of a small boy picking the most expensive toy in the shop.

'Let him have the dago,' shouted the gentlemen on the hotel roof and Jock Heyns eyed them nervously; it was clear that they were about to add a few more bottles to the argument.

'All right,' he agreed hastily. 'The first challenger, at—' he glanced at Barnard and repeated after him, 'two hundred and fifty-five pounds – Mr Felezardo da Silva Fernandes.'

In a storm of hoots and applause the Portuguese waddled down off the veranda and into the ring. Sean had seen Candy at the dining-room window and he waved to her. She blew him a two-handed kiss and at that instant Trevor

240

Heyns, the timekeeper, hit the bucket which served as a gong and Sean heard Duff's warning shout. Instinctively he started to duck. There was a flash of lightning inside his skull and he found himself sitting in amongst the legs of the first line of spectators.

'The bastard King hit me,' Sean complained loudly. He shook his head and was surprised to find it still attached to his body. Someone poured a glass of beer over him and it steadied him. He felt his anger flaming up through his body.

'Six,' counted Jock Heyns.

The Portuguese was standing at the ropes. 'Come back, Leetle Sheet, I haf some more for you, not half.'

Sean's anger jumped in his throat.

'Seven, eight.'

Sean gathered his legs under him.

'I kiss your mother.' Fernandes puckered his lips and smacked them. 'I love your sister, like this.' He demonstrated graphically.

Sean charged. With the full weight of his run behind it, his fist thudded into the Portuguese's mouth, then the ropes caught Sean and catapulted him back into the crowd once more.

'You weren't even in the ring, how could you hit him?' protested one of the spectators who had broken Sean's fall. He had money on Fernandes.

'Like this!' Sean demonstrated. The man sat down heavily and had nothing further to say. Sean hurdled the ropes. Jock Heyns was halfway through his second count when Sean interrupted him by lifting the reclining Portuguese to his feet, using the tangled bush of his hair as a handle. He balanced the man on his unsteady legs and hit him again.

'One, two, three . . .' resignedly Jock Heyns began his third count, this time he managed to reach ten.

241

There was a howl of protest from the crowd and Jock Heyns struggled to make himself heard above it.

'Does anyone want to lodge a formal objection?'

It seemed that there were those who did.

'Very well, please step into the ring. I can't accept shouted comments.' Jock's attitude was understandable – he stood to lose a considerable sum if his decision were reversed. But Sean was patrolling the ropes as hungrily as a lion at feeding time. Jock waited a decent interval, then held up Sean's right arm.

'The winner – ten minutes for refreshments before the next bout. Will the keepers please come and fetch their property.' He gestured towards the Portuguese.

'Nice going, laddie, unorthodox perhaps but beautiful to watch.' Duff took Sean's arm and led him to a chair on the veranda.

'Three more to go, then we can call it a day.' He handed Sean a glass.

'What's this?'

'Orange juice.'

'I'd prefer something a little stronger.'

'Later, laddie.'

Duff collected the Portuguese purse and dropped it into the valise while that gentleman was being carried from the ring by his straining sponsors and laid to rest at the far end of the veranda.

Mr Anthony Blair was next. His heart was not in the encounter. He moved prettily enough on his feet but always in the direction best calculated to keep him out of reach of Sean's fists.

'The boy's a natural long-distance champ.'

'Watch it, Courtney, he'll run you to death.'

'Last lap, Blair, once more round the ring and you've done five miles.'

The chase ended when Sean, now sweating gently, herded him in a corner and there dispatched him.

The third challenger had by this time developed a pain in his chest.

'It hurts like you wouldn't believe it,' he announced through gritted teeth.

'Does it sort of gurgle in your lungs as you breathe?' asked Francois.

'Yes, that's it – gurgles like you wouldn't believe it.'

'Pleurisy,' diagnosed du Toit with more than a trace of envy in his voice.

'Is that bad?' the man asked anxiously.

'Yes it is. Page one hundred and sixteen. The treatment is—'

'Then I won't be able to fight. Hell, that's bad luck,' the invalid complained cheerfully.

'It's exceptionally bad luck,' agreed Duff. 'It means you'll have to forfeit your purse money.'

'You wouldn't take advantage of a sick man?'

'Try me,' Duff suggested pleasantly.

The fourth contestant was a German. Big, blond and happy-faced. He stumbled three or four times on his way to the ring, tripped over the ropes and crawled to his corner on hands and knees; once there he was able to regain his feet with a little help from the ring post. Jock went close to him to smell his breath and before he could dodge, the German caught him in a bear hug and led him into the opening steps of a waltz. The crowd loved it and there were no objections when at the end of the dance Jock declared Sean the winner on a technical knockout. More correctly the decision should have gone to Candy who had provided the free drinks.

'We can close down the circus now if you want to, laddie,' Duff told Sean. 'You've made enough to keep the Candy Deep afloat for another couple of months.'

'I haven't had a single good fight out of the lot of them. But I like the looks of this last one. The others were for business; this one I'll have just for the hell of it.'

'You've been magnificent – now you deserve a little fun,' agreed Duff.

'Mr Timothy Curtis. Heavyweight champion of Georgia, U.S.A.' Jock introduced him.

Gideon Barnard put his weight at two hundred and ten pounds, the same as Sean's. Sean shook his hand and from the touch of it knew he was not going to be disappointed.

'Glad to know you.' The American's voice was as soft as his grip was hard.

'Your servant, sir,' said Sean and hit the air where the man's head had been an instant before. He grunted as a fist slogged into his chest under his raised right arm and backed away warily. A soft sigh blew through the crowd and they settled down contentedly. This was what they had come to see.

The red wine was served early; it flew in tiny drops every time a punch was thrown or received. The fight flowed smoothly around the square of trampled grass. The sound of bone on flesh was followed immediately by the growl of the crowd and the seconds between were filled with the hoarse breathing of the two men and the slither, slither of their feet.

'Yaaaa!' Through the tense half silence ripped a roar like that of a mortally wounded foghorn. Sean and the American jumped apart startled, and turned with everyone else to face Candy's Hotel. Fernandes was with them again; his mountain-wide hairiness seemed to fill the whole veranda. He picked up one of Candy's best tables and holding it across his chest tore off two of its legs as though they were the wings of a roasted chicken.

'Francois, the bag!' shouted Sean. Francois snatched it up and threw it high over the heads of the crowd. Sean held his breath as he followed its slow trajectory, then he blew out again with relief as he saw Mbejane field the pass and vanish around the corner of the Hotel.

'Yaaaa!' Fernandes gave tongue again. With a table leg in each hand he charged the crowd that stood between him and Sean; it scattered before him.

'Do you mind if we finish this some other time?' Sean asked the American.

'Of course not. Any time at all. I was just about to leave myself.'

Duff reached through the ropes and caught Sean's arm.

'There's someone looking for you – or had you noticed?'

'It might just be his way of showing friendliness.'

'I wouldn't bet on it – are you coming?'

Fernandes rumbled to a halt, braced himself and threw. The table leg whirred like a rising pheasant an inch over Sean's head, ruffling his hair with the wind of its passage.

'Lead on, Duff.' Sean was uncomfortably conscious of the fact that Fernandes was again in motion towards him, still armed with a long oak, and that three very thin ropes were all that stood between them. The speed that Sean and Duff turned on them made Mr Blair's earlier exhibition seem like that of a man with both legs in plaster. Fernandes, carrying top weight as he was, never looked like catching them.

Francois came up to the Candy Deep just after midday with the news that the Portuguese, after beating three of his sponsors into insensibility, had left on the noon coach back to Kimberley.

Duff uncocked his rifle. 'Thanks, Franz, we were waiting lunch for him. I thought he might call on us.'

'Have you counted the takings?'

'Yes, your commission is in that paper bag on the table.'

'Thanks, man, let's go down and celebrate.'

'You go and have one for us.'

'Hey, Duff, you promised—' Sean started.

'I said later – in three or four weeks' time. Now we've got a little work to do, like digging a trench fifty feet deep and three hundred yards long.'

'We could start first thing tomorrow.'

'You want to be rich, don't you?' asked Duff.

'Sure, but—'

'You want nice things, like English suits, French champagne and—'

'Yes, but—'

'Well, stop arguing, get off your fat arse and come with me.'

– 12 –

The Chinese use firecrackers to keep the demons away. Duff and Sean applied the same principle. They kept the mill running; as long as its clunking carried across the valley to the ears of their creditors all was well. Everyone accepted the fact that they were working a payable reef and left them alone, but the money they fed into the front of the mill had halved its value by the time it came out of the other side in those pathetic little yellow pellets.

In the meantime they cut their trench, tearing into the earth in a race against Settlement Day. They fired dynamite and as the last stones dropped back out of the sky they were in again, coughing with the fumes, to clear the loosened rock and start drilling the next set of holes. It was summer, the days were long, and while it was light they worked. Some evenings they lit the last fuses by lantern light.

Sand fell through the hour-glass faster than they had bargained for, the money dribbled away and on the fifteenth of February Duff shaved himself, changed his shirt and went to see Candy about another loan. Sean watched him walk away down the slope. They had sold the horses a week before, and he said a small prayer – the first for many years.

Duff came back in the late morning. He stood on the edge of the trench and watched Sean tamping in the charges for the next cut. Sean's back was shiny with sweat; each individual muscle standing out in relief, swelling and subsiding as he moved.

'That's the stuff, laddie, keep at it.'

Sean looked up with dust-reddened eyes. 'How much?' he asked.

'Another fifty, and this is the last – or so she threatens.'

Sean's eyes fastened on the package Duff held under his arm.

'What's that?'

He could see the stains seeping through the brown paper and the saliva flooded out from under his tongue.

'Prime beef chops – no mealie meal porridge for lunch today.' Duff grinned at him.

'Meat.' Sean caressed the word. 'Underdone – bleeding a little as you bite it, a trace of garlic, just enough salt.'

'And you beside me, singing in the wilderness,' agreed Duff. 'Cut out the poetry, light those fuses and let's go and eat.'

An hour later they walked side by side along the bottom of their trench, Mbejane and his Zulus crowding behind them. Sean belched. 'Ah, pleasant memory, I'll never be able to look another plate of mealie meal in the face again.'

They reached the end, where the freshly broken earth and rock lay piled. Sean felt the thrill start in his hands, tingle up his arms and squeeze his lungs. Then Duff's fingers were biting into his shoulder; he could feel them trembling.

It looked like a snake, a fat grey python crawling down one wall of the trench, disappearing under the heap of new rubble and out the other side.

Duff moved first, he knelt and picked up a piece of the reef, a big grey mottled lump of it and he kissed it.

'It must be it, hey, Duff? It must be the Leader?'

'It's the end of the rainbow.'

'No more mealie meal,' Sean said softly and Duff laughed. Then Sean laughed. Wildly, crazily, together they howled their triumph.

– 13 –

'Let me hold it again,' said Sean.

Duff passed it across to him.

'Hell, it's heavy.'

'There's nothing heavier,' agreed Duff.

'Must be all of fifty pounds.'

Sean held the bar in two hands, it was the size of a cigar box. 'More!'

'We've retrieved all our losses in two days' working.'

'And some to spare, I'd say.'

Sean placed the gold bar on the table between them. It shone with little yellow smiles in the lantern light and Duff leaned forward and stroked it, its surface felt knobbly from the rough casting.

'I can't keep my hands off it,' he confessed sheepishly.

'I can't either!' Sean reached out to touch it. 'We'll be able to pay Candy out for the claims in another week or two.'

Duff started. 'What did you say?'

'I said we'd be able to pay Candy out.'

'I thought I wasn't hearing things.' Duff patted his arm indulgently. 'Listen to me, laddie, I'll try and put it simply. How long have we got the option on these claims for?'

'Three years.'

'Correct – now the next question. How many people on these fields have any money?'

Sean looked mystified. 'Well, we have now and – and . . .'

'No one else, that is until Hradsky gets back,' Duff finished for him.

'What about the Heyns brothers? They've cut open the Leader Reef.'

'Certainly, but it won't do them any good, not until their machinery arrives from England.'

'Go on!' Sean wasn't quite sure where Duff was leading.

'Instead of paying Candy out now we are going to use this' – he patted the gold bar – 'and all its little brothers to buy up every likely claim we can lay our hands on. For a start there are Doc Sutherland's claims between us and the Jack and Whistle. Then we are going to order a couple of big ten-stamp mills and when those are spilling out gold we'll use it to buy land, finance brick works, engineering shops, transport companies and the rest. I've told you before there are more ways of making gold than digging for it.'

Sean was staring at him silently.

'Have you got a head for heights?' asked Duff.

Sean nodded.

'You're going to need it, because we are going up where the eagles fly – you are about to be a party to the biggest financial killing this country has ever seen.'

Sean lit one of Candy's cigars; his hand was a little unsteady.

'Don't you think it would be best to – well – not try and go too quickly. Hell, Duff, we've only been working the Leader for two days—'

'And we've made a thousand pounds,' Duff interrupted him. 'Listen to me, Sean, all my life I've been waiting for an opportunity like this. We're the first in on this field, it's

249

as wide open as the legs of a whore. We're going to go in and take it.'

The next morning Duff had the good fortune to find Doc Sutherland early enough to talk business with him, before he began the day's drinking. Another hour would have been too late. As it was Doc knocked over his glass and fell out of his chair before he finally signed away twenty-five claims to Sean and Duff. The ink was hardly dry on the agreement before Duff was riding down to Ferrieras Camp to look for Ted Reynecke who held the claims on the other side of the Cousin Jock. Up on the Candy Deep Sean nursed the mill and bit his nails. Within seven days Duff had bought over one hundred claims and committed them to forty thousand pounds in debts.

'Duff, you're going mad.' Sean pleaded with him. 'We'll lose everything again.'

'How much have we pulled out of the Candy Deep so far?'

'Four thousand.'

'Ten per cent of what we owe in ten days – and with a miserable little four-stamp mill at that. Hold on to your hat, laddie, tomorrow I'm going to sign up for the forty claims on the other side of the Jack and Whistle. I would have had them today but that damned Greek is holding out for a thousand pounds apiece. I'll have to give it to him, I suppose.'

Sean clutched his temples.

'Duff – please, man, we're in over our necks already.'

'Stand back, laddie, and watch the wizard work.'

'I'm going to bed – I suppose I'll have to take your shift again in the morning if you're determined to spend tomorrow ruining us.'

'That's not necessary, I've hired that Yankee – Curtis. You know, your sparring partner. It turns out he's a miner and he's willing to work for thirty a month. So you can come to town with me and watch me make you rich. I'm meeting the Greek at Candy's Hotel at nine o'clock.'

– 14 –

At nine o'clock Duff was talking and Sean sat silently on the edge of his chair; at ten the Greek had still not put in an appearance. Duff was moody and Sean was garrulous with relief. At eleven Sean wanted to go back to the mine.

'It's an omen, Duff, God looked down and he saw us sitting here all ready to make a terrible mistake. "No," he said, "I can't let them do it – I'll have the Greek break a leg – I can't let it happen to such nice boys."'

'Why don't you go and join a Trappist monastery?' Duff checked his watch. 'Come on, let's go!'

'Yes, sir!' Sean stood up with alacrity. 'We'll get back in plenty of time to clean the tables before lunch.'

'We're not going home, we're going to look for the Greek.'

'Now listen, Duff.'

'I'll listen later – come on.'

They rode across to the Bright Angels, left the horses outside and walked in together. It was dark in the canteen after the sunshine outside, but even in the gloom a group at one of the tables caught their attention immediately. The Greek sat with his back to them; the line of his parting seemed to be drawn with white chalk and a ruler through the oily black waves of his hair. Sean's eyes switched from him to the two men that sat across the table from him. Jews, there was no mistaking it, but there any similarity ended. The younger one was thin with smooth olive skin drawn tight across the bold bones of his cheeks; his lips were very red and his eyes, fringed with girl's lashes, were toffee-brown and melting. In the chair beside him was a man with a body that had been shaped in wax then held near a hot flame. Shoulders rounded to the verge of deformity drooped down over a pear-shaped body; with difficulty they supported the great Taj Mahal domed head. His hair was styled in the fashion of Friar Tuck, thick only around the ears. But the eyes – the flickering yellow eyes – there was nothing comical about them.

'Hradsky,' hissed Duff, then his expression changed. He smiled as he walked across to the table.

'Hello, Nikky, I thought we had an appointment.'

The Greek twisted quickly in his chair.

'Mr Charleywood, I'm sorry, I was held up.'

'So I see, the woods are full of highwaymen.'

Sean saw the flush start to come up out of Hradsky's collar then sink back again.

'Have you sold?' Duff asked.

The Greek nodded nervously.

'I'm sorry, Mr Charleywood, but Mr Hradsky paid my price and no haggling – cash money, too!'

Duff let his eyes wander across the table.

'Hello, Norman. How's your daughter?'

This time the flush escaped from Hradsky's shirt and flooded over his face. He opened his mouth, his tongue clucked twice, then he closed it again.

Duff smiled, he looked at the younger Jew. 'Say it for him, Max.'

The toffee eyes dropped to the table top. 'Mr Hradsky's daughter is very well.'

'I believe she married soon after my involuntary departure from Kimberley.'

'That is correct.'

'Wise move, Norman, much wiser than having your bully boys run me out of town. That wasn't very nice of you.'

252

No one spoke.

'We must get together some time and have a chat about old times. Until then, fa – fa – fare ye we – we – well.'

On the way back to the mine Sean asked, 'He's got a daughter? If she looks like him you were lucky to escape.'

'She didn't – she was like a bunch of ripe grapes with the bloom on them.'

'I can hardly credit it.'

'Neither could I. The only conclusion I could reach was that Max did that job for him as well.'

'What's the story about Max?'

'He's the Court Jester. Rumour has it that after Hradsky has finished hanging it out, Max shakes it for him.'

Sean laughed and Duff went on, 'But don't underestimate Hradsky. His stutter is his only weakness and with Max to talk for him he's overcome that. Beneath that monumental skull is a brain as quick and merciless as a guillotine. Now that he's arrived on this goldfield there's going to be some action; we'll have to gallop to keep up with him.'

Sean thought for a few seconds, then, 'Talking about action, Duff, now that we've lost the Greek's claims and won't have to use all our ready money satisfying him, let's give some thought to ordering new machinery to work the claims we have got.'

Duff grinned at him.

'I sent a telegram to London last week. There'll be a pair of brand new ten-stamp mills on the water to us before the end of the month.'

'Good God, why didn't you tell me?'

'You were worried enough as it was – I didn't want to break your heart.'

Sean opened his mouth to blast Duff out of the saddle. Duff winked at him before he could talk and Sean's lips trembled. He felt the laughter in his throat, he tried to stop it but it swamped him.

'How much is it going to cost us?' he howled through his mirth.

'If you ask that question once more, I'll strangle you,' Duff laughed back at him. 'Rest content in the knowledge that if we're going to have enough to honour the bills of lading when those mills arrive at Port Natal, we'll have to run a mountain of Leader Reef through our little rig during the next few weeks.'

'What about the payments on the new claims?'

'That's my department – I'll worry about that.'

And so their partnership crystallized; their relationship was established over the weeks that followed. Duff with his magic tongue and his charming, lopsided grin was the one who negotiated, who poured the oil on the storm waters churned up by impatient creditors. He was the storehouse of mining knowledge which Sean tapped daily, he was the conceiver of schemes, some wild, others brilliant. But his fleeting nervous energy was not designed to bring them to fruition. He lost interest quickly and it was Sean who finally rejected the least likely Charleywood brain children and adopted the others that were more deserving; once he had made himself stepfather to them he reared them as though they were his own. Duff was the theorist, Sean the practician. Sean could see why Duff had never found success before, but at the same time he recognized that without him he would be helpless. He watched with profound admiration the way that Duff used the barely sufficient flow of gold from the Candy Deep to keep the mill running, pay the tradesmen, meet the claim monies as they fell due and still save enough for the new machinery. He was a man juggling with live coals: hold one too long and it burns, let one fall and all fall. And Duff, deep-down-uncertain Duff, had a wall to put his back against. His speech never showed it but his eyes did when he looked at Sean. Sometimes he felt small next to Sean's big body and bigger determination, but it was a good feeling: like being on a friendly mountain.

They put up new buildings around the mill: storerooms, a smelting house and cabins for Sean and Curtis. Duff was sleeping at the Hotel again. The location for the Natives sprawled haphazard down the back slope of the ridge, retreating a little each week as the white mountain of the mine dump grew and pushed it back. The whole valley was changing. Hradsky's new mills arrived and stood up along the ridge, tall and proud until their own dumps dwarfed them. Johannesburg, at first a mere pattern of surveyors' pegs, sucked the scattered encampments onto her grassy chequerboard and arranged them in a semblance of order along her streets.

The Diggers' Committee, its members tired of having to scrape their boots every time they went indoors, decreed public latrines be erected. Then, flushed with their own audacity, they built a bridge across the Natal Spruit, purchased a water cart to lay the dust on the streets of Johannesburg and passed a law prohibiting burials within half a mile of the city centre. Sean and Duff as members of the Committee felt it their duty to demonstrate their faith in the goldfield, so they bought twenty-five plots of ground in Johannesburg, five pounds each to be paid within six months. Candy recruited all her customers and in one weekend of frantic effort they razed her Hotel to the ground, packed every plank and sheet of iron onto their wagons, carried it a mile down the valley and re-erected it on her own land in the centre of the township. During the party she gave them on that Sunday night they nearly succeeded in dismantling it for the second time. Each day the roads from Natal and the Cape fed more wagons, more men into the Witwatersrand goldfield. Duff's suggestion that the Diggers' Committee levy a guinea a head from all newcomers to help finance the public works was reluctantly rejected, the general feeling being that if it led to civil rebellion there were more newcomers than Committee members and no one fancied being on the losing side.

One morning, when he came out to the mine, Duff brought a telegram with him. He handed it to Sean without comment. Sean read it. The machinery had arrived.

'Good God, it's three weeks early.'

'They must have had a downhill sea, or a following wind or whatever it is that makes ships go faster,' muttered Duff.

'Have we got enough to pay the bill?' asked Sean.

'No.'

'What are we going to do?'

'I'll go and see the little man at the bank.'

'He'll throw you out in the street.'

'I'll get him to give us a loan on the claims.'

'How the hell are you going to do that – we haven't paid for them yet.'

'That's what you call financial genius. I'll simply point out to him that they're worth five times what we bought them for.' Duff grinned. 'Can you and Curtis carry on here without me for today while I go and arrange it?'

'You arrange it and I'll happily give you a month's holiday.'

When Duff came back that afternoon he carried a paper with him. It had a red wax seal in the bottom corner, across the top it said 'Letter of Credit' and in the middle, standing out boldly from the mass of small print, was a figure that ended in an impressive string of noughts.

'You're a bloody marvel,' said Sean.

'Yes, I am rather, aren't I?' agreed Duff.

The Heyns brothers' machinery was on the same ship. Jock and Duff rode down to Port Natal together, hired a hundred wagons and brought it all back in one load.

'I'll tell you what I'll do with you, Jock, I'll wager you that we get our mills producing before you do. Loser pays for the transport on the whole shipment,' Duff challenged him when they reached Johannesburg where, in Candy's new bar-room, they were washing the dust out of their throats.

'You're on!'

'I'll go further, I'll put up a side bet of five hundred.'

Sean prodded Duff in the ribs.

'Gently, Duff – we can't afford it.' But Jock had already snapped up the bet.

'What do you mean we can't afford it?' whispered Duff. 'We've got nearly fifteen hundred pounds left on the letter of credit.'

Sean shook his head. 'No, we haven't.'

Duff pulled the paper from his inside pocket and tapped Sean's nose with it. 'There – read for yourself.'

Sean took it out of Duff's hand.

'Thanks, old chap, I'll go and pay the man now.'

'What man?'

'The man with the wagons.'

'What wagons?'

'The wagons that you and Jock hired in Port Natal. I've bought them.'

'The hell you say!'

'It was your idea to start a transport business. Just as soon as they've offloaded they'll be on their way again to pick up a shipment of coal from Dundee.'

257

Duff grinned at him. 'Don't you ever forget an idea? All right, laddie, off you go – we'll just have to win the bet, that's all.'

One of the mills they placed on the Candy Deep, the other on the new claims beyond the Cousin Jock Mine. They hired two gangs from among the unemployed in Johannesburg. Curtis supervised one of them and Sean the other, while Duff darted back and forth keeping an eye on both. Each time he passed the Cousin Jock he spent a few minutes checking Trevor and Jock's progress.

'They've got the edge on us, Sean; their boilers are up and holding pressure already,' he reported fretfully, but the next day he was smiling again.

'They didn't mix enough cement in the platform – it started to crumble as soon as they put the crusher on it. They'll have to cast it again. That set them back three or four days.'

The betting down in the canteens fluctuated sharply with each change of fortune. Francois came up to the Candy Deep one Saturday afternoon. He watched them work, made a suggestion or two, then remarked, 'They're giving three-to-one against you at the Bright Angels; they reckon the Heynses will be finished by next weekend.'

'Go down and put another five hundred pounds on for me,' Duff told him, and Sean shook his head despairingly.

'Don't worry, laddie, we can't lose – that amateur mining engineer, Jock Heyns, has assembled his crusher jaws all arse-about-face. I only noticed it this morning – he's in for a surprise when he tries to start up. He'll have to strip the whole damn rig.'

Duff was right – they brought both their mills into production a comfortable fifteen hours before the Heyns brothers. Jock rode over to see them with his jaw on his chest. 'Congratulations.'

'Thanks, Jock, did you bring your cheque book?'

'That's what I came to talk about. Can you give me a little time?'

'Your credit's good,' Sean assured him, 'come and have a drink and let me sell you some coal.'

'Ah, yes, I heard your wagons arrived back this morning. What price are you charging?'

'Fifteen pounds a hundredweight.'

'Good God. You bloody bandit, I bet it cost you less than five shillings a hundredweight.'

'A man's entitled to a reasonable profit,' protested Sean.

It had been a long hard pull up to the top of the hill but Sean and Duff had arrived at last and from there it was downhill all the way. The money poured in.

The geological freak that had bowed the Leader Reef away from the Main across the Candy Deep claims had, at the same time, enriched it – injected it full of the metal. Francois was there one evening when they put the ball of amalgam into the retort. His eyes bulged as the mercury boiled away; he stared at the gold the way a man watches a naked woman.

'*Gott!* I'm going to have to call you two thunders "Mister" from now on.'

'Have you ever seen richer reef, Francois?' Duff gloated.

Francois shook his head slowly. 'You know my theory about the reef being the bed of an old lake – well this bears it out. The kink in your reef must have been a deep trench along the bottom of the lake. It would have acted as a natural gold trap. Hell, man, what luck. With your eyes closed you have picked the plum out of the pudding. The Jack and Whistle is half as rich as this.'

Their overdraft at the bank dropped like a barometer in a hurricane; the tradesmen started greeting them with a smile; they gave Doc Sutherland a cheque which would have kept even him in whisky for a hundred years. Candy kissed them both when they paid her out in full, plus interest at seven per cent. Then she built herself a new Hotel, double storied, with a crystal chandelier in the dining-room and a magnificent bedroom suite on the second floor done out in maroon and gold. Duff and Sean rented it immediately but with the express understanding that if ever the Queen visited Johannesburg they would allow her to use it. In anticipation Candy called it the Victoria Rooms.

Francois, with a little persuasion, agreed to take over the running of the Candy Deep. He moved his possessions, one chest of clothes and four chests of patent medicines, across from the Jack and Whistle. Timothy Curtis was the manager of the mill on the new claims; they named it the Little Sister Mine. Although not nearly as rich as the Candy Deep it was producing a sweet fortune each month, for Curtis worked as well as he fought.

By the end of August Sean and Duff had no more creditors: the claims were theirs, the mills were theirs and they had money to invest.

'We need an office of our own here in town. We can't run this show from our bedrooms,' complained Sean.

'You're right,' agreed Duff, 'we'll build on that corner plot nearest the market square.' The plan was for a modest little four-room building, but it finally expanded to two stories, stinkwood floors, oak panelling and twenty rooms. What they couldn't use they rented.

'The price of land has trebled in three months,' said Sean, 'and it's still moving.'

'You're right – now's the time to buy,' Duff agreed. 'You're starting to think along the right lines.'

'It was your idea.'

'Was it?' Duff looked surprised.

'Don't you remember your "up where the eagles fly" speech?'

'Don't you forget anything?' asked Duff.

They bought land: one thousand acres at Orange Grove

and another thousand around Hospital Hill. Their transport wagons, now almost four hundred strong, plied in daily from Port Natal and Lourenço Marques. Their brickfields worked twenty-four hours a day, seven days a week, to try to meet the demand for building materials.

It took Sean almost a week to dissuade Duff from building an Opera House but he succeeded and instead they joined most of the other members of the Diggers' Committee in financing a different type of pleasure palace. At Duff's suggestion they called it the Opera House. They recruited the performers not from the great companies of Europe but from the dock areas of Capetown and Port Natal and chose as the conductor a Frenchwoman of vast experience named Blue Bessie after the colour of her hair. The Opera House provided entertainment on two levels. For the members of the Committee and the other emergent rich there was a discreet side entrance, a lavishly furnished lounge where one could buy the finest champagne and discuss the prices on the Kimberley Stock Exchange, and beyond the lounge were a series of tastefully decorated retiring-rooms. For the workers there was a bare corridor to queue in, no choice for your money and a five-minute time limit. In one month the Opera House produced more gold than the Jack and Whistle mine.

By December there were millionaires in Johannesburg: Hradsky, the Heyns brothers, Karl Lochtkamper, Duff Charleywood, Sean Courtney and a dozen others. They owned the mines, the land, the buildings and the city: the aristocracy of the Witwatersrand, knighted with money and crowned with gold.

A week before Christmas, Hradsky, their unacknowledged but undoubted king, called them all to a meeting in one of the private lounges of Candy's Hotel.

'Who the hell does he think he is,' complained Jock Heyns, 'ordering us round like a bunch of kaffirs.'

'*Verdammt Juden!*' agreed Lochtkamper.

But they went, every last man of them, for whatever Hradsky did had the smell of money about it and they could no more resist it than a dog can resist the smell of a bitch in season.

Duff and Sean were the last to arrive and the room was already hazed with cigar smoke and tense with expectation. Hradsky sagged in one of the polished leather armchairs with Max sitting quietly beside him; his eyes flickered when Duff walked in but his expression never changed. When Duff and Sean had found chairs Max stood up. 'Gentlemen, Mr Hradsky has invited you here to consider a proposition.'

They leaned forward slightly in their chairs and there was a glitter in their eyes like hounds close upon the fox.

'From time to time it is necessary for men in your position to find capital to finance further ventures and to consolidate past gains; on the other hand those of us who have money lying idle will be seeking avenues for investment.' Max cleared his throat and looked at them with his sad brown eyes.

'Up to the present there has been no meeting-place for these mutual needs such as exists in the other centres of the financial world. Our nearest approach to it is the Stock Exchange at Kimberley which, I'm sure you will agree, is too far removed to be of practical use to us here at Johannesburg. Mr Hradsky has invited you here to consider the possibility of forming our own Exchange and, if you accept the idea, to elect a chairman and governing body.'

Max sat down and in the silence that followed they took up the idea, each one fitting it into his scheme of thinking, testing it with the question 'How will I benefit?'.

'*Ja*, it's dom fine idea.' Lochtkamper spoke first.

'Yes, it's what we need.'

'Count me in.'

While they schemed and bargained, setting the fees, the

place and the rules, Sean watched their faces. The faces of bitter men, happy men, quiet ones and big bull-roarers but all with one common feature – that greedy glitter in the eyes. It was midnight before they finished.

Max stood up again.

'Gentlemen, Mr Hradsky would like you to join him in a glass of champagne to celebrate the formation of our new enterprise.'

'This I can't believe; the last time he paid for drinks was back in 'sixty,' declared Duff. 'Quickly somebody – find a waiter before he changes his mind.'

Hradsky hooded his eyes to hide the hatred in them.

– 16 –

With its own Stock Exchange and bordel Johannesburg became a city. Even Kruger recognized it; he deposed the Diggers' Committee and sent in his own police force, sold monopolies for essential mining supplies to members of his family and Government, and set about revising his tax laws with special attention to mining profits. Despite Kruger's efforts to behead the gold-laying goose, the city grew, overflowed the original Government plots and spread brawling and blustering out into the surrounding veld.

Sean and Duff grew with it. Their way of life changed swiftly; their visits to the mines fell to a weekly inspection and they left it to their hired men. A steady river of gold poured down from the ridge to their offices on Eloff Street, for the men they hired were the best that money could find.

Their horizons closed in to encompass only the two panelled offices, the Victoria Rooms and the Exchange. Yet within that world Sean found a thrill that he had never dreamed existed. He had been oblivious to it during the first feverish months; he had been so absorbed in laying the foundations that he could spare no energy for enjoying or even noticing it.

Then one day he felt the first voluptuous tickle of it. He had sent to the bank for a land title document he needed, expecting it to be delivered by a junior clerk – but instead the sub-manager and a senior clerk filed respectfully into his office. It was an exquisite physical shock and it gave him a new awareness. He noticed the way men looked at him as he passed them on the street. He realized suddenly that over fifteen hundred human beings depended on him for their livelihood.

There was satisfaction in the way a path cleared for him and Duff as they crossed the floor of the Exchange each morning to take their places in the reserved leather armchairs of the members' lounge. When Duff and he leaned together and talked quietly before the trading began, even the other big fish watched them. Hradsky with his fierce eyes hooded by sleepy lids, Jock and Trevor Heyns, Karl Lochtkamper – any of them would have given a day's production from their mines to overhear those conversations.

'Buy!' said Sean.

'Buy! Buy! Buy!' clamoured the pack and the prices jumped as they hit them, then slumped back as they sucked their money away and put it to work elsewhere.

Then one March morning in 1886 the thrill became so acute it was almost an orgasm. Max left the chair at Norman Hradsky's side and crossed the lounge towards them. He stopped in front of them, lifted his sad eyes off the patterned carpet and almost apologetically proffered a loose sheaf of papers.

'Good morning, Mr Courtney. Good morning, Mr Charleywood. Mr Hradsky has asked me to bring this new share issue to your attention. Perhaps you would be interested in these reports, which are, of course, confidential, but he feels they are worthy of your support.'

You have power when you can force a man who hates you to ask for your favours. After the first advance by Hradsky they worked together often. Hradsky never acknowledged their existence by word or look. Each morning Duff called a cheerful greeting across the full width of the lounge, 'Hello, chatterbox,' or 'Sing for us, Norman.'

Hradsky's eyes would flicker and he would sag a little lower into his chair, but before the bell started the day's trading Max would stand up and come across to them, leaving his master staring into the empty fireplace. A few soft sentences exchanged and Max would walk back to Hradsky's side.

Their combined fortunes were irresistible: in one wild morning's trading alone they added another fifty thousand to their store of pounds.

An untaught boy handles his first rifle like a toy. Sean was twenty-two. The power he held was a more deadly weapon than any rifle, and much sweeter, more satisfying to use. It was a game at first with the Witwatersrand as a chessboard, men and gold for pieces. A word or a signature on a slip of paper would set the gold jingling and the men scampering. The consequences were remote and all that mattered was the score, the score chalked up in black figures on a bank statement. Then in that same March he was made to realize that a man wiped off the board could not be laid back in the box with as much compassion as a carved wooden knight.

Karl Lochtkamper, the German with a big laugh and a happy face, laid himself open. He needed money to develop a new property on the east end of the Rand; he borrowed and signed short-term notes on his loans, certain that he could extend them if necessary. He borrowed secretly from men he thought he could trust. He was vulnerable and the sharks smelt him out.

'Where is Lochtkamper getting his money?' asked Max.

'Do you know?' asked Sean.

'No, but I can guess.'

Then the next day Max came back to them again.

'He has eight notes out. Here is the list,' he whispered sadly. 'Mr Hradsky will buy the ones that have a cross against them. Can you handle the rest?'

'Yes,' said Sean.

They closed on Karl on the last day of the quarter; they called the loans and gave him twenty-four hours to meet them. Karl went to each of the three banks in turn.

'I'm sorry, Mr Lochtkamper, we have loaned over our budget for this quarter.'

'Mr Hradsky is holding your notes – I'm sorry.'

'I'm sorry, Mr Lochtkamper, Mr Charleywood is one of our directors.'

Karl Lochtkamper rode back to the Exchange. He walked across the floor and into the lounge for the last time. He stood in the centre of the big room, his face grey, his voice bitter and broken.

'Let Jesus have this much mercy on you when your time comes. Friends! My friends! Sean, how many times haf we drunk together? And you, Duff, was it yesterday you shook my hand?'

Then he went back across the floor, out through the doors. His suite in the Great North Hotel wasn't fifty yards from the Exchange. In the members' lounge they heard the pistol shot quite clearly.

That night Duff and Sean got drunk together in the Victoria rooms.

'Why did he have to do it? Why did he have to kill himself?'

'He didn't,' answered Duff. 'He was a quitter.'

'If I'd known he was going to do that – my God, if only I'd known.'

'Damn it, man, he took a chance and lost – it's not our fault. He would have done the same to us.'

'I don't like this – it's dirty. Let's get out, Duff.'

'Someone gets knocked down in the rush and you want to cry "enough!"'

'It's different now somehow, it wasn't like this at the start.'

'Yes, and it'll be different in the morning. Come on, laddie, I know what you need.'

'Where are we going?'

'To the Opera House.'

'What will Candy say?'

'Candy doesn't have to know.'

Duff was right; it was different in the morning. There was the usual hurly-burly of work at the office and some tense action at the Exchange. He thought about Karl only once during the day and somehow it didn't seem to matter so much. They sent him a nice wreath.

He had faced the reality of the game he was playing. He had considered the alternative which was to get out with the fortune he had already made; but to do that would mean giving up the power he held. The addiction was already seated too deeply, he could not deny it. So his subconscious opened, sucked in his conscience and swallowed it deep down into its gut. He could feel it struggling there sometimes, but the longer it stayed swallowed the more feeble those struggles became. Duff comforted him: Duff's words were like a gastric juice that helped to digest that lump in the gut and he had not yet learned that what Duff said and what Duff did were not necessarily what Duff believed.

Play the game without mercy, play to win.

Duff stood with his back to the fireplace in Sean's office smoking a cheroot while they waited for the carriage to take them up to the Exchange. The fire behind him silhouetted his slimly tapered legs with the calves encased in polished black leather. He still wore his top coat, for the winter morning was cold. It fell open at his throat to show a diamond that sparkled and glowed in his cravat.

'. . . you get used to a woman somehow,' he was saying. 'I've known Candy four years now and yet it seems I've been with her all my life.'

'She's a fine girl,' Sean agreed absently as he dipped his pen and scribbled his signature on the document in front of him.

'I'm thirty-five now,' Duff went on. 'If I'm ever to have a son of my own . . .'

Sean laid down the pen deliberately and looked up at him; he was starting to grin.

'The man said to me once "They take you into their soft little minds" and again he said "They don't share, they possess". Is this a new tune I hear?'

Duff shifted uneasily from one foot to the other.

'Things change,' he defended himself. 'I'm thirty-five . . .'

'You're repeating yourself,' Sean accused and Duff smiled weakly.

'Well, the truth is . . .'

He never finished the sentence; hooves beat urgently in the street outside and both their faces swung in the direction of the window.

'Big hurry!' said Sean coming quickly to his feet. 'Big trouble!' He crossed to the window. 'It's Curtis, and by his face it's not good news he brings.'

There were voices outside the door raised in agitation and the quick rush of feet, then Timothy Curtis burst into the room without knocking. He wore a miner's overall and splattered gumboots. 'We've hit a mud rush on the ninth level.'

'How bad?' Duff snapped.

'Bad enough – it's flooded right back to number eight.'

'Jesus, that will take two months at least to clear,' Sean exclaimed. 'Does anyone else in town know – have you told anyone?'

'I came straight here – Cronje and five men were up at the face when it blew.'

'Get back there immediately,' ordered Sean, 'but ride quietly, we don't want the whole world to know there's trouble. Don't let a soul off the property. We must have time to sell out.'

'Yes, Mr Courtney.' Curtis hesitated. 'Cronje and five others were hit by the rush. Shall I send word to their wives?'

'Can't you understand English? I don't want a whisper of this to get out before ten o'clock. We've got to have time.'

'But, Mr Courtney—' Curtis was appalled. He stood staring at Sean and Sean felt the sick little stirring of guilt. Six men drowned in treacle-thick mud ... He made an irresolute gesture with his hands.

'We can't—' He stopped and Duff cut in.

'They're dead now, and they'll be just as dead when we tell their wives at ten o'clock. Get going, Curtis.'

They sold their shares in the Little Sister within an hour of the start of trading and a week later they bought them back at half the price. Two months later the Little Sister was back on full production again.

18

They split their land at Orange Grove into plots and sold them, all but a hundred acres and on that they started building a house. Into the designing of it they poured their combined energy and imagination. With money Duff seduced the horticulturist of the Capetown Botanical Gardens and brought him up by express coach. They showed him the land.

'Make me a garden,' said Duff.

'The whole hundred acres?'

'Yes.'

'It'll cost a pretty penny.'

'That is no problem.'

The carpets came from Persia, the wood from the Knysna forests and the marble from Italy. On the gates at the entrance to the main drive they engraved the words 'At Xanadu did Kublai Khan a stately pleasure dome decree'. As the gardener had predicted, it all cost a pretty penny. Each afternoon when the Exchange closed they would drive up together and watch the builders at work. One day Candy came with them and they showed it off to her like two small boys.

'This will be the ballroom.' Sean bowed to her. 'May I have the pleasure of this dance?'

'Thank you, sir.' She curtsied, then swept away on his arm across the unsanded boards.

'This will be the staircase,' Duff told her, 'marble – black and white marble – and there on the main landing in a glass case will be Hradsky's head, beautifully mounted with an apple in his mouth.'

They climbed laughing up the rough concrete ramp.

'This is Sean's room – the bed is being made of oak,

thick oak to withstand punishment.' They trooped with linked arms down the passage.

'And this is my room – I was thinking of a solid gold bath but the builder says it's too heavy and Sean says it's too vulgar. Look at that view; from here you can see out across the whole valley. I could lie in bed in the mornings and read the prices on the Exchange floor with a telescope.'

'It's lovely,' Candy said dreamily.

'You like it?'

'Oh, yes.'

'It could be your room too.'

Candy started to blush and then her face tightened with annoyance. 'He was right – you are vulgar.'

She started for the door and Sean fumbled for his cigars to cover his embarrassment. With two quick steps Duff caught her and turned her to face him. 'You sweet idiot, that was a proposal.'

'Let me go.' Near to tears she twisted in his hands. 'I don't think you're funny.'

'Candy – I'm serious. Will you marry me?'

The cigar dropped out of Sean's mouth but he caught it before it hit the ground. Candy was standing very still, her eyes fastened on Duff's face.

'Yes or no – will you marry me?'

She nodded once slowly and then twice very fast.

Duff looked at Sean over his shoulder. 'Leave us, laddie.'

On the way back to town Candy had regained her voice. She chattered happily and Duff answered her with his lopsided grin. Sean hunched morosely in one corner of the carriage. His cigar was burning unevenly and he threw it out of the window.

'You'll let me keep the Victoria rooms, I hope, Candy.'

There was a silence.

'What do you mean?' asked Duff.

271

'Two's company,' Sean answered.

'Oh, no,' Candy exclaimed.

'It's your house as well.' Duff spoke sharply.

'I give it to you – a wedding present.'

'Oh, shut up,' Duff grinned, 'it's big enough for all of us.'

Candy crossed quickly to Sean's seat and put her hand on his shoulder.

'Please – we've been together a long time. We'd be lonely without you.'

Sean grunted.

'Please!'

'He'll come,' said Duff.

'Please.'

'Oh, well—' Sean frowned ungraciously.

– 19 –

They went racing at Milnerton. Candy with a hat full of ostrich feathers, Sean and Duff with pearl grey toppers and gold heads on their canes.

'You can pay for your wedding gown by putting fifty guineas on Trade Wind! She can't lose—' Duff told Candy.

'What about Mr Hradsky's new filly? I've heard she's a good bet,' Candy asked and Duff frowned.

'You want to go over to the enemy?'

'I thought you and Hradsky were almost partners.' Candy twirled her parasol. 'From the rumours I've heard you work with him all the time.'

Mbejane slowed the carriage as they ran into the crush of pedestrians and coaches outside the Turf Club gates.

'Well you've heard wrong both times. His Sun Dancer will never hold Trade Wind over the distance, she's bred too light in the legs. Frenchified with Huguenot blood; she'll fade within the mile. And as far as Hradsky being our partner, we throw him an occasional bone. Isn't that right, Sean?'

Sean was watching Mbejane's back. The Zulu, in loin clothes only and his spears laid carefully on the boards at his feet, was handling the horses with an easy familiarity. They cocked their ears back to catch his voice, deep and soft, as he talked to them.

'Isn't that right, Sean?' Duff repeated.

'Of course,' agreed Sean vaguely. 'You know – I think I'll get Mbejane a livery. He looks out of place in those skins.'

'Well, some of the other horses from the same stud were stayers. Sun Honey won the Cape Derby twice and Eclipse showed up the English stock in the Metropolitan Handicap last year,' Candy argued.

'Huh,' Duff smiled his superiority, 'well, you can take my word for it that Trade Wind will walk the main race today and he'll be back in his stable before Sun Dancer sees the finishing post.'

'Maroon and gold – the same as our racing colours,' Sean muttered thoughtfully. 'That would go very well with his black skin, perhaps a turban with an ostrich feather in it.'

'What the hell are you talking about?' complained Duff.

'Mbejane's livery.'

They left the carriage in the reserved area and went through to the members' grandstand, Candy sailing prettily between her escorts.

'Well, Duff, we've got the nicest looking woman here today.'

'Thank you.' Candy smiled up at Sean.

'Is that why you keep trying to look down the front of her dress?' challenged Duff.

'You filthy-minded beast.' Sean was shocked.

'Don't deny, it,' Candy teased, 'but I find it very flattering – you're welcome.'

They moved through the throng of butterfly-coloured dresses and stiffly-suited men. A ripple of greetings moved with them.

'Morning, Mr Courtney.' The accent was on the 'Mister'. 'How's your Trade Wind for the big race?'

'Put your pants on him.'

'Hello, Duff, congratulations on your engagement.'

'Thanks, Jock, it's time you took the plunge as well.'

They were rich, they were young, they were handsome and all the world admired them. Sean felt good, with a pretty girl on his arm and a friend walking beside him.

'There's Hradsky – let's go across and engage in a little hog-baiting,' Duff suggested.

'Why do you hate him so much?' Candy asked softly.

'Look at him and answer your own question. Have you ever seen anything more pompous, joyless and unlovable?'

'Oh, leave him alone, Duff, don't spoil the day. Let's go down to the paddock.'

'Come on!' Duff steered them across to where Hradsky and Max were standing alone by the rail of the track.

'Salome, Norman, and peace to you also, Maximilian.' Hradsky nodded and Max murmured sadly; his lashes touched his cheeks as he blinked.

'I noticed you two chatting away and thought I would come across and listen to your stimulating repartee.'

He received no answer and went on. 'I saw your new filly exercising on the practice track yesterday evening and I said to myself, Norman's got a girl friend – that's what it is – he's bought a hack for his lady. But now they tell me you are going to race her. Oh, Norman, I wish you'd consult me before you do these silly things. You're an impetuous little devil at times.'

'Mr Hradsky is confident that Sun Dancer will make a reasonable showing today,' Max murmured.

'I was about to offer you a side bet, but being a naturally

kind-hearted person, I feel it would be taking an unfair advantage.'

A small crowd had gathered round them listening with anticipation. Candy tugged gently at Duff's elbow trying to lead him away.

'I thought five hundred guineas would be acceptable to Norman.' Duff shrugged. 'But let's forget it.'

Hradsky made a fierce little sign with his hands and Max interpreted smoothly. 'Mr Hradsky suggests a thousand.'

'Rash, Norman, extremely rash.' Duff sighed. 'But I suppose I must accommodate you.'

They walked down to the refreshment pavilion. Candy was quiet awhile, then she said, 'An enemy like Mr Hradsky is a luxury that even you two gods can't afford. Why don't you leave him alone?'

'It's a hobby of Duff's,' explained Sean as they found seats at one of the tables. 'Waiter – bring us a bottle of Pol Roger.'

Before the big race they went down to the paddock. A steward opened the wicket gate for them and they passed into the ring of circling horses. A gnome in silk of maroon and gold came to meet them and touched his cap then stood awkwardly, fingering his whip.

'He looks good this morning, sir.' The little man nodded at Trade Wind. There was a dark patch of sweat on the horse's shoulder and he mouthed the snaffle, lifting his feet delicately. Once he snorted and rolled his eyes in mock terror.

'He's got an edge on him, sir, eager kind of – if you follow me.'

'I want you to win, Harry,' said Duff.

'So do I, sir, I'll do my best.'

'There's a thousand guineas for you if you do.'

'A thousand—' the jockey repeated on an outgoing breath.

Duff looked across to where Hradsky and Max were standing talking to their trainer. He caught Hradsky's eye, glanced significantly at Hradsky's honey-coloured filly and shook his head sympathetically.

'Win for me, Harry,' he said softly.

'That I will, sir!'

The groom led the big stallion across to them and Sean flicked the jockey up into the saddle.

'Good luck.'

Harry settled his cap and gathered up the reins; he winked at Sean, his hobgoblin face wrinkling in a grin.

'There's no better luck than a thousand guineas, sir, if you follow me.'

'Come on.' Duff caught Candy's arm. 'Let's get a place at the rail.'

They hustled her out of the paddock and across the members' enclosure. The rail was crowded but a place opened for them respectfully and no one jostled them.

'I can't understand you two,' Candy laughed breathlessly. 'You make an extravagant bet, then you fix it so you can get nothing even if you win.'

'Money's not the problem,' Duff assured her.

'He won that much from me at Klabejas last night,' Sean commented. 'If Trade Wind beats the filly his prize will be the look on Hradsky's face – the loss of a thousand guineas will hurt him like a kick between the legs.'

The horses came parading past, stepping high next to the grooms who held them, then they turned free and cantered back, dancing sideways, throwing their heads, shining in the sunlight like the bright silk upon their backs. They moved away round the curve of the track.

The crowd rustled with excitement, a bookmaker's voice carried over the buzz.

'Twenty-to-one bar two. Sun Dancer at fives. Trade Wind even money.'

Duff showed his teeth as he smiled. 'That's right, you tell the people.'

Candy twisted her gloves nervously and looked up at Sean.

'You there in the grandstand – can you see what they're doing?'

'They're in line now, moving up together – it looks as though they'll get away first time,' Sean told her without taking his binoculars from his eyes. 'Yes, there they go – they're away!'

'Tell me, tell me,' commanded Candy, pounding Sean's shoulder.

'Harry's showing in front already – can you see the filly, Duff?'

'I saw a flash of green in the pack – yes, there she is lying sixth or seventh.'

'What horse is that next to Trade Wind?'

'That's Hamilton's gelding, don't worry about him, he won't last to the turn.'

The frieze of horses, their heads going like hammers and the dust lifting pale and thin behind them, were framed by the guide rail and the white mine dumps beyond them. Like a string of dark beads they moved up the back stretch and then bunched in the straight.

'Trade Wind's still there – I think he's making ground – the gelding's finished and no sign of the filly yet.'

'Yes! There she is, Duff, wide on the outside. She's moving up.'

'Come on, my darling—' Duff half whispered. 'Let's see you foot it now.'

'She's clear of the pack – she's coming up, Duff, she's coming up fast,' Sean warned.

'Come on, Trade Wind, hold her off,' Duff pleaded. 'Keep her there, boy.'

The pounding of the hooves reached them now, a sound

277

like distant surf, but rising sharply. The colours showed, emerald green above a honey skin and maroon and gold leading on the bay.

'Trade Wind – come on Trade Wind,' shrieked Candy. Her hat flopped over her eyes as she hopped; she ripped it off impatiently and her hair tumbled to her shoulders.

'She's catching him, Duff!'

'Give him the whip, Harry, for Christ's sake – the whip, man.'

The hoof beats crescendoed, thundered up to them, then passed. The filly's nose was at Harry's boot, creeping steadily forward, now level with Trade Wind's heaving shoulder.

'The whip, God damn you,' screamed Duff, 'give him the whip.'

Harry's right arm moved, fast as a mamba – crack, crack; they heard the whip above the howling crowd, above the drumming of hooves and the bay jumped at its sting. Like a pair in harness the two horses swept over the finishing line.

'Who won?' Candy asked as though she were in pain.

'I couldn't see, damn it,' Duff answered.

'Nor could I—' Sean took out his handkerchief and wiped his forehead. 'That didn't do my heart any good – as Francois would say. Have a cigar, Duff.'

'Thanks – I need one.'

Everyone in the crowd was turned to face the board above the judges' box and an uneasy silence held them.

'Why do they take such a long time to make up their minds?' complained Candy. 'I'm so upset that I can only last a minute before I visit the Ladies' Room.'

'The numbers are going up,' shouted Sean.

'Who is it?' Candy jumped to try and see over the heads of the crowd then stopped hurriedly with an expression of alarm on her face.

'Number Sixteen,' bellowed Duff and Sean together, 'it's Trade Wind!'

Sean punched Duff in the chest and Duff leaned over and snapped Sean's cigar in half. Then they caught Candy between them and hugged her. She let out a careful shriek and fought her way out of their arms. 'Excuse me,' she said and fled.

'Let me buy you a drink.' Sean lit the mutilated stump of his cigar.

'No, it's my honour, I insist.' Duff took his arm and they walked with big satisfied grins towards the pavilion. Hradsky was sitting at one of the tables with Max. Duff walked up behind him, lifted his top hat off his head with one hand and with the other ruffled Hradsky's few remaining hairs.

'Never mind, Norman, you can't win all the time.'

Hradsky turned slowly. He retrieved his hat and smoothed back his hair, his eyes glittered yellow.

'He's going to talk,' whispered Duff excitedly.

'I agree with you, Mr Charleywood, you can't win all the time,' said Norman Hradsky. It came out quite clearly with only a small catch on the 'c's' – they were always difficult letters for him. He stood up, put his hat back on his head and walked away.

'I will have a cheque delivered to your office early on Monday morning,' Max told them quietly without taking his eyes off the table. Then he stood up and followed Hradsky.

Sean came through from the bathroom, his beard in wild disorder and a bath-towel round his waist.

> 'The famous Duke of York
> He had ten thousand men
> He marched them up to the top of the hill
> And he marched them down again.'

He sang as he poured bay rum from a cut-glass bottle into his cupped hands and rubbed it into his hair. Duff sat in one of the gilt chairs watching him. Sean combed his hair carefully then smiled at himself in the mirror.

'You magnificent creature,' Sean told his reflection.

'You're getting fat,' Duff grunted.

Sean looked hurt. 'It's muscle.'

'You've got a backside on you like a hippopotamus.'

Sean removed his towel and turned his back to the mirror; he surveyed it over his shoulder.

'I need a heavy hammer to drive a long nail,' he protested.

'Oh, no,' groaned Duff. 'Your wit at this time of the morning is like pork for breakfast, heavy on the stomach.'

Sean took a silk shirt out of his drawer, held it like a toreador's cape, made two passes and swirled it onto his back with a half veronica.

'Olé!' applauded Duff wryly. Sean pulled on his trousers and sat to fit his boots.

'You're in a nice mood this morning,' he told Duff.

'I've just come through an emotional hurricane!'

'What's the trouble?'

'Candy wants a church wedding.'

'Is that bad?'

'Well, it's not good.'

'Why?'

'Is your memory so short?'

'Oh, you mean your other wife.'

'That's right, my other wife.'

'Have you told Candy about her?'

'Good God, no.' Duff looked horrified.

'Yes, I see your problem – what about Candy's husband? Doesn't that even the score between you?'

'No, he has gone to his reward.'

'Well, that's convenient. Does anyone else know you're married already?' Duff shook his head.

'What about Francois?'

'No, I never told him.'

'Well, what's your problem – take her down to the church and marry her.'

Duff looked uncomfortable.

'I don't mind marrying a second time in a magistrate's court, it would only be a couple of old Dutchmen I'd be cheating, but to go into a church—' Duff shook his head.

'I'd be the only one who'd know,' said Sean.

'You and the headman.'

'Duff,' Sean beamed at him. 'Duff, my boy, you have scruples – this is amazing!'

Duff squirmed a little in his chair.

'Let me think.' Sean held his forehead dramatically. 'Yes, yes, it's coming to me – that's it.'

'Come on, tell me.' Duff sat on the edge of his chair.

'Go to Candy and tell her it's all fixed, not only are you prepared to marry her in a church but you're even going to build your own church.'

'That's wonderful,' Duff murmured sarcastically, 'that's the way out of my difficulties all right.'

'Let me finish.' Sean started filling his silver cigar case. 'You also tell her that you want a civil ceremony as well – I

281

believe that's what royalty do. Tell her that, it should win her over.'

'I still don't follow you.'

'Then you build your own chapel up at Xanadu – we can find a distinguished-looking character, dress him up in a dog collar and teach him the right words. That keeps Candy happy. Immediately after the service the priest takes the coach for Capetown. You take Candy down to the magistrate's office and that keeps you happy.'

Duff looked stunned then slowly his face broke into a great happy smile. 'Genius – pure inspired genius.'

Sean buttoned his waistcoat. 'Think nothing of it. And now if you'll excuse me I'll go and do some work – one of us has to make sufficient to allow you to indulge these strange fancies of yours.'

Sean shrugged on his coat, picked up his cane and swung it. The gold head gave it a balance like a handmade shotgun. The silk next to his skin and the halo of bay rum round his head made him feel good.

He went down the stairs. Mbejane had the carriage waiting for him in the Hotel yard. The body tilted slightly at Sean's weight and the leather upholstery welcomed him with a yielding softness. He lit his first cigar of the day and Mbejane smiled at him.

'I see you, Nkosi.'

'I see you also, Mbejane, what is that lump on the side of your head?'

'Nkosi, I was a little drunk, otherwise that ape of Basuto would never have touched me with his fighting stick.'

Mbejane rolled the carriage smoothly out of the yard and into the street.

'What were you fighting about?'

Mbejane shrugged. 'Must a man have a reason to fight?'

'It is usual.'

'It is in my memory that there was a woman,' said Mbejane.

'That is also usual – who won this fight?'

'The man bled a little, his friends took him away. The woman, when I left, was smiling in her sleep.'

Sean laughed, then ran his eyes over the undulating plain of Mbejane's bare back. It was definitely not in keeping. He hoped his secretary had remembered to speak to the tailor. They pulled up in front of his offices. One of his clerks hurried down off the veranda and opened the door of the carriage.

'Good morning, Mr Courtney.'

Sean went up the stairs with his clerk running ahead of him like a hunting dog.

'Good morning, Mr Courtney,' another polite chorus from the row of desks in the main office. Sean waved his cane at them and went through into his own office. His portrait leered at him from above the fireplace and he winked at it.

'What have we this morning, Johnson?'

'These requisitions, sir, and the pay cheques, sir, and development reports from the engineers, sir, and . . .'

Johnson was a greasy-haired little man in a greasy-looking alpaca coat; with each 'sir' he made a greasy little bow. He was efficient so Sean hired him, but that didn't mean he liked him.

'You got a stomach ache, Johnson?'

'No, sir.'

'Well, for God's sake, stand up straight, man.'

Johnson shot to attention.

'Now let's have them one at a time.'

Sean dropped into his chair. At this time of the day came the grind. He hated the paper work and so he tackled it with grim concentration, making random checks on the long rows of figures, trying to associate names with faces and querying requisitions that appeared exorbitant until finally he wrote his signature between the last of Johnson's carefully pencilled crosses and threw his pen onto the desk.

'What else is there?'

'Meeting with Mr Maxwell from the Bank at twelve-thirty, sir.'

'And then?'

'The agent for Brooke Bros. at one, and immediately after that Mr MacDougal, sir, then you're expected up at the Candy Deep mine.'

'Thank you, Johnson, I'll be at the Exchange as usual this morning if anything out of the ordinary comes up.'

'Very good, Mr Courtney. Just one other thing.' Johnson pointed at the brown paper parcel on the couch across the room. 'From your tailor.'

'Ah!' Sean smiled. 'Send my servant in here.' He walked across and opened the parcel. Within a few minutes Mbejane filled the doorway.

'Nkosi?'

'Mbejane – your new uniform.' Sean pointed at the clothes laid out on the couch. Mbejane's eyes switched to the gold and maroon finery, his expression suddenly dead.

'Put it on – come on, let's see how you look.'

Mbejane crossed to the couch and picked up the jacket. 'These are for me?'

'Yes, come on, put it on.' Sean laughed.

Mbejane hesitated, then slowly he loosened his loin cloth and let it drop. Sean watched him impatiently as he buttoned on the jacket and pantaloons, then he walked in a critical circle around the Zulu.

'Not bad,' he muttered, and then in Zulu, 'Is it not beautiful?'

284

Mbejane wriggled his shoulders against the unfamiliar feel of the cloth and said nothing.

'Well, Mbejane, do you like it?'

'When I was a child I went with my father to trade cattle at Port Natal. There was a man who went about the town with a monkey on a chair, the monkey danced and the people laughed and threw money to it. That monkey had such a suit as this. Nkosi, I do not think he was a very happy monkey.'

The smile slipped off Sean's face. 'You would rather wear your skins?'

'What I wear is the dress of a warrior of Zululand.'

There was still no expression on Mbejane's face. Sean opened his mouth to argue with him but before he could speak he lost his temper.

'You'll wear that uniform,' he shouted. 'You'll wear what I tell you to wear and you'll do it with a smile, do you hear me?'

'Nkosi, I hear you.' Mbejane picked up his loin cloth of leopard tails and left the office. When Sean went out to the carriage Mbejane was sitting on the driver's seat in his new livery. All the way to the Exchange his back was stiff with protest and neither of them spoke. Sean glared at the doorman of the Exchange, drank four brandies during the morning, rode back to his office again at noon scowling at Mbejane's still protesting back, shouted at Johnson, snapped at the bank manager, routed the representative from Brooke Bros. and drove out to the Candy Deep in a high old rage. But Mbejane's silence was impenetrable and Sean couldn't re-open the argument without sacrifice of pride. He burst into the new administrative building of the Candy Deep and threw the staff into confusion.

'Where's Mr du Toit?' he roared.

'He's down the Number Three shaft, Mr Courtney.'

285

'What the hell is he doing down there? He's supposed to be waiting for me here.'

'He didn't expect you for another hour, sir.'

'Well, get me some overalls and a mining helmet, don't just stand there.'

He clapped the tin hat on his head and stamped his heavy gumboots across to the Number Three shaft. The skip dropped him smoothly five hundred feet into the earth and he climbed out at the tenth level.

'Where's Mr du Toit?' he demanded of the shift boss at the lift station.

'He's up at the face, sir.'

The floor of the drive was rough and muddy; his gumboots squelched as he set off down the tunnel. His carbide lamp lit the uneven rock walls with a flat white light and he felt himself starting to sweat. Two natives pushing a cocopan back along the railway lines forced him to flatten himself against one wall to allow them to pass and while he waited he felt inside his overalls for his cigar case. As he pulled it out it slipped from his hand and plunked into the mud. The cocopan was gone by that time so he stooped to pick up the case. His ear came within an inch of the wall and a puzzled expression replaced his frown of annoyance. The rock was squeaking. He laid his ear against it. It sounded like someone grinding his teeth. He listened to it for a while trying to guess the cause; it wasn't the echo of shovels or drills, it wasn't water. He walked another thirty yards or so down the drive and listened again. Not so loud here but now the grinding noise was punctuated with an occasional metallic snap like the breaking of a knife blade. Strange; very strange; he had never heard anything like it before. He walked on down the drive, his bad mood lost in his preoccupation with this new problem. Before he reached the face he met Francois.

'Hello, Mr Courtney.' Sean had long since given up

trying to stop Francois calling him that. 'Gott, I'm sorry I wasn't there to meet you. I thought you were coming at three.'

'That's all right, Francois, how are you?'

'My rheumatism's been giving me blazes, Mr Courtney, but otherwise I'm all right. How's Mr Charleywood?'

'He's fine.' Sean couldn't restrain his curiosity any longer. 'Tell me something, Franz, just now I put my ear against the wall of the drive and I heard an odd noise, I couldn't make out what it was.'

'What kind of noise?'

'A sort of grinding, like – like . . .' Sean searched for words to describe it, 'like two pieces of glass being rubbed together.'

Francois's eyes flew wide open and then began to bulge, the colour of his face changed to grey and he caught Sean's arm.

'Where?'

'Back along the drive.'

The breath jammed in Francois's throat and he struggled to speak through it, shaking Sean's arm desperately.

'Cave-in!' he croaked. 'Cave-in, man!'

He started to run but Sean grabbed him. Francois struggled wildly.

'Francois, how many men up at the face?'

'Cave-in.' Francois's voice was now hysterically shrill. 'Cave-in.' He broke Sean's grip and raced away towards the lift station, the mud flying from his gumboots. His terror infected Sean and he ran a dozen paces after Francois before he stopped himself. For precious seconds he wavered with fear slithering round like a reptile in his stomach; go back to call the others and perhaps die with them or follow Francois and live. Then the fear in his belly found a mate, a thing just as slimy and cold; its name was shame, and shame it was that drove him back towards the face. There

287

were five blacks and a white man there, bare-chested and shiny with sweat in the heat. Sean shouted those two words at them and they reacted the way bathers do when someone on the beach shouts 'shark'. The same moment of paralysed horror, then the panic. They came stampeding back along the tunnel. Sean ran with them, the mud sucked at his heavy boots and his legs were weak with easy living and riding in carriages. One by one the others passed him.

'Wait for me,' he wanted to scream. 'Wait for me.' He slipped on the greasy footing, scraping his shoulder on the rough wall as he fell, and dragged himself up again, mud plastered in his beard, the blood humming in his ears. Alone now he blundered on down the tunnel. With a crack like a rifle shot one of the thick shoring timbers broke under the pressure of the moving rock and dust smoked from the roof of the tunnel in front of him. He staggered on and all around him the earth was talking, groaning, protesting, with little muffled shrieks. The timbers joined in again, crackling and snapping, and as slowly as a theatre curtain the rock sagged down from above him. The tunnel was thick with dust that smothered the beam of his lamp and rasped his throat. He knew then that he wasn't going to make it but he ran on with the loose rock starting to fall about him. A lump hit his mining helmet and jarred him so that he nearly fell. Blinded by the swirling dust fog he crashed at full run into the abandoned cocopan that blocked the tunnel, he sprawled over the metal body of the trolley with his thighs bruised from the collision.

'Now I'm finished,' he thought, but instinctively he pulled himself up and started to grope his way around the cocopan to continue his flight. With a roar the tunnel in front of him collapsed. He dropped on his knees and crawled between the wheels of the cocopan, wriggling under the sturdy steel body just an instant before the roof above him collapsed also. The noise of the fall around him seemed

288

to last for ever, but then it was over and the rustling and grating of the rock as it settled down was almost silence in comparison. His lamp was lost and the darkness pressed as heavily on him as the earth squeezed down on his tiny shelter. The air was solid with dust and he coughed; he coughed until his chest ached and he tasted salty blood in his mouth. There was hardly room to move, the steel body of the trolley was six inches above him, but he struggled until he managed to open the front of his overalls and tear a piece off the tail of his shirt. He held the silk like a surgical mask across his mouth and nose. It strained the dust out of the air so he could breathe. The dust settled; his coughing slowed and finally stopped. He felt surprise that he was still alive and cautiously he started exploring. He tried to straighten out his legs but his feet touched rock. He felt with his hands, six inches of head room and perhaps twelve inches on either side, warm mud underneath him and rock and steel all around. He took off his helmet and used it as a pillow. He was in a steel coffin buried five hundred feet deep. He felt the first flutter of panic. 'Keep your mind busy, think of something, think of anything but the rock around you, count your assets,' he told himself. He started to search his pockets, moving with difficulty in the cramped space.

'One silver cigar case with two Havanas.' He laid it down next to him.

'One box of matches, wet.' He placed it on top of the case.

'One pocket watch.'

'One handkerchief, Irish linen, monogrammed.'

'One comb, tortoiseshell – a man is judged by his appearance.' He started to comb his beard but found immediately that though this occupied his hands it left his mind free. He put the comb down next to his matches.

'Twenty-five pounds in gold sovereigns—' He counted

them carefully, 'yes, twenty-five. I shall order a bottle of good champagne.' The dust was chalky in his mouth so he went on hurriedly, 'And a Malay girl from the Opera. No, why be mean – ten Malay girls. I'll have them dance for me, that'll pass the time. I'll promise them a sovereign each to bolster their enthusiasm.'

He continued the search, but there was nothing else. 'Gumboots, socks, well-cut trousers, shirt torn I'm afraid, overalls, a tin hat, and that's all.'

With his possessions laid out carefully beside him and his cell explored he had to start thinking. First he thought about his thirst. The mud in which he lay was too thick to yield water. He tried straining it through his shirt without success, and then he thought about air. It seemed quite fresh and he decided that sufficient was filtering in from the loosely packed rock around him to keep him alive.

To keep him alive – alive until the thirst killed. Until he died curled up like a foetus in the warm womb of the earth. He laughed, a worm in a dark warm womb. He laughed again and recognized it as the beginnings of panic, he thrust his fist into his mouth to stop himself, biting down hard on his knuckles. It was very quiet, the rock had stopped moving.

'How long will it take? Tell me, Doctor. How long have I got?'

'Well, you are sweating. You'll lose moisture quite rapidly. I'd say about four days,' he answered himself.

'What about hunger, Doctor?'

'Oh, no, don't worry about that, you'll be hungry, of course, but the thirst will kill you.'

'And typhoid, or is it typhus, I can never remember. What about that, Doctor?'

'If there were dead men trapped in here with you there'd be a good chance, but you're alone, you know.'

'Do you think I'll go mad, Doctor, not immediately, of course, but in a few days?'

'Yes, you'll go mad.'

'I've never been mad before, not that I know of anyway, but I think it will help to go mad now, don't you?'

'If you mean, will it make it easier, well, I don't know.'

'Ah! now you're being obscure – but I follow you. You mean in that sleep of madness what dreams will come? You mean, will madness be more real than reality? You mean, will dying mad be worse than dying thirsty? But then I may beat the madness. This cocopan might buckle under the strain, after all there must be thousands of tons of rock bearing down on it. That's quite clever, you know, Doctor; as a medical man you should appreciate it. Mother Earth was saved but, alas, the child was stillborn, she bore down too hard.' Sean had spoken aloud, and now he felt foolish. He picked up a piece of stone and tapped the cocopan with it.

'It sounds firm enough. A most pleasing noise, really.' He beat harder on the metal body – one, two, three, one, two, three – then dropped the stone. Soft as an echo, distant as the moon, he heard his taps repeated. His whole body stiffened at the sound, and he started to shiver with excitement. He snatched up the stone: three times he rapped, and three times the answer came back to him.

'They heard me, sweet merciful Christ, they heard me.' He laughed breathlessly. 'Dear Mother Earth, don't bear down, please don't bear down. Just be patient. Wait a few days and by Caesarean they'll take this child out of your womb.'

Mbejane waited until Sean disappeared down the Number Three shaft before he took off his new jacket. He folded it

291

carefully on the driver's seat next to him. He sat and enjoyed the feel of the sun on his skin for a while, then he climbed off the carriage and went to the horses. He took them one at a time to the trough for water then returned them to their harnesses, buckling them in loosely. He picked up his spears from the footboard and moved across to a patch of short grass next to the administrative building. He sat down and went to work on the blade, humming softly to himself as he honed. At last he ran an expert thumb along each edge, grunted, shaved a few hairs off his forearm, smiled contentedly and laid his spears beside him in the grass. He lay back and the sun warmed him to sleep.

The shouting woke him. He sat up and automatically checked the height of the sun. He had slept an hour or more. Duff was shouting and Francois, mud-splattered and frightened-looking, was answering him. They were standing together in front of the administrative building. Duff's horse was sweating. Mbejane stood up and went across to them; he listened closely, trying to understand their staccato voices. They went too fast for him, but something was wrong, that much he knew.

'It's caved in almost to the Number Ten lift station,' Francois said.

'You left him in there,' accused Duff.

'I thought he was following me, but he turned back.'

'What for – why did he turn back?'

'To call the others—'

'Have you started clearing the drive?'

'No, I was waiting for you.'

'You stupid bloody idiot, he might be alive in there . . . every minute is vital.'

'But he hasn't a chance, Mr Charleywood, he must be dead.'

'Shut up, damn you.'

Duff swung away from him and started running towards

292

the shaft. There was a crowd gathered beneath the high steel structure of the head gear, and suddenly Mbejane knew it was Sean. He caught up with Duff before he reached the shaft.

'Is it the Nkosi?'

'Yes.'

'What has happened?'

'The rock has fallen on him.'

Mbejane pushed his way into the skip next to Duff and neither of them spoke again until they reached the tenth level. They went down the drive, only a short way before they reached the end. There were men there with crowbars and shovels standing undecided, waiting for orders, and Mbejane shouldered a path through them. He and Duff stood together in front of the new wall of broken rock that sealed the tunnel, and the silence went on and on. Then Duff turned on the white shift-boss.

'Were you at the face?'

'Yes.'

'He went back to call you, didn't he?'

'Yes.'

'And you left him there?'

The man couldn't look at Duff.

'I thought he was following us,' he muttered.

'You thought only of your own miserable skin,' Duff told him, 'you filthy little coward, you slimy yellow bastard, you . . .'

Mbejane caught Duff's arm and Duff stopped his tirade. They all heard it then – clink, clink, clink.

'It's him – it must be him,' whispered Duff, 'he's alive!' He snatched a crowbar from one of the natives and knocked against the side of the tunnel. They waited, their breathing the only sound, until the answer came back to them louder and sharper than before. Mbejane took the crowbar out of Duff's hands. He thrust it into a crack in the rock jam and his back muscles bunched as he heaved. The bar bent like a liquorice stick, he threw it away and went at the stone with his bare hands.

'You!' Duff snapped at the shift-boss. 'We'll need timber to shore up as we clear the fall – get it.' He turned to the natives. 'Four of you working on the face at one time – the rest of you carry the stone away as we loosen it.'

'Do you want any dynamite?' asked the shift-boss.

'And bring the rock down a second time? Use your brains, man. Go and get that timber and call Mr du Toit while you're at the surface.'

In four hours they cleared fifteen feet of tunnel, breaking the larger slabs of stone with sledge hammers and prising the pieces out of the jam. Duff's body ached and his hands were raw. He had to rest. He walked slowly back to the lift station and there he found blankets and a huge dish of soup.

'Where did this come from?'

'Candy's Hotel, sir. Half Johannesburg is waiting at the head of the shaft.'

Duff huddled into a blanket and drank a little of the soup. 'Where's du Toit?'

'I couldn't find him, sir.'

Up at the face Mbejane worked on. The first four natives came back to rest and fresh men took their place. Mbejane led them, grunting an order occasionally but otherwise reserving his strength for the assault on the rock. For an hour Duff rested and when he returned to the head of the tunnel Mbejane was still there. Duff watched him curl his arms round a piece of stone the size of a beer keg, brace his legs and tear the stone out of the jam. Earth and loose rock followed it, burying Mbejane's legs to the knees, and Duff jumped forward to help him.

Another two hours and Duff had to rest again. This time he led Mbejane back with him, gave him a blanket and made him drink a little soup. They sat next to each other with their backs against the wall of the tunnel and blankets over their shoulders. The shift-boss came to Duff.

'Mrs Rautenbach sent this down for you, sir.'

It was a half-bottle of brandy.

'Tell her, thank you.' Duff pulled the cork with his teeth and swallowed twice. It brought the tears into his eyes – he offered the bottle to Mbejane.

'It is not fitting,' Mbejane demurred.

'Drink.'

Mbejane drank, wiped the mouth of the bottle carefully on his blanket and handed it back. Duff took another swallow and offered it again but Mbejane shook his head.

'A little of that is strength, too much is weakness. There is work to do now.'

Duff corked the bottle.

'How long before we reach him?' asked Mbejane.

'Another day, maybe two.'

'A man can die in two days,' mused the Zulu.

'Not one with a body like a bull and a temper like a devil,' Duff assured him. Mbejane smiled and Duff went on groping for his words in Zulu.

'You love him, Mbejane?'

'Love is a woman's word.'

Mbejane inspected one of his thumbs; the nail was torn loose, standing up like a tombstone; he took it between his teeth, pulled it off and spat it onto the floor of the drive. Duff shuddered as he watched.

'Those baboons will not work unless they are driven.' Mbejane stood up. 'Are you rested?'

'Yes,' lied Duff, and they went back to the face.

Sean lay in the mud with his head on the hard pillow of the helmet. The darkness was as solid as the rock around him. He tried to imagine where the one ended and the other began – by doing that he could stop himself feeling his thirst so strongly. He could hear the ring of hammer on stone and the rattle of rock falling free but it never seemed to come any closer. The whole side of his body was stiff and sore but he could not turn over, his knees caught on the cocopan every time he tried and the air in his little cave was starting to taste stale – his head ached. He moved again, restlessly, and his hand brushed the small pile of sovereigns. He struck at them, scattering them into the mud. They were the bait that had led him into this trap. Now he would give them, and all the millions of others, for just the feel of the wind in his beard and the sun in his face. The darkness clung to him, thick and cloying as black treacle; it seemed to fill his nose, his throat and eyes, smothering him. He groped and found the matchbox. For a few seconds of light he would burn up most of the precious oxygen in his cave and call it fair exchange – but the box was sodden. He struck match after match but the wet heads crumbled without a spark and he threw them away and clenched his eyelids to keep the darkness out. Bright colours formed in front of his closed eyes, moving and rearranging themselves until suddenly and very clearly they formed a picture of Garrick's face. He hadn't thought about his family for months, he had been too busy reaping the golden harvest, but now memories crowded back. There were so many things he had forgotten. Everything else had become unimportant when compared with power and gold – even lives, men's lives, had meant nothing. But now it was his own life, teetering on the edge of the black cliff.

The sound of the sledge-hammers broke into his thoughts again. There were men on the other side of the blocked tunnel trying to save him, working their way into the treacherous rock pile which might collapse again at any minute. People were more valuable than the poisonous metal, the little gold discs that lay smugly beside him in the mud while men struggled to save him.

He thought of Garry, crippled by his careless shotgun, father to the bastard he had sired, of Ada whom he had left without a word of goodbye, of Karl Lochtkamper with the pistol in his hand and half his head splattered across the floor of his bedroom, of other nameless men dead or broken because of him.

Sean ran his tongue across his lips and listened to the hammers; he was certain they were nearer now.

'If I get out of here, it'll be different. I swear it.'

Mbejane rested for four hours in the next thirty-six. Duff watched the flesh melt off him in sweat. He was killing himself. Duff was worn out; he could no longer work with his hands but he was directing the teams who were shoring up the reclaimed tunnel. By the second evening they had cleared a hundred feet of the drive. Duff paced it out and when he reached the face he spoke to Mbejane.

'How long since you last signalled to him?'

Mbejane stepped back with a sledge-hammer in his tattered hands; its shaft was sticky and brown with blood.

'An hour ago and even then it sounded as though there were but the length of a spear between us.'

Duff took a crowbar from one of the other natives and tapped the rock. The answer came immediately.

'He's hitting something made of iron,' Duff said. 'It sounds as though he's only a few feet away. Mbejane, let these other men take over. If you wish you can stay and watch but you must rest again now.'

For answer Mbejane lifted the hammer and swung it against the face. The rock he hit cracked and two of the natives stepped up and levered it loose with their crowbars. At the back of the hole it left in the wall they could see the corner of the cocopan. Everyone stared at it, then Duff shouted.

'Sean, Sean, can you hear me?'

'Stop talking and get me out of here.' Sean's voice was hoarse with thirst and dust, and muffled by the rock.

'He's under the cocopan.'

'It's him.'

'Nkosi, are you all right?'

'We've found him.'

The shouts were picked up by the men working behind them in the drive and passed back to those waiting at the lift station.

'They've found him – he's all right – they've found him.'

Duff and Mbejane jumped forward together, their exhaustion completely forgotten. They cleared the last few lumps of rock and with their shoulders touching knelt and peered under the cocopan.

'Nkosi, I see you.'

'I see you also, Mbejane, what took you so long?'

'Nkosi, there were a few small stones in the way.'

Mbejane reached under the cocopan and with his hands under Sean's armpits pulled him out.

'What a hell of a place you chose to go to ground in, laddie. How are you feeling?'

'Give me some water and I'll be all right.'

'Water – bring water,' shouted Duff.

Sean gulped it, trying to drink the whole mug in one mouthful. He coughed and it shot out of his nose.

'Easy, laddie, easy.' Duff thumped his back. Sean drank the next mugful more slowly and finished panting from the effort.

'That was good.'

'Come on, we've got a doctor waiting up on top.' Duff draped a blanket over his shoulders. Mbejane picked Sean up across his chest.

'Put me down, damn you, I haven't forgotten how to walk.'

Mbejane set him down gently, but his legs buckled like those of a man just out of bed from a long illness and he clutched at Mbejane's arm. Mbejane picked him up again and carried him down to the lift station. They rode up in the skip into the open.

'The moon's shining. And the stars – my God, they're beautiful.' There was wonder in Sean's voice; he sucked the night air into his lungs but it was too rich for him and he started coughing again. There were people waiting at the head of the shaft and they crowded round them as they stepped out of the skip.

'How is he?'

'Are you all right, Sean?'

'Doc Symmonds is waiting in the office.'

'Quickly, Mbejane,' said Duff, 'get him out of the cold.'

One on either side of him they hurried Sean across to the administrative building and laid him on the couch in Francois's office. Symmonds checked him over, looked down his throat and felt his pulse.

'Have you got a closed carriage here?'

'Yes,' Duff answered.

'Well, wrap him up warmly and get him home to bed. With the dust and bad air he's been breathing there's serious danger of pneumonia. I'll come down with you and give him a sedative.'

'I won't need one, Doc,' Sean grinned at him.

'I think I know what's best for you, Mr Courtney.' Doctor Symmonds was a young man. He was the fashionable doctor among the rich of Johannesburg and he took it very seriously.

'Now if you please, we'll get you to your hotel.' He started to pack his instruments back into his valise.

'You're the doctor,' Sean agreed, 'but before we go will

you have a look at my servant's hands, they're in a hell of a mess. There's hardly any meat left on them.'

Doctor Symmonds did not look up from what he was doing. 'I have no Kaffir practice, Mr Courtney, I'm sure you'll find some other doctor to attend to him when we get back to town.'

Sean sat up slowly, he let the blankets slip off his shoulders. He walked across to Doctor Symmonds and held him by the throat against the wall. The doctor had a fine pair of waxed moustaches and Sean took one of them between the thumb and forefinger of his free hand: he plucked it out like feathers from the carcass of a dead fowl and Doctor Symmonds squealed.

'Starting now, Doctor, you have a Kaffir practice,' Sean told him. He pulled the handkerchief out of Symmonds' top pocket and dabbed at the little drops of blood on the doctor's bare upper lip.

'Be a good fellow – see to my servant.'

– 21 –

When Sean woke the next morning the hands of the grandfather clock across the bedroom pointed at the top of their dial. Candy was in the room opening the curtains and with her were two waiters, each with a loaded tray.

'Good morning, how is our hero this morning?' The waiters put down their trays and went out as she came across to Sean's bed.

Sean blinked the sleep out of his eyes. 'My throat feels as though I've just finished a meal of broken glass.'

'That's the dust,' Candy told him and laid her hands on his forehead. Sean's hand sneaked round behind her and she squeaked as he pinched her. Standing well away from the bed she rubbed her bottom and made a face at him.

'There's nothing wrong with you!'

'Good, then I'll get up.' Sean started to pull back the bedclothes.

'Not until the doctor's had a look at you, you won't.'

'Candy, if that bastard puts one foot in this room I'll punch him so hard in the mouth his teeth will march out of his backside like soldiers.'

Candy turned to the breakfast trays to cover her smile. 'That's no way to talk in front of a lady. But don't worry, it isn't Symmonds.'

'Where's Duff?' Sean asked.

'He's having a bath, then he's coming to eat breakfast with you.'

'I'll wait for him, but give me a cup of coffee in the meantime, there's a sweetheart.'

She brought the coffee to him. 'Your savage has been camping on my trail all morning, he wants to see you. I've just about had to put an armed guard on this room to keep him out.'

Sean laughed. 'Will you send him in, Candy?'

She went to the door and stopped with a hand on the latch.

'It's nice to have you back, Sean, don't do anything silly like that again, will you?'

'That's a promise,' Sean assured her.

Mbejane came quickly and stood in the doorway. 'Nkosi, is it well with you?'

Sean looked at the iodine-stained bandages on his hands and the maroon and gold livery without answering. Then he rolled on his back and stared at the ceiling. 'I sent for my servant and instead there comes a monkey on a chain.'

Mbejane stood still, his face expressionless but for the hurt in his eyes.

'Go – find my servant. You will know him by his dress which is that of a warrior of Zululand.'

It took a few seconds for the laughter to start rolling around in Mbejane's belly; it shook his shoulders and creased the corners of his mouth. He closed the door very softly behind him and when he came back in his loin cloth Sean grinned at him.

'Ah! I see you, Mbejane.'

'And I see you also.'

He stood by the bed and they talked. They spoke little of the cave-in and not at all of Mbejane's part in the rescue. Between them it was understood, words could only damage it. Perhaps they would talk of it later, but not now.

'Tomorrow, will you need the carriage?' Mbejane asked at last.

'Yes – go now. Eat and sleep.' Sean reached out and touched Mbejane's arm. Just that small physical contact – that almost guilty touching – and Mbejane left him.

Then Duff came in in a silk dressing-gown and they ate eggs and steak from the trays and Duff sent down for a bottle of wine just to rinse the dust out of their throats once more.

'They tell me Francois is still down at the Bright Angels – he's been on the drink ever since he got out of that shaft. When he sobers up he can come to the office and collect his pay packet.'

Sean sat up. 'You're going to fire him?'

'I'm going to fire him so high he'll only touch ground when he reaches Capetown.'

'What the hell for?' demanded Sean.

'What for?' Duff echoed. 'What for? For running – that's what for.'

'Duff, he was in a cave-in at Kimberley, wasn't he?'

302

'Yes.'

'Broke his legs, didn't you say?'

'Yes.'

'Shall I tell you something? If it were to happen to me a second time I'd run as well.'

Duff filled his wine glass without answering.

'Send down to the Bright Angels, tell him alcohol is bad for the liver – that should sober him – tell him unless he's back at work by tomorrow morning we'll dock it off his pay,' Sean said. Duff looked at him with a puzzled expression. 'What is this?'

'I had some time to think while I was down in that hole. I decided that to get to the top you don't have to stamp on everyone you meet.'

'Ah, I understand.' Duff gave his lopsided grin. 'A good resolution – New Year in August. Well, that's all right, you had me worried there, I thought a rock had fallen on your head. I also make good resolutions.'

'Duff, I don't want Francois fired.'

'All right, all right – he stays on. If you like we can open a soup kitchen at the office and turn Xanadu into a home for the aged.'

'Oh, go and burst. I just don't think it's necessary to fire Francois, that's all.'

'Who's arguing? I agreed with you, didn't I? I have deep respect for good resolutions. I make them all the time.'

Duff pulled his chair up to the bed. 'Quite by chance I happen to have a pack of cards with me.' He took them out of his dressing-gown pocket. 'Would you care for a game of Klabejas?'

Sean lost fifty pounds before he was saved by the arrival of the new doctor. The doctor tapped his chest and tut-tutted, looked down his throat and tut-tutted, wrote out a prescription and confined him to bed for the rest of the day.

He was just leaving when Jock and Trevor Heyns arrived. Jock had a bunch of flowers which he presented to Sean in an embarrassed fashion.

Then the room began to fill in earnest: the rest of the crowd from the Exchange arrived, someone had brought a case of champagne, a poker game started in one corner and a political meeting in another.

'Who does this Kruger think he is, anyway – God or something? You know what he said last time we went to see him about getting the vote, he said "Protest, protest – I have the guns and you have not!"'

'Three Kings wins – you *are* holding cards!'

' – you wait and see. Consolidated Wits. will hit thirty shillings by the end of the month.'

' – and the taxes – they're putting another twenty per cent on dynamite.'

' – a new piece at the Opera, Jock's got a season ticket on her – no one else has had a look in yet.'

'All right, you two – stop that. If you want to fight go outside – this is a sick room.'

'This bottle's empty – break open a new one, Duff.'

Sean lost another hundred to Duff and then a little after five Candy came in. She was horrified. 'Out, all of you, out!'

The room emptied as quickly as it had filled and Candy wandered around picking up cigar butts and empty glasses.

'The vandals! Someone's burnt a hole in the carpet and look at this – champagne spilt all over the table.'

Duff coughed and started pouring himself another drink.

'Don't you think you've had enough of that, Dufford?'

Duff put down his glass. 'And it's time you went and changed for dinner.' Duff winked sheepishly at Sean, but he went.

Duff and Candy came back to his room after supper and had a liqueur with him.

'Now to sleep,' Candy commanded and went across to draw the curtains.

'It's still early,' protested Duff with no effect. Candy blew the lamp out.

Sean was not tired, he had lain in bed all day and now his brain was overactive. He lit a cigar and smoked, listening to the street noises below his window and it was past midnight before he finally drifted off. When he woke, he woke screaming, for the darkness was on him again and the blankets pressed down on him suffocating him. He fought them off and stumbled blindly across the room. He had to have air and light. He ran into the thick velvet curtains and they closed around his face; he tore himself free and hit the french windows with his shoulder; they burst open and he was out on the balcony, out in the cold air with the moon fat and yellow in the sky above him. His gasping slowed until he was breathing normally again. He went back inside and lit the lamp, then he went through to Duff's empty bedroom. There was a copy of *Twelfth Night* on the bedside table and he took it back to his own room. He sat with the lamp at his elbow and forced his eyes to follow the printed words even though they made no sense. He read until the dawn showed grey through the open windows, then he put down the book. He shaved, dressed and went down the back stairs into the hotel yard. He found Mbejane in the stables.

'Put a saddle on the grey.'

'Where are you going, Nkosi?'

'To kill a devil.'

'Then I will come with you.'

'No, I will be back before midday.'

He rode up to the Candy Deep and tied his horse outside the administration buildings. There was a sleepy clerk in the front offices.

'Good morning, Mr Courtney. Can I help you?'

'Yes. Get me overalls and a helmet.'

Sean went to the Number Three shaft. There was a frost on the ground that crunched as he walked on it and the sun had just cleared the eastern ridge of the Witwatersrand. Sean stopped at the hoist shed and spoke to the driver.

'Has the new shift gone on yet?'

'Half an hour ago, sir.' The man was obviously surprised to see him. 'The night shift finished blasting at five o'clock.'

'Good – drop me down to the fourteenth level.'

'The fourteenth is abandoned now, Mr Courtney, there's no one working there.'

'Yes, I know.'

Sean walked across to the head of the shaft. He lit his carbide lamp and while he waited for the skip he looked out across the valley. The air was clear and the sun threw long shadows. Everything stood out in sharp relief. He had not been up this early in the morning for many months and he had almost forgotten how fresh and delicately coloured a new day was. The skip stopped in front of him. He took a deep breath and stepped into it. When he reached the fourteenth level he got out and pushed the recall signal for the skip and he was alone in the earth again. He walked up the tunnel and the echo of his footsteps went with him. He was sweating and a muscle in his cheek started to jerk; he reached the face and set the carbide lamp down on a ledge of rock. He checked to make sure his matches were in his pocket, then he blew out the lamp. The darkness came squeezing down on him. The first half hour was the worst. Twice he had the matches in his hand ready to strike but he stopped himself. The sweat formed cold wet patches under his arms and the darkness filled his open mouth and choked him. He had to fight for each lungful of air, suck in, hold it, breathe out. First he regulated his breathing and then slowly, slowly his mind came under control and he knew he had won. He waited another ten minutes breathing

306

easily and sitting relaxed with his back against the side of the tunnel, then he lit the lamp. He was smiling as he went back to the lift station and signalled for the skip. When he reached the surface he stepped out and lit a cigar; he flicked the match into the square black opening of the shaft.

'So much for you, little hole.'

He walked back towards the administration building. What he could not know was that the Number Three shaft of the Candy Deep was to take something from him just as valuable as his courage and that, next time, what it took it would not give back. But that was many years ahead.

– 22 –

By October Xanadu was nearly finished. The three of them drove out to it as usual one Saturday afternoon.

'The builder is only six months behind schedule – now he says he'll be finished by Christmas and I haven't found the courage yet to ask him which Christmas,' Sean remarked.

'It's all the alterations Candy has thought up,' Duff said. 'She's got the poor man so confused he doesn't know whether he's a boy or a girl.'

'Well, if you'd consulted me in the first place it would have saved a lot of trouble,' Candy told them.

The carriage turned in through the marble gates and they looked around them. Already the lawns were smooth and green and the jacaranda trees lining the drive were shoulder high.

'I think it's going to live up to its name – that gardener's doing a good job,' Sean spoke with satisfaction.

'Don't you call him a gardener to his face or we'll have a strike on our hands. He's a horticulturist,' Duff smiled across at him.

'Talking about names,' Candy interrupted, 'don't you think Xanadu is – well, a bit outlandish?'

'No, I do not,' Sean said. 'I picked it myself. I think it's a damn good name.'

'It's not dignified – why don't we call it Fair Oaks?'

'Firstly, because there isn't an oak tree within fifty miles and secondly because it's already called Xanadu.'

'Don't get cross, it was just a suggestion.'

The builder met them at the top of the drive and they began the tour of the house. That took an hour, then they left the builder and went out into the garden. They found the gardener with a gang of natives near the north boundary.

'How's it going, Joubert?' Duff greeted him.

'Not bad, Mr Charleywood, but it takes time you know.'

'You've done a damn fine job so far.'

'It's kind of you to say so, sir.'

'When are you going to start laying out my maze?'

The gardener looked surprised; he glanced at Candy, opened his mouth, closed it again and looked once more at Candy.

'Oh, I told Joubert not to worry about the maze.'

'Why did you do that? I wanted a maze – ever since I visited Hampton Court as a child I've wanted my own maze.'

'They're silly things,' Candy told him. 'They just take up a lot of space and they're not even nice to look at.'

Sean thought Duff was going to argue, but he didn't. They talked to the gardener a little longer, then they walked back across the lawns in front of the house towards the chapel.

'Dufford, I've left my parasol in the carriage, would you mind getting it for me?' Candy asked.

When Duff was gone Candy took Sean's arm.

'It's going to be a lovely home. We're going to be very happy here.'

'Have you two decided on a date yet?' Sean asked.

'We want the house finished first so we can move straight in. I think we'll make it some time in February next year.'

They reached the chapel and stopped in front of it.

'It's a sweet little church.' Candy spoke dreamily. 'And such a nice idea of Dufford's – a special church of our own.'

Sean shuffled uncomfortably. 'Yes,' he agreed, 'it's a very romantic idea.' He glanced over his shoulder and saw Duff coming back with the parasol.

'Candy – it's none of my business. I don't know anything about marriage, but I know about training horses – you break them to the halter before you put the saddle on their backs.'

'I don't follow you.' Candy looked puzzled. 'What are you trying to say?'

'Nothing – just forget it. Here comes Duff.'

When they got back to the hotel there was a note at the reception desk for Sean. They went through into the main lounge and Candy went off to check the menu for dinner. Sean opened the envelope and read the note:

'I should like to meet you and Mr Charleywood to discuss a matter of some importance. I will be at my hotel after dinner this evening and hope that it will be convenient for you to call on me then. N. Hradsky.'

Sean passed the note across to Duff.

'What do you suppose he wants?'

'He has heard of your deadly skill as a Klabejas player. He wants to take lessons,' Duff answered.

'Shall we go?'

'Of course. You know I can't resist Norman's exhilarating company.'

309

It was a superb dinner. The crayfish, packed in ice, had come up from Capetown by express coach.

'Candy – Sean and I are going across to see Hradsky. We might be back a little late,' Duff told her when they were finished.

'As long as it's Hradsky,' Candy smiled at him. 'Don't get lost – I have my spies at the Opera House you know.'

'Shall we take the carriage?' Duff asked Sean, and Sean noticed that he hadn't laughed at Candy's joke.

'It's only two blocks, we might as well walk.'

They walked in silence. Sean felt his dinner settling down comfortably inside him, he belched softly and took another puff from his cigar. When they had almost reached the Grand National Hotel Duff spoke.

'Sean . . .' He stopped.

'Yes?' Sean prompted him.

'About Candy . . .' He stopped again.

'She's a fine girl,' Sean prompted again.

'Yes, she's a fine girl.'

'Is that all you wanted to say?'

'Well – oh! never mind. Let's go and see what Saul and David want.'

Max met them at the door of Hradsky's suite.

'Good evening, gentlemen, I am so pleased you could come.'

'Hello, Max.' Duff went past him to where Hradsky was standing in front of the fireplace.

'Norman, my dear fellow, how are you?'

Hradsky nodded an acknowledgement and Duff took hold of the lapels of Hradsky's coat and adjusted them carefully; then he picked an imaginary piece of fluff off his shoulder.

'You have a way with clothes, Norman. Don't you agree that Norman has a way with clothes, Sean? I know of no

310

one else who can put on a twenty-guinea suit and make it look like a half-filled bag of oranges.' He patted Hradsky's arm affectionately. 'Yes, thank you – I will have a drink.' He went across to the liquor cabinet and poured one for himself. 'Now, what can you gentlemen do for me?'

Max glanced at Hradsky and Hradsky nodded.

'I will come to the point immediately,' said Max. 'Our two groups of companies are the largest on the Witwatersrand.'

Duff put his glass back on top of the cabinet and dropped his grin. Sean sat down in one of the armchairs, his expression also serious; both of them could guess what was coming.

'In the past,' continued Max, 'we have worked together on numerous occasions and we have both benefited from it. The next logical step, of course, is to combine our strength, pool our resources and go on together to new greatness.'

'I take it that you are proposing a merger?'

'Precisely, Mr Courtney, a merger of these two vast financial ventures.'

Sean leaned back in his chair and started to whistle softly. Duff picked up his glass again and took a sip.

'Well, gentlemen, what are your feelings on the subject?' asked Max.

'Have you got a proposal worked out, Max, something definite for us to think about?'

'Yes, Mr Courtney, I have.' Max went to the stinkwood desk which filled one corner of the room and picked up a sheaf of papers. He carried it across to Sean. Sean scanned through it.

'You've done quite a bit of work here, Max. It's going to take us a day or two to work out exactly what you are offering.'

'I appreciate that, Mr Courtney. Take as long as you

wish. We have worked for a month to draw up that scheme and I hope our labours have not been in vain. I think you will find our offer very generous.'

Sean stood up.

'We'll contact you again in the next few days, Max. Shall we go, Duff?'

Duff finished his drink.

'Goodnight, Max, look after Norman. He's very precious to us, you know.'

They went to their building on Eloff Street. Sean let them in through one of the side doors, lit the lamps in his office and Duff pulled up an extra chair to the desk. By two o'clock the following morning they understood the essentials of Hradsky's offer. Sean stood up and went to open one of the windows, for the room was thick with cigar smoke. He came back and flopped onto the couch, arranged a cushion behind his head and looked at Duff.

'Let's hear what you've got to say.'

Duff tapped his teeth with a pencil while he arranged his words.

'Let's decide first if we want to join with him.'

'If he makes it worth our while, we do,' Sean answered.

'I agree with you – but only if he makes it worth our while.' Duff laid back in his chair. 'Now the next point. Tell me, laddie, what is the first thing that strikes you about this scheme of Norman's?'

'We get nice-sounding titles and fat cash payments and Hradsky gets control,' Sean answered.

'You have laid your finger on the heart of it – Norman wants control. More than money, Norman wants control, so that he can sit at the top of the pile, look down on everyone else and say, "All right, you bastards, what if I do stutter?"'

Duff stood up, he walked round the desk and stopped in front of Sean's couch.

312

'Now for my next question. Do we give him control?'

'If he pays our price, then we give him control,' Sean answered. Duff turned away and went across to the open window.

'You know I rather like the feeling of being top man myself,' he said thoughtfully.

'Listen, Duff, we came here to make money. If we go in with Hradsky we'll make more,' Sean said.

'Laddie, we've got so much now that we could fill this room waist deep in sovereigns. We've got more than we'll ever be able to spend and I like being top man.'

'Hradsky's more powerful than we are – let's face up to that. He's got his diamond interests as well, so you're not top man even now. If we join him you still won't be top man but you'll be a damn sight richer.'

'Unassailable logic,' Duff nodded. 'I agree with you then. Hradsky gets control but he pays for it; we'll put him through the wringer until he's dry.'

Sean swung his legs off the couch. 'Agreed – now let's take this scheme of his by the throat, tear it to pieces and build it up again to suit ourselves.'

Duff looked at his watch. 'It's after two o'clock. We'll leave it now and start on it when we're fresh in the morning.'

They had their lunch brought down to the office the next day, and ate it at the desk. Johnson, who had been sent up to the Stock Exchange with instructions to keep an eye on prices and call them immediately if anything out of the ordinary happened, reported back after high change.

'It's been as quiet as a graveyard all day, sir, there's all sorts of rumours flying about. Seems someone saw the lights burning in this office at two o'clock this morning. Then when you didn't come to the Exchange but sent me instead – well, I can tell you, sir, there were a lot of questions asked.' Johnson hesitated, then his curiosity got the better of him.

'Can I help you at all, sir?' He started sidling across towards the desk.

'I think we can manage on our own, Johnson. Shut the door as you go out, please.'

At half-past seven they decided it was enough for one day and they went back to the hotel. As they walked into the lobby Sean saw Trevor Heyns disappear into the lounge and heard his voice.

'Here they are!'

Almost immediately Trevor appeared again with his brother.

'Hello, boys.' Jock appeared surprised to see them. 'What are you doing here?'

'We live here,' said Duff.

'Oh, yes, of course. Well, come and have a drink with us.' Jock smiled expansively.

'And then you can pump us and find out what we've been doing all day,' Duff suggested.

Jock looked embarrassed. 'I don't know what you mean, I just thought we'd have a drink together, that's all.'

'Thanks all the same, Jock, we've had a hard day. I think we'll just go on up to bed,' Duff said. They were halfway across the lobby before Duff turned back to where the two brothers were standing.

'I'll tell you boys something,' he said in a stage whisper. 'This is really big – it's so big it takes a while for the mind to grasp it. When you two realize that it's been right there under your noses all the time, you're going to kick yourselves.'

They left the Heyns brothers in the lobby staring after them and went up the stairs.

'That wasn't very kind,' Sean laughed. 'They won't sleep for a week.'

When neither Sean nor Duff put in an appearance at the Exchange the next morning, the rumours surged round the members' lounge and the prices started running amok. Reliable information that Sean and Duff had struck a rich new goldfield across the vaal sent the prices up like rocketing snipe; then twenty minutes later the denial came in and clipped fifteen shillings a share off the Courtney-Charleywood stock. Johnson ran backwards and forwards between the office and the Exchange all morning. By eleven he was so tired he could hardly talk.

'Don't worry any more, Johnson,' Sean told him. 'Here's a sovereign – go down to the Grand National and buy yourself a drink, you've had a hard morning.'

One of Jock Heyns's men, who had been detailed off to watch the Courtney-Charleywood offices, followed Johnson down to the Grand National and heard him place his order with the barman. He raced back to the Exchange and reported to Jock.

'Their head clerk has just gone and ordered himself a bottle of French champagne,' he panted.

'Good God!' Jock nearly jumped out of his chair and beside him Trevor signalled frantically for his clerk.

'Buy,' he whispered in the man's ear. 'Buy every scrap of their script you can lay your hands on.'

Across the lounge Hradsky settled down a little further in his chair; he clasped his hands contentedly over the front of his stomach and he very nearly smiled.

By midnight Sean and Duff had completed their counter-proposal to Hradsky's offer.

'How do you think Norman will react to it?' asked Sean.

'I hope his heart is strong enough to stand the shock,'

Duff grinned. 'The only reason that his jaw won't hit the floor is that his great gut will be in the way.'

'Shall we go down to his hotel now and show him?' suggested Sean.

'Laddie, laddie.' Duff shook his head sorrowfully. 'After all the time I've spent on your education, and you still haven't learned.'

'What do we do then?'

'We send for him, laddie, we make him come to us. We play him on the home ground.'

'How does that help?' Sean asked.

'It gives us an advantage immediately – it makes him remember that he's the one doing the asking.'

Hradsky came down to their office at ten o'clock the next morning; he came in state driven behind a four-in-hand and attended by Max and two secretaries. Johnson met them at the front door and ushered them into Sean's office.

'Norman, dear old Norman, I'm delighted to see you,' Duff greeted him and, fully aware of the fact that Hradsky never smoked, Duff thrust a cheroot between his lips. When everyone was seated Sean opened the meeting.

'Gentlemen, we have spent some time examining your proposition and in the main we find it just, fair and equitable.'

'Hear, hear,' Duff agreed politely.

'At the outset I want to make it quite clear,' Sean went on, 'that Mr Charleywood and myself feel strongly that the union of our two ventures is desirable – nay! essential. If you will forgive the quotation, "*ex unitate vires*".'

'Hear, hear – hear, hear.' Duff lit his cigar.

'As I was saying, we have examined your proposition and we accept it readily and happily, with the exception of a few minor details which we have listed.' Sean picked up the thick pile of paper. 'Perhaps you would care to glance

316

through it and then we can proceed to the drawing-up of a formal agreement.'

Max accepted the sheaf gingerly. 'If you want privacy, Mr Charleywood's office which adjoins this room is at your disposal.'

Hradsky took his band next door and an hour later when he led them back again they looked like a party of pallbearers. Max was on the verge of tears, he cleared the lump from his throat.

'I think we should examine each item separately,' he said sadly, and three days later they shook hands on the deal.

Duff poured the drinks and gave each man a glass. 'To the new company, Central Rand Consolidated. It has been a long confinement, gentlemen, but I think we have given birth to a child of which we can be proud.'

Hradsky had control, but it had cost him dearly.

Central Rand Consolidated had its christening party on the main floor of the Johannesburg Stock Exchange; ten per cent of the shares were put out for sale to the public. Before the day's dealings began the crowd had overflowed the Stock Exchange building and jammed in the street for a block in each direction. The President of the Exchange read the prospectus of Central Rand Consolidated; in the cathedral hush his every word carried clearly to the members' lounge. The bell rang and still the hush persisted. Hradsky's authorized clerk broke the silence timidly. 'I sell C.R.C.'s.'

It was nearly a massacre; two hundred men were trying to buy shares from him simultaneously. First his jacket and then his shirt disintegrated beneath the clutching hands; he lost his spectacles, crushed to powdered glass beneath the trampling feet. Ten minutes later he managed to fight his way out of the crowd and report to his masters, 'I was able to sell them, gentlemen.'

Sean and Duff laughed. They had reason to laugh, for in

317

those ten minutes their thirty per cent holding in C.R.C. had appreciated in value by half a million pounds.

– 24 –

That year Christmas dinner at Candy's Hotel was considerably better than it had been five years previously. Seventy-five people sat down to it at one table and by three o'clock, when it ended, only half of them were able to stand up. Sean used the banisters to get up the stairs and at the top he told Candy and Duff solemnly, 'I love you – I love you both desperately – but now I must sleep.' He left them and set off down the corridor bouncing against the walls like a trick billiard shot until he ricocheted through the door into his suite.

'You'd better make sure he's all right, Dufford.'

'A case of the blind drunk leading the blind drunk,' said Duff indistinctly, and also employing the wall to wall route followed Sean down the corridor. Sean was sitting on the edge of his bed wrestling with one of his boots.

'What you trying to do, laddie, break your ankle?'

Sean looked up and smiled beatifically. 'Come in, come in – all four of you. Have a drink.'

'Thanks, I brought my own.'

Duff closed the door behind him like a conspirator and produced a bottle from under his coat. 'She didn't see me – she didn't know her little Dufford had a big beautiful bottle in his inside pocket.'

'Would you mind helping me with this damn boot?' Sean asked.

'That's a very good question,' said Duff seriously as he set a course across the room for one of the armchairs. 'I'm glad you asked it.' He reached the chair and dropped into it. 'The answer, of course, is, Yes! I would mind.'

Sean let his foot drop and lay back on the bed.

'Laddie, I want to talk to you,' Duff said.

'Talk's free – help yourself.'

'Sean, what do you think of Candy?'

'Lovely pair of titties,' Sean opined.

'Sure, but a man cannot live by titties alone.'

'No, but I suppose she's also got the other basic equipment,' Sean said drowsily.

'Laddie, I'm being serious now – I want your help. Do you think I am doing the right thing – this marriage business, I mean.'

'Don't know much about marriage.' Sean rolled over on his face.

'She's calling me Dufford already – did you notice that, laddie? That's an omen, that's an omen of the most frightful portent. Did you notice, hey?' Duff waited a second for an answer which he didn't receive. 'That's what the other one used to call me. "Dufford," she'd say – I can hear it now – "Dufford, you're a pig".'

Duff looked hard at the bed. 'Are you still with me?'

No answer.

'Sean, laddie, I need your help.'

Sean snored softly.

'Oh, you drunken oaf,' said Duff miserably.

– 25 –

Xanadu was finished by the end of January and the wedding was set for the twentieth of February. Duff sent the Commandant and the entire police force of Johannesburg an invitation: in return they put a twenty-four hour a day guard on the ballroom of Xanadu where the wedding gifts were laid out on long trestle tables. Sean drove up with Duff and Candy on the afternoon of the

319

tenth, as Duff put it, to make the latest count of the booty. Sean gave the constable on duty a cigar and then they went through into the ballroom.

'Look, oh look,' squealed Candy. 'There's a whole lot of new presents!'

'This one's from Jock and Trevor.' Sean read the card.

'Open quickly, please, Dufford, let's see what they've given us.'

Duff prised the lid off the case and Sean whistled softly.

'A solid gold dinner service,' gasped Candy. She picked up one of the plates and hugged it to her chest. 'Oh, I just don't know what to say.'

Sean examined the other boxes. 'Hey, Duff, this one will make you specially happy – "Best wishes, N. Hradsky".'

'This I must see,' said Duff with the first enthusiasm he had shown in a month. He unwrapped the parcel.

'A dozen of them!' Duff hooted gleefully. 'Norman, you priceless little Israelite, a whole dozen dish towels.'

'It's the thought that counts,' laughed Sean.

'Dear old Norman, how it must have hurt him to shell out for them! I'll have him autograph them and I'll frame them and hang them in the front hall.'

They left Candy to arrange the presents and they went out into the garden.

'Have you got this mock priest organized?' asked Duff.

'Yes, he's at a hotel in Pretoria. He's in training now – he'll be able to rattle through the service like an old hand when the time comes.'

'You don't think that faking it is just as bad as doing it properly?' asked Duff dubiously.

'It's a hell of a time to think of that now,' said Sean.

'Yes, I suppose it is.'

'Where are you going for the honeymoon?' Sean asked.

'We'll coach down to Capetown and take the mail boat

to London, then a month or so on the Continent. Be back here about June.'

'You should have a good time.'

'Why don't you get married as well?'

'What for?' Sean looked surprised.

'Well, don't you feel as though you're letting the old firm down a bit – me going into this alone?'

'No,' said Sean. 'Anyway, who is there to marry?'

'What about that lass you brought to the races last Saturday; she's a lovely piece of work.'

Sean raised an eyebrow. 'Did you hear her giggle?'

'Yes, I did,' admitted Duff. 'You couldn't very well miss it.'

'Can you imagine that giggle coming at you across the breakfast table?' Sean asked.

Duff shuddered. 'Yes, I see your point. But as soon as we get back I'll have Candy start picking you out a suitable female.'

'I've got a better idea, you let Candy run your life and I'll run my own.'

'That, laddie, is what I'm very much afraid is going to happen.'

Hradsky reluctantly agreed that the activities of the group – the mines, the workshops, the transport companies, all of them – should be suspended on the twentieth to allow their employees to attend Duff's nuptials. This meant that half the businesses on the Witwatersrand would shut down for the day. Consequently, most of the independent companies decided to close as well. On the eighteenth the wagons carrying the food and liquor started caravanning up the hill to Xanadu. Sean, in a burst of benevolence, that night invited the entire company from the Opera House to the wedding. He remembered it vaguely the next morning and went down to cancel the invitation but Blue Bessie told him that most of the girls had already gone into town to buy new dresses.

'The hell with it then – let them come. I just hope Candy doesn't guess who they are, that's all.'

On the night of the nineteenth Candy gave them the use of the dining-room and all the downstairs lounges of the Hotel for Duff's bachelor party. Francois arrived with a masterpiece made up in the mine workshops – an enormous ball and chain. This was formally locked onto Duff's leg and the party began.

Afterwards there was a school of thought that maintained that the building contractor commissioned to repair the damage to the Hotel was a bandit and that the bill for just under a thousand pounds that he presented was nothing short of robbery. However, none of them could deny that the Bok-Bok game in the dining-room, played by a hundred men, had done a certain amount of damage to the furniture and fittings; nor that the chandelier had not been able to support Mr Courtney's weight and on the third swing had come adrift from the ceiling and knocked a moderately large hole through the floor. Neither did anyone dispute the fact that after Jock Heyns had tried unsuccessfully for half an hour to shoot a glass off the top of his brother's head with champagne corks, the resulting ankle-deep lake of wine in the one lounge made it necessary for the floor to be relaid. Nevertheless they felt that a thousand was a little bit steep. On one point, however, everyone agreed – it was a memorable party.

At the beginning Sean was worried that Duff's heart wasn't in it for Duff stood by the bar with the metal ball under one arm listening to the lewd comments with a lopsided grin fixed on his face. After seven or eight drinks Sean stopped worrying about him and went off to have his way with the chandelier. At midnight Duff talked Francois into releasing him from his chains and he slipped out of the room. No one – least of all Sean – noticed him go.

Sean could never remember how he got up to bed that night but next morning he was tactfully awakened by a waiter with a coffee tray and a note.

'What time is it?' asked Sean as he unfolded the note.

'Eight o'clock, baas.'

'No need to shout,' muttered Sean. His eyes focused with difficulty for the pain in his head was pushing them out of their sockets.

'Dear Best Man,
    This serves as a reminder that you and Duff have an appointment at eleven o'clock. I am relying on you to get him there, whole or in pieces. Love Candy.'

The brandy fumes in the back of his throat tasted like chloroform, he washed them out with coffee and lit a cigar which started him coughing, and every cough nearly took the top off his head. He stubbed out the cigar and went to the bathroom. Half an hour later he felt strong enough to wake Duff. He went across the sitting-room and pushed open Duff's door; the curtains in the room were still drawn. He pulled them open and was nearly blinded by the sunlight that poured in through them. He turned to the bed and frowned with surprise. He walked slowly across and sat on the edge of it.

'He must have slept in Candy's room,' Sean muttered as he looked at the unused pillows and neatly tucked blankets. It took a few seconds for him to find the fault in his reasoning.

'Then why did she write that note?' He stood up, feeling the first twinge of alarm. A picture of Duff, drunk and helpless lying out in the yard or knocked over the head by

323

one of the busy Johannesburg footpads came very clearly to mind. He ran across the bedroom and into the sitting-room. Halfway to the door he saw the envelope propped up on the mantelpiece and he took it down.

'What is this, a meeting of the authors' guild?' he muttered. 'The place is thick with letters.'

The paper crackled as he opened it and he recognized Duff's back sloping hand.

'The first the worst, the second the same. I'm not going through with it. You're the best man so make my excuses to all the nice people. I'll be back when the dust has settled a little. D.'

Sean sat down in one of the armchairs, he read through it twice more. Then he exploded.

'Damn you, Charleywood – "make my excuses". You craven bastard. Walk out and leave me to sweep up the mess.'

He rushed across the room with his dressing-gown flapping furiously round his legs. 'You'll make your own damned excuses – even if I have to drag you back on the end of a rope.'

Sean ran down the back stairs. Mbejane was in the stable yard talking to three of the grooms.

'Where is Nkosi Duff?' Sean roared.

They stared at him blankly.

'Where is he?' Sean's beard bristled.

'The baas took a horse and went for a ride,' answered one of the grooms nervously.

'When?' bellowed Sean.

'In the night – perhaps seven, eight hours ago. He should be back soon.'

Sean stared at the groom, breathing heavily. 'Which way did he go?'

'Baas, he did not say.'

Eight hours ago – he could be fifty miles away by now. Sean turned and went back to his room. He threw himself on the bed and poured another cup of coffee.

'This is going to break her up badly—' He imagined the tears and the chaos of undisciplined grief.

'Oh, hell – damn you to hell, Charleywood.' He sipped the coffee and thought about going as well – taking a horse and getting as far away as possible. 'It's no mess of my making – I want no part of it.' He finished the coffee and started dressing. He looked in the mirror to comb his hair and saw Candy standing alone in the chapel, waiting while the silence turned to murmuring and then to laughter.

'Charleywood, you pig,' Sean scowled. 'I can't let her go up there – it'll be bad enough without that. I'll have to tell her.'

He picked up his watch from the dressing-table, it was past nine.

'Damn you, Charleywood.'

He went down the passage and stopped outside Candy's door. He could hear women's voices inside and he knocked before he went in. There were two of Candy's friends and the coloured girl Martha. They stared at him.

'Where's Candy?'

'In the bedroom – but you mustn't go in. It's bad luck.'

'It's the worst bloody luck in the world,' agreed Sean. He knocked on the bedroom door.

'Who is it?'

'Sean.'

'You can't come in – what do you want?'

'Are you decent?'

'Yes, but you mustn't come in.'

He opened the door and looked in on a confusion of squealing females.

'Get out of here' – he said harshly – 'I have to speak to Candy alone.'

They fled and Sean closed the door behind them. Candy was in a dressing-gown. Her face was quick with anticipation; her hair was pulled back and hung shiny and soft. She was beautiful, Sean realized. He looked at the frothy pile of her wedding-dress on the bed.

'Candy, bad news – I'm afraid. Can you take it?' He spoke almost roughly – hating it, hating every second of it.

He saw the bloom on her face wither until her expression was dead – blank and dead as a statue.

'He's gone,' said Sean. 'He's run out on you.'

Candy picked up a brush from her dressing-table and started stroking it listlessly through her hair. It was very quiet in the room.

'I'm sorry, Candy.'

She nodded without looking at him; instead she was looking down the lonely corridor of the future. It was worse than tears would have been, that silent acceptance. Sean scratched the side of his nose – hating it.

'I'm sorry – I wish I could do something about it.' He turned to the door.

'Sean, thank you for coming and telling me.' There was no emotion in her voice; like her face it was dead.

'That's all right,' Sean said gruffly.

He rode up to Xanadu. There were people clustered about the marquees on the lawn; by the quality of their laughter he could tell they were drinking already. The sun was bright and as yet not too hot, the band was playing from the wide veranda of the mansion, the women's dresses were gay against the green of the lawns. 'Gala day' fluttered the flags above the tents. 'Gala day' shouted the laughter.

Sean rode up the drive, lifting his hand in brief acknowledgement of the greetings that were shouted to him. From

326

the vantage point of his horse's back he spotted Francois and Martin Curtis, glasses in hand, standing near the house talking to two of the Opera girls. He gave his horse to one of the native grooms and strode across towards them.

'Hello, boss,' called Curtis. 'Why so glum – you're not the one getting married.' They all laughed.

'Francois, Martin, come with me please.'

'What's the trouble, Mr Courtney?' Francois asked as he led them aside.

'The party's over,' Sean said grimly. 'There'll be no wedding.'

They gaped at him.

'Go around and tell everybody. Tell them they'll get their presents back.'

He turned to leave them.

'What's happened, boss?' Curtis asked.

'Just tell them that Candy and Duff changed their minds.'

'Do you want us to send them home?'

Sean hesitated. 'Oh, the hell with it – let them stay – let them all get sick drunk. Just tell them there'll be no wedding.'

He went up to the house. He found the pseudo-priest waiting nervously in the downstairs study. The man's Adam's apple had been rubbed raw by the starch-stiff dog collar.

'We won't need you,' Sean told him.

He took out his cheque book, sat down at the desk and filled in a cheque form.

'That's for your trouble. Now get out of town.'

'Thank you, Mr Courtney, thank you very much.' The man looked mightily relieved; he started for the door.

'My friend,' Sean stopped him. 'If you ever breathe a word about what we planned to do today, I'll kill you. Do I make myself clear?'

327

Sean went through to the ballroom, he slipped a small stack of sovereigns into the constable's hand.

'Get all these people out of here.' He gestured with his head at the crowds that were wandering among the tables looking at the gifts. 'Then lock the doors.'

He found the chef in the kitchen. 'Take all this food outside – give it to them now. Then lock up the kitchens.'

He went round the house closing the doors and drawing the curtains. When he walked into the study there was a couple on the big leather couch and the man's hand was under the girl's skirts; she was giggling.

'This isn't a whore house,' Sean shouted at them and they left hurriedly. He sank into one of the chairs. He could hear the voices and the laughter from outside on the lawn, the band was playing a Strauss waltz. It irritated him and he scowled at the marble fireplace. His head was aching again and the skin of his face felt dry and tight from the night's debauch.

'What a mess – what a bloody mess,' he said aloud. After an hour he went out and found his horse. He rode out along the Pretoria Road until he had passed the last houses, then he turned off into the veld. He cantered into the sea of grass with his hat pushed back on his head so the sun and the wind could find his face. He sat relaxed and loose in the saddle and let his horse pick its own way. In the late afternoon he came back to Johannesburg and left his horse with Mbejane in the stableyard. He felt better; the exercise and the fresh air had cleared his head and helped him to see things in truer perspective. He ran himself a deep hot bath, climbed into it and while he soaked the last of his anger at Duff smoothed out. He had control of himself again. He got out of the bath and towelled, then he slipped on his gown and went through to the bedroom. Candy was sitting on his bed.

'Hello, Sean.' She smiled at him, a brittle smile. Her hair was a little tangled now, her face was pale and unrouged. She had not changed from the dressing-gown he had seen her in that morning.

'Hello, Candy.' He picked up the cut-glass bottle of bay rum and rubbed some into his hair and beard.

'You don't mind me coming to see you, do you?'

'No, of course not.' He started combing his hair. 'I was about to come and see you myself.'

She drew her legs up under her in the double-jointed manner of women that is impossible for a man to copy.

'Can I have a drink, please?'

'I'm sorry – I thought you never touched the stuff.'

'Oh, today is special.' She laughed too gaily. 'It's my wedding day, you know.'

He poured the brandy without looking at her. He hated this suffering and he felt his anger at Duff coming back strongly. Candy took the drink and sipped it. She pulled a face. 'It tastes awful.'

'It'll do you good.'

'To the bride,' she said and drank it down quickly.

'Another one?' asked Sean.

'No thanks.' She stood up and went across to the window. 'It's getting dark now – I hate the darkness. Darkness distorts things so; what is bad in the daylight is unbearable at night.'

'I'm sorry, Candy, I wish I could help you.'

She whirled and came to him, her arms circled tight round his neck and her face pale and frightened pressed to his chest.

'Oh, Sean, please hold me – I'm so afraid.'

He held her awkwardly.

'I don't want to think about it. Not now, not now in the darkness,' she whispered. 'Please help me. Please help me not to think about it.'

'I'll stay with you. Don't get yourself upset. Come and sit down. I'll get you another drink.'

'No, no,' she clung to him desperately. 'I don't want to be alone. I don't want to think. Please help me.'

'I can't help you – I'll stay with you but that's all I can do.' Anger and pity mixed together in Sean like charcoal and saltpetre; his fingers tightened hard on her shoulders, digging into the flesh until they met bone.

'Yes, hurt me. That way I'll forget for a while. Take me to the bed and hurt me, Sean, hurt me deep.'

Sean caught his breath. 'You don't know what you're saying, that's crazy talk.'

'It's what I want – to forget for a little. Please, Sean, please.'

'I can't do that, Candy, Duff's my friend.'

'He's finished with me and I with him. I'm your friend too. Oh, God, I'm so alone. Don't you leave me too. Help me, Sean, please help me.'

Sean felt his anger slide down from his chest and flare up, cobra-headed, from his thighs. She felt it also.

'Yes, oh please, yes.'

He picked her up and carried her to the bed. He stood over her while he tore off his gown. She moved on the bed, shedding her clothing and spreading herself to meet him, to take him in and let him fill the emptiness. He covered her quickly bayoneting through the soft veil and into the warmth of her body. There was no desire in it, it was cruel and hard drawn out to the frontiers of endurance. For him an expression of anger and pity; for her an act of renunciation. Once was not enough. Again and yet again he took her, until there were brown smudges on the bedclothes from his bleeding back, until her body ached and they lay entwined, wet and tired from the fury of it. In the quiescence of after-passion Sean spoke softly. 'It didn't help, did it?'

330

'Yes, it did.' Physical exhaustion had weakened the barriers that held back her grief. Still holding onto him, she started to cry.

A street lamp outside the room threw a silver square of light on the ceiling. Sean laid on his back and watched it, listening to Candy's sobs. He recognized the moment they reached their climax and followed their decline into silence. They slept then and later before the day woke together as if by arrangement.

'You are the only one who can help him now,' Candy said.

'Help him do what?' asked Sean.

'Find what he is looking for. Peace, himself – whatever you want to call it. He's lost, you know, Sean. He's lost and lonely, almost as lonely as I am. I could have helped him, I'm sure I could.'

'Duff lost?' Sean asked cynically. 'You must be mad!'

'Don't be so blind, Sean, don't be misled by the big talk and the grand manner. Look at the other things.'

'Like what?' asked Sean.

She didn't answer for a while. 'He hated his father, you know.'

'I guessed as much from the little he told me.'

'The way he revolts at any discipline. His attitude to Hradsky, to women, to life. Think about it, Sean, and then tell me if he acts like a happy man.'

'Hradsky did him a disservice once – he just doesn't like him,' Sean defended Duff.

'Oh, no – it's much deeper than that. In a way Hradsky is an image of his father. He's so broken up inside, Sean, that's why he clings to you. You can help him.'

Sean laughed outright. 'Candy, my dear, we like each other that's all, there are no deep and dark motives in our friendship. Don't you start getting jealous of me now.'

Candy sat up and the blankets slipped down to her waist.

331

She leaned towards Sean and her breasts swung forward, heavy, round and silver-white in the half light.

'There's a strength in you, Sean, a kind of solid sureness in you that you haven't discovered yet. Duff has recognized it and so will other unhappy people. He needs you, he needs you very badly. Look after him for me, help him to find what he seeks.'

'Nonsense, Candy,' Sean muttered with embarrassment.

'Promise me you'll help him.'

'It's time you went back to your room,' Sean told her. 'People will start talking.'

'Promise me, Sean.'

'All right, I promise.'

Candy slipped out of the bed. She dressed quickly. 'Thank you, Sean, goodnight.'

– 26 –

For Sean, Johannesburg was poorer without Duff: the streets were not so busy, the Rand Club was drearier and the thrills at the Stock Exchange not so intense. However, there was work to do; his share and Duff's as well.

It was late every evening when the conferences with Hradsky and Max ended and he went back to the Hotel. In the reaction from the day's tension, when his brain was numb and his eyes burned, there was little energy to spare for regret. Yet he was lonely. He went to the Opera House and drank champagne with the crowd there. One of the girls did the Can-Can on the big table in the centre of the room and when she stopped in front of Sean and Trevor Heyns, with her forehead touching her knees and her petticoats hanging forward over her shoulders, Sean let Trevor whip her pants down – a week before he would have punched Trevor in the nose rather than concede the honour. It wasn't so much fun any more. He went home early.

The following Saturday noon Curtis and Francois came into the office for the weekly progress meeting. When they had finished and Hradsky had left, Sean suggested, 'Come along with me, we'll go and have a pot or twelve at the Grand National Bar, baptize the weekend so to speak.'

Curtis and Francois fidgeted in their chairs.

'We had arranged to meet some of the other boys down at the Bright Angels, boss.'

'That's fine, I'll come along with you,' said Sean eagerly, the prospect of being with ordinary men again was suddenly very attractive to him. He felt sickened of the company of those who shook his hand and smiled at him while they waited for a chance to wipe him off the board. It would be good to go along with these two and talk mining and not stocks and shares, to laugh with men who didn't give a damn if C.R.C.'s hit sixty shillings on Monday. He'd get a little drunk with Francois and Curtis; later on perhaps he'd have a fight – an honest, snorting, stand-up fight. God, yes, it would be good to be with men who were clean inside – even if there was dirt under their nails and the armpits of their shirts were stained with sweat.

Curtis glanced quickly at Francois. 'There'll be just a crowd of roughnecks down there, boss, all the diggers come in on a Saturday.'

'That's fine,' said Sean. 'Let's go.'

He stood up and buttoned his dove-grey coat; the lapels were edged in black watered silk and matched the black pearl pin in his tie. He picked up his cane from the desk.

'Come on – let's get moving.'

They ran into the noise from the Bright Angels a block before they reached the building. Sean grinned and quickened his step like an old gun dog with the scent of the bird in its nostrils again. Francois and Curtis hurried along on either side of him. There was a big digger standing on the bar counter. Sean recognized him as one of his men from the Little Sister Mine; the man's body was tilted back to balance the weight of the demijohn he held to his lips and his throat jerked regularly as he swallowed. The crowd around his feet were chanting:

'Drink it, down, down, down, down.'

The digger finished, he threw the bottle against the far wall and belched like an air-locked geyser. He bowed to acknowledge the applause and then he caught sight of Sean standing in the doorway. He wiped his mouth guiltily with the back of his hand and jumped down off the counter. The other men in the crowd turned and saw Sean and the noise tapered off. They spread out along the bar in silence. Sean led Francois and Curtis into the room. He placed a pile of sovereigns on the counter.

'Set them up, barman, take the orders. Today is Saturday and it's time to tie the dog loose.'

'Cheers, Mr Courtney.'

'Good luck, sir.'

'*Gezondheid*, Mr Courtney.'

Their voices were subdued with respect.

'Drink up, men, there's plenty more where that came from.' Sean stood with Francois and Curtis at the bar. They laughed at his jokes. His voice was loud with good fellow-ship and his face flushed with happiness. He bought more drinks. After a while his bladder started making its presence felt and he went through the back door into the washrooms. There were men talking in there; he stopped before he rounded the edge of the screen into the room. '. . . what's he want to come here for, hey? This isn't the mucking Rand Club.'

'Shh! He'll hear you, man, do you want to lose your job?'

'I don't give a damn. Who does he think he is – "Drink up, boys, there's plenty more where that came from – I'm

the boss, boys, do as you're told, boys, kiss my arse, boys.'"
Sean stood paralysed.

'Pipe down, Frank, he'll go just now.'

'The sooner the better, say I, the big dandy bastard with his ten-guinea boots and gold cane. Let him go back where he belongs.'

'You're drunk, man, don't talk so loud.'

'Sure I'm drunk, drunk enough to go in there and tell him to his face . . .'

Sean backed out through the door and walked slowly across the bar to Francois and Curtis.

'I hope you'll excuse me; I've just remembered there's something I've got to do this afternoon.'

'That's too bad, boss.' Curtis looked relieved. 'Perhaps some other time, hey?'

'Yes, perhaps some other time.'

They were pleased to see him when he went up to the Rand Club. Three men nearly fought one another to buy him a drink.

– 27 –

He had dinner with Candy that night and over the liqueurs he told her about it. She listened without interruption until he finished.

'They didn't want me there, I don't see what I've done to them that they should dislike me that way.'

'And it worries you?' she asked.

'Yes, it worries me. I've never had people feel like that towards me before.'

'I'm glad it worries you.' She smiled gently at him. 'One day you're going to grow into quite a nice person.'

'But why do they hate me?' Sean followed his original line of thought.

'They're jealous of you – you say this man said, "ten-guinea boots and gold cane" – that is what's behind it. You're different from them now, you're rich. You can't expect them to accept that.'

'But I've never done anything to them,' he protested.

'You don't have to. One thing I've found in this life – for everything you get you have to pay a price. This is part of the payment you have to make for success.'

'Hell, I wish Duff was here,' said Sean.

'Then Duff would explain to you that it doesn't matter, wouldn't he?' said Candy. '"Who gives a damn for them, laddie, the unwashed herd? We can do without them,"' she mimicked. Sean scratched the side of his nose and looked down at the table.

'Please, Sean, don't ever let Duff teach you that people don't matter. He doesn't believe it himself – but he's so convincing. People are important. They are more important than gold or places or – or anything.'

Sean looked up at her. 'I realized that once; when I was trapped in the Candy Deep. I saw it very clearly then in the darkness and the mud. I made a resolution.' He grinned sheepishly. 'I told myself I'd never hurt anyone again if I could help it. I really meant it, Candy. I felt it so strongly at the time – but, but . . .'

'Yes, I think I understand. That's a big resolution to make and a much bigger one to keep. I don't think any single experience is enough to change a person's way of thinking. It's like building a wall brick by brick. You add to it a little at a time until at last it's finished. I've told you before, Sean, that you have a strength in you. I think one day you'll finish building your wall – and when you do, it will have no weak spots.'

The next Tuesday Sean rode up to Xanadu for the first time since Duff had left. Johnson and four of the clerks from the office were at work in the ballroom, packing and labelling the presents.

'Nearly finished, Johnson?'

'Just about, Mr Courtney, I'll send a couple of wagons up tomorrow morning to fetch this lot.'

'Yes, do that. I don't want them lying around here any longer.'

He went up the marble staircase and stood on the top landing. The house had a dead feeling to it: new and sterile, it was waiting for people to come into it and bring it to life. He went down the corridor, stopping to look at the paintings that Candy had chosen. They were oils in soft pastels, woman's colours.

'We can do without these – I'll get some with fire in them, scarlets and blacks and bright blues.'

He pushed open the door to his own bedroom. This was better: vivid Persian rugs on the floor, walls panelled in dark satiny wood and a bed like a polo field. He lay on the bed and looked up at the scrolled ornate plaster ceiling.

'I wish Duff were back – we can do some real living in this house.' He went downstairs again.

Johnson was waiting at the foot of the stairs. 'All finished, sir.'

'Good man! Off you go, then.'

He went through into the study and walked across to the gun rack. He took down a Purdey shotgun, carried it to the french windows and looked at it in the light. His nostrils flared a little at the nostalgic smell of gun oil. He brought the gun up to his shoulder, felt the true exciting balance of it and enjoyed it. He swung the barrels in an arc across the room, following the flight of an imaginary bird, and suddenly Duff's face was in his sights. Sean was taken so by surprise that he stood with the gun trained at Duff's head.

'Don't shoot, I'll come quietly,' said Duff solemnly.

Sean lowered the shotgun and carried it back to the rack.

'Hello.'

'Hello,' Duff answered, still standing in the doorway. Sean made a pretence of fitting the gun into the rack with his back to Duff.

'How are you, laddie?'

'Fine! Fine!'

'How's everybody else?'

'To whom do you refer, in particular?' Sean asked.

'Candy, for one.'

Sean considered the question. 'Well, you could have damaged her more by feeding her into a stamp mill.'

'Bad, hey?'

'Bad,' agreed Sean.

They stood in silence for a while.

'I take it that you are not very well disposed towards me either,' Duff said at last.

Sean shrugged his shoulders and moved across to the fireplace.

'Dufford, you're a pig,' he said conversationally.

Duff winced. 'Well, it was nice knowing you, laddie. I suppose from here on our paths diverge?'

'Don't drivel, Duff, you're wasting time. Pour the drinks and then you can tell me what it feels like being a pig. Also I want to discuss with you those paintings Candy has plastered along the upstairs corridor. I don't know whether to give them away or burn them.'

Duff straightened up from leaning against the door jamb; he tried to stop the relief showing on his face but Sean went on quickly, 'Before we close the lid on the subject and bury it, I want to tell you this. I don't like what you did. I can see why you did it, but I don't like it. That's my piece said. Have you got anything to add to it?'

'No,' said Duff.

'All right then. I think you'll find a bottle of Courvoisier right at the back of the cabinet behind the whisky decanter.'

Sean went down to Candy's Hotel that evening and found Candy in her office.

'He's back, Candy.'

'Oh!' Candy caught her breath. 'How is he, Sean?'

'A little chastened, but not much.'

'I didn't mean that – I meant is he well?'

'The same as ever. He had the grace to ask how you were,' said Sean.

'What did you tell him?' asked Candy.

Sean shrugged and sat down in the chair next to her desk. He looked at the tall stacks of sovereigns that Candy was counting.

'Is that last night's bar takings?' he asked, avoiding her question.

'Yes,' she answered absently.

'You're rich – will you marry me?' he smiled.

Candy stood up and walked across to the window.

'I suppose you two will be moving up to Xanadu now,' she said. Sean grunted and she went on quickly. 'The Heyns brothers will take over the Victoria rooms – they've spoken to me about it already, so don't worry about that. You'll have fun up there, it will be marvellous for you. I bet you'll have parties every night and crowds of people. I don't mind, I've gotten used to the idea now.'

Sean stood up and went to her, he took her gently by the elbow and turned her to face him. He gave her the silk handkerchief out of his top pocket to blow her nose.

'Do you want to see him again, Candy?'

She shook her head, not trusting her voice.

'I'll look after him like I promised.' He gave her a hug and turned to go.

'Sean,' she called after him. He looked back. 'You'll come to see me sometimes. We could have dinner and talk a little. You'll still be my friend, won't you?'

'Of course, Candy, of course, my dear.'

She smiled damply. 'If you pack your things and Duff's I'll have them sent up to Xanadu for you.'

– 29 –

Sean looked across the boardroom table at Duff, seeking his support. Duff blew a thick ring of cigar smoke. It spun and expanded like a ripple in a pond before it hit the table top and disintegrated. Duff wasn't going to back him up, Sean realized bitterly. They had argued half the previous night. He had hoped that Duff might still change his mind. Now he knew he wouldn't. He made one last appeal.

'They have asked for a ten per cent wage increase. I believe they need it – prices have soared in this town, but wages have remained the same. These men have wives and children, gentlemen, can't we take that into account?'

Duff blew another smoke ring and Hradsky pulled his watch from his pocket and looked at it pointedly. Max coughed and interrupted. 'I think we've been over that before, Mr Courtney. Could we put it to the vote now?'

Sean watched Hradsky's hand go up against him. He

didn't want to look at Duff. He didn't want to see him vote with Hradsky, but he forced himself to turn his head. Duff's hands were on the table in front of him. He blew another smoke ring and watched it hit the table top.

'Those in favour of the motion?' asked Max, and Duff and Sean raised their right hands together. Sean realized then how much it would have meant if Duff had voted against him. Duff winked at him and he couldn't help grinning.

'That is thirty votes for, and sixty against,' declared Max. 'Therefore Mr Courtney's motion falls to the ground. I will inform the Mineworkers' Union of the decision. Now is there any other business before we close the meeting?'

Sean walked with Duff back to his own office.

'The only reason I supported you was because I knew Hradsky would win anyway,' said Duff pleasantly. Sean snorted.

'He's right, of course,' Duff went on unperturbed as he held open the door to Sean's office. 'A ten per cent wage increase would jump the group working costs up ten thousand a month.'

Sean kicked the door closed behind them and didn't answer.

'For God's sake, Sean, don't carry this goodwill-towards-men attitude to absurdity. Hradsky's right – Kruger is likely to slap another one of his taxes on us at any moment and we've got to finance all that new development on the East Rand. We can't let production costs creep up now.'

'All right,' gruffed Sean. 'It's all settled. I just hope we don't have a strike on our hands.'

'There are ways of dealing with strikes. Hradsky has got the police on our side and we can have a couple of hundred men up from Kimberley in no time at all,' Duff told him.

'Damn it, Duff, it's wrong. You know it's wrong. That

grotesque Buddha with the little eyes knows it's wrong. But what can I do? Damn it, what can I do?' Sean exploded. 'I feel so bloody helpless.'

'Well, you're the one who wanted to give him control.' Duff laughed at him. 'Stop trying to change the world and let's go home.'

Max was waiting for them in the outer office. He looked nervous. 'Excuse me, gentlemen, could I have a word with you?'

'Who's talking,' Sean asked abruptly, 'you or Hradsky?'

'It's a private matter, Mr Courtney.' Max dropped his voice.

'Can't it wait until tomorrow?' Sean pushed past him and kept going for the door.

'Please, Mr Courtney, it's of the utmost importance.'

Max plucked desperately at Sean's arm.

'What is it, Max?' Duff asked.

'I have to speak to you alone,' Max dropped his voice again and glanced unhappily at the street door.

'Well, speak then,' Duff encouraged him. 'We're alone now.'

'Not here. Can you meet me later?'

Duff raised an eyebrow. 'What is this, Maximilian, don't tell me you are selling dirty pictures.'

'Mr Hradsky is waiting for me at the hotel. I told him I was coming to find some papers, he'll get suspicious if I don't go back immediately.' Max was nearly in tears; his Adam's apple played hide-and-seek behind his high collar, bobbing out and disappearing again. Duff was suddenly very interested in what Max had to say.

'You don't want Norman to know about this?' he asked.

'My goodness, no.' Max came closer to tears.

'When do you want to meet us?'

'Tonight, after ten o'clock when Mr Hradsky has retired.'

'Where?' asked Duff.

'There's a side road round the east end of the Little Sister Mine dump. It's not used any more.'

'I know it,' said Duff. 'We'll ride along there about half past ten.'

'Thank you, Mr Charleywood, you won't regret it.' Max scampered for the door and disappeared.

Duff adjusted his beaver at the correct angle, then he prodded Sean in the belly with the point of his cane.

'Smell it – suck it in.' Duff sniffed appreciatively and Sean did the same.

'I don't smell a thing,' Sean declared.

'The air is thick with it,' Duff told him. 'The sweet smell of treachery.'

They left Xanadu just after half past nine. Duff insisted on wearing a black opera cloak.

'Atmosphere is vital, laddie, you can't go to a rendezvous like this dressed in dirty khaki pants and *veldschoen*. It would ruin the whole thing.'

'Well, I'm damned if I'm going to get into fancy dress. This is a very good suit. It will have to do.'

'Can't I persuade you to wear a pistol in your belt?' asked Duff wistfully.

'No,' laughed Sean.

'No?' Duff shook his head. 'You're a barbarian, laddie. No taste, that's your trouble.'

They avoided the main streets on their way through Johannesburg and met the Cape road half a mile beyond the town. There was only a minute slice of moon left in the dark bowl of the sky. The stars, however, were big and by their light the white mine dumps, each the size of a large hill, stood out like pustules on the earth's face.

Despite himself, Sean felt a little breathless with excitement – Duff's zest was always infectious. They cantered

343

with their stirrups almost touching, Duff's cloak billowing out behind him and the breeze of their passage fanning the tip of Sean's cigar to a fierce red spark.

'Slow down, Duff, the turning's just about here somewhere. It's overgrown, we'll miss it.'

They reined to a walk.

'What's the time?' asked Duff.

Sean drew on his cigar and held his watch close to the glow. 'A quarter after ten. We're early.'

'My bet is Maximilian will be there before us – here's the road.' Duff turned his horse onto it and Sean followed him. The Little Sister Mine dump rose up next to them, steep and white in the starlight. They skirted it but its bulk threw a shadow over them. Duff's horse snorted and shied and Sean gripped with his knees as his own horse danced sideways. Max had stepped out from a scraggy cluster of bushes next to the road.

'Well met by moonlight, Maximilian,' Duff greeted him.

'Please bring your horses off the road, gentlemen.' Max was still showing signs of the afternoon's agitation. They tied their horses next to Max's among the bushes and walked across to join him.

'Well, Max, what's new? How are the folks?' Duff asked.

'Before we go any further in this matter, I want you gentlemen to give me your word of honour that, whether anything comes of it or not, you will never say a word to anybody of what I tell you tonight.' Max was very pale, Sean thought, or perhaps it was just the starlight.

'I agree to that,' said Sean.

'Cross my heart,' said Duff.

Max opened the front of his coat and brought out a long envelope. 'I think if I show you these first it will make it easier to explain my proposition.'

Sean took the envelope from him. 'What are they, Max?'

'The latest statements from all four banks at which Mr Hradsky deals.'

'Matches, Sean, give us a light, laddie,' said Duff eagerly.

'I have a lantern with me,' Max said and he squatted down to light it. Sean and Duff squatted with him and spread the bank statements in the circle of yellow light. They examined them in silence until at last Sean rocked back on his heels and lit another cigar.

'Well, I am glad I don't owe that much money,' Sean announced. Sean folded up the sheets and put them back in the envelope. He slapped the envelope into the palm of his free hand and started chuckling. Max reached across, took it from him and placed it carefully back inside his coat.

'All right, Max, spell it out for us,' said Sean. Max leaned forward and blew out the lantern. What he had to say was easier said in darkness.

'The large cash payment that Mr Hradsky had to make to you gentlemen and the limitation of output from his diamond mines in terms of the new cartel agreements in the diamond industry have forced him to borrow heavily on all his banks.' Max stopped and cleared his throat. 'The extent of this borrowing you have seen. Of course, the banks demanded security for the loans and Mr Hradsky has given them his entire holding of C.R.C. shares. The banks have set a limit on the shares of thirty-five shillings each. As you know C.R.C.'s are currently quoted at ninety shillings, which leaves a wide margin of safety. However, if the shares were to suffer a setback and fall in price to thirty-five shillings the banks would sell. They would dump every single share that Mr Hradsky owns in C.R.C.'s onto the market.'

'Go on, Max,' said Duff. 'I'm beginning to like the sound of your voice.'

'It occurred to me that if Mr Hradsky were temporarily absent from Johannesburg – say if he went on a trip to England to buy new machinery or something of that nature – it would be possible for you gentlemen to force the price of C.R.C.'s down to thirty-five shillings. Done correctly it would only take three or four days to accomplish. You could sell short and start rumours that the Leader Reef had pinched out at depth. Mr Hradsky would not be here to defend his interests and as soon as C.R.C.'s hit thirty-five shillings the banks would off-load his shares. The price would crash and you, with ready cash available, would be in a position to buy up C.R.C. shares at a fraction of their actual value. There is no reason why you shouldn't gain control of the group and make a couple of million to boot.'

There was another silence. It lasted a long time before Sean asked, 'What do you get out of it, Max?'

'Your cheque for one hundred thousand pounds, Mr Courtney.'

'Wages are going up,' remarked Sean. 'I thought the standard pay for this type of work was thirty pieces of silver. The rate, I believe, was set by a countryman of yours.'

'Shut up,' snapped Duff, then more pleasantly to Max, 'Mr Courtney likes his little jokes. Tell me, Max, is that all you want – just the money? I'll be frank with you – it doesn't ring true. You must be a moderately rich man as it is.'

Max stood up quickly and started towards the horses. He hadn't reached them before he swung around. His face was in darkness but his voice was naked as he screamed at them.

'Do you think I don't know what they call me – "The Court Jester", "Hradsky's tongue", "Lick-arse". Do you think I like it? Do you think I enjoy crawling to him every minute of every day? I want to be free again. I want to be a man again.' His voice choked off and his hands came up and covered his face. He was sobbing. Sean couldn't watch him and even Duff looked down at the ground in embarrassment. When Max spoke again it was in his usual soft and sad voice.

'Mr Courtney, if you wear your yellow waistcoat to the office tomorrow, I will take it as a sign that you intend to follow my suggestion and that my terms are acceptable to you. I will then make the necessary arrangements to ensure Mr Hradsky's absence from the country.' He untied his horse, mounted and rode away down the track towards the Cape Road. Neither Sean nor Duff moved to stand up. They listened to the hoof-beats of Max's horse fade into the darkness, before Duff spoke. 'Those bank statements were genuine – I had a good look at the seals.'

'And even more genuine was Max's emotion.' Sean flicked his cigar away into the bushes. 'No one could act that well. It made me feel quite sick listening to him. Hell, how can a man so cold-bloodedly betray his trust?'

'Laddie, let's not turn this into a discussion of Max's morals. Let's concern ourselves with the facts. Norman has been delivered into our hands, neatly trussed, spiced with garlic and with a sprig of parsley behind each ear. I say let's cook him and eat him.'

Sean smiled at him. 'Give me a few good reasons. I want you to convince me. The way I feel towards him after that meeting this afternoon, I shouldn't be surprised if I convince easily.'

'One.' Duff held up a finger. 'Norman deserves it.'

Sean nodded.

'Two.' Another of Duff's fingers came up. 'If we gain control we can run things the way we want. You can indulge your good resolution and give everybody a pay rise and I'll be top man again.'

'Yes!' Sean tugged at his moustache thoughtfully.

'Three. We came here to make money, we'll never get another opportunity like this. And my last reason, but the most potent – you look so beautiful in that yellow waistcoat, laddie, I wouldn't miss seeing you in it tomorrow morning, not for a thousand C.R.C. shares.'

'It is rather natty,' admitted Sean. 'But listen, Duff, I don't want another Lochtkamper business. Messy, you know.'

Duff stood up.

'Norman's a big boy, he wouldn't do that. Anyway, he'll still be rich – he's got his diamond mines. We'll only be relieving him of his responsibilities on the Witwatersrand.'

They walked across to the horses. Sean had his foot in the stirrup when he stiffened and exclaimed, 'My God, I can't do it. It's all off.'

'Why?' Duff was alarmed.

'I spilt gravy on that waistcoat – I can't possibly wear it tomorrow. My tailor would murder me.'

– 30 –

There was no problem in arranging for Hradsky's absence – someone had to go to London. There was machinery to buy for the new areas on the East Rand and they had to select two engineers from the hundred or so applicants waiting in England. Not ungraciously, Hradsky allowed himself to be elected for the job.

'We'll give him a farewell party,' Duff suggested to Sean during dinner that night. 'Well, not really a farewell party – but a wake.'

Sean started whistling the 'Dead March' and Duff tapped it out on the table with the handle of his knife.

'We'll have it at Candy's Hot—' Duff cut himself short. 'We'll have it here. We'll really lay it on for poor old Norman so afterwards he'll be able to say, "The bastards may have cleaned me out, but they certainly gave me a grand party".'

'He doesn't like parties,' said Sean.

'That's an excellent reason why we should give him one,' agreed Duff.

A week later when Hradsky and Max left on the morning coach for Port Natal there were fifty members of the Johannesburg Stock Exchange still in full evening dress from the night's party to wave him goodbye. Duff made a touching, if somewhat slurred, little speech and presented Hradsky with a bouquet of roses. Nervous of the crowd that milled about them, the horses bolted when the driver cracked his whip and Max and Hradsky were thrown together in an undignified heap on the rear seat of the coach. The crowd cheered them out of sight. With an arm around his shoulder Sean led Duff across the street to the office and deposited him in one of the deep leather armchairs.

'Are you sober enough to talk sense?' Sean asked dubiously.

'Sure. Always at your service as the lady said to the customer.'

'I managed to have a word with Max last night,' Sean told him. 'He will send us a telegram from Port Natal when he and Hradsky are safely on the mailboat. We won't start anything until we receive it.'

'Very wise – you're the wisest chap I know,' Duff grinned happily.

'You'd better go to bed,' Sean told him.

'Too far,' said Duff. 'I'll sleep here.'

It was another ten days before Max's telegram arrived. Sean and Duff were eating lunch in the Rand Club when it was delivered to their table. Sean slit open the envelope and read the message to Duff.

'Sailing four o'clock this afternoon. Good luck. Max.'

349

'I'll drink to that.' Duff lifted his wine glass.

'Tomorrow,' said Sean, 'I'll go up to the Candy Deep and tell Francois to pull all the men out of the bottom levels of the mine. No one's to be allowed in.'

'Put a guard at the fourteenth level,' suggested Duff. 'That'll make it more impressive.'

'Good idea,' agreed Sean. He looked up as someone passed their table and suddenly he started to smile. 'Duff, do you know who that is?'

'Who are you talking about?' Duff looked bewildered.

'That chap who's just gone out into the lounge – there he is, going into the lavatories.'

'Isn't that Elliott, the newspaper fellow?'

'Editor of the *Rand Mail*,' nodded Sean. 'Come with me, Duff.'

'Where are we going?'

'To get a bit of cheap publicity.'

Duff followed Sean out of the dining-room, across the lounge and into the men's lavatories. The door of one of the closets was closed and as they walked in someone farted softly behind it. Sean winked at Duff and went across to the urinal. As he addressed himself to it he said, 'Well, all we can hope for now, Duff, is that Norman will be able to work a miracle in England. Otherwise—' He shrugged his shoulder. Duff picked up his cue.

'We're taking a hell of a chance relying on that. I still say we should sell out now. C.R.C.'s were at ninety-one shillings this morning so it's obvious that the story hasn't leaked out yet. But when it does you won't be able to give the bloody shares away. I say we should get out while the going's good.'

'No,' Sean disagreed. 'Let's wait until we hear from Norman. It's taking a bit of a chance, I know, but we have a responsibility to the men working for us.' Sean took Duff's arm and led him out of the lavatory again; at the door he added the cherry to the top of the pie. 'If and when C.R.C. collapses there are going to be thousands of men out of work – do you realize that?'

Sean closed the door behind them and they grinned delightedly at each other.

'You're a genius, laddie,' whispered Duff.

'I'm happy to say I agree with you,' Sean whispered back.

The next morning Sean woke with the knowledge that something exciting was going to happen that day. He lay and savoured the feeling before he sent his mind out to hunt for the reason. Then he sat up suddenly and reached for the newspaper that lay folded on the coffee tray beside his bed. He shook it open and found what he was looking for on the front page, big headlines: *Is all well with the Central Rand Consolidated? Norman Hradsky's mystery journey*. The story itself was a masterpiece of journalistic evasion. Seldom had Sean seen anyone write so fluently or convincingly on a subject about which he knew nothing. 'It is suggested', 'Usually reliable sources report' and 'There is reason to believe' – all the old phrases of no significance. Sean groped for his slippers and padded down the corridor to Duff's room.

Duff had all the blankets and most of the bed; the girl was curled up like a pink anchovy on the outskirts. Duff was snoring and the girl whimpered a little in her sleep. Sean tickled Duff's lips with the tassel of his dressing-gown cord, Duff's nose twitched and his snores gurgled into silence. The girl sat up and looked at Sean with eyes wide but vacant from sleep.

'Quickly, run,' Sean shouted at her, 'the rebels are coming.'

She leapt straight into the air and landed three feet from the bed quivering with panic. Sean ran a critical eye over her. A pretty filly, he decided, and made a mental note to take her for a trot just as soon as Duff put her out to grass.

351

'All right,' he reassured her, 'they've gone away now.'

She became aware of her nakedness and Sean's frank appraisal of it. She tried to cover it with hands too small for the task. Sean picked up Duff's gown from the foot of the bed and handed it to her.

'Go and have a bath or something, sweetheart, I want to talk to Mr Charleywood.'

With the gown on she recovered her composure and told him severely, 'I didn't have any clothes on, Mr Courtney.'

'I would never have guessed,' said Sean politely.

'It's not nice.'

'You are too modest – I thought it was better than average. Off you go now, there's a good girl.' With a saucy flick of her head she disappeared into the bathroom and Sean transferred his attention to Duff. Duff had held grimly onto the threads of sleep throughout the exchange but he let go when Sean whacked him across the backside with the folded newspaper. Like a tortoise coming out of its shell his head emerged from the blankets. Sean handed him the paper and sat down on the edge of the bed. He watched Duff's face crease into laughter lines before he spoke.

'You better get down to the Editor's office and shout at him a little – just to confirm his suspicions. I'll go up to the Candy Deep and close all the bottom levels. I'll meet you back at the Exchange at opening time and don't forget to clean that grin off your face before you show it round town. Try and look haggard, it shouldn't be difficult for you.'

When Sean arrived at the Stock Exchange building the crowd had filled the street outside. Mbejane eased the landau into it and it opened to give them a passage. Sean scowled straight ahead and ignored the questions which were shouted at him from all around. Mbejane stopped the carriage outside the main entrance and four police con-stables held back the mob while Sean hurried across the pavement and through the double doors. Duff was there

352

ahead of him, the centre of a turbulent circle of members and brokers. He saw Sean and waved frantically over the heads of his inquisitors. That was sufficient to switch their attention from Duff to Sean and they flocked to him, ringing him in with anxious angry faces. Sean's hat was knocked forward over his eyes and a button popped off his coat as one of them caught hold of his lapels.

'Is it true?' the man shouted, spittle flying from his lips into Sean's face. 'We've got a right to know if it's true.'

Sean swung his cane in a full overarm stroke onto the man's head and sent him tottering backwards into the arms of those behind him.

'Back, you bastards,' he roared at them using both the point and the edge of his cane to beat them away, scattering them across the floor until he stood alone, glowering at them with the cane still twitching restlessly in his hand.

'I'll make a statement later on. Until then, behave yourselves.' He adjusted his hat, picked the loose thread where the button had been from his coat and stalked across to join Duff. He could see Duff's grin starting to lift the corner of his mouth and he cautioned him silently with his eyes. Grim-faced they walked through into the members' lounge.

'How's it going your end?' Duff kept his voice low.

'Couldn't be better.' Sean contrived a worried expression. 'I've got an armed guard on the fourteenth level. When this bunch hear about that, they'll really start frothing at the mouth.'

'When you make your statement, let it ring with obvious false confidence,' Duff instructed. 'If it goes on like this we'll have the shares down to thirty-five shillings within an hour of opening.'

Five minutes before opening time Sean stood in the President's box and made his address to his fellow members, Duff listened to him with mounting admiration. Sean's hearty reassurances and verbal side-stepping were enough to strike despair into the souls of the most hardened optimists. Sean finished his speech and climbed down from the box amid a gloomy lack of applause. The bell rang and the brokers stood singly or in small disconsolate groups about the floor. The first tentative offer was made. 'I sell C.R.C.'

But there was no rush to buy. Ten minutes later there was a sale recorded at eighty-five shillings, six shillings lower than the previous day's closing price. Duff leaned across to Sean. 'We'll have to start selling some of our own shares to get things moving, otherwise everybody's going to keep sitting on the fence.'

'That's all right,' Sean nodded, 'we'll buy them back later at a quarter of the price. But wait until the news about the Candy Deep gets out.'

It was just before ten o'clock when that happened. The reaction was sharp. In one quick burst of selling C.R.C.'s dropped to sixty shillings. But there they hung, fluctuating nervously in the chaos of hope and doubt.

'We'll have to sell now,' whispered Duff, 'they are short of script. We'll have to give it to them otherwise the price will stick here.'

Sean felt his hands trembling and he clenched them in his pockets. Duff was showing signs of the strain as well, there was a nerve jumping in his cheek and his eyes had receded into their sockets a little. This was a game with high stakes.

'Don't overdo it – sell thirty thousand.'

The price of C.R.C.'s sagged under the weight but levelled out at forty-five shillings. There was still another hour until high change and Sean's whole body was screwed up tight with tension. He felt the cold patches of sweat under his arms.

'Sell another thirty thousand,' he ordered his clerk and

even to himself his voice sounded wheezy. He stubbed out his cigar in the copper ashtray next to his chair; it was already half full of butts. It was no longer necessary for either of them to act worried. This time the price stuck at forty shillings and the sale of sixty thousand more of their shares failed to move it down more than a few shillings.

'Someone's buying up,' muttered Sean uneasily.

'It looks like it,' agreed Duff. 'I'll lay odds it's that bloody Greek Efthyvoulos. It looks as if we'll have to sell enough to glut him before they'll drop any further.'

By high change Duff and Sean had sold three-quarters of their holdings in C.R.C.'s and the price still stood stubbornly at thirty-seven and sixpence. So tantalizingly close to the magic figure that would release a flood of Hradsky's shares onto the unprepared market, but now they were nearing the stage when they would no longer have any shares with which to force the price down that last two and sixpence.

The market closed and left Duff and Sean sitting limply in their armchairs, shaken and tired as prizefighters at the end of the fifteenth round. Slowly the lounge emptied but still they sat on. Sean leaned across and put his hand on Duff's shoulder. 'It's going to be all right,' he said. 'Tomorrow it will be all right.'

They looked at each other and they exchanged strength, each of them drawing it from the other until they were both smiling. Sean stood up. 'Come on, let's go home.'

Sean went to bed early and alone. Although he felt drained of energy, sleep was a long time coming to him and when it did it was full of confused dreams and punctuated with sharp jerks back into wakefulness. It was almost a relief to see the dawn define the windows as grey squares and to be released from his unrewarding rest. At breakfast he drank a cup of coffee and found that his stomach was unable to accept the plateful of steak and eggs that was offered it for it was already screwing up tight in anticipation of the day ahead. Duff was edgy and tired-looking as well; they spoke only a little during the meal and not at all in the carriage when Mbejane drove them down to the Exchange.

The crowd was outside the Stock Exchange again. They forced their way through it and into the building; they took their seats in the lounge and Sean looked round at the faces of his fellow members. In each of them were the marks of worry, the same darkness round the eyes and the jerkiness in movement. He watched Jock Heyns yawn extravagantly and had to do the same; he lifted his hand to cover his mouth and found it was trembling again. He laid the hand on the arm of his chair and kept it still. Across the lounge Bonzo Barnes caught Sean's eye and looked away quickly, then he also gaped into a cavernous yawn. It was the tension. In the years ahead Sean would see men yawn like that while they waited for the dawn to send them against the Boer guns. Duff leaned across to him and broke his line of thought.

'As soon as the trading starts, we'll sell. Try and panic them. Do you agree?'

'Sudden death,' Sean nodded. He couldn't face another morning of that mental agony. 'Couldn't we offer shares at thirty-two shillings and sixpence and get it over with?' he asked.

Duff grinned at him. 'We can't do that, it's too obvious – we'll just have to go on offering to sell at best and let the price fall on its own.'

'I suppose you're right – but we'll play our high cards now and dump the rest of our shares as soon as the market opens. I don't see how the price can possibly hold after that.'

Duff nodded. He beckoned to their authorized clerk who was waiting patiently at the door of the lounge and when the man came up to them he told him, 'Sell one hundred thousand C.R.C.'s at best.'

The clerk blinked but he jotted the order down on his pad and went out onto the main floor where the other brokers were gathering. It was a few minutes from the bell.

'What if it doesn't work?' Sean asked. The tightness in his belly was nauseating him.

'It must work – it's got to work,' Duff whispered as much to himself as to Sean. He was twisting his fingers round the head of his cane and chewing against clenched teeth. They sat and waited for the bell and when it rang Sean jumped then reached sheepishly for his cigar case. He heard their clerk's voice, raised sharply, 'I sell C.R.C.'s,' and then the confused mumble of voices as the trading started. Through the lounge door he saw the recorder chalk up the first sale. 'Thirty-seven shillings.'

He drew hard on his cigar and lay back in his chair forcing himself to relax, ignoring the restless tapping of Duff's fingers on the arm of the chair next to him. The recorder wiped out the figures and wrote again. 'Thirty-six shillings.'

Sean blew out cigar smoke in a long jet. 'It's moving,' he whispered and Duff's hand clenched on the arm of the chair, his knuckles paling from the pressure of his grip.

'Thirty-five.' The elusive number at last. Sean heard Duff sigh next to him and his voice, 'Now! watch it go, laddie, now the banks will come on. Get ready, laddie, get ready now.'

'Thirty-four and six,' wrote the recorder.

'They must come in now,' said Duff again. 'Get ready to get rich, laddie.'

Their clerk was coming back across the floor and into the lounge. He stopped in front of their chairs. 'I managed to sell them, sir.'

Sean straightened up quickly. 'So soon?' he asked.

'Yes, sir, three big sales and I got rid of them all. I'm afraid the last was only at thirty-four and sixpence.'

Sean stared back at the board. The figure was still at thirty-four and sixpence.

'Duff, something's going on here. Why haven't the banks come in yet?'

'We'll force them to off-load.' Duff's voice was unnaturally hoarse. 'We'll force the bastards.' He pulled himself half out of his chair and snarled at the clerk.

'Sell another one hundred thousand at thirty shillings.' The man's face went slack with surprise. 'Hurry, man, do you hear me? What are you waiting for?' The clerk backed away from Duff, then he turned and scurried out of the lounge.

'Duff, for God's sake.' Sean grabbed his arm. 'Have you gone mad?'

'We'll force them,' muttered Duff. 'They'll have to sell.'

'We haven't got another hundred thousand shares.' Sean jumped up. 'I'm going to stop him.' He ran across the lounge but before he reached the door he saw the sale being chalked up on the board at thirty shillings. He pushed his way across the crowded floor until he reached his clerk. 'Don't sell any more,' he whispered.

The man looked surprised. 'I've sold them already, sir.'

'The whole hundred thousand?' There was horrified disbelief in Sean's voice.

'Yes, sir, someone took the lot in one batch.'

Sean walked back across the floor in a daze. He sank into the chair beside Duff.

'They're sold already.' He spoke as though he didn't believe himself.

'We'll force them, we'll force them to sell,' muttered Duff again and Sean turned to him with alarm. Duff was sweating in little dewdrops across his forehead and his eyes were very bright.

'Duff, for God's sake,' Sean whispered to him, 'steady, man.' Sean knew that they were watched by everybody in the lounge. The watching faces seemed as large as those seen through a telescope and the buzz of their voices echoed strangely in his ears. Sean felt confused: everything seemed to be in slow motion like a bad dream. He looked through into the trading floor and saw the crude number thirty still chalked accusingly against C.R.C. Where were the banks? Why weren't they selling?

'We'll force them, we'll force the bastards,' Duff said again. Sean tried to answer him but the words wouldn't come. He looked back across the trading floor and now he knew it was a bad dream for Hradsky and Max were there, walking across the floor towards the members' lounge. Men were crowding around them and Hradsky was smiling and holding up his hands as if to fend off their questions. They came through into the lounge and Hradsky went to his chair by the fireplace. He lowered himself into it with his shoulders sagging forward and his waistcoat wrinkled tightly around the full bag of his belly. He was still smiling and Sean thought that his smile was one of the most unnerving things he had ever seen. He watched it with flesh-crawling fascination and beside him Duff was just as still and stricken. Max spoke quickly to Hradsky and then he stood up and walked across to Sean and Duff. He stopped in front of them.

'The clerk informs us that you have contracted to sell to Mr Hradsky five hundred thousand shares in C.R.C.'s at an average price of thirty-six shillings.' Max's lashes drooped sadly onto his cheeks. 'The total issue of C.R.C.'s, as you know, is one million shares. During the last two days Mr Hradsky was able to purchase another seventy-five thousand shares apart from the ones you sold to him. This makes his total holdings of C.R.C.'s almost six hundred thousand shares. It seems therefore that you have sold shares that don't exist. Mr Hradsky foresees that you will have some difficulty in fulfilling your contract.'

Sean and Duff went on staring at him. He turned to leave them and Duff blurted out. 'But the banks – why didn't the banks sell?'

Max smiled a mournful little smile. 'The day he reached Port Natal Mr Hradsky transferred sufficient funds from his accounts there to liquidate his overdrafts in Johannesburg. He sent you that telegram and returned here immediately. We only arrived an hour ago.'

'But – but, you lied to us. You tricked us!'

Max inclined his head. 'Mr Charleywood, I will not discuss honesty with a man who does not understand the meaning of the word.' He went back to Hradsky's side. Everyone in the lounge had heard him and while Duff and Sean went on sitting amongst the ruins of their fortune the struggle to buy C.R.C. shares started on the main floor. In five minutes the price was over ninety shillings and still climbing. When it reached one hundred shillings, Sean touched Duff's arm.

'Let's go.' They stood up together and started for the door of the members' lounge. As they passed Hradsky's chair he spoke.

'Yes, Mr Charleywood, you can't win all the time.' It came out quite clearly with only a slight catch on the 'c's' – they were always difficult letters for Norman Hradsky.

Duff stopped, he turned to face Hradsky, his mouth open as he struggled to find a reply. His lips moved, groping, groping for words – but there were none. His shoulders drooped, he shook his head and turned away. He stumbled once at the edge of the floor. Sean held his arm and guided him through the excited jabber of brokers. No one took any notice of the two of them. They were bumped and jostled before they were through the crush and out onto the pavement. Sean signalled Mbejane to bring the carriage.

They climbed into it and Mbejane drove them up to Xanadu.

They went through into the drawing-room.

'Get me a drink, please, Sean.' Duff's face was grey and crumpled-looking. Sean poured two tumblers half full of brandy and carried one across to Duff. Duff drank and then sat staring into the empty glass.

'I'm sorry – I lost my head. I thought we'd be able to buy those shares for dirt, when the banks started selling.'

'It doesn't matter,' Sean's voice was tired. 'We were smashed before that happened. Christ! What a well-laid trap it was!'

'We couldn't have known. It was so damn cunning, we couldn't have guessed, could we, Sean?' Duff was trying to excuse himself.

Sean kicked off his boots and loosened his collar. 'That night up at the mine dump – I would have staked my life Max wasn't lying.' He lay back in the chair and stirred his brandy with a circular movement of his hand. 'Christ, how they must have laughed to see us stampede into the pitfall!'

'But we aren't finished, Sean, we aren't completely finished, are we?' Duff was pleading with him, begging for a peg to hang his hope on. 'We'll come out of this all right, you know we will, don't you? We'll save enough out of the wreckage to start again. We'll build it all up again, won't we, Sean?'

'Sure,' Sean laughed brutally. 'You can get a job down at the Bright Angels cleaning out the spittoons and I'll get one at the Opera House playing the piano.'

'But – but – there'll be something left. A couple of thousand even. We could sell this house.'

'Don't dream, Duff, this house belongs to Hradsky. Everything belongs to him.' Sean flicked the brandy that was left in his glass into his mouth and swallowed it. He stood up quickly and went across to the liquor cabinet. 'I'll

361

explain it to you. We owe Hradsky a hundred thousand shares that don't exist. The only way we can deliver them is to buy them from him first and he can set his own price on them. We're finished, Duff, do you know what that means? Smashed! Broken!' Sean poured brandy into his glass, slopping a little on the sideboard. 'Have another drink on Hradsky, it's his brandy now.' Sean swept his arm round the room, pointing at the rich furniture and heavy curtains. 'Take a last look at this lot. Tomorrow the Sheriff will be here to attach it; then through the due processes of the law it will be handed to its rightful owner – Mr Norman Hradsky.' Sean started back towards his chair and then he stopped.

'The due processes of the law,' he repeated softly. 'I wonder – it might just work.'

Duff sat up eagerly in his chair. 'You've got an idea?'

Sean nodded. 'Well, half an idea anyway. Listen, Duff, if I can save a couple of thousand out of this do you agree that we get out of here?'

'Where to – where will we go?'

'We were facing north when we started. It's as good a direction as any. They say there's gold and ivory beyond the Limpopo for those who want it.'

'But, why can't we stay here? We could play the stock market.' Duff looked uncertain, almost afraid.

'Damn it, Duff, we're finished here. It's a different story playing the market when you are paying the fiddler and calling the tune, but with a mere thousand or so we'd be among the dogs fighting for the scraps under Hradsky's table. Let's get out and start again. We'll go north, hunt ivory and prospect for a new reef. We'll take a couple of wagons and find another fortune. I bet you've forgotten how it feels to sit on a horse and handle a rifle, to have the wind in your face and not a whore or a stockbroker within five hundred miles.'

362

'But it means leaving everything we've worked for,' Duff groaned.

'Sweet merciful heavens, man, are you blind or just plain stupid?' Sean stormed at him. 'You don't own anything, so how the hell can you leave something you haven't got? I'm going down to see Hradsky and try to make a deal with him. Are you coming?'

Duff looked at him without seeing him, his lips were trembling and he was shaking his head. At last he was realizing the position they were in and the impact of it had dazed him. The higher you ride the further there is to fall.

'All right,' said Sean. 'Wait for me here.'

Hradsky's suite was full of talking, laughing men. Sean recognized most of them as the courtiers who used to cluster round the throne on which he and Duff had sat. The King is dead, long live the King! They saw him standing in the doorway and the laughter and loud voices fizzled out. He saw Max take two quick steps to the stinkwood desk in the corner, pull open the top drawer and drop his hand into it. He stood like that watching Sean. One by one the courtiers picked up their hats and canes and hurried out of the room. Some of them mumbled embarrassed greetings as they brushed passed Sean. Then there were only the three of them left: Sean standing quietly in the doorway, Max behind the desk with his hand on the pistol and Hradsky in the chair by the fireplace watching through yellow, half-hooded eyes.

'Aren't you going to invite me in, Max?' Sean asked and Max glanced quickly at Hradsky, saw his barely perceptible nod and looked back at Sean. 'Come in, please, Mr Courtney.'

Sean pushed the door shut behind him. 'You won't need the gun, Max, the game is over.'

'And the score is in our favour, is it not, Mr Courtney?'

Sean nodded. 'Yes, you've won. We are prepared to make over to you all the C.R.C. shares we hold.'

Max shook his head unhappily. 'I'm afraid it's not quite as easy as that. You have undertaken to sell us a certain number of shares and we must insist upon delivery in full.'

'Just where do you suggest we get them?' Sean asked.

'You could buy them on the Stock Exchange.'

'From you?'

Max shrugged but made no reply.

'So you are going to twist the knife, are you?'

'You put it very poetically, Mr Courtney,' agreed Max.

'Have you considered the consequences of forcing us into bankruptcy?'

'I will admit freely that the consequences to you do not concern us.'

Sean smiled. 'That was not very nice, Max, but I was talking about it from your point of view. Sequestration orders, creditors' meetings – you can rest assured that the liquidator appointed will be a member of the *Volksraad* or a relative of one. There will be court actions and counter actions, enforced sale of the shares in the estate and costs to pay. A liquidator with any sense at all could string it out for three or four years, all the time drawing a handsome commission. Have you thought about that, Max?'

The narrowing of Max's eyes showed that he hadn't. He looked at Hradsky with a trace of helplessness in his face, and Sean took a little comfort from that look.

'Now what I suggest is this – you let us draw ten thousand, take our horses and personal belongings. We in exchange will give you the rest. Shares, bank accounts, property, everything. You cannot possibly get more out of it if you force us into bankruptcy.'

Hradsky gave Max a message in their private facial code and Max interpreted it to Sean.

364

'Would you mind waiting outside, please, while we discuss this offer of yours.'

'I'll go down and have a drink in the bar,' said Sean. He pulled his watch from his waistcoat pocket and checked the time. 'Will twenty minutes be enough?'

'Ample, thank you, Mr Courtney.'

Sean had his drink by himself although the bar was nowhere near empty. This was not an arrangement of his own choosing, but he was flying the fever flag of failure and so he had to take an isolation berth at one end of the bar while all the other ships steered wide of him. No one looked in his direction and the conversation that went on round him was carefully arranged so as to exclude him. While he waited out the twenty minutes he amused himself by imagining the reactions of these his friends if he were to ask them for a loan. This helped to take the sting out of their snubs but still he felt it rankling. He looked at his watch again. The twenty minutes were up. Sean walked back along the counter towards the door. Jock and Trevor Heyns saw him coming, they turned away abruptly and immediately became absorbed in staring at the bottle-lined shelves behind the bar counter. Sean stopped level with Jock and cleared his throat deferentially. 'Jock, could you spare a minute?'

Jock turned slowly. 'Ah, Sean. Yes, what is it?'

'Duff and I are leaving the Rand. I have something for you, just something to remember us by. I know Duff would want you to have it too.'

Jock reddened with embarrassment. 'That's not necessary,' he said and started to turn back to his drink.

'Please, Jock.'

'Oh, all right,' Jock's voice was irritable. 'What is it?'

'This,' Sean said and stepped forward, moving his weight behind the fist. Jock's large and whisky-flushed nose was a target to dream about. It was not one of Sean's best punches, he was out of training, but it was good enough to send Jock in a spectacular back-somersault over the counter. Dreamily Sean picked up Jock's glass and emptied it over Trevor's head.

'Next time you meet me smile and say "Hello",' he told Trevor. 'Until then – stay out of mischief.'

He went up the stairs to Hradsky's suite in much better spirits. They were waiting for him.

'Give me the word, Max,' Sean could even grin at him.

'Mr Hradsky has very generously—'

'How much?' Sean cut him short.

'Mr Hradsky will allow you to take fifteen hundred and your personal effects. As part of the agreement you will give an undertaking not to embark on any business venture on the Witwatersrand for a period of three years.'

'That will be too soon,' said Sean. 'Make it two thousand and you've got a deal.'

'The offer is not open to discussion.'

Sean could see they meant it. They didn't have to bargain; it was a statement.

'All right, I accept.'

'Mr Hradsky has sent for his lawyer to draw up the agreement. Would you mind waiting, Mr Courtney?'

'Not at all, Max, you forget I am a gentleman of leisure now.'

Sean found Duff still sitting in the chair where he had left him in the drawing-room of Xanadu. The bottle clutched in his hand was empty and he was unconscious. He had spilt brandy down the front of his waistcoat and three of the buttons were undone. Huddled in the big chair, his body seemed to have shrunk and the curly hair hanging onto his forehead softened the gaunt lines of his face. Sean loosened his fingers from the neck of the bottle and Duff moved restlessly, muttering and twisting his head.

'Bedtime for small boys,' said Sean. He lifted him out of the chair and hung him over one shoulder.

Duff sicked up copiously.

'That's the way, show Hradsky what you think of his bloody carpet,' Sean encouraged him. 'Give him another one for luck, but not on my boots.'

Duff did as he was bid and, chuckling, Sean carried him up the stairs. At the top he stopped and with Duff still bundled over one shoulder tried to analyse his own feelings. Damn it, he felt happy. It was ridiculous to feel so happy in the midst of disaster. He went on down the passage still wondering at himself and into Duff's room. He dropped Duff on the bed and stripped his clothes off, then he rolled him under the blankets. He brought the enamel wash basin from the bathroom and placed it next to the bed.

'You may need this – sleep well. There's a long ride ahead of us tomorrow.'

He stopped again at the top of the stairs and looked down their marble slope into the splendour of the lobby. He was leaving all of it and that was nothing to feel happy about. He laughed aloud. Perhaps it was because he had faced complete annihilation and at the last instant had changed it into something less; by avoiding the worst he had made defeat into a victory. A pathetic little victory to be sure, but at least they were no worse off now than they had been when they had arrived on the Rand. Was that the reason? Sean thought about it and found that it wasn't the whole truth. There was also a feeling of release. That was another part of it. To go on his way: north to a new land. He felt the tingle of anticipation.

'Not a whore or a stockbroker within five hundred miles,' he said aloud and grinned. He gave up trying to find words for his feeling. Emotion was so damned elusive: as soon as you cornered it, it changed its shape and the net of words which you had ready to throw over it was no longer suitable. He let it go free to range through his body, accepting and enjoying it. He ran down the stairs, out through the kitchens and into the stableyard.

'Mbejane!' he shouted, 'where the hell are you?'

The clatter of a stool overturning in the servants' quarters and the door of one of the rooms burst open.

'Nkosi – what is it?' The urgency of Sean's voice had alarmed Mbejane.

'Which are the six best horses we have?'

Mbejane named them, making no attempt to hide his curiosity.

'Are they all salted against the Nagana?'*

'All of them, Nkosi.'

'Good – have them ready before tomorrow's light. Two with saddles, the others to carry the packs.'

Mbejane turned on his smile. 'Could it be we are going hunting, Nkosi?'

'It could easily be,' Sean agreed.

'How long will we be gone, Nkosi?'

'How long is for ever? Take leave of all your women,

---

* Sleeping sickness. Salting involved deliberate exposure to the sting of the tsetse fly. Animals that recovered were then immune.

bring your kaross and your spears and we will see where the road leads.'

Sean went back to his bedroom. It took him half an hour to pack. The pile of discarded clothing in the centre of the room grew steadily and what he kept made only half a horseload. He crammed it into two leather valises. He found his sheepskin coat in the back of one of the closets and threw it over a chair with his leather breeches and slouch hat, ready to wear in the morning. He went down to the study and made his selection from the gun rack, ignoring the fancy doubles and obscure calibres. He took down a pair of shotguns and four Mannlichers.

Then he went to tell Candy goodbye. She was in her suite but she opened quickly to his knock.

'Have you heard?' he asked her.

'Yes, the whole town knows. Oh! Sean, I'm so sorry – please come in.' She held the door open for him. 'How is Duff?'

'He'll be all right – right now he's both drunk and asleep.'

'I'll go to him,' she said quickly. 'He'll need me now.'

For answer Sean raised an eyebrow and looked at her until she dropped her eyes.

'No, you're right, I suppose. Perhaps later, when he's got over the first shock.' She looked up at Sean and smiled. 'I suppose you need a drink. It must have been hell for you as well.' She went across to the cabinet. She had on a blue gown and it clung to the womanish thrust of her hips and did not go high enough to cover the cleft of her breasts. Sean watched her pour his drink and bring it to him. She was lovely, he thought.

'Till we meet again, Candy.' Sean lifted his glass.

Her eyes went wide and very blue. 'I don't understand. Why do you say that?'

'We're going, Candy, first thing tomorrow.'

369

'No, Sean – you're joking.' But she knew he wasn't. There wasn't much to say after that. He finished his drink and they talked for a while, then he kissed her.

'Be happy, please,' he ordered her.

'I'll try. Come back one day soon.'

'Only if you promise to marry me.' He smiled at her and she caught hold of his beard and tugged his head from side to side.

'Get away with you – before I hold you to that.' He left her then because he knew she was going to weep and he didn't want to watch it.

The next morning Duff packed his gear under Sean's direction. He followed each instruction with a dazed obedience, answering when Sean spoke but otherwise withdrawn in a protective shell of silence. When he had finished Sean made him pick up his bags and marched him down to where the horses waited in the chill gloom of not-yet day. With the horses were men, four shapes in the darkness. Sean hesitated before going out into the yard.

'Mbejane,' he called. 'Who are these with you?'

They came forward into the light that poured through the doorway and Sean chuckled.

'Hlubi, of the noble belly! Nonga! And is it you, Kandhla?' Men who had worked beside him in the trenches of the Candy Deep, had plied the spades that had uncovered his fortune, had plied the spears that protected it from the first predators. Happy at his recognition of them, for it had been many years, they crowded forward smiling as widely and whitely as only a Zulu can.

'What brings you three rogues together so early in the day?' Sean asked, and Hlubi answered for them.

'Nkosi, we heard talk of a trek and our feet burned, we heard talk of hunting and we could not sleep.'

'There is no money for wages,' Sean spoke gruffly to cover the sudden rush of affection he felt for them.

370

'We made no talk of wages,' Hlubi answered with dignity. Sean nodded, it was the reply he had expected. He cleared his throat and went on.

'You would come with me when you know that I have the Tagathi on me?' He used the Zulu word for witchcraft. 'You would follow me knowing that behind me I leave a spoor of dead men and sorrow?'

'Nkosi,' Hlubi was grave as he answered. 'Something always dies when the lion feeds – and yet there is meat for those that follow him.'

'I hear the chatter of old women at a beer drink,' Mbejane observed drily. 'There is no more to say and the horses grow restless.'

They rode down the driveway of Xanadu between the jacaranda trees and the smooth wide lawns. Behind them the mansion was grey and unlighted in the half darkness. They took the Pretoria road, climbed to the ridge and checked their horses at the crest. Sean and Duff looked back across the valley. The valley was filled with early morning mist, and the mine headgears probed up out of it. They watched the mists turn to gold as the low sun touched them and a mine hooter howled dismally.

'Couldn't we stay for just a week longer – perhaps we could work something out?' Duff asked softly.

Sean sat silently staring at the golden mist. It was beautiful. It hid the scarred earth and it hid the mills – it was a most appropriate cloak for that evil, greedy city. Sean turned his horse away towards Pretoria and slapped the loose end of his reins across its neck.

– III –

The Wilderness

– 1 –

They stayed five days in Pretoria, just long enough to buy the wagons and commission them, and when they left on the morning of the sixth day they went north on the Hunters Road. The wagons moved in column urged on by the Zulus and a dozen new servants that Sean had hired. They were followed by a mixed bag of black and white urchins and stray dogs; men called good luck after them and women waved from the verandas of the houses which lined the road. Then the town was behind them and they were out into the veld with only a dozen of the more adventurous mongrels still following them.

They made fifteen miles the first day and when they camped that night beside the ford of a small stream, Sean's back and legs ached from his first full day in the saddle in over five years. They drank a little brandy and ate steaks grilled over wood embers, then they let the fire die and sat and looked at the night. The sky was a curtain at which a barrel of grape-shot had been fired, riddling it with the holes through which the stars shone. The voices of the servants made a hive murmur as a background to the wailing of a jackal in the darkness beyond the firelight. They went to their living wagon early and for Sean the feel of rough blankets instead of silk sheets and the hardness of a straw mattress were not sufficient to keep him long from sleep.

From an early start the following morning they put another twenty miles behind them before outspan that night and twenty more the next day. The push and urgent drive were habits Sean had acquired on the Rand when every minute was vital and the loss of a day was a disaster. They were habits that stuck, and he pushed the caravan northward as impatiently as he would have chivvied the men on the Candy Deep who were cutting a drive to intersect the Reef. Then one morning, when they were inspanning the oxen at the usual hour of dawn, Mbejane asked him, 'Do we go to meet someone, Nkosi?'

'No. Why do you ask?'

'When a man moves fast there is usually a reason. I was seeking the reason for our haste.'

'The reason is—' Sean stopped. He looked around him quickly as if to find it, then he cleared his throat and scratched the side of his nose, ' – outspan an hour before high sun,' he finished abruptly and went to his horse. He and Duff rode out a mile or two ahead of the wagons that day, then instead of keeping to the track or hurrying back to chase up the caravan Sean suggested, 'Let's ride across to that kopje over there. We'll leave the horses at the bottom and climb up to the top.'

'What for?' asked Duff.

'For the hell of it – come on.'

They hobbled the horses and set off up the steep side of the kopje, picking their way over the tumbled boulders and through the tangle of tree trunks. They were sweating and blowing hard when they came out on the summit and found a place with shade and a flat rock ledge on which to sit. Sean gave Duff a cheroot and they smoked and looked out across the land that was spread like a map below them.

Here the grasslands of the high veld were starting to blend into the forests and hilly country of the bushveld. There were vleis open as wheatfields, ending suddenly against a hill or bounded by haphazard plantations of tall trees. From the height at which they sat they could trace the courses of underground rivers by the dark green and superior height of the trees that grew above them. Everything else was the colour of Africa – brown, a thousand different shades of brown. Pale brown grass on red brown soil, with twisted, chocolate-brown tree trunks reaching up to the moving masses of brown leaves at their tips. Flickering indefinite brown were the herds of springbok that fed amongst the trees and on the slopes of the bare bulging brown hills, and the brown land reached away vast and unhurried into immeasurable distance, unmarred by the scratchings of man: tranquil and dignified in its immensity.

'It makes me feel small, but sort of safe – as though no one will notice me here,' said Duff, then laughed self-consciously.

'I know what you mean,' Sean answered him. He saw that for the first time since they had left the Rand the strain was gone from Duff's face. They smiled at each other and leaned back against the rock face behind them. They watched their wagons, far below them, coil into the tight circle of the laager and the cattle turned free move out to graze. The sun sank and the shadows stretched out longer and longer across the land. At last they went down the hill and found their horses. That night they stayed later than usual next to the fire and though they talked little there was the old feeling between them again. They had discovered a new reef that was rich with the precious elements of space and time. Out here there was more of those two treasures than a man could use in a dozen lifetimes. Space to move, to ride or to fire a rifle; space spread with sunlight and wind, grass and trees, but not filled with them. There was also time. This was where time began: it was a quiet river, moving but not changed by movement; draw on it as much as you would and still it was always full. It was measured by the seasons but not restricted by them, for the summer that was now standing back to let autumn pass was

377

the same summer that had flamed a thousand years before and would flame again a thousand years hence. In the presence of so much space and time all striving was futile.

From then on their lives took their tempo from the leisurely turning of wagon-wheels. Sean's eyes which had been pointing straight ahead along the line of travel now turned aside to look about him. Each morning he and Duff would leave the wagons and wander out into the bush. Sometimes they would spend the day panning for gold in the sands of a stream, another day they would search for the first signs of elephant, but mostly they just rode and talked or lay hidden and watched the herds of game that daily became more numerous. They killed just enough to feed themselves, their servants and the pack of dogs that had followed them when they left Pretoria. They passed the little Boer settlement at Pietersburg and then the Zoutpansberg climbed up over the horizon, its sheer sides dark with rain forest and high rock cliffs. Here under the mountains they spent a week at Louis Trichardt, the most northerly permanent habitation of white men.

In the town they spoke with men who had hunted to the north of the mountains, across the Limpopo. These were taciturn brown-faced Boers with tobacco-stained beards – big men with the peace of the bush in their eyes. In their courteous, unhurried speech Sean sensed a fierce possessive love of the animals that they hunted and the land through which they moved so freely. They were a different breed from the Natal Afrikanders and those he had met on the Witwatersrand, and he conceived the respect for them that would grow stronger in the years ahead when he would have to fight them.

There was no way through the mountains, they told him, but wagons could pass around them. The western passage skirted the edge of the Kalahari desert and this was bad country where the wagon wheels sank into the sandy

378

soil and the marches between water became successively longer. To the east there was good rich forest land, well watered and stocked with game: low country, hotter the nearer one went to the coast, but the true bushveld where a man could find elephant.

So Sean and Duff turned east and, holding the mountains always in sight at their left hand, they went down into the wilderness.

– 2 –

Within a week's trek they saw elephant sign: trees broken and stripped of their bark. Although it was months old – the trees already dried out – nevertheless Sean felt the thrill of it and that night spent an hour cleaning and oiling his rifles. The forest thickened until the wagons had to weave continually between the trunks of the trees. But there were clearings in the forest – open vleis filled with grass where buffalo grazed like herds of domestic cattle and white tick birds squawked about them. This country was well watered with streams as clear and merry as a Scottish trout stream, but the water was blood-warm and the banks thick with bush. Along the rivers, in the forest and in the open were the herds of game: impala twisting and leaping away at the first approach with their crumpled horns laid back, kudu with big ears and soft eyes, black sable antelope with white bellies and horns curved like a naval cutlass, zebra trotting with the dignity of fat ponies, while about them frolicked their companions, the gnu, waterbuck, nyala, roan antelope and – at last – elephant.

Sean and Mbejane were ranging a mile ahead of the wagons when they found the spoor. It was fresh, so fresh that sap still oozed from the mahoba-hoba tree where the bark had been prised loose with the tip of a tusk and then stripped off. The wood beneath was naked and white.

'Three bulls,' said Mbejane. 'One very big.'

'Wait here.' Sean spun his horse and galloped back to the column. Duff lay on the driver's seat of the first wagon rocking gently to its motion, his hat covering his face and his hands behind his head.

'Elephant! Duff,' Sean yelled. 'Not an hour ahead of us. Get saddled up, man!'

Duff was ready in five minutes. Mbejane was waiting for them; he had already worked the spoor a short distance and picked up the run of it and now he went away on it. They followed him, riding slowly side by side.

'You've hunted elephant before, laddie?' asked Duff.

'Never,' said Sean.

'Good grief!' Duff looked alarmed. 'I thought you were an expert. I think I'll go back and finish my sleep, you can call me when you've had a little more experience.'

'Don't worry,' Sean laughed with excitement. 'I know all about it; I was raised on elephant stories.'

'That sets my heart at ease,' Duff murmured sarcastically and Mbejane glanced over his shoulder at them, not trying to conceal his irritation.

'Nkosi, it is not wise to talk now for we will soon come up with them.'

So they went on in silence: passing a knee-high pile of yellow dung that looked like the contents of a coir mattress, following the oval pad marks in the dust and the trail of torn branches.

It was a good hunt, this first one. The small breeze held steadily into their faces and the spoor ran straight and hot. They closed in, each minute strengthening the certainty of the kill. Sean sat stiff and eager in the saddle with his rifle across his lap, his eyes restlessly moving over the frieze of

380

bush ahead of him. Mbejane stopped suddenly and came back to Sean's stirrup.

'Here they halted for the first time. The sun is hot and they will rest but this place was not to their liking and they have moved on. We will find them soon now.'

'The bush becomes too thick,' Sean grunted; he eyed the untidy tangle of catbush into which the spoor had led them. 'We will leave the horses here with Hlubi and go in on foot.'

'Laddie,' Duff demurred. 'I can run much faster on horseback.'

'Off!' said Sean and nodded to Mbejane to lead. They moved forward again. Sean was sweating and the drops clung heavily to his eyebrows and trickled down his cheeks; he brushed them away. The excitement was an indigestible ball in his stomach and a dryness in his throat.

Duff sauntered casually next to Sean with that small half smile on his face, but there was a quickness in his breathing. Mbejane cautioned them with a gesture of his hand and they stopped. Minutes passed slowly and then Mbejane's hand moved again, pink-palmed eloquence.

'It was nothing,' said the hand. 'Follow me.'

They went on again. There were Mopani flies swarming at the corners of Sean's eyes, drinking the moisture, and he blinked them away. Their buzzing was so loud in his ears that he thought it must carry to their quarry. His every sense was tuned to its limit: hearing magnified, vision sharp and even his sense of smell so clear that he could pick up the taint of dust, the scent of a wild flower and Mbejane's faintly musky body-smell.

Suddenly in front of him Mbejane was still; his hand moved again gently, unmistakably.

'They are here,' said the hand.

Sean and Duff crouched behind him, searching with eyes

381

that could see only brown bush and grey shadows. The tension coarsened their breathing and Duff was no longer smiling. Mbejane's hand came up slowly and pointed at the wall of vegetation in front of them. The seconds strung together like beads on the string of time and still they searched.

An ear flapped lazily and instantly the picture jumped into focus. Bull elephant, big and very close, grey among grey shadow. Sean touched Mbejane's arm. 'I had seen it,' said that touch.

Slowly Mbejane's hand swivelled and pointed again. Another wait, another searching and then a belly rumbled, a great grey belly filled with half-digested leaves. It was a sound so ridiculous in the silence that Sean wanted to laugh – a gurgling sloshy sound – and Sean saw the other bull. It was standing in shadow also, with long yellow ivory and small eyes tight-closed. Sean put his lips to Duff's ear.

'This one is yours,' he whispered. 'Wait until I get into position for the other,' and he began moving out to the side, each step exposing a little more of the second bull's flank until the shoulder was open to him and he could see the point of the elbow beneath the baggy, wrinkled skin. The angle was right; from here he could reach the heart. He nodded at Duff, brought his rifle up – leaning forward against the recoil, aiming close behind the massive shoulder – and he fired.

The gunfire was shockingly loud in the confined thorn bush; dust flew in a spurt from the bull's shoulder and it staggered from the strike of the bullet. Beyond it the third elephant burst from sleep into flight and Sean's hands moved neatly on his weapon, ejecting and reloading, swinging up and firing again. He saw the bullet hit and he knew it was a mortal wound. The two bulls ran together and the bush opened to them and swallowed them: they were gone, crashing away wounded, trumpeting in pain.

382

Sean ran after them, dodging through the catbush, oblivious to the sting of the thorns that snatched at him as he passed.

'This way, Nkosi,' Mbejane shouted beside him. 'Quickly or we will lose them.' They sprinted after the sounds of flight – a hundred yards, two hundred, panting now and sweating in the heat. Suddenly the catbush ended and in front of them was a wide riverbed with steep banks. The river sand was blindingly white and in the middle was a sluggish trickle of water. One of the bulls was dead, lying in the stream with the blood washing off him in a pale brown stain. The other bull was trying to climb the far bank; it was too steep for him and he slid back wearily. The blood dripped from the tip of his trunk, and he swung his head to look at Sean and Mbejane. His ears cocked back defiantly and he began his charge, blundering towards them through the soft river sand.

Sean watched him come and there was sadness in him as he brought up his rifle, but it was the proud regret that a man feels when he watches hopeless courage. Sean killed with a brain shot, quickly.

They climbed down the bank into the riverbed and went to the elephant; it knelt with its legs folded under it and its tusks driven deep into the sand with the force of its fall. The flies were already clustering at the little red mouths of the bullet wounds. Mbejane touched one of the tusks and then he looked up at Sean.

'It is a good elephant.' He said no more, for this was not the time to talk. Sean leaned his rifle against the bull's shoulder; he felt in his top pocket for a cheroot and stood with it unlit between his teeth. He would kill more elephant, he knew, but always this would be the one he would remember. He stroked his hand over the rough skin and the bristles were stiff and sharp.

'Where is Nkosi Duff?' Sean remembered him suddenly. 'Did he also kill?'

'He did not shoot,' answered Mbejane.

'What!' Sean turned quickly to Mbejane. 'Why not?'

Mbejane sniffed a pinch of snuff and sneezed, then he shrugged his shoulders.

'It is a good elephant,' he said again, looking down at it.

'We must go back and find him.' Sean snatched up his rifle and Mbejane followed him. They found Duff sitting alone in the catbush with his rifle propped beside him and a water-bottle to his lips. He lowered the bottle as Sean came up and saluted him with it.

'Hail! the conquering hero comes.' There was something in his eyes that Sean could not read.

'Did you miss yours?' Sean asked.

'Yes,' said Duff, 'I missed mine.' He lifted the bottle and drank again. Suddenly and sickeningly Sean was ashamed for him. He dropped his eyes, not wanting to acknowledge Duff's cowardice.

'Let's get back to the wagons,' he said. 'Mbejane can come with packhorses for the tusks.'

They did not ride together on the way home.

– 3 –

It was almost dark when they arrived back at the laager. They gave their horses to one of the servants and washed in the basin that Kandhla had ready for them, then they went to sit by the fire. Sean poured the drinks, fussing over the glasses to avoid looking at Duff. He felt awkward. They'd have to talk about it and he searched his brain for a way to bring it into the open. Duff had shown craven and Sean started to find excuses for him – he may have had a misfire or he may have been unsighted by Sean's shot. At all events Sean determined not to let it stay like this, sour and brooding between them. They'd talk it out then forget it. He carried Duff's glass to him and smiled at him.

'That's right, try and cover it with a grin,' Duff lifted his glass. 'To our big brave hunter. Dammit, laddie, how could you do it?'

Sean stared at Duff. 'What do you mean?'

'You know what I mean, you're so damned guilty you can't even look me in the face. How could you kill those bloody great animals – but even worse how could you *enjoy* doing it?'

Sean subsided weakly into his chair. He couldn't tell which of his emotions was uppermost – relief or surprise. Duff went on quickly.

'I know what you're going to say, I've heard the arguments before – from my dear father. He explained it to me one evening after we'd ridden down a fox. When I say "we", I mean twenty horsemen and forty hounds.'

Sean had not yet rallied from the shock of finding himself in the dock after preparing himself to play the role of prosecutor.

'Don't you like hunting?' he asked incredulously. The way he might have asked, 'don't you like eating?'

'I'd forgotten what it was like. I was carried away by your excitement, but when you started to kill them it all came back to me.' Duff sipped his brandy and stared into the fire. 'They never had a chance. One minute they were sleeping and the next you were ripping them with bullets the way the hounds ripped that fox. They didn't have a chance.'

'But, Duff, it wasn't meant to be a contest.'

'Yes, I know, my father explained that to me. It's a ritual – a sacred rite to Diana. He should have explained it to the fox as well.'

Sean was getting angry now. 'We came out here to hunt ivory – and that's what I'm doing.'

'Tell me that you killed those elephant only for their

385

teeth, laddie, and I'll call you a liar. You loved it. Christ!
You should have seen your face and the face of your damned
heathen.'

'All right! I like hunting and the only other man I ever
met who didn't was a coward,' Sean shouted at him.

Duff's face paled and he looked up at Sean. 'What are
you trying to say?' he whispered. They stared at each other
and in the silence Sean had to choose between letting his
temper run or keeping Duff's friendship, for the words that
would spoil it for ever were crowding into his mouth. He
made his hands relax their grip on the arms of his chair.

'I didn't mean that,' he said.

'I hope you didn't.' Duff's grin came precariously back
onto his face. 'Tell me why you like hunting, laddie. I'll try
and understand but don't expect me to hunt with you
again.'

It was like explaining colour to a blind man, describing
the lust of the hunter to someone who was born without it.
Duff listened in agonized silence as Sean tried to find the
words for the excitement that makes a man's blood sing
through his body, that heightens his senses and allows him
to lose himself in an emotion as old as the urge to mate.
Sean tried to show him how the nobler and more beautiful
was the quarry, the stronger was the compulsion to hunt
and kill it, that it had no conscious cruelty in it but was
rather an expression of love: a fierce possessive love. A
devouring love that needed the complete and irrevocable
act of death for its consummation. By destroying something,
a man could have it always as his own: selfish perhaps, but
then instinct knows no ethics. It was all very clear to Sean,
so much a part of him that he had never tried to voice it
before and now he stumbled over the words, gesticulating
in helpless inarticulateness, repeating himself, coming at
last to the end and knowing by the look on Duff's face that
he had failed to show it to him.

'And you were the gentleman who fought Hradsky for the rights of man,' Duff said softly, 'the one who always talked about not hurting people.'

Sean opened his mouth to protest but Duff went on. 'You get ivory for us and I'll look for gold – each of us to what he is best suited. I'll forgive you your elephants as you forgave me my Candy – still equal partners. Agreed?'

Sean nodded and Duff held up his glass.

'It's empty,' he said. 'Do me a favour, laddie.'

– 4 –

There was never any after-taste to their disputes, no rankling of unspoken words or lingering of doubt. What they had in common they enjoyed, where there were differences they accepted them. So when after each hunt the packhorses brought the tusks into the camp there was no trace of censure in Duff's face or voice; there was only the genuine pleasure of having Sean back from the bush. Sometimes it was a good day and Sean would cut the spoor, follow, kill and be back in the laager the same night. But more often, when the herd was moving fast or the ground was hard or he could not kill at the first approach, he would be gone for a week or more. Each time he returned they celebrated, drinking and laughing far into the night, lying late in bed the next morning, playing Klabejas on the floor of the wagon between their cots or reading aloud out of the books that Duff had brought with him from Pretoria. Then a day or two later Sean would be gone again, with his dogs and his gunboys trotting behind him.

This was a different Sean from the one who had whored it up at the Opera House and presided over the panelled offices in Eloff Street. His beard, no longer groomed and shaped by a barber, curled onto his chest. The doughy colour of his face and arms had been turned by the sun to the rich brown of a newly-baked loaf. The seat of his pants that had been stretched to danger point across his rump now hung loosely; his arms were thicker and the soft swell of fat had given way to the flatness and bulge of hard muscle. He walked straighter, moved quicker and laughed more easily.

In Duff the change was less noticeable. He was lean and gaunt-faced as ever, but now there was less of the restlessness in his eyes. His speech and movements were slower and the golden beard he was growing had the strange effect of making him appear younger. Each morning he left the wagons, taking one of the servants with him, and spent the days wandering in the bush, tapping with his prospecting hammer at the occasional outcrops of rock or squatting beside a stream and spinning the gravel in his pan. Every evening he came back to camp and analysed the bag of rock samples he had collected during the day; then he threw them away, bathed and set out a bottle and two glasses on the table beside the fire. While he ate his supper he listened and waited for the dogs to bark, for the sound of horses in the darkness and Sean's voice. If the night remained silent he put the bottle away and climbed up into his wagon. He was lonely then, not with a deep loneliness but just enough to add relish to Sean's return.

Always they moved east, until gradually the silhouette of the Zoutpansberg softened as the mountains became less steep and began to fade into the tail of the range. Scouting along their edge Sean found a pass and they took the wagons up and over and down into the Limpopo valley beyond. Here the country changed character again; it became flat, the monotony of thorn scrub relieved only by the baobab trees with their great, swollen trunks crowned in a little halo of branches. Water was scarce and Sean rode ahead from each camp to find the next waterhole before they moved. However, the hunting was good for the game was concentrated on the isolated drinking places, and before they were halfway from the mountains to the Limpopo Sean had filled another wagon with ivory.

'We'll be coming back this way, I suppose?' Duff asked.

'I suppose so,' agreed Sean.

'Well then, I don't see any point in carrying a ton of ivory with us. Let's bury it and we can pick it up on our way back.'

Sean looked at him thoughtfully. 'About once in every year you come up with a good idea – we'll do exactly that.'

The next camp was a good one. There was water – an acre of muddy liquid not as heavily salted with elephant urine as some of the previous ones had been; there was shade provided by a grove of wild fig trees and the grazing was of a quality that promised to restore the condition that the oxen had lost since crossing the mountains. They decided to make it a rest camp: bury the ivory, do some repairs and maintenance on the wagons and let the servants and animals fatten up a little. The first task was to dig a hole large enough to contain all the hundred-odd tusks they had accumulated and it was evening on the third day before they finished.

– 5 –

Sean and Duff sat together inside the laager and watched the sun go down, bleeding below the land, and after it had gone the clouds were oyster and lilac-coloured in the brief twilight. Kandhla threw wood on the fire and it burnt up fiercely. They ate grilled kudu liver, and thick steaks with a rind of yellow fat on them, and they drank brandy with their coffee. The conversation lagged into contented silence for they were both tired. They sat staring into the fire, too lazy to make the effort required for bed. Sean watched the fire pictures form in the coals, the faces and the phantoms flickering and fading. He saw a tiny temple have its columns pulled out from under it by a fiery Samson and collapse in a shower of sparks – a burning horse changed magically into a dragon of blue flame. He looked away to rest his eyes and when he turned back there was a small black scorpion scuttling out from under the loose bark on one of the logs. It lifted its tail like the arm of a flamenco dancer and the flames that ringed it shone on its glossy body armour. Duff was also watching it, leaning forward with his elbows on his knees.

'Will he sting himself to death before the flames reach him?' he asked softly. 'I have heard that they do.'

'No,' said Sean.

'Why not?'

'Only man has the intelligence to end the inevitable; in all other creatures the instinct of survival is too strong,' Sean answered him, and the scorpion crabbed sideways from the nearest flames and stopped again with its raised sting jerking slightly. 'Besides he's immune to his own poison so he has no choice.'

'He could jump down into the fire and get it over with,' murmured Duff, subdued by the little tragedy.

The scorpion started its last desperate circuit of the closing ring. Its tail drooped and the grip of its claws was unsteady on the rough bark; it was shrivelling with the heat, its legs curling up and its tail subsiding. The flames caressed it with swift yellow hands and smeared its shiny body with the dullness of death. The log tipped sideways and the speck was gone.

'Would you?' asked Sean. 'Would you have jumped?'

Duff sighed softly. 'I don't know,' he said and stood up. 'I'm going to pump out my bilges and crawl into bed.' He

390

walked away and went to stand at the edge of the circle of firelight.

Since they had left Pretoria the small voices of the jackals had yapped discreetly around each outspan – they were so much a part of the African night that they went unnoticed – but now suddenly there was a difference. Only one jackal spoke, and with a voice that stammered shrilly – a sound of pain, a crazy hysterical shrieking that made Sean's skin prickle. He scrambled to his feet and stood staring undecided into the darkness. The jackal was coming towards the camp, coming fast – and suddenly Sean knew what was happening.

'Duff!' he called. 'Come back here! Run, man, run!'

Duff looked back at Sean helplessly, his hands held low in front of him and his water arcing down, curving silver in the firelight from his body to the ground.

'Duff!' Sean's voice was a shout. 'It's a rabid jackal. Run, damn you, run!' The jackal was close now, very close, but at last Duff started to move. He was halfway back to the fire before he tripped. He fell and rolled over and brought his feet up under his body to rise. His head turned to face the darkness from which it would come. Then Sean saw it. It flitted out of the shadows like a grey moth in the bad light and went straight for where Duff knelt. Sean saw him try to cover his face with his hands as the jackal sprang at him. One of the dogs twisted out of Mbejane's hand and brushed past Sean's legs. Sean snatched up a piece of firewood and sprinted after it, but already Duff was on his back, his arms flailing frantically as he tried to push away the terrier-sized animal that was slashing at his face and hands. The dog caught it and dragged it off, worrying it, growling through locked jaws. Sean hit the jackal with the club – breaking its back. He swung again and again, beating its body into shapelessness before he turned to Duff. Duff was on his feet now. He had unwound the scarf from his neck and was mopping with it at his face but the blood dribbled down his chin and blotched the front of his shirt. His hands were trembling. Sean led him close to the fire, pulled Duff's hands down and examined the bites. His nose was torn and the flesh of one cheek hung open in a flap.

'Sit down!'

Duff obeyed, holding the scarf to his face again. Sean went quickly to the fire: with a stick he raked embers into a pile, then he drew his hunting-knife and thrust the blade into the coals.

'Mbejane,' he called, without taking his eyes off the knife. 'Throw that jackal onto the fire. Put on plenty of wood. Do not touch its body with your hands. When you have done that tie up that dog and keep the others away from it.' Sean turned the knife in the fire. 'Duff, drink as much of that brandy as you can.'

'What are you going to do?'

'You know what I've got to do.'

'He bit my wrist as well.' Duff held up his hand for Sean to see the punctures, black holes from which the blood oozed watery and slow.

'Drink.' Sean pointed at the brandy bottle. For a second they looked at each other and Sean saw the horror moving in Duff's eyes: horror of the hot knife and horror of the germs which had been injected into him. The germs that must be burnt out before they escaped into his blood, to breed and ferment there until they ate into his brain and rode him to a screaming, gibbering death.

'Drink,' said Sean again. Duff took up the bottle and lifted it to his mouth. Sean stooped and pulled the knife out of the fire. He held the blade an inch from the back of his hand. It was not hot enough. He thrust it back into the coals.

'Mbejane, Hlubi, stand on each side of the Nkosi's chair.

392

Be ready to hold him.' Sean loosened his belt, doubled the thick leather and handed it to Duff. 'Bite on this.'

He turned back to the fire and this time when he drew the knife its blade was pale pink. 'Are you ready?'

'The work you are about to do will break the hearts of a million maids.' A last hoarse attempt at humour from Duff.

'Hold him,' said Sean.

Duff gasped at the touch of the knife – a great shuddering gasp – and his back arched, but the two Zulus held him down remorselessly. The edges of the wound blackened and hissed as Sean ran the blade in deeper. The stink of burning brought the vomit into his throat. He clenched his teeth. When he stepped back Duff hung slackly in the Zulus' hands, sweat had soaked his shirt and wet his hair. Sean heated the knife again and cleaned the bites in Duff's wrist while Duff moaned and writhed weakly in the chair. He smeared axle grease over the burns and bandaged the wrist loosely with strips torn from a clean shirt. They lifted Duff into the wagon and laid him on his cot. Sean went out to where Mbejane had tied the dog. He found scratches beneath the hair on its shoulder. They put a sack over its head to stop it biting and Sean cauterized its wounds also.

'Tie it to the far wagon, do not let the other dogs near it, see it has food and water,' he told Mbejane.

Then he went back to Duff. Delirious with pain and brandy Duff did not sleep at all that night and Sean stayed by his cot until the morning.

About fifty yards from the laager under one of the wild fig trees the servants built Duff a hut. The framework was of poles and over it they stretched a tarpaulin. They made a bed for him and brought his mattress and blankets from the wagon. Sean joined four trekchains together, forging new links and hammering them closed. He passed one end of the chain round the base of the fig tree and riveted it back up on itself. Duff sat in the shade of a wagon and watched them work. His hurt hand was in a sling and his face was swollen, the wound crusty-looking and edged in angry red. When he was finished with the chain, Sean walked across to him.

'I'm sorry, Duff, we have to do it.'

'They abolished the slave trade some time ago – just in case you didn't know.' Duff tried to grin with his distorted face. He stood up and followed Sean to the hut. Sean looped the loose end of the chain round Duff's waist. He locked it with a bolt through two of the links then flattened the end of the bolt with a dozen strokes of the hammer.

'That should hold you.'

'An excellent fit,' Duff commended him. 'Now let us inspect my new quarters.'

Sean followed him into the hut. Duff lay down on the bed. He looked very tired and sick.

'How long will it take before we know?' he asked quietly.

Sean shook his head. 'I'm not sure. I think you should stay here at least a month – after that we'll allow you back into society.'

'A month – it's going to be fun. Lying here expecting any minute to start barking like a dog and lifting my leg against the nearest tree.'

Sean didn't laugh. 'I did a thorough job with the knife.

It's a thousand to one you'll be all right. This is just a precaution.'

'The odds are attractive – I'll put a fiver on it.' Duff crossed his ankles and stared up at the roof. Sean sat down on the edge of the bed. It was a long time before Duff ended the silence.

'What will it be like, Sean? Have you ever seen someone with rabies?'

'No.'

'But you've heard about it, haven't you? Tell me what you've heard about it,' Duff persisted.

'For Chrissake, Duff, you're not going to get it.'

'Tell me, Sean, tell me what you know about it.' Duff sat up and caught hold of Sean's arm.

Sean looked steadily at him for a moment before he answered. 'You saw that jackal, didn't you?'

Duff sank back onto his pillows. 'Oh, my God!' he whispered.

Together they started the long wait. They used another tarpaulin to make an open shelter next to the hut and under it they spent the days that followed.

In the beginning it was very bad. Sean tried to pull Duff out of the black despair into which he had slumped, but Duff sat for hours at a time gazing out into the bush, fingering the scabs on his face and only occasionally smiling at the banquet of choice stories that Sean spread for him. But at last Sean's efforts were rewarded – Duff began to talk. He spoke of things he had never mentioned before and listening to him Sean learned more about him than he had in the previous five years. Sometimes Duff paced up and down in front of Sean's chair with the chain hanging down behind him like a tail; at other times he sat quietly, his voice filled with longing for the mother he had never known.

' – there was a portrait of her in the upper gallery, I used to spend whole afternoons in front of it. It was the kindest face I had ever seen—'

Then it hardened again as he remembered his father, 'that old bastard'.

He talked of his daughter. ' – she had a fat chuckle that would break your heart. The snow on her grave made it look like a big sugar-iced cake, she would have liked that—'

At other times his voice was puzzled as he examined some past action of his, angry as he remembered a mistake or a missed opportunity. Then he would break off and grin self-consciously. 'I say, I am talking a lot of drivel.'

The scabs on his face began to dry up and come away, and more often now his old gaiety bubbled to the surface.

On one of the poles that supported the tarpaulin roof he started a calendar, cutting a notch for each day. It became a daily ceremony. He cut each notch with the concentration of a sculptor carving marble and when he had finished he would stand back and count them aloud as if by doing so he could force them to add up to thirty, the number that would allow him to shed his chain.

There were eighteen notches on the pole when the dog went mad. It was in the afternoon. They were playing Klabejas. Sean had just dealt the cards when the dog started screaming from among the wagons. Sean knocked over his chair as he jumped up. He snatched his rifle from where it leant against the wall and ran down to the laager. He disappeared behind the wagon to which the dog was tied and almost immediately Duff heard the shot. In the abrupt and complete stillness that followed, Duff slowly lowered his face into his hands.

It was nearly an hour before Sean came back. He picked up his chair, set it to the table and sat down.

'It's you to call – are you going to take on?' he asked as he picked up his cards. They played with grim intensity, fixing their attention on the cards, but both of them knew that there was a third person at the table now.

'Promise you'll never do that to me,' Duff blurted out at last.

Sean looked up at him. 'That I'll never do what to you?'

'What you did to that dog.'

The dog! The bloody dog. He should never have taken a chance with it, he should have destroyed it that first night.

'Just because the dog got it doesn't mean that you—'

'Swear to me,' Duff interrupted fiercely, 'swear you won't bring the rifle to me.'

'Duff, you don't know what you're asking. Once you've got it—' Sean stopped; anything he said would make it worse.

'Promise me,' Duff repeated.

'All right, I swear it then.'

– 7 –

It was worse now than it had been in the beginning. Duff abandoned his calendar and with it the hope that had been slowly growing stronger. If the days were bad then the nights were hell, for Duff had a dream. It came to him every night – sometimes two or three times. He tried to keep awake after Sean had left, reading by the light of a lantern; or he lay and listened to the night noises, the splash and snort of buffalo drinking down at the waterhole, the liquid half-warble of night birds or the deep drumming of a lion. But in the end he would have to sleep and then he dreamed.

He was on horseback riding across a flat brown plain: no hills, no trees, nothing but lawnlike grass stretching away on all sides to the horizon. His horse threw no shadow – he always looked for a shadow and it worried him that there never was one. Then he would find the pool – clear water, blue and strangely shiny. The pool frightened him but he could not stop himself going to it. He would kneel beside it and look into the water; the reflection of his own face looked up at him – animal-snouted, shaggy-brown with wolf teeth, white and long. He would wake then and the horror of that face would last until morning.

Nearly desperate with his own utter helplessness, Sean tried to help him. Because of the accord they had established over the years and because they were so close to each other, Sean had to suffer with him. He tried to shut himself off from it; sometimes he succeeded for an hour or even half a morning, but then it came back with a stomach-swooping shock. Duff was going to die – Duff was going to die an unspeakable death. Was it a mistake to let someone get too deep inside you, so that you must share his agony in every excruciating detail? Didn't a man have enough of his own that he must share the full measure of another's suffering?

By then the October winds had started, the heralds of the rain: hot winds full of dust, winds that dried the sweat on a man's body before it had time to cool him, thirsty winds that during daylight brought the game to the water-hole in full view of the camp.

Sean had half a case of wine hoarded under his cot. That last evening he cooled four bottles, wrapping them in wet sacking. He took them up to Duff's shelter just before supper and set them on the table. Duff watched him. The scars on his face were almost completely healed now, glassy red marks on his pale skin.

'Chateau Olivier,' said Sean and Duff nodded.

'It's a good wine – most probably travel-sick.'

'Well, if you don't want it, I'll take it away again,' said Sean.

'I'm sorry, laddie,' Duff spoke quickly. 'I didn't mean to be ungrateful. This wine suits my mood tonight. Did you know that wine is a sad drink?'

'Nonsense!' Sean disagreed as he twisted the corkscrew into the first cork. 'Wine is gay.' He poured a little into Duff's glass and Duff picked it up and held it towards the fire so the light shone through it.

'You see only the surface, Sean. A good wine has the elements of tragedy within it. The better the wine the more sad it is.'

Sean snorted. 'Explain yourself,' he invited.

Duff put his glass down on the table again and stared at it. 'How long do you suppose this wine has taken to reach its present perfection?'

'Ten or fifteen years, I suppose,' Sean answered.

Duff nodded. 'And now all that remains is to drink it – the work of years destroyed in an instant. Don't you think that is sad?' Duff asked softly.

'My God, Duff, don't be so damned morbid.'

But Duff wasn't listening to him. 'Wine and mankind have this in common. They can find perfection only in age, in a lifetime of seeking. Yet in the finding they find also their own destruction.'

'So you think that if a man lives long enough he will reach perfection?' Sean challenged him, and Duff answered him still staring at the glass.

'Some grapes grew in the wrong soil, some were diseased before they went to the press and some were spoiled by a careless vintner – not all grapes make good wine.' Duff picked up his glass and tasted from it, then he went on. 'A man takes longer and he must find it not within the quiet confines of the cask but in the cauldron of life; therefore his is the greater tragedy.'

'Yes, but no one can live for ever,' Sean protested.

'So you think that makes it less sad?' Duff shook his

head. 'You're wrong, of course. It does not detract from it, it enhances it. If only there were some escape, some way of ensuring that what is good could endure instead of this complete hopelessness.'

Duff lay back in his chair, his face pale and gaunt-looking. 'Even that I could accept, if only they had given me more time.'

'I've had enough of this talk. Let's discuss something else. I don't know what you're worrying about. You're not fit to drink yet, you've got another twenty or thirty years to go,' Sean said gruffly and Duff looked up at him for the first time.

'Have I, Sean?'

Sean couldn't meet his eyes. He knew Duff was going to die. Duff grinned his lopsided grin and looked down again at his glass. Slowly the grin disappeared and he spoke again.

'If only I had more time, I could have done it. I could have found the weak places and fortified them. I could have seen the answers.' His voice rose higher. 'I could have! I know I could have! Oh God, I'm not ready yet. I need more time.' His voice was shrill and his eyes wild and haunted. 'It's too soon – it's too soon!'

Sean couldn't stand it, he jumped up and caught Duff's shoulders and shook him.

'Shut up, God damn you, shut up,' he shouted at him. Duff was panting, his lips were parted and quivering. He touched them with the tips of his fingers as though to stop them.

'I'm sorry, laddie, I didn't mean to let go like that.' Sean dropped his hands from Duff's shoulders.

'Both of us are too damned edgy,' he said. 'It's going to be all right, you wait and see.'

'Yes – it will be all right.' Duff ran his fingers through his hair, combing it back from his eyes. 'Open another bottle, laddie.'

400

8

That night after Sean had gone to bed, Duff had his dream again. The wine he had drunk slowed him down and prevented him from waking. He was trapped in his fancy, struggling to escape into wakefulness but only reaching the surface before he sank back to dream that dream again.

Sean went up to Duff's shelter the next morning early. Although the night's coolness still lingered under the spreading branches of the wild figs the rising day promised to blow dry and burn hot. The animals could sense it. The trek oxen were clustered among the trees and a small herd of eland was moving from the waterhole. The bull, with his short thick horns and the dark tuft on his forehead, was leading his cows away to find shade. Sean stood in the doorway of the hut and waited while his eyes adjusted themselves to its gloom. Duff was awake.

'Get out of bed or you'll have bed sores to add to your happiness.'

Duff swung his feet off the litter and groaned.

'What did you put in that wine last night?' He massaged his temples gently. 'I've got a hundred hobgoblins doing a Cossack dance around the roof of my skull.'

Sean felt the first twinge of alarm. He put his hand on Duff's shoulder feeling for the heat of fever, but Duff was quite cool. He relaxed.

'Breakfast's ready,' said Sean. Duff played with his porridge and barely tasted the grilled eland liver. He kept screwing his eyes up against the glare of the sun and when they had finished their coffee he pushed back his chair.

'I'm going to take my tender head to bed.'

'All right.' Sean stood up as well. 'We're a bit short of meat. I'll go and see if I can get a buck.'

'No, stay and talk to me,' Duff said quickly. 'We can have a few hands of cards.'

They hadn't played in days and Sean agreed readily. He sat on the end of Duff's bed and within half an hour he had won thirty-two pounds from him.

'You must let me teach you this game sometime,' he gloated.

Petulantly, Duff threw his hand in. 'I don't feel like playing any more.' He pressed his fingers to his closed eyelids. 'I can't concentrate with this headache.'

'Do you want to sleep?' Sean gathered up the cards and put them in their box.

'No. Why don't you read to me?'

Duff picked up a leather-bound copy of *Bleak House* from the table beside the bed and tossed it into Sean's lap.

'Where shall I start?' Sean asked.

'It doesn't matter, I know it almost by heart.' Duff lay back and closed his eyes. 'Start anywhere.'

Sean read aloud. He stumbled on for half an hour with his tongue never quite catching the rhythm of the words. Once or twice he glanced up at Duff, but Duff lay still with a faint sheen of sweat on his face and the scars very noticeable. He was breathing easily. Dickens is a powerful sleeping-draught for a hot morning and Sean's eyelids sagged down and his voice slowed and finally stopped. The book slid off his lap.

The small tinkle of Duff's chain disturbed him; he awoke and looked at the bed. Duff crouched apelike. The madness was a fire in his eyes and his cheeks twitched. A yellowish froth coated his teeth and formed a thin line of scum along his lips.

'Duff—' Sean said, and Duff lunged at him with fingers hooked and a noise in his throat that was not human nor yet animal. It was a sound that jellied Sean's stomach and took the strength from his legs.

'Don't!' screamed Sean, and the chain caught on one of the posts of the bed, jerking Duff back sprawling onto the bed before he could sink his teeth into Sean's paralysed body.

Sean ran. He ran out of the hut and into the bush. He ran with terror trembling in his legs and choking his breath. He ran with his heart taking its beat from his racing feet and his lungs pumping in disordered panic. A branch ripped across his cheek and the sting of it served to steady him. His feet slowed – he stopped and stood gasping, staring back towards the camp. He waited while his body settled and he forced his terror down until it was only a sickening sensation in his stomach. Then he circled through the thorn bush and approached the laager from the side farthest away from Duff's shelter. The camp was empty, the servants had fled in the same terror that had driven Sean. He remembered that his rifle was still in the hut beside Duff's bed. He slipped into his wagon and quickly opened the case of unused rifles. His hands were unsteady again as he fumbled with the locks, for the chain might have parted and at every second he expected to hear that inhuman sound behind him. He found his bandolier hanging on the end of his cot and he took cartridges from it. He loaded the rifle and cocked it. The weight of steel and wood in his hands gave him comfort. It made him a man again.

He jumped down out of the wagon and with the rifle held ready he went cautiously out of the circle of wagons. The chain had held. Duff stood in the shade of the wild fig plucking at it. He was making a sound like a new-born puppy. His back was turned to Sean and he was naked, his torn clothing scattered about him. Sean walked slowly towards him. He stopped outside the reach of the chain.

'Duff!' Sean called uncertainly. Duff spun and crouched, the froth was thick in his golden beard; he looked at Sean and his teeth bared. Then he charged screaming until the chain caught him and threw him onto his back once more. He scrambled to his feet and fought the chain, his eyes fastened hungrily on Sean. Sean backed away. He brought up the rifle and aimed between Duff's eyes.

Swear to me. Swear to me you won't bring the rifle to me.

Sean's aim wavered. He kept moving backwards. Duff was bleeding now. The steel links had smeared the skin off his hips, but still he pulled against them fighting to get at Sean – and Sean was shackled just as effectively by his promise. He could not end it. He lowered the rifle and watched in impotent pity.

Mbejane came to him at last.

'Come away, Nkosi. If you will not end it, come away. He no longer has need of you. The sight of you inflames him.'

Duff still struggled and screamed against his chain. From his torn waist the blood trickled down and clung in the hair of his legs with the stickiness of molten chocolate. With each jerk of his head the froth sprayed from his mouth and splattered his chest and arms.

Mbejane led Sean back into the laager. The other servants were there and Sean roused himself to give orders.

'I want everyone away from here. Take blankets and food – go camp on the far side of the water. I will send for you when it is over.' He waited until they had gathered their belongings and as they were leaving he called Mbejane back. 'What must I do?' he asked.

'If a horse breaks a leg?' Mbejane answered him with a question.

'I gave him my word,' Sean shook his head desperately, still facing towards the sound of Duff's raving.

'Only a rogue and a brave man can break an oath,' Mbejane answered simply. 'We will wait for you.' He turned and followed the others. When they were gone Sean hid in one of the wagons and through a tear in the canvas he watched Duff. He saw the idiotic shaking of his head, the curious shambling gait as he moved around the circle of the chain. He watched when the pain made him roll on the ground and claw at his head, tearing out tufts of hair and leaving long scratches down his face. He listened to the sounds of insanity: the bewildered bellows of pain, the senseless giggling and that growl, that terrible growl.

A dozen times he sighted along the rifle barrel, holding his aim until the sweat ran into his eyes and blurred them and he had to take the butt from his shoulder and turn away.

Out there on the end of the chain, its exposed flesh reddening in the sun a piece of Sean was dying. Some of his youth, some of his laughter, some of his carefree love of life – so he had to creep back to the hole in the canvas and watch.

The sun reached its peak and started down again and the thing on the chain grew weaker. It fell and was a long time crawling on its hands and knees before it regained its feet again.

An hour before sunset Duff had his first convulsion. He was standing facing Sean's wagon, swinging his head from side to side, his mouth working silently. The convulsion took him and he stiffened; his lips pulled up grinning, showing his teeth, his eyes rolled back and disappeared leaving only the whites, and his body started to bend backwards. That beautiful body, still slim as a boy's with the long moulded legs, bending tighter and tighter until with a brittle crack the spine snapped and he fell. He lay wriggling, moaning softly and his trunk was twisted at an impossible angle from the broken spine.

Sean jumped from the wagon and ran to him: standing over him he shot Duff in the head and turned away. He flung his rifle from him and heard it clatter on the hard earth. He walked back to his wagon and took a blanket off

405

Duff's cot. He came back and wrapped Duff in it, averting his eyes from the mutilated head. He carried him to the shelter and laid him on the bed. The blood soaked through the blanket, spreading on the cloth, like ink spilled on blotting-paper. Sean sank down on the chair beside the bed.

Outside the darkness gathered and became complete. Once in the night a hyena came and snuffled at the blood outside on the earth, then it moved away. There was a pride of lions hunting in the bush beyond the waterhole; they killed two hours before dawn and Sean sat in the darkness and listened to their jubilant roaring.

In the morning, Sean stood up stiffly from his chair and went down to the wagons. Mbejane was waiting beside the fire in the laager.

'Where are the others?' Sean asked.

Mbejane stood up. 'They wait where you sent them. I came alone – knowing you would need me.'

'Yes,' said Sean. 'Get two axes from the wagon.'

They gathered wood, a mountain of dry wood, and packed it around Duff's bed – then Sean put fire to it. Mbejane saddled a horse for Sean and he mounted up and looked down at the Zulu.

'Bring the wagons on to the next waterhole. I will meet you there.'

Sean rode out of the laager. He looked back only once and saw that the breeze had spread the smoke from the pyre in a mile long smudge across the tops of the thorn trees.

9

Like a bag of pus at the root of an infected tooth the guilt and grief rotted in Sean's mind. His guilt was double-edged. He had betrayed Duff's trust, and he had lacked the courage to make the betrayal worthwhile. He had waited too long. He should have done it at the beginning, cleanly and quickly, or he should not have done it at all. He longed with every fibre of his body to be given the chance to do it again, but this time the right way. He would gladly have lived once more through all that horror to clear his conscience and clean the stain from the memory of their friendship.

His grief was a thing of emptiness, an aching void – so immense that he was lost in it. Where before there had been Duff's laughter, his twisted grin and his infectious zest there was now only a grey nothingness. No glimmer of sun penetrated it and there were no solid shapes in it.

The next waterhole was shallow soup in the centre of a flat expanse of dry mud the size of a polo field. The mud was cracked in an irregular chequered pattern forming small brickettes, each the size of a hand. A man could have jumped across the water without wetting his feet. Scattered thickly round its circumference were the droppings of the animals that had drunk there. Back and forth across its surface, changing direction as the wind veered, a few loose feathers sailed. The water was brackish and dirty. It was a bad camp. On the third day Mbejane went to Sean's wagon. Sean lay in his cot. He had not changed his clothes since leaving Duff. His beard was beginning to mat, sticky with sweat for it was hot as an oven under the wagon canvas.

'Nkosi, will you come and look at the water. I do not think we should stay here.'

'What is wrong with it?' Sean asked without interest.

'It is dirty, I think we should go on towards the big river.'

'Do whatever you think is right.' Sean rolled away from him, his face towards the side of the wagon.

So Mbejane took the wagon-train down towards the Limpopo. It was two days later that they found the ribbon of dark green trees that lined the banks. Sean stayed in his cot throughout the trek, jolting over the rough ground, sweating in the heat but oblivious to all discomfort. Mbejane put the wagons into laager on the bank above the riverbed, then he and all the other servants waited for Sean to come to life again. Their talk round the fire at nights was baited with worry and they looked often towards Sean's living wagon, where it stood unlit by lantern, dark as the mood of the man that lay within.

Like a bear coming out of its cave at the end of winter, Sean came out of the wagon at last. His clothes were filthy. The dogs hurried to meet him, crowding round his knees, begging for attention and he did not notice them. Vaguely he answered the greetings of his servants. He wandered down the bank into the riverbed.

The summer had shrunk the Limpopo into a sparse line of pools strung out down the centre of the watercourse. The pools were dark olive green. The sand around them was white, glaring snowfield white, and the boulders that choked the barely moving river were black and polished smooth. The banks were steep, half a mile apart and walled in with trees. Sean walked through the sand, sinking to his ankles with each step. He reached the water and sat down at the edge, he dabbled his hand in it and found it warm as blood. In the sand next to him was the long slither mark of a crocodile, and a troop of monkeys were shaking the branches of a tree on the far bank and chattering at him. A pair of Sean's dogs splashed across the narrow neck between two pools and went off to chase the monkeys. They went half-heartedly with their tongues flapping at the corners of their mouths for it was very hot in the whiteness of the riverbed. Sean stared into the green water. It was lonely without Duff; he had only his guilt and his sorrow for company. One of the dogs that had stayed with him touched his cheek with its cold nose. Sean put his arm round its neck and the dog leaned against him. He heard footsteps in the sand behind him, he turned and looked up. It was Mbejane.

'Nkosi, Hlubi has found elephant not an hour's march up stream. He has counted twenty who show good ivory.'

Sean looked back at the water. 'Go away,' he said.

Mbejane squatted down beside him with his elbows on his knees. 'For whom do you mourn?' he asked.

'Go away, Mbejane, leave me alone.'

'Nkosi Duff does not need your sorrow – therefore I think that you mourn for yourself.' Mbejane picked up a pebble and tossed it into the pool.

'When a traveller gets a thorn in his foot,' Mbejane went on softly, 'and he is wise he plucks it out – and he is a fool who leaves it and says "I will keep this thorn to prick me so that I will always remember the road upon which I have travelled." Nkosi, it is better to remember with pleasure than with pain.' Mbejane lobbed another pebble into the pool, then he stood up and walked back to the camp. When Sean followed him ten minutes later he found a saddle on his horse, his rifle in the scabbard and Mbejane and Hlubi waiting with their spears. Kandhla handed him his hat, he held it by the brim, turning it in his hands. Then he clapped it onto his head and swung up onto the horse.

'Lead,' he ordered.

During the next weeks Sean hunted with a single-mindedness that left no time for brooding. His returns to the wagons were short and intermittent; his only reasons for returning at all were to bring in the ivory and change his horse. At the end of one of these brief visits to camp and as Sean was about to mount up for another hunt, even Mbejane complained. 'Nkosi, there are better ways to die than working too hard.'

'You look well enough,' Sean assured him, although Mbejane was now as lean as a greyhound and his skin shone like washed anthracite.

'Perhaps all men look healthy to a man on horseback,' Mbejane suggested and Sean stopped with one foot in the stirrup. He looked at Mbejane thoughtfully, then he lowered his leg again. 'We hunt on foot now, Mbejane, and the first to ask for mercy earns the right to be called "woman" by the other.'

Mbejane grinned; the challenge was to his liking. They crossed the river and found spoor before midday – a small herd of young bulls. They followed it until nightfall and slept huddled together under one blanket, then they went on again next morning. On the third day they lost the spoor in rocky ground and they cast back towards the river. They picked up another herd within ten miles of the wagons, went after them and killed that evening – three fine bulls, not a tusk between them under fifty pounds weight. A night march back to the wagons, four hours' sleep and they were away again. Sean was limping a little now and on the second day out, during one of their infrequent halts, he pulled off his boot. The blister on his heel had burst and his sock was stiff with dried blood. Mbejane looked at him expressionlessly. 'How far are we from the wagons?' asked Sean.

'We can be back before dark, Nkosi.' Mbejane carried Sean's rifle for him on the return. Not once did his mask of solemnity slip. Back in camp Kandhla brought a basin of hot water and set it in front of Sean's chair. While Sean soaked his feet in it his entire following squatted in a circle about him. Every face wore an expression of studied concern and the silence was broken only by the clucking sounds of

Bantu sympathy. They were loving every minute of it and Mbejane, with the timing of a natural actor, was building up the effect, playing to his audience. Sean puffed at a cheroot, scowling to stop himself laughing. Mbejane cleared his throat and spat into the fire. Every eye was on him; they waited breathlessly.

'Nkosi,' said Mbejane, 'I would set fifty head of oxen as your marriage price – if you were my daughter.'

One instant more of silence, then a shout of laughter. Sean laughed with them at first, but after a while when Hlubi had nearly staggered into the fire and Nonga was sobbing loudly on Mbejane's shoulder with tears of mirth streaming down his cheeks, Sean's own laughter stopped. It wasn't *that* funny.

He looked at them sourly – at their wide open pink mouths and their white teeth, at their shaking shoulders and heaving chests and suddenly it came to him very clearly that they were no longer laughing at him. They were laughing for the joy of it. They were laughing because they were alive. A chuckle rattled up Sean's throat and escaped before he could stop it, another one bounced around inside his chest and he lay back in his chair, opened his mouth and let it come. The hell with it, he was alive, too.

In the morning when he climbed out of his wagon and limped across to see what Kandhla was cooking for breakfast, there was a faint excitement in him again, the excitement of a new day. He felt good. Duff's memory was still with him, it always would be, but now it was not a sickening ache. He had plucked out the thorn.

10

They moved camp three times in November, keeping to the south bank of the river, following it back towards the west. Slowly the wagons which they had emptied of ivory beside the waterhole began to fill again, for the game was concentrated along the river. The rest of the land was dry but now each day there was promise of relief.

The clouds that had been scattered across the sky began to crowd together, gathering into rounded dark-edged masses or rearing proudly into thunderheads. All of nature seemed impressed by their growing importance. In the evenings the sun dressed them in royal purple and during the day the whirlwinds did dervish dances for their entertainment. The rains were coming. Sean had to make a decision, cross the Limpopo and cut himself off from the south when the river flooded, or stay where he was and leave the land beyond undisturbed. It wasn't a difficult decision. They found a place where the banks flattened out a little on both sides of the river. They unloaded the first wagon and double-teamed it; then with everybody shouting encouragement the oxen galloped down the steep slope into the riverbed. The wagon bounced behind them until it hit the sand where it came to a halt, tilted at an abandoned angle, with its wheels sunk axle-deep into the sand.

'Onto the spokes,' shouted Sean. 'They flung themselves on the wheels and strained to keep them turning, but half the oxen were down on their knees, powerless in the loose footing.

'Damn it to hell.' Sean glared at the wagon. 'Outspan the oxen and take them back. Get out the axes.'

It took them three days to lay a bridge of corduroyed branches across the river and another two to get all the wagons and ivory to the far bank. Sean declared a holiday when the last wagon was manhandled into the laager and the whole camp slept late the next morning. The sun was high by the time Sean descended from his wagon. He was still muzzy and a little liverish from lying abed. He yawned wide and stretched like a crucifix. He ran his tongue round his mouth and grimaced at the taste, then he scratched his chest and the hair rasped under his fingers.

'Kandhla, where's the coffee? Don't you care that I am near dead from thirst?'

'Nkosi, the water will boil very soon.'

Sean grunted and walked across to where Mbejane squatted with the other servants by the fire watching Kandhla.

'This is a good camp, Mbejane.' Sean looked up at the roof of leaves above them. It was a place of green shade, cool in the late morning heat. Christmas beetles were squealing in the wide stretched branches.

'There is good grazing for the cattle,' Mbejane agreed; he stretched out his hand towards Sean.

'I found this in the grass – someone else has camped here.' Sean took it from him and examined it, a piece of broken china with a blue fig-leaf pattern. It was a shock to Sean, that little fragment of civilization in the wilderness; he turned it in his fingers and Mbejane went on. 'There are the ashes of an old fire there against the shuma tree and I found the ruts where wagons climbed the bank at the same place as ours.'

'How long ago?'

Mbejane shrugged. 'A year perhaps. Grass has grown in the wagon tracks.'

Sean sat down in his chair, he felt disturbed. He thought about it and grinned as he realized he was jealous; there were strangers here in the land he was coming to regard as his own, those year-old tracks gave him a feeling of being

413

in a crowd. Also there was the opposite feeling, that of longing for the company of his own kind. The sneaking desire to see a white face again. It was strange that he could resent something and yet wish for it simultaneously.

'Kandhla, am I to have coffee now or at supper tonight?'

'Nkosi, it is done.' Kandhla poured a little brown sugar into the mug, stirred it with a stick and handed it to him. Sean held the mug in both hands, blowing to cool it, then sipping and sighing with each mouthful. The talk of his Zulus passed back and forth about the circle and the snuff-boxes followed it, each remark of worth being greeted with a solemn chorus of 'It is true, it is true,' and the taking of snuff. Small arguments jumped up and fell back again into the leisurely stream of conversation. Sean listened to them, occasionally joining in or contributing a story until his stomach told him it was time to eat. Kandhla started to cook, under the critical supervision and with the helpful suggestions of those whom idleness had made garrulous. He had almost succeeded in grilling the carcass of a guinea-fowl to the satisfaction of the entire company, although Mbejane felt that he should have added a pinch more salt, when Nonga, sitting across the fire from him, jumped to his feet and pointed out towards the north. Sean shaded his eyes and looked.

'For Chrissake,' said Sean.

'Ah! ah! ah!' said his servants.

A white man rode towards them through the trees; he cantered with long stirrups, slouched comfortably, close enough already for Sean to make out the great ginger beard that masked the bottom half of his face. He was a big man; the sleeves of his shirt rolled high around thick arms.

'Hello,' shouted Sean and went eagerly to meet him. The rider reined in at the edge of the laager. He climbed stiffly out of the saddle and grabbed Sean's outstretched hand. Sean felt his finger-bones creak in the grip.

414

'Hello, man! How goes it?' He spoke in Afrikaans. His voice matched the size of his body and his eyes were on a level with Sean's. They pumped each other's arms mercilessly, laughing, putting sincerity into the usual inanities of greeting.

'Kandhla – get out the brandy bottle,' Sean called over his shoulder, then to the Boer, 'Come in, you're just in time for lunch. We'll have a dram to celebrate. Hell, it's good to see a white man again!'

'You're on your own, then?'

'Yes – come in, man, sit down.'

Sean poured drinks and the Boer took one up.

'What's your name?' he asked.

'Courtney – Sean Courtney.'

'I'm Jan Paulus Leroux – glad to meet you, meneer.'

'Good health, meneer,' Sean answered him and they drank. Jan Paulus wiped his whiskers on the palm of his hand and breathed out heavily, blowing the taste of the brandy back into his mouth.

'That was good,' he said and held out his mug. They talked excitedly, tongues loose from loneliness, trying to say everything and ask all the questions at once – meetings in the bush are always like this. Meanwhile the tide was going out in the bottle and the level dropped quickly.

'Tell me, where are your wagons?' Sean asked.

'An hour or two behind. I came ahead to find the river.'

'How many in your party?' Sean watched his face, talking just for the sound of it.

'Ma and Pa, my little sister and my wife – which reminds me – you had better move your wagons.'

'What?' Sean looked puzzled.

'This is my outspan place,' the Boer explained to him. 'See, there are the marks of my fire – this is my camp.'

The smile went out of Sean's voice. 'Look around you,

415

Boer, there is the whole of Africa. Take your pick – anywhere except where I am sitting.'

'But this is my place.' Jan Paulus flushed a little. 'I always camp at the same place when I return along a spoor.'

The whole temper of their meeting had changed in a few seconds. Jan Paulus stood abruptly and went to his horse. He stooped and tightened the girth, hauling so savagely on the strap that the animal staggered off balance. He flung himself onto its back and looked down at Sean.

'Move your wagons,' he said. 'I camp here tonight.'

'Would you like to bet on that?' Sean asked grimly.

'We'll see!' Jan Paulus flashed back.

'We certainly shall,' agreed Sean.

The Boer wheeled his horse and rode away. Sean watched his back disappear among the trees and only then did he let his anger slip. He rampaged through the laager working himself into a fury, pacing out frustrated circles, stopping now and then to glare out in the direction from which the Boer's wagons would come – but under all the external signs of indignation was his unholy anticipation of a fight. Kandhla brought him food, hurrying along behind him with the plate. Sean waved him away impatiently and continued his pugnacious patrol. At last a trek whip popped in the distance and an ox lowed faintly, to be answered immediately by Sean's cattle. The dogs started barking and Sean crossed to one of the wagons on the north side of the laager and leaned against it with assumed nonchalance. The long line of wagons wound out of the trees towards him. There were bright blobs of colour on the high box seat of the lead wagon. Women's dresses! Ordinarily they would have made Sean's nostrils flare like those of a stud stallion, but now his whole attention was concentrated on the larger of the two outriders. Jan Paulus cantered ahead of his father, and Sean, with his fists clenched into bony hammers at his sides, watched him come. Jan Paulus sat straight in the saddle; he stopped his horse a dozen paces from Sean and shoved his hat onto the back of his head with a thumb as thick and as brown as a fried sausage; he tickled his horse a little with his spurs to make it dance and he asked with mock surprise, 'What, *Rooi Nek*, still here?'

Sean's dogs had rushed forward to meet the other pack and now they milled about in a restrained frenzy of mutual bottom-smelling, stiff-limbed with tension, backs abristle and legs cocking in the formal act of urination.

'Why don't you go and climb a tree? You'll feel more at home there,' Sean suggested mildly.

'Ah! so?' Jan Paulus reared in his stirrups. He kicked loose his right foot, swung it back over his horse's rump to dismount and Sean jumped at him. The horse skittered nervously, throwing the Boer off balance and he clutched at the saddle. Sean reached up, took a double handful of his ginger beard and leaned back on it with all his weight. Jan Paulus came over backwards with his arms windmilling, his foot caught in the stirrup and he hung suspended like a hammock, held at one end to the plunging horse and at the other by his chin to Sean's hands. Sean dug his heels in, revelling in the Boer's bellows.

Galvanized into action by Sean's example, the dogs cut short the ceremony and went at each other in a snarling, snapping shambles; the fur flew like sand in a Kalahari dust-storm.

The stirrup-leather snapped; Sean fell backwards and rolled to his feet just in time to meet Jan Paulus's charge. He smothered the punch that the Boer bowled overarm at him, but the power behind it shocked him; then they were chest to chest and Sean felt his own strength matched. They strained silently with their beards touching and their eyes inches apart. Sean shifted his weight quickly and tried for a fall, but smoothly as a dancer Jan Paulus met and held him. Then it was his turn; he twisted in Sean's arms and

Sean sobbed with the effort required to stop him. Oupa Leroux joined in by driving his horse at them, scattering the dogs, his hippo-hide sjambok hissing as he swung it.

'Let it stand! you thunders, give over – hey! Enough, let it stand!'

Sean shouted with pain as the lash cut across his back and at the next stroke Jan Paulus howled as loudly. They let go of each other and massaging their whip-weals retreated before the skinny old white-beard on the horse.

The first of the wagons had come up now and two hundred pounds of woman, all in one package, called out from the box seat, 'Why did you stop them, Oupa?'

'No sense in letting them kill each other.'

'Shame on you – so you must spoil the boys' fun. Don't you remember how you loved to fight? Or are you now so old you forget the pleasures of your youth? Leave them alone!'

Oupa hesitated, swinging the sjambok and looking from Sean to Jan Paulus.

'Come away from there, you old busybody,' his wife ordered him. She was solid as a granite kopje, her blouse packed full of bosom and her bare arms brown and thick as a man's. The wide brim of her bonnet shaded her face but Sean could see it was pink and pudding-shaped, the kind of face that smiles more easily than it frowns. There were two girls on the seat beside her but there was no time to look at them. Oupa had pulled his horse out of the way and Jan Paulus was moving down on him. Sean went up on his toes, crouching a little, preoccupied with the taste he had just had of the other's strength, watching Jan Paulus close in for the main course and not too certain he was going to be able to chew this mouthful.

Jan Paulus tested Sean with a long right-hander but Sean rolled his head with it and the thick pad of his beard cushioned the blow; he hooked Jan Paulus in the ribs under his raised arm and Jan Paulus grunted and circled away.

Forgetting his scruples, Oupa Leroux watched them with rising delight. It was going to be a good fight. They were well matched – both big men, under thirty, quick and smooth on their feet. Both had fought before and that often; you could tell it by the way they felt each other out, turning just out of reach, moving in to offer an opening that a less experienced man might have attempted and regretted, then dropping back.

The fluid, almost leisurely pattern of movement exploded. Jan Paulus jumped in, moving left, changed direction like the recoil of a whip lash and used his right hand again; Sean ducked under it and laid himself open to Jan Paulus's left. He staggered back from its kick, bleeding where it had split the flesh across his cheek-bone, and Jan Paulus followed him eagerly, his hands held ready, searching for the opening. Sean kept clear, instinct moving his feet until the blackness faded inside his head and he felt the strength in his arms again. He saw Jan Paulus following him and he let his legs stay rubbery; he dropped his hands and waited for Jan Paulus to commit himself. Too late Jan Paulus caught the cunning in Sean's eyes and tried to break from the trap, but clenched bone raked his face. He staggered away and now he was bleeding also.

They fought through the wagons with the advantage changing hands a dozen times. They came together and used their heads and their knees, they broke and used their fists again. Then locked chest to chest once more they rolled down the steep bank into the riverbed of the Limpopo. They fought in the soft sand and it held their legs, it filled their mouths when they fell and clung like white icing-sugar to their hair and beards. They splashed into one of the pools and they fought in the water, coughing with the agony of it in their lungs, floundering like a pair of bull hippos, their movements slowing down until they knelt facing each other, no longer able to rise, the water running from them and the only sound their gasping for air.

Not sure whether the darkness was actuality or a fantasy of fatigue, for the sun had set by the time they were finished, Sean watched Jan Paulus starting to puke, retching with a tearing noise to bring up a small splash of yellow bile. Sean crawled to the edge of the pool and lay with his face in the sand. There were voices echoing in his ears and the light of a lantern – the light was red – filtered through the blood that had trickled into his eyes. His servants lifted him and he hardly felt them. The light and the voices faded into blackness as he slipped over the edge of consciousness.

The sting of iodine woke him and he struggled to sit up but hands pushed him down.

'Gently, gently, the fight is over.' Sean focused his one eye to find the voice. The pinkness of Ouma Leroux hung over him. Her hands touched his face and the antiseptic stung him again. He exclaimed through puffed lips.

'So! Just like a man,' Ouma chuckled. 'Your head nearly knocked off without a murmur but one touch of medicine and you cry like a baby.'

Sean ran his tongue round inside his mouth; one tooth loose but all the others miraculously present. He started to lift his hand to touch his closed eye but Ouma slapped it down impatiently and went on working over him.

'Glory, what a fight!' She shook her head happily. 'You were good, *kerel*, you were very good.'

Sean looked beyond her and saw the girl. She was standing in shadow, a silhouette against the pale canvas. She was holding a basin. Ouma turned and dipped the cloth in it, washing out the blood before she came back to his face. The wagon rocked under her weight and the lantern that hung from the roof swung, lighting the girl's face from the side. Sean's legs straightened on his cot and he moved his head slightly to see her better.

'Be still, *jong*,' Ouma commanded. Sean looked past her at the girl at the full serene line of her lips and the curve of her cheek. He saw the pile of her hair fluff up in happy disarray and then, suddenly – penitent – slide down behind her neck, curl over her shoulder and hang to her waist in a plait as thick as his wrist.

'Katrina, do you expect me to reach right across to the basin each time? Stand closer, girl.'

She stepped into the light and looked at Sean. Green, laughing, almost bubbling green was the colour of her eyes. Then she dropped them to the basin. Sean stared at her, not wanting to miss the moment when she would look up again.

'My big bear,' Ouma spoke with grudging approval. 'Steal our camp site, fight my son and ogle my daughter. If you go on like this I might have to knock the thunder out of you myself. Glory, but you are a dangerous one! Katrina, you had better go back to our wagons and help Henrietta see to your brother. Leave the basin on the chest there.'

She looked at Sean once more before she left. There were secret shadows in the green – she didn't have to smile with her mouth.

– 11 –

Sean woke to the realization that something was wrong. He started to sit up but the pain checked him: the stiffness of bruised muscle and the catch of half-dried scab. He groaned and the movement hurt his lips. Slowly he swung his legs off the cot and roused himself to take stock of the damage. Dark through the hair of his chest showed a heel imprint of Jan Paulus's boot. Sean prodded round it gently, feeling for the give of a broken rib; then, satisfied with that area, he went on to inspect the raw graze that wrapped round onto his back, holding his left arm high and peering closely at the broken skin. He picked a bit of blanket fluff from the scab. He stood up, only to freeze as a torn muscle in his shoulder knifed him. He started to swear then softly, monotonously, and he kept it up all through the painful business of climbing down out of the wagon.

His entire following watched his descent – even the dogs looked worried. Sean reached the ground and started to shout.

'What the hell—' He stopped hurriedly as he felt his lip crack open again and start to bleed.

'What the hell' – he said again, keeping his lips still – 'are you doing standing round like a bunch of women at a beer drink – is there no work here? Hlubi, I thought I sent you out to look for elephant.' Hlubi went. 'Kandhla, where's breakfast? Mbejane, get me a basin of water and my shaving-mirror.' Sean sat in his chair and morosely inspected his face in the mirror.

'If a herd of buffalo had stampeded across it they would have done less damage.'

'Nkosi, it is nothing compared to his face,' Mbejane assured him.

'Is he bad?' Sean looked up.

'I have spoken to one of his servants. He has not left his bed yet and he lies there, growling like a wounded lion in a thicket; but his eyes are as tightly closed as those of a new cub.'

'Tell me more, Mbejane. Say truly, was it a good fight?'

Mbejane squatted down next to Sean's chair. He was silent a moment as he gathered his words.

'When the sky sends its cloud impis against the peaks of the Drakensberg, with thunder and the spears of lightning, it is a thing to thrill a man. When two bull elephants fight unto death there is no braver show in all the veld. Is this not so?'

Sean nodded, his eyes twinkling.

'Nkosi, hear me when I tell you these things were as the play of little children beside this fight.'

Sean listened to the praises. Mbejane was well versed in the oldest art of Zululand and when he had finished he looked at Sean's face. It was happy. Mbejane smiled and took a fold of paper out of his loin cloth. 'A servant from the other camp brought this while you slept.'

Sean read the note. It was written in a big round school-girl hand and worded in High Dutch. He liked that writing. It was an invitation to dinner.

'Kandhla, get out my suit and my number one boots.' He picked up the mirror again. There wasn't very much he could do about his face – trim the beard, perhaps, but that was all. He laid the mirror down and looked up stream to where the Leroux wagons were half hidden among the trees.

Mbejane carried a lantern in front of Sean. They walked slowly to enable Sean to limp with dignity. When they reached the other laager, Jan Paulus climbed stiffly out of his chair and nodded an equally stiff greeting. Mbejane had lied – except for a missing tooth there was little to choose between their faces. Oupa slapped Sean's back and pressed a tumbler of brandy into his hand. He was a tall man, but twenty thousand suns had burnt away his flesh and left only stringy muscle, had faded his eyes to a pale green and toughened his skin to the texture of a turkey's neck. His beard was yellowish-white with still a touch of ginger round the mouth. He asked Sean three questions without giving him time to answer the first, then he led him to a chair.

Oupa talked, Sean listened and Jan Paulus sulked. Oupa talked of cattle and hunting and the land to the north. After a few minutes Sean realized that he was not expected to take part in the conversation: his few tentative efforts

423

were crushed under Oupa's verbal avalanche. So Sean listened half to him and half to the whisper of women's voices from the cooking fires behind the laager. Once he heard her laugh. He knew it was her for it was the rich sound of the thing that he had seen in her eyes. At last the women's business with food and pots was finished and Ouma led the girls to where the men sat. Sean stood up and saw that Katrina was tall, with shoulders like a boy. As she walked towards him the movement pressed her skirt against her legs – they were long but her feet were small. Her hair was red-black and tied behind her head in an enormous bun.

'Ah, my battling bear,' Ouma took Sean's arm, 'let me present my daughter-in-law, Henrietta – here is the man that nearly killed your husband.' Jan Paulus snorted from his chair and Ouma laughed, her bosom wobbling merrily. Henrietta was a small dark-eyed girl. *She doesn't like me*, Sean guessed instantly. He bowed slightly and took her hand. She pulled it away.

'This is my youngest daughter, Katrina. You met her last night.'

She does like me. Her fingers were long and square-tipped in his. Sean risked his lips with a smile.

'Without her ministrations I might have bled to death,' he said. She smiled straight back at him but not with her mouth.

'You wear your wounds well, maneer, the blue eye has an air of distinction.'

'That will be enough from you, girl,' Oupa spoke sharply. 'Go and sit by your mother.' He turned to Sean. 'I was telling you about this horse – I said to the fellow, "He's not worth five pounds let alone fifteen, look at those hocks, thin as sticks." So he says to me, trying to get me away, you follow, he says, "Come and look at the saddle." But I can see he's worried—'

424

The thin cotton of the girl's blouse could hardly contain the impatient push of her breasts. Sean thought that he had never seen anything so wonderful.

There was a trestle-table next to the cooking fire; they went to it at last. Oupa said grace. Sean watched him through his lashes. Oupa's beard waggled as he spoke and at one point he thumped the table to emphasize the point he was making to the Almighty. His 'amen' had such an impressive resonance that Sean had to make an effort to stop himself applauding and Oupa fell back spent.

'Amen,' said Ouma and ladled stew from a pot the size of a bucket. Henrietta added pumpkin fritters and Katrina stacked slices of fresh mealie bread on each plate. A silence fell on the table, spoiled only by the clank of metal on china and the sound of Oupa breathing through his nose.

'Mevrouw Leroux, I have waited a long time to taste food like this again.' Sean mopped up the last bit of gravy with a piece of mealie bread. Ouma beamed.

'There's plenty more, meneer. I love to see a man eat. Oupa used to be a great trencherman. My father made him take me away for he could not afford to feed him every time he came courting.' She took Sean's plate and filled it. 'You look to me like a man who can eat.'

'I think I'll hold my own in most company,' Sean agreed.

'So?' Jan Paulus spoke for the first time. He passed his plate to Ouma. 'Fill it up, please, Mother, tonight I am hungry.'

Sean's eyes narrowed, he waited until Jan Paulus had his plate back in front of him, then he took up his fork deliberately. Jan Paulus did the same.

'Glory,' said Ouma happily. 'Here we go again. Oupa, you may have to go out and shoot a couple of buffalo before dinner is finished tonight.'

'I will bet one sovereign on Jan Paulus,' Oupa challenged

425

his wife. 'He is like an army of termites. I swear that if there was nothing else he'd eat the canvas off the wagons.'

'All right,' agreed Ouma. 'I've never seen the Bear eat before, but it seems to me he has plenty of room to put it.'

'Your woollen shawl against my green bonnet that Jan Paulus gives up first,' Katrina whispered to her sister-in-law.

'When Jannie has finished the stew he'll eat the English man,' Henrietta giggled. 'But it's a pretty bonnet – I'll take the wager.'

Plateful for plateful, Ouma measuring out each ladle with scrupulous fairness, they ate against each other. The talk round the table dwindled and halted.

'More?' asked Ouma each time the plates were clean, and each time they looked at each other and nodded. At last the ladle scraped the bottom of the pot.

'That's the end of it, my children, we will have to call it another draw.'

The silence went on after she had spoken. Sean and Jan Paulus sat very still looking at their respective plates. Jan Paulus hiccupped, his expression changed. He stood up and went into the darkness.

'Ah! listen! listen!' crowed Ouma. They waited and then she exploded into laughter. 'The ungrateful wretch, is that what he thinks of my food? Where's your sovereign, Oupa?'

'Wait, you greedy old woman, the game's not finished yet.' He turned and stared at Sean. 'To me it looks as though your horse is nearly blown.'

Sean closed his eyes. The sounds of Jan Paulus's distress came to him very clearly.

'Thank you for a—' He didn't have time to finish. He wanted to get far away so the girl couldn't hear him.

426

12

The following morning during breakfast Sean thought about his next move. He would write an invitation to dinner and then he would deliver it himself. They would have to ask him to stay for coffee and then, if he waited, there would be a chance. Even Oupa would have to stop talking sometime and Ouma might relax her vigilance. He was sure there'd be a chance to talk to the girl. He didn't know what he would say to her but he'd worry about that when the time came. He climbed into the wagon and found pencil and paper in his chest. He went back to the table and spread the paper in front of him. He chewed the end of the pencil and stared out into the bush. Something moved against the trees. Sena put the pencil down and stood up. The dogs barked then stopped as they recognized Hlubi. He was coming at a trot – he was coming with news. Sean waited for him.

'A big herd, Nkosi, with many showing ivory. I saw them drink at the river and then go back into the bush, feeding quietly.'

'When?' asked Sean to gain time. He was searching for a plausible excuse to stay in camp – it would have to be good to satisfy Mbejane who was already saddling one of the horses.

'Before the sun this morning,' answered Hlubi and Sean was trying to remember which was his sore shoulder – he couldn't hunt with a sore shoulder. Mbejane led the horse into the laager. Sean scratched the side of his nose and coughed.

'The tracker from the other camp follows close behind me, Nkosi, he too has seen the herd and brings the news to his master. But I, being as swift as a springbok when I run, have outdistanced him,' Hlubi ended modestly.

'Is that so?' For Sean it changed the whole problem, he couldn't leave the herd to that red-headed Dutchman. He ran across to the wagon and snatched his bandolier from the foot of the cot. His rifle was already in the scabbard.

'Are you tired, Hlubi?' Sean buckled the heavy ammunition belt across his chest. The sweat had run in oily streaks down the Zulu's body; his breathing was deep and quick.

'No, Nkosi.'

'Well, then, lead us to these elephant of yours, my fleet-footed springbok.' Sean swung up onto his horse. He looked over his shoulder at the other camp. She would still be there when he came back.

Sean was limited to the speed of Hlubi's feet while the two Leroux had only to gallop along the easy spoor left by Sean's party and they caught up with him before he had gone two miles.

'Good morning to you,' Oupa greeted him as he drew level and pulled his horse in to a trot. 'Out for a morning's ride, I see.'

Sean made the best of it with a grin. 'If we are all to hunt then we must hunt together. Do you agree?'

'Of course, meneer.'

'And we must share the bag equally, one third to each man.'

'That is always the way.' Oupa nodded.

'Do you agree?' Sean turned in his saddle towards Jan Paulus. Jan Paulus grunted. He showed little inclination to open his mouth since he had lost his tooth.

They found the spoor within an hour. The herd had wrecked a road through the thick bush along the river. They had stripped the bark from the saplings and left them naked and bleeding. They had knocked down bigger trees to reach the tender top leaves and they had dropped their great piles of dung in the grass.

428

'We need no trackers to follow this.' Jan Paulus had the first excitement on him. Sean looked at him and wondered how many elephant had died in front of his rifle. A thousand perhaps, and yet the excitement was on him again now.

'Tell your servants to follow us. We'll go ahead. We'll catch them within an hour.' He smiled at Sean, gap-toothed, and Sean felt the excitement lift the hair on his own forearms. He smiled back.

They cantered in a rough line abreast, slack-reined to let the horses pick their own way among the fallen trees. The river bush thinned out as they moved north and soon they were into parkland. The grass brushed their stirrups and the ground beneath it was firm and smooth.

They rode without talking, leaning forward in their saddles, looking ahead. The rhythmic beat of hooves was a war drum. Sean ran his fingers along the row of bullets strapped across his chest, then he drew his rifle, checked the load and thrust it back into its scabbard.

'There!' said Oupa and Sean saw the herd. It was massed among a grove of fever trees a quarter of a mile ahead.

'Name of a name,' Paulus whistled. 'There must be two hundred at least.'

Sean heard the first pig-squeal of alarm, saw ears fan out and trunks lift. Then the herd bunched together and ran with their backs humped, a thin screen of dust trailing behind them.

'Paulus take the right flank. You, meneer, in the middle and I'll ride left,' shouted Oupa.

Sean jammed his hat down over his ears and his horse jumped under him as he hit it with his heels. Like a thrown trident the three horsemen hurled themselves at the herd. Sean rode into the dust. He picked an old cow elephant from the moving mountain range in front of him and pressed his horse so close upon her that he could see the bristles in her tail tuft and the erosion of her skin, wrinkled as an old man's scrotum. He touched his hand to his horse's neck and it plunged – from full gallop to standstill in half a dozen strides. Sean threw his feet free of the stirrups and hit the ground, loose-kneed to ride the shock. The cow's spine was a line of lumps beneath the grey skin – Sean broke it with his first bullet and she dropped, sliding on her hindquarters like a dog with worms. His horse started to run again before he was properly in the saddle and everything became movement and noise, dust and the smell of burnt powder. Chase them, coughing in the dust. Close with them. Off the horse and shoot. Wet blood on grey skin. Slam, slam of the rifle – its barrel hot, recoiling savagely. Sweat in the eyes, stinging. Ride. Shoot again. Two more down, screaming, anchored by paralysed legs. Blood-red as a flag. Load, cramming cartridges into the rifle. Ride. Chase them, shoot again and again. The bullets striking on flesh with a hollow sound, then up and ride again. Ride – until the horse could no longer keep up with them and he had to let them go. He stood holding his horse's head, the dust and the thirst closed his throat. He could not swallow. His hands trembled in reaction. His shoulder was aching again. He untied his silk scarf, wiped his face with it and blew the mud out of his nose, then he drank from his water-bottle. The water tasted sweet.

The hunt had led from parkland into mopani bush. It was very thick, shiny green leaves hanging to the ground and pressing close around him. The air was still and warm to breathe. He turned back along the line of the chase. He found them by their squealing. When they saw him they tried to charge, dragging themselves towards him – using the front legs only and groping with their trunks. They sagged into stillness after the head shot. This was the bad part. Sean worked quickly. He could hear the other rifles in the mopani forest around him and when he came to one of the long clearings among the trees he saw Jan Paulus walking towards him, leading his horse.

'How many?' called Sean.

'*Gott*, man, I didn't count. What a killing, hey? Have you got a drink for me? I dropped my water-bottle somewhere.'

Jan Paulus's rifle was in its saddle scabbard. The reins were slung over his shoulder and his horse followed him with its head drooping from exhaustion. The clearing was walled in with the dense mopani trees and a wounded elephant broke into the open. It was lung shot – the side of its chest painted with froth – and when it squealed the blood sprayed in a pink spout from the end of its trunk. It went for Jan Paulus, streaming the black battle ensigns of its ears. His horse reared, the reins snapped, it turned free and galloped away, leaving him full in the path of the charge. Sean went up onto his horse's back without touching stirrups. His horse threw its head, dancing in a tight circle, but he dragged it around and drove it to intercept the charge.

'Don't run, for God's sake, don't run!' he shouted as he cleared his rifle from the scabbard. Jan Paulus heard him. He stood with his hands at his sides, his feet apart and his body braced. The elephant heard Sean shout also and it swung its head and Sean saw the first hesitation in its run. He fired, not trying to pick his shot, hoping only to hurt it, to bring it away from Jan Paulus. The bullet slapped into it with the sound of a wet towel flicked against a wall. The elephant turned, clumsy with the weakness of its shattered lungs. Sean gathered his horse beneath him and wheeled it away and the elephant followed him.

Sean fumbled as he reloaded, his hands were slippery with sweat. One of the brass shells slipped through his fingers, tapped against his knee and dropped into the grass under his horse's hooves. The elephant gained on him. He

431

loosened his bed-roll from the saddle and let it fall – they would sometimes stop to savage even a fallen hat, but not this one. He turned in the saddle and fired into it. It squealed again so close upon him that the blown blood splattered into his face. His horse was almost finished; he could feel its legs flopping with every stride and they were nearly at the end of the clearing racing towards the solid wall of green mopani. He pushed another round into the breech of his rifle and swung his body across the saddle. He slid down until his feet touched the ground and he was running next to his horse. He let go and was flung forward, but he fought to keep his balance, his body jarring with the force of his run. Then, still on his feet, he turned for his first steady shot. The elephant was coming in fast, almost on top of him, hanging over him like a cliff. Its trunk coiled on its chest and the curves of its ivory were lifted high.

It's too close, much too close, I can't hit the brain from here.

He aimed at the hollow in its forehead just above the level of its eyes. He fired and the elephant's legs folded up; its brain burst like an overripe tomato within the bone castle of its skull.

Sean tried to jump aside as the massive body came skidding down upon him, but one of its legs hit him and threw him face down into the grass. He lay there. He felt sick, for his stomach was still full of warm oily fear.

After a while he sat up and looked at the elephant. One of its tusks had snapped off flush with the lip. Jan Paulus came, panting from his run. He stopped next to the elephant and touched the wound in its forehead, then he wiped his fingers on his shirt.

'Are you all right, man?'

He took Sean's arm and helped him to his feet; then he picked up Sean's hat and dusted it carefully before handing it to him.

13

In the three-sided shelter formed by the belly and out-thrust legs of one of the dead elephants they made their camp that night. They drank coffee together and Sean sat between the two Leroux with his back against the rough skin of the elephant's belly. The silhouettes of the tree against the night sky were deformed by the shapes of the vultures that clustered in them and the darkness was ugly with the giggling of hyena. They had set a feast for the scavengers. They spoke little for they were tired, but Sean could feel the gratitude of the men who sat beside him and before they rolled into their blankets Jan Paulus said gruffly, 'Thank you, *kerel.*'

'You might be able to do the same for me one day.'

'I hope so, *ja*! I hope so.'

In the morning Oupa said, 'It's going to take us three or four days to cut out all this ivory.' He looked up at the sky. 'I don't like these clouds. One of us had better ride back to camp to fetch more men and wagons to carry the ivory.'

'I'll go.' Sean stood up quickly.

'I was thinking of going myself.' But Sean was already calling to Mbejane to saddle his horse and Oupa couldn't really argue with him, not after yesterday.

'Tell Ouma to take the wagons across the river,' he acquiesced. 'We don't want to be caught on this side when the river floods. Perhaps you wouldn't mind helping her.'

'No,' Sean assured him. 'I don't mind at all.'

His horse was still tired from the previous day's hunt and it was three hours before he reached the river.

He tied his horse on the bank and went down to one of the pools. He stripped off his clothes and lowered himself into the water. He scrubbed himself with handfuls of the coarse sand and when he waded out of the pool and dried on his shirt his skin was tingling. He rode along the bank and the temptation to gallop his horse was almost unbearable. He laughed to himself a little.

'The field's almost clear, though I wouldn't put it past that suspicious old Dutchman to follow me.'

He laughed again and thought about the colour of her eyes, green as *crème-de-menthe* in a crystal glass, and the shape of her bosom. The muscles in his legs tightened and the horse lengthened its stride in response to the pressure of his knees. 'All right, run then,' Sean encouraged it, 'I don't insist on it, but I would be grateful.'

He went to his own wagons first and changed his sweaty shirt for a fresh one, his leather breeches for clean calico and his scuffed boots for soft polished leather. He scrubbed his teeth with salt and dragged a comb through his hair and beard. He saw in the mirror that the battle damage to his face was fading and he winked at his image. 'How can she resist you?' He gave his moustache one more twirl, climbed out of the wagon and was immediately aware of a most uncomfortable feeling in his stomach. He walked towards the Leroux laager thinking about it, and he recognized it as the same feeling he used to have when Waite Courtney called him to the study to do penance for his boyhood sins.

'That's odd,' he muttered. 'Why should I feel like that?' His confidence faded and he stopped. 'I wonder if my breath smells – I think I'd better go back and get some cloves.' He turned with relief, knew it as cowardice and stopped again. 'Get a grip on yourself. She's only a girl, an uneducated little Dutch girl. You've had fifty finer women.'

'Name me two,' he shot back at himself.

'Well, there was – Oh! for Chrissake, come on.' Resolutely he set off for the Leroux's laager again.

She was sitting in the sun within the circle of wagons. She was leaning forward on the stool and her newly-washed hair fell thickly over her face almost to the ground. With each stroke of the brush it leapt like a live thing and the sun sparkled the red lights in it. Sean wanted to touch it – he wanted to twist fistfuls of it round his hands and he wanted to smell it, it would smell warm and slightly milky like a puppy's fur. He stepped softly towards her but before he reached her she took the shiny mass with both hands and threw it back over her shoulders – a startled flash of green eyes, one despairing wail, 'Oh, no! not with my hair like this.' A swirl of skirts that sent the stool flying and she was gone into her wagon. Sean scratched the side of his nose and stood awkwardly.

'Why are you back so soon, meneer?' she called through the canvas. 'Where are the others? Is everything all right?'

'Yes, they're both fine. I left them and came to fetch wagons to carry the ivory.'

'Oh, that's good.' Sean tried to interpret the inflection of her voice: was it good that they were fine, or good that he had left them? So far the indications were favourable; her confusion at seeing him boded well.

'What's wrong?' Ouma bellowed from one of the other wagons. 'It's not Oupa, don't tell me something has happened to him?' The wagon rocked wildly and her pink face, puckered with sleep, popped out of the opening. Sean's reassurances were smothered by her voice.

'Oh, I knew this would happen. I had a feeling. I shouldn't have let him go.'

'Paulus, oh, Jan Paulus – I must go to him. Where is he?'

Henrietta came running from the cooking fire behind the wagons and then the dogs started barking and the servants added their chatter to the confusion. Sean tried to shout them all down and watch Katrina emerging from her wagon at the same time. She had disciplined her hair now – it had a green ribbon in it and hung down her back. She was laughing and she helped him to quieten Ouma and Henrietta.

They brought him coffee, then they sat round him and listened to the story of the hunt. Sean went into detail on the rescue of Jan Paulus and was rewarded by a softening of the dislike in Henrietta's eyes. By the time Sean had finished talking it was too late to start moving the wagons across the river. So he talked some more, it was most agreeable to have three women as an attentive audience, and then they ate supper.

With ostentatious tact Ouma and Henrietta retired early to their respective living wagons and left Sean and Katrina sitting by the fire. At carefully-spaced intervals there was a stage cough from Ouma's wagon, a reminder that they were not entirely alone. Sean lit a cheroot and frowned into the fire searching desperately for something intelligent to say, but all his brain could dredge up was, 'Thank God, Oupa isn't here.' He sneaked a glance at Katrina: she was staring into the fire as well and she was blushing. Instantly Sean felt his own cheeks starting to heat up. He opened his mouth to talk and made a squawking noise. He shut it again.

'We can speak in English if you like, meneer.'

'You speak English?' Sean's surprise brought his voice back.

'I practise every night – I read aloud out of my books.'

Sean grinned at her delightedly – it was suddenly very important that she could speak his language. The dam, holding back all the questions that there were to ask and all the things there were to say, burst and the words came pouring out over each other. Katrina fluttered her hands when she couldn't find the word she wanted and then lapsed back into Afrikaans. They killed the short taut silences with a simultaneous rush of words, then laughed together in confusion. They sat on the edges of their chairs and watched each other's faces as they talked. The moon came up, a red rain moon, and the fire faded into a puddle of ashes.

436

'Katrina, it's long past the time decent people were asleep. I'm sure Meneer Courtney is tired.'

They dropped their voices to a whisper, drawing out the last minutes.

'In just one minute, girl, I'm coming out to fetch you to bed.'

They walked to her wagon and with each step her skirts brushed against his leg. She stopped with one hand on the wagon step. She wasn't as tall as he'd imagined, the top of her head came to his chin. The seconds slid by as he hesitated, reluctant to touch, strangely frightened to test the delicate thread they had spun together lest he destroy it before it became strong. Slowly he swayed towards her and something surged up inside him as he saw her chin lift slightly and the lashes fall over her eyes.

'Goodnight, Meneer Courtney.' Ouma's voice again, loud and with an edge to it. Sean started guiltily.

'Goodnight, mevrouw.'

Katrina touched his arm just above the elbow, her fingers were warm.

'Goodnight, meneer, I shall see you in the morning.'

She rustled up the steps and slipped through the opening of the canvas. Sean scowled at Ouma's wagon.

'Thanks very much – and if there is ever anything I can do for you, please don't hesitate to ask.'

– 14 –

They started moving the wagons early next morning. There was no time to talk to Katrina in the bustle of inspanning and working the wagons across the corduroy bridge. Sean spent most of the morning in the riverbed and the white sand bounced the heat up at him. He threw off his shirt and sweated like a wrestler. He trotted beside Katrina's wagon when they ran it through the riverbed. She looked once at his naked chest and arms; her cheeks darkened in the shadow of her bonnet and she dropped her eyes and didn't look at him again. With only the two wagons that were going back to fetch the ivory still on the north bank and the rest safely across, Sean could relax. He washed in one of the pools, put on his shirt and went across to the south bank looking forward to a long afternoon of Katrina's company.

Ouma met him. 'Thank you, my dear, the girls have made you a parcel of cold meat and a bottle of coffee to eat on your way.' Sean's face went slack. He had forgotten all about that stinking ivory; as far as he was concerned Oupa and Paulus could keep the lot of it.

'Don't worry about us any more now, maneer. I know how it is with a man who is a man. When there's work to do everything else comes after.'

Katrina put the food in his hands. Sean looked for a sign from her. One sign and he'd defy even Ouma.

'Don't be too long,' she whispered. The thought that he might shirk work had obviously not even occurred to her. Sean was glad he hadn't suggested it.

It was a long ride back to the elephant.

'You've taken your time, haven't you?' Oupa greeted him with sour suspicion. 'You'd better get to work if you don't want to lose some of your share.'

Taking out the tusks was a delicate task: a slip of the axe would scar the ivory and halve its value. They worked in the heat with a blue haze of flies around their faces, settling on their lips and crawling into their nostrils and eyes. The carcasses had started to rot and the gases ballooned their bellies and escaped in posthumous belches. They sweated as they worked and the blood caked their arms to the elbows, but each hour the wagons filled higher until on the

438

third day they loaded the last tusk. Sean reckoned his share at twelve hundred pounds, the equivalent of a satisfactory day on the Stock Exchange.

He was in a good mood on the morning that they started back to the camp, but it deteriorated as the day wore on and they struggled with the heavily-loaded wagons. The rain seemed to have made up its mind at last and now the sky's belly hung down as heavily as that of a pregnant sow. The clouds trapped the heat beneath them and the men panted and the oxen complained mournfully. At mid-afternoon they heard the first far thunder.

'It will be on us before we pass the river,' fretted Oupa. 'See if you can't get some pace out of those oxen.'

They reached Sean's camp an hour after dark and threw his share of the ivory out of the wagons almost without stopping; then they went down to the river and across the bridge to the south bank.

'My mother will have food ready,' Jan Paulus called back to Sean. 'When you have washed come across and eat with us.'

Sean had supper with the Leroux, but his attempts to get Katrina by herself were neatly countered by Oupa whose suspicions were now confirmed. The old man played his trump card immediately after supper and ordered Katrina to bed. Sean could only shrug helplessly in reply to Katrina's appealing little glance. When she had gone Sean went back to his own camp. He was dizzy with fatigue and he fell onto his cot without bothering to undress.

The rains opened their annual offensive with a midnight broadside of thunder. It startled Sean to his feet before he was awake. He pulled open the front of the wagon and heard the wind coming.

'Mbejane, get the cattle into the laager. Make sure all the canvas is secure.'

'It is done already, Nkosi. I have lashed the wagons together so the oxen cannot stampede and I have—' Then the wind whipped his voice away.

It came out of the east and it frightened the trees so they thrashed their branches in panic; it drummed on the wagon canvas and filled the air with dust and dry leaves. The oxen turned restlessly within the laager. Then came the rain: stinging like hail, drowning the wind and turning the air to water. It swamped the sloping ground that could not drain it fast enough, it blinded and it deafened. Sean went back to his cot and listened to its fury. It made him feel drowsy. He pulled the blankets up to his chin and slept.

In the morning he found his oilskins in the chest at the foot of his cot. They crackled as he pulled them on. He climbed out of the wagon. The cattle had churned the inside of the laager to calf-deep mud and there was no chance of a fire for breakfast. Although the rain was still falling the noise was out of proportion to its strength. Sean paused in his inspection of the camp; he thought about it and suddenly he knew that it was the flood voice of the Limpopo that he heard. Sliding in the mud, he ran out of the laager and stood on the bank of the river. He stared at the mad water. It was so thick with mud it looked solid and it raced so fast it appeared to be standing still. It humped up over piles of submerged rock, gullied through the deeps and hissed in static waves through the shallows. The branches and tree trunks in it whisked past so swiftly that they did little to dispel the illusion that the river was frozen in this brown convulsion.

Reluctantly Sean lifted his eyes to the far bank. The Leroux's wagons were gone.

'Katrina,' he said with the sadness of the might-have-been, then again, 'Katrina,' with the sense of his loss melting in the flame of his anger; and he knew that his wanting was not just the itch that is easily scratched and forgotten, but that it was the true ache, the one that gets into your hands and your head and your heart as well as your loins. He couldn't let her go. He ran back to his wagon and threw his clothes onto the cot.

'I'll marry her,' he said and the words startled him. He stood naked, with an awed expression on his face.

'I'll marry her,' he said again; it was an original thought and it frightened him a little. He took a pair of shorts out of his chest and put his legs into them; he pulled them up and buttoned the fly.

'I'll marry her!' He grinned at his own daring. 'I'm damned if I won't!' He buckled his belt on and tied a pair of *veldschoen* to it by their laces. He jumped down into the mud. The rain was cold on his bare back and he shivered briefly. Then he saw Mbejane coming out of one of the other wagons and he ran.

'Nkosi, Nkosi, what are you doing?' Sean put his head down and ran faster with Mbejane chasing him out onto the bank of the river.

'It's madness ... let us talk about it first,' Mbejane shouted. 'Please, Nkosi, please.' Sean slipped in the mud and slithered down the bank. Mbejane jumped down after and caught him at the edge of the water, but the mud had coated Sean's body like grease and Mbejane couldn't hold him. Sean twisted out of his hands and sprang far out. He hit the water flat and swam on his back trying to avoid the undertow. The river swept him away. A wave slapped into his mouth and he doubled up to cough; immediately the river caught him by the heels and pulled him under the surface. It let him go again, just long enough to snatch air then it stirred him in a whirlpool and sucked him under once more. He came up beating at the water with his arms, then it tumbled him over a cascade and he knew by the pain in his chest that he was drowning. He swooped down a chute of swift water between rocks and it didn't matter anymore. He was too tired. Something scraped against his chest and he put out his hand to protect himself; his fingers closed round a branch and his head lifted out of the water. He drank air and then he was clinging to the branch, still alive and wanting to live. He started kicking, edging across the current, riding the river with his arms around the log.

One of the eddies beneath the south bank swung the log in, under the branches of a tree. He reached up, caught them and dragged himself out. He knelt in the mud and water came gushing up out of him, half through his mouth and half through his nose. He had lost his *veldschoen*. He belched painfully and looked at the river. How fast was it moving, how long had he been in the water? He must be fifteen miles below the wagons. He wiped his face with his hand. It was still raining. He stood shakily and faced upstream.

It took him three hours to reach the spot opposite his wagons. Mbejane and the others waved in wild relief when they saw him, but their shouts could not carry across the river. Sean was cold now and his feet were sore. The tracks of the Leroux wagons were dissolving in the rain. He followed them and at last the pain in his feet healed as he saw the flash of canvas in the rain mist ahead of him.

'Name of a name,' shouted Jan Paulus. 'How did you cross the river?'

'I flew, how else?' said Sean. 'Where's Katrina?'

Paulus started to laugh, leaning back in the saddle. 'So that's it then, you haven't come all this way to say goodbye to me.'

Sean flushed. 'All right, laughing boy. That's enough merriment for today . . . Where is she?'

Oupa came galloping back towards them. He asked his first question when he was fifty yards away and his fifth as he arrived. From experience Sean knew there was no point

442

in trying to answer them. He looked beyond the two Leroux and saw her coming. She was running back from the lead wagon, her bonnet hanging from its ribbon around her throat and her hair bouncing loosely with each step. She held her skirts out of the mud, her cheeks flushed darker than the brown of her face and her eyes were very green. Sean ducked under the neck of Oupa's horse and went wet, muddy and eager to meet her.

Then the shyness stopped them and they stood paces apart. 'Katrina, will you marry me?'

She went pale. She stared at him then turned away, she was crying and Sean felt the bottom drop out of his stomach.

'No,' shouted Oupa furiously. 'She won't marry you. Leave her alone, you big baboon. You've made her cry. Get out of here. She's only a baby. Get out of here.' He forced his horse between them.

'You hold your mouth, you old busybody.' Ouma came panting back to join the discussion. 'What do you know about it anyway? Just because she's crying doesn't mean she doesn't want him.'

'I thought he was going to let me go,' sobbed Katrina. 'I thought he didn't care.'

Sean whooped and tried to dodge around Oupa's horse.

'You leave her alone,' shouted Oupa desperately, manoeuvring his horse to cut Sean off. 'You made her cry. I tell you she's crying.'

Katrina was undoubtedly crying. She was also trying to get around Oupa's horse.

'*Vat haar*,' shouted Jan Paulus. 'Get her, man, go and get her!'

Ouma caught the horse by the reins and dragged it away: she was a powerful woman. Sean and Katrina collided and held tight.

443

'Hey, that's it, man.' Jan Paulus jumped off his horse and pounded Sean's back from behind. Unable to protect himself Sean was driven forward a pace with each blow.

Much later Oupa muttered sulkily, 'She can have two wagons for her dowry.'

'Three!' said Katrina.

'Four!' said Ouma.

'Very well, four. Take your hands off him, girl. Haven't you any shame?' Hastily Katrina dropped her arm from Sean's waist. Sean had borrowed a suit of clothing from Paulus and they were all standing round the fire. It had stopped raining but the low clouds were prematurely bringing on the night.

'And four of the horses,' Ouma prompted her husband.

'Do you want to beggar me, woman?'

'Four horses,' repeated Ouma.

'All right, all right ... four horses.' Oupa looked at Katrina, his eyes were stricken. 'She's only a baby, man, she's only fifteen years.'

'Sixteen,' said Ouma.

'Nearly seventeen,' said Katrina, 'and anyway you've promised, Pa, you can't go back on your word now.'

Oupa sighed; then he looked at Sean and his face hardened.

'Paulus, get the Bible out of my wagon. This big baboon is going to swear an oath.'

Jan Paulus put the Bible on the tailboard of the wagon. It was thick and the cover was of black leather, dull with use.

'Come here,' Oupa said to Sean. 'Put your hand on the book ... don't look at me. Look up, man, look up. Now say after me, "I do most solemnly swear to look after this woman" – don't gobble, speak slower – "until I can find a priest to say the proper words. Should I fail in this then I ask you, God, to blast me with lightning, sting me with

444

serpents, burn me in eternal fire – "' Oupa completed the list of atrocities, then he grunted with satisfaction and tucked the Bible under his arm. 'He won't have a chance to do all that to you . . . I'll get you first.'

Sean shared Jan Paulus's wagon that night; he wasn't in a mood for sleep and anyway Jan Paulus snored. It was raining again in the morning, depressing weather for farewells. Jan Paulus laughed, Henrietta cried and Ouma did both. Oupa kissed his daughter.

'Be a woman like your mother,' he said, then he scowled at Sean.

'Remember, just you remember!'

Sean and Katrina stood together and watched the trees and the curtain of rain hide the wagon train. Sean held Katrina's hand. He could feel the sadness on her; he put his arm round her and her dress was damp and cold. The last wagon disappeared and they were alone in a land as vast as solitude. Katrina shivered and looked up at the man beside her. He was so big and overpoweringly male; he was a stranger. Suddenly she was frightened. She wanted to hear her mother's laugh and see her brother and father riding ahead of her wagon, the way it had always been.

'Oh, please, I want . . .' She pulled out from his arm. She never finished that sentence, for she looked at his mouth and his lips were full and burnt dark by the sun – they were smiling. Then she looked at his eyes and her panic smoothed away. With those eyes watching over her she was never to feel frightened again, not until the very end and that was a long time away. Going into his love was like going into a castle, a thick-walled place. A safe place where no one else could enter. The first feeling of it was so strong that she could only stand quietly and let the warmth wrap her.

That evening they outspanned Katrina's wagons back at the south bank of the river. It was still raining. Sean's servants waved and signalled to them, but the brown water bellowed down between them cutting off all sound and hope of passage. Katrina looked at the water. 'Did you really swim that, meneer?'

'So fast that I hardly got wet.'

'Thank you,' she said.

Despite the rain and smoky fire Katrina served up a meal as good as one of Ouma's. They ate it in the shelter of the tarpaulin beside her wagon. The wind guttered the hurricane lamp, flogged the canvas and blew a fine haze of rain in on them. It was so uncomfortable that when Sean suggested that they go into the wagon Katrina barely hesitated before agreeing. She sat on the edge of her cot and Sean sat on the chest opposite her. From an awkward start their conversation was soon running as fast as the river outside the wagon.

'My hair is still wet,' Katrina exclaimed at last. 'Do you mind if I dry it while we talk?'

'Of course not.'

'Then let me get my towel out of the chest.'

They stood up at the same time. There was very little space in the wagon. They touched. They were on the cot. The movement of his mouth on hers, the warm taste of it, the strong pleading of his fingers at the nape of her neck and along her spine – all these things were strangely confusing. She responded slowly at first, then faster with bewildered movements of her own body and little graspings at his arms and shoulders. She did not understand and she did not care. The confusion spread through her whole body and she could not stop it, she did not want to. She reached up and her fingers went into his hair. She pulled his face down on hers. His teeth crushed her lips – sweet, exciting pain. His hand came round from her back and enclosed a fat round breast. Through the thin cotton he found the erectness of her nipple and rolled it gently between his fingers. She reacted like a filly feeling the whip for the first time. One instant she lay under the shock of his touch and then her convulsive heave caught him by surprise. He went backwards off the cot and his head cracked against the wooden chest. He sat on the floor and stared up at her, too surprised even to rub the lump on his head. Her face was flushed and she pushed the hair back from her forehead with both hands. She was shaking her head wildly in her effort to speak through her gasping. 'You must go now, meneer – the servants have made a bed for you in one of the other wagons.'

Sean scrambled to his feet. 'But, I thought . . . surely we are . . . well, I mean.'

'Keep away from me,' she warned anxiously. 'If you touch me again tonight, I'll . . . I'll bite you.'

'But, Katrina, please, I can't sleep in the other wagon.' The thought appalled him.

'I'll cook your food, mend your clothes . . . everything! But until you find a priest . . .' She didn't go on, but Sean got the idea. He started to argue. It was his introduction to Boer immovability and at last he went to find his own bed. One of Katrina's dogs was there before him – a three-quarters-grown brindle hound. Sean's attempts to persuade it to leave were as ill-fated as had been his previous arguments with its mistress. They shared the bed. During the night a difference of opinion arose between them as to what constituted a half-share of the blankets. From it the dog earned its name – Thief.

447

Sean determined to show Katrina just how strongly he resented her attitude. He would be polite but distant. Five minutes after they had sat down to breakfast the next morning this demonstration of disapproval had deteriorated to the stage where he was unable to take his eyes off her face and he was talking so much that breakfast lasted an hour.

The rain held steady for three more days and then it stopped. The sun came back, as welcome as an old friend, but it was another ten days before the river regained its sanity. Time, rain or river meant very little to the two of them. They wandered out into the bush together to pick mushrooms; they sat in camp and when Katrina was working Sean followed her around. Then, of course, they talked. She listened to him. She laughed at the right places and gasped with wonder when she was meant to. She was a good listener. As for Sean, if she had repeated the same word over and over the sound of her voice alone would have held him entranced. The evenings were difficult. Sean would start getting restless and make excuses to touch her. She wanted him to, but she was frightened of the confusion that had so nearly trapped her the first night. So she drew up a set of rules and put them to him. 'Do you promise not to do anything more than kiss me?'

'Not unless you say I can,' Sean agreed readily.

'No.' She saw the catch in that.

'You mean, I must never do anything but kiss you even if you say I can?'

She started to blush. 'If I say so in the daytime, that's different . . . but anything I say at night doesn't count, and if you break your promise I'll never let you touch me again.'

Katrina's rules stood unchanged by the time the river

had dropped enough for the wagons to be taken across to the north bank. The rains were resting, gathering their strength, but soon they would set in once more. The river was full but no longer murderous. Now was the time to cross. Sean took the oxen across first, swimming them in a herd. Holding on to one of their tails he had a Nantucket sleigh-ride across the river and when he reached the north bank there was a joyous welcome awaiting him.

They took six thick coils of unused rope from the stores wagon and joined them together. With the end of the rope round his waist Sean made one of his horses tow him back across the river, Mbejane paying out the line to him as he went. Then Sean supervised Katrina's servants as they emptied all the water barrels and lashed them to the sides of the first wagon to serve as floats. They ran the wagon into the water, tied on the rope and adjusted the barrels so that the wagon floated level. Sean signalled to Mbejane and waited until he had made the other end of the rope fast to a tree on the north bank. Then they pushed the wagon into the current and watched anxiously as it swung across the river like a pendulum, the current driving it but the tree anchoring it. It hit the north bank a distance the exact width of the river downstream of the tree, and Sean's party cheered as Mbejane and the other servants ran down the bank to retrieve it. Mbejane had a team of oxen standing ready and they dragged it out. Sean's horse towed him across the river again to fetch the rope.

Sean, Katrina and all her servants rode across on the last wagon. Sean stood behind Katrina with his arms round her waist, ostensibly to steady her, and the servants shouted and chattered like children on a picnic.

The water piled up brown against the side of the wagon, tilting it and making it roll, and with an exhilarating swoop they shot across the river and crashed into the far bank. The impact tumbled them overboard, throwing them into the knee-deep water beside the bank. They scrambled ashore. The water streamed out of Katrina's dress, her hair melted wetly over her face; she had mud on one cheek and she was gasping with laughter. Her sodden petticoats clung to her legs, tripping her, and Sean picked her up and carried her to his own laager. His servants shouted loud encouragement after him and Katrina shrieked genteelly to be put down, but held tight round his neck with both arms.

– 17 –

Now that the rains had changed every irregularity in the land into a waterhole and sowed new green grass where before had been dust and dry earth, the game scattered away from the river. Every few days Sean's trackers came into camp to report that there were no elephant. Sean condoled with them and sent them out again. He was well satisfied; there was a new quarry now, more elusive and therefore more satisfying than an old bull elephant with a hundred and fifty pounds of ivory on each side of his face. Yet to call Katrina his quarry was a lie. She was much more than that.

She was a new world – a place of endless mysteries and unexpected delights, an enchanting mixture of woman and child. She supervised the domestic routine with deceptive lack of fuss. With her there, suddenly his clothes were clean and had their full complement of buttons; the stew of boots and books and unwashed socks in his wagon vanished. There were fresh bread and fruit preserves on the table; Kandhla's eternal grilled steaks gave way to a variety of dishes. Each day she showed a new accomplishment. She could ride astride, though Sean had to turn his back when she mounted and dismounted. She cut Sean's hair and made as good a job of it as his barber in Johannesburg. She had a medicine chest in her wagon from which she produced remedies for every ailing man or beast in the company. She handled a rifle like a man and could strip and clean Sean's Mannlicher. She helped him load cartridges, measuring the charges with a practised eye. She could discuss birth and procreation with a clinical objectivity and a minute later blush all over when he looked at her that way. She was as stubborn as a mule, haughty when it suited her, serene and inscrutable at times and at others a little girl. She would push a handful of grass down the back of his shirt and run for him to chase her, giggle for minutes at a secret thought, play long imaginative games in which the dogs were her children and she talked to them and answered for them. Sometimes she was so naive that Sean thought she was joking until he remembered how young she was. She could drive him from happiness to spitting anger and back again within the space of an hour. But, once he had won her confidence and she knew that he would play to the rules, she responded to his caresses with a violence that startled them both. Sean was completely absorbed in her. She was the most wonderful thing he had ever found and, best of all, he could talk to her. He told her about Duff. She saw the extra cot in his wagon and found clothing that was obviously too small for him. She asked about it and he told her all of it and she understood.

The days became weeks. The cattle grew fat, their skins sleek and tight. Katrina planted a small vegetable garden and reaped a crop from it. Christmas came and Katrina baked a cake. Sean gave her a kaross of monkey skins that Mbejane had worked on in secret. Katrina gave Sean handsewn shirts, each with his initials embroidered on the top pocket, and she relaxed the rules a fraction.

Then when the new year had begun and Sean hadn't killed an elephant in six weeks, Mbejane headed a deputation from the gunboys. The question he had to ask, though tactfully disguised, was simply, 'Did we come here to hunt, or what?'

They broke camp and moved north again and the strain was showing on Sean at last. He tried to sweat it out by long days of hunting but this didn't help for conditions were so bad that they added to his irritability. The grass in most places was higher than a mounted man's head, its sharp edges cut as he passed through it. But the grass seeds were the worst: half an inch long and barbed like an arrow they worked their way quickly through clothing and into the skin. In the humid heat the small wounds they made festered within hours. Then there were the flies. Hippo-flies, greenheaded flies, sand-flies all with one thing in common – they stung. The soft skin behind the ears was their favourite place. They'd creep upon him, settle so lightly he wouldn't feel it – then, ping with the red-hot needle. Always wet, sometimes with sweat, other times with rain, Sean would close with a herd of elephant. He would hear them moving in the long grass around him and see the white canopy of egrets fluttering over them, but it was seldom he could get a shot at them. If he did he had to stand in the centre of a storm of blundering bodies. Often they would be following a herd, almost upon them, when Sean would lose interest and they'd all go back to camp. He couldn't keep away.

He was miserable, his servants were miserable, and Katrina was happy as a bird at daybreak. She had a man, she was mistress of a household which she ran with confidence and, because her senses were not yet as seasoned as Sean's, she was physically content. Even with Sean's strict adherence to the rules, their evenings in her wagon would end for her with a sigh and a shudder and she would go dreamy-eyed to bed and leave Sean with a burning devil inside of him. The only person Sean could complain to was Thief. He would lie with his snout buried in Sean's armpit, with at least his share of the blankets over him, and listen quietly.

The Zulus could see what the trouble was but they didn't understand it. They didn't discuss it, of course, but if one of them spread his hands expressively or coughed in a certain way the others knew what he meant. Mbejane came closest to actually putting it into words. Sean had just thrown a tantrum. It was a matter of a lost axe and who was responsible. Sean lined them up and expressed doubts as to their ancestry, present worth and future prospects, then he stormed off to his wagon. There was a long silence and Hlubi offered his snuff-box to Mbejane.

Mbejane took a pinch and said, 'It's a stupid stallion that doesn't know how to kick down a fence.'

'It is true, it is true,' they agreed, and there the matter rested.

– 18 –

A week later they reached the Sabi river. The mountains on the far side were blue-grey with distance and the river was full – brown and full.

The next morning was fresh and cool from the night's rain. The camp smelt of wood-smoke, cattle and wild mimosa. From one of the ostrich eggs that Mbejane had found the day before, Katrina made an omelette the size of a soup-plate. It was flavoured with nutmeg and chunks of mushroom, yellow and rich. Afterwards there were scones and wild honey, coffee and a cheroot for Sean.

'Are you going out today?' Katrina asked.

'Uh huh.'

'Oh!'

'Don't you want me to?'

'You haven't stayed in camp for a week.'

'Don't you want me to go?'

She stood up quickly and started clearing the table. 'Anyway you won't find any elephant . . . you haven't found anything for ages.'

'Do you want me to stay?'

'It's such a lovely day.' She signed to Kandhla to take the plates away.

'If you want me to stay, ask me properly.'

'We could look for mushrooms.'

'Say it,' said Sean.

'All right then, please!'

'Mbejane! Take the saddle off that horse, I won't be using him.'

Katrina laughed. She ran to her wagon, skirts swirling around her legs, calling to the dogs. She came back with her bonnet on and a basket in her hand. The dogs crowded round them, jumping up and barking.

'Go on . . . seek up then,' Sean told them and they raced ahead, circling back barking, chasing one another. Sean and Katrina walked holding hands. The brim of Katrina's bonnet kept her face in shadow, but even then her eyes when she looked at him were bright green. They picked the new mushrooms, round and hard, brown and slightly sticky on top, fluted underneath delicately as a lady's fan. In an hour they had filled the basket and they stopped under a marula tree. Sean lay on his back. Katrina broke off a blade of grass and tickled his face with it until he caught her wrist and pulled her down onto his chest. The dogs watched them, sitting around them in a circle, their tongues hanging out pink and wet.

'There's a place in the Cape, just outside Paarl. The mountains stand over it and there's a river . . . the water's very clear, you can see the fish lying on the bottom,' said Katrina. Her ear was against his chest and she was listening to his heart. 'Will you buy me a farm there one day?'

454

'Yes,' said Sean.

'We'll build a house with a wide veranda and on Sundays we'll drive to church with the girls and the little ones in the back and the bigger boys riding next to the buggy.'

'How many will there be?' asked Sean. He lifted the side of her bonnet and looked at her ear. It was a very pretty ear, in the sunlight he could see the fine fur on the lobe.

'Oh lots . . . boys mostly, but a few girls.'

'Ten?' suggested Sean.

'More than that.'

'Fifteen?'

'Yes, fifteen.'

They lay and thought about it. To Sean it seemed a fairly well-rounded number.

'And I'll keep chickens, I want lots of chickens.'

'All right,' said Sean.

'You don't mind?'

'Should I?'

'Some people mind chickens, some people don't like them at all,' said Katrina. 'I'm glad you don't mind them. I've always wanted them.'

Stealthily Sean advanced his mouth towards her ear but she felt him move and sat up.

'What are you doing?'

'This,' said Sean and his arm shot out.

'No, Sean, they're watching us.' She waved her hand at the dogs.

'They'll understand,' said Sean and then they were both quiet for a long time.

The dogs burst out together in full hunting chorus. Katrina sat up and Sean turned his head and saw the leopard. It stood fifty yards away on the edge of the thick bush along the river bank watching them, poised elegantly in tights of black and gold, long and small-bellied. It moved then, blurring with speed, touching the ground as lightly as a swallow touches the water when it drinks in flight. The dogs went after it in a pack, Thief leading them, his voice cracking with excitement.

'Back, come back,' shouted Sean. 'Leave it, damn you, come back.'

'Stop them, Sean, go after them. We'll lose them all.'

'Wait here,' Sean told her.

He ran after the sound of the pack. Not shouting, saving his wind. He knew what would happen and he listened for it. He heard the tone of the hunt change – sharper now. Sean stopped and stood panting, peering ahead. The dogs were not moving. The sound of their barking was steady in volume.

'The swine has stopped; he's going to take them.'

He started running again and almost immediately heard the first dog scream. He kept running. He found the dog lying where the leopard had flung it – the old bitch with white ears, her stomach was stripped out. Sean went on. The tan ridgeback next, disembowelled, still alive and crawling to meet him. He ran on; always the hunt was out of sight ahead of him but he kept after it. He no longer stopped to help the dogs that had been mauled. Most of them were dead before he reached them. The saliva thickened in his mouth, his heart jumped against his ribs and he reeled as he ran.

Suddenly he was in the open and the hunt was spread out before him. There were three dogs left. One of them was Thief. They were circling the leopard, belling him, darting in at his back legs, snapping, then jumping back as the leopard spun snarling. The grass was short and green in the clearing. The sun was directly overhead: it threw no shadow, it lit everything with a flat, even light. Sean tried to shout but his throat wouldn't let the sound out. The leopard dropped onto its back and lay with the sprawled grace of a sleeping cat, its legs open and its belly exposed.

The dogs hung back, hesitating. Sean shouted again but his voice still would not carry. That creamy yellow belly, soft and fluffy, was too much temptation. One of the dogs went for it, dipping its head, its mouth open. The leopard closed on it like a spring trap. It caught and held the dog with its front paws and its back legs worked quickly. The dog yammered at the swift surgeon strokes and then it was thrown aside, its bowels hanging out. The leopard relaxed again to show the yellow bait of its belly. Sean was close now and this time the two dogs heard his shout. The leopard heard it also. It flashed to its feet and tried to break, but the instant it turned Thief was at it, slashing at its back legs forcing it to swing and crouch.

'Here, boy, leave him! Here, Thief, come here!'

Thief took Sean's shout as encouragement. He danced just out of reach of the flicking paws, shrilly taunting the leopard. The hunt was finely balanced now. Sean knew if he could get the dogs to slacken their attack the leopard would run. He went forward a pace, stooped to pick up a stone to throw at Thief and his movement tipped the balance. When he straightened up the leopard was watching him and he felt the eel of fear move in his stomach. It was going to come for him. He knew it by the way its ears flattened against its head and its shoulders bunched like loaded springs. Sean dropped the stone and reached for the knife on his belt.

The leopard's lips peeled back. Its teeth were yellow, its head with the ears flattened was like a snake's. It came fast and low against the ground, brushing the dogs aside. Its run was long-reaching, smoothly beautiful. It snaked towards him, fast over the short grass. It came into the air, lifting high, very fast and very smoothly. Sean felt the shock and the pain together. The shock threw him backwards and the pain sucked the breath from his lungs. Its claws hooked into his chest, he felt them scrape his ribs. He held its mouth from his face, his forearm against its throat and he smelt the overripe grave smell of its breath. They rolled together in the grass, its front claws still holding in the flesh of his chest, and he felt its back legs coming up to rake his stomach. He twisted desperately to keep clear of them, using his knife at the same time, slipping the blade into its back. The leopard screamed, its back legs came up again; he felt the claws go into his hip and tear down his thigh. The pain was deep and strong and he knew he was badly hurt. The legs came up again. This time they would kill him.

Thief locked his teeth in the leopard's leg before the claws could catch in Sean's flesh, he dragged back, digging in with his front feet, holding the leopard stretched out across Sean's body. Sean's vision was dissolving into blackness and bright lights. He pushed the knife into the leopard's back, close to the spine and pulled it down between the ribs the way a butcher cuts a chop. The leopard screamed again with its body shuddering and its claws curling in Sean's flesh. Sean cut again, deep and long – and again, then again. Tearing at it, mad with the pain, its blood gushed out and mixed with his and he rolled away from it. The dogs were worrying it, growling. It was dead. Sean let the knife slip out of his hand and touched the tears in his leg. The blood was dark red, pouring with the thickness of treacle, much blood. He was looking down a funnel of darkness. The leg was far away, not his – not his leg.

'Garry,' he whispered. 'Garry, oh God! I'm sorry. I slipped, I didn't mean it, I slipped.' The funnel closed and there was no leg – only darkness. Time was a liquid thing, all the world was liquid, moving in darkness. The sun was dark and only the pain was steady, steady as a rock in the dark moving sea. He saw Katrina's face indistinct in the darkness. He tried to tell her how sorry he was. He tried to tell her it was an accident, but the pain stopped him. She was crying. He knew she would understand so he went back into the dark sea. Then the surface of the sea boiled and he choked in the heat, but always the pain was there like a rock to hold onto. The steam from the sea coiled up around him and it hardened into the shape of a woman and he thought it was Katrina, then he saw its head was a leopard's head and its breath stank like the rotting of a gangrenous leg.

'I don't want you – I know who you are,' he shouted at it. 'I don't want you. It's not my child,' and the thing broke into steam, twisting grey steam, and came back gibbering at him on a chain that tinkled, frothing yellow from the grey misty mouth, and terror came with it. He twisted and covered his face, holding onto the pain for the pain was real and steady.

Then after a thousand years the sea froze and he walked on it and the white ice stretched away wherever he looked. It was cold and lonely on the ice. There was a small wind, a cold small wind, the wind whispered across the ice and its whispering was a sad sound, and Sean held his pain, hugging it close to him for he was lonely and only the pain was real. Then there were other figures moving around him on the ice, dark figures all hurrying one way, crowding him, pushing him along with them and he lost his pain, lost it in the desperate hurrying press. And though they had no faces, some of the figures wept and others laughed and they hurried forward until they came to the place where the crevasse split across the ice in front of them. The crevasse was wide and deep and its sides were white, then pale-green shading to blue and at last to infinite blackness, and some of the figures threw themselves joyfully into it singing as they fell. Others clung to edges, their formless faces full of fear, and still others stepped off into the void, tiredly, like travellers at the end of a long journey. When Sean saw the crevasse he began to fight, throwing himself back against the crowd that bore him forward, carrying him to the edge of the pit, and his feet slid over the edge. He clawed with his fingers at the slippery edge of the ice. He fought and he shouted as he fought for the dark drop sucked at his legs. Then he lay quietly and the crevasse had closed and he was alone. He was tired – wasted and terribly tired. He closed his eyes and the pain came back to him, throbbing softly in his leg.

He opened his eyes and he saw Katrina's face. She was pale and her eyes were big and heavily underscored in blue. He tried to lift his hand to touch her face but he couldn't move.

'Katrina,' he said. He saw her eyes go green with surprise and happiness.

'You've come back. Oh, thank God. You've come back.'

Sean rolled his head and looked at the canvas of the wagon tent.

'How long?' he asked. His voice was a whisper.

'Five days . . . Don't talk – please, don't talk.'

Sean closed his eyes. He was very tired so he slept.

– 19 –

Katrina washed him when he woke. Mbejane helped her lift and turn him, his big pink-palmed hands very gentle as he handled the leg. They washed the smell of fever off him and changed the dressings. Sean watched Katrina as she worked and every time she looked up they smiled at each other. Once he used a little of his strength to ask Mbejane, 'Where were you when I needed you?'

'I slept in the sun, Nkosi, like an old woman,' Mbejane half-laughed, half-apologized. Katrina brought him food and when he smelt it he was hungry. He ate it all and then he slept again.

Mbejane built a shelter with open sides and a roof of thatch. He sited it in the shade on the bank of the Sabi. Then he made a bed of poles and laced leather thongs. They carried Sean from the wagon, Katrina fussing around them until they had laid him in the shelter. Katrina went back to the wagon for pillows and when she returned she found Thief and Sean settling down comfortably.

'Sean, get that monster out of there – those blankets have just been washed.'

Thief flattened his body and hid his head in Sean's armpit.

'It's all right, he's quite clean,' Sean protected him.

'He smells.'

'He does not.' Sean sniffed at Thief. 'Well, not much anyway.'

'You two!' She put the pillows under Sean's head and went round to his leg. 'How does it feel?'

'It's fine,' said Sean. Thief inched himself up the bed until he reached the pillows.

In the slow slide of days Sean's body healed and the well of his strength filled. The moving air under the shelter dried the scabs off his chest and leg, but there would be scars. In the mornings, after breakfast, Sean held court from his couch. Katrina sat on the end of the bed and his servants squatted around him. First they talked over domestic matters – the health of the oxen, mentioning them by name, discussing their eyes, hooves and stomachs. There was a tear in the canvas of one wagon. The single remaining bitch was in season – was Thief man enough for the job yet? There was meat to kill – perhaps the Nkosikaze would take the rifle later today. Hlubi had caught four barbel of medium size in his fish trap, and here the talk turned to the bush around them. A lion had killed a buffalo below the first bend in the river – there you could see the vultures. During the night a herd of cow elephant had drunk a mile upstream. Each item was considered by the meeting. Everyone felt free to comment or argue against any view which conflicted with his own. When everything had been said Sean gave them their tasks for the day and sent them away. Then he and Katrina could be alone.

From the shelter they could see the full sweep of the river, with the crocodiles lying on the white sandbars and the kingfishers plopping into the shallows. They sat close to each other and they talked of the farm they would have. Sean would grow grapes and breed horses and Katrina would keep chickens. By the next rainy season they would have filled all the wagons; one more trip after that and they would have enough to buy the farm.

Katrina kept him in bed long after he was strong enough to leave it. She mothered him and he loved it. Shamelessly, in the fashion of the male, he accepted her attentions and even exaggerated his injuries a little. Finally but reluctantly Katrina let him up. He stayed in camp a week more, until his legs stopped wobbling, then one evening he took his rifle and went with Mbejane to shoot fresh meat. They went slowly, Sean favouring his leg, and he shot a young eland not far from the laager. Sean sat against a msasa tree and smoked a cheroot while Mbejane went back to fetch servants to carry the meat. Sean watched them butcher the carcass; there were slabs of white fat on the meat. They slung it on poles and carried it between them, two men to a pole, and when they got back to camp Sean found Katrina in one of her inscrutable moods. When he talked to her at supper she answered him from far away and afterwards by the fire she sat detached from him. She was very lovely and Sean was puzzled and a little resentful. At last he stood up.

'It's time for bed – I'll see you to your wagon.'

'You go. I'll sit a little longer.'

Sean hesitated. 'Is there something wrong? Have I done something wrong?'

'No,' she said quickly. 'No. I'm all right. You go to bed.'

He kissed her cheek. 'If you need me I'll be close. Goodnight, sleep sweet.'

He straightened up. 'Come on, Thief,' he said. 'Time for bed.'

'Leave Thief with me, please.' Katrina caught the skin at the back of the dog's neck and restrained him.

'Why?'

'I just feel like company.'

'Then I'll stay as well.' Sean moved to sit down again.

'No, you go to bed.' She sounded desperate and Sean looked hard at her.

'Are you sure you're all right?'

'Yes, please go.'

He went to his wagon and looked back at her. She was sitting very straight, holding the dog. He climbed into the wagon. The lamp was lit and he stopped in surprise when he saw his cot. There were sheets on it, not just the rough blankets. He ran his hand over the smooth fabric; it was crisp from new ironing. He sat on the cot and pulled off his boots. He undid his shirt and threw it onto the chest, then he lay back and looked up at the lamp.

'There's something bloody funny going on here,' he said.

'Sean' – her voice just outside the wagon. Sean jumped up and opened the flap. 'Can I come in?'

'Yes, of course.' He gave her his hand and lifted her into the wagon. He looked at her face. She was frightened.

'There *is* something wrong,' he said.

'No, don't touch me. There's something I've got to tell you. Sit down on the cot.'

Sean watched her face. He was worried.

'I thought I loved you when I came away with you. I thought we had for ever to be together.' She swallowed

463

painfully. 'Then I found you there in the grass – torn and dead. Before our life together had begun you were dead.'

Sean saw the pain come back into her eyes; she was living it again. He put out his hand to her but she held his wrist.

'No, wait . . . please let me finish. I have to explain to you. It's very important.'

Sean dropped his hand and she went on speaking quickly.

'You were dead and I, too, was dying inside. I felt empty. There was nothing left. Nothing . . . just the hollowness inside and the dry dead feeling on the outside. I touched your face and you looked at me. I prayed then, Sean, and I prayed through the days when you fought the rotting of your body.'

She knelt in front of him and held him around the waist.

'Now we are alive and together again, but I know that it cannot be for ever. A day more, a year, if we are lucky, twenty. But not for ever. I see how small I have been to us. I want to be your wife.'

He bent to her quickly but she pulled away and stood up. She slipped the buttons and her clothing fell away. She loosed her hair and let it drop shiny bright down the whiteness of her body.

'Look at me, Sean, I want you to look at me. This and my love I can give you . . . is it enough?'

There was smoothness, hollow and swell, hair like black fire and soft light on soft skin. He saw the flush from her cheeks spread onto her breasts until they glowed, pink and shy but proud in their perfection. He looked no further. He took her to him and covered her nakedness with his big body. She was trembling and he put her between the sheets and gentled her with his voice until the trembling stopped and she lay with her face pressed up under his beard into his neck.

'Show me how ... I want to give everything to you. Please show me how,' she whispered.

So they married each other and their marriage was a comingling of many things. There was the softness of the wind in it and wanting, the way the baked earth wants the rain. There was pain sharp and swift, movement like running horses, sound low as voices in the night but glad as a greeting, joy climbing on eagles' wings, the triumphant surge and burst of wild water on a rock shore and then there was stillness and warmth within and the snuggling of drowsy puppies, and sleep. Yet it did not end in the sleep, it went on to another seeking and finding, another union and a stranger mystery in the secret depths of her body.

– 20 –

In the morning she brought her Bible to him.

'Hey, hey,' protested Sean, 'I've already sworn one oath.' Katrina laughed at him, the memory of the night still warm and happy inside her. She opened the book at its fly leaf.

'You've got to write your name in it ... here, next to mine.'

She watched him, standing next to his chair with her hip touching his shoulder.

'And your date of birth,' she said.

Sean wrote: 'Ninth Jan. 1862.' Then he said: 'What's this "date of death" ... do you want me to fill that in as well?'

'Don't talk like that,' she said quickly and touched the wooden table.

Sean was sorry he'd said it. He tried to cover up. 'There's only space for six children.'

'We can write the others in the margin. That's what Ma

did . . . hers even go over onto the first page of Genesis. Do you think we'll get that far, Sean?'

Sean smiled at her. 'The way I feel now we should reach the New Testament without much trouble.'

They had made a good start. By June the rains were over and Katrina walked with her shoulders back to balance her load. There was a good feeling in the camp. Katrina was more woman than child now. She was big and radiant, pleased with the awe her condition inspired in Sean. She sang to herself often and sometimes in the night she would let him share in it. She would let him pull the nightdress back from the mound of her stomach and lay his ear against the tight-stretched, blue-veined skin. He listened to the suck and gurgle and felt the movement against his cheek. When he sat up his eyes would be full of the wonder of it and she would smile proudly at him and take his head on her shoulder and they would lie together quietly. In the daytime things were right as well. Sean laughed with the servants and hunted without the intensity of before.

They moved north along the Sabi river. Sometimes they camped for a month at one place. The game came back to the rivers as the veld dried out and once more the ivory started piling up in the wagons.

One afternoon in September Sean and Katrina left the camp and walked along the bank. The land was brown again and smelt of dry grass. The river was pools and white sand.

'Hell, it's hot.' Sean took off his hat and wiped the sweat off his forehead. 'You must be cooking under all those clothes.'

'No, I'm all right.' Katrina was holding his arm.

'Let's have a swim.'

'You mean with no clothes on?' Katrina looked shocked.

'Yes, why not?'

'It's rude.'

466

'Come on.' He took her down the bank protesting every step and at a place where boulders screened the water he prised her out of her dress. She was laughing and gasping and blushing all at the same time. He carried her into the pool and she sat down thankfully with the water up to her chin.

'How's that feel?' Sean asked.

She let her hair down and it floated out round her, she wriggled her toes in the sand and her stomach showed through the water like the back of a white whale.

'It's nice,' she admitted. 'It feels like silk underwear against my skin.'

Sean stood over her with only his hat on. She looked at him.

'Sit down,' she said uncomfortably and looked away from him.

'Why?' he asked.

'You know why . . . you're rude, that's why.'

Sean sat down beside her.

'You should be used to me by now.'

'Well, I'm not.'

Sean put his arm round her under the water.

'You're lovely,' he said. 'You're my fancy.'

She let him kiss her ear.

'What's it going to be?' He touched the ripe swelling. 'Boy or girl?' This was currently the favourite topic of conversation.

'Boy.' She was very definite.

'What shall we call him?'

'Well, if you don't find a *predikant* soon we'll have to call him the name you're always giving to the servants.'

Sean stared at her. 'What do you mean?'

'You know what you call them when you're cross.'

'Bastard,' said Sean, then really concerned, 'Hell, I hadn't thought of that! We'll have to find a priest. No child

467

of mine will be a bastard. We'll have to go back to Louis Trichardt.'

'You've got about a month,' Katrina warned him.

'My God, we'll never make it. We've left it too late.' Sean's face was ghastly. 'Wait, I've got it. There are Portuguese settlements across the mountains on the coast.'

'Oh, Sean, but they're Roman Catholics.'

'They all work for the same boss.'

'How long will it take to cross the mountains?' Katrina asked doubtfully.

'I don't know. Perhaps two weeks to reach the coast on horseback.'

'On horseback?' Katrina looked still more doubtfully.

'Oh hell . . . you can't ride!' Sean scratched the side of his nose. 'I'll have to go and fetch one. Will you stay on your own? I'll leave Mbejane to look after you.'

'Yes, I'll be all right.'

'I won't go if you don't want me to. It's not that important.'

'It is important, you know it is. I'll be all right, truly I will.'

Before he left the next morning Sean took Mbejane aside. 'You know why you're not coming with me, don't you?'

Mbejane nodded, but Sean answered his own question. 'Because there is more important work for you to do here.'

'At night,' said Mbejane, 'I will sleep beneath the Nkosikazi's wagon.'

'You'll sleep?' asked Sean threateningly.

'Only once in a while and then very lightly,' Mbejane grinned.

'That's better,' said Sean.

Sean said goodbye to Katrina. There were no tears, she understood necessity and helped him to a quiet acceptance of it. They stood a long while beside their wagon, holding each other, their lips almost touching as they whispered together and then Sean called for his horse. Hlubi followed him leading the packhorse when he crossed the Sabi and when Sean reached the far bank he turned and looked back. Katrina was still standing by their wagon and behind her hovered Mbejane. In her bonnet and green dress she looked very young. Sean waved his hat over his head and then set off towards the mountains.

The forests dwindled into grassland as they climbed and each night was colder than the last. Then, in its turn the grassland conceded to the sheer bluffs and misty gorges of the mountain back. Sean and Hlubi struggled upwards, following the game trails, losing them, turning back from impassable cliffs, scouting for a pass, leading the horses over the steep pitches and at night sitting close to the fire and listening to the baboons barking in the kranses around them. Then suddenly, in the middle of a morning that was bright as a cut diamond, they were at the top. To the west the land lay spread out like a map and the distance they had travelled in a week was pathetically small. By straining his eyes and his imagination Sean could make out the dark-green belt of the Sabi watercourse. To the east the land merged with a blueness that was not the sky and for a while he failed to recognize it. Then – 'The sea,' he shouted and Hlubi laughed with him for it was a godlike feeling to stand above the world. They found an easier route down the eastern slopes and followed it onto the coastal plain. At the bottom of the mountains they came to a native village. To see cultivated lands and human dwellings again was a small shock to Sean. He had come to accept the fact that he and his retinue were the only people left on earth.

The entire population of the village fled when they saw him. Mothers snatched up a child in each hand and ran as fast as their menfolk – memories of the slave-traders still persisted in this part of Africa. Within two minutes of his arrival Sean again had the feeling that he was the only person left on earth. With the contempt of the Zulu for every other tribe in Africa, Hlubi shook his head sadly.

'Monkeys,' he said.

They dismounted and tied their horses under the big tree that was the centre of the village. They sat in the shade and waited. The huts were grass beehives, their roofs blackened with smoke, and a few chickens picked and scratched at the bare earth between them. Half an hour later Sean saw a black face watching him from the edge of the bush and he ignored it. Slowly the face emerged, followed closely by a reluctant body. With a twig, Sean went on drawing patterns in the dust between his feet. Out of the corner of his eye he watched the hesitant approach. It was an old man with stork thin legs and one eye glazed into a white jelly by tropical ophthalmia. Sean concluded that his fellows had picked him to act as ambassador on the grounds that of all their number he would be the least loss.

Sean looked up and gave him a radiant smile. The old man froze and then his lips twitched into a sickly grin of relief. Sean stood up, dusted his hands on the sides of his breeches and went to shake the old man's hand. Immediately the bush around them swarmed with people, they poured back into the village jabbering and laughing: they crowded round Sean and felt his clothing, peered into his face and exclaimed delightedly. It was obvious that most of them had never seen a white man before. Sean was trying to shake off One-Eye, who still had a possessive hold on Sean's right hand, and Hlubi leaned disdainfully against the

470

tree, taking no part in the welcome. One-Eye ended the confusion by screeching at them in a voice rusty with age. The courage he had displayed earlier now earned its reward. At his command a dozen of the younger women scampered off and came back with a carved wooden stool and six earthenware pots of native beer. By the hand, on which he had not for an instant relaxed his grip, One-Eye led Sean to the stool and made him sit; the rest of the villagers squatted in a circle round him and one of the girls brought the biggest beer-pot to Sean. The beer was yellow and it bubbled sullenly. Sean's stomach shied at the sight of it. He glanced at One-Eye who was watching him anxiously, he lifted the pot and sipped. Then he smiled with surprise; it was creamy and pleasantly tart.

'Good,' he said.

'Goot,' chorused the villagers.

'Your health,' said Sean.

''ealt,' said the village as one man, and Sean drank deep. One of the girls took another beer-pot to Hlubi. She knelt in front of him and shyly offered it. She had a plaited-grass string around her waist from which a small kilt hung down in front, but her stern was completely exposed and her bosoms were the size and shape of ripe melons. Hlubi looked at them until the girl hung her head, then he lifted the beer-pot.

Sean wanted a guide to the nearest Portuguese settlement. He looked at One-Eye and said, 'Town? Portagee?'

One-Eye was almost overcome by Sean's attention. He grabbed Sean's hand again before he could pull it away and shook it vigorously.

'Stop that, you bloody fool,' said Sean irritably and One-Eye grinned and nodded, then without releasing Sean's hand he began an impassioned speech to the other villagers. Sean meanwhile was searching his memory for the name of one of the Portuguese ports on this coast.

'Nova Sofala,' he shouted as he got it.

One-Eye broke off his speech abruptly and stared at Sean.

'Nova Sofala,' said Sean again pointing vaguely towards the east and One-Eye showed his gums in his biggest grin yet.

'Nova Sofala,' he agreed pointing with authority and then it was only a matter of minutes before it was understood between them that he would act as guide. Hlubi saddled the horses, One-Eye fetched a grass sleeping mat and a battle-axe from one of the huts. Sean mounted and looked at Hlubi to do the same but Hlubi was acting strangely.

'Yes?' Sean asked with resignation. 'What is it?'

'Nkosi.' Hlubi was looking at the branches of the tree above them. 'The Old One could lead the packhorse.'

'You can take it in turns,' said Sean.

Hlubi coughed and transferred his eyes to the fingernails of his left hand.

'Nkosi, is it possible that you will return to this village on the way back from the sea?'

'Yes, of course,' said Sean, 'we'll have to leave the Old One here. Why do you ask?'

'I have a thorn in my foot, Nkosi, it gives me pain. If you do not require me I will wait here for you. Perhaps the thorn wound will have healed by then.' Hlubi looked up at the tree again and shuffled his feet with embarrassment. Sean had not noticed him limping and he was puzzled as to why Hlubi should start malingering now. Then Hlubi could not stop himself from glancing at where the girl stood in the circle of villagers. Her kilt was very small and from the sides gave her no cover at all. Understanding came to Sean and he chuckled.

'The thorn you have is painful, but it's not in your foot.'

472

Hlubi shuffled his feet again. 'You said they were monkeys . . . have you changed your mind?' Sean asked.

'Nkosi, they are indeed monkeys,' Hlubi sighed. 'But very friendly monkeys.'

'Stay then . . . but do not weaken yourself too much. We have mountains to cross on the way home.'

– 22 –

One-Eye led the packhorse – this made him very proud. Through tall grass, mangrove swamp and thick hot jungle, then through white coral sand and the curving stems of palm trees, they came at last to the sea. Nova Sofala was a fort with brass cannon and thick walls. The sea beyond it was muddy brown from the estuary that flowed into it.

The sentry at the gates said, 'Madre de Dio' when he saw Sean, and took him to the Commandant. The Commandant was a small man with fever-yellowed face and a tired, sweat-darkened tunic. The Commandant said, 'Madre de Dio,' and shot his chair back from his desk. It took some time for him to realize that contrary to appearance this dirty, bearded giant was not dangerous. The Commandant could speak English and Sean laid his problem before him.

For a certainty he could be of assistance. There were three Jesuit missionaries in the fort, freshly arrived from Portugal and eager for employment. Sean could take his pick but first he must bath, eat dinner with the Commandant and help him sample the wines that had arrived on the same boat as the missionaries. Sean thought that was a good idea.

At dinner he met the missionaries. They were young men, pink-faced still, for Africa had not yet had a chance

473

to mark them. All three of them were willing to go with him and Sean selected the youngest – not for his appearance but rather for his name. 'Father Alphonso' had a heroic ring to it. The Jesuits went early to bed and left the Commandant, the four junior officers and Sean to the port. They drank toasts to Queen Victoria and her family and to the King of Portugal and his family. This made them thirsty so they drank to absent friends, then to each other. The Commandant and Sean swore a mutual oath of friendship and loyalty and this made the Commandant very sad. He cried and Sean patted his shoulder and offered to dance the Dashing White Sergeant for him. The Commandant said that he would esteem it as a very great honour and furthermore he would be delighted. He himself did not know this dance but perhaps Sean would instruct him. They danced on the table. The Commandant was doing very well until in his enthusiasm he misjudged the size of the table. Sean helped the junior officers put him to bed and in the morning Sean, Father Alphonso and One-Eye started back towards the mountains.

Sean was impatient of any delay now; he wanted to get back to Katrina. Father Alphonso's English was on a par with Sean's Portuguese. This made conversation difficult, so Alphonso solved the problem by doing all the talking. At first Sean listened but when he decided that the good father was trying to convert him he no longer bothered. Alphonso did not seem put out – he just went on talking and clinging to the horse with both hands while his cassock flapped about his legs and his face sweated in the shade of his wide-brimmed hat. One-Eye followed them like an ancient stork.

It took them two days back to One-Eye's village and their entry was a triumphal procession. Father Alphonso's face lit up when he saw so many prospective converts. Sean could see him mentally rubbing his hands together, and he decided to keep going before Alphonso forgot the main object of the expedition. He gave One-Eye a hunting-knife in payment for his services. One-Eye sat down under the big tree in the centre of the village, his own thin legs no longer able to support his weight and the knife clutched to his chest.

'Hlubi, you've had enough of that . . . come on now!' Sean had not dismounted and was restlessly waiting for Hlubi to say his farewells to three of the village girls. Hlubi had displayed traditional Zulu taste – all three of them were big-breasted, big-bottomed and young. They were also crying.

'Come on, Hlubi . . . what's the trouble?'

'Nkosi, they believe that I have taken them for my wives.'

'What made them think that?'

'Nkosi, I do not know.' Hlubi broke the armhold that the plumpest and youngest had around his neck, he snatched up his spears and fled. Sean and Alphonso galloped after him. The villagers shouted farewells and Sean looked back and saw One-Eye still sitting at the base of the big tree.

The pace which Sean set was at last telling on Alphonso. His verbal spring-tides slackened and he showed a measure of reluctance to let his backside touch the saddle; he rode crouched forward on his horse's neck with his buttocks in the air. They crossed the mountains and went down the other side; the ground levelled out into the Sabi Valley and they rode into the forest. On the ninth day out from Nova Sofala they reached the Sabi river. It was late afternoon. Flocks of guinea-fowl were drinking in the riverbed. They went up in a blue haze of whirling wings as Sean led his party down the bank. While the horses watered Sean spoke with Hlubi.

'Do you recognize this part of the river?'

'Yes, Nkosi, we are two hours' march upstream from the wagons ... we held too far to the north coming through the forest.'

Sean looked at the sun, it was on the tree-tops.

'Half an hour's light left ... and there's no moon tonight.'

'We could wait until morning,' Hlubi suggested hopefully. Sean ignored him and motioned to Alphonso to mount up. Alphonso was prepared to debate the advisability of moving on. Sean took a handful of his cassock and helped him into the saddle.

– 23 –

In the darkness the lantern burning in Katrina's wagon glowed through the canvas and guided them the last half mile into camp. Thief bayed them welcome and Mbejane ran out at the head of the other servants to take Sean's horse. His voice was loud with worry and relief.

'Nkosi, there is little time ... it has begun.'

Sean jumped off his horse and ran to the wagon. He tore open the canvas flap.

'Sean.' She sat up. Her eyes were very green in the lantern light, but they were dark-ringed. 'Thank God, you've come.'

Sean knelt beside her cot and held her. He said certain things to her and she clung to him and moved her lips across his face. The world receded and left one wagon standing in darkness, lit by a single lamp and the love of two people.

Suddenly she stiffened in his arms and gasped. Sean held her, his face suddenly helpless and his big hands timid and uncertain on her shoulders.

'What can I do, my fancy? How can I help you?'

Her body relaxed slowly and she whispered, 'Did you find a priest?'

'The priest!' Sean had forgotten about him. Still holding onto her he turned his head and bellowed, 'Alphonso ... Alphonso. Hurry, man.'

Father Alphonso's face in the opening of the wagon was pale with fatigue and grimy with dust.

'Marry us,' said Sean. 'Quickly, man, che-cha, chop-chop ... you savvy?'

Alphonso climbed into the wagon. The skirts of his cassock were torn and his knees were white and bony through the holes. He stood over them and opened his book. 'Ring?' he asked in Portuguese.

'I do,' said Sean.

'No! No! Ring?' Alphonso held up a finger and made an encircling gesture. 'Ring?'

'I think he wants a wedding ring,' whispered Katrina.

'Oh, my God,' said Sean. 'I'd forgotten about that.' He looked round desperately. 'What can we use? Haven't you got one in your chest or something?'

Katrina shook her head, opened her lips to answer but closed them again as another pain took her. Sean held her while it lasted and when she relaxed he looked up angrily at Alphonso.

'Marry us ... damn you. Don't you see there's no time for all the trimmings?'

'Ring?' said Alphonso again. He looked very unhappy.

'All right, I'll get you a ring.' Sean leapt out of the wagon and shouted at Mbejane.

'Bring my rifle, quickly.'

If Sean wanted to shoot the Portuguese that was his business and Mbejane's duty was to help him. He brought Sean the rifle. Sean found a gold sovereign in the pouch on his belt, he threw it on the ground and held the muzzle of the rifle on it. The bullet punched a ragged hole through it.

477

He tossed the rifle back to Mbejane, picked up the small gold circle and scrambled back into the wagon.

Three times during the service the pains made Katrina gasp and each time Sean held her tight and Alphonso increased the speed of his delivery. Sean put the punctured sovereign on Katrina's finger and kissed her. Alphonso gabbled out the last line of Latin and Katrina said, 'Oh, Sean, it's coming.'

'Get out,' Sean told Alphonso and made an expressive gesture towards the door – thankfully Alphonso went.

It did not take long then, but to Sean it was an eternity – like that time when they had taken Garrick's leg. Then in a slippery rush it was finished. Katrina lay very quiet and pale, while on the cot below her, still linked to her, purple-blotched and bloody lay the child that they had made.

'It's dead,' croaked Sean. He was sweating and he had backed away against the far wall of the wagon.

'No.' Katrina struggled up fiercely. 'No, it's not . . . Sean, you must help me.'

She told him what to do and at last the child cried.

'It's a boy,' said Katrina softly. 'Oh, Sean . . . it's a boy.' She was more beautiful than he had ever seen her before; pale and tired and beautiful.

– 24 –

Sean's protests were in vain – Katrina left her bed the next morning and squeezed into one of her old dresses. Sean hovered between her and the child on the cot.

'I'm still so *fat*,' she lamented.

'Fancy, please stay in bed another day or two.'

She pulled a face at him and went on struggling with the lacing of her bodice.

'Who's going to look after the baby?'

'I will!' said Sean earnestly. 'You can tell me what to do.'

Arguing with Katrina was like trying to pick up quick-silver with your fingers, not worth the effort. She finished dressing and took up the child.

'You can help me down the steps.' She smiled at him. Sean and Alphonso set a chair for her in the shade of one of the big shuma trees and the servants came to see the child. Katrina held him in her lap and Sean stood over them in uncertain possession. For Sean it seemed unreal yet ... too much for his mind to digest in so short a time. He grinned dazedly at the steady stream of comment from his servants and his arm was limp when Alphonso shook his hand for the twentieth time that morning.

'Hold your child ... Nkosi. Let us see you with him on your arm,' called Mbejane and the other Zulus took up the cry. Sean's expression changed slowly to one of apprehension.

'Pick him up, Nkosi.'

Katrina proffered the bundle and a hunted look came into Sean's eyes.

'Have no fear, Nkosi, he has no teeth, he cannot harm you,' Hlubi encouraged him. Sean held his first-born awkwardly and assumed the hunchbacked posture of the new father. The Zulus cheered him and slowly Sean's face relaxed and his smile was a glow of pride.

'Mbejane, is he not beautiful?'

'As beautiful as his father,' Mbejane agreed.

'Your words are a blade with two edges,' laughed Sean. He looked at the child closely. It wore a cap of dark hair, its nose was flat as a bulldog's, its eyes were milky-grey and its legs were long, skinny and red.

'How will you name him?' asked Hlubi. Sean looked at Katrina.

'Tell them,' he said.

'He shall be called Dirk,' she said in Zulu.

'What is the meaning?' asked Hlubi, and Sean answered him.

'It means a dagger . . . a sharp knife.'

There was immediate nodded approval from all the servants. Hlubi produced his snuff-box and passed it among them and Mbejane took a pinch.

'That,' he said, 'is a good name.'

– 25 –

Paternity, the subtle alchemist, transformed Sean's attitude to life within twelve hours. Never before had anything been so utterly dependent upon him, so completely vulnerable. That first evening in their wagon he watched Katrina sitting cross-legged on her cot, stooping forward over the child to give it her breast. Her hair hung in a soft wing across one cheek, her face was fuller, more matronly and the child in her lap fed with a red face and small wheezings. She looked up at him and smiled and the child tugged her breast with its tiny fists and hunting mouth.

Sean crossed to the cot, sat beside them and put his arm around them. Katrina rubbed her cheek against his chest and her hair smelt warm and clean. The boy went on feeding noisily. Sean felt vaguely excited as though he were on the threshold of a new adventure.

A week later, when the first rain clouds built up in the sky, Sean took the wagons across the Sabi and onto the slopes of the mountains to escape the heat of the plains. There was a valley he had noticed when he and Hlubi had made their journey to the coast. The valley bottom was covered with short sweet grass and cedar trees grew along a stream of clean water. Sean took them to this place.

Here they would wait out the rainy season and when it was finished and the baby was strong enough to travel they could take the ivory south and sell it in Pretoria. It was a happy camp. The oxen spread out along the valley, filling it with movement and the contented sound of their lowing; there was laughter among the wagons and at night when the mist slumped down off the mountains the camp fire was bright and friendly. Father Alphonso stayed with them for nearly two weeks. He was a pleasant young man and although he and Sean never understood what the other was saying yet they managed well enough with sign language. He left at last with Hlubi and one of the other servants to escort him back over the mountains, but before he did he managed to embarrass Sean by kissing him goodbye. Sean and Katrina were sorry to see him go. They had grown to like him and Katrina had almost forgiven him his religion.

The rains came with the usual flourish and fury. Weeks drifted into months. Happy months, with life centring around Dirk's cot. Mbejane had made the cot for him out of cedarwood and one of Katrina's chests produced the sheets and blankets for it. The child grew quickly: each day he seemed to occupy more of his cot, his legs filled out, his skin lost its blotchy-purple look and his eyes were no longer a vague milky-blue. There was green in them now – they would be the same colour as his mother's.

To fill the long lazy days Sean started to build a cabin beside the stream. The servants joined in and from a modest first plan it grew into a thing of sturdy plastered walls and neatly thatched roof with a stone fireplace at one end. When it was finished Sean and Katrina moved into it. After their wagon with its thin canvas walls, the cabin gave a feeling of permanence to their love. One night, when the rain hissed down in darkness outside and the wind whined at the door like a dog wanting to be let in, they spread a mattress in front of the fireplace and there in the moving firelight they started another baby.

Christmas came, and after it the New Year. The rains stuttered and stopped and still they stayed on in their valley. Then at last they had to go, for their supplies of basic stores – powder, salt, medicines, cloth – were nearly finished. They loaded the wagons, inspanned and left in the early morning. As the line of wagons wound down the valley towards the plains Katrina sat on the box-seat of the lead wagon holding Dirk on her lap and Sean rode beside her. She looked back – the roof of their cabin showed brown through the branches of the cedar trees. It seemed forlorn and lonely.

'We must come back one day, we've been so happy here,' she said softly. Sean leaned out of the saddle towards her and touched her arm.

'Happiness isn't a place, my fancy, we aren't leaving it here, we're taking it with us.'

She smiled at him. The second baby was starting to show already.

– 26 –

They reached the Limpopo river at the end of July and found a place to cross. It took three days to unload the wagons, work them through the soft sand and then carry the ivory and stores across. They finished in the late afternoon of the third day and by then everyone was exhausted. They ate an early supper and an hour after sunset the Zulus were rolled in their blankets, and Sean and Katrina were sleeping arms-around and head-on-chest in the wagon. In the morning Katrina was quiet and a little pale. Sean didn't notice it until she told him that she felt tired and was going to lie down – immediately he was all attentive. He helped her into the wagon and settled the pillows under her head.

'Are you sure you're all right?' he kept asking.

'Yes . . . it's nothing, I'm just a bit tired. I'll be all right,' she assured him. She appreciated his concern but was relieved when finally he went to see to the business of reloading the wagons for Sean's ministrations were always a little clumsy. She wanted to be left alone, she felt tired and cold.

By midday the wagons were loaded to Sean's satisfaction. He went to Katrina's wagon, lifted the canvas and peeped in. He expected her to be asleep. She was lying on the cot with her eyes open and two of the thick grey blankets wrapped around her. Her face was as pale as a two-day corpse. Sean felt the first leap of alarm. He scrambled into the wagon.

'My dear, you look ghastly. Are you sick?' He put his hand on her shoulder and she was shivering. She didn't answer him, instead her eyes moved from his face to the floor near the foot of the bed and Sean's eyes followed hers. Katrina's luxury was her chamberpot; it was a massive china thing with red roses hand-painted on it. She loved it dearly and Sean used to tease her when she was perched on top of it. Now the pot stood near the foot of the bed and when Sean saw what was in it his breathing stopped. It was half full of a liquid the colour of milk stout. 'Oh, my God,' he whispered. He went on staring at it, standing very still while a gruesome snatch of doggerel he remembered hearing sung in the canteens of the Witwatersrand began trotting through his brain like an undertaker's hack.

> Black as the Angel,
> Black as disgrace
> When the fever waters flow
> They're as black as the ace.

483

Roll him in a blanket
Feed him on quinine
But all of us we know
It's the end of the line.

Black as the Angel
Black as disgrace
Soon we'll lay him down below
And chuck dirt in his face.

He raised his head and looked steadily at her, searching for the signs of fear. But just as steadily she looked back at him.

'Sean, it's blackwater.'

'Yes . . . I know,' Sean said, for there was nothing to be gained by denial, no room for extravagant hope. It was blackwater fever: malaria in its most malignant form, attacking the kidneys and turning them to fragile sacks of black blood that the slightest movement could rupture. Sean knelt by her cot. 'You must lie very still.' He touched her forehead lightly with the tips of his fingers and felt the heat of her skin.

'Yes,' she answered him, but already the expression in her eyes was blurring and she made the first restless movement of delirium. Sean put his arm across her chest to hold her from struggling.

By nightfall Katrina was deep in the nightmare of malaria. She laughed, she screamed in senseless terror, she shook her head and fought him when he tried to make her drink. But she had to drink, it was her one chance, to flush out her kidneys that she might live. Sean held her head and forced her.

Dirk started crying, hungry and frightened by the sight of his mother.

'Mbejane!' shouted Sean, his voice pitched high with

desperation. Mbejane had waited all afternoon at the entrance of the wagon.

'Nkosi, what can I do?'

'The child . . . can you care for him?'

Mbejane picked up the cot with Dirk still in it. 'Do not worry about him again. I will take him to the other wagon.'

Sean turned his whole attention back to Katrina. The fever built up steadily within her. Her body was a furnace, her skin was dry and with every hour she was wilder and her movements more difficult to control.

An hour after dark Kandhla came to the wagon with a pot of steaming liquid and a cup. Sean's nose wrinkled as he caught the smell of it.

'What the hell is that?'

'I have stewed the bark from a maiden's breast tree . . . the Nkosikazi must drink it.'

It had the same musty smell as boiling hops and Sean hesitated. He knew the tree. It grew on high ground, it had a diseased-looking lumpy bark and each lump was the size and shape of a breast surmounted by a thorn.

'Where did you get it? I have seen none of these trees near the river.' Sean was marking time while he decided whether to make Katrina drink the brew. He knew these Zulu remedies, what they didn't kill they sometimes cured.

'Hlubi went back to the hills where we camped four days ago . . . he brought the bark into the camp an hour ago.'

A thirty-mile round journey in something under six hours – even in his distress Sean could smile.

'Tell Hlubi the Nkosikazi will drink his medicine.'

Kandhla held her head and Sean forced the evil-smelling liquid between her lips – he made her finish the whole potful. The juice of the bark seemed to relieve the congestion of her kidneys; four times before morning she passed frothy black water. Each time Sean held her gently, cushioning her body from any movement that might have killed

485

her. Gradually her delirium became coma; she lay huddled and still in the cot, shaken only by the brief fits of shivering. When the morning sun hit the wagon canvas and lit the interior, Sean saw her face, and he knew that she was dying. Her skin was an opaque yellowish white, her hair had lost its glow and was lifeless as dry grass. Kandhla brought another pot of the medicine and they fed it to her. When the pot was empty Kandhla said, 'Nkosi, let me lay a mattress on the floor beside the Nkosikazi's bed. You must sleep and I will stay here with you and wake you if the Nkosikazi stirs.'

Sean looked at him with haunted eyes. 'There will be time to sleep later, my friend.' He looked down at Katrina and went on softly. 'Perhaps, very soon there will be time.'

Suddenly Katrina's body stiffened and Sean dropped on his knees beside her cot. Kandhla hovered anxiously behind him. It took Sean a while to understand what was happening and then he looked up at Kandhla.

'Go! Go quickly!' he said and the suffering in his voice sent Kandhla stumbling blindly from the wagon. Sean's second son was born that morning and while Kandhla watched over Katrina Sean wrapped the child in a blanket, took him into the veld and buried him. Then he went back to Katrina and stayed with her while days and nights blended together into a hopeless muddle of grief. As near as Katrina was to death, that near was Sean to insanity. He never moved out of the wagon, he squatted on the mattress next to her cot, wiping the perspiration from her face, holding a cup to her lips or just sitting and watching her. He had lost his child and before his eyes Katrina was turning into a wasted yellow skeleton. Dirk saved him. Mbejane brought the boy to him and he romped on the mattress, crawling into Sean's lap and pulling his beard. It was the one small glimmer of light in the darkness.

27

Katrina survived. She came back slowly from the motionless coma that precedes death and with her hesitant return Sean's despair changed to hope and then to a wonderful relief. Her water was no longer black but dark pink and thick with sediment. She was aware of him now and, although she was so weak that she could not lift her head off the pillow, her eyes followed him as he moved about the wagon. It was another week before she learned about the baby. She asked him, her voice a tired whisper, and Sean told her with all the gentleness of which he was capable. She did not have the strength for any great show of emotion; she laid quietly staring up at the canvas above her head and her tears slid down across her yellow cheeks.

The damage that the fever had done to her body was hardly credible. Her limbs were so thin that Sean could completely encircle her thigh with one hand. Her skin hung in loose yellow folds from her face and body and pink blood still stained her water. This was not all: the fever had sucked all the strength from her mind. She had nothing left to resist the sorrow of her baby's death, and the sorrow encased her in a shell through which neither Sean nor Dirk could reach her. Sean struggled to bring her back to life, to repair the terrible damage to her mind and body. Every minute of his time he employed in her service.

He and the servants scoured the veld for thirty miles around the laager to find delicacies to tempt her appetite, wild fruits, honey, giraffe marrows, the flesh of a dozen animals: kabobs of elephant heart and duiker liver, roasted iguana lizard as white and tender as a plump pullet, golden fillets of the yellow-mouthed bream from the river. Katrina picked at them listlessly then turned away and lay staring at the canvas wall of the cot.

Sean sat beside her and talked about the farm they would buy, trying vainly to draw her into a discussion of the house they would build. He read to her from Duff's books and the only reaction he received was a small quivering of her lips when he read the words 'death' or 'child'. He talked about the days on the Witwatersrand, searching his mind for stories that might amuse her. He brought Dirk to her and let him play about the wagon. Dirk was walking now, his dark hair had started to curl and his eyes were green. Dirk, however, could not be too long confined in the wagon. There was too much to do, too much to explore. Before long he would stagger to the entrance and issue the imperial summons: 'Bejaan! Bejaan!'

Almost immediately Mbejane's head would appear in the opening and he would glance at Sean for permission.

'All right, take him out then . . . but tell Kandhla not to stuff him full of food.'

Quickly, before Sean changed his mind, Mbejane would lift Dirk down and lead him away. Dirk had nearly two dozen Zulus to spoil him. They competed hotly for his affections, no effort was too much – dignified Mbejane down on his hands and knees being ridden mercilessly in and out among the wagons, Hlubi scratching himself under the arms and gibbering insanely in his celebrated imitation of a baboon while Dirk squealed with delight, fat Kandhla raiding Katrina's store of fruit preserves to make sure Dirk was properly fed and the others keeping in the background, anxious to join the worship but fearful of incurring the jealousy of Mbejane and Hlubi. Sean knew what was happening but he was powerless to prevent it. His time was completely devoted to Katrina.

For the first time in his life Sean was giving more than just a superficial part of himself to another human being. It was not an isolated sacrifice: it went on throughout the months it took for Katrina to regain sufficient of her strength to enable her to sit up in bed without assistance; it continued through the months that she needed before Sean judged it safe to resume the trek towards the south. They built a litter for her – Sean would not risk the jarring of the wagon – and the first day's trek lasted two hours. Four of the servants carried the litter and Katrina lay in it, protected from the sun by a strip of canvas spread above her head. Despite the gentleness with which the Zulus handled her, at the end of the two hours Katrina was exhausted. Her back ached and she was sweating in small beads from her yellow skin. The next week they travelled two hours daily and then gradually increased the time until they were making a full day's journey.

They were halfway to the Magaliesberg, camped at a muddy waterhole in the thorn flats, when Mbejane came to Sean.

'There is still one wagon empty of ivory, Nkosi.'

'The others are full,' Sean pointed out.

'Four hours' march from this place there is enough ivory buried to fill those wagons.'

Sean's mouth twisted with pain. He looked away towards the south-east and he spoke softly. 'Mbejane, I am still a young man and yet already I have stored up enough ugly memories to make my old age sad. Would you have me steal from a friend not only his life but his share of ivory also?'

Mbejane shook his head. 'I asked, that is all.'

'And I have answered, Mbejane. It is his . . . let it lie.'

28

They crossed the Magaliesberg and turned west along the mountain range. Then, two months after they had left the Limpopo river, they reached the Boer settlement at Louis Trichardt. Sean left Mbejane to outspan the wagons on the open square in front of the church and he went to search for a doctor. There was only one in the district. Sean found him in his surgery above the general dealer's store and took him to the wagons. Sean carried his bag for him and the doctor, a greybeard and unused to such hardships, trotted to keep up with Sean. He was panting and pouring sweat by the time they arrived. Sean waited outside while the doctor completed his examination and when he finally made his descent from the wagon Sean fell on him impatiently. 'What do you think, man?'

'I think, meneer, that you should give hourly thanks to your Maker.' The doctor shook his head in amazement. 'It seems hardly possible that your wife could have survived both the fever and the loss of the child.'

'She is safe then, there's no chance of a relapse?' Sean asked.

'She is safe now . . . but she is still a very sick woman. It may take a year before her body is fully mended. There is no medicine I can give you. She must be kept quiet, feed her well and wait for time to cure her.' The doctor hesitated. 'There is other damage—' He tapped his forehead with his forefinger. 'Grief is a terrible destroyer. She will need love and gentleness and after another six months she will need a baby to fill the emptiness left by the one she lost. Give her those three things, meneer, but most of all give her love.' The doctor hauled his watch from his waistcoat and looked at it. 'Time! There is so little time. I must go, there are others who need me.' He held out his hand to Sean. 'Go with God, meneer.'

Sean shook his hand. 'How much do I owe you?'

The doctor smiled, he had a brown face and his eyes were pale blue; when he smiled he looked like a boy. 'I make no charge for words. I wish I could have done more.' He hurried away across the square and when he walked you could see that his smile lied, he was an old man.

'Mbejane,' said Sean. 'Get a big tusk out of the wagon and take it to the doctor's room above the store.'

Katrina and Sean went to the morning service in the church next day. Katrina could not stand through the hymns. She sat quietly in her pew, watching the altar, her lips forming the words of the hymn and her eyes full of her sorrow.

They stayed on for three more days in Louis Trichardt and they were made welcome. Men came to drink coffee with them and see the ivory and the women brought them eggs and fresh vegetables, but Sean was anxious to move south. So on the third day they started the last stage of their trek.

Katrina regained her strength rapidly now. She took over the management of Dirk from the servants, to their ill-concealed disappointment, and soon she left her litter and rode on the box seat of the lead wagon again. Her body filled out and there was colour showing once more through the yellow skin of her cheeks. Despite the improvement to her body the depression of her mind still persisted and there was nothing that Sean could do to lift it.

A month before the Christmas of 1895 Sean's wagon train climbed the low range of hills above the city and they looked down into Pretoria. The jacaranda trees that filled every garden were in bloom – masses of purple – and the busy streets spoke well of the prosperity of the Transvaal

491

Republic. Sean outspanned on the outskirts of the city, simply pulling the wagons off the road and camping beside it, and once the camp was established and Sean had made certain that Katrina no longer needed his help he put on his one good suit and called for his horse. His suit had been cut to the fashion of four years previously and had been made to encompass the belly he had acquired on the Witwatersrand. Now it hung loosely down his body but bunched tightly around his thickened arms. His face was burnt black by the sun and his beard bushed down onto his chest and concealed the fact that the stiff collar of his shirt could no longer close around his neck. His boots were scuffed almost through the uppers, there was not a suspicion of polish on them and they had completely lost their shape. Sweat had soaked through his hat around the level of the band and left dark greasy marks; the brim drooped down over his eyes so he had to wear it pushed onto the back of his head. There was, therefore, some excuse for the curious glances that followed him that afternoon as he rode down Church Street with a great muscular savage trotting at his one stirrup and an overgrown brindle hound at the other. They pushed their way between the wagons that cluttered the wide street; they passed the Raadsaal of the Republican Parliament, passed the houses standing back from the road in their spacious purple and green gardens and came at last to the business area of the city that crowded round the railway station. Sean and Duff had bought their supplies at a certain general dealer's stores and now Sean went back to it. It was hardly changed – the signboard in front had faded a little but still declared that I. Goldberg, Importer & Exporter, Dealer in Mining Machinery, Merchant & Wholesaler, was prepared to consider the purchase of gold, precious stone, hides and skins, ivory and other natural produce. Sean swung down from the saddle and tossed his reins to Mbejane. 'Unsaddle, Mbejane. This may take time.'

Sean stepped up onto the sidewalk, lifted his hat to two passing ladies and went through into the building where Mr Goldberg conducted his diverse activities. One of the assistants hurried to meet him, but Sean shook his head and the man went back behind the counter. He had seen Mr Goldberg with two customers at the far end of the store. He was content to wait. He browsed around among the loaded shelves of merchandise, feeling the quality of a shirt, sniffing at a box of cigars, examining an axe, lifting a rifle down off the rack and sighting at a spot on the wall, until Mr Goldberg bowed his customers through the door and turned to Sean. Mr Goldberg was short and fat. His hair was cropped short and his neck bulged over the top of his collar. He looked at Sean and his eyes were expressionless while he rifled through the index cards of his memory for the name. Then he beamed like a brilliant burst of sunlight. 'Mr Courtney, isn't it?'

Sean grinned. 'That's right. How are you, Izzy?' They shook hands. 'How's business?'

Mr Goldberg's face fell. 'Terrible, terrible, Mr Courtney. I'm a worried man.'

'You look well enough on it.' Sean prodded his stomach. 'You've put on weight.'

'You can joke, Mr Courtney, but I'm telling you it's terrible. Taxes and worry, taxes and worry.' Mr Goldberg sighed, 'And now there's talk of war.'

'What's this?' Sean frowned.

'War, Mr Courtney, war between Britain and the Republic.'

Sean's frown dissolved and he laughed. 'Nonsense, man, not even Kruger could be such a bloody fool! Get me a cup of coffee and a cigar and we'll go through to your office and talk business.'

Mr Goldberg's face went blank and his eyelids drooped almost sleepily.

'Business, Mr Courtney?'

'That's right, Izzy, this time I'm selling and you're buying.'

'What are you selling, Mr Courtney?'

'Ivory!'

'Ivory?'

'Twelve wagon loads of it.'

Mr Goldberg sighed sadly. 'Ivory's no good now, the bottom's fallen out of it. You can hardly give it away.' It was very well done; if Sean had not been told the ruling prices two days before he might have been convinced.

'I'm sorry to hear that,' he said. 'If you're not interested, I'll see if I can find someone else.'

'Come along to my office anyway,' said Mr Goldberg. 'We can talk about it. Talk costs nothing.'

Two days later they were still talking about it. Sean had fetched his wagons and had off-loaded the ivory in the back yard of the store. Mr Goldberg had personally weighed each tusk and written the weights down on a sheet of paper. He and Sean had added the columns of figures and agreed on the total. Now they were in the last stages of agreeing the price.

'Come on, Izzy, we've wasted two days already. That's a fair price and you know it ... let's get it over with,' Sean growled.

'I'll lose money on this,' protested Mr Goldberg. 'I've got to make a living, every man's got to live.'

'Come on.' Sean held out his right hand. 'Let's call it a deal.'

Mr Goldberg hesitated a second longer, then he put his pudgy hand in Sean's fist and they grinned at each other, both well satisfied. One of Mr Goldberg's assistants counted out the sovereigns, stacking them in piles of fifty along the counter, then Sean and Mr Goldberg checked them and agreed once more. Sean filled two canvas bags with the gold, slapped Mr Goldberg's back, helped himself to another cigar and headed heavily laden for the bank.

'When are you going into the veld again?' Mr Goldberg called after him.

'Soon!' said Sean.

'Don't forget to get your supplies here.'

'I'll be back,' Sean assured him.

Mbejane carried one of the bags and Sean the other. Sean was smiling and streamers of cigar smoke swirled back from his head as he strode along the sidewalk. There's something in the weight of a sack of gold that makes the man who holds it stand eight feet tall.

That night as they lay together in the darkness of the wagon Katrina asked him.

'Have we enough money to buy the farm yet, Sean?'

'Yes,' said Sean. 'We've got enough for the finest farm in the whole Cape peninsular ... and, after one more trip, we'll have enough to build the house and the barns, buy the cattle, lay out the vineyard and still have some left over.'

Katrina was silent for a moment then, 'So we are going back into the bushveld again?'

'One more trip,' said Sean. 'Another two years and then we'll go down to the Cape.' He gave her a hug. 'You don't mind, do you?'

'No,' she said. 'I think I'd like that. When will we leave?'

'Not just yet awhile,' Sean laughed. 'First we're going to have some fun.' He hugged her again, her body was still painfully thin; he could feel the bones of her hips pressed against him.

'Some pretty clothes for you, my fancy, and a suit for me that doesn't look like a fancy dress. Then we'll go out and see what this burg has to offer in the way of entertainment—' He stopped as the idea swelled up in his mind. 'Damn it! I know what we'll do. We'll hire a carriage and go across to Jo'burg. We'll take a suite at the Grand National Hotel and do some living. Bath in a china bath, sleep in a real bed; you can have your hair prettied-up and I'll have my beard trimmed by a barber. We'll eat crayfish and penguin eggs ... I can't remember when I last tasted pork or mutton ... we'll wash it down with the old bubbling wine and waltz to a good band—' Sean raced on and when he stopped for breath Katrina asked softly, 'Isn't the waltz a very sinful dance, Sean?'

Sean smiled in the darkness. 'It certainly is!'

'I'd like to be sinful just once ... not too much; just a little with you to see what it's like.'

'We will be,' said Sean, 'as wicked as hell.'

– 29 –

The next day Sean took Katrina to the most exclusive ladies' shop in Pretoria. He chose the material of half a dozen dresses. One of them was to be a ball gown in canary-yellow silk. It was extravagance and he knew it, but he didn't care once he saw the flash of guilty delight in Katrina's cheeks and the old green sparkle in her eyes. For the first time since the fever she was living again. He spilled out his sovereigns with thankful abandon. The sales girls were delighted with him, they crowded round him with trays of feminine accessories.

'A dozen of those,' said Sean and, 'yes, those will do.' Then a flash of green on the racks across the room caught his eye – it was Katrina's green.

'What's that?' He pointed and two sales girls nearly knocked each other down in the rush to get it for him. The winner carried the shawl back to him and Sean took it and placed it around Katrina's shoulders. It was a beautiful thing.

'We'll take it,' said Sean and Katrina's lips quivered – then suddenly she was crying, sobbing brokenly. The excitement had been too much. There was immediate consternation among the shop assistants, they flapped around Sean like hens at feeding time while he picked Katrina up and carried her out to the hired carriage. At the door he paused and spoke over his shoulder.

'I want those dresses finished by tomorrow evening. Can you do it?'

'They'll be ready, Mr Courtney, even if my girls have to work all night on them.'

He took Katrina back to the wagons and laid her on her cot.

'Please forgive me, Sean, I've never done that in my life before.'

'It's all right, my fancy, I understand. Now you just go to sleep.'

The following day Katrina stayed at the camp resting, while Sean went to see Mr Goldberg again and buy from him the stores they would need for the next expedition. It took another day to load the wagons and by then Katrina seemed well enough to make the trip to Johannesburg.

They left in the early afternoon. Mbejane driving, Sean and Katrina sitting close together on the back seat holding hands under the travelling rug and Dirk bouncing round the interior of the carriage, pausing now and then to flatten his face against a window and keeping up a flow of comment in the peculiar mixture of English, Dutch and Zulu that Sean called Dirkese. They reached Johannesburg long before Sean expected to. In four years the town had doubled its size and had spread out into the veld to meet them. They followed the main road through the new areas and came to the centre. There were changes here as well but it was, in the main, the way he remembered it. They threaded their way through the babble of Eloff Street, and around them, mingling with the crowds on the sidewalks, were the ghosts of the past. He heard Duff laugh and twisted quickly in his seat to place the sound; a dandy in a boater hat with gold fillings in his teeth laughed again from a passing carriage and Sean heard that it was not Duff's laugh. Very close, but not the same. All of it was like that – similar but subtly changed, nostalgic but sad with the knowledge of loss. The past was lost – and he knew then that you can never go back. Nothing is the same, for reality can exist at one time only and in one place only. Then it dies and you have lost it and you must go on to find it at another time and in another place.

They took a suite at the Grand National, with a sitting-room and two bedrooms, a private bathroom and a balcony that looked out over the street – over the rooftops to where the headgears and white dumps stood along the ridge. Katrina was exhausted. They had supper sent up to the room early and when they had eaten Katrina went to bed and Sean went down alone to drink a nightcap at the bar. The bar-room was crowded. Sean found a seat in the corner and sat silently in the jabber of conversation. In it, but no longer a part of it.

They had changed the picture above the bar – it used to be a hunting print; but now it was a red-coated general, impressively splattered with blood, taking leave of his staff in the middle of a battlefield. The staff looked bored. Sean let his eyes wander on along the dark panelled walls. He remembered – there was so much to remember! Suddenly he blinked. Near the side door was a star-shaped crack in the wooden panelling. Sean started to grin and put down his glass and massaged the knuckles of his right hand. If Oakie Henderson hadn't ducked under that punch it would have taken his head off.

Sean signalled to the barman. 'Another brandy, please.'

While the man was pouring, Sean asked, 'What happened to that panel near the door?'

The man glanced up and then back at the bottle. 'Some fellow put his fist through it in the old days. Boss left it like that, sort of souvenir, you know.'

'He must have been quite a fellow . . . that wood's an inch thick. Who was he?' Sean asked expectantly.

The man shrugged. 'One of the drifters. They come and they go. Make a few pounds, piss it against the wall and then go back where they came from.' He looked at Sean with bored eyes. 'That'll be half a dollar, mate.' Sean drank the brandy slowly, turning the glass in his hands between sips and watching the liquor cling to its sides like thin oil. By a cracked panel in a bar-room they shall remember you.

And now I shall go to bed, he decided, this is no longer my world. My world is upstairs sleeping – I hope! He smiled a little to himself and finished the brandy in his glass.

'Sean' – a voice at his ear and a hand on his shoulder as he turned to leave. 'My God, Sean, is it really you?'

Sean stared at the man beside him. He did not recognize the neatly clipped beard and the big sun-burned nose with the skin peeling off the tip, but suddenly he knew the eyes.

'Dennis, you old rogue. Dennis Petersen from Ladyburg. That's right isn't it?'

'You didn't recognize me!' laughed Dennis. 'So much for our friendship – you disappear without a word and ten years later you don't even know me!'

Now they were both laughing.

'I thought they would have hanged you long ago—' Sean defended himself. 'What on earth are you doing in Johannesburg?'

'Selling beef – I'm on the committee of the Beef Growers' Association.' There was pride in Dennis's voice. 'I have been up here negotiating the renewal of our contracts.'

'When are you going back?'

'My train leaves in an hour.'

'Well, there's time for a drink before you go – what will it be?'

'I'll have a small brandy, thanks.'

Sean ordered the drinks and they took them up and stood, suddenly awkward in the awareness that ten years were between their once complete accord.

'So, what have you been doing with yourself?' Dennis ended the pause.

'This and that, you know – a bit of mining, just come back from the bushveld. Nothing very exciting.'

'Well, it's good to see you again anyway. Your health.'

'And yours,' said Sean, and then suddenly he realized that here was news of his family – news he had been without for many years.

'How's everyone at Ladyburg – your sisters?'

'Both married – so am I, with four sons,' and the pride was in Dennis's voice again.

'Anyone I know?' asked Sean.

'Audrey – you know old Pye's daughter.'

'No!' Sean ripped out the word, and then quickly, 'That's wonderful, Dennis. I'm pleased for you – she was a lovely girl.'

'The best,' agreed Dennis complacently. He had the sleek well-fed, well-cared for look of a married man, fatter in the face and his stomach starting to show. I wonder if I have it yet, Sean thought. 'Of course, old man Pye's dead now – that's one creditor he couldn't buy off. Ronnie's taken over the bank and the store.'

'The bat-eared bush rat,' said Sean and knew immediately that he had said the wrong thing. Dennis frowned slightly. 'He's family now, Sean. A very decent chap really – and a clever business man.'

'I'm sorry, I was joking. How's my mother?' Sean changed

500

the subject by asking the question that had been in the forefront of his mind and he had picked the right topic. Dennis's expression softened immediately – you could see the warmth in his eyes.

'The same as ever. She's got a dress shop now, next door to Ronnie's store. It's a gold mine – no one would think of buying anywhere else but at Aunt Ada's. She's godmother to my two eldest, I guess she's godmother to half the kids in the district,' and then his expression hardened again. 'The least you could have done was write to her sometime, Sean. You can't imagine the pain you have caused her.'

'There were circumstances.' Sean dropped his eyes to his glass.

'That's no excuse – you have a duty which you neglected. There is no excuse for it.'

You little man. Sean lifted his head and looked at him without trying to disguise his annoyance. You pompous, preaching little man peering out at the world one-eyed through the keyhole of your own self-importance. Dennis had not noticed Sean's reaction and he continued. 'That's a lesson a man must learn before he grows up – we all have our responsibilities and our duties. A man grows up when he faces those duties, when he accepts the burdens that society places on him. Take my own case: despite the vast amount of work I have on the farms – I now own Mahoba's Kloof as well – and despite the demands made on me by my family, yet I have time to represent the district on the committee of the Beef Growers' Association, I am a member of the Church Council and the village management board, and I have every reason to believe that next month I will be asked to accept the office of mayor.' Then he looked steadily at Sean. 'What have *you* done with your life so far?'

'I've lived it,' Sean answered, and Dennis looked a little perplexed – then he gathered himself.

'Are you married yet?'

'I was – but I sold her to the Arab slavers up north.'

'You did what?'

'Well,' grinned Sean, 'she was an old wife and the price was good.'

'That's a joke, hey? Ha, ha!' You couldn't fool good old Dennis – Sean laughed out loud. This unbelievable little man!

'Have a drink, Dennis,' he suggested.

'Two is my limit, thanks, Sean.' Dennis pulled the gold hunter from his waistcoat pocket and inspected it. 'Time to go – I'm afraid. Nice seeing you again.'

'Wait,' Sean stopped him. 'My brother – how's Garry?'

'Poor old Garry.' Dennis shook his head solemnly.

'What's wrong with him?' Sean's voice was sharp with his sense of dread.

'Nothing – ' Dennis reassured him quickly. 'Well, I mean nothing more than ever was.'

'Why did you say "poor old Garry" then?'

'I don't really know – except that everybody says it. It's habit, I suppose – he's just one of those people you say *poor old* in front of.'

Sean suppressed his irritation, he wanted to know. He had to know.

'You haven't answered me – how is he?'

Dennis made a significant gesture with his right hand. 'Looking into the bottle quite a bit these days – not that I blame him with that woman he married. You were well out of it there if I may say so, Sean.'

'You may,' Sean acquiesced, 'but is he well? How are things at Theunis Kraal?'

'We all took a bit of a beating with the rindepest* but Garry – well, he lost over half of his herds. Poor old Garry, everything happens to him.'

* An epidemic cattle disease.

'My God – fifty per cent!'

'Yes – but, of course, Ronnie helped him out. Gave him a mortgage on the farm to tide him over.'

'Theunis Kraal bonded again,' groaned Sean. 'Oh Garry, Garry.'

'Yes – well.' Dennis coughed uneasily. 'Well, I think I'd better be going. *Totsiens*, Sean.' He held out his hand. 'Shall I tell them I saw you?'

'No,' said Sean quickly. 'Just leave it stand.'

'Very well then.' Dennis hesitated. 'Are you all right, Sean? I mean' – he coughed again – 'are you all right for money?'

Sean felt his unhappiness dissolve a little; this pompous little man was going to offer him a loan. 'That's very good of you, Dennis. But I've got a couple of pounds saved up – enough to eat on for a few days,' he spoke seriously.

'All right then.' Dennis looked mightily relieved. 'All right then – *totsiens*, Sean,' and he turned and walked quickly out of the bar. As he left the room so he went out of Sean's mind, and Sean was thinking of his brother again.

Then suddenly Sean decided. I will go back to Ladyburg when this next trip is over. The dream farm outside Paarl would not lose anything in being transplanted to Natal – and he suddenly longed to sit in the panelled study at Theunis Kraal again, and to feel the mist come cold down the escarpment in the mornings, and see the spray blowing off the white falls in the wind. He wanted to hear Ada's voice again and to explain to her, knowing she would understand and forgive.

But more, much more it was Garry – poor old Garry. I must go back to him – ten years is a long time and he will have lost the bitterness. I must go back to him – for his sake and for Theunis Kraal. With the decision made, Sean finished his drink and went up the stairs to his suite.

Katrina was breathing softly in her sleep, the dark mass

of her hair spread out on the pillow. While he undressed he watched her and slowly the melancholy dissolved. Gently he pulled back the blankets on his side of the bed and just then Dirk whimpered from the next room. Sean went through to him. 'All right, what's the trouble?'

Dirk blinked owlishly and searched for an excuse, then the relief flooded into his face and he produced the one that creaked with age. 'I want a drink a water.'

The delay while Sean went through to the bathroom gave Dirk an opportunity to rally his forces and when Sean came back he opened the offensive in earnest.

'Tell me a story, Daddy.' He was sitting up now, bright-eyed.

'I'll tell you a story about Jack and a Nory—' said Sean.

'Not that one—' protested Dirk. The saga of Jack and his brother lasted five seconds and Dirk knew it. Sean sat down on the edge of the bed and held the glass for him.

'How about this one? There once was a king who had everything in the world . . . but when he lost it he found out that he had never had anything and that he now had more than he ever had before.'

Dirk looked stunned.

'That's not a very good one,' he gave his opinion at last.

'No,' said Sean. 'It isn't . . . is it? But I think we should be charitable and admit that it's not too bad for this time of night.'

30

Sean woke feeling happy. Katrina was sitting up in bed filling cups from a pewter coffee pot and Dirk was hammering at the door to be let in. Katrina smiled at him. 'Good morning, meneer.'

Sean sat up and kissed her. 'How did you sleep, fancy?'

'Well, thank you,' but there were dark rings under her eyes. Sean went across to the bedroom door.

'Prepare to receive cavalry,' he said and swung it open. Dirk's charge carried him onto the bed and Sean dived after him. When two men are evenly matched, weight will usually decide and within seconds Dirk had straddled Sean's chest, pinning him helplessly and Sean was pleading for quarter.

After breakfast Mbejane brought the carriage round to the front of the hotel. When the three of them were settled in it, Sean opened the small window behind the driver's seat and told Mbejane, 'To the office first. Then we have to be at the Exchange by ten o'clock.'

Mbejane grinned at him. 'Yes, Nkosi, then lunch at the Big House.' Mbejane had never been able to master the word Xanadu.

They went to all the old places. Sean and Mbejane laughing and reminiscing at each other through the window. There was a panic at the Exchange, crowds on the pavement outside. The offices on Eloff Street had been refaced and a brass plate beside the front door carried the roll of the subsidiaries of Central Rand Consolidated. Mbejane stopped the carriage outside and Sean boasted to Katrina. She sat silently and listened to him, suddenly feeling inadequate for a man who had done so much. She misinterpreted Sean's enthusiasm and thought he regretted the past and wished he were back.

'Mbejane, take us up to the Candy Deep,' Sean called at last. 'Let's see what's happening there.'

The last five hundred yards of the road was overgrown and pitted with disuse. The administration block had been demolished and grass grew thick over the foundations. There were new buildings and headgears half a mile farther along the ridge, but here the reef had been worked out and abandoned. Mbejane pulled up the horses in the circular drive in front of where the offices had stood. He jumped down and held their heads while Sean helped Katrina out of the carriage. Sean lifted Dirk and sat him on his shoulder and they picked their way through the waist-high grass and piles of bricks and rubbish towards the Candy Deep Number Three Shaft.

The bare white concrete blocks that had held the machinery formed a neat geometrical pattern in the grass. Beyond them reared the white mine dump; some mineral in the powdered rock had leaked out in long yellow stains down its sides. Duff had once had the mineral identified. It was of little commercial value, used occasionally in the ceramics industry. Sean had forgotten the name of it; it sounded like the name of a star – Uranus perhaps.

They came to the shaft. The edges of it had crumbled and the grass hung into it, the way an unkempt moustache hangs into an old man's mouth. The headgear was gone and only a rusty barbed-wire fence ringed the shaft. Sean bent his knees: keeping his back straight for Dirk still sat on his shoulder, he picked up a lump of rock the size of a man's fist and tossed it over the fence. They stood quietly and listened to it clatter against the sides as it fell. It fell for a long time and when at last it hit the bottom the echo rang faintly up from a thousand feet below.

'Throw more!' commanded Dirk, but Katrina stopped him.

'No, Sean, let's go. It's an evil place.' She shuddered slightly. 'It looks like a grave.'

'It very nearly was,' said Sean softly, remembering the darkness and the rock pressing down upon him.

'Let's go,' she said again, and they went back to where Mbejane waited with the carriage.

Sean was gay at lunch, he drank a small bottle of wine, but Katrina was tired and more miserable than she had been since they left Louis Trichardt. She had begun to realize the type of life he had led before she met him and she was frightened that now he wanted to return to it. She had only known the bush and the life of the Trek-Boer. She knew she could never learn to live like this. She watched as he laughed and joked during the meal, she watched the easy assurance with which he commanded the white head waiter, the way he picked his way through the maze of cutlery that was spread out on the table before them and at last she could hold it in no longer.

'Let's go away, let's go back into the bush.'

Sean stopped with a loaded fork halfway to his mouth. 'What?'

'Please, Sean, the sooner we go the sooner we'll be able to buy the farm.'

Sean chuckled. 'A day or two more won't make any difference. We're starting to have fun. Tonight I'll take you dancing – we were going to be sinful, remember?'

'Who will look after Dirk?' she asked weakly.

'Mbejane will—' Sean looked at her closely. 'You have a good sleep this afternoon and tonight we'll go out and tie the dog loose.' He grinned at the memories that expression invoked.

When Katrina woke from her rest that evening she found the other part of the reason for her depression. For the first time since the baby her periodic bleeding had started again, the tides of her body and mind were at their lowest ebb. She said nothing to Sean, but bathed and put on the yellow gown. She brushed her hair furiously, dragging the brush through it until her scalp tingled, but still it hung dull and lifeless – as dull as the eyes that looked back at her out of the yellow face in the mirror.

Sean came up behind her and leaned over her to kiss her cheek. 'You look,' said he, 'like a stack of gold bars five-and-a-half feet high.' But he realized that the yellow gown had been a mistake: it matched too closely the fever colour of her skin. Mbejane was waiting in the sitting-room when they went through.

'It may be late before we return,' Sean told him.

'That is of no account, Nkosi.' Mbejane's face was as impassive as ever, but Sean caught a sparkle of anticipation in his eyes and realized that Mbejane could hardly wait to get Dirk to himself.

'You are not to go into his room,' Sean warned.

'What if he cries, Nkosi?'

'He won't ... but if he does see what he wants, give it to him then leave him to sleep.'

Mbejane's face registered his protest.

'I'm warning you, Mbejane, if I come home at midnight and find him riding you round the room I'll have both your hides for a kaross.'

'His sleep shall be unspoiled, Nkosi,' lied Mbejane.

In the hotel lobby Sean spoke to the receptionist. 'Where can we find the best food in this town?' he asked.

'Two blocks down, sir, the Golden Guinea. You can't miss it.'

'It sounds like a gin palace.' Sean was dubious.

'I assure you, sir, that you'll have no complaint when you get there. Everyone goes there. Mr Rhodes dines there when he's in town, Mr Barnato, Mr Hradsky—'

'Dick Turpin, Cesare Borgia, Benedict Arnold,' Sean

continued for him. 'All right, you have convinced me. I'll take a chance on having my throat cut.'

Sean went out through the front entrance with Katrina on his arm. The splendour of the Golden Guinea subdued even Sean a little. A waiter with a uniform like a major-general's led them down a marble staircase, across the wide meadow of carpet between the group of elegant men and women to a table that even in the soft light dazzled with its bright silver and snowy linen. Chandeliers of crystal hung from the vaulted ceiling, the band was good, and the air was rich with the fragrance of perfume and expensive cigars.

Katrina stared helplessly at the menu until Sean came to her rescue and ordered the meal in a French accent that impressed her but not the waiter. The wine came and with it Sean's high spirits returned. Katrina sat quietly opposite him and listened. She tried to think of something witty to answer him with; in their wagon or alone in the veld they could talk for hours at a time but here she was dumb.

'Shall we dance?' Sean leaned across the table and squeezed her hand. She shook her head.

'Sean, I couldn't. Not with all these people watching. I'd only make a fool of myself.'

'Come on, I'll show you how . . . it's easy.'

'No, I couldn't, truly I couldn't.'

And to himself Sean had to admit that the dance floor of the Golden Guinea on a Saturday night was not the best place for a waltz lesson. The waiter brought the food, great steaming dishes of it. Sean addressed himself to it and the one-sided conversation wilted. Katrina watched him, picking at the too rich food herself, acutely conscious of the laughter and voices around them, feeling out of place and desperately miserable.

'Come on, Katrina,' Sean smiled at her. 'You've hardly touched your glass. Be a devil and get a little of that in you to warm you up.'

509

Obediently she sipped the champagne. She didn't like the taste. Sean finished the last of his crayfish thermidor and, leaning back in his chair glowing with wine and good food, said, 'Man . . . I only pray the chef can keep the rest of the meal up to that standard.' He belched softly behind his fingers and ran his eyes contentedly round the room. 'Duff used to say that a well-cooked crayfish was proof that—'

Sean stopped abruptly. He was staring at the head of the marble staircase – a party of three had appeared there. Two men in evening dress hovering attentively on each side of a woman. The woman was Candy Rautenbach. Candy with her blonde hair piled on top of her head. Candy with diamonds in her ears and at her throat, her bosom overflowing her gown as white as the frothy head on a beer tankard. Candy with bright blue eyes above a red mouth, Candy poised and lovely. Laughing, she glanced towards him and her eyes met his across the room. She stared in open disbelief, the laughter frozen on her lips, then suddenly her poise was gone and she was running down the stairs towards him, holding her skirts up to her knees, her escorts cantering after her in alarm, waiters scattering out of her path and every head in the room turning to watch her. Sean pushed back his chair, stood up to meet her and Candy reached him and jumped up to throw her arms around his neck. There was a long incoherent exchange of greetings and at last Sean prised her loose from his neck and turned her to face Katrina. Candy was flushed and panting with excitement; with every breath her bosom threatened to spring out of her bodice, and she was still holding on to Sean's arm.

'Candy, I want you to meet my wife, Katrina. My dear, this is Candy Rautenbach.'

'How do you do.' Katrina smiled uncertainly and Candy said the wrong thing.

'Sean, you're joking! You married?'

Katrina's smile faded. Candy noticed the change and went on quickly, 'But I must applaud your choice. I am so pleased to meet you, Katrina. We must get together sometime and I'll tell you all about Sean's terrible past.'

Candy was still holding Sean's arm and Katrina was watching her hand – the long tapered fingers against the dark cloth of Sean's suit. Sean saw the direction of Katrina's eyes and tried tactfully to disengage himself but Candy held on. 'Sean, these are my two current beaux.' They were standing to heel behind her like well-trained gundogs. 'They are both so nice I can't make up my mind about them. Harry Lategaan and Derek Goodman. Boys, this is Sean Courtney. You've heard lots about him.'

They shook hands all round.

'Do you mind if we join you?' asked Derek Goodman.

'I'd be upset if you didn't!' said Sean. The men spread out to find chairs while Candy and Katrina studied each other. 'Is this your first visit to Johannesburg, Mrs Courtney?' Candy smiled sweetly. *I wonder where Sean found her, she's thin as a stick and that complexion! – that accent! He could have done better for himself – he could have had his pick.*

'Yes, we won't be here very long though.' *She's a harlot. She must be – her breasts half-naked and the paint on her face and the way she touches Sean. She must have been his mistress. If she touches him again I'll – I'll kill her.*

Sean came back to the table carrying a chair and set it down for Candy. 'Candy's one of my old friends, my dear, I'm sure you two will like each other.'

'I'm sure we will,' said Candy but Katrina didn't answer and Candy turned back to him. 'Sean, how wonderful it is to see you again. You look so well ... as sunburnt and handsome as the first time I met you. Do you remember that day you and Duff came to eat at the Hotel?'

A shadow fell across Sean's face at the mention of Duff's name. 'Yes, I remember.' He looked round and snapped his fingers for the waiter. 'Let's have some more champagne.'

'I'll get it,' Candy's escorts cut in simultaneously and then started wrangling good-naturedly as to whose turn it was.

'Is Duff with you tonight, Sean?' Candy asked.

'Candy, didn't Derek get the drinks last time? It's my turn now.' Harry sought her support. Candy ignored them and looked at Sean for a reply but he turned and went round the table to the seat beside Katrina.

'I say, old girl, can I have the first dance?' asked Derek.

'I'll spin you for it, Derek, winner pays but gets first dance,' Harry suggested.

'You're on.'

'Sean, I said is Duff here tonight?' Candy looked at him across the table.

'No, he's not. Listen, you two, how about letting me in on this.' Sean avoided her eyes and joined in the haggle with Harry and Derek. Candy bit her lip – she wanted to press Sean further. She wanted to know about Duff – then suddenly she turned on her smile again. She wasn't going to plead with him.

'What is this?' She tapped Harry's shoulder with her fan. 'Am I going to be the prize in a game of chance? Derek will pay for the wine and Sean gets first dance.'

'I say old girl, that's a bit rough, you know.' But Candy was already standing up.

'Come on, Sean, let's see if you can still tread a stately measure.'

Sean glanced at Katrina. 'You don't mind, do you ... just one dance?'

Katrina shook her head.

I hate her. She's a harlot. Katrina had never in her life spoken the word out loud, she had seen it only in her Bible,

512

but now it gave her a fierce pleasure to think it. She watched Sean and Candy walk arm-in-arm to the dance floor.

'Would you care to dance, Mrs Courtney?' said Derek. Katrina shook her head again without looking at him. She was staring at Sean and Candy. She saw Sean take her in his arms and a cold lump settled in her stomach. Candy was looking up into Sean's face, laughing at him, her arm on his shoulder, her hand in his.

She's a harlot. Katrina felt her tears very near the surface and thinking that word held them back. Sean swirled Candy into a turn – Katrina stiffened in her chair, her hands clenching in her lap – their legs were touching, she saw Candy arch her back slightly and press her thighs against Sean. Katrina felt as though she were suffocating, jealousy had spread up cold and tight through her chest.

I could go and pull him away, she thought. *I could stop him doing that. He has no right. It's as though the two of them are doing – doing it together. I know they have before, I know it now – Oh God, make them stop it. Please make them stop.*

At last Sean and Candy came back to the table. They were laughing together and when he reached her chair Sean dropped his hand on Katrina's shoulder. She moved away from it but Sean seemed not to notice. Everybody was having a good time. Everybody except Katrina. Harry and Derek were jostling for position. Sean's big laugh kept booming out and Candy was sparkling like the diamonds she wore. Every few minutes Sean turned to Katrina and tried to draw her into the conversation but Katrina stubbornly refused to be drawn. She sat there hating them all. Hating even Sean – for the first time she was unsure of him, jealous and frightened for him. She stared down at her hands on the tablecloth in front of her and saw how bony they were, chapped and reddened by the sun and wind, ugly compared to Candy's. She pulled them quickly into her lap and leaned across towards Sean. 'Please, I want to go back to the hotel. I don't feel well.'

Sean stopped in the middle of a story and looked at her with a mixture of concern and dismay. He didn't want to leave and yet he knew she was still sick. He hesitated one second and then he said, 'Of course, my fancy, I'm sorry. I didn't realize—' He turned to the others. 'We'll have to be going ... my wife's not too strong ... she's just had one hell of a go of blackwater.'

'Oh, Sean, must you?' Candy couldn't hide her disappointment. 'There's still so much to talk about.'

'I'm afraid so. We'll get together another night.'

'Yes,' agreed Katrina quickly, 'next time we come to Johannesburg we'll see you.'

'Oh, I don't know ... perhaps before we go,' Sean demurred. 'Some night next week. How about Monday?'

Before Candy could answer Katrina interrupted. 'Please, Sean, can we go now. I'm very tired.' She started towards the stairs but looked back to see Candy jump up and take Sean's arm, hold her lips close to his ear and whisper a question. Sean answered her tersely and Candy turned back to the table and sat down. When they were out on the street Katrina asked, 'What did she say to you?'

'She just said goodbye,' muttered Sean and Katrina knew he was lying. They didn't talk again on the way back to the hotel. Katrina was preoccupied with her jealousy and Sean was thinking about what Candy had asked and what he had answered.

'Sean, where's Duff? You must tell me.'

'He's dead, Candy.'

The second before she turned back to the table Sean had seen her eyes.

31

Sean woke with a headache and Dirk's jumping on his chest did not help to ease it at all. Sean had to bribe him off with the promise of sweets. Dirk, sensing his advantage, raised his price to a packet of bull's eyes and two lollipops, the kind with red stripes, before he allowed Katrina to lead him away to the bathroom. Sean sighed and settled back under the blankets. The pain moved up and crouched just behind his eyes. He could taste stale champagne on his own breath and his skin smelt of cigar smoke. He drowsed back in half sleep and the ache faded a little.

'Sean, it's Sunday you know. Are you coming to church with us?' Katrina asked coldly from the bedroom door. Sean squeezed his eyelids tighter closed.

'Sean!' No answer.

'Sean!' He opened one eye.

'Are you going to get up?'

'I don't feel very well,' he croaked. 'I think I have a touch of malaria.'

'Are you coming?' Katrina demanded remorselessly. Her feelings towards him had not softened during the night.

'I don't feel up to it this morning, truly I don't. I'm sure the Good Lord will understand.'

'Thou shalt not take the Lord's name in vain,' Katrina warned him with ice in her voice.

'I'm sorry.' Sean pulled the blankets up to his chin defensively. 'But truly, fancy, I can't get up for another couple of hours. My head would burst.'

Katrina turned back into the sitting-room and Sean heard her speak to Dirk in a voice purposely pitched to reach him.

'Your father's not coming with us. We will have to go

down to breakfast by ourselves. Then we will have to go to church on our own.'

'But,' Dirk pointed out, 'he's going to buy me a packet of bull's eyes and *two* lollipops with red stripes.' In Dirk's opinion that levelled the score. Sean heard the door of the suite close and Dirk's voice receded down the passage. Sean relaxed slowly and waited for the ache behind his eyes to diminish. After a while he became aware of the coffee tray on the table beside the bed and he weighed the additional pain that the effort of sitting up would involve against the beneficial effect of a large cup of coffee. It was a difficult decision but in the end he carefully raised his body to a sitting position and poured a cupful. There was a small jug of fresh cream on the tray. He took it in his right hand and was just about to add a little to the cup when there was a knock on the sitting-room door.

'Come in!' called Sean. He supposed it was the waiter coming to collect the tray. Sean searched his mind for a really scathing remark to send him on his way. He heard the sitting-room door open.

'Who is it?' he asked. There were quick footsteps and then Sean started so violently that the cream slopped out of the jug onto his sheets and his new nightshirt.

'Good God, Candy, you shouldn't have come here.' Sean was in a frenzy of agitation. He put the jug back on the tray with nervous haste and wiped ineffectually at the mess on his nightshirt with his hands. 'If my wife ... Did anyone see you? You mustn't stay. If Katrina knows you've been here she'll ... well I mean, she won't understand.'

Candy's eyes were puffy and rimmed with red. She looked as though she hadn't slept. 'It's all right, Sean, I waited across the street until I saw your wife leave. One of my servants followed her, she went to the Dutch church on Commissioner Street and there the service lasts about fifty

516

years.' She came into the room and sat down on the edge of his bed.

'I had to talk to you alone. I couldn't let you go without knowing about Duff. I want you to tell me about it . . . everything about it. I promise not to cry, I know how you hate it.'

'Candy, let's not torture ourselves with it. He's dead. Let's remember him alive.' Sean had forgotten his headache for its place had been taken by pity for her and worry at the position in which she had placed him.

'Tell me, please. I must know. I'd never rest again if I didn't,' she said quietly.

'Candy, don't you see that it doesn't matter? The way in which he went is not important. All that you need to know is he's gone.' Sean's voice faded but went on softly almost to himself, 'He's gone, that is the only thing that matters, he's gone and left us richer for knowing him and a little poorer for having lost him.'

'Tell me,' she said again and they looked at each other, their emotions locked behind expressionless faces. Then Sean told her, his words limping at first, then faster and stronger as the horror of it came back to him. When he had finished she said nothing. She sat on the edge of the bed staring down at the patterned carpet. Sean moved closer to her and put his arm around her.

'There is nothing we can do. That's the thing about death, there is nothing you can do to make it change its mind.'

She leaned against him, against the comfort of his big body and they sat silently until suddenly Candy pulled away from him and smiled her gay brittle smile.

'And now tell me about you. Are you happy? Was that your son with Katrina? He's a lovely child.'

With relief Sean followed her away from the memory of

Duff. They talked about each other, filling in the blanks from the time they had last met until suddenly Sean returned to reality.

'Good God, Candy, we've been talking for ages. Katrina will be back at any moment. You had better run.'

At the door she turned, buried her fingers in his beard and tugged his head from side to side. 'If she ever throws you out, you magnificent brute, here's somebody who'll have a place for you.'

She stood up on her toes and kissed him. 'Be happy,' she commanded and the door closed softly behind her.

Sean rubbed his chin, then he pulled off his nightshirt, screwed it into a ball, tossed it through the open door of the bedroom and went to the bathroom. He was towelling himself and whistling the waltz that the band had played the night before, sweating a little in the steamy warmth of the bathroom when he heard the front door open. 'Is that you, Fancy?'

'Daddy! Daddy! Mummy got sweets for me.' Dirk hammered on the bathroom door, and Sean wrapped the towel round his waist before opening it.

'Look! Look at all my sweets,' gloated Dirk. 'Do you want one, Pa?'

'Thank you, Dirk,' Sean put one of the huge striped humbugs in his mouth, moved it to one side and spoke around it.

'Where's your Mummy?'

'There.' Dirk pointed at the bedroom. He closed the sweet packet carefully. 'I'll keep some for Bejaan,' he announced.

'He'll like that,' Sean said and went across to the bedroom. Katrina lay on the bed; as soon as he saw her he knew something was desperately wrong. She lay staring up at the ceiling, her eyes unseeing, her face as yellow and set as that of a corpse. Two quick strides carried him to her.

He touched her cheek with his fingers and the sense of dread settled on him again, heavily, darkly.

'Katrina?' There was no response. She lay still without a flicker of life in her eyes. Sean swung round and ran out of the suite, down the corridor to the head of the stairs. There were people in the lobby below him and he yelled over their heads to the clerk behind the desk.

'Get a doctor, man, as fast as you can ... my wife's dying.'

The man stared up at him blankly. He had a neck too thin for his high stiff collar and his black hair was parted down the centre and polished with grease.

'Hurry, you stupid bastard, get moving,' roared Sean. Everybody in the lobby was looking at him. He still wore only a small towel around his waist and, heavy with water, his hair hung down over his forehead.

'Move, man! Move!' Sean was dancing with impatience. There was a heavy stone vase on the banister at Sean's side, he picked it up threateningly and the clerk jerked out of his trance and scuttled for the front door. Sean ran back to the suite.

Dirk was standing by Katrina's bed, his face distorted by the humbug it contained and his eyes large with curiosity. Sean snatched him up, carried him through to the other bedroom and locked the door on his outraged howls. Dirk was unused to being handled in that manner. Sean went back to Katrina and knelt beside her bed. He was still kneeling there when the doctor arrived. Tersely Sean explained about the blackwater, and the doctor listened then sent him to wait in the sitting-room. It was a long wait before the doctor came through to him and Sean sensed that behind his professional poker face the man was puzzled.

'Is it a relapse?' Sean demanded.

'No, I don't think so. I've given her a sedative.'

'What's wrong with her? What is it?' Sean pursued him and the doctor hedged.

'Has your wife had some sort of shock ... some bad news, something that could have alarmed her? Has she been under nervous strain?'

'No ... she's just come back from church. Why? What's wrong?' Sean caught the doctor's lapels and shook him in his agitation.

'It appears to be some sort of paralytic hysteria. I've given her laudanum. She'll sleep now and I'll come back to see her this evening.'

The doctor was trying to loosen Sean's hands from his jacket. Sean let him go and pushed past him to the bedroom.

The doctor called again just before dark. Sean had undressed Katrina and put her into the bed, but apart from that she had not moved. Her breathing was shallow and fast despite the drug she had been given. The doctor was baffled.

'I can't understand it, Mr Courtney. There is nothing I can find wrong with her apart from her general run-down condition. I think we'll just have to wait and see. I don't want to give her any more drugs.'

Sean knew the man could be of no more help to him and he hardly noticed when he left with a promise to come again in the morning. Mbejane gave Dirk his bath, fed him and put him to bed and then he slipped quietly out of the suite and left Sean alone with Katrina. The afternoon of worry had tired Sean. He left the gas burning in the sitting-room and stretched out on his own bed. After a while he slept.

When the rhythm of his breathing changed Katrina looked across at him. Sean lay fully clothed on top of his blankets, one thickly-muscled arm thrown above his head and his tension betrayed by the twitching of his lips and the frown that puckered his face. Katrina stood up and moved across to stand over him, lonely as she had never been in the solitude of the bush, hurt beyond the limits of physical pain and with everything that she believed in destroyed in those few minutes that it had taken for her to discover the truth.

She looked down at Sean and with surprise realized that she still loved him, but now the security that she had found with him was gone. The walls of her castle had proved paper. She had felt the first cold draughts blowing in through them as she watched him reliving his past and regretting it. She had felt the walls tremble and the wind howl stronger outside when he danced with that woman – then, they had collapsed into ruin around her. Standing in the half-darkened room, watching the man she trusted so completely and who just as completely had betrayed her, she went carefully over the ground again to make sure there was no mistake.

That morning, she and Dirk had stopped at the sweet shop on the way back from church. It was almost opposite the hotel. It had taken Dirk a long time to select his tuppenny worth. The profusion of wares on display unmanned him and reduced him to a state of dithering indecision. Finally, with the assistance of the proprietor and a little prompting from Katrina, his purchases were made and packed into a brown paper bag. They were just about to go when Katrina looked out through the large front window of the shop and saw Candy Rautenbach leaving the hotel. She came quickly down the front steps, glanced about her, crossed the street to a waiting carriage and her coachman whisked her away. Katrina had stopped the instant she caught sight of her. A pang of last night's jealousy returned, for Candy looked very lovely even in the morning sunlight. It was not until Candy's carriage disappeared that Katrina began to question her presence at their hotel at eleven o'clock on a Sunday morning. Her jealousy was a bayonet thrust up under her ribs: it made her catch her breath. Vividly she remembered Candy's whispered question as they left the Golden Guinea the previous night. She remembered the way Sean had answered and the way he had lied about it afterwards. Sean knew that Katrina would go to church that morning. How simple it all was! Sean had arranged to meet her, he had refused to accompany Katrina and while Katrina was out of the way that harlot had gone to him.

'Mummy, you're hurting me.' Unconsciously she had tightened her grip on Dirk's hand. She hurried out of the shop, dragging Dirk with her. She almost ran across the hotel lobby, up the stairs and along the passage. The door was closed. She opened it and the smell of Candy's perfume met her. Her nostrils flared at it. There was no mistaking it, she remembered it from the previous evening – the smell of fresh violets. She heard Sean call from the bathroom, Dirk ran across the room and hammered on the door.

'Daddy! Daddy! Mummy got sweets for me.'

She put her Bible down on top of the writing desk and moved across the thick carpet with the smell of violets all around her. She stood in the doorway of the bedroom. Sean's nightshirt lay on the floor, there were still damp stains on it. She felt her legs begin to tremble. She looked up and saw the stains on the bed, grey on the white sheets. She felt giddy, her cheeks burned; she only just managed to reach her own bed.

32

She knew there was no mistake. Sean had taken that woman in such a casually blatant manner – in their own bedroom, almost before her eyes, that his rejection of her could hardly have been more final if he had slapped her face and thrown her into the street. Weakened by fever, depressed by the loss of her child and the phase of her cycle, she had not the resilience to fight against it. She had loved him but she had proved insufficient for him. She could not stay with him: the stubborn pride of her race would not allow it. There was only one alternative.

Timidly she bent over him and as she kissed him she smelt the warm man-smell of his body and felt his beard brush her cheek. Her determination wavered; she wanted to throw herself across his chest, lock her arms around his neck and plead with him. She wanted to ask for another chance. If he could tell her how she had failed him she could try to change, if only he could show her what she had done wrong. Perhaps if they went back into the bush again – She dragged herself away from his bed. She pressed her knuckles hard against her lips. It was no use. He had decided and even if she begged him to take her back there would always be this thing between them. She had lived in a castle and she would not change it now for a mud hut. Driven by the trek whip of her pride she moved quickly across to the wardrobe. She put on a coat and buttoned it – it reached to her ankles and covered her nightdress; she spread the green shawl over her head, winding the loose end around her throat. Once more she looked across at Sean. He slept with his big body sprawled and the frown still on his face.

In the sitting-room she stopped beside the writing desk. Her Bible lay where she had left it. She opened the front cover, dipped the pen and wrote. She closed the book and went to the door. There she hesitated once more and looked back at Dirk's bedroom. She could not trust herself to see him again. She lifted an end of the shawl to cover her mouth, then she went out into the passage and closed the door softly behind her.

– 33 –

Sean was surprised to find himself fully dressed and lying on top of his bed when he woke next morning. It was still half dark outside the hotel windows and the room was cold. He propped himself up on one elbow and rubbed at his eyes with the back of a clenched fist. Then he remembered and he swung his legs off the bed and looked at Katrina's bed. The blankets were thrown back and it was empty. Sean's first feeling was relief, she had recovered enough to get up on her own. He went through to the bathroom, stumbling a little from the stiffness of uneasy sleep. He tapped on the closed door.

'Katrina?' he questioned and then again louder. 'Katrina, are you in there?'

The handle turned when he tried it and the door swung open without resistance. He blinked at the empty room, white tiles reflecting the uncertain light, a towel thrown across a chair where he had left it. He felt the first twinge of alarm. Dirk's room – the door was still locked, the key on the outside. He flung it open. Dirk sat up in bed, his face flushed, his curls standing up like the leaves of a sisal bush. Sean ran out into the passage, along it and looked down into the lobby. There was a light burning behind the reception desk. The clerk slept with his head on his arms, sitting forward on his chair snoring. Sean went down the stairs three at a time. He shook the clerk.

'Has anybody been out through here during the night?' Sean demanded.

'I . . . I don't know.'

'Is that door locked?' Sean pointed at the front door.

'No, sir, there's a night latch on it. You can get out but not in.'

Sean ran out onto the pavement. Which way, which way to search for her? Which way had she gone? Back to Pretoria to the wagons? Sean thought not. She would need transport and she had no money to hire it. Why should she leave without waking him, leave Dirk, leave her clothing and disappear into the night? She must have been unbalanced by the drugs the doctor had given her. Perhaps there was something in his theory that she had suffered a shock, perhaps she was wandering in her nightdress through the streets with no memory, perhaps – Sean stood in the cold grey Transvaal morning, the city starting to murmur into wakefulness around him, the questions crowding into his head and finding there no answers with which to mate.

He turned and ran back through the hotel, out of the rear door into the stable yard.

'Mbejane,' he shouted. 'Mbejane, where the hell are you?'

Mbejane appeared quickly from the stall where he was currying one of the hired horses.

'Nkosi.'

'Have you seen the Nkosikazi?'

Mbejane's face creased into a puzzled frown. 'Yesterday—'

'No, man,' shouted Sean. 'Today, last night . . . have you seen her?'

Mbejane's expression was sufficient reply.

Sean brushed impatiently past him and ran into the stable. He snatched a saddle off the rack and threw it onto the back of the nearest horse. While he clinched the girth and forced a bit between its teeth he spoke to Mbejane.

'The Nkosikazi is sick. She has left during the night. It is possible that she walks as one who still sleeps. Go quickly among your friends and tell them to search for her, tell them that there's ten pounds in gold for the one who finds her. Then come back here and care for Dirk until I return.'

Sean led the horse from the stable and Mbejane hurried off to spread the word. Sean knew that within minutes half the Zulus in Johannesburg would be looking for Katrina – tribal loyalty and ten pounds in gold were strong incentives. He swung up onto the horse and galloped out of the yard. He tried the Pretoria road first. Three miles out of town a native herd boy grazing sheep beside the road convinced him that Katrina had not passed that way. He turned back. He paid a visit to the police station at Marshal Square. The Commandant remembered him from the old days; Sean could rely on his cooperation. Sean left him and rode fast through the streets that were starting to fill with the bustle of a working day. He hitched his horse outside the hotel and took the front steps three at a time. The clerk had no news for him. He ran up the stairs and along the passage to his suite. Mbejane was feeding Dirk his breakfast. Dirk beamed at Sean through a faceful of egg and spread his arms to be picked up but Sean had no time for him.

'Has she come back?'

Mbejane shook his head. 'They will find her, Nkosi. Fifty men are searching for her now.'

'Stay with the child,' said Sean and went down to his horse. He stood beside it ready to mount but not knowing which way to go. 'Where the hell has she got to?' he demanded aloud. In her night clothes with no money, where the hell had she gone?

He mounted and rode with aimless urgency through the streets, searching the faces of the people along the sidewalks, turning down the sanitary lanes and peering into backyards and vacant plots. By midday he had tired his horse and worked himself into a ferment of worry and bad temper. He had searched every street in Johannesburg, made a nuisance of himself at the police station and sworn at the hotel clerk, but there was still no sign of Katrina. He was riding down Jeppe Street for the fifth time when the imposing double-storey of Candy's Hotel registered through his preoccupation.

'Candy,' he whispered. 'She can help.'

He found her in her office among Persian rugs and gilt furniture, walls covered with pink and blue patterned wallpaper, a mirrored ceiling hung with six crystal waterfalls of chandeliers and a desk with an Indian mosaic top. Sean pushed aside the little man in the black alpaca coat who tried to stop him entering and burst into the room. Candy looked up and her small frown of annoyance smoothed as she saw who it was.

'Sean . . . oh, how nice to see you.' She came round from behind the desk, the bell tent of her skirts covering the movement of her legs so she seemed to float. Her skin was smooth white and her eyes were happy blue. She held out her hand to him, but hesitated as she saw his face. 'What is it, Sean?'

He told her in a rush and she listened and when he had finished she rang the bell on her desk.

'There's brandy in the cabinet by the fireplace,' she said, 'I expect you are in need of one.'

The little man in the alpaca coat came quickly to the bell. Sean poured himself a large brandy and listened to Candy giving orders.

'Check the railway station. Telegraph the coach stages on each of the main roads. Send someone up to the hospital. Check the registers of every hotel and boarding-house in town.'

'Very well, madame.' The little man bobbed his head as he acknowledged each instruction and then he was gone.

Candy turned back to Sean.

'You can pour a drink for me also and then sit down and simmer down. You're behaving just the way she wanted you to.'

'What do you mean?' demanded Sean.

'You are being given a little bit of wifely discipline, my dear. Surely you have been married long enough to recognize that?'

Sean carried the glass across to her and Candy patted the sofa next to her.

'Sit down,' she said. 'We'll find your little Cinderella for you.'

'What do you mean ... wifely discipline?' he demanded again.

'Punishment for bad behaviour. You may have eaten with your mouth open, answered back, taken more than your share of the blankets, not said good morning with the right inflection or committed one of the other mortal sins of matrimony, but—' Candy sipped her drink and gasped slightly, 'I see that time has not given you a lighter hand with the brandy bottle. One Courtney tot always did equal an imperial gallon ... but, as I was saying, my guess is that little Katy is having an acute attack of jealousy. Probably her first, seeing that the two of you have spent your whole married life out in the deep sticks and she has never had an opportunity of watching the Courtney charm work on any other female before.'

'Nonsense,' said Sean. 'Who's she got to be jealous of?'

'Me,' said Candy. 'Every time she looked at me the other night I felt as though I'd been hit in the chest with an axe.' Candy touched her magnificent bosom with her fingertips, skilfully drawing Sean's attention to it. Sean looked at it. It was deeply cleft and smelt of fresh violets. He shifted restlessly and looked away.

'Nonsense,' he said again. 'We're just old friends, almost like—' he hesitated.

'I hope, my dear, that you weren't going to say "brother and sister" . . . I'll not be party to any incestuous relationship . . . or had you forgotten about that?'

Sean had not forgotten. Every detail of it was still clear. He blushed and stood up.

'I'd better be going,' he said. 'I'm going to keep looking for her. Thanks for your help, Candy, and for the drink.'

'Whatever I have is yours, m'sieur,' she murmured, lifting an eyebrow at him, enjoying the way he blushed. 'I'll let you know as soon as we hear anything.'

The assurance that Candy had given him wore thinner as the afternoon went by with no news of Katrina. By nightfall Sean was again wild with worry, it had completely swamped his bad temper and even anaesthetized his fatigue. One by one Mbejane's tribesmen came in to report a blank score, one by one the avenues Candy's men were exploring proved empty, and long before midnight Sean was the only hunter left. He rode hunched in the saddle, a lantern in his hand, riding the ground that had already been covered a dozen times, visiting the mining camps along the ridge, stopping to question late travellers he met along the network of roads between the mines. But the answer was always the same. Some thought he was joking: they laughed until they saw that his face was haunted and dark-eyed in the lantern light, then they stopped laughing and moved hurriedly on. Others had heard about the missing woman; they started to question him, but as soon as Sean realized they could not help him, he pushed past them and went on searching. At dawn he was back at the hotel. Mbejane was waiting for him.

'Nkosi, I have had food ready for you since last night. Eat now and sleep a little. I will send the men out to search again today, they will find her.'

'Tell them, I will give one hundred pounds to the one who finds her.' Sean passed his hand wearily across his face. 'Tell them to hunt the open veld beyond the ridges, she may not have followed a road.'

'I will tell them . . . but now you must eat.'

Sean blinked his eyes, they were red-veined and each had a little lump of yellow mucus in the corner.

'Dirk?' he asked.

'He is well, Nkosi, I have stayed with him all the while.' Mbejane took Sean firmly by the arm. 'There is food ready. You must eat.'

'Saddle me another horse,' said Sean. 'I will eat while you do it.'

Without sleep, unsteady in the saddle as the day wore on, Sean widened the circle of his search until he was out into the treeless veld and the mine headgears were small spidery triangles on the horizon.

A dozen times he met Zulus from the city, big black men in loin cloths, moving at their businesslike trot, hunting the ground like hounds. There was a concealed sympathy behind their greetings.

'Mbejane has told us, Nkosi. We will find her.' And Sean left them and rode on alone, more alone than he had ever been in his life before. After dark he rode back into Johannesburg, the faint flutter of hope inside him stilled as he limped stiffly into the gas-lit lobby of the hotel and saw the pity in the reception clerk's face.

'No word, I'm afraid, Mr Courtney.'

Sean nodded. 'Thanks anyway. Is my son all right?'

'Your servant has taken good care of him, sir. I sent dinner up to him an hour ago.'

The stairs seemed endless as he climbed them. By God, he was tired – sick-tired and sick with worry. He pushed open the door of his suite and Candy stood up from a chair across the room. The hope flared up in him again.

'Have you—' he started eagerly.

'No,' she said quickly. 'No, Sean, I'm sorry.' He flopped into one of the chairs and Candy poured a drink for him from a decanter that was waiting on the writing desk. He smiled his thanks and took a big gulp at the glass. Candy lifted his legs one at a time and pulled off his boots, ignoring his faint protest. Then she took up her own glass and went to sit across the room from him.

'I'm sorry I joked yesterday,' she apologized softly. 'I don't think I realized how much you love her.' She lifted her glass to him. 'Here's a speedy end to the search.'

Sean drank again, half a glass at a swallow.

'You do love her, don't you?' Candy asked.

Sean answered her sharply. 'She's my wife.'

'But it's not only that,' Candy went on recklessly, knowing his anger was just below the surface of his fatigue.

'Yes, I love her. I'm just learning how much, I love her as I'll never be able to love again.' He drained his glass and stared at it, his face grey under the brown and his eyes dark with unhappiness. 'Love,' he said. 'Love,' mouthing the word, weighing it. 'They've dirtied that word . . . they sell love at the Opera House . . . they have used that word so much that now when I want to say "I love Katrina" it doesn't sound what I mean.' Sean hurled the glass against the far wall, it shattered with a crack and a tingle and Dirk stirred in the bedroom. Sean dropped his voice to a fierce whisper. 'I love her so it screws my gut, I love her so that to think of losing her now is like thinking of dying.'

He clenched his fists and leaned forward in his chair. 'I'll not lose her now, by Christ, I'll find her and when I do I'll tell her this. I'll tell her just like I'm telling you.' He stopped and frowned. 'I don't think I've ever said to her "I love you." I've never liked using that word. I've said "Marry me" and "You're my fancy," but I've never said it straight before.'

'Perhaps that's part of the reason she ran away, Sean,

perhaps because you never said it she thought you never felt it.' Candy was watching him with a strange expression – pity and understanding and a little yearning.

'I'll find her,' said Sean, 'and this time I'll tell her . . . if it's not too late.'

'You'll find her and it won't be too late. The earth can't have swallowed her, and she'll be glad to hear you say it.' Candy stood up. 'You must rest now, you have a hard day ahead of you.'

Sean slept fully dressed in the chair in the sitting-room. He slept brokenly, his mind struggling and kicking him back to half wakefulness every few minutes. Candy had turned the gas low before she left and its light fell in a soft pool onto the writing desk beneath it. Katrina's Bible lay where she had left it and each time Sean started awake the fat, leather-covered book caught his eye. Some time before dawn he woke for the last time and knew he could not sleep again.

He stood up and his body still ached and his eyes felt gritty. He moved across to the gas lamp and turned it up high, he let his hand drop from the lamp onto the Bible. Its leather was cool and softly polished beneath his fingers. He opened the front cover and caught his breath with a hiss.

Beneath Katrina's name, in her carefully rounded writing, the ink still freshly blue, *she had filled in the date of death*.

The page magnified slowly in front of his eyes until it filled the whole field of his vision. There was a rushing sound in his ears, the sound of a river in flood, but above it he heard voices, different voices.

'Let's go, Sean, it looks like a grave.'

'But more than anything she needs love.'

'The earth can't have swallowed her.'

And his own voice, 'If it's not too late, if it's not too late.'

The morning light was gathering strength as he reached the ruins of the old Candy Deep office block. He left his horse and ran through the grass towards the mine dump. The wind was small and cold; it moved the tops of the grass and went on to where Katrina's green shawl was caught on the barbed wire fence that ringed the shaft. In the wind the shawl flapped its wings like a big green bird of prey.

Sean reached the fence and looked down into the mouth of the shaft. At one place the grass had been torn away from the edge as though someone had snatched at it as they fell.

Sean loosed the shawl from the spikes of the barbed wire, he balled the heavy material in his fists, then he held it out over the shaft and let it drop. It spread out as it floated down into the blackness, and it was the bright green of Katrina's eyes.

'Why?' whispered Sean. 'Why have you done this to us, my fancy?' He turned away and walked back to his horse, stumbling carelessly in the rough footing.

Mbejane was waiting for him in the hotel suite.

'Get the carriage,' Sean told him.

'The Nkosikazi – ?'

'Get the carriage,' Sean repeated.

Sean carried Dirk downstairs. He paid his bill at the reception desk and went out to where Mbejane had the carriage ready. He climbed up into it and held Dirk on his lap.

'Drive back to Pretoria,' Sean said.

'Where's Mummy?' Dirk demanded.

'She's not coming with us.'

'Are we going alone?' Dirk insisted and Sean nodded wearily.

'Yes, Dirk, we are going alone.'

'Is Mummy coming just now?'

'No, Dirk. No, she's not.'

It was finished, Sean thought. It was all over – all the

dreams and the laughter and the love. He was too numbed to feel the pain yet – it would come later.

'Why are you squeezing me so hard, Daddy?'

Sean slackened his grip and looked down at the child on his lap. It was not finished, he realized; it was only a new beginning.

But first I must have time for this to heal: time – and a quiet place to lie up with this wound. The wagons are waiting and I must go back into the wilderness.

Perhaps after another year I will have healed sufficiently to start again, to go back to Ladyburg with my son, back to Ladyburg, and to Ada and to Garry – he thought. Then suddenly and sickeningly he felt the pain again, and the deep raw ache of it frightened him. *Please God*, prayed Sean who had never prayed before, *please God give me the strength to endure it.*

'Are you going to cry, Daddy? You look like you're going to cry.' Dirk was watching Sean's face with solemn curiosity. Sean pulled the child's head gently against his shoulder and held it there.

If tears could pay both our debts, thought Sean, if with my tears I could buy for you an indulgence from all pain, if by weeping now I could do all your weeping for you – then I would cry until my eyes were washed away.

'No, Dirk,' he answered. 'I am not going to cry – crying never helps very much.'

And Mbejane took them to where the wagons waited at Pretoria.

Visit **www.panmacmillan.com** to read more about all our books and to buy them. You will also find features, author interviews and news of any author events, and you can sign up for e-newsletters so that you're always first to hear about our new releases.